Dynamic Macroeconomics

Dynamic Macroeconomics

George Alogoskoufis

The MIT Press
Cambridge, Massachusetts
London, England

This book was set in Times New Roman by Westchester Publishing Services. Printed and bound in the United States of America.

Library of Congress Cataloging-in-Publication Data

Names: Alogoskoufis, George, author.
Title: Dynamic macroeconomics / George Alogoskoufis.
Description: Cambridge, MA : MIT Press, [2019] | Includes bibliographical references and index.
Identifiers: LCCN 2018060935 | ISBN 9780262043014 (hardcover : alk. paper)
Subjects: LCSH: Macroeconomics—Mathematical models. | Equilibrium (Economics)—Mathematical models.
Classification: LCC HB172.5 .A396 2019 | DDC 339—dc23
LC record available at https://lccn.loc.gov/2018060935

10 9 8 7 6 5 4 3 2 1

To Spyros, Athinais, and Danae

Contents

List of Figures and Table xxi
Preface xxvii

1 Introduction 1
1.1 The Nature and Evolution of Macroeconomics 2
1.1.1 Pre-Keynesian Macroeconomics 2
1.1.2 Classical and Keynesian Macroeconomics 4
1.1.3 Microeconomic Foundations of Macroeconomics 6
1.1.4 Deterministic and Stochastic Dynamic General Equilibrium Models 7
1.2 Key Facts about Long-Run Economic Growth 11
1.2.1 Cross-Country Differences in Per Capita Output and Income 11
1.2.2 Evolution of Per Capita Output and Income over Time 13
1.2.3 Economic Growth and Convergence since 1820 14
1.3 Key Facts about Aggregate Fluctuations 18
1.3.1 Frequency, Severity, and Duration of Recessions 18
1.3.2 Unemployment in Booms and Recessions 20
1.3.3 Trends and Fluctuations in the Price Level and Inflation 22
1.3.4 Monetary Policy and Government Debt 26
1.3.5 Monetary Policy and Inflation in the Postwar Period 31
1.4 Conclusion 32

2 The Intertemporal Approach 33
2.1 Models, Variables, and Functions 34
2.2 General Equilibrium in a One-Period Competitive Model 36
2.2.1 Endowments, Preferences, and the Optimal Behavior of Households 36
2.2.2 The Production Function and the Profit-Maximizing Behavior of Firms 38
2.2.3 The Cobb-Douglas Production Function 40
2.2.4 General Equilibrium in the One-Period Model 40
2.3 Savings and Investment in a Two-Period Competitive Model 42
2.3.1 The Representative Household in a Two-Period Model 42
2.3.2 Implications of the Euler Equation for Consumption 45
2.3.3 The Case of a Constant Elasticity of Intertemporal Substitution 46
2.3.4 Firms, Technology, and the Optimal Output Path 48

2.3.5 General Equilibrium in the Two-Period Model 49
2.3.6 Diagrammatic Exposition of the Intertemporal Equilibrium 53
2.3.7 Implications for Growth and Business Cycle Theory 55
2.4 Consumption and Labor Supply in a One-Period Competitive Model 56
2.4.1 The Optimal Choice of Consumption and Labor Supply 56
2.4.2 Income and Substitution Effects on Labor Supply 58
2.4.3 The Frisch Elasticity of Labor Supply 60
2.4.4 The Production Function and the Optimal Decisions of Firms 61
2.4.5 General Equilibrium and the Determination of Output and Employment 61
2.5 Consumption and Labor Supply in a Two-Period Competitive Model 62
2.5.1 Optimal Consumption and Labor Supply in a Two-Period Model 63
2.5.2 Intertemporal Substitution in Consumption and Labor Supply 64
2.5.3 Optimal Production Decisions of Firms 65
2.5.4 General Equilibrium and the Determination of Output and Employment 66
2.5.5 Implications for Business Cycle Theory 68
2.6 Money, Prices, and Inflation in a Two-Period Competitive Model 69
2.6.1 The Representative Household and the Demand for Money 69
2.6.2 The Classical Dichotomy and the Neutrality of Money 71
2.6.3 The Two-Period Competitive Model and Classical Monetary Theory 74
2.7 Fiscal Policy in a Two-Period Competitive Model 74
2.7.1 Government Expenditure and Taxes in a One-Period Economy 74
2.7.2 Income Taxes and Labor Supply 76
2.7.3 Government Expenditure, Taxes, and Debt in a Two-Period Economy 77
2.7.4 Ricardian Equivalence between Tax and Debt Finance 78
2.7.5 Income Taxation and Aggregate Savings and Investment 81
2.7.6 Implications for Fiscal Policy and Government Debt 81
2.8 The Treatment of Time and the Intertemporal Approach 82
2.9 Conclusion 84

3 Savings, Investment, and Economic Growth 85
3.1 The Solow Growth Model 87
3.1.1 The Neoclassical Production Function 87
3.1.2 The Cobb-Douglas Production Function 89
3.1.3 Population Growth and Technical Progress 90
3.1.4 Savings, Capital Accumulation, and Economic Growth 90
3.1.5 The Balanced Growth Path and the Convergence Process 92
3.1.6 The Rate of Growth of Capital and Output 93
3.1.7 Significance of the Inada Conditions 95
3.2 Competitive Markets, the Real Interest Rate, and Real Wages 96
3.3 The Savings Rate and the Golden Rule 97
3.3.1 The Savings Rate and the Balanced Growth Path 98
3.3.2 The Savings Rate, the Golden Rule, and Dynamic Inefficiency 99
3.3.3 The Elasticity of Steady State Output with Respect to the Savings Rate 101

3.4 Total Factor Productivity and Population Growth 102
3.4.1 Dynamic Effects of Total Factor Productivity in the Solow Model 103
3.4.2 Dynamic Effects of Population Growth in the Solow Model 104
3.5 Speed of Convergence toward the Balanced Growth Path 104
3.6 The Process of Economic Growth and the Solow Model 106
3.6.1 The Kaldor Stylized Facts of Economic Growth 107
3.6.2 Differences in Per Capita Output and Income between Developed and Less Developed Economies 108
3.6.3 Conditional Convergence 110
3.7 Convergence with a Cobb-Douglas Production Function 110
3.8 Dynamic Simulations of a Calibrated Solow Model 111
3.8.1 The Solow Model in Discrete Time 112
3.8.2 The Calibrated Solow Model 113
3.8.3 Dynamic Simulations of the Model 114
3.9 Conclusion 117

4 The Representative Household Model of Optimal Growth 119
4.1 The Optimal Intertemporal Path of Consumption 121
4.2 The Ramsey Model of Economic Growth 124
4.2.1 The Production Function 124
4.2.2 The Utility Function of the Representative Household 125
4.2.3 The Accumulation of Capital and the Optimality of the Decentralized Competitive Equilibrium 126
4.2.4 Conditions for Utility Maximization by the Representative Household 128
4.2.5 The Euler Equation for Consumption 129
4.2.6 The Intertemporal Budget Constraint of the Representative Household 130
4.2.7 The Transversality Condition with an Infinite Time Horizon 132
4.2.8 The Consumption Function of the Representative Household with an Infinite Horizon 133
4.3 Dynamic Adjustment and the Balanced Growth Path 135
4.3.1 Dynamic Adjustment toward the Balanced Growth Path 135
4.3.2 The Balanced Growth Path and the Modified Golden Rule 138
4.3.3 Effects of a Permanent Increase in the Pure Rate of Time Preference 139
4.3.4 Effects of a Permanent Increase in Total Factor Productivity 141
4.3.5 Effects of a Permanent Increase in the Rate of Growth of Population 142
4.4 Properties of the Adjustment Path and the Speed of Convergence 143
4.5 Dynamic Simulations of a Calibrated Ramsey Model 146
4.5.1 The Ramsey Model in Discrete Time 146
4.5.2 The Calibrated Ramsey Model 148
4.5.3 Dynamic Simulations of the Model 149
4.6 Conclusion 152

5 Overlapping Generations Models of Growth 153
5.1 The Diamond Model 154
5.1.1 Definitions 155
5.1.2 The Production Function 155

5.1.3 The Intertemporal Utility Function of Households 155
5.1.4 Markets and the Behavior of Households 156
5.1.5 Capital Accumulation and the Dynamic Adjustment of the Economy 157
5.1.6 A Simplified Diamond Model with Logarithmic Preferences and Cobb-Douglas Technology 159
5.1.7 The Speed of Adjustment in the Simplified Diamond Model 163
5.1.8 Welfare Implications of the Diamond Model and the Possibility of Dynamic Inefficiency 164
5.1.9 Dynamic Simulations of a Calibrated Diamond Model 165
5.2 The Blanchard-Weil Model 169
5.2.1 Definitions 169
5.2.2 The Production Function 170
5.2.3 The Intertemporal Utility Function of Households and Household Consumption 170
5.2.4 Aggregation across Generations 172
5.2.5 The Model in Terms of Efficiency Units of Labor 173
5.2.6 The Balanced Growth Path and the Adjustment Path 173
5.3 Dynamic Simulations of a Calibrated Blanchard-Weil Model 177
5.3.1 The Blanchard-Weil Model in Discrete Time 178
5.3.2 Dynamic Simulations of the Model 178
5.4 Conclusion 182

6 Fiscal Policy and Economic Growth 183
6.1 The Government Budget Constraint 185
6.1.1 Government Deficits, Debt, and Solvency 185
6.2 Ricardian Equivalence and the Ramsey Model 187
6.2.1 Ricardian Equivalence between Government Debt and Taxes 187
6.2.2 Government Expenditure, Taxes, and Debt in the Ramsey Model 188
6.3 Dynamic Effects of Fiscal Policy in the Blanchard-Weil Model 191
6.3.1 The Blanchard-Weil Model with Government Expenditure and Debt 191
6.3.2 Government Debt, Taxes, and Redistribution across Generations 192
6.3.3 Dynamic Simulations of Fiscal Policy in a Calibrated Blanchard-Weil Model 194
6.4 Dynamic Effects of Distortionary Taxation 201
6.4.1 Distortionary and Nondistortionary Taxes 201
6.4.2 Dynamic Effects of Capital Income and Business Gross Profits Taxation 203
6.4.3 Dynamic Simulations of Increases in Capital Income and Business Gross Profits Taxation 205
6.5 Conclusion 206

7 Money, Inflation, and Economic Growth 209
7.1 Private Consumption and Money Demand in a Representative Household Model 211
7.1.1 Money in the Utility Function of Households 211
7.1.2 Nominal and Real Interest Rates and the Opportunity Cost of Real Money Balances 212

7.1.3 First-Order Conditions for an Optimum 212
7.1.4 The Money Demand Function 213
7.1.5 Growth Rate of the Money Supply and Inflation 214
7.1.6 The Euler Equation for Consumption 215
7.2 Aggregate Capital Accumulation in a Ramsey Model with Money 216
7.2.1 The Production Function, the Real Interest Rate, and the Real Wage 216
7.2.2 The Inflation Tax and the Accumulation of Capital 216
7.3 Effects of the Growth Rate of the Money Supply in the Ramsey Monetary Model 218
7.3.1 The Balanced Growth Path in the Ramsey Model with Money 219
7.3.2 The Superneutrality of Money and Inflation 220
7.3.3 The Welfare Costs of Inflation in a Ramsey Model 221
7.4 Effects of Monetary Growth in an OLG Model 222
7.4.1 The Blanchard-Weil Model with Money 223
7.4.2 Real Effects of the Growth Rate of the Money Supply 224
7.4.3 A Dynamic Simulation of the Effects of a Rise in the Growth Rate of the Money Supply in a Calibrated Blanchard-Weil Model 227
7.5 Conclusion 229

8 Externalities, Human Capital, and Technical Progress 231
8.1 Externalities from Capital Accumulation and Economic Growth 232
8.1.1 Definitions 233
8.1.2 The Production Function 233
8.1.3 Externalities from the Accumulation of Capital 234
8.1.4 Determination of the Real Interest Rate and the Real Wage 237
8.1.5 The Savings Rate and the Endogenous Growth Rate 238
8.1.6 Externalities and Endogenous Growth in the Ramsey Model 239
8.1.7 The Suboptimality of the Competitive Equilibrium with Externalities Due to Capital Accumulation 241
8.1.8 Externalities and Endogenous Growth in the Blanchard-Weil Model 242
8.1.9 Fiscal Policy and Endogenous Growth 245
8.1.10 Convergence in Exogenous and Endogenous AK Growth Models 247
8.2 Investment in Human Capital and Economic Growth 248
8.2.1 The Extended Solow Model and the Share of Spending on Education and Training 249
8.2.2 The Balanced Growth Path in the Extended Solow Model 250
8.2.3 Endogenous Growth in the Extended Solow Model 251
8.2.4 The Jones Model of Human Capital Accumulation 252
8.2.5 The Lucas Model of Human Capital Accumulation and Endogenous Growth 253
8.2.6 A Detailed Analysis of the Lucas Model 254
8.3 Ideas, Innovations, and Technical Progress 258
8.3.1 Key Features of Ideas and Innovations 258
8.3.2 Key Elements of an Ideas-and-Innovations Growth Model 259
8.3.3 Endogenous Determination of the Rate of Technical Progress 261
8.3.4 The Balanced Growth Path with Endogenous Technical Progress 261
8.4 Unified Growth Theory and the Transition from Stagnation to Growth 262

8.5 Institutions and Long-Run Growth 263
8.6 The New Stylized Facts of Economic Growth 265
8.7 Conclusion 266

9 Dynamic Stochastic Models under Rational Expectations 269
9.1 A Stochastic Expectational Model of a Competitive Market 271
9.1.1 Absence of Uncertainty and Perfect Foresight 272
9.1.2 Uncertainty and Adaptive Expectations 273
9.1.3 The Rational Expectations Hypothesis 275
9.2 Rational Expectations for Linear Autoregressive Processes 277
9.3 First-Order Linear Expectational Models 279
9.3.1 The Method of Repeated Substitutions 279
9.3.2 The Method of Factorization 281
9.3.3 The Method of Undetermined Coefficients 282
9.3.4 Two Additional Economic Examples 282
9.3.5 Alternative Assumptions about the Evolution of Exogenous Variables 284
9.3.6 The Expectational Competitive Market Model Revisited 286
9.4 Second-Order Linear Expectational Models 286
9.4.1 The Method of Factorization 287
9.4.2 The Method of Undetermined Coefficients 288
9.4.3 An Economic Example of a Second-Order System 290
9.5 Multivariate Linear Models with Rational Expectations 291
9.5.1 The Blanchard-Kahn Method 291
9.5.2 Other Solution Methods 293
9.5.3 A Second-Order Example of the Blanchard-Kahn Method 293
9.6 Rational Expectations and Learning 295
9.7 Conclusion 295

10 Consumption and Portfolio Choice under Uncertainty 297
10.1 Consumption and Portfolio Choice 298
10.1.1 The Random Walk Model of Consumption 301
10.1.2 The Consumption Capital Asset Pricing Model 302
10.2 Full Analysis of Consumption and Portfolio Choice 303
10.2.1 The Case of Logarithmic Preferences 303
10.2.2 Quadratic Preferences and Certainty Equivalence 305
10.2.3 The Permanent-Income Hypothesis with Quadratic Preferences 306
10.2.4 The Consumption CAPM with Quadratic Preferences 307
10.2.5 The Efficient Markets Hypothesis 308
10.3 Precautionary Savings and Borrowing Constraints 310
10.4 Conclusion 311

11 Investment and the Cost of Capital 313
11.1 Optimal Investment with Convex Adjustment Costs 315
11.1.1 The Choice of Optimal Investment 315
11.1.2 The Case of Zero Adjustment Costs 317

11.1.3 The Investment Function with Convex Adjustment Costs 317
11.1.4 The Determinants of q 317
11.1.5 Dynamic Adjustment of q and the Capital Stock K 318
11.2 Optimal Investment under Uncertainty 320
11.2.1 The Value of a Firm under Uncertainty 321
11.2.2 The Lucas-Prescott Model of Investment under Uncertainty 323
11.2.3 Rational Expectations Equilibrium and Aggregate Investment in the Lucas-Prescott Model 325
11.3 Conclusion 327

12 Money, Interest, and Prices 329
12.1 The Functions of Money 331
12.2 The Supply of Money and Central Banks 332
12.2.1 Central Banks and Their Functions 332
12.2.2 Central Banks and the Money Supply 333
12.3 The Demand for Money 336
12.4 Nominal Interest Rates and Short-Run Equilibrium in the Money Market 339
12.5 The Long-Run Neutrality of Money 343
12.5.1 Monetary Growth, Inflation, and Nominal Interest Rates in the Long Run 345
12.5.2 The Welfare Cost of Inflation 346
12.5.3 The Long-Run Neutrality of Money and Monetary Reforms 346
12.6 Money and the Price Level in Dynamic General Equilibrium Models 347
12.6.1 The Samuelson OLG Model 347
12.6.2 Money in the Utility Function of a Representative Household 351
12.6.3 Cash in Advance in a Representative Household Model 353
12.6.4 Cash in Advance in an OLG Model 355
12.7 Nominal and Real Interest Rates and the Money Supply 357
12.7.1 Money in the Utility Function of a Representative Household 357
12.7.2 Cash in Advance in a Representative Household Model 359
12.7.3 Cash in Advance in an OLG Model 359
12.7.4 The Liquidity Effect in Representative Household Models 360
12.8 Interest Rate Pegging and Price Level Indeterminacy 361
12.8.1 Interest Rate Pegging and Price Level Indeterminacy in Representative Household Models 361
12.8.2 The Wicksell Solution to the Problem of Price Level Indeterminacy 362
12.8.3 The Fiscal Theory of the Price Level 363
12.8.4 The Pigou Effect and Price Level Determinacy in OLG Models 364
12.9 Money Growth, Seigniorage, and Inflation 364
12.9.1 Relations between Monetary Growth, Seigniorage, and Inflation 365
12.9.2 The Seigniorage Laffer Curve 367
12.9.3 The Demand for Seigniorage and Equilibrium with High Inflation 368
12.9.4 The Transition to Hyperinflation 368
12.9.5 How Can High Inflation and Hyperinflation Be Tackled? 371
12.10 Conclusion 372

13 The Stochastic Growth Model of Aggregate Fluctuations 375
13.1 The Stochastic Growth Model 376
13.1.1 Extending the Ramsey Model to Account for Aggregate Fluctuations 377
13.1.2 The Representative Firm 377
13.1.3 The Representative Household 378
13.1.4 Exogenous Population Growth, Efficiency of Labor, and Government Expenditure 378
13.1.5 Labor Supply of the Representative Household 380
13.1.6 Intertemporal Substitution in Labor Supply 381
13.1.7 Uncertainty and the Behavior of the Representative Household 382
13.2 A Simplified Version of the Stochastic Growth Model 383
13.2.1 Fluctuations of Output in the Simplified Stochastic Growth Model 384
13.2.2 The Simplified Stochastic Growth Model and the Evidence on Aggregate Fluctuations 385
13.3 A Log-Linear Approximation to the General Stochastic Growth Model 386
13.3.1 The Steady State 387
13.3.2 Log-Linearizing the Model around the Steady State 388
13.4 Solving the Log-Linear Stochastic Growth Model 390
13.4.1 Aggregate Fluctuations around the Steady State 391
13.4.2 A Dynamic Simulation of the Log-Linear Stochastic Growth Model 391
13.5 Conclusion 393

14 Perfectly Competitive Models with Flexible Prices 395
14.1 A Perfectly Competitive Model without Capital 396
14.1.1 The Representative Household 396
14.1.2 The Representative Firm 397
14.1.3 General Equilibrium 398
14.2 Monetary Factors in a Perfectly Competitive Model 400
14.2.1 An Exogenous Path for the Money Supply 400
14.2.2 An Exogenous Path for the Nominal Interest Rate 401
14.2.3 An Inflation-Based Nominal Interest Rate Rule 401
14.2.4 Optimal Monetary Policy 402
14.3 Imperfect Information and the Nonneutrality of Money 403
14.3.1 Competitive Equilibrium under Imperfect Information about the Price Level 403
14.3.2 The Determination of Output and Employment 406
14.3.3 The Real Effects of Monetary Shocks in a Rational Expectations Equilibrium 407
14.3.4 Optimal Monetary Policy in the Lucas Model 410
14.3.5 The New Classical Model and the Great Depression 410
14.3.6 Models of Informational Frictions and Rational Inattention 411
14.4 Conclusion 411

15 **Keynesian Models and the Phillips Curve 413**
15.1 The Original Keynesian Models 415
15.1.1 The Keynesian Cross 416
15.1.2 The IS-LM Model 419
15.1.3 The AD-AS Model 422
15.1.4 The Impact of Aggregate Demand Policies 424
15.2 The Samuelson Multiplier Accelerator Model 427
15.3 The Theory of Discretionary Monetary and Fiscal Policy 429
15.3.1 The Tinbergen-Theil Theory of Discretionary Aggregate Demand Policies 431
15.3.2 Monetary and Fiscal Policy with a Full Employment Target 431
15.3.3 Monetary and Fiscal Policy with a Full Employment Target and a Price Level Target 432
15.4 The Phillips Curve and Inflationary Expectations 435
15.4.1 The Phillips Curve and the Trade-off between Inflation and Unemployment 435
15.4.2 Instability of the Phillips Curve and Inflationary Expectations 437
15.5 The Natural Rate of Unemployment and Aggregate Demand Policies 439
15.5.1 The Path of Inflation and Unemployment under Adaptive Expectations 440
15.5.2 Rules versus Discretion in Aggregate Demand Policy 444
15.5.3 Inflation and Unemployment under Rational Expectations 446
15.6 Conclusion 447

16 **A Model of Imperfect Competition and Staggered Pricing 449**
16.1 An Imperfectly Competitive Model of Aggregate Fluctuations 451
16.1.1 The Representative Household 452
16.1.2 The Representative Firm and Optimal Pricing 454
16.1.3 Full Price Flexibility and the Natural Rate 455
16.1.4 Inefficiency of the Natural Rate 456
16.2 Staggered Price Adjustment and Aggregate Fluctuations 457
16.2.1 Optimal Pricing with Staggered Price Adjustment 459
16.2.2 Equilibrium in the Market for Goods and Services and the New Keynesian IS curve 461
16.2.3 Labor Market Equilibrium and the New Keynesian Phillips Curve 462
16.2.4 The Imperfectly Competitive Model with Staggered Pricing and the Taylor Rule 463
16.2.5 Real and Monetary Shocks and Aggregate Fluctuations 464
16.2.6 The Divine Coincidence and Optimal Monetary Policy in the New Keynesian Model with Staggered Pricing 468
16.2.7 A Dynamic Simulation of the Model 469
16.3 The Rotemberg Model of Convex Costs of Price Adjustment 470
16.4 Conclusion 473

17 **A Model of Unemployment and Nominal Wage Contracts 475**
17.1 Alternative Views of the Labor Market and Equilibrium Unemployment 477
17.2 Households and Optimal Consumption and Money Demand 478

17.3 Firms and Optimal Pricing and Production 481
17.4 Wage Setting and Employment in a Model with Insiders and Outsiders 483
17.4.1 Wage Determination, Unemployment Persistence, and the Phillips Curve 485
17.4.2 The Relation between Output and Unemployment Persistence 487
17.4.3 The Phillips Curve in Terms of Deviations of Output from Its Natural Rate 488
17.5 The Implications of Staggered Pricing 489
17.5.1 Optimal Pricing with Staggered Price Adjustment 490
17.5.2 Inflation and Unit Labor Costs under Staggered Pricing 491
17.6 An Extended New Keynesian Phillips Curve: Combining Staggered Pricing with Periodic Nominal Wage Contracts 492
17.7 Inflation and Aggregate Fluctuations under a Taylor Rule 494
17.7.1 New Neoclassical Synthesis IS-LM Functions 494
17.7.2 The Natural and Equilibrium Real Interest Rate 494
17.7.3 Equilibrium Fluctuations with Exogenous Preference and Productivity Shocks 495
17.7.4 Does Staggered Pricing Matter for Inflation Persistence? 500
17.7.5 Inflation Stabilization and the Divine Coincidence 501
17.8 The Optimal Taylor Rule 502
17.8.1 Optimal Inflation Policy 502
17.9 A Dynamic Simulation of the Effects of Monetary and Real Shocks 504
17.10 Conclusion 506

18 Matching Frictions and Equilibrium Unemployment 509
18.1 The Matching Function 510
18.1.1 The Probability of Filling a Vacancy and Labor Market Tightness 511
18.1.2 The Probability of the Unemployed Finding a Job 511
18.2 Flows into and out of Employment, Equilibrium Unemployment, and the Beveridge Curve 512
18.3 Firms and the Creation of Vacancies 513
18.3.1 The Present Value of Net Expected Profits from an Existing Job 514
18.3.2 The Present Value of Net Expected Profits from a Vacancy and the Creation of Vacancies 515
18.3.3 Free Entry and the Job Creation Condition 516
18.4 The Behavior of Unemployed Job Seekers 517
18.4.1 The Permanent Income of an Unemployed Job Seeker 518
18.4.2 The Permanent Income of an Employed Worker 518
18.4.3 Comparing the Permanent Income of the Employed and the Unemployed 518
18.5 Wage Bargaining and the Wage Equation 519
18.6 Wage Determination and Equilibrium Unemployment 521
18.7 Determinants of Equilibrium Unemployment, Real Wages, and Labor Market Tightness 523
18.7.1 An Increase in Labor Productivity 523
18.7.2 An Increase in Unemployment Benefits 525

18.7.3 An Increase in the Real Interest Rate 527
18.7.4 An Increase in the Probability of Job Destruction 527
18.8 Dynamic Adjustment to the Steady State 527
18.8.1 The Dynamic Adjustment of Unemployment and Vacancies 530
18.8.2 Numerical Simulations of the Model 532
18.9 Matching Models and Nominal Rigidities 534
18.10 Conclusion 535

19 The Macroeconomic Implications of Financial Frictions 539
19.1 The Role of Finance and Financial Markets 539
19.1.1 Financial Frictions and Financial Intermediation 541
19.1.2 The Risks of Financial Intermediation, Leverage, and the External Finance Premium 542
19.1.3 The Links between the Financial Sector and Real Activity in the Presence of Frictions 543
19.2 Financial Frictions in a New Keynesian Model with Staggered Pricing 544
19.3 Financial Frictions in a Model with Unemployment Persistence and Nominal Wage Contracts 546
19.4 Conclusion 548

20 The Role of Monetary Policy 551
20.1 Rules versus Discretion in Monetary Policy 552
20.2 Rules, Discretion, and Credibility in a New Keynesian Model 554
20.2.1 The Social Welfare Loss from Inflation and Unemployment 555
20.2.2 Monetary Policy under Discretion: The Problem of Credibility 556
20.2.3 Monetary Policy under a Fixed Inflation Rule 559
20.2.4 Central Bank Constitutions 559
20.2.5 Reputation as a Solution to the Problem of Inflationary Bias 560
20.3 Optimal Monetary Policy in the Presence of Stochastic Shocks 562
20.4 The Mechanics of Monetary Policy 564
20.4.1 Financial Markets and Open Market Operations 565
20.4.2 The Term Structure of Interest Rates 566
20.5 Optimal Monetary Policy and the Taylor Rule 567
20.6 Monetary Policy Shocks and the Optimal Policy Rule 569
20.7 Monetary Policy, Financial Frictions, and the Zero Lower Bound on Interest Rates 571
20.7.1 The Liquidity Trap 572
20.7.2 Monetary Policy at the Zero Lower Bound 573
20.7.3 The Zero Lower Bound and Unconventional Monetary Policy 574
20.8 Conclusion 576

21 Fiscal Policy and Government Debt 579
21.1 Tax Smoothing and Government Debt Accumulation 581
21.1.1 The Barro Tax-Smoothing Model 581
21.1.2 Steady State Implications of Tax Smoothing 583
21.2 Keynesian Stabilization Policy, Automatic Stabilizers, and Fiscal Implications of the Zero Lower Bound 585

21.3 Optimal Dynamic Ramsey Taxation 586
21.4 Fiscal Policy and Politics 589
21.4.1 Distributional Considerations and Politics 589
21.4.2 Electoral Factors and Partisan Differences 590
21.5 The Burden of High Government Deficits and Debt 592
21.6 A Model of Government Debt Crises 593
21.6.1 The Calvo Model 593
21.6.2 Multiple Equilibria and Self-Fulfilling Prophecies 598
21.7 Conclusion 600

22 Bubbles, Multiple Equilibria, and Sunspots 601
22.1 Bubbles in Linear Rational Expectations Models 602
22.1.1 Bubbles versus Fundamentals 603
22.1.2 Deterministic versus Stochastic Bubbles 604
22.1.3 Bubbles as Self-Fulfilling Prophecies in Inherently Unstable Models 605
22.1.4 Higher-Order Linear Models 607
22.2 Bubbles in Models of Stock and Money Markets 607
22.2.1 Stock Market Bubbles 607
22.2.2 Money Market Bubbles, the Price Level, and Inflation 609
22.3 Ruling Out Unstable Bubbles 611
22.4 Indeterminacy, Self-Fulfilling Prophecies, and Sunspots 612
22.4.1 The Samuelson OLG Model with Money, Revisited 614
22.4.2 Other Models of Indeterminacy and Sunspots in Macroeconomics 619
22.5 Conclusion 620

23 The Interaction of Events and Ideas in Dynamic Macroeconomics 623
23.1 The Financial Crisis and Recent Developments in Dynamic Macroeconomics 624
23.2 The Interaction of Events and Ideas and the Role of Empirical Macroeconomics 626
23.3 Policy Evaluation and DSGE Models 628
23.4 Conclusion 629

Appendixes 631

A Variables, Functions, and Optimization 633
A.1 Models, Variables, and Functions 633
A.1.1 Functions 634
A.1.2 Derivatives and Partial Derivatives of Functions 635
A.1.3 Maxima and Minima of Functions 642
A.2 Mathematical Optimization under Constraints 644
A.2.1 Constrained Optimization in the Case of a Function of One Variable 644
A.2.2 Optimal Consumption under an Income Constraint 645
A.2.3 The Lagrange Method 647
A.3 Some Useful Functional Forms 651
A.3.1 The Two-Factor CES Production Function and the Elasticity of Substitution 652

A.3.2 Special Cases of the CES Production Function 653
A.3.3 The CES Production Function and the Solow Model of Economic Growth 653
A.3.4 The CES Utility Function 655
A.3.5 Additively Separable Utility and the CEIS Utility Function 655

B Linear Models and Linear Algebra 659
B.1 Linear Models 659
B.2 Elements of Linear Algebra 660
B.2.1 Matrix Addition, Subtraction, and Multiplication 661
B.2.2 The Inverse of a Square Matrix 661
B.3 An Example with Two Endogenous Variables 663
B.3.1 Cramer's Rule 664
B.3.2 The Augmented Matrix and Gauss-Jordan Elimination 664
B.3.3 Diagonalization, Eigenvalues, and Eigenvectors 665
B.3.4 Solving a System with Two Endogenous and Two Exogenous Variables 665

C Ordinary Differential Equations 667
C.1 Definitions 667
C.2 First-Order Linear Differential Equations 669
C.2.1 Constant Coefficients 669
C.2.2 Variable Right-Hand Side 670
C.2.3 Variable Coefficients 671
C.2.4 Homogeneous and Nonhomogeneous Differential Equations 671
C.2.5 Convergence and Stability of First-Order Differential Equations 672
C.3 Second-Order Linear Differential Equations 673
C.3.1 Homogeneous Equations with Constant Coefficients 673
C.3.2 Nonhomogeneous Equations with Constant Coefficients 674
C.4 A Pair of First-Order Linear Differential Equations 675
C.4.1 The Method of Substitution 675
C.4.2 The Method of Eigenvalues 676
C.5 A System of *n* First-Order Linear Differential Equations 678
C.5.1 Eigenvalues and Eigenvectors 679
C.5.2 Solving the *n*th-Order System of Linear Differential Equations 679

D Difference Equations 683
D.1 Lag Operators and Difference Equations 683
D.2 First-Order Linear Difference Equations 686
D.3 Second-Order Linear Difference Equations 687
D.4 A Pair of First-Order Linear Difference Equations 689
D.5 A System of *n* First-Order Linear Difference Equations 690

E Methods of Intertemporal Optimization 693
E.1 The Form of Dynamic Optimization Problems 693
E.2 The Method of Optimal Control 694
E.3 The Optimal Control Method in Continuous Time 696

E.4 Dynamic Programming and the Bellman Equation 697
E.5 An Example Based on Optimal Savings in Continuous Time 700

F Random Variables and Stochastic Processes 703
F.1 Probability 703
F.2 Random Variables and Probability Distributions 704
F.2.1 Discrete Probability Distributions 704
F.2.2 Continuous Probability Distributions 705
F.2.3 Mathematical Expectation, Variance, and Higher Moments 706
F.2.4 Some Useful Probability Distributions 707
F.2.5 Convergence of Random Variables 712
F.2.6 The Law of Large Numbers 713
F.2.7 The Central Limit Theorem 714
F.2.8 Joint Probability Distributions 714
F.3 Stochastic Processes 715
F.4 Univariate Linear Stochastic Processes in Discrete Time 716
F.4.1 The White Noise Process 717
F.4.2 Moving Average Stochastic Processes 717
F.4.3 Autoregressive Stochastic Processes 718
F.4.4 Autoregressive Moving Average Stochastic Processes 720
F.5 Vector Stochastic Processes and Vector Autoregressions 720

References 723
Index 743

List of Figures and Table

Figures

1.1 Distribution of countries by per capita GNI, 2012 12
1.2 Long-run growth of (natural log) per capita GDP in the United Kingdom, the United States, and Japan 16
1.3 Long-run growth of (log) per capita GDP in the major European economies 17
1.4 Recessions (shaded areas) and (log) per capita GDP in the United States 19
1.5 Recessions (shaded areas) and (log) per capita GDP in the United Kingdom 20
1.6 Recessions (shaded areas) and the unemployment rate in the United States 21
1.7 Recessions (shaded areas) and the unemployment rate in the United Kingdom 22
1.8 Evolution of the price level in the United States 23
1.9 Evolution of the price level in the United Kingdom 24
1.10 Evolution of consumer price index (CPI) inflation in the United States 25
1.11 Evolution of CPI inflation in the United Kingdom 26
1.12 Money growth and inflation in 110 countries, 1960–1990 27
1.13 Money growth and real GDP growth in 110 countries, 1960–1990 28
1.14 Evolution of US federal debt as a percentage of GDP 29
1.15 Evolution of UK public debt as a percentage of GDP 30
2.1 Equilibrium capital accumulation in a two-period economy 51
2.2 Intertemporal equilibrium in a two-period economy 53
2.3 Optimal consumption and leisure in a one-period economy 58
2.4 Income and substitution effects on labor supply 59
3.1 The production function in intensive form 89
3.2 Equilibrium in the Solow model 93
3.3 Determination of the growth rate 94
3.4 Implications of a rise in the savings rate 98
3.5 Impulse response function of a rise in the savings rate 99
3.6 Implications of a rise in total factor productivity 103
3.7 Implications of a rise in population growth 104
3.8 Convergence in the Solow model in discrete time 113
3.9 Impulse response functions of the Solow model following a permanent increase in the savings rate of 1% 115

3.10 Impulse response functions of the Solow model following a permanent increase in total factor productivity of 1% 116
3.11 Impulse response functions of the Solow model following a permanent increase in the rate of population growth of 1% 117
4.1 The balanced growth path and dynamic adjustment in the Ramsey model 136
4.2 Short- and long-run effects of a permanent increase in the pure rate of time preference 140
4.3 Impulse response function of consumption and capital stock following a permanent increase at t_0 in the pure rate of time preference 141
4.4 Short- and long-run effects of a permanent increase in total factor productivity 142
4.5 Effects of a permanent increase in the population growth rate 143
4.6 Impulse response functions of the calibrated Ramsey model for a 1% permanent drop in the pure rate of time preference 150
4.7 Impulse response functions of the calibrated Ramsey model for a 1% permanent increase in total factor productivity 151
5.1 Multiple equilibria in the Diamond model 158
5.2 Unique balanced growth path in the simplified Diamond model 160
5.3 Effects of a permanent rise in the pure rate of time preference 161
5.4 Effects of a permanent rise in total factor productivity 162
5.5 Impulse response functions of the Diamond model for a permanent rise in the pure rate of time preference of 1% 167
5.6 Impulse response functions of the Diamond model, for a permanent rise in total factor productivity of 1% 168
5.7 The balanced growth path and the adjustment path for the Blanchard-Weil model 174
5.8 Short- and long-run effects of an increase in the pure rate of time preference in the Blanchard-Weil model 176
5.9 Short- and long-run effects of an increase in the rate of population growth in the Blanchard-Weil model 177
5.10 Impulse response functions for a 1% increase in the pure rate of time preference in the calibrated Blanchard-Weil model 179
5.11 Impulse response functions for a 1% increase in the population growth rate in the calibrated Blanchard-Weil model 180
5.12 Impulse response functions for a 1% increase in total factor productivity in the calibrated Blanchard-Weil model 181
6.1 Primary government expenditure in the Ramsey model 190
6.2 Primary government expenditure and debt in the Blanchard-Weil model 192
6.3 An increase in government debt in the Blanchard-Weil model 193
6.4 An increase in primary government expenditure in the Blanchard-Weil model 194
6.5 A tax-financed increase of primary government expenditure in the calibrated Blanchard-Weil model 197
6.6 A debt-financed increase of primary government expenditure in the calibrated Blanchard-Weil model 198
6.7 A debt-financed tax cut in the calibrated Blanchard-Weil model 199
6.8 Short- and long-run effects of capital income taxation in the Ramsey model 203
6.9 Dynamic effects of a 10% tax on interest income in the calibrated Ramsey model 204

6.10 Dynamic effects of a 10% tax on business profits, before interest and depreciation, in the calibrated Ramsey model 205
7.1 The demand for real money balances and the welfare cost of inflation 222
7.2 The balanced growth path and the adjustment path in the Blanchard-Weil model with money 225
7.3 Dynamic effects of an increase in the growth rate of money supply in the Blanchard-Weil model with money 226
7.4 Dynamic simulation of an increase in the growth rate of money supply in a calibrated Blanchard-Weil model with money 228
8.1 The aggregate production function for different values of β 235
8.2 Determination of the consumption-to-output ratio and the endogenous growth rate in the Blanchard-Weil model 244
8.3 Determination of private consumption and the growth rate with government expenditure and debt 246
8.4 The path of per capita output in exogenous and endogenous growth models 248
9.1 The cobweb model under adaptive expectations 274
11.1 Adjustment cost of investment 316
11.2 Determination of q and the capital stock K 319
11.3 Dynamic effects of a permanent rise in the real interest rate 320
11.4 Dynamic effects of a permanent rise in total factor productivity 321
12.1 The demand for money and the nominal interest rate 337
12.2 An increase in real income and the demand for money 338
12.3 Short-run equilibrium in the money market 339
12.4 The short-run effects of a rise in the money supply: the liquidity effect 340
12.5 The short-run effects of an exogenous rise in real income 341
12.6 Equilibrium in the money market with interest rate pegging 342
12.7 Money demand indeterminacy in the Samuelson OLG model 350
12.8 The seigniorage Laffer curve 367
12.9 Equilibrium with high inflation 369
12.10 Equilibria with high inflation and the transition to hyperinflation 372
13.1 Dynamic simulation of the stochastic growth model following a 1% persistent shock to productivity 392
15.1 Exogenous investment and government expenditure: the Keynesian cross 418
15.2 Aggregate output and the nominal interest rate: the IS-LM model 420
15.3 Aggregate output and the price level: the AD-AS model 423
15.4 Aggregate demand disturbances and their effects on aggregate output and the price level 425
15.5 Aggregate supply disturbances and their effects on aggregate output and the price level 426
15.6 Convergence of real output for different values of the accelerator 430
15.7 The Phillips curve 436
15.8 The Phillips curve and the socially optimal combination of inflation and unemployment 437
15.9 Shifts of the Phillips curve due to inflationary expectations 438
15.10 Continuous shifts of the Phillips curve due to rising inflationary expectations 442

15.11 Determination of steady state inflation and unemployment under discretion and commitment to an inflation rule 445
16.1 Impulse response functions of the staggered pricing model following a contractionary monetary shock 470
16.2 Impulse response functions of the staggered pricing model following a positive productivity shock 471
17.1 Impulse response functions following a 1% unanticipated temporary positive shock to the nominal interest rate 505
17.2 Impulse response functions following a 1% unanticipated persistent positive shock to productivity 506
18.1 The Beveridge curve and equilibrium unemployment 514
18.2 The job creation condition 517
18.3 The determination of real wages and labor market tightness 522
18.4 Labor productivity and equilibrium unemployment 524
18.5 Unemployment benefits and equilibrium unemployment 526
18.6 The real interest rate and equilibrium unemployment 528
18.7 The probability of job destruction and equilibrium unemployment 529
18.8 Dynamic adjustment of unemployment and vacancies 531
18.9 Dynamic adjustment of unemployment and vacancies to an increase in the job destruction rate 533
18.10 Dynamic adjustment of unemployment and vacancies to an increase in the replacement rate 534
18.11 Dynamic adjustment of unemployment and vacancies to an increase in the real interest rate 534
20.1 Inflation and lack of credibility under a discretionary policy 557
20.2 The liquidity trap 572
21.1 Expected default and the debt holding condition 595
21.2 The actual probability of default and the cumulative distribution of the primary surplus 596
21.3 Determination of the interest factor and the probability of default for a low rate of return of the safe asset 597
21.4 Determination of the interest factor and the probability of default for a high rate of return of the safe asset 599
22.1 Deterministic bubbles 604
22.2 A stochastically bursting bubble versus a deterministic bubble 606
22.3 Equilibrium consumption in the Samuelson OLG model 616
22.4 Saddle point equilibrium money balances in the Samuelson OLG model 618
22.5 Multiple convergence paths for money balances in the Samuelson OLG model 619
22.6 Multiple equilibria, sunspots, and cycles in the Samuelson OLG model 620
A.1 Utility as a function of consumption 636
A.2 Output as a function of capital and labor 637
A.3 Isoquants: capital labor combinations that produce given amounts of output 638
A.4 Output as a function of the capital stock, for a given level of employment of labor 639
A.5 Utility and marginal utility: the derivative of the utility function 640
A.6 Stationary points: maxima, minima, and points of inflection 643
A.7 Maximization with a binding and a nonbinding constraint 646
A.8 Maximization of consumer utility subject to an income constraint 647

A.9 Optimal choice of a consumption bundle 651
F.1 The uniform distribution 709
F.2 The CDF of the continuous uniform distribution 710
F.3 The normal distribution 711
F.4 The CDF of the standard normal distribution 712

Table

1.1 Per capita GDP and average annual growth rates over time, various countries 15

Preface

Macroeconomics deals with the structure, behavior and performance of economies in their entirety. It concentrates on aggregate variables, such as output and income (gross domestic product), unemployment rates, price indices, and inflation. It studies the structure and interrelations among economy-wide markets for output, labor, capital, and financial instruments and their implications for aggregate economic performance.

Macroeconomics mainly focuses on the determinants of long-run economic growth in living standards and the causes and implications of short-term fluctuations in economic aggregates.

This book is an advanced treatment of modern macroeconomics using a sequence of dynamic general equilibrium models, which are based on intertemporal optimization on the part of economic agents, such as households, firms, and the government. The book also analyzes and discusses the role of monetary and fiscal policy in the context of such dynamic models.

The intertemporal approach, based on the use of dynamic general equilibrium models, is currently the dominant approach to macroeconomics. This approach is adopted in this text. The book is addressed to advanced undergraduate as well as first-year graduate students of economics. It is also suitable for trained economists who wish to deepen and broaden their grasp of dynamic macroeconomics. It highlights the potential but also some limitations of the modern intertemporal approach.

Chapter 1 serves as an introduction and overview, providing a brief survey of the evolution of macroeconomics, as well as presenting the key facts about long-run economic growth and aggregate fluctuations. Accounting for these key facts is the main objective of the dynamic macroeconomic models that are analyzed in the rest of the book.

Chapter 2 introduces the main elements of the intertemporal approach to macroeconomics by means of two-period competitive general equilibrium models. Two-period models are the simplest possible intertemporal models. They help highlight both the strengths and the weaknesses of modern intertemporal macroeconomics without the need for advanced mathematical methods.

These two-period models are used to address issues such as savings and capital accumulation, intertemporal substitution in consumption and labor supply, the distinction between real and nominal variables, the classical dichotomy and the neutrality of money, monetary growth and inflation, Ricardian equivalence between debt and tax finance of public expenditure, and the effects of distortionary taxation. These are themes that recur again and again in macroeconomics. The two-period models of chapter 2 thus set the stage for the more advanced infinite-horizon dynamic and dynamic stochastic models that are the workhorses of modern theories of economic growth and aggregate fluctuations.

The remainder of the book is divided into 21 chapters, presenting models of economic growth, aggregate fluctuations, and monetary and fiscal policy.

The process of long-run economic growth is analyzed in chapters 3–8.

Chapter 3 introduces and discusses the basic neoclassical model of savings, investment, and economic growth. This model was developed by Solow [1956] and Swan [1956]. It is based on a neoclassical production function and an exogenous savings and investment rate. The model highlights the role of physical capital accumulation, technical progress, and population growth for the process of economic growth.

Chapter 4 presents and analyzes the model of the representative household. In this model, which was first put forward by Ramsey [1928] and later developed by Cass [1965] and Koopmans [1965], savings and investment are chosen optimally by a representative household with an infinite time horizon. The household is assumed to be able to borrow and lend freely in competitive capital markets.

Overlapping generations models of growth are presented in chapter 5. These are models in which different generations of households coexist. Younger households enter the economy with human capital as their only asset, because no intergenerational transfers of capital or financial assets take place. Overlapping generations models were first developed by Allais [1947], Samuelson [1958], and Diamond [1965], and later by Blanchard [1985] and Weil [1989].

Chapter 6 discusses models that highlight the intertemporal effects of fiscal policy, focusing on the effects of government consumption and the ways it is financed, such as through taxation and government debt.

Chapter 7 discusses models that focus on the intertemporal effects of the money supply and monetary growth. Monetary models help determine the evolution not only of real variables but also of nominal variables, expressed in money terms, such as the price level, nominal wages, inflation, and nominal interest rates.

More general growth models based on externalities, human capital accumulation, and endogenous technical change are discussed in chapter 8.

Chapters 9–12 introduce decision making under uncertainty in the context of dynamic stochastic models. These chapters highlight the role of expectations in macroeconomics. Chapter 9 introduces dynamic stochastic models under rational expectations, while chapters 10 and 11 focus on models of the microeconomic foundations of consumption under uncertainty and investment and the cost of capital. Chapter 12 is an extended treatment of the role of money, alternative general equilibrium models with money, and the relation between the need for seigniorage and inflation.

Chapters 13–19 present and analyze alternative dynamic stochastic general equilibrium models of aggregate fluctuations. Such models are the basis of the new neoclassical synthesis, which is the dominant modern approach to the study of aggregate fluctuations.

Chapter 13 presents the stochastic growth model of aggregate fluctuations, and chapter 14 analyzes perfectly competitive models without capital. These are benchmark new classical models, based on competitive markets and perfectly flexible wages and prices.

Chapter 15 introduces and discusses the basic Keynesian model and the Phillips curve. Two new Keynesian dynamic stochastic models of aggregate fluctuations are then presented. Keynesian models assume distortions in the adjustment of wages and prices. Chapter 16 presents an imperfectly competitive model with staggered pricing; chapter 17 introduces an alternative new Keynesian model with periodic wage setting by labor market insiders. Chapter 18 focuses on labor market frictions and analyzes a matching model of the determination of the so-called natural rate of unemployment. Chapter 19 focuses on financial frictions and their macroeconomic implications.

Chapters 20 and 21 delve deeper into the roles of monetary and fiscal policy. The role and effectiveness of monetary policy is analyzed in chapter 20, whereas fiscal policy and the determination and implications of government debt are analyzed in chapter 21.

Chapter 22 focuses on dynamic stochastic models with bubbles, multiple macroeconomic equilibria, self-fulfilling prophecies, and sunspots. Such models allow for a different view of aggregate fluctuations than the standard dynamic stochastic general equilibrium models of the new neoclassical synthesis examined in chapters 13–19, which are usually based on a unique equilibrium.

Finally, chapter 23 discusses the current state of macroeconomics, highlighting the role of theoretical models and their interactions with empirical macroeonomics. It also discusses the impact of the financial crisis and the Great Recession of 2008–2009. The incorporation of labor market and financial frictions into dynamic stochastic general equilibrium models seems to be the main direction in which macroeconomics has been heading ever since.

Dynamic Macroeconomics is predominantly based on the intertemporal approach. The book presents and analyzes dynamic and dynamic stochastic general equilibrium models, in which households and firms (but also the government and the central bank) make their decisions taking full account of their intertemporal effects. The dynamic element of time, the element of uncertainty about stochastic shocks, and the techniques of intertemporal optimization permeate modern macroeconomics and are central to the analysis of the models in this book.

There are two exceptions to this rule about relying on models of intertemporal optimization. Chapter 3 contains an extensive discussion of the Solow model, which, from the perspective of the intertemporal approach, is an ad hoc general equilibrium model. In the

Solow model, the savings rate is assumed exogenous and is not derived from intertemporal optimization on the part of households. However, this model is pivotal for the theory of economic growth and provides the foundation for examining the implications of optimizing growth models, such as the representative household and overlapping generations model. The Solow model also provides the link to models with externalities, human capital accumulation, and endogenous growth. It is thus important that the Solow model and the role of savings and investment are fully analyzed and understood early on.

The second exception is chapter 15, which contains a full presentation and discussion of traditional Keynesian models, such as the Keynesian cross, the IS-LM model, the AD-AS model, and models of the Phillips curve. First sketched in the *General Theory* of Keynes [1936] and later developed by Hicks [1937], Modigliani [1944], Samuelson [1948], Hansen [1949], Patinkin [1956], and others, these models are the basis on which macroeconomics was originally developed as a separate subdiscipline of economics. They led to the original neoclassical synthesis and are the foundation of the new neoclassical synthesis and the distinction between the new classical and the new Keynesian approaches to intertemporal macroeconomics. It is thus crucial that the properties, the strengths, and the weaknesses of these traditional Keynesian models are fully understood.

Even though they belong to previous generations of macroeconomic models, the Solow model and the traditional Keynesian models serve as the basis through which the student of modern macroeconomics can appreciate the strengths, weaknesses, and policy implications of the intertemporal approach. Unlike the traditional approach to macroeconomics, the intertemporal approach is based on dynamic and dynamic stochastic models derived from explicit microeconomic foundations.

In the dynamic general equilibrium growth models that are discussed in this book, the optimal and mutually compatible decisions of households, firms, and the government (or central bank) help determine key macroeconomic aggregates. These aggregates include output and income, employment, consumption, investment, government expenditure and taxes, the stock of physical and human capital, the stock of government debt, the price level, real and nominal wages, real and nominal interest rates, and inflation. The performance of the economy depends on which distortions are present and how they are addressed by government policy.

In the models of aggregate fluctuations, such as the new classical, and the new Keynesian dynamic stochastic general equilibrium models presented here, fluctuations in aggregate real and nominal variables are the result of the individually optimal and mutually compatible reactions of households, firms, and the government and central bank to stochastic real or monetary disturbances.

Several elements differentiate this book from other advanced texts on macroeconomics. First, many of the concepts and the characteristics of intertemporal macroeconomics are introduced at an early stage (chapter 2) in the context of two-period intertemporal general equilibrium models, which can be analyzed with minimal mathematical superstructure. This allows the student to gain a fundamental understanding of the issues at stake early on and relatively easily.

Second, the book focuses on a full analysis of a limited number of key intertemporal models. For example, in growth theory, the focus is on the representative household and overlapping generations models, variants of which are combined with different assumptions about technology, externalities from capital accumulation, human capital accumulation, and endogenous technical progress. In the theory of aggregate fluctuations, the focus is on essentially four models. They are the stochastic growth model and three short-run models of aggregate fluctuations: a new classical model without capital, an imperfectly competitive new Keynesian model with staggered pricing and an alternative new Keynesian model with periodic wage contracts. Such models form the basis of what has been termed the *new neoclassical synthesis* and are analyzed fully.

A third distinguishing element of the approach adopted in this book is that the models are stripped down to essentials, so that they can be fully solved and analyzed. Thus, most of the models used can be reduced to second-order dynamic systems whose solutions can be fully characterized, either algebraically or with the help of simple two-dimensional phase diagrams. This approach allows students to focus on the dynamic properties of the models and gain a deep understanding of the economics of these dynamic processes. A variety of exercises scattered throughout the text encourages students to try their hand at solving versions of the main dynamic models that define modern macroeconomics.

But because dynamic simulation techniques are an important element of modern dynamic macroeconomics and policy analysis (especially for higher-dimensional models), the dynamic models used in the book are also simulated numerically, and their impulse response functions are plotted and discussed. This is something intended to help students of this text gain a better grasp of the dynamic properties of the models themselves. In addition, such simulations allow for an assessment of the quantitative significance of the various effects highlighted in the theoretical models. They help determine which effects are quantitatively significant and which are not. Finally, the simulations demonstrate to students of this text how to set up and simulate dynamic and dynamic stochastic general equilibrium macroeconomic models, something that should familiarize them with the techniques and prepare them to analyze higher-dimensional, more complicated, and more realistic models.[1]

Modern macroeconomics is not based on a single generally accepted and all-encompassing model. For this reason, this book is eclectic. It treats macroeconomics as applied and policy-oriented general equilibrium analysis, based on various alternative, relatively simple aggregate dynamic or dynamic stochastic models. We examine a plurality of

1. The dynamic simulations of the various models are carried out through the use of the software platform Dynare (dynare.org), in conjunction with the programming language Matlab (mathworks.com). The Dynare programs used for carrying out the simulations are available through the dedicated website for the book (dynamic macroeconomics.com).

models, each of which is suitable for investigating specific issues and addressing specific questions, but may be unsuitable for other issues or questions. The book highlights both the potential strengths as well as the limitations of alternative models.[2]

However, some key unifying principles in the models are adopted. The most important of these principles is the assumption that economic agents base their decisions on intertemporal optimization of some well-defined objective function under appropriate constraints. Thus, for the most part, we examine dynamic general equilibrium models with explicit intertemporal microeconomic foundations. Where there are theoretical disagreements, alternative approaches are juxtaposed, their pros and cons are analyzed, and their compatibility with the empirical evidence is also briefly discussed.

Key facts about long-run economic growth and aggregate fluctuations are presented in chapter 1. Additional facts are also presented as we move to the particular models in the relevant chapters and they relate to the specific issues these models seek to explain. The discussion of these facts facilitates the process of evaluating the relevance and usefulness of the theoretical models in the rest of this book.

However, note that the rigorous and full empirical evaluation and testing of alternative theories and models is beyond the scope of this book. The present text, although concerned with models that account for the key stylized facts about macroeconomic phenomena, is a text on macroeconomic theory, not empirical or applied macroeconomics. Texts that focus on empirical macroeconomics and macroeconometrics could complement the present text for empirically inclined students and economists, and should indeed be consulted, as macroeconomics ultimately relies on the interactions between theory and evidence.[3]

The book assumes introductory knowledge of economic theory and mathematics for economists. The main mathematical techniques needed to analyze optimizing dynamic macroeconomic models are fully reviewed in the appendixes. These appendixes assume some basic prior knowledge of the material contained in mathematical textbooks for economists but are for the most part self-contained. They discuss some useful functional forms for the production and utility functions used in macroeconomics, derivatives and partial derivatives, optimization under constraints and the Lagrange method, linear algebra and the solution of linear models, solution methods for linear differential and difference equations, dynamic optimization techniques, and random variables and stochastic processes.

The book has emerged from my lectures over more than 30 years at Birkbeck College, University of London, and the Athens University of Economics and Business, both at

2. As noted by Keynes [1938], in a letter to Roy Harrod, "economics is a science of thinking in terms of models, joined to the art of choosing models which are relevant to the contemporary world." See Rodrik [2015] for a similarly eclectic approach to the role of models in economics in general, and the rules for setting up models and evaluating them.

3. Good examples of such texts are Favero [2001], Canova [2007], DeJong and Chetan [2011], and Herbst and Schorfheide [2015].

advanced undergraduate and postgraduate levels. The past 50 years have been a period of impressive progress for dynamic macroeconomics, which has transformed the discipline. The book traces this evolution and the current trends in macroeconomics, and is thus suitable for advanced undergraduates, professional economists, and graduate students in the first year of degrees leading to an MSc or a PhD in economics or related subjects, such as finance.

I thank a number of people who have contributed to this book, both directly and indirectly.

First and foremost, I thank my PhD advisors during 1979–1981 at the London School of Economics: George Akerlof, Steve Nickell, and Chris Pissarides. They had a great positive influence on my training as a macroeconomist and on my attitude as an academic economist, which has stood me well over the years. I owe them a lot.

More recently, my biggest debt is to successive generations of students, and especially the students in the master's and PhD programs in economics at the Athens University of Economics and Business over the past decade. They have suffered through successive versions of my lecture notes between 2009 and 2016, provided useful feedback, and helped improve the original notes.

The Fletcher School at Tufts University was an ideal academic environment that allowed me to complete and improve the manuscript between 2016 and 2018.

Various colleagues have contributed through comments and discussions that have helped bring about improvements in the book. I particularly thank Marios Angeletos, Yannis Ioannides, Michael Klein, Tryphon Kollintzas, Athanasios Orphanides, Apostolis Philippopoulos, and Plutarchos Sakellaris. Olivier Blanchard reviewed an early version of the full manuscript and provided helpful comments and much needed encouragement.

I thank Emily Taber, the MIT Press economics acquisitions editor, for putting this manuscript through a very efficient editorial process. I also acknowledge the very helpful comments and suggestions of eight anonymous reviewers in the prepublication process. These reviews have been extremely useful and have led to a much improved manuscript. The copy editor, Cyd Westmoreland, and the production editor, Erin Davis, have also helped improve the final manuscript, through a very efficient editing process.

Throughout the long years of writing, revising, and rewriting, my wife Dika has provided much needed support and encouragement, as she has done through the many years of our common life. I cannot thank her enough.

I remain solely responsible for all remaining errors.

George Alogoskoufis
Fletcher School, Tufts University; and Athens University of Economics and Business

1

Introduction

Macroeconomics focuses on the analysis of economies in their entirety. It seeks to provide answers to some of the most important economic and social concerns, such as the ones relating to economic growth, fluctuations in output, employment, and inflation, and the role of monetary and fiscal policy.

Why are some countries "rich" and others "poor"? What determines the improvement of living standards and the process of economic growth? Why are there recessions and upswings in economic activity? What are the causes and consequences of inflation? What are the determinants and consequences of unemployment and its fluctuations? What are the possibilities for government policy to promote economic growth, counter recessions, and maintain low inflation and unemployment?

These and a host of related questions have occupied social thinkers even before economics was founded as a separate discipline, following the publication of Adam Smith's pathbreaking 1776 book, *The Wealth of Nations*. Smith sought to systematically analyze the causes of differences in wealth and living standards across countries. In the process, he founded economics as an academic discipline that was separate from the other social sciences. Following the publication in 1936 of *The General Theory of Employment, Interest and Money* by John Maynard Keynes, macroeconomics eventually emerged as a separate subdiscipline of economics.[1]

Macroeconomics uses relatively simple, aggregate, general equilibrium models that focus on the operation of three sets of markets. The first is the market for goods and services. Such goods and services are typically assumed to consist of a homogeneous *final output*. The second is the set of markets for factors of production, which are usually assumed to

1. The term "macroeconomics," coined by Frisch [1933], only prevailed beginning in the 1950s. For example, in the first edition of the most successful introductory economics textbook of the postwar period, Samuelson [1948], the terms "macroeconomics" and "microeconomics" were not used at all. Samuelson titled the (unabashedly Keynesian) macroeconomic section of his textbook "Determination of National Income and Its Fluctuations," and the (unabashedly neoclassical) microeconomic section "The Composition and Pricing of National Income." However, by the third edition, in 1955, Samuelson uses the terms "macroeconomics" and "microeconomics" repeatedly to distinguish between the two main subdisciplines of economics.

be mainly *capital and labor*. The third is the set of markets for *financial assets*, such as interest-yielding securities and money.

In the context of macroeconomic models, the main groups of agents assumed to be making choices are households, firms, and the government, or independent government agencies, such as a central bank.

Through their choices and their market interactions, economic agents determine macroeconomic outcomes, such as the volume of production and consumption, employment and unemployment, investment and capital accumulation, real wages and real interest rates, taxes and government debt, the price level and inflation, and nominal wages and interest rates.

1.1 The Nature and Evolution of Macroeconomics

The subject matter of macroeconomics is usually divided into two distinct areas: (1) the analysis of long-run economic growth, which is the main focus of Smith [1776] and other classical economists, and (2) the analysis of aggregate fluctuations, which is the main focus of Hume [1752], subsequent monetary and other business cycle theorists, and, of course, Keynes [1936].

1.1.1 Pre-Keynesian Macroeconomics

Macroeconomics did not exist as a separate field of economics before the publication of the *General Theory* in 1936. However, at least three important theoretical streams foreshadowed it.

One was the analysis of *long-run economic growth*, an important concern of classical economists, such as Smith, Malthus, Ricardo, and Mill. The classical economists sought to explain economic growth in terms of population growth; the accumulation of capital; and the increase in the efficiency of production, as determined by the division of labor and technical progress. These factors interacted with the availability of land, a factor of production that was assumed to be in fixed supply. The classical theory of economic growth, focusing on the production and distribution of income, is essentially macroeconomic in nature.[2]

The second stream of pre-Keynesian macroeconomics is *monetary theory*. Monetary theory was quite advanced even before the emergence of classical economics. Hume [1752] provides important examples of advanced monetary analysis more than 20 years before Smith. By the early twentieth century, monetary theory had established the quantity theory of money, the classical dichotomy between real and nominal variables, and some monetary explanations of the business cycle. The quantity theory of money suggests that increases in

2. See Samuelson [1978] for an analysis of the canonical classical model of economic growth that synthesizes the views of Smith [1776], Malthus [1798], Ricardo [1817], and Mill [1848].

the money supply lead, at least eventually, to equiproportional increases in the general level of prices. The classical dichotomy suggests that, at least in the long run, real variables are determined purely by nonmonetary factors.

Monetary theories of the business cycle attribute the business cycle to the short-term real effects of monetary factors interacting with the gradual adjustment of wages and prices (Hume [1752], Thornton [1802]), with misperceptions between changes in relative prices and the price level (Mill, [1833, 1848]) and with temporary deviations of the interest rate from its equilibrium value (Fisher [1896], Wicksell [1898], von Mises [1912]). Various monetary schools of thought had evolved by the latter part of the nineteenth century and still existed in the early part of the twentieth century.[3]

The third stream foreshadowing macroeconomics consists of various types of *real business cycle theories*. Apart from the dominant monetary theories, there were alternative theories that attempt to explain aggregate fluctuations in terms of overinvestment, underconsumption, excess indebtedness, psychology, technology, or harvest and agricultural cycles. These theories are also essentially macroeconomic in nature.[4]

The term "macroeconomics" predates the *General Theory* and has to be credited to Frisch [1933, p. 2], who defines it as follows:

> When we approach the study of business cycles with the intention of carrying through an analysis that is truly dynamic and determinate, we are naturally led to distinguish between two types of analyses: the micro-dynamic and the macro-dynamic types.... The macro-dynamic analysis ... tries to give an account of the fluctuations of the whole economic system taken in its entirety.

In any event, the *General Theory,* as codified in the IS-LM framework of Hicks [1937], and later by Modigliani [1944], Samuelson [1948], Hansen [1949], Patinkin [1956], and others, eventually prevailed over previous approaches during the 1940s and the 1950s and was pivotal in the establishment of macroeconomics as a separate field of economics.[5]

3. These include Irving Fisher of the Yale School (see I. Fisher [1896, 1911, 1930]), the Cambridge School (Pigou [1917], Keynes [1923], Marshall [1923]), the Stockholm School (Wicksell [1898]), and the Austrian School (von Mises [1912]). Monetary theories of aggregate fluctuations included, among others, those of Pigou [1913], Hawtrey [1919], Marshall [1923], and Keynes [1923]. These economists, like Hume and Thornton before them, stressed the short-run real effects of money when there is partial adjustment of nominal wages and prices. I. Fisher [1896], Wicksell [1898], and von Mises [1912], among others, also stress monetary factors in aggregate fluctuations through short-run deviations of the market interest rate from the Wicksellian "natural" (equilibrium) rate of interest, which causes fluctuations in the real interest rate. Humphrey [1991] discusses how many otherwise "classical" monetary economists had suggested reasons for the short-run nonneutrality of money.

4. Pre-Keynesian *trade cycle* or *business cycle* theories are surveyed and analyzed extensively by Haberler [1937].

5. It is again useful to quote Frisch [1933, p. 3], who also wrote that "as far as I know no determinate macro-dynamic analysis is yet to be found in the literature." This statement was about the state of the pre-Keynesian business-cycle models, which were mainly heuristic and nonrigorous. The IS-LM framework was given its name by Hansen [1949] and was popularized by Hansen [1953]. The IS curve is the equilibrium relation between investment I and savings S, and the LM curve is the equilibrium relation between the demand for money L and the supply of money M. See chapter 15 for more details.

Macroeconomics gradually integrated the three theoretical streams mentioned above and experienced explosive growth during the rest of the twentieth century. In its evolution over the years, macroeconomics has displayed continuity but also significant controversies, changes of direction, and outright scientific revolutions.[6]

1.1.2 Classical and Keynesian Macroeconomics

Following the Keynesian revolution of the 1930s, macroeconomics originally evolved with little reliance on underlying microeconomic theory. For the most part, in the aftermath of the trauma of the Great Depression and the scathing attack by Keynes [1936] on classical economics, macroeconomics based on solid microeconomic principles was dismissed as classical macroeconomics. In the increasingly dominant paradigm of Keynesian macroeconomics, during the 1950s and the 1960s, most key aggregate relations (such as the consumption function, the investment function, and the relation between inflation and unemployment) were postulated rather than derived from explicit choice–theoretic microeconomic foundations. Surprisingly, this applied not only to the short-run Keynesian model of aggregate fluctuations but also to models of long-run economic growth.

To a large extent, the instability and knife-edge conditions characterizing the early post-Keynesian models of economic growth (those by Harrod [1939] and Domar [1946]) were due to their unsatisfactory microeconomic foundations, such as the postulates of a constant savings rate and the assumed absence of long-run substitution possibilities between capital and labor in the production of goods and services.

The neoclassical Solow [1956] and Swan [1956] model of economic growth—which was based on a much more general production function allowing for substitution between capital and labor—also relied on a postulated Keynesian consumption function that was based on the assumption of the *General Theory* that consumption is an exogenous fraction of current income.

It took some time before Cass [1965] and Koopmans [1965] rediscovered and extended the Ramsey [1928] *representative household* model of optimal savings and reestablished the link between growth theory and optimizing households. At around the same time, Diamond [1965] extended the Samuelson [1958] model of *overlapping generations*, which was a different type of optimizing general equilibrium model of aggregate savings. Diamond used this model to analyze economic growth and the effects of government debt.

6. For the concept of scientific revolutions, see Kuhn [1962]. Macroeconomics itself was established through such a revolution, the Keynesian revolution (Klein [1947]). The Keynesian orthodoxy was later challenged by the monetarist counterrevolution (Johnson [1971]), the rational expectations revolution (Begg [1982]), to end up with the revolution implied by the adoption of dynamic stochastic general equilibrium models. For recent scholarly analyses of the key theoretical developments in macroeconomics since Keynes, see Woodford [1999], Blanchard [2000], and DeVroey [2016].

Both the representative household model and the overlapping generations model are dynamic general equilibrium models with explicit microeconomic foundations and are widely used in macroeconomics to this day.[7]

The Keynesian approach to aggregate fluctuations, which became totally dominant in the 1950s and the 1960s, suffers from insufficient microeconomic foundations to an even greater extent than growth theory. This applies to both *theoretical models* (such as the IS-LM framework of Hicks [1937], as adapted by Hansen [1949] and the models of Samuelson [1939] and Modigliani [1944]) and *econometric models* (such as the Klein [1950] and Klein and Goldberger [1955] models).[8]

For example, the IS-LM framework of Hicks [1937] is essentially a static short-run general equilibrium model of income and interest rate determination, based on ad hoc *General Theory* postulates, such as the positive consumption-income relation, the negative investment–interest rate relation, and liquidity preference.

Even the multiplier-accelerator model of Samuelson [1939], probably the most influential early dynamic business cycle model based on Keynesian principles, relies on a simple postulated consumption function, with consumption being a linear function of past income and investment a constant multiple of the change in consumption. The marginal propensity to consume out of past income defines the *multiplier*, and the marginal propensity to invest, following a change in consumption, defines the *accelerator*. Yet neither the multiplier nor the accelerator was derived from an optimizing microeconomic model for households and firms.[9]

The same also applied, although to a lesser extent, to the so-called *neoclassical synthesis*, which is a combination of the IS-LM framework with an aggregate short-run supply function that depends on the assumption of short-run rigidity of nominal wages and prices.[10]

This state of affairs was of significant concern to many economists, including the protagonists of the development of the Keynesian models themselves, who were unhappy with the weakness of the microeconomic foundations of many of the postulated macroeconomic relations. As a result, many sought to provide better links between macroeconomics and microeconomics.

7. We analyze the Solow model in chapter 3, the representative household model in chapter 4, and the overlapping generations models in chapter 5.

8. It has to be noted that Klein [1950] expends a lot of effort on providing microeconomic foundations for his econometric model of the United States. For the most part, the 45 pages of chapter II are devoted to economic theory, with profit-maximizing firms and utility-maximizing households. However, when shifting from economic theory to his statistical models, Klein uses the theory relatively loosely, as a rationalization of "simple" aggregate behavioral equations.

9. We analyze the various traditional Keynesian models and the Samuelson multiplier-accelerator model in chapter 15.

10. The term "neoclassical synthesis" was first used in the 1955 edition of Samuelson [1948]. Modigliani [1944] and Patinkin [1956] develop this synthesis, which was nonetheless derived from the *General Theory* itself. The neoclassical synthesis is presented in chapter 15.

1.1.3 Microeconomic Foundations of Macroeconomics

Beginning in the 1950s, the various attempts to provide better microeconomic foundations for macroeconomics gradually started to bear fruit.

Modigliani and Brumberg [1954] and Friedman [1957] provide dynamic microeconomic foundations for the consumption function, based on intertemporal considerations. From these efforts came the *life cycle* and *permanent income* theories of consumption, which differ from the simple static Keynesian consumption function.[11]

Jorgenson [1963] introduces the *flexible accelerator* model of investment, based on profit maximization by firms and the assumption of adjustment costs for the capital stock. His contribution and that of Tobin [1969] led to the modern optimizing *q theories of investment*.[12]

Baumol [1952], Tobin [1956], Friedman [1956], Patinkin [1956], Samuelson [1958], and others derive the *demand for money* from the optimizing behavior of households and firms.[13]

More importantly, Patinkin [1956] sought to base the whole model of the neoclassical synthesis on a better microeconomic footing, consistent with developments in Walrasian general equilibrium theory. The program of Patinkin was carried forward by Clower [1965], Leijonhufvud [1968], and the so-called *non-Walrasian equilibrium modeling* of Barro and Grossman [1971], Muellbauer and Portes [1978], and others.

These are only some of the early attempts to provide microeconomic foundations for the postulated key relations of Keynesian macroeconomic models.

The most celebrated case of an empirical relationship with inadequate microeconomic foundations is probably the *Phillips curve*. This was an inverse empirical relation between inflation and unemployment, discovered by Phillips [1958]. Initially, very little theory underpinned the Phillips curve, which was interpreted simply as an adjustment equation for wages, depending on the excess demand for labor. The Phillips curve was incorporated in Keynesian models as the missing aggregate supply function, where it helped determine the extent to which changes in aggregate demand were translated into changes in wages and prices or changes in real output and employment. Samuelson and Solow [1960] were quick to suggest that aggregate demand policies could, in principle, be used to select the socially desirable combination of inflation and unemployment along the Phillips curve.

However, in the late 1960s, the Phillips curve appeared to break down. Rises in inflation resulted in only temporary reductions in unemployment. Phelps [1967] and Friedman [1968] were able to explain the breakdown of the Phillips curve, and even to anticipate it to a certain extent, in terms of shifts in inflationary expectations. They used the first

11. We analyze deterministic and stochastic versions of these theories of consumption in chapters 4 and 10.

12. We analyze optimizing models of investment and the cost of capital in chapter 11.

13. We analyze optimizing general equilibrium models of the demand for money and the determination of the price level, the nominal interest rate, and inflation in chapters 7 and 12.

rudimentary optimizing models of inflation and unemployment, which resulted in the so-called *expectations-augmented Phillips curve* and the *natural rate hypothesis*.[14]

An important research effort, seeking to provide firm dynamic microeconomic foundations for the Phillips curve, followed almost immediately afterward. The contributions in Phelps [1970] kickstarted this program. The rational expectations revolution followed suit, when Lucas [1972] applied the *rational expectations hypothesis* of Muth [1961] to a general equilibrium model of the Phillips curve. Up until then, the standard expectations hypothesis used in macroeconomics was the hypothesis of *adaptive expectations*.[15]

Gradually, the focus shifted to *dynamic stochastic general equilibrium* (DSGE) models of aggregate fluctuations, based on dynamic optimization by households and firms, following the ideas of Lucas [1977] and the important early such model by Kydland and Prescott [1980, 1982]. These models were initially in the classical tradition and led to what is now termed *new classical* macroeconomics, or *real business cycle theory*.[16]

Alternative DSGE models were also developed in the monetary and Keynesian tradition of gradual adjustment of prices and nominal wages. These alternative models emphasized both real and nominal distortions, such as labor market imperfections and nominal wage contracts, or imperfect competition and staggered pricing in product markets. Mankiw and Romer [1991] is an early collection of papers in what is now termed *new Keynesian* macroeconomics. These models can account for fluctuations caused by monetary factors as well as real factors. They can also justify a stabilizing role for monetary policy not only for inflation but also for fluctuations in real output and employment.[17]

1.1.4 Deterministic and Stochastic Dynamic General Equilibrium Models

Both the new classical and the new Keynesian approaches coexist today, in the context of what Goodfriend and King [1997] have termed the "new neoclassical synthesis." This synthesis is based on DSGE models, which may or may not satisfy the conditions for optimality of the Arrow-Debreu model. They share many common elements but are also characterized by important differences with regard to their accounts of aggregate fluctuations and their implications for monetary policy.[18]

14. We discuss developments involving the Phillips curve and the role of stabilization policy in Keynesian models in chapter 15.

15. We discuss the rational expectations hypothesis and compare it to the adaptive expectations hypothesis in chapter 9.

16. See King and Rebelo [1999] for an overview of such models. We discuss the *stochastic growth model* in chapter 13 and a competitive equilibrium model without capital in chapter 14. Both are models in the new classical tradition.

17. Woodford [2003a] and Gali [2008] are based on such models. I introduce and analyze two alternative new Keynesian models in chapters 16 and 17.

18. See Arrow and Debreu [1954], Debreu [1959], and Arrow [1964] for the Arrow-Debreu model of competitive equilibrium.

In a different development, after a long pause, growth theory has displayed significant progress since the 1980s in the context of what has been called "new growth theory." This work has focused on the exploration of the implications of increasing returns to scale, the role of human capital accumulation, and endogenous technical progress. A more recent literature has emphasized the interactions between fertility and technical progress as a choice between the quantity and quality of children. This has resulted in the development of the so-called unified growth theory, which, unlike previous theories, can also explain the transition from stagnation to growth in the early nineteenth century. Yet another stream in the literature emphasizes the role of institutions in providing appropriate incentives for the accumulation of physical and human capital and for research and development that leads to technical progress.[19]

In seeking to explain long-run economic growth and fluctuations in aggregate economic activity, modern macroeconomics is *dynamic*. The element of time is indispensable for understanding and explaining both types of phenomena. In seeking to explain aggregate fluctuations, modern macroeconomics is also *stochastic*: It explains aggregate fluctuations in terms of the response of dynamic economic systems to random disturbances. Stochastic growth models have also been developed. Hence, both the new neoclassical synthesis and the new growth theory combine dynamic and stochastic elements.[20]

The dynamic stochastic approach to aggregate fluctuations follows a tradition that was also founded in the 1930s, by mathematical economists and statisticians, such as Frisch [1933] and Slutsky [1937]. This tradition, which initially evolved independently of the *General Theory*, was subsequently followed and extended in various directions by econometricians, such as Tinbergen [1937], Haavelmo [1944] and the Cowles Commission, and Burns and Mitchell [1946]. The development of early Keynesian macroeconometric models by Klein [1950], Klein and Goldberger [1955], and others applied this tradition to the framework of the *General Theory*.[21]

The way in which modern macroeconomics approaches and analyzes aggregate fluctuations owes a lot to the following important observation by Lucas [1977, pp. 9–10]:

> Technically, movements about trend in gross national product in any country can be well described by a stochastically disturbed difference equation of very low order. These movements do not exhibit

19. The new growth theory sprang to life as a result of three important papers: by P. M. Romer [1986, 1990] and Lucas [1988]. It is introduced and discussed in chapter 8. Unified growth theory is surveyed in Galor [2011], and the role of institutions is surveyed in Acemoglu et al. [2005].

20. One cannot help noticing the proliferation of the adjective "new" to describe the theories that have emerged since the 1980s: "new classical" and "new Keynesian" macroeconomics, "new neoclassical synthesis," "new growth theory," and so on. There is little doubt that these theories are based on older foundations. However, the DSGE models used are new and improved versions of the simpler and more ad hoc older models. We take up this subject again in chapter 23, the final chapter of this book.

21. The term "econometrics" is also due to Frisch, who was one of the founders of the Econometric Society and the academic journal *Econometrica*.

> uniformity of either period or amplitude, which is to say, they do not resemble the deterministic wave motions which sometimes arise in the natural sciences. Those regularities which are observed are in the co-movements among different aggregative time series. ... One is led by the facts to conclude that, with respect to the qualitative behavior of co-movements among series, business cycles are all alike. To theoretically inclined economists, this conclusion should be attractive and challenging, for it suggests the possibility of a unified explanation of business cycles, grounded in the general laws governing market economies, rather than in political or institutional characteristics specific to particular countries or periods.

This observation by Lucas, based on the foundations laid out by Frisch [1933], Slutsky [1937], and Burns and Mitchell [1946], brought about significant changes in the way in which all schools of thought in modern macroeconomics approach and try to explain aggregate fluctuations.

The traditional Keynesian macroeconomic and macroeconometric models, from the 1950s to the 1970s, were deemed to have weaknesses in the detailed study of aggregate fluctuations and the impact of monetary and fiscal policy in relation to the criteria of Lucas. The most important of these weaknesses was that the macroeconomic relationships assumed in traditional models were not explicitly drawn from well-defined microeconomic foundations, based on intertemporal optimization on the part of households and firms. Therefore, one could not easily interpret their parameters and be confident in their stability. This became the basis of the Lucas critique of econometric policy evaluation. Lucas [1976, p. 41] concluded that

> Given that the structure of all econometric model consists of optimal decision rules of economic agents, and that optimal decision rules vary systematically with changes in the structure of series relevant to the decision maker, it follows that any change in policy will systematically alter the structure of econometric models.

Lucas arrived at this conclusion after having demonstrated the fragility of traditional econometric models of aggregate consumption, investment, and the Phillips curve. Pursuing this critique—and the quest for dynamic microeconomic foundations in macroeconomic models—the macroeconomics of aggregate fluctuations shifted to the study of DSGE models with explicit dynamic microeconomic foundations.

Modern macroeconomics is now almost entirely based on such dynamic general equilibrium models, which may be either deterministic or stochastic. For the study of economic growth, the main models are variants of the representative household model (due to Ramsey [1928], Cass [1965], and Koopmans [1965]) and overlapping generations models (such as the Diamond [1965] and Blanchard [1985]–Weil [1989] models). These are chiefly deterministic dynamic general equilibrium models, although stochastic elements can be added to them. Models used for the study of aggregate fluctuations combine elements from both new classical and new Keynesian DSGE models to form the basis of the new neoclassical synthesis. Naturally, such models form the backbone of the present book. I present the main theories of economic growth and aggregate fluctuations through a sequence of such dynamic models, based on intertemporal optimization on the part of economic agents. For the most part, these models are transformed into linear or log-linear systems of equations. In chapter 22, we also discuss an alternative approach to aggregate fluctuations based on nonlinear overlapping generations models that result in endogenous cycles, self-fulfilling prophecies, and sunspots (Azariadis [1981], Azariadis and Guesnerie [1986], Benhabib and Farmer [1999]). For completeness, I also discuss some of the important precursors to these dynamic general equilibrium models.[22]

The models presented and analyzed in this book are treated as tools for understanding the main macroeconomic phenomena of long-run economic growth, aggregate fluctuations, inflation and unemployment, and the role of monetary and fiscal policies. The book highlights both their potential strengths as well as their limitations.

It is worth keeping in mind that modern macroeconomics is not based on a single, generally accepted, all-encompassing model. For this reason, this book is eclectic and treats macroeconomics as applied and policy-oriented general equilibrium analysis, based on various alternative, relatively simple aggregate dynamic models. We examine a plurality of models, each of which is suitable for investigating specific issues and addressing specific questions but may be unsuitable for other issues or questions.[23]

Some key unifying principles are found in the models that we adopt. The most important of these principles is the assumption that economic agents base their decisions on intertemporal optimization of some well-defined objective function under appropriate constraints. Thus, for the most part, we rely on dynamic general equilibrium models with explicit intertemporal microeconomic foundations. Where there are theoretical disagreements, alternative approaches are juxtaposed, their pros and cons are analyzed, and their compatibility with the empirical evidence is also briefly discussed.

Before we turn to the theory and the models themselves, it is worth looking at the key empirical facts concerning long-run economic growth and aggregate fluctuations. These key facts are what macroeconomics seeks to explain and account for.

We start with some of the key facts about long-run economic growth and then move on to some of the key facts about aggregate fluctuations. Additional facts are also presented as we move to particular models in the relevant chapters and the specific issues these models seek to explain. Knowledge of these key facts will facilitate the process of evaluating the relevance and usefulness of the theoretical models in the rest of this book.[24]

22. For example, in chapter 3, I devote a lot of space to the Solow [1956] model, even though its consumption function is postulated and not derived from explicit microeconomic foundations. I also devote chapter 15 to the traditional Keynesian models and the Phillips curve because of their significance for the development of macroeconomics and to compare their structure and implications with the new Keynesian models of chapters 16 and 17.

23. See Keynes [1938] and, more recently, Rodrik [2015] for a similarly eclectic approach to the role of models in economics in general and to the rules for setting up models and evaluating them.

24. It is worth repeating that the rigorous and full empirical evaluation and testing of alternative theories and models is outside the scope of the present text. This is a text on macroeconomic theory, not empirical or applied

1.2 Key Facts about Long-Run Economic Growth

To examine the key facts about long-run economic growth, we first review current cross-country differences in living standards and then survey the evolution of living standards over time for some economies.[25]

Living standards are usually measured by annual gross national income (GNI) per capita or annual gross domestic product (GDP) per capita. However, to perform cross-country comparisons, per capita income must be measured in comparable units. This requires the transformation of per capita incomes in a common currency, usually the US dollar. To adjust for differences in purchasing power among countries, we use exchange rates that reflect such differences. These exchange rates ensure purchasing power parity (PPP) and are called PPP-adjusted exchange rates. Thus, to compare GNI per capita or GDP per capita among different countries, these indexes are measured in PPP-adjusted, or international, dollars. For comparisons over time, we must also adjust for inflation in each country by using real per capita income or output.[26]

1.2.1 Cross-Country Differences in Per Capita Output and Income

The world today consists of countries characterized by very large differences in both the standard of living of their inhabitants and the rate of growth of their living standards.

For example, in the United States, annual per capita GNI in 2012 was $52,220, whereas the annual per capita income of the Congo, one of the poorest economies, was only $710, of comparable purchasing power. The Congo had a per capita income that was just 1.4% of the US per capita income.

The World Bank publishes comparable data, in international US dollars, measuring the per capita GNIs of 214 countries of the world. For 2012, the relevant data exist for 184 countries. The average per capita GNI of countries classified as high-income economies

macroeconomics. Texts on empirical macroeconomics and macroeconometrics exist and could complement the present text for empirically inclined economists. Good examples of such texts are Favero [2001], Canova [2007], DeJong and Chetan [2011], and Herbst and Schorfheide [2015].

25. The key facts discussed in this section are the essential facts about long-run growth. Additional facts, which require some prior theoretical background, will be discussed in chapters 3 and 8. For a fuller and up-to-date survey of the key empirical facts about economic growth, see Jones [2016].

26. GDP is defined as the market value of final goods and services produced in an economy over a given period, say, a quarter or a year. Measuring how GDP changes over time or conducting cross-country comparisons requires separating out differences in prices and differences in quantities of goods and services. In contrast, GNI is defined as the value of income of domestic residents over a period of time. This may differ from GDP to the extent that there is income from abroad. For the exact methodology of measuring GDP and GNI for intertemporal and cross-country comparisons, see the World Bank website (www.worldbank.org), Summers and Heston [1991], or Maddison [1982]. World Bank data, the data of the Penn World Tables (which are based on the Summers and Heston methodology), and the data of the Maddison Project (based on the Maddison methodology) are revised at regular intervals. For the Maddison Project, see Bolt and van Zanden [2014].

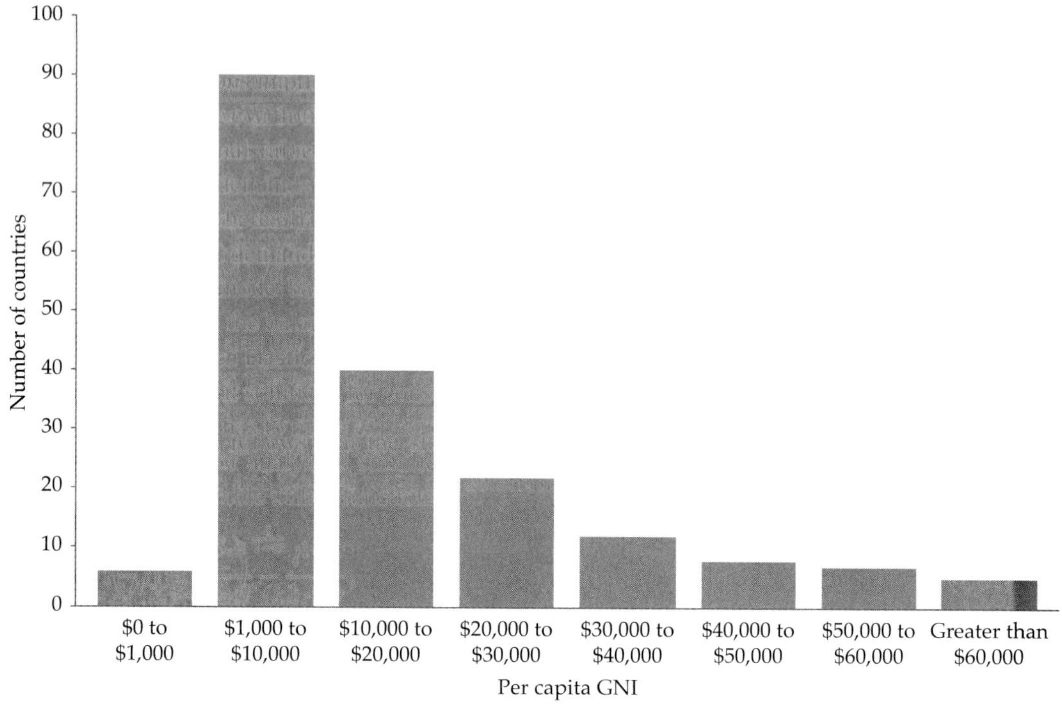

Figure 1.1
Distribution of countries by per capita GNI, 2012.

was $39,903, whereas the average per capita GNI of low-income economies was $1,870. The per capita income of high-income (developed) economies was thus on average 20 times higher than that of low-income, or least-developed, economies. The average per capita income of middle-income economies was equal to $9,075. The per capita income of high-income (developed) economies is thus on average 4 times higher than that of middle-income economies.

The number of countries with per capita GNI in a particular income bracket, measured in international US dollars, is depicted in figure 1.1.

Five countries (Qatar, Macau, Singapore, Bermuda, and Norway) had GNIs per capita greater than $60,000. Seven countries (United Arab Emirates, Luxembourg, Switzerland, Saudi Arabia, Oman, the United States, and Hong Kong) had GNIs per capita between $50,000 and $60,000. Eight developed European economies, as well as Australia and Canada, had GNIs per capita between $40,000 and $50,000. Twelve countries (including France, Great Britain, Japan, Italy, S. Korea, Spain, New Zealand, and Israel) had GNIs per capita between $30,000 and $40,000. Twenty-two countries (including Greece, Cyprus, and Russia) had GNIs per capita between $20,000 and $30,000. Forty countries (including

Turkey, Brazil, and China) had GNIs per capita between \$10,000 and \$20,000. Ninety countries, about half of the 184, had GNIs per capita between \$1,000 and \$10,000. These included India, with per capita GNI of \$5,080. Finally, six countries in sub-Saharan Africa had per capita GNIs of less than \$1,000.

These numbers suggest the extent of the disparities in per capita output and income. An adequate theory of economic growth ought to be able to account for such wide disparities.

1.2.2 Evolution of Per Capita Output and Income over Time

Reliable data on the per capita outputs and incomes of various countries and their growth rates before 1820 is extremely rare.

The estimates of Maddison [1982], based on heroic assumptions, suggest that the average growth rate of real world GDP per capita in the two centuries between 1500 and 1700 AD was only 0.04% per year. In the period 1700–1820, it was slightly higher, at just 0.07% per year. Even in Western Europe, for which 1500–1820 was a period of relative economic prosperity compared to other world regions, the average growth rate of GDP per capita did not exceed 0.14% per year.

Before 1500, all indications suggest that the standard of living, despite large cyclical fluctuations, displayed no long-term trend.

A second feature of the period before 1820 is that income differences between countries were very small compared to today. According to the estimates of Bairoch [1993], the differences in living standards between the richest and the poorest countries did not exceed 1.5–2.0 to 1. Moreover, Bairoch estimates that there were no significant differences in living standards between Rome in the first century AD, the Arab caliphates in the tenth century, China in the eleventh century, India in the seventeenth century, and Europe in the early eighteenth century.

In the fifteenth century (before the economic boom in Europe), China, the Ottoman Empire, the Incas, and the Aztecs seem to have had a higher standard of living than did Western Europe. However, economic growth in Western Europe picked up after 1500, while China entered a long period of economic decline.[27]

The average growth rate of world per capita output increased between 1820 and 1870, reaching 0.5% per year. Between 1870 and 1950, the average growth rate doubled to 1.1%,

27. Between the eighth and twelfth centuries, China experienced a unprecedented period of economic and cultural prosperity. It was in this period that gunpowder, printing, and the hydraulic hose reel were invented. Coal was used in the production of steel, and a series of canals and waterways for water supply and transportation of products was constructed. The magnetic compass was invented in that period, and the imperial fleet of China had reached as far as the eastern coast of Africa by the early fifteenth century. However, China gradually withdrew from the world economy, following a switch to a policy of introversion, and around 1750, the standard of living in Europe had overtaken the Chinese standard of living. One hundred years later, in the nineteenth century, China was unable to defend itself during the Opium Wars against Great Britain, and in the twentieth century, it had become one of the least-developed economies of the world.

and since 1950, it has doubled again to more than 2%. Between 1950 and the early twenty-first century, many countries have seen their standards of living more than triple.[28]

As a result, in the high-income countries of today, real per capita output and income is, depending on the country, between 10 and 30 times higher than it was 200 years ago.

The increase in per capita output and income is not and has not been uniform. Table 1.1 presents relevant data based on Maddison [1982] and the Maddison Project. After centuries of stagnation in the average standard of living of all countries of the world, the average growth rate began to rise in Europe and its former colonies, such as the United States, Canada, and Australia, from the early nineteenth century. In other countries, such as Japan, the growth process started later.

However, growth has been uneven. In 1820, the more-developed countries of today had a per capita GDP which was about three times the per capita GDP of the less-developed countries. In 2012, this factor was about 20 times higher. The former colonies of Western Europe (United States, Canada, Australia, and New Zealand), often termed Western offshoots, in 1820 had a slightly lower standard of living compared to Western Europe itself. In 1950, they had twice the per capita income of Western Europe. Japan surpassed the standard of living of Eastern Europe, Latin America, the former Soviet Union, and Western Europe in the second half of the twentieth century. China, which had become one of the poorest countries in the world in 1950, in 2010 had a per capita income that was more than double the per capita income of India and Africa. Latin America, parts of Asia, and Africa have been generally left behind.

1.2.3 Economic Growth and Convergence since 1820

Figure 1.2 depicts the long-run evolution of (the natural log of) per capita GDP in the United Kingdom, the United States, and Japan.[29]

In 1800, British per capita GDP was more than 60% higher than in the United States. At the beginning of the twentieth century, US per capita GDP had surpassed the corresponding British one, because of the higher growth rate in the United States during the nineteenth century. The two World Wars led to a widening of the gap between the two countries, even though the Great Depression of the 1930s was more severe in the United States than in Britain. After World War II, US per capita output has remained consistently higher than in Britain and the other major industrial economies.

28. The number of years required for a magnitude like per capita output or income to double in value depends on its growth rate. If per capita real income grows at $g\%$ per year, it takes approximately $70/g$ years for it to double. Thus, if g is 1%, it takes 70 years for per capita real income to double; if g is 2%, it takes 35 years; if g is 3%, it takes 23 years, and so on. This rule of 70 is derived from $100 \times \ln 2 = 69.3$, which is approximately equal to 70, and from the approximation that $g\%$ is approximately equal to $\ln(1 + g\%)$. For growth rates higher than 5%, most economists prefer to use the rule of 72, because dividing 72 by the growth rate is a more accurate approximation for growth rates between 5% and 10%.

29. In what follows, log refers to natural logarithms.

Table 1.1
Per capita GDP and average annual growth rates over time, various countries.

Country	Year 1500	1800	1850	1900	1950	2000
Great Britain/United Kingdom	1,086 0.07%	2,097 0.2%	2,330 0.2%	4,492 1.3%	6,939 0.9%	21,046 2.2%
France			1,597	2,876 1.2%	5,186 1.2%	20,392 2.8%
Germany			1,428	2,985 1.5%	3,881 0.5%	18,944 3.2%
Holland		2,609	2,355 −0.2%	3,329 0.7%	5,996 1.2%	22,148 2.6%
Western Europe			1,627	2,959 1.2%	4,517 0.8%	19,298 2.9%
United States		1,296	1,849 0.7%	4,091 1.6%	9,561 1.7%	28,702 2.2%
Western offshoots			1,801	4,015 1.6%	9,268 1.7%	27,574 2.2%
Japan			681	1,180 1.1%	1,921 1.0%	20,481 4.8%
China			600	545 −0.02%	448 −0.4%	3,421 4.1%
India			533	599 0.4%	619 0.07%	1,882 2.2%
Brazil			683	678 −0.01%	1,672 1.8%	5,418 2.4%
Argentina			1,251	2,875 1.7%	4,987 1.1%	8,410 1.05%

Source: "Maddison Project Database 2018."
Note: Per capita GDP in 1990 international dollars.

GDP per capita in Japan, for which continuous annual estimates exist only after 1870, has been consistently lower than the British and US levels in the nineteenth century. In 1870, it was only 23% of the corresponding British level and only 30% of the American level. By 1913, on the eve of World War I, it had risen to 28% of the British per capita GDP but had fallen to 26% of the US per capita GDP. Japan had experienced slightly higher growth than Britain but lower growth than that of the United States. By 1939, on the eve of World War II, GDP per capita in Japan had risen to 45% of the corresponding value in Britain, and to 43% of that for the United States. Japan experienced much higher growth than did Britain and the United States during World War I and the interwar years. Japanese per capita output fell precipitously in the aftermath of World War II, much more than in Britain and the United States. However, since the end of World War II, Japan has experienced

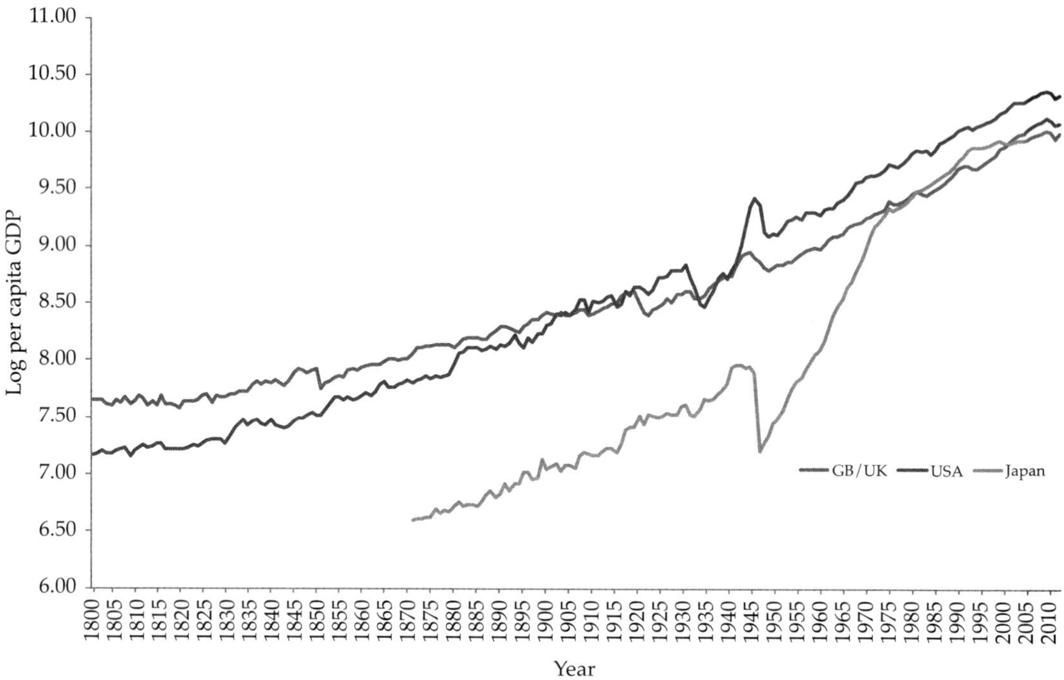

Figure 1.2
Long-run growth of (natural log) per capita GDP in the United Kingdom, the United States, and Japan.

extremely high growth, and by the mid-1970s, the Japanese GDP per capita had converged to the British value. Since the early 1980s, Japanese growth has slowed down, and British growth picked up, with the result that Britain has again surpassed the living standards of Japan.

Figure 1.3 depicts the long-run evolution of per capita GDP in the four major European economies: Britain (the United Kingdom), France, Germany, and Italy. France, Germany, and Italy had lower per capita GDP than that of Britain throughout the nineteenth century and the first half of the twentieth century. France and Germany experienced a slow process of convergence until the eve of World War I, and faster convergence in the interwar period. In the aftermath of World War II, convergence was much more rapid, and by the early 1970s, per capita GDP did not differ by much in these four economies.

Both figures 1.2 and 1.3 display the significant rise of the rate of economic growth in the post–World War II period. In the 60 years between 1950 and 2010, the real per capita GDP of the United States more than tripled. In fact, it rose by about 3.2 times, from $9,561 (in 1990 prices) in 1950, to $30,491 in 2010. Its average annual growth rate was about 2% per year. The major developed European economies displayed even higher growth. The average

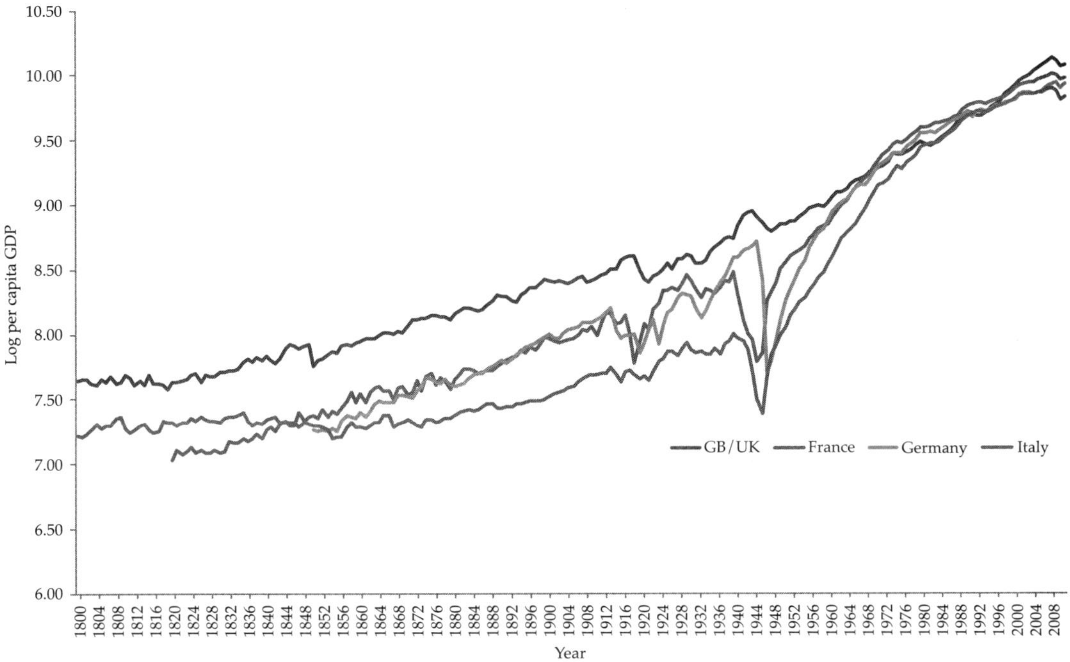

Figure 1.3
Long-run growth of (log) per capita GDP in the major European economies.

annual growth rates of real per capita GDP in Britain was 2.1%, slightly higher than in the United States. Italy achieved an average annual growth rate of 3.0%, Germany 2.8%, and France 2.4%. As a result, there was significant convergence of the per capita GDP of the major European economies to that of the United States. The average annual growth rate of per capita income in Japan was 4.1% in the same period, significantly higher than in the United States and the major European economies.

However, even during these 60 years, the less-developed economies have not demonstrated a uniform tendency toward convergence with the per capita incomes of the developed economies. Some developing economies, particularly in the rest of Western Europe and Southeast Asia, have achieved impressive increases in per capita income compared to 1950 and significant convergence with the living standards of the developed economies. However, other economies, particularly in Latin America, the rest of Asia, and Africa, have failed to display significant convergence; in fact, some of them have fallen dramatically behind.[30]

30. Crafts and O'Rourke [2014] present and try to account for the twentieth century growth experience of some additional economies in their effort to explain the growth experience of the past century.

1.3 Key Facts about Aggregate Fluctuations

Historically, the process of economic growth has been anything but smooth. As can be seen from both figures 1.2 and 1.3, GDP per capita displays significant fluctuations around its long-run trend. The explanation of these fluctuations in economic activity is the second main area of macroeconomics, besides long-run economic growth.

In accounting for the key facts about aggregate fluctuations, I present evidence mainly from the United States and the United Kingdom. These two countries have long and relatively consistent time series for the relevant variables, and, to a large extent, it is the experience of these two countries that has contributed to the development of macroeconomics as we know it. However, where appropriate, I present evidence for other countries as well.[31]

1.3.1 Frequency, Severity, and Duration of Recessions

Figure 1.4 presents the evolution of the log of real GDP per capita in the United States from 1854 to 2014. Figure 1.5 shows the evolution of the log of real GDP per capita in the United Kingdom from 1820 to 2014. The gray shaded areas indicate years of recession. Recessions are generally defined as periods in which there is a contraction in economic activity, with real GDP falling rather than rising.

In the United States, the Business Cycle Dating Committee of the National Bureau of Economic Research (NBER) is generally considered to be the authority for dating US recessions. The NBER defines an economic recession as "a significant decline in economic activity spread across the economy, lasting more than a few months, normally visible in real GDP, real income, employment, industrial production, and wholesale-retail sales (nber.org/cycles)." In the United Kingdom, recessions are generally defined as two consecutive quarters of negative economic growth, as measured by the seasonally adjusted quarter-on-quarter figures for real GDP. The same definition of a recession applies for all member states of the European Union and is the most widely used international definition of a recession.

As can be seen from figure 1.4, there were 54 years of recession in the United States between 1854 and 2014, and 107 years of no recession. In periods of recession, per capita GDP usually falls or remains stagnant. In the 161 years between 1854 and 2014, a recession occurred, on average, in 1 out of every 3 years. After World War II, a drop in the frequency of US recessions occurred. There were 14 years of recession between 1946 and 2014. In the 69 postwar years, a recession occurred, on average, in 1 out of every 4.9 years.

31. For more formal econometric approaches to the stylized facts regarding business cycles in the United States and the United Kingdom, see Hodrik and Prescott [1997] and Blackburn and Ravn [1992], among others. For international evidence, see Backus and Kehoe [1992] and Basu and Taylor [1999], among others.

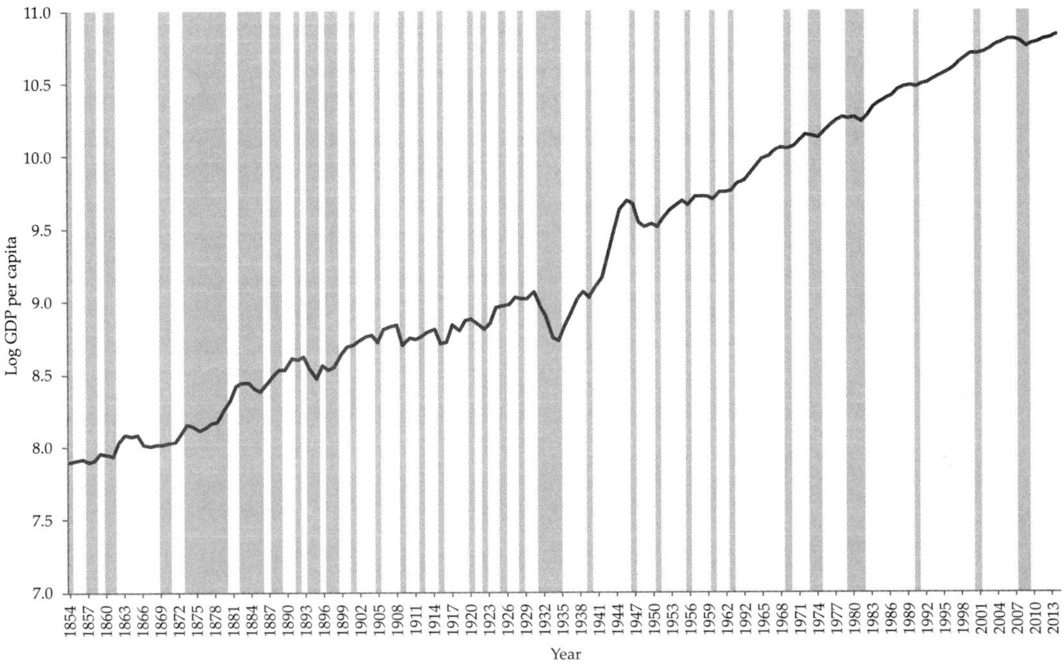

Figure 1.4
Recessions (shaded areas) and (log) per capita GDP in the United States.

In the United Kingdom (figure 1.5), there were 41 years of recession between 1820 and 2014, and 154 years of no recession. In the 195 years between 1820 and 2014, a recession occurred on average in 1 out of every 4.75 years. In the post–World War II period, there were 13 years of recession, with a recession occurring in 1 out of every 5.3 years on average.

What is also clear from figures 1.4 and 1.5 is that not all recessions are alike. Many recessions are short and shallow, but a few deep and quite prolonged ones also occur.

The longest US recession was that of the 1870s, while the deepest and second-longest recession was the Great Depression of the 1930s. The recessions of the 1890s were the deepest recessions before the onset of the Great Depression. In the post–World War II period, the most severe recessions were the ones of the early 1970s and early 1980s, as well as the recent recession of 2008–2009. In the United Kingdom, deep and long recessions occurred in the 1840s, in the aftermath of the two World Wars, in the early and late 1970s and the early 1980s, in the early 1990s, as well as in 2008–2009.[32]

32. For an extensive discussion of the available empirical evidence with regard to the key shocks driving aggregate fluctuations, see Ramey [2016].

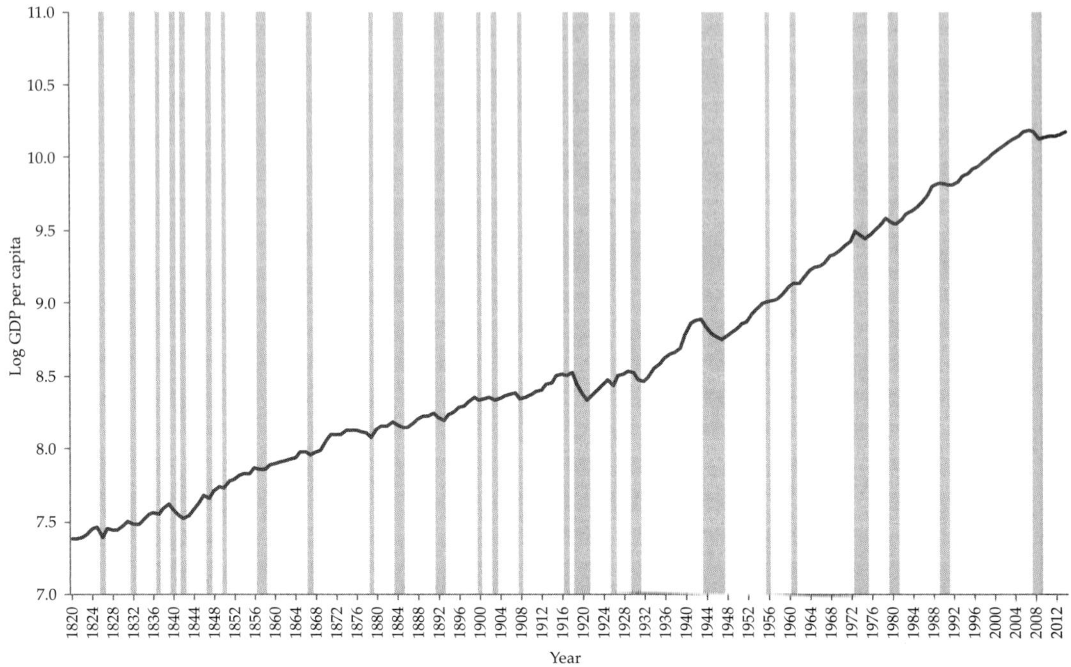

Figure 1.5
Recessions (shaded areas) and (log) per capita GDP in the United Kingdom.

1.3.2 Unemployment in Booms and Recessions

One of the key characteristics of recessions is that they are associated with falls in employment and persistent rises in *unemployment rates*.[33]

Figures 1.6 and 1.7 depict the evolution of unemployment rates in the United States and the United Kingdom, respectively. As is clear from both figures, large and prolonged rises in unemployment rates occur during recessions. On many occasions, the rise in unemployment continues even after the end of the recession, and the return of unemployment to lower levels is often quite slow.

The rise in unemployment is considered by many as the most significant economic and social cost of recessions, along with the general fall in real incomes.

Whereas in the pre–World War II period, unemployment in the United States tended to fluctuate around a rate slightly below 5% of the labor force, during the Great Depression, unemployment reached almost 25% of the labor force. The average unemployment rate in

33. Unemployment rates are measured as the number of those who declare themselves as unemployed (i.e, who are actively seeking a job), divided by the labor force, defined as the sum of the numbers of the employed and the unemployed.

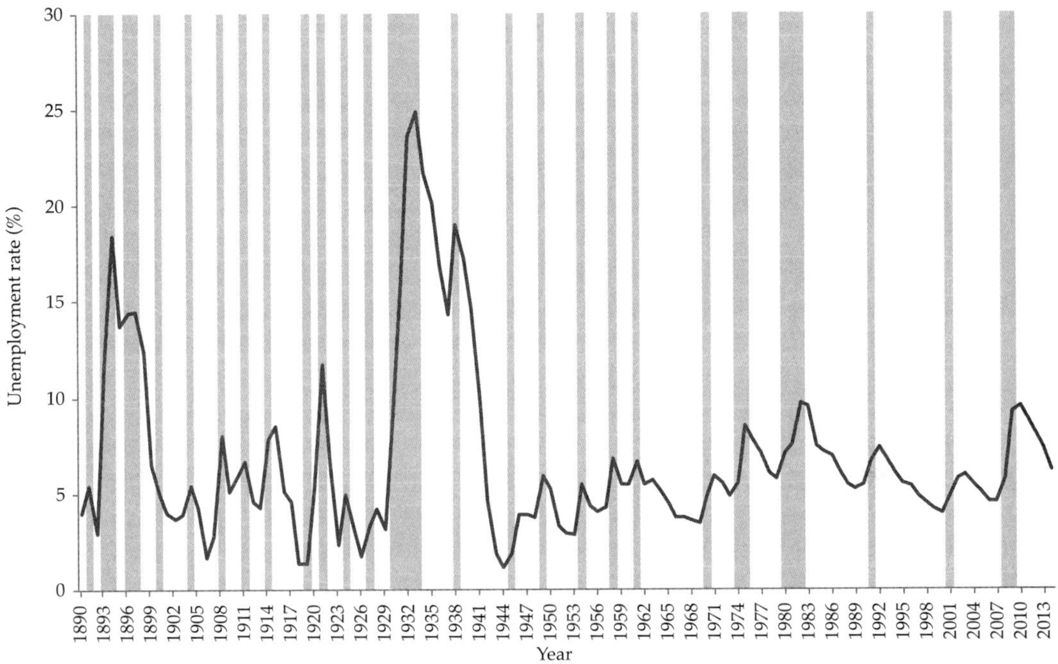

Figure 1.6
Recessions (shaded areas) and the unemployment rate in the United States.

the 1930s was 18.8% of the US labor force, higher than the peak unemployment rate of 18.4% in the previously deepest recession of the 1890s.[34]

In the post–World War II period, fluctuations in the US unemployment rate are smaller but significant nonetheless. In the recession of the 1970s, unemployment rose from 4.9% of the labor force in 1973 to a peak of 8.5% in 1975. In the recession of the early 1980s, unemployment rose from 5.8% of the labor force in 1979 to 9.7% in 1982. In the recession of 2008–2009, unemployment rose from 4.6% of the labor force in 2007 to 9.6% in 2010.

The UK experience is not too different. Unemployment rates as high as 7–10% were not uncommon in the recessions of the nineteenth century. In the recession of the early 1920s, unemployment rose to 12.1%, and in the Great Depression of the early 1930s, it rose to a peak of 15.3% in 1932.

In the post–World War II period unemployment in the United Kingdom was remarkably low for many years. However, following the recession of the early 1970s, it started creeping up. From 2.2% of the labor force in 1973, it rose to 5.1% in 1977. It is remarkable that it

34. Darby [1976] and C. Romer [1986] have provided lower revised estimates of the pre–World War II unemployment rates in the United States, but the general picture does not change.

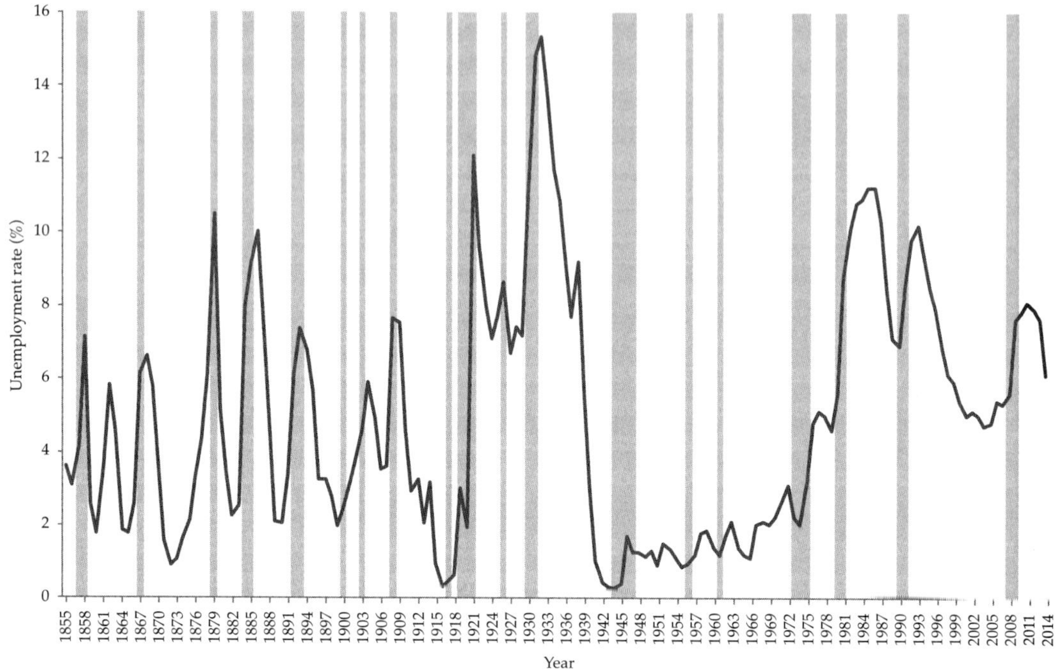

Figure 1.7
Recessions (shaded areas) and the unemployment rate in the United Kingdom.

continued rising even after the recovery had started. From 4.6% in 1979, it rose significantly during the recession of the early 1980s. It peaked at 11.2% of the labor force in 1985, long after the recovery had started. The same pattern was repeated in the recession of the early 1990s, and the deep recession of 2008–2009. In the early 1990s, the unemployment rate rose from 7.1% in 1989 to 10.2% in 1993, after the recession had ended; in the last recession, it rose from 5.3% in 2007 to a peak of 8.1% in 2011, 2 years after the end of the recession.

The sustained and persistent rise in unemployment, along with the sustained drop in real incomes, is thus one of the key characteristics of recessions, and one of the most important reasons that macroeconomics is concerned with aggregate fluctuations. Unemployment not only rises during recessions, but it also persists, and on many occasions, it peaks after a recession has turned into recovery. Thereafter, it falls only gradually during the recovery.

1.3.3 Trends and Fluctuations in the Price Level and Inflation

A third key macroeconomic variable that concerns both the general public and policymakers is the price level, and its rate of change, the rate of inflation. The price level and its rate of change is what determines the purchasing power of money incomes. Figures 1.8 and 1.9 depict the evolution of the price level in the United States and the United Kingdom,

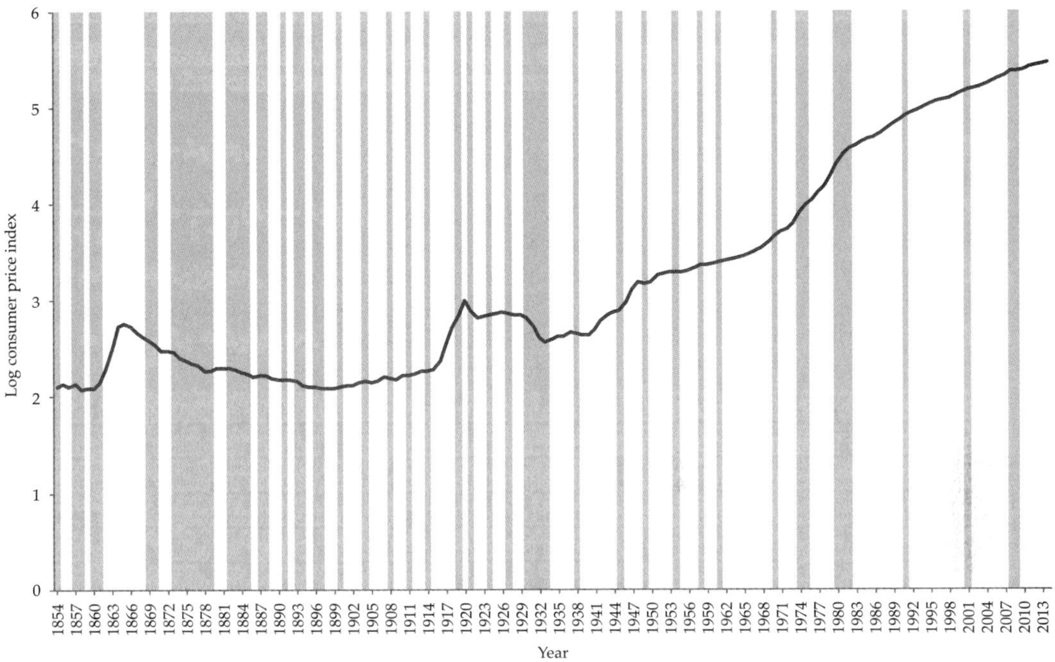

Figure 1.8
Evolution of the price level in the United States (shaded areas indicate recessions).

respectively, as measured by the index of consumer prices, while figures 1.10 and 1.11 depict the evolution of inflation.

Some interesting facts emerge from these figures with regard to the evolution of the price level and inflation.

The first fact is that before World War II, the price level did not display a marked upward trend, as it did after World War II. If anything, there were long periods of a falling price level, both during the gold standard period and in the interwar years. Inflation was a temporary phenomenon, associated with wars, such as the American Civil War of 1861–1865, World War I, or periods of economic boom. In contrast, the price level tended to fall during recessions, which were thus also periods of deflation.

Average annual inflation during 1854–1913 was only 0.6% in the United States, and average annual inflation during 1821–1913 in the United Kingdom was negative, −0.2% (figures 1.10 and 1.11). The price level in the United Kingdom was on a slightly negative trend until World War I. Had it not been for the American Civil War, the United States would probably also have been characterized by falling prices.

During the American Civil War, US inflation averaged approximately 15% per year, with peak inflation rates of about 25% in both 1863 and 1864. During World War I, average annual inflation was equal to 9.7% in the United States and to 15.3% in the United Kingdom.

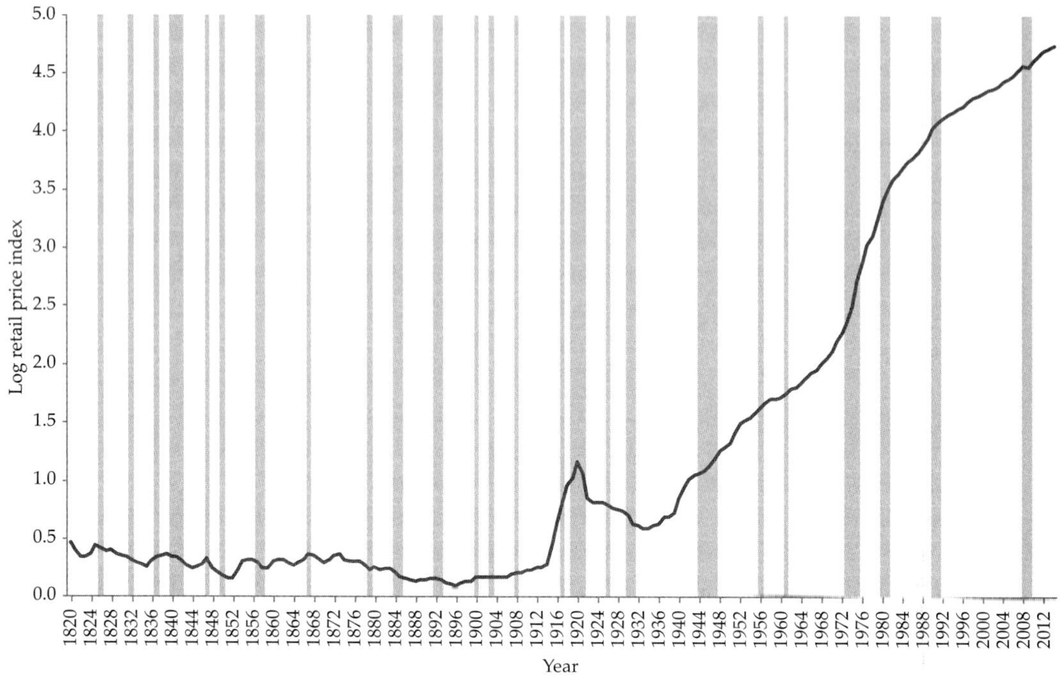

Figure 1.9
Evolution of the price level in the United Kingdom (shaded areas indicate recessions).

During the interwar period (1919–1939), deflation occurred in both countries. Prices in the United States were falling by 0.2% per year on average, whereas prices in the United Kingdom were falling by 0.9% per year on average.

As can be seen from figures 1.8–1.11, after World War II, the price level displays a significant positive trend in both the United States and the United Kingdom. Average inflation has been positive and periodically high in both countries throughout the post–World War II period.

In addition, the negative impact of recessions on the price level and inflation, which was a regular characteristic of the pre–World War II period, does not seem to hold as firmly in the postwar period. The recessions of the 1970s and the early 1980s are associated with an increase rather than a decrease in inflation, a phenomenon that has been described as *stagflation*.

What stands out when trying to explain the long-run trends of the price level and inflation is (1) the very high correlation of inflation and the rate of growth of the money supply and (2) the total lack of correlation of economic growth and the growth of the money supply.

Figure 1.12 shows the close correlation between inflation and the rate of growth of the money supply, as measured by a broad measure of the money stock (M2) in 110 countries,

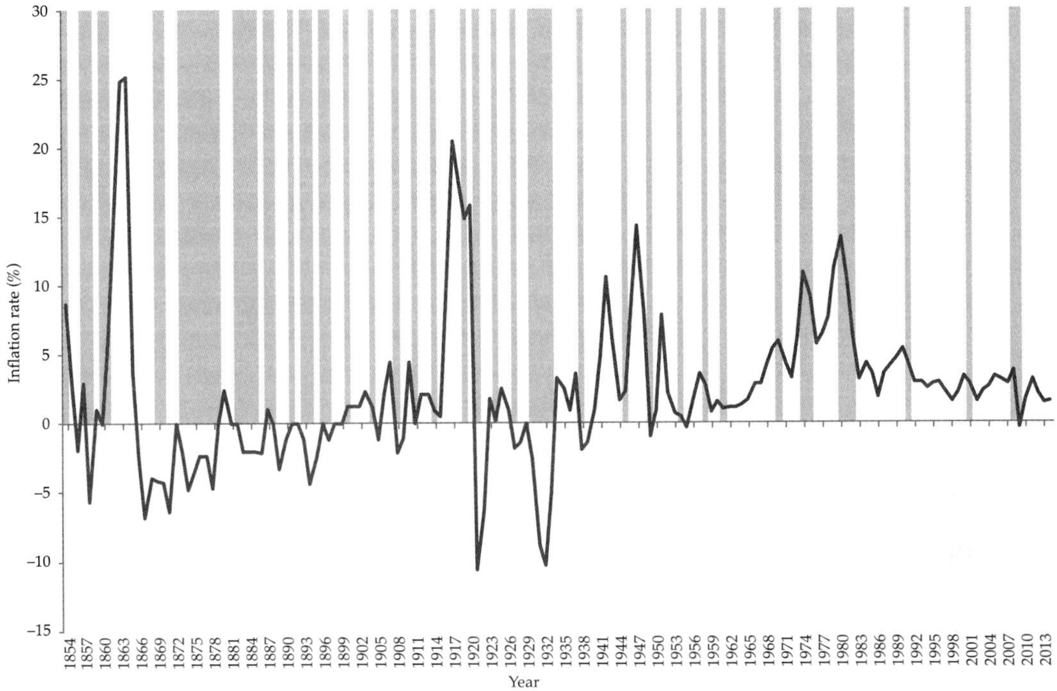

Figure 1.10
Evolution of consumer price index(CPI) inflation in the United States (shaded areas indicate recessions).

for 1960–1990. The correlation coefficient is equal to 0.95. In figure 1.13, one can see the complete absence of any correlation between the growth rate of real GDP and the rate of growth of the money supply. The correlation coefficient is -0.014 and is not statistically significant.

These two facts—the almost complete correlation of money growth and inflation and the total absence of any correlation between money growth and economic growth—form the empirical basis of the assumption of the *long-run neutrality of money*, characteristic of both models of economic growth and models of aggregate fluctuations. This long-run neutrality of money is one of the main predictions of the *quantity theory of money*. As Lucas [1996, p. 668] has commented:

> The prediction that prices respond proportionally to changes in money in the long run, deduced by Hume in 1752 (and by many other theorists, by many different routes, since), has received ample—I would say decisive—confirmation, in data from many times and places. The observation that money changes induce output changes in the same direction receives confirmation in some data sets but is hard to see in others. Large-scale reductions in money growth can be associated with large-scale depressions or, if carried out in the form of a credible reform, with no depression at all.

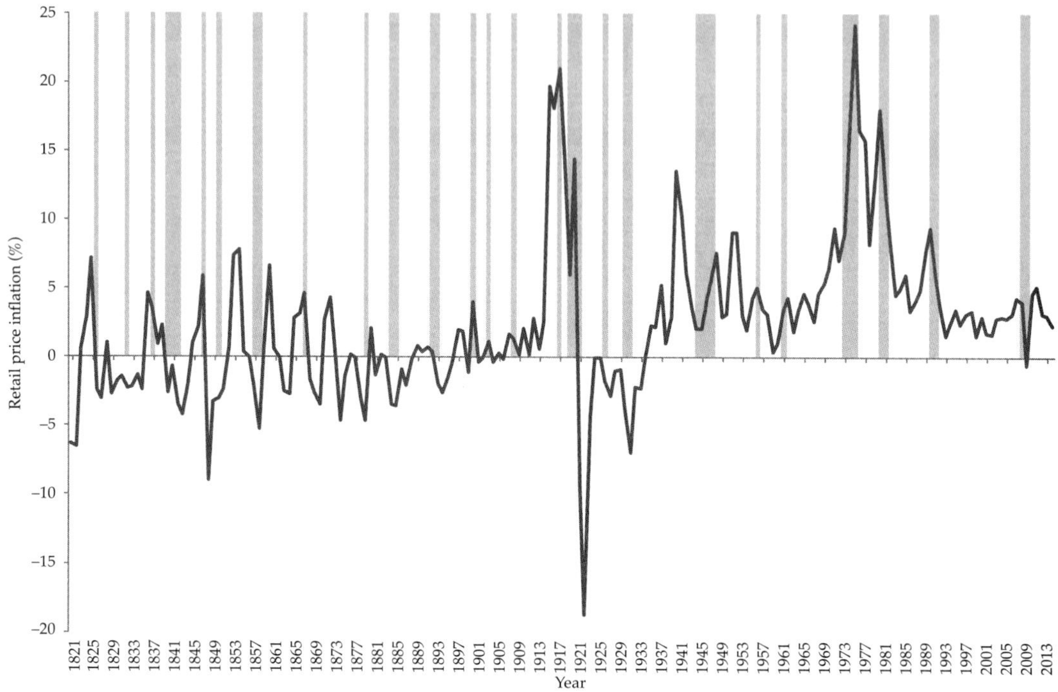

Figure 1.11
Evolution of CPI inflation in the United Kingdom (shaded areas indicate recessions).

As we shall see when we discuss models of the determination of inflation in the relevant chapters 7, 12, and 20, one cannot explain the evolution of the price level and inflation without reference to monetary policy and its relation to fiscal policy and the aims of stabilization policy.

1.3.4 Monetary Policy and Government Debt

At the risk of running a bit ahead of our discussion in the relevant chapter, I provide a short explanation of the trends in prices and inflation depicted in figures 1.8–1.11. A fuller explanation will have to wait for the analysis of models of inflation and monetary policy in chapters 7, 12, and 20, and the determination of fiscal policy and government debt in chapters 6 and 21.

There was no systematic inflation and the price level did not display a particular trend until World War I, because for most of this period, both the United States and the United Kingdom had adopted metallic monetary systems, based on precious metals (specie), such as gold and silver. Such metallic systems constrained the rate of growth of the money supply. When they were forced to temporarily abandon such systems, as during wars, both countries sought to return to such systems as soon as possible.

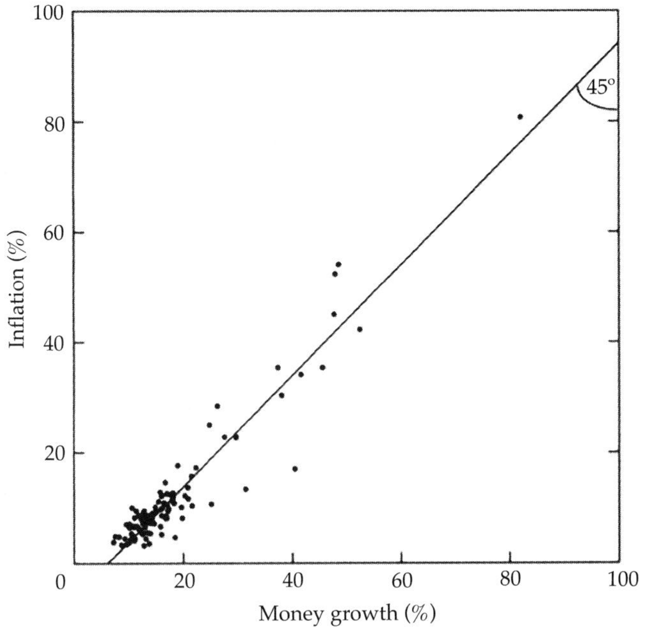

Figure 1.12
Money growth and inflation in 110 countries, 1960–1990. Adapted from McCandles and Weber [1995].

Britain had been on a de facto gold standard since the early eighteenth century. The United States had been on a silver standard until 1834, on a bimetallic standard until 1861, and on an effective gold standard since 1879.

During the Napoleonic Wars of 1803–1815 in the United Kingdom and the American Civil War of 1861–1865 in the United States, the convertibility to specie was suspended. Thus, the link of the money supply to gold and silver was relaxed through the issuance of nonconvertible paper currency. The Bank of England issued nonconvertible sterling banknotes, and the United States issued nonconvertible *greenbacks*. The issuance of nonconvertible banknotes was used to finance these countries' respective war and resulted in large increases in the money supply. The increase in the money supply resulted in a rise in the price level through inflation. Yet in both countries, the suspension of convertibility was always considered to be temporary. Sterling convertibility was restored in 1821, and dollar convertibility was finally restored in 1879.

What happened during the Napoleonic Wars and the American Civil War is an example of the use of *seigniorage* (i.e., revenue from money creation) to partly finance temporary increases in government expenditure. Government expenditure rises significantly during a war, and money creation is one of the ways to finance this temporarily increased expenditure. The other is *government debt*.

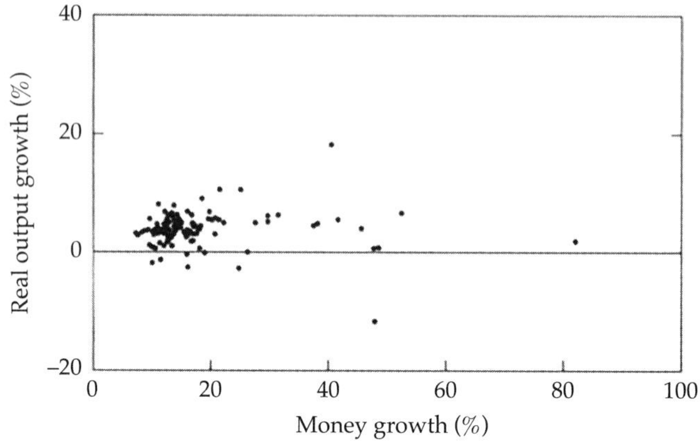

Figure 1.13
Money growth and real GDP growth in 110 countries, 1960–1990. Adapted from McCandles and Weber [1995].

Figure 1.14 depicts the federal debt of the US government as a percentage of GDP since 1792. With a few exceptions, episodes of significant increase in the ratio of federal debt to GDP are associated with recessions and major wars, such as the American Civil War and the two great wars of the twentieth century (during 1914–1918 and 1939–1945). Major recessions, such as the Great Depression of the early 1930s and the Great Recession of 2008–2009, are also associated with significant hikes in government debt.

Wars require significant rises in government expenditure. Governments, instead of raising taxes, resort to temporary borrowing and inflationary finance to minimize the economic and political disadvantages of significant hikes in taxes. The same happens during recessions. Recessions result in a temporary fall in tax revenues, because of the reduction in economic activity, and temporary increases in expenditure on unemployment insurance and social protection.

Hence, both wars and recessions result in rises in government deficits and debts and, in the case of wars, they result in increases in revenue from money creation. We shall examine the relationship between war finance, inflation, and government debt in various parts of the book (mainly in chapters 12 and 21).

The United States had remained on the gold standard during World War I. In addition, in 1913, the Federal Reserve System was created and assumed the role of the central bank of the United States. The money supply increased less in the United States than in the United Kingdom during World War I, as the war affected the US economy and federal government expenditure less than in the case of Britain. As a result, the need for seigniorage was not as large in the United States.

Figure 1.15 depicts UK public debt as a percentage of GDP since 1792. Significant rises in the ratio of British public debt to GDP are associated with major wars, such as

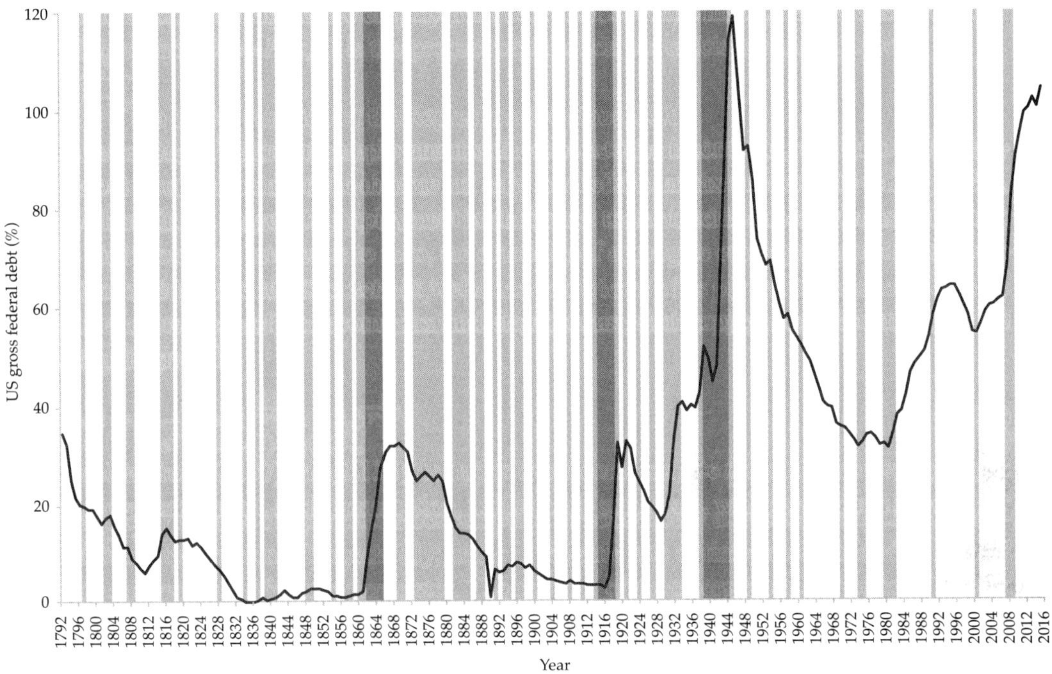

Figure 1.14
Evolution of US federal debt as a percentage of GDP (dark shaded areas indicate major wars; light shaded areas indicate recessions).

the Napoleonic Wars (1803–1815) and the two great wars of the twentieth century. As in the case of the United States, they are also associated with recessions, such as the Great Depression of the early 1930s and the Great Recession of 2008–2009.

During World War I, the United Kingdom resorted to both government debt and money creation when convertibility to gold was suspended. The reason was again to help finance the war without disruptive rises in taxes.

However, after the war, the major aim of UK postwar financial policy became the return to gold at the prewar parity. Thus, from the early 1920s, UK monetary policy was extremely deflationary so as to reverse the wartime rise of the price level and allow sterling to return to the gold standard at the prewar parity to gold and the US dollar.

The 1920s was a period of monetary instability for many European economies. Germany, and other economies in Central Europe, experienced hyper inflations that totally disrupted their payments system. The underlying cause was the need to pay war reparations and the excessive use of seigniorage (see chapter 12).

The United Kingdom returned to the gold standard in 1925, after a prolonged period of deflation. However, when the Great Depression struck, the United Kingdom was forced to

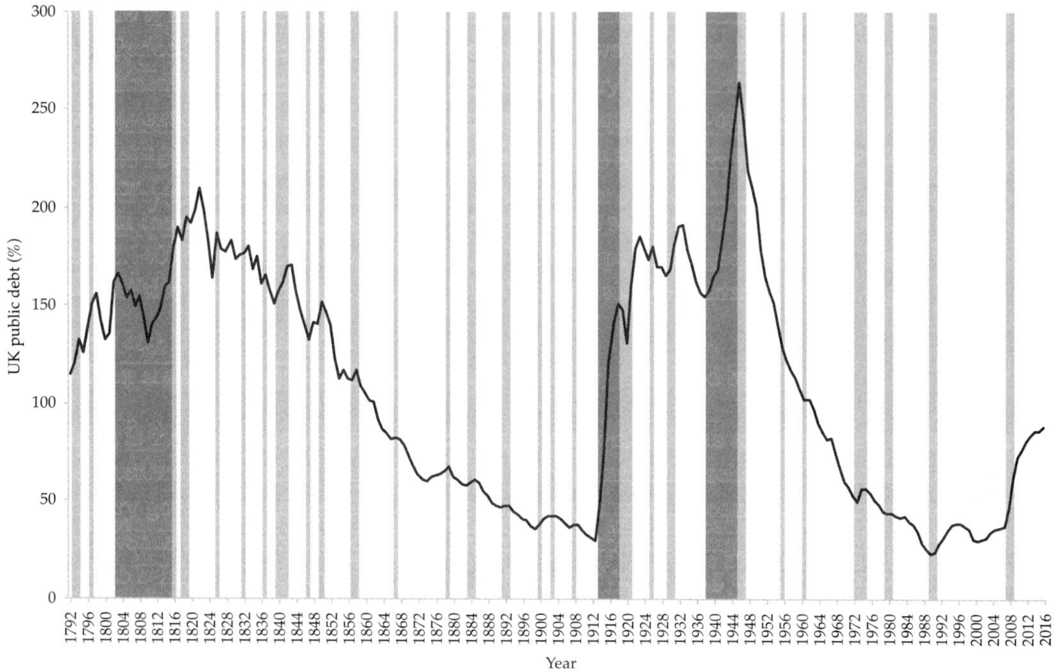

Figure 1.15
Evolution of UK public debt as a percentage of GDP (dark shaded areas indicate major wars; light shaded areas indicate recessions).

again abandon the gold standard, which it duly did in 1931. The United States, which had maintained the gold standard during the war, also allowed the dollar to be gradually devalued by about 40% against gold in both 1933 and 1934. From $20.67 an ounce, the price of gold rose to $35 an ounce.

The gold standard changed permanently in 1934, as gold coinage was discontinued in the United States, and significant holdings of gold coins or bullion by the public were made illegal. Thus, convertibility only remained for the purposes of foreign payments. This change had important consequences for monetary policy and inflation, especially in the post–World War II period.

To explain the change in the behavior of prices and inflation during World War II and especially in the postwar period, one must thus again refer to monetary policy. Both the United States and the United Kingdom resorted to significant increases in the money supply to finance part of the cost of World War II. As a result, the price level and inflation rose, despite extensive price controls during the war.

1.3.5 Monetary Policy and Inflation in the Postwar Period

The nature of monetary policy changed after World War II. The Bretton Woods system of fixed but adjustable exchange rates, which was agreed upon in 1944 by the United States, the United Kingdom, and a host of other countries, was quite different from the international gold standard. Although the United States undertook to maintain a fixed price of gold at $35 an ounce and managed to do so until 1968, convertibility existed only among central banks, and for the purpose of foreign payments. Domestic convertibility to gold was not restored in any of the industrial economies. The United Kingdom and other industrial economies undertook to maintain a fixed exchange rate vis-à-vis the dollar, but the system allowed for currency devaluations in the case of "fundamental disequilibrium."

Monetary policy in the post–World War II period, free from the constraints of convertibility and influenced by Keynesian macroeconomics, was directed toward the goal of maintaining high employment. This was partly because no country was prepared to see a return to the unemployment rates of the 1930s.

As we shall see in the relevant chapters (chapters 15 and 20), if a central bank seeks to keep unemployment at a very low rate, it can eventually lead to high inflation through an increase in inflationary expectations. Until the 1980s, the Federal Reserve, the Bank of England, and other central banks sought to maintain low nominal interest rates. The money supply accommodated changes in the demand for money, caused either by real output growth or by inflation. The goal of maintaining low unemployment took higher precedence relative to the prewar period, which contributed to a rise in the average rate of inflation.

When the Bretton Woods system collapsed in the early 1970s, monetary policy became even more conducive to inflation. Inflation, which until the late 1960s was persistently positive but relatively low, increased significantly in the 1970s, a period also characterized by two recessions and low growth. As mentioned earlier, the term *stagflation* was invented to explain this phenomenon. It was only after the restrictive monetary policies of the early 1980s in the United States, the United Kingdom, and other industrial economies, that inflation returned to low levels, as their monetary authorities changed the primary emphasis of monetary policy from low unemployment to low inflation.

To summarize, neither the long-run evolution nor the fluctuations of the price level and inflation can be analyzed without reference to monetary and fiscal factors and policies. In periods of temporarily high government expenditure, such as wars, monetary policy is subordinated to fiscal policy, as governments finance a large part of the increased expenditure through money creation and government debt. Money creation results in inflation, which is higher during wars.

In the period before World War II, when most developed countries were on the gold or silver standard, their price levels did not display a significant upward trend, and average inflation was close to zero. This was because the requirement of convertibility constrained the rate of growth of the money supply to be very low. Periods of war often resulted in suspension of convertibility and temporarily high inflation, as monetary policy was subordinated to the financing needs of national treasuries, and so the rate of growth of the money supply increased significantly. Periods of recession were usually associated with deflation and moderate increases in government debt.

In the post–World War II period, the stance of monetary policy appears to have become more accommodative, leading to a positive trend for the price level and permanently positive inflation. Inflation increased significantly in the 1970s, when the system of floating exchange rates further freed up national monetary policies to pursue high employment targets.

Since the early 1980s, the problem of high inflation has been addressed in the main industrial economies, as national central banks shifted the focus of monetary policy from low unemployment to low inflation. The negative link between inflation and recessions was also broken in the post–World War II period, as the recessions of the 1970s were characterized by rises in inflation, resulting in stagflation.

But some countries continue to be plagued by high inflation rates. The underlying reason for their problems is the same as that which caused inflation to rise in wartime in both the United States and the United Kingdom. This is none other than the need to finance part of government expenditure through seigniorage, as other methods of finance do not suffice. Thus, the problem of high and persistent inflation in some countries (or even the problem of hyperinflation) has its roots in the inadequacies of those countries' fiscal systems, or their temporary collapse because of wars, civil wars, revolutions, or extreme forms of political and economic instability. Models that can explain episodes of very high inflation and hyperinflation are analyzed in chapter 12.

1.4 Conclusion

This introductory chapter provides a brief overview of the evolution and the current state of macroeconomics as well as some key facts about long-run economic growth and fluctuations in output, unemployment, and inflation.

It thus sets the stage for an examination and assessment of the main macroeconomic models of long-run growth and aggregate fluctuations that are presented in the remainder of this book.

2

The Intertemporal Approach

The intertemporal approach is the dominant theoretical approach in modern macroeconomics. Hence, it is the main theme of this text. By way of introduction, it is worth laying out the main elements of this approach in the context of the simplest possible intertemporal macroeconomic models. This is the main function of the present chapter.

The intertemporal approach is fully grounded on neoclassical microeconomics, as it is based on the assumption that households maximize their intertemporal utility and firms maximize the present value of their profits, subject to the appropriate resource, technological, market, and information constraints.

The approach is also based on the concept of *general intertemporal equilibrium*, either through the operation of fully competitive markets or through markets subjected to various distortions relative to the competitive model. Relative prices (such as real interest rates and real wages) and nominal magnitudes (such as the price level, inflation, and nominal interest rates) are assumed to be determined through appropriate general equilibrium concepts, which depend on market structure and assumptions about price and wage flexibility.

Intertemporal, or dynamic, general equilibrium models are thus based on the resource, technological, market, and informational possibilities of households, firms, and the government, who choose the optimal path of consumption, production, employment, and investment. These possibilities are described by appropriate intertemporal budget constraints. The analysis of the role of money and the interrelated intertemporal budget constraints of the private and public sectors illuminate the role of monetary and fiscal policy and the possibilities of the government and government agencies (such as central banks) to affect and improve on macroeconomic outcomes. The properties of intertemporal models depend on the equilibrium concept used, the nature of the assumed market and informational distortions, and the assumptions adopted about the degree of price and wage flexibility.

In this chapter, we focus on competitive economies lasting for only two periods, period 1 (the *present*) and period 2 (the *future*). The two-period competitive model is the simplest possible intertemporal general equilibrium model and can be analyzed with the help of relatively simple mathematical tools. We thus use it to investigate some salient characteristics of the intertemporal approach, avoiding the mathematical complexity and other complications that sometimes emerge in multiperiod dynamic general equilibrium models.

As will become apparent in the remainder of this book, many properties of the two-period model carry over to multiperiod intertemporal models, such as infinite-horizon models. In addition, many models that are based on market distortions (such as transactions costs, externalities, increasing returns to scale, and imperfect or asymmetric information) can be best understood when juxtaposed with simple competitive intertemporal models.

We start by investigating general competitive equilibrium in a one-period macroeconomic model with exogenous capital and labor endowments. Then we investigate intertemporal general equilibrium in a two-period competitive macroeconomic model, which allows for savings and investment. We also investigate extensions of the two-period model to examine intertemporal substitution in labor supply, the role of money and monetary policy, and the role of fiscal policy.

Many themes examined through the two-period models of this chapter will be revisited and expanded on in the context of the infinite-horizon models used to analyze economic growth, aggregate fluctuations, and the role of monetary and fiscal policy in the remainder of this book. Therefore, the investment required to understand the two-period intertemporal model has high payoffs.

2.1 Models, Variables, and Functions

Before I introduce the intertemporal approach, it is worth briefly reviewing the nature of mathematical models in macroeconomics.

Scientific models can be thought of as imaginary, simplified versions of the aspect of the world being studied. They are based on a set of simplifying assumptions about the real world phenomenon being studied, and their analysis helps in the derivation of the logical implications of these assumptions for both the model, and, hopefully, for the real world phenomenon under study. If the simplifying assumptions are not critical for the properties of the model relative to the real world phenomenon, then the predictions and properties of the model carry over to the real world.[1]

Macroeconomic *models* are thus simplified representations of economies, which allow us to analyze their salient characteristics. Although there is no inherent reason why a model must be mathematical, mathematical models ensure internal consistency in our reasoning about actual economies. They also allow us to handle a greater degree of complexity than nonmathematical models and also to assess the quantitative significance of various factors. It is for these reasons that macroeconomic models are expressed in mathematical form.

1. See Rodrik [2015], and in particular, chapter 1, for an informed discussion of the role of models and the role of simplifying assumptions in economics.

Mathematical macroeconomic models consist of variables, functions, and parameters. They are meant to describe the outcome of the behavior and the interactions of economic agents, such as households, firms, the government, and government agencies (such as central banks).

The behavioral rules of economic agents can be postulated directly or derived by making assumptions about the preferences and constraints faced by these agents and then using the main postulates of rational choice on which microeconomics is based. Methods of mathematical optimization allow us to model the behavior of agents that maximize their objective functions under appropriate constraints. Thus, households are assumed to follow rules that maximize their utility functions under appropriate budget and market constraints, while firms are assumed to follow rules that maximize an appropriately defined profit function under the relevant technological and market constraints. Similar considerations apply to the government and government agencies.

Mathematical economic models typically take the form of systems of equations, designed to describe the structure of the economy in question and the behavior of economic agents.

The equations relate variables to one another and are meant to be *behavioral relations*, *accounting identities*, or *equilibrium conditions*. *Variables* refer to economic magnitudes that can take different values. There is an important distinction between *endogenous variables* (i.e., variables whose values are determined by the model itself) and *exogenous variables*, whose values are determined outside the model and are taken as exogenously given.

Another important element of mathematical models is a set of *parameters*, usually assumed constant and exogenously given. Parameters relate to the objective functions and constraints of economic agents, and they eventually determine the relations among endogenous and exogenous variables in the model.

Equations in mathematical models take the form of *mathematical functions*, which describe the relation of a particular variable to other variables in the model. Functions can be linear or nonlinear.

Variables and parameters of functions are usually defined in terms of *real numbers*. Real numbers can be thought of as points on an infinitely long line called the "number line" or "real line," where the points corresponding to integers are equally spaced. Any real number can be determined by a possibly infinite decimal representation, such as that of 8.632. The real line can be thought of as a part of the complex plane, and complex numbers include real numbers.[2]

Examples of such intertemporal macroeconomic models follow in the remainder of this chapter.

2. Appendix A contains a more general treatment of mathematical concepts related to mathematical models, such as variables, functions, and optimization.

2.2 General Equilibrium in a One-Period Competitive Model

To gain a better understanding of the intertemporal approach, and its differences from non-intertemporal approaches, we first analyze a one-period competitive macroeconomic model without savings and investment.

In this model, we assume that there is a continuum of identical households with the same capital and labor endowments and the same preferences. Households live only for one (the current) period. We can thus analyze the behavior of the *representative household* with a one-period horizon. We shall maintain the concept of a representative household throughout this chapter. We also assume a continuum of identical competitive firms, who hire capital and labor from households and produce a homogeneous output. Because all firms are identical and trade at the same factor and output prices in competitive markets, we only analyze the behavior of one of them, the *representative firm*.

2.2.1 Endowments, Preferences, and the Optimal Behavior of Households

The representative household lives for one period and is characterized by its *endowments* and its *preferences*. We assume that the representative household is endowed with one unit of capital and one unit of labor. Its endowment of capital and labor can be rented to private firms at a competitive rental price of capital r and a competitive real wage w, respectively. Capital and labor are used by competitive firms in the production of a single good y, which has the same characteristics as the capital endowment of the household. The household can use the income from the rental of its capital and labor endowments for consumption, and it can also consume its capital endowment at the end of the period.

Denoting the stock of capital rented to private firms by k, the volume of labor services rented out by l, and the volume of consumption by c, the resource constraints of the representative household are given by

$$c \leq 1 + rk + wl, \tag{2.1}$$

$$k \leq 1, \tag{2.2}$$

$$l \leq 1. \tag{2.3}$$

(2.1) indicates that consumption cannot exceed the sum of the income and the capital endowment of the household. (2.2) and (2.3) indicate that the household cannot rent out more than its one unit of endowment of capital and labor.[3]

We assume that the preferences of the representative household are described by a continuous, twice differentiable, concave utility function u, which depends on the volume of consumption c of the single good:

3. Note that the household can consume all of its capital endowment, although it may choose to rent out part of it. This is why the budget constraint (2.1) has this form instead of the form $c \leq (1+r)k + wl$.

$$u(c). \tag{2.4}$$

The utility function (2.4) satisfies

$$u' = \frac{\partial u}{\partial c} > 0, u'' = \frac{\partial^2 u}{\partial c^2} < 0. \tag{2.5}$$

Thus, the marginal utility of consumption is assumed positive but diminishing. The assumption of a strictly positive marginal utility at all levels of consumption implies that the preferences of the representative household are characterized by *nonsatiation*. Hence, the representative household always prefers more to less consumption.

The Lagrange function for the problem of the maximization of (2.4), subject to the constraints (2.1), (2.2), and (2.3), can be written as

$$\mathcal{L} = u(c) - \lambda_1 (c - 1 - rk - wl) - \lambda_2(k - 1) - \lambda_3(l - 1), \tag{2.6}$$

where λ_1, λ_2, λ_3 are the Langrange multipliers for the constraints (2.1), (2.2), and (2.3), respectively.[4]

The first-order conditions for a maximum are

$$\lambda_1 = u', \tag{2.7}$$

$$\lambda_2 = \lambda_1 r, \tag{2.8}$$

$$\lambda_3 = \lambda_1 w. \tag{2.9}$$

The interpretation of these first-order conditions is straightforward. (2.7) implies that the shadow price of the budget constraint (2.1), λ_1, will be positive, because the marginal utility of consumption is always positive. Hence, the household will consume all its current income plus its capital endowment at the end of the period. The budget constraint (2.1) will be satisfied with equality.

Because λ_1 is positive, (2.8) and (2.9) imply that λ_2 and λ_3 will also be positive for a positive real rental price of capital r and a positive real wage w. Hence the household will commit its full capital and labor endowment for rental and productive use. The resource constraints (2.2) and (2.3) will thus also be satisfied with equality.

Hence, from the assumption of nonsatiation, embodied in (2.4) and (2.5), the household will rent out its full capital and labor endowment as long as it earns a positive rental price r for capital and a positive real wage w for labor. It will also consume all of its income plus its capital endowment. As a result, the household will choose c to maximize (2.4), subject to the constraints (2.1), (2.2), and (2.3) holding with equality. As a result, the supply of capital and labor to firms and consumption demand will be equal to, respectively,

4. See appendix A for an introduction to utility maximization and the Lagrange method.

$$k = 1, \tag{2.10}$$

$$l = 1, \tag{2.11}$$

$$c = 1 + r + w. \tag{2.12}$$

Thus, by maximizing its utility subject to its endowments and its budget constraint, the representative household will commit its full endowments to rental and production; and it will consume all its current income plus the endowment that can be consumed, such as the capital stock.

This completes the discussion of the optimal decisions of the representative household.

Exercise 2.1 Assume that the representative household is endowed with k_0 units of capital and l_0 units of labor. Derive the quantities of capital and labor rented out to private firms, assuming that the household maximizes utility subject to the relevant resource constraints in this case.

2.2.2 The Production Function and the Profit-Maximizing Behavior of Firms

Output is produced by competitive firms, who rent the factors of production (such as capital and labor services) from households through competitive factor markets. All firms have access to the same technology and factor markets, and they produce a homogeneous output y, through the following *neoclassical production function*:

$$y = AF(k, l). \tag{2.13}$$

A is an exogenous technological parameter denoting *total factor productivity*, and F is a continuous, twice differentiable, quasi-concave function. The factors of production are capital k and labor l. We assume that F is characterized by positive but diminishing returns to each factor of production, but constant returns to scale.

From the assumptions we have made, the first and second derivatives of the production function satisfy

$$\begin{aligned} F_k &= \frac{\partial F}{\partial k} > 0, F_l = \frac{\partial F}{\partial l} > 0, \\ F_{kk} &= \frac{\partial^2 F}{\partial k^2} < 0, F_{kl} = \frac{\partial^2 F}{\partial k \partial l} > 0, \\ F_{ll} &= \frac{\partial^2 F}{\partial l^2} < 0, F_{lk} = \frac{\partial^2 F}{\partial l \partial k} > 0. \end{aligned} \tag{2.14}$$

The marginal product of both factors of production is positive but diminishing. In addition, the marginal product of each factor is a positive function of the employment of the other factor.

Constant returns to scale imply that if all factors of production are multiplied by any nonnegative real number—say, μ—the scale of production is also multiplied by μ. Thus, (2.13) also satisfies

$$\mu y = AF(\mu k, \mu l) \tag{2.15}$$

for any $\mu \geq 0$.

Because of the assumption of constant returns to scale, we can multiply all factors by $1/l$, and the production function can be written as

$$\hat{y} = AF(\hat{k}, 1) = Af(\hat{k}), \tag{2.16}$$

where $\hat{y} = y/l$ is output per worker, and $\hat{k} = k/l$ is capital per worker.

Because of the assumptions about the original production function, the per-worker production function f satisfies the following properties:

$$f(0) = 0, f'(\hat{k}) = \frac{\partial f}{\partial \hat{k}} > 0, f''(\hat{k}) = \frac{\partial^2 f}{\partial \hat{k}^2} < 0. \tag{2.17}$$

Thus, the marginal, and average, product of capital per worker is positive and declining.

Firms are assumed to maximize profits $\mathcal{P}$. Hence, they choose capital and labor to maximize

$$\mathcal{P} = AF(k, l) - rk - wl = l(Af(\hat{k}) - r\hat{k} - w). \tag{2.18}$$

From the first-order conditions for a maximum, we have

$$r = AF_k = Af'(\hat{k}), \tag{2.19}$$

$$w = AF_l = Af(\hat{k}) - \hat{k}Af'(\hat{k}). \tag{2.20}$$

Firms will employ capital and labor up to the point where (i) the marginal product of capital is equal to the rental price of capital r and (ii) the marginal product of labor is equal to the real wage w.

Note that because of the assumption of constant returns to scale, factor payments are equal to total output, and firms make zero profits. From (2.19) and (2.20), it follows that

$$rk + wl = kAf'(\hat{k}) + lAf(\hat{k}) - kAf'(\hat{k}) = lAf(\hat{k}) = AF(k, l). \tag{2.21}$$

Thus, because of constant returns to scale, the labor and capital income of households add up to total output.

Because firms operate in competitive markets, they all face the same factor prices. Because they are also assumed to have access to the same technology, they will all choose the same quantities of capital and labor. Thus, we can confine our analysis to the problem of the *representative firm*. To derive explicit solutions for factor demands and output supply by the representative firm, we have to make explicit assumptions about the production function.

2.2.3 The Cobb-Douglas Production Function

For analytical simplicity, we confine our analysis to the *Cobb-Douglas production function* of the form[5]

$$y = Ak^{\alpha} l^{1-\alpha}, \tag{2.22}$$

where $0 < \alpha < 1$ is a fixed parameter denoting the output elasticity of capital, and $1 - \alpha$ is the output elasticity of labor.

We can easily confirm that the Cobb-Douglas production function (2.22) satisfies all the assumptions we have made about the neoclassical production function in (2.14) and (2.15). The Cobb-Douglas production function (2.22) is a continuous, twice differentiable, quasi-concave homogeneous function, characterized by constant returns to scale. The marginal product of both factors of production is positive but diminishing, and the marginal product of each factor is a positive function of the employment of the other factor.

From the marginal productivity conditions (2.19) and (2.20) and the Cobb-Douglas production function (2.22), it follows that

$$r = \alpha Ak^{\alpha-1} l^{1-\alpha} = aA\hat{k}^{\alpha-1}, \tag{2.23}$$

$$w = (1-\alpha)Ak^{\alpha} l^{-\alpha} = (1-\alpha)A\hat{k}^{\alpha}. \tag{2.24}$$

This completes our discussion of the optimal behavior of the representative firm.

2.2.4 General Equilibrium in the One-Period Model

We next turn to the discussion of general equilibrium. Equilibrium employment, output, consumption, real wages, and the real rental price of capital will be determined by (i) the equality of the supply of factors of production by households and the demand for factors of production by firms and (ii) the equality of the demand for and the supply of output.

Because the supply of capital and labor has been shown to be equal to the endowments of the representative household, which have both been assumed to be exogenously given and equal to unity, it follows that capital per worker in production will also be equal to unity. We thus have that

$$k = 1, l = 1, \hat{k} = 1. \tag{2.25}$$

5. This production function was first put forward by Cobb and Douglas [1928] to fit empirical equations for production, employment, and the capital stock in US manufacturing. It has since been known as the Cobb-Douglas production function, although this functional form was first explored in the nineteenth century by economists such as von Thunen, Marshall, Clark, Wicksell, and Wicksteed. See Humphrey [1997] for a discussion of the evolution of algebraic production functions before Cobb and Douglas [1928]. More general production functions, such as the CES production function, are introduced in appendix A.

The equilibrium real rental price of capital will be determined in the market for capital, and the equilibrium real wage will be determined in the market for labor, by the equality of the demand and supply for capital and labor.

Substituting (2.25) in (2.23) and (2.24), we find that the equilibrium real rental price of capital and the equilibrium real wage are determined by

$$\begin{aligned} \bar{r} &= \alpha A, \\ \bar{w} &= (1-\alpha)A, \end{aligned} \tag{2.26}$$

where a bar above a variable denotes its equilibrium value.

The equilibrium rental price of capital will be equal to total factor productivity times the share of capital in production, while the equilibrium real wage will be equal to total factor productivity times the share of labor in production. These are the marginal products of capital and labor for a capital-labor ratio equal to one, as implied by our assumptions about the endowments of the representative household.

Note that because the capital and labor endowments have been assumed equal to unity, equilibrium output supply will be equal to total factor productivity and will be given by

$$\bar{y} = A. \tag{2.27}$$

Also note that, as shown in (2.21), because of the assumption of constant returns to scale, factor payments to households exhaust output. Firms pay to households the rental price on the capital stock r plus the real wage w. From (2.25), (2.26), and (2.27), one can confirm that, because the endowments are equal to unity, the income of the representative household is equal to

$$\bar{r} + \bar{w} = \alpha A + (1-\alpha)A = A = \bar{y}. \tag{2.28}$$

From (2.28), the aggregate income of the representative household is equal to aggregate output.

Equilibrium consumption is then determined by the optimal consumption function (2.12) of the representative household as

$$\bar{c} = 1 + \bar{r} + \bar{w} = 1 + A. \tag{2.29}$$

From (2.29), households consume all current output plus their initial capital endowment.

This completes the determination of the main macroeconomic variables in the one-period competitive macroeconomic model analyzed in this section. The equilibrium depends on the preferences and the endowments of the representative household and on the technology of production used by the representative firm.

Because of the assumption of nonsatiation, households optimally supply their full endowments of capital and labor to be used for production, and they consume both their current income and their capital endowment.

In equilibrium, the main determinants of real variables are the endowments and preferences of households, the parameters of the technology of production (such as total factor productivity A), and the share of capital α in the case of the Cobb-Douglas production process.

Exercise 2.2 Assume that the representative household is endowed with k_0 units of capital and l_0 units of labor. Derive equilibirum production, consumption, the real interest rate, and the real wage, assuming that households maximize utility subject to the relevant resource constraints, firms maximize profits, and product and factor markets are competitive. Assume a Cobb-Douglas production function of the form of (2.22). Discuss how the equilibrium depends on factor endowments, preferences, and technological parameters.

2.3 Savings and Investment in a Two-Period Competitive Model

The problem of households in the one-period model is relatively simple. Commit your full endowments of capital and labor to production, earn the maximum possible income, and consume all your income plus the endowments that can be consumed, such as the capital stock.

We next turn to a presentation of the simplest possible intertemporal general equilibrium model. This is a two-period model, first analyzed explicitly by Fisher [1930], one of the pioneers of intertemporal macroeconomics. As we shall see, the representative household in a two-period model faces a much wider choice set than in the one-period model.

In a two-period model, the household has to make intertemporal decisions, the most important of which is the savings and investment decision in the first period.

2.3.1 The Representative Household in a Two-Period Model

Assume a representative household, which lives for two periods, say, period 1 (the *present*) and period 2 (the *future*). As in the one-period model, the representative household is characterized by its endowments and preferences.

Assume that the representative household is endowed with one unit of capital in period 1 and one unit of labor for each of periods 1 and 2. Also assume that there is no uncertainty and that the household has *perfect foresight* of developments in period 2.[6]

In period 1, its endowment of capital and labor can be rented to private firms at a competitive rental price of capital r_1 and a competitive real wage w_1. Capital and labor are used by competitive firms in the production of a single good y_1. The household can use the income

6. The assumption of perfect foresight will be maintained in all intertemporal models in which there is no uncertainty. In models with uncertainty about the future, it will be replaced by the assumption of *rational expectations*.

from the rental of its capital and labor endowments in period 1 for either consumption or investment.

In period 2, the household's capital stock is equal to its initial capital endowment plus its investment from the first period. It again decides to rent its capital stock and its labor endowment at a competitive rental price of capital r_2 and a competitive real wage w_2. At the end of period 2, the representative household consumes its period 2 income plus the capital stock carried over from period 1.

Thus, the main decision of households, apart from the decision to rent out their full endowments of capital and labor to maximize income in each of the two periods, is how much to consume in period 1 relative to period 2. As we shall see, this depends on the future return of investment. Hence, unlike the one-period model, in which the rental price of capital is a pure rent for a fixed endowment, in the two-period intertemporal model, the second-period interest rate acts as an incentive for savings and investment.

The representative household is assumed to maximize the following intertemporal utility function:

$$U(c_1, c_2) = u(c_1) + \frac{1}{1+\rho} u(c_2), \tag{2.30}$$

where u is a continuous, twice differentiable, concave per period utility function, which depends on the volume of consumption in the period. It has the same properties as the utility function (2.4). Here, $\rho > 0$ is the pure rate of time preference, which is a measure of household impatience (i.e., of how much the household prefers current to future utility). Because this is a positive parameter, other things being equal, the household is assumed to be impatient: It prefers current to future utility. The utility function (2.30) is characterized by time separability, as intertemporal utility is the weighted sum of per period utilities.[7]

The utility function (2.30) is maximized subject to the following sequence of *budget constraints*:

$$1 + r_1 k_1 + w_1 l_1 - c_1 = k_2,$$

$$c_2 = (1 + r_2) k_2 + w_2 l_2.$$

Because households are assumed to be endowed with one unit of initial capital k_1 and one unit of labor l per period, and by the assumption of nonsatiation (i.e., they will supply their full endowments for rental in every period), it follows that $k_1 = 1$, $l_1 = l_2 = 1$. The sequence of budget constraints can thus be written as

7. Time separability of utility means that past consumption does not influence current and future utility. This form of preferences does not restrict the size of intertemporal substitution effects. See Barro and King [1984] for the implications of time separability in more general models.

$$(1+r_1)+w_1-c_1=k_2, \tag{2.31}$$

$$c_2=(1+r_2)k_2+w_2, \tag{2.32}$$

where (2.31) is the budget constraint that applies for period 1. The extent to which the initial capital endowment (assumed equal to unity) plus first-period capital and labor income exceed first-period consumption determines the second-period capital stock k_2. In other words, first-period savings $r_1+w_1-c_1$ are equal to first-period investment k_2-1. (2.32) is the budget constraint that applies for period 2. Because this is the last period, the household consumes all of its current income plus the capital stock k_2 carried over from the first period.

The sequence of budget constraints (2.31) and (2.32) can be combined in a single *intertemporal budget constraint* by using (2.31) to substitute for the period 2 capital stock in (2.32). Then one can show that the intertemporal budget constraint can be expressed as

$$c_1+\frac{1}{1+r_2}c_2=(1+r_1)+w_1+\frac{1}{1+r_2}w_2, \tag{2.33}$$

which is derived from the combination of the sequence of budget constraints (2.31) and (2.32) and is therefore equivalent to them. It states that the present value of consumption is equal to the sum of the period 1 capital stock and its real rent r_1 plus the present value of labor income. Present values are calculated using the period 2 real interest rate r_2, which is the rate of return on savings and investment. Recall that the period 1 real rental price of capital r_1 is a pure economic rent, in the sense that it is the compensation of a factor of production in fixed supply. Real wages are also pure real rents in this model, as labor supply is inelastic.

The right-hand side of (2.33) can be viewed as the *wealth* of the representative household, consisting of its initial endowment of capital plus the present value of income from its capital and labor endowments.

The problem of the representative household is then to maximize the intertemporal utility function (2.30), subject to the intertemporal budget constraint (2.33). The Lagrange function for this problem can be written as

$$\mathcal{L}=u(c_1)+\frac{1}{1+\rho}u(c_2)-\lambda\left(c_1+\frac{1}{1+r_2}c_2-1-r_1-w_1-\frac{1}{1+r_2}w_2\right), \tag{2.34}$$

where λ is the associated Lagrange multiplier. The economic interpretation of λ is that it is the shadow price, or marginal value of household wealth. As long as λ is positive, the value of a marginal addition to the wealth of the representative household is positive.

From the first-order conditions for a maximum, it follows that

$$u'(c_1)=\lambda, \tag{2.35}$$

$$\frac{1}{1+\rho}u'(c_2)=\frac{\lambda}{1+r_2}. \tag{2.36}$$

Thus, at the optimum, λ (the marginal value of wealth of the representative household) is equal to the marginal utility of first-period consumption. At the optimum, the household is indifferent between consuming and saving an extra unit of income or wealth. Discounted by the second-period real interest rate, λ is also equal to the marginal utility of second-period consumption. At the optimum, the household has no further incentive to shift consumption from period 1 to period 2, or vice versa.

Dividing (2.36) by (2.35), one gets that at the optimum:

$$\frac{1}{1+\rho}\frac{u'(c_2)}{u'(c_1)}=\frac{1}{1+r_2}. \tag{2.37}$$

(2.37) is known as the *Euler equation for consumption*. Its economic interpretation is that the marginal rate of substitution between future and current consumption is equal to the marginal rate of transformation of future consumption into current consumption, or the opportunity cost (price) of future consumption. This opportunity cost is equal to the inverse of 1 plus the real interest rate r_2.

Note that the marginal rate of substitution between current and future consumption depends on the concavity of the per period utility function u, ensuring that indifference curves between current and future consumption will be convex with respect to the origin.

2.3.2 Implications of the Euler Equation for Consumption

The Euler equation for consumption (2.37) can be rewritten as

$$\frac{u'(c_2)}{u'(c_1)}=\frac{1+\rho}{1+r_2}. \tag{2.38}$$

(2.38) indicates that the ratio of consumption in the two periods depends solely on the relationship between the real interest rate and the pure rate of time preference of the household. The household will smooth its consumption between the two periods by adjusting its savings and investment, according to the relation between the real interest rate and the pure rate of time preference.

If $\rho=r_2$, then $u'(c_1)=u'(c_2)\Leftrightarrow c_1=c_2$. If the real interest rate is equal to the pure rate of time preference of the household, then the return on savings is equal to the rate at which the household values the present over the future, and there will be complete *consumption smoothing*.

If $\rho>r_2$, then $u'(c_1)<u'(c_2)\Leftrightarrow c_1>c_2$. If the real interest rate is lower than the pure rate of time preference of the household, then the return on savings is lower than the rate at which the household values the present over the future, savings will be lower, and consumption will be higher in the first period than in the second period.

If $\rho<r_2$, then $u'(c_1)>u'(c_2)\Leftrightarrow c_1<c_2$. If the real interest rate is higher than the pure rate of time preference of the household, then the return on savings is higher than the rate

at which the household values the present over the future, savings will be higher, and consumption will be lower in the first period than in the second period.

2.3.3 The Case of a Constant Elasticity of Intertemporal Substitution

To further analyze how the consumption path depends on the real interest rate, we will use a special but widely used utility function: the utility function with a *constant elasticity of intertemporal substitution* (CEIS) of consumption. This takes the form

$$u(c) = \frac{c^{1-\theta} - 1}{1-\theta}, \tag{2.39}$$

where $1/\theta$ is the *elasticity of intertemporal substitution of consumption*. This utility function is quite general, and versions of it are used extensively throughout this book.[8]

The elasticity of intertemporal substitution of consumption is defined as the percentage change in the ratio of consumption in period 2, relative to consumption in period 1, divided by the percentage change in the marginal rate of substitution between consumption in the two periods, with utility being held constant. It is a measure of the curvature of the intertemporal indifference curves, or the ease with which households can substitute consumption intertemporally. For the utility function (2.39), from the definition above, it can easily be confirmed that this elasticity is constant and is given by $1/\theta$.

The marginal rate of substitution (MRS) is given by

$$MRS = \frac{1}{1+\rho}\frac{u'(c_2)}{u'(c_1)} = \frac{1}{1+\rho}\left(\frac{c_2}{c_1}\right)^{-\theta}.$$

Hence, the elasticity of intertemporal substitution is given by

$$\frac{\partial\,(c_2/c_1)}{\partial MRS}\frac{MRS}{c_2/c_1} = \frac{1+\rho}{\theta}\left(\frac{c_2}{c_1}\right)^{\theta+1}\frac{1}{1+\rho}\left(\frac{c_2}{c_1}\right)^{-\theta-1} = \frac{1}{\theta}.$$

In the case where the elasticity of intertemporal substitution is equal to unity, (2.39) is not defined. By using L'Hopital's rule, one can show that for $\theta = 1$, (2.39) takes the form of logarithmic utility:[9]

$$u(c_t) = \ln c_t. \tag{2.40}$$

8. In models with uncertainty, (2.39) is also called the *constant relative risk aversion* utility function, and θ is interpreted as the coefficient of constant relative risk aversion. See appendix A for a more general discussion of this functional form.

9. The essence of L'Hopital's rule is that if the first derivative of a function is defined at the limit $\theta = 1$ and is the first derivative of another known function, then the original function tends to that other known function as θ tends to unity. See appendix A.

Thus, logarithmic utility is a special case of (2.39) when the elasticity of intertemporal substitution of consumption is equal to unity.

For the CEIS utility function (2.39), the Euler equation for consumption can be written as

$$\frac{1}{1+\rho}\left(\frac{c_2}{c_1}\right)^{-\theta} = \frac{1}{1+r_2}. \tag{2.41}$$

From (2.41), consumption in the first period satisfies

$$c_1 = \left(\frac{1+\rho}{1+r_2}\right)^{\frac{1}{\theta}} c_2, \tag{2.42}$$

which describes the determination of first-period consumption as a function of the real interest rate and second-period consumption. Combined with the intertemporal budget constraint (2.33), this equation can fully determine the consumption path as a function of the path of real interest rates and real wages.

From (2.42) and the intertemporal budget constraint (2.33), consumption in the first period is determined by

$$c_1 = \frac{(1+\rho)^{1/\theta}}{(1+\rho)^{1/\theta} + (1+r_2)^{(1-\theta)/\theta}}\left(1+r_1+w_1+\frac{w_2}{1+r_2}\right). \tag{2.43}$$

(2.43) is the household consumption function. In the first period, the household consumes a fraction of its total wealth, given by the right-hand side of its intertemporal budget constraint (2.33). The fraction consumed depends on the pure rate of time preference, the second-period real interest rate, and the elasticity of intertemporal substitution $1/\theta$.

It is straightforward to show that the higher the pure rate of time preference ρ is, the higher will be the fraction of its wealth that the household consumes in the first period. This is logical, as the more impatient the household is, the more willing it will be to bring utility and consumption forward.

It is also straightforward to show that if the elasticity of intertemporal substitution of consumption is higher than unity (i.e., if $\theta < 1$), then the second-period real interest rate r_2 has a negative impact on the fraction of its wealth that the household consumes in the first period. This is because the intertemporal substitution effect is stronger than the income (wealth) effect. Hence, higher real interest rates induce higher savings in this case, as they reduce the relative price of future consumption.

The opposite happens if the elasticity of intertemporal substitution of consumption is lower than unity (i.e., if $\theta > 1$). Then the second-period real interest rate has a positive impact on the fraction of its wealth that the household consumes in the first period. Higher real interest rates induce lower savings, as the intertemporal substitution effect is weaker than the income effect in this case.

In the case where the intertemporal elasticity of substitution is equal to unity (i.e., logarithmic preferences), the fraction of its wealth that the household consumes in the first period is independent of the second-period real interest rate and only depends on the pure rate of time preference. It is given by $(1+\rho)/(2+\rho)$. In this case, the intertemporal substitution effect of real interest rates exactly cancels out the income effect.

To fully determine the path of real interest rates and real wages, as well as household wealth, in this two-period model, we have to examine the optimizing behavior of firms and impose the competitive equilibrium conditions.

2.3.4 Firms, Technology, and the Optimal Output Path

As in the one-period model of section 2.2, we assume that output is produced by competitive firms, who rent the factors of production from households through competitive factor markets. All firms have access to the same technology and face the same factor prices. They produce a homogeneous output y, through the neoclassical production function

$$y_t = A_t F(k_t, l_t) = A_t f(\hat{k}_t) l_t, \tag{2.44}$$

where t is a discrete time index taking the values 1 and 2, and $\hat{k} = k/l$. We maintain the assumption that F is characterized by diminishing returns to each factor of production but constant returns to scale, satisfying the properties given in (2.14)–(2.17). Note that A, the exogenous technological parameter denoting total factor productivity, as do the factors of production, capital k and labor l, also depends on the time period. Hence, total factor productivity may differ between periods 1 and 2.

Firms are assumed to maximize profits in both periods. Hence, in every period, they choose capital and labor to maximize

$$\mathcal{P}_t = A_t f(\hat{k}_t) l_t - r_t k_t - w_t l_t. \tag{2.45}$$

From the first-order conditions for a maximum, we have

$$r_t = A_t f'(\hat{k}_t), \tag{2.46}$$

$$w_t = A_t f(\hat{k}_t) - \hat{k}_t A_t f'(\hat{k}_t). \tag{2.47}$$

Thus, in every period, $t = 1, 2$, firms will employ capital and labor up to the point where the marginal product of capital is equal to the rental price of capital r, and up to the point where the marginal product of labor is equal to the real wage w. Note that because of the assumption of constant returns to scale, factor payments are equal to total output in every period.

Because firms operate in competitive markets, where they all face the same factor prices, and because they are also assumed to share the same technology, they will all choose the same quantities of capital and labor. Thus, we can again confine our analysis to the problem of the *representative firm*.

For analytical simplicity, let us employ a Cobb-Douglas production function of the form

$$y_1 = Ak_1^{\alpha} l_1^{1-\alpha}, y_2 = A(1+g)k_2^{\alpha} l_2^{1-\alpha}, \tag{2.48}$$

where $g \geq 0$ is the exogenous *rate of technical progress* between periods 1 and 2. Hence, g measures the rate of increase in total factor productivity between the two periods.

From the marginal productivity conditions (2.46) and (2.47) and the Cobb-Douglas production function (2.48), it follows that

$$\begin{aligned} r_1 &= \alpha A k_1^{\alpha-1} l_1^{1-\alpha} = \alpha A \hat{k}_1^{\alpha-1}, \\ r_2 &= \alpha A(1+g) k_2^{\alpha-1} l_2^{1-\alpha} = \alpha A(1+g)\hat{k}_2^{\alpha-1}, \end{aligned} \tag{2.49}$$

$$\begin{aligned} w_1 &= (1-\alpha)Ak_1^{\alpha} l_1^{-\alpha} = (1-\alpha)A\hat{k}_1^{\alpha}, \\ w_2 &= (1-\alpha)A(1+g)k_2^{\alpha} l_2^{-\alpha} = (1-\alpha)A(1+g)\hat{k}_2^{\alpha}, \end{aligned} \tag{2.50}$$

where $\hat{k} = k/l$.

This completes our discussion of the optimal behavior of the representative firm.

2.3.5 General Equilibrium in the Two-Period Model

We can now turn to the discussion of general equilibrium. Equilibrium employment, output, consumption, investment, real wages, and the real rental price of capital in each of the two periods will be determined by the equality of the supply of factors of production by households and the demand for factors of production by firms, and the supply of output by firms and the demand for output by households.

Because the supply of capital and labor in period 1 has been shown to be equal to the endowments of the representative household, which are both assumed to be equal to unity, it follows that capital per worker in production in period 1 will also be equal to unity:

$$\hat{k}_1 = 1. \tag{2.51}$$

The real rental price of capital will be determined in the market for capital, and the real wage will be determined in the market for labor, by the equality of the demand and supply for capital and labor. Substituting (2.51) in (2.49) and (2.50), we get that the equilibrium rental price of capital and the real wage in period 1 will be given by

$$\bar{r}_1 = \alpha A, \tag{2.52}$$

$$\bar{w}_1 = (1-\alpha)A, \tag{2.53}$$

where a bar above a variable again denotes its equilibrium value.

Note that because the capital and labor endowments have been assumed equal to unity in period 1, equilibrium output supply in period 1 is equal to total factor productivity and is given by

$$\bar{y}_1 = A. \tag{2.54}$$

Also note that, because of the assumption of constant returns to scale, factor payments to households exhaust output. Firms pay to households the rental price on the capital stock r plus the real wage w. Hence, from (2.52), (2.53), and (2.54), the income of the representative household in period 1 is equal to

$$\bar{r}_1 + \bar{w}_1 = \alpha A + (1-\alpha)A = A = \bar{y}_1. \tag{2.55}$$

The aggregate income of the representative household is thus equal to aggregate output.

Equilibrium consumption in period 1 cannot be determined unless we also analyze equilibrium in period 2, as savings depend on the real interest rate in period 2, which is determined by the marginal productivity of capital in period 2.

In period 2, the endowment of labor continues to be equal to 1. However, the period 2 capital stock may differ from the initial endowment, as a result of savings and investment by the representative household. Thus, although equilibrium factor prices and output in period 1 are determined as a function of the initial endowments of capital and labor and the technology of production in period 1, consumption in period 1 cannot be determined unless we consider the determination of general equilibrium in period 2 as well.

Because the labor endowment in period 2 is equal to unity, it follows that capital per worker will be equal to

$$\hat{k}_2 = k_2. \tag{2.56}$$

Thus, the key is to determine the capital stock in period 2, which will depend on savings and investment in period 1.

The optimal capital stock for period 2 is determined at the point where the marginal rate of substitution between period 2 and period 1 consumption is equal to the marginal rate of transformation, which is equal the inverse of 1 plus the real interest rate of period 2. The condition that determines the capital stock is then (2.43), the Euler equation for consumption. We can rewrite it as

$$\frac{1}{1+\rho}\left(\frac{c_1}{c_2}\right)^{\theta} = \left(\frac{1}{1+r_2}\right), \tag{2.57}$$

which is the optimality condition that determines the equilibrium capital stock in period 2. Because both c_1 and c_2 depend on the period 2 capital stock through the household budget constraints, and r_2 also depends on the period 2 capital stock through the relevant marginal productivity condition, we need to invoke both the household budget constraints and the marginal productivity condition to determine the equilibrium capital stock.

From the household budget constraints (2.31) and (2.32), after substituting for the equilibrium variables in period 1 from (2.52), (2.53), and (2.54), we have that

$$c_1 = 1 + A - k_2, \tag{2.58}$$

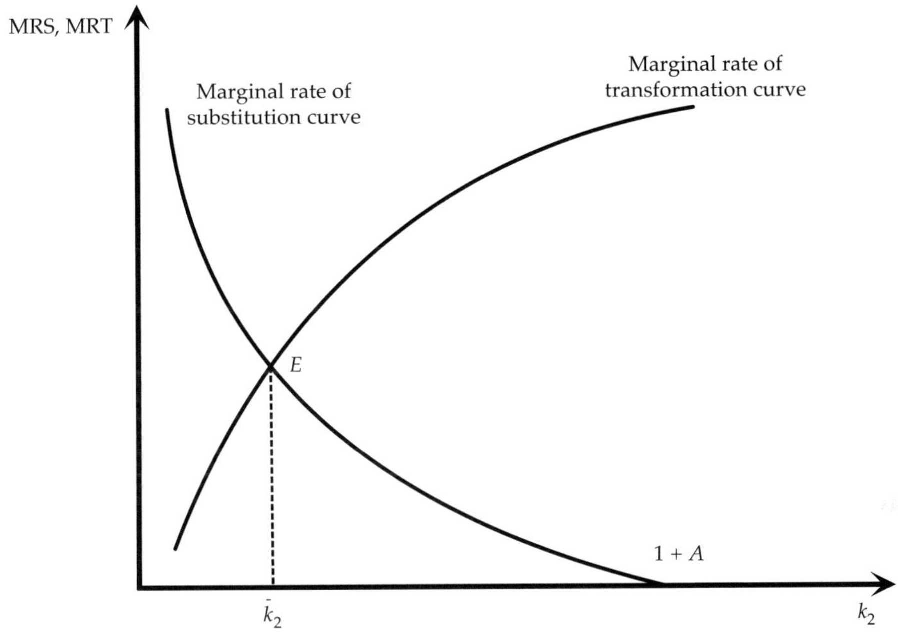

Figure 2.1
Equilibrium capital accumulation in a two-period economy.

$$c_2 = k_2 + A(1+g)k_2^{\alpha}. \tag{2.59}$$

From the period 2 marginal productivity condition (2.49) for the real interest rate, we have that

$$r_2 = \alpha A(1+g)k_2^{\alpha-1}. \tag{2.60}$$

Using (2.58), (2.59), and (2.60) to substitute for c_1, c_2, and r_2 in the optimality condition (2.57), the equilibrium capital stock in period 2 is determined by

$$\frac{1}{1+\rho}\left(\frac{1+A-\bar{k}_2}{\bar{k}_2+A(1+g)\bar{k}_2^{\alpha}}\right)^{\theta} = \frac{1}{1+\alpha A(1+g)\bar{k}_2^{\alpha-1}}, \tag{2.61}$$

where $\bar{k}_2$ is the equilibrium capital stock that satisfies equation (2.61). This is a highly nonlinear equation, which cannot be solved analytically. Its interpretation is nonetheless straightforward, and the determination of the equilibrium capital stock can be analyzed with the help of a simple diagram, as in figure 2.1.

The downward-sloping curve in figure 2.1 depicts the left-hand side of (2.61), which is the marginal rate of substitution between period 2 and period 1 consumption. This is a negative function of the second-period capital stock, because as consumers reduce period 1 consumption to increase investment, the marginal utility of first-period consumption rises relative to the marginal utility of period 2 consumption, and hence the marginal rate of substitution falls.

The upward-sloping curve depicts the right-hand side of (2.61), which is the marginal rate of transformation between consumption in periods 2 and 1, again as a function of the second-period capital stock. As investment in the second-period capital stock increases, the real interest rate in period 2 falls, because of the diminishing marginal productivity of capital; hence the marginal rate of transformation between consumption in periods 2 and 1 increases.

The equilibrium capital stock is determined at the intersection of the two curves, where the marginal rate of substitution is equal to the marginal rate of transformation.

If the period 2 capital stock is higher than the equilibrium capital stock, the real interest rate would be lower, and households would immediately reduce savings and investment, reducing the capital stock to its equilibrium value. If the capital stock is lower than the equilibrium capital stock, the real interest rate would be higher, and households would immediately increase savings and investment, increasing the capital stock to its equilibrium value.

To put it differently, the second-period equilibrium capital stock is the stock for which the second-period real interest rate induces households to provide sufficient savings and investment in the first period, so that this capital stock will be attained in the second period.

Note that from (2.61), the optimal second-period capital stock depends on preference parameters, such as the pure rate of time preference ρ and the elasticity of intertemporal substitution of consumption $1/\theta$, as well as technological parameters, such as A, g, and α. Obviously, it depends on initial endowments as well, which have been normalized to unity.

Having determined the optimal second-period capital stock from (2.61), the rest of the equilibrium variables follow from the household budget constraints (2.58) and (2.59), and the marginal productivity conditions (2.49) and (2.50) for period 2. We thus have that

$$\bar{c}_1 = 1 + A - \bar{k}_2, \tag{2.62}$$

$$\bar{c}_2 = \bar{k}_2 + A(1+g)\bar{k}_2^{\alpha}, \tag{2.63}$$

$$\bar{r}_2 = \alpha A(1+g)\bar{k}_2^{\alpha-1}, \tag{2.64}$$

$$\bar{w}_2 = (1-\alpha)A(1+g)\bar{k}_2^{\alpha}. \tag{2.65}$$

All these variables are determined as functions of the preference, technological, and endowment parameters that determine the second-period capital stock.

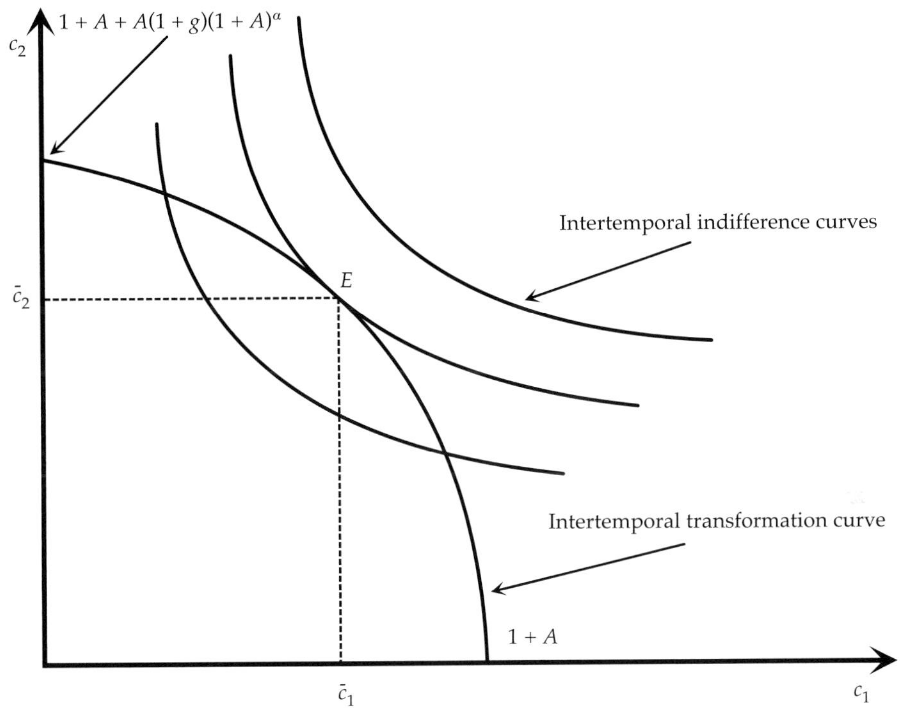

Figure 2.2
Intertemporal equilibrium in a two-period economy.

Exercise 2.3 Assume that the representative household is endowed with k_0 units of capital and l_0 units of labor and lives for two periods. Derive equilibirum production, consumption, the real interest rate, and the real wage for each period, assuming that households maximize utility subject to the relevant resource constraints, firms maximize profits, and product and factor markets are competitive. Assume a CEIS intertemporal utility function of the form (2.30) and (2.39), and a Cobb-Douglas production function of the form (2.22). Discuss how the equilibrium depends on factor endowments, preferences, and technological parameters.

2.3.6 Diagrammatic Exposition of the Intertemporal Equilibrium

The full intertemporal equilibrium in our two-period model can be analyzed through the use of a simple diagram, as shown in figure 2.2.

The preferences of the representative household are depicted by the indifference curves between consumption in period 1 and consumption in period 2. The slope of these intertemporal indifference curves is the marginal rate of substitution between consumption in the two periods.

With a CEIS utility function, as we have assumed, intertemporal household utility is given by

$$\frac{c_1{}^{1-\theta}}{1-\theta}+\frac{1}{1+\rho}\frac{c_2{}^{1-\theta}}{1-\theta}. \tag{2.66}$$

The slope of the indifference curves can be found by totally differentiating the intertemporal utility function (2.66) with respect to c_1 and c_2 and setting the total differential to zero, so that utility remains constant:

$$c_1^{-\theta}dc_1+\frac{1}{1+\rho}c_2^{-\theta}dc_2=0. \tag{2.67}$$

From (2.67), it follows that the slope of the indifference curve is given by

$$\frac{dc_1}{dc_2}=-\frac{1}{1+\rho}\left(\frac{c_2}{c_1}\right)^{-\theta}. \tag{2.68}$$

Thus, the slope of indifference curves is equal to the marginal rate of substitution between consumption in the two periods. It is negative and decreasing in the ratio c_1/c_2.

The budget constraint of the representative household is depicted as the intertemporal transformation curve, which shows the maximum consumption that can be attained in one period, subject to a given level of consumption in the other period. The intertemporal transformation curve is essentially the budget constraint of the representative household and depends on endowments and technological possibilities.

Note that if the household maximizes first-period consumption by consuming its capital endowment and all its period 1 income in the first period (i.e., by consuming $1+A$ in the first period), then second-period capital and consumption are equal to zero, as there is no capital and no production in the second period. If first-period consumption is equal to zero, then the second-period capital stock is maximized at $1+A$, and second-period consumption is maximized at $1+A+A(1+g)(1+A)^{\alpha}$. The intertemporal transformation curve shows all other feasible combinations in between these two extremes.

The slope of the intertemporal transformation curve can be found by totally differentiating the intertemporal budget constraint (2.33) and setting the total differential to zero:

$$\frac{dc_1}{dc_2}=-\frac{1}{1+r_2}=-\frac{1}{1+aA(1+g)k_2^{\alpha-1}}. \tag{2.69}$$

This is a negative and decreasing function of the capital stock in period 2 (i.e., a negative but increasing function of the ratio c_1/c_2). Hence, the transformation curve is concave to the origin.

Equilibrium is at point E in Figure 2.2, where the transformation curve is tangential to the highest possible indifference curve. This point is the only intertemporal equilibrium for this model, and it is the only point where the Euler equation for consumption (2.57) is satisfied.

Because of the assumption of nonsatiation, the representative household will always choose points on the intertemporal transformation curve. For any point other than E, the household can increase its intertemporal utility by changing its consumption pattern. The only point where the household has no incentive to change its consumption pattern is point E.

2.3.7 Implications for Growth and Business Cycle Theory

The two-period model of savings and investment that we have examined in this section can be seen as the basis of most optimizing one-sector models of economic growth and of competitive models of aggregate fluctuations.

The representative household model of economic growth, one of the workhorses of growth theory, is nothing more than an extension of the two-period model to economies that last for an infinite number of periods. In fact, this extension was accomplished by Ramsey [1928], even before the publication of the two-period model by Fisher [1930].

The Ramsey infinite horizon representative household model of optimal growth is analyzed in chapter 4. Models of overlapping generations (such as the Diamond [1965] and the Blanchard [1985] and Weil [1989] models, which are analyzed in chapter 5) are also based on the two-period intertemporal model of Fisher [1930]. Essentially, they are an extension of the representative household model to economies in which households have different birth dates. However, as we shall see, overlapping generations models do not share the optimality properties of the two-period representative household model or the infinite horizon Ramsey model with perfect markets. The reason is that in the overlapping generations model without intergenerational links, current generations do not take the welfare of future generations into account, and hence savings are lower that what would be socially optimal.

As we shall see in chapters 4–9, which rely on versions of either representative household or overlapping generations models, the invididual household optimality conditions of the two-period model, such as the Euler equation for consumption, recur again and again in these infinite horizon growth models. Hence, their basic properties are related to those of the two-period model, although, obviously, these multiperiod models also have richer and more diverse predictions and implications. However, to the extent that there is no intergenerational altruism, overlapping generations models imply suboptimally low savings.

The two-period representative household model forms the basis of competitive equilibrium theories of business cycles, in the form of the stochastic growth model presented in chapter 13. However, in addition to going beyond the two-period model, this requires introducing the consumption-leisure choice and uncertainty in the form of stochastic real disturbances.

2.4 Consumption and Labor Supply in a One-Period Competitive Model

Up to now we have assumed that the household provides a unit of labor inelastically. Yet in many contexts, it is appropriate to treat employment as a choice variable for households, much like consumption. Hence, it is worth investigating the properties of models in which households choose not only the path of consumption and savings but also the path of employment. This results in richer models of the labor market, in which labor supply reacts endogenously to changes in real wages, and real wages are no longer just rents.

As before, we start our analysis with a one-period model, in which households choose both consumption and labor supply. This helps contrast the resulting equilibrium with the intertemporal equilibrium in models with more than one period.

2.4.1 The Optimal Choice of Consumption and Labor Supply

Assume an economy in which the representative household lives for one period and is endowed with one unit of time. For analytical simplicity, we concentrate on the case in which labor is the only factor of production and there is no capital.

Time can be used for leisure activities z, which yield utility to the household, or rented out as labor l to private firms at a competitive wage rate w, and is used in the production of the single good. Denoting the volume of consumption by c, the budget constraints of the representative household are given by

$$z+l=1, \tag{2.70}$$

$$c=wl. \tag{2.71}$$

Assume that the preferences of the representative household are described by a continuous, twice differentiable, quasi-concave utility function u, whose arguments are the volume of consumption and the amount of leisure time:

$$u(c,z). \tag{2.72}$$

From the quasi-concavity of the utility function, it follows that

$$u_c=\frac{\partial u}{\partial c}>0, u_z=\frac{\partial u}{\partial z}>0, u_{cc}=\frac{\partial^2 u}{\partial c^2}\leq 0, u_{zz}=\frac{\partial^2 u}{\partial z^2}\leq 0. \tag{2.73}$$

From the assumption of nonsatiation, the household will use all its time, either as leisure z or as labor services l. Thus, the household will choose l to maximize (2.72), subject to the constraints (2.70) and (2.71). Substituting (2.70) in the utility function, the problem of the representative household can be restated as the maximization of

$$u(c,1-l), \tag{2.74}$$

subject to

$$c = wl. \tag{2.75}$$

The Lagrange function for this problem can be written as

$$\mathcal{L} = u(c, 1 - l) - \lambda\,(c - wl)\,, \tag{2.76}$$

where λ is the Langrange multiplier for the budget constraint (2.75). From the first-order conditions for a maximum, it follows that

$$u_c = \lambda, \tag{2.77}$$

$$u_z = \lambda w. \tag{2.78}$$

The interpretation of these two first-order conditions is straightforward. At the optimum, the marginal utility of consumption is equal to the marginal valuation of income λ, while the marginal utility of leisure is equal to the marginal valuation of income λ times the real wage w. Hence, at the optimum, the household cannot increase its utility by either increasing or decreasing its labor supply at the expense (or in favor) of leisure.

Dividing (2.78) by (2.77), we get the optimality condition that the marginal rate of substitution between consumption and leisure is equal to the real wage, which is the opportunity cost of leisure:

$$\frac{u_z}{u_c} = w. \tag{2.79}$$

As one can confirm by totally differentiating the utility function (2.74) and keeping the level of utility constant, the ratio of the marginal utilities of leisure and consumption in (2.79) is equal to the marginal rate of substitution between consumption and leisure:

$$\frac{dc}{dz} = -\frac{u_z}{u_c}. \tag{2.80}$$

The optimum is shown diagrammatically in figure 2.3. The utility function of the representative household is depicted by the indifference map, consisting of convex-to-the-origin indifference curves. The budget constraint is depicted by the negatively sloped straight line. The slope of the indifference curves is the marginal rate of substitution between consumption and leisure, and the slope of the budget constraint is (minus) the real wage w.

The optimum is at point E, where the budget constraint is tangential to the highest possible indifference curve. At point E, the marginal rate of substitution between consumption and leisure is equal to the real wage. The household cannot attain a higher level of utility by substituting away from (or toward) more leisure compared to point E.

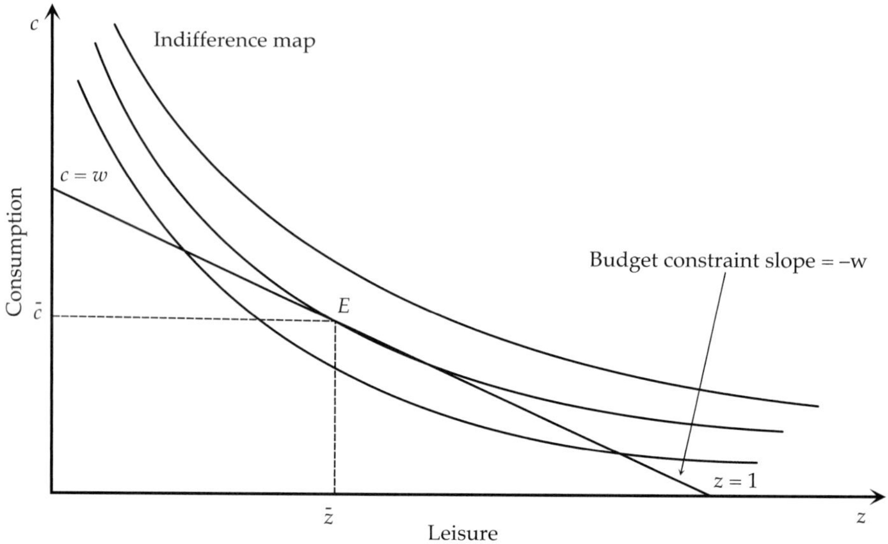

Figure 2.3
Optimal consumption and leisure in a one-period economy.

2.4.2 Income and Substitution Effects on Labor Supply

The effects of changes in the real wage on consumption and labor supply can be analyzed with the help of figure 2.4.

In figure 2.4, we assume that originally the economy is at the equilibrium point E. We consider the impact of a reduction of the real wage from w to w'. The budget constraint shifts to one with a smaller slope, and the economy will shift to E' with lower consumption, because for consumption, the income and the substitution effects are both negative.

Whether labor supply will also fall depends on the relative strength of the income and substitution effects. The income effect points to a reduction in the demand for leisure and an increase in labor supply: The income of the household is now lower, and the household demands less of both consumption and leisure at a lower real income. The substitution effect works in the opposite direction: The opportunity cost of leisure has gone down, and leisure has become relatively less expensive. The substitution effect points to an increase in the demand for leisure and a reduction in labor supply.

In figure 2.4, the substitution effect dominates, and at the new equilibrium E', the "Marshallian" demand for leisure (which depends on both the income and the substitution effect) has gone up, and labor supply has gone down.

There are at least three ways to isolate the income from the substitution effect of any change in the real wage: The Hicks [1939] method, the Slutsky [1915] method, and the Frisch [1932] method. The Hicks method relies on the assumption of compensating the

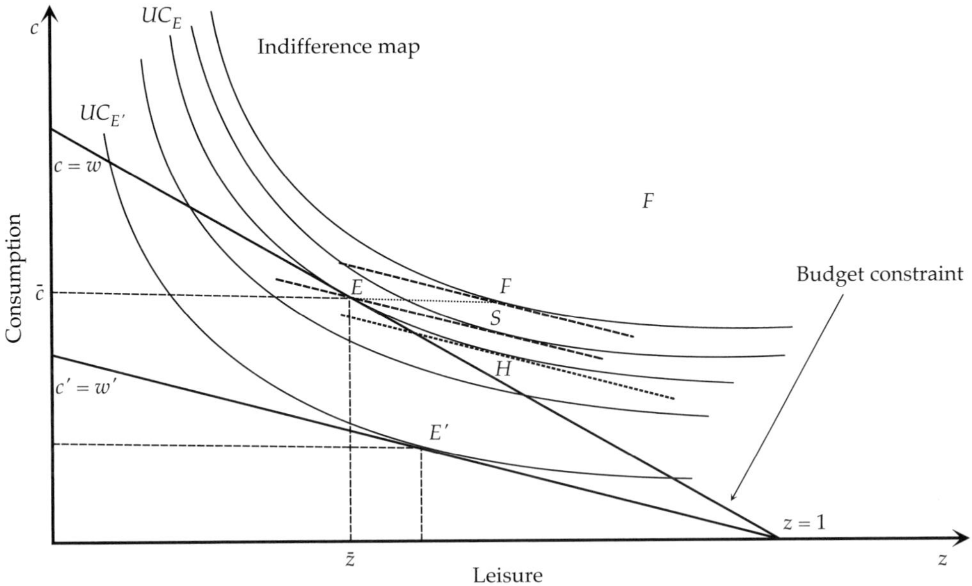

Figure 2.4
Income and substitution effects on labor supply.

household to achieve the original level of utility after the change in the real wage. The Slutsky method relies on the assumption of compensating the household to buy the original consumption-leisure bundle after the change in the real wage. The Frisch method relies on the assumption of compensating the household to maintain the same marginal utility of wealth following the change in the real wage. With separable preferences, this is equivalent to assuming that the level of consumption remains unchanged.

The Hicksian substitution effect, which is theoretically the most satisfactory of the three methods, is measured from the movement from E to H, along the original indifference curve in figure 2.4. At point H, the marginal rate of substitution between consumption and leisure is equal to the new lower real wage, but we have assumed that the household has been compensated to achieve the original level of utility. This measures the Hicksian compensated demand for leisure, or equivalently, the compensated supply of labor.

The Slutsky substitution effect is measured from the movement from E to S, along a line that passes through the original consumption-leisure bundle but has the slope of the new budget constraint. At point S, the marginal rate of substitution between consumption and leisure is equal to the new lower real wage, but we have assumed that the household has been compensated so that it can select the original bundle if it wants to. This measures the Slutsky compensated demand for leisure (or supply of labor).

The movement from point E to point F measures the Frisch demand for leisure (or supply of labor) and is based on the assumption that the household is compensated to achieve the same level of consumption (not utility) as in the original equilibrium, following the decline in the real wage. With time-separable preferences, the same level of consumption implies the same marginal value of wealth.

Marshallian demands are the actual market demands for leisure, following a change in the real wage, whereas Hicksian, Slutskian, and Frischian demands are alternative measures of compensated demands based on different approaches to the isolation of the substitution effect.

2.4.3 The Frisch Elasticity of Labor Supply

To derive explicit solutions for consumption demand and labor supply by the representative household, one has to make explicit assumptions about the utility function.

For reasons of analytical simplicity, we confine our analysis to the following class of additively separable utility functions:

$$u(c, 1-l) = \frac{c^{1-\theta}}{1-\theta} - \frac{l^{1+\gamma}}{1+\gamma}, \tag{2.81}$$

where θ and γ are nonnegative parameters. (2.81) is an additively separable extension of (2.39), the CEIS utility function used in section 2.3.3. It is additively separable in utility from consumption and leisure.

From (2.81), the marginal rate of substitution between consumption and leisure (i.e., the slope of the indifference curves) is given by

$$-\frac{u_z}{u_c} = -\frac{l^{\gamma}}{c^{-\theta}}. \tag{2.82}$$

From the optimality condition that the marginal rate of substitution between consumption and leisure must be equal to the real wage, it follows that

$$\frac{l^{\gamma}}{c^{-\theta}} = w. \tag{2.83}$$

From (2.83), solving for employment, one can see that the elasticity of labor supply with respect to the real wage, holding consumption constant, is equal to $1/\gamma$. This is a Frisch [1932]–compensated elasticity, called the *Frisch elasticity of labor supply*.

Hence, the two parameters θ and γ of the utility function (2.81) can be interpreted as the inverse of the elasticity of intertemporal substitution of consumption and the inverse of the Frisch elasticity of labor supply, respectively.

2.4.4 The Production Function and the Optimal Decisions of Firms

Output is produced by competitive firms, who rent labor services from households in competitive labor markets. Firms have access to the same technology and labor markets, and they produce a homogeneous output y through the following linear production function:

$$y = Al, \tag{2.84}$$

where A is an exogenous parameter denoting total factor productivity and possibly a fixed factor of production such as land. Because labor is the only variable factor of production, (2.84) is characterized by constant returns to scale.[10]

Firms are competitive and are assumed to maximize profits. Hence, they choose labor to maximize

$$Al - wl. \tag{2.85}$$

From the first-order conditions for a maximum, we have

$$A = w. \tag{2.86}$$

Because firms operate in competitive markets, they all face the same real wage. Because they are also assumed to share the same technology, they will all choose the same quantity of labor. Thus, we can confine our analysis to the problem of the representative firm.

Note that, because of the assumption of constant returns to scale, wage payments to households exhaust output. Firms pay to households the real wage bill wl. Because the real wage w is equal to A, we have

$$wl = Al = y. \tag{2.87}$$

The income of the representative household is thus equal to aggregate output.

2.4.5 General Equilibrium and the Determination of Output and Employment

To determine the employment rate (and through the employment rate, the rest of the endogenous variables), we must consider the equilibrium conditions in product and labor markets. Hence we must combine the optimal decisions of firms with the optimal decisions of households, which will allow us to determine all the endogenous variables.

Using the definition of household income in (2.87) and the budget constraint of the representative household (2.75), we have that consumption is also a function of the employment rate:

$$c = Al, \tag{2.88}$$

10. In fact, the assumption of a production function linear in employment is made for simplicity and to maintain constant returns to scale.

which is the *equilibrium condition in the product market*, ensuring that the consumption decisions of households are compatible with the production decisions of firms. It implies that consumption is equal to total output.

The equilibrium real wage is the one that makes the employment decisions of households, as determined by (2.83), equal to the employment decisions of firms, as determined by (2.86). So these equations imply that

$$\frac{l^{\gamma}}{c^{-\theta}}=A, \tag{2.89}$$

which is the *equilibrium condition in the labor market*, ensuring that the real wage w is compatible with the employment decisions of both households and firms.

Solving (2.88) and (2.89) simultaneously, we can determine the equilibrium employment rate. The solution for l is given by

$$\bar{l}=A^{\frac{1-\theta}{\gamma+\theta}}, \tag{2.90}$$

where $\bar{l}$ denotes equilibrium employment.

From (2.90), equilibrium employment will be a positive function of total factor productivity only if $\theta<1$ (i.e., only if $1/\theta$, the intertemporal elasticity of substitution of consumption, is greater than unity). Note that if the intertemporal elasticity of substitution of consumption is equal to unity, then equilibrium employment is equal to unity as well.

Equilibrium real wages and equilibrium output and consumption are determined by

$$\bar{w}=A, \tag{2.91}$$

$$\bar{y}=\bar{c}=A^{\frac{\gamma+1}{\gamma+\theta}}. \tag{2.92}$$

The equilibrium real wage is equal to the exogenous total factor productivity, which is equal to the marginal product of labor for a linear production function.

Equilibrium output and consumption will be positive functions of total factor productivity. If the intertemporal elasticity of substitution of consumption is higher than unity (i.e., $\theta<1$), then the elasticity of equilibrium aggregate output and consumption with respect to total factor productivity is greater than unity as well, as higher productivity induces higher employment by households and vice versa.

2.5 Consumption and Labor Supply in a Two-Period Competitive Model

We next turn to an intertemporal, two-period model of consumption and labor supply. For reasons of analytical simplicity, as in the model of section 2.4, we abstract from capital accumulation.

Thus, the representative household chooses consumption and employment in both periods, given its endowments of time in periods 1 and 2, a competitive real interest rate for its savings, and competitive real wages in periods 1 and 2.

2.5.1 Optimal Consumption and Labor Supply in a Two-Period Model

Assume a representative household that lives for two periods, 1 and 2. Also assume that the representative household is endowed with one unit of labor for each of periods 1 and 2. In both periods, its endowment of time can either be used as leisure (which yields utility to the household) or rented as labor to private firms at competitive real wages w_1 and w_2. Labor is used by competitive firms in the production of a single good in both periods y_1 and y_2.

The household can use its labor income for consumption in each period. Savings from period 1 to 2 can be lent in competitive financial markets at a competitive real interest rate r. Obviously, there are no savings in period 2. There is also no uncertainty, and the household has perfect foresight.

The representative household is assumed to maximize the intertemporal utility function

$$U=\frac{c_1^{1-\theta}}{1-\theta}-\frac{l_1^{1+\gamma}}{1+\gamma}+\frac{1}{1+\rho}\left(\frac{c_2^{1-\theta}}{1-\theta}-\frac{l_2^{1+\gamma}}{1+\gamma}\right), \tag{2.93}$$

subject to the intertemporal budget constraint

$$c_1+\frac{c_2}{1+r}=w_1 l_1+\frac{w_2 l_2}{1+r}. \tag{2.94}$$

The first-order conditions for the maximum are

$$c_1^{-\theta}=\lambda, \tag{2.95}$$

$$\frac{c_2^{-\theta}}{1+\rho}=\frac{\lambda}{1+r}, \tag{2.96}$$

$$l_1^{\gamma}=\lambda w_1, \tag{2.97}$$

$$\frac{l_2^{\gamma}}{1+\rho}=\frac{\lambda}{1+r}w_2, \tag{2.98}$$

where λ is the Lagrange multiplier of the constraint (2.94). Its economic interpretation is that it measures the marginal value of household wealth.

The economic interpretation of these first-order conditions is straightforward. (2.95) implies that the marginal utility of first-period consumption is equal to the marginal value of wealth. (2.96) implies that the marginal utility of second-period consumption is equal to the discounted marginal value of wealth. (2.97) implies that the marginal utility of first-period leisure is equal to the opportunity cost of leisure (i.e., the real wage in period 1 multiplied by the marginal value of wealth). Finally, (2.98) implies that the marginal utility of second-period leisure is equal to the opportunity cost of leisure (i.e., the real wage in period 2 multiplied by the discounted marginal value of wealth). The discount factor is inversely related to the real interest rate r.

2.5.2 Intertemporal Substitution in Consumption and Labor Supply

Eliminating λ between (2.95) and (2.96) gives us the Euler equation for consumption:

$$\frac{1}{1+\rho}\left(\frac{c_2}{c_1}\right)^{-\theta} = \frac{1}{1+r}. \tag{2.99}$$

This is the same as the Euler equation for consumption (2.41) in the model with exogenous labor supply and has the same interpretation. At the optimum, the marginal rate of substitution between future and current consumption is equal to the marginal rate of transformation of future consumption into current consumption (or the opportunity cost [price] of future consumption). This rate is equal to the inverse of one plus the real interest rate r.

Eliminating λ between (2.97) and (2.98) gives us a corresponding Euler equation for labor supply:

$$\frac{1}{1+\rho}\left(\frac{l_2}{l_1}\right)^{\gamma} = \frac{1}{1+r}\frac{w_2}{w_1}. \tag{2.100}$$

This is a new optimality condition relative to the two-period model with exogenous labor supply. At the optimum, the marginal rate of substitution between future and current leisure (employment) is equal to the marginal rate of transformation of future leisure into current leisure (or the opportunity cost [price] of future leisure). This opportunity cost is the discounted future real wage relative to the current real wage.

(2.100) suggests that the household will not only engage in intertemporal substitution in consumption, as suggested by (2.99), but also in intertemporal substitution in labor supply. When discounted future wages are higher than current wages, the household will reduce its current labor supply in favor of future labor supply, and vice versa.

The importance of (2.100) is that fluctuations of employment over time will not only depend on fluctuations in real wages but also on fluctuations in the real interest rate.[11]

Eliminating λ between (2.95) and (2.97), and (2.96) and (2.98), respectively, gives us the optimality conditions for the choice between consumption and leisure in each period (i.e., the marginal rate of substitution between consumption and leisure must be equal to the real

11. Intertemporal substitution in labor supply was put forward as an explanation for employment fluctuations in an important paper by Lucas and Rapping [1969], in the context of a competitive model of the labor market. It has since served as an important building block in "new classical" models of aggregate fluctuations.

wage in both periods):

$$\frac{l_1^\gamma}{c_1^{-\theta}} = w_1, \tag{2.101}$$

$$\frac{l_2^\gamma}{c_2^{-\theta}} = w_2. \tag{2.102}$$

These are the same conditions as in the static model of section 2.3.

This completes our examination of the optimal decisions of the representative household.

2.5.3 Optimal Production Decisions of Firms

Assume that output is produced by competitive firms and that labor is the only factor of production. The production functions of firms are given by

$$y_1 = Al_1, y_2 = A(1+g)l_2, \tag{2.103}$$

where $A > 0$ is total factor productivity in period 1, and $g \geq 0$ is the growth rate of total factor productivity between periods 1 and 2. Here, g is an exogenous parameter measuring technical progress. This is the same technology as assumed in the one-period model with endogenous labor supply, the only difference being that total factor productivity is allowed to grow between periods.

Firms are assumed to maximize profits. Hence, in each period, they choose labor to maximize

$$Al_1 - w_1 l_1, A(1+g)l_2 - w_2 l_2. \tag{2.104}$$

From the first-order conditions for a maximum, we have

$$w_1 = A, w_2 = A(1+g). \tag{2.105}$$

Because firms operate in competitive markets, they all face the same real wage. Because they are also assumed to share the same technology, they will all choose the same quantity of labor. Thus, we can confine our analysis to the problem of the representative firm.

Note that, because of the assumption of constant returns to scale, wage payments to households exhaust output. Firms pay to households the real wage bill wl in each period. The real wage w is equal to total factor productivity, so that

$$w_1 l_1 = Al_1 = y_1, w_2 l_2 = A(1+g)l_2 = y_2. \tag{2.106}$$

The income of the representative household is equal to aggregate output in each of the two periods.

2.5.4 General Equilibrium and the Determination of Output and Employment

To determine the employment rates in each period (and through the employment rates, the rest of the endogenous variables), we must consider the equilibrium conditions in product, labor, and financial markets. Hence we must combine the optimal decisions of firms with the optimal decisions of households. This will allow us to determine all the endogenous variables.

Because there is no capital (i.e., an outside asset for savings), households that wish to save in period 1 can only lend to households that wish to borrow in period 1. However, because all households have the same endowments and preferences, and they face the same real wages and real interest rate, all households will wish to be either a net lender or a net borrower at any given interest rate. As there cannot be an equilibrium with either positive or negative savings, the interest rate adjusts to ensure that the representative household consumes all its current income in every period, and there are no savings. This is the equilibrium condition in financial and product markets, which determines the real interest rate. If there were an outside asset, like capital, then the equilibrium condition would have been that savings are equal to investment.

Using the definition of household income (2.106) and the budget constraint of the representative household (2.75), we get that consumption in every period is also a function of the employment rate:

$$c_1 = Al_1, c_2 = A(1+g)l_2. \tag{2.107}$$

These are the *equilibrium conditions in the product market*, ensuring that the consumption decisions of households are compatible with the production decisions of firms. They imply that consumption is equal to total output in every period.

Equilibrium employment makes the employment decisions of households (as given by (2.101) and (2.102)) equal to the employment decisions of firms (as given by (2.105)). As a result, we have

$$\frac{l_1^{\gamma}}{c_1^{-\theta}} = A, \frac{l_2^{\gamma}}{c_2^{-\theta}} = A(1+g), \tag{2.108}$$

which is the set of *equilibrium conditions in the labor market*, ensuring that the real wage w is compatible with the employment decisions of both households and firms in every period.

Solving (2.107) and (2.108) simultaneously, we can determine the equilibrium employment rates. The solutions for the equilibrium l_1 and l_2 are given by

$$\bar{l}_1 = A^{\frac{1-\theta}{\gamma+\theta}}, \bar{l}_2 = (A(1+g))^{\frac{1-\theta}{\gamma+\theta}}, \tag{2.109}$$

where $\bar{l}$ denotes equilibrium employment. From (2.109), equilibrium employment will be a positive function of productivity A and productivity growth g only if $\theta < 1$ (i.e., only if $1/\theta$, the intertemporal elasticity of substitution of consumption, is greater than unity).

If the intertemporal elasticity of substitution of consumption is greater than unity, then the period with higher productivity will be the period with higher employment as well, as households will wish to work more and so have higher income and consumption. The intertemporal substitution effect is stronger than the income effect in this case. The opposite happens if the intertemporal elasticity of substitution of consumption is less than unity.

Note that if the intertemporal elasticity of substitution of consumption is equal to unity or if the Frisch elasticity of labor supply is equal to zero, then equilibrium employment is constant and equal to unity and does not depend on productivity or productivity growth.

Because there is no outside asset as an outlet for savings, the equilibrium real interest rate adjusts to ensure that consumption is equal to income in both periods. From the Euler equation for consumption (2.99), the equilibrium conditions that consumption is equal to current income in each period (2.107), and the equation for equilibrium employment (2.109), the equilibrium real interest rate is determined by

$$1+\bar{r}=(1+\rho)(1+g)^{\theta\frac{\gamma+1}{\gamma+\theta}}. \tag{2.110}$$

This equation defines the equilibrium real interest rate that ensures that the intertemporal decisions of the representative household are consistent, in the sense that savings are equal to investment. Because there is no capital in this model and investment is equal to zero, the equilibrium real interest rate ensures that savings are equal to zero.

The equilibrium real interest rate is a positive function of the pure rate of time preference and also of the rate of growth of productivity. Thus, both the preferences of the representative household and the technology of production affect the equilibrium real interest rate.

For a given rate of growth of productivity, the real interest rate increases with increasing θ (i.e., it decreases with decreasing intertemporal elasticity of substitution of consumption $1/\theta$). The more difficult it is for households to substitute consumption intertemporally, the higher the equilibrium real interest rate will be.

By taking the logarithm of the real interest rate, the equilibrium condition (2.110) can be approximated by

$$\bar{r}\simeq\rho+\theta g\frac{\gamma+1}{\gamma+\theta}. \tag{2.111}$$

If the intertemporal elasticity of substitution of consumption $1/\theta$ is equal to unity, then the equilibrium real interest rate is equal to $\rho+g$, the sum of the pure rate of time preference and the growth rate of productivity.

Equilibrium real wages and equilibrium output and consumption are determined by

$$\bar{w}_1=A, \bar{w}_2=A(1+g), \tag{2.112}$$

$$\bar{y}_1=\bar{c}_1=A^{\frac{\gamma+1}{\gamma+\theta}}, \bar{y}_2=\bar{c}_2=(A(1+g))^{\frac{\gamma+1}{\gamma+\theta}}. \tag{2.113}$$

The equilibrium real wage is equal to the exogenous total factor productivity, which for a linear production function is equal to the marginal productivity of labor. Thus, real wages grow at a rate g between periods 1 and 2.

Equilibrium output and consumption are also positive functions of total factor productivity. If the intertemporal elasticity of substitution of consumption is higher than unity (i.e., $\theta < 1$), then the elasticity of equilibrium aggregate output and consumption with respect to total factor productivity is greater than unity as well, as higher productivity induces higher employment from households, and vice versa.

Exercise 2.4 Assume that the representative household is endowed with l_0 units of labor in each period and lives for two periods. There is no capital. Derive equilibirum production, consumption, the real interest rate, and the real wage for each period, assuming that households maximize utility subject to the relevant resource constraints, firms maximize profits, and product and factor markets are competitive. Assume a CEIS intertemporal utility function of the form (2.93) and production functions of the form (2.103). Discuss how the equilibrium depends on the labor endowment, preferences, and technological parameters. How are your conclusions modified if the elasticity of intertemporal substitution of consumption is equal to unity?

2.5.5 Implications for Business Cycle Theory

The two-period model of consumption and labor supply that we have examined in this section is the basis of most dynamic stochastic general equilibrium (DSGE) models of aggregate fluctuations.

The stochastic growth model analyzed in chapter 13 (which is the basis of most real business cycle models) and the new classical model of aggregate fluctuations without capital (analyzed in chapter 14) are direct extensions of the two-period model of consumption and labor supply to economies that last for an infinite number of periods. These models are subject to random disturbances to total factor productivity. However, much like the two-period model of this section, these models assume full and perfectly competitive markets, and the absence of market distortions, such as wage and price rigidity. As we shall see in chapters 13 and 14, the optimality conditions of the two-period model, such as the Euler equation for consumption and the individual optimality conditions for labor supply, recur again and again in these infinite-horizon competitive models. Hence, the key properties of these infinite-horizon competitive models are quite closely related to the two-period model.

New Keynesian models of aggregate fluctuations are extensions of the two-period model to monetary economies that are characterized by both real and nominal distortions and disturbances in product and labor markets. Such new Keynesian models relax the assumptions of full and competitive markets, as well as the assumption of perfect wage and price flexibility. They imply that the resulting macroeconomic equilibria are suboptimal. Such models are analyzed in chapters 16 and 17.

A more recent development is the extension of new Keynesian models to models including financial distortions as well. This was a direct result of the financial crisis of 2008–2009. Models of fully efficient financial markets are gradually giving way to models of financial frictions and the absence of perfect capital markets. Such models are introduced and discussed in chapter 19 on financial frictions.

2.6 Money, Prices, and Inflation in a Two-Period Competitive Model

In the models we have presented so far, money has no role. Yet money performs very important functions in an economy. Money is a unit of account, in terms of which market prices are defined and quoted; a means of payments, which reduces transaction costs; and the most liquid store of value.

In this section, we allow for the role of money as a unit of account and a means of payments in a two-period intertemporal model. We assume that transactions can only take place through the intermediation of money (i.e., by paying *cash in advance*) and that all prices are quoted in terms of money.

In models with money, one can draw the distinction between *real variables*, defined in terms of physical quantities (such as the ones we have analyzed so far), and *nominal variables*, defined in money units (such as the stock of money, price level, inflation, nominal output, nominal wages, and nominal interest rates).

2.6.1 The Representative Household and the Demand for Money

We focus on the two-period model without capital, analyzed in section 2.5. The representative household in endowed with one unit of labor for each of periods 1 and 2. It is also endowed with one unit of money m at the beginning of period 1, which it has to return at the end of the period, and one plus an extra μ units of money in period 2, which it again has to return at the end of the period. It is assumed that $-1 < \mu < 1$.

Money can be thought of as a separate commodity that is a generally accepted unit of account and means of payments. It could be *commodity money*, in the form of coins, or *paper money*, in the form of banknotes. It could even be *digital money*. The stock of money cannot be consumed, and therefore yields no direct utility. For simplicity, we assume that it cannot be carried over from period to period. It can only be used for current economic transactions. The household uses money to buy commodities for consumption, and its labor income is also paid with money.

The representative household is assumed to maximize the following intertemporal utility function:

$$U = \frac{c_1^{1-\theta}}{1-\theta} - \frac{l_1^{1+\gamma}}{1+\gamma} + \frac{1}{1+\rho}\left(\frac{c_2^{1-\theta}}{1-\theta} - \frac{l_2^{1+\gamma}}{1+\gamma}\right). \tag{2.114}$$

Its intertemporal budget constraint is given by

$$p_1c_1 + \frac{p_2c_2}{1+i} = p_1w_1l_1 + \frac{p_2w_2l_2}{1+i}, \tag{2.115}$$

where p_1 is the money (nominal) price of consumption goods in period 1, p_2 is the money price of consumption goods in period 2, p_1w_1 is the nominal wage in period 1, p_2w_2 is the nominal wage in period 2, and i is the nominal interest rate (i.e., the interest rate expressed in terms of money).

The timing of transactions is assumed to be as follows. In period 1, the household uses its money endowment to buy commodities that cost p_1c_1. At the end of the period, it is paid its money wages $p_1w_1l_1$ with money. At the end of the period, it also has to repay its money endowment. In period 2, it uses the money it has received for this period, which is one plus the additional money endowment of μ, to buy commodities that cost p_2c_2; at the end of period 2, it is paid its money wages $p_2w_2l_2$. At the end of period 2, it also has to repay its money endowmnent.[12]

The household has to pay money up front to purchase commodities for consumption. In addition, the household receives money for its labor services in the form of money wages. Hence, there are four additional constraints, usually called *cash in advance constraints*. These take the form

$$p_1c_1 \le m = 1, \tag{2.116}$$

$$p_2c_2 \le m(1+\mu) = 1+\mu, \tag{2.117}$$

$$p_1w_1l_1 \ge m = 1, \tag{2.118}$$

$$p_2w_2l_2 \ge m(1+\mu) = 1+\mu. \tag{2.119}$$

The Lagrange function for this problem is given by

$$\mathcal{L} = \tfrac{c_1^{1-\theta}}{1-\theta} - \tfrac{l_1^{1+\gamma}}{1+\gamma} + \tfrac{1}{1+\rho}\left(\tfrac{c_2^{1-\theta}}{1-\theta} - \tfrac{l_2^{1+\gamma}}{1+\gamma}\right) - \lambda_1\left(p_1\left(c_1 - w_1l_1\right) + \tfrac{p_2}{1+i}\left(c_2 - w_2l_2\right)\right) - \\ -\lambda_2\left((p_1c_1 - 1) + (1 - p_1w_1l_1) - \tfrac{1}{1+i}\left((p_2c_2 - 1 + \mu) + (1 + \mu - p_2w_2l_2)\right)\right), \tag{2.120}$$

where the Lagrange multiplier λ_1 measures the marginal value of household wealth, and λ_2 measures the marginal value of money. The marginal value of money for period 2 is discounted at the nominal interest rate i. Given the assumption of nonsatiation, the marginal value of money will be nonnegative, as the household will try to buy goods

12. The timing could, of course, be the opposite. Households receive money from firms in exchange for their labor services at the beginning of the period, and use the money to buy goods at the end of the period.

until it exhausts its money stock endowment, given that money does not yield utility directly.

From the first-order conditions for a maximum, we get that

$$c_1^{-\theta} = (\lambda_1 + \lambda_2) p_1, \tag{2.121}$$

$$\frac{1}{1+\rho} c_2^{-\theta} = \frac{1}{1+i} (\lambda_1 + \lambda_2) p_2, \tag{2.122}$$

$$l_1^{\gamma} = (\lambda_1 + \lambda_2) p_1 w_1, \tag{2.123}$$

$$l_2^{\gamma} = \frac{1}{1+i} (\lambda_1 + \lambda_2) p_2 w_2. \tag{2.124}$$

The interpretation of these first-order conditions is straightforward. (2.121) suggests that the marginal utility of period 1 consumption is equal to the marginal value of wealth plus the marginal value of money, multiplied by the period 1 money price of consumption goods. (2.122) suggests that the marginal utility of period 2 consumption is equal to the discounted marginal value of wealth plus the discounted marginal value of money, multiplied by the period 2 money price of consumption goods. (2.123) suggests that the marginal utility of period 1 leisure is equal to the marginal value of wealth plus the marginal value of money, multiplied by the period 1 money price of leisure, which is none other than the period 1 nominal wage. And (2.124) suggests that the marginal utility of period 2 leisure is equal to the discounted marginal value of wealth plus the discounted marginal value of money, multiplied by the period 2 money price of leisure, which is the nominal wage in period 2.

Given the assumption of nonsatiation, the intertemporal budget constraint (2.115) and the cash in advance constraints (2.116)–(2.119) will also be satisfied with equality. As a result, the demand for money in every period will be proportional to household consumption and/or income, whichever is higher. Thus, the demand for money in this model is determined by a simple version of the *quantity theory of money*.[13]

2.6.2 The Classical Dichotomy and the Neutrality of Money

Eliminating $\lambda_1 + \lambda_2$ between (2.121) and (2.122) gives us the Euler equation for consumption:

$$\frac{1}{1+\rho} \left(\frac{c_2}{c_1} \right)^{-\theta} = \frac{1}{1+i} \frac{p_2}{p_1} = \frac{1+\pi}{1+i}, \tag{2.125}$$

13. There are other ways of motivating the demand for money other than the particular way assumed in this chapter. The two main approaches used in the literature are the *cash in advance approach*, a version of which is used in this chapter, and the *money in the utility function approach*, where it is assumed that money yields utility because of its liquidity services. The latter approach is introduced in chapter 7, and we return to the similarities and differences between the two approaches in chapter 12, where we examine more general intertemporal models of the money market.

where $\pi = (p_2/p_1) - 1$ is the rate of change of money prices (i.e., the inflation rate) between periods 2 and 1. The second equality in (2.125) defines the inverse of one plus the real interest rate.

As first defined by Fisher [1896], the relationship between the real interest rate r and the nominal interest rate i is given by

$$1 + r = \frac{1+i}{1+\pi}. \tag{2.126}$$

This equation is the exact form of the so-called *Fisher equation*, which states that the real interest rate is defined by the ratio of one plus the nominal interest rate and one plus expected inflation.[14]

Note that for a low r and a low inflation rate π, we have

$$\ln \frac{1+i}{1+\pi} \simeq i - \pi, \ln(1+r) \simeq r.$$

Hence, (2.126) implies that

$$r \simeq i - \pi. \tag{2.127}$$

(2.127) is the approximate form of the Fisher equation, which is often used in place of (2.126) and is relatively accurate only when inflation rates are low.

From (2.125) and (2.126), the Euler equation for consumption in the two-period model with money has the same form as the Euler equation for consumption in the two-period models without money. The marginal rate of substitution between period 2 and period 1 consumption is equal to the inverse of one plus the real interest rate.

Eliminating $\lambda_1 + \lambda_2$ between (2.121) and (2.123) and between (2.122) and (2.124) gives us the optimality conditions for the choice between consumption and leisure in each period. These are the same as equations (2.101) and (2.102) in the two-period model without money. The marginal rate of substitution between consumption and leisure is equal to the real wage in each period.

Finally, dividing the intertemporal budget constraint of the representative household (2.115) by p_1 and using the definition of the real interest rate from (2.125), we get back to (2.94), the intertemporal budget constraint of the representative household in the model without money.

14. To quote from Fisher [1896, p. 58]: "When prices are rising or falling, money is depreciating or appreciating relative to commodities. Our theory would therefore require high or low interest according as prices are rising or falling, provided we assume that the rate of interest in the commodity standard should not vary." The rate of interest in the commodity standard is the real interest rate, and rising or falling prices are expected inflation. The Fisher equation was further elaborated in Fisher [1930], where it was made even clearer that Fisher was referring to expected inflation.

Hence, making the same assumptions about the behavior of firms as in the model without money, the evolution of real variables in the monetary model of this section and the non-monetary model of section 2.5 will be exactly the same. The evolution of real variables will be determined as in equations (2.109)–(2.113) in section 2.5.4.

The existence of money and monetary growth does not affect the optimal decision rules of either households or firms concerning the determination of real variables. Money matters for nominal but not for real variables. This property is called the classical dichotomy and implies the neutrality of money. It is a property characterizing both static and intertemporal general equilibrium models with optimizing households and firms.

From the cash in advance constraints (2.116) and (2.117) and the determination of equilibrium real consumption and output from (2.113), equilibrium nominal prices will be determined by

$$\bar{p}_1 = \frac{m}{\bar{c}_1} = \frac{1}{\bar{c}_1} = A^{-\frac{\gamma+1}{\gamma+\theta}}, \bar{p}_2 = \frac{m(1+\mu)}{\bar{c}_2} = \frac{1+\mu}{\bar{c}_2} = \frac{1+\mu}{(1+g)^{(\gamma+1)/(\gamma+\theta)}} A^{-\frac{\gamma+1}{\gamma+\theta}}. \tag{2.128}$$

Thus, equilibrium nominal prices are equal to the ratio of the money stock to equilibrium real output and consumption.

Equilibrium inflation is determined by

$$\bar{\pi} = \frac{1+\mu}{(1+g)^{(\gamma+1)/(\gamma+\theta)}} - 1 \simeq \mu - \frac{\gamma+1}{\gamma+\theta} g. \tag{2.129}$$

From (2.129), we have that if the intertemporal elasticity of substitution of consumption is equal to unity, then the equilibrium inflation rate is equal to the difference between the rate of growth of the money supply μ and the aggregate growth rate g. Otherwise, equilibrium inflation is equal to the difference between the rate of growth of the money supply and a multiple $(\gamma+1)/(\gamma+\theta)$ of the growth rate.

Equilibrium nominal wages will be equal to the product of equilibrium prices from (2.128) and equilibrium real wages from (2.112).

From (2.127), (2.129), and (2.110), the equilibrium nominal interest rate is equal to

$$\bar{i} = \bar{r} + \bar{\pi} = \rho + (\theta - 1)\frac{\gamma+1}{\gamma+\theta} g + \mu. \tag{2.130}$$

From (2.130), if the intertemporal elasticity of substitution of consumption is equal to unity, then the equilibrium nominal interest rate is equal to pure rate of time preference plus the rate of growth of the money supply. Otherwise, productivity growth also affects the equilibrium nominal interest rate.

2.6.3 The Two-Period Competitive Model and Classical Monetary Theory

The two-period model with money analyzed in this section embodies most of the basic postulates of *classical monetary theory*. This model implies the *quantity theory of money* in the form of the cash in advance constraints (2.116)–(2.119). Households demand money to purchase goods, and they accept money in payment for their labor services.

The model also implies the *classical dichotomy*, whereby real factors determine real variables (such as output, employment, real wages, and the real interest rate), and monetary factors determine only nominal and monetary variables (such as the price level and nominal wages, and interest rates) as well as inflation. Through the classsical dichotomy, the model thus implies the *neutrality of money*.

We shall examine extensions of the two-period monetary model to growth models where households have an infinite horizon in chapter 7. In chapter 12, we also examine stochastic general equilibrium models of money demand, introducing uncertainty. In chapters 14–17, we examine the role of money in new classical and new Keynesian DSGE models of aggregate fluctuations. Because of the assumption of nominal price and wage sluggishness, new Keynesian models do not imply classical neutrality in the short run, and they imply than even nominal disturbances can generate fluctuations in real variables, such as output and employment. In chapters 19 and 20, we take an integrated and detailed look at the role of monetary policy in the context of models with nominal rigidities and financial frictions.

The main predictions of extended intertemporal models with full and competitive markets are closely related to the properties of the two-period intertemporal model with money, such as the model examined in this section. The new Keynesian models discussed in chapters 16, 17, 19, and 20 are based on the sluggish adjustment of prices and nominal wages and imply short-run deviations from the neutrality of money and a significant role for monetary policy as a stabilization policy instrument. The intertemporal models with financial frictions discussed in chapters 19 and 20 also imply a modified role for monetary policy, but through channels other than the adjustment of nominal interest rates.

2.7 Fiscal Policy in a Two-Period Competitive Model

Up to this point we have not allowed for the existence of government expenditure and taxes. In this section, we introduce the government and examine how fiscal policy (i.e., government expenditure, taxes, and government debt) affect the economy. The aim is to examine intertemporal aspects of fiscal policy, in the context of a two-period model. However, by way of comparison, it is useful to first consider fiscal policy in the context of a one-period competitive economy.

2.7.1 Government Expenditure and Taxes in a One-Period Economy

Assume a one-period economy in which the representative household is endowed with one unit of capital and one unit of labor. Its endowment of capital and labor can be rented to private firms at a competitive rental price of capital r and a competitive real wage w. Capital and labor are used by competitive firms in the production of a single good y. The household can use the income from the rental of its capital and labor endowments for consumption, and it can also consume its capital endowment at the end of the period.

The government can tax the representative household and spend the proceeds on buying the single good y itself. Government expenditure is denoted by c_g. Because this is a one-good economy, government expenditure is on goods that yield utility to the representative household and are perfect substitutes for private consumption. The government pays for government expenditure by imposing a *lump sum tax* on the representative household, which is denoted by τ.

Because the economy lasts for only one period, the value of taxes must be equal to government expenditure. In this one-period model, the government cannot spend more than its tax revenue, as it would not have the ability to pay, and it will not spend less, as this would imply a waste of resources. Its budget constraint is thus given by

$$c_g = \tau. \tag{2.131}$$

The problem of the representative household is to maximize its utility function u, which depends on the volume of both private and public consumption, subject to its budget constraint and the choice of government expenditure and taxes by the government. Thus, the representative household chooses private consumption c to maximize

$$u(c + c_g), \tag{2.132}$$

subject to

$$c = 1 + rk + wl - \tau = 1 + r + w - \tau. \tag{2.133}$$

The last equality in (2.133) is the result of imposing the condition that the household commits to production its full endowments of capital and labor, each of which is equal to unity. As we have already shown, this follows from the assumption of nonsatiation.

From the first-order conditions for a maximum, and after taking account of the optimal behavior of the representative firm (as in the case of subsection 2.2.4) and the government budget constraint (2.131), equilibrium private consumption is given by

$$\bar{c} = 1 + \bar{y} - \tau = 1 + A - c_g, \tag{2.134}$$

where A denotes total factor productivity. In equilibrium, because taxes are equal to government expenditure, government expenditure displaces private consumption one for one, without affecting any other real variables.

Substituting the government budget constraint (2.131) into (2.134), equilibrium aggregate output is given by

$$\bar{y} = \bar{c} + c_g - 1 = A. \tag{2.135}$$

This is the same as in the model of subsection 2.2.1 without government expenditure and taxes. One can also show that the equilibrium real rental price of capital and the real wage are given by (2.26), as in the one-period model without a government.

Hence, the only real effect of government expenditure and taxes in this economy would be a one-for-one substitution of public for private consumption, without any other real effects. Aggregate output and employment are the same as in the case where government expenditure and taxes are equal to zero.

The same would apply in this model if taxes were not lump sum but proportional to household income. Suppose that taxes on the representative household are given by

$$\tau = t_y(rk + wl) = t_y(r + w), \tag{2.136}$$

where $0 < t_y < 1$ is the income tax rate.

Because both the capital and labor endowments are fixed, income taxes would have no effects on the utilization of either capital or labor. The representative household would still commit its full endowments to production. Therefore, income taxes do not imply any distortions in this case. Equilibrium aggregate consumption and output would be the same as in the absence of government expenditure and income taxation. They would be given by (2.135).

Private consumption would be equal to the disposable income of the household plus its capital endowment, but there would be no other real effects from government expenditure and taxes.

2.7.2 Income Taxes and Labor Supply

An income tax would only be distortionary and affect equilibrium employment, output, and consumption, in the case where labor supply is endogenous, as in the model of section 2.4.

Assuming an income tax at a rate t_y in the one-period model of section 2.4, with endogenous labor supply, results in equilibrium employment being equal to

$$\bar{l} = A^{\frac{1-\theta}{\gamma+\theta}} (1 - t_y)^{\frac{1}{\gamma+\theta}}. \tag{2.137}$$

Thus, the presence of income taxation is *distortionary* in this model, as it reduces the net of tax equilibrium real wage and has a negative effect on labor supply and equilibrium aggregate employment.

The only cases in which income taxation would not have a negative impact on labor supply and aggregate employment are the cases in which either the Frisch elasticity of labor supply $1/\gamma$ is equal to zero or the intertemporal elasticity of substitution of consumption $1/\theta$ is equal to zero. In either of these two cases, labor supply is independent of the net of tax real wage.

The elasticity of aggregate employment with respect to the income tax rate is given by

$$-\frac{t_y}{1-t_y}.$$

The elasticity of aggregate employment with respect to the income tax rate is not only negative but also increasing in the income tax rate. As the income tax rate tends to unity (100%), the elasticity of aggregate employment with respect to the income tax rate tends to infinity. As the income tax rate tends to zero, the elasticity of aggregate employment with respect to the income tax rate tends to zero as well.

In the presence of an income tax and endogenous labor supply, equilibrium aggregate output is given by

$$\bar{y}=\bar{c}+c_g-1=A^{\frac{\gamma+1}{\gamma+\theta}}(1-t_y)^{\frac{1}{\gamma+\theta}}. \tag{2.138}$$

It is clear from (2.137) and (2.138) that a positive income tax rate t_y results in lower aggregate employment, output, and consumption, unlike lump sum taxes, which would not affect labor supply.

2.7.3 Government Expenditure, Taxes, and Debt in a Two-Period Economy

We next turn to an analysis of fiscal policy in the two-period model of section 2.3. In this two-period model, labor supply is exogenous, but the savings decision is endogenous. Both the representative household and the government have to make intertemporal decisions. As we have seen, the most important such decision for the household is the savings and investment decision in the first period. For the government, the most important intertemporal decision is whether to finance government expenditure in the first period through taxes or borrowing (government debt).

We assume a government that wishes to finance a stream of primary government expenditure c_{g1}, c_{g2} over two periods. The sequence of government budget constraints is as follows:

$$d_1=c_{g1}-\tau_1, \tag{2.139}$$

$$-d_1=c_{g2}+r_2d_1-\tau_2, \tag{2.140}$$

where (2.139) is the period 1 budget balance, which could be a deficit or surplus. To the extent that government expenditure is higher than taxes in the first period, the government runs a budget deficit equal to d_1. This deficit is financed by one-period *bonds* (i.e., government debt equal to d_1).

(2.139) is the period 2 budget balance. If the government has run a deficit in the first period, then in the second period, it has to run a surplus equal to the deficit of the first period, because the second is the last period and the government has to repay its debt. Thus, tax revenue τ_2 must be sufficient to cover period 2 government expenditure and repayment of the debt. Period 2 government expenditure consists of two elements. First, interest payments on government debt from period 1, plus period 2 primary government expenditure c_g. *Primary government expenditure* is defined as government expenditure other than interest payments on existing government debt. The period 2 government budget constraint is thus given by equation (2.140).

As in the case of the representative household, the sequence of budget constraints (2.139) and (2.140) can be combined into a single intertemporal budget constraint. Using (2.139) to substitute for government debt in (2.140), after a simple rearrangement, we get

$$c_{g1} + \frac{c_{g2}}{1+r_2} = \tau_1 + \frac{\tau_2}{1+r_2}, \tag{2.141}$$

which is the *government intertemporal budget constraint*. It has an interpretation similar to the intertemporal budget constraint of the representative household. The present value of primary government expenditure in the two periods must be equal to the present value of tax revenue in the two periods. Thus, in an intertemporal setting, the government does not have to balance the government budget in every period, as long as its intertemporal budget constraint of the form of (2.141) is satisfied. It can run a government deficit or surplus in the first period, provided that this is reversed in the second period.

2.7.4 Ricardian Equivalence between Tax and Debt Finance

What are the implications of the government intertemporal budget constraint for the behavior of the economy? Does the method of financing first-period primary expenditure matter?

To address these questions, let us consider the intertemporal budget constraint of the representative household in this case. In the presence of government expenditure and taxes, the intertemporal budget constraint of the representative household is affected by the taxes that have to be paid and is given by

$$c_1 + \frac{1}{1+r_2}c_2 = 1 + (r_1 + w_1 - \tau_1) + \frac{1}{1+r_2}(w_2 - \tau_2). \tag{2.142}$$

Substituting the present value of taxes from the government budget constraint (2.141) into the household intertemporal budget constraint (2.142), we get that the household intertemporal budget constraint is given by

$$c_1 + \frac{1}{1+r_2}c_2 = 1 + (r_1 + w_1 - c_{g1}) + \frac{1}{1+r_2}(w_2 - c_{g2}). \tag{2.143}$$

From (2.143) it is clear that only the present value of primary government expenditure affects the intertemporal budget constraint of the representative household. The method of financing primary government expenditure (i.e., tax versus debt finance) has no effect on the household intertemporal budget constraint.

What about the intertemporal utility function of the representative household? In the presence of government expenditure, this is given by

$$U=\frac{\left(c_1+c_{g1}\right)^{1-\theta}}{1-\theta}+\frac{1}{1+\rho}\frac{\left(c_2+c_{g2}\right)^{1-\theta}}{1-\theta}, \tag{2.144}$$

where it is assumed that government expenditure is not wasteful. In fact, government expenditure affects the utility of the representative household in the same way as private consumption. The representative household chooses private consumption to maximize the intertemporal utility function (2.144), subject to the intertemporal budget constraint (2.143).

Note that the method of financing primary government expenditure does not appear either in the utility function of the representative household or in the intertemporal budget constraint. Hence, the only fiscal policy parameters that can affect the optimal decisions of the representative household and the behavior of the economy are related to the path of primary government expenditure. The method of financing the path of government expenditure cannot affect the optimal savings and investment decisions of the representative household. Debt and tax finance are equivalent.

This result, which was first alluded to by Ricardo [1817], is called *Ricardian equivalence* between debt and tax finance of government expenditure. In effect, the representative household realizes that debt finance is nothing more than a postponement of taxes to the future. Lower current taxes will result in higher future taxes with the same present value. Hence, the only thing that matters for the optimal savings and investment decisions of the representative household is the present value of primary government expenditure that needs to be financed, not the distribution of financing between the two periods. At the end of the two periods, the representative household will need to pay taxes with present value equal to the present value of the stream of primary government expenditure.[15]

The first-order conditions for a maximum of (2.144) subject to the intertemporal budget constraint (2.143) are given by

$$\left(c_1+c_{g1}\right)^{-\theta}=\lambda, \tag{2.145}$$

$$\frac{1}{1+\rho}\left(c_2+c_{g2}\right)^{-\theta}=\frac{\lambda}{1+r_2}, \tag{2.146}$$

where λ is the Lagrange multiplier measuring the marginal value of wealth.

15. Ricardian equivalence was brought to the forefront of macroeconomics by Barro [1974], who addressed the question of whether government bonds are considered as wealth by households who internalize the welfare of future generations. We return to this issue in chapter 6.

Eliminating λ between equations (2.145) and (2.146), we get the familiar Euler equation for consumption. Consumption is now the sum of private and government consumption:

$$\frac{1}{1+\rho}\left(\frac{c_2+c_{g2}}{c_1+c_{g1}}\right)^{-\theta}=\frac{1}{1+r_2}. \tag{2.147}$$

Taking into account the behavior of the representative firm, which is not affected by government expenditure and taxes, the product market equilibrium conditions in the two periods require that output is equal to the sum of private and public consumption plus investment in every period, which implies that

$$y_1=A=c_1+c_{g1}+(k_2-1), \tag{2.148}$$

$$y_2=A(1+g)k_2^{\alpha}=c_2+c_{g2}-k_2. \tag{2.149}$$

Furthermore, from the marginal productivity condition of the second period, we have that

$$r_2=\alpha Ak_2^{\alpha-1}. \tag{2.150}$$

Using (2.148), (2.149), and (2.150) to substitute for the sum of private and public consumption in the two periods, and the period 2 real interest rate in the Euler equation (2.147), we get that the equilibrium period 2 capital stock will be determined by solving

$$\frac{1}{1+\rho}\left(\frac{1+A-\bar{k}_2}{\bar{k}_2+A(1+g)\bar{k}_2^{\alpha}}\right)^{\theta}=\frac{1}{1+\alpha A(1+g)\bar{k}_2^{\alpha-1}}, \tag{2.151}$$

where $\bar{k}_2$ denotes the equilibrium capital stock in period 2. Equilibrium investment in period 1 is equal to $\bar{k}_2-1$, and equilibrium investment in period 2 is equal to $-\bar{k}_2$, as the household consumes its capital stock at the end of period 2.

Equation (2.151) is the same as (2.61), which is from the two-period model without government expenditure. Hence, equilibrium investment and the equilibrium period 2 capital stock will not be affected by either government expenditure or the method of financing it. The evolution of real output, aggregate savings, and investment will be the same as in the case where there is no government expenditure, government debt, or taxes.

The only effect of the path of government expenditure in this model is the displacement of an equal amount of private consumption. Since government consumption is assumed to be a perfect substitute for private consumption, neither aggregate savings and investment nor the evolution of real output are affected by the path of government expenditure, debt, or taxes.

This is a striking result. It is due to the assumptions that government expenditure is a perfect substitute for private consumption and that taxes are lump sum (i.e., they do not distort the savings and investment decisions of households). This result would not hold if either government expenditure were an imperfect substitute for private consumption, or if taxes were distortionary and affected the real interest rate faced by households.

2.7.5 Income Taxation and Aggregate Savings and Investment

Although Ricardian equivalence holds for lump sum taxes, an income tax would be distortionary in this model, as it would affect equilibrium savings and investment and second-period output and consumption.

Assuming an income tax rate of t_y, results in the Euler equation for consumption (2.151) amended to

$$\frac{1}{1+\rho}\left(\frac{1+A-\bar{k}_2}{\bar{k}_2+A(1+g)\bar{k}_2^{\alpha}}\right)^{\theta}=\frac{1}{1+(1-t_y)\alpha A(1+g)\bar{k}_2^{\alpha-1}}. \tag{2.152}$$

The net of tax real interest rate will be lower at the level of savings and investment without an income tax. Households would thus reduce savings and investment, and the economy will end up with a lower capital stock and output in period 2. Consumption in period 1 will rise relative to consumption in period 2, and savings, investment, and the capital stock in period 2 will be lower.

Thus, with income taxation, the method of financing government expenditure and the level of government expenditure itself will matter for the determination of first-period savings and investment and second-period output and consumption. Ricardian equivalence will no longer hold.

If we allowed for endogenous labor supply as well, income taxation would also distort labor supply decisions, as in the one-period model of subsection 2.7.2.

2.7.6 Implications for Fiscal Policy and Government Debt

The two-period model of fiscal policy analyzed in this section embodies many of the properties of more general intertemporal models of fiscal policy.

Ricardian equivalence is also a property of the infinite horizon, representative household model of economic growth, analyzed in chapter 6. However, in this model, there are full and perfect markets. As we shall see in chapter 6, Ricardian equivalence is not an implication of overlapping generations models of economic growth, in which current generations do not internalize the welfare of future generations. More generally, market distortions (such as the absence of perfect markets for the welfare of future generations) distortionary taxes, or financial distortions lead to a rejection of pure Ricardian equivalence and to potential differences between tax and debt finance of government expenditure. For example, distortionary taxes result in real effects from fiscal policy in all models with endogenous savings or endogenous labor supply.

We return to the impact of distortionary taxation in chapter 6, when we examine capital income taxation and economic growth. In chapter 21, we introduce more general intertemporal models of fiscal policy and investigate the relation between distortionary taxes and the accumulation of government debt.

2.8 The Treatment of Time and the Intertemporal Approach

The two-period intertemporal models examined in this chapter are obviously simplified and restrictive examples. One of the main simplifications is with regard to the treatment of time, which is confined to two time periods only. Yet the models can be extended in a straightforward manner by allowing for additional time periods.

For example, one could assume that time is an integer belonging to any subset of the set of integers $\mathbb{Z}$, from minus infinity to plus infinity. Put in mathematical terms, with an infinite number of time periods, we can assume that

$$t = -\infty, \ldots, -2, -1, 0, 1, 2, \ldots, \infty,$$

or

$$t \in \mathbb{Z},$$

where $\mathbb{Z}$ is the full set of integers. Intertemporal analysis could also be confined to any subset of the set of integers $\mathbb{Z}$, such as the set of positive natural numbers $\mathbb{N}$, or any finite subset of $\mathbb{Z}$ or $\mathbb{N}$.

For example, the two-period intertemporal utility function (2.30) of the representative household could be extented to T periods, and take the form

$$U = \sum_{t=0}^{T} \left(\frac{1}{1+\rho}\right)^{t} u\left(c_t\right). \tag{2.153}$$

Similarly, the two-period intertemporal budget constraint of the representative household (2.33) could be extended to T periods and takes the form

$$\sum_{t=1}^{T} \left(\frac{1}{1+r}\right)^{t-1} c_t = 1 + r + \sum_{t=1}^{T} \left(\frac{1}{1+r}\right)^{t-1} w_t, \tag{2.154}$$

where r is the real interest rate, assumed constant.

When time is expressed in terms of integers, it refers to discrete time periods, such as days, weeks, months, quarters, and years. Such intertemporal analysis is termed *discrete time* analysis.

Discrete time views values of variables as occurring at distinct, separate points in time, or equivalently, as being unchanged between these points. Thus, an economic variable that depends on time jumps from one value to another as time moves from one time period to the next. For example, the change of variable x between period t and period $t+1$ is denoted by

$$\Delta x_{t+1} = x_{t+1} - x_t,$$

where Δ is called the *first difference operator*.

This view of time corresponds to a digital clock that displays a fixed reading of 12:00 pm for one minute, then jumps to a new fixed reading of 12:01 pm for the next minute, then to 12:02 pm, and so on. In this framework, each variable of interest is measured once in each time period. The number of measurements between any two time periods is finite. Measurements are typically made at sequential integer values of the discrete variable, time.

Another way to treat time is as a continuous variable. *Continuous time analysis* views variables as taking a particular value for potentially only an infinitesimally short amount of time. Between any two points in time, there are an infinite number of other points in time. The continuous variable time, denoted by t, ranges over the entire set of real numbers $\mathbb{R}$, or, depending on the context, over some subset of it, such as the nonnegative real numbers. Hence, in continuous time models it is assumed that

$$t \in \mathbb{R}.$$

We can think of continuous time as the limit of discrete periods of duration Δt, where Δt tends to zero. For example, the change Δ in a variable x between periods t and $t + \Delta t$ can be written as

$$\Delta x_t = x_{t+\Delta t} - x_t.$$

Dividing by Δt and letting it tend to zero, we get

$$\dot{x}(t) = \lim_{\Delta t \to 0} \left(\frac{x_{t+\Delta t} - x_t}{\Delta t} \right).$$

A dot above a variable denotes its first derivative with respect to time, when time is a continuous real variable.

In continuous time, the T-period intertemporal utility function (2.153) takes the form

$$U = \int_{t=0}^{T} e^{-\rho t} u\left(c(t)\right) dt, \tag{2.155}$$

where t is assumed continuous in the interval $[0, T]$. The integral is the limit of the sum, when the length of the time intervals tend to zero.

Similarly, in continuous time, the T-period intertemporal budget constraint (2.154) takes the form

$$\int_{t=0}^{T} e^{-rt} c(t) dt = 1 + \int_{t=0}^{T} e^{-rt} w(t) dt. \tag{2.156}$$

In subsequent chapters, we use the common convention that t is written as a subscript in an analysis using discrete time and is treated as an argument (in parentheses) in an analysis using continuous time. We will use both ways of defining time. Growth models will be analyzed mostly in continuous time, whereas stochastic models of aggregate fluctuations will be analyzed mostly in discrete time.

The two types of intertemporal analysis are equivalent, but depending on the context, one of the two methods is either analytically or notationally more convenient.

2.9 Conclusion

In this chapter, we focused on equilibrium outcomes in competitive economies lasting for only two periods, to highlight some of the main themes of the intertemporal approach to macroeconomics.

We first analyzed the properties of general equilibrium in a one-period competitive macroeconomic model with exogenous capital and labor endowments. We then investigated intertemporal general equilibrium in a competitive two-period macroeconomic model with fixed capital and labor endowments. We also investigated extensions of the two-period model to examine intertemporal substitution in labor supply, the role of money, and the role of fiscal policy. In all models, we assumed full and competitive markets.

The two-period competitive model is the simplest possible intertemporal model, and we have used it to investigate some of the salient characteristics of the intertemporal approach when perfect competitive markets exist. As will become apparent in the remainder of this book, many of the properties of the two-period model carry over to competitive market models, in which economies last for more than two periods, such as the infinite-horizon competitive representative household model. However, models that are based on market distortions (such as transactions costs, externalities, uncertainty, increasing returns to scale, asymmetric information, or nominal wage and price rigidities) can be best understood in juxtaposition to competitive intertemporal models, such as the ones analyzed in this chapter. Hence, the models presented in this chapter should be understood as ideal types, against which more realistic models of absence of markets, market distortions, and gradual adjustment of nominal wages and prices are to be compared.

Many of the macroeconomic themes examined through the two-period models of this chapter will be revisited in the context of the intertemporal models without perfect markets used in the remainder of this book.

3

Savings, Investment, and Economic Growth

In this chapter, we go beyond the two-period model and begin our investigation of the determinants of long-run economic growth in economies that exist for a large number of periods. In fact, we focus on economies with an infinite horizon and examine the relationship between savings, investment, capital accumulation, and economic growth.

The starting point for the analysis of this process is the Solow [1956] model. This is a model of an infinite-horizon economy. It is based on a neoclassical production function, such as the one postulated in chapter 2, but instead of optimizing households, it is based on the assumption that the savings rate is exogenous and constant. Given that in a closed economy, aggregate savings are always equal to investment, the process of capital accumulation depends on the savings rate, which in equilibrium determines the investment rate.[1]

In this model, capital accumulation per employee continues until savings per employee is equated with the depreciation and the additional investment per employee required to maintain a constant ratio of capital to labor. The growth rate of population and the growth rate of the number of employees is assumed to be exogenous in this model.

The model also allows for exogenous technical progress, which raises the efficiency of labor continuously. In this case, capital accumulation per efficiency unit of labor continues until savings per efficiency unit of labor is equated to depreciation plus the additional investment required to provide for population growth and technical progress.

In the long-run equilibrium of this infinite-horizon model, alternatively referred to as the *steady state* or the *balanced growth path*, economic growth is exogenous and equal to the rate of population growth plus the rate of technical progress. Essentially, on the balanced growth path, per capita output grows at the exogenous rate of technical progress.

During the adjustment process toward the balanced growth path, an economy that has an initial capital stock lower than its steady state value experiences a growth rate that is higher than its long-run growth rate. Capital accumulates at a rate that exceeds the sum of the rate of growth of population and the rate of technical progress, and so does output. For

1. This model is often referred to as the "Solow-Swan model," as a similar analysis was published in the same year by Swan [1956].

an economy that has an initial capital stock that is higher than its steady state value, the growth rate during the transition is below the long-run growth rate, as capital accumulates at a rate that falls short of the sum of the rate of population growth and the rate of technical progress.

This model predicts that economies converge to a unique balanced growth path. A "poor" economy and a "rich" one (in terms of initial capital stock) converge to the same balanced growth path, provided that they are characterized by the same savings rate and the same technological and demographic parameters.

However, if two economies have different savings rates, total factor productivity, initial labor efficiency, rates of population growth or depreciation rate of capital, they will converge to different balanced growth paths. Convergence in this model is thus conditional. The balanced growth path depends on the structural characteristics of economies, such as their savings and investment rates, total factor productivity, the rate of population growth, and the rate of technical progress.

This model predicts that an economy with a higher savings (and investment) rate will be characterized by higher steady state capital and output per worker. Furthermore, it predicts a positive impact on capital and output per worker from higher total factor productivity and initial labor efficiency, and a negative impact from the rate of population growth, the rate of technical progress, and the depreciation rate of capital.

The Solow model is a key model and an important reference point for the theory of economic growth. Although it is not an intertemporal model in which households determine savings and investment optimally, and although the basic model has other theoretical and empirical weaknesses, this model provides a very useful, simple, and flexible framework for the analysis of the growth process, and it has stood the test of time well.

From the point of view of modern intertemporal macroeconomics, it has two main weaknesses. First, the assumption of an exogenous savings rate. This weakness is addressed by extensions of the model to optimizing models in which households choose savings in an individually optimal fashion. The representative household model of chapter 4 and the overlapping generations models of chapter 5 are such optimizing dynamic general equilibrium models, which retain most of the characteristics of the Solow model.

The second weakness is that the accumulation of physical capital, which is the main engine of economic growth in the Solow model, cannot fully explain either the long-term growth of output per worker and per capita income that has been observed in developed economies, or the large differences in labor productivity and living standards per head between developed and less developed economies. Only a small part of these differences can be explained by the accumulation of physical capital. Most of it is accounted for by differences in total factor productivity and technical progress, which in the Solow model are considered exogenous parameters. In this sense, the Solow model, like all models that rely on similar assumptions about technology and technical progress, shows us how to overcome its weaknesses, first, by introducing human as well as physical capital, and second, by trying to explain technical progress endogenously. Such extensions are introduced in chapter 8.

3.1 The Solow Growth Model

To account for the process of economic growth, the Solow model focuses on the determination of three main aggregate endogenous variables: total output Y, total physical stock K, and aggregate consumption C. Two additional endogenous variables, the real wage w and the real interest rate r, are determined if one assumes competitive markets for factors of production. The number of employees L is assumed proportional to an exogenously evolving total population, and the efficiency of labor h is assumed to evolve exogenously as well, growing at a constant rate of exogenous technical progress.

Thus, the rate of growth in the number of employees is equal to the population growth rate n and is considered exogenous. The rate of growth in the efficiency of labor is equal to the rate of exogenous technical progress g.

The model explains the level and rate of growth of output and physical capital as functions of these exogenous factors (n and g), the savings rate s (which is also considered exogenous), total factor productivity, and the exogenous rate of depreciation of capital δ. Once the capital stock, output, consumption, and investment are determined, one can derive the real interest rate r (renumeration of capital) and real wages w (remuneration of labor), as these depend on the ratio of capital to total labor efficiency. Obviously, all endogenous variables are determined simultaneously in a dynamic general equilibrium.

3.1.1 The Neoclassical Production Function

A key assumption that differentiates the Solow model from the models of economic growth that preceded it is the *neoclassical production function*. This function, as we discussed in chapter 2, implies a positive but finite elasticity of substitution between factors of production. Thus, at each point in time t, the economy is assumed to possess a stock of capital, number of employees, and labor efficiency that are combined to produce output through this production function. This production function is assumed to take the form

$$Y(t) = AF(K(t), h(t)L(t)), \tag{3.1}$$

where A is a positive constant denoting total factor productivity, and F is a continuous, twice differentiable quasi-concave function. We assume, as in chapter 2, that F is characterized by positive but diminishing returns to each factor of production but constant returns to scale. Hence, F is also a linearly homogeneous function.

Growth models that preceded the Solow model, such as the Harrod [1939]–Domar [1946] model, were based on a fixed proportions production function without the possibility of substitution between capital and labor. Such a production function was also used by Leontieff [1941] and is called the Leontieff production function. However, these earlier models did not necessarily imply covergence to a balanced growth path because of the lack of substitutability between capital and labor.

It is worth noting the following five characteristics of the neoclassical production function. First, time t enters the production function solely through the factors of production $K(t)$ and $h(t)L(t)$. Output can change over time only through changes in the quantity or efficiency of factors of production.

Second, technical progress is assumed to increase only the efficiency of labor $h(t)$. This is called *labor augmenting technical progress*, or *Harrod neutral technical progress*.

Third, the production function is characterized by *constant returns to scale*. Multiplying all factors of production by any nonnegative real number multiplies the scale of production by the same nonnegative real number. Thus, (3.1) satisfies

$$\mu Y(t) = AF\left(\mu K(t), \mu h(t)L(t)\right)$$

for any $\mu \geq 0$. Because of the assumption of constant returns to scale, the production function can be rewritten as

$$y(t) = Af\left(k(t)\right), \tag{3.2}$$

where $y = Y/hL$ is output per efficiency unit of labor, $k = K/hL$ is capital per efficiency unit of labor, and $f(k) = F(k, 1)$ is the production function per efficiency unit of labor. Equation (3.2) is often referred to as the production function in *intensive form*. The intensity of production (output per efficiency unit of labor) depends on the intensity of capital (capital per efficiency unit of labor).

Fourth, it is assumed that the production function has the following properties:

$$f(0) = 0, f' = \frac{\partial f}{\partial k} > 0, f'' = \frac{\partial^2 f}{\partial k^2} < 0.$$

The marginal product of capital per efficiency unit of labor is positive but declining. The production function in intensive form, with these additional assumptions, is depicted in figure 3.1.

Fifth, it is assumed that

$$\lim_{k\to 0} f'(k) = \infty, \ \lim_{k\to\infty} f'(k) = 0.$$

These final assumptions are called the *Inada conditions*. The Inada conditions ensure that the marginal product of capital is very high when capital intensity is low, and very low when capital intensity is high. These conditions are necessary and sufficient in order to prove the global uniqueness of the balanced growth path.[2]

2. See Inada [1964].

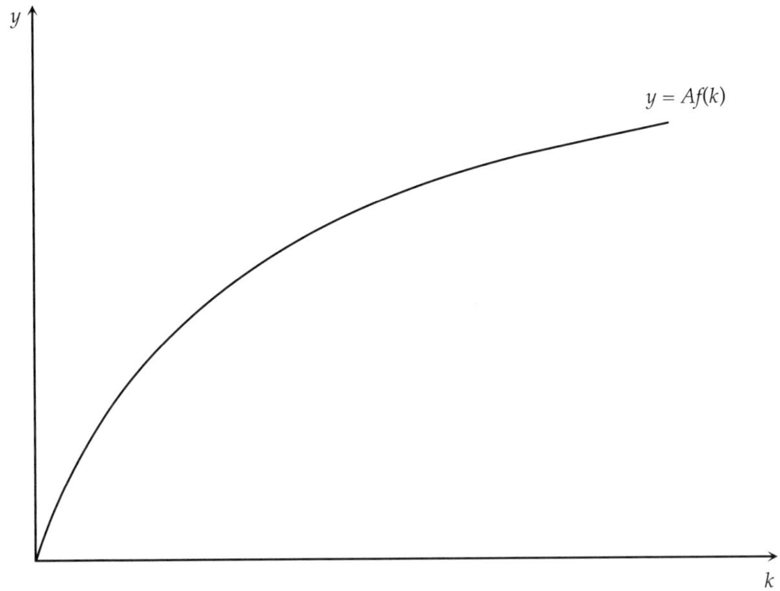

Figure 3.1
The production function in intensive form.

3.1.2 The Cobb-Douglas Production Function

A particular production function that is often used in the theory of growth, but also more generally in macroeconomics, is the Cobb-Douglas production function. As already discussed in chapter 2, it takes the form

$$AF(K(t), h(t)L(t)) = AK(t)^{\alpha}(h(t)L(t))^{1-\alpha}, \tag{3.3}$$

where $A > 0$, $0 < \alpha < 1$, α is the elasticity of production with respect to capital, and $1-\alpha$ is the corresponding elasticity with respect to labor.

The Cobb-Douglas production function in intensive form is given by

$$y(t) = Af(k(t)) = Ak(t)^{\alpha}. \tag{3.4}$$

One can easily confirm that the Cobb-Douglas production function (3.3) satisfies all the assumptions we have made about the neoclassical production function. The marginal product of capital and labor are positive and declining, and the Inada conditions are satisfied.

In addition, for the Cobb-Douglas production function, labor augmenting technical progress (Harrod neutral) does not differ from capital augmenting technical progress, or technical progress that augments both factors (Hicks neutral). The reason is that in the

Cobb-Douglas production function, the factors of production enter multiplicatively, and thus, it does not matter which of the factors of production is multiplied by technical progress.[3]

3.1.3 Population Growth and Technical Progress

We analyze the Solow model in continuous time, assuming that t is a continuous variable, where $t \in [0, \infty)$.[4] Assume that the number of employees is a constant fraction of total population and grows continuously at a constant, exogenous rate of population growth n. Thus, employment evolves over time according to

$$L(t) = L(0)e^{nt}, \tag{3.5}$$

where $L(0)$ is the number of employees at time 0, and e is the base of natural logarithms. Also assume that the efficiency of labor also grows continuously at a constant exogenous rate of technical progress g:

$$h(t) = h(0)e^{gt}, \tag{3.6}$$

where $h(0)$ is the efficiency of labor at time 0.

From (3.5) and (3.6), it follows that

$$\dot{L}(t) = \frac{dL(t)}{dt} = nL(t), \tag{3.7}$$

$$\dot{h}(t) = \frac{dh(t)}{dt} = gh(t). \tag{3.8}$$

A dot over a variable denotes its first derivative with respect to time (i.e., its change over time).[5]

3.1.4 Savings, Capital Accumulation, and Economic Growth

The output produced accrues to households as income, which is either consumed or saved. In the Solow model, the share of income which is saved and invested in any instant is assumed to be an exogenous parameter, denoted by s.

3. In appendix A, we discuss a more general functional form, the CES (constant elasticity of substitution) production function, put forward by Arrow et al. [1961]. It is shown that the CES production function encompasses the Cobb-Douglas, the Leontieff, and the linear production function as special cases but does not necessarily satisfy the Inada conditions.

4. In section 3.8, we also analyze the Solow model in discrete time, where $t = 0, 1, 2, \dots$ is an integer that refers to discrete time periods, such as years, months, weeks, or days.

5. Technically, (3.7) and (3.8) are first-order linear differential equations, whose solution is given by (3.5) and (3.6), respectively. For an introduction to ordinary differential equations, see appendix C.

Aggregate consumption C, is thus given by

$$C(t) = (1 - s)Y(t). \tag{3.9}$$

The demand for total output consists of consumption plus gross investment:

$$Y(t) = C(t) + I(t), \tag{3.10}$$

where $I(t)$ is gross investment. Equation (3.10) is an equilibrium condition in the product market, stating that total production (output supply) is equal to the demand for output.

Gross investment consists of additions to the capital stock plus replacement investment and is given by

$$I(t) = \dot{K}(t) + \delta K(t), \tag{3.11}$$

where $0 < \delta < 1$ is the rate of depreciation of the capital stock, assumed to be a constant exogenous parameter. Thus, δ is the instantaneous rate at which the capital stock declines over time because of wear and tear.

Substituting the consumption function (3.9) and the definition of gross investment (3.11) in the equilibrium condition (3.10), we get

$$Y(t) = (1 - s)Y(t) + \dot{K}(t) + \delta K(t). \tag{3.12}$$

Solving (3.12) for the change in the capital stock yields

$$\dot{K}(t) = sY(t) - \delta K(t). \tag{3.13}$$

From (3.13), the accumulation of capital is determined by the difference between savings and replacement investment. To the extent that savings is higher than replacement investment, the capital stock grows over time. If savings is lower than replacement investment, the capital stock is reduced over time.

Dividing (3.13) through by hL and taking into account that L grows at rate n and h grows at rate g, we get

$$\dot{k}(t) = sy(t) - (n + g + \delta)k(t), \tag{3.14}$$

which is the capital accumulation equation expressed in efficiency units of labor. To the extent that savings per efficiency unit of labor is higher than the investment required to keep capital per efficiency unit of labor constant, capital per efficiency unit of labor grows over time. In the opposite case, it declines over time.

Using the production function in intensive form, (3.2), to replace y in (3.14), we get

$$\dot{k}(t) = sAf(k(t)) - (n + g + \delta)k(t). \tag{3.15}$$

The nonlinear differential equation (3.15) is the key equation determining the accumulation of capital in the Solow model. It suggests that the change over time in capital per efficiency unit of labor is determined by the difference of two terms that both depend on the level of capital per efficiency unit of labor. The first term is *current savings and investment per efficiency unit of labor*, and the second term is *steady state investment per efficiency unit of labor*. Steady state, or long-run equilibrium, investment is defined as the investment rate that keeps capital per efficiency unit of labor constant.

3.1.5 The Balanced Growth Path and the Convergence Process

Given that the aggregate labor force, in efficiency terms, is increasing at an exogenous rate $n+g$, and that a fraction δ of the capital stock needs to be replaced at every moment due to depreciation, the investment required to keep the capital stock per efficiency unit of labor constant is given by $(n+g+\delta)k$. This we denote as steady state investment.

Steady state capital per efficiency unit of labor is thus determined by the condition that

$$\dot{k}(t)=0, \Rightarrow sf(k(t))=(n+g+\delta)k(t). \tag{3.16}$$

Denote by k^* the capital stock per efficiency unit of labor k that satisfies (3.16). One can easily deduce that k^* is constant and independent of time. It defines the so-called balanced growth path or steady state of the model, as all other steady state variables in this model depend on k^*.

On the steady state (or balanced growth) path, the capital stock, output, consumption, and investment per efficiency unit of labor are constant. The per capita steady state capital stock, output, consumption, and investment are of course not constant, as they are all growing at the exogenous rate of technical progress g. The aggregate steady state capital stock, output, consumption, and investment are growing at the rate $g+n$, which is the sum of the rate of population growth and the rate of technical progress.

The determination of k^* and the dynamic adjustment of k toward k^* are depicted in figure 3.2. The straight line depicts steady state investment $(n+g+\delta)k$. The curved line $sAf(k)$ depicts current savings and investment. At the point k^*, current savings and investment are equal to steady state savings and investment. Also depicted in Figure 3.2 is the production function in intensive form $Af(k)$, which relates output per efficiency unit of labor to capital per efficiency unit of labor.

To the left of k^*, current investment is higher than steady state investment, and k is increasing over time. To the right of k^*, current investment is lower than steady state investment, and k is declining over time. The equilibrium at k^* is unique and globally stable. Irrespective of initial conditions, the economy converges to k^*, which is the steady state capital stock per efficiency unit of labor.

Exercise 3.1 Assuming a Cobb-Douglas production function, as in (3.4), derive the steady state capital stock per efficiency unit of labor in the Solow model, as represented in (3.16). Also derive steady state output and consumption per efficiency unit of labor. How do these steady state variables depend on the savings rate s, total factor productivity A, the rate of technical progress g, the rate of growth of population n, and the depreciation rate δ? Discuss.

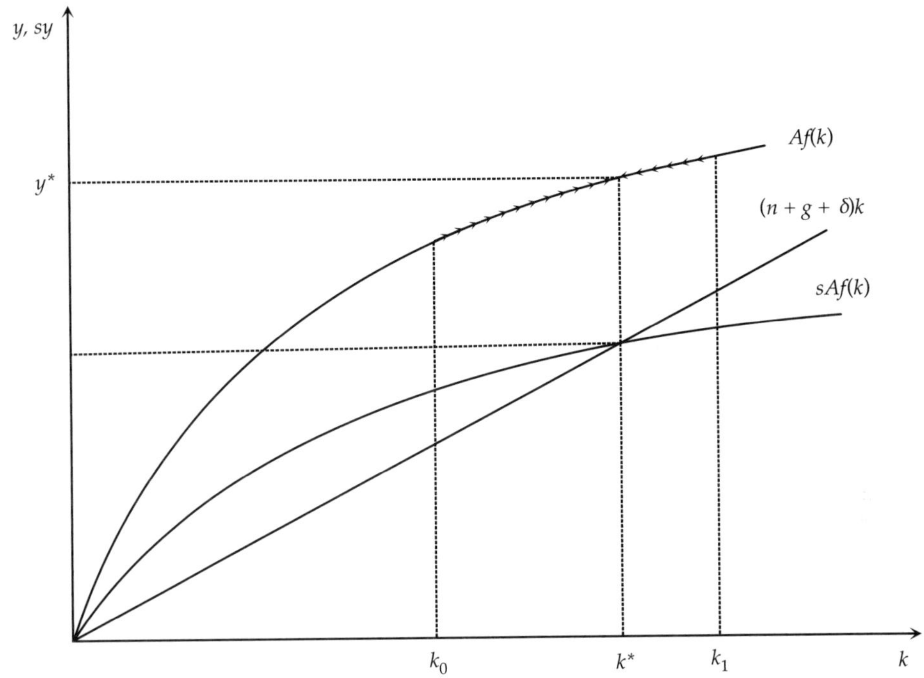

Figure 3.2
Equilibrium in the Solow model.

3.1.6 The Rate of Growth of Capital and Output

To examine the behavior of the growth rate of capital per efficiency unit of labor in the Solow model, we can divide both sides of equation (3.15) by $k(t)$. We then find that the growth rate of capital per efficiency unit of labor is given by

$$\gamma_k(t) = \frac{\dot{k}(t)}{k(t)} = s\frac{Af(k(t))}{k(t)} - (n+g+\delta).$$

The growth rate of capital (per efficiency unit of labor) in the Solow model depends on the difference of the average product of capital, multiplied by the savings rate, from the sum of population growth, the rate of technical progress and the depreciation rate. If savings per unit of capital exceed steady state investment per unit of capital, then capital per efficiency unit of labor displays positive growth, as the capital stock increases at a rate higher than $n+g$. In the opposite case, capital per efficiency unit of labor displays negative growth, as the capital stock either falls or grows at a rate lower than $n+g$. In the steady state, capital per efficiency unit of labor is constant, as the capital stock grows at a rate equal to $n+g$. The determination of the growth rate is depicted in figure 3.3.

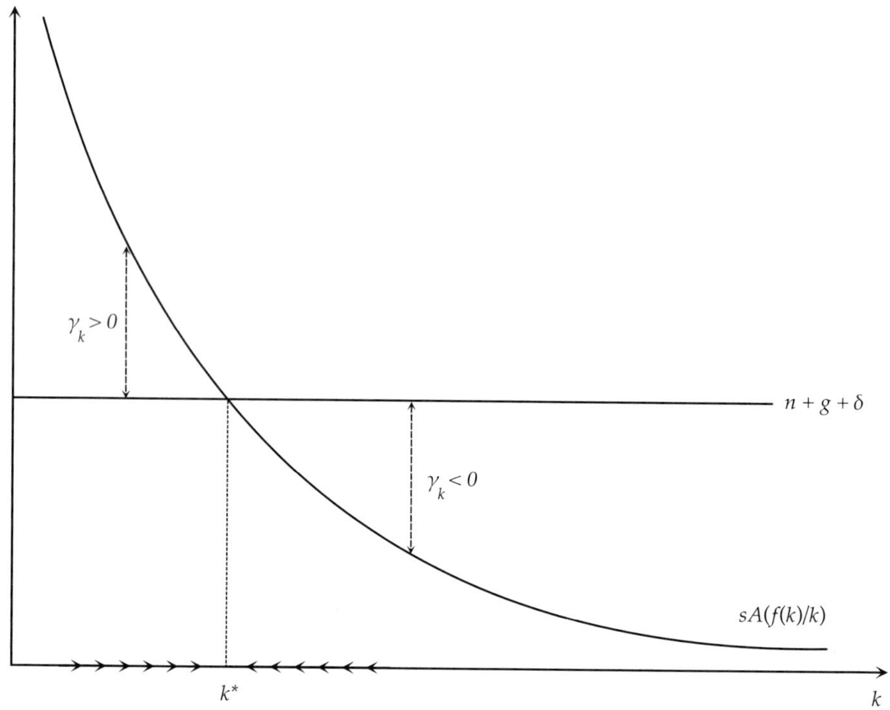

Figure 3.3
Determination of the growth rate.

The downward sloping curve depicts savings per unit of capital. As capital per efficiency unit of labor increases, savings per unit of capital fall, because the marginal and average product of capital is decreasing. This curve approaches infinity as capital tends to zero, and it approaches zero as capital tends to infinity, because of the Inada conditions. The straight line $n+g+\delta$ depicts steady state investment per unit of capital. It is the investment required to keep capital per efficiency unit of labor constant. Because of the Inada conditions, the two curves intersect at a positive capital stock per efficiency unit of labor, which is the steady state capital stock k^*. To the left of k^*, the growth rate of k is positive and declining, and to the right of k^*, the growth rate of k is positive and increasing. At k^*, the balanced growth path, the growth rate of k is equal to zero, and the capital stock itself grows at the exogenous rate $n+g$.

From the production function, the growth rate of output per efficiency unit of labor is given by

$$\gamma_y(t) = \frac{\dot{y}(t)}{y(t)} = Af'(k(t))\frac{\dot{k}(t)}{k(t)}.$$

Because the marginal product of capital is positive, the growth rate of output per efficiency unit of labor has the same sign as the growth rate of capital per efficiency unit of labor.

To the left of k^*, output per efficiency unit of labor grows at a positive and declining rate. In fact, the growth rate of output declines at a faster rate than the growth rate of capital because of the declining marginal product of capital. To the right of k^*, output per efficiency unit of labor grows at a negative and increasing rate. In fact, the growth rate of output increases at a faster rate than the growth rate of capital because of the increasing marginal product of capital. At k^*, the growth rate of output per efficiency unit of labor is zero, and total output increases at the exogenous rate $n+g$.

Because consumption is a constant fraction of output in this model, the growth rate of consumption is equal to the growth rate of output γ_y.

From the above analysis, it follows that the Solow growth model does not explain the rate of long-run economic growth (i.e., the rate of economic growth on the balanced growth path), as this is equal to the sum of two exogenous parameters, g and n. It also does not explain the growth rate of per capita income and consumption along the balanced growth path, as this is equal to the rate of exogenous technical progress g.

What the Solow model does explain is the level of the per capita capital stock and per capita output and income, the level of per capita consumption and real wages, and the real interest rate on the balanced growth path. These depend on all the parameters of the model, as we shall shortly see.

In addition, the Solow growth model explains the process of convergence toward the balanced growth path. The process of convergence predicted by the model is the result of the accumulation of physical capital. The growth rate of output (or output per capita) in the convergence process differs from the long-run growth rate $g + n$ or g, to the extent that, during the convergence process, the economy accumulates capital at a different rate than $g+n$. Note that the convergence process is asymptotic, in the sense that the steady state (or balanced growth path) is the limit as time goes to infinity.

Exercise 3.2 Assuming a Cobb-Douglas production function, as in exercise 3.1, derive the equations describing the evolution of steady state output per head and consumption per head in the Solow model. Also derive the equations describing the evolution of aggregate steady state output and consumption. What are the determinants of the growth rates of per capita and aggregate output and consumption?

3.1.7 Significance of the Inada Conditions

One can use (3.16) to show that if the Inada conditions are not satisfied, a steady state may not exist. Assume that as capital per efficiency unit of labor tends to infinity, the marginal product of capital remains positive, and the average product of capital converges not to zero but to a positive value (say, ω), where

$$\omega > \frac{n+g+\delta}{s}.$$

Thus, from (3.16), the growth rate of capital per efficiency unit of labor also does not converge to zero, and k^* does not exist. In such a case, capital per efficiency unit of labor grows continuously, and the Solow model becomes an *endogenous growth model*, with the long-run growth rate of capital per efficiency unit of labor being

$$\gamma_k = s\omega - (n+g+\delta) > 0.$$

In the opposite case, assume that as capital per efficiency unit of labor tends to zero, the marginal product of capital does not tend to infinity (as required by the Inada conditions) but instead to a level that makes the average product of capital equal to χ, where

$$\chi < \frac{n+g+\delta}{s}.$$

From (3.16), and the properties of the production function, k will be driven to zero, and a steady state will not exist.

As is shown in appendix A, the CES production function does not necessarily satisfy the Inada conditions and thus may not be compatible with the existence of a steady state capital stock and output per efficiency unit of labor.

3.2 Competitive Markets, the Real Interest Rate, and Real Wages

As we have studied it so far, the Solow model assumes a single domestic firm and one national household, which owns this firm. However, because of the constant returns to scale hypothesis, all the properties of this model go through when one assumes competitive markets with many identical firms and households.

Suppose we have many households owning capital and supplying one unit of labor per member. Firms rent capital and labor in competitive capital and labor markets. The interest rate is $r(t)$, and the real wage (per efficiency unit of labor) is $w(t)$. Each firm uses capital and labor and produces according to a production function that, in intensive form, is given by (3.2). Each firm pays the return on capital to households holding its shares and real wages to its workers.

The conditions for profit maximization on the part of firms are that the marginal product of capital equals the user cost of capital (the real interest rate plus the depreciation rate) and that the marginal product of labor equals the real wage. Therefore it holds that

$$Af'(k(t)) = r(t) + \delta, \tag{3.17}$$

$$Af(k(t)) - k(t)Af'(k(t)) = w(t). \tag{3.18}$$

It is easy to see that when (3.17) and (3.18) are satisfied, firms have zero profits, and factor payments exhaust real output. This is a consequence of constant returns to scale.

The total household income per efficiency unit of labor is equal to gross output and is given by

$$(r(t)+\delta)\,k(t)+w(t).$$

The condition equating savings and investment per efficiency unit of labor is given by

$$\dot{k}(t)=s\left((r(t)+\delta)\,k(t)+w(t)\right)-(n+g+\delta)k(t). \tag{3.19}$$

Substituting (3.17) and (3.18) in (3.19), we have the basic accumulation equation of the Solow model:

$$\dot{k}(t)=sAf(k(t))-(n+g+\delta)k(t).$$

Consequently, the Solow model is compatible with the existence of competitive markets for goods, labor, and capital.

In the process of adjustment toward the balanced growth path from the left (i.e., when the initial capital per efficiency unit of labor is less than its steady state value), real wages are rising and real interest rates are falling, reflecting the evolution of the falling marginal product of capital and the rising marginal product of labor.

On the balanced growth path, the real wage (per efficiency unit of labor) remains constant, and the same happens with the real interest rate. However, the real wage per employee, along with all other per capita variables, is growing at a rate g, the exogenous rate of technical progress.

Exercise 3.3 Assuming a Cobb-Douglas production function, as in exercise 3.1, and competitive product and factor markets, derive and discuss the conditions determining the real interest rate and the real wage in the Solow model. Also derive and discuss the steady state real interest rate and the steady state real wage per efficiency unit of labor, as functions of the savings rate and the other parameters of the model. What is the growth rate of real wages per worker in the steady state?

3.3 The Savings Rate and the Golden Rule

One can prove that a rise in the savings rate results in an increase in steady state capital and output, in both aggregate and per capita terms. It can also be shown that the rate of growth of the aggregate capital stock, output, and income rise temporarily above the steady state or long-run rate of economic growth $g+n$. Similarly, following a rise in the savings rate, the rate of growth of the per capita capital stock and per capita output and income rise temporarily above the rate of technical progress g, which determines the steady state growth rate of per capita magnitudes. The relevant analysis is presented in figure 3.4.

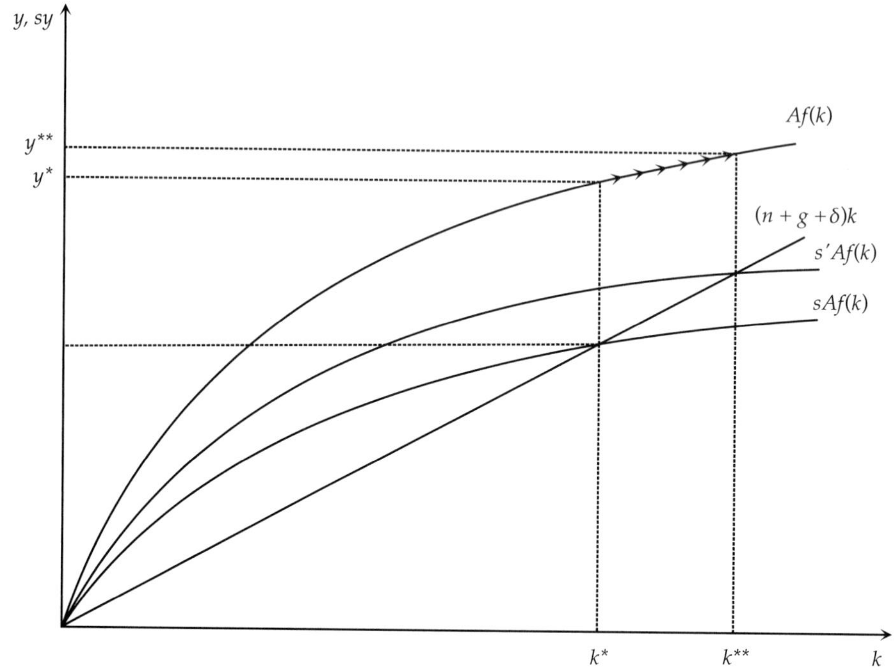

Figure 3.4
Implications of a rise in the savings rate.

3.3.1 The Savings Rate and the Balanced Growth Path

Assume that the initial balanced growth path is at (y^*, k^*) in figure 3.4. A rise in the savings rate from s to s' leads to an increase in savings and investment that initiates a process of capital accumulation, which gradually causes an increase in output and income per efficiency unit of labor. The economy starts converging to a new balanced growth path (y^{**}, k^{**}), which is characterized by both higher capital and higher income. During the adjustment process, savings and investment exceed equilibrium investment, and the rate of growth exceeds the long-run growth rate $g+n$.

The process of convergence toward the new balanced growth path over time is depicted in figure 3.5, which shows the so-called impulse response function of the Solow model to a change in the savings rate.[6]

The rise in the savings rate leads to investment that exceeds the level required to maintain the capital stock per effective unit of labor at its initial steady state level k^*. Capital starts

6. An impulse response refers to the response of any dynamic system to some external impulse. The impulse response function describes the reaction of the system as a function of time (or possibly as a function of some other independent variable that parameterizes the dynamic behavior of the system). Impulse response functions are plotted for most of the dynamic models analyzed in this book.

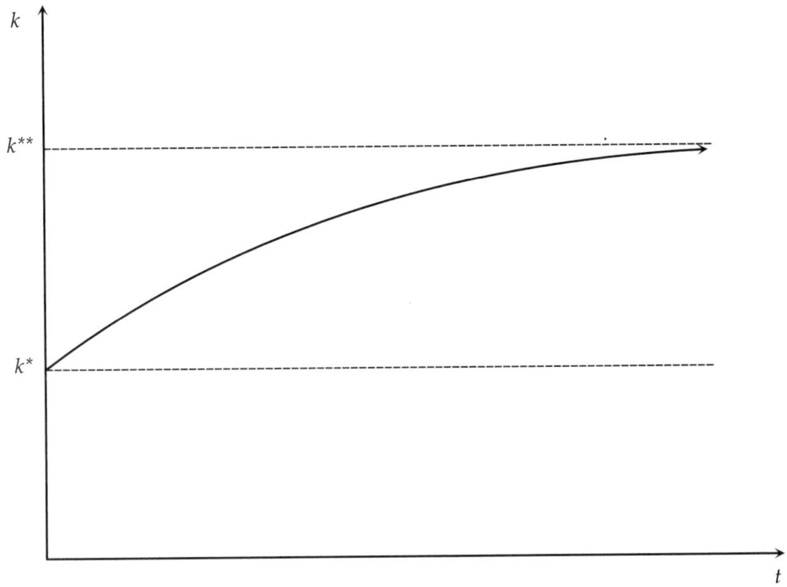

Figure 3.5
Impulse response function of a rise in the savings rate.

accumulating at a faster rate, leading to parallel rises in output and income per effective unit of labor, and the process continues until the economy gradually converges to the new balanced growth path k^{**}. This process of convergence is asymptotic.[7]

3.3.2 The Savings Rate, the Golden Rule, and Dynamic Inefficiency

Capital and income increase definitely and unequivocally following a rise in the savings rate. What happens to consumption is more uncertain, as a rise in the savings rate reduces consumption for any given level of income. Initially, as capital, output, and income are given, a rise in the savings rate causes a temporary fall in consumption. Capital output and income gradually rise, and so does consumption. Whether consumption per capita on the new balanced growth path will be higher or lower than on the original balanced growth path depends on the difference between the marginal product of capital and $n+g+\delta$. The latter is the marginal increase in steady state investment. Consumption will be higher on the new balanced growth path if the marginal product of capital is higher than $n+g+\delta$, and it will be lower in the opposite case.

7. The term "asymptotic" means that a variable approaches its steady state value arbitrarily closely as t tends to infinity.

To see this, recall that steady state consumption is given by

$$c^* = Af(k^*) - (n+g+\delta)k^*. \tag{3.20}$$

It follows that the change in steady state consumption following a rise in the savings rate is given by

$$\frac{\partial c^*}{\partial s} = \left(Af'(k^*) - (n+g+\delta)\right)\frac{\partial k^*}{\partial s}. \tag{3.21}$$

Because the last term on the right-hand side of (3.21) has been shown to be positive, the impact of the change in the savings rate on steady state consumption per effective unit of labor depends on the difference between the marginal product of capital $Af'(k^*)$ and the equilibrium investment rate $n+g+\delta$. Another way to express this is to say that the change in steady state consumption depends on the difference between the net (of depreciation) marginal product of capital $Af'(k^*)-\delta$ and the long-run growth rate $g+n$.

If the net marginal product of capital is lower than the long-run growth rate, then the extra product from the accumulation of capital will not be sufficient to fund the higher equilibrium investment rate, and consumption will have to go down. If the net marginal product of capital is higher than the long-run growth rate, then the extra product from the accumulation of capital will be more than sufficient to fund the higher equilibrium investment rate, and consumption will also increase.

In the special case where the net marginal product of capital on the original balanced growth path is exactly equal to the long-run growth rate, equilibrium consumption will remain unchanged following an infinitesimally small rise in the savings rate. In this case, equilibrium consumption is at its highest possible level, and the value of k^* that corresponds to this case is referred to as the *golden rule capital stock*.[8]

The *golden rule savings rate* is defined as the savings rate that implies a steady state capital stock (per effective unit of labor) that maximizes steady state consumption (per effective unit of labor). Because the welfare of households is usually assumed to depend on consumption, the maximization of steady state consumption per effective unit of labor is a proxy for the maximization of steady state consumer welfare.

From (3.20), the first-order conditions for the maximization of steady state consumption require

$$Af'(k^*) = n+g+\delta \Rightarrow Af'(k^*) - \delta = n+g. \tag{3.22}$$

From (3.22), the steady state capital stock that maximizes steady state consumption is the one that results in a net marginal product of capital equal to the long-run growth rate. This is

8. The significance of the golden rule for the Solow growth model and growth theory was first highlighted by Phelps [1961], although the concept was previously alluded to by John von Neumann and Maurice Allais.

what determines the golden rule capital stock. Because the net marginal product of capital is equal to the real interest rate in a competitive equilibrium, the golden rule capital stock is the one for which the real interest rate is equal to the steady state growth rate:

$$r = n + g.$$

If the savings rate is such that the steady state capital stock is higher than the golden rule capital stock, then the economy is said to be characterized by *dynamic inefficiency*. Steady state consumption and presumably, consumer welfare could be increased by reducing the savings rate, consuming more, and accumulating less capital. By reducing the savings rate, households will be able to enjoy higher steady state consumption, despite the reduction in steady state capital and output.

Thus, an increase in the savings rate is not necessarily always desirable in the Solow model, even though it results in an increase in steady state capital and income. It is only desirable as long as the savings rate is below the golden rule rate (i.e., the rate that maximizes steady state consumption per efficiency unit of labor). In such a case, an increase in the savings rate increases steady state consumption.

A major problem with the Solow model is that, because the savings rate is assumed exogenous, there is nothing in the model that can help exclude the possibility of *dynamic inefficiency* (that is, a suboptimally high savings rate). It is therefore worth keeping in mind than an increase in the savings rate is not necessarily desirable from the point of view of consumer welfare. It is only desirable in the case of dynamic efficiency, that is, when the real interest rate exceeds the steady state growth rate.[9]

Exercise 3.4 Assuming a Cobb-Douglas production function, as in exercise 3.1, derive and discuss the condition determining the golden rule capital stock in the Solow model. What should be the objective of policy with regard to the savings rate if the economy is characterized by dynamic inefficiency?

3.3.3 The Elasticity of Steady State Output with Respect to the Savings Rate

One can show that in the Solow model, the long-run elasticity of output with respect to the savings rate is equal to the ratio of the share of capital to the share of labor in total output. To prove this, we start from the change in steady state output following a change in the savings rate. This is equal to

$$\frac{\partial y^*}{\partial s} = Af'(k^*)\frac{\partial k^*}{\partial s}, \tag{3.23}$$

9. This discussion highlights the difficulties arising in ad hoc dynamic models that do not address the optimizing behavior of households. There is nothing in the Solow model that would help us assess the welfare of consumers, as we do not know the utility function of the representative household.

where k^* is defined by,

$$sAf(k^*) = (n+g+\delta)k^*. \tag{3.24}$$

Differentiating (3.24) with respect to s, we get

$$\frac{\partial k^*}{\partial s} = \frac{Af(k^*)}{(n+g+\delta) - sAf'(k^*)}. \tag{3.25}$$

Substituting (3.25) into (3.23) results in

$$\frac{\partial y^*}{\partial s} = \frac{Af'(k^*)Af(k^*)}{(n+g+\delta) - sAf'(k^*)}. \tag{3.26}$$

From (3.26) and (3.24), the long-run elasticity of output with respect to the savings rate is given by

$$\begin{aligned}\frac{s}{y^*}\frac{\partial y^*}{\partial s} &= \frac{s}{Af(k^*)}\frac{Af'(k^*)Af(k^*)}{(n+g+\delta) - sAf'(k*)} \\ &= \frac{(n+g+\delta)k^*f'(k^*)}{f(k^*)(n+g+\delta)[1-k^*f'(k^*)/f(k^*)]} \\ &= \frac{k^*f'(k^*)}{f(k^*)[1-k^*f'(k^*)/f(k^*)]}.\end{aligned} \tag{3.27}$$

Equation (3.27) can be rewritten as

$$\frac{s}{y^*}\frac{\partial y^*}{\partial s} = \frac{k^*f'(k^*)/f(k^*)}{1-[k^*f'(k^*)/f(k^*)]} = \frac{\alpha_K(k^*)}{1-\alpha_K(k^*)}, \tag{3.28}$$

where $\alpha_K(k^*)$ is the elasticity of total output with respect to capital at the steady state. With competitive markets, factor incomes are equal to their marginal products. In such a case, the elasticity of total output with respect to capital is equal to the ratio of the share of capital to the share of labor in total output. A commonly accepted estimate of the share of capital in total output is about $1/3$. Using this estimate, the long-run elasticity of total output with respect to the savings rate is equal to $1/2$.

3.4 Total Factor Productivity and Population Growth

The savings rate is of course one of the parameters affecting per capita output, income, and consumption in the Solow model. All the other parameters also affect the evolution of per capita output, income, and consumption, both on the balanced growth path and on the convergence path. In this section, we concentrate on two additional parameters: total factor productivity A and population growth n.

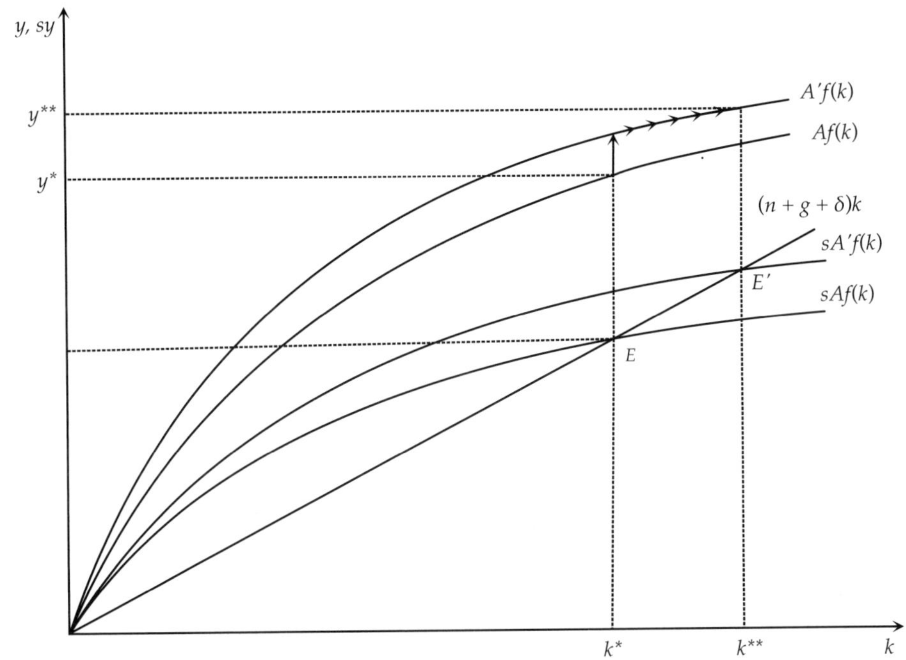

Figure 3.6
Implications of a rise in total factor productivity.

3.4.1 Dynamic Effects of Total Factor Productivity in the Solow Model

Figure 3.6 shows the dynamic effects of a one-off increase in total factor productivity A in the Solow model. An increase in total factor productivity raises total output for given factor inputs, such as capital and labor. Through the savings function, it also raises aggregate savings and investment. Hence, as shown in figure 3.6, a one-off increase in total factor productivity results in a gradual accumulation of capital and a shift from the initial balanced growth path k^* to a new balanced growth path k^{**} with higher capital and output per efficiency unit of labor.

An increase in total factor productivity has both direct and indirect effects on output per efficiency unit of labor. It raises output for given capital per efficiency unit of labor and also causes additional capital accumulation through higher savings and investment. Hence, the elasticity of steady state per capita output with respect to total factor productivity is higher than unity, because of the induced accumulation of capital.

The Solow model thus implies that economies with higher total factor productivity will not only have higher per capita incomes but also higher capital per worker, which will further increase their per capita income.

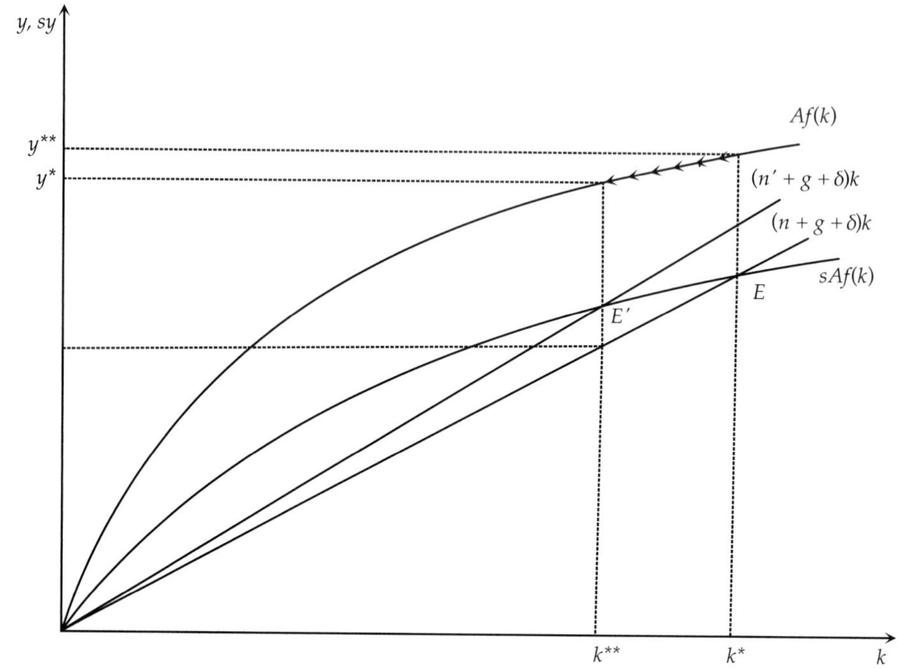

Figure 3.7
Implications of a rise in population growth.

3.4.2 Dynamic Effects of Population Growth in the Solow Model

Figure 3.7 shows the dynamic effects of a one-off increase in the rate of growth of population n in the Solow model. A rise in the population growth rate raises the steady state investment rate (i.e., the investment required to maintain a constant capital stock per efficiency unit of labor). For a given level of savings, this leads to decumulation of capital, as the initial steady state savings are lower than the new steady state investment. The decumulation of capital reduces equilibrium investment until a new balanced growth path is reached, in which equilibrium investment is equal to savings. In the new steady state, both capital and output (as well as consumption) per efficiency unit of labor will be lower. Hence, a higher growth rate of population results in lower per capita income and consumption on the balanced growth path. This is a direct implication of the assumption of an exogenous savings rate in the Solow model.

3.5 Speed of Convergence toward the Balanced Growth Path

How fast does the economy converge to the balanced growth path from an initial condition that is not on this path? This is a theoretically and empirically interesting question worth answering.

In the neighborhood of the balanced growth path, the speed of convergence of k toward k^* depends on their difference. On the basis of widely accepted values for the parameters of the model, one can show that the speed of convergence in the Solow model is about 4% per year. As a result, the Solow model predicts that it should take slightly more than 17 years to close half of any given gap between k and k^*, and therefore any given gap between y and y^*.

To derive the speed of convergence, we start from the basic accumulation equation of the Solow model:

$$\dot{k}(t) = sAf(k(t)) - (n+g+\delta)k(t). \tag{3.29}$$

Steady state capital (per effective unit of labor) k^* is determined from (3.29) for $\dot{k}(t) = 0$. To determine the speed at which $k(t)$ approaches k^*, we linearize (3.29) around k^*. From the linear Taylor approximation of the nonlinear differential equation (3.29) around k^*, we get

$$\dot{k}(t) \simeq \left(\frac{\partial \dot{k}}{\partial k}\right)_{k=k^*} (k(t) - k^*), \tag{3.30}$$

where the first derivative is taken from (3.29). Equation (3.30) can be written as

$$\dot{k}(t) \simeq -\lambda(k(t) - k^*), \tag{3.31}$$

where $\lambda = -\left(\frac{\partial \dot{k}}{\partial k}\right)_{k=k^*} = -[sAf'(k^*) - (n+g+\delta)]$, which implies that around the steady state k^*, k approaches k^* with a speed that depends on its distance from k^*. The rate at which $k(t) - k^*$ is reduced is approximately constant and equal to λ. We refer to λ as the *speed of convergence*.

Solving the linear first-order differential equation (3.31), we get that

$$k(t) \simeq k^* + e^{-\lambda t}(k(0) - k^*), \tag{3.32}$$

where $k(0)$ is the initial value of k.

To calculate the speed of convergence λ in terms of the structural parameters of the model, rearrange the definition of λ in (3.31) as

$$\begin{aligned} \lambda &= (n+g+\delta) - sAf'(k^*) \\ &= (n+g+\delta)\left[1 - \frac{k^* f'(k^*)}{f(k^*)}\right] \\ &= (n+g+\delta)[1 - \alpha_K(k^*)], \end{aligned} \tag{3.33}$$

where $\alpha_K(k^*)$ is the share of capital in total income at the steady state. To proceed from the initial expression in (3.33), note that in the steady state, $sAf(k^*) = (n+g+\delta)k^*$, which can be used to eliminate s. To get to the final expression in terms of the share of capital, note that in a competitive equilibrium, the return on capital is equal to its marginal product.

Widely accepted annual estimates of $n+g+\delta$ suggest a value of about 6%. For example, this would be the result with $n=1\%, g=2\%$, and $\delta=3\%$. With the share of capital estimated at about 1/3, (3.33) implies an annual speed of convergence of about 4%.

Thus, on the basis of these estimates, the Solow model implies that each year, roughly 4% of the gap between the current capital stock (and income) and the steady state capital stock (and income) is closed through the process of capital accumulation.

From (3.32), which is the solution of the linearized differential equation (3.31), we can estimate how many years it will take with this speed of convergence to close a particular percentage of the gap between $k(0)$ and k^*. To calculate the number of years required to cover half of the initial difference, we need to calculate the time span t that satisfies

$$e^{-\lambda t}=0.5$$

for $\lambda=4\%$. This suggests that $t=-\ln(0.5)/\lambda=0.69/\lambda=0.69/0.04=17.3$. Thus, for an annual speed of convergence of 4%, it would take 17.3 years to cover half of any initial difference between the initial capital stock (and real income) and its steady state value. This is often referred to as the *half-life* of the convergence process.

To calculate the number of years required to cover two-thirds of the initial difference, we need to calculate the time span t that satisfies

$$e^{-\lambda t}=0.333$$

for $\lambda=4\%$. This suggests that $t=-\ln(0.333)/\lambda=2.1/\lambda=2.1/0.04=27.5$. Thus, it would take 27.5 years to cover two-thirds of any difference between the initial capital stock (and real income) and its steady state value.

Econometric evidence from, among others, Mankiw et al. (1992) suggests that the speed of convergence for many economies in the postwar period was on average about 2% per year. Thus, the speed of convergence predicted by the Solow model, based on the parameter estimates we used, is on the high side compared with the econometric evidence. We shall return to this issue in chapter 8.

3.6 The Process of Economic Growth and the Solow Model

The Solow model, like any other economic model, is based on relatively simple and, many would claim, largely unrealistic assumptions. However, it constitutes a significant improvement on previous models, which did not rely on the neoclassical production function. Such were, for example, the models of Harrod [1939] and Domar [1946], which were based on Leontieff [1941] production functions with constant coefficients and a zero elasticity of substitution between capital and labor.

The question is whether the model of Solow (and all models based on similar assumptions about the technology of production) can offer an adequate and satisfactory account of the actual process of economic growth. To answer this question, we must delve a little deeper into the main empirical facts about long-run growth.

3.6.1 The Kaldor Stylized Facts of Economic Growth

An important early codification of the main empirical features pertaining to long run growth, is due to Kaldor [1961], who based them on the long-run growth experience of Great Britain and the United States. According to Kaldor, a growth theory should be consistent with the following six stylized facts about long-run growth:

1. Per capita GDP is growing over time, and the growth rate is not declining.[10]
2. Physical capital per worker is growing over time.
3. The long run-rate of return on capital is roughly constant.
4. The long-run capital-output ratio is roughly constant.
5. The shares of labor and capital in GDP do not display a long-term trend.
6. The growth rate of labor productivity varies substantially across countries.

These stylized facts continue to be accepted today, with the addition of some newer ones.[11]

At a general level, the Solow model is roughly consistent with all the above stylized empirical characteristics. However, the process of physical capital accumulation, which is the main engine of economic growth in the Solow model, is not sufficient as an explanation of either the long-run growth of output per worker that has been observed historically in almost all developed economies of the world or the large differences in output per worker between developed and less developed economies.

Only a small part of these phenomena can be explained by the accumulation of physical capital. The largest part appears to be due to technical progress and to differences in total factor productivity and the efficiency of labor, which are considered exogenous in the Solow model.[12]

10. In fact, as we saw in chapter 1, this only applies since the Industrial Revolution and the early nineteenth century.

11. Jones and Romer [2010] have recently codified some additional stylized facts that a satisfactory theory of economic growth must be able to account for. We shall examine these additional stylized facts in chapter 8.

12. Kaldor, who was quite critical of neoclassical theory, considered the Solow model to be incompatible with at least some of the stylized facts that he identified, mainly stylized facts 1, 2, and 6. He was critical because the Solow model is compatible with these facts only when one assumes exogenous technical progress, which drives the efficiency of labor, per capita income, per capita consumption, and real wages along the balanced growth path. Without the assumption of exogenous technical progress, the Solow growth model cannot account for all the Kaldor stylized facts.

3.6.2 Differences in Per Capita Output and Income between Developed and Less Developed Economies

The Solow model identifies three sources of differences in per capita income and output per worker between countries or between periods: first, differences in capital per worker; second, differences in total factor productivity and labor efficiency; and third, differences in initial conditions.

To simplify the analysis of the impact of each of these differences, let us use the Solow model and assume a Cobb-Douglas production function.

In the Solow model based on the Cobb-Douglas production function, capital per efficiency unit of labor on the balanced growth path is defined by the condition

$$sA\left(k^*\right)^{\alpha} = (n+g+\delta)k^*. \tag{3.34}$$

From (3.34), it follows that the steady state capital stock per efficiency unit of labor is given by

$$k^* = \left(\frac{sA}{n+g+\delta}\right)^{\frac{1}{1-\alpha}}. \tag{3.35}$$

From (3.35) and the production function (3.4), output per efficiency unit of labor is given by

$$y^* = A\left(k^*\right)^{\alpha} = A\left(\frac{sA}{n+g+\delta}\right)^{\frac{\alpha}{1-\alpha}}. \tag{3.36}$$

The per capita product on the balanced growth path is thus given by

$$\hat{y}^*(t) = \frac{Y^*(t)}{L(t)} = y^*h(t) = A\left(k^*\right)^{\alpha}h(0)e^{gt}, \tag{3.37}$$

where a hat over a variable denotes the per capita magnitude.

Based on (3.37), differences in capital per worker, for realistic estimates of the parameters of the model, cannot explain the differences in output per worker that we observe in the real world. For example, let us assume that we want to explain a ratio x in output per worker between two economies, economy 1 (a developed economy) and economy 2 (a less developed economy). From (3.37), assuming that all other parameters except for the capital stock are the same between the two economies, we must have that

$$\frac{\hat{y}_1(t)}{\hat{y}_2(t)} = \frac{A\hat{k}_1(t)^{\alpha}\left(h(0)e^{gt}\right)^{1-\alpha}}{A\hat{k}_2(t)^{\alpha}\left(h(0)e^{gt}\right)^{1-\alpha}} = \left(\frac{\hat{k}_1(t)}{\hat{k}_2(t)}\right)^{\alpha} = x. \tag{3.38}$$

To explain this ratio, capital per worker should differ by x to the power $1/\alpha$, where α is the share of capital in domestic income. Since α is of the order of 1/3, to explain why

GDP per worker in developed countries is currently 20 times higher than in less developed countries, capital per worker should be 8,000 times (20 raised to the third power) higher. But this is not the case. In developed economies, capital per worker is only 20–30 times higher than in less developed economies. Thus, we cannot account for differences in per capita output and income solely on the basis of differences in the per capita capital stock.

We can certify this indirectly as well. If the differences in output per worker were due only to differences in physical capital per worker, then we should observe huge differences in the rate of return to capital between periods and between countries. However, such huge differences in the rate of return to capital do not exist.

To explain the large differences between developed and less developed countries on the balanced growth path, we should allow for other differences, such as disparities in total factor productivity and the efficiency of labor. Allowing for such differences in (3.38), we have that

$$\frac{\hat{y}_1(t)}{\hat{y}_2(t)}=\frac{A_1\hat{k}_1(t)^\alpha(h_1(0)e^{gt})^{1-\alpha}}{A_2\hat{k}_2(t)^\alpha(h_2(0)e^{gt})^{1-\alpha}}=\frac{A_1\hat{k}_1(t)^\alpha(h_1(0))^{1-\alpha}}{A_2\hat{k}_2(t)^\alpha(h_2(0))^{1-\alpha}}=x. \tag{3.39}$$

Differences in total factor productivity and the initial efficiency of labor, along with those in physical capital per worker, can explain almost all differences in output per worker that we observe in the real world. For example, if the developed countries have capital per worker 30 times higher than the less developed countries have, a total factor productivity that is three times that of the less developed countries ($A_1=3A_2$), and three times the initial efficiency of labor ($h_1(0)=3h_2(0)$), then (3.39) predicts that, along the balanced growth path, their output per worker and their per capita income will be about 20 times higher than those of the less developed countries.

However, total factor productivity and the efficiency of labor are not explained by the Solow model but are instead considered as exogenous. Therefore, one could say that this model does not explain the process of long-run growth; it only assumes such growth.[13]

This is why this model, like all models based on similar assumptions about the technology of production and technical progress, is often referred to as an *exogenous growth model*. It assumes that total factor productivity A, the initial efficiency of labor $h(0)$, and the rate of technical progress g are all exogenous parameters.

13. Mankiw et al. [1992] have generalized the Solow model, attributing differences in the efficiency of labor to investment in human capital (education of the labor force). However, they retain the assumption that total factor productivity increases at an exogenous rate g. The generalized Solow model that they put forward is analyzed in chapter 8, and it seems to explain the growth experience of 98 non-oil producing countries after 1960 fairly well. See also Jones [2002] and chapter 8 for other generalized models for economic growth that rely on investment in both physical and human capital.

3.6.3 Conditional Convergence

Our analysis in subsection 3.6.2 makes it clear that the process of convergence predicted by the Solow model does not entail convergence to the same per capita income for all economies. The per capita income to which an economy converges is determined by (3.36) and (3.37) to be

$$\hat{y}^*(t) = A(k^*)^\alpha h(0)e^{gt} = A\left(\frac{sA}{n+g+\delta}\right)^{\frac{\alpha}{1-\alpha}} h(0)e^{gt}. \tag{3.40}$$

If parameters such as the rate of savings and investment s, total factor productivity A, the population growth rate n, the depreciation rate δ, and the initial efficiency of labor $h(0)$ differ between two economies, these economies will converge toward different levels of per capita income, even if along the balanced growth path, per capita income is growing at the same rate of technological progress g.

Convergence toward different levels of per capita income, which depend on the parameters characterizing the structure of different economies, is called *conditional convergence*. The per capita income toward which economies converge in the Solow model (and in the other exogenous growth models that we shall analyze in the next few chapters) depends on their specific structural characteristics. Not all economies converge to the same per capita income. Each economy converges to the per capita income determined by its own technological, demographic, and savings (investment) parameters.

3.7 Convergence with a Cobb-Douglas Production Function

The Solow model with a Cobb-Douglas production function can be solved analytically not only for the steady state variables, as we have done so far, but also for their evolution during the process of convergence. This is because the first-order differential equation that characterizes the convergence process in this case has the form of a *Bernoulli equation*, which can be converted to a linear differential equation in the capital-output ratio, and thus solved analytically.

With a Cobb-Douglas production function, output per efficiency unit of labor is given by

$$y(t) = Ak(t)^\alpha.$$

Therefore, the adjustment of capital per efficiency unit of labor is given by

$$\dot{k}(t) = sAk(t)^\alpha - (n+g+\delta)k(t). \tag{3.41}$$

This is a Bernoulli equation, which can be converted to a linear differential equation if we define a new variable z:[14]

$$z(t) = \frac{k(t)}{y(t)} = \frac{1}{A}k(t)^{1-\alpha}. \tag{3.42}$$

This variable is none other than the capital-output ratio. From (3.42), it follows that

$$\dot{z}(t) = \frac{\partial z(t)}{\partial k(t)}\dot{k}(t) = \frac{1-\alpha}{A}k(t)^{-\alpha}\dot{k}(t). \tag{3.43}$$

By substituting (3.41) into (3.43) we get

$$\dot{z}(t) = (1-\alpha)s - \lambda z(t), \tag{3.44}$$

where $\lambda = (1-\alpha)(n+g+\delta)$. The parameter λ is just the speed of convergence. (3.44) is a first-order linear differential equation in the variable z (the capital output ratio) and can be solved as

$$z(t) = \frac{s}{n+g+\delta} + \left(z_0 - \frac{s}{n+g+\delta}\right)e^{-\lambda t}. \tag{3.45}$$

Substituting from the definition of the capital-output ratio with a Cobb-Douglas production function, the convergence process of capital and output per efficiency unit of labor is given by

$$k(t) = \left[\frac{As}{n+g+\delta}\left(1-e^{-\lambda t}\right) + {k_0}^{1-\alpha}e^{-\lambda t}\right]^{\frac{1}{1-\alpha}}, \tag{3.46}$$

$$y(t) = A\left[\frac{As}{n+g+\delta}\left(1-e^{-\lambda t}\right) + \left(\frac{y_0}{A}\right)^{\frac{1-\alpha}{\alpha}}e^{-\lambda t}\right]^{\frac{\alpha}{1-\alpha}}. \tag{3.47}$$

As time tends toward infinity, the limit of (3.46) and (3.47) is the balanced growth path, as determined by (3.35) and (3.36).

3.8 Dynamic Simulations of a Calibrated Solow Model

To further investigate the process of dynamic adjustment that characterizes the Solow model, we can simulate, for specific numerical values of the parameters, the transition from a balanced growth path to another path when there is an exogenous permanent change in

14. This solution method is analyzed in Chiang [1974] and is also discussed in Jones [2002] and Barro and Sala-i Martin [2004].

particular parameters (such as the savings rate, total factor productivity, or the rate of growth of population).

To simulate the model numerically, let us convert it from a continuous-time model to a discrete-time model.

3.8.1 The Solow Model in Discrete Time

Instead of assuming that time is a continuous variable, time is now measured as successive discrete time periods, where $t=0, 1, 2, \ldots$. The variable x_t indicates the variable x in period t.

Population and the efficiency of labor grow at constant exogenous rates n and g per period, respectively. Thus, we have

$$L_t = L_0(1+n)^t, \tag{3.48}$$

$$h_t = h_0(1+g)^t. \tag{3.49}$$

The production function is given by

$$Y_t = AF(K_t, h_t L_t) \tag{3.50}$$

and is characterized by constant returns to scale and diminishing returns of individual factors.

As in the case of continuous time, we assume that the consumption function is characterized by a fixed savings rate s:

$$C_t = (1-s)Y_t = (1-s)AF(K_t, h_t L_t). \tag{3.51}$$

The accumulation of capital is determined by

$$K_{t+1} - K_t = AF(K_t, h_t L_t) - C_t - \delta K_t = sAF(K_t, h_t L_t) - \delta K_t. \tag{3.52}$$

Thus, in discrete time, the accumulation of capital per efficiency unit of labor is given by

$$k_{t+1} = \frac{1}{(1+n)(1+g)} \left(sAf(k_t) + (1-\delta)k_t \right). \tag{3.53}$$

It can easily be shown diagrammatically (see figure 3.8) that the difference equation (3.53) converges to a unique equilibrium.

In figure 3.8, the curve depicts the accumulation equation (3.53), and the 45° straight line the steady state equilibrium condition $k_t = k_{t+1)} = k^*$. The process of convergence is determined by (3.53), and the equilibrium toward which the economy converges determines the balanced growth path.[15]

15. Note that (3.53) is a nonlinear first-order difference equation that can be analyzed diagrammatically.

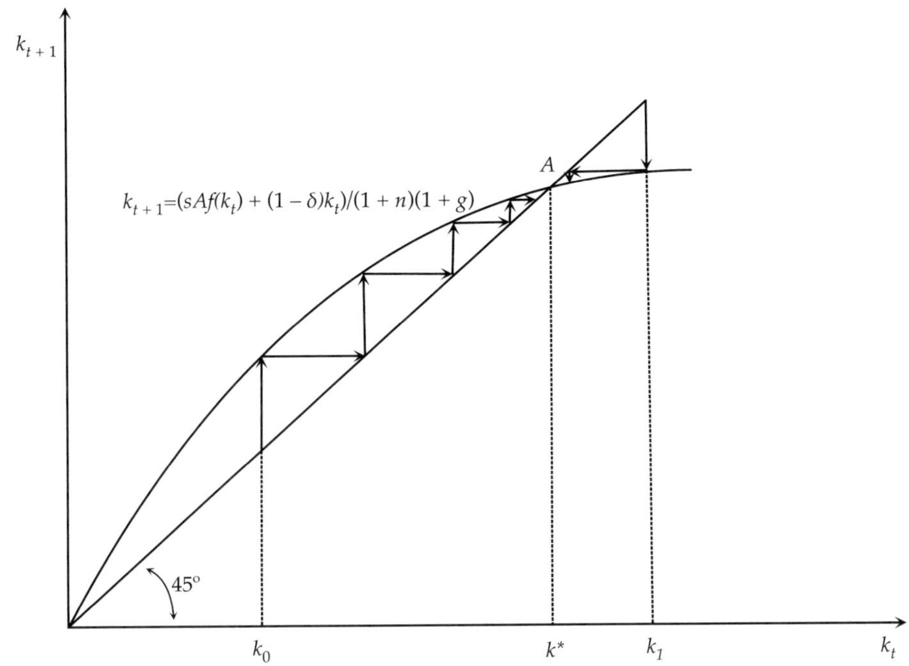

Figure 3.8
Convergence in the Solow model in discrete time.

3.8.2 The Calibrated Solow Model

For the purposes of simulation, let us use a calibrated version of the model, assuming that the production function is Cobb-Douglas:

$$y_t = Af(k_t) = Ak_t^{\alpha}, \tag{3.54}$$

where $A > 0$ is total factor productivity, and $0 < \alpha < 1$ is the exponent (share) of capital in the production function. $1 - \alpha$ is the exponent of labor.

Substituting (3.54) in (3.53), the capital accumulation equation is given by

$$k_{t+1} = \frac{1}{(1+n)(1+g)} \left(sAk_t^{\alpha} + (1-\delta)k_t \right). \tag{3.55}$$

From (3.55), the steady state capital stock, per efficiency unit of labor, is given by

$$k^* = \left(\frac{sA}{(1+n)(1+g) - (1-\delta)} \right)^{\frac{1}{1-\alpha}}. \tag{3.56}$$

The remaining variables are all functions of k, and their steady state values are functions of k^*. Output is given by (3.54), and steady state output is given by

$$y^* = A\left(\frac{sA}{(1+n)(1+g)-(1-\delta)}\right)^{\frac{\alpha}{1-\alpha}}. \tag{3.57}$$

Consumption is given by

$$c_t = (1-s)Ak_t^{\alpha}. \tag{3.58}$$

Finally, the real interest rate and the real wage are given by

$$r_t = \alpha Ak_t^{\alpha-1} - \delta, \tag{3.59}$$

$$w_t = (1-\alpha)Ak_t^{\alpha}. \tag{3.60}$$

Simulating (3.55) numerically, for specific parameter values, we can calculate the dynamic adjustment of capital toward the balanced growth path. The dynamic adjustment of the other variables can then be calculated from (3.54), (3.58), (3.59), and (3.60).

3.8.3 Dynamic Simulations of the Model

The calibrated model relies on the following values of the initial parameters: $A = 1$, $\alpha = 0.333$, $s = 0.30$, $n = 0.01$, $g = 0.02$, and $\delta = 0.03$. These are the same as the values used to calculate the speed of convergence in section 3.5.

Figure 3.9 shows the impulse response functions of the calibrated Solow model following a permanent increase in the savings rate s of 1%. In the simulation shown, the economy is on the initial balanced growth path, and after period 1, the savings rate increases permanently and unexpectedly by 1%, from 0.30 (i.e., 30%) to 0.303 (30.3%). The increase in the savings rate leads to a decrease in consumption, a gradual accumulation of capital, a gradual increase in production, a gradual increase in real wages and a gradual fall in real interest rates. The reason for increasing real wages is the gradual increase in the marginal product of labor caused by the accumulation of capital. The reason for the gradual reduction in the real interest rate is the gradual reduction of the marginal product of capital caused by the accumulation of capital. The economy gradually converges toward a new balanced growth path. In this new balanced growth path, capital per efficiency unit of labor is higher by approximately 1.5%, output and real wages by 0.5%, consumption by 0.07% (due to the increase in the savings rate), and the real interest rate has fallen by 0.07 percentage points.

Figure 3.10 presents the impulse response functions of the model following an increase in total factor productivity A of 1%. In this simulation, the economy is on the initial balanced growth path, and after period 1, total factor productivity A increases permanently

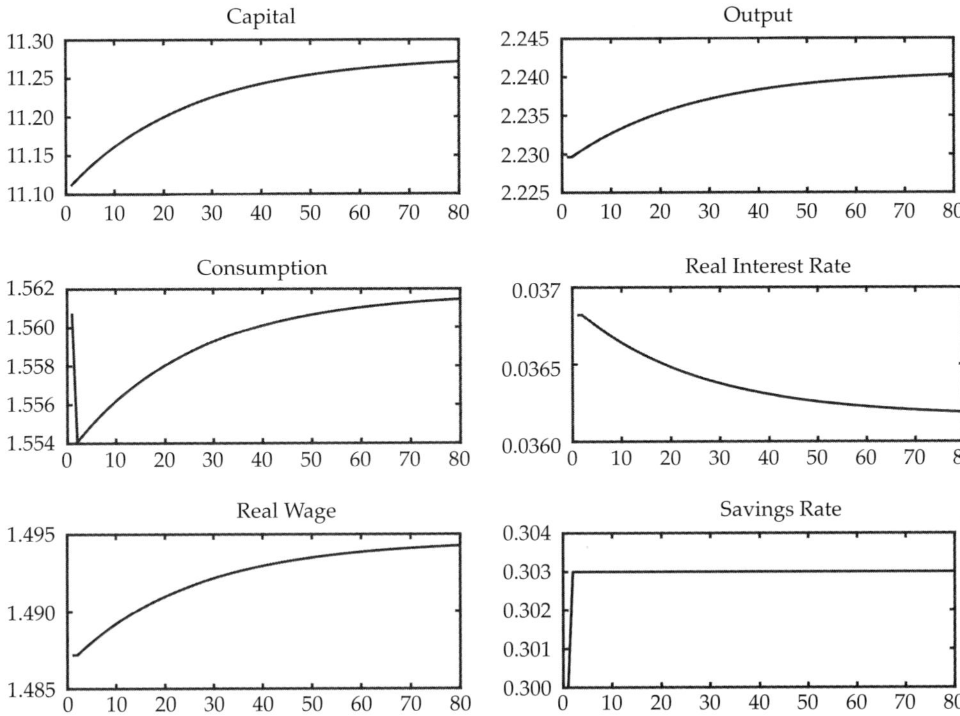

Figure 3.9
Impulse response functions of the Solow model following a permanent increase in the savings rate of 1%.

and unexpectedly by 1%, from 1 to 1.01. This increase leads immediately to an increase in output, consumption, savings, the marginal product of labor (real wage), and the marginal product of capital (real interest rate). The increase in savings causes a gradual accumulation of capital, which leads to a further gradual increase in output and consumption, a further gradual increase in real wages, but a gradual fall in real interest rates. The reason for the gradual decrease of the real interest rate is the gradual reduction of the marginal product of capital caused by the accumulation of capital. The economy gradually converges to a new balanced growth path. Steady state capital per efficiency unit of labor increases by about 1.5%, output, consumption and real wages also increase by 1.5%, while the real interest rate, after the initial increase, returns to its original equilibrium. Because the production function is assumed to be Cobb-Douglas, the equilibrium real interest rate is independent of total factor productivity A. An increase in total factor productivity by 1% leads to an increase in real income by 1.5% (i.e., more than 1%) because the increase in total factor productivity causes an increase in savings and capital accumulation, which in turn causes additional secondary increases in real output, income, and consumption. These results can

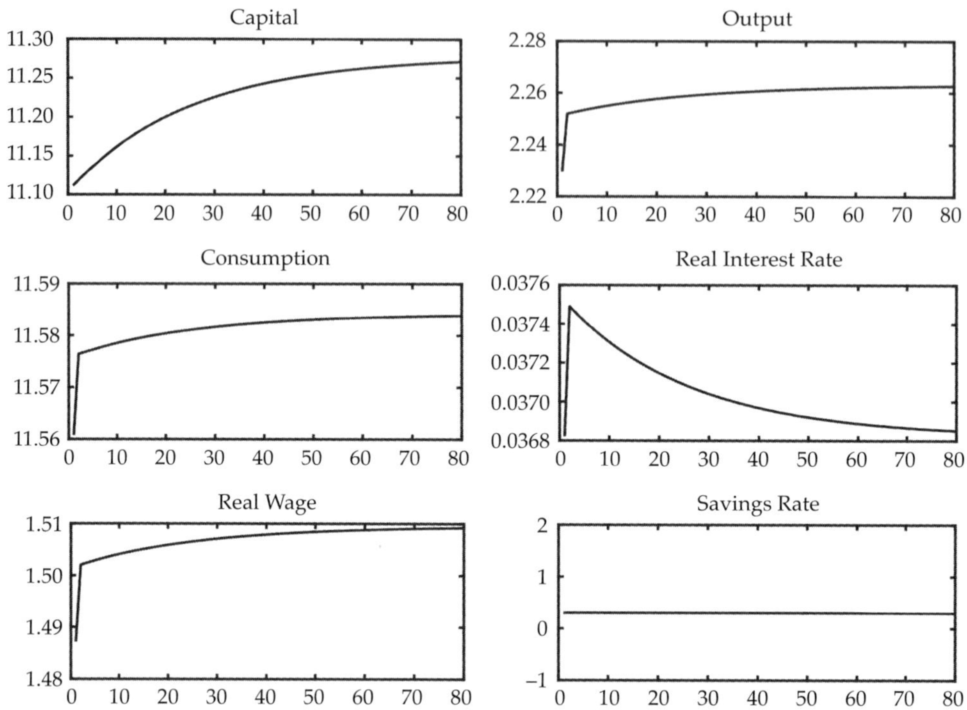

Figure 3.10
Impulse response functions of the Solow model following a permanent increase in total factor productivity of 1%.

be confirmed by examining (3.57), where the elasticity of steady state output with respect to total factor productivity A is equal to $1/(1-\alpha) > 1$.

Finally, figure 3.11 shows the impulse response functions of the model following an increase in the rate of population growth n by 1%. In this simulation, the economy is on the initial balanced growth path, and after period 1, the rate of growth of population n increases permanently and unexpectedly by 1%, from 1% to 1.01%. This increase leads to a gradual decumulation of capital and a gradual decline in output, consumption, and the real wage (the marginal product of labor). The real interest rate (marginal product of capital) gradually increases. The economy gradually converges to a new balanced growth path. On this path, capital per efficiency unit of labor is lower by about 0.25%; output, consumption, and real wages are lower by 0.08%; and the real interest rate has increased from 3.68% to 3.69%. The negative effects of an increase in population growth on steady state per capita income and consumption in the Solow model are not insignificant, but neither are they huge.

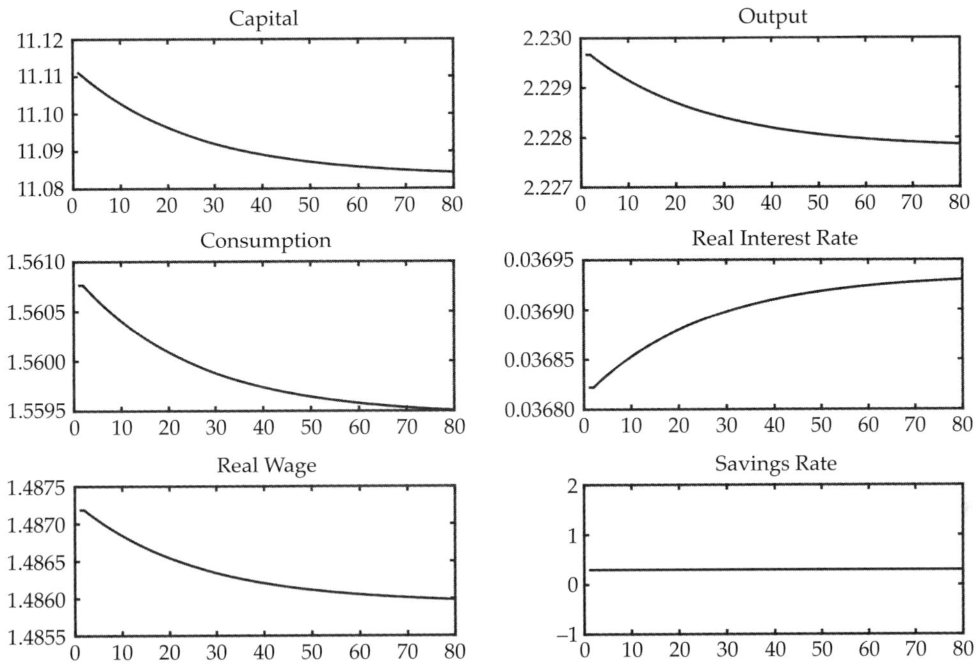

Figure 3.11
Impulse response functions of the Solow model following a permanent increase in the rate of population growth of 1%.

3.9 Conclusion

The Solow model is a key model in the theory of economic growth. Although it is rooted in older models and has theoretical and empirical weaknesses, this model provides an extremely useful, relatively simple, and flexible framework for the analysis of the process of economic growth.

However, the process of physical capital accumulation (which is the main engine of economic growth in the Solow model) cannot fully explain either the long-run growth of output per worker that has been observed in developed economies or the large differences in output per worker between developed and less developed economies. In fact, only a small part of these phenomena can be explained by the accumulation of physical capital. To explain the rest, one has to rely on total factor productivity, the efficiency of labor, and technical progress, which are considered exogenous in the Solow model.

In this sense, the Solow model (and any model that makes similar assumptions about technology and technical progress) shows us how to overcome its weaknesses and try to explain total factor productivity, labor efficiency, and technical progress. Extensions of the Solow model to address such weaknesses are examined in chapter 8.

Another theoretical weakness of the Solow model is the assumption that the savings rate is exogenous. At the time that the Solow model first appeared, this was a widely accepted assumption. However, the assumption is not satisfactory, as it does not take into account the underlying determinants of household savings behavior.

In the next two chapters, we examine two alternative classes of dynamic general equilibrium models of savings behavior, where savings result from the optimal intertemporal behavior of households that have access to competitive capital markets. These two classes of models, which are essential building blocks of modern intertemporal macroeconomics, are the representative household and the overlapping generations classes of models.

4

The Representative Household Model of Optimal Growth

The representative household class of models is a family of dynamic general equilibrium models that is based on the assumption that the dynamic path of aggregate consumption is decided in an optimal fashion by identical households. In the most widely used model in this class, the Ramsey model, all households are assumed to have an infinite time horizon and free access to the capital market, at a given, competitively determined, real interest rate. In other respects, the Ramsey model has a lot in common with the Solow [1956] neoclassical model of economic growth.

Historically, the representative household growth model predates the Solow growth model. The first such model is due to Ramsey [1928], who set out to analyze the optimal savings behavior of a household with a long time horizon and access to the capital market. However, because the calculus-of-variations methods employed by Ramsey were unfamiliar to the majority of economists of the time, the Ramsey model remained in relative obscurity for many years. It resurfaced in the 1960s, with the restatement and extensions of Cass [1965] and Koopmans [1965]. It has since evolved as one of the key models in intertemporal macroeconomics. It is being used widely both in the theory of economic growth and the theory of aggregate fluctuations, in the form of the stochastic growth model.[1]

It is worth mentioning that, around the same time as Ramsey, the problem of the optimal intertemporal choice of consumption by a representative household was also analyzed by Fisher [1930]. Fisher employed a two-period dynamic model, which was in many respects similar to (but much less demanding mathematically than) the Ramsey model. The Fisher model, variants of which we have already analyzed in chapter 2, belongs to the representative household class of models but has a restricted two-period time structure.[2]

Assumptions about technology and market structure in the representative household growth model are similar to those of the Solow model. What differs is the assumption about

1. The stochastic growth model is presented and analyzed in chapter 13.

2. The Fisher model has also been used as the basic building block of a nonrepresentative household class of optimizing dynamic models, such as the Allais [1947], Samuelson [1958], and Diamond [1965] models of overlapping generations. We will discuss overlapping generations models in chapter 5.

the determination of savings. Instead of the fixed and exogenous savings rate of the Solow model, in the representative household model, savings are determined as a result of optimal intertemporal consumption behavior of forward-looking households. Consequently, savings behavior is determined endogenously and is individually optimal.

The representative household model is thus theoretically more satisfactory than the Solow model, as it is based on full intertemporal optimization. It is a dynamic general equilibrium model in which the path of the economy depends solely on parameters related to the preferences of households, the technology of production, population growth, and market structure. Instead of assuming an exogenous savings rate, the model explains savings behavior as the outcome of the optimizing behavior of households. Moreover, as the typical form of the model assumes complete and competitive markets and identical households, the Ramsey model determines not only the privately optimal but also the socially optimal savings behavior, in the sense of the maximization of social welfare.

The savings rate in the Ramsey growth model is not constant, as in the Solow model, but is a function of the state of the economy. Given that the savings rate is one of the key determinants of the accumulation of capital and of the dynamic evolution of all other real variables, the fact that the savings rate is determined optimally is extremely important. For example, in the representative household model, there is no possibility of dynamic inefficiency, in the sense of an excessively high savings rate that would lead the economy to a level of capital beyond the golden rule. The representative household chooses its individually optimal level of savings, which, because of the assumption of full competitive markets, is also socially optimal. As it turns out, the steady state capital stock in this model is below the golden rule capital stock, because of the assumption of a positive pure rate of time preference. This optimal steady state capital stock defines the so-called modified golden rule.

One of the main differences of the Ramsey representative household model from the Solow model is related to the effects of population growth on per capita income. As shown in chapter 3, in the Solow model, the rate of population growth has a negative impact on per capita output and income on the balanced growth path. This is because the savings rate is an exogenous constant. In the Ramsey model, because of the optimal savings behavior of the representative household, the rate of population growth does not affect per capita income on the balanced growth path. Instead, the household internalizes the welfare of future generations, and the optimal savings rate responds to the rate of growth of population in a way that does not affect capital accumulation and therefore per capita capital and income.

However, the Ramsey model is also an exogenous growth model, similar in this respect to the Solow model. As for the Solow model, the Ramsey model determines the level of the per capita capital stock, per capita output and consumption, per capita real wages, and the real interest rate on both the balanced growth path and the convergence path toward the balanced growth path. However, it does not determine the per capita steady state growth rate, which is treated as an exogenous parameter (i.e., the exogenous rate of technical progress).

4.1 The Optimal Intertemporal Path of Consumption

To introduce the problem of the optimal intertemporal choice of consumption, in chapter 2 we assumed a household that lives only for two periods and maximizes an intertemporal utility function that depends on the level of consumption in each of the two periods. This type of two-period dynamic model was first analyzed by Fisher [1930] and also forms the basis of the Diamond [1965] overlapping generations model (analyzed in chapter 5).

We now extend the two-period analysis to the problem of a household with a long time horizon equal to T. This is the problem posed and solved by Ramsey [1928]. We assume that time is continuous and that the representative household has a finite time horizon equal to T.

The household supplies a unit of labor per instant and has a exogenous flow of labor income equal to w. It can borrow and lend freely in the capital market at a real interest rate r. The household has an initial endowment of an interest yielding asset equal to $a(0)$. It is assumed to maximize the following intertemporal utility function:

$$U = \int_{t=0}^{T} e^{-\rho t} u(c(t))dt, \tag{4.1}$$

subject to

$$\dot{a}(t) = ra(t) + w - c(t), \tag{4.2}$$

$$a(0) \geq 0, \tag{4.3}$$

$$a(T) \geq 0, \tag{4.4}$$

where u is the instantaneous utility function of the household, which depends on consumption of goods and services (u is twice differentiable and concave); and ρ is the pure rate of time preference, the rate at which the household discounts future utilities. (4.2) is the asset accumulation equation, (4.3) defines the initial assets of the household, and (4.4) is a terminal condition that ensures that the household respects its intertemporal budget constraint. The household cannot end up with negative assets at the end of its horizon T. A condition such as (4.4) is called a *transversality condition*.

From the maximum principle, the first-order conditions for the maximization of (4.1), subject to the accumulation constraint (4.2), are the same as the first-order conditions for the maximization of the current-value Hamilton function, or "Hamiltonian", which for this problem is defined by[3]

3. See appendix E for the mathematics of intertemporal optimization in continuous time, and their application to the representative household problem.

$$\mathcal{H}(t) = u(c(t)) + \lambda(t)(ra(t) + w - c(t)), \tag{4.5}$$

where $\lambda(t)$ is the current value multiplier of the asset accumulation constraint; $\lambda(t)$ can be interpreted as the shadow price of the marginal instantaneous change of household assets at time t.

The Hamilton function is thus defined as the sum of the instantaneous utility of consumption plus the value of the change in the assets of the household, priced at the shadow price $\lambda(t)$. An optimal plan must maximize the Hamilton function at each instant t, provided that the shadow value is chosen correctly. The first-order conditions for the maximization of the Hamilton function coincide with the first-order conditions for the maximization of (4.1), subject to the sequence of the accumulation equations (4.2).

The first-order conditions for the maximization of the current-value Hamilton function are given by

$$\frac{\partial \mathcal{H}(t)}{\partial c(t)} = 0 \Rightarrow u'(c(t)) = \lambda(t), \tag{4.6}$$

$$-\frac{\partial \mathcal{H}(t)}{\partial a(t)} = \dot{\lambda}(t) - \rho\lambda(t) \Rightarrow \dot{\lambda}(t) = -(r - \rho)\lambda(t), \tag{4.7}$$

$$\frac{\partial \mathcal{H}(t)}{\partial \lambda(t)} = \dot{a}(t) \Rightarrow \dot{a}(t) = ra(t) + w - c(t). \tag{4.8}$$

From (4.6), on the optimal path, we see that the multiplier $\lambda(t)$ (which is the value of the marginal increase in assets) is equal to the marginal utility of consumption. Thus, the household is indifferent between one extra unit of consumption and one extra unit of savings. Equation (4.7) shows that on the optimal path, the real interest rate plus the expected marginal increase in the value of assets (capital gain) is equal to the pure rate of time preference of the household. Finally, (4.8) is the asset accumulation equation.

We can use the first-order conditions (4.6) and (4.7) to characterize the behavior of consumption along the optimal path. Differentiating (4.6) with respect to time, we get

$$\dot{\lambda}(t) = u''(c(t))\dot{c}(t). \tag{4.9}$$

Substituting (4.6) and (4.9) into (4.7) results in

$$\dot{c}(t) = -\frac{u'(c(t))}{u''(c(t))}(r - \rho), \tag{4.10}$$

which is the *Euler equation for consumption*. It is nothing more than the expression in continuous time of the typical condition for optimality: The marginal rate of intertemporal substitution of consumption is equal to the marginal rate of intertemporal transformation of current to future consumption. The interpretation of (4.10) is analogous to that of the Euler equation for the two-period problem already analyzed in chapter 2.[4]

Because the second derivative of the instantaneous utility function is assumed to be negative (i.e., the marginal utility is declining with consumption), the change in consumption will have the same sign as the difference between the real interest rate and the pure rate of time preference. If the real interest rate is higher than the pure rate of time preference, then consumption will be continuously increasing. In the opposite case, consumption will be continuously decreasing. If the real interest rate is equal to the pure rate of time preference, then consumption will be constant on the optimal path.

If we assume that the instantaneous utility function of the household has the form of (2.39), with a constant elasticity of intertemporal substitution of consumption $1/\theta$, then (4.10) takes the form

$$\frac{\dot{c}(t)}{c(t)} = \frac{1}{\theta}(r - \rho), \tag{4.11}$$

which implies that the optimal consumption of the household increases, remains constant, or decreases, depending on whether the real interest rate exceeds, equals, or falls short of the pure rate of time preference, respectively.

Exercise 4.1 Derive equation (4.11) from an intertemporal optimization problem of a representative household with a CEIS utility function.

This optimality rule is logical. The higher the real interest rate is relative to the pure rate of time preference, the greater will be the incentive for the representative household to reduce current consumption and invest in assets with a rate of return r (and so enjoy higher future consumption). So if the real interest rate is higher than the pure rate of time preference, consumption per capita will be growing along the optimal path. If the real interest rate is lower than the pure rate of time preference, consumption per capita will be declining along the optimal path. Finally, if the real interest rate is equal to the pure rate of time preference, consumption will be constant along the optimal path. In this last case, there will be full consumption smoothing.

Equation (4.11) also highlights the role of the elasticity of intertemporal substitution $1/\theta$. The higher the elasticity of intertemporal substitution is, the easier it will be for the household, in utility terms, to substitute consumption over time (and thus the easier it is to substitute current for future consumption). Consequently, for a given difference between the real interest rate and the pure rate of time preference, the growth rate of per capita

4. This interpretation of equation (4.10) is sometimes referred to as the *Keynes-Ramsey rule*, because this type of Euler equation was presented by Ramsey in his classic 1928 *Economic Journal* article, accompanied by the interpretation above, which Ramsey partly attributed to Keynes, then editor of the *Journal*.

consumption is higher, the higher the elasticity of intertemporal substitution. We can now proceed to incorporate the optimal consumption behavior of a representative household in a full-blown growth model.

4.2 The Ramsey Model of Economic Growth

As with the Solow model, in the Ramsey representative household model, we focus on the following set of endogenous variables: Y, aggregate output (or y, output per efficiency unit of labor); K, aggregate stock of (physical) capital (or k, capital per efficiency unit of labor); C, aggregate consumption (or c, consumption per efficiency unit of labor); r, real interest rate; and $\hat{w} = wh$ real wage per worker (or w, real wage per efficiency unit of labor).

The exogenous variables and exogenous parameters in the model are defined as follows: t, time (a continuous exogenous variable); L, aggregate population and employment (an exogenous variable that depends on time); h, efficiency of labor (an exogenous variable that depends on time); n, rate of growth of population (exogenous parameter); g, rate of technical progress (exogenous parameter); δ, rate of depreciation of capital (exogenous parameter); and ρ, pure rate of time preference of households (exogenous parameter).

4.2.1 The Production Function

At each instant, the economy has a stock of capital, a given labor force, and given labor efficiency, which are combined to produce output. The production function has the form

$$Y(t) = AF\left(K(t), h(t)L(t)\right). \tag{4.12}$$

This production function has all the properties of the neoclassical production function assumed in the Solow model. The marginal product of all inputs is positive but decreasing, there are constant returns to scale, and the Inada conditions are satisfied.[5]

As in the Solow model, let us assume that population growth and the efficiency of labor evolve according to

$$L(t) = L_0 e^{nt}, \tag{4.13}$$

$$h(t) = h_0 e^{gt}, \tag{4.14}$$

where L_0 and h_0 denote population and the efficiency of labor at time 0.

Due to the assumption of constant returns to scale, the production function can be expressed in intensive form (i.e., per efficiency unit of labor) as

$$y(t) = Af(k(t)), \tag{4.15}$$

5. See the discussion of the neoclassical production function in chapters 2 and 3 and appendix A.

where $y = Y/hL$ is output per efficiency unit of labor, $k = K/hL$ is capital per efficiency unit of labor, and $f(k) = F(k, 1)$ is the production function per efficiency unit of labor.

4.2.2 The Utility Function of the Representative Household

All households in this economy are assumed to be identical. Thus, we shall eventually focus our attention on the behavior of only one of them: the representative household. Households are indexed by j, where j is uniformly distributed between zero and 1. Thus, $j \in [0, 1]$.

The utility function of household j depends on the level of its per capita consumption. The household is assumed to have an infinite time horizon and to maximize the intertemporal utility function[6]

$$U_j = \int_{t=0}^{\infty} e^{-\rho t} u(c_j(t)) L_j(t) dt, \tag{4.16}$$

where $c_j(t)$ denotes the per capita consumption of household j at instant t; u is the instantaneous utility function of household j; and ρ is the pure rate of time preference of household j, an exogenous preference parameter. The number of members of the household is given by $L_j(t)$ and is the same for all households. Thus, it follows that the relation between the members of individual households j and total population is given by

$$L_j(t) = \frac{L(t)}{\int_0^1 dj} = L_0 e^{nt}.$$

We assume that the instantaneous utility function of the household takes the form

$$u(c_j(t)) = \frac{c_j(t)^{1-\theta}}{1-\theta}, \tag{4.17}$$

where $\theta > 0$, and $\rho - n - (1-\theta)g > 0$. This functional form is the constant elasticity of intertemporal substitution utility function already introduced in chapter 2 and in subsection 4.2.1, with $1/\theta$ being the elasticity of intertemporal substitution of consumption.

The assumption that $\rho - n - (1-\theta)g > 0$ is sufficient to ensure that the intertemporal utility function (4.16) is well defined and converges to a finite value. This assumption is also sufficient to ensure that the economy eventually converges to a steady state, or balanced growth path.

As already mentioned, as θ tends to unity, one can prove, using l'Hopital's rule, that the utility function tends to the logarithmic utility function. That is, in the case $\theta = 1$,

6. The assumption of the infinite horizon is justified on the grounds that households are dynasties in economies that go on forever. Without this assumption, the model does not possess a steady state.

we have

$$u(c_j(t)) = \ln c_j(t).$$

Because all households are the same, we shall henceforth drop the subscript j and concentrate not on average household consumption, but on consumption per efficiency unit of labor. If $c_j(t)$ is the average consumption per member of household j, and all households are the same, then it follows that

$$c_j(t) = \hat{c}(t), \forall j,$$

where $\hat{c}(t)$ is per capita consumption at instant t.

Then consumption per efficiency unit of labor $c(t)$ is defined by

$$c(t) = \frac{\hat{c}(t)}{h(t)}. \tag{4.18}$$

Substituting equation (4.18) into equation (4.17) and the resulting equation in equation (4.16), and then taking into account that $h(t)$ and $L(t)$ increase at exogenous rates g and n, respectively, we arrive at an intertemporal utility function of the representative household, expressed in terms of consumption per efficiency unit of labor:

$$U = B \int_{t=0}^{\infty} e^{-\beta t} \frac{c(t)^{1-\theta}}{1-\theta} dt, \tag{4.19}$$

where $B = h_0^{1-\theta} L_0 > 0$, and $\beta = \rho - n - (1-\theta)g > 0$.

The representative household thus maximizes (4.19), which is equivalent to (4.16), subject to the constraint that its savings result in the accumulation of real assets, which take the form of physical capital.

4.2.3 The Accumulation of Capital and the Optimality of the Decentralized Competitive Equilibrium

As in the Solow model, the accumulation of capital per efficiency unit of labor in the economy is determined by

$$\dot{k}(t) = Af(k(t)) - c(t) - (n + g + \delta)k(t). \tag{4.20}$$

Equation (4.20) shows that the change in aggregate physical capital per efficiency unit of labor is determined by the difference of two terms: current investment (savings) per efficiency unit of labor minus equilibrium investment (i.e., the investment required to maintain capital per efficiency unit of labor at its current level).

A social planner who seeks to maximize the intertemporal utility of the representative household (4.19), subject to the constraint (4.20), would thus determine the savings behavior that maximizes social welfare. The question is whether (4.20) is also the budget constraint facing the representative household itself in a decentralized competitive equilibrium. If so, the optimal savings behavior of the representative household would also maximize social welfare, and the decentralized equilibrium would be socially optimal. To answer this question, one needs to consider the budget constraint facing the representative household in a decentralized competitive economy.

Assume a competitive economy, in which each member of the representative household provides a unit of labor, and savings take the form of investment in physical capital. The real wage per worker equals the real wage per efficiency unit of labor $w(t)$ times the efficiency of labor $h(t)$. Consequently, the per capita labor income of the household at time t equals

$$w(t)h(t),$$

where $w(t)$ is the real wage per efficiency unit of labor.

Households rent their capital stock to competitive firms in a competitive capital market. The per capita income from capital of the representative household is given by

$$\frac{(r(t)+\delta)\,K(t)}{L(t)},$$

where $r(t)+\delta$ is the rental price of capital in the competitive capital market.

Consequently, in a decentralized competitive economy, the accumulation of capital per efficiency unit of labor is determined by the savings of the representative household, and is given by

$$\begin{aligned}\dot{k}(t) &= (r(t)+\delta)\,k(t)+w(t)-c(t)-(n+g+\delta)k(t)\\ &= r(t)k(t)+w(t)-c(t)-(n+g)k(t).\end{aligned} \tag{4.21}$$

The representative household takes the evolution of $w(t)$ and $r(t)+\delta$ as given, as these are determined in competitive labor and capital markets. In such markets, capital and labor are paid their respective marginal product. Thus,

$$\begin{aligned}r(t)+\delta &= Af'(k(t)),\\ w(t) &= Af(k(t))-k(t)Af'(k(t)).\end{aligned} \tag{4.22}$$

Substituting the pair of equations (4.22) into (4.21), we end up with (4.20). Hence, the budget constraint faced by the representative household, in the form of the asset accumulation equation (4.21), is the same as the budget constraint (4.20) faced by the economy as a whole and by the hypothetical social planner.

In this model, due to the assumption of competitive markets, maximizing the intertemporal utility function of a representative household is essentially under the same constraint as the one that would be used by a social planner (i.e., the economywide budget constraint (4.20)). The problem of the representative household is the same as that of a hypothetical omnipotent social planner.

Consequently, the competitive equilibrium in the model of the representative household is fully optimal. A decentralized competitive equilibrium in which each household maximizes its own utility function over time, under its private budget constraint, would lead to the same outcome as that of an omnipotent social planner who had as her objective the maximization of the intertemporal utility function of the representative household, under the appropriate aggregate budget constraint.

In the case of the representative household model with full and competitive markets, we have an application of the *first theorem of welfare economics*: When markets are competitive and complete, and there are no externalities, the decentralized equilibrium is optimal, because it maximizes social welfare.

4.2.4 Conditions for Utility Maximization by the Representative Household

To find the first-order conditions for the maximization of (4.19) under the accumulation equation (4.21), we define the current value Hamilton function as

$$\mathcal{H}(t)=\left(\frac{c(t)^{1-\theta}}{1-\theta}\right)+\lambda(t)(r(t)k(t)+w(t)-c(t)-(n+g)k(t)), \tag{4.23}$$

where $\lambda(t)$ is the multiplier of the Hamilton function; $\lambda(t)$ can be interpreted as the "shadow price" of the marginal instantaneous change of the capital stock at t (marginal investment).

The Hamilton function is thus defined as the sum of the instantaneous utility of consumption plus the value of the change in the capital stock, priced at the shadow price $\lambda(t)$. An optimal plan must maximize the Hamilton function at each instant t, provided that the shadow value is chosen correctly. From the maximum principle, the first-order conditions for the maximization of the Hamilton function coincide with the first-order conditions for the maximization of (4.19), subject to the sequence of the accumulation equations (4.21).

The first-order conditions for the maximization of the Hamilton function are

$$\frac{\partial\mathcal{H}(t)}{\partial c(t)}=0, \tag{4.24}$$

$$\frac{\partial\mathcal{H}(t)}{\partial\lambda(t)}=\dot{k}(t), \tag{4.25}$$

$$-\frac{\partial\mathcal{H}(t)}{\partial k(t)}=\dot{\lambda}(t)-\beta\lambda(t). \tag{4.26}$$

Here (4.24) implies

$$\lambda(t) = c(t)^{-\theta}, \tag{4.27}$$

and (4.26) implies

$$\dot{\lambda}(t) = -\lambda(t)\,(r(t) - \beta - n - g) = -\lambda(t)\,(r(t) - \rho - \theta g)\,. \tag{4.28}$$

Finally, (4.25) implies the capital accumulation equation (4.21).

Equation (4.27) suggests that consumption must be chosen at each instant so that its marginal utility is equal to the shadow price of the marginal unit of savings invested in capital. At each instant, goods must be equally valuable at the margin, either as consumption or as investment.

Equation (4.28) implies that capital gains (i.e., the rate of change of the shadow price of capital $\lambda(t)$) must be equal to the difference between the discount factor of the household β and the rate of return of capital per efficiency unit of labor $r(t) - n - g$. This condition essentially ensures that the total rate of return of a marginal unit of capital, including capital gains, is equal to the discount factor of the household β.

This interpretation can be confirmed by rearranging (4.28) as

$$\left(r(t) + \frac{\dot{\lambda}(t)}{\lambda(t)} - n - g\right) = \beta.$$

It is straightforward to show that if a social planner maximized the intertemporal utility function of the representative household, subject to the economywide capital accumulation condition (4.20), then the relevant first- order conditions would be (4.27) and

$$\dot{\lambda}(t) = -\lambda(t)\left(Af'(k(t)) - \delta - \rho - \theta g\right).$$

By the definition of the real interest rate in (4.21), (4.28) is exactly the same as the equation above, which confirms that the competitive equilibrium maximizes social welfare in this model.

4.2.5 The Euler Equation for Consumption

We can examine the first-order conditions by eliminating $\lambda(t)$ between (4.27) and (4.28). Taking the first derivative of (4.27) with respect to time, after using (4.28) and the definition of β, we end up with the following differential equation for c:

$$\frac{\dot{c}(t)}{c(t)} = \frac{1}{\theta}\,(r(t) - \rho - \theta g) = \frac{1}{\theta}\,(r(t) - \rho) - g, \tag{4.29}$$

which is the Euler equation for consumption per efficiency unit of labor. The growth rate of consumption per capita is positive if the real interest rate exceeds the pure rate of time preference of the representative household. In addition, the higher the elasticity of intertemporal substitution of consumption is, the higher the growth rate of consumption will be for a given difference between the real interest rate and the pure rate of time preference of the representative household. In equation (4.29), g has a negative impact because c is consumption per efficiency unit of labor, and its denominator increases at a rate g (the exogenous rate of technical progress). This is why g must be subtracted.

If (4.29) is rewritten in terms of per capita consumption, we would have

$$\frac{\dot{\hat{c}}(t)}{\hat{c}(t)} = \frac{1}{\theta}\left(r(t) - \rho\right),$$

where $\hat{c}$ is per capita consumption. This equation is the same as (4.11) and has the same interpretation.

In what follows, we concentrate on the Euler equation for consumption per efficiency unit of labor (4.29). If the economy is on a balanced growth path, consumption per head will be growing at the exogenous rate of technical progress g, and consumption per efficiency unit of labor will be constant. Thus, from (4.29), the real interest rate on the balanced growth path will be equal to $\rho + \theta g$. As we shall see below, there is a unique constant real interest rate that is consistent with a balanced growth path in this model.

4.2.6 The Intertemporal Budget Constraint of the Representative Household

Equation (4.29) determines the rate of change of consumption on the optimal path. To determine the level of consumption on the optimal path, one must solve the two differential equations (4.29) and (4.21), which determine the optimal path of consumption and capital accumulation of the representative household.

Let us first solve the capital accumulation equation of the representative household (4.21). This is a first-order linear differential equation with variable coefficients. As a result, its solution for any $T \geq 0$ takes the form[7]

$$e^{-\left(\int_{v=0}^{T} r(v)dv-(n+g)T\right)}k(T) + \int_{t=0}^{T} e^{-\left(\int_{v=0}^{t} r(v)dv-(n+g)t\right)}c(t)dt$$

$$= k(0) + \int_{t=0}^{T} e^{-\left(\int_{v=0}^{t} r(v)dv-(n+g)s\right)}w(t)dt, \tag{4.30}$$

which describes the intertemporal budget constraint of the representative household with horizon T. This intertemporal budget constraint implies that at time 0, the present value of labor income between time 0 and time T, plus the initial capital stock at time 0, must be equal to the present value of consumption between time 0 and time T, plus the

7. For how to solve first-order linear differential equations, see appendix C.

present value of the capital stock at time T. The term that includes the integral of interest rates is a term that converts one unit of income, consumption, or capital at time t to its present value at time 0. If the real interest rate is fixed at r, then the term would simplify to $-rt$.

We can define the *average real interest rate* between time 0 and time t as

$$\bar{r}(t) = \frac{1}{t}\int_{v=0}^{t} r(v)dv. \tag{4.31}$$

With this definition of the average real interest rate, (4.30) can be written as

$$e^{-(\bar{r}(T)-n-g)T}k(T) + \int_{t=0}^{T} e^{-(\bar{r}(t)-n-g)t}c(t)dt$$

$$= k(0) + \int_{t=0}^{T} e^{-(\bar{r}(t)-n-g)t}w(t)dt. \tag{4.32}$$

If the horizon of the household were T, then the optimal capital stock at instant T would be equal to zero. If the capital stock at T were positive, then the household could increase its utility by consuming the rest of its capital just before T, and hence the path would not be optimal. Thus, a positive capital stock at T would not be optimal. If the capital stock at T were negative, then the household would be accumulating unsustainable debts (negative capital) along the optimal path, which would be violating its intertemporal budget constraint. We should therefore assume that on the optimal path, $k(T) = 0$. A similar assumption was made in the two-period model of chapter 2, when we assumed that the household consumes its remaining capital in period 2.

This type of condition is called a *transversality condition*, and it ensures that the present value of consumption of the household cannot exceed or fall short of its total wealth. Total wealth consists of the initial capital stock of the household plus the present value of its labor income. Thus, because we must have that $k(T) = 0$, for a finite time horizon T, the intertemporal budget constraint of the representative household takes the form

$$\int_{t=0}^{T} e^{-(\bar{r}(t)-n-g)t}c(t)dt = k(0) + \int_{t=0}^{T} e^{-(\bar{r}(t)-n-g)t}w(t)dt.$$

Taking into account the transversality condition, the intertemporal budget constraint implies that at time 0, the present value of labor income between time 0 and time T, plus the initial capital stock at time 0, must be equal to the present value of consumption between time 0 and time T. The question that arises is: What is the transversality condition when the horizon of the household is infinite, as we have assumed?

4.2.7 The Transversality Condition with an Infinite Time Horizon

If the time horizon of the household is infinite, as we have been assuming, then we should take the limit of (4.32) as T tends to infinity. In this case, the first term on the left in (4.32) should tend to zero. That is, we should have

$$\lim_{T\to\infty} e^{-(\bar{r}(T)-n-g)T}k(T)=0. \tag{4.33}$$

If this condition is not satisfied (for example, if the above limit is positive), then the household could increase its intertemporal utility along the optimal path by consuming a larger part of its capital. If the above limit is negative, then the household would be accumulating unsustainable debts (negative capital) along the optimal path, which is not consistent with its intertemporal budget constraint. Therefore, the only optimal path consistent with the intertemporal budget constraint of the representative household is the one that satisfies (4.33), which requires that the present value of its capital stock tends to zero as time tends to infinity.

Condition (4.33) is the *infinite-horizon transversality condition*. It is satisfied as long as the capital stock per efficiency unit of labor does not increase (or decrease) at a rate faster than $r-n-g$, which is the same as saying that the aggregate capital stock does not increase (or decrease) at a rate faster than r.

As already mentioned (and is proved explicitly in section 4.3), the real interest rate on the balanced growth path is equal to $\rho+\theta g$. As a result, if the economy is on the balanced growth path, the transversality condition takes the form

$$\lim_{T\to\infty} e^{-\beta T}k(T)u'(c(T))=\lim_{T\to\infty} e^{-\beta T}k(T)=0, \tag{4.34}$$

given that $u'(c(T))>0$. Equation (4.34) is the transversality condition on the balanced growth path.

Given that the transversality condition (4.33) must be satisfied, the intertemporal budget constraint of a representative household with an infinite time horizon takes the form

$$\int_{t=0}^{\infty} e^{-(\bar{r}(t)-n-g)t}c(t)dt=k(0)+\int_{t=0}^{\infty} e^{-(\bar{r}(t)-n-g)t}w(t)dt, \tag{4.35}$$

which implies that the present value of consumption of a representative household with an infinite time horizon equals its total wealth, defined as its initial capital stock (physical capital) plus the present value of current and future labor income (human capital).

4.2.8 The Consumption Function of the Representative Household with an Infinite Horizon

If we solve (integrate) the differential equation describing the Euler equation for consumption (4.29), then we find that consumption at time t is defined by

$$c(t)=c(0)e^{\frac{1}{\theta}(\bar{r}(t)-\rho-\theta g)t}. \tag{4.36}$$

Substituting (4.36) in the intertemporal budget constraint (4.35) and solving for $c(0)$ yields

$$c(0)=\gamma(0)\left(k(0)+\tilde{w}(0)\right), \tag{4.37}$$

where

$$\tilde{w}(0)=\int_{t=0}^{\infty}e^{-(\bar{r}(t)-n-g)t}w(t)dt \tag{4.38}$$

is the present value of labor income, and

$$\gamma(0)=\left(\int_{t=0}^{\infty}e^{\left(\frac{\bar{r}(t)(1-\theta)-\rho+\theta n}{\theta}\right)t}dt\right)^{-1} \tag{4.39}$$

is the proportion of total wealth consumed in period 0.

Equation (4.37), along with definitions (4.38) and (4.39), determines the level of consumption for the representative household. Consumption at time 0 is a proportion $\gamma(0)$ of total wealth. (4.37) allows us to deduce the properties of the consumption function of the representative household.

The representative household consumes a share of its total wealth equal to $\gamma(0)$. This share depends on the evolution of the average future real interest rates, the pure rate of time preference rate ρ, the elasticity of intertemporal substitution of consumption $1/\theta$, and the population growth rate n.

The impact of the average real interest rate on the proportion of total wealth that is consumed depends on the elasticity of intertemporal substitution of consumption $1/\theta$. An increase in average real interest rates has two kinds of effects on the average consumption to total wealth ratio: an intertemporal substitution effect and an income effect. The *intertemporal substitution effect* induces the household to substitute current for future consumption, as it increases the cost of current consumption relative to future consumption. This tends to decrease current consumption. The *income effect* of an increase in real interest rates increases income from capital and tends to increase both current and future consumption. This tends to increase current consumption.

If the elasticity of intertemporal substitution of consumption is greater than one (i.e., $\theta<1$), then consumption as a proportion of total wealth decreases when real interest rates rise and savings increase, because the negative intertemporal substitution effect is stronger than the positive income effect. In such a case, the intertemporal substitution effect prevails. If the elasticity of intertemporal substitution is less than unity ($\theta > 1$), then consumption as a proportion of total wealth increases when interest rates rise, because the positive income effect is stronger than the negative intertemporal substitution effect. Finally, if $\theta = 1$, which is the case with logarithmic preferences, the two results cancel each other out, and consumption as a proportion of total wealth is independent of the path of real interest rates. These effects are exactly the same as in the two-period model analyzed in chapter 2.

It is worth deriving the consumption function when the real interest rate is fixed at r, as happens in the steady state. In this case, (4.39) takes the form

$$\gamma(0) = \left(\int_{t=0}^{\infty} e^{\frac{1}{\theta}(r(1-\theta)-\rho+\theta n)t}\right)^{-1}$$
$$= \frac{r(1-\theta)-\rho+\theta n}{\theta\left(\lim_{t\to\infty} e^{\frac{1}{\theta}(r(1-\theta)-\rho+\theta n)t} - \lim_{t\to 0} e^{\frac{1}{\theta}(r(1-\theta)-\rho+\theta n)t}\right)}$$
$$= \frac{1}{\theta}\left(\rho - \theta n - r(1-\theta)\right).$$

For $\gamma(0)$ to be positive, we must have that $r < (\rho - \theta n)/(1-\theta)$. On the balanced growth path, the real interest rate is constant and equal to $r = \rho + \theta g$. As a result, on the balanced growth path, the share of total wealth that is consumed is equal to

$$\gamma(0) = (\rho - n - (1-\theta)g) = \beta.$$

From the assumptions we have made to ensure a well-defined intertemporal optimization problem for the representative household (see equation (4.19)), this share is positive.

In the case where $\theta = 1$ (i.e., logarithmic preferences), from (4.39), the share of consumption to total wealth is given by

$$\gamma(0) = \left(\int_{t=0}^{\infty} e^{-(\rho-n)t}\right)^{-1} = \frac{\rho - n}{-\lim_{t\to\infty} e^{-(\rho-n)t} + \lim_{t\to 0} e^{-(\rho-n)t}} = \rho - n.$$

Given that we have assumed that $\rho > n$, with a unitary elasticity of intertemporal substitution of consumption, the share of consumption in total wealth is equal to the difference between the pure rate of time preference and the population growth rate.

Finally, it is important to note that the overall impact of real interest rates on consumption is not limited to the impact on the propensity to consume out of total wealth. An increase in real interest rates leads to a decrease in the present value of future labor income, reducing the overall wealth of the representative household and leading to a reduction in consumption, even if the elasticity of intertemporal substitution is equal to one.

Essentially, the effects of real interest rates on the present value of income from employment (i.e., the wealth effects of real interest rates) reinforce the negative substitution effect on current consumption.

4.3 Dynamic Adjustment and the Balanced Growth Path

We can now move on to the question of how the balanced growth path is determined and the analysis of the dynamic adjustment of consumption, capital, and other real variables in the Ramsey model of the representative household.

The dynamic adjustment of the economy in the model is described by equations (4.20) for the accumulation of capital and (4.29) for the rate of growth of consumption. We have two first-order differential equations in two variables, k and c. We can use the two differential equations (4.20) and (4.29) to fully analyze the dynamic adjustment of the economy.

Equation (4.20) is given by

$$\dot{k}(t) = Af(k(t)) - c(t) - (n + g + \delta)k(t),$$

which describes the accumulation of capital per efficiency unit of labor.

Equation (4.29) can be modified to, assuming $r_t = Af'(k(t)) - \delta$,

$$\frac{\dot{c}(t)}{c(t)} = \frac{1}{\theta}\left(Af'(k(t)) - \delta - \rho - \theta g\right), \tag{4.29'}$$

which is the Euler equation for consumption per efficiency unit of labor. On the right-hand side of (4.29′), we have have used (4.22) to substitute for the real interest rate it terms of the marginal product of capital minus the depreciation rate of capital δ.

Once we determine the path of the capital stock and consumption, the paths of all other real variables (namely, output, the real interest rate, and the real wage) follow from the production function (4.15) and the marginal productivity conditions (4.22), which only depend on capital per effective unit of labor.

The solution of the second-order system of nonlinear differential equations (4.20) and (4.29′) can be described diagrammatically with the help of a phase diagram.

4.3.1 Dynamic Adjustment toward the Balanced Growth Path

The capital stock (per efficiency unit of labor) that ensures $\dot{c}(t) = 0$ (i.e., constant consumption per efficiency unit of labor) is determined by (4.29′) from the equalization of the marginal product of capital with the pure rate of time preference, plus the depreciation rate, plus the rate of technical progress g multiplied by θ. This defines the steady state real interest rate and the steady state capital stock in this model:

$$Af'(k) = \rho + \delta + \theta g. \tag{4.40}$$

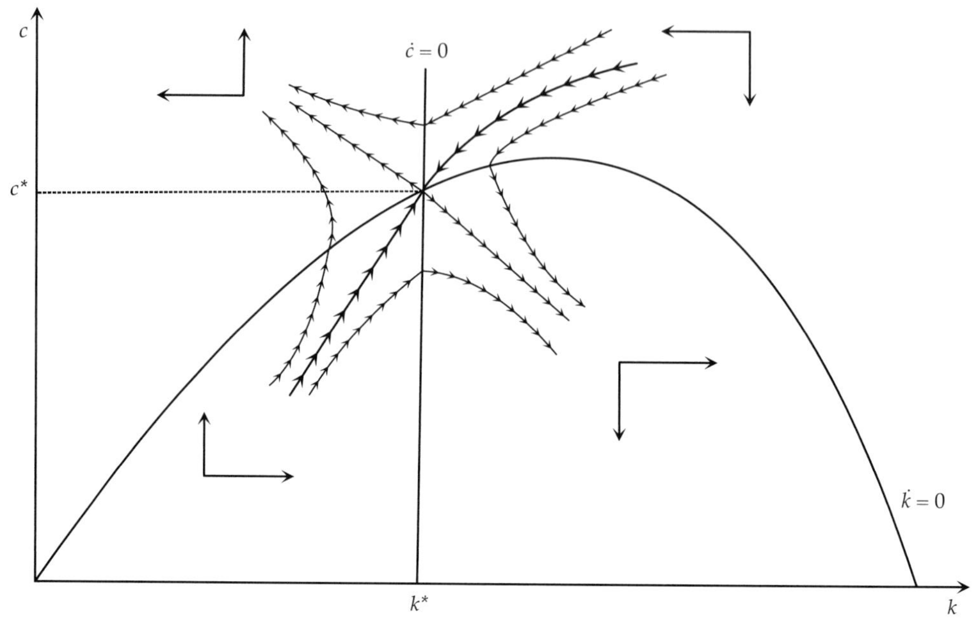

Figure 4.1
The balanced growth path and dynamic adjustment in the Ramsey model.

Note that (4.40) implies that the steady state capital stock depends only on the parameters of the production function and four other parameters: the pure rate of time preference ρ, the depreciation rate δ, the inverse of the elasticity of intertemporal substitution in consumption θ, and the rate of technical progress g. Only technological and preference parameters affect the steady state per capita capital stock and, by means of the production function, the steady state per capita income. Note that the rate of growth of population n, unlike in the Solow model, does not affect steady state per capita capital and income.

Figure 4.1 depicts (4.40) as the vertical line $\dot{c}=0$. We shall call it the *steady state consumption locus*, because along it, consumption per efficiency unit of labor is constant. This condition defines the steady state capital stock k^*. If the capital stock is lower than k^*, then the real interest rate is higher than $\rho+\theta g$, and from (4.29), consumption per efficiency unit of labor is rising. Hence the vertical arrows depicting rising consumption to the left of k^* in figure 4.1. If the capital stock is higher than k^*, then the real interest rate is lower than $\rho+\theta g$, and from (4.29), consumption per efficiency unit of labor is falling. Hence the vertical arrows depicting falling consumption to the right of k^*.

For $\dot{k}(t)=0$ in (4.20), one can derive the relation between consumption and the capital stock (per efficiency unit of labor) that ensures a constant capital stock (per efficiency unit of labor). This is given by

$$c=Af(k)-(n+g+\delta)k, \tag{4.41}$$

which is depicted as the $\dot{k}=0$ curve in figure 4.1. Let us call it the *steady state capital locus*, because along it, the capital stock per efficiency unit of labor is constant. Because of the properties of the production function $Af(k)$, it is upward sloping up to the point $Af'(k)=n+g+\delta$, and downward sloping after that point. Thus, it achieves its maximum at the golden rule capital stock, for which the real interest rate is equal to the steady state growth rate $n+g$.

If consumption is higher than the level implied by (4.41), then savings are lower than the savings required to maintain a constant capital stock per efficiency unit of labor, and the capital stock per efficiency unit of labor is declining. Hence the left-pointing horizontal arrows above the constant capital curve in figure 4.1. If consumption is lower than the level implied by (4.41), then savings are higher than the savings required to maintain a constant capital stock per efficiency unit of labor, and the capital stock per efficiency unit of labor is increasing. Hence the right-pointing horizontal arrows above the constant capital curve in figure 4.1.

When (4.40) and (4.41) are satisfied simultaneously, the economy is on a balanced growth path, as both the capital stock and consumption per efficiency unit of labor are constant, which is equivalent to saying that per capita consumption and the per capita capital stock grow at the exogenous rate of technical progress g. The remaining real variables (such as output, the real wage, and the real interest rate) are also on a balanced growth path, because by the production function and the marginal productivity conditions, they depend solely on the capital stock per efficiency unit of labor.

The balanced growth path (or steady state equilibrium) at (k^*, c^*) is unique. It is shown in figure 4.1, which depicts both (4.40) and (4.41) geometrically. Figure 4.1 also depicts the adjustment path leading to the steady state. In each section of figure 4.1, adjustment paths are determined by the direction of the resultant of the adjustment in consumption and capital. Thus, if both consumption and capital are rising in a section of the graph, then the economy moves toward the northeast. If both consumption and capital are falling in a section of the graph, then the economy moves toward the southwest. If consumption is rising and capital falling, the economy moves toward the northwest, and in the opposite case, toward the southeast. Both of these directions move the economy away from the steady state.

The steady state (k^*, c^*) is called a saddle point: A unique adjustment path, the saddle path, leads to this saddle point, as the capital stock k is a predetermined (state) variable, and consumption c is a control variable. The saddle path goes through the northeast and the southwest parts of the diagram. For any initial value of k, consumption adjusts immediately to ensure that the economy is put on the unique saddle path leading to the steady state (the balanced growth path). All other adjustment paths, some of which are also depicted in figure 4.1, eventually diverge and lead the economy away from the balanced growth path, violating the transversality condition (4.33).

On the adjustment path, if the capital stock (per efficiency unit of labor) is lower that k^*, consumption is also lower than c^*, and the economy accumulates capital at a rate higher than $n+g$. During this process, capital and consumption per efficiency unit of labor are rising.

The opposite happens if the initial capital stock (per efficiency unit of labor) is higher than k^*. Then the capital stock and consumption per efficiency unit of labor are falling.

Consequently, the behavior of the economy on the adjustment path resembles in many ways the behavior of the economy in the Solow model. There is convergence toward a unique long-run equilibrium (steady state or balanced growth path), regardless of initial conditions.

The difference is that in the Ramsey model, savings behavior is not exogenous, but endogenous and optimal. At any point in time, the representative household chooses its consumption to maximize its intertemporal utility. Due to competitive markets, the optimal individual behavior of the representative household also maximizes social welfare. Both the short-run equilibrium (on the adjustment path) and the long-run equilibrium (on the balanced growth path) are not only Pareto efficient but also consistent with the maximization of social welfare.

It is worth looking into the properties of the steady state, or balanced growth path, in more detail. Although the capital stock, output, and consumption per efficiency unit of labor are constant, the per capita capital stock, output, and consumption increase continuously at rate g (the exogenous rate of technical progress). The real interest rate is fixed on the balanced growth path, as is the real wage per efficiency unit of labor. However, the real wage per employee $w(t)h(t)$ grows at rate g, which causes a continuous increase in labor efficiency.

In the process of adjustment toward the balanced growth path from the left (i.e., when the initial capital stock per efficiency unit of labor is less than k^*), per capita output and per capita consumption are rising faster than g, the real interest rate is on a downward path (because of the falling marginal product of capital), and the real wage per employee is rising faster than g (because of the rising marginal product of labor). The opposite happens in the process of adjustment to the balanced growth path from the right (i.e., when the initial capital stock per efficiency unit of labor is higher than k^*).

4.3.2 The Balanced Growth Path and the Modified Golden Rule

The balanced growth path in the representative household model is similar to the balanced growth path in the Solow model. The capital stock, output, and consumption per efficiency unit of labor are constant. Consequently, the savings ratio $s = (y - c)/y$ is also constant on the balanced growth path. The aggregate capital stock, aggregate output, and total consumption are growing at the rate $n + g$. The per capita capital stock, per capita output, and per capita consumption are growing at the rate g.

Consequently, most of the central predictions of the Solow model regarding the determinants of long-term growth are not dependent on the assumption of a constant exogenous savings rate. Even when the savings rate is endogenous, as in the Ramsey model, the exogenous rate of technical progress remains the sole determinant of the long-term growth rate of output, consumption, and real wages per capita.

The main difference between the Ramsey and Solow models regarding the balanced growth path is that in the Ramsey model, it is not possible for the capital stock on the balanced growth path to exceed the capital stock that corresponds to the golden rule. In the Solow model, with a sufficiently high savings rate, there may be *dynamic inefficiency* (i.e., the capital stock may end up higher than the one that corresponds to the golden rule). In such a case, it is possible to reduce the capital stock and increase consumption and social welfare. This possibility does not exist in the Ramsey model, because the optimization of intertemporal utility by the representative household rules it out.

In fact, in the representative household model, capital per efficiency unit of labor on the balanced growth path is always lower than the golden rule. This is because the representative household has a positive pure rate of time preference and discounts future utility. Thus, the representative household does not seek to maximize per capita consumption on the balanced growth path, as assumed in the derivation of the golden rule. Instead, it maximizes an intertemporal utility function that (given the positive pure rate of time preference) places a greater weight on current consumption relative to future consumption.

As can be seen from equation (4.40), which defines the steady state capital stock k^*, or from figure 4.1, the steady state capital stock in the Ramsey model is lower than that corresponding to the golden rule, because the steady state real interest rate is equal to $\rho + \theta g$, which is higher than $n + g$. The steady state in the Ramsey model is often referred to as the *modified golden rule*.

Exercise 4.2 Assuming a Cobb-Douglas production function, derive the steady state of the representative household model from the system of differential equations (4.20) and (4.29). Discuss the determinants of all steady state variables. Also, analyze the stability of the system by linearizing the system around the steady state. Compare the steady state of the representative household model to the steady state corresponding to the golden rule. What determines the growth rate of per capita output, consumption, and real wages in the steady state?

4.3.3 Effects of a Permanent Increase in the Pure Rate of Time Preference

Figure 4.2 analyzes the impact of an increase in the pure rate of time preference of the representative household. It is assumed that the economy is initially on the balanced growth path (k^*, c^*) corresponding to the initial pure rate of time preference, and that at time t_0, the pure rate of time preference increases permanently and unexpectedly.

An increase in the pure rate of time preference rate leads to a shift of the steady state consumption line to the left. On the new balanced growth path (c^{**}, k^{**}), both consumption and capital will be lower. At time t_0, consumption increases to c_0 (because the capital stock is fixed) and puts the economy on the saddle path corresponding to the new balanced growth path. Because savings are lower than equilibrium investment, the economy begins to decumulate capital and gradually adjusts toward the new balanced growth path.

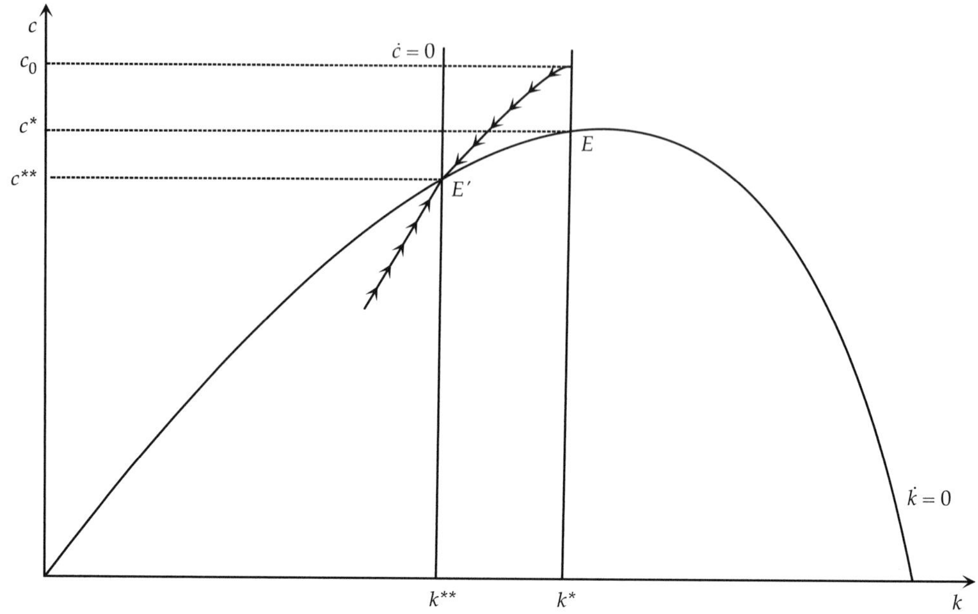

Figure 4.2
Short- and long-run effects of a permanent increase in the pure rate of time preference.

Figure 4.3 illustrates the impulse response function of consumption and capital per efficiency unit of labor after the increase in the pure rate of time preference. Consumption originally increases, which starts the process of gradual decumulation of capital per efficiency unit of labor, a gradual reduction in consumption, and a convergence to a new balanced growth path. This new balanced growth path is associated with lower capital and consumption compared to the previous path.

A decrease in the pure rate of time preference would have the opposite effects. On the new balanced growth path, both consumption and the capital stock will be higher. Consumption initially falls, the economy begins to accumulate capital, and there is gradual convergence toward the new balanced growth path with a higher capital stock and consumption per efficiency unit of labor.

The pure rate of time preference is a key determinant of savings behavior and steady state capital, output, and consumption in this model. The higher it is, the lower the inclination of the representative household will be to save for the future, and the lower the level of capital, output, and consumption will be on the balanced growth path.

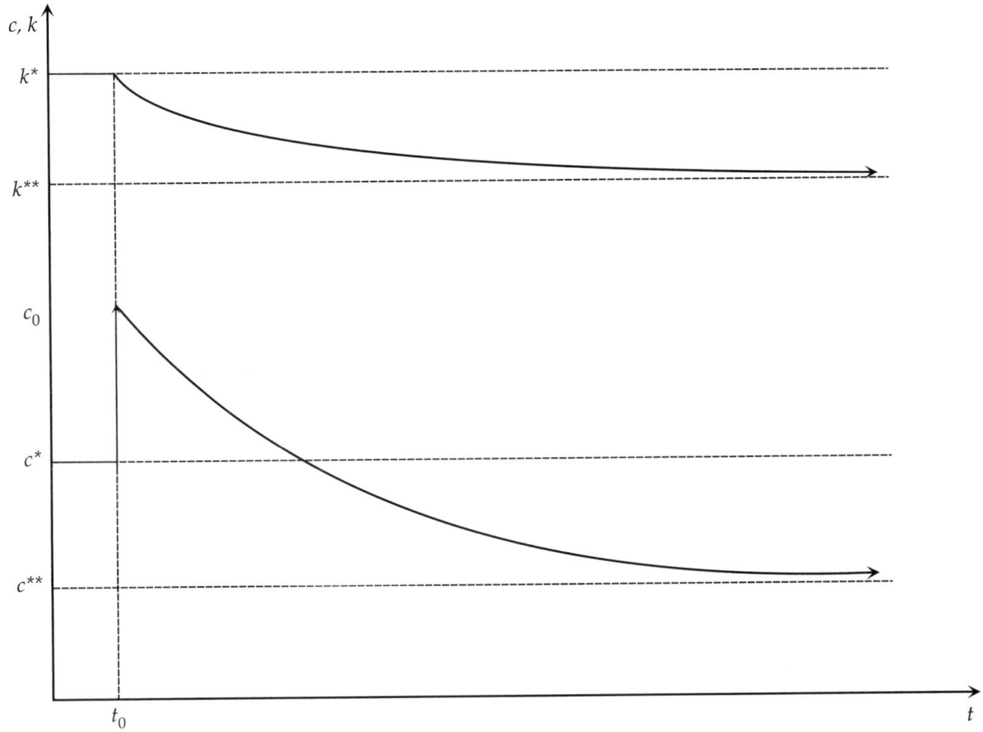

Figure 4.3
Impulse response function of consumption and capital stock following a permanent increase at t_0 in the pure rate of time preference.

4.3.4 Effects of a Permanent Increase in Total Factor Productivity

Figure 4.4 shows the impact of a permanent one-off increase in total factor productivity A. It is assumed that the economy is initially on the balanced growth path (k^*, c^*), corresponding to the initial total factor productivity, and that at time t_0, total factor productivity increases permanently and unexpectedly.

An increase in total factor productivity leads to a shift of the steady state consumption locus to the right and to an upward shift in the locus of steady state capital. On the new balanced growth path (c^{**}, k^{**}), both consumption and capital will be higher. At time t_0, consumption increases to c_0 (because the capital stock is fixed) and puts the economy on the saddle path corresponding to the new balanced growth path. Because savings are higher than equilibrium investment, the economy begins to accumulate capital and gradually adjusts toward the new balanced growth path.

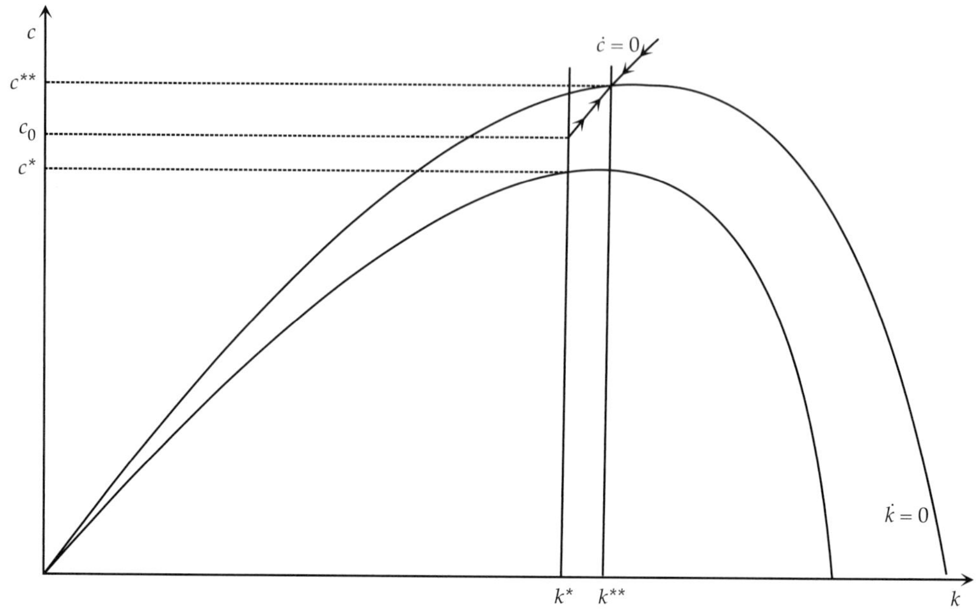

Figure 4.4
Short- and long-run effects of a permanent increase in total factor productivity.

4.3.5 Effects of a Permanent Increase in the Rate of Growth of Population

As already shown by equation (4.40), on the balanced growth path, per capita capital and income are independent of the rate of growth of population. However, steady state consumption per capita depends negatively on the rate of growth of population, as can be seen from equation (4.41). A rise in the rate of growth of population calls for an increase in per capita savings to finance the higher steady state investment required to maintain a constant capital stock per efficiency unit of labor.

This result can also be shown diagramatically, with the help of figure 4.5. An increase in the population growth rate leads to a downward shift of the steady state capital locus but does not affect the steady state consumption locus ($\dot{c} = 0$). On the new balanced growth path, only consumption will be lower. At time t_0, consumption jumps immediately to c^{**}. The capital stock is not affected, because savings increase immediately to match the higher equilibrium investment.

Thus, because of the optimal savings behavior of the representative household, which internalizes the welfare of future generations, an increase in the population rate of growth does not affect per capita capital and income on the balanced growth path. This is because savings immediately match the extra equilibrium investment required as a result of the higher population growth. This behavior is a major difference between the Ramsey representative household model and the Solow model with an exogenous savings rate. As we shall see in

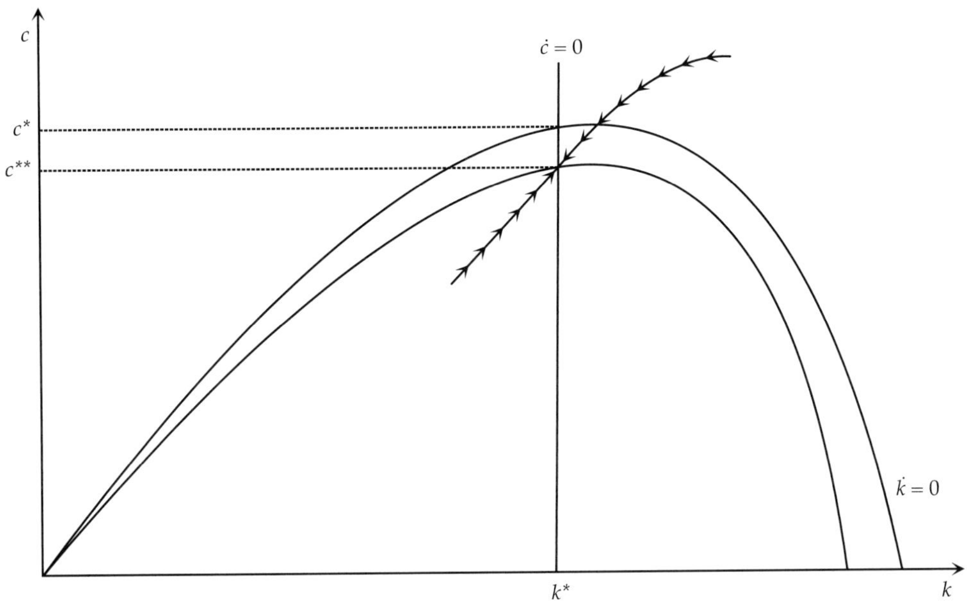

Figure 4.5
Effects of a permanent increase in the population growth rate.

chapter 5, it is also a major difference between the representative household and overlapping generations models as well.

4.4 Properties of the Adjustment Path and the Speed of Convergence

To algebraically analyze the convergence of the economy toward the balanced growth path, let us replace the pair of nonlinear differential equations (4.20) and (4.29) with linear approximations around the balanced growth path. Take the first-order Taylor approximations of (4.20) and (4.29) around the balanced growth path $k=k^*$ and $c=c^*$:

$$\dot{c} \simeq \left.\frac{\partial \dot{c}}{\partial k}\right|_{k^*,c^*}[k-k^*]+\left.\frac{\partial \dot{c}}{\partial c}\right|_{k^*,c^*}[c-c^*], \tag{4.42}$$

$$\dot{k} \simeq \left.\frac{\partial \dot{k}}{\partial k}\right|_{k^*,c^*}[k-k^*]+\left.\frac{\partial \dot{k}}{\partial c}\right|_{k^*,c^*}[c-c^*]. \tag{4.43}$$

The system of linear differential equations (4.42) and (4.43) can be written as

$$\dot{\tilde{c}} \simeq \frac{\partial \dot{c}}{\partial k}\tilde{k}+\frac{\partial \dot{c}}{\partial c}\tilde{c}, \tag{4.44}$$

$$\dot{\tilde{k}} \simeq \frac{\partial \dot{k}}{\partial k}\tilde{k} + \frac{\partial \dot{k}}{\partial c}\tilde{c}, \tag{4.45}$$

where $\tilde{c} = c - c^*$, and $\tilde{k} = k - k^*$.

From (4.29), we have

$$\dot{c} = \left\{\left[Af'(k) - \delta - \rho - \theta g\right]/\theta\right\} c. \tag{4.46}$$

Using (4.46) to evaluate the derivatives in (4.44), we get

$$\dot{\tilde{c}} \simeq \frac{Af''(k^*)c^*}{\theta}\tilde{k}. \tag{4.47}$$

Correspondingly, from (4.20), we have

$$\dot{k} = Af(k) - c - (n + g + \delta)k, \tag{4.48}$$

and using (4.48) to evaluate the derivatives in (4.45), we get

$$\dot{\tilde{k}} \simeq \left[Af'(k^*) - (n + g + \delta)\right]\tilde{k} - \tilde{c} = [(\rho + \theta g) - (n + g)]\,\tilde{k} - \tilde{c} = \beta\tilde{k} - \tilde{c}, \tag{4.49}$$

where $\beta = \rho - n - (1 - \theta)g$.

With two simple divisions on each side of (4.47) and (4.49), we can re-write them as

$$\frac{\dot{\tilde{c}}}{\tilde{c}} \simeq \frac{Af''(k^*)c^*}{\theta}\frac{\tilde{k}}{\tilde{c}}, \tag{4.50}$$

$$\frac{\dot{\tilde{k}}}{\tilde{k}} \simeq \beta - \frac{\tilde{c}}{\tilde{k}}. \tag{4.51}$$

Expressions (4.50) and (4.51) imply that the rates of change of the distance of consumption and the capital stock from their steady state values depend only on the ratio of their respective distances from their steady state values.

The roots of the system of differential equations (4.47) and (4.49) are determined by

$$\mu = \frac{\beta \pm \left[\beta^2 - 4Af''(k^*)c^*/\theta\right]^{1/2}}{2}. \tag{4.52}$$

Only the negative root leads the system to the balanced growth path. We thus have that

$$\mu_1 = \frac{\beta - \left[\beta^2 - 4Af''(k^*)c^*/\theta\right]^{1/2}}{2}. \tag{4.53}$$

Assuming a Cobb-Douglas production function of the form $Af(k)=Ak^{\alpha}$, (4.53) can be written as

$$\mu_1=\frac{1}{2}\left(\beta-\left\{\beta^2+\frac{4}{\theta}\frac{1-\alpha}{\alpha}(\rho+\delta+\theta g)\left[\rho+\delta+\theta g-\alpha(n+g+\delta)\right]\right\}^{1/2}\right), \qquad (4.54)$$

where α is the exponent of capital in the Cobb-Douglas production function.

Equation (4.54) expresses the speed of adjustment of the economy toward the balanced growth path as a function of structural parameters related to the preferences of the representative household, the technology of production, population growth, the rate of technical progress, and the depreciation rate of the capital stock.

To get a quantitative feel for the speed of adjustment, let us assume, as in the Solow model, that $\alpha = 1/3$. Let us also assume that $\theta=1$ and that, per year, $\rho=2\%$, $n=1\%$, $g=2\%$, $\delta=3\%$. The assumption about θ implies logarithmic preferences. With these assumptions, the annual real interest rate on the balanced growth path is equal to 4%, and the savings rate on the balanced growth path is 28.5%. And β turns out to be 1% per year.

Using these parameter values and equation (4.54), the speed of adjustment toward the balanced growth path turns out to be −7.9% per year. The half-life of the adjustment process (i.e., the time it takes to cover half the distance between any initial position and the balanced growth path) is 8.8 years. With the same assumptions about parameters, the speed of adjustment in the Solow model is −4% per year, and the half-life of the adjustment process is 17.3 years.

Adjustment in the representative household model is thus faster than in the corresponding Solow model for similar parameter values. The reason is that in this model, the savings rate is not constant but a negative function of the capital stock k. When the capital stock is lower than k^*, the savings rate is higher than the steady state savings rate, speeding up capital accumulation. When the capital stock is higher than k^*, the savings rate is lower than the steady state savings rate, speeding up the decumulation of capital. In contrast, the savings rate in the Solow model is assumed to be constant along the adjustment path.

Apart from the fact that savings behavior is optimal in the Ramsey model, this model in other respects has the same theoretical weaknesses as the Solow model. The rate of technical progress, which determines long-run growth in per capita output, income, real wages, consumption, and the capital stock is exogenously given rather than determined by the model.

As with the Solow model, what the Ramsey model does explain is the level (not the growth rate) of per capita output, income, real wages, consumption, and the capital stock on the balanced growth path. It also explains the adjustment process toward the balanced growth path.

4.5 Dynamic Simulations of a Calibrated Ramsey Model

To gain a better insight into the quantitative aspects of the process of adjustment in the Ramsey model, we can use numerical simulations for specific values of the parameters of the model. Such simulations help visualize how the calibrated Ramsey model adjusts from one balanced growth path to another when a particular parameter changes exogenously. As with the Solow model in chapter 3, we shall concentrate on changes in two such parameters: the pure rate of time preference of the representative household (a preference shock) and total factor productivity (a technological shock). To simulate the model numerically, we will convert it from a continuous-time model to a discrete time model.

4.5.1 The Ramsey Model in Discrete Time

Instead of assuming that time is a continuous variable, time is now measured as successive time periods, where $t=0, 1, 2, \ldots$. The variable x_t indicates the variable x in period t. Population and the efficiency of labor grow at constant exogenous rates n and g per period, respectively. Thus, we have

$$L_t = L_0(1+n)^t,$$

$$h_t = h_0(1+g)^t,$$

The intertemporal utility function of the representative household in given by

$$U = \sum_{t=0}^{\infty} \left(\frac{1}{1+\rho}\right)^t u(\hat{c}_t)L_t = L_0 \sum_{t=0}^{\infty} \left(\frac{1+n}{1+\rho}\right)^t u(\hat{c}_t), \tag{4.55}$$

where $\hat{c}$ is per capita consumption.

We assume, as in the continuous time case, that the single-period utility function u has the form of the constant elasticity of intertemporal substitution utility function:

$$u(\hat{c}_t) = \frac{\hat{c}_t^{1-\theta}}{1-\theta}. \tag{4.56}$$

With this assumption, after expressing consumption per efficiency unit of labor c, we get

$$U = B \sum_{t=0}^{\infty} \beta^t \frac{{c_t}^{1-\theta} - 1}{1-\theta}, \tag{4.57}$$

where $B = {h_0}^{1-\theta} L_0$, and $\beta = \frac{(1+n)(1+g)^{1-\theta}}{(1+\rho)} < 1$. The maximization of (4.57) takes place under the capital accumulation constraint by the representative household. Expressed in terms of efficiency units of labor, this constraint is given by

$$k_{t+1} = \frac{1}{(1+n)(1+g)} \left((1+r_t)k_t + w_t - c_t \right). \tag{4.58}$$

We thus assume that the representative household maximizes (4.57) under the sequence of constraints (4.58). The Lagrange function for this problem is given by

$$\mathcal{L} = \sum_{t=0}^{\infty} \beta^t \left(B \frac{{c_t}^{1-\theta}}{1-\theta} + \lambda_t \left((1+r_t)k_t + w_t - c_t - (1+n)(1+g)k_{t+1} \right) \right), \tag{4.59}$$

where λ_t is the sequence of Lagrange multipliers. The first-order conditions for the maximization of (4.59) are given by

$$\lambda_t = B{c_t}^{-\theta}, \tag{4.60}$$

$$\lambda_t = \beta \frac{1+r_{t+1}}{(1+n)(1+g)} \lambda_{t+1} = \frac{1+r_{t+1}}{(1+\rho)(1+g)^{-\theta}} \lambda_{t+1}, \tag{4.61}$$

Combining (4.60) and (4.61), we get

$$\frac{c_{t+1}}{c_t} = \left(\frac{1+r_{t+1}}{(1+\rho)(1+g)^{\theta}} \right)^{1/\theta} = \left(\frac{1+r_{t+1}}{(1+\rho)} \right)^{1/\theta} \frac{1}{(1+g)}, \tag{4.62}$$

which is the Euler equation for consumption in the discrete-time Ramsey model.

Assuming a competitive capital market, the real interest rate will be given by

$$r_{t+1} = Af'(k_{t+1}) - \delta, \tag{4.63}$$

and substituting (4.63) into (4.62), we get

$$\frac{c_{t+1}}{c_t} = \left(\frac{1+Af'(k_{t+1}) - \delta}{(1+\rho)(1+g)^{\theta}} \right)^{1/\theta} = \left(\frac{1+Af'(k_{t+1}) - \delta}{(1+\rho)} \right)^{1/\theta} \frac{1}{(1+g)}. \tag{4.64}$$

As a result, the balanced growth path $c_{t+1} = c_t = c^*$ requires a capital stock k^*, the marginal product of which satisfies

$$Af'(k^*) = (1+\rho)(1+g)^{\theta} - (1-\delta). \tag{4.65}$$

To calculate equilibrium consumption, we utilize the capital accumulation equation (4.58). After substituting for the real interest rate and the real wage, this constraint can be expressed as

$$c_t = Af(k_t) - (1+n)(1+g)k_{t+1} + (1-\delta)k_t. \tag{4.66}$$

In the steady state (balanced growth path), we have

$$c^* = Af(k^*) - (n + g(1+n) + \delta)\, k^*, \tag{4.67}$$

which determines steady state consumption, in the sense that savings are equal to the equilibrium investment that maintains the capital stock at its steady state value k^*.

The dynamic adjustment toward this steady state is described by the system of nonlinear difference equations (4.64) and (4.66).

4.5.2 The Calibrated Ramsey Model

To simulate the model numerically, we assume, as in the case of the simulations of the Solow model, that the production function is Cobb-Douglas of the form

$$y_t = Ak_t^{\alpha}, \tag{4.68}$$

where $A > 0$ is total factor productivity, $0 < \alpha < 1$ is the exponent (share) of capital in the production function, and $1 - \alpha$ is the exponent of labor.

The real interest rate and the real wage per efficiency unit of labor are given by the marginal productivity conditions

$$r_t = \alpha A k_t^{\alpha-1} - \delta, \tag{4.69}$$

$$w_t = (1-\alpha) A k_t^{\alpha}. \tag{4.70}$$

The pair of nonlinear adjustment equations for capital and consumption per efficiency unit of labor are obtained by adapting (4.64) and (4.66) for the Cobb-Douglas production function:

$$k_{t+1} = \frac{1}{(1+n)(1+g)} \left(Ak_t^{\alpha} + (1-\delta)k_t - c_t\right), \tag{4.71}$$

$$\frac{c_{t+1}}{c_t} = \left(\frac{1 + \alpha A k_{t+1}^{\alpha-1} - \delta}{(1+\rho)}\right)^{\frac{1}{\theta}} \frac{1}{(1+g)}. \tag{4.72}$$

The steady state values for the capital stock, output, consumption, real wages, and the real interest rate can be calculated by setting $c_t = c_{t+1} = c^*$ and $k_t = k_{t+1} = k^*$ in (4.71) and (4.72), and using (4.68), (4.69), and (4.70) to calculate output, the real interest rate, and the real wage:

$$k^* = \left(\frac{\alpha A}{(1+\rho)(1+g)^{\theta} - (1-\delta)}\right)^{\frac{1}{1-\alpha}}, \tag{4.73}$$

$$c^* = A\left(k^*\right)^{\alpha} - ((1+n)(1+g) - (1-\delta))\, k^*, \tag{4.74}$$

$$y^* = A(k^*)^{\alpha} = A\left(\frac{\alpha A}{(1+\rho)(1+g)^{\theta} - (1-\delta)}\right)^{\frac{\alpha}{1-\alpha}}, \tag{4.75}$$

$$r^* = \rho + \theta g, \tag{4.76}$$

$$w^* = (1-\alpha)y^* = (1-\alpha)A\left(\frac{\alpha A}{(1+\rho)(1+g)^{\theta} - (1-\delta)}\right)^{\frac{\alpha}{1-\alpha}}. \tag{4.77}$$

From (4.73) and (4.75), note that the rate of growth of population does not affect the steady state capital stock and steady state output and income. This is because the representative household internalizes the welfare of future generations in its optimal savings decision. Only steady state consumption is affected by the rate of growth of population, which is unlike the Solow model, where the savings rate is exogenous.

From (4.74) and (4.75), the steady state savings rate is equal to

$$s^* = \frac{y^* - c^*}{y^*} = \alpha \frac{(1+n)(1+g) - (1-\delta)}{(1+\rho)(1+g)^{\theta} - (1-\delta)}. \tag{4.78}$$

The optimal steady state savings rate will be a positive function of the rate of growth of population. It will also be smaller than the share of capital α, assuming that we have chosen the discount factor of the representative household to be smaller than unity:

$$\beta = \frac{(1+n)(1+g)^{1-\theta}}{(1+\rho)} < 1.$$

Simulating the system of the two nonlinear difference equations (4.71) and (4.72) numerically for specific values of the parameters, we can calculate the dynamic adjustment of capital and consumption toward the balanced growth path. The dynamic adjustment of the other variables can then be calculated from (4.68), (4.69), and (4.70).

4.5.3 Dynamic Simulations of the Model

The parameter values used in the simulations are as follows: $A=1$, $\alpha=0.333$, $\rho=0.02$, $\theta=1$, $n=0.01$, $g=0.02$, $\delta=0.03$. These values are consistent with the values that we used in the simulations of the Solow model and those used to calculate the speed of adjustment of both models.

As in the case of the Solow model, we consider two alternative scenarios: a permanent drop in the pure rate of time preference of the representative household ρ by 1% (from 0.02

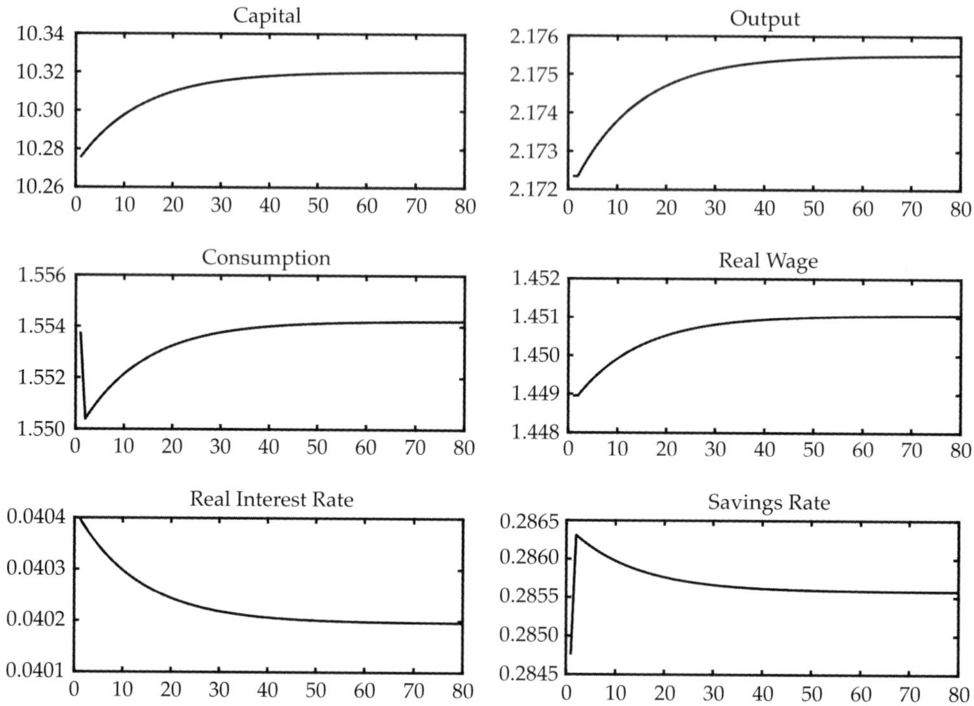

Figure 4.6
Impulse response functions of the calibrated Ramsey model for a 1% permanent drop in the pure rate of time preference.

to 0.019), and a permanent increase in total factor productivity A by 1% (from 1 to 1.01). The results of the simulations are presented in figures 4.6 and 4.7.

In the simulation of figure 4.6, the economy is on its original balanced growth path, and after period 1, the pure rate of time preference of the representative household ρ falls permanently and unexpectedly by 1%, from 0.02 to 0.019. This leads directly to a drop in consumption, a rise in the savings rate, a gradual accumulation of physical capital, a gradual increase in output and real wages, and a gradual decline in the real interest rate. The reason for rising real wages is the gradual increase of the marginal product of labor caused by the accumulation of capital. The reason for the declining real interest rate is that the marginal product of capital gradually declines because of the accumulation of capital. The economy gradually converges to a new balanced growth path. On the new balanced growth path, capital per efficiency unit of labor is higher by around 0.4%, output and real wages by 0.15%, consumption by 0.03% (due to the decline in the savings rate). The real interest rate has declined by 0.01 percentage points, the same as the increase in the pure rate of time preference. The steady state savings rate rises slightly, from 28.5% to 28.6%.

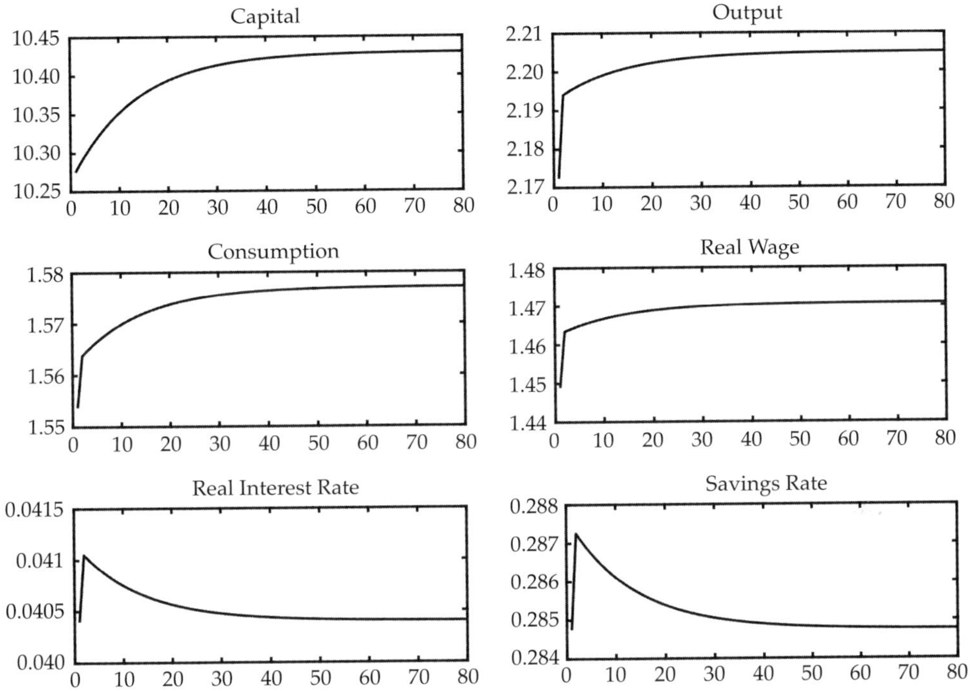

Figure 4.7
Impulse response functions of the calibrated Ramsey model for a 1% permanent increase in total factor productivity.

In the simulation of figure 4.7, the economy is initially on its original balanced growth path. After period 1, total factor productivity A rates rises permanently and unexpectedly by 1%, from 1 to 1.01. This increase leads to an immediate increase in production, consumption, savings, and the marginal product of both labor (the real wage) and capital (the real interest rate). The increase in savings causes a gradual accumulation of capital, which leads to a further gradual increase in production, consumption, and the real wage, but a gradual fall in real interest rates. The reason for the falling real interest rate is the gradual reduction of the marginal product of capital caused by the accumulation of capital. The economy gradually converges to a new balanced growth path. On this path, capital per efficiency unit of labor has increased by about 1.5%; output, consumption, and real wages are also higher by 1.5%; and the real interest rate has returned to its original equilibrium. The steady state real interest rate only depends on the pure rate of time preference of the representative household, the elasticity of intertemporal substitution, and the rate of technical progress. The increase in total factor productivity by 1% leads to an increase in real income by 1.5% (i.e., more than 1%) because the increase in total factor productivity causes a temporary rise in the savings rate and accumulation of capital, which in turn induces additional increases in real incomes and consumption. As can be seen from the steady state equation for output (4.75), the elasticity of steady state output with respect to total factor productivity is equal to $1/(1-\alpha) > 1$.

4.6 Conclusion

The Ramsey model of a representative household is a very important reference model not only for the theory of economic growth but also more generally for modern dynamic macroeconomics. As it is based on the assumption of intertemporal optimization by a representative household and firms operating in competitive markets, this model describes the socially optimal choice of savings and the socially optimal growth path.

This model is a dynamic general equilibrium model whose significance for dynamic macroeconomics is comparable to the significance of the competitive Arrow-Debreu general equilibrium model for microeconomics and general equilibrium theory.

In other respects, the Ramsey model has properties and weaknesses similar to the Solow model. It does not explain the determinants of the long-run growth rate, because it assumes exogenous technical progress. However, it determines the level of per capita output and income, consumption, real wages, and real interest rates as functions of preference and technological parameters and population growth. It also determines the adjustment process toward the balanced growth path as a function of those same parameters.

The Ramsey model is based on the assumption that all households are identical and as a result have identical savings behavior. An alternative class of models is based on the assumption that there are overlapping generations of households. As young households enter the economy and elderly households pass away, there is a succession of generations. This succession means that at any point in time, the economy is populated by households that belong to different generations. The savings behavior of households belonging to different generations varies, if current generations do not internalize the welfare of future generations, so these models do not necessarily imply the homogeneity or economic efficiency that characterizes the basic representative household model. We investigate the properties of such overlapping generations models in the next chapter.

5

Overlapping Generations Models of Growth

The representative household model is based on the assumption that all households are identical and that they internalize the welfare of future generations. An alternative class of models allows for households to differ and for the absence of such intergenerational links. As young households are being born and old households die, there is a succession of overlapping generations. At any given time, households represent different generations. The savings behavior across generations generally differs, as households belonging to different generations have differences in accumulated wealth. Thus, such models do not necessarily imply the homogeneity or economic efficiency that characterizes the basic representative household model.

The standard model in this category is the overlapping generations (OLG) model of Diamond [1965]. This model, which is a generalization of the two-period Fisherian model, is analyzed in discrete time (i.e., we assume that time is divided into discrete time periods rather than being a continuous variable). In each time period, two types of households coexist. The young, who are in the first period of their lives, and the old, who are in the second and last period of their lives. Young households supply labor but own no capital. Thus, they only earn labor income. Old households are not working and consume the income from the capital they accumulated during their first period of life, as well as their capital stock itself, because they are in the last period of life and are not concerned with the welfare of future generations. In the following period, the old households have passed away, young households have become old, and a new generation of young households has entered the economy.

In the Diamond OLG model, no generation of households internalizes the welfare of future generations. Thus, the competitive equilibrium is not socially optimal.[1]

1. The model of two overlapping generations of Diamond [1965] is based on the two-period model of Fisher [1930] and bears many similarities to an earlier model put forward by Allais [1947]. It is also closely related to a model of three overlapping generations, first presented and analyzed by Samuelson [1958], to explain the demand for money as a store of value. OLG models are also known as Samuelson-Diamond models, because the important contribution of Allais was in French and was initially ignored. See Malinvaud [1987]. We will analyze the Diamond growth model in this chapter, a simplified version of the Samuelson OLG monetary model in chapter 12, where

The production technology and the structure of markets is similar to that assumed in the Solow and Ramsey models. There are many competitive firms, the technology of production is described by a neoclassical production function, capital and labor markets are competitive, and capital and labor are paid their marginal product.

The Diamond model is analyzed in discrete time, but a more recent category of OLG models, due to Blanchard [1985] and Weil [1989], is usually analyzed in continuous time. In this more recent class of OLG models, new households are being born continuously. All households, irrespective of their time of birth, have an infinite time horizon. In the original Blanchard [1985] version of these models, at every instant there is also a constant probability of death, which is independent of the age of households. In the model of Weil, the probability of death is zero.

What emerges is that the differences of these OLG models from a representative household model do not depend on the assumption of a positive probability of death but on the assumption that current generations do not internalize the welfare of future generations. Thus, generations that have been born at different times in the past, and thus hold different amounts of accumulated assets, have differences in their savings behavior.

Savings behavior in OLG models is not socially optimal, as in the representative household model. Moreover, in economies without a representative household, comparing utility across different generations of households is largely arbitrary. Furthermore, in OLG models, it is theoretically possible that the competitive equilibrium is not even Pareto efficient, as the possibility of dynamic inefficiency cannot be ruled out a priori. In any case, in models of overlapping generations, policy interventions that can improve social efficiency can be justified, because the competitive equilibrium is not necessarily optimal.[2]

5.1 The Diamond Model

In the Diamond [1965] model, each household lives for only two periods. New households are being born in each period. Thus, in each period, the model assumes the coexistence of two overlapping generations of households: the young, who are in their first period of life, and the old, who are in the second period of life. The young supply labor and earn labor income, whereas the old do not participate in the labor market and live off their savings.[3]

---

we analyze general equilibrium models with money, and a more general version of the Samuelson OLG monetary model in chapter 22, when we discuss multiple equilibria and sunspots. Barro [1974] has extended the Diamond model to a model where households are also concerned about the welfare of their offspring, converting it effectively to a representative household model.

2. See Weil [2008] for a relatively recent survey of OLG models and their policy implications.

3. The time period in the Diamond [1965] model, as in the Fisher [1930] model for that matter, can be thought of as being equal to one half of the life expectancy of an adult (i.e., about 30 years).

5.1.1 Definitions

The definitions of the variables are analogous to those we have used so far. As with the Solow and Ramsey models, we focus on the following set of endogenous variables: Y, aggregate output (or y, output per efficiency unit of labor); K, aggregate (physical) capital stock (or k, capital per efficiency unit of labor); C, aggregate consumption (or c, consumption per efficiency unit of labor); r, real interest rate; and $\hat{w}$ real wage per worker (or w, real wage per efficiency unit of labor).

The exogenous variables and exogenous parameters in the model are defined as follows: t, time (a discrete exogenous variable); L, population of the young generation (an exogenous variable that depends on time); h, efficiency of labor (an exogenous variable that depends on time); n, rate of growth of population (exogenous parameter); g, rate of technical progress (exogenous parameter); δ, rate of depreciation of capital (exogenous parameter); ρ, pure rate of time preference of households (exogenous parameter); and θ, inverse of the elasticity of intertemporal substitution.

5.1.2 The Production Function

The technology of production is described by a neoclassical production function, analogous to the one we assumed in the Solow and Ramsey models. The production function has all the properties of the neoclassical production function assumed in the Solow model. The marginal product of all inputs is positive but decreasing, there are constant returns to scale, and the Inada conditions are satisfied (see chapters 3 and 4):

$$Y_t = AF(K_t, h_t L_t). \tag{5.1}$$

Because of the assumption of constant returns to scale, the production function can be rewritten as

$$y_t = Af(k_t), \tag{5.2}$$

where $y = Y/hL$ is output per efficiency unit of labor, $k = K/hL$ is capital per efficiency unit of labor, and $f(k) = F(k, 1)$ is the production function per efficiency unit of labor.

5.1.3 The Intertemporal Utility Function of Households

In period t, L_t households are being born, and population grows at an exogenous rate n:

$$L_t = (1+n)L_{t-1}. \tag{5.3}$$

The young (i.e., those in the first period of life) work, while the old (those in the second period of life) do not. Thus, each household supplies a unit of labor when young and allocates labor income between consumption of the first period and savings. In the second period of life, old households consume their savings plus the interest on their savings. Thus, each generation chooses savings to solve a Fisherian problem.

The utility function of a household born in period t is defined by

$$U_t = \frac{c_{1t}^{1-\theta}}{1-\theta} + \frac{1}{1+\rho}\frac{c_{2t+1}^{1-\theta}}{1-\theta}, \tag{5.4}$$

where $0 < \theta < 1$, $\rho > -1$, and c_{1t}, c_{2t+1} denote consumption in the first and second period of life, respectively. Equation (5.4) is the constant elasticity of intertemporal substitution utility function, known to us from chapter 2. Here, θ is the coefficient of constant relative risk aversion, and $1/\theta$ is the constant elasticity of intertemporal substitution of consumption.

5.1.4 Markets and the Behavior of Households

Production takes place by many competitive firms, each with a production function like (5.1). Output, capital, and labor markets are competitive. Capital and labor are paid their marginal products, and because of constant returns to scale, firms make zero profits. The real interest rate and the real wage are determined by

$$r_t = Af'(k_t) - \delta, \tag{5.5}$$

$$w_t = Af(k_t) - k_t Af'(k_t), \tag{5.6}$$

where $Af'(k_t)$ is the marginal product of capital.

Each young household allocates its labor income $w_t h_t$ between consumption and savings. As a result, the capital stock of period $t+1$ is equal to the aggregate savings of period t:

$$K_{t+1} = L_t(w_t h_t - c_{1t}). \tag{5.7}$$

This capital stock is combined in production with the labor supplied by the generation born in period $t+1$, and the economy continues from period to period.

In the second period of life, the household born in period t consumes all its interest income plus the savings it has accumulated in the first period of life. Thus, consumption in the second period of life of a household born in period t is given by

$$c_{2t+1} = (1 + r_{t+1})(w_t h_t - c_{1t}). \tag{5.8}$$

Maximizing (5.4) under the budget constraint (5.8) and rearranging the first-order conditions, we get the following expression for the ratio of consumption in the two periods:

$$\frac{c_{2t+1}}{c_{1t}} = \left(\frac{1 + r_{t+1}}{1+\rho}\right)^{1/\theta}, \tag{5.9}$$

which is the first-order condition of the Fisher model of chapter 2 and is analogous to the Euler equation for consumption in the Ramsey model analyzed in chapter 4. Consumption in the second period of life is higher or lower than consumption in the first period of life, depending on whether the real interest rate exceeds or falls short of the pure rate of time preference. The elasticity of intertemporal substitution of consumption determines the elasticity of the effect.

Using (5.8) and (5.9) to solve for c_{1t}, we get

$$c_{1t} = \frac{(1+\rho)^{1/\theta}}{(1+\rho)^{1/\theta} + (1+r_{t+1})^{(1-\theta)/\theta}} w_t h_t. \tag{5.10}$$

Young households consume a share of their labor income that depends on their preferences and the real interest rate. We can rewrite (5.9) as

$$c_{1t} = (1 - s\,(r_{t+1}))\, w_t h_t,$$

where s is the savings rate of young households, defined as

$$s(r) = \frac{(1+r)^{(1-\theta)/\theta}}{(1+\rho)^{1/\theta} + (1+r)^{(1-\theta)/\theta}}. \tag{5.11}$$

Equation (5.11) suggests that the savings rate is a positive function of the real interest rate r only if θ is lower than unity (i.e., if the elasticity of intertemporal substitution of consumption $1/\theta$ is higher than unity). Only in this case does the substitution effect dominate the negative income effect. If θ is greater than unity, the savings rate is a negative function of r, as the income effect dominates. In the special case that θ is equal to one (i.e., logarithmic preferences), the savings rate is independent of the real interest rate and is equal to $1/(2+\rho)$.[4]

We can now aggregate the savings behavior of the two overlapping generations and determine capital accumulation and the dynamic adjustment of this economy.

5.1.5 Capital Accumulation and the Dynamic Adjustment of the Economy

The aggregate capital stock in each period is equal to the savings of young households of the previous period, because the old households of the previous period consumed all their capital and the young households of the current period own no capital. Thus, we have

$$K_{t+1} = s(r_{t+1}) L_t w_t h_t. \tag{5.12}$$

Expressing (5.12) in efficiency units of labor, dividing by $h_{t+1}L_{t+1}$, we get

$$k_{t+1} = \frac{1}{(1+n)(1+g)} s(r_{t+1}) w_t. \tag{5.13}$$

4. These conditions are the same as the conditions discussed in the Fisher and Ramsey models in chapters 2 and 4.

Substituting for r and w from (5.5) and (5.6) yields

$$k_{t+1} = \frac{1}{(1+n)(1+g)} s(Af'(k_{t+1}) - \delta) \left(f(k_t) - k_t f'(k_t) \right). \tag{5.14}$$

This equation determines the dynamic behavior of capital per efficiency unit of labor. Because output, the real interest rate, real wages, and savings only depend on capital per efficiency unit of labor, (5.14) determines the dynamic evolution of all other endogenous variables.

As with previous models, the first question that arises is whether a steady state equilibrium point k^* exists, and, if it does, whether the economy converges to this steady state. Equation (5.14) is a nonlinear first-order difference equation in the capital stock per efficiency unit of labor. Because of nonlinearity, there is the possibility of *multiple equilibria*. Figure 5.1 highlights this possibility for a general form of the production function.

The 45° line is the locus of equilibrium points, for which,

$$k_{t+1} = k_t.$$

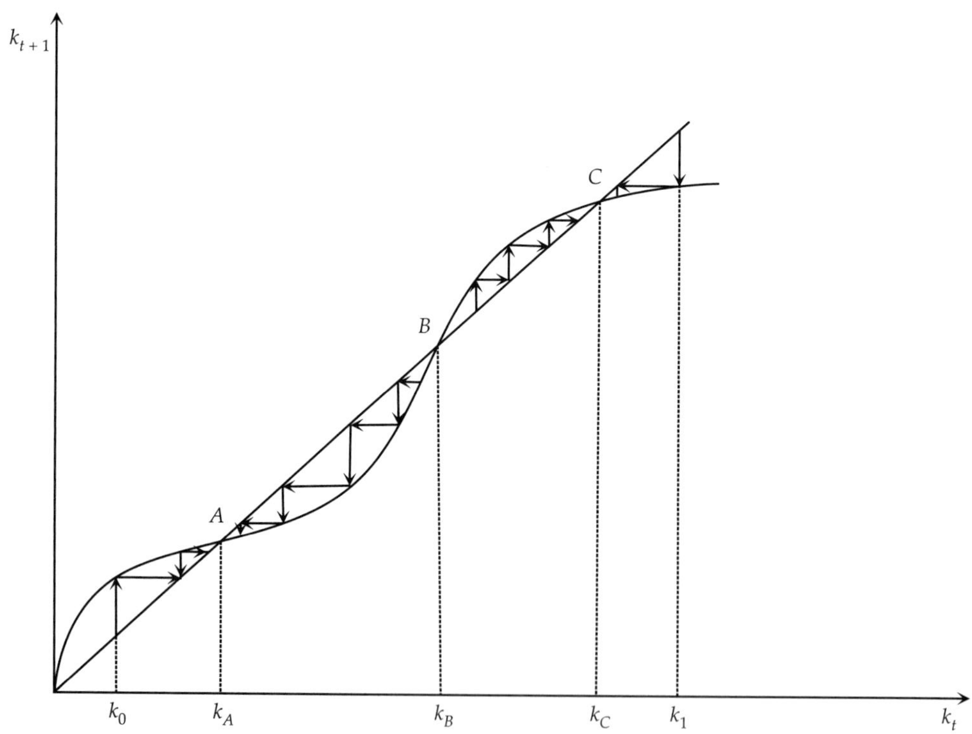

Figure 5.1
Multiple equilibria in the Diamond model.

The nonlinear curve is the geometric version of a possible general form of (5.14). As shown in figure 5.1, there are at least three possible equilibria for this general form of the curve: A, B, and C. Of these, A and C are locally stable, and B is unstable. Which equilibrium is reached by the economy depends on initial conditions.

If the initial capital per efficiency unit of labor is equal to k_0, then the economy will converge to equilibrium A. If the initial capital per efficiency unit of labor is higher than B, then the economy will converge to C. Thus, at least two potential stable equilibria exist, depending on initial conditions. There is no guarantee that the economy will converge to a unique balanced growth path as in the Solow and Ramsey models.

Consequently, the Diamond model differs from the models examined so far, in that it can result in *multiple balanced growth paths* in its general form. There is no unique balanced growth path toward which an economy will converge regardless of initial conditions. Thus, which equilibrium will prevail can depend on initial conditions.

As illustrated in figure 5.1, an economy with a low initial capital stock will converge to a balanced growth path like A, which is characterized by low capital and output per efficiency unit of labor. Per capita income in the balanced growth path will therefore be lower than in an economy that has a high initial capital stock (greater than that corresponding to point B) and converges to a balanced growth path like C, which is characterized by a higher capital stock and output per efficiency unit of labor.[5]

5.1.6 A Simplified Diamond Model with Logarithmic Preferences and Cobb-Douglas Technology

The Diamond model can be simplified significantly if one assumes logarithmic preferences ($\theta = 1$) and a Cobb-Douglas production function ($Af(k) = Ak^{\alpha}$). Then (5.6) and (5.12) simplify to

$$w_t = (1-\alpha)Ay_t^{\alpha},$$

$$s(r) = \frac{1}{2+\rho}.$$

In this case, the real wage is a constant share of output, and the savings rate is independent of the real interest rate. Substituting in (5.13), the adjustment equation for capital per efficiency unit of labor takes the form

$$k_{t+1} = \frac{1}{(1+n)(1+g)}\frac{1}{2+\rho}(1-\alpha)Ak_t^{\alpha}. \tag{5.15}$$

5. Moreover, the equilibrium that eventually prevails may, under some conditions, depend on self-fulfilling expectations, or sunspots, or the economy may be characterized by endogenous cyclical fluctuations, even though there are no exogenous random shocks. Balanced growth is therefore not guaranteed, and the balanced growth path, if it exists, may depend on initial conditions. We shall postpone our discussion of self-fulfilling expectations, sunspots, and endogenous cycles to chapter 22. See Azariadis [1993] for an extensive textbook treatment of these issues.

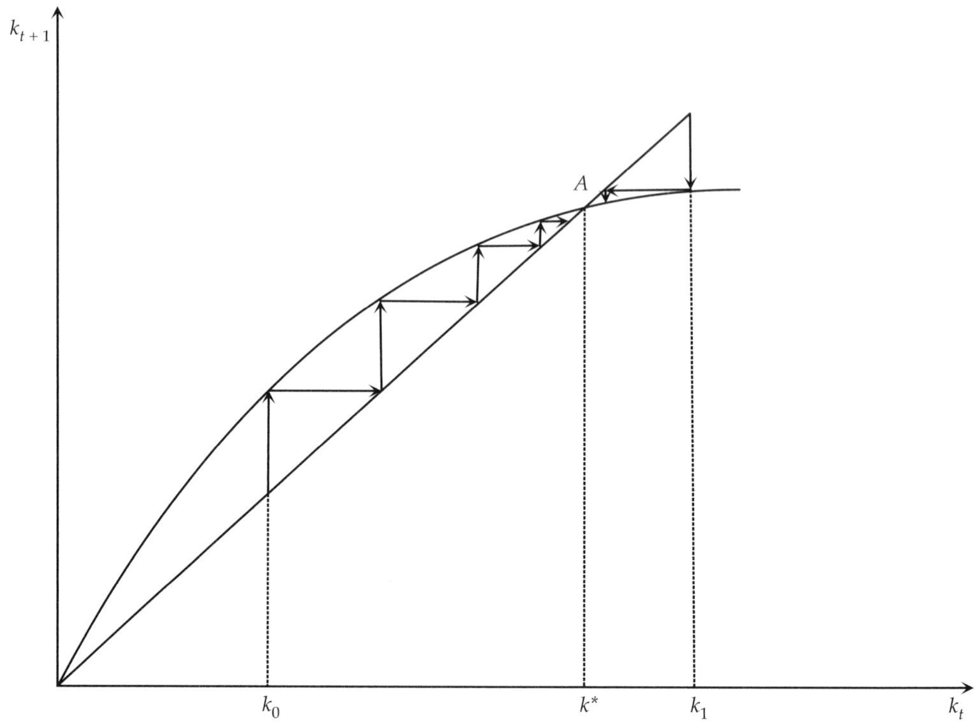

Figure 5.2
Unique balanced growth path in the simplified Diamond model.

One can show, as in figure 5.2, that in this case, a unique balanced growth path exists, because of the constant savings rate and the properties of the Cobb-Douglas production function. The Diamond economy converges to this unique balanced growth path k^* independently of the initial conditions, as long as the initial capital stock is positive.

The properties of this simplified Diamond model are analogous to those of the Solow and Ramsey models. On the unique balanced growth path, the savings rate is constant. Output, consumption, and the real wage per worker grow at a rate g, while the capital output ratio and the real interest rate are constant.

Figure 5.3 examines the impact of a previously unanticipated permanent increase in the pure rate of time preference in the simplified Diamond model. This has the effect of reducing the savings of the young generation, which leads to a lower level of capital in the following period compared with the initial equilibrium level k^*. This decline sets in motion a process of capital decumulation until the economy converges to the new equilibrium k^{**}, in which the capital stock per efficiency unit of labor is lower. Consequently, as in the Ramsey model, an increase in the pure rate of time preference in the simplified Diamond model eventually leads to an equilibrium with a lower capital stock and real output per efficiency unit of labor.

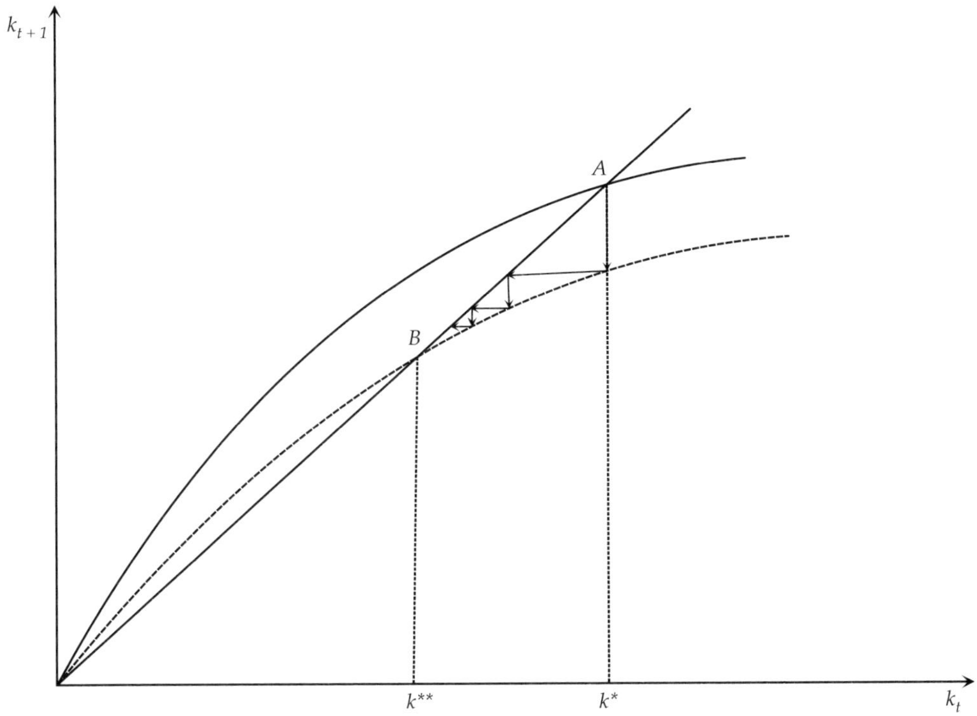

Figure 5.3
Effects of a permanent rise in the pure rate of time preference.

A decrease in the pure rate of time preference has the opposite effects. In the new balanced growth path, both consumption and capital per efficiency unit of labor will be higher. Consumption will initially fall; the economy will begin accumulating additional capital; and on the new balanced growth path, the economy will end up with a higher capital stock and real output and income per efficiency unit of labor.

As in the representative household model, the pure rate of time preference is a key determinant of the savings rate. The higher it is, the smaller will be the savings of the young as well as the overall savings rate. Recall that in this model, it is only the young that save, as the old have negative savings, because they consume both their current income and their capital.

An increase in the population growth rate n or an increase in the rate of exogenous technical progress g has similar effects to an increase in the pure rate of time preference, leading to a lower capital stock and real output and income per efficiency unit of labor. The analysis would be similar to the analysis in figure 5.3.

Note that, with regard to the rate of growth of population, the Diamond OLG model has different predictions than the Ramsey representative household model. In the Diamond

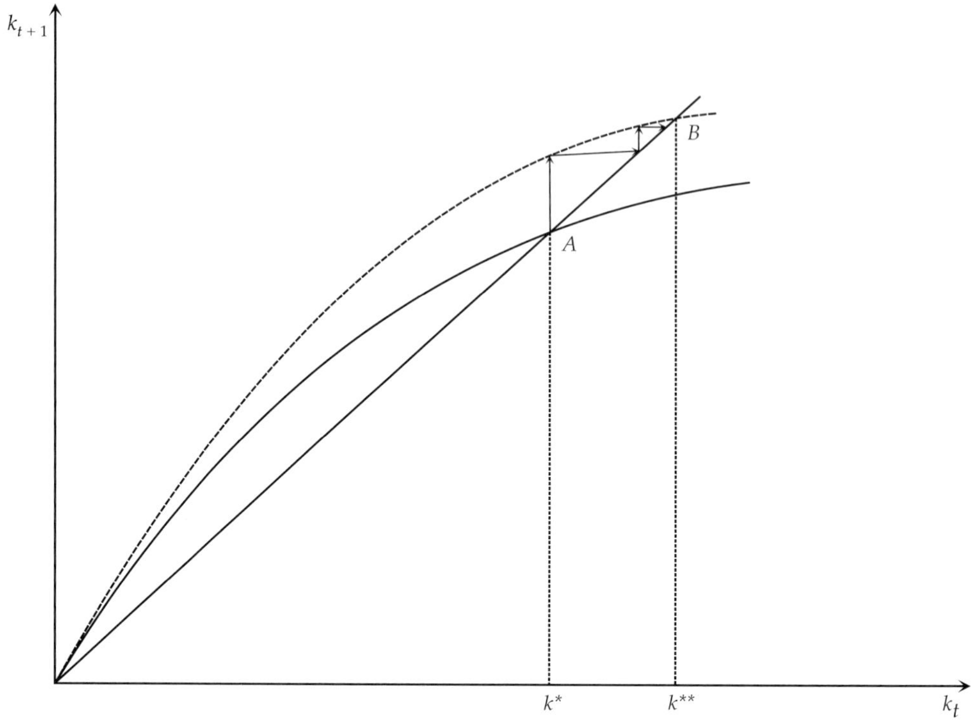

Figure 5.4
Effects of a permanent rise in total factor productivity.

model, an increase in the rate of population growth, which leads to an increase in steady state investment, is not matched by a equal increase in savings through an adjustment of the savings rate. This is because current generations do not internalize the welfare of future generations, as in the case with the representative household model. Hence, an increase in the rate of population growth leads to a decline in the capital stock, so that steady state investment adjusts to savings. This is a major difference between representative household and OLG models and is something that we shall also encounter in chapter 6 and 7, when we discuss the effects of government debt or monetary policy in growth models.

Figure 5.4 analyzes the impact of a previously unanticipated permanent rise in total factor productivity A. This causes an immediate increase in income and savings for a given capital stock per efficiency unit of labor. The rise in aggregate savings leads to capital accumulation, until the capital stock approaches its new higher steady state value at k^{**}. Consequently, after a permanent increase in total factor productivity, the economy converges to a new balanced growth path, with higher steady state capital, output, and income per efficiency unit of labor.

5.1.7 The Speed of Adjustment in the Simplified Diamond Model

As for the Solow and Ramsey models, it is worth exploring the quantitative as well as the qualitative properties of the simplified Diamond model. From (5.15), the economy is on the balanced growth path k^* when

$$k^* = \frac{1}{(1+n)(1+g)} \frac{1}{2+\rho}(1-\alpha)A(k^*)^\alpha.$$

Solving for the steady state capital per efficiency unit of labor k^*, we get

$$k^* = \left(\frac{(1-\alpha)A}{(1+n)(1+g)(2+\rho)} \right)^{1/(1-\alpha)}. \tag{5.16}$$

From the production function, steady state output per efficiency unit of labor y^* is then equal to

$$y^* = A(k^*)^\alpha = A^{1/(1-\alpha)} \left(\frac{(1-\alpha)}{(1+n)(1+g)(2+\rho)} \right)^{\alpha/(1-\alpha)}. \tag{5.17}$$

Equation (5.17) determines output per efficiency unit of labor on the balanced growth path and its dependence on technological and population growth parameters (such as A, α, g, and n), as well as on parameters of the preferences of households (such as ρ). From estimates of the values of the various parameters, we can get quantitative estimates for the long-term effects of various changes in the parameters on steady state output. Note that because in this model the length of the time period equals half the life expectancy of an adult, the choice of parameters should take account of this fact. For example, n must be calculated not as the annual rate of population increase but as the population growth rate over 30 years. Similar choices have to be made for other parameters, such as g and ρ.

To find the speed of adjustment toward the balanced growth path, we take a linear approximation of (5.15) around the steady state capital stock, $k = k^*$. This is given by

$$k_{t+1} = k^* + \left(\frac{dk_{t+1}}{dk_t} \right)_{k_t = k^*} (k_t - k^*). \tag{5.18}$$

From (5.15) and (5.17) we have that

$$\left(\frac{dk_{t+1}}{dk_t} \right)_{k_t = k*} = \alpha \frac{(1-\alpha)A}{(1+n)(1+g)(2+\rho)} (k*)^{\alpha-1} = \alpha. \tag{5.19}$$

The speed of adjustment therefore depends on only one parameter, the exponent (share) of capital in the Cobb-Douglas production function. If α equals 1/3, then in each period, the capital stock per efficiency unit of labor moves 2/3 of the distance that separates it from the value corresponding to the balanced growth path. If the period is 30 years, this amounts to about 2% per year.

Recall that in this model, under the assumption of logarithmic preferences, the savings rate is constant only for the young generation. The negative savings of the old generation are not a constant percentage of its income but instead increase in absolute terms as the capital stock per efficiency unit of labor increases. This is because of diminishing returns to capital accumulation that reduce the old generation's interest income. As a result, in the simplified Diamond model, total savings as a percentage of total income (the aggregate savings rate) are a negative function of capital per efficiency unit of labor k. The same applies to the representative household model with a Cobb-Douglas production function and logarithmic preferences.

5.1.8 Welfare Implications of the Diamond Model and the Possibility of Dynamic Inefficiency

The greatest difference between the representative household model and the OLG model is perhaps related to its welfare implications and the efficiency of the equilibrium. We saw that in the Ramsey model, competitive equilibrium leads to the maximization of welfare of the representative household. In OLG models, a representative household does not exist, and therefore it is not clear how we would evaluate the welfare implications of the competitive equilibrium. If we define social welfare as a weighted average of the welfare of the different generations, there is no reason to expect that the competitive equilibrium would lead to the maximization of that weighted average.

The minimum efficiency criterion we have in economics is Pareto efficiency, which states that it is impossible to make someone better off without making somebody else worse off. But even the simplified Diamond model does not necessarily satisfy this criterion. Theoretically, the capital stock on the balanced growth path can exceed that which satisfies Pareto efficiency and corresponds to the golden rule. Thus, the Diamond model may even be characterized by *dynamic inefficiency*. Therefore, a social planner could, if the economy ends up with more capital than the golden rule, theoretically increase the level of consumption (and therefore the level of welfare of all generations) by reducing savings and the aggregate capital stock.

To see how this possibility can arise, we focus on the simplified Diamond model with logarithmic preferences and a Cobb-Douglas production function.

The steady state capital stock is given by (5.16). Its marginal product is given by

$$Af'(k^*) = \alpha A(k^*)^{\alpha-1} = \frac{\alpha}{1-\alpha}(1+n)(1+g)(2+\rho). \tag{5.20}$$

On the balanced growth path, the capital stock that satisfies the golden rule has a marginal product equal to the growth rate. It must satisfy

$$Af'(k_{GR}) = aA(k_{GR})^{\alpha-1} = (1+n)(1+g) - 1, \tag{5.21}$$

where GR stands for the golden rule value.

For a sufficiently small α, the marginal product of the steady state capital stock, as given by (5.20), could be smaller than the marginal product corresponding to the golden rule, which is given by (5.21). This would mean that the steady state capital stock is higher than the golden rule capital stock. As a result, a social planner could increase the current consumption and welfare of all generations by reducing savings and the steady state capital stock to the level corresponding to the golden rule. As we have already discussed in the case of the Solow model, a steady state in which the marginal product of capital is lower than the long-term growth rate of the economy results in dynamic inefficiency.

How likely is dynamic inefficiency in the case of the simplified Diamond model? The answer is largely an empirical matter. Staying in the confines of the model, let us assume that the share of capital in total income α is equal to 1/3, the annual population growth rate n is 1%, the annual rate of technical progress g is 2%, and that the annual pure rate of time preference ρ is 2%. These are the empirical assumptions that we have made so far. Also assume that the time period in the Diamond model is equal to 30 years. Thus, over 30 years, $n = 0.348$, $g = 0.811$, and $\rho = 0.811$.

Under these assumptions, the marginal product of steady state capital from (5.20) is equal to 4.44. From (5.21), the marginal product of the capital stock that corresponds to the golden rule is equal to 1.44. Thus, based on these empirical estimates of the parameters, the possibility of dynamic inefficiency does not arise in the simplified Diamond model. With the assumptions about n, g, and ρ that we have made, the share of capital should be lower than 1/6 instead of 1/3 for the possibility of dynamic inefficiency to arise.

In any case, when Abel et al. [1989] explored the possibility of dynamic inefficiency empirically for the US economy and six other developed economies, they concluded that the marginal product of capital comfortably exceeds the long-run growth rate, a finding that rules out the possibility of dynamic inefficiency for the developed economies.

On the basis of these observations and the available empirical evidence, the possibility of dynamic inefficiency, although theoretically interesting, does not seem likely. Besides, it would mean that there is excess saving, which is in contrast with other empirical features of developed market economies, such as current account deficits in many of them.

5.1.9 Dynamic Simulations of a Calibrated Diamond Model

To further investigate the process of dynamic adjustment characterizing the simplified Diamond model, we can simulate, for specific calibrated values of the parameters of the model, the process of dynamic adjustment from one balanced growth path to another, when there is an exogenous permanent change in specific parameters. As for the Ramsey model, let us shall concentrate on changes in the pure rate of time preference and total factor productivity.

But we shall also report on the effects of a rise in the rate of growth of population, which only affects per capita consumption and not per capita output or capital in the Ramsey model.

In the simulation, it is assumed that the production function has the usual Cobb-Douglas form, $Af(k) = Ak^{\alpha}$, and that the intertemporal elasticity of substitution in consumption is equal to unity. The evolution of total private consumption can be derived from the consumption functions of young and old households. The evolution of the real interest rate and real wages per efficiency unit of labor can be derived from the usual marginal productivity conditions (5.5) and (5.6) for a Cobb-Douglas production function.

The model was simulated for the following parameter values: $A = 1$, $\alpha = 1/3$, $\theta = 1$, $\rho = 0.811$, $n = 0.348$, $g = 0.811$, $\delta = 1.427$. Unlike the previous models, which assumed that the time period is a calendar year, here the time period is 30 years, the half-life of a generation. An annual rate of 1% is converted into a 30-year rate of 34.8%, an annual rate of 2% is converted into a 30-year rate of 81.1%, and an annual rate of 3% is converted into a 30-year rate of 142.7%.

We consider two alternative scenarios: a permanent increase in the pure rate of time preference of households ρ by 1% and a permanent increase in total factor productivity A by 1%. The results of the simulations are presented in figures 5.5 and 5.6.

In figure 5.5, the economy is on its original balanced growth path, and after period 1, the pure rate of time preference of the young generation ρ rises by 1%, from 0.811 to 0.819, where it remains thereafter. This increase leads directly to an increase in consumption of the young, a decline in the savings rate, a gradual decumulation of capital, a gradual decline in output and real wages, and a gradual increase in the real interest rate. The reason for the decline in real wages is the gradual reduction of the marginal product of labor; the reason for the increasing real interest rate is the gradual increase in the marginal product of capital. Both trends are caused by the declining capital stock. The economy gradually converges to a new balanced growth path. On this new path, capital per efficiency unit of labor is lower by about 0.9% compared to the original path, output and real wages are lower by 0.3%, consumption is lower by 0.3%, and the real interest rate has increased by 1.1%. The steady state savings rate for the economy as a whole, which is endogenous in this model, has declined slightly, from 13.31% to 13.30%. This drop is due to the slight fall in the savings rate of the young. Recall that the savings rate of the young, with logarithmic preferences, is independent of the real interest rate and only depends on the pure rate of time preference, as it is equal to $1/(2 + \rho)$.

A similar simulation has also been conducted, in which the rate of population growth n rises by 1% (from 0.348 to 0.351). The dynamic path is similar to the simulation for the pure rate of time preference, but the steady state effects are smaller. Per capita output and real wages fall by only 0.1%, about one-third of the effects of a similar rise in the pure rate of time preference. Per capita capital falls by 0.4% and per capita consumption by 0.2%. The effects are quantitatively smaller, because there is no additional negative effect through

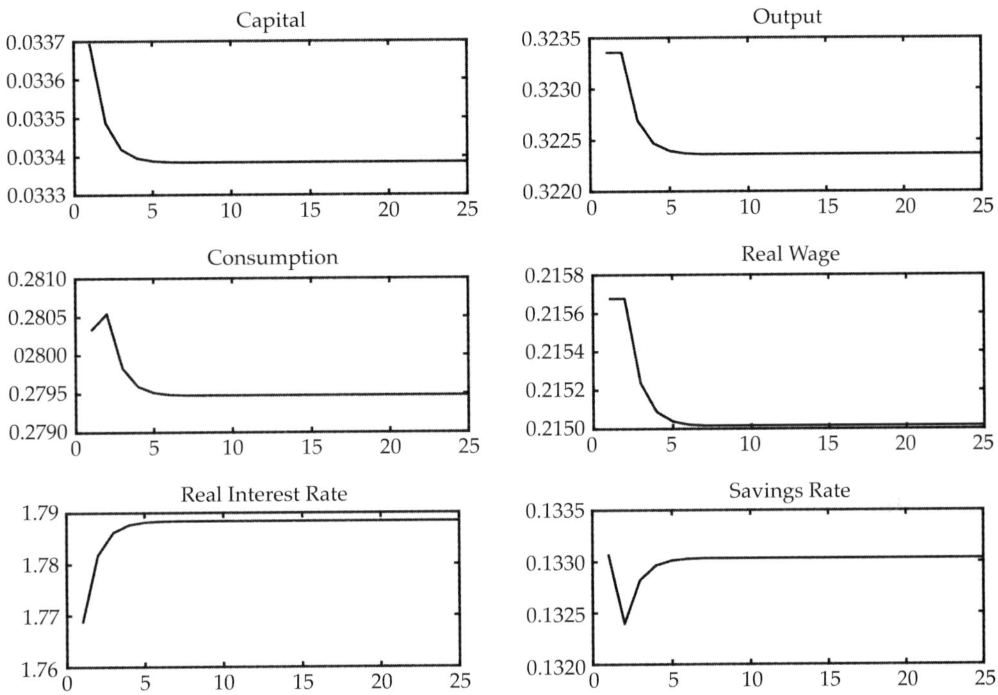

Figure 5.5
Impulse response functions of the Diamond model for a permanent rise in the pure rate of time preference of 1%.

the decline in the savings rate of the young generation, which occurs for the case with the decline in the pure rate of time preference.

In the simulation shown in figure 5.6, the economy is on its original balanced growth path, and after period 1, total factor productivity A rises permanently by 1%, from 1 to 1.01. This increase leads immediately to an increase in production, consumption, savings, and the marginal product of both labor (real wage) and capital (real interest rate). The increase in savings causes a gradual accumulation of capital, which leads to a further gradual increase in production, consumption, and the real wage, and a gradual decline in the real interest rate. The reason for the declining real interest rate is the gradual reduction of the marginal product of capital caused by the accumulation of capital. The economy gradually converges to a new balanced growth path. On this new path, capital per efficiency unit of labor is increased by about 1.5%; output, consumption, and real wages have also increased by 1.5%; whereas the real interest rate has returned to very near its original equilibrium. An increase in productivity by 1% leads to an increase in real output by 1.5% (i.e., more than 1%) because higher total productivity causes a temporary increase in the savings rate and capital accumulation,

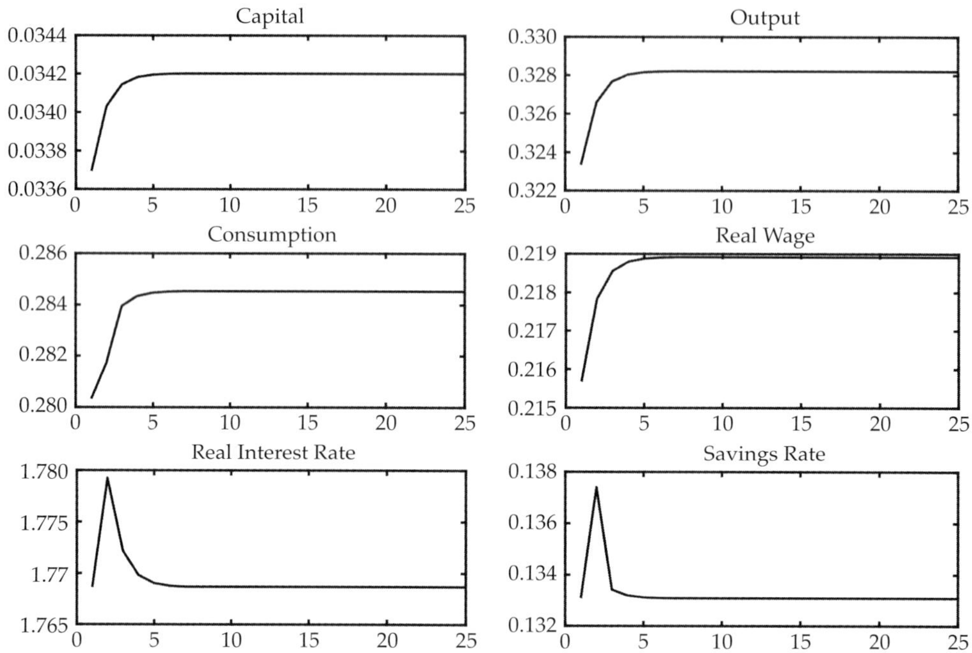

Figure 5.6
Impulse response functions of the Diamond model, for a permanent rise in total factor productivity of 1%.

which causes secondary increases in the capital stock, real output, consumption, and real wages.

As we can see from these simulations, the dynamic behavior of the simplified Diamond OLG model is qualitatively similar to that of the Ramsey model of a representative household. Although the models differ in the specific assumptions they make about the determination of aggregate savings, they result in qualitatively similar properties regarding the process of adjustment toward the balanced growth path. In addition, despite the prediction that the savings rate is not constant along the adjustment path, as assumed in the Solow model, in all other respects, the predictions of the Diamond and Ramsey models about the adjustment path are very similar to the predictions of the Solow model.

However, the Diamond model has one important difference from the representative household model. The rate of population growth affects the steady state per capita output and capital stock negatively, as in the Solow model with an exogenous savings rate. The reason is that current generations do not take into account the welfare of future generations, and thus they do not adjust their savings by enough to allow for a higher population growth.

5.2 The Blanchard-Weil Model

We now turn to an alternative OLG model, the model of Blanchard [1985] and Weil [1989], also known as the model of *perpetual youth*.[6]

In the Blanchard-Weil model, it is assumed that new households are being born continuously, with each household having an infinite time horizon. All generations of households supply labor and have the same efficiency of labor, regardless of their date of birth. Consequently, all households have the same labor productivity, present value of labor income, and (infinite) time horizon. For this reason, this model is often referred to as the model of perpetual youth. This model bears many similarities to the Ramsey representative household model, but it is an OLG model like the Diamond model, in that current generations do not internalize the welfare of future generations.[7]

In the original version of this model by Blanchard [1985], at any instant there is a constant probability of death, which is independent of the age of households. In the model of Weil [1989], the probability of death is zero (i.e., households not only have an infinite time horizon but discount the future only by using the pure rate of time preference and not the probability of death).

What emerges from the model of perpetual youth is that the main differences between the predictions of OLG models and representative household models result from differences in the age of different households and not the possibility of death.[8]

Technology and market structure in this model is similar to the previous models we have analyzed so far. We have competitive markets and a neoclassical production function with constant returns to scale.

5.2.1 Definitions

The definitions of the variables are analogous to those we have used so far. As with the Solow, Ramsey, and Diamond models, we shall focus on the following set of endogenous variables: Y, aggregate output (or y, output per efficiency unit of labor); K, aggregate (physical) capital stock (or k, capital per efficiency unit of labor); C aggregate consumption (or c, consumption

6. This model, augmented with a positive probability of death, was first presented by Blanchard [1985] and was based to some extent on the model of Yaari [1965].

7. There are variations of this model in which productivity and labor income is a negative function of the age of the household. The properties of these variants of the model are closer to some of the properties of the Diamond model, in the sense that the possibility of dynamic inefficiency may arise. See Blanchard and Fischer [1989].

8. In the perpetual youth model, accumulated savings depend on the date of birth of households. This causes differences in the savings behavior of households depending on their date of birth, because households of different generations have different accumulated stocks of nonhuman capital. This results in direct effects of the aggregate capital stock (and other assets, such as government bonds) on the behavior of aggregate consumption. Buiter [1988] has an extensive discussion of this point.

per efficiency unit of labor); r real interest rate; and $\hat{w}$, real wage per worker (or w, real wage per efficiency unit of labor).

The exogenous variables and exogenous parameters in the model are defined as follows: t, time (a continuous exogenous variable); L, total population and employment (an exogenous variable that depends on time); h, efficiency of labor (an exogenous variable that depends on time); n, rate of growth of population (exogenous parameter); g, rate of technical progress (exogenous parameter); δ, rate of depreciation of capital (exogenous parameter); and ρ, pure rate of time preference of households (exogenous parameter).

With regard to L and h, we also assume that

$$\lim_{t\to-\infty}(L(t))=1,\ \lim_{t\to-\infty}(h(t))=1.$$

5.2.2 The Production Function

Production takes place on the basis of technological possibilities described by a neoclassical production function, similar to the one assumed in the Solow, Ramsey, and Diamond models:

$$Y(t)=AF(K(t),h(t)L(t)). \tag{5.22}$$

The production function is characterized by constant returns to scale, so it can be written as

$$y(t)=Af(k(t)), \tag{5.23}$$

where $y=Y/hL$, output per efficiency unit of labor; $k=K/hL$, capital stock per efficiency unit of labor; and $f(k)=F(k,1)$, production function per efficiency unit of labor.

5.2.3 The Intertemporal Utility Function of Households and Household Consumption

Following Weil [1989], let us assume that households have an infinite time horizon (i.e., that they are dynasties) but differ in their birth dates. Each instant, nL new households are born. New households have no connection with old households whatsoever. The typical household born at time j chooses the path of its current and future consumption to maximize the intertemporal utility function:

$$U_j=\int_{t=j}^{\infty}e^{-\rho t}u\left(c(j,t)\right)dt, \tag{5.24}$$

where $c(j,t)$ is consumption of household j at instant t, u is the instantaneous concave utility function, and ρ is the pure rate of time preference.

Following Blanchard [1985] and Weil [1989], we shall assume that the instantaneous utility function is logarithmic. This is equivalent to assuming a unitary elasticity of intertemporal substitution of consumption:

$$u\left(c(j,t)\right)=\ln c(j,t). \tag{5.25}$$

All households have a constant number of members (assumed to be equal to one), with each supplying one unit of labor. All households, irrespective of their date of birth, can borrow and lend freely at the market-determined real interest rate r.

Moreover, we assume that there exist a large number of competitive firms, each with a production function similar to (5.22). Markets are competitive, and therefore the real interest rate and the real wage are defined by the marginal productivity conditions

$$r(t) = Af'(k(t)) - \delta, \tag{5.26}$$

$$w(t) = Af(k(t)) - k(t)Af'(k(t)), \tag{5.27}$$

where $f'(k)$ is the marginal product of capital. Therefore, household j maximizes (5.24) under the constraint

$$\dot{k}(j,t) = r(t)k(j,t) + w(t)h(t) - c(j,t), \tag{5.28}$$

where $k(j,j) = 0$.

From the first-order conditions for a maximum, we can derive the Euler equation for consumption of household j:

$$\dot{c}(j,t) = (r(t) - \rho)c(j,t). \tag{5.29}$$

Integrating (5.29) over time and using the fact that the present value of consumption is equal to initial assets plus the present value of labor income for all households, we get the following consumption function:

$$c(j,t) = \rho(k(j,t) + W(j,t)), \tag{5.30}$$

where

$$W(j,t) = \int_{v=t}^{\infty} e^{-\int_{x=t}^{v} r(x)dx} w(v)h(v)dv = \hat{W}(t). \tag{5.31}$$

Here, $\hat{W}(t)$ is the present value at time t of labor income (human capital). From (5.31), we can confirm that the present value of labor income is the same for all households, irrespective of their birth date, because the real wage is the same for all households, as is labor efficiency, and all households supply one unit of labor per instant.

From (5.30), we can see that the average and marginal propensity to consume wealth (the sum of nonhuman and human capital) is the same for all households and is equal to the pure rate of time preference. This is a consequence of logarithmic preferences and the assumption that there is no population growth in households.[9]

9. Compare the consumption function (5.30) with those for the representative household derived in chapter 4.

5.2.4 Aggregation across Generations

The aggregate variables $C(t)$, $K(t)$, and $W(t)$ are determined by the integral of the variables that correspond to every generation of households at time t (i.e., for every $j \leq t$). For every generation j, its size, equal to ne^{nj}, is taken into account. Obviously, younger generations are more numerous than older generations. As a result, aggregate consumption and aggregate physical and human capital are given by

$$C(t) = \int_{j=-\infty}^{t} ne^{nj} c(j,t) dj, \tag{5.32}$$

$$K(t) = \int_{j=-\infty}^{t} ne^{nj} k(j,t) dj, \tag{5.33}$$

$$W(t) = \int_{j=-\infty}^{t} ne^{nj} W(j,t) dj = e^{nt}\, \bar{W}(t). \tag{5.34}$$

From (5.30) and (5.32), it follows that

$$C(t) = \rho(K(t) + W(t)), \tag{5.35}$$

and (5.35) gives

$$\dot{C}(t) = \rho(\dot{K}(t) + \dot{W}(t)). \tag{5.36}$$

From (5.28) and (5.33), it follows that

$$\dot{K}(t) = r(t)K(t) + w(t)h(t)e^{nt} - C(t), \tag{5.37}$$

and from (5.34), we have

$$\dot{W}(t) = (r(t) + n)W(t) - w(t)h(t)e^{nt}. \tag{5.38}$$

Finally, (5.35) to (5.38) yield

$$\dot{C}(t) = (r(t) + n - \rho)C(t) - n\rho K(t). \tag{5.39}$$

Equation (5.39) describes the evolution of aggregate consumption over time. To the extent that the real interest rate exceeds the pure rate of time preference, all households accumulate capital, which leads to an increase in their consumption. In addition, because of the addition of new households at rate n, aggregate consumption increases because of the additional consumption of these households. Finally, because a proportion n of households (the youngest generation born at t) own no capital, one has to subtract from their consumption that part corresponding to the possession of capital. This explains why the last term $n\rho K(t)$ in (5.39) has a minus sign. Generation t consumes only $\rho W(t)$, because it owns no capital.

5.2.5 The Model in Terms of Efficiency Units of Labor

Consumption and the capital stock per efficiency unit of labor are defined as

$$c(t) = \frac{C(t)}{h(t)L(t)} = C(t)e^{-(n+g)t}, \tag{5.40}$$

$$k(t) = \frac{K(t)}{h(t)L(t)} = K(t)e^{-(n+g)t}. \tag{5.41}$$

From (5.40) and (5.41), it follows that

$$\dot{c}(t) = [r(t) - \rho - g]c(t) - n\rho k(t). \tag{5.42}$$

Using (5.26) to substitute for the real interest rate in (5.42), consumption per efficiency unit of capital evolves according to

$$\dot{c}(t) = [Af'(k(t) - \delta) - \rho - g]c(t) - n\rho k(t). \tag{5.43}$$

From (5.37) and (5.41), and using the constant return to scale property of the production function and the marginal productivity conditions (5.26) and (5.27) for the real interest rate and the real wage, we get the following accumulation equation for capital per efficiency unit of labor:

$$\dot{k}(t) = Af(k(t)) - c(t) - (n + g + \delta)k(t). \tag{5.44}$$

This is the usual accumulation equation, which defines the change in the capital stock per efficiency unit of labor as the difference between savings and steady state investment $(n + g + \delta)k$.

We can now use (5.43) and (5.44) to analyze both the balanced growth path and the process of adjustment toward the balanced growth path.

5.2.6 The Balanced Growth Path and the Adjustment Path

We now analyze the balanced growth path and the adjustment path using a phase diagram analogous to that used for the Ramsey model. On the balanced growth path, we have that

$$\dot{c}(t) = \dot{k}(t) = 0.$$

From (5.43), the condition for constant consumption per efficiency unit of labor is given by

$$c(t) = \frac{n\rho k(t)}{Af'(k(t)) - \delta - \rho - g}. \tag{5.45}$$

From (5.44), the condition for constant capital per efficiency unit of labor is given by

$$c(t) = Af(k(t)) - (n + g + \delta)k(t). \tag{5.46}$$

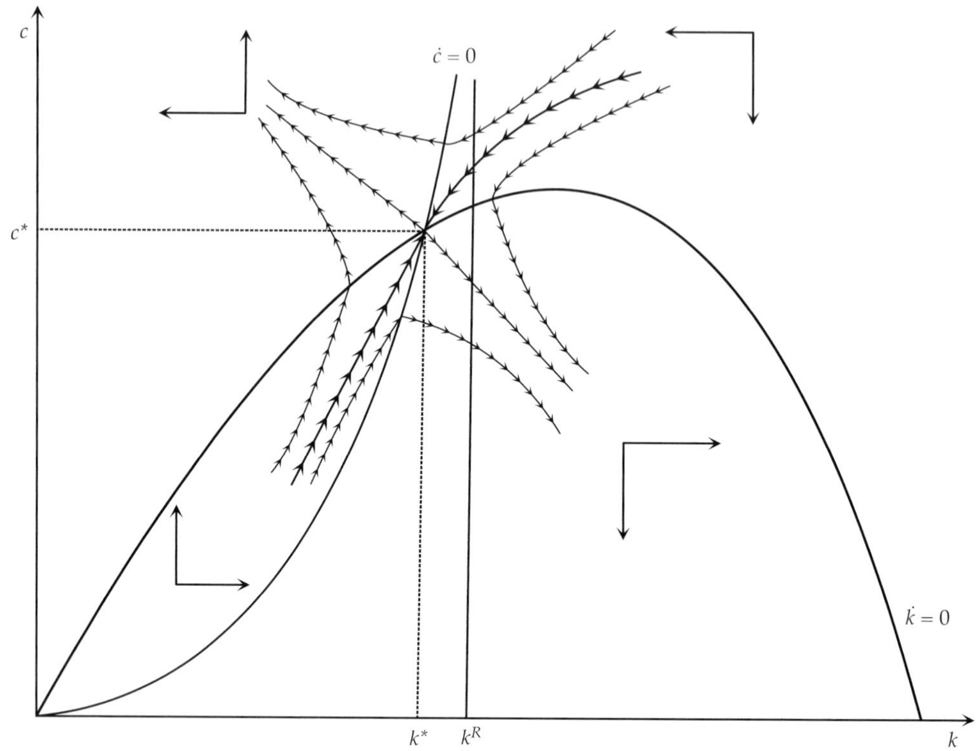

Figure 5.7
The balanced growth path and the adjustment path for the Blanchard-Weil model.

The balanced growth path (steady state) is defined by the simultaneous satisfaction of conditions (5.45) and (5.46).

The geometric depiction of both the balanced growth path and the adjustment path in this model is presented in figure 5.7. The balanced growth path is determined at the point (k^*, c^*), where (5.45) and (5.46) are simultaneously satisfied. In the figure, (5.45) is depicted by the $\dot{c} = 0$ curve (the steady state consumption curve), and (5.46) is depicted by the $\dot{k} = 0$ curve (the steady state capital curve). The balanced growth path is a saddle point, and only one adjustment path leads to the balanced growth path. All other paths do not satisfy the relevant transversality condition.

Note that the balanced growth path lies to the left of the balanced growth path that would prevail in the case of a representative household (k^R in figure 5.7). In the steady state of the model of overlapping generations with perpetual youth, both the capital stock and the level of consumption (per efficiency unit of labor) are lower than the values corresponding to the modified golden rule. This is because current generations do not internalize the welfare of future generations, and they end up saving less than a representative household that takes the welfare of future generations into account. For this reason, and despite competitive markets, the balanced growth path in the model of perpetual youth is not socially efficient in the sense of maximizing social welfare. Redistributing capital to favor the new generations would result in higher consumption and output per efficiency unit of labor. However, the possibility of dynamic inefficiency does not arise in this model. The capital stock cannot be higher than the level corresponding to the golden rule.

As in the Ramsey model, a unique saddle path leads to the steady state. Because consumption is not a predetermined variable but the capital stock is, from any initial position, consumption will directly adjust to put the economy on the unique saddle path leading to the steady state. To the left of k^*, consumption is lower than its steady state value, and the economy accumulates capital. During this process, capital and consumption per efficiency unit of labor are increasing. The opposite occurs if the initial capital stock is to the right of the steady state capital stock. Both the capital stock and consumption per efficiency unit of labor are higher than in the steady state and are decreasing on the unique saddle path.

Exercise 5.1 Assuming a Cobb-Douglas production function, derive the steady state of the Blanchard-Weil OLG model from the system of differential equations (5.43) and (5.44). Discuss the determinants of all steady state variables. Also analyze the stability of the system by linearizing the system around the steady state. Compare the steady state of the Blachard-Weil OLG model to that corresponding to the comparable representative household model. What determines the growth rate of per capita output, consumption, and real wages in the steady state?

Figure 5.8 shows the effects of an increase in the pure rate of time preference of households. An increase in pure rate of time preference leads to a shift of the steady state consumption function to the left. At the new equilibrium (c^{**}, k^{**}), both consumption and the capital stock per efficiency unit of labor will be lower. When the shift occurs, consumption increases from c^* to c_0 and puts the economy on the saddle path corresponding to the new balanced growth path. Savings are lower than equilibrium investment, and the economy starts to decumulate capital, gradually adapting to the new balanced growth path, with lower consumption and capital per efficiency unit of labor.

A decrease in the pure rate of time preference has the opposite effect. At the new equilibrium, both consumption and capital will be higher. When the shift occurs, consumption decreases, the economy begins to accumulate additional capital, and it gradually adjusts to the new balanced growth path with higher capital and consumption per efficiency unit of labor.

We thus see that in this model, the pure rate of time preference is a key factor determining savings behavior and the balanced growth path. The higher it is, the less households of all generations will save, as they prefer more utility from consumption today relative to utility from future consumption.

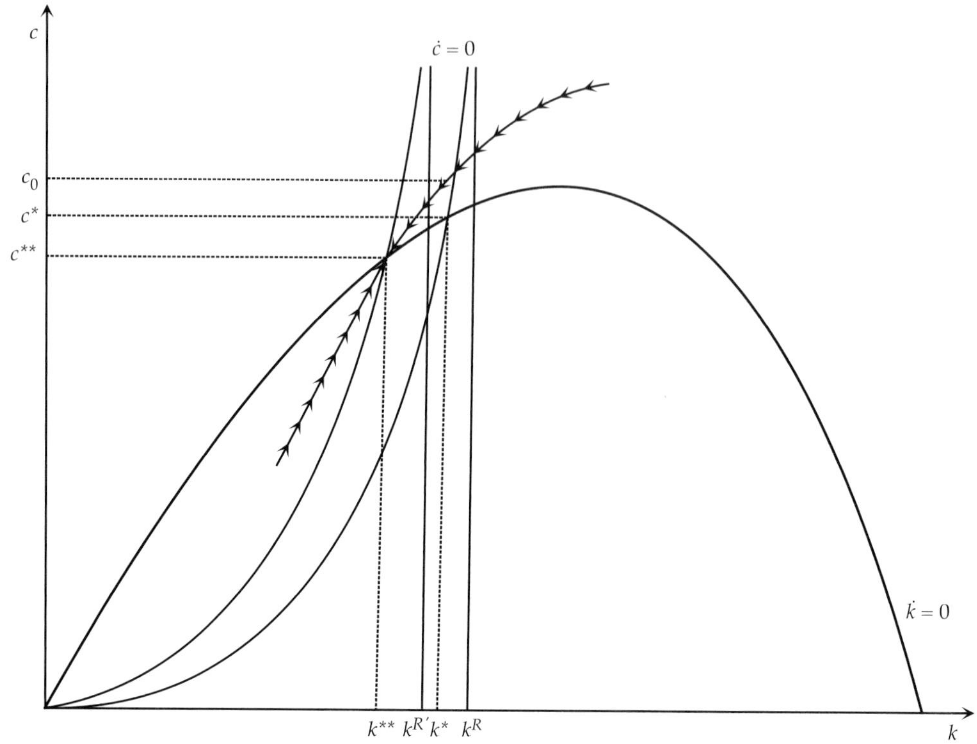

Figure 5.8
Short- and long-run effects of an increase in the pure rate of time preference in the Blanchard-Weil model.

The short- and long-run effects of a previously unanticipated permanent increase in the rate of population growth n are analyzed in figure 5.9. The Blanchard-Weil OLG model differs from the Ramsey representative household model in the effects of a change in population growth n. In the Ramsey model, population growth occurs in the representative household and is internalized by the savings behavior of the representative household. Thus, as already shown, population growth affects only consumption and not capital per effective unit of labor. In the Blanchard-Weil model, population growth is external to existing households, as it takes the form of additional households. Therefore, population growth is not internalized. As a result, an increase in population growth results in an insufficient increase in savings, which results in the decumulation of capital. On the new balanced growth path, both consumption and the capital stock go down as a result of higher population growth. In this respect, the Blanchard-Weil model resembles the Solow and Diamond models, in which population growth has a negative impact on per capita income.

A rise in population growth shifts the steady state consumption curve up and the steady state capital accumulation locus down. In the new balanced growth path, both consumption

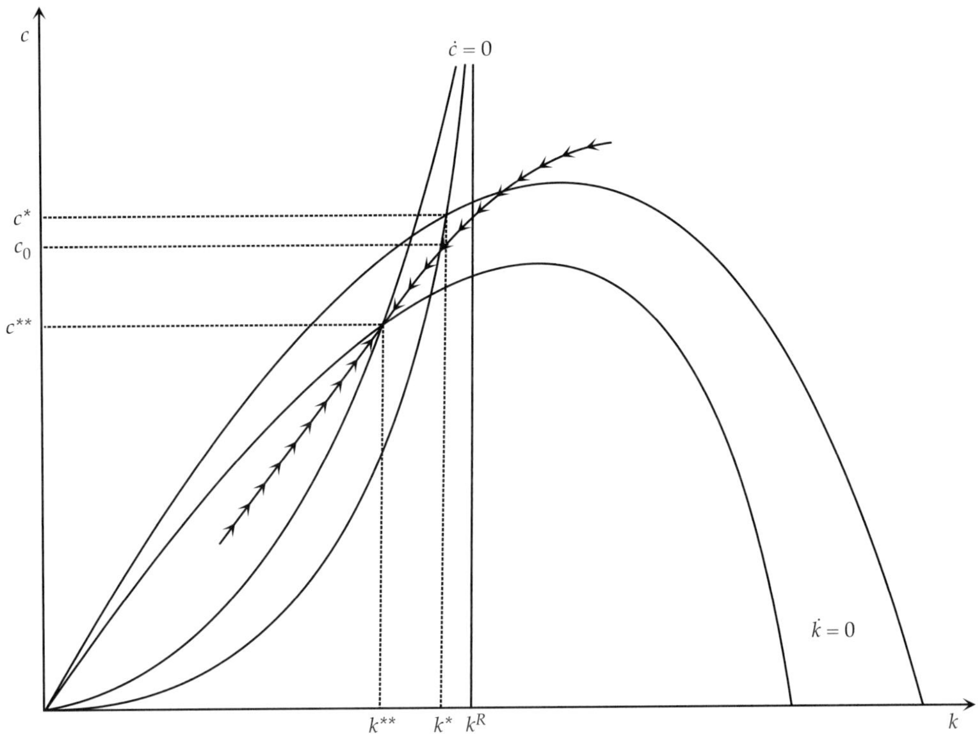

Figure 5.9
Short- and long-run effects of an increase in the rate of population growth in the Blanchard-Weil model.

and the capital stock per efficiency unit of labor are lower. When the shift occurs, consumption declines, but not by enough to prevent the decumulation of capital, as in the case of the representative household model. The reason is that current generations do not internalize the welfare of future generations. Thus, the economy adjusts along the new saddle path, on which savings are lower than steady state investment. The economy continues to decumulate capital and gradually adapts toward the new balanced growth path (c^{**}, k^{**}), with lower consumption and capital per efficiency unit of labor.

5.3 Dynamic Simulations of a Calibrated Blanchard-Weil Model

It is illuminating to investigate further the dynamic properties of the Blanchard-Weil model and get a quantitative feel for the effects of the various parameters. To do so, let us simulate specific cases of the process of dynamic adjustment from one balanced growth path to another when there is an exogenous permanent change in specific parameters (such as the pure rate of time preference, total factor productivity, or population growth). To simulate the model, we shall convert it from a continuous time model to a discrete time model.

5.3.1 The Blanchard-Weil Model in Discrete Time

It is straigthforward to show that, in terms of efficiency units of labor, the discrete time versions of the consumption growth equation (5.43) and the capital accumulation equation (5.44) of the Blanchard-Weil model take the form

$$c_{t+1} = \frac{1+f'(k_{t+1})-\delta}{(1+\rho)(1+g)}c_t - \frac{n\rho}{(1+n)(1+g)(1+\rho)}k_t,$$

$$k_{t+1} = \frac{1}{(1+n)(1+g)}(f(k_t)+(1-\delta)k_t - c_t).$$

For a Cobb-Douglas production function $y_t = A(k_t)^{\alpha}$, these equations can be rewritten as

$$c_{t+1} = \frac{1+\alpha A k_{t+1}^{\alpha-1}-\delta}{(1+\rho)(1+g)}c_t - \frac{n\rho}{(1+n)(1+g)(1+\rho)}k_t, \tag{5.47}$$

$$k_{t+1} = \frac{1}{(1+n)(1+g)}\left(Ak_t^{\alpha}+(1-\delta)k_t - c_t\right). \tag{5.48}$$

Equations (5.47) and (5.48) determine the adjustment path for consumption and capital per efficiency unit of labor. After we determine the adjustment path for these two variables, the path of real output can be calculated from the production function, and the paths of the real interest rate and the real wage are then obtained from the marginal productivity conditions for capital and labor.

5.3.2 Dynamic Simulations of the Model

The parameter values used to calibrate the model are $A=1$, $\alpha=0.333$, $\rho=0.02$, $n=0.01$, $g=0.02$, $\delta=0.03$. These values are the same as the ones used for the Ramsey model in chapter 4. They are also consistent with the values used for the Solow model in chapter 3 and the Diamond model in the first part of this chapter.

We consider three alternative scenarios. A permanent increase in the pure rate of time preference of the households ρ by 1% (from 0.02 to 0.0202), a permanent rise in the rate of population growth n by 1% (from 0.01 to 0.0101), and a permanent increase in total factor productivity A by 1% (from 1 to 1.01). The results of the simulations are presented in figures 5.10–5.12.

In the simulation shown in figure 5.10, the economy is on its original balanced growth path, and after period 1, the pure rate of time preference of households ρ rises permanently and unexpectedly by 1% (from 0.02 to 0.0202). This increase leads directly to an increase in consumption which then declines, a decline in the savings rate, a gradual decumulation of physical capital, a gradual decline in output, a gradual decline in real wages, and a gradual increase in the real interest rate. The reason for declining real wages is the gradual reduction of the marginal product of labor caused by the falling capital stock; the real interest rate

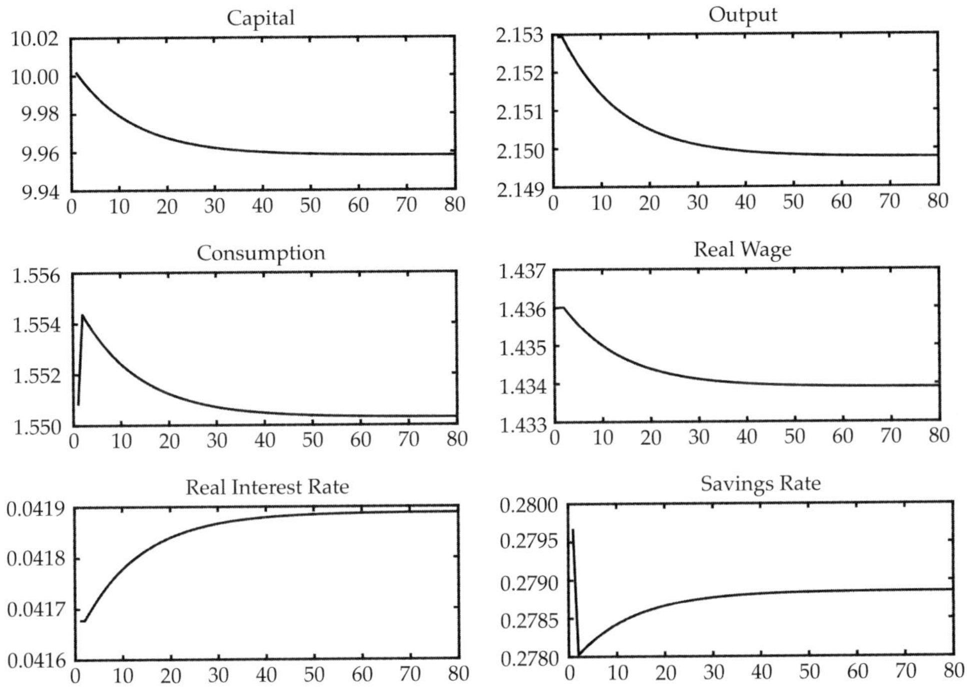

Figure 5.10
Impulse response functions for a 1% increase in the pure rate of time preference in the calibrated Blanchard-Weil model.

increases, because the marginal product of capital gradually increases due to the decumulation of capital. The economy gradually converges to a new balanced growth path. On this new path, capital per efficiency unit of labor is lower by about 0.4%, output and real wages by 0.1%, consumption by 0.03% (due to the decline in the savings rate). The real interest rate has increased by 0.02 the same as the increase in the pure rate of time preference. The steady state savings rate, which is endogenous in this model, falls from 28.0% to 27.9%.

In the simulation shown in figure 5.11, the economy is on its original balanced growth path, and after period 1, the rate of population growth n rises permanently and unexpectedly by 1% (from 0.01 to 0.0101). This increase leads directly to a decline in consumption; an increase in the savings rate; but a gradual decumulation of capital, as the decline in consumption is smaller than the one required to keep capital per efficiency unit of labor constant. The gradual decline in capital leads to a gradual decline in output, a gradual decline in real wages, and a gradual increase in the real interest rate. The reason for declining real wages is the gradual reduction of the marginal product of labor caused by the falling capital stock. The real interest rate increases, because the marginal product of capital gradually increases due to the decumulation of capital. The economy gradually converges to a new

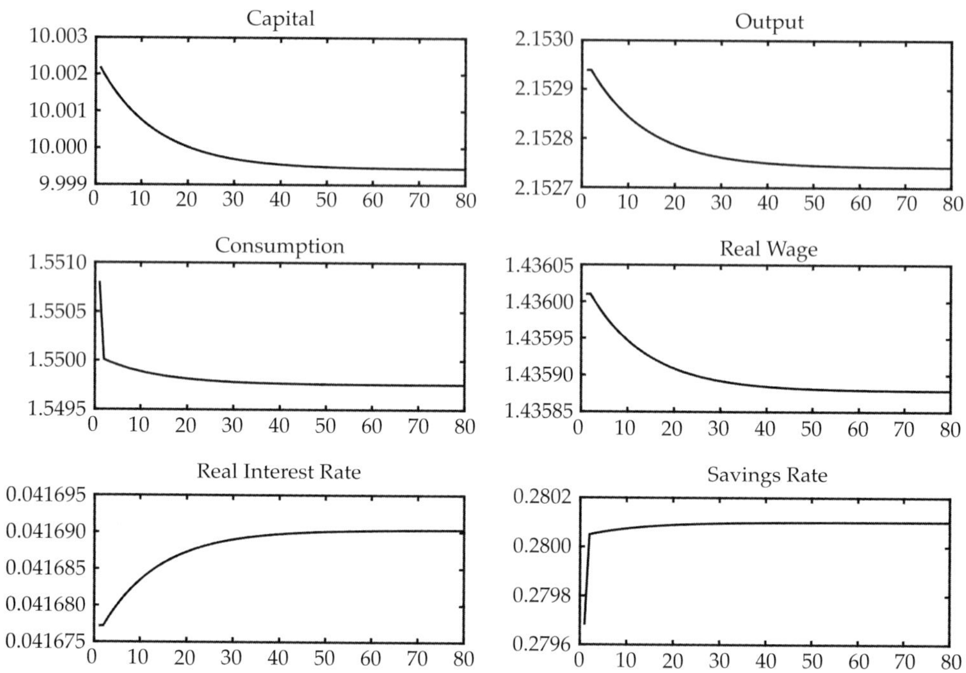

Figure 5.11
Impulse response functions for a 1% increase in the population growth rate in the calibrated Blanchard-Weil model.

balanced growth path. On the new balanced growth path, capital per efficiency unit of labor is lower by about 0.03%, output and real wages by 0.01%, consumption by 0.07% (due to the increase in the savings rate), while the real interest rate has increased by 0.01 percentage points. The steady state savings rate, which is endogenous in this model, rises from 27.97% to 28.01%.

In the simulation shown in figure 5.12, the economy is initially on its original balanced growth path. After period 1, total factor productivity A rates rises permanently and unexpectedly by 1% (from 1 to 1.01). This increase leads to an immediate increase in production, consumption, savings, and the marginal product of both labor (the real wage) and capital (the real interest rate). The increase in savings causes a gradual accumulation of capital, which leads to a further gradual increase in production and consumption, a further gradual increase in the real wage, but a gradual fall in real interest rates. The reason for the falling real interest rate is the gradual reduction of the marginal product of capital caused by the accumulation of capital. The economy gradually converges to a new balanced growth path. On this path, capital per efficiency unit of labor has increased by about 1.5%, output, consumption, and real wages are also higher by 1.5%, while the real interest rate has returned to a level very near its original equilibrium. The increase in total factor productivity by

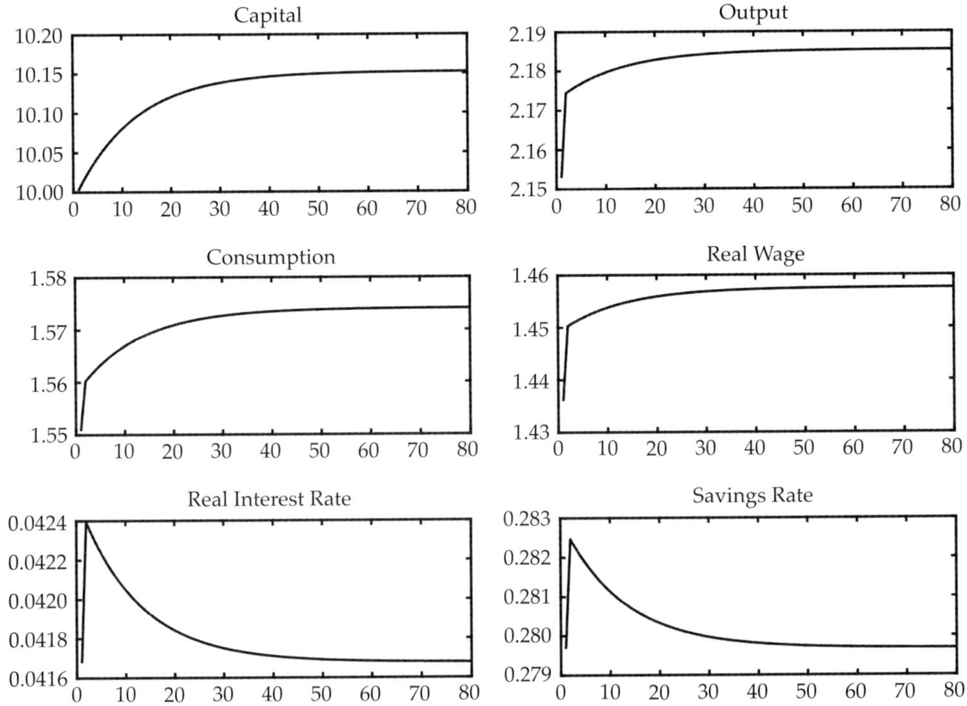

Figure 5.12
Impulse response functions for a 1% increase in total factor productivity in the calibrated Blanchard-Weil model.

1% leads to an increase in real income by 1.5% (i.e., more than 1%), because productivity growth causes a temporary increase in the savings rate and capital accumulation, which in turn causes additional induced increases in real incomes and consumption.

The dynamic behavior of the OLG model of Blanchard and Weil is similar to the dynamic behavior of the representative household model and the Diamond OLG model.

However, note that, as the theoretical analysis suggests, the savings rate in the OLG model is lower than that in the corresponding representative household model. For exactly the same parameter values, the steady state savings rate in the perpetual youth model is 28%, whereas the corresponding savings rate in the representative household model of chapter 4 is equal to 28.5.

The higher savings rate in the representative household Ramsey model results in a higher steady state capital stock, real output, consumption, and real wages, compared to the Blanchard-Weil OLG model. In contrast, the steady state real interest rate is lower in the representative household model.

For the initial values of the parameters used in the simulations, capital per efficiency unit of labor on the balanced growth path is equal to 10.275 in the representative household model and only 10.002 in the corresponding OLG model (higher by 2.73%). Real income per efficiency unit of labor is equal to 2.172 in the representative household model, compared to 2.153 in the corresponding OLG model (higher by 0.9%). The same applies to steady state real wages, which are higher by 0.9% in the representative household model. The difference in consumption is 0.2% for the model of the representative household because of the higher savings rate. Finally, due to the lower capital stock per efficiency unit of labor, the real interest rate on the balanced growth path is 4.2% in the OLG model, compared to 4% in the corresponding representative household model.

As we see from these simulations, the dynamic behavior of the Blanchard-Weil OLG model is qualitatively similar to the dynamic behavior of the Ramsey and Diamond models. In addition, despite the prediction that the savings rate is not constant along the adjustment path (as assumed in the Solow model), in all other respects, the predictions of the Blanchard-Weil model about the adjustment path are very similar to the predictions of the Solow model.

5.4 Conclusion

Aggregate savings behavior in OLG models is not characterized by social efficiency, as it is in the representative household model. Besides, in economies where there is no representative household, comparing welfare across different households is largely arbitrary.

In any case, although the dynamic behavior of OLG models is largely similar to that of the representative household model, there is no guarantee of efficiency OLG models. Thus, in these models, there is scope for policy interventions that would result in greater social efficiency, as the competitive equilibrium does not necessarily lead to optimal results. Furthermore, in the Diamond model, it is theoretically possible to have dynamic inefficiency, although empirical considerations suggest that this possibility is unlikely.

Because the competitive equilibrium does not result in an optimal savings behavior in OLG models, such models also have different properties than the representative household model regarding both the short- and the long-run effects of budgetary (fiscal) policies and monetary policies that affect the rate of growth of the money supply. These are questions that we shall investigate in the next two chapters.

6

Fiscal Policy and Economic Growth

This chapter introduces the government into the exogenous growth models we have analyzed so far. We first discuss the intertemporal budget constraint of the government and the conditions for government debt sustainability. Then we analyze the impact of the path of lump sum taxes, primary government expenditure, and government debt in the representative household model and an OLG model. Finally, we analyze the short- and long-term effects of distortionary taxes on labor and capital income, consumption, and business profits before interest and depreciation.

As demonstrated in chapter 2, the intertemporal government budget constraint is defined in a way that is similar to the intertemporal budget constraint of a household that can borrow and lend freely at the market interest rate. It requires the equality of the present value of current and future tax revenue to the sum of the current stock of government debt plus the present value of current and future primary government expenditure. Primary government expenditure is defined as government expenditure excluding interest payments on government debt, and present values are calculated using the market interest rate.

As we will see in the present chapter, the intertemporal budget constraint of a government with an infinite horizon does not prevent it from having debt or even from increasing the level of its debt. It means, however, that the limit of the present value of government debt, as time tends to infinity, cannot be positive. For example, if the real interest rate is positive, a positive but constant real government debt—which means that the government never repays it—satisfies the government budget constraint. Even if government debt increases continuously, the government budget constraint is satisfied to the extent that the real interest rate exceeds the growth rate of real government debt.

When the government budget constraint was introduced in the two-period representative household model of chapter 2, it was shown that the only aspect of it that matters for the choice of the optimal path of private consumption is the present value of primary government expenditure. The method of financing primary government expenditure (i.e., the breakdown between government debt and the path of nondistortionary taxes) does not affect the optimal path of consumption of the representative household. This property has become known as

Ricardian equivalence between taxes and government debt, and holds in the infinite-horizon Ramsey model as well. The stock of government bonds held by the representative household is not considered as part of its total wealth and does not affect its consumption path. The representative household realizes that the bonds will be financed by future taxes equal in present value to the stock of the existing government debt, and, as the household internalizes the welfare of future generations, it treats debt and (lump sum) taxes equivalently. In the absence of financial frictions, when households and the government borrow on the same terms, Ricardian equivalence is a key characteristic of representative household models in general.

Ricardian equivalence does not apply to OLG models. The stock of government debt affects aggregate savings, as current generations realize that part of the present value of future taxes required to finance the stock of government debt will be paid by future generations. In OLG models, current generations do not internalize the welfare of future ones. Thus, current generations treat part of the existing stock of government debt that they hold as part of their wealth, because it exceeds the present value of their own future taxes. As a result, debt and tax finance are not equivalent in OLG models, and Ricardian equivalence does not hold.

In OLG models, both the stock of real government debt and real primary government expenditure affect private and aggregate savings and the accumulation of capital. Rises in real government debt or real primary government expenditure reduce savings and capital accumulation, and they also have negative effects on the steady state capital stock, output, private consumption, and real wages. This is because current generations know that part of the increase in future tax revenues needed to finance a higher level of primary government expenditure (or interest payments on the increased debt) will be shouldered by future generations. Aggregate savings are thus affected negatively by an increase in real government debt or an increase in real primary government expenditure. This leads to an adjustment process with declining capital stock and private consumption and a lower steady state level of capital, output, and consumption per head.

Taxes are usually distortionary, as they affect incentives for savings, investment, and labor supply. In the representative household and OLG models that we have considered, labor supply is exogenously given and does not depend on net of tax real wages. Consequently, tax rates on labor income or (time-invariant) consumption taxes do not cause distortions in labor supply and savings, and they do not affect either the adjustment path or the balanced growth path. In contrast, capital income taxation and taxes on business earnings before interest and depreciation have a negative impact on savings and investment. Such taxes affect savings and capital accumulation negatively and as a result, have a negative impact on the steady state capital stock, steady state output and income, steady state real wages, and steady state private consumption.

6.1 The Government Budget Constraint

For a household that can borrow and lend freely at a market-determined interest rate, the intertemporal budget constraint requires that the present value of its current and future consumption cannot exceed the value of its current assets plus the present value of its future labor income. The intertemporal budget constraint of a government that can borrow and lend freely at a market-determined interest rate is defined accordingly: The present value of current and future primary government expenditure cannot exceed the value of current government assets plus the present value of current and future tax receipts.

6.1.1 Government Deficits, Debt, and Solvency

Consider a government that chooses a stream of primary government expenditure $C_g(t)$, a stream of taxes $T(t)$, and has a stock of outstanding government debt $D(t)$. Government expenditure can be financed by either taxes or the accumulation of government debt. Government debt accumulates according to

$$\dot{D}(t) = r(t)D(t) + C_g(t) - T(t), \tag{6.1}$$

where $r(t)$ is the real interest rate at time t.

The right-hand side of (6.1) denotes the *government deficit*, the extent to which current taxes fall short of total government expenditure. A government deficit means that the government is accumulating government debt.

The solution of the differential equation (6.1) for the accumulation of government debt gives us the *government intertemporal budget constraint* in the form[1]

$$\lim_{t\to\infty} e^{-R(t)}D(t) + \int_{t=0}^{\infty} e^{-R(t)}C_g(t)dt = -D(0) + \int_{t=0}^{\infty} e^{-R(t)}T(t)dt, \tag{6.2}$$

where $R(t) = \int_{s=0}^{t} r(s)ds$.

The intertemporal budget constraint of the government (6.2) states that at any initial time 0, as time goes to infinity, the present value of primary government expenditure plus the present value of government debt must be equal to the present value of tax revenues minus the initial level of government debt.

Clearly, a solvent government cannot maintain a government debt with a positive present value as time goes to infinity. The present value of its debt should be tending to zero, or even become negative. Hence, the condition for a solvent government is that the first term

1. Equation (6.1) is a first-order differential equation with variable coefficients, similar to the asset accumulation equation of the representative household in chapter 4. For how to solve it, see appendix C on ordinary differential equations.

of (6.2) on the left tends to a nonpositive number:

$$\lim_{t\to\infty} e^{-R(t)}D(t) \leq 0. \tag{6.3}$$

Expression (6.3) is the *transversality condition* that any solvent government must satisfy. The present value of government debt cannot be positive as time goes to infinity. Thus, (6.3) denotes the limits to the accumulation of government debt.

From (6.2) and (6.3), the intertemporal government budget constraint for a solvent government can be written as

$$\int_{t=0}^{\infty} e^{-R(t)}C_g(t)dt \leq -D(0) + \int_{t=0}^{\infty} e^{-R(t)}T(t)dt. \tag{6.4}$$

As in the case of the representative household model in chapter 4, we can define the average real interest rate between time 0 and time t as

$$\bar{r}(t) = \frac{1}{t}\int_{s=0}^{t} r(s)ds = \frac{1}{t}R(t).$$

With this definition, (6.4) can also be written as

$$\int_{t=0}^{\infty} e^{-\bar{r}(t)t}C_g(t)dt \leq -D(0) + \int_{t=0}^{\infty} e^{-\bar{r}(t)t}T(t)dt. \tag{6.5}$$

The government budget constraint does not stop the government from having debt continuously, or even from increasing the stock of its debt. However, the present value of future government debt as time goes to infinity cannot possibly be positive. As for households, this restriction implies that the government must satisfy the transversality condition (6.3), which can also be written as

$$\lim_{t\to\infty} e^{-R(t)}D(t) = \lim_{t\to\infty} e^{-\bar{r}(t)t}D(t) \leq 0.$$

For example, if the real interest rate is positive, a positive constant stock of real government debt—which means that the government never pays it back—satisfies the transversality condition and therefore the government budget constraint. Even if the stock of real government debt is increasing over time, the budget constraint of the government and the transversality condition (6.3) are satisfied, as long as the growth rate of real government debt does not exceed the average real interest rate. Let us call the transversality condition (6.3) the *sustainability criterion* for fiscal policy. To the extent that it is satisfied, a government is solvent, and its fiscal policy is sustainable.

Apart from the overall government deficit, it is also worth defining another measure of fiscal policy, $C_g(t) - T(t)$, which is called the *primary government deficit*. This measures the extent to which current taxes fall short of *primary* government expenditure, which excludes interest payments on outstanding debt. The primary deficit is a very informative index of the contribution of fiscal policy to the evolution of government debt. For example, we can write the intertemporal government budget constraint (6.4) as

$$\int_{t=0}^{\infty} e^{-\bar{r}(t)t}\left[T(t)-C_g(t)\right]dt \geq D(0). \tag{6.6}$$

Expressed in this form, the government budget constraint requires that the current stock of government debt must be smaller than or equal to the present value of current and future primary surpluses (negative primary deficits). A government that has a positive level of debt must be committed to a policy of future primary surpluses that, in present-value terms, are at least as high as its current stock of debt. Otherwise, it does not satisfy its intertemporal budget constraint, and its fiscal policy is not sustainable.

Whether the government budget constraint (in the sense that we have defined it) is satisfied determines whether a given budgetary policy is sustainable over time. Real government debt cannot be growing at a rate higher than the real interest rate. When it does, the government follows an unsustainable budgetary policy.

In what follows, we shall concentrate on budgetary policies that satisfy the sustainability criterion (6.3), which is the same as satisfying the intertemporal budget constraint (6.4).

6.2 Ricardian Equivalence and the Ramsey Model

Let us now introduce the government in the Ramsey model of a representative household that we analyzed in chapter 4. Assume that the government engages in primary spending and finances this primary spending through a combination of debt and taxes that satisfies the government budget constraint (6.4).

6.2.1 Ricardian Equivalence between Government Debt and Taxes

When there are taxes and a stock of government debt, the intertemporal budget constraint of the representative household implies that the present value of its (private) consumption cannot exceed the value of its current assets (capital plus government bonds) plus the present value of its disposable labor income (i.e., its after-tax labor income). Thus, the intertemporal budget constraint of the representative household is given by

$$\int_{t=0}^{\infty} e^{-\bar{r}(t)t}C(t)dt \leq K(0)+D(0)+\int_{t=0}^{\infty} e^{-\bar{r}(t)t}\left[W(t)-T(t)\right]dt, \tag{6.7}$$

where $C(t)$ is the real consumption of the representative household at time t; $W(t)$ is its real labor income at time t; $K(0)$ is its initial stock of capital; and $D(0)$ the initial stock of government bonds, held as assets by the representative household. Expression (6.7) can be rewritten as

$$\int_{t=0}^{\infty} e^{-\bar{r}(t)t} C(t)dt \leq K(0) + D(0) + \int_{t=0}^{\infty} e^{-\bar{r}(t)t} W(t)dt - \int_{t=0}^{\infty} e^{-\bar{r}(t)t} T(t)dt. \tag{6.8}$$

Assume that the government satisfies its intertemporal budget constraint (6.4) exactly, in the sense that the present value of future taxes minus its initial debt is equal to the present value of primary government expenditure. Substituting (6.4) in (6.8), we get

$$\int_{t=0}^{\infty} e^{-\bar{r}(t)t} C(t)dt \leq K(0) + \int_{t=0}^{\infty} e^{-\bar{r}(t)t} W(t)dt - \int_{t=0}^{\infty} e^{-\bar{r}(t)t} C_g(t)dt, \tag{6.9}$$

which suggests that we can express the intertemporal budget constraint of the representative household as a function of the present value of primary government expenditure without any reference to the method of financing it. A given present value of primary government expenditure has the same impact on the intertemporal budget constraint of the representative household, irrespective of whether it is financed by government debt or by taxes. All that matters for the intertemporal budget constraint of the representative household is the presence of government expenditure, as taxes and debt have the same present value as primary government expenditure.

Because the path of tax revenue or the original debt does not affect the budget constraint or the preferences of the representative household, the path of tax revenue or the level of government debt cannot possibly affect private consumption. Thus, (6.9) leads us to conclude that the only aspect that matters for the course of private consumption is the present value of primary government expenditure and not the method of financing it (i.e., through taxes or government debt).

This result is demonstrated in an important paper by Barro [1974], and it has since been known as *Ricardian equivalence* between debt and taxes. It is a result we also demonstrated for the two-period model of chapter 2.[2]

Government bond holdings by the representative household are not considered a net addition to its wealth, as the representative household realizes that its bond holdings will be financed by future taxes of equal present value.

6.2.2 Government Expenditure, Taxes, and Debt in the Ramsey Model

We can analyze the Ricardian equivalence result in a different way, by introducing the government in the full Ramsey model of chapter 4.

2. The term "Ricardian equivalence" is due to Buchanan [1976] who, commenting on the Barro [1974] paper, pointed out that the possible equivalence between debt and taxes was first raised and highlighted by Ricardo [1817].

The Euler equation for consumption is not affected by introducing the government. It is given by

$$\dot{c}(t) = \frac{1}{\theta}[Af'(k(t)) - \delta - \rho - \theta g]c(t). \tag{6.10}$$

The capital accumulation equation takes the form

$$\dot{k}(t) = Af(k(t)) - c(t) - c_g(t) - (n + g + \delta)k(t). \tag{6.11}$$

Total savings in (6.11) are now defined by the difference between total income and total consumption (private and public).

Finally, government debt evolves according to (6.1). Expressing government debt accumulation per efficiency unit of labor, we get

$$\dot{d}(t) = [c_g(t) - \tau(t)] + [Af'(k(t)) - \delta - (n + g)]d(t), \tag{6.12}$$

where c is private consumption, k the stock of capital, d the stock of government debt, c_g primary government expenditure, and τ taxes, all defined in real terms per efficiency unit of labor. In (6.12), the marginal productivity condition $r(t) = Af'(k(t)) - \delta$ has been used to substitute out for the real interest rate.

Let us examine policies with exogenous and constant primary government expenditure per efficiency unit of labor. Thus, assume that the government stabilizes primary government expenditure at

$$c_g(t) = \bar{c}_g, \tag{6.13}$$

where $\bar{c}_g$ is a constant target level of primary government expenditure (per efficiency unit of labor).

Further assume that the government uses taxes to stabilize government debt per efficiency unit of labor. From (6.12) and (6.13), this requires a tax policy of the form

$$\tau(t) = \bar{c}_g + \left[Af'(k(t)) - \delta - n - g\right]\bar{d}, \tag{6.14}$$

where $\bar{d}$ is a constant target level of government debt (per efficiency unit of labor). Equation (6.14) implies that taxes are equal to the level of primary government expenditure plus the part of the interest payments on government debt that must be financed by taxes, so that debt per efficiency unit of labor remains constant.

In the representative household model, the real interest rate converges to $\rho + \theta g$, so that taxes per efficiency unit of labor converge to the steady state value

$$\bar{\tau} = \bar{c}_g + [\rho - n - (1 - \theta)g]\bar{d} \geq \bar{c}_g. \tag{6.15}$$

Steady state taxes are equal to the level of primary government expenditure plus the part of the interest payments on government debt that must be financed by taxes, so that debt

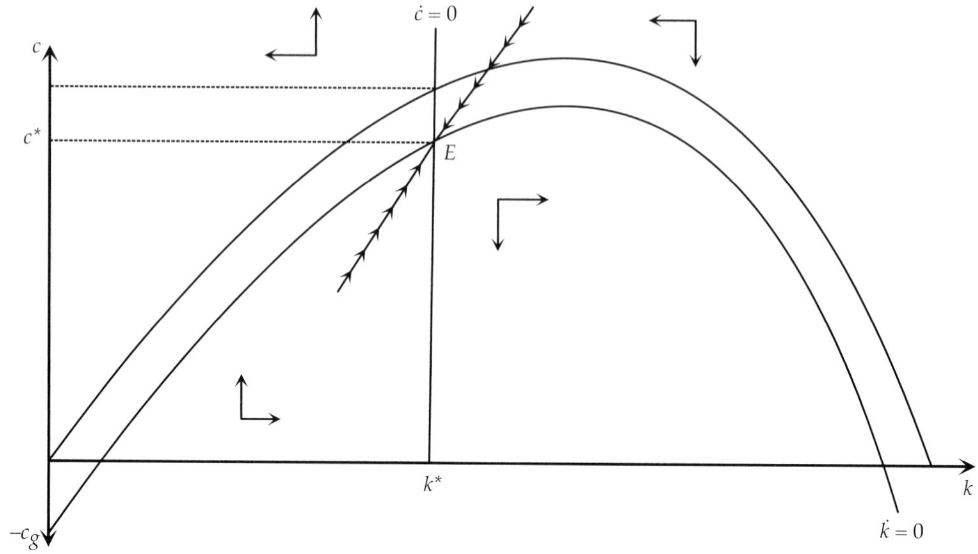

Figure 6.1
Primary government expenditure in the Ramsey model.

per efficiency unit of labor remains constant. This part is equal to the difference between the steady state real interest rate and the steady state growth rate. If the target debt level is positive, then steady state taxes must be higher than steady state primary government expenditure in order to finance interest payments on government debt. Thus, with a positive level of steady state government debt, the government runs a *primary surplus* on the balanced growth path. Equations (6.13) and (6.14) imply a sustainable fiscal policy, because the government satisfies its intertemporal budget constraint.

The evolution of capital and savings per efficiency unit of labor is described by the Euler equation for consumption (6.10) and the capital accumulation equation (6.11) for constant primary government expenditure per efficiency unit of labor, as in (6.13). Thus, the capital accumulation equation is given by

$$\dot{k}(t) = Af(k(t)) - c(t) - \bar{c}_g - (n + g + \delta)k(t). \tag{6.16}$$

The balanced growth path and the dynamic adjustment path are presented in figure 6.1. For comparison, the figure also shows the equilibrium for zero primary government expenditure, which lies above E. It is clear from figure 6.1 that primary government expenditure only leads to an equal reduction in private consumption without any other effect on real variables. An increase in primary government expenditure causes an equal reduction in private consumption due to the increase in the present value of future taxes (which reduces the present value of disposable labor income of the representative household). The stock of government debt has no effect at all on private consumption, because the method of financing government expenditure does not affect the intertemporal budget constraint of the representative household.

If the economy is out of steady state, the adjustment takes place along the unique saddle path that leads to the steady state. To the left of k^*, the economy is accumulating capital, which leads to a gradual increase in private consumption per efficiency unit of labor. To the right of k^*, the economy is decumulating capital, which leads to a gradual decline in private consumption per efficiency unit of labor.

In conclusion, in the representative household model, primary government expenditure, government debt, and taxes do not affect aggregate savings and the balanced growth path, nor do they change the adjustment path toward the steady state. Primary government expenditure crowds out an equal amount of private consumption and has no other effects on either the balanced growth path or the adjustment path. Aggregate savings and the accumulation of capital are not affected by the level of primary government expenditure, in either the short or the long run. In addition, the method of financing government expenditure (i.e., the steady state level of government debt per efficiency unit of labor) has no effect on either the steady state or the adjustment path. These Ricardian equivalence results were also proven for the two-period representative household model in chapter 2.

6.3 Dynamic Effects of Fiscal Policy in the Blanchard-Weil Model

We next examine the impact of fiscal policy in the Blanchard-Weil OLG model. The basic model was analyzed in chapter 5. Here, we introduce the government to this model.

6.3.1 The Blanchard-Weil Model with Government Expenditure and Debt

The Blanchard-Weil model with constant government expenditure $\bar{c}_g$, and government debt $\bar{d}$, per efficiency unit of labor, as implied by (6.13) and (6.14), is described by the following two differential equations:

$$\dot{k}(t) = Af(k(t)) - c(t) - \bar{c}_g - (n+g+\delta)k(t), \tag{6.17}$$

$$\dot{c}(t) = [Af'(k(t)) - \delta - \rho - g]c(t) - n\rho[k(t) + \bar{d}]. \tag{6.18}$$

All variables are expressed per efficiency unit of labor. In these equations, c is private consumption, k is physical capital, $\bar{d}$ is government debt, and $\bar{c}_g$ is primary government expenditure. Equation (6.17) describes the accumulation of physical capital as the difference between aggregate savings and equilibrium investment, and (6.18) describes the behavior of consumers.

The only difference from the Ramsey model of section 6.2 is in equation (6.18) for the adjustment of private consumption. Because new entrants to the economy do not have

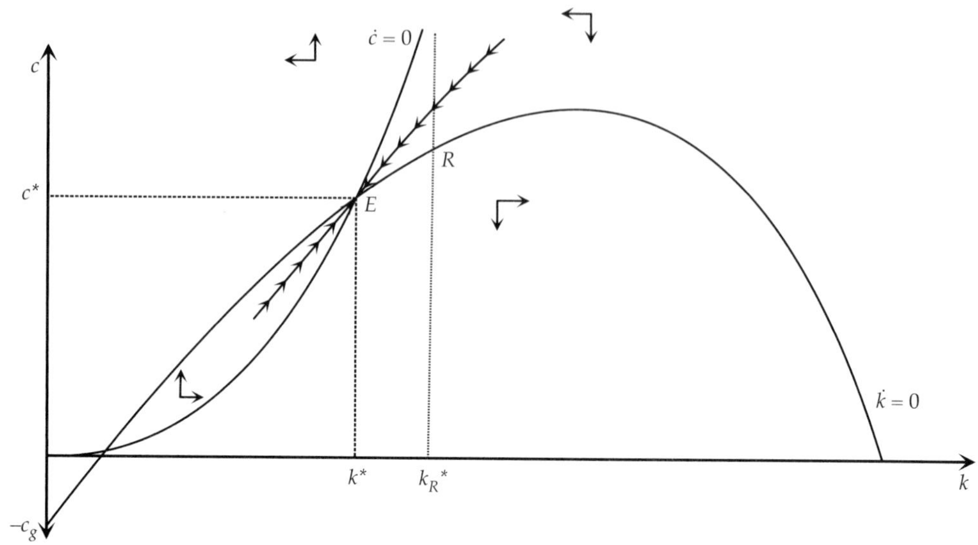

Figure 6.2
Primary government expenditure and debt in the Blanchard-Weil model.

accumulated savings in the form of either capital k or government bonds $\bar{d}$, the change in private consumption depends negatively on $k+\bar{d}$ multiplied by the product of the proportion of new entrants in total population n and their propensity ρ to consume out of wealth. The term $\rho(k+\bar{d})$ measures the difference between the average consumption of the old generations and that of the new generation born at t. It is a reflection of the fact that current generations do not internalize the welfare of future generations in this model, unlike in the representative household model.

6.3.2 Government Debt, Taxes, and Redistribution across Generations

The behavior of the model is analyzed in figure 6.2. The balanced growth path is at point E, where both (6.17) and (6.18) are satisfied for constant consumption and capital per efficiency unit of labor. A unique saddle path leads to the balanced growth path. One can see that E implies lower consumption and capital per efficiency unit of labor than the corresponding representative household model at point R. Point R is the balanced growth path of a corresponding economy with $n=0$ in (6.18), which is the balanced growth path of a representative household economy.

With the help of the phase diagram in figure 6.3, one can easily show that a previously unanticipated permanent one-off increase in government debt leads to a reduction of both steady state capital and steady state private consumption. When government debt rises in a one-off fashion, consumption rises to point E_0 on the new saddle path, as current generations

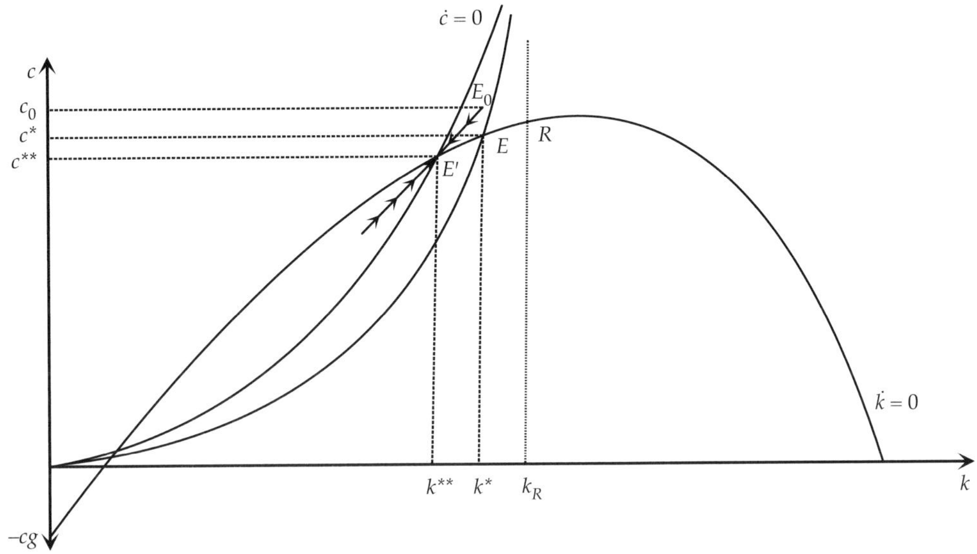

Figure 6.3
An increase in government debt in the Blanchard-Weil model.

treat their higher bond holdings as an increase in their wealth. This initiates a process of decumulation of capital and declining private consumption, which leads the economy toward the new balanced growth path at E′.

With the help of figure 6.4, one can show that a permanent increase in primary government expenditure financed by a rise in autonomous taxes also leads to lower steady state capital and private consumption. When the increase in government expenditure occurs, private consumption falls, as current generations react to the increase in the present value of their taxes. However, the anticipated increase in the present value of taxes for current generations is lower than the increase in the present value of primary government expenditure. This is because part of the future tax burden will be shouldered by future generations. Thus, private consumption falls by less than the increase in primary government expenditure, and total savings fall relative to equilibrium investment. This starts a process of capital decumulation and declining consumption on the new saddle path, which leads the economy to a new balanced growth path with lower steady state capital, output, and consumption per effective unit of labor.

As one can deduce from this analysis, in an OLG model, both the level of government debt and taxes and the primary government expenditure affect the balanced growth path. Ricardian equivalence does not hold, because current generations know that part of the increase in the present value of taxes required to finance an increase in government debt (or primary government expenditure) will be borne by future generations. Thus, total

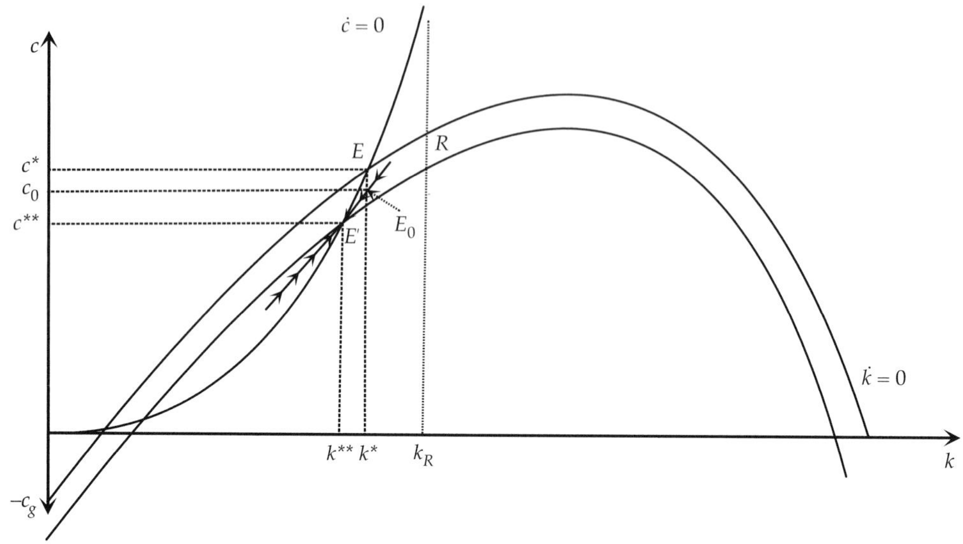

Figure 6.4
An increase in primary government expenditure in the Blanchard-Weil model.

savings and capital accumulation are affected, as government debt and expenditure policies essentially redistribute wealth across generations.[3]

Exercise 6.1 Introduce the government budget constraint in the simplified Diamond model of chapter 5 with logarithmic preferences and a Cobb-Douglas production function. Assume that taxes are lump sum and are levied on the young. Primary government expenditure, taxes, and government debt per worker grow at the rate of technical progress. Analyze the effects of a tax-financed permanent one-off increase in the level of government expenditure that leaves government debt on its previous path. Government expenditure per worker continues growing at the rate of technical progress after this permanent shift. Again, analyze the effects of a tax-financed permanent increase in the level of government debt that leaves primary government expenditure on its previous path. Government debt per worker continues growing at the rate of technical progress after this permanent shift. How would your conclusions be modified if this were a representative household model?

6.3.3 Dynamic Simulations of Fiscal Policy in a Calibrated Blanchard-Weil Model

The fiscal policies we have considered so far are restricted to one-off permanent increases in either primary government expenditure or government debt, per efficiency unit of labor.

3. This property of OLG models was first noted in the model of Diamond [1965]. In fact, as its title highlights, the Diamond paper was primarily about the effects of government debt on capital accumulation and economic growth.

This has allowed us to eliminate the dynamics of government debt accumulation and keep our model simple and analytically tractable (in that it consists of two differential equations, with one state and one control variable).

We shall now examine a more realistic description of fiscal policy in the Blanchard-Weil model, where the government chooses a level of primary government expenditure and autonomous taxes. The model then allows taxes and government debt to adjust gradually, in a way that satisfies the government budget constraint. Thus, we again assume that the government has a fixed target for primary government expenditure:

$$c_g(t) = \bar{c}_g. \tag{6.19}$$

However, let us now assume that the government changes taxes to stabilize government debt per efficiency unit of labor only gradually and not immediately, as in equation (6.14). To do this, it uses a *tax-smoothing policy* of the form

$$\tau(t) = \bar{\tau} + \psi d(t), \tag{6.20}$$

where $\bar{c}_g \geq \bar{\tau} > 0$, and $\psi > r_E - n - g > 0$. In (6.20), $\bar{\tau}$ denotes autonomous taxes (per efficiency unit of labor), $\psi > 0$ is the induced stabilizing reaction of taxes to the level of government debt, and r_E is the steady state real interest rate in the Blanchard-Weil model. As the government accumulates debt, taxes increase gradually to stabilize government debt per efficiency unit of labor. According to (6.20), taxes have two components: an autonomous component and a debt-induced component, which serves to stabilize government debt. This is a more realistic depiction of the actual response of taxes to government debt and is consistent with the tax smoothing observed in most economies.[4]

Substituting (6.19) and (6.20) in (6.12), government debt per efficiency unit of labor evolves according to

$$\dot{d}(t) = [\bar{c}_g - \bar{\tau}] + [r(t) - (n+g) - \psi]d(t). \tag{6.21}$$

Three parameters now describe fiscal policy: $\bar{c}_g$, primary government expenditure per efficiency unit of labor; $\bar{\tau}$, autonomous taxes; and ψ, the responsiveness of taxes to government debt.

The differential equation (6.21) will be stable if the responsiveness of taxes to government debt ψ is higher than $r(t) - n - g$, which, as we have assumed, will certainly apply in the steady state.

Let us now consider the simulation of a calibrated version of the Blanchard-Weil model, assuming a Cobb-Douglas production function of the form Ak^{α}, as in the previous simulations. We thus consider the simulation of a discrete time version of the model described

4. We shall delve deeper into the rationale for tax smoothing in chapter 21 on fiscal policy and the determination of government debt.

by (6.17) and (6.18), using a Cobb-Douglas production function; the marginal productivity conditions for the determination of real wages and the real interest rate; and the assumptions about fiscal policies embodied in (6.19), (6.20), and (6.21). This will allow us to get both a qualitative and a quantitative assessment of the full dynamic effects of tax-versus debt-financed increases in government expenditure, as well as debt-financed cuts in autonomous taxes.

The parameter values in the simulations are as follows: $A=1$, $\alpha=0.333$, $\rho=0.02$, $\theta=1$, $n=0.01$, $g=0.02$, $\delta=0.03$. These values are the same as the ones used in previous simulations, such as the simulations discussed in chapters 3, 4, and 5. As for the parameters of fiscal policy, let us assume that $\bar{c_g}=0.5$, $\bar{\tau}=0.45$, and $\psi=0.075$.[5]

We consider three alternative fiscal policy shocks. First, a 10% tax-financed increase in primary government expenditure (from 0.5 to 0.55; see figure 6.5). This policy does not result in an increase in government debt. Second, a 10% debt-financed increase in primary government expenditure (from 0.5 to 0.55; see figure 6.6). This policy results in an increase in government debt but also eventually in taxes, through the induced stabilizing reaction of taxes to the rise in government debt. Third, a debt-financed cut in autonomous taxes by 0.05 (see figure 6.7). This last shock amounts to a temporary tax cut equivalent to a 10% increase in governement expenditure. This tax reduction causes an increase in government debt and eventually, by means of equation (6.20), causes an increase in total taxes, because of the induced stabilizing reaction of taxes to the rise in government debt.

Figure 6.5 depicts the effects of a permanent tax-financed increase in primary government expenditure by 0.05 (10% of its original level). This increase reduces private consumption expenditure immediately because of the increase in autonomous taxes. However, as part of the future autonomous taxes will be paid by future generations, the reduction of private consumption by current generations is lower than the increase in primary government expenditure, and total savings fall. This starts a process of decumulation of capital that leads the economy to a new steady state, with lower capital, output, private consumption, and real wages per efficiency unit of labor, as well as a higher real interest rate.

However, note that the effects of an tax-financed increase in primary government expenditure on steady state nonfiscal real variables are extremely small. A 10% increase in real primary government expenditure (such as the one we have considered) reduces steady state real per capita output (and real wages) by only 0.07% and increases the steady state real interest rate by only 0.01 percentage points (i.e., from 4.24% to 4.25%). The steady state aggregate savings rate is reduced from 27.7% to 27.6%, again a very small decline.

Figure 6.6 depicts the effects of a debt-financed increase in primary government expenditure by 0.05 (10% of its original level). This increase also reduces private consumption

5. With these parameters for fiscal policy, there is a positive initial government debt, because zero debt would imply a primary deficit.

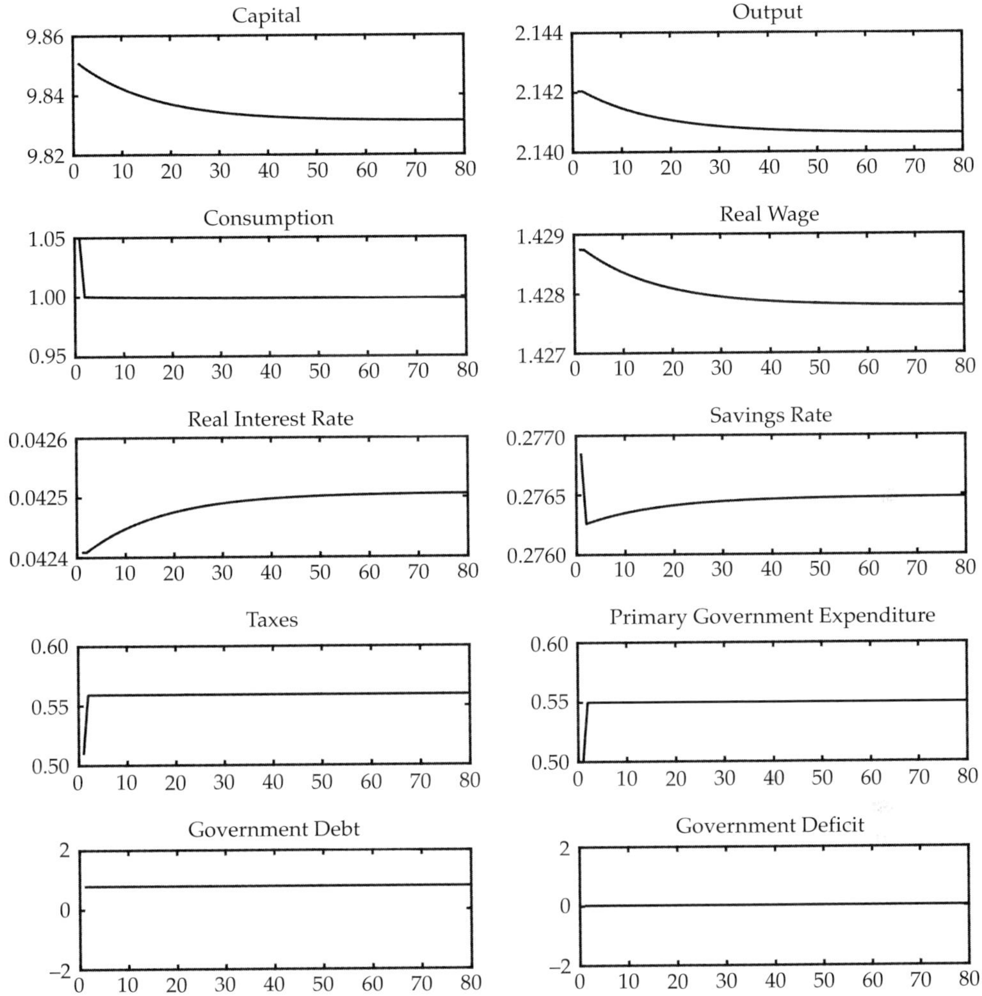

Figure 6.5
A tax-financed increase of primary government expenditure in the calibrated Blanchard-Weil model.

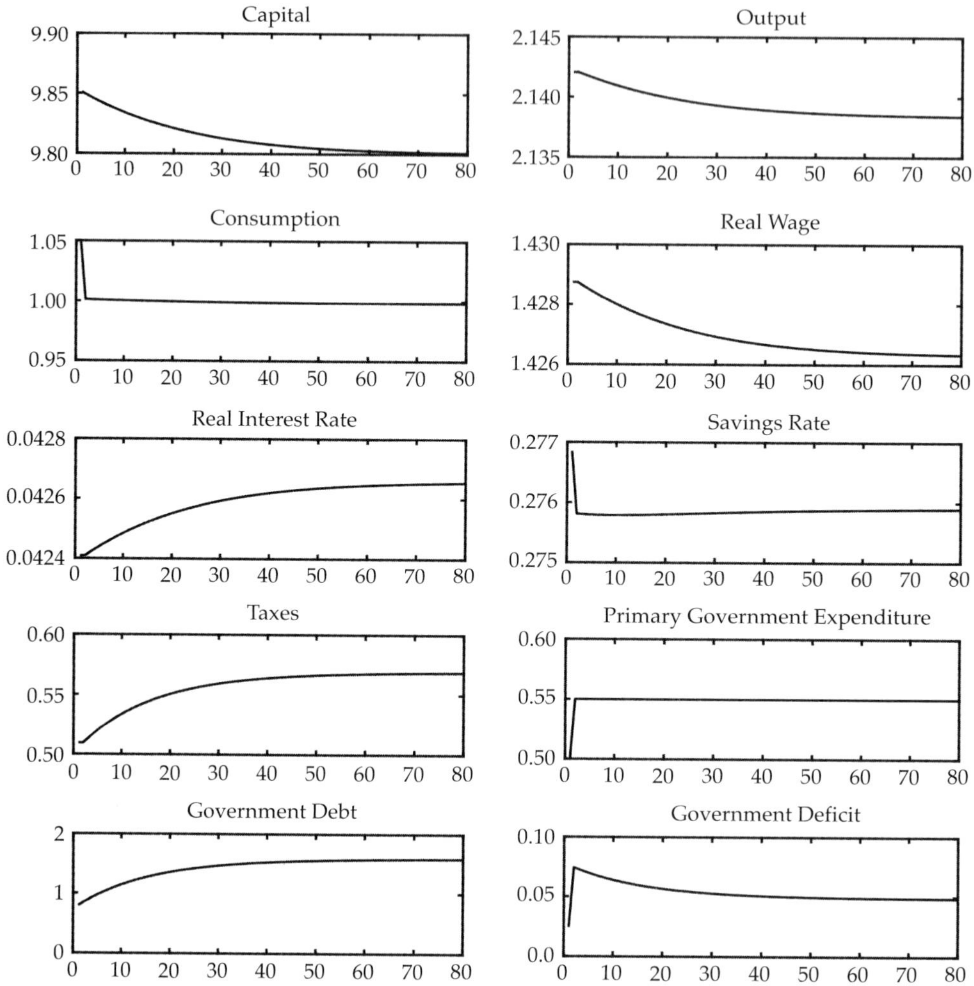

Figure 6.6
A debt-financed increase of primary government expenditure in the calibrated Blanchard-Weil model.

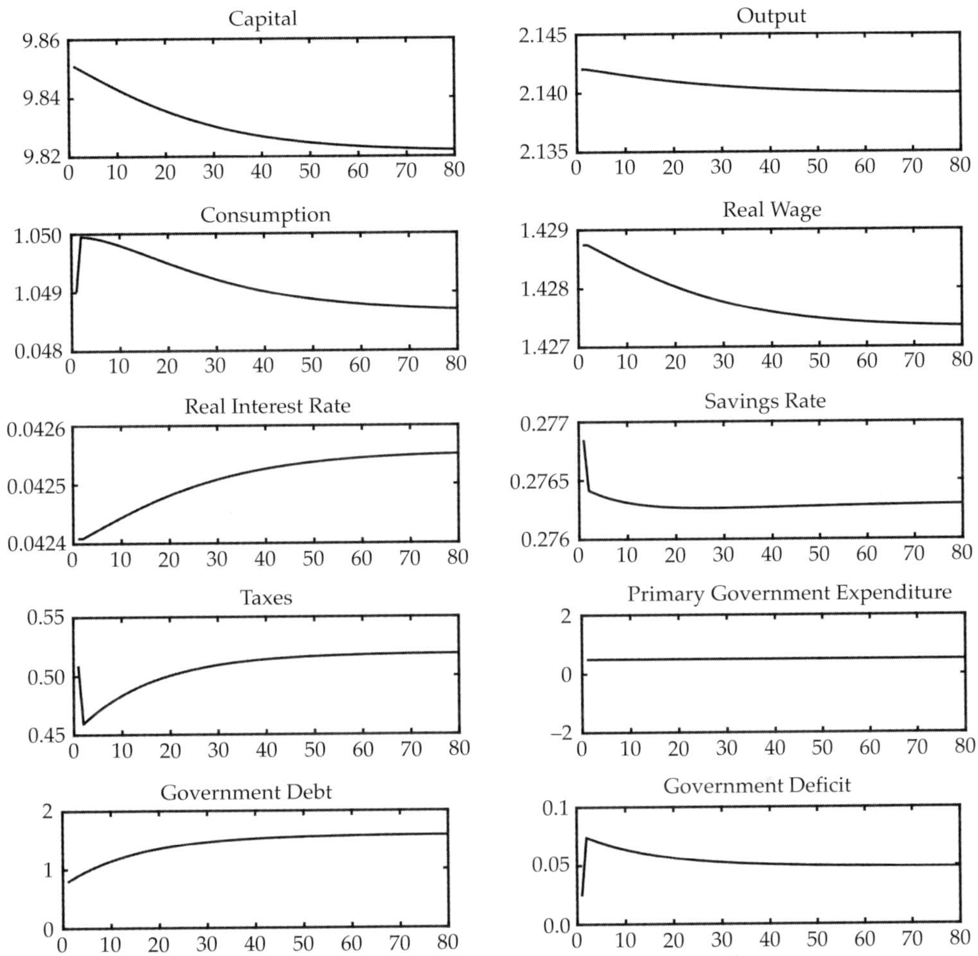

Figure 6.7
A debt-financed tax cut in the calibrated Blanchard-Weil model.

expenditure immediately, because of the anticipated future increase in taxes that will be required for debt to be eventually stabilized. However, as part of the future taxes will be paid by future generations, the reduction of private consumption by current generations is lower than the increase in primary government expenditure, and total savings fall. This starts a process of decumulation of capital that leads the economy to a new steady state with lower capital, output, private consumption, and real wages per efficiency unit of labor, as well as a higher real interest rate. Government debt is also increasing in the process and ends up at more than double its initial level.

Again, note that the effects of a debt-financed increase in primary government expenditure on nonfiscal steady state real variables are extremely small, although larger than for a tax-financed increase. A 10% increase in real primary government expenditure (such as the one we have considered) reduces steady state real per capita output (and real wages) by only 0.17% and increases the steady state real interest rate by only 0.03 percentage points (i.e., from 4.24% to 4.27%). The steady state aggregate savings rate is reduced from 27.7% to 27.6%, again a very small decline. However, the steady state debt to GDP ratio more than doubles, rising from 79% of GDP to 159% of GDP. Thus, although the real effects of a debt-financed increase in primary government expenditure on per capita real output and the real interest rate are almost three times as high as the effect of an equivalent tax-financed increase, they remain extremely small.

Finally, figure 6.7 depicts the effects of debt-financed cut in autonomous taxes by 0.05 (10% of the level of primary government expenditure). This cut increases private consumption expenditure immediately, because current generations anticipate that the future increases in taxes that will be required for the debt to be stabilized will be paid in part by future generations. The increase in private consumption and the associated reduction in savings start a process of decumulation of capital that leads the economy to a new steady state, with lower capital, output, private consumption, and real wages per efficiency unit of labor, as well as a higher real interest rate. Government debt is also increasing in the process and ends up being more than double its initial level.

The effects of a debt-financed cut in autonomous taxes on nonfiscal real variables are also extremely small. A 10% reduction in autonomous taxes reduces steady state real per capita output (and real wages) by only 0.10% and increases the steady state real interest rate by only 0.02 percentage points (from 4.24% to 4.26%). The steady state aggregate savings rate is reduced from 27.7% to 27.6%, again a very small decline. Thus, the real effects of a debt-financed cut in autonomous taxes are extremely small—even smaller than a debt-financed rise in primary government expenditure. However, the steady state debt to GDP ratio more than doubles, rising from 79% of GDP to 159% of GDP.

The results of these simulations are extremely informative. They suggest that although Ricardian equivalence does not hold in OLG models, the deviations from Ricardian equivalence imply very small real effects on steady state real variables (such as the savings rate, or per capita real output, real wages, and real interest rates).

This observation should not be very surprising, as the non-Ricardian effects in OLG models depend on the product of two quantitatively small parameters: population growth (which is assumed to take place through the entry of new generations) and the pure rate of time preference (which determines the proportion of total assets consumed by households). With a population growth rate of 1% per year and a pure rate of time preference of 2% per year (as assumed in the simulations), the product of the two is only 0.02%, a very small number indeed.[6]

6.4 Dynamic Effects of Distortionary Taxation

Until now we have assumed that taxation takes the form of lump sum taxes that do not distort factor prices and relative prices faced by households and business firms. However, lump sum taxes, are a very rare breed. Most forms of taxation, such as income and consumption taxes, are levied in ways that distort the incentives of households and firms to work, save, and invest. In this section, we investigate the dynamic effects of such distortionary taxes in the representative household model of economic growth.

6.4.1 Distortionary and Nondistortionary Taxes

To keep things simple, assume that the government runs a continuously balanced budget and has no government debt. The government engages in primary government expenditure and transfers to households, and it levies taxes on income from capital and labor, business profits before interest and depreciation, and on the consumption of households. Thus, at every instant, the government budget constraint per efficiency unit of labor is given by

$$\bar{c}_g + v(t) = \tau_w w(t) + \tau_k r(t)k(t) + \tau_c c(t) + \tau_f\,(f(k(t)) - w(t)), \tag{6.22}$$

where c_g is primary government expenditure, v is real transfers to households and firms, τ_w is the tax rate on labor income, τ_k is the tax rate on capital income, τ_c is the tax rate on consumption, and τ_f is the tax rate on firms' profits before interest and depreciation. All variables, apart from tax rates and the real interest rate r, are defined per efficiency unit of labor.

The existence of income and consumption tax rates and government transfers affects the intertemporal budget constraints of both households and firms (and thus their optimal savings and investment decisions). The first-order condition for the maximization of profits by

6. The empirical evidence on the long-run effects of government deficits and debts is generally mixed. But it is not necessarily inconsistent with approximate Ricardian equivalence of the kind implied by OLG models or models with other distortions (such as liquidity constraints). See Bernheim [1987, 1989], Barro [1989], and especially Seater [1993] for surveys of the empirical evidence.

firms now takes the form

$$(1-\tau_f)Af'(k(t))=r(t)+\delta. \tag{6.23}$$

Firms now equate the post-tax marginal product of capital with the pre-tax user cost of capital $r+\delta$, because taxes are levied on profits before interest and depreciation.

The Euler equation for consumption of the representative household now takes the form

$$\dot{c}(t)=\frac{1}{\theta}[(1-\tau_k)r(t)-\rho-\theta g]c(t). \tag{6.24}$$

Because income from capital is taxed, it is the net-of-tax real interest rate that drives savings decisions.

From (6.23) and (6.24), it follows that

$$\dot{c}(t)=\frac{1}{\theta}[(1-\tau_k)\left((1-\tau_f)Af'(k(t))-\delta\right)-\rho-\theta g]c(t). \tag{6.25}$$

The accumulation equation for capital is not affected by the existence of distortionary taxes, because the government budget constraint (6.22) shows that the revenue from distortionary taxes minus transfers is equal to primary government expenditure. Thus, the accumulation of capital (per efficiency unit of labor) is determined by the usual accumulation equation of the form

$$\dot{k}(t)=Af(k(t))-c(t)-\bar{c}_g-(n+g+\delta)k(t). \tag{6.26}$$

The behavior of the economy is determined by (6.25) and (6.26). The only distortionary taxes that enter these two equations are the tax rate τ_k on interest income and the tax rate τ_f on the profits of firms before interest and depreciation.

The tax rate τ_w on labor income does not affect the behavior of the economy. The reason is that we have assumed that labor supply is inelastic: Every household member supplies one unit of labor, irrespective of the real wage. If labor supply were elastic, then taxes on labor income would imply distortions and have real effects.

In addition, the consumption tax τ_c does not enter the Euler equation for consumption, as we have assumed that this tax rate is constant and does not affect the intertemporal substitution of consumption (savings). And because labor supply is also assumed to be exogenous, the tax rate on consumption does not affect labor market incentives, as there is no substitution between consumption and leisure.

Thus in the Ramsey model with inelastic labor supply, as we have assumed throughout, the only distortionary taxes are those on income from capital and those on profits of business firms before interest and depreciation. All other taxes are nondistortionary.

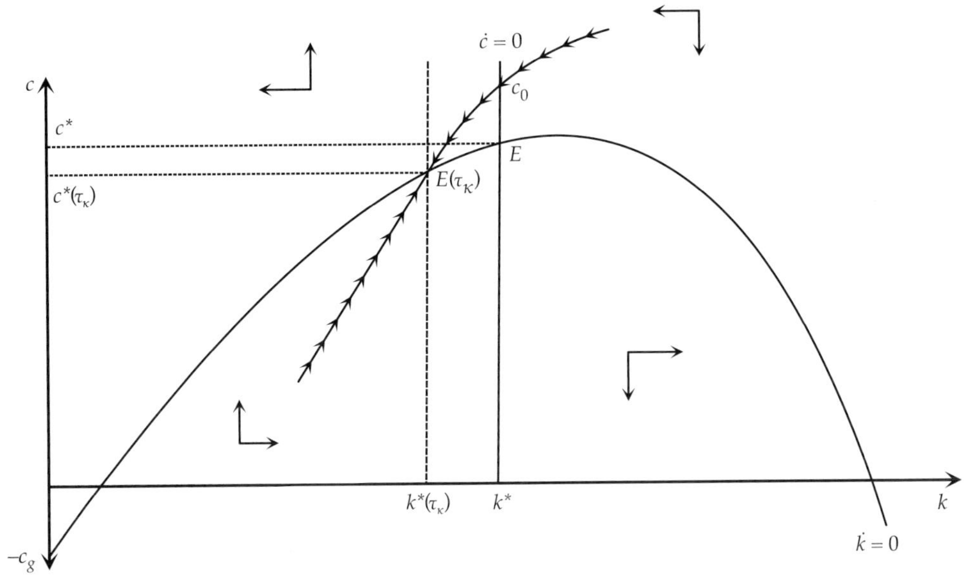

Figure 6.8
Short- and long-run effects of capital income taxation in the Ramsey model.

6.4.2 Dynamic Effects of Capital Income and Business Gross Profits Taxation

The dynamic effects of capital income taxes are analyzed in figure 6.8. Assume that initially, the taxation of income from capital is zero and the economy is at the balanced growth path E. The government announces a previously unanticipated capital income tax at a rate τ_k. The proceeds are returned to households in the form of transfer payments.

The steady state consumption line moves to the left, because on the new balanced growth path, the pre-tax real interest rate must rise, something that requires a lower steady state capital stock per efficiency unit of labor. As the capital stock is a predetermined variable, the pre-tax real interest rate is also a predetermined variable. The introduction of the tax thus causes a reduction in post-tax real interest rates for households. Consumption rises to c_0, and savings fall immediately. The economy enters into a process of capital decumulation, rising real interest rates, and falling consumption. In the new balanced growth path at $E(\tau_k)$, the capital stock per efficiency unit of labor is lower, and so is total output and private consumption.

A similar process will take place if there is an increase in the tax rate on business profits before interest and depreciation (gross profits). This will initially cause a fall in the real interest paid out to households, a temporary increase in private consumption, a process of decumulation of capital, and adjustment to a new balanced growth path. This new path

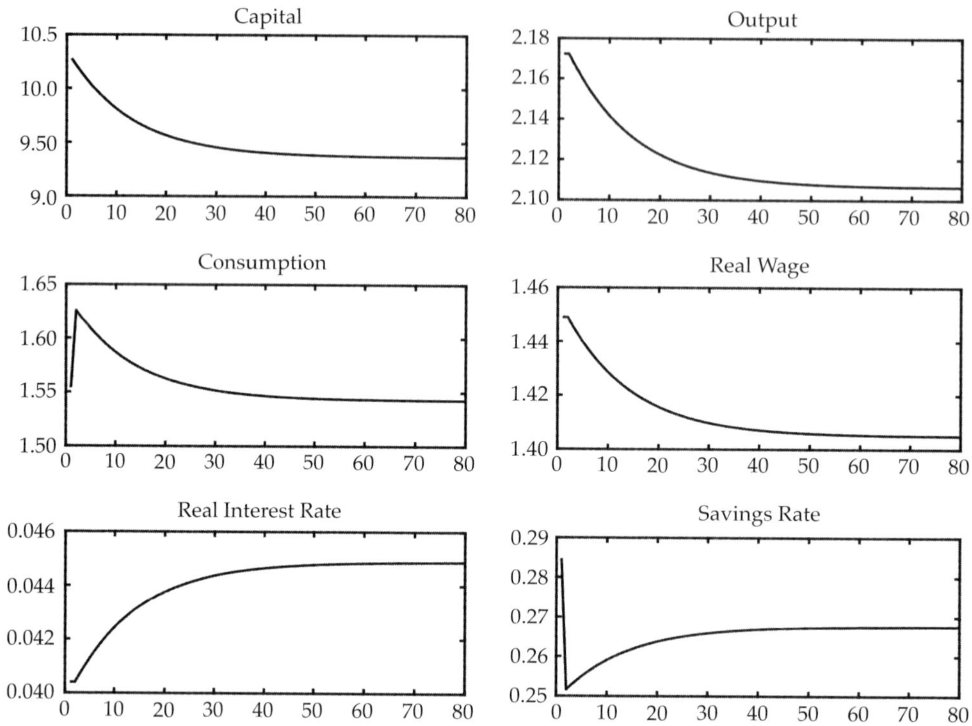

Figure 6.9
Dynamic effects of a 10% tax on interest income in the calibrated Ramsey model.

will have a lower capital stock, lower output and income, lower real wages, and lower consumption per efficiency unit of labor.

The dynamic effects of distortionary taxation would be qualitatively similar in OLG models, such as the model of Blanchard and Weil.

Exercise 6.2 Introduce distortionary taxes in the Blanchard-Weil OLG model, and analyze the impact of a proportional income tax levied on the labor and capital income of households. The tax proceeds are returned to households without affecting the distribution of income. Assume that initially, the taxation of income from capital is zero and the economy is on the balanced growth path. The government announces a previously unanticipated income tax at a rate τ. Primary government expenditure and debt remain at their previous path.

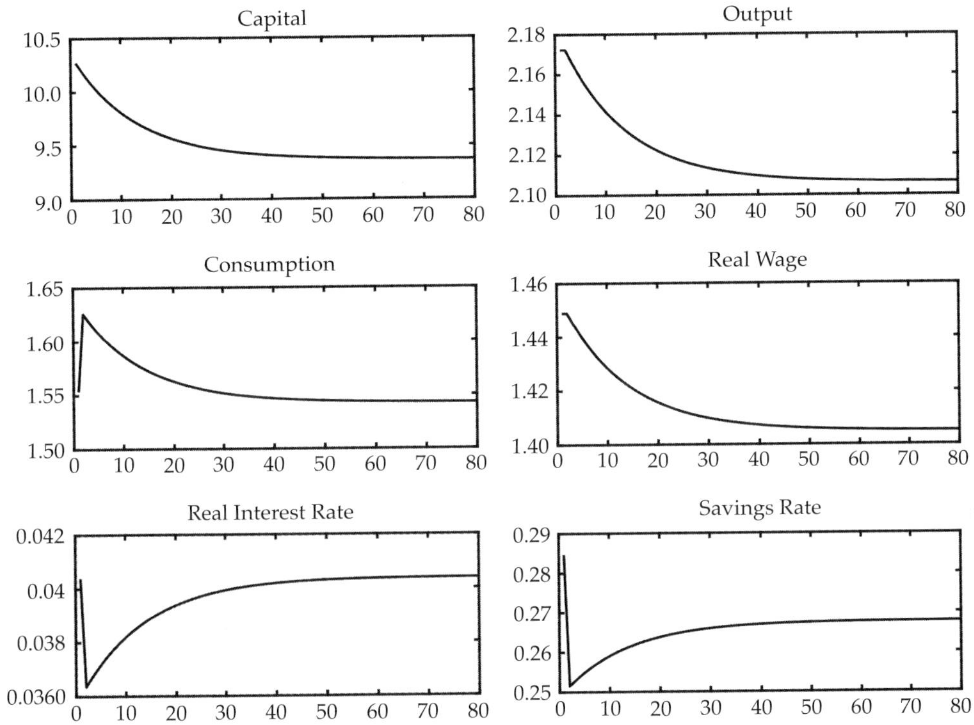

Figure 6.10
Dynamic effects of a 10% tax on business profits, before interest and depreciation, in the calibrated Ramsey model.

6.4.3 Dynamic Simulations of Increases in Capital Income and Business Gross Profits Taxation

To quantitatively examine the dynamic effects of an increase in capital income taxation in the Ramsey model, we can simulate, for the specific values of the parameters of the model assumed so far, the transition from a balanced growth path without capital income taxation to a balanced growth path after the introduction of capital income taxation.

The parameter values used in the simulations are the same as those used in the simulations of the Ramsey model in chapter 4. Thus, we assume a Cobb-Douglas production function, and the parameters take the values $A=1$, $\alpha=0.333$, $\rho=0.02$, $\theta=1$, $n=0.01$, $g=0.02$, $\delta=0.03$.

In the simulation depicted in figure 6.9, the economy is on its original balanced growth path, without capital income taxation. In period 1, the government imposes a previously unanticipated 10% tax on interest income (increase of τ_k). This increase, as predicted theoretically in the analysis of figure 6.8, leads to a decrease in the net real interest rate enjoyed by households. This decreased rate causes an increase in consumption and a fall in the savings rate, which initiate a process of capital decumulation, a gradual decline in real output and real wages, and a gradual increase in the pre-tax real interest rate.

The reduction in real wages and the increase in the pre-tax real interest rate are a result of the declining capital stock, which causes a falling marginal product of labor and a rising marginal product of capital. The economy gradually converges to a new balanced growth path. On this path, capital per efficiency unit of labor is lower by approximately 8.9% compared to the original balanced growth path, output and real wages are lower by 3.0%, consumption is lower by 0.7% (due to the decline in the savings rate), and the (pre-tax) real interest rate has increased by 0.44 percentage points (or approximately 10%). The steady state savings rate, which is endogenous in this model, falls from 28.5% to 26.8%.

The dynamic real effects of a 10% tax on on business profits before interest and depreciation are exactly the same. The only real variable that behaves differently is the pre-tax real interest rate, which initially falls and then gradually returns to its original steady state value through the decumulation of capital. The results of this simulation are presented in figure 6.10.

As one can deduce from these simulations, even a relatively low rate of capital income taxation or taxation of business net income (before interest and depreciation) causes relatively large declines in per capita output and income, as it leads to a significant reduction of savings and capital accumulation.

6.5 Conclusion

In this chapter, we first discussed the intertemporal government budget constraint and analyzed the conditions for government debt sustainability. We also analyzed the dynamic effects of government debt and primary government expenditure in the representative household model of Ramsey and the OLG model of Blanchard and Weil. We finally analyzed the dynamic impact of distortionary taxes.

In the representative household model without distortionary taxes, fiscal policy has no effects on either the convergence process or the balanced growth path. The only fiscal variable that matters for the path of private consumption is the present value of primary government expenditure, which reduces the present value of private consumption by exactly the same amount. The method of financing primary government expenditure—such as government debt and (nondistortionary) taxes—does not affect private consumption or the adjustment and balanced growth path of all other real variables. This result is known as Ricardian equivalence between lump sum taxes and government debt. Holdings of government bonds by the representative household are not considered as wealth and do not affect household consumption, because the representative household realizes that government bonds will be financed by future taxes of equal present value.

The Ricardian equivalence result does not apply to OLG models. The levels of government debt and primary government expenditure affect both the balanced growth path and the adjustment path. This is because current generations realize that part of the future taxes that will finance primary government expenditure (or interest on the government debt) will be shouldered by future generations. Consequently, both primary government expenditure and government debt lead to a reduction in aggregate savings and to a reduction of steady state capital and private consumption. However, a dynamic simulation of the Blanchard-Weil OLG model suggests that the effects of deviations from Ricardian equivalence are quantitatively small in this model.

We also analyzed the dynamic impact of distortionary taxes, as taxes are rarely nondistortionary. In the representative household and OLG models that we have considered, labor supply is exogenous. Consequently, tax rates on income from employment or constant consumption tax rates do not affect employment and savings. As a result, they do not affect either the adjustment path or the balanced growth path. However, tax rates on capital income or business earnings before interest and depreciation are distortionary. They have negative effects on private savings and investment, the accumulation of capital, and per capita real output and real wages. A dynamic simulation of a calibrated Ramsey model suggests that these effects of capital income taxation may be quantitatively significant.

7

Money, Inflation, and Economic Growth

In the long-run growth models we have presented so far, there is no role for money. Yet money performs very important functions in an economy. Money is a unit of account, in terms of which prices are defined; a means of payments, which reduces transaction costs; and the most liquid store of value.

In this chapter, we allow for the role of money in the growth models analyzed so far. We first consider a representative household model, in which real money balances enter the utility function of households. Then we analyze a corresponding OLG model.[1]

In models with money, one can draw the distinction between *real variables* (such as the ones we have analyzed so far) and *nominal variables* (such as the stock of money, the price level, inflation, nominal output, nominal wages, and nominal interest rates). Whereas real variables are measured in physical or money-free terms, all nominal variables are expressed in terms of money.

By assuming that money enters the utility function of households, we can derive a money demand function from microeconomic foundations, as a result of the solution of an intertemporal optimization problem by households.

Based on this particular approach to money demand, we will see that the demand for real money balances is proportional to aggregate consumption and depends negatively on the nominal interest rate. Because money is a nominal asset that pays no interest, the nominal interest rate measures the opportunity cost of holding real money balances. The demand for nominal money balances is proportional to the price level, a property that implies the *neutrality of money*. The stock of nominal money balances does not affect any real variables in these models, only the price level.

1. The approach to the derivation of money demand in the continuous time models of this chapter is the so-called *money in the utility function* approach. It is based on the assumption that real money balances yield utility due to their liquidity services and was first utilized in macroeconomics by Patinkin [1956]. This approach contrasts with an alternative one, used in chapter 2, called *cash in advance*. The cash in advance approach emphasizes the role of money as a means of payments, which reduces transaction costs, eliminating the need for a double coincidence of wants between buyers and sellers (Clower [1967]). As shown by Feenstra [1986], both approaches are functionally equivalent. We compare the two approaches in chapter 12, which has a fuller treatment of alternative partial and general equilibrium approaches to money demand and the money market.

We also analyze the determination of inflation, the nominal interest rate and other nominal variables, and the intertemporal effects of the growth rate of the money supply on the path of economic growth.

Monetary conditions in modern economies are determined by central banks. The central bank may affect both interest rates and the money supply through a variety of policy instruments at its disposal. The money supply consists of the quantity of bank notes (and coins) in circulation and the stock of deposits in commercial banks. Thus, central banks can affect the money supply both directly and indirectly. In this chapter, we concentrate on the dynamic effects of the growth rate of the money supply, assuming that the money supply is fully controlled by the central bank. More general and more detailed treatments of the money market and the role of central banks is postponed until chapters 12 and 20.

In the representative household model, the dynamic path of all real variables (with the exception of the stock of real money balances) turns out to be independent of either the level or the rate of growth of the money supply. These chiefly affect nominal variables, such as the level of prices, inflation, and nominal interest rates. The level of the money supply affects no real variables, only the level of prices. This property is known as the *neutrality of money*. The rate of growth of the money supply only affects inflation and nominal interest rates. The demand for real money balances, which depends negatively on the nominal interest rate, is thus the only real variable that is affected by the growth rate of the money supply. This is because this growth rate affects the opportunity cost of holding real money balances. To put it differently, the growth rate of the money supply imposes an inflation tax on the real money balances held by households. The independence of the path of all real variables—apart from the path of real money balances—from the growth rate of the money supply is known as the *superneutrality of money*.

In OLG models, the growth rate of the money supply affects the path of all real variables, because in OLG models, holdings of real money balances differ among generations. Thus, when the growth rate of the money supply increases, older generations, which hold higher real money balances, reduce their asset holdings and their consumption more than younger generations do, because they pay a higher inflation tax. As a result, aggregate consumption falls, and aggregate savings rise. This leads to a higher accumulation of capital, which has a positive effect on the growth path.[2]

The differences in the effects of the growth rate of the money supply between representative household and OLG models arise for the same reason that government debt has no real effects in representative household models, whereas it has real effects in OLG models.

2. The literature on money and economic growth originated with Tobin [1965]. Sidrauski [1967] first used a representative household model to demonstrate the superneutrality of money (i.e., that the rate of growth rate of the money supply does not affect the path of real variables on the adjustment path or the balanced growth). The literature has since expanded exponentially. Weil [1987b, 1991] analyzed the role of money in an OLG model and demonstrated that the superneutrality of money does not apply in such models.

Ricardian equivalence and the superneutrality of money are closely linked, as the growth rate of the money supply is essentially an inflation tax on real money balances.

In OLG models, this inflation tax and government debt have different effects on current and future generations, and thus they affect aggregate savings. An increase in government debt redistributes taxes from current to future generations, causing an increase in the consumption of current generations, whereas an increase in the growth rate of the money supply redistributes taxes from future to current generations, causing a reduction in the consumption of current generations. This redistribution among generations and its effects on aggregate savings are thus the reason for the nonexistence of Ricardian equivalence and the superneutrality of money in OLG models.

7.1 Private Consumption and Money Demand in a Representative Household Model

Assume, as in the Ramsey model of chapter 4, a competitive economy in which all households are identical. Households are indexed by j, where j is uniformly distributed between zero and 1. Thus, $j \in [0, 1]$. We therefore focus on the behavior of only one of them, the representative household.

The number of members of each household is equal to $L(t)$ and is growing at an exogenous rate n, which is also the growth rate of population $L(t)$. Labor supply and employment is equal to $L(t)$, and the efficiency of labor $h(t)$ grows at an exogenous rate of technical progress g. The instantaneous utility function of households depends on consumption of goods and services, and on holdings of real money balances.

7.1.1 Money in the Utility Function of Households

Household j selects a path of consumption and real money balances to maximize the following intertemporal utility function:

$$U_j = \int_{t=0}^{\infty} e^{-\rho t} u\left(c_j(t), m_j(t)\right) L(t) dt. \tag{7.1}$$

The maximization takes place under the instantaneous budget constraint

$$\dot{a}_j(t) = \left(r(t) - n\right) a_j(t) + w(t)h(t) - \tau(t)h(t) - c_j(t) - \left(r(t) + \pi(t)\right) m_j(t), \tag{7.2}$$

and the transversality condition

$$\lim_{t \to \infty} e^{-\int_{s=0}^{t} (r(s)-n) ds} a_j(t) = 0, \tag{7.3}$$

where ρ is the pure rate of time preference of households, and u is a quasi-concave instantaneous utility function that depends on consumption and real money balances (assumed positive). In addition, $c_j(t)$ denotes average consumption per person of household j at time t, $m_j(t)$ denotes average per person real money balances of household j at time t, $a_j(t)$ is average assets per person (nonhuman wealth) of household j at time t, $w(t)$ denotes the real wage per efficiency unit of labor at time t, $h(t)$ is labor efficiency per worker, $\tau(t)$ denotes average taxes (minus transfers) per efficiency unit of labor at time t, $r(t)$ is the real interest rate at time t, n is the population growth rate (equal to the growth rate of members per household), and $\pi(t)$ is inflation (which is equal to expected inflation).

Real money balances provide utility because of their liquidity services: they facilitate payments (the exchange of goods and services) and reduce transaction costs. The instantaneous utility function is assumed to take the form

$$u_j(t) = u\left(c_j(t), m_j(t)\right) = \gamma \frac{c_j(t)^{1-\theta}}{1-\theta} + (1-\gamma)\frac{m_j(t)^{1-\theta}}{1-\theta}, \tag{7.4}$$

where $1/\theta$ is the intertemporal elasticity of substitution of consumption and real money balances, and γ is the share of consumption in the utility of the household. This utility function, which is a generalization of the constant elasticity of intertemporal substitution (CEIS) utility function we used previously, is additively separable: The elasticity of substitution between consumption and real money balances is equal to unity.

7.1.2 Nominal and Real Interest Rates and the Opportunity Cost of Real Money Balances

Unlike other assets held by households (such as capital or government bonds), the nominal yield of money is equal to zero, because money balances do not pay interest. Moreover, when there is a positive inflation rate $\pi(t)$, real (inflation adjusted) money balances depreciate at the inflation rate $\pi(t)$.

Therefore, the opportunity cost of holding real money balances is equal to the sum of the real return of interest-yielding assets plus the expected inflation rate. This is defined as the nominal interest rate $i(t)$, which is determined by

$$i(t) = r(t) + \pi(t). \tag{7.5}$$

This relationship between nominal and real interest rates is the Fisher equation introduced and discussed in chapter 2. It was first highlighted by Irving Fisher in 1896.[3]

7.1.3 First-Order Conditions for an Optimum

Maximizing (7.1) under the constraint (7.2) by forming the relevant Hamilton function yields the following first-order conditions:

$$\gamma c_j(t)^{-\theta} = \lambda_j(t), \tag{7.6}$$

3. See Fisher [1896] or Fisher [1930], chapter 2.

$$(1-\gamma)m_j(t)^{-\theta}=\lambda_j(t)(r(t)+\pi(t)), \tag{7.7}$$

$$\dot{\lambda}_j(t)=-\,(r(t)-\rho)\,\lambda_j(t), \tag{7.8}$$

where $\lambda_j(t)$ is the current value multiplier of the relevant current value Hamilton function, and its economic interpretation is that it measures the shadow value of marginal savings (assets) of the household. The asset accumulation constraint (7.2) and the transversality condition (7.3) must also be satisfied.

From (7.6), $\lambda_j(t)$, which is the shadow value of marginal savings, is equal to the current marginal utility of consumption. At the optimum, the marginal value of savings must be equal to the marginal utility of consumption, and the household must be indifferent between consumption and savings.

From (7.7), the current marginal utility of real money balances is equal to the marginal utility of consumption $\lambda_j(t)$ times the opportunity cost of holding real money balances. At the optimum, the marginal value of holding real money balances must be equal to the opportunity cost of holding money, evaluated in terms of the marginal utility of consumption. Thus, at the optimum, the household should be indifferent between substituting consumption for the utility services of money.

Finally, from (7.8), the marginal utility of consumption falls at a rate equal to the difference between the real interest rate and the pure rate of time preference. This is another way of saying that the expected real return on savings, including capital gains on assets, is equal to the pure rate of time preference of the household. This can be seen by rearranging (7.8):

$$r(t)+\frac{\dot{\lambda}_j(t)}{\lambda_j(t)}=\rho.$$

As shown below, we can now use the first-order conditions to derive the money demand function and the Euler equation for consumption.

7.1.4 The Money Demand Function

Dividing (7.7) by (7.6) and solving for real money balances, we can derive a function for the demand for real money balances by the representative household:

$$m_j(t)=\left(\frac{\gamma}{1-\gamma}(r(t)+\pi(t))\right)^{-\frac{1}{\theta}}c_j(t). \tag{7.9}$$

We can use (7.9) to deduce aggregate money demand. Multiplying both sides of (7.9) by $L(t)$, we get

$$\frac{M(t)}{P(t)}=\left(\frac{\gamma}{1-\gamma}(r(t)+\pi(t))\right)^{-\frac{1}{\theta}}C(t), \tag{7.10}$$

where $M(t)$ is the aggregate nominal money supply, $P(t)$ is the price level, and $C(t)$ is aggregate real consumption of goods and services. Equation (7.10) describes the aggregate money demand function in this model. Aggregate money demand is proportional to the price level and aggregate real consumption, and it depends negatively on the nominal interest rate. Put differently, the elasticity of aggregate money demand with respect to the price level and aggregate private consumption is equal to one, whereas the elasticity of aggregate money demand with respect to the nominal interest rate is equal to $-1/\theta$, the elasticity of intertemporal substitution.

Equation (7.10) is characterized by homogeneity of degree one with respect to the price level, because households demand money for its purchasing power. For a given aggregate real consumption and nominal interest rates, doubling the money supply would cause a doubling of the price level. This property is known as the neutrality of money.

Expressing real money balances per efficiency unit of labor, we have

$$m(t) = \left(\frac{\gamma}{1-\gamma} (r(t) + \pi(t)) \right)^{-\frac{1}{\theta}} c(t), \tag{7.11}$$

where $c = C/hL$, $m = (M/P)/hL$, and h is the efficiency of labor.

7.1.5 Growth Rate of the Money Supply and Inflation

One can use (7.10) or (7.11) to determine the price level and inflation, assuming that the aggregate nominal money supply and its rate of growth μ are determined by the government or a government agency, such as a central bank.

From (7.10) and (7.5), it follows that

$$\frac{M(t)}{P(t)C(t)} = \left(\frac{\gamma}{1-\gamma} i(t) \right)^{-\frac{1}{\theta}}. \tag{7.12}$$

For given aggregate real consumption and nominal interest rates, the level of the nominal money supply determines the level of prices. From (7.12), it follows that

$$\left(\mu - \pi(t) - \frac{\dot{C}(t)}{C(t)} \right) = -\frac{1}{\theta} \frac{\dot{i}(t)}{i(t)}. \tag{7.13}$$

Thus, from (7.13), inflation is determined to be

$$\pi(t) = \mu - \frac{\dot{C}(t)}{C(t)} + \frac{1}{\theta} \frac{\dot{i}(t)}{i(t)}. \tag{7.14}$$

For a given rate of growth in private consumption and fixed nominal interest rates, the inflation rate $\pi(t)$ is determined by the rate of growth of the money supply. For example, in a steady state where the growth rate of consumption in equal to $g+n$, and inflation and nominal interest rates are constant, inflation would be determined by

$$\pi = \mu - g - n. \tag{7.15}$$

Equation (7.15) is the basis of the monetary approach to the determination of inflation. In the long run, inflation is determined by the difference between the growth rate of the money supply and the long-run growth rate of aggregate output and consumption.

7.1.6 The Euler Equation for Consumption

Turning now to the first-order conditions for consumption, from (7.6) and (7.8), it follows that

$$\dot{c}_j(t) = \frac{1}{\theta}\left(r(t) - \rho\right) c_j(t), \tag{7.16}$$

which is the standard Euler equation for consumption in a representative household model. In this monetary model, it does not differ from the corresponding equation in a real model, such as the one examined in chapter 4.

The real money balances and the nominal interest rate do not appear in (7.16) because of the assumption of additively separable preferences of the household for consumption and real money balances. With additively separable preferences, the marginal utility of consumption in (7.6) does not depend on real money balances or the determinants of their demand (such as the nominal interest rate).

It is straightforward to show that without additively separable preferences, the marginal utility of consumption in (7.6) depends on real money balances as well, and (7.16) does not generally follow.

For example, consider a nonadditively separable CES instantaneous utility function of the form

$$u(c_j(t), m_j(t)) = \left(\gamma c_i(t)^{(\sigma-1)/\sigma} + (1-\gamma) m_i(t)^{(\sigma-1)/\sigma}\right)^{\sigma/(\sigma-1)},$$

where σ is the elasticity of substitution between consumption and real money balances. The first-order condition (7.6) would then take the form

$$\frac{\partial u}{\partial c_j} = \frac{\gamma}{\gamma c_j(t)^{(\sigma-1)/\sigma} + (1-\gamma) m_j(t)^{(\sigma-1)/\sigma}} c_j(t)^{1/\sigma} = \lambda_j(t).$$

With an elasticity of substitution σ different from unity (i.e., nonadditively separable preferences), the marginal utility of consumption depends on real money balances as well.

In any case, in what follows, we shall continue assuming additively separable preferences between consumption and real money balances, mainly for reasons of analytical simplicity. In this case, (7.16) holds. From (7.16), the evolution of aggregate consumption C and consumption per efficiency unit of labor c are determined by

$$\dot{C}(t) = \frac{1}{\theta}\left(r(t) - \rho + \theta n\right) C(t), \tag{7.17}$$

$$\dot{c}(t) = \frac{1}{\theta}\left(r(t) - \rho - \theta g\right) c(t), \tag{7.18}$$

where g is the rate of exogenous technical progress.

From (7.17) and (7.18), the rate of growth of aggregate consumption (or consumption per efficiency unit of labor) only depends on real variables and not the money supply or its rate of growth.

7.2 Aggregate Capital Accumulation in a Ramsey Model with Money

We next turn to the determinants of capital accumulation, output, and other real variables, such as the real interest rate and real wages.

7.2.1 The Production Function, the Real Interest Rate, and the Real Wage

As in the previous models, assume that output per efficiency unit of labor is determined by

$$y(t) = Af(k(t)), \tag{7.19}$$

where f is a neoclassical production function with all the usual properties. Once the capital stock per efficiency unit of labor is determined, output is determined by the production function (7.19).

We have already assumed an exogenous rate of growth of population n and an exogenous rate of technical progress g. The depreciation rate of the capital stock will be assumed equal to δ, where $1 > \delta > 0$.

In a competitive equilibrium, assuming that firms maximize profits, the real interest rate $r(t)$ and the real wage per efficiency unit of labor $w(t)$ will be determined by the usual marginal productivity conditions:

$$r(t) = Af'(k(t)) - \delta, \tag{7.20}$$

$$w(t) = Af(k(t)) - k(t)Af'(k(t)). \tag{7.21}$$

7.2.2 The Inflation Tax and the Accumulation of Capital

We shall assume that the assets of household j in equation (7.2) consist of capital, government bonds, and money,

$$a_j(t) = k_j(t) + d_j(t) + m_j(t), \tag{7.22}$$

where k_j, d_j, and m_j denote physical capital, real government bonds, and real money balances, respectively, held by an average member of household j.

Substituting (7.22) in (7.2), after multiplying by $L(t)$, we get an accumulation equation for total household assets in the economy:

$$\dot{K}(t)+\dot{D}(t)+\left(\dot{\frac{M(t)}{P(t)}}\right)=r(t)\left(K(t)+D(t)+\frac{M(t)}{P(t)}\right)+w(t)h(t)L(t) \\ -T(t)-C(t)-(r(t)+\pi(t))\frac{M(t)}{P(t)}. \tag{7.23}$$

The rate of growth of real money balances is given by $\mu-\pi(t)$. Thus, we have

$$\left(\dot{\frac{M(t)}{P(t)}}\right)=(\mu-\pi(t))\frac{M(t)}{P(t)}. \tag{7.24}$$

Substituting (7.24) into (7.23) and solving for the accumulation of physical capital and real government bonds, we get

$$\dot{K}(t)+\dot{D}(t)=r(t)K(t)+w(t)h(t)L(t)+r(t)D(t)-T(t)-\mu\frac{M(t)}{P(t)}-C(t). \tag{7.25}$$

The aggregate accumulation of capital and real government bonds by households depends on the difference between aggregate household disposable income and aggregate household consumption. The disposable income of households consists of their total asset and labor income minus taxes $T(t)$ and the inflation tax imposed by the government through the growth rate of the money supply. Government revenue from the monopoly of issuing money, usually referred to as *seigniorage*, is equal to $\mu(M(t)/P(t))$ and comprises a tax on real money balances held by households.

Equation (7.25) describes the budget constraint of households. The government budget constraint in an economy in which the government has the monopoly of money creation is described by

$$\dot{D}(t)=C_g(t)+r(t)D(t)-T(t)-\mu\frac{M(t)}{P(t)}, \tag{7.26}$$

which suggests that the government accumulates debt to the extent that primary government expenditure C_g plus the real interest expenditure on existing debt rD exceeds total taxes (minus transfers) T plus the inflation tax $\mu(M/P)$.

Substituting the government budget constraint (7.26) into the household budget constraint (7.25), we end up with the well-known equation for aggregate capital accumulation:

$$\dot{K}(t)=r(t)K(t)+w(t)h(t)L(t)-C_g(t)-C(t). \tag{7.27}$$

Only primary government expenditure, and not the way it is financed, appears in the aggregate capital accumulation equation. Debt, taxes, and seigniorage revenue do not affect the accumulation of capital.

Expressing both sides of (7.27) per efficiency unit of labor (i.e., dividing by $h(t)L(t)$), we get

$$\dot{k}(t) = r(t)k(t) + w(t) - c(t) - c_g(t) - (n+g)k(t)$$
$$= Af(k(t)) - c(t) - c_g(t) - (n+g+\delta)k(t). \tag{7.28}$$

The economy accumulates capital per efficiency unit of labor when total savings per efficiency unit of labor exceed the investment required to maintain a constant capital stock per efficiency unit of labor. This is the same as the capital accumulation equation in the Ramsey model without money. The existence of money and money demand also does not affect the accumulation of real capital.

7.3 Effects of the Growth Rate of the Money Supply in the Ramsey Monetary Model

The evolution of real variables in the Ramsey model with money is determined by the Euler equation for consumption (7.18) and the capital accumulation equation (7.28). These two determine the paths of private consumption and the capital stock.

All other real variables are functions of the capital stock (per efficiency unit of labor) or private consumption. Output is determined by the production function (7.19). The real interest rate and real wage are determined by the marginal productivity conditions, which are only a function of capital per effective unit of labor k. The demand for real money balances is determined by the money demand function (7.11), the nominal interest rate is determined by the Fisher equation (7.5), and inflation is determined by equation (7.14).

As for the government, let us make similar assumptions to the ones made in chapter 6. Assume that the government chooses a constant level of primary expenditure $\bar{c}_g$ and government debt $\bar{d}$ per efficiency unit of labor, and it uses taxes to satisfy the government budget constraint. The government also chooses, through the central bank, a constant rate of growth μ for the money supply. All seigniorage revenue accrues to the government budget.

Under these assumptions, private consumption and the accumulation of capital are determined by the pair of differential equations

$$\dot{c}(t) = \frac{1}{\theta}(Af'(k(t)) - \delta - \rho - \theta g)c(t), \tag{7.29}$$

$$\dot{k}(t) = Af(k(t)) - c(t) - \bar{c}_g - (n+g+\delta)k(t). \tag{7.30}$$

As one can see from (7.29) and (7.30), neither the stock of money nor the growth rate of the money supply affects the evolution of private consumption (savings) or the accumulation of capital (investment). The determination of consumption and the capital stock is the same as in a model without money. The only government policy variable that appears to affect the economy is real primary government expenditure.

The model is the same as the Ramsey model without money in chapter 6. The growth rate of the money supply affects inflation, nominal interest rates, and the demand for money, but no other real variables (such as output, consumption, the capital stock, real wages, and real interest rates). This can be seen by examining the balanced growth path.

7.3.1 The Balanced Growth Path in the Ramsey Model with Money

As in the Ramsey model without money, it is straightforward to prove that the economy possesses a unique balanced growth path and a unique saddle path leading to the balanced growth path.

On the balanced growth path, all variables that have been defined per efficiency unit of labor remain constant, and the same applies to interest rates (real and nominal) and inflation.

From (7.29), on the balanced growth path, the real interest rate must be equal to the pure rate of time preference plus the exogenous rate of technical progress multiplied by the inverse of the intertemporal elasticity of substitution. Therefore, steady state capital per efficiency unit of labor is determined by the condition

$$Af'(k^*) = \rho + \theta g + \delta. \tag{7.31}$$

Steady state consumption per efficiency unit of labor is determined by the steady state version of (7.30) to be

$$c^* = Af(k^*) - \bar{c}_g - (n + g + \delta)k^*. \tag{7.32}$$

Primary government expenditure has a one-to-one negative effect on private consumption and does not affect the steady state capital stock or steady state output.

Real output per efficiency unit of labor on the steady state is determined by the production function (7.19):

$$y^* = Af(k^*). \tag{7.33}$$

The steady state real interest rate and the real wage per efficiency unit of labor are determined by the marginal productivity conditions:

$$r^* = \rho + \theta g, \tag{7.34}$$

$$w^* = Af(k^*) - k^* Af'(k^*). \tag{7.35}$$

Equations (7.31)–(7.35) determine the evolution of all real variables on the balanced growth path, with the exception of real money balances. Capital, output, the real wage, and consumption per efficiency unit of labor are constant on the balanced growth path, as is the real interest rate. All per capita variables grow at the exogenous rate of technical progress g.

In this model, the method of financing government expenditure, the money stock, and the growth rate of the money supply do not affect the balanced growth path. Thus, Ricardian equivalence, the neutrality of money, and the superneutrality of money hold in a representative household model.

7.3.2 The Superneutrality of Money and Inflation

The superneutrality of money was first analyzed by Sidrauski [1967], who demonstrated that in a representative household model, the growth rate of the money supply does not affect real variables on the balanced growth path.

On the balanced growth path, the inflation rate is determined by the difference between the growth rate of the money supply from the long-term growth rate $n+g$. This can be seen from the inflation determination equation (7.14). Assuming a constant growth rate of the money supply, the inflation rate on the balanced growth path equals

$$\pi^* = \mu - (n+g), \tag{7.36}$$

where $n+g$ is the steady state growth rate of total private consumption (and output).

Moving from (7.14) to (7.36) we have assumed that the nominal interest rate is constant on the balanced growth path. From the Fisher equation (7.5), the steady state nominal interest rate is indeed constant and equal to

$$i^* = r^* + \pi^* = \rho + \theta g + \mu - (n+g) = \rho + (\theta - 1)g - n + \mu. \tag{7.37}$$

Finally, real money balances per efficiency unit of labor are also constant on the balanced growth path. They are determined from the money demand equation (7.11) and are given by

$$m^* = \left(\frac{1-\gamma}{\gamma}\frac{1}{i^*}\right)^{\frac{1}{\theta}} c^* = \left(\frac{1-\gamma}{\gamma}\frac{1}{\rho + (\theta-1)g - n + \mu}\right)^{\frac{1}{\theta}} c^*. \tag{7.38}$$

Note that the elasticity of money demand with respect to the nominal interest rate is equal to the elasticity of intertemporal substitution $1/\theta$.

The higher the growth rate of the money supply is, given the other structural parameters of the model, the higher the inflation rate and the nominal interest rate and the lower the stock of real money balances on the balanced growth path will be.

A permanent increase in the growth rate of the money supply by 5 percentage points causes an increase in inflation and in nominal interest rates by 5 percentage points as well. It also causes a decrease in the demand for real money balances. In a representative household model, real money balance is the only real variable affected by the growth rate of the money supply on the balanced growth path. As mentioned at the start of this chapter, this has been termed the superneutrality of money.

It also follows that the neutrality of money holds in this model, as the level of the money supply only affects the price level and not real variables. From the definition of real money balances per efficiency unit of labor, we have

$$\frac{M(t)}{P(t)} = m^* h_0 L_0 e^{(g+n)t}, \tag{7.39}$$

where h_0 and L_0 are the efficiency of labor and the labor force at time 0, respectively. Real money balances are also growing at a rate $g+n$ on the balanced growth path. From (7.39), the only effect of a rise in the money stock is an equiproportionate rise in the price level. Thus, the neutrality of money also holds in this model.

Exercise 7.1 Derive the steady state for all real and nominal variables using the model consisting of equations (7.11), (7.18)–(7.21), and (7.28). Assume a Cobb-Douglas production function, a unitary intertemporal elasticity of substitution of consumption, constant government expenditure and government debt per efficiency unit of labor, and a constant growth rate of the money supply. Discuss how the various exogenous parameters of the model affect real and nominal steady state variables. By linearizing the model around the steady state, analyze and discuss the properties of the adjustment path.

7.3.3 The Welfare Costs of Inflation in a Ramsey Model

Does the superneutrality of money mean that inflation does not matter in a representative household model? Far from it. Inflation implies a distortion in that the demand for real money balances, and therefore, the liquidity services of money decrease as the rate of inflation and nominal interest rates increase. Hence, the welfare of the representative household goes down with the rate of inflation, as the representative household economizes on real money balances and enjoys lower liquidity services.

The analysis of the welfare costs of inflation can be simplified by using the steady state money demand function (7.38). This is depicted graphically in figure 7.1 for a given steady state consumption per efficiency unit of labor.

The figure compares two equilibria. At one of them, inflation is zero, and the nominal interest rate is equal to the real steady interest rate $\rho+\theta g$. At the other, the positive inflation rate is π. The welfare cost of inflation is measured by the area of the gray triangle in figure 7.1, which is the loss of consumer surplus that does not translate into a higher inflation tax. This is the net welfare cost of inflation, which measures the reduction in the welfare of the representatitve household that does not translate into higher government revenue from inflation. One can easily show that the higher the inflation rate is, the higher the welfare cost of inflation will be.

Hence, inflation matters in the representative household model: It causes a reduction in the demand for real money balances and thus lower liquidity services from money. To the extent that the liquidity services of money yield utility, this reduction implies a welfare cost.[4]

4. This approach to the welfare costs of inflation, developed by Bailey [1956] and extended by Friedman [1969], treats real money balances as a consumption good and inflation as a tax on real balances. Fischer [1981] and Lucas

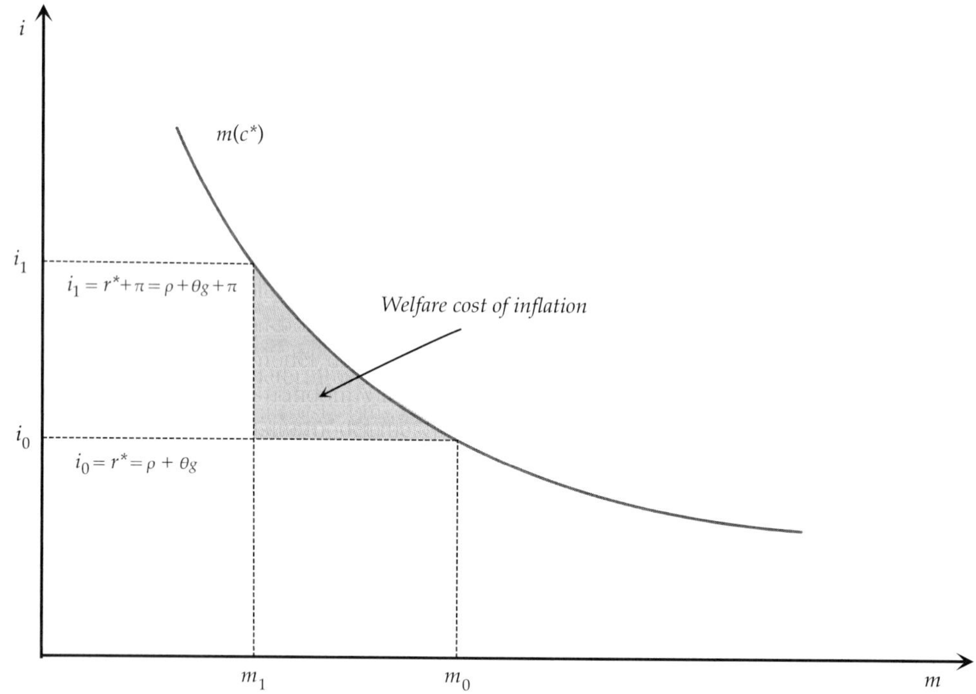

Figure 7.1
The demand for real money balances and the welfare cost of inflation.

7.4 Effects of Monetary Growth in an OLG Model

We next turn to the analysis of the impact of the growth rate of the money supply in the OLG model of Blanchard and Weil.

We assume, as in the Blanchard-Weil model of chapter 5, that the economy consists of overlapping generations of households born at different times in the past. Each generation has an infinite time horizon. At each instant t, $nL(t)$ households are born, where $L(t)$ is total population at time t, and n is the growth rate of the number of households and the overall population. Each household has one member and provides one unit of labor. Consequently, the growth rate of the labor force is also n. Unlike the representative household model,

[1981] find the cost of inflation to be relatively low, between 0.3–0.5% of GDP. Lucas [2000] revised his estimate upward, to slightly less than 1% of GDP. The cost is low but not insignificant, and it appears to rise significantly for high-inflation economies. We shall return to this issue in chapter 12, when we discuss alternative approaches to the demand for money and the macroeconomics of high inflation and hyperinflation.

OLG models do not internalize the welfare of future generations. We now assume that the instantaneous utility function of households depends on both consumption and real money balances, because of the liquidity services of holding money.

7.4.1 The Blanchard-Weil Model with Money

The household born at time j chooses a path for consumption and real money balances to maximize the intertemporal utility function

$$U_j = \int_{s=j}^{\infty} e^{-\rho s} u\left(c(j,s), m(j,s)\right) ds, \tag{7.40}$$

subject to the instantaneous asset accumulation equation

$$\dot{a}(j,s) = r(s)a(j,s) + w(s)h(s) - \tau(s) - c(j,s) - (r(s) + \pi(s))\, m(j,s) \tag{7.41}$$

and the transversality condition

$$\lim_{t\to\infty} e^{-\int_{s=j}^{t} r(s)ds} a(j,t) = 0. \tag{7.42}$$

The variables and parameters are defined as in the case of the representative household model: ρ is the pure rate of time preference of households, and u is a quasi-concave instantaneous utility function; $c(j,s)$ denotes the consumption of the household born at time j at time s; $m(j,s)$ is real money balance of the household born at time j at time s; $a(j,s)$ denotes average assets of the household born at time j at time s; $w(s)$ denotes the real wage per efficiency unit of labor at time t, assumed to the same for all households; $h(s)$ denotes labor efficiency per worker; $\tau(s)$ denotes average taxes (minus transfers) per household at time s; $r(s)$ is the real interest rate at time s; and $\pi(s)$ is inflation, which is equal to expected inflation.

Assuming that the instantaneous utility function u takes the form of (7.4) with an intertemporal elasticity of substitution equal to unity (as in chapter 5), we can write the instantaneous utility function as[5]

$$u(c(j,s), m(j,s)) = \gamma \ln c(j,s) + (1-\gamma) \ln m(j,s). \tag{7.43}$$

From the first-order conditions for a maximum and assuming that the assets of households consist of physical capital, government bonds, and money, we can derive the aggregate money demand function, the equation describing the evolution of aggregate consumption,

5. Logarithmic preferences are assumed, because this allows us to obtain exact aggregation. It implies little loss of generality.

and the equation describing capital accumulation:[6]

$$\frac{M(t)}{P(t)}=\frac{1-\gamma}{\gamma}\frac{1}{r(t)+\pi(t)}C(t), \tag{7.44}$$

$$\dot{C}(t)=(r(t)-\rho+n)\,C(t)-n\rho\gamma\left(K(t)+D(t)+\frac{M(t)}{P(t)}\right), \tag{7.45}$$

$$\dot{K}(t)=r(t)K(t)+w(t)h(t)L(t)-C(t)-C_g(t). \tag{7.46}$$

Expressing (7.44), (7.45), and (7.46) per efficiency unit of labor and assuming that the government has a constant target for primary government expenditure and government debt per efficiency unit of labor (as well as a constant target for the rate of growth of the money supply), we get

$$m(t)=\frac{1-\gamma}{\gamma}\frac{1}{r(t)+\pi(t)}c(t), \tag{7.47}$$

$$\dot{c}(t)=\left(r(t)-\rho-g-\frac{n\rho(1-\gamma)}{r(t)+\pi(t)}\right)c(t)-n\rho\gamma(k(t)+\bar{d}), \tag{7.48}$$

$$\dot{k}(t)=r(t)k(t)+w(t)-c(t)-\bar{c}_g-(n+g)k(t), \tag{7.49}$$

where in (7.48), we have used (7.47) to substitute for the stock of real money balances per efficiency unit of labor. $\bar{d}$ is government debt per efficiency unit of labor, assumed constant.

Using the marginal productivity conditions to replace the real interest rate and the real wage per efficiency unit of labor, (7.48) and (7.49) can be written as

$$\dot{c}(t)=\left(Af'(k(t))-\delta-\rho-g-\frac{n\rho(1-\gamma)}{f'(k(t))-\delta+\pi(t)}\right)c(t)-n\rho\gamma\left(k(t)+\bar{d}\right), \tag{7.50}$$

$$\dot{k}(t)=Af(k(t))-c(t)-\bar{c}_g-(n+g+\delta)k(t). \tag{7.51}$$

Equations (7.50) and (7.51) can be used to analyze both the balanced growth path and the adjustment path in terms of the exogenous parameters of the model and the policy variables describing government expenditure, government debt, and the growth rate of the money supply.

7.4.2 Real Effects of the Growth Rate of the Money Supply

From (7.50) and (7.51), we have on the balanced growth path

$$c^*=\frac{n\rho\gamma}{Af'(k^*)-\delta-\rho-g-\frac{n\rho(1-\gamma)}{Af'(k^*)-\delta+\mu-(n+g)}}\left(k^*+\bar{d}\right), \tag{7.52}$$

6. See chapter 5 on how aggregation takes place in the Blanchard-Weil model.

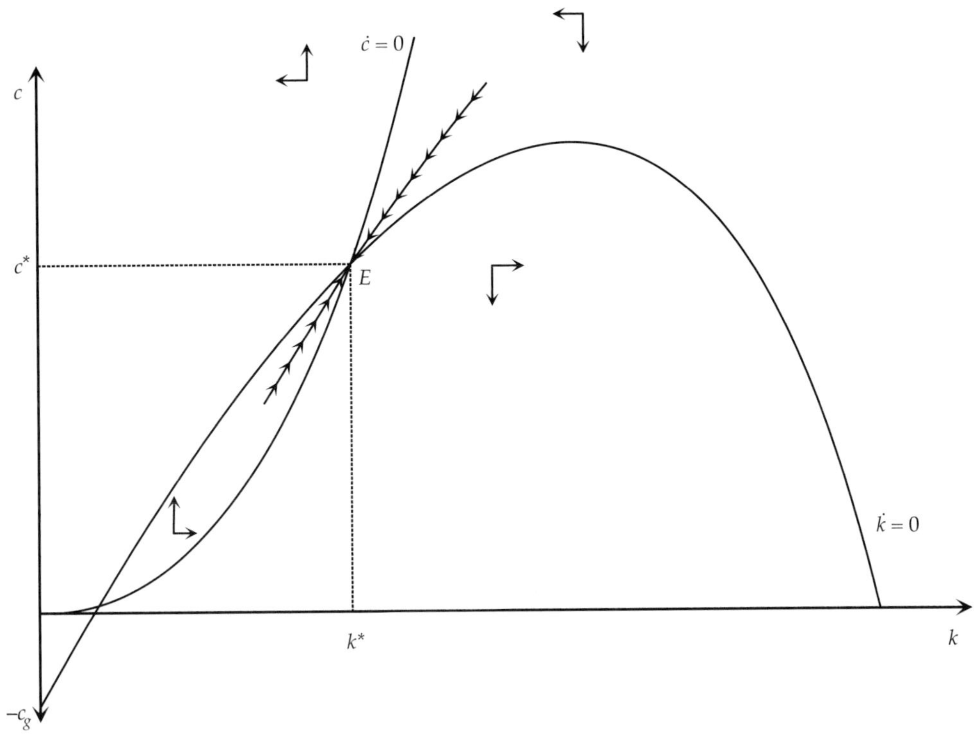

Figure 7.2
The balanced growth path and the adjustment path in the Blanchard-Weil model with money.

$$c^* = Af(k^*) - \bar{c}_g - (n+g+\delta)k^*. \tag{7.53}$$

Equations (7.52) and (7.53) jointly determine real private consumption and real capital per efficiency unit of labor on the balanced growth path as a function of parameters of technology, household preferences, the population growth rate, and the rate of exogenous technical progress, as well as the parameters describing fiscal and monetary policy.

The balanced growth path and the relevant unique saddle path are shown graphically in figure 7.2. In the figure, $\dot{c}=0$ is the steady state consumption function (7.52), and $\dot{k}=0$ is the steady state capital accumulation function (7.53). The balanced growth path and the adjustment path have the usual properties that characterize the model of Blanchard and Weil. The balanced growth path is a saddle point. The new element here is the impact of the growth rate of the money supply on private consumption.[7]

7. See Weil [1987b, 1991].

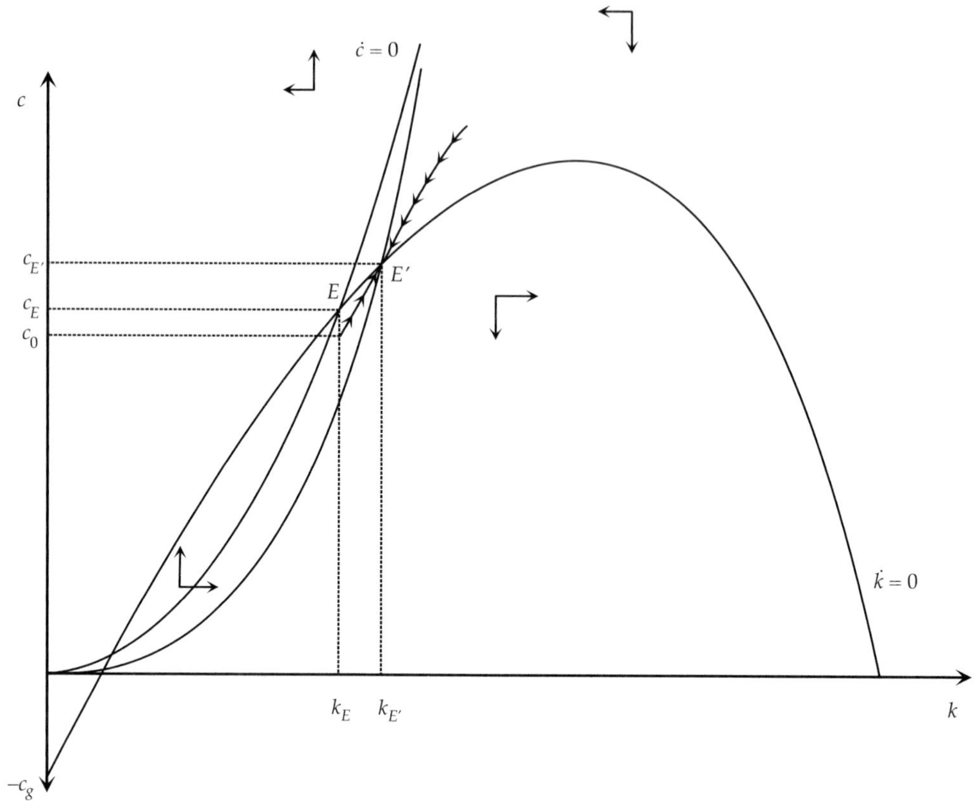

Figure 7.3
Dynamic effects of an increase in the growth rate of money supply in the Blanchard-Weil model with money.

A permanent increase in the growth rate of the money supply μ leads to a permanent increase in inflation and nominal interest rates. This in turn leads to a reduction in the demand for real money balances. In this model, the decline in real money balances leads to a corresponding reduction in private consumption by current generations, thus increasing aggregate savings and causing the accumulation of physical capital.

The relevant analysis is shown in figure 7.3. A previously unanticipated permanent increase in the rate of growth of the money supply, which leads to an increase in inflation, results in a heavier inflation tax for the current generations. These generations hold higher real money balances compared to future generations, who do not hold real money balances. This causes a reduction in their current consumption, an increase in aggregate savings, and the initiation of a process of accumulation of physical capital. At the time of the implementation of the policy, consumption falls from c_E to c_0. The economy adjusts toward a new balanced growth path E$'$, which implies higher capital, output, and consumption per efficiency unit of labor, due to the substitution toward physical capital caused by higher inflation. In this model, the superneutrality of money does not apply, because the inflation tax impacts different generations differently, and the redistribution it causes in favor of future generations reduces current consumption and increases savings by current generations.

Thus, as with Ricardian equivalence, the superneutrality of money does not apply in an OLG model like that of Blanchard and Weil model, because in this model current generations do not internalize the welfare of future generations.

7.4.3 A Dynamic Simulation of the Effects of a Rise in the Growth Rate of the Money Supply in a Calibrated Blanchard-Weil Model

To gain some insights into the quantitative impact of the growth rate of the money supply in the OLG model of Blanchard-Weil, let us examine simulations of the model for specific parameter values, assuming the usual Cobb-Douglas production function of the form

$$y(t) = Ak(t)^{\alpha}. \tag{7.54}$$

Consequently, the model being simulated consists of discrete time versions of (7.50) for the evolution of private consumption, (7.51) for the accumulation of capital, (7.54) for the production function, (7.47) for the money demand function, the marginal productivity conditions (7.20) and (7.21) for the real interest rate and real wages, the Fisher equation (7.5) for the nominal interest rate, and (7.14) for inflation. Where the marginal product of capital or labor appears, this is derived from the production function (7.54).

The simulations use the usual parameter values, as in chapters 3–6. For γ, the share of consumption in the utility function, we use a value equal to 97.5%. With regard to the parameters of fiscal policy it is assumed, as in chapter 6, that, $\bar{c}_g = 0.5$ and $\bar{d} = 0.5$. Thus, the paramerer values used are $A = 1$, $\alpha = 0.333$, $\rho = 0.02$, $n = 0.01$, $g = 0.02$, $\delta = 0.03$, $\gamma = 0.975$, $\bar{c}_g = 0.5$, $\bar{d} = 0.5$.

Figure 7.4 shows the dynamic effects of a permanent change in the growth rate of the money supply from 5% to 10% in the calibrated Blanchard-Weil model. In the simulation, this change is accompanied by corresponding reductions in taxes, which are continuously equal to the increase in the inflation tax on real money balances. There is thus no impact on primary government expenditure or government debt.

The change in the growth rate of the money supply from 5% to 10% reduces private consumption expenditure immediately, due to the reduction in the real money balances of current generations. This causes an increase in savings and initiates a process of capital accumulation that leads the economy toward a new balanced growth path with a higher capital stock, higher output, higher private consumption, and higher real wages per efficiency unit of labor. In contrast, the real interest rate falls. Inflation rises by five percentage points, the same as the rise in the rate of growth of the money supply, and roughly the same happens to nominal interest rates.

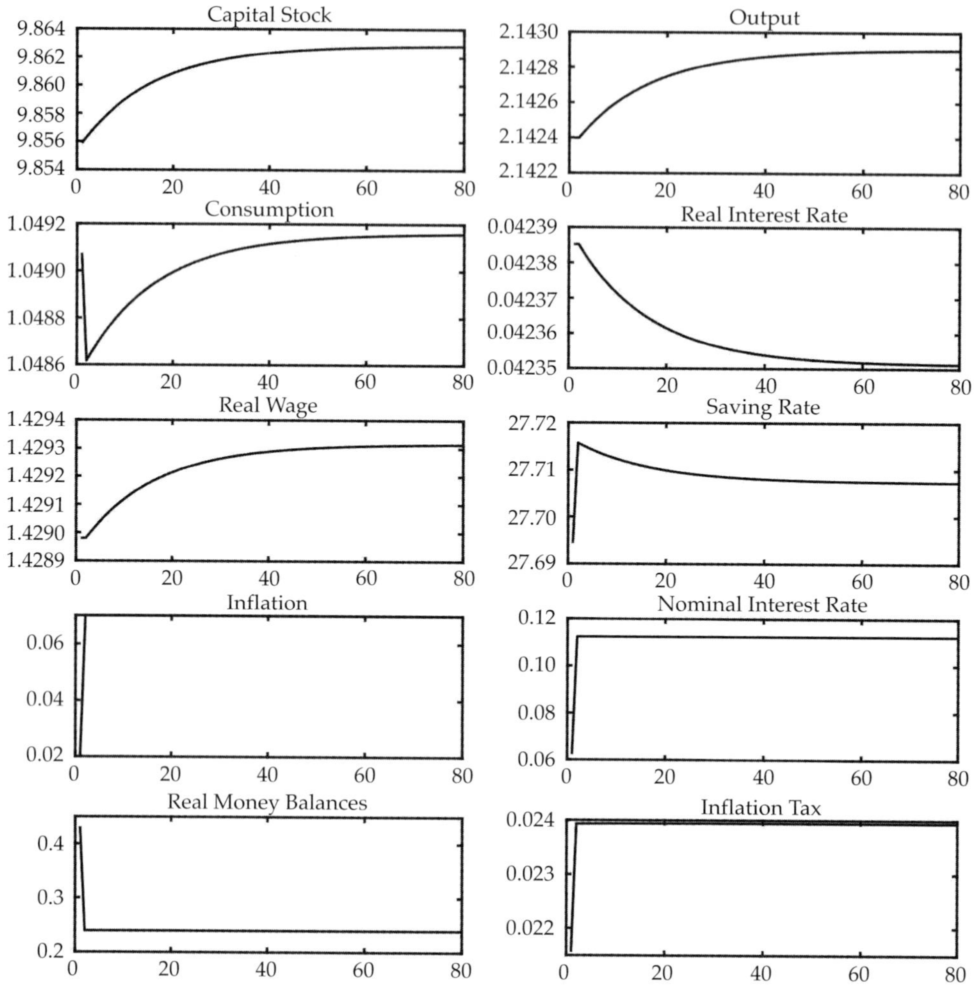

Figure 7.4
Dynamic simulation of an increase in the growth rate of money supply in a calibrated Blanchard-Weil model with money.

However, note that the impact of a change in the growth rate of the money supply on the real economy is extremely small. A doubling of the rate of growth of the money supply from 5% to 10% leads to an increase in steady state real per capita income (and real wages) of only 0.02%, and a reduction in the real interest rate by only 0.005 percentage points (i.e., from 4.239% to 4.234%). The overall savings rate in the balanced growth path rises from 27.69% to 27.70%, again a very slight increase. In contrast, inflation rises by five percentage points (from 2% to 7%), and nominal interest rates rise from 6.24% to 11.24%. The rise in the nominal interest rate is due to the rise in inflation, because the fall in the real interest rate is negligible. The rise in nominal interest rates results in a fall of the demand for real money balances by 44.5%. This is the only significant real effect of the doubling of the rate of growth of the money supply. All other real effects are miniscule.

We see therefore that, as with deviations from Ricardian equivalence, deviations from the superneutrality of money in OLG models (such as the Blanchard-Weil model) are quantitatively limited. The changes are small, because these deviations depend on the product of two quantitatively small parameters: the rate of growth of population (which determines the rate of entry of new generations in the economy) and the pure rate of time preference of households (which determines the percentage of total household wealth that is consumed). With the assumptions made, for a population growth rate of 1% per year and a pure rate of time preference of 2%, their product is equal to just 0.02%.

7.5 Conclusion

In this chapter, we have analyzed the impact of money and the growth rate of the money supply in optimizing models of economic growth. Initially we analyzed the role of money in a representative household model, in which money enters the utility function of the representative household. We then analyzed money's role in a corresponding OLG model.

In growth models with money, one can analyze the determination of both real and nominal variables (such as the price level, inflation, and nominal interest rates) and examine the dynamic impact of the growth rate of the money supply. This is a major advantage of monetary over real models.

In the representative household model, the growth rate of the money supply has virtually no real effects, apart from reducing the demand for real money balances, because money does not pay interest. The balanced growth path of all other real variables is independent of the growth rate of the money supply, which only affects inflation, nominal interest rates, and the demand for real money balances by households. This result is known as the superneutrality of money.

In an OLG model, the growth rate of the money supply has real effects, as it has a different impact on the holdings of real money balances and on the level of consumption of different generations. When the growth rate of the money supply increases, older generations, which hold higher real money balances, pay a higher inflation tax than do younger generations.

Therefore, current aggregate consumption falls, and savings increase. This leads to a higher accumulation of capital and a transition to a balanced growth path with higher capital per efficiency unit of labor. However, dynamic simulations suggest that these deviations from the superneutrality of money are quantitatively small for plausible parameter values.

The differences in the effects of the growth rate of the money supply between the two categories of models are due to the same reasons that government debt has real effects in OLG models, while it does not in a representative household model. In the representative household model, neither government debt nor the growth rate of the money supply causes a redistribution of the tax burden among generations. However, in an OLG model, both government debt and the rate of growth of the money supply are associated with a redistribution of the tax burden among generations. An increase in government debt redistributes the tax burden from current to future generations, causing an increase in consumption by current generations and a fall in savings and the accumulation of capital. An increase in the growth rate of the money supply redistributes the tax burden from future to current generations, causing a reduction of aggregate private consumption and an increase in savings and the accumulation of capital.

As is the case with the effects of government debt, the quantitative significance of the effects of the growth rate of the money supply on real variables is small in OLG models with competitive capital markets. This is because they depend on the product of two quantitatively small parameters: the rate of growth of population and the pure rate of time preference.

Both representative household and OLG models imply that the growth rate of the money supply mainly affects long-run inflation and nominal interest rates; it has quantitatively insignificant effects on per capita real output, consumption, and the capital stock. The only real variable that is affected significantly is the stock of real money balances, which depends negatively on the nominal interest rate. These conclusions are in accordance with the predictions of the two-period intertemporal model with money (analyzed in chapter 2). They are also in accordance with the evidence on the effects of the rate of monetary growth across countries discussed in chapter 1 (see figures 1.12 and 1.13). There it was shown that, although a very strong empirical association exists between monetary growth and inflation, the association between monetary and real growth is insignificant. As we shall see in chapter 12, these conclusions are consistent with a wide variety of other monetary models with flexible prices.

8

Externalities, Human Capital, and Technical Progress

In this chapter, we examine growth models in which the efficiency of labor is no longer entirely exogenous, but may be influenced by positive externalities from the accumulation of physical capital, by the accumulation of human capital, or even by the endogenous generation of new ideas and innovations. Under certain conditions, these models can lead to endogenous growth, unlike the models that we have analyzed so far.[1]

Initially we consider a growth model that is based on the assumption of positive externalities from aggregate capital accumulation on labor efficiency. The main idea that drives this model is learning by doing, an idea introduced into growth models by Arrow [1962]. This assumption can, under certain conditions, lead to endogenous growth, as in P. M. Romer [1986].

In the learning-by-doing model, labor efficiency is a function of both exogenous technical progress and aggregate capital per worker. Thus, the efficiency of labor, which is the same for all firms, depends on capital per worker in the rest of the economy. Because of learning by doing, the accumulation of aggregate capital increases labor productivity both directly and indirectly, through knowledge spillovers that have a direct effect on the efficiency of labor. It is assumed here that knowledge is like a public good and that the accumulation of knowledge depends on the accumulation of aggregate capital.

An important consequence of this approach is that diminishing returns from capital accumulation set in more slowly, and that under certain conditions, there may even be constant or increasing returns from capital accumulation. In these latter circumstances, growth becomes endogenous and is determined by the rate of accumulation of aggregate physical capital.

To analyze the impact of the savings behavior of households in the process of endogenous growth, we combine this approach with the assumptions of the Solow model for a

1. Throughout the chapter, we mainly address effects on the efficiency of labor, but all the results would go through if instead we considered effects on total factor productivity. As we use a Cobb-Douglas production function throughout this chapter, labor augmenting technical progress (Harrod neutral) and total factor productivity augmenting technical progress (Hicks neutral) are equivalent.

fixed savings and investment rate, as well as with the savings assumptions of the Ramsey representative household model and the OLG model of Blanchard and Weil.

We then consider an alternative class of growth models that emphasizes the dependence of labor efficiency on education and training, and the accumulation of *human capital.*

We start with a generalized Solow model, in which the accumulation of human capital is the result of spending on education and training. The model is due to Mankiw et al. [1992] and generalizes the Solow model in two dimensions. First, labor efficiency depends in part on exogenous technical progress and in part on the accumulated human capital of workers. Second, the accumulation of human capital depends on spending on education and training, which is treated as a fixed, endogenous share of total output. Thus, in this model, there is investment in both physical and human capital. Under certain conditions, this generalized Solow model can also lead to endogenous growth.

We also consider an alternative model in which investment in human capital depends not on the share of income spent on education and training, but on the amount of time devoted to education and training. These models (Lucas [1988], Jones [2002]) assume that workers spend part of their time in education and training and that this investment of their time increases their human capital and the efficiency of labor. Under certain conditions, these models can also lead to endogenous growth.

Finally, we examine a class of models in which technical progress is the result of investment in research and development. These models also emphasize the externalities associated with the production of new ideas and innovations that increase labor efficiency. Although models of research and development have existed since the late 1960s, their full economic implications for the functioning of markets were developed in the early 1990s, based on the work of Romer [1990]. Under certain conditions, these models can also lead to endogenous growth.

Note that endogenous-growth models do not necessarily imply convergence in per capita output, as in the corresponding exogenous-growth models. Initial conditions matter for the evolution of per capita output and income. However, the available empirical evidence from postwar international data (see Mankiw et al. [1992] and Barro [1997a]) suggests that the issue of convergence of per capita incomes cannot be dismissed easily. The convergence observed can be explained by broader exogenous-growth models, in which there is learning by doing, or accumulation of human capital and ideas and innovations, but not to an extent that completely neutralizes the diminishing returns from the accumulation of physical and human capital.

8.1 Externalities from Capital Accumulation and Economic Growth

We start with a class of models in which physical capital accumulation leads to improved labor efficiency through a process of learning by doing. It is assumed in these models that the accumulation of aggregate capital implies a direct externality that leads to higher efficiency of labor, as a higher aggregate capital stock implies a higher stock of accumulated experience of all workers in the production process. This is what Arrow [1962] termed *learning by doing*.

In this class of models, capital has both direct effects on labor productivity and also indirect effects through the accumulated economywide efficiency of workers. The indirect impact of capital accumulation on labor efficiency is an example of a positive externality. Knowledge spillovers, which are a positive function of the aggregate capital stock, increase the efficiency of labor. It is assumed here that knowledge is like a public good and that the accumulation of knowledge depends on the accumulation of aggregate capital.

8.1.1 Definitions

The definitions of the variables are analogous to those we have used in previous models. However, the efficiency of labor is now an endogenous variable that depends on the accumulation of physical capital. We thus define: Y, aggregate output (or $\hat{y}$, output per worker); K, aggregate (physical) capital stock (or $\hat{k}$, capital per worker); h, efficiency of labor, or "human capital" per worker (an endogenous variable that depends on the accumulation of aggregate capital per worker); C, aggregate consumption (or $\hat{c}$, consumption per worker); r, real interest rate; and $\hat{w}$, real wage per worker.

The exogenous variables and exogenous parameters in the model are defined as follows: t, time (a discrete exogenous variable); L, population and labor force (an exogenous variable that depends on time); n, rate of growth of population (exogenous parameter); g, rate of technical progress (exogenous parameter); δ, rate of depreciation of capital (exogenous parameter); ρ, pure rate of time preference of households (exogenous parameter); s the savings rate (in the Solow model); α, the exponent of capital in a Cobb-Douglas production function; and A, total factor productivity.

8.1.2 The Production Function

Production of goods and services takes place through a large number of competitive firms. The production function of firm i is given by

$$Y_i(t) = AF(K_i(t), h(t)L_i(t)), i = 1, 2, \ldots. \tag{8.1}$$

The production function is characterized by constant returns to scale and satisfies the usual conditions of a neoclassical production function. We can thus write the production function as

$$\hat{y}_i(t) = Af(\hat{k}_i(t), h(t)), \tag{8.2}$$

where $\hat{y}_i = Y_i/L_i$ is output per worker of firm i; $\hat{k}_i = K_i/L_i$ is physical capital per worker of firm i; and h is efficiency of labor, or human capital per worker in firm i, assumed to be the same for all firms.

In what follows we assume a Cobb-Douglas production function of the form

$$Y_i(t) = AK_i(t)^{\alpha}(h(t)L_i(t))^{1-\alpha}, \tag{8.3}$$

where $0 < \alpha < 1$ is the direct elasticity of output with respect to the capital stock, and A is total factor productivity. Those two parameters, as well as the efficiency of labor h, are assumed to be the same for all firms.

8.1.3 Externalities from the Accumulation of Capital

Unlike the growth models we have analyzed so far, where labor augmenting technical progress was assumed exogenous, we will assume that the aggregate efficiency of labor is a function of both time and the aggregate capital stock per worker in the economy. This dependence is justified on the basis of the learning by doing concept of Arrow [1962]. Economies with a high capital stock per worker are characterized by higher labor efficiency as well, because of the accumulated experience of workers in the production process.

As noted by Arrow [1962, p. 156],

> I advance the hypothesis here that technical change in general can be ascribed to experience, that it is the very activity of production which gives rise to problems for which favorable responses are selected over time. ... I therefore take ... cumulative gross investment (cumulative production of capital goods) as an index of experience. Each new machine produced and put into use is capable of changing the environment in which production takes place, so that learning is taking place with continually new stimuli. This at least makes plausible the possibility of continued learning in the sense, here, of a steady rate of growth in productivity.

Thus, on the basis of this observation, assume that the efficiency of labor is determined by

$$h(t) = \left(\frac{K(t)}{L(t)}\right)^{\beta} \left(e^{gt}\right)^{1-\beta}, \tag{8.4}$$

where $0 \leq \beta \leq 1$. K is the aggregate capital stock (an index of experience), and L is aggregate employment of labor. From (8.4), a higher aggregate capital stock per worker implies a higher efficiency of labor for all workers in the economy, irrespective of the capital stock used by the firm that employs the particular worker. The parameter β measures the elasticity of labor efficiency with respect to the aggregate capital stock per worker, and g is the exogenous rate of technical progress.

Substituting (8.4) in (8.3) and aggregating the production of all firms, we can derive the aggregate production function:

$$Y(t) = A(K(t))^{\alpha+\beta(1-\alpha)}(e^{gt}L(t))^{1-(\alpha+\beta(1-\alpha))}. \tag{8.5}$$

From (8.5), it follows that aggregate output per worker is given by

$$\hat{y}(t) = A(\hat{k}(t))^{\alpha+\beta(1-\alpha)}\left(e^{gt}\right)^{1-\alpha-\beta(1-\alpha)}, \tag{8.6}$$

where $\hat{y} = Y/L$ and $\hat{k} = K/L$.

The shape of this production function is depicted in figure 8.1 for different values of the parameter β. For $\beta = 0$, there is no effect of the aggregate accumulation of capital on labor efficiency, and we are back to an aggregate Cobb-Douglas production function without externalities. The efficiency of labor depends only on the exogenous rate of technical progress g. For $0 < \beta < 1$, the accumulation of capital implies a positive externality on the efficiency of labor, but the aggregate marginal product of capital tends to fall as the economy accumulates more capital per worker. Capital accumulation per worker leads to diminishing returns, although the productivity of capital declines at a slower rate than if there were no externalities. For $\beta = 1$, the aggregate marginal product of capital is constant, equal to total factor productivity A, and not affected by the accumulation of capital. There are no diminishing returns to capital accumulation, as the aggregate marginal product of capital is constant.

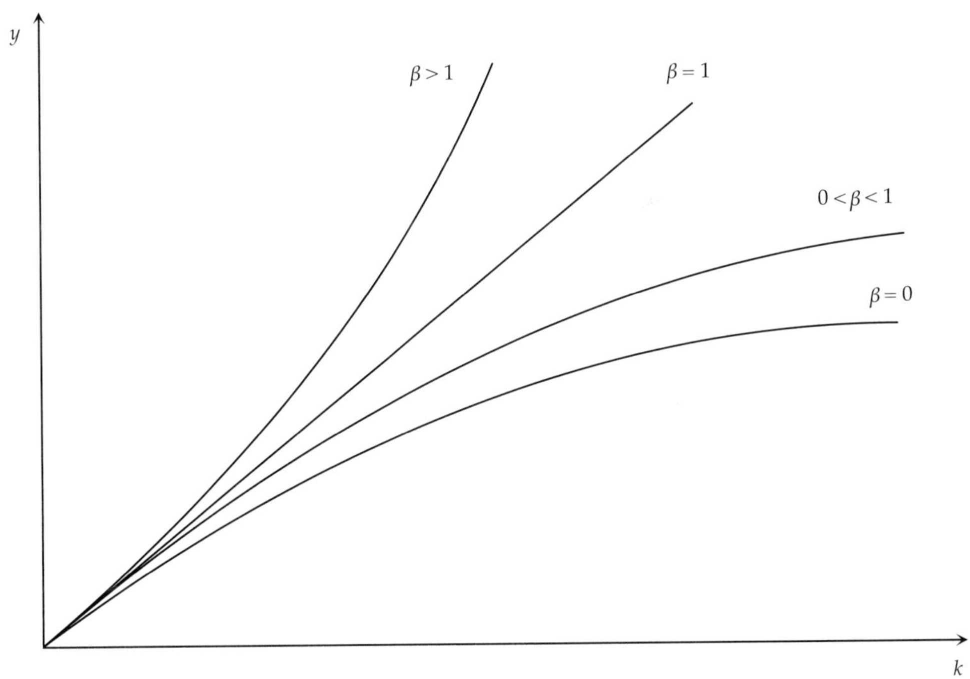

Figure 8.1
The aggregate production function for different values of β.

Finally, for $\beta > 1$, the marginal product of capital increases with capital accumulation, but this assumption violates the condition of constant returns to scale for the aggregate economy.

In the case $\beta < 1$, the properties of the exogenous-growth models we have analyzed so far do not change by much. There are decreasing returns to capital accumulation, and the economy converges to a balanced growth path that can be analyzed in the same way as the exogenous-growth models in previous chapters. However, if $\beta \geq 1$, then (8.6) leads to endogenous growth.

In what follows, we concentrate on the special case $\beta = 1$, which implies endogenous growth without violating the assumption of constant returns to scale. In the special case $\beta = 1$, (8.5) and (8.6) take the form

$$Y(t) = AK(t), \tag{8.7}$$

$$\hat{y}(t) = A\hat{k}(t), \tag{8.8}$$

where (8.8) implies that aggregate output per worker is a linear function of capital per worker. The marginal and average productivity of capital is constant. Because of the linearity of the aggregate production function, the rate of growth of output per worker (or per capita income) g is equal to the rate of growth of capital per worker. The accumulation of capital per worker does not lead to diminishing returns. It thus follows that

$$\frac{\dot{\hat{y}}(t)}{\hat{y}(t)} = \frac{\dot{\hat{k}}(t)}{\hat{k}(t)} = g, \tag{8.9}$$

where g is now endogenous and is determined by the rate of accumulation of capital.

For the same reason, from (8.7), the rate of growth of aggregate output $g + n$ is determined by the share of net investment in total output. As a result, we have that

$$g + n = \dot{Y}(t)/Y(t) = \dot{K}(t)/K(t) = (I(t)/K(t)) - \delta = A(I(t)/Y(t)) - \delta, \tag{8.10}$$

where I denotes gross investment in physical capital, and δ is the depreciation rate.[2]

2. This endogenous-growth model belongs to a class of models known as AK models from the form of the aggregate production function (8.7). The AK model with learning by doing was analyzed by P. M. Romer [1986], and we shall refer to it as the Arrow-Romer model. An alternative AK model that is widely used is due to Rebelo [1991], who demonstrates that as long as there is a core of capital goods whose production does not involve nonreproducible factors, endogenous growth is compatible with production technologies that exhibit constant returns to scale. The simplest Rebelo [1991] model is a two-sector model in which consumption goods are produced using both capital and labor, but capital goods are produced using only capital. In this class of models, there are no externalities through knowledge spillovers, but in competitive equilibrium aggregate output turns out to be proportional to the capital stock. Because the Rebelo model is not based on externalities, its policy implications are different from those of the Arrow-Romer model.

8.1.4 Determination of the Real Interest Rate and the Real Wage

Assuming that firms operate under perfect competition, they maximize profits by taking the prices of inputs as given. Profit maximization implies that the real interest rate will be equal to the marginal product of capital for individual firms, and the real wage will equal the marginal product of labor for individual firms. From the point of view of each individual firm, the efficiency of labor is exogenously given. Thus, from (8.3), the net marginal product of capital for each individual firm is given by

$$\alpha A\hat{k}_i(t)^{\alpha-1}h(t)^{1-\alpha}-\delta.$$

Substituting $h(t)$ from (8.4) and assuming that $\beta=1$, we get the marginal productivity condition

$$r(t)=\alpha A\hat{k}_i(t)^{\alpha-1}\hat{k}(t)^{1-\alpha}-\delta, \tag{8.11}$$

where $r(t)$ is the real interest rate, and the expression on the right-hand side is the net marginal product of capital from the vantage point of each individual firm. Equation (8.11) implies that all firms will select the same capital per worker, as they face the same real interest rate and the same labor efficiency per worker. Therefore, $\hat{k}_i(t)=\hat{k}(t), \forall i$. As a result, the real interest rate will be equal to

$$r(t)=\alpha A-\delta. \tag{8.12}$$

The real interest rate is constant and equal to the private marginal product of capital, as calculated by each individual firm. Because of its small size, each competitive firm does not internalize the effects of its own choice of capital per worker on the aggregate capital stock per worker in the economy, treating labor efficiency as exogenously given. Labor efficiency depends on the aggregate capital stock per worker and not on the firm-specific capital per worker. This externality explains why each firm underestimates the social marginal product of capital and why the real interest rate, as determined in competitive markets, is lower than the social (aggregate) marginal product of capital. We shall return to this market failure in section 8.1.7 below, when we discuss the efficiency of the competitive equilibrium.[3]

In competitive equilibrium, the real wage will be equal to the marginal product of labor as calculated by each individual firm. It is thus determined by

$$\hat{w}(t)=(1-\alpha)A\hat{k}_i(t)^{\alpha}\hat{k}(t)^{1-\alpha}=(1-\alpha)A\hat{k}(t)=(1-\alpha)\hat{y}(t), \tag{8.13}$$

where $\hat{w}(t)$ is the real wage per worker, and the property that in the competitive equilibrium $\hat{k}_i(t)=\hat{k}(t), \forall i$, has been used.

3. This market failure does not arise in the benchmark AK model of Rebelo [1991] without externalities.

The real wage is a constant share of output per worker. If output per worker is growing at a rate g, then the real wage per worker will also be growing at a rate g.

Note that this endogenous-growth model predicts a constant real interest rate and growing real wages per worker, in agreement with the Kaldor stylized facts analyzed in chapter 3.

However, unlike the exogenous-growth models we have analyzed so far, this model does not predict convergence. As we shall see, the growth rate is constant and endogenously determined. Therefore, two economies that have different initial capital stocks per worker will not experience convergence to the same per capita output and income, even if they have the same technological and population parameters and the same preferences of consumers. They will have the same endogenous growth rate, but conditional convergence does not occur in such an endogenous-growth model.[4]

8.1.5 The Savings Rate and the Endogenous Growth Rate

Let us first assume that, as in the Solow model, consumer behavior is described by a constant savings rate. Per capita consumption is thus given by

$$\hat{c}(t) = (1 - s)\hat{y}(t), \tag{8.14}$$

where s is the exogenous savings rate.

In equilibrium, total output will be equal to consumption plus gross investment. In per capita terms, we have

$$\hat{y}(t) = \hat{c}(t) + \dot{\hat{k}}(t) + (n + \delta)\hat{k}(t). \tag{8.15}$$

Combining (8.8), (8.14), and (8.15), the change in the capital stock per worker will be given by

$$\dot{\hat{k}}(t) = s\hat{y}(t) - (n + \delta)\hat{k}(t) = (sA - n - \delta)\hat{k}(t). \tag{8.16}$$

Dividing both sides of (8.16) by $\hat{k}(t)$, we get

$$g = \frac{\dot{\hat{k}}(t)}{\hat{k}(t)} = sA - (n + \delta). \tag{8.17}$$

Equation (8.17) determines the endogenous growth rate g. The higher the exogenous savings (and investment) rate s and total factor productivity A are, the higher the growth rate of per capita income will be. However, population growth and the depreciation rate have a negative impact on the endogenous growth rate.

In this model, the savings rate plays a similar role to its role in the exogenous-growth Solow model. In the latter model, the savings rate has a positive impact on steady state capital k^* and output per effective unit of labor y^*, and the transitional growth rate during

4. This is demonstrated in section 8.1.10.

the convergence process toward the steady state, but it does not affect the long-term growth rate, which is equal to the exogenous rate of technical progress g. In this endogenous-growth Arrow-Romer-Solow model, with positive externalities from capital accumulation, the savings rate s determines the gross investment rate (and through the gross investment rate, the endogenous growth rate), because the accumulation of capital does not imply diminishing returns for the marginal product of capital, and growth continues forever.

Therefore, in this endogenous-growth model, economies characterized by different stocks of initial capital will not converge to the same per capita income, even if they have identical savings rate, total factor productivity, rate of population growth, and depreciation rate. They will simply have the same steady state growth rate, without converging to the same per capita income on the balanced growth path. Their initial differences will be maintained forever.

8.1.6 Externalities and Endogenous Growth in the Ramsey Model

As already mentioned, the assumption of an exogenous savings rate is not theoretically satisfactory. The savings rate is determined by underlying factors associated with the preferences and constraints of households.

How is the endogenous growth determined in a representative household model, where households maximize the intertemporal utility from consumption? Assume a representative household, which maximizes the intertemporal utility function

$$U=\int_{t=0}^{\infty} e^{-(\rho-n)t}\frac{\hat{c}(t)^{1-\theta}-1}{1-\theta}dt, \tag{8.18}$$

subject to the household budget constraint

$$\dot{\hat{k}}(t)=r(t)\hat{k}(t)+\hat{w}(t)-\hat{c}(t)-n\hat{k}(t). \tag{8.19}$$

Variables in (8.18) and (8.19) are defined per capita. Income per capita is capital income per capita plus labor income per capita. Each household member supplies one unit of labor.

From the first-order conditions for a maximum, we get the Euler equation for consumption (see chapter 4):

$$\frac{\dot{\hat{c}}(t)}{\hat{c}(t)}=\frac{1}{\theta}\left(r(t)-\rho\right). \tag{8.20}$$

Given that the real interest rate is constant and equal to $\alpha A-\delta$, from (8.12), the rate of growth of per capita consumption is also constant and is given by

$$\frac{\dot{\hat{c}}(t)}{\hat{c}(t)}=\frac{1}{\theta}\left(\alpha A-\delta-\rho\right)=g. \tag{8.21}$$

This determines the endogenous growth rate g, as on a balanced growth path, all per capita variables grow at the same rate. If that were not so, either consumption or investment would eventually grow to be equal to output.

From (8.21), a higher pure rate of time preference of households, relative to the private marginal product of capital to firms (the real interest rate), results in a lower endogenous growth rate of per capita income and consumption. This is because a higher pure rate of time preference of households implies lower savings and a lower rate of accumulation of capital. In contrast, a higher total factor productivity A or a higher private contribution of capital to output α leads to a higher endogenous growth rate, as both result in a higher equilibrium real interest rate and higher savings and capital accumulation rates. For the opposite reason, the depreciation rate δ has a negative impact on the endogenous growth rate.

To find the savings rate, we use (8.8) and (8.15). These equations imply that

$$\dot{\hat{k}}(t) = A\hat{k}(t) - \hat{c}(t) - (n+\delta)\hat{k}(t). \tag{8.22}$$

Equation (8.22) is the aggregate equilibrium condition of equality of total output to consumption plus investment. Dividing through by $\hat{k}(t)$ yields

$$\frac{\dot{\hat{k}}(t)}{\hat{k}(t)} = A - n - \delta - \left(\frac{\hat{c}(t)}{\hat{k}(t)}\right) = g. \tag{8.23}$$

From (8.23) it follows that

$$\left(\frac{\hat{c}(t)}{\hat{k}(t)}\right) = A - n - \delta - g. \tag{8.24}$$

From (8.24) and the aggregate production function (8.8), the share of consumption to total output is equal to

$$\left(\frac{\hat{c}(t)}{\hat{y}(t)}\right) = \left(\frac{\hat{c}(t)}{A\hat{k}(t)}\right) = \left(1 - \frac{n+g+\delta}{A}\right). \tag{8.25}$$

From (8.25) and (8.21), the aggregate savings rate is equal to

$$s = 1 - \left(\frac{\hat{c}(t)}{\hat{y}(t)}\right) = \frac{n+g+\delta}{A} = \frac{1}{\theta A}\left(\alpha A - (1-\theta)\delta - \rho + \theta n\right). \tag{8.26}$$

The savings rate in this endogenous-growth Ramsey model is constant, because the real interest rate is constant. It depends positively on the determinants of the real interest rate $\alpha A - \delta$, the rate of population growth n, and the elasticity of intertemporal substitution in consumption $1/\theta$, and negatively on the pure rate of time preference of households ρ. The effect of the depreciation rate of capital on the endogenous savings rate depends on the elasticity of intertemporal substitution in consumption. If the latter is equal to one, which implies $\theta = 1$, then the depreciation rate of capital has no effect on the savings rate. If the elasticity of intertemporal substitution in consumption is greater than one ($\theta < 1$), then the depreciation rate of capital has a negative effect on the savings rate. The opposite happens if the elasticity of intertemporal substitution is less than one ($\theta > 1$).

These effects are analogous to the steady state effects in the Ramsey exogenous-growth model. The main difference in the Arrow-Romer-Ramsey endogenous-growth model has to do with the determinants of the endogenous growth rate in (8.21) and the fact that there is no conditional convergence in this model. Another difference is that, because of the existence of positive externalities in the Arrow-Romer-Ramsey model, the competitive equilibrium is socially suboptimal, as it does not maximize social welfare.

8.1.7 The Suboptimality of the Competitive Equilibrium with Externalities Due to Capital Accumulation

In chapter 4, we have already demonstrated that in the exogenous-growth Ramsey model without externalities, the competitive equilibrium maximizes social welfare. Does this result carry over to the Ramsey model with externalities from capital accumulation, as in the endogenous-growth model we have analyzed? The existence of externalities would immediately suggest that the answer is no.

To examine the nature of the suboptimality of the competitive equilibrium, let us assume there is a social planner who maximizes (8.18) under the macroeconomic constraint (8.22) instead of the private constraint (8.19). From the first-order conditions for a maximum, the Euler equation for the social planner would take the form

$$\frac{\dot{\hat{c}}(t)}{\hat{c}(t)} = \frac{1}{\theta}(A - \delta - \rho) = g^* > \frac{1}{\theta}(\alpha A - \delta - \rho) = g.$$

From the above inequality, we can deduce that the endogenous growth rate in the competitive economy is lower than the socially efficient growth rate. This is because the competitive real interest rate ($\alpha A - \delta$) underestimates the social net marginal product of capital ($A - \delta$), which, because of the positive externality from capital accumulation, is higher than the private net marginal product of capital. Because the positive externality from capital accumulation is not reflected in the real interest rate, households have a smaller incentive to save and accumulate capital, and, as a result, the savings rate, the investment rate, and the growth rate of the economy are lower than what would be socially optimal.

Thus, the competitive equilibrium is suboptimal and could be improved on by a social planner who would choose savings and capital accumulation, taking the externality into account. Various other policies, such as the subsidization of capital, could improve efficiency in this case.

Exercise 8.1 Assume a competitive representative household model in which the production technology is as in (8.5), with $0 < \beta < 1$. Derive the steady state, and discuss the properties of the steady state and the adjustment path. How does the steady state compare with the steady state of a model without externalities from learning by doing? Is the speed of adjustment higher or lower, and how does it depend on the strength of the externalities from capital accumulation? What determines the long-run growth rate in this model? Discuss the optimality properties of the competitive equilibrium.

8.1.8 Externalities and Endogenous Growth in the Blanchard-Weil Model

We next turn to the determinants of endogenous growth in an OLG model with externalities from capital accumulation. We shall utilize the Blanchard-Weil model, where population growth comes from the entry of new households. The number of members of each household is constant, and the rate of entry of new households is equal to n. Every household has an infinite time horizon.

The household born at instant j maximizes the intertemporal utility function

$$U_j = \int_{t=j}^{\infty} e^{-\rho t} u\left(c(j,t)\right) dt, \tag{8.27}$$

where $c(j,t)$ is consumption at instant t of the household born at instant j, u is the instantaneous utility function of the household, and ρ is pure rate of the time preference of the household.

Following Blanchard [1985] and Weil [1989], we shall assume that the instantaneous utility function is logarithmic:

$$u\left(c(j,t)\right) = \ln c(j,t). \tag{8.28}$$

All households supply one unit of labor and receive a real wage $\hat{w}$, and to the extent that they have accumulated savings, they also receive capital income. Household j thus maximizes (8.27) under the constraint

$$\dot{k}(j,t) = r(t)k(j,t) + w(t) - c(j,t), \tag{8.29}$$

where $k(j,j) = 0$.

From the first-order conditions, and after aggregation, we get the following equation for the evolution of aggregate consumption:[5]

$$\dot{C}(t) = (r(t) + n - \rho)C(t) - n\rho K(t). \tag{8.30}$$

From (8.30), after division by $L(t)$, the evolution of per capita consumption is described by

$$\dot{\hat{c}}(t) = [r(t) - \rho]\hat{c}(t) - n\rho\hat{k}(t). \tag{8.31}$$

5. See chapter 5 for a detailed derivation of aggregate consumption in the Blanchard-Weil model.

Dividing (8.31) by per capita income $\hat{y}(t)$, and after replacing the real interest rate from (8.12) and the capital output ratio from (8.8), we get the following equation for the evolution of the ratio of private consumption to total output:

$$\dot{\bar{c}}(t) = (r(t) - \rho - g)\bar{c}(t) - n\rho\bar{k}(t) = (\alpha A - \delta - \rho - g)\bar{c}(t) - n\rho A^{-1}, \tag{8.32}$$

where for any variable X, we define its ratio to total output Y as

$$\bar{x} = \frac{X}{Y}.$$

From the per capita capital accumulation equation (8.22), we get

$$g = (1 - \bar{c}(t))\, A - n - \delta. \tag{8.33}$$

Equation (8.33) suggests that the aggregate growth rate $g + n$ is equal to the net savings (=investment) rate times total factor productivity, minus the depreciation rate. Because of constant returns to capital accumulation, total factor productivity is equal to the (constant) average and marginal product of capital.

From (8.32) and (8.33), we can determine the two endogenous variables, that is, the growth rate and the savings rate. Given that neither is a predetermined variable, the equilibrium is achieved instantaneously.

For a constant ratio of private consumption to output, (8.32) implies

$$\bar{c}(t) = \frac{n\rho A^{-1}}{\alpha A - \delta - \rho - g}. \tag{8.34}$$

The higher the growth rate is, the greater will be the ratio of private consumption to total output for a given difference between the real interest rate and the pure rate of time preference of households.

Solving (8.33) and (8.34) for the endogenous growth rate, we get that

$$g = aA - \delta - \rho - \frac{n\rho}{(1 - n - \delta)A}. \tag{8.35}$$

From (8.35), it follows that the endogenous growth rate in an Arrow-Romer-Blanchard-Weil model is lower than that in the corresponding Arrow-Romer-Ramsey model. The reason is that savings, and therefore capital accumulation and growth, are lower in the former model, because current generations do not internalize the welfare of future generations.

The difference between the two models can be depicted graphically, with the help of figure 8.2. The nonlinear relationship (8.34) between the consumption rate and the growth rate is represented by the positively sloped curve in figure 8.2. Obviously, as g tends to $\alpha A - \delta - \rho$, the ratio of private consumption to total income tends to infinity.

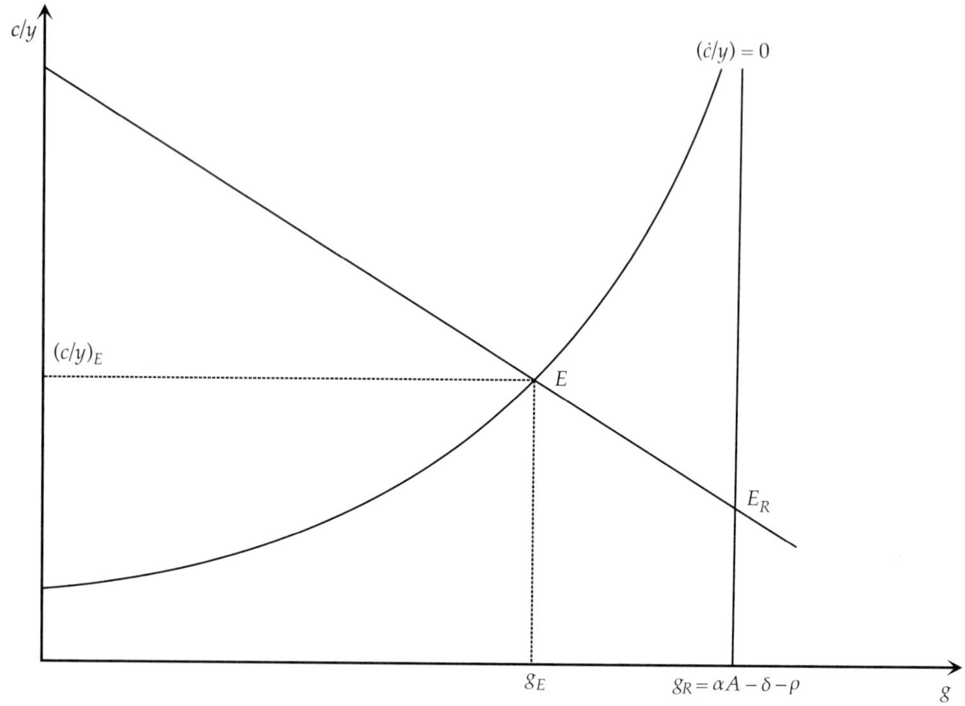

Figure 8.2
Determination of the consumption-to-output ratio and the endogenous growth rate in the Blanchard-Weil model.

The capital accumulation equation (8.33) is represented by the negatively sloped line. The higher the ratio of private consumption to total income is, the smaller will be the savings rate, the investment rate, and the endogenous growth rate.

The equilibrium is determined at the intersection of the two loci (point E in the figure). Because neither private consumption nor the rate of economic growth is a predetermined variable, the economy jumps directly to the equilibrium at E. Note that the equilibrium ratio of private consumption to output is greater than in the corresponding representative household model and the endogenous growth rate is lower. The equilibrium in the corresponding representative household model ($n = 0$) is determined at point E_R.

The Arrow-Romer-Blanchard-Weil model implies two externalities that reduce the long-run growth rate. One arises because current generations do not internalize the welfare of future generations and thus save less than would be socially optimal, and the second arises because firms do not internalize the effects of their capital stock decisions on the aggregate capital stock and hence on the efficiency of labor. The corresponding Arrow-Romer-Ramsey model implies only the latter of the two externalities.

8.1.9 Fiscal Policy and Endogenous Growth

When we introduce the government, the effects of fiscal policy are analogous to the effects in the exogenous-growth Blanchard-Weil model. The exogenous-growth version of the model determines the capital stock and consumption per efficiency unit of labor, whereas the endogenous-growth version determines the growth rate and the ratio of consumption to total output.

Assuming that the government stabilizes the government debt to output ratio and that it selects a fixed ratio of primary government expenditure to total output, the endogenous-growth Blanchard-Weil model takes the following form:

$$\dot{\bar{c}}(t) = (r(t) - \rho - g)\bar{c}(t) - n\rho(\bar{k}(t) + \bar{b}) = (\alpha A - \delta - \rho - g)\bar{c}(t) - n\rho(A^{-1} + \bar{d}),$$
$$\bar{c}(t) = 1 - \bar{c}_g - (n + g + \delta)A^{-1}. \tag{8.36}$$

The top equation in (8.36) is the aggregate private consumption function, when households hold assets in both capital and government bonds, and is derived from (8.32). The bottom equation is derived from (8.33) with the addition of primary government expenditure; it describes the capital accumulation rate, which is equal to the endogenous growth rate, as a result of total domestic savings.

The additional assumption that the government selects a constant government debt and primary expenditure to output ratio takes the form

$$\bar{c}_g = \frac{c_g(t)}{y(t)}, \quad \bar{d} = \frac{d(t)}{y(t)}.$$

The model of (8.36) determines the ratio of private consumption to total output $\bar{c}$, and the growth rate g.

The equilibrium is depicted in figure 8.3. The dashed positively sloped curve depicts the top equation in (8.36), for a constant ratio of private consumption to total output, and is given by

$$\bar{c}(t) = \frac{n\rho(A^{-1} + \bar{d})}{(\alpha A - \delta - \rho - g)}. \tag{8.37}$$

The higher the growth rate is, the greater the ratio of private consumption to total output will be, for a given difference between the real interest rate and the pure rate of time preference of households. The nonlinear relationship is represented by the dashed upward-sloping curve in figure 8.3. As g tends to $\alpha A - \delta - \rho$, the ratio of private consumption to total output tends to infinity.

For a positive ratio of government debt to output, this curve lies above the corresponding curve for zero government debt (solid curve). Current households consider government debt

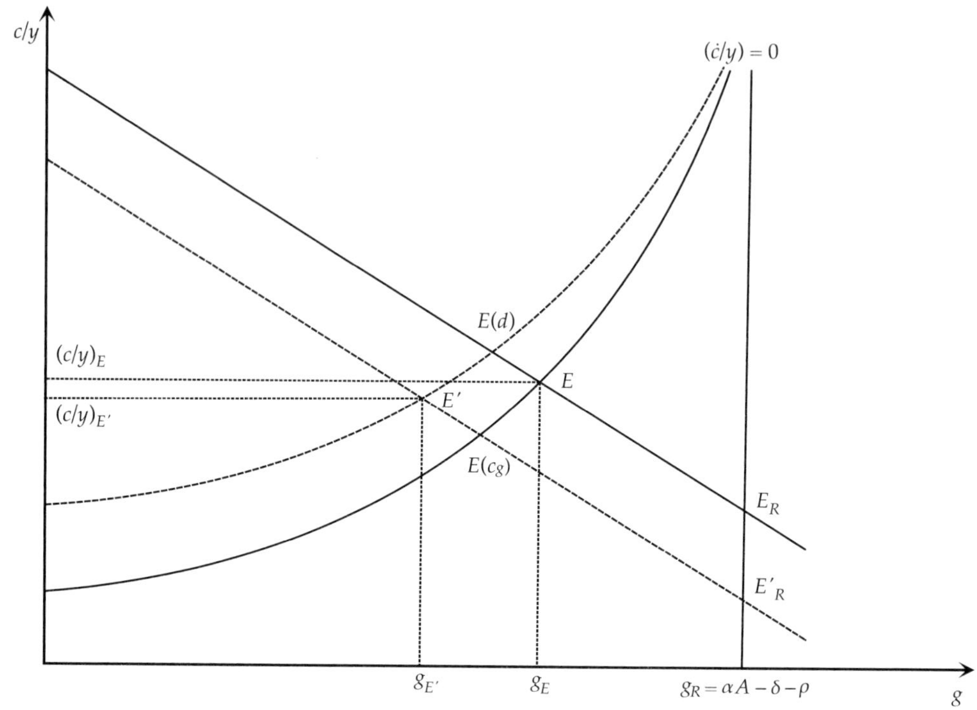

Figure 8.3
Determination of private consumption and the growth rate with government expenditure and debt.

as part of their wealth and thus consume more relative to income, because they know that part of the future taxes to finance government debt will be paid by future generations.

The dashed negatively sloped straight line represents the negative relationship between growth (capital accumulation) and the private consumption ratio, because the higher the ratio of private consumption to output is, the lower the ratio of savings and investment to total output will be. With a positive ratio of primary government expenditure to total output, this line is below the corresponding line for zero primary government expenditure.

It is evident that both the ratio of government debt to output and that of primary government expenditure to output have a negative impact on the endogenous growth rate g. The reason is that both government debt and primary government expenditure cause a reduction in total savings and capital accumulation and thus reduce the growth rate. The equilibrium with government expenditure and taxes is at point E', which implies a lower growth rate.

Government debt causes an increase in private consumption by current generations, reducing the rate of accumulation of capital and the growth rate (point $E(d)$ in figure 8.3). Primary government expenditure causes a decline in private consumption that is not fully offsetting, reducing total savings, the rate of capital accumulation, and the growth rate (point $E(c_g)$ in figure 8.3). The combination of the two results in even greater reduction in the endogenous rate of economic growth.

In the corresponding representative household model (with $n=0$), the rate of economic growth is not affected by the level of government debt and primary government expenditure. The endogenous growth rate is determined by the difference of the real interest rate of the pure rate of time preference (point E_R in figure 8.3). Primary government expenditure crowds out an equal amount of private consumption and thus does not affect aggregate savings. Government debt does not affect private consumption, as it is considered equivalent to the present value of future taxes for the representative household (point E'_R in figure 8.3).

Exercise 8.2 Analyze the impact of capital income taxation in the Ramsey and Blanchard-Weil endogenous-growth models. Assume logarithmic preferences and a Cobb-Douglas technology with learning by doing. How does a tax rate τ_K on interest income affect the steady state growth rate? Assume in your analysis that government expenditure and public debt per head are constant, and that the government redistributes receipts from the capital income tax back to households in a lump sum fashion.

8.1.10 Convergence in Exogenous and Endogenous AK Growth Models

We have already seen that, unlike in exogenous growth models, in endogenous growth models of the AK variety (such as those examined in this section), there is no convergence process.

In exogenous growth models, any two economies characterized by the same parameters describing the technology of production, household preferences, and economic policy will converge to the same balanced growth path, even if they start from different initial conditions. In endogenous growth models, they will have the same endogenous growth rate, but they will not converge to the same per capita income. Their initial differences will remain forever.

The analysis of this difference is presented in figure 8.4, where it is assumed that two otherwise identical economies are characterized by different initial conditions. Economy 1 has initially less capital and output per worker in relation to economy 2. In terms of the production technology, the preferences of consumers, and fiscal policy, the two economies are identical.

If the two economies are characterized by the conditions that apply to an exogenous growth model, then they both converge to the balanced growth path $\bar{y}^*(t)$. Initially, economy 1 will have a higher growth rate of output per head than economy 2. Gradually the two economies will converge to the balanced growth path $\bar{y}^*(t)$ and will be characterized by the same per capita output and the same growth rate of per capita output.

If the two economies are characterized by the conditions that apply to an endogenous growth model, then their initial differences will remain. Economies 1 and 2 will be characterized by the same rate of growth of per capita output, but their initial percentage differences in per capita output, per capita consumption, and real wages will persist. Economy 1 will

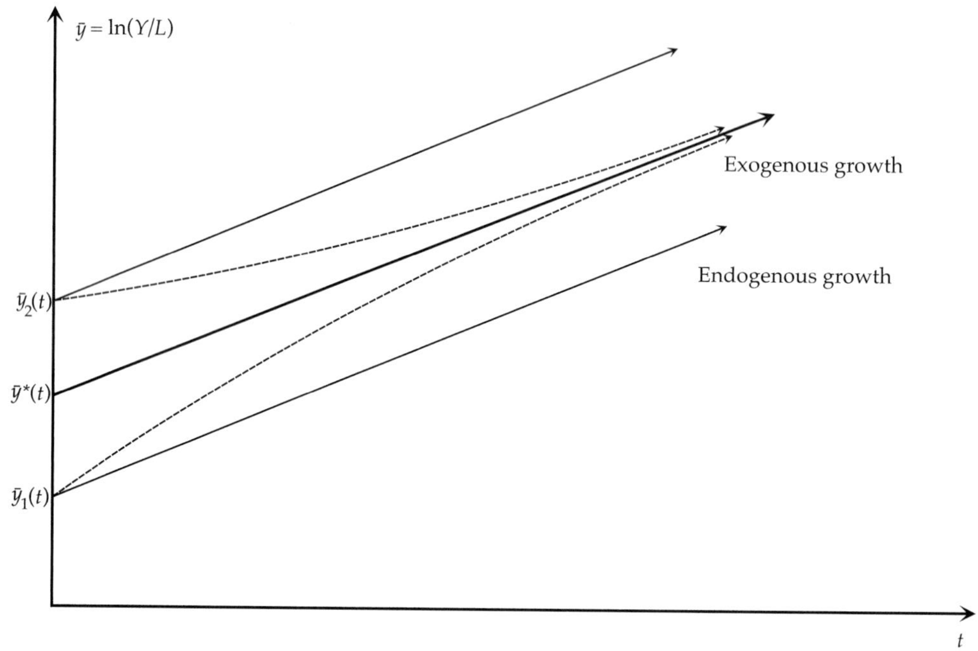

Figure 8.4
The path of per capita output in exogenous and endogenous growth models.

follow the balanced growth path $\bar{y}_1(t)$, and economy 2 the balanced growth path $\bar{y}_2(t)$. Their per capita output, consumption, and real wages will grow at the same rate, but they will not converge.

The paths of per capita output of two such economies (in logarithms), under exogenous and under endogenous growth, are illustrated in figure 8.4.

Note that the available empirical evidence from postwar international experience indicates that conditional convergence cannot be dismissed easily, casting doubts on the applicability of endogenous growth models. However, this does not mean that externalities of the learning-by-doing variety do not exist, as such externalities are also compatible with exogenous growth models, as long as they do not lead to constant returns to the accumulation of physical capital.[6]

8.2 Investment in Human Capital and Economic Growth

In the learning-by-doing endogenous-growth model that we presented in the previous section, endogenous growth is essentially a by-product of the accumulation of physical

6. For example, see Mankiw et al. [1992] and Barro [1997a].

capital, because it is assumed that labor efficiency is a function of the aggregate physical capital stock per worker.

An alternative class of growth models emphasizes the education and training of workers and the accumulation of human capital implied by such activities. In this section, we consider some alternative models in which the efficiency of labor depends on investment in human capital through education and training.

8.2.1 The Extended Solow Model and the Share of Spending on Education and Training

We start with a model in which the accumulation of human capital is the result of spending on education and training. The model is due to Mankiw et al. [1992] and is a generalization of the Solow model to allow for the accumulation of human as well as physical capital. The efficiency of labor depends partly on exogenous technical progress and partly on the stock of human capital, which accumulates due to investment in education and training.

Firms are competitive, and their production technology is Cobb-Douglas, of the form

$$Y(t) = AK(t)^{\alpha}\left(\hat{h}(t)L(t)\right)^{1-\alpha}, \tag{8.38}$$

where $0 < \alpha < 1$, and $\hat{h}(t)$ denotes the efficiency of labor at instant t.

Assume that the efficiency of labor is a function of human capital per worker h and exogenous technical progress. This function takes the form

$$\hat{h}(t) = (h(t))^{\gamma}\left(e^{gt}\right)^{1-\gamma}, \tag{8.39}$$

where h is human capital per worker, resulting from accumulated education and training, and $0 \leq \gamma \leq 1$ is a parameter that measures the relative contribution of human capital to the efficiency of labor. A fraction $1-\gamma$ of the efficiency of labor depends on technical progress, which grows at an exogenous rate g.

Substituting (8.39) in (8.38), we get the following aggregate production function:

$$Y(t) = AK(t)^{\alpha}H(t)^{\gamma(1-\alpha)}\left(e^{gt}L(t)\right)^{(1-\gamma)(1-\alpha)}, \tag{8.40}$$

where $H = hL$ is aggregate human capital.

We assume, generalizing the Solow model, that total household income is either consumed or invested in physical capital or invested in human capital. The percentage of output and income invested in physical capital equals s_K, and the percentage invested in human capital equals s_H. These percentages are considered exogenous, in the same way that the savings rate is assumed exogenous in the Solow model. Furthermore, assume that δ, the depreciation rate, is the same for both physical and human capital. With these assumptions, the accumulation equations for physical and human capital are given by

$$\dot{K}(t) = s_K Y(t) - \delta K(t), \tag{8.41}$$

$$\dot{H}(t) = s_H Y(t) - \delta H(t). \tag{8.42}$$

If $\gamma = 0$, then we get the familiar neoclassical production function, as spending on education and training does not contribute to labor efficiency of workers, which is a simple function of time (exogenous technical progress).

If $0 < \gamma < 1$, we have a generalized model of exogenous growth, in which the per capita capital stock and output on the balanced growth path are positive functions of both the proportion of total income spent on physical capital accumulation s_K, and the proportion spent on education and training s_H.

In this case, the equilibrium condition in the goods and services market is given by

$$Y(t) = C(t) + \dot{K}(t) + \dot{H}(t) + \delta\left(K(t) + H(t)\right), \tag{8.43}$$

which, in conjunction with (8.41) and (8.42), implies a consumption function of the form

$$C(t) = (1 - s_K - s_H)Y(t). \tag{8.44}$$

In the case where $0 < \gamma < 1$, we can divide (8.40), (8.41), and (8.42) by the number of workers L times the exogenous labor efficiency e^{gt}, and the model takes the form

$$\tilde{y}(t) = A\tilde{k}(t)^{\alpha}\tilde{h}(t)^{\gamma(1-\alpha)}, \tag{8.45}$$

$$\dot{\tilde{k}}(t) = s_K\tilde{y}(t) - (n + g + \delta)\tilde{k}(t), \tag{8.46}$$

$$\dot{\tilde{h}}(t) = s_H\tilde{y}(t) - (n + g + \delta)\tilde{h}(t), \tag{8.47}$$

where $\tilde{y}(t) = \frac{Y(t)}{e^{gt}L(t)}$, $\tilde{k}(t) = \frac{K(t)}{e^{gt}L(t)}$, and $\tilde{h}(t) = \frac{H(t)}{e^{gt}L(t)}$. These variables are defined respectively as output, physical capital, and human capital, per exogenous efficiency unit of labor.

8.2.2 The Balanced Growth Path in the Extended Solow Model

On the balanced growth path, all per capita variables grow at the rate of exogenous technical progress g. It therefore follows that

$$s_K\tilde{y}^* = s_K A\left(\tilde{k}^*\right)^{\alpha}\left(\tilde{h}^*\right)^{\gamma(1-a)} = (n + g + \delta)\tilde{k}^*, \tag{8.48}$$

$$s_H\tilde{y}^* = s_H A\left(\tilde{k}^*\right)^{\alpha}\left(\tilde{h}^*\right)^{\gamma(1-a)} = (n + g + \delta)\tilde{h}^*. \tag{8.49}$$

From (8.48), (8.49), and the production function (8.45), it follows that

$$\tilde{k}^* = \frac{s_K}{s_H}\tilde{h}^*. \tag{8.50}$$

From (8.50), it follows that on the balanced growth path, the ratio of physical to human capital is constant, and equal to the ratio of the investment rates in physical and human capital, respectively. This follows because equilibrium investment on the balanced growth path is a proportion $n+g+\delta$ of both physical and human capital, per exogenous efficiency unit of labor.

Substituting (8.50) in the production function and solving (8.48) and (8.49) results in

$$\tilde{h}^* = \left(\frac{A\left(s_K{}^{\alpha} s_H{}^{1-\alpha}\right)}{n+g+\delta} \right)^{\frac{1}{(1-\gamma)(1-\alpha)}}, \tag{8.51}$$

$$\tilde{k}^* = \left(\frac{A\left(s_K{}^{1-\gamma(1-\alpha)} s_H{}^{\gamma(1-\alpha)}\right)}{n+g+\delta} \right)^{\frac{1}{(1-\gamma)(1-\alpha)}}, \tag{8.52}$$

$$\tilde{y}^* = \left(\frac{A\left(s_K{}^{\alpha} s_H{}^{\gamma(1-\alpha)}\right)}{(n+g+\delta)^{\alpha+\gamma(1-\alpha)}} \right)^{\frac{1}{(1-\gamma)(1-\alpha)}}. \tag{8.53}$$

From (8.53), per capita output on the balanced growth path is given by

$$\hat{y}^*(t) = \tilde{y}^* e^{gt} = \left(\frac{A\left(s_K{}^{\alpha} s_H{}^{\gamma(1-\alpha)}\right)}{(n+g+\delta)^{\alpha+\gamma(1-\alpha)}} \right)^{\frac{1}{(1-\gamma)(1-\alpha)}} e^{gt}, \tag{8.54}$$

where $\hat{y}(t) = \frac{Y(t)}{L(t)}$.

The level of per capita output on the balanced growth path depends positively on total factor productivity A, the shares of output invested in physical and human capital (s_K and s_H), and negatively on the population growth rate n, the rate of exogenous technical progress g, and the depreciation rate δ. The growth rate of per capita output on the balanced growth path is equal to the rate of exogenous technical progress g.

Thus, in the case $0 < \gamma < 1$, we have an extended Solow model of exogenous growth. In this model, human capital accumulation plays a role similar to that of physical capital accumulation in the original Solow model. As the accumulation of human capital causes an increase in the marginal productivity of physical capital and vice versa, the convergence process continues for longer. But eventually, the economy converges to a balanced growth path where growth in per capita income is equal to the exogenous rate of technical progress.

8.2.3 Endogenous Growth in the Extended Solow Model

If $\gamma = 1$ in (8.39), there is no exogenous technical progress. The efficiency of labor only depends on accumulated human capital. In this case, the model is an endogenous growth model. Setting $\gamma = 1$ in the production function (8.40) we get

$$\hat{y}(t) = A\hat{k}(t)^{\alpha}\hat{h}(t)^{1-\alpha}, \tag{8.55}$$

where $\hat{y} = Y/L$, $\hat{k} = K/L$, and $\hat{h} = H/L$.

In this model, the balanced growth path is defined by

$$\frac{\hat{k}^*(t)}{\hat{h}^*(t)} = \frac{s_K}{s_H}, \tag{8.56}$$

$$g = \frac{\dot{\hat{y}}^*(t)}{\hat{y}^*(t)} = A s_K^{\alpha} s_H^{1-\alpha} - (n+\delta). \tag{8.57}$$

On the balanced growth path, the ratio of physical to human capital is stabilized at the ratio of the investment rates in physical and human capital. Because both physical and human capital are growing at the same rate, we have endogenous growth. The accumulation of physical capital causes an increase in income, which in turn causes an increase in human capital through expenditure on education and training. This in turn leads to a further rise in output, which causes new investment in physical capital. The parallel accumulation of physical and human capital leads to endogenous growth.

The endogenous growth rate depends positively on total factor productivity A and a weighted average of the income ratios invested in physical and human capital s_K and s_H. The growth rate of population n and the depreciation rate δ have a negative impact on the endogenous growth rate.

In all other respects, the properties of the endogenous growth, extended Solow model are similar to those of the learning-by-doing model of Arrow and Romer, as analyzed in section 8.1. The main difference is that in this extended Solow model, the accumulation of human capital is not a simple by-product of physical capital accumulation but the result of explicit investment on human capital through education and training.

8.2.4 The Jones Model of Human Capital Accumulation

We next consider an alternative model, in which human capital depends on the time span devoted to education and training. We assume that workers spend part of their time v in education and training and that this investment of time involves a rate of return ψ. The model is analyzed in Jones [2002].

The production technology is described by the production function (8.38). The efficiency of labor per employee is determined by

$$\hat{h}(t) = h(v, \psi)e^{gt}, \tag{8.58}$$

where the function $h(v, \psi)$ determines human capital per worker as a function of the time span v devoted to education and training, and the rate of return of investment in human capital ψ.

A plausible form of this function is the exponential function. Let us therefore assume that

$$h(v, \psi) = e^{\psi v}. \tag{8.59}$$

The exponential form is plausible, because it implies that the proportional change in the function with respect to the time devoted to education and training is equal to the rate of return ψ. From (8.59), we get

$$\frac{\partial h(v,\psi)}{\partial v} = \psi e^{\psi v} = \psi h(v,\psi). \tag{8.60}$$

Substituting (8.59) in (8.58) and the resulting equation in the production function (8.38), we get that output per worker is determined by

$$\hat{y}(t) = A\hat{k}(t)^{\alpha}(e^{\psi v}e^{gt})^{1-\alpha}. \tag{8.61}$$

Combining (8.61) with the savings assumption of the Solow model (i.e., that there is an exogenous constant savings rate), per capita output on the balanced growth path is determined by

$$\hat{y}^{*}(t) = A\left(\frac{sA}{n+g+\delta}\right)^{\frac{\alpha}{1-\alpha}} e^{\psi v}e^{gt}. \tag{8.62}$$

Per capita output on the balanced growth path is a positive function of the amount of time spent on education and training v and the rate of return on investment in human capital ψ. However, in all other respects, this model is an exogenous growth model, similar to the Solow model.

8.2.5 The Lucas Model of Human Capital Accumulation and Endogenous Growth

An alternative model of investment in human capital is the endogenous growth model of Lucas [1988], which is based in part on Uzawa [1965].

Lucas assumed that labor efficiency is equal to human capital per worker:

$$\hat{h}(t) = h(t). \tag{8.63}$$

With regard to the production of human capital per worker, he assumed that this depends on the existing stock of human capital per worker times the proportion of nonleisure time that workers devote to education and training. He thus assumed that

$$\dot{h}(t) = \zeta(1-u(t))h(t) - (n+\delta)h(t). \tag{8.64}$$

According to (8.64), only human capital is required for the production of human capital. Here u is defined as the proportion of the nonleisure time of households that is devoted to the production of goods and services, and $1-u$ is the proportion of time devoted to education and training. Education and training results in the accumulation of human capital. In addition, ζ is the productivity of human capital in the production of new human capital, n is the population growth rate, and δ the depreciation rate of human capital (assumed for simplicity to be equal to that of physical capital).

On the balanced growth path, u will be constant at u^*. Taking the integral of (8.64) and substituting in (8.63), we get

$$\hat{h}(t) = h(t) = e^{(\zeta(1-u*)-(n+\delta))t}. \tag{8.65}$$

Lucas assumed that u is chosen by a representative household to maximize its intertemporal utility of consumption. As a result, the choice of u depends both on the preferences of the representative household and on the technological parameters characterizing the production of goods and services and human capital.

From the form of (8.65), it follows that the endogenous growth rate is equal to $g = \zeta(1-u^*) - (n+\delta)$, which works like the exogenous rate of technical progress in exogenous growth models. The higher is the steady state proportion of nonleisure time devoted to education and training, the higher the endogenous growth rate will be. In the Lucas model, $1-u^*$ is chosen endogenously, and in conjunction with the exogenous ζ, δ, and n, it determines the steady state growth rate of per capita output.

8.2.6 A Detailed Analysis of the Lucas Model

In what follows, we proceed to analyze in detail the Lucas [1988] model. The dynamic analysis of this model has been generalized by Caballe and Santos [1993], Faig [1995], and Mulligan and Sala-i Martin [1993].

As in the Ramsey model, the representative household is assumed to maximize

$$U = \int_{t=0}^{\infty} e^{-(\rho-n)t} \frac{c(t)^{1-\theta}}{1-\theta} dt, \tag{8.66}$$

subject to the following constraints:

$$y(t) = Ak(t)^{\alpha}(u(t)h(t))^{1-\alpha}, \tag{8.67}$$

$$\dot{k}(t) = y(t) - c(t) - (n+\delta)k(t), \tag{8.68}$$

$$\dot{h}(t) = \zeta(1-u(t))h(t) - (n+\delta)h(t), \tag{8.69}$$

where c is consumption per capita, y is output per capita, k is the stock of physical capital per capita, h is the stock of human capital per capita, and u is the proportion of nonleisure time spent on the production of goods and services. Thus, $1-u$ is the proportion of nonleisure time spent on the accumulation of human capital.

Equation (8.67) is the production function for goods and services, (8.68) the accumulation equation for physical capital, and (8.69) the accumulation equation (production function) for human capital. Let us assume constant returns to scale in both the goods and services sector and the human capital sector. Building on the model of Uzawa [1965], Lucas assumed that only human capital is used in the production of human capital.

In these equations, ρ is the pure rate of time preference of the representative household, $1/\theta$ is the elasticity of intertemporal substitution in consumption, A is total factor productivity in the production of goods and services, α is the elasticity of output of goods and services with respect to physical capital, ζ is total factor productivity in the production of human capital, and δ is the depreciation rate of both types of capital.

From (8.69), the growth rate of human capital per worker is given by

$$\frac{\dot{h}(t)}{h(t)} = \zeta(1 - u(t)) - (n + \delta). \tag{8.70}$$

On the balanced growth path, the growth rate of human capital per worker is constant and equal to the growth rate of all other per capita variables. Given that the growth rate is determined by u, to determine the growth rate, we must consider how the representative household selects it.

The current-value Hamilton function for the problem of the representative household takes the form

$$\mathcal{H} = \frac{c^{1-\theta}}{1-\theta} + \lambda\left(Ak^{\alpha}(uh)^{1-\alpha} - c - (n+\delta)k\right) + \mu\left(\zeta(1-u)h - (n+\delta)h\right), \tag{8.71}$$

where we have omitted the time index and substituted out the production function of goods and services (8.67). The shadow price of physical capital λ and the shadow price of human capital μ are the two multipliers of the Hamilton function, corresponding to the constraints (8.68) and (8.69).

From the first-order conditions for an optimum, we have

$$c^{-\theta} = \lambda, \tag{8.72}$$

$$\lambda(1-\alpha)A(k/(uh))^{\alpha} = \mu\zeta, \tag{8.73}$$

$$\dot{\lambda} = -\left(\alpha Ak^{\alpha-1}(uh)^{1-\alpha} - \delta - \rho\right)\lambda, \tag{8.74}$$

$$\dot{\mu} = -\left(\zeta(1-u) - \delta - \rho\right)\mu - \lambda\left((1-\alpha)uAk^{\alpha}(uh)^{-\alpha}\right). \tag{8.75}$$

The interpretations of these first-order conditions are straightforward. Equation (8.72) suggests that on the margin, goods and services must be equally valuable in their two uses of consumption and investment, respectively. Equation (8.73) suggests that nonleisure time must be equally valuable in its two uses: production of goods and services and production of human capital. The differential equations (8.74) and (8.75) describe the evolution of the shadow prices of physical and human capital as a result of the accumulation of both types of capital.

From (8.72)–(8.75) and the accumulation equations (8.68) and (8.69), we can determine the endogenous variables. From (8.72) and (8.74), we can derive the familiar Euler equation for consumption:

$$\frac{\dot{c}}{c} = \frac{1}{\theta}\left(\alpha A k^{\alpha-1}(uh)^{1-\alpha} - \delta - \rho\right). \tag{8.76}$$

From (8.73) and (8.75), it follows that

$$\frac{\dot{\mu}}{\mu} = -\left(\zeta - \delta - \rho\right). \tag{8.77}$$

From the capital accumulation equation (8.68), the rate of growth of the per capita capital stock is given by

$$\frac{\dot{k}}{k} = Ak^{\alpha-1}(uh)^{1-\alpha} - \frac{c}{k} - (\delta + n). \tag{8.78}$$

From the human capital accumulation equation (8.69), we have

$$\frac{\dot{h}}{h} = \zeta(1-u) - (\delta + n). \tag{8.79}$$

Taking the logarithm of (8.73) and differentiating with respect to t, we get

$$\frac{\dot{u}}{u} = \frac{1}{\alpha}\left(\frac{\dot{\lambda}}{\lambda} - \frac{\dot{\mu}}{\mu}\right) + \frac{\dot{k}}{k} - \frac{\dot{h}}{h}. \tag{8.80}$$

Substituting (8.75), (8.77), (8.78), and (8.79) in (8.80), after some rearrangement, we get

$$\frac{\dot{u}}{u} = \zeta\left(\frac{1-\alpha}{\alpha} + u\right) - \frac{c}{k}. \tag{8.81}$$

On the balanced growth path, we have that

$$\frac{\dot{c}}{c} = \frac{\dot{k}}{k} = \frac{\dot{h}}{h} = -\frac{1}{\theta}\frac{\dot{\mu}}{\mu} = g^*, \tag{8.82}$$

where g^* is the steady state endogenous growth rate.

From the steady state versions of (8.77) and (8.79), we can determine g^* and $1-u^*$ as

$$g^* = \frac{1}{\theta}\left(\zeta - \delta - \rho\right), \tag{8.83}$$

$$1-u^* = \frac{1}{\theta}\left(1 - \frac{1}{\zeta}\left(\rho - (\theta-1)\delta - \theta n\right)\right). \tag{8.84}$$

The remaining endogenous variables on the balanced growth path, such as the ratio of physical to human capital and the ratio of aggregate consumption to the physical capital stock, can be determined by substituting in the steady state versions of (8.76) and (8.78).

From (8.83) and (8.84), the higher the productivity of human capital in the production of human capital, the higher the proportion of its nonleisure time that the household will devote to education and training. As a result, the endogenous growth rate is higher as well. In contrast, the higher the pure rate of time preference of households, the lower the endogenous growth rate and the proportion of its time that the household will devote to education and training, as opposed to the production of goods and services. This is because of higher discounting of the future, which makes education and training less attractive. Finally, a higher elasticity of intertemporal substitution in consumption results in a higher endogenous growth rate and a higher proportion of nonleisure time devoted to education and training.

In the special case where the elasticity of intertemporal substitution is equal to unity ($\theta = 1$), the equations describing the determination of the endogenous growth rate and the time devoted to education and training simplify to

$$g^* = (\zeta - \delta - \rho),$$

$$1 - u^* = 1 - \frac{1}{\zeta}(\rho - n).$$

The time devoted to the accumulation of human capital is a positive function of productivity in the production function of human capital and a negative function of the discount factor of the representative household $\rho - n$.

To go beyond the analysis of the balanced growth path and describe the transitional dynamics of the model, we can define

$$\omega = \frac{h}{k}, \psi = \frac{c}{k}. \tag{8.85}$$

From the definitions in (8.85), and (8.76), (8.78), (8.79), and (8.81), the transitional dynamics of the model are described by

$$\frac{\dot{\omega}}{\omega} = \zeta(1-u) - A(u\omega)^{1-\alpha} + \psi, \tag{8.86}$$

$$\frac{\dot{\psi}}{\psi} = A\left(\frac{\alpha - \theta}{\theta}\right)(u\omega)^{1-\alpha} + \psi + \frac{\theta - 1}{\theta}\delta + n - \frac{1}{\theta}\rho, \tag{8.87}$$

$$\frac{\dot{u}}{u} = \zeta\left(\frac{1-\alpha}{\alpha} + u\right) - \psi. \tag{8.88}$$

The system of the three differential equations (8.86), (8.87), and (8.88) determines the transitional dynamics of the three endogenous variables ω, ψ, and u.

In the steady state, we have

$$\frac{\dot{\omega}}{\omega}=\frac{\dot{\psi}}{\psi}=\frac{\dot{u}}{u}=0. \tag{8.89}$$

Thus, (8.86) – (8.89) determine the steady state endogenous variables ω, ψ, and u.

8.3 Ideas, Innovations, and Technical Progress

We next turn to a final category of growth models, in which technical progress is a result of ideas and innovations that lead to higher total factor productivity or labor efficiency.

These models emphasize the externalities involved in generating new ideas and innovations that increase the efficiency of production. Just as the learning-by-doing model of Arrow emphasizes the externalities from capital accumulation, so the ideas-and-innovations models emphasize the externalities of the production of ideas and innovations.

Models in this category are sometimes called research and development (R&D) models. Although they date from the late 1960s, the microeconomic foundations of these models and their implications for the functioning of markets were developed in the early 1990s, inspired by the work of Romer [1990]. Under certain conditions, these models can lead to endogenous growth as well.[7]

8.3.1 Key Features of Ideas and Innovations

A crucial assumption of such models is that ideas and innovations can improve the efficiency of production, either through total factor productivity or through labor efficiency.

These models recognize that, unlike most other goods and services, the use of an idea or an innovation by a particular firm (or employee) does not prevent the use of the same idea or innovation by other firms or workers. The use of a particular idea or innovation is *nonrivalrous*, in contrast to the use of a particular machine or a specific employee. From the time an idea or innovation has been produced, anyone with knowledge of this idea can use it, independently of how many others use it simultaneously. If a firm uses a specific machine or a particular employee, it automatically excludes any other firm from simultaneously using the same machine or employee. The property of nonrivalry gives ideas and innovations the character of a quasi-public good.

But in contrast to purely public goods, the use of an idea can be partially excludable by law. This allows the producer of an idea to charge for the use of her idea. For example, if an idea or innovation is legally covered by a patent, then a firm or an employee who wants to use this idea or innovation will have to pay a fee to the holder of the patent.

7. For R&D models of the 1960s, see Uzawa [1965], Phelps [1966], Shell [1966], and Nordhaus [1969]. For models that build on the ideas of Romer [1990], see Grossman and Helpman [1991], Aghion and Howitt [1992], and Jones [1995].

The use of ideas and innovations is not rivalrous, but the degree of excludability that can be achieved varies considerably among ideas and innovations. For example, the use of an encrypted television signal is easily excludable, whereas the use of computer software is excludable only with greater difficulty.

Purely public goods and services are both nonrivalrous and nonexcludable. Other goods and services, such as ideas that can be covered by copyright laws, may be nonrivalrous but may also be excludable. Consequently, the producers of goods and services that use an idea or innovation may be charged for the benefits arising from their use.

The production of nonrivalrous and nonexcludable goods and services implies externalities, which are not reflected in the remuneration of producers of these goods and services. Goods and services that result in positive externalities, such as ideas and innovations, will be produced in smaller quantities than would be socially desirable. And goods and services that result in negative externalities, such as pollution of the environment, will be produced in larger quantities than would be socially desirable.

If the use of ideas and innovations is both nonrivalrous and nonexcludable, then the market will produce fewer ideas and innovations than would be socially desirable. However, if the use of ideas and innovations can be made excludable by the protection of laws on copyright or a patent, then the production of ideas and innovations can rise, as producers of ideas and innovations will be paid for the value of their product.

In the analysis that follows, we shall ignore many of the microeconomic characteristics of the markets for ideas and innovations and will focus on a simple growth model in which technological progress is simply the result of the production of new ideas and innovations.[8]

8.3.2 Key Elements of an Ideas-and-Innovations Growth Model

To present the key elements of a growth model based on the production of ideas and innovations, we start with the production function of goods and services. Assume a Cobb-Douglas production function, of the form

$$Y(t) = AK(t)^{\alpha}\left(H(t)L_y(t)\right)^{1-\alpha}, \tag{8.90}$$

where H is the existing aggregate stock of ideas and innovations that affects the efficiency of labor in the goods and services sector, and L_y is the number of workers who are employed in the goods and services sector.

Apart from goods and services, the economy produces new ideas and innovations. The new ideas and innovations produced per instant are proportional to the number of research workers (i.e., those employed in the production of ideas and innovations). This relationship can be written as

8. Due to the increasing returns implied by ideas and innovations, the assumption of perfect competition is no longer appropriate, and one should ideally use models of imperfect competition. See Romer [1990].

$$\dot{H}(t) = h(H(t), L_h(t))L_h(t), \tag{8.91}$$

where L_h is the number of workers employed in the production of ideas and innovations (whom we call research workers or researchers) and $h(\cdot)$ is the average productivity of research workers.

Assume that the average productivity of research workers is a positive function of the total stock of ideas and innovations and a negative function of the number of research workers. The existing stock of ideas and innovations makes every researcher more productive. However, assume that this effect is subject to diminishing returns. In contrast, as the number of researchers increases, the probability of duplication of effort (that is, the probability of simultaneous production of the same idea or innovation by more than one researcher) increases. Thus, the average productivity of research workers falls with the number of researchers.

In particular, we will assume that the productivity function of research workers, with the characteristics highlighted above, takes the form

$$h(H(t), L_h(t)) = hH(t)^{\beta} L_h(t)^{\gamma - 1}, \tag{8.92}$$

where $h > 0$, $0 < \beta < 1$, and $0 < \gamma < 1$.

Substituting (8.92) in (8.91), we can express the production function of ideas and innovations as

$$\dot{H}(t) = hH(t)^{\beta} L_h(t)^{\gamma}. \tag{8.93}$$

This production function implies that the existing stock of ideas and innovations has diminishing returns in the production of new ideas and innovations, because the higher the existing stock of ideas and innovations is, the more difficult it will be to discover new ones. It also implies that the number of research workers is also associated with diminishing returns, as the likelihood of duplication of effort in the production of new ideas and innovations is growing with the number of research workers.

The total number of workers in the economy is the sum of workers employed in the production of goods and services and research workers employed in the generation of new ideas and innovations. Consequently, we have

$$L(t) = L_y(t) + L_h(t). \tag{8.94}$$

To keep the model simple, assume, as in the Solow model, that the savings rate is a constant proportion of output s_Y, and that the number of research workers is a constant fraction of the total number of workers s_H. In addition, assume that the growth rate of the population and the labor force is exogenous and equal to n. It therefore follows that

$$\dot{L}(t) = nL(t), \tag{8.95}$$

$$\dot{K}(t) = s_Y Y(t) - \delta K(t), \tag{8.96}$$

$$L_h(t) = s_H L(t), \tag{8.97}$$

$$L_y(t) = (1 - s_H) L(t). \tag{8.98}$$

We can now examine the behavior of the model.

8.3.3 Endogenous Determination of the Rate of Technical Progress

To determine the rate of technical progress g, substitute (8.97) in (8.93) and divide by the total stock of ideas and innovations H:

$$\frac{\dot{H}(t)}{H(t)} = (h s_H{}^{\gamma}) H(t)^{\beta - 1} L(t)^{\gamma}. \tag{8.99}$$

On the balanced growth path, the rate of technical progress will be constant. Taking the logarithm of (8.99) and then taking the first derivative of the resulting log-linear equation with respect to time, it follows that the rate of technical progress on the balanced growth path will be given by

$$g = \frac{\gamma n}{1 - \beta}. \tag{8.100}$$

The rate of technical progress on the balanced growth path, denoted by g, will be proportional to the population growth rate n. The reason is that the population growth rate determines the growth rate of research workers, who contribute to the generation of new ideas and innovations.

The only other parameters that determine the endogenous rate of technical progress are the parameters of the production function of new ideas and innovations, β and γ. Both have a positive impact on the endogenous rate of technical progress. The higher the elasticity of production of new ideas and innovations is with respect to the existing stock of ideas and innovations (β) and with respect to the number of research workers (γ), the higher the rate of technical progress on the balanced growth path will be. Thus, this model attributes technical progress to population growth and to the parameters of the production function of new ideas and innovations.[9]

8.3.4 The Balanced Growth Path with Endogenous Technical Progress

On the balanced growth path, all per capita variables grow at the endogenous rate of technical progress g, as given by (8.100). Variables per efficiency unit of labor are determined in a way similar to the corresponding Solow model. One can show that, on the balanced growth

9. For an empirical investigation of how population growth affects technical progress in historical perspective, see Kremer [1993].

path, we have

$$k^* = \left(\frac{s_Y A (1 - s_H)^{1-\alpha}}{n + g + \delta} \right)^{\frac{1}{1-\alpha}}, \tag{8.101}$$

$$y^* = A(1 - s_H)^{1-\alpha} (k^*)^\alpha, \tag{8.102}$$

$$c^* = (1 - s_Y) y^*, \tag{8.103}$$

$$H^*(t) = \left(\frac{(1 - \beta)h}{\gamma n} \right)^{\frac{1}{1-\beta}} (s_H L(0))^{\frac{\gamma}{1-\beta}} e^{\left(\frac{\gamma n}{1-\beta}\right)t}, \tag{8.104}$$

where $k = K/(HL)$, $y = Y/(HL)$, $c = C/(HL)$, and the superscript * denotes the value of the corresponding variable on the balanced growth path.

On the balanced growth path, the model behaves exactly as the Solow model does, except that the rate of technical progress g is determined endogenously and depends on population growth and the parameters that characterize the production function of new ideas and innovations.

8.4 Unified Growth Theory and the Transition from Stagnation to Growth

The models we have analyzed in this and the preceding chapters aim to explain the process of economic growth since the takeoff in economic growth following the industrial revolution. They have little if anything to say about the long centuries of economic stagnation that preceded this period, as documented in chapter 1. They also have very little to say about the reasons for the transition from stagnation to economic growth and about why some countries have been successful in creating the conditions for sustained growth whereas others have not.

A recent development in the theory of economic growth is the so-called *unified growth theory*. Unified growth theory aims to explain both the process of economic growth after 1820 and the centuries of economic stagnation that preceded it.[10]

Unified growth theory first concentrates on the conditions that prevailed in the Malthusian era, when technological innovations or new resources (such as land) resulted in an increase in population rather than an increase in per capita income and living standards. Thus, unified growth theory treats population growth as endogenous.

The theory then attempts to explain the transition from stagnation to growth, following the industrial revolution: because of the high rate of technological innovation and other

10. See, among others, Galor and Weil [1999, 2000], Lucas [2002], Hansen and Prescott [2002], and Galor [2005; 2011].

social developments, this transition resulted in a demographic transition from high to low population growth rates, allowing for a sustained rise in living standards. This process was facilitated by social changes that emphasized education and training and the accumulation of human capital.

Unified growth theory combines historical and empirical research with theoretical growth models to explain both the Malthusian process of economic fluctuations that led to fluctuations in population growth rates (but more or less stagnant living standards) and the post-Malthusian takeoff in living standards in the industrial economies.

As suggested by Galor [2011, p. 2]:

> Unified Growth Theory explores the fundamental factors that have contributed to the remarkable transition from stagnation to growth and examines their significance for the understanding of the contemporary growth process of developed and less developed economies.

Unified growth theory does not necessarily clash with or refute the models of economic growth that we have examined. However, it treats them as partial and incomplete accounts of the process of economic growth and as accounts that are mainly relevant for the post-Malthusian era in industrial economies. It emphasizes the interaction between technical progress and population growth, which are treated as endogenous variables (and not as exogenous parameters, as they are treated in most of the models that we have examined).

8.5 Institutions and Long-Run Growth

The models we have presented in this book explain long-run economic growth as a result of the accumulation of physical and human capital and technological change. Then why don't all countries adopt policies that are friendly to such processes? If they did, then the large differences in per capita income between the developed and less-developed world would gradually disappear.

One of the reasons that has been put forward, along with geography and cultural differences, is the role of institutions. The role of institutions has been emphasized by economic historians for a long time, as they have treated the accumulation of physical and human capital and technological progress as only the proximate and not the fundamental determinants of long-run economic growth. As North and Thomas [1973, p. 2] put it: "the factors we have listed (innovation, economies of scale, education, capital accumulation, etc.) are not causes of growth; they *are* growth" (italics in original). Factor accumulation and innovation are only *proximate* causes of growth. In North and Thomas's view, and in the view of many other economic historians, the fundamental explanation of comparative growth is differences in institutions. Of primary importance to economic outcomes are economic and political institutions, such as civil and property rights, the existence and the imperfections of markets, the nature of the political system, and so forth.

Economic and political institutions are important, because they influence the structure of economic incentives. Without the protection of property rights, individuals will not have the incentive to invest in physical or human capital or to adopt more efficient technologies. Economic institutions are also important because they help allocate resources to their most efficient uses, and they determine who gets the profits, revenues, and residual rights of control. When markets are missing or ignored, potential gains from trade are unexploited, and resources are misallocated. Societies with economic institutions that facilitate and encourage factor accumulation, innovation, and the efficient allocation of resources will prosper.[11]

Economists have also turned their attention to the role of institutions, as exemplified by the pioneering empirical study of Acemoglu et al. [2001] and the literature that it sparked. In recent years, some authors have formalized these ideas investigating the effects of institutions on the process of long-run growth. Three basic premises of this approach are as follows.

First, economic institutions matter for economic growth, because they shape the incentives to invest in physical and human capital and technology and to improve the organization of production. Although cultural and geographical factors may also matter for economic performance, differences in economic institutions are the major source of cross-country differences in economic growth and prosperity. Economic institutions not only determine the aggregate economic growth potential of the economy but also an array of economic outcomes, including the distribution of resources in the present and the future.

Second, economic institutions are treated as endogenous. They are determined collectively, in large part for their economic consequences. Not all individuals and groups will prefer the same set of economic institutions, because different economic institutions lead to different distributions of resources. Consequently, there will typically be conflicts of interest among various groups and individuals over the choice of economic institutions. These conflicts of interest are resolved through the political process.

Third, the distribution of political power in society is also treated as endogenous. Similarly to economic institutions, political institutions determine the constraints on and the incentives of the key actors in the political sphere. Political power can be either de jure (institutional) or de facto. The de facto power of particular groups depends on their economic resources, which determine both their ability to use (or misuse) existing political institutions and also their option to hire and use force against other groups.

There are two sources of persistence in the behavior of such a system. First, political institutions are durable, and typically, a sufficiently large change in the distribution of political power is necessary to cause a change in political institutions (such as, a transition from dictatorship to democracy). Second, when a particular group is rich relative to others, this

11. North [1990] is an important contribution to this historical literature, which has been recently surveyed by Crafts and O'Rourke [2014].

will increase its de facto political power and enable it to push for economic and political institutions favorable to its interests. This will tend to entrench the initial disparity in relative wealth. Despite these tendencies for persistence, the framework also emphasizes the potential for change. In particular, "shocks," including changes in technologies and the international environment, can modify the balance of (de facto) political power in society. Such shocks can lead to major changes in political institutions and therefore in economic institutions and economic growth.[12]

8.6 The New Stylized Facts of Economic Growth

As mentioned in chapter 3, in 1961, Nicholas Kaldor highlighted six stylized facts to summarize the patterns that economists had discovered in national income accounts and to check the growth models being developed to explain them. Jones and Romer [2010] attempted to redo this exercise to investigate how much progress has been made. They came up with additional stylized facts that a satisfactory growth model should account for. Their list of additional stylized facts is as follows:

1. *Increases in the extent of the market*. Increased flows of goods, ideas, finance, and people, via globalization, as well as urbanization, have increased the extent of the market for all workers and consumers.

2. *Accelerating growth*. For thousands of years, growth in both population and per capita GDP has accelerated, rising from virtually zero to the relatively rapid rates observed in the past century.

3. *Variation in growth rates*. The variation in the growth rate of per capita GDP increases with the distance from the technology frontier.

4. *Large income and total factor productivity differences*. Differences in measured inputs explain less than half of the enormous cross-country differences in per capita GDP.

5. *Increases in human capital per worker*. Human capital per worker is rising dramatically throughout the world.

6. *Long-run stability of relative wages*. The rising quantity of human capital, relative to unskilled labor, has not been matched by a sustained decline in its relative price.

Whereas Kaldor's original facts were accounted for almost entirely using the neoclassical growth model, the facts highlighted by Jones and Romer reveal the broader reach of modern growth theory. To capture these facts, a growth model must consider the interaction between ideas, institutions, population, and human capital.

12. See Acemoglu et al. [2005] and Ogilvie and Carus [2014] for surveys of this literature. Acemoglu and Robinson [2012] apply such a framework to the explanation of differences in prosperity among nations.

Two of the major facts of growth—its acceleration over the very long run and the extraordinary rise in the extent of the market associated with globalization—are readily understood as reflecting the defining characteristic of ideas: their nonrivalry.

The next two major facts—the enormous income and total factor productivity differences across countries and the stunning variation in growth rates for countries far behind the technology frontier—testify to the importance of institutions and institutional change.

The final two facts of Jones and Romer parallel two of Kaldor's original observations, but Kaldor's emphasis was on physical capital, whereas the emphasis in modern growth theory is on human capital. Human capital per worker is rising rapidly, and this occurs despite no systematic trend in the wage premium associated with education.

According to Jones and Romer, these facts also reveal important complementarities among the key endogenous variables. The virtuous circle between population and ideas accounts for the acceleration of growth. Institutions may have their most important effects on cross-country income differences by hindering the adoption and utilization of ideas from throughout the world. Institutions like public education and the university system are surely important for understanding the growth in human capital. And institutions are themselves based on ideas—inventions that shape the allocation of resources—and the search for better institutions is unending. Finally, the rising extent of the market, which raises the return to ideas and to the human capital that is a fundamental input to the production of ideas, may help explain why the college wage premium has not fallen systematically, despite the huge increases in the ratio of college graduates to high school graduates.

8.7 Conclusion

In this chapter, we have analyzed growth models that do not rely solely on physical capital accumulation and exogenous technical progress. Instead, they are based on external effects from the accumulation of physical capital (learning by doing), or on investment in human capital (education and training), or even on the endogenous generation of technical progress through ideas and innovations. Under certain conditions, such models can generate endogenous growth.

Endogenous growth models do not necessarily imply convergence, as do the corresponding exogenous growth models. However, the available empirical evidence from postwar international experience (see, for example, Mankiw et al. [1992] and Barro [1997a]) indicates that the issue of conditional convergence of per capita incomes of the various economies cannot be dismissed easily. Convergence can be explained by generalized models that include learning by doing, accumulation of human capital, and endogenous technical progress, but not to a degree that would completely neutralize the diminishing returns from the accumulation of physical capital.

Consequently, such generalized exogenous growth models could, in principle, explain most aspects of the process of economic growth that cannot be explained by the original Solow model or the corresponding representative household or OLG models.

The analysis of these generalized growth models helps explain additional stylized facts about economic growth, such as those recently summarized by Jones and Romer [2010, p. 242]. To quote from their conclusions:

> The virtuous circle between population and ideas accounts for the acceleration of growth. Institutions may have their most important effects on cross-country income differences by hindering the adoption and utilization of ideas from throughout the world. Institutions like public education and the university system are surely important for understanding the growth in human capital. And institutions are themselves ideas—inventions that shape the allocation of resources—and the search for better institutions is unending.

The emphasis here is on the accumulation of physical and human capital, and endogenous technical progress as the proximate determinants of living standards and the growth process in the long run. But one needs to understand why some countries succeed and others fail to raise living standards and promote economic growth. The evolving literature on the political conditions and institutions that are conducive or nonconducive to long-run growth has already shed some light on these questions and continues to do so.

This chapter concludes our examination of the key macroeconomic models of long-run economic growth. We shall next turn to stochastic models and the rational expectations hypothesis, before moving on to stochastic models of consumption, investment, and money demand as a prelude to the analysis of models of aggregate fluctuations.[13]

13. For comprehensive surveys of the extensive recent literature on economic growth and other additional models, including political economy models, see *The Handbook of Economic Growth*, edited by Aghion and Durlauf [2005] and Aghion and Durlauf [2014], as well as the excellent presentations in the books by Acemoglu [2009]; Aghion and Howitt [2009]; Barro and Sala-i Martin [2004]; and, on unified growth theory, Galor [2011].

9

Dynamic Stochastic Models under Rational Expectations

In this chapter, we consider uncertainty about the future, the concept of dynamic stochastic models, and the hypothesis of rational expectations. Dynamic stochastic models (and an appropriate expectations hypothesis) are indispensable if one is to model conditions in which there is uncertainty about the future. Unlike the deterministic models with perfect foresight that we have used so far, in which there was no uncertainty about the future, a more realistic treatment of dynamic macroeconomics requires the modeling of uncertainty and uncertain expectations about the future. Thus, models need not only be dynamic but also stochastic, in the sense that they encompass uncertainty. This chapter introduces the basic concepts and presents the properties and alternative solution methods for such dynamic stochastic models under rational expectations.[1]

Dynamic stochastic models can be contrasted with dynamic deterministic models, which do not allow for uncertainty. A dynamic deterministic model consists of a set of differential or difference equations that describe exactly how the system will evolve over time. Thus, there is no uncertainty about the evolution of such a model economy, unless the model is characterized by multiple equilibria. The two-period models of chapter 2, and the infinite-horizon growth models of chapters 3–8 are examples of such deterministic models. A static stochastic model allows for uncertainty and describes the interactions of random variables. A dynamic stochastic model describes the dynamic interactions among stochastic processes, which constitute the dynamic equivalents of random variables. If a dynamic stochastic model is solved several times, it will not produce identical results because of differences

1. The concept of rational expectations is due to Muth [1961] and was introduced to macroeconomics by Lucas [1972]. It has since become the dominant expectations hypothesis in macroeconomics, replacing the concept of adaptive expectations, which was used until then. The adaptive expectations hypothesis was first used, though not under this name, in the work of Fisher [1911] and later in the work of Koyck [1954]. In received its major impetus as a result of the work of Cagan [1956] on hyperinflation, and subsequently Friedman [1957] on the permanent income hypothesis. As we shall see in chapter 15, before the mid-1970s, it was also used extensively to model the role of expectations in models of the relation between inflation and unemployment (i.e., the Phillips curve).

in its stochastic elements. Different runs of a dynamic stochastic model are different realizations of a stochastic process and will in general result in different outcomes. Stochastic models embody both randomness and uncertainty.[2]

Thus, instead of describing a process that can only evolve in one way (as in the case of solutions of deterministic systems of ordinary differential or difference equations), a dynamic stochastic model exhibits indeterminacy due to randomness. Even if the initial conditions (or starting points) are known, there are several, often infinitely many, directions in which the process can evolve over time.

Like random variables and stochastic processes, dynamic stochastic models can be defined and analyzed in both continuous and discrete time. In the case of discrete time, a dynamic stochastic model determines a sequence of endogenous random variables as functions of exogenous random variables, stochastic processes, and a set of parameters. The approach we take is to model these random variables as random functions of the time index. The random variables of a dynamic stochastic model exhibit dynamic stochastic interdependence.

We start with a simple expectational model of a competitive market, to illustrate the differences between deterministic and stochastic models and also highlight the role of the treatment of expectations. This is a model in which demand is a function of the current price, but supply has to be determined one period in advance, based on the prior expectations of firms about the current price. In addition, supply is subject to a random disturbance, that is not known when supply decisions are made. Hence, prior expectations about the current price partly determine the supply of the commodity in question. The market clears at a price that equates this partly predetermined stochastic supply with current market demand. This simple expectational model has played a very important role in the study of expectations in economics, which is the reason we will examine it here at some length.

We move on to distinguish between two expectations hypotheses. *Adaptive expectations*, which was the main expectations hypothesis used in macroeconomics before the 1970s, and *rational expectations*, which is the key expectations hypothesis used since then. We then demonstrate how the dynamic properties of the simple expectational stochastic model differ under the two alternative expectations hypotheses.

We then proceed to illustrate general solution methods for dynamic stochastic models with rational expectations, applying them to models of exogenous univariate stochastic processes and first- and second-order linear stochastic models with one endogenous and one exogenous variable. We apply these methods to both the expectational competitive market model and two additional simple economic models, one from finance and one from monetary economics.

2. See appendix F for an introduction to random variables and stochastic processes, which are the building blocks of dynamic stochastic models.

The final part of the chapter introduces multivariate rational expectations models and briefly discusses the conditions for unique solutions and the alternative solution methods used.

In subsequent chapters, the solution methods introduced in this chapter are applied extensively to dynamic stochastic models of aggregate consumption, investment, money, and aggregate fluctuations.

9.1 A Stochastic Expectational Model of a Competitive Market

In this section, we consider a simple expectational model of a competitive market to illustrate the differences between deterministic and stochastic models and to highlight the importance of the treatment of expectations.

This is a log-linear model, in which demand is a function of the current price, but supply decisions are made one period in advance, based on the prior expectations of firms for the current price. Hence, the expectations about the current price, based on information available one period in advance, partly determine the supply of the commodity in question. In addition, there is a stochastic supply shock, which cannot be known in advance. Ex post, the market clears at a price that equates this partly predetermined supply with current market demand.

This simple expectational model, known as the *cobweb model* because of its dynamic properties under adaptive expectations, has played a very important role in the study of market cycles and expectations in economics.[3]

The model consists of log-linear demand and supply functions, and an equilibrium condition requiring that the current price adjusts to equate demand and supply.

The supply of the commodity is question is determined by

$$q_t^s = a + bp_t^e + v_t, \tag{9.1}$$

where q_t^s denotes the logarithm of the supply of commodity Q in period t, and p_t^e is the expectation of suppliers about the logarithm of the market price at t, based on information they possess in the previous period $t-1$. In addition, a and b are constant positive parameters, and v_t is a stochastic supply shock. It is assumed that suppliers have to make their supply decisions before the current market price is known and that supply is a positive function of

3. This model has been used to describe agricultural markets because of the lag between planting and harvesting. Kaldor [1934] labeled it the cobweb model, because the pattern of convergence to equilibrium under adaptive expectations resembles a cobweb. Ezekiel [1938], Buchanan [1939], and Nerlove [1958] analyzed the model under various forms of adaptive expectations. The model has since been used extensively, as it has applications in other markets as well. Muth [1961] used this particular model to introduce the concept of rational expectations, arguing that rational producers would not be making systematic mistakes in their formation of expectations, as implied by the adaptive expectations hypothesis.

the expected price. The parameter b is the elasticity of supply with respect to the expected price.

The demand for the commodity is determined by

$$q_t^d = c - dp_t, \tag{9.2}$$

where q_t^d denotes the logarithm of the demand for commodity Q in period t, p_t is the logarithm of the market price at t, and c and d are constant positive parameters. It is assumed that demand is a negative function of the current price; d is the elasticity of demand with respect to the current price.

The market being competitive, equilibrium is determined by the equality of demand and supply. Thus, the equilibrium condition is that

$$q_t^s = q_t^d = q_t, \tag{9.3}$$

where q_t is the equilibrium quantity.

From (9.1)–(9.3), the equilibrium price is determined by

$$p_t = \frac{c-a}{d} - \frac{b}{d}p_t^e - \frac{1}{d}v_t. \tag{9.4}$$

From (9.4), the equilibrium price depends negatively on the prior expectation of the equilibrium price by suppliers. The higher the expected price is the higher the supply will be, and therefore the lower the resulting equilibrium price will be. To solve for the market equilibrium in terms of the market fundamentals (like the parameters a, b, c, d, and the supply shock v_t), we must make an assumption about the formation of expectations.

9.1.1 Absence of Uncertainty and Perfect Foresight

If there is no uncertainty, and suppliers know the supply shock with certainty, a natural assumption about the formation of expectations in this case is the assumption of perfect foresight. In fact, this is the assumption we have been utilizing in the optimizing deterministic models of chapters 2–8. Because everybody knows everything with certainty, suppliers can form a perfect prediction of the equilibrium price, and in this case, $p_t^e = p_t$. Hence, equilibrium prices and quantities under perfect foresight are given by

$$\begin{aligned} p_t &= \frac{c-a}{b+d} - \frac{1}{b+d}v_t, \\ q_t &= \frac{cb+da}{b+d} + \frac{d}{b+d}v_t. \end{aligned} \tag{9.5}$$

Because there is no uncertainty about either the parameters a, b, c, d or the supply shock v_t, suppliers can forecast the equilibrium price perfectly, and the model becomes equivalent to a simple demand and supply competitive model, in which the price moves immediately to clear the market.

If v_t is a random variable or a stochastic process, the model is *stochastic*, and prices and quantities fluctuate randomly, as they are driven by the stochastic process followed by the exogenous supply shock v_t. Otherwise, the model is *deterministic*. For example, in the case of a deterministic model where the supply shock is constant and equal to zero, equilibrium prices and quantities are also constant:

$$p_t = \bar{p} = \frac{c-a}{b+d}, \qquad q_t = \bar{q} = \frac{cb+da}{b+d}. \tag{9.6}$$

9.1.2 Uncertainty and Adaptive Expectations

What if there is uncertainty about the evolution of the supply shock v_t? Then suppliers, not knowing the market price, which will depend on the unknown supply shock, will have to form expectations about the price in advance.

The key hypothesis traditionally made about the formation of expectations under uncertainty is the hypothesis of *adaptive expectations*.

The adaptive expectations hypothesis is an empirically motivated short-cut to the formation of expectations, postulating that agents adapt their expectations gradually to correct for past expectational errors. It was the key expectational hypothesis for many decades before the appearance of the rational expectations hypothesis.

In the context of our simple competitive model, the adaptive expectations hypothesis postulates that supplier's expectations about the market price evolve according to

$$p_t^e - p_{t-1}^e = (1-\lambda)(p_{t-1} - p_{t-1}^e). \tag{9.7}$$

Equation (9.7) implies that if the equilibrium price in the previous period was higher than the previously expected equilibrium price, the expected equilibrium price for next period will be revised upward. In the equation, $0 \leq \lambda \leq 1$ measures the degree of inertia in the revision of expectations. If $\lambda = 1$, there is full inertia, and expectations are never revised. This is the case of *static expectations*, implying that $p_t^e = p_{t-1}^e$ for all t. If $\lambda = 0$, there is no inertia, and expectations are fully revised and are therefore equal to the previous price. In the context of our model, this case of fully adaptive expectations implies that

$$p_t^e = p_{t-1}. \tag{9.8}$$

Substituting the fully adaptive expectations hypothesis (9.8) for the expected price in the expectational equilibrium price equation (9.4), we get that the equilibrium price is

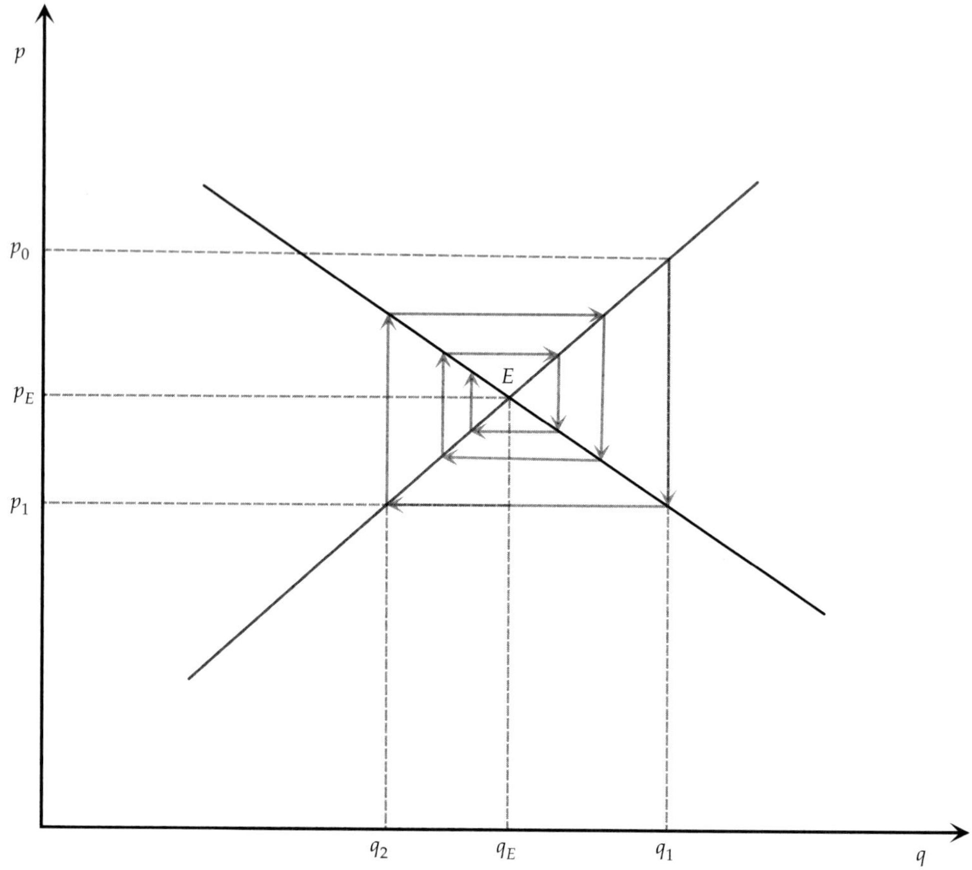

Figure 9.1
The cobweb model under adaptive expectations.

determined by

$$p_t = \frac{c-a}{d} - \frac{b}{d}p_{t-1} - \frac{1}{d}v_t. \tag{9.9}$$

This is a stochastic first-order difference equation that determines the equilibrium price as a negative function of the previous equilibrium price. In the absence of shocks, the equilibrium price will display oscillations. High prices today cause an increase in supply and low prices tomorrow, and vice versa. It was this type of behavior of prices (and quantities) that led Kaldor [1934] to name this model the *cobweb model*, as the diagrammatic representation of this type of price and quantity adjustment looks like a cobweb.

This cobwed is depicted in figure 9.1. The pair of equilibrium price and quantity, if the expectations of suppliers are correct, is determined at point E and is given by (p_E, q_E).

If, however, the initial price in period 0 is equal to p_0, above the equilibrium price, supply in period 1 will be equal to q_1, above the equilibrium quantity. For this higher quantity to be sold, the price in period 1 must fall to p_1, which is below the equilibrium price. At the low p_1, the quantity supplied in period 2 will fall below the equilibrium quantity, at q_2, prompting the price to rise above the equilibrium price in period 2. The process will continue, and in the example shown in figure 9.1, prices and quantities will eventually converge, in a cobweb fashion, to the equilibrium pair (p_E, q_E).

In the absence of supply shocks, the oscillations will lead to convergence to an equilibrium price only if the root of the difference equation (9.9) is less than unity in absolute terms:

$$\left|\frac{b}{d}\right| < 1. \tag{9.10}$$

This condition requires that the elasticity of supply with respect to the expected price b is lower (in absolute terms) than the elasticity of demand with respect to the current price d. If the elasticities are equal, there will be nonconvergent oscillations; if the supply elasticity exceeds the demand elasticity, the oscillations will diverge, and the model will be unstable.[4]

In general, in the presence of supply shocks, and if (9.10) is satisfied, the solution of the difference equation (9.9) takes the form

$$p_t = \frac{c-a}{b+d} - \frac{1}{d}\sum_{i=0}^{\infty}\left(-\frac{b}{d}\right)^i v_{t-i}. \tag{9.11}$$

Equilibrium prices (and quantities) are a geometrically distributed lag of current and past supply shocks, with alternating signs. If the supply shocks are stochastic, equilibrium prices and quantities will be stochastic as well. It is important to note that current prices and quantities are backward looking, because of the assumption of adaptive expectations, which make future expectations a function of past prices.

9.1.3 The Rational Expectations Hypothesis

The rational expectations hypothesis was introduced by Muth [1961], who illustrated its significance using a version of the particular expectational market model introduced in section 9.12.

Muth [1961, p. 316] argued that

> expectations, since they are informed predictions of future events, are essentially the same as the predictions of the relevant economic theory. ... we call such expectations "rational." ... The hypothesis can be rephrased a little more precisely as follows: that expectations of firms (or, more generally, the subjective probability distribution of outcomes) tend to be distributed, for the same

4. See Ezekiel [1938], Buchanan [1939], and Nerlove [1958] for a more general analysis of this model under various forms of adaptive expectations.

information set, about the prediction of the theory (or the "objective" probability distributions of outcomes).

Rational expectations are thus defined as the mathematical expectations for the future evolution of a stochastic variable, based on the model determining this variable and a given information set.

Thus defined, the rational expectation of a variable x in period $t+1$, based on available information in period t, is the mathematical expectation of the variable at $t+1$, conditional on the information set available at t:

$$E_t x_{t+1} = E(x_{t+1} \,|I_t) \,, \tag{9.12}$$

where

$$I_t = \{x_{t-i}, z_{t-i}, i = 0, 1, 2, \ldots, \infty\}. \tag{9.13}$$

Here I_t is the set of available information, which consists of current and past values of the variable x itself, as well as the current and past values of a set of variables z, which affect and thus can help predict the future values of x. Note that this definition of the information set does not involve loss of memory, as whatever is known in period t is also known in period $t+1$ and all future periods.

More generally, we define the rational expectation of a variable x at $t+s$, based on available information at t, as

$$E_t x_{t+s} = E(x_{t+s} \,|I_t). \tag{9.14}$$

In what follows, let us simplify the notation by using $E_t x_{t+s}$ in place of $E(x_{t+s} \,|I_t)$.

Note that to define rational expectations for a variable more precisely, it is not enough to specify the information set. One also needs to specify the model determining how this variable evolves over time.

Imposing the rational expectations hypothesis on our competitive market model implies that the formation of expectations about prices will take account of the price determination process itself. Hence, expectations will be formed taking into account the price determination equation (9.4).

Applying the rational expectations hypothesis to (9.4), by taking the rational expectation of the market price conditional on information available up to period $t-1$, implies that

$$p_t^e = E_{t-1} p_t = \frac{c-a}{d+b} - \frac{1}{d+b} E_{t-1} v_t. \tag{9.15}$$

Hence, the rational expectation of the equilibrium price is equal to the equilibrium price in the absence of supply shocks, adjusted for the rational expectation of the impact of the supply shock, based on information available in period $t-1$.

Substituting for this rational expectation in the expectational price equation (9.4), we have that the equilibrium price is given by

$$p_t = \frac{c-a}{b+d} - \frac{1}{d(b+d)}\left(b(v_t - E_{t-1}v_t) + dv_t\right). \tag{9.16}$$

Supply shocks depress the equilibrium price, because they increase supply relative to demand. However, to the extent that the shocks are unexpected, they have an additional depressing effect, because suppliers have overestimated the equilibrium price and hence have increased supply by more than they would have done otherwise.

In the case where supply shocks are fully expected, there are no unanticipated shocks, and we are back to the perfect foresight case described by (9.5). In the case where supply shocks are fully unexpected, the rational expectations solution takes the form

$$p_t = \frac{c-a}{b+d} - \frac{1}{d}v_t.$$

The unexpected supply shock reduces the equilibrium price, but there is no cobweb pattern.

The rational expectations solution in general differs from the solution under adaptive expectations, as it does not depend on the whole history of past supply shocks but only on whatever information is required at $t-1$ to form a rational expectation of the supply shock in period t. In addition, there is no cobweb under rational expectations, as expectations about current prices do not depend only on past prices, as postulated by the adaptive expectations hypothesis. However, to fully solve the model under rational expectations, we need to assume a model for the evolution of the exogenous supply shock v_t. This model will be the one used to calculate the rational expectation of prices on the basis of past information.

We have already solved the model for perfectly anticipated and perfectly unanticipated supply shocks. In the case of partly anticipated supply shocks, one has to make specific assumptions about the stochastic process determining the evolution of such shocks. Let us postpone this discussion until we examine how rational expectations of a stochastic process are computed. We thus turn to the discussion of solution methods for more general stochastic models of exogenous shocks and more general dynamic stochastic models under rational expectations.

9.2 Rational Expectations for Linear Autoregressive Processes

We begin with the method for computing the rational expectations solution for the simplest dynamic stochastic model, that of a univariate stochastic process. Exogenous shocks in macroeconomics are often assumed to follow such processes. Then we shall examine more general models, according to which an endogenous variable depends on expectations for its evolution in the future as well as on an exogenous variable. Even more general models of a system of endogenous and exogenous variables can be solved by similar methods.

Let us assume a variable x, which follows a linear first-order autoregressive stochastic process of the form

$$x_t = (1-\lambda)\bar{x} + \lambda x_{t-1} + \varepsilon_t, \tag{9.17}$$

where $\bar{x}$ is a constant (the mean of the variable x), and ε is a white noise stochastic process, with zero mean and constant variance.[5]

Define the deviation of x from its mean as

$$\hat{x}_t = x_t - \bar{x} \tag{9.18}$$

From (9.17) and (9.18) we get that

$$\hat{x}_t = \lambda \hat{x}_{t-1} + \varepsilon_t. \tag{9.19}$$

By repeated substitutions, it is easy to see that

$$E_t\hat{x}_{t+1} = \lambda\hat{x}_t, E_t\hat{x}_{t+2} = \lambda^2\hat{x}_t, \ldots, E_t\hat{x}_{t+s} = \lambda^s\hat{x}_t. \tag{9.20}$$

The rational expectation of a first-order linear autoregressive stochastic process depends only on its current value and has a coefficient that depends only on λ.

If the stochastic process (9.17) is stationary (i.e., if., $-1 < \lambda < 1$), then the impact of the current value of the variable on its rational expectation at time $t+s$ is decreasing with s. As s approaches infinity, the limit of the rational expectation is given by

$$\lim_{s\to\infty} E_t\hat{x}_{t+s} = \lim_{s\to\infty} \lambda^s\hat{x}_t = 0. \tag{9.21}$$

Equations (9.21) and (9.18) imply that

$$\lim_{s\to\infty} E_t x_{t+s} = \bar{x}. \tag{9.22}$$

In this sense, the mean of the stationary stochastic process x, which is its long-run equilibrium value, is also the limit to which rational expectations about its future evolution converge over time.

If the process is nonstationary (for example, a random walk for which $\lambda = 1$), then (9.20) is transformed to

$$E_t x_{t+1} = x_t, E_t x_{t+2} = x_t, \ldots, E_t x_{t+s} = x_t. \tag{9.23}$$

5. See appendix F for an introduction to random variables and stochastic processes.

In this case, the rational expectation for the future value of x is the current value of x, independently of s, as the variable is a random walk and does not converge to a long-run equilibrium.

These methods generalize to higher-order stationary and nonstationary autoregressive moving-average processes.[6]

Exercise 9.1 Compute the rational expectations solution for a second-order, linear, autoregressive process of the form

$$\hat{x}_t = a\hat{x}_{t-1} + b\hat{x}_{t-2} + \varepsilon_t,$$

where $a, b > 0$, $a + b < 1$, and ε_t is a white noise process.

How are your conclusions modified if $a + b = 1$?

9.3 First-Order Linear Expectational Models

We now turn to the rational expectations solution of a linear stochastic model in which a variable y depends on the rational expectation of its future value and on another exogenous stochastic variable x. The model is described by a first-order linear expectational difference equation of the form

$$y_t = aE_t y_{t+1} + bx_t. \tag{9.24}$$

The rational expectations hypothesis implies that economic agents know that the variable y is determined by the expectational difference equation (9.24). We also assume that all economic agents have access to the same information set.

Various methods are available for the solution of (9.24). All methods are based on the *law of iterated expectations*, which requires that the current expectation of the future expectation of a future value of a variable is nothing more than the current expectation of the future value of the variable. That is,

$$E_t\left(E_{t+z}x_{t+s}\right) = E_t x_{t+s}, \tag{9.25}$$

for $z, s \geq 1$, and $z \leq s$.

9.3.1 The Method of Repeated Substitutions

The simplest method for solving (9.24) is the method of repeated substitutions, a method that we also used to find the rational expectations for the simple first-order autoregressive process in the previous section. From (9.24) and (9.25), we have

$$E_t y_{t+1} = aE_t\left(E_{t+1}y_{t+2}\right) + bE_t x_{t+1} = aE_t y_{t+2} + bE_t x_{t+1}. \tag{9.26}$$

6. See, for example, the classic text by Box and Jenkins [1976] on forecasting with stationary autoregressive moving average models and nonstationary integrated autoregressive moving average models.

Substituting (9.26) in (9.24), we get

$$y_t = a^2 E_t y_{t+2} + abE_t x_{t+1} + bx_t.$$

Repeatedly substituting the future expectations of y, for T future periods, we get

$$y_t = a^{T+1} E_t y_{t+T+1} + b \sum_{s=0}^{T} a^s E_t x_{t+s}. \quad (9.27)$$

To have convergence of the last term of (9.27) as T tends to infinity, the absolute value of a must be less than one, and the expected value of x should not increase too quickly. If the expected value of x increases exponentially, its growth rate should not exceed $(1/a) - 1$. Under these conditions, it follows that

$$\lim_{T \to \infty} a^{T+1} E_t y_{t+T+1} = 0. \quad (9.28)$$

Then a solution of (9.24) can be derived from (9.27):

$$y_t = b \sum_{s=0}^{\infty} a^s E_t x_{t+s}. \quad (9.29)$$

Note that (9.29) satisfies the condition (9.28) and is thus a solution of (9.24). It suggests that the current value of the endogenous variable y is the discounted sum of the expected future values of the exogenous variable x, with a discount rate equal to a. This solution is usually called the *fundamental solution*.

However, note that (9.29) is not the only solution of (9.24). The fundamental solution is based only on the minimum number of variables (x in our case), the so-called fundamentals, and satisfies (9.28). If (9.28) is not satisfied, then there exist a host of other, *nonfundamental, solutions*.

Suppose there is an alternative solution to (9.24) that consists of (9.29) plus an additional variable z. This solution takes the form

$$y_t = b \sum_{s=0}^{\infty} a^s E_t x_{t+s} + z_t. \quad (9.30)$$

One can easily demonstrate that if the variable z satisfies

$$z_t = aE_t z_{t+1},$$

or equivalently,

$$E_t z_{t+1} = \frac{z_t}{a},$$

then (9.30) is also a solution of (9.24).

However, because $a < 1$, the mathematical expectation of the future z explodes over time. This can be proven by taking the limit of the mathematical expectation as time tends to infinity:

$$\lim_{s\to\infty} E_t z_{t+s} = \lim_{s\to\infty} \left(\frac{1}{a}\right)^s z_t = \pm\infty,$$

depending on whether z is positive or negative.

Solutions based on nonfundamental variables such as z are called *bubbles*, as opposed to solutions like (9.29), which are based only on the fundamentals. In the rest of this and in most subsequent chapters, we will focus on the fundamental solutions, ignoring bubbles. We shall return to bubbles in chapter 22.

Besides the method of repeated substitutions, two other methods can be used to solve (9.24): the method of factorization and the method of undetermined coefficients. These methods are simpler to use in more complex dynamic models, for which the method of repeated substitutions soon becomes unwieldy. However, we can also apply them to the simple case of (9.24).

9.3.2 The Method of Factorization

The factorization method requires the use of the *future mathematical expectations operator F*. We define the future mathematical expectations operator F for a variable x, as

$$F^s x_t = E_t x_{t+s},$$

for $s = \ldots, -1, 0, 1, 2, \ldots$. Note that this operator is conditional on the information set available in period t, which does not change when the operator is raised to different powers.

It follows that for $s = 0$, $Fx_t = x_t$; for $s = 1$, $Fx_t = E_t x_{t+1}$, $F^2 x_t = E_t x_{t+2}$, and so forth. In addition, for $s = -1$, $F^{-1} x_t = x_{t-1}$; for $s = -2$, $F^{-2} x_t = x_{t-2}$, and so forth. Thus, the future mathematical expectations operator is the inverse of the lag operator L, which we have used for the solution of difference equations.

Using the future mathematical expectations operator and assuming that $-1 < a < 1$, (9.24) can be written as

$$y_t = aFy_t + bx_t = \frac{b}{1 - aF} x_t = b \sum_{s=0}^{\infty} a^s F^s x_t = b \sum_{s=0}^{\infty} a^s E_t x_{t+s}. \tag{9.31}$$

Equation (9.31) is the same as the fundamental solution (9.29) that we found using the method of repeated substitutions. Hence, using the factorization method, one can arrive at the fundamental solution in a few simple steps.

9.3.3 The Method of Undetermined Coefficients

The method of undetermined coefficients consists of using a presumed functional form of a solution with undetermined coefficients, obtaining the mathematical expectation of the presumed solution, replacing this for the expectation in (9.24), and comparing the coefficients of the resulting equation with the undetermined coefficients of the presumed solution. If the form of the presumed solution is correct, this method will suffice to determine the undetermined coefficients.

For example, if our guess is that the solution has the form

$$y_t = \sigma \sum_{s=0}^{\infty} \mu^s E_t x_{t+s}, \tag{9.32}$$

where σ and μ are undetermined coefficients, then

$$E_t y_{t+1} = \sigma \sum_{s=0}^{\infty} \mu^s E_t x_{t+s+1}. \tag{9.33}$$

Substituting (9.33) in (9.24) and comparing coefficients between the resulting equation and (9.32), we find that $\sigma = b$ and $\mu = a$. This confirms our presumption of (9.32), and the solution is exactly the same as with the two other methods.

The choice of method to be used to solve models with rational expectations depends on the ease of application. In simple models, the method of repeated substitutions can easily be applied, but in more complex models, the method is not easy to use, and the two other methods are preferable.

9.3.4 Two Additional Economic Examples

To see how these methods are applied, we shall use two simple economic models that result in equations of the form (9.24).

Stock Prices in Efficient Capital Markets In our first model, we assume a capital market in which investors are risk neutral. They choose between a common stock with an uncertain return and a safe asset with a certain rate of return r. In equilibrium, arbitrage will ensure that the expected rate of return of the stock will be equal to the rate of return of the safe asset:

$$\frac{E_t p_{t+1} - p_t}{p_t} + \frac{d_t}{p_t} = r, \tag{9.34}$$

where p is the price of the stock in the capital market, and d is the dividend. The expected rate of return of the stock is equal to the expected capital gain plus the dividend as a proportion of the stock price. In equilibrium in an efficient capital market, this cannot differ from the rate of return of the safe asset r. Equation (9.34) can be rearranged as

$$p_t = \frac{1}{1+r}\left(E_t p_{t+1} + d_t\right), \tag{9.35}$$

which has the form of (9.24), with $0 < a = b = 1/(1+r) < 1$.

The solution of (9.35) gives us the stock price as a function of expected future dividends:

$$p_t = \frac{1}{1+r}\sum_{s=0}^{\infty}\left(\frac{1}{1+r}\right)^s E_t d_{t+s}, \tag{9.36}$$

Thus, the stock price is the present value of the current and expected future dividends, discounted by the rate of return of the safe asset.

The Cagan Model of Money Demand In our second model, we assume that consumers and firms decide between holding money and goods in the face of inflation. Money is a nominal asset whose real value is affected negatively by inflation. In this case, the demand for money is a negative function of expected inflation, and money market equilibrium requires that

$$\frac{M_t}{P_t} = \exp\left(-\alpha\left(\frac{E_t P_{t+1} - P_t}{P_t}\right)\right), \tag{9.37}$$

where M is the nominal money supply, P is the price level, and $\alpha > 0$ is the semi-elasticity of money demand with respect to expected inflation. This model was first used by Cagan [1956] to explain hyperinflation.[7]

Taking logarithms on both sides and denoting the logarithm of the nominal money supply by m and the logarithm of the price level by p, the model can be written in log-linear form as[8]

$$m_t - p_t = -\alpha(E_t p_{t+1} - p_t). \tag{9.38}$$

Solving for p_t results in

$$p_t = \frac{\alpha}{1+\alpha}E_t p_{t+1} + \frac{1}{1+\alpha}m_t. \tag{9.39}$$

Equation (9.39) has the form of (9.24), with

$$a = \frac{\alpha}{1+\alpha}, b = 1 - a.$$

The fundamental solution takes the form

7. A full analysis of this model is given in chapter 12.

8. Recall that, for a small x, $\ln(1+x)$ is approximately equal to x.

$$p_t = \frac{1}{1+\alpha} \sum_{s=0}^{\infty} \left(\frac{\alpha}{1+\alpha} \right)^s E_t m_{t+s}. \tag{9.40}$$

The current price level depends on the discounted expectations about the evolution of the money supply in the future, with a discount factor equal to $0 < \alpha/(1+\alpha) < 1$. Thus, it is the full expected future path of the money supply, and not just the current money supply, that determines the price level in this model.

9.3.5 Alternative Assumptions about the Evolution of Exogenous Variables

The solution of equation (9.24) (for example, (9.29)) is based on the discounted rational expectations about the future path of the exogenous variable x. To have a closed-form solution for the variable y, we must make additional assumptions about the evolution of the exogenous variable x. The final closed-form solution depends on such assumptions.

We shall examine two alternative examples to demonstrate this point.

Our first assumption is that the exogenous variable x is expected to remain constant at the level x_0. From (9.29), the endogenous variable y is determined by

$$y_t = b \sum_{s=0}^{\infty} a^s E_t x_{t+s} = b \sum_{s=0}^{\infty} a^s x_0 = \frac{b}{1-a} x_0. \tag{9.41}$$

This is the assumption usually made in deterministic models with perfect foresight, such as the growth models of chapters 3–8. If x changes permanently and unexpectedly from x_0 to x_1, then y jumps immediately from the initial equilibrium value, $y_0 = (b/(1-a))x_0$, to the new equilibrium value, $y_1 = (b/(1-a))x_1$. Equation (9.41) can also be used to analyze the impact of an anticipated future change in the constant level of the exogenous variable.

Let us assume that at time t_0, it is announced that from a future period t_1 onward, the variable x will rise from x_0 to a new constant level x_1. In this case, the path of the endogenous variable y will be as follows:

$$y_t = \frac{b}{1-a} x_0, t < t_0,$$

$$y_t = \frac{b}{1-a} x_0 + a^{t_1 - t} \frac{b}{1-a} \left(x_1 - x_0 \right), t_0 \leq t < t_1,$$

$$y_t = \frac{b}{1-a} x_1, t \geq t_1.$$

At the time of the announcement t_0, variable y jumps up, as the expectations about the future path of x change. Until the change is implemented at time t_1, y continues rising gradually, as the impact of the higher x_1 after period t_0 rises, compared to the impact of the lower x_0 in the interval $t_1 - t$. After period t_1, the endogenous variable y is stabilized at the higher level corresponding to the higher x_1.

If x is the dividend, as in our first example, then the share price will rise immediately after the announcement of a future dividend increase and will continue rising as the expected dividend increase approaches. When the increase in the dividend materializes, the stock price stops growing and is stabilized at the new higher level, corresponding to the higher dividend.

If x is the money supply, as in our second example, the price level will rise immediately after the announcement of a future increase in the money supply, and it will continue rising until the rise in the money supply materializes. The price level will then be stabilized at its new higher level.

The second case that we analyze is based on the assumption that the exogenous variable x follows a first-order linear autoregressive stochastic process, as in (9.17). In this case, we have

$$y_t = b\sum_{s=0}^{\infty} a^s E_t x_{t+s} = \frac{b}{1-a}\bar{x} + b\sum_{s=0}^{\infty} (a\lambda)^s (x_t - \bar{x}), \tag{9.42}$$

which converges to

$$y_t = \frac{b}{1-a}\bar{x} + \frac{b}{1-a\lambda}(x_t - \bar{x}).$$

Thus, (9.42) can be written as

$$y_t - \bar{y} = \frac{b}{1-a\lambda}(x_t - \bar{x}), \tag{9.43}$$

where $\bar{y} = \frac{b}{1-a}\bar{x}$ is the steady state value of y.

This case is relevant for stochastic models, such as the models examined in this and subsequent chapters, and especially the models of aggregate fluctuations in chapters 13–22.

In the stock price model, (9.43) tells us that the price of the stock will be a function only of the current dividend. This is because if dividends follow a first-order autoregressive stochastic process (as we have assumed), the current dividend is the only element required to predict future dividends. Because dividends follow an AR(1) process, the price of the stock will also follow an AR(1) process.

Similarly, in the money demand model, (9.43) tells us that the price level will be determined only by the current money supply. This is because if the money supply follows a first-order autoregressive stochastic process (as assumed), the current money supply is the only element required to predict the future course of the money supply.

Exercise 9.2 Derive and discuss the rational expectations solution of the stock market model and the money demand model, assuming that the dividend and the money supply process follow a second-order autoregressive process of the form

$$\hat{x}_t = a\hat{x}_{t-1} + b\hat{x}_{t-2} + \varepsilon_t,$$

where $\hat{x}_t$ denotes either the deviation of the dividend (in the stock market model) or the money supply (in the money demand model) from its long-run equilibrium level. Assume that $a, b > 0$, $a + b < 1$, and ε_t is a white noise process. How is your solution modified if $a + b = 1$?

9.3.6 The Expectational Competitive Market Model Revisited

Returning to the expectational competitive market model of section 9.1, let us assume that the supply shock v_t follows a first-order autoregressive process of the form

$$v_t = \lambda v_{t-1} + \varepsilon_t, \tag{9.44}$$

where $0 < \lambda < 1$, and ε_t is a white noise process. Then, from (9.16) and (9.44), the closed-form rational expectations solution for the equilibrium price is given by

$$\begin{aligned} p_t &= \frac{c-a}{b+d} - \frac{1}{d(b+d)}(b(v_t - \lambda v_{t-1}) + dv_t) = \\ &= \frac{c-a}{b+d} - \frac{1}{d}v_t + \frac{b\lambda}{d(b+d)}v_{t-1}. \end{aligned} \tag{9.45}$$

The current supply shock depresses the equilibrium price, as it increases current supply. But the past supply shock boosts the price, because by positively affecting prior expectations about the current supply shock, it induces firms to reduce supply, as it reduces their expectation about the current price. Note that the dynamics of the market price differ from the case of adaptive expectations in equation (9.11), and there is no cobweb pattern in this case either.

9.4 Second-Order Linear Expectational Models

We next turn to the methods of solving a second-order dynamic stochastic linear model under rational expectations. In this model, we assume that an endogenous variable y depends on the rational expectation of its future value y_{t+1}, an exogenous stochastic variable x, and also on its own lagged value y_{t-1}. This model combines rational expectations about the future value of the variable with the impact of lagged values of the variable. As we shall see in future chapters, the model often arises in macroeconomics. Our model is linear and takes the form

$$y_t = aE_t y_{t+1} + by_{t-1} + cx_t, \tag{9.46}$$

where $a, b > 0$, and $a + b < 1$.

This model, which is essentially a second-order difference equation, can be solved using either the factorization method or the method of undetermined coefficients. Of course, both methods result in the same fundamental solution.

9.4.1 The Method of Factorization

Using the future expectations operator F, (9.46) can be written as

$$y_t = aFy_t + bF^{-1}y_t + cx_t, \tag{9.47}$$

where F^{-1}, the inverse of the future expectations operator, is the same as the lag operator.

Moving all terms that contain y to the left-hand side, we get

$$y_t\left(1 - aF - bF^{-1}\right) = cx_t. \tag{9.48}$$

The left-hand side of (9.48) can be multiplied and divided by $-F/a$, which results in

$$-aF^{-1}y_t\left(F^2 - \frac{1}{a}F + \frac{b}{a}\right) = cx_t.$$

This can be rewritten as

$$y_t\left(F^2 - \frac{1}{a}F + \frac{b}{a}\right) = -\frac{c}{a}Fx_t. \tag{9.49}$$

Equation (9.49) can be factorized as

$$y_t(F-\lambda)(F-\mu) = y_t\left(F^2 - (\lambda+\mu)F + \lambda\mu\right) = -\frac{c}{a}Fx_t, \tag{9.50}$$

where λ and μ are the two roots of the characteristic polynomial of

$$F^2 - \frac{1}{a}F + \frac{b}{a}. \tag{9.51}$$

From (9.50), we know that $\lambda + \mu = 1/a$, $\lambda\mu = b/a$. It is simple to show that one root is smaller than unity, and the other is greater than unity. The characteristic polynomial of (9.51) is given by

$$\Phi(\phi) = \phi^2 - \frac{1}{a}\phi + \frac{b}{a}. \tag{9.52}$$

To show that one root is smaller than unity, calculate the characteristic polynomial for $\phi = 0$ and $\phi = 1$:

$$\Phi(0) = \frac{b}{a} > 0, \Phi(1) = -\frac{1-a-b}{a} < 0.$$

Hence, there is one root (let us assume it is λ) between zero and one, for which $\Phi(\lambda)=0$.

The second root μ is determined by

$$\mu = \frac{b}{a\lambda}.$$

We have $\mu > 1$, if $\lambda < (b/a)$. This is actually true, because

$$\Phi\left(\frac{b}{a}\right) = -\frac{b(1-a-b)}{a^2} < 0.$$

Therefore, we have that $\lambda < (b/a) < 1$, and $\mu > 1$.

The model is saddlepath stable, as it has one predetermined variable, y_{t-1} and one non-predetermined variable, the rational expectation $E_t(y_{t+1})$. Dividing both sides of (9.50) by $F(\mu - F)$, we get

$$y_t\left(1-\lambda F^{-1}\right) = \frac{c}{a}\frac{1}{\mu - F}x_t = \frac{c}{a\mu}\frac{1}{1-\mu^{-1}F}x_t = \frac{\lambda c}{b}\frac{1}{1-\mu^{-1}F}x_t, \tag{9.53}$$

where the last part of (9.53) makes use of the equality $a\mu = b/\lambda$. This follows from (9.50). From (9.53), it follows that

$$y_t = \lambda y_{t-1} + \frac{\lambda c}{b}\frac{1}{1-\mu^{-1}F}x_t = \lambda y_{t-1} + \frac{\lambda c}{b}\sum_{s=0}^{\infty}\left(\frac{1}{\mu}\right)^s E_t x_{t+s}, \tag{9.54}$$

which is the fundamental solution of (9.46). As in the case of (9.29), (9.54) suggests that the current value of the endogenous variable y depends on the discounted sum of the expected future values of the exogenous variable x, with a discount factor equal to $1/\mu < 1$. It also depends on its own lagged value, with a coefficient equal to $\lambda < 1$.

The factorization method is perhaps a more effective method of solving equations of the form (9.46) than the method of repeated substitutions. An alternative is the method of undetermined coefficients.

9.4.2 The Method of Undetermined Coefficients

To apply the method of undetermined coefficients, as in the case of the first-order model, we assume that the solution of (9.46) takes the form

$$y_t = \phi y_{t-1} + \psi\sum_{s=0}^{\infty}\omega^s E_t x_{t+s} \tag{9.55}$$

with undetermined coefficients ϕ, ψ, and ω. From (9.55), the rational expectation of the future y is given by

$$E_t y_{t+1} = \phi y_t + \psi\sum_{s=1}^{\infty}\omega^{s-1}E_t x_{t+s}. \tag{9.56}$$

Substituting (9.56) in (9.46), we get

$$y_t = \frac{b}{1-a\phi}y_{t-1} + \frac{c}{1-a\phi}x_t + \frac{a\psi}{1-a\phi}\sum\nolimits_{s=1}^{\infty} \omega^{s-1} E_t x_{t+s}. \tag{9.57}$$

Comparing coefficients between (9.57) and (9.55), we can solve for the undetermined coefficients:

$$\begin{aligned} \phi &= \frac{b}{1-a\phi}, \\ \psi &= \frac{c}{1-a\phi}, \\ \omega &= \frac{a}{1-a\phi}. \end{aligned} \tag{9.58}$$

From the first equation in (9.58), ϕ will be the smaller root of the polynomial

$$\Phi(\phi) = \phi^2 - \frac{1}{a}\phi + \frac{b}{a}. \tag{9.59}$$

This is none other than the characteristic polynomial (9.52), analyzed in the factorization method. There are two roots, λ and μ, where $0 < \lambda < 1$, and $\mu > 1$. The roots satisfy

$$\lambda + \mu = \frac{1}{a}, \lambda\mu = \frac{b}{a}. \tag{9.60}$$

From (9.58)–(9.60), we get

$$\begin{aligned} \phi &= \lambda < 1, \\ \psi &= \frac{\lambda c}{b}, \\ \omega &= \frac{1}{\mu} < 1. \end{aligned} \tag{9.61}$$

As a result, the fundamental solution is given by

$$y_t = \lambda y_{t-1} + \frac{\lambda c}{b}\sum\nolimits_{s=0}^{\infty} \left(\frac{1}{\mu}\right)^s E_t x_{t+s}, \tag{9.62}$$

which is the same as (9.54), arrived at through the method of factorization.

9.4.3 An Economic Example of a Second-Order System

As an economic example of a second-order system, we return to the model of the capital market with risk-neutral investors. Investors choose between a stock and a safe asset with a rate of return r. In equilibrium, arbitrage will ensure that the expected rate of return of the stock will be equal to the rate of return of the safe asset:

$$\frac{E_t p_{t+1} - p_t}{p_t} + \frac{d_t}{p_t} = r, \tag{9.63}$$

where p is the price of the stock, and d is the dividend. The expected rate of return of the stock is equal to the expected capital gain plus the dividend as a proportion of the stock price.

We now assume that the firm has a known dividend policy of the form

$$d_t = d_0 + \delta p_{t-1}, \tag{9.64}$$

where $0 < \delta < r$. Dividends per share are a constant d_0 plus a percentage of the price of the share in the previous period. Presumably this is a policy adopted by the firm and is intended to boost the price of the share.

Substituting (9.64) in (9.63) and solving for the price of the share, we get

$$p_t = \frac{1}{1+r}(E_t p_{t+1} + \delta p_{t-1} + d_0). \tag{9.65}$$

Because of the dependence of current dividends on the stock price of the previous period, (9.65) is a second-order equation, like (9.46), with $0 < a = c = 1/(1+r) < 1$, $0 < b = \delta/(1+r) < 1$, and $a + b < 1$. In this case, x_t is a constant equal to d_0.

Using either the factorization method or the method of undetermined coefficients, the solution of (9.65) gives us the stock price as a function of the past stock price and the constant part of dividends d_0:

$$p_t = \lambda p_{t-1} + \frac{\lambda}{\delta}\frac{1}{1-\mu^{-1}F}d_0 = \lambda p_{t-1} + \frac{\lambda}{\delta}\sum_{s=0}^{\infty}\left(\frac{1}{\mu}\right)^s d_0. \tag{9.66}$$

The two roots λ and μ lie on either side of unity and satisfy $\lambda + \mu = 1 + r$ and $\lambda\mu = \delta$. Assume that λ is the smaller root. Note that in the case where $\delta = 0$, we have $\lambda = 0$, and $\mu = 1 + r$. With $\delta = 0$, we are back to the first-order case.

One can show from (9.66) and the definitions of the two roots that because d_0 is constant, the stock price evolves according to

$$p_t = \lambda p_{t-1} + (1-\lambda)\frac{d_0}{r-\delta}. \tag{9.67}$$

The stock price converges to a steady state stock price, which is defined by

$$\bar{p} = \frac{d_0}{r - \delta}. \tag{9.68}$$

The steady state stock price is indeed higher than in the case where $\delta = 0$, and the dividend policy of a positive δ does indeed raise the price of the stock.

9.5 Multivariate Linear Models with Rational Expectations

Solution methods for more general multivariate linear models with rational expectations have been analyzed by Blanchard and Kahn [1980], Klein [2000], and Sims [2002]. McCallum [1983], Binder and Pesaran [1995], Uhlig [1999], and Christiano [2002] have generalized the method of undetermined coefficients for the multivariate case. Finally, Judd [1998], Schmitt-Grohe and Uribe [2004], and others have developed so-called perturbation methods, which are also appropriate for nonlinear models.

In what follows we shall concentrate on linear models and the important solution method of Blanchard and Kahn [1980].

9.5.1 The Blanchard-Kahn Method

Blanchard and Kahn [1980] consider the solution of the following multivariate linear model:

$$\mathbf{A}_1 \begin{pmatrix} \mathbf{x}_{t+1} \\ E_t \mathbf{y}_{t+1} \end{pmatrix} = \mathbf{A}_2 \begin{pmatrix} \mathbf{x}_t \\ \mathbf{y}_t \end{pmatrix} + \mathbf{A}_3 \mathbf{z}_t, \tag{9.69}$$

where $\mathbf{x}_t$ is an $(n \times 1)$ vector of predetermined variables at t, $\mathbf{y}_t$ is an $(m \times 1)$ vector of non-predetermined variables at t, and $\mathbf{z}_t$ is a $(k \times 1)$ vector of exogenous variables at t. The z values can be stochastic. Also, $E_t \mathbf{y}_{t+1}$ is the vector of rational expectations held at t, $\mathbf{A}_1$ and $\mathbf{A}_2$ are $(n+m) \times (n+m)$ matrices, and $\mathbf{A}_3$ is an $(n+m) \times k$ matrix.

A predetermined variable at $t+1$ is a function of variables known at t, whereas a non-predetermined variable at $t+1$ is a function of variables known at $t+1$. That is why at time t, the system can only determine the expectation of the non-predetermined variable at time $t+1$.

The equations of the system are ordered so that the coefficients of the non-predetermined variables occupy the last rows of the matrices $\mathbf{A}_1$, $\mathbf{A}_2$, and $\mathbf{A}_3$.

If the matrix $\mathbf{A}_1$ is invertible, then the first-order difference system (9.69) can be written as

$$\begin{pmatrix} \mathbf{x}_{t+1} \\ E_t \mathbf{y}_{t+1} \end{pmatrix} = \mathbf{A}_1{}^{-1} \mathbf{A}_2 \begin{pmatrix} \mathbf{x}_t \\ \mathbf{y}_t \end{pmatrix} + \mathbf{A}_1{}^{-1} \mathbf{A}_3 \mathbf{z}_t = \mathbf{A} \begin{pmatrix} \mathbf{x}_t \\ \mathbf{y}_t \end{pmatrix} + \mathbf{B} \mathbf{z}_t. \tag{9.70}$$

The matrix $\mathbf{A} = \mathbf{A}_1{}^{-1} \mathbf{A}_2$ can be decomposed into its Jordan canonical form, $\mathbf{A} = \mathbf{P} \Lambda \mathbf{P}^{-1}$, where Λ is a matrix with the eigenvalues of the matrix $\mathbf{A}$ on its diagonal, ordered from smallest to largest, and $\mathbf{P}$ is a matrix of the corresponding right eigenvectors.

Blanchard and Kahn [1980] prove that the system has a unique solution if there are n eigenvalues inside the unit circle (i.e., less than unity) and m eigenvalues outside the unit circle (i.e., greater than unity). The eigenvalues inside the unit circle correspond to the predetermined variables, and the eigenvalues outside the unit circle to the non-predetermined expectational variables. Then the system displays saddle path stability. The Blanchard-Kahn condition is not satisfied

1. if the number of unstable eigenvalues (roots) exceeds the number of non-predetermined variables (resulting in no solution, or explosive paths as the transversality condition is violated), or
2. if the number of unstable roots is less than the number of non-predetermined variables (yielding multiple equilibria).

Rewriting (9.70) using the Jordan canonical form, multiplying both sides by $\mathbf{P}^{-1}$, and defining $\mathbf{P}^{-1}\mathbf{B} = \mathbf{R}$, yields

$$\mathbf{P}^{-1}\begin{pmatrix} \mathbf{x}_{t+1} \\ E_t\mathbf{y}_{t+1} \end{pmatrix} = \Lambda\mathbf{P}^{-1}\begin{pmatrix} \mathbf{x}_t \\ \mathbf{y}_t \end{pmatrix} + \mathbf{R}\mathbf{z}_t, \tag{9.71}$$

where

$$\Lambda = \begin{pmatrix} \Lambda_1 & \\ & \Lambda_2 \end{pmatrix},$$

and Λ_1 denotes the stable eigenvalues and Λ_2 the unstable ones.

By defining

$$\mathbf{P}^{-1}\begin{pmatrix} \mathbf{x}_{t+1} \\ E_t\mathbf{y}_{t+1} \end{pmatrix} = \begin{pmatrix} \tilde{\mathbf{x}}_{t+1} \\ E_t\tilde{\mathbf{y}}_{t+1} \end{pmatrix}, \mathbf{P}^{-1}\begin{pmatrix} \mathbf{x}_t \\ \mathbf{y}_t \end{pmatrix} = \begin{pmatrix} \tilde{\mathbf{x}}_t \\ \tilde{\mathbf{y}}_t \end{pmatrix},$$

where the matrix $\mathbf{P}^{-1}$ is partitioned as

$$\mathbf{P}^{-1} = \begin{pmatrix} \mathbf{P}_{11} & \mathbf{P}_{12} \\ \mathbf{P}_{21} & \mathbf{P}_{22} \end{pmatrix},$$

we end up with the transformed system

$$\begin{pmatrix} \tilde{\mathbf{x}}_{t+1} \\ E_t\tilde{\mathbf{y}}_{t+1} \end{pmatrix} = \begin{pmatrix} \Lambda_1 & \\ & \Lambda_2 \end{pmatrix}\begin{pmatrix} \tilde{\mathbf{x}}_t \\ \tilde{\mathbf{y}}_t \end{pmatrix} + \begin{pmatrix} \mathbf{R}_1 \\ \mathbf{R}_2 \end{pmatrix}\mathbf{z}_t, \tag{9.72}$$

where (9.72) is a decoupled system of equations of the form

$$\tilde{x}_{i,t+1} = \lambda_i\tilde{x}_{i,t} + R_1 z_t, \tag{9.73}$$

$$E_t\tilde{y}_{j,t+1} = \lambda_j\tilde{y}_{j,t} + R_2 z_t, \tag{9.74}$$

for $i=1,2,\ldots,n$, $j=1,2,\ldots,m$; λ_i is the eigenvalue corresponding to the predetermined variable i; and λ_j is the eigenvalue corresponding to the non-predetermined variable j. The equations (9.73) are solved backward, and the equations (9.74) are solved forward.

9.5.2 Other Solution Methods

The Klein [2000] and Sims [2002] solution methods are variations of the Blanchard and Kahn [1980] solution method. In the Klein [2000] solution method, z_t is assumed to be a zero-mean vector autoregression. The solution method uses a Schur decomposition of the matrices $\mathbf{A}_1$ and $\mathbf{A}_2$, in (9.69) but is otherwise similar to Blanchard and Kahn [1980].

In the Sims [2002] solution method, the rational expectations variables are replaced by their observed values minus their innovation error. No distinction is then required between predetermined and non-predetermined variables. This solution method is based on so-called QZ factorizations of the matrices $\mathbf{A}_1$ and $\mathbf{A}_2$ in (9.54), which, for the Sims solution method, is rewritten as

$$\mathbf{A}_1\begin{pmatrix}\mathbf{x}_{t+1}\\ \mathbf{y}_{t+1}\end{pmatrix}=\mathbf{A}_2\begin{pmatrix}\mathbf{x}_t\\ \mathbf{y}_t\end{pmatrix}+\mathbf{A}_3\mathbf{z}_t+\mathbf{A}_1\begin{pmatrix}0\\ I\end{pmatrix}\mathbf{e}_{t+1}, \tag{9.75}$$

where $\mathbf{e}_{t+1}=\mathbf{y}_{t+1}-E_t\mathbf{y}_{t+1}$.

Other solution methods rely on a generalization of the method of undetermined coefficients by McCallum [1983], Binder and Pesaran [1995], Uhlig [1999], and Christiano [2002]. Various perturbation methods, also appropriate for nonlinear models, were introduced by Judd [1998], Schmitt-Grohe and Uribe [2004], and others.

9.5.3 A Second-Order Example of the Blanchard-Kahn Method

Let us return now to the share price determination model and see how it can be solved using the Blanchard-Kahn method. The model is the one discussed in section 9.4.3, in which dividends depend on the share price of the previous period. It is described by (9.63) and (9.64). These equations can be rewritten as

$$E_t p_{t+1}=-d_t+(1+r)p_t, \tag{9.76}$$

$$d_{t+1}=d_0+\delta p_t, \tag{9.77}$$

where (9.64) has been shifted forward one period.

The system of (9.76) and (9.77) can be written in matrix form as

$$\begin{pmatrix}d_{t+1}\\ E_t p_{t+1}\end{pmatrix}=\begin{pmatrix}0 & \delta\\ -1 & 1+r\end{pmatrix}\begin{pmatrix}d_t\\ p_t\end{pmatrix}+\begin{pmatrix}1\\ 0\end{pmatrix}d_0. \tag{9.78}$$

Equation (9.78) has the form of (9.70) of the general Blanchard Kahn model. The system will be stable if the coefficient matrix $\mathbf{A}$ has one eigenvalue that is less than one (corresponding to the predetermined variable d) and one eigenvalue greater than one (corresponding to the non-predetermined variable p). To find the eigenvalues, set

$$\det(\mathbf{A}-\rho\mathbf{I})=\det\begin{pmatrix} 0-\rho & \delta \\ -1 & (1+r)-\rho \end{pmatrix}=0, \tag{9.79}$$

which implies that

$$\rho^2-(1+r)\rho+\delta=0. \tag{9.80}$$

This is identical to the characteristic polynomial corresponding to the second-order difference equation (9.65). One can show that the characteristic polynomial (9.80) has two roots (say, λ and μ), which lie on either side of unity. The roots satisfy $\lambda+\mu=1+r$, and $\lambda\mu=\delta$, where λ is assumed to be the smaller root.

The Jordan decomposition of the coefficient matrix is given by

$$\begin{pmatrix} 0 & \delta \\ -1 & 1+r \end{pmatrix}=\frac{1}{\delta(\mu-\lambda)}\begin{pmatrix} \delta & \delta \\ \lambda & \mu \end{pmatrix}\begin{pmatrix} \lambda & 0 \\ 0 & \mu \end{pmatrix}\begin{pmatrix} \mu & -\delta \\ -\lambda & \delta \end{pmatrix}. \tag{9.81}$$

Thus, the model in (9.78) can be rewritten as

$$\begin{pmatrix} \mu & -\delta \\ -\lambda & \delta \end{pmatrix}\begin{pmatrix} d_{t+1} \\ E_t p_{t+1} \end{pmatrix}=\begin{pmatrix} \lambda & 0 \\ 0 & \mu \end{pmatrix}\begin{pmatrix} \mu & -\delta \\ -\lambda & \delta \end{pmatrix}\begin{pmatrix} d_t \\ p_t \end{pmatrix}+ \\ +\begin{pmatrix} \mu & -\delta \\ -\lambda & \delta \end{pmatrix}\begin{pmatrix} 1 \\ 0 \end{pmatrix}d_0. \tag{9.82}$$

By defining

$$\tilde{d}_{t+1}=\mu d_{t+1}-\delta E_t p_{t+1}, E_t\tilde{p}_{t+1}=\delta E_t p_{t+1}-\lambda d_{t+1},$$

$$\tilde{d}_t=\mu d_t-\delta p_t, \tilde{p}_t=\delta p_t-\lambda d_t,$$

we can rewrite (9.82) as

$$\begin{pmatrix} \tilde{d}_{t+1} \\ E_t\tilde{p}_{t+1} \end{pmatrix}=\begin{pmatrix} \lambda & 0 \\ 0 & \mu \end{pmatrix}\begin{pmatrix} \tilde{d}_t \\ \tilde{p}_t \end{pmatrix}+\begin{pmatrix} \mu \\ -\lambda \end{pmatrix}d_0. \tag{9.83}$$

Equation (9.83) is a decoupled system of difference equations that can be solved. Once the solutions are obtained, one can use the definitions in (9.83) to solve for p_t and d_t, noting that

$$d_t=\frac{1}{\mu-\lambda}\left(\tilde{d}_t+\tilde{p}_t\right), \tag{9.84}$$

$$p_t=\frac{1}{\delta}\left(\left(1-\frac{\lambda}{\mu-\lambda}\right)\tilde{p}_t-\frac{\lambda}{\mu-\lambda}\tilde{d}_t\right). \tag{9.85}$$

This completes the solution.

9.6 Rational Expectations and Learning

The rational expectations hypothesis assumes that agents fully utilize the information available to them and that they also know the parameters of the model that determines the variables about which they form expectations. An alternative hypothesis is that agents learn over time about the values of the parameters of the model that determines the relevant variables. This learning approach to the modeling of expectations formation in macroeconomics assumes that agents adapt their expectations on the basis of new data.

Learning models have some differences from rational expectations models. First, they provide a boundedly rational approach as to how full rational expectations can be reached. Second, learning acts as a selection device in models with multiple rational expectations equilibria. Third, the learning dynamics themselves may be of interest. Although there are various approaches to learning in macroeconomics, the emphasis usually is on adaptive learning schemes, in which agents use statistical or econometric techniques in self-referential stochastic systems.

This adaptive learning approach to the formation of expectations is surveyed by Evans and Honkapohja [1999] and is analyzed extensively in Evans and Honkapohja [2001].

9.7 Conclusion

This chapter introduces the concepts of dynamic stochastic models and rational expectations. Dynamic stochastic models and an appropriate expectations hypothesis (such as rational expectations) are indispensable for modeling conditions in which there is uncertainty about the future and agents exploit all available information. Unlike the deterministic models with perfect foresight used in previous chapters, in which there was no uncertainty about the future, a more realistic treatment of dynamic macroeconomics requires the modeling of uncertainty and uncertain expectations about the future.

We started with a simple expectational model of a competitive market, which illustrates the difference between deterministic and stochastic models and also highlights the role of the treatment of expectations. We distinguished between two expectations hypotheses: adaptive expectations and rational expectations. We determined that the dynamic behavior of the model differs under the two alternative expectational hypotheses.

Finally, we discussed general solution methods for dynamic stochastic models with rational expectations for both exogenous stochastic processes and more general first- and second-order linear models with one endogenous and one exogenous variable. We applied these methods to examples from finance and monetary economics, and also briefly discussed the conditions for unique solutions of multivariate rational expectations models and their alternative solution methods.

The methods illustrated in this chapter are indispensable for understanding and solving dynamic stochastic general equilibrium models and will prove extremely useful in the chapters that follow.

10

Consumption and Portfolio Choice under Uncertainty

In this chapter, we examine dynamic models of consumer choice under uncertainty. We continue, as in the Ramsey model, to take the decision of the household with regard to labor supply as given, assuming that each household provides a unit of labor per period. We also assume that the household can borrow and lend freely in competitive capital markets.

In intertemporal models with free borrowing and lending, consumption does not depend on current household income but on total household wealth, which consists of its current portfolio of assets plus the present value of expected future labor income. In this sense, consumption smooths temporary changes in income, as it depends on the so-called permanent income.[1]

Analyzing the consumption function of a representative household under certainty in chapter 4, we concluded that the household consumes a proportion of its total wealth that depends on the evolution of interest rates, the pure rate of time preference, the elasticity of intertemporal substitution in consumption, and the population growth rate.

Under certainty, the impact of interest rates on the propensity to consume out of total wealth depends on the elasticity of intertemporal substitution. An increase in interest rates has two kinds of effects on the propensity to consume out of total wealth. First, it induces the household to substitute future for current consumption, as it increases the cost of current consumption relative to future consumption. This is the result of intertemporal substitution in consumption. Second, an increase in interest rates increases household income from capital, inducing the household to increase both current and future consumption. This is the income effect. If the intertemporal elasticity of substitution is greater than one, the propensity to consume out of total wealth decreases when interest rates rise, because the substitution effect prevails over the income effect. If the intertemporal elasticity of substitution is less than unity, the propensity to consume out of total wealth increases when interest rates rise, because the income effect prevails over the substitution effect. Finally, in the case

1. See Friedman [1957], or the "life cycle income" of the household in Modigliani and Brumberg [1954].

where the intertemporal elasticity of substitution of consumption is equal to one (which corresponds to logarithmic preferences), the two results cancel each other out, and the propensity to consume out of total wealth is independent of the path of real interest rates. It is instead equal to the difference between the pure rate of time preference and the population growth rate.

In addition, an increase in real interest rates leads to a decrease in the present value of future labor income, reducing the overall wealth of the household and leading to lower consumption, even in the case where the elasticity of intertemporal substitution is equal to one. Essentially, the wealth effect of real interest rates on the present value of income from employment reinforces the substitution effect on current consumption.

The choice of consumption under conditions of uncertainty is linked to the portfolio allocation decisions of the household (Samuelson [1969], Merton [1969]).

Under uncertainty, consumption generally depends on the same factors as under certainty only in the case of quadratic preferences, which guarantee certainty equivalence. In the case of quadratic preferences, we can derive the permanent income model of consumption (sections 10.2 and 10.3).

In all other cases, under uncertainty, we cannot go beyond the first-order conditions and solve explicitly for consumption, unless we make further restrictive assumptions about the preferences of households or the variability of labor income.

With regard to portfolio choice, this approach results in the *consumption capital asset pricing model*. This model suggests that, under quadratic preferences, the expected return premium of a risky asset is proportional to the covariance of its return with consumption. The factor of proportionality is sometimes referred to as a "consumption beta" and can be used to explain the valuation of risky assets.

Keep in mind that under uncertainty, the permanent income hypothesis and the consumption capital asset pricing model rely on very restrictive assumptions. In addition, empirical studies suggest two puzzles that throw doubt on the validity of this model. One is the excess sensitivity of consumption to changes in current income, and the second is the equity premium puzzle (see sections 10.2.4 and 10.2.5).

Thus, although the intertemporal model of consumption under uncertainty is a useful framework for modeling consumption and portfolio allocation decisions, one may need to go beyond the permanent income hypothesis and the consumption capital asset pricing model and consider less restrictive set-ups, with precautionary savings, incomplete markets for securities, asymmetric information, and borrowing constraints.

10.1 Consumption and Portfolio Choice

The problem of how consumers choose between consumption and saving under uncertainty, in conjunction with the allocation of their portfolio among different assets, was first analyzed in an intertemporal setting by Samuelson [1969] and Merton [1969]. In what follows, we discuss the approach of Samuelson, who analyzed the problem in discrete time.[2]

Assume a household that at time 0, maximizes an intertemporal utility function of the form

$$E_0\left(\sum_{t=0}^{T-1}\left(\frac{1}{1+\rho}\right)^t u(C_t)\right), \tag{10.1}$$

where E_0 denotes a mathematical expectation based on the set of available information available at time 0; ρ is the pure rate of time preference of the household; and u a one-period utility function, depending on the level of current consumption C_t.

The household is uncertain regarding its future income from employment and the future returns of its portfolio of assets. The evolution of the value of the household portfolio of assets is described by

$$A_{t+1} = (A_t + Y_t - C_t)\left[(1+r_t)\omega_t + (1+x_t)(1-\omega_t)\right], \tag{10.2}$$

where A_t is the value of the portfolio of assets of the household in the beginning of period t; Y_t is labor income, which is assumed to be a random variable whose value is known in period t. Gross savings of the household are defined by $A_t + Y_t - C_t$. The household allocates its gross savings between a safe asset with certain return r_t, and a risky asset with uncertain return x_t (x_t is assumed to be a random variable whose value is known in period t). The portfolio allocation decision of the household is determined by the percentage ω of its assets that is invested in the safe asset. The term in brackets in (10.2) thus denotes the average rate of return of the household's portfolio.

The household chooses a consumption and portfolio allocation plan for period 0, knowing that it will be able to choose a new plan in the following period 1 on the basis on new information, a new plan in the following period 2, and so on, until the penultimate period $T-1$. The easiest method of solving dynamic optimization problems under uncertainty is the method of stochastic dynamic programming.[3]

Dynamic programming converts multiperiod problems into a sequence of simpler two-period selection problems. The first step is the introduction of a value function $V_t(A_t)$, which is defined as

2. To understand stochastic models and decision making under uncertainty, one must be aware of the concepts of random variables and stochastic process, as well as the concept of rational expectations. Appendix F introduces random variables and stochastic processes in discrete time, and chapter 9 discusses the concept of rational expectations and solution methods of linear stochastic models under rational expectations.

3. See appendix E for methods of intertemporal optimization.

$$V_t(A_t) = \max E_t \left(\sum_{s=t}^{T-1} \left(\frac{1}{1+\rho} \right)^{s-t} u(C_s) \right) \tag{10.3}$$

under the constraint (10.2).

The value function in period t is the discounted present value of the expected utility of the household, calculated under the assumption that the household follows the optimal program of consumption and portfolio allocation. This optimal value depends on the value of the portfolio of the household at the beginning of period t, which is the only state variable affecting the household. The value function depends of course on the conditional joint probability distribution of the random variables that describe the future labor income of the household and the uncertain rate of return of the risky asset, as well as the rate of return of the safe asset and the length of time between t and $T-1$. This dependence is indicated by the time index for the value function, and it shows that the value function may be changing over time.

From (10.3), the value function satisfies the following recursive equation, which is known as the *Bellman equation*:

$$V_t(A_t) = \max_{\{C_t, \omega_t\}} \left\{ u(C_t) + \frac{1}{1+\rho} E_t \left[V_{t+1}(A_{t+1}) \right] \right\}. \tag{10.4}$$

The value function in period t is equal to the maximum utility of consumption in period t plus the discounted expected value function in period $t+1$.

The first-order conditions for the maximization of the right-hand side of (10.4) under the constraint (10.2) are

$$u'(C_t) = E_t \left[\frac{1}{1+\rho} \left((1+r_t)\omega_t + (1+x_t)(1-\omega_t) \right) V'_{t+1}(A_{t+1}) \right], \tag{10.5}$$

$$E_t \left[V'_{t+1}(A_{t+1})(r_t - x_t) \right] = 0. \tag{10.6}$$

In (10.6), we have made use of the fact that the discounted gross savings of the household, which are equal to $(A_t - Y_t - C_t)/(1+\rho)$, are known in period t.

Applying the *envelope theorem* to (10.4) (i.e., the effects of a small change in the value of the portfolio of assets A_t on both sides of (10.4)), we get that

$$V'_t(A_t) = E_t \left[\frac{1}{1+\rho} \left((1+r_t)\omega_t + (1+x_t)(1-\omega_t) \right) V'_{t+1}(A_{t+1}) \right]. \tag{10.7}$$

From (10.5) and (10.7), it follows that

$$V'_t(A_t) = u'(C_t). \tag{10.8}$$

The marginal value of the household portfolio of assets in the application of the optimal program is equal to the marginal utility of consumption. As a result, we can use (10.8) to substitute the marginal utility of future consumption for the marginal value of the future portfolio of assets in the first-order conditions (10.5) and (10.6):

$$u'(C_t) = E_t\left[\frac{1}{1+\rho}\left((1+r_t)\omega_t + (1+x_t)(1-\omega_t)\right)u'_{t+1}(C_{t+1})\right], \tag{10.9}$$

$$E_t\left[u'(C_{t+1})(1+r_t)\right] = E_t\left[u'(C_{t+1})(1+x_t)\right]. \tag{10.10}$$

Substituting (10.10) in (10.9), the two conditions take the form

$$u'(C_t) = \frac{1+r_t}{1+\rho}E_t\left[u'(C_{t+1})\right], \tag{10.11}$$

$$u'(C_t) = \frac{1}{1+\rho}E_t\left[(1+x_t)\,u'(C_{t+1})\right]. \tag{10.12}$$

Conditions (10.11) and (10.12) have a simple interpretation, which is a generalization of the interpretation of the Euler equation for consumption in the Ramsey problem. Recall that the Euler equation for consumption in the Ramsey problem suggests that the marginal rate of substitution between the levels of consumption in the two periods must be equal to the marginal rate of transformation.

In the case of (10.11), assume that the household reduces its consumption by an infinitesimally small amount dC in period t, invests the amount in the safe asset, and consumes the return in the next period $t+1$. The reduction in its utility in period t is equal to $u'(C_t)$, which is the left-hand side of (10.11). The increase in its expected utility in period $t+1$ is equal to the right-hand side of (10.11). In the application of the optimal program, this infinitesimal reallocation does not affect the value of the plan, and as a result, (10.11) holds. For the same reason, (10.12) holds under the assumption that the household invests in the risky asset, rather than the safe asset in its portfolio.

10.1.1 The Random Walk Model of Consumption

Equations (10.11) and (10.12) are just first-order conditions and do not describe the full solution of the problem. Nevertheless, they suggest strong restrictions for the dynamic behavior of consumption. Equation (10.11) implies that

$$\frac{1+r_t}{1+\rho}u'(C_{t+1}) = u'(C_t) + \varepsilon_{t+1}, \tag{10.13}$$

where $E_t(\varepsilon_{t+1}) = 0$.

Equation (10.13) suggests that, given the marginal utility of consumption $u'(C_t)$, no additional information is available in period t that could help predict $u'(C_{t+1})$, the future marginal utility of consumption.

Assuming that the utility function is quadratic in consumption and that the rate of return of the safe asset is equal to the pure rate of time preference, then (10.13) takes the form[4]

$$C_{t+1} = C_t + \varepsilon_{t+1}. \tag{10.14}$$

The model implies that consumption follows a random walk process. Given the level of consumption in period t, no other variable known in period t helps predict consumption in period $t+1$. This prediction of the model was first highlighted by Hall [1978], who also investigated it empirically.

10.1.2 The Consumption Capital Asset Pricing Model

Conditions (10.11) and (10.12) can also be used to determine the rate of return of the risk-free asset and the expected rate of return (and hence the price) of the risky asset. To do so requires that all individual households are alike, (i.e., that there is a representative household).

From (10.11), the rate of return of the risk-free asset will satisfy

$$1 + r_t = (1+\rho)\frac{u'(C_t)}{E_t\left[u'(C_{t+1})\right]}. \tag{10.15}$$

From (10.12), it follows that

$$u'(C_t) = \frac{1}{1+\rho}\left\{E_t\left(1+x_t\right)E_t\left(u'(C_{t+1})\right) + \mathrm{Cov}_t\left(1+x_t, u'(C_{t+1})\right)\right\}. \tag{10.16}$$

Cov denotes the covariance of two random variables.

From (10.16), the expected rate of return of the risky asset will satisfy

$$E_t\left(1+x_t\right) = (1+\rho)\frac{u'(C_t)}{E_t\left(u'(C_{t+1})\right)} - \frac{\mathrm{Cov}_t\left(1+x_t, u'(C_{t+1})\right)}{E_t\left(u'(C_{t+1})\right)}. \tag{10.17}$$

From (10.15) and (10.17), the expected return premium of the risky asset is given by

$$E_t\left(x_t\right) - r_t = -\frac{\mathrm{Cov}_t\left(1+x_t, u'(C_{t+1})\right)}{E_t\left(u'(C_{t+1})\right)}. \tag{10.18}$$

The expected return premium of the risky asset depends on the covariance of the rate of return of the risky asset with the marginal utility of consumption. Given that the marginal utility of consumption is negatively correlated with consumption, because of decreasing marginal utility, the expected return premium of the risky asset will depend positively on the covariance of the rate of return of this asset with consumption. Risky assets whose returns are positively correlated with consumption will tend to have a higher expected return relative to the risk-free asset.

4. For a quadratic utility of the form $u(C_t) = (1/2)C_t{}^2$, it follows that $u'(C_t) = C_t$.

This model of the determination of expected asset returns is known as the *consumption capital asset pricing model* (consumption CAPM).

10.2 Full Analysis of Consumption and Portfolio Choice

From the first-order conditions, one cannot fully describe the behavior of consumption and savings, apart from specific cases. One can come up with specific solutions for two special cases. The first is the case of insurable income risk, and the second is the case of quadratic utility functions.

As demonstrated by Merton [1971], if labor income can be insured, we can deduce specific solutions for consumption for a broad class of utility functions, the hyperbolic absolute risk aversion (HARA) utility functions. This class includes isoelastic utility functions with constant relative risk aversion, the exponential utility function with constant absolute risk aversion, and quadratic utility functions.

One way to derive the specific solution is to use the *Bellman principle of optimality*, which says that for any value of the state variable (the portfolio of assets in this case) at a given time, the solution for the future must be optimal. Using this principle and the value function, the solution can be found through backward induction. For example, in period $T-2$, for any value of the portfolio of assets A_{T-2}, the household faces a two-period problem. After solving this problem, take a step back, and solve the problem of the period $T-3$, having already identified the value of the value function of $T-2$. Then move on and solve the same problem inductively for the $T-4$ period, and so on.

In the case of an infinite time horizon, take the limit of the solution to the problem of T periods as T tends to infinity. Alternatively, we can also solve the problem of infinite periods directly. For example, if the consumer has an infinite time horizon, the safe interest rate is fixed, and the uncertain return x_t is distributed according to an independent uniform probability distribution, then the value function is independent of time and only depends on the state variable A_t. Therefore, we can assume its form, derive the consumption function, and verify whether our assumption was correct.

HARA utility functions allow us to infer analytical solutions, because the value function belongs to the same family as the utility function, and all that remains is to infer the parameters of the value function.

10.2.1 The Case of Logarithmic Preferences

Consider the simple case, in which

$$u(C_t) = \ln C_t. \tag{10.19}$$

Using the result of Merton that the value function has the same functional form as the utility function for HARA utility functions, we assume that the value function takes the form

$$V(A_t) = a \ln(A_t) + b, \tag{10.20}$$

where a and b are constant parameters to be determined. This conjecture allows us to formulate the maximization problem in period t as

$$\max \ln(C_t) + \frac{1}{1+\rho} E_t\left[a \ln(A_{t+1}) + b\right] \tag{10.21}$$

under the constraint[5]

$$A_{t+1} = (A_t - C_t)\left[(1+r)\omega_t + (1+x_t)(1-\omega_t)\right]. \tag{10.22}$$

Solving for consumption C and the share of the portfolio invested in the safe asset ω, we get

$$C_t = \left(1 + \frac{a}{1+\rho}\right)^{-1} A_t, \tag{10.23}$$

$$E_t\left[(r - x_t)((1+r)\omega + (1+x_t)(1-\omega))^{-1}\right] = 0, \tag{10.24}$$

where (10.23) determines consumption as a linear function of the value of the total portfolio of assets of the household. Equation (10.24) determines indirectly the optimal proportion invested in the safe asset ω as a constant, due to the assumption that the return of the risky asset x is distributed according to a uniform independent probability distribution. The proportion ω is independent of the total value of the portfolio of assets.

To find a and b, substitute (10.22), (10.23), and (10.24) in the value function (10.21) and compare coefficients with (10.20). The parameter b is a complex but not economically significant constant, which depends on all the parameters of the model. The parameter a is determined to be $(1+\rho)/\rho$. Substituting this value in the consumption function (10.23), we get

$$C_t = \frac{\rho}{1+\rho} A_t. \tag{10.25}$$

In conclusion, assuming that labor income is insurable and the utility function is logarithmic, we get a consumption function analogous to the case of certainty. Consumption is a linear function of the total value of the portfolio of the household, and the marginal propensity to consume out of wealth depends only on the pure rate of time preference and not on the real interest rate or the rate of return of the risky asset. Changes in future nonlabor income (dividends and interest) affect consumption only through their impact on total wealth.

5. Because we assume that labor income risk is insurable, we concentrate on the case in which labor income Y is zero.

10.2.2 Quadratic Preferences and Certainty Equivalence

The second case we examine is the case of quadratic preferences. We initially assume that the portfolio consists only of the safe asset. The maximization problem of the household is

$$\max E_0\left[\sum_{t=0}^{T-1}\left(\frac{1}{1+\rho}\right)^t\left(aC_t-bC_t^2\right)\right] \tag{10.26}$$

under the constraints

$$A_{t+1}=(1+r)\left(A_t+Y_t-C_t\right), A_T\geq 0. \tag{10.27}$$

From the first-order conditions for a maximum, we have

$$E_tC_{t+1}=\frac{r-\rho}{1+r}\frac{a}{2b}+\frac{1+r}{1+\rho}C_t. \tag{10.28}$$

In what follows, assume that $r=\rho$. In this case, (10.28) takes the form

$$E_tC_{t+1}=C_t, \tag{10.29}$$

which implies that

$$E_0C_t=C_0, t=1,2,\ldots,T-1. \tag{10.30}$$

Because of the equality between the real interest rate and the pure rate of time preference, the optimal consumption path is such that there is *perfect consumption smoothing.* The optimal path of consumption is such that expected consumption is constant along the optimal path.

The budget constraint (10.27) implies that

$$A_T=A_0(1+r)^T+\sum_{t=0}^{T-1}(1+r)^{T-t}(Y_t-C_t). \tag{10.31}$$

Because the household does not derive utility from its portfolio directly, but only from its consumption, its consumption in the last period will be such that $A_T=0$. Using this transversality condition in (10.31), the intertemporal budget constraint of the household will be

$$\sum_{t=0}^{T-1}\left(\frac{1}{1+r}\right)^t C_t=A_0+\sum_{t=0}^{T-1}\left(\frac{1}{1+r}\right)^t Y_t. \tag{10.32}$$

According to (10.32), the present value of consumption of the household is equal to the value of its initial portfolio plus the present value of expected labor income. The household knows at time 0 that the budget constraint (10.32) should be satisfied but does not know future labor income. Accordingly, at time 0, the household aims to satisfy

$$E_0\left[\sum_{t=0}^{T-1}\left(\frac{1}{1+r}\right)^t C_t\right]=A_0+E_0\left[\sum_{t=0}^{T-1}\left(\frac{1}{1+r}\right)^t Y_t\right], \tag{10.33}$$

which suggests that the expected present value of consumption is equal to the value of the original portfolio of household plus the present value of expected labor income.

Substituting (10.30) in (10.33) and taking the limit as T tends to infinity results in

$$C_0=\frac{r}{1+r}\left(A_0+E_0\left[\sum_{t=0}^{\infty}\left(\frac{1}{1+r}\right)^t Y_t\right]\right). \tag{10.34}$$

Consumption is constant and is a fixed percentage of the total wealth of the household, including the present value of expected labor income. In every period, the household consumes a constant fraction of its total wealth, depending on the real interest rate (or the pure rate of time preference), so that expected total wealth remains constant.

10.2.3 The Permanent-Income Hypothesis with Quadratic Preferences

From (10.30), the change in consumption from period to period is determined only by the revision of expectations regarding labor income:

$$C_t-C_{t-1}=\frac{r}{1+r}\sum_{i=0}^{\infty}\left(\frac{1}{1+r}\right)^i\left(E_tY_{t+i}-E_{t-1}Y_{t+i}\right). \tag{10.35}$$

For example, assume that labor income follows a stationary first-order autoregressive stochastic process (i.e., an AR(1) process) of the form

$$Y_t=a+\lambda Y_{t-1}+\varepsilon_t, \tag{10.36}$$

where $a>0$ is a positive intercept, λ is the autoregressive parameter and satisfies $0<\lambda<1$, and ε is a white noise process measuring the current innovation in labor income. Then one can show from (10.31) that the change in current consumption depends only on the current innovation in labor income ε. This is because (10.36) implies that

$$E_tY_t-E_{t-1}Y_t=\varepsilon_t,$$

$$E_tY_{t+1}-E_{t-1}Y_{t+1}=\lambda\varepsilon_t.$$

By repeated substitutions we get

$$E_tY_{t+i}-E_{t-1}Y_{t+i}=\lambda^i\varepsilon_t,$$

so that expected future innovations in current income depend only on the current innovation, with geometrically declining weights, determined by the autoregressive parameter λ.

Thus, assuming (10.36), when one calculates the geometric progression in (10.35) using the prediction formula above, the change in consumption is determined by

$$C_t - C_{t-1} = \frac{r}{1+r-\lambda}\varepsilon_t. \tag{10.37}$$

The coefficient of the transitory innovation in income ε is smaller than unity, because λ is less than unity. Equation (10.37) incorporates the predictions of the permanent-income hypothesis of Friedman [1957] and the life cycle hypothesis of Modigliani and Brumberg [1954] that consumption smooths out transitory changes in income.

If λ is equal to unity, then disturbances in labor income ε are of a permanent nature, and the coefficient of (10.37) is also equal to unity. Permanent changes in labor income lead to equal permanent changes in household consumption.

Empirical studies of the permanent income hypothesis suggest that aggregate consumption displays excess sensitivity to changes in current income, compared to the predictions of this hypothesis. This evidence suggests that one may have to go beyond the permanent-income hypothesis to adequately account for aggregate consumption.[6]

10.2.4 The Consumption CAPM with Quadratic Preferences

Assuming quadratic preferences, as we have in (10.26), the marginal utility of consumption is given by

$$u'(C_t) = a - bC_t. \tag{10.38}$$

The marginal utility of consumption is thus a negative linear function of consumption.

Substituting for the marginal utility of consumption in (10.18), we get

$$E_t(x_t) - r_t = \frac{2b\text{Cov}_t(1+x_t, C_{t+1})}{a - bE_tC_{t+1}}. \tag{10.39}$$

This confirms that under quadratic preferences, the expected return premium of a risky asset is proportional to the covariance of its return with consumption. This factor of proportionality is sometimes referred to as a *consumption beta*, from a regression of consumption growth on asset returns. Thus, a central prediction of the consumption CAPM is that the return premium of a risky asset is proportional to its consumption beta.[7]

6. The more recent empirical literature on the permanent-income hypothesis is huge. Tests based on aggregate data include the original paper of Hall [1978], Flavin [1981, 1985], Hansen and Singleton [1982, 1983], Campbell and Mankiw [1989, 1991], and others. Attanasio [1999] surveys both aggregate and disaggregated studies.

7. See Merton [1973], Lucas [1978], and Breeden [1979]. The original CAPM of Sharpe [1964] and Lintner [1965] assumes that investors are concerned with the mean and variance of the return of their portfolio, rather than the mean and variance of consumption. That version of the model thus focused on so-called market betas, that is, coefficients from regressions of asset returns on the returns of a market portfolio.

However, empirical studies suggest an *equity premium puzzle*, that is, a much bigger difference between the average return of equities (the risky asset) and government bonds (the safe asset) than would be suggested by the consumption CAPM.[8]

10.2.5 The Efficient Markets Hypothesis

When the CAPM is combined with rational expectations on the part of investors, one gets a version of the *efficient markets hypothesis* (EMH). This hypothesis states that market participants make full use of available information in forming their expectations and therefore, the price of an asset fully reflects all available information.[9]

To demonstrate the logic of the EMH, assume a capital market in which investors choose between a common stock and a safe asset with a rate of return r. In equilibrium, optimality will ensure that the expected rate of return of the stock x will be equal to the rate of return of the safe asset plus a risk premium, as in (10.39). For simplicity, assume that both the rate of return of the safe asset r and the risk premium, denoted by σ, are constant:

$$E_t(x_t) = \frac{E_t p_{t+1} - p_t}{p_t} + \frac{d_t}{p_t} = r + \sigma, \tag{10.40}$$

where p is the price of the stock in the capital market, and d is the dividend. The expected rate of return of the stock $E_t(x_t)$ is equal to the expected capital gain plus the dividend as a proportion of the stock price. In equilibrium in an efficient capital market, this cannot differ from the rate of return of the safe asset r plus the risk premium σ.

Equation (10.40) can be rearranged as

$$p_t = \frac{1}{1+r+\sigma}\left(E_t p_{t+1} + d_t\right). \tag{10.41}$$

Under rational expectations, the fundamental solution of (10.41) gives us the stock price as the present value of current and expected future dividends, discounted by the sum of the rate of return of the safe asset and the risk premium σ:[10]

$$p_t = \frac{1}{1+r+\sigma}\sum_{s=0}^{\infty}\left(\frac{1}{1+r+\sigma}\right)^s E_t d_{t+s}. \tag{10.42}$$

To find closed-form solutions, assume that dividends follow a stationary AR(1) process of the form

8. See the important paper of Mehra and Prescott [1985], which has generated a large theoretical and empirical literature on this issue.

9. The roots of the EMH can be traced back to Bachelier [1900]. Its modern reincarnation is due to Fama [1965], Samuelson [1965], and especially Fama [1970].

10. See chapter 9 for the solution of first-order linear models with rational expectations, as is equation (10.41).

$$d_t = (1-\lambda)\bar{d} + \lambda d_{t-1} + \varepsilon_t, \tag{10.43}$$

where $\bar{d}$ is the steady state dividend, $0 < \lambda < 1$ is the degree of persistence of deviations of current dividends from the steady state dividend, and ε_{t+1} is a white noise process.

From (10.42) and (10.43), the fundamental solution is given by

$$p_t = \frac{\bar{d}}{r+\sigma} + \frac{1}{1+r+\sigma-\lambda}\left(d_t - \bar{d}\right). \tag{10.44}$$

From (10.44) and (10.43) it follows that

$$p_t = (1-\lambda)\frac{\bar{d}}{r+\sigma} + \lambda p_{t-1} + \frac{1}{1+r+\sigma-\lambda}\varepsilon_t. \tag{10.45}$$

Thus the stock market price, based on fundamentals, is an AR(1) process itself, with mean equal to the present value of the steady state dividend $\bar{d}/(r+\sigma)$.

From (10.45), it follows that

$$E_t p_{t+1} = (1-\lambda)\frac{\bar{d}}{r+\sigma} + \lambda p_t. \tag{10.46}$$

From (10.46), the current stock price fully reflects all available information about dividends. Hence, the only information relevant for predicting future stock prices is the current stock price itself. Only unanticipated changes in dividends (i.e., new information) can cause the future stock price to deviate from the currently expected future stock price.

Note that if dividends are nonstationary and follow a random walk (i.e., if $\lambda = 1$), then the stock price is a random walk itself, determined by

$$p_t = p_{t-1} + \frac{1}{r+\sigma}\varepsilon_t. \tag{10.47}$$

Equation (10.46) is modified accordingly and can be written as

$$E_t p_{t+1} = p_t. \tag{10.48}$$

If dividends follow a random walk process, stock prices follow a random walk process as well. In any case, the EMH suggests that no other variable apart from current stock prices helps predict future stock prices.[11]

As with the consumption CAPM itself, the evidence on the EMH is generally mixed. The problem is that most empirical tests test a joint hypothesis: a model of asset pricing (such as the consumption CAPM) and the EMH. Thus it is hard to determine whether negative statistical tests imply rejection of the particular asset pricing model or the EMH. Both Fama

11. For a general treatment of asset pricing and the CAPM, see Cochrane [2005].

and Shiller survey the empirical evidence in their Nobel lectures. Fama [2014] interprets the evidence as generally favorable to the EMH, but Shiller [2014] interprets the evidence as rejecting the EMH in favor of the alternative hypothesis of behavioral finance.[12]

10.3 Precautionary Savings and Borrowing Constraints

The assumption of quadratic preferences is quite restrictive. When preferences are not quadratic, certainty equivalence does not hold, and uncertainty about noninsurable labor income generally affects consumption. To see this, consider, for example, the first-order condition (10.11) with a constant risk free rate r:

$$u'(C_t) = \frac{1+r}{1+\rho} E_t\left[u'(C_{t+1})\right]. \tag{10.49}$$

So long as consumers are risk averse (i.e., so long as $u'' < 0$), increased uncertainty in the form of an increase in the variance of consumption decreases expected utility. But the effect of increased uncertainty on behavior depends on whether it affects the expected marginal utility of consumers through the first-order condition (10.49).

As long as utility is quadratic, marginal utility is linear in consumption, and $u''' = 0$. Thus, in the case of quadratic utility the variance of consumption has no effect on expected marginal utility and thus no effect on optimal behavior. After all, this is why certainty equivalence holds with quadratic preferences. In the general case, however, for most plausible utility functions, $u''' > 0$. Then marginal utility is convex in consumption, and an increase in uncertainty increases expected marginal utility. Thus, from (10.49), increased variability of future consumption would require an increase in expected future consumption relative to current consumption. Uncertainty leads consumers to defer consumption and thus be more prudent. The effects of prudence on savings were first analyzed by Leland [1968] and subsequently by Sandmo [1970] and Dreze and Modigliani [1972].

However, in general, it is almost impossible to solve for optimal consumption in the presence of prudent behavior. A case that can be solved analytically is the case of constant absolute risk aversion, which implies a utility function of the form

$$u(C_t) = -\frac{1}{\theta} e^{-\theta C_t}, \tag{10.50}$$

where θ is the coefficient of absolute risk aversion. This case has been analyzed in Caballero [1990].

12. Behavioral finance is the application of psychology to financial behavior. For surveys of models of behavioral finance see, among others, Shleifer [2000] and Shiller [2003]. Thaler [2015] is a more general nontechnical introduction to behavioral economics, and Akerlof [2007] considers the implications of behavioral economics for macroeconomics (in particular, consumption and investment behavior, the Phillips curve, and Ricardian equivalence).

Nonquadratic preferences and precautionary savings are not the only deviations from the permanent income hypothesis that have been considered in the literature. Other deviations that have been considered are incomplete markets and liquidity (borrowing) constraints, asymmetric information, and departures from full optimization. These extensions have been motivated by empirical weaknesses of the permanent income hypothesis and the consumption CAPM and are surveyed extensively in Attanasio [1999]. Financial frictions (i.e., deviations from perfect financial markets) are discussed in chapter 19.

10.4 Conclusion

In this chapter, we have examined the determination of household consumption under conditions of uncertainty, in conjunction with the determination of the allocation of the portfolio of the household among alternative assets (Samuelson [1969], Merton [1969]).

Under conditions of uncertainty, for a household that can borrow and lend freely in the capital market, consumption generally depends on the same factors as under certainty: the current and expected future rates of assets, the current and expected future labor income, and the total value of the portfolio and human wealth of the household.

Consumption does not depend on current household income but on total wealth, which consists of the value of its portfolio plus the present value of current and expected future labor income. In this sense, consumption smooths out temporary changes in income, as it depends on permanent or life cycle income (Modigliani and Brumberg [1954], Friedman [1957]).

However, the permanent income hypothesis cannot explain many of the features of individual or aggregate consumption patterns, especially the excess sensitivity of consumption to changes in current income. In addition, the consumption CAPM and the EMH, which are associated predictions of stochastic intertemporal models of consumption, seem to be refuted by the equity premium puzzle and excess volatility tests. The literature has thus examined models of behavioral finance, or models that result in precautionary savings, markets that are incomplete and households that are also subject to borrowing constraints (see Attanasio [1999]). Such models of consumption are quite diverse and complex. So far, they have not been adequately integrated into DSGE macroeconomic models. The financial crisis of 2008–2009 has, however, sparked a renewal of interest in financial market frictions. The literature on financial market frictions and their macroeconomic implications is introduced and discussed in chapter 19.

11

Investment and the Cost of Capital

In this chapter, we turn to the investment decisions of firms and discuss the main neoclassical model of investment under convex adjustment costs. This model is known as the "q model" of investment, where q is the ratio of the market value of installed capital relative to its replacement value. We discuss the model both under conditions of certainty and under uncertainty.

So far we have been assuming that firms choose their capital stock so that the marginal product of capital equals the user cost of capital, as determined by the real interest rate and the rate of depreciation. This theory in fact determines the optimal capital stock and not the optimal rate of investment. Investment flows determine how quickly a firm moves from its current to the optimal capital stock. When firms can adjust their capital stock immediately and without cost, the capital stock jumps immediately to its optimal level. This is the assumption we have been using implicitly so far.[1]

In fact, however, the change of the capital stock involves adjustment costs. A firm that chooses to raise its stock of productive capital should rent or buy additional space, buy and install new equipment, and train employees to use the extra equipment. In addition, there are delivery lags and installation costs, making it more costly to adjust the capital stock quickly. All these costs are in addition to the cost of buying additional capital goods. In general, it is to be expected that these adjustment costs will be convex (i.e., they will depend on the size of investment). The higher the absolute level of investment (i.e., the addition to the existing capital stock or the subtraction from it), the greater will be the average adjustment cost of installing (or deinstalling) an additional unit of capital.

In the presence of adjustment costs, the investment decisions of firms will thus not only depend on present conditions (such as the relation of the user cost of capital to the marginal product of capital) but also on past and expected future decisions. The problem of the firm becomes truly dynamic. Jorgenson [1963] assumed that, precisely because of the

1. The investment rate is defined as a finite rate in the growth models of chapters 3–8 because of the assumption that in a closed economy, the investment rate is equal to the savings rate. Thus, it is the savings rate and not the investment decisions of firms that constrains the investment rate in these models.

existence of adjustment costs, firms are not immediately but only gradually adjusting their stock of capital toward its optimal level, as determined by the user cost of capital and the marginal product of capital. He thus postulated an investment function that determines current investment as a fraction of the difference between the current and the optimal capital stock.

However, Jorgenson did not derive the speed of adjustment, and thus the flow of investment, from a fully dynamic optimization problem. This was accomplished later by Lucas [1967], Gould [1968], and Treadway [1969], who, instead of postulating the investment function (as Jorgensen had done), solved for the optimal investment function from the dynamic problem of a firm maximizing the present value of its profits, subject to convex costs of adjusting its capital stock. Soon afterward, Lucas and Prescott [1971] extended this framework to examine the determination of investment under uncertainty.[2]

An alternative approach to the problem of investment was that of Tobin [1969], who compared the ratio of the market value of installed capital of a firm to the replacement cost of capital, naming this ratio q. Tobin argued that if the already installed capital stock of a firm has higher value than the cost of replacing the capital goods that compose it (i.e., if q is greater than one), then it will be profitable for the firm to invest (i.e., to purchase and install additional capital goods). Tobin argued that the rate of investment will be an increasing function of q. The ratio of the value of the already installed capital stock to its replacement cost has since been called "Tobin's q." However, much like Jorgenson, Tobin did not derive his investment function from a dynamic optimization problem.

Several years later, Abel [1982] and Hayashi [1982] showed that Tobin's q theory and the theory of adjustment costs for investment of Jorgenson (as modeled by Lucas, Prescott, Gould, and Treadway) can be combined in a unified framework. This synthesis of the two theories is now considered as the main neoclassical dynamic model of investment.

The firm does not choose the level of its capital stock by equating the marginal product of capital to the sum of the real interest rate and the depreciation rate at any given time. It instead chooses the amount of investment, taking into account the adjustment costs of the capital stock. Because marginal adjustment costs are assumed to increase with the amount of investment, investment results in a gradual optimal adjustment of the capital stock toward its steady state value. On the adjustment path, the firm takes into account both the current and future effects of its investment decisions. Thus, investment depends on both current and expected future developments in the value of the marginal product of capital and the user cost of capital.

2. These models of investment are sometimes referred to as "flexible accelerator" models of investment, in contrast to earlier "fixed accelerator" models, which modeled investment as a constant multiple of the change in output or consumption. For a survey of these earlier accelerator models, see Knox [1952]. The most famous application of the earlier accelerator models in economics has been the paper of Samuelson [1939], which combined the multiplier and the accelerator to characterize output fluctuations in a Keynesian model. We shall analyze the Samuelson multiplier accelerator model along with other traditional Keynesian models in chapter 15.

11.1 Optimal Investment with Convex Adjustment Costs

Let us consider a competitive firm producing a good Y. The production function of the firm is given by

$$Y(t) = AF(K(t)), \tag{11.1}$$

where A is total factor productivity, and K is the capital stock. The production function is characterized by diminishing returns. The market price of output and the capital stock are equal to unity.[3]

To change its capital stock, the firm must undertake gross investment I. The change in its capital stock is thus determined by

$$I(t) = \dot{K}(t) + \delta K(t), \tag{11.2}$$

where δ is a constant depreciation rate.

Assume that the instantaneous cost of gross investment for the firm is equal to

$$I(t) + \psi(I(t)), \tag{11.3}$$

where ψ is a convex function, for which it holds that $\psi(0) = 0$, $\psi' > 0$, and $\psi'' \geq 0$. The convex function ψ measures the installation (adjustment) cost of gross investment. It is assumed that the higher the size of gross investment is, the higher the marginal installation cost will be. The total cost of gross investment is thus equal to the cost of buying the relevant capital goods plus the installation (adjustment) cost.

Figure 11.1 depicts the adjustment (installation) cost as a function of the size of gross investment of the firm. The installation cost rises as the absolute volume of gross investment rises. If the second derivative is positive, the installation cost rises at an increasing rate. The adjustment cost function is assumed symmetric. Thus, what applies to positive investment also applies to negative investment. The instantaneous profits of the firm are thus equal to

$$\mathcal{P}(t) = Y(t) - I(t) - \psi(I(t)). \tag{11.4}$$

11.1.1 The Choice of Optimal Investment

Assume that at time 0, the firm chooses an investment path that maximizes the present value of current and future profits. Assuming an infinite time horizon, the present value of the profits of the firm is equal to

$$\mathcal{V}(0) = \int_{t=0}^{\infty} e^{-rt}\left(Y(t) - I(t) - \psi(I(t))\right)dt, \tag{11.5}$$

3. To simplify the analysis, we assume that capital is the only factor of production. The nature of the results does not depend on this simplifying assumption.

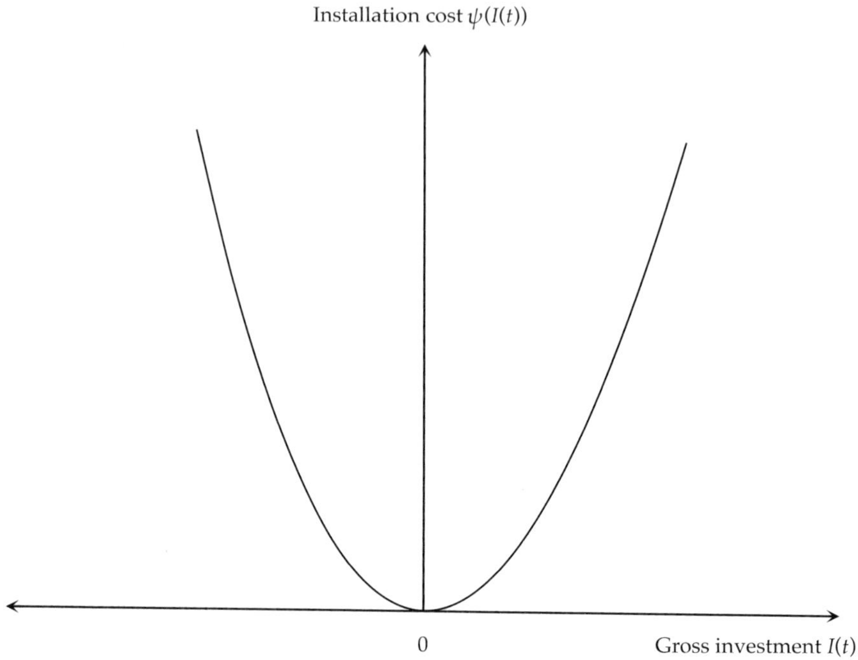

Figure 11.1
Adjustment cost of investment.

where r is the real interest rate, assumed exogenous and constant. The present value (11.5) is maximized under the constraint of the production function (11.1) and the investment function (11.2), which links gross investment to the accumulation of capital.

The current-value Hamilton function of this problem is defined by

$$\mathcal{H} = (AF(K(t)) - I(t) - \psi(I(t))) + q(t)(I(t) - \delta K(t)), \tag{11.6}$$

where $q(t)$ is the multiplier of the capital accumulation constraint (11.2) and represents the shadow value of an additional unit of capital at instant t.

From the first-order conditions for a maximum, it follows that

$$q(t) = 1 + \psi'(I(t)) = 1 + \psi'\left(\dot{K}(t) + \delta K(t)\right), \tag{11.7}$$

$$\left(r + \delta - \frac{\dot{q}(t)}{q(t)}\right) q(t) = A\frac{\partial F(K(t))}{\partial K(t)} = AF_K(K(t)). \tag{11.8}$$

The interpretation of this form of the first-order conditions is straightforward. Condition (11.7) determines the optimal shadow value of an additional unit of capital q as equal to the marginal cost of investment. This is equal to the purchase price of capital goods (assumed equal to unity) plus the marginal installation (adjustment) cost $\psi'(I(t))$.

Condition (11.8) requires that at the optimum, the firm will invest until the *user cost of capital* (on the left-hand side) is equal to the *marginal product of capital* (on the right-hand side). The user cost of capital is the real interest rate, plus the depreciation rate, minus the expected appreciation rate of the capital stock, all multiplied by the shadow value of capital $q(t)$.

11.1.2 The Case of Zero Adjustment Costs

In the case of zero adjustment costs, the marginal adjustment cost of the capital stock ψ' is equal to zero. In this case, conditions (11.7) and (11.8) imply

$$q(t) = 1,$$

$$r + \delta = AF_K\left(K(t)\right).$$

These are the usual first-order conditions that we have utilized so far. The variables q and K jump immediately to their equilibrium values. The shadow value of capital is continuously equal to unity (i.e., the purchase price of capital goods and the capital stock adjust immediately to the level where the marginal product of capital is equal to the real interest rate plus the depreciation rate, $r + \delta$). There is no investment flow, as the capital stock adjusts immediately. Without adjustment costs, this model does not determine gross investment but only the equilibrium capital stock.

11.1.3 The Investment Function with Convex Adjustment Costs

Let us now return to the general case, where there is a strictly convex adjustment cost function for the capital stock. From (11.7), it follows that investment is a positive function of $q - 1$. Solving (11.7) for I, we get

$$I(t) = \left(\psi'\right)^{-1}\left(q(t) - 1\right). \tag{11.9}$$

Gross investment depends only on the difference of the shadow price of installed capital q from unity, as assumed by Tobin. This dependence is positive, because the marginal cost of investment is positive. For this reason, the theory that depends on rising adjustment costs of investment is referred to as the q theory of investment.

11.1.4 The Determinants of q

We have already defined q as the shadow price of an additional unit of installed capital. We next turn to the determinants of q. From the first-order condition (11.7), q is equal to the marginal cost of investment. We have already used this condition to derive the investment function (11.9).

To analyze the determinants of q, we must look into the second first-order condition (11.8). This can be rewritten as

$$\dot{q}(t) = (r + \delta)q(t) - AF_K\left(K(t)\right). \tag{11.10}$$

Equation (11.10) is a first-order linear differential equation with variable coefficients. Its solution takes the form

$$q(t) = \int_{s=t}^{\infty} e^{-(r+\delta)(s-t)} AF_K\left(K(s)\right) ds. \tag{11.11}$$

From (11.11), it follows that q is the present value of all future marginal products of capital. As a result, q depends negatively on the real interest rate and the depreciation rate, as well as on factors that reduce the marginal product of capital (such as the capital stock). In contrast, q depends positively on factors that increase the marginal product of capital (such as total factor productivity).

In equilibrium, q is determined so that both first-order conditions are satisfied. Thus, in equilibrium, the marginal cost of investment is equal to the expected present value of future marginal products of capital. This condition determines optimal investment.

11.1.5 Dynamic Adjustment of q and the Capital Stock K

The determination of the shadow price of an additional unit of capital q, and the stock of capital K, can be inferred from the differential equations (11.7) and (11.8). Because both of these differential equations are nonlinear, their solution can be described by a phase diagram, as in figure 11.2.

For a constant capital stock, (11.7) implies that

$$q = 1 + \psi'\left(\delta K\right). \tag{11.12}$$

The higher the stock of capital is, the higher will be the shadow value q implied by (11.12), as depreciation investment will be higher. Equation (11.12) is depicted as the curve with a positive slope in figure 11.2 and can be interpreted as the *constant capital stock condition*. When q is higher than the level implied by (11.12), the capital stock increases, as gross investment is higher than depreciation investment. The opposite happens when q is lower than the level implied by (11.12): Then the capital stock decreases.

For a constant q, (11.8) implies that

$$q = \frac{1}{r+\delta} AF_K(K), \tag{11.13}$$

so, the higher the stock of capital is, the lower the shadow value of capital q will be, as the marginal product of capital is a negative function of the stock of capital. Equation (11.13), which is the curve with a negative slope in figure 11.2, can be seen as the *constant gross investment condition*. When K (the stock of capital) is higher than the level implied by (11.13), then the marginal product of capital is lower than what would be required by (11.13), and q increases, so that the user cost of capital is also lower. Thus, investment is low but increasing over time. The opposite happens when the capital stock is lower than the level implied by (11.13).

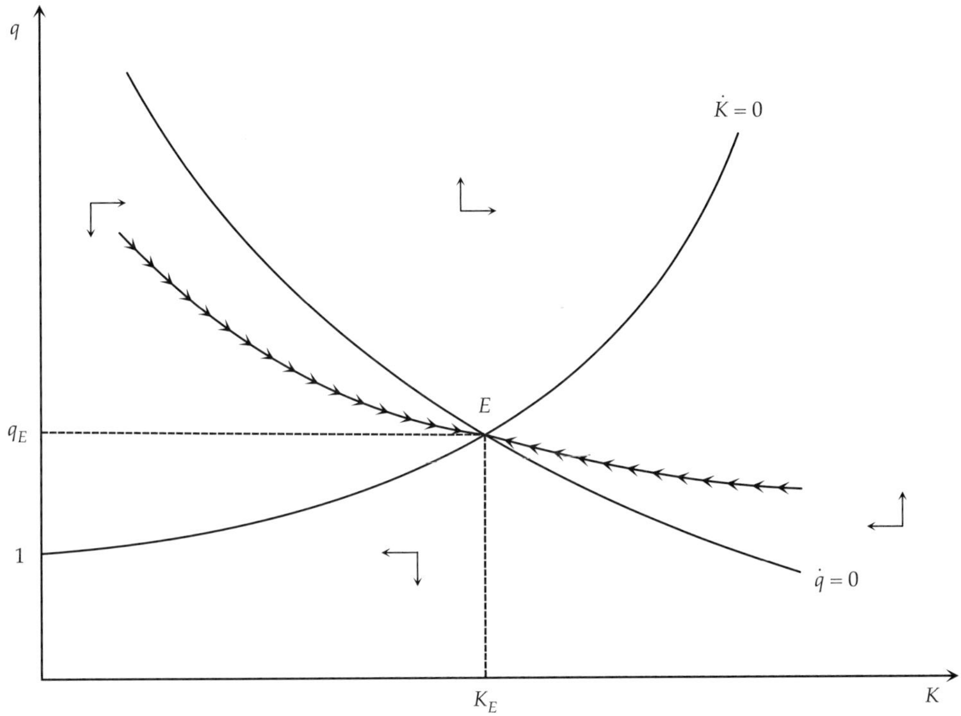

Figure 11.2
Determination of q and the capital stock K.

The steady state is determined at the intersection of the two curves (11.12) and (11.13). This steady state equilibrium is a saddle point, because q is a non-predetermined variable and K is a predetermined variable. The adjustment path is unique and is depicted in figure 11.2.

Figure 11.3 shows the effects of a permanent increase in the real interest rate. This leads to increase in the user cost of capital and a downward shift of the constant investment condition. Because the capital stock is predetermined in the short run, the change leads to an immediate reduction of q and investment, and a gradual reduction of the stock of capital. As the capital stock decreases, the marginal product of capital gradually increases, which causes a gradual increase in both q and investment. At the new steady state E', both the stock of capital and q are at a lower level than at the initial steady state E.

Figure 11.4 shows the effects of a permanent increase in total factor productivity A, which leads to an increase in the marginal product of capital and a shift upward of the constant investment condition. Because the capital stock is predetermined in the short run, the result is an immediate increase of q and investment, and a gradual increase of the stock of capital. As the capital stock increases, the marginal product of capital gradually falls, causing a

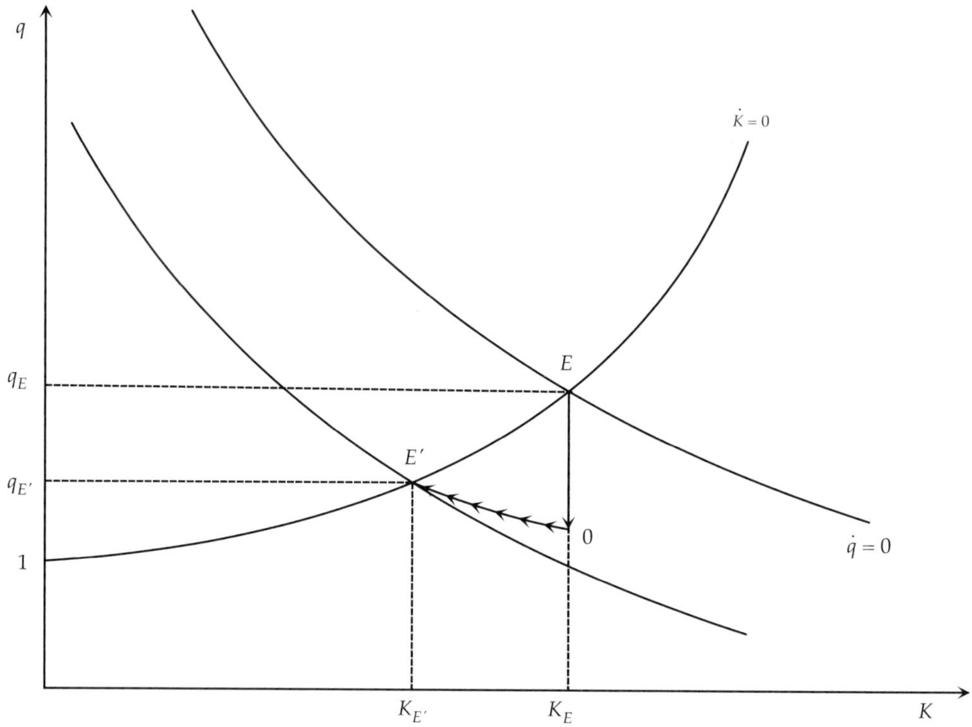

Figure 11.3
Dynamic effects of a permanent rise in the real interest rate.

gradual reduction of both q and investment. At the new steady state E', both the stock of capital and q (investment) are at a higher level than at the initial steady state E.

The dynamics depicted in figures 11.2–11.4 describe the basic neoclassical model of investment with convex adjustment costs. This model can be generalized so that the adjustment cost function depends not only on gross investment but also on the stock of capital. It can also be generalized to simultaneously analyze investment and labor demand. Finally, it can also be generalized to allow for product market imperfections, as well as to the case of uncertainty.

11.2 Optimal Investment under Uncertainty

We now turn to the case of investment under uncertainty. As in the case of consumption, uncertainty introduces additional problems. Just as under certainty, we shall assume that the firm chooses its investment path to maximize its value to its owners. The value is equal to the present value of the profits that the firm generates.

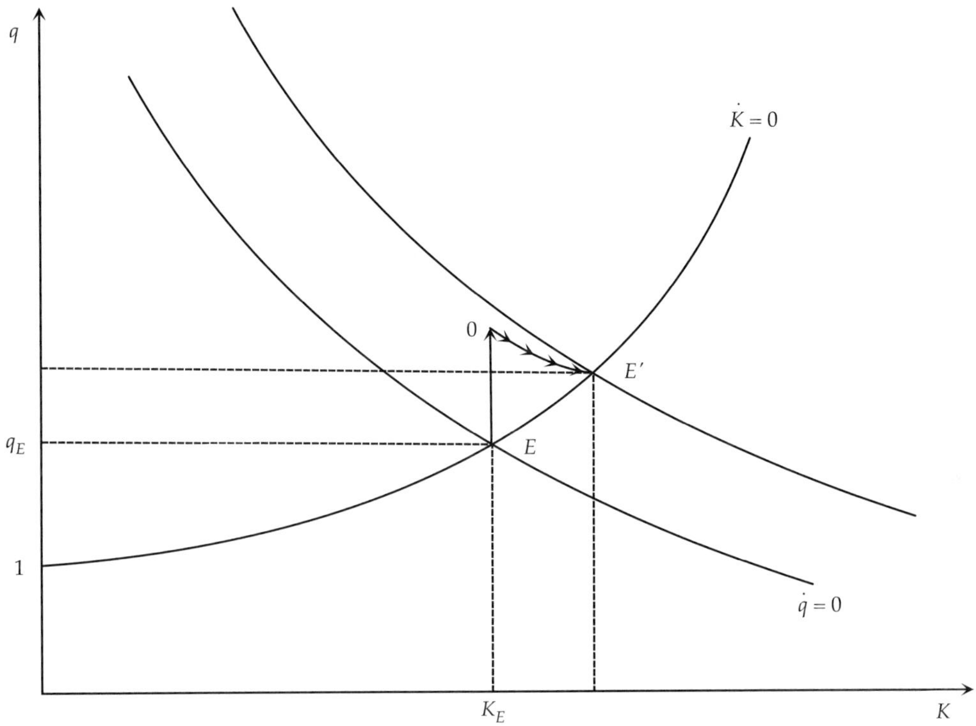

Figure 11.4
Dynamic effects of a permanent rise in total factor productivity.

11.2.1 The Value of a Firm under Uncertainty

Under certainty, the problem of maximizing the present value of the profits of the firm is easily defined. But under uncertainty, the question that arises is: What is the discount rate at which firms should discount future profits?

Let us assume that $\mathcal{V}_t$ is the value of the firm in period t, and $\mathcal{P}_t$ is its per period revenue, net of investment expenditures. Then the rate of return $1+\pi_t$ from holding the firm for one period is given by

$$1+\pi_t = \frac{\mathcal{V}_{t+1}+\mathcal{P}_t}{\mathcal{V}_t}. \tag{11.14}$$

For a household that invests in the firm under uncertainty, the rate of return from holding the firm $1+\pi_t$, and hence V_t and Π_t, must satisfy

$$u'(C_t) = \frac{1}{1+\rho}E_t\left[(1+\pi_t)\,u'(C_{t+1})\right] = \frac{1}{1+\rho}E_t\left[\left(\frac{\mathcal{V}_{t+1}+\mathcal{P}_t}{\mathcal{V}_t}\right)u'(C_{t+1})\right]. \tag{11.15}$$

Equation (11.15) is similar to the first-order condition (10.12) for investing in a risky asset in the problem analyzed in chapter 10. The returns generated by the firm in each state of nature are weighted by the marginal utility of consumption in that state. The discount factor that must be applied must take into account the correlation of the firm's profits with the marginal utility of consumption at each state.

Solving the first-order condition (11.15) recursively forward and assuming away bubbles, we get the fundamental solution for the value of the firm $\mathcal{V}_t$:

$$\mathcal{V}_t = E_t\left(\sum_{s=1}^{\infty}\left(\frac{1}{1+\rho}\right)^s \frac{u'(C_{t+s})}{u'(C_t)}\mathcal{P}_{t+s}\right). \tag{11.16}$$

This equation shows that the value of the firm is equal to the present discounted value of expected future profits. The discount rate for each period and for each state of nature is the marginal rate of substitution between consumption at time t and consumption at that period and that state of nature. The implication is that the higher the correlation between a firm's profits and consumption is, the higher will be the discount factor applied and the lower the value of the firm.

In practice, it is often assumed that firms maximize the present discounted value of profits by using a deterministic discount rate. For firms opting to do this, (11.16) becomes

$$\mathcal{V}_t = E_t\left(\sum_{s=1}^{\infty}\left(\prod_{z=1}^{s}\frac{1}{1+r_{t+z}}\right)\mathcal{P}_{t+s}\right), \tag{11.17}$$

where r_{t+z} is a deterministic interest rate in period $t+z$. Although widely used, a specification such as (11.17) is generally inappropriate, because it suggests that at each date, the same discount factor is used to evaluate returns in different states of nature.

An equation such as (11.17) can be justified only under very specific assumptions. One assumption that can be used to justify it is the assumption of risk neutrality on the part of consumers. If consumers are risk neutral, so their utility is linear in consumption and their marginal utility of consumption is constant, then the discount rate is not only deterministic but also constant, and it equals the pure rate of time preference ρ. Thus, in the case of risk neutrality, (11.17) simplifies further to

$$\mathcal{V}_t = E_t\left(\sum_{s=1}^{\infty}\left(\frac{1}{1+\rho}\right)^s \mathcal{P}_{t+s}\right). \tag{11.18}$$

Another set of assumptions that can be used to justify a deterministic discount rate is to assume that investment decisions do not affect the relative distribution of returns across states of nature but only the scale of the firm. In this case, the firm can use a constant discount rate, equal to the risk free rate, plus a risk premium that reflects the specific risk associated with the firm's activities.

Both sets of assumptions are unlikely to hold in general, but they are often used as convenient approximations. However, they are good approximations only when considerations of risk aversion are not central to the problem analyzed.

11.2.2 The Lucas-Prescott Model of Investment under Uncertainty

We next turn to an examination of the investment decisions of a competitive firm under uncertainty, assuming that the objective of the firm is to maximize value as defined in (11.18), with a deterministic discount rate. The model we analyze is a linear quadratic variant of the class of models introduced by Lucas and Prescott [1971]. It is similar in many respects to the q model analyzed in section 11.1.

Assume a competitive firm i that takes market prices as given. Its profit in period t is defined by

$$\mathcal{P}_{it} = \left(p_t Y_{it} - I_{it} - \frac{\psi}{2} (I_{it})^2 \right), \tag{11.19}$$

where p is the competitive relative price of its output Y; I is gross investment; and ψ is a constant positive parameter measuring the strength of investment adjustment costs, which are quadratic in gross investment. The relative price of investment goods is normalized to unity.

Output is produced using capital, through a linear production function of the form

$$Y_{it} = AK_{it}, \tag{11.20}$$

where A is total factor productivity, assumed to be constant and the same for all firms.

The relation between gross investment and the evolution of the capital stock is determined by

$$K_{it+1} = I_{it} + (1 - \delta) K_{it}, \tag{11.21}$$

where δ is the constant depreciation rate, and i is uniformly distributed in the interval [0, 1]. Thus, industry output is given by

$$Y_t = \int_{i=0}^{1} Y_{it} di. \tag{11.22}$$

Because all firms face the same technology and the same market prices, the output of all firms will be the same. Thus, from now on, we treat Y as the output of the representative firm. The same goes for all other variables, such as investment and the capital stock.

Under the assumptions we have made, the representative firm maximizes its expected present value

$$\mathcal{V}_t = E_t \left(\sum_{s=1}^{\infty} \left(\frac{1}{1+r} \right)^s \left(p_{t+s} A K_{t+s} - I_{t+s} - \frac{\psi}{2} (I_{t+s})^2 \right) \right), \tag{11.23}$$

subject to the sequence of accumulation equations (11.21). The stochastic processes driving the market price and productivity are taken as given.

The Lagrange function of this problem is defined by

$$E_t\left(\sum_{s=1}^{\infty}\left(\frac{1}{1+r}\right)^s\left(\begin{array}{l}\left(p_{t+s}AK_{t+s}-I_{t+s}-\frac{\psi}{2}(I_{it+s})^2\right)+\\+q_{t+s}\left(I_{t+s}+(1-\delta)K_{t+s}-K_{t+s+1}\right)\end{array}\right)\right), \tag{11.24}$$

where q_{t+s} is the sequence of Lagrange multipliers of the capital accumulation constraints.

From the first-order conditions for a maximum, we get the two familiar first-order conditions:

$$q_t = 1+\psi I_t, \tag{11.25}$$

$$(1+r)q_t-(1-\delta)E_t q_{t+1} = E_t p_{t+1}A. \tag{11.26}$$

Equations (11.25) and (11.26) have interpretations similar to the that of the corresponding conditions (11.7) and (11.8) in the deterministic case analyzed in section 11.1. Equation (11.25) requires that at the optimum, the firm equates the shadow value of an addition to its capital stock q to the marginal cost of investment. The latter consists of the price of purchasing capital goods (assumed to be equal to one) plus the adjustment cost of investment.

Equation (11.26) requires that the user cost of capital, as measured by the term on the left-hand side, is equal to the expected future value of the marginal product of capital, as measured by the term on the right-hand side. Solving (11.26) forward for q, we get

$$q_t = \frac{1}{1+r}E_t\sum_{s=0}^{\infty}\left(\frac{1-\delta}{1+r}\right)^s p_{t+s+1}A, \tag{11.27}$$

So q turns out to be the discounted value of all expected future values of the marginal product of capital. It depends positively on the expected future evolution of the relative price for the product of the firm and the marginal productivity of capital A. It also depends negatively on the discount rate r and the depreciation rate δ.

To determine investment, we can solve (11.25) for investment:

$$I_t = \frac{1}{\psi}\left(q_t-1\right). \tag{11.28}$$

From (11.28), investment depends positively on the difference of q from unity, which is the purchase price of investment goods. Substituting (11.27) in (11.28), investment of the representative firm will be determined by

$$I_t = \frac{1}{\psi}\left(\frac{1}{(1+r)}\left(E_t\sum_{s=0}^{\infty}\left(\frac{1-\delta}{1+r}\right)^s p_{t+s+1}A\right)-1\right). \tag{11.29}$$

Investment thus depends positively on the discounted value of all expected future changes in the value of the marginal product of capital; it depends negatively on the real interest rate, the depreciation rate, and the adjustment cost parameter ψ.

From (11.29), the capital stock of the representative firm evolves according to

$$K_{t+1} = (1-\delta)K_t + \frac{1}{\psi}\left(\frac{1}{(1+r)}\left(E_t \sum\nolimits_{s=0}^{\infty}\left(\frac{1-\delta}{1+r}\right)^s p_{t+s+1}A\right) - 1\right). \tag{11.30}$$

To say more about the determination of investment and the capital stock, one must make specific assumptions about the stochastic process driving the market price of output.

Although for each competitive firm, the price of output is taken as given, for the industry, the market price will be determined endogenously from the equation of total demand for its product and industry supply. Industry supply will depend on investment and the evolution of the capital stock. This is something that Lucas and Prescott [1971] took explicitly into account, solving for the equilibrium price endogenously as a function of the capital stock, and characterizing the evolution of the capital stock and the equilibrium price in a *rational expectations equilibrium*.

11.2.3 Rational Expectations Equilibrium and Aggregate Investment in the Lucas-Prescott Model

Assume that industry demand is linear in the price and is given by

$$Y_t = D - bp_t + v_t, \tag{11.31}$$

where $D > 0$, $b > 0$ are constant parameters; D measures the size of the market; b the price responsiveness of demand; and v is a stochastic disturbance to industry demand.

From (11.31), and after substituting for output from the production function, the competitive (relative) price is determined as

$$p_t = \frac{1}{b}(D - Y_t + v_t) = \frac{1}{b}(D - AK_t + v_t). \tag{11.32}$$

We can use (11.32) to substitute for the expected equilibrium price in the capital accumulation equation (11.30) and solve for the evolution of the capital stock as a function of only exogenous shocks.

Note that using the forward shift operator, $Fp_t = E_t(p_{t+1})$, (11.30) can be written as

$$K_{t+1} = (1-\delta)K_t + \frac{1}{\psi}\left\{\frac{1}{(1+r)}\left(E_t \sum\nolimits_{s=0}^{\infty}\left(\frac{1-\delta}{1+r}\right)^s F^{s+1}p_tA\right) - 1\right\}.$$

The above can be rewritten as

$$K_{t+1} = (1-\delta)K_t + \frac{1}{\psi}\left\{\frac{AFp_t}{(1+r)-(1-\delta)F} - 1\right\}. \tag{11.33}$$

Multiplying both sides of (11.33) by $(1+r)-(1-\delta)F$ and collecting the terms containing K on the left-hand side, after using (11.32) to substitute out for p_t, we get

$$\left(F^2-\frac{(1+r)+(1-\delta)^2+(A^2/\psi b)}{(1-\delta)}F+(1+r)\right)K_t=$$

$$=-\frac{1}{\psi(1-\delta)}\left(\frac{A}{b}(D+Fv_t)-(r+\delta)\right). \tag{11.34}$$

The characteristic polynomial of the quadratic equation involving F on the left-hand side has two roots that lie on either side of unity. We can thus rewrite (11.34) as

$$(F-\lambda)(F-\mu)K_t=-\frac{1}{\psi(1-\delta)}\left(\frac{A}{b}(D+Fv_t)-(r+\delta)\right), \tag{11.35}$$

where $\lambda<1$ is the smaller root, and $\mu>1$ the larger root. It follows from (11.34) that $\lambda=(1+r)/\mu$, as the roots satisfy

$$\lambda+\mu=\frac{(1+r)+(1-\delta)^2+(A^2/\psi b)}{(1-\delta)}>2, \lambda\mu=1+r.$$

From (11.35), the capital stock follows:

$$K_{t+1}=\lambda K_t+\frac{\lambda}{\psi(1-\delta)(1+r-\lambda)}\left(\frac{AD}{b}-(r+\delta)\right)+$$

$$+\frac{A}{b}\frac{\lambda}{\psi(1-\delta)(1+r)}E_t\sum\nolimits_{s=0}^{\infty}\left(\frac{\lambda}{1+r}\right)^s v_{t+s+1} \tag{11.36}$$

Equation (11.36) shows that the evolution of the industry capital stock in rational expectations equilibrium depends on current expectations about the whole future path of disturbances to industry demand and on parameters such as the discount rate r, the productivity of capital A, the adjustment cost parameter ψ, the depreciation rate δ, the size of the market D, and the price responsiveness of industry demand b. The root λ depends only on the discount rate and technological parameters.

To get a closed-form solution, we must make assumptions about the exogenous stochastic process driving industry demand. Assume that v follows a stationary AR(1) process of the form

$$v_t=\theta v_{t-1}+\varepsilon_t, \tag{11.37}$$

where $0<\theta<1$, and ε_t is a white noise process.

Under this assumption, (11.36) implies that

$$K_{t+1}=\lambda K_t+\frac{\lambda}{\psi(1-\delta)(1+r-\lambda)}\left(\frac{AD}{b}-(r+\delta)\right)+$$

$$+\frac{A}{b}\frac{\lambda\theta}{\psi(1-\delta)(1+r-\lambda\theta)}v_t. \tag{11.38}$$

Investment and the evolution of the capital stock depend only on the current shock to aggregate demand, because the current shock is a sufficient statistic for all future shocks to industry demand.

Thus, the structure of the full Lucas-Prescott model is as follows. The representative firm chooses investment—and implicitly, the capital stock and output—to maximize the present value of its profits, taking as given the market price of its output, the exogenous relative price of capital goods, and exogenous productivity A. To compute the full equilibrium, once investment and output of the representative firm are determined, industry output is replaced in the industry demand function to solve for the equilibrium price in terms of the exogenous stochastic process driving industry demand. The full rational expectations equilibrium is thus described by a pair of interrelated capital accumulation and price equations, which are consistent with continuous market clearing in a competitive industry.

This model can be ammended in various directions. First, one could introduce additional shocks, such as shocks to total factor productivity. Second, one could introduce labor in the production function and study interactions between investment and labor demand. Third, one could introduce business taxes. Fourth, one could introduce externalities from capital accumulation. Finally, one could assume imperfect rather than perfect competition.[4]

11.3 Conclusion

In this chapter, we have examined the main neoclassical model of investment under convex adjustment costs. This model is known as the q model of investment, where q is the ratio of the market value of installed capital relative to its replacement value. We analyzed the model both under conditions of certainty and of uncertainty.

In rational expectations equilibrium, the evolution of investment and the capital stock depends on current expectations about the whole future path of disturbances to demand and parameters such as the discount rate, total factor productivity, the adjustment cost function, the depreciation rate, the size of the market, and the price responsiveness of industry demand. The speed of adjustment of the capital stock depends on the discount rate and technological parameters.

The model can be generalized in various directions by introducing additional shocks, such as shocks to total factor productivity and allowing for labor in the production function, business taxes, externalities from capital accumulation, and imperfect competition.

4. An alternative competitive version of the linear quadratic Lucas and Prescott [1971] model can be found in Sargent [1987].

12

Money, Interest, and Prices

The existence of money in a modern economy is usually taken for granted. It performs three main functions. First, it is a unit of account; second, it is a universally accepted means of payment; and third, it is a store of value.

In models without money, one can only analyze the determination of real variables, such as the quantities of goods and services produced and consumed, and their relative prices. But in models with money, one can also determine nominal variables, such as the price level, nominal income, the level of nominal wages, nominal interest rates, and inflation. These nominal variables are expressed in terms of money.

In this chapter, we focus on the money market to analyze the supply and the demand for money and the determination of nominal variables.

Monetary conditions in modern economies are determined by central banks. A central bank can affect, through a variety of policy instruments at its disposal, both interest rates and the money supply. The money supply consists of the quantity of bank notes (and coins) in circulation and the stock of deposits in commercial banks. Thus, central banks can indirectly affect the money supply, although they usually operate through short-term interest rates, intervening in the money market and determining nominal interest rates. If the central bank follows a policy of pegging interest rates, the stock of money in the economy is determined indirectly by the demand for money, as the money supply adapts to demand, so that it is consistent with the target of the central bank regarding nominal interest rates.

The demand for money depends on three main factors. The first factor is the price level. The higher the level of prices is, the higher will be the amount of money that households and firms will want to hold for their current and future transactions. The demand for money is usually assumed to be proportional to the price level. This demand stems from the roles of money as both a unit of account and a means of payment.

The second factor is the volume of transactions, usually measured by aggregate real output and income. When the volume of transactions increases, households and firms will need more money to carry out their increased transactions. This determines the demand for real money balances, and it stems from the role of money as a means of payments.

The third factor is the level of nominal interest rates. Banknotes pay no interest. In contrast, demand deposits and current accounts in commercial banks, even when they pay interest, yield a very low return compared to the yields of less-liquid assets that are not means of payments, such as time deposits, treasury bills, and bonds. In what follows, we shall maintain the assumption that money pays no interest. Thus, as interest rates rise, households and firms will want to hold a smaller part of their assets in the form of money compared to interest-yielding assets, such as bonds and other less-liquid assets. Consequently, the demand for money will be assumed to depend negatively on the level of nominal interest rates.

In this chapter, we first review the basic functions of money and the factors that determine the supply and the demand for money. We analyze the concept of short-run equilibrium in the money market, assuming that the central bank follows a policy of either targeting the money supply or pegging nominal interest rates. We also discuss the notion of the long-run neutrality of money.[1]

We then focus on some dynamic general equilibrium models with money. We analyze the determination of the price level and nominal interest rates and dicuss the long-run relationship between the money supply, the price level, and inflation.

Finally, we examine incentives for increasing the money supply and the effects of continuous increases of the money supply on inflation. The most important motive for sustained large increases in the money supply by governments has been the incentive to finance government expenditure that could not be financed by other methods (such as additional taxes or government bonds). This monetary source of revenue for the government is called *seigniorage*.

We first analyze the case in which the maximum income from seigniorage in equilibrium is adequate for the financing needs of a government, although these financing needs are large. In such a case, an economy will end up in an equilibrium with high inflation. Second, we analyze the case in which the maximum revenue from seigniorage is not sufficient for the financing needs of the government. In this case, an economy will end up with a hyperinflation, which is a disequilibrium phenomenon. The government will try to increase the rate of growth of the money supply continuously. This accelerating rate of growth of the money supply will eventually result in hyperinflation.

The main cause of all episodes of sustained high inflation or even hyperinflation has been the need of governments to use their privilege of printing money to obtain significant amounts of seigniorage.

1. For an advanced up-to-date textbook entirely devoted to monetary theory and policy, see Walsh [2017].

12.1 The Functions of Money

What are the functions of money in an economy, and why do households and firms hold money? The answer is that money performs three important functions.

First, money is a *unit of account*. In a monetary economy, all prices are determined and quoted in terms of the monetary unit. Otherwise, economic agents would have to calculate all the relative prices of goods and services to conduct their transactions. For example, in an economy with N goods plus money, households and firms have to calculate N money prices. Without money, economic agents would need to calculate $N(N-1)/2$ relative prices to make their transactions. As the number of goods and services increases, the number of relative prices to be calculated grows exponentially. For example, if there are 5 goods and services, there are 5 money prices, and 10 relative prices of goods between them. With 10 goods and services, there are 10 money prices, and and 45 relative prices of all goods and services. With 100 goods and services, there are 100 money prices, and 4,950 relative prices between goods and prices. With 1,000 goods and services, there are 1,000 money prices, and 499,500 relative prices between goods and prices. Money therefore helps simplify the calculation of prices and values and thus facilitates economic transactions through its function as a unit of account.

Second, money is a generally accepted *means of payment*. Being accepted by all, money greatly facilitates economic transactions and drastically reduces their costs. Without money, to complete a transaction, the seller of a product or service would have to find a buyer who would be prepared to offer in return another good or service that the seller wishes to acquire. This requires a double coincidence of wants in all economic transactions. Transactions or this kind are called *barter*, which implies large transactions costs on the part of economic agents to find suitable counterparties to their transactions. A modern economy would immediately cease functioning if there were no generally accepted medium of exchange and payments, because transaction costs would become prohibitive. This is probably the most important role of money.

Third, money is a *store of value* (i.e., a means of holding wealth) and is indeed the asset that is characterized by greater liquidity than any other asset, as it can be used directly for payments for the acquisition of goods and services. This is a key feature of money, because if money were not a store of value and lost its value quickly, it would not be generally accepted as a means of payments. And because money is the only store of value that is also a means of payments, by definition, it is the most liquid store of value. However, as a means of holding wealth, money does not pay interest, unlike other, less-liquid assets.

All three functions of money—as a unit of account, a means of payments, and a store of value—determine its social role in an economy and help explain why households and firms attach such great importance to money.

We now turn to the determinants of the supply and the demand for money.

12.2 The Supply of Money and Central Banks

The supply of money in a modern economy consists of the sum of banknotes, coins, and deposits in current (checking) accounts in commercial banks held by households and firms. This definition of the money supply is usually known as M1. It emphasizes the more-liquid assets held by households and firms, which usually do not yield interest. However, there are broader definitions of the money supply (M2, M3, and M4) that include less-liquid assets, such as time deposits, repurchase agreements (repos), and certificates of deposit.[2]

Deposits of credit institutions and other institutions participating in the interbank market and the foreign exchange market are not considered to be part of the money supply. These deposits are not used for the transactions of the general public.

12.2.1 Central Banks and Their Functions

The aggregate money supply of an economy, whether defined narrowly or broadly, is critically influenced by the actions of central banks. A *central bank* (sometimes known as a *reserve bank*, or *monetary authority*) is an institution, usually public, that manages the currency in an economy (namely, its money supply and interest rates in so-called money markets). Central banks also usually oversee the domestic commercial banking system. In contrast to a commercial bank, a central bank possesses a monopoly on issuing notes and coins, which serve as the state's legal tender.

The primary function of a central bank is to control the nation's monetary conditions, through active duties, such as issuing notes and coins, managing short-term interest rates, setting reserve requirements for commercial banks, and acting as a lender of last resort to the banking sector (and possibly the state) during times of financial crisis. These duties usually determine a country's monetary policy.

Central banks usually also have supervisory powers, intended to prevent bank runs and to reduce the risk that commercial banks and other financial institutions engage in reckless or fraudulent behavior. Central banks in most developed nations are institutionally designed to be independent from political interference. Still, limited control by the executive and legislative bodies usually exists.

Prior to the seventeenth century, money was mostly *commodity money*, typically gold, silver, or bronze coins. Bronze coins were used for low-denomination transactions, and silver and gold coins for higher-denomination transactions. However, promises to pay (bank notes) circulated widely and were accepted as money at least 500 years earlier in both Europe and Asia. Paper currency first developed during the Tang Dynasty in China in the seventh century, although true paper money did not appear until the eleventh century, during the Song Dynasty. The usage of paper currency later spread throughout the Mongol empire. European explorers like Marco Polo introduced the concept to Europe during the thirteenth

2. See Mishkin [2016, chapter 3] for a more detailed discussion of alternative definitions of money.

century. Paper money originated in two forms: drafts, which were receipts for precious metals held on account, and bills, which were issued with a promise to convert to precious metals at a later date.

As the first public bank to offer accounts not directly convertible to coin, the Bank of Amsterdam, established in 1609, is considered to be the precursor to modern central banks. The central bank of Sweden ("Sveriges Riksbank" or simply "Riksbanken") was founded in Stockholm from the remains of the failed bank Stockholms Banco in 1664 and answered to parliament (known as the Riksdag of the Estates). One role of the Swedish central bank was lending money to the government. The establishment of the Bank of England, the model for most modern central banks, was devised by Charles Montagu, First Earl of Halifax, in 1694. He proposed a loan of 1.2 million to the government. In return, the subscribers would be incorporated as The Governor and Company of the Bank of England, with long-term banking privileges, including the issue of notes. The Royal Charter was granted on July 27, 1694, through the passage of the Tonnage Act of that year.

Although some scholars would point to the 1694 establishment of the Bank of England as the origin of central banking, the Bank of England did not originally have the same functions as a modern central bank (namely, to regulate the value of the national currency, to finance the government, to be the sole authorized distributor of banknotes, and to function as a lender of last resort for banks suffering a liquidity crisis). The modern central bank evolved slowly through the eighteenth and nineteenth centuries before reaching its current form.[3]

12.2.2 Central Banks and the Money Supply

The determination of the money supply by central banks is not a simple process. It depends on the rules under which the central bank participates in money and asset markets and regulates the financial system, on its relations with the government, and on the goals envisaged in its charter.[4]

The *monetary base* in an economy is defined as the sum of coins and banknotes held by the public plus the reserves of commercial banks held at the central bank. Thus, the monetary

3. See Goodhart [1988], Capie et al. [1994], and Fischer [1994], for the evolution of the role of central banks.

4. There is an extensive literature on the transmission mechanisms of monetary policy in economies with developed financial and fiscal systems, going back at least to Fisher [1896] and Wicksell [1898]. The views of Keynes, as they evolved, can be found in Keynes [1923, 1936]. The views of the Keynesians are summarized in the IS-LM framework of Hicks [1937]. A more sophisticated Keynesian view is Tobin [1969], and the dominant monetarist view is Friedman [1970]. The subsequent literature is extensive. See, for example, Friedman [1975], Modigliani and Papademos [1980], Papademos and Modigliani [1983], Mishkin [1995], Taylor [1995], Bernanke and Gertler [1995], and Meltzer [1995], for a variety of views about the transmission mechanism. In what follows, and until chapters 19 and 20, we shall focus on a simplified monetary policy transmission mechanism that depends on the effects of changes in the money supply on nominal and real interest rates and asset prices, through open market operations. Other channels, such as the credit channel, will be discussed when we discuss financial frictions in chapter 19.

base B is equal to

$$B = C + R, \tag{12.1}$$

where C is currency (coins and notes) held by the nonbank public (households and firms), and R is the reserves of commercial banks. An alternative name for the monetary base is *high-powered money*, sometimes denoted as M_0.

The monetary base is the monetary aggregate that a central bank can control better than any other aggregate, as the central bank decides how much currency to issue and can also control the reserves of commercial banks either directly or indirectly.

The *money supply* is defined as the total of coins and banknotes held by the public plus deposits of households and firms in commercial banks. Thus, the money supply M is determined by

$$M = C + D, \tag{12.2}$$

where D denotes deposits in commercial banks. If D refers to deposits in checking (current) accounts only, then the money supply is narrowly defined, a definition known as M_1. If D refers to deposits in checking accounts and savings and time deposits, the money supply is more broadly defined, a definition known as M_2. If longer-term deposits, institutional money market funds, short-term repurchase, and other liquid assets are included in deposits, then the money supply is yet more broadly defined, a definition known as M_3.

The relationship between the monetary base and the money supply is given by

$$M = \frac{C + D}{C + R} B = \frac{c + 1}{c + r} B = mB, \tag{12.3}$$

where m is the so-called money multiplier. The money multiplier depends on two crucial parameters: the ratio of currency to deposits chosen by the nonbank public ($c = C/D$) and the reserve ratio of commercial banks ($r = R/D$).

To the extent that these two ratios are stable, there is a stable proportional relationship between the monetary base and the money supply. Thus, by controlling the monetary base, the central bank can control the money supply. To the extent that either the ratio of currency to deposits of the nonbank public or the reserve ratio of commercial banks are volatile, the control of the money supply by the central bank entails difficulties, because of the volatility of the money multiplier. However, the central bank can still exercise some control over the money multiplier through minimum reserve requirements for commercial banks and other instruments (such as short-term interest rates) that may affect the currency-deposit ratio of the nonbank public or the reserve ratio of commercial banks.

It is clear from the above that the central bank is not the only institution that affects the money supply. The behavior of the nonbank public (in choosing to hold money in the form of either currency or deposits) and the behavior of commercial banks (in deciding the ratio of their reserves to their deposits) also affect the money supply. A reduction in the reserve ratio of commercial banks causes an increase in the money multiplier and the money supply for a given monetary base.

Thus, ultimately, the money supply is determined by three factors:

1. the number of notes and coins issued by the central bank;
2. the choices of the nonbank public between holding money in the form of notes and coins and deposits in commercial banks; and
3. the choices of commercial banks between holding reserves with the central bank against their deposits, versus lending to the nonbank public (households and firms) or investing in other interest yielding assets (such as shares and bonds).

Because the central bank can largely determine the monetary base (and indirectly, the cash deposit ratio of the nonbank public and the reserve ratio of commercial banks) it can, to some extent, exert indirect control on the money supply. However, bank regulation and financial innovations in payments are important factors that determine bank-created money, and they are among the reasons the money multiplier may be unstable and not easily controlled by central banks. As noted by Bernanke [2006, p. 2] at the beginning of his term as chairman of the Federal Reserve Board, "In practice, the difficulty has been that, deregulation, financial innovation, and other factors have led to recurrent instability in the relationships between various monetary aggregates and other nominal variables."

The main economic goals of a central bank are usually stated in its statutes. They are the control of inflation; the stability of the financial system; and in some cases, the support of the general economic policies of the government. In what follows, we shall ignore many of the institutional details that relate to how a central bank operates and will instead make two alternative simple assumptions.

First, let us assume that the central bank has full control of the money supply. This is an assumption with a long history in macroeconomic analysis, although it is not particularly realistic.

Alternatively, let us assume that the central bank follows a policy of determining (pegging) the nominal interest and committing to providing unlimited credit to households, businesses, and commercial banks at this rate. This policy of interest rate determination (which many find to be a more realistic description of how central banks operate in modern economies) means that the money supply is determined by the demand for money at the nominal interest rate determined by the central bank. Although rules for the money supply are sometimes mentioned, most of our analysis of monetary policy in chapters 14–20 will be in terms of interest rate rules.

12.3 The Demand for Money

The demand for money by households and firms depends on three main factors. The first factor is the price level. The higher the level of prices is, the higher will be the amount of money that households and firms want to hold for their current and future transactions. For example, if the price level were to double, then for a household or a firm to buy the same amount of goods and services would require twice as much money. The demand for money is thus usually assumed to be proportional to the price level.

The second factor is the volume of transactions. When the volume of transactions, usually measured by aggregate real output, increases, households and firms will need more money to carry out their increased transactions.

The third factor is the level of interest rates. Banknotes pay no interest. Demand deposits and current (checking) accounts, even when they pay interest, pay a very low rate compared to the yields of less-liquid assets, such as time deposits, treasury bills, or bonds. As interest rates rise, households and firms want to hold a smaller part of their assets in low- (or zero-) yielding money, in relation to assets that pay interest. Consequently, the demand for money will depend negatively on the nominal interest rate, as the nominal interest rate measures the opportunity cost of holding money.

The money demand function is usually expressed as

$$\frac{M^d}{P} = m(Y, i), \tag{12.4}$$

where M^d denotes nominal money demand, P is the price level, Y is real aggregate income (GDP), i is the nominal interest rate, and m is a function increasing in real aggregate income and decreasing in the nominal interest rate. The demand for money is assumed to be proportional to the price level, in the sense that an increase in the price level requires an increase in the quantity of money by the same proportion to carry out the same volume of transactions. Thus the demand for money is a demand for *real money balances*, that is, a given amount of purchasing power or liquidity.[5]

Assuming that the demand for money function has a unitary elasticity with respect to real aggregate income, it takes the form of the quantity theory equation

$$\frac{M^d}{P} = Y\kappa(i),$$

5. A demand for money in this form was first introduced by Keynes [1936] and was termed *liquidity preference*. The classic optimizing partial equilibrium models of money demand for transaction purposes, which also depend on the nominal interest rate, are due to Baumol [1952] and Tobin [1956]. The restatement of the quantity theory of money by Friedman [1956] also results in money demand functions that depend on interest rates.

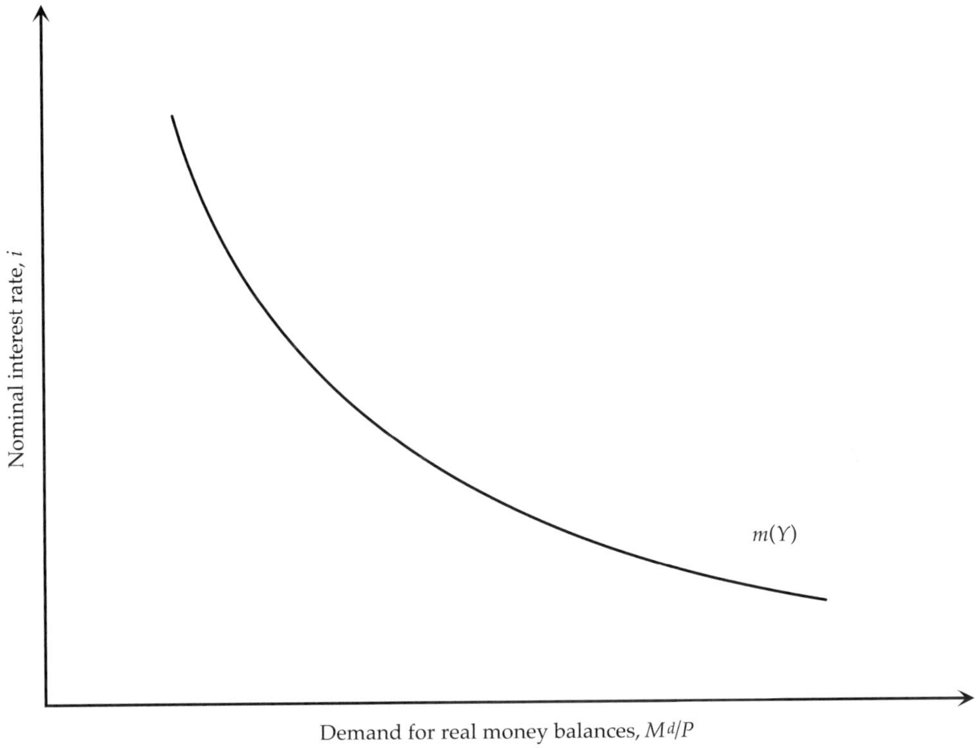

Figure 12.1
The demand for money and the nominal interest rate.

where κ is a decreasing function of the nominal interest rate. The quantity theory equation is a special case of (12.4), in which the demand for real money balances is proportional to aggregate real income.[6]

The demand for real money balances as a function of the nominal interest rate is depicted in figure 12.1. The relationship between real money demand and the nominal interest rate is negative, because holding money becomes more expensive as interest rates rise (recall that money does not pay interest). Therefore, households and firms reduce the amount of money holdings and increase holdings of securities and other interest-yielding assets.

The position of the money demand function in figure 12.1 depends on the level of real income, which determines the volume of transactions in goods and services. For given nominal interest rates, an increase in real income will increase the demand for money

6. The quantity theory equation is the basis of the quantity theory of money, which states that, in the long run, the general price level of goods and services is directly proportional to the amount of money in circulation.

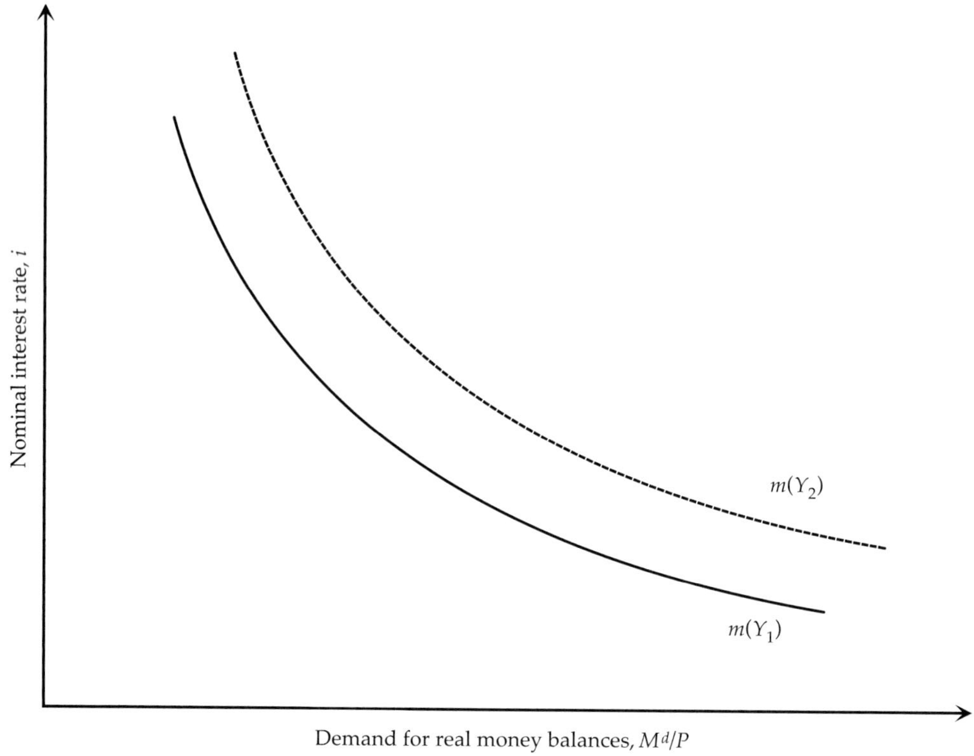

Figure 12.2
An increase in real income and the demand for money.

as it will increase the amount of money required by households and firms to carry out their increased transactions. The money demand curve will move to the right, as shown in figure 12.2.

A similar shift may occur if there is an exogenous increase in liquidity preference on the part of households and firms. For example, because of increased uncertainty or any other reason, if households and firms desire to hold more money for a given real income and nominal interest rate, then the demand for money will shift to the right, as in the case of an increase in real income depicted in figure 12.2.

As already mentioned, households and firms hold money because of the liquidity it provides. How much money households and firms wish to hold depends proportionately on the price level. The demand for money is not a demand for a certain amount of nominal money but for a certain amount of purchasing power. This demand depends positively on the volume of economic transactions (as measured by aggregate real income) and negatively on the opportunity cost of holding money (as measured by the nominal interest rate). These three factors—the price level, the volume of economic transactions as measured by aggregate output and income) and the nominal interest rate—are the factors that affect the demand for money.

12.4 Nominal Interest Rates and Short-Run Equilibrium in the Money Market

Equilibrium in the money market means that the existing money supply is willingly held by households and firms. Thus, the equilibrium condition in the money market is for the money supply to be equal to money demand:

$$\frac{M^s}{P} = \frac{M^d}{P} = m(Y, i). \tag{12.5}$$

Short-run equilibrium in the money market is depicted in figure 12.3. It is assumed that the central bank controls the money supply and fixes it at some constant level, and that aggregate real income and the price level are given. Therefore, in the short run, the only

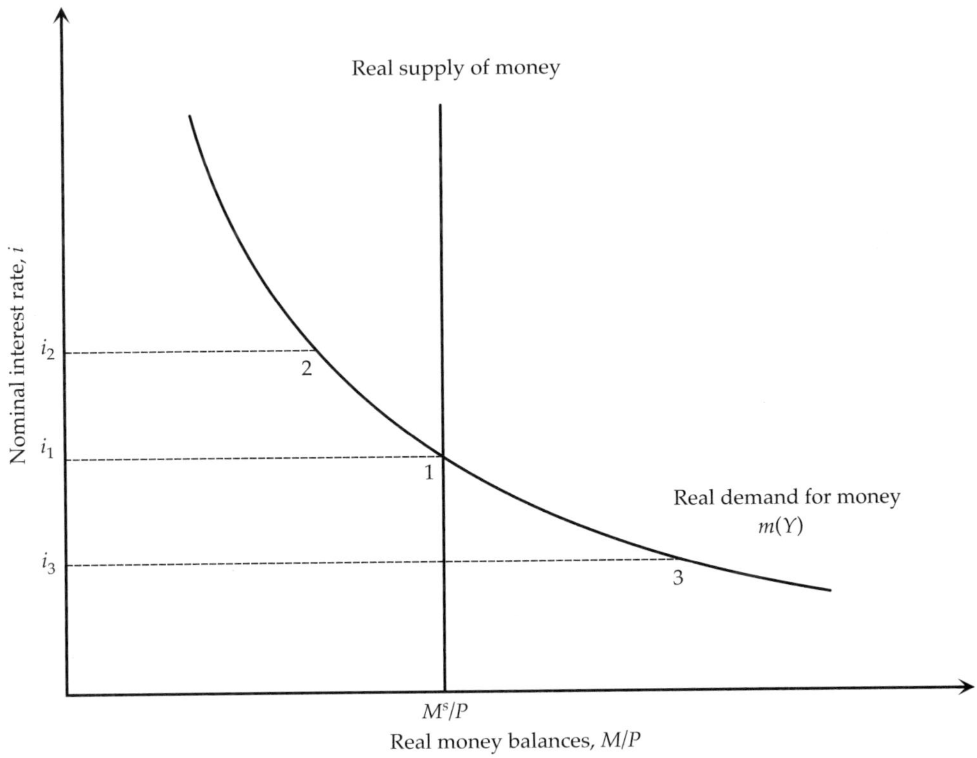

Figure 12.3
Short-run equilibrium in the money market.

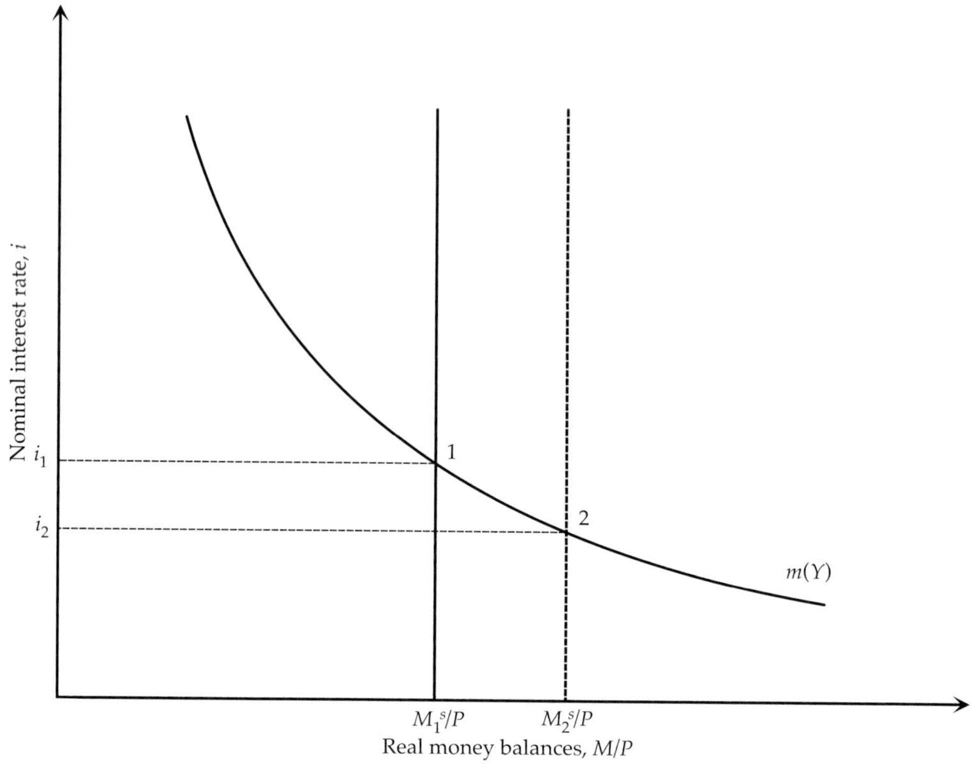

Figure 12.4
The short-run effects of a rise in the money supply: the liquidity effect.

variable that can adjust to equilibrate the money market is the nominal interest rate. The money market equilibrates at the nominal interest rate at which, for given aggregate real income and the price level, the demand for money becomes equal to the supply of money by the central bank.

As shown in figure 12.4, an increase in the money supply causes a reduction in the nominal interest rate, because an increase in the money supply creates excess liquidity in the domestic money market. Households and firms shift this excess liquidity to interest-bearing assets, raising their prices and reducing their yield. This reduces the level of nominal interest rates. In the new equilibrium, given the price level and real income, households and firms voluntarily hold the increased supply of money, as the opportunity cost of holding money (i.e., the nominal interest rate) has fallen.

The negative short-term effect of the money supply on the level of nominal interest rates is often referred to as the *liquidity effect*. The more liquidity the central bank injects into the money market in the form of increasing the money supply, the lower the nominal interest

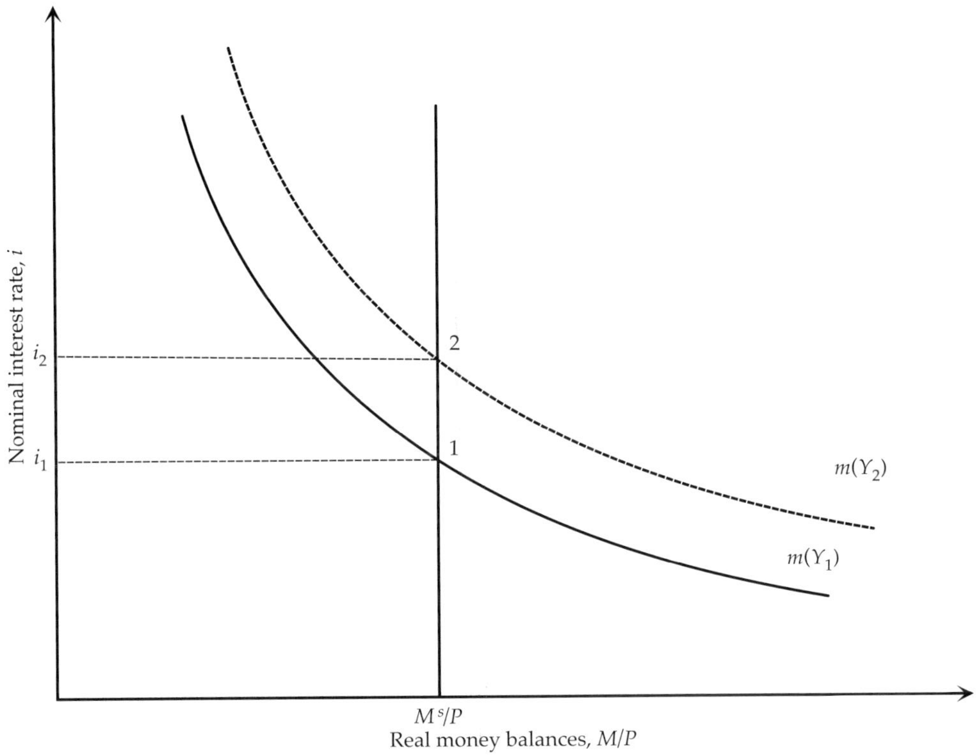

Figure 12.5
The short-run effects of an exogenous rise in real income.

rate will be. Conversely, a decrease in the money supply would reduce liquidity and cause an increase in the nominal interest rate.

Figure 12.5 shows the impact of an increase in money demand. This can be either autonomous (increased demand for liquidity on the part of households and firms) or due to an increase in real income. The latter case is the one shown in figure 12.5.

An increase in real income from Y_1 to Y_2 raises money demand because of the increase in transactions that have to be financed. Given the money supply and the price level, this creates an excess demand for money for transaction purposes. As households and firms try to move out of interest-yielding assets by liquidating them (to acquire greater liquidity for transaction purposes), the prices of these assets fall, leading to higher nominal interest rates. The money market will equilibrate at higher nominal interest rates, which will reduce the excess demand for money arising from the increased transactions.

Similar effects also apply to the case of an autonomous increase in the price level or an autonomous increase in liquidity preference by households and firms. Given the nominal money supply, an autonomous increase in the price level reduces real money balances, requiring an increase in the nominal interest rate for money demand to adjust to the lower supply of real money balances. The same would apply if liquidity preference by households or firms increased, say, because of a shift in preferences or an increase in uncertainty.

Finally, suppose that the central bank follows a policy of pegging the nominal interest rate rather than fixing the money supply. The central bank stabilizes the nominal interest rate at the level i_0, by committing to lend (supply) any quantity of money demanded at this nominal interest rate. In this case, the money supply in the economy is determined by money demand. An increase in the price level or real income (or liquidity preference) causes an increase in the money supply, because the central bank is prepared to provide unlimited liquidity at the nominal interest rate i_0. As shown in figure 12.6, when the central bank follows a policy of stabilization of the nominal interest rate, an increase in money demand automatically leads to a higher money supply and vice versa.

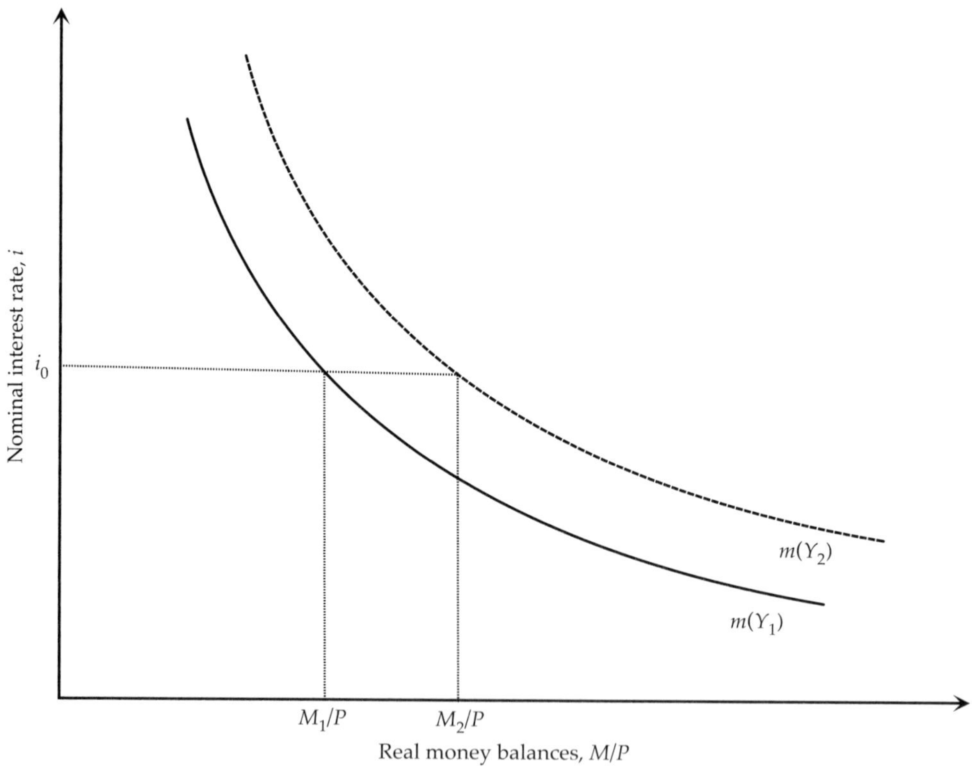

Figure 12.6
Equilibrium in the money market with interest rate pegging.

12.5 The Long-Run Neutrality of Money

Our analysis so far has been based on the simplifying assumption that real income and the price level are exogenously given. For this reason, the only variable that could adjust to equilibrate the money market was the nominal interest rate. This may be realistic in the very short run (as interest rates are generally more flexible than the prices of goods and services and real income), but it is not realistic in the medium and long run.

Beyond the very short run, the price level also adjusts. We can see the direction of this adjustment by rearranging the equilibrium condition in the money market and solving (12.5) with respect to the price level:

$$P = \frac{M^S}{m(Y, i)} \tag{12.6}$$

Equation (12.6) indicates that the price level depends on the money supply and the two factors that determine the demand for money (i.e., aggregate real income and the nominal interest rate).

The price level can rise if there is an increase in the money supply, a decline in real income, an increase in the nominal interest rate, or some other extraneous factor that autonomously reduces the demand for money.

To explain *inflation* in the long run (i.e., continuous increases in the price level), the focus has to be on continuous increases in the money supply. As we saw in chapter 7, in the process of balanced growth, real incomes grow at a steady rate, while real interest rates are stabilized. Nominal interest rates are equal to the real interest rate plus expected inflation. Thus, in a steady state with constant inflation, the nominal interest rate is also constant.

Expressed differently, in the steady state, aggregate real income and the real interest rate are on their balanced growth paths. With constant inflation, nominal interest rates are also constant. Thus, the factors affecting the demand for money are given, and the level of the money supply determines the price level without affecting the evolution of real variables. This property is called the *long-run neutrality of money*.

The proportional long-run relationship between the money supply and the price level has been analyzed since the sixteenth century, on the basis of the quantity theory of money, according to which the quantity of money demanded is proportional to the volume of transactions (aggregate real income) and the price level. Among the first who analyzed the relationship between the money supply and the price level was Copernicus, who, in a memorandum of 1517, used the quantity theory to explain the large increase in the price level in the early sixteenth century, following the import of gold and silver, used in the coinage of money, from the New World. The quantity theory of money has since been refined by many analysts and economists, such as Hume [1752] and Mill [1848], as an explanation of the determination of the price level.

Algebraically, the quantity theory of money took two alternative forms (see Humphrey [1984]). First, the form of the equation of exchange, $MV = PY$, where V is the velocity of money (Newcomb [1885], Fisher [1911]). Alternatively, according to the Cambridge School, it took the form of a money demand function, $M = kPY$, where k is the percentage of income held in the form of money (Pigou [1917], Keynes [1923]). After World War II, the quantity theory of money was restated by Milton Friedman and formed the basis of *monetarism*.[7]

To support the long-run neutrality of money, we should be able to prove that the money supply does not affect real output or real interest rates in the long run. This is both an empirical and a theoretical matter.

The evidence (including that presented in figures 1.12 and 1.13 in chapter 1) generally supports the long-run neutrality of money.

In addition, the long-run neutrality of money applies to all theoretically consistent general equilibrium models with flexible prices. The determinants of the level of equilibrium real income and other real variables are the available resources; technology; preferences; the functioning of markets; and the economic institutions that determine total factor productivity, the productivity of specific factors, and the efficiency of economic exchange. In general equilibrium models, real output and income and other real variables do not depend on the level of the nominal money supply. Although money is an important economic institution, the existence of which guarantees the efficiency of economic exchange, in other respects, the quantity of money is merely a veil, simply determining nominal variables (such as the price level).[8]

In dynamic general equilibrium models, such as the ones examined in chapter 7, we must distinguish between the neutrality and the superneutrality of money. The neutrality of money refers to the effects of a one-off change in the money supply, and the super neutrality of money refers to the effects of a change in the rate of growth of the money supply.

The neutrality of money applies to all dynamic general economic equilibrium models with flexible prices. However, as we saw in chapter 7, the growth rate of the money supply affects inflation and long-term nominal interest rates, and it thus affects real money demand.

In a representative household model, the growth rate of the money supply does not affect any other real variable apart from real money balances. Consequently, it could be argued that the superneutrality of money applies to representative household models. This is the case of the Sidrauski [1967] model analyzed in chapter 7. In overlapping generations (OLG) models, the superneutrality of money does not apply, as the growth rate of the money supply affects savings and the accumulation of capital, and thus all other real variables on the steady

7. See Friedman [1956] and Friedman and Schwartz [1963].

8. See Pigou [1941] for an early exposition of this viewpoint.

growth path. This is the case with the Weil [1987b, 1991] model, also analyzed in chapter 7. Yet, as we saw for the dynamic simulations of the Blanchard-Weil model, even in OLG models, deviations from the superneutrality of money are not significant for output growth and the evolution of other real variables.

12.5.1 Monetary Growth, Inflation, and Nominal Interest Rates in the Long Run

In the same way that a permanent increase in the money supply causes a long-run increase in the price level by the same proportion, monetary growth (in the form of continuous increases in the money supply that exceed the long-run growth rate of output), causes continuous price inflation. Inflation in the long run is determined by the difference between the long-run growth rate of the money supply and the long-run growth rate of money demand, which is equal to the long-run growth rate of output. Thus, as we saw in chapter 7, long-run inflation is determined by

$$\pi = \mu - g - n,$$

where π is inflation, μ the growth rate of the money supply, and $g + n$ the growth rate of output and demand for real money balances, assumed exogenous. This relation is derived by taking the growth rates of prices, money, and output in the money market equilibrium condition (12.5), assuming a unitary elasticity of money demand with respect to real output, an exogenous rate of technical progress and population growth, a constant growth rate of the money supply, and a constant long-run nominal interest rate. These assumption are all compatible with the long-run growth monetary models of chapter 7.

The positive one-to-one relation between monetary growth and inflation implied by the above relation is related to the neutrality of money. A high growth rate of the money supply by the central bank results in long-run inflation without affecting either the growth rate of output or real interest rates.

However, long-run inflation affects the level of nominal interest rates, as investors in bonds and other interest-yielding nominal securities seek to be compensated for the loss in the real value of their assets through inflation. Thus, in an economy with nonzero long-run inflation, nominal interest rates are determined by the Fisher equation, which states that the nominal interest rate is equal to the real rate of return on capital, plus expected inflation. As we saw in chapters 2 and 7, the Fisher equation takes the form

$$i = r + \pi,$$

where r is the equilibrium real interest rate, equal to the real rate of return on capital.

As there is a one-to-one relationship between long-run monetary growth and inflation, so there is a one-to-one relationship between long-run inflation and nominal interest rates in the Fisher equation. Thus, economies with high monetary growth will tend to have high long-run inflation, and those with high long-run inflation will tend to have high long-run nominal interest rates.

12.5.2 The Welfare Cost of Inflation

Economies with high inflation will tend to have high nominal interest rates. High nominal interest rates will result in a reduction in money demand. Thus, such economies will be associated with lower real money balances in the long run. This will result in a loss of consumer surplus from the use of money, which is the welfare cost of inflation.

The welfare cost of inflation was analyzed in chapter 7 with the help of figure 7.1. A higher long-run inflation rate causes nominal interest rates to rise. This reduces money demand and real money balances in the long run, and it creates a welfare cost in the form of loss of consumer surplus. Essentially, in high-inflation economies, households and firms hold smaller quantities of money for their transactions, because of the higher opportunity cost of holding money implied by higher inflation. This forces them to make more transactions to convert interest-yielding assets into money, and thus implies a welfare cost in the form of higher transactions costs.

We shall return to this issue when we discuss high inflation and hyperinflation in section 12.9.1.

12.5.3 The Long-Run Neutrality of Money and Monetary Reforms

An alternative way to think about the neutrality of money is to consider the impact of a very radical change in the money supply. Such radical changes take place in times of monetary reforms. Such historical examples exist, which suggest that, after a monetary reform, the price level adjusts immediately to the new monetary standard.

For example, in May 1954, a radical monetary reform took place in postwar Greece. A new drachma was created, which amounted to 1,000 old drachmas. Essentially this reform was equivalent to a direct reduction in the money supply to one thousandth of the old money supply. As one would expect on the basis of equation (12.6), the price level in Greece fell immediately to one thousandth of the price level before the reform. Something that had a price of 1,500 drachmas before the reform fell in price to 1.5 (new) drachmas after the reform. Nothing else changed, other than the level of prices.

Similar monetary reforms involving the redefinition of the value of a national currency have taken place in the European economies that were affected by hyperinflation in the 1920s, and more recently in many other countries. Mexico redefined the peso in January 1993 by creating a new peso, equal to 1,000 old pesos. The price level fell to one thousandth of the old price level. Turkey redefined the lira in January 2005 by creating a new turkish lira, equal to 1,000,000 old liras, and the price level fell to one millionth of the previous price level. Argentina and Brazil have also gone through a number of such monetary reforms. The creation of the euro was also a monetary reform of this nature, as the euro replaced national currencies of different denominations, causing immediate changes in the price level related to the conversion rates to the new currency for all countries that adopted the euro.

Gradual increases in the money supply in the long run have effects similar to such monetary reforms. The tripling of the money supply over a decade has the same long-run effects as a monetary reform in which a currency unit is replaced with three units of a new currency.

Thus, although a short-term change in the money supply can cause equilibrating changes in nominal interest rates, in the longer term, what adjusts to equilibrate the money market is the price level. Nominal interest rates return to their long-run equilibrium value, determined by the real interest rate plus expected long-run inflation, as suggested by the Fisher equation.

12.6 Money and the Price Level in Dynamic General Equilibrium Models

To shed further light on the determinants of money demand, the role of money, and also the long-run neutrality of money, let us analyze a series of alternative dynamic and dynamic stochastic general equilibrium models, in which prices are flexible and the demand for money results from the optimizing behavior of households and firms. For simplicity, we shall consider *endowment economies*, in which output is exogenously given.

As we shall see, the long-run neutrality of money is a property that characterizes all the models examined, although these models have different properties regarding the role of money and the operation of the money market, the determination of the price level, the liquidity effect, and the implications of interest rate rules.

12.6.1 The Samuelson OLG Model

We start with a simple version of the OLG model of Samuelson [1958], in which the demand for money arises solely from its role as a store of value.

Assume that the economy consists of successive generations of households, each of which lives for two periods. Every household has exogenous income Y_1 in the first period of life and Y_2 in the second period. This income is in the form of a perishable good that cannot be transferred from period to period. The only nonperishable commodity is money, which can be used as a store of value. Normalize the size of each generation to 1 and abstract from population growth, assuming it is equal to zero.

The utility function of the household in the generation born at time t depends on the consumption of goods in the first and second periods of life. Consequently, the household born in period t maximizes the utility function

$$U_t = u(C_{1t}) + \beta u(C_{2t+1}) \tag{12.7}$$

under the constraints

$$P_t C_{1t} + M = P_t Y_1, \tag{12.8}$$

$$P_{t+1} C_{2t+1} = M + P_{t+1} Y_2. \tag{12.9}$$

C_1 is household consumption in the first period; C_2 is consumption in the second period; u is a concave utility function; and $\beta = 1/(1+\rho)$ is the discount factor, where ρ is the pure rate of time preference. In these equations, M is the money supply, carried over by the household from the first to its second period of life. The money supply is equal to the savings of households in their first period of life. Finally, P_t is the money price of the consumption good in period t, and P_{t+1} the money price of the consumption good in period $t+1$.

Assume for simplicity that the household utility function is logarithmic and takes the form

$$\ln C_{1t} + \beta \ln C_{2t+1}. \tag{12.10}$$

From the maximization of (12.10) under the constraints (12.8) and (12.9) it follows that the consumption of the young in period t is determined by

$$P_t C_{1t} = \frac{1}{1+\beta}\left(P_t Y_1 + P_{t+1} Y_2\right). \tag{12.11}$$

The old generation in period t (those who are in their second period of life) consumes all its current income, plus its savings (i.e., the quantity of money carried over from the previous period):

$$P_t C_{2t} = M + P_t Y_2. \tag{12.12}$$

The equilibrium condition in the goods market implies that

$$C_{1t} + C_{2t} = Y_1 + Y_2. \tag{12.13}$$

From (12.11)–(12.13) it thus follows that

$$(1+\beta)M = \beta Y_1 P_t - Y_2 P_{t+1}. \tag{12.14}$$

Solving (12.14) for the demand for real money balances yields

$$\frac{M}{P_t} = \frac{1}{1+\beta}\left(\beta Y_1 - \frac{P_{t+1}}{P_t} Y_2\right). \tag{12.15}$$

From (12.15), it follows that, if there exists a constant equilibrium price level P^*, it should satisfy

$$\frac{M}{P^*} = \frac{1}{1+\beta}\left(\beta Y_1 - Y_2\right). \tag{12.16}$$

The condition for a positive equilibrium price level, and thus a positive demand for real money balances, is that

$$\frac{\beta Y_1}{Y_2} > 1. \tag{12.17}$$

The demand for money, and hence the price level, will be positive only if the discounted first-period income of households exceeds the second-period income. It is only then that savings, and hence money demand, will be positive.

In the Samuelson model, money improves welfare, because it allows households to engage in intertemporal trade and smooth consumption over time. In the absence of money, consumption in each period would have to be equal to current income for all generations. Such an equilibrium would be clearly suboptimal compared to the equilibrium of a monetary economy that allows for consumption smoothing.

To examine the dynamic adjustment of the price level, we can substitute (12.16) in (12.14). The resulting adjustment equation for the price level takes the form

$$P_{t+1} - P^* = \frac{\beta Y_1}{Y_2}(P_t - P^*). \tag{12.18}$$

Because the price level is a non-predetermined variable, the condition for the stability of the dynamic adjustment to the equilibrium price level P^* is (12.17) (i.e., that the root of the difference equation (12.18) is greater than one). Consequently, the condition for the existence of a positive equilibrium price level coincides with the condition for the stability of the equilibrium. If (12.17) is satisfied, then a positive equilibrium price level exists. In addition, the equilibrium is a saddle point (i.e., dynamically stable).

The Samuelson OLG model is one of the simplest dynamic general equilibrium models that generates a positive demand for money as a store of value. The neutrality of money follows immediately. From equation (12.16), an increase in the money supply M will cause an increase in the equilibrium price level P^* by the same percentage. Moreover, in this model, because the price level is a non-predetermined variable, the increase in the price level happens immediately.

However, the Samuelson model also has some weaknesses as a model of money demand. Its first weakness is that the equilibrium just described, which entails a positive demand for money, is not unique. There is a second, suboptimal equilibrium with zero money demand. Thus, the demand for money in this model is extremely fragile. To examine this issue, we can divide both sides of (12.14) by M and solve the resulting equation for M/P_{t+1}:

$$\frac{M}{P_{t+1}} = \frac{M}{P_t}\frac{Y_2}{\beta Y_1 - (1+\beta)(M/P_t)}. \tag{12.19}$$

From (12.19), it follows that there are two equilibria for money demand. One is given by (12.16), and the second is the zero solution:

$$\frac{M}{P^{**}} = 0. \tag{12.20}$$

The equilibrium with a price level P^* is locally stable and well defined, but the system is globally indeterminate, because there are an infinite number of adjustment paths that,

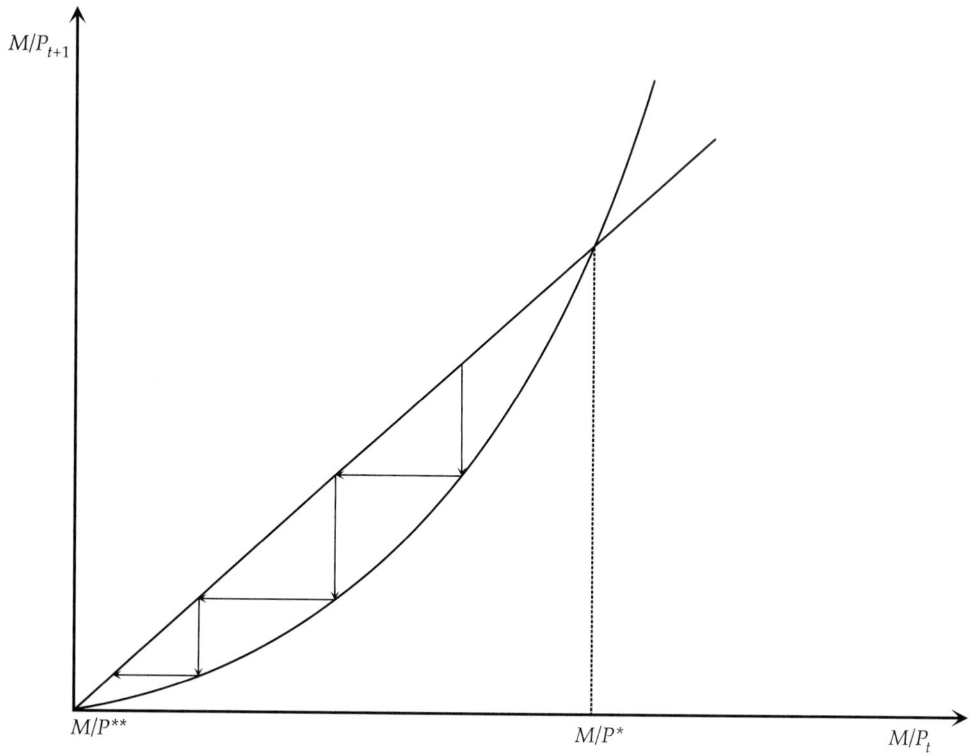

Figure 12.7
Money demand indeterminacy in the Samuelson OLG model.

starting with a price level above P^*, converge to the price level P^{**} (i.e., infinity). This global indeterminacy is analyzed in figure 12.7.

Note that this global indeterminacy does not arise if the income of the second period is equal to zero (i.e., if the exogenous household income only occurs during the first period of life). In this case, (12.15) simplifies to

$$\frac{M}{P_t} = \frac{\beta}{1+\beta} Y_1. \tag{12.21}$$

This implies a unique equilibrium for the price level.

The second major weakness of this model is that it has no alternative store of value. The only outlet for savings in this model is holding money. However, if there is an alternative asset that pays interest (e.g., bonds or capital), then money would be ostracized from this economy, because its only role is as a store of value, and money does not pay interest. In other words, in the presence of bonds or capital, the demand for money would be equal to zero, because bonds and capital are interest-yielding stores of value, in contrast to money.

Two categories of alternative dynamic general equilibrium models generate a positive demand for money and do not have the weaknesses of the Samuelson OLG model. These two categories, which were first mentioned in chapter 7, are models in which money enters the utility function of households (called money in the utility function models), and models in which economic transactions can only take place through the mediation of money (called cash in advance models).

12.6.2 Money in the Utility Function of a Representative Household

We have already introduced this class of models in the context of the money and growth models in chapter 7. This class of models originates with Patinkin [1956], Sidrauski [1967], and Brock [1974, 1975]. Unlike the Samuelson [1958] OLG model, in this class of models, money can coexist with interest-yielding assets (such as bonds), because it yields direct utility to households, due to its liquidity properties, which facilitate economic transactions.

We will focus on money demand in an endowment economy in which, as in the Samuelson model, real income is exogenous, and there is no capital.

A representative household has an intertemporal expected utility function of the form

$$U_t = E_t \sum_{s=t}^{\infty} \beta^{s-t} u\left(C_s, \frac{M_s}{P_s}\right), \tag{12.22}$$

where E_t is the mathematical expectations operator, on the basis of information available in period t; C is real consumption of goods and services; M is the quantity of nominal money balances held by the household; P is the price level; and u is a quasi-concave periodic utility function, which is homogeneous of degree one in its two arguments, consumption and real money balances.

The representative household maximizes its intertemporal utility function under the sequence of budget constraints

$$C_t + \frac{M_t}{P_t} + \frac{B_t}{P_t} = Y_t - T_t + \frac{M_{t-1}}{P_t} + \frac{(1+i_{t-1})B_{t-1}}{P_t}, \tag{12.23}$$

where Y is the real income of the household, assumed exogenous; T is per capita taxes net of transfers; B is the nominal value of bonds held by the household; and i the nominal interest rate.

The Lagrange function corresponding to this problem can be written as

$$E_t \sum_{s=t}^{\infty} \beta^{s-t} \left(u\left(C_s, \frac{M_s}{P_s}\right) + \right.$$
$$\left. + \lambda_s \left(\frac{M_{s-1}}{P_s} + \frac{(1+i_{s-1})B_{s-1}}{P_s} + Y_s - T_s - C_s - \frac{M_s}{P_s} - \frac{B_s}{P_s} \right) \right). \tag{12.24}$$

The first-order conditions for a maximum with respect to C, B, and M imply

$$\lambda_t = \frac{\partial u}{\partial C_t}, \tag{12.25}$$

$$\frac{\lambda_t}{P_t} = \beta(1+i_t)E_t\left(\frac{\lambda_{t+1}}{P_{t+1}}\right), \tag{12.26}$$

$$\frac{\lambda_t}{P_t} = \frac{1}{P_t}\frac{\partial u}{\partial M_t} + \beta E_t\left(\frac{\lambda_{t+1}}{P_{t+1}}\right). \tag{12.27}$$

These first-order conditions have the usual interpretations. Equation (12.25) is the static first-order condition, according to which the marginal utility of consumption in any period should equal the "shadow value" of marginal savings λ. Essentially, the household should be indifferent at the margin between consumption and savings.

Equation (12.26) is the dynamic first-order condition that the total expected real return on savings should equal the pure rate of time preference of the household. This can be seen if we take the logarithm of (12.26), which yields

$$i_t - E_t(\ln P_{t+1} - \ln P_t) + E_t(\ln \lambda_{t+1} - \ln \lambda_t) \simeq -\ln \beta \simeq \rho. \tag{12.28}$$

The left-hand side of (12.28) is the total expected real return on savings, taking into account expected inflation and expected capital gains from a change in λ. The right-hand side is the pure rate of time preference of the household, because $\beta = 1/(1+\rho)$.

Finally, (12.27) is the dynamic first-order condition that the marginal utility of real money balances equals the difference of the pure rate of time preference from the expected real return of money, taking into account expected inflation and expected capital gains from a change in λ.

From these three first-order conditions, we can derive the demand for money. Assume that the per period utility function takes the form

$$u = \ln\left(\gamma(C_t)^{\varepsilon} + (1-\gamma)\left(\frac{M_t}{P_t}\right)^{\varepsilon}\right)^{\frac{1}{\varepsilon}}, \tag{12.29}$$

where $1/(1-\varepsilon)$ is the elasticity of substitution between consumption and real money balances. Under this assumption, using the first-order conditions (12.25)–(12.27), the demand for money function takes the form

$$\frac{M_t}{P_t} = \left(\frac{\gamma}{1-\gamma}\frac{i_t}{1+i_t}\right)^{-\frac{1}{1-\varepsilon}} C_t. \tag{12.30}$$

The money demand function depends negatively on the nominal interest rate and positively on total consumption. The negative dependence on the nominal interest rate arises because, with higher nominal interest rates, the opportunity cost of holding money compared to bonds is higher, which reduces the demand for money.

As in the model of Samuelson, for given income, consumption, and nominal interest rate, a one-off increase in the money supply leads to an increase in the price level by the same percentage. As can be seen from (12.30), the neutrality of money holds in this model as well.

12.6.3 Cash in Advance in a Representative Household Model

The basic idea of models in which money is the only means of payment is that to complete any economic transaction, payment must be in the form of money (in particular, cash), which the buyer holds in advance of the completion of the transaction. This idea is due to Clower [1967], and its integration into general equilibrium models leads to a class of models known as *cash in advance models*.

The restriction that the transaction must be paid with money held in advance imposes a cost of holding money, because otherwise, economic agents could hold an interest-yielding asset, such as bonds.

The cash in advance constraint can take several forms, depending on the assumptions made about the sequencing of transactions. A simple traditional way of expressing this constraint is given by

$$P_tC_t \leq M_{t-1}, \tag{12.31}$$

where M_{t-1} is the stock of money accumulated until the end of period $t-1$. The problem with this version of the constraint is that someone who enters the economy in period t would not be able to consume at all, because she holds no money.

An alternative hypothesis is that each period consists of two different subperiods. In the first subperiod, agents visit a financial market (say, a bank), where they can swap interest-bearing assets with money, or borrow cash. In the second subperiod, they deal in markets for goods and services, which are liable to the cash in advance constraint (see Lucas [1980, 1982] and Helpman [1981]). This allows the following two-part form of the constraint:

$$A_t = M_t + B_t, \tag{12.32}$$

$$P_tC_t \leq M_t, \tag{12.33}$$

where A is the stock of all nominal assets of the household, M is nominal money balances and B is the value of nominal bonds held by the household.

In the second subperiod, households also receive their exogenous real income Y and pay their taxes (net of transfers) T. As a result, the nominal assets of the household in the beginning of the following period are determined by

$$A_{t+1} = M_t + (1+i_t)B_t + P_t(Y_t - T_t - C_t) = (1+i_t)A_t - i_tM_t + P_t(Y_t - T_t - C_t). \tag{12.34}$$

The representative household thus maximizes the intertemporal expected utility function

$$U_t = E_t \sum_{s=t}^{\infty} \beta^{s-t} u(C_s), \tag{12.35}$$

under the sequence of budget constraints (12.34) and the cash in advance constraint (12.33). The Lagrange function is given by

$$E_t \sum_{s=t}^{\infty} \beta^{s-t} \left(u(C_s) + \nu_s \left(\frac{M_s}{P_s} - C_s \right) + \right.$$
$$\left. + \lambda_s \left((1+i_s)\frac{A_t}{P_t} + Y_s - T_s - C_s - i_s \frac{M_t}{P_t} - \frac{A_{s+1}}{P_s} \right) \right), \tag{12.36}$$

where ν_s and λ_s are the two sequences of Lagrange multipliers.

The first-order conditions for a maximum imply that

$$\lambda_t + \nu_t = \frac{\partial u}{\partial C_t} = u'(C_t), \tag{12.37}$$

$$\frac{\lambda_t}{P_t} = \beta E_t \left((1+i_{t+1}) \frac{\lambda_{t+1}}{P_{t+1}} \right), \tag{12.38}$$

$$\nu_t = \lambda_t i. \tag{12.39}$$

The interpretation of these first-order conditions is straightforward. Equation (12.37) is the static first-order condition that on the optimal path, the marginal utility of consumption must be equal to the shadow value of savings λ plus the shadow value of money ν. The shadow value of money results from the restriction that cash in advance is required to buy consumer goods.

Equation (12.38) is the dynamic first-order condition that the total expected real return on savings, including expected inflation and expected capital gains, equals the pure rate of time preference of the household.

Finally, (12.39) is the static first-order condition stipulating that the shadow value of money equals the shadow value of savings times the opportunity cost of holding money, which is none other than the nominal rate (because money pays no interest).

Combining (12.37)–(12.39), one gets

$$\frac{u'(C_t)}{P_t} = \beta(1+i_t)E_t \left(\frac{u'(C_{t+1})}{P_{t+1}} \right). \tag{12.40}$$

Equation (12.40) is a monetary form of the usual Euler equation for consumption in this model, in which consumption requires money payments in advance. Assuming logarithmic preferences, we have

$$\frac{\partial u}{\partial C_t} = \frac{1}{C_t}. \tag{12.41}$$

Under the assumption of logarithmic preference, (12.40) can be written as

$$\frac{1}{P_t C_t} = \beta(1+i_t)E_t\left(\frac{1}{P_{t+1}C_{t+1}}\right). \tag{12.42}$$

The cash in advance constraint implies that

$$\frac{M_t}{P_t} = C_t, \tag{12.43}$$

which is a version of the simple quantity equation. Equation (12.43) determines the demand for money function in this model. Monetary neutrality holds in this model as well.

Finally, substituting (12.43) in (12.42), we get

$$\frac{1}{1+i_t} = \beta E_t\left(\frac{M_t}{M_{t+1}}\right). \tag{12.44}$$

The nominal interest rate depends positively on the pure rate of time preference ρ (which determines β) and the expected rate of change of the money supply (which determines expected inflation).

12.6.4 Cash in Advance in an OLG Model

We now examine the implications for money demand of a cash in advance constraint in a variant of the Samuelson OLG models. In this model, money is both a means of payment and a store of value, unlike the original Samuelson model, in which money was only a store of value.[9]

The household born at the beginning of period t lives for two periods, period t and period $t+1$. She receives income Y_t in the first period of life, and consumes in both periods.

The intertemporal utility function of the household is given by

$$U_t = \ln C_{1t} + \beta \ln C_{2t+1}. \tag{12.45}$$

In each period of life, the household is subject to a cash in advance constraint of the form

$$P_t C_{1t} \leq M_{1t},$$

$$P_{t+1} C_{2t+1} \leq M_{2t+1}. \tag{12.46}$$

9. In chapter 7 we analyzed the Blanchard-Weil OLG growth model, with money in the utility function of households, and showed that in such a model, the superneutrality of money does not hold.

Aggregate consumption and the money supply in each period are given by

$$\begin{aligned} C_t &= C_{1t} + C_{2t}, \\ M_t &= M_{1t} + M_{2t}. \end{aligned} \tag{12.47}$$

Total assets of households are equal to A, and we assume that young households are born with zero assets. As a result, all assets belong to the old households. For simplicity, assume that taxes T are only paid by young households out of the exogenous income Y.

Given that old households receive no current income, their consumption is equal to their assets:

$$C_{2t} = \frac{A_t}{P_t}. \tag{12.48}$$

Note that because of the cash in advance constraint, the old households need to convert their assets into money to purchase consumer goods.

Given that young households hold no assets, they need to borrow at the current interest rate and to convert their loan into money, in order to finance their consumption. As a result, for young households, the following constraints must hold:

$$\begin{aligned} M_{1t} &= P_t C_{1t}, \\ B_{1t} &= -P_t C_{1t}. \end{aligned} \tag{12.49}$$

The assets of young households at the end of their first period of life will be equal to

$$A_{t+1} = M_{1t} + (1+i_t)B_{1t} + P_t\left(Y_t - T_t - C_{1t}\right) = P_t\left(Y_t - T_t - (1+i_t)C_{1t}\right). \tag{12.50}$$

From (12.48) and (12.50), it follows that

$$C_{2t+1} = \frac{A_{t+1}}{P_{t+1}} = \frac{P_t\left(Y_t - T_t - (1+i_t)C_{1t}\right)}{P_{t+1}}. \tag{12.51}$$

Introducing (12.51) in the utility function (12.45), we find that young households will choose consumption in their first period of life to maximize

$$U_t = \ln C_{1t} + \beta \ln\left(\frac{P_t\left(Y_t - T_t - (1+i_t)C_{1t}\right)}{P_{t+1}}\right). \tag{12.52}$$

From the first-order conditions for the maximization of (12.52), it follows that

$$C_{1t} = \frac{1}{1+\beta}\frac{Y_t - T_t}{1+i_t}. \tag{12.53}$$

From (12.48) and (12.53), aggregate consumption is given by

$$C_t = C_{1t} + C_{2t} = \frac{1}{1+\beta}\frac{Y_t - T_t}{1+i_t} + \frac{A_t}{P_t}. \tag{12.54}$$

From the equilibrium condition in the market for goods and services, we have

$$C_t = Y_t = \frac{1}{1+\beta}\frac{Y_t - T_t}{1+i_t} + \frac{A_t}{P_t}. \tag{12.55}$$

Given the cash in advance constraints (12.46), it also follows that

$$M_t = P_t Y_t. \tag{12.56}$$

Money demand is thus determined by a simple quantity equation, and the neutrality of money holds in this model as well. Substituting (12.55) in (12.56), we can solve for the price level and the nominal interest rate.

12.7 Nominal and Real Interest Rates and the Money Supply

We next turn to the determinants of the nominal interest rate in the general equilibrium models presented. We will concentrate on three of the models: the model with money in the utility function of a representative household, the representative household model with a cash in advance constraint, and the OLG model with a cash in advance constraint. In all three models, money demand is positive, even if consumers have the option of holding interest-bearing assets, such as bonds.

12.7.1 Money in the Utility Function of a Representative Household

The money demand function in this model is given by (12.30). For simplicity and comparability with the other two models, let us consider the case of logarithmic preferences ($\varepsilon = 0$).

With logarithmic preferences, the first-order conditions for the maximization of the utility function of the representative household are given by

$$\lambda_t = \frac{\gamma}{C_t}, \tag{12.57}$$

$$\frac{\lambda_t}{P_t} = \beta(1+i_t)E_t\left(\frac{\lambda_{t+1}}{P_{t+1}}\right), \tag{12.58}$$

$$\frac{\lambda_t}{P_t} = \frac{1-\gamma}{M_t} + \beta E_t\left(\frac{\lambda_{t+1}}{P_{t+1}}\right). \tag{12.59}$$

From (12.57) and (12.58) it follows that

$$\frac{1}{P_t C_t} = \beta(1+i_t) E_t \left(\frac{1}{P_{t+1} C_{t+1}} \right) \tag{12.60}$$

Equation (12.60) is the Euler equation for consumption in a representative household economy with money.

From (12.57) and (12.59) it follows that

$$\frac{1}{P_t C_t} = \frac{1-\gamma}{\gamma} \frac{1}{M_t} + \beta E_t \left(\frac{1}{P_{t+1} C_{t+1}} \right). \tag{12.61}$$

The rational expectations solution of (12.61) takes the form

$$\frac{1}{P_t C_t} = \frac{1-\gamma}{\gamma} \sum_{s=t}^{\infty} \beta^{s-t} E_t \left(\frac{1}{M_s} \right). \tag{12.62}$$

Given that $C_t = Y_t = Y$, which is exogenous, (12.62) determines the equilibrium price level as a function of expectations about the future evolution of the money supply.

Substituting (12.62) in the money demand equation (12.30) for $\varepsilon = 0$ and solving for the nominal interest rate yields

$$\frac{1+i_t}{i_t} = \frac{\gamma}{1-\gamma} \frac{M_t}{P_t C_t} = \sum_{s=t}^{\infty} \beta^{s-t} E_t \left(\frac{M_t}{M_s} \right). \tag{12.63}$$

The nominal interest rate is determined by the current money supply and expectations about the future development of the money supply, discounted at a rate that depends on the pure rate of time preference of the household.

Assume that the expected growth rate of the money supply is constant and equal to μ. From (12.63), we get

$$\begin{aligned} \frac{1+i_t}{i_t} &= \sum_{s=t}^{\infty} \beta^{s-t} \left(\frac{1}{1+\mu} \right)^{s-t} = \\ &= \sum_{s=t}^{\infty} \left(\frac{1}{(1+\rho)\,(1+\mu)} \right)^{s-t} = \frac{(1+\rho)(1+\mu)}{(1+\rho)(1+\mu)-1}. \end{aligned} \tag{12.64}$$

From (12.64), it follows that

$$i_t = (1+\rho)(1+\mu) - 1 \simeq \rho + \mu. \tag{12.65}$$

Consequently, from (12.65), the higher the growth rate of money supply μ is, the higher will be the nominal interest rate i, as the expected future inflation rate will be higher.

Note that the steady state real interest rate in this model is equal to ρ. For $\mu = 0$, (12.65) implies $i = \rho$. In this case, because the expected future inflation rate is equal to zero, the nominal interest rate equals the equilibrium real interest rate (i.e., the pure rate of time preference of the representative household).

Note that if $\mu = -\rho/(1+\rho)$ (i.e., if the money supply is reduced at this rate), the nominal interest rate is driven to zero. As argued by Friedman [1969], a zero nominal interest rate has attractive properties and, in the absence of other distortions, leads to the optimum quantity of money, in the sense that the opportunity cost of holding money is equal to its marginal cost of production, which is equal to zero.[10]

12.7.2 Cash in Advance in a Representative Household Model

In the representative household model in which money demand results from the cash in advance constraint, under the assumption of logarithmic preferences, the nominal interest rate is determined by equation (12.44). Assuming that the growth rate of money supply is equal to μ, (12.44) implies

$$\frac{1}{1+i_t} = \beta\left(\frac{1}{1+\mu}\right) = \frac{1}{(1+\rho)(1+\mu)}. \tag{12.66}$$

From (12.66), the nominal interest rate is determined by (12.65), just as in the representative household model with money in the utility function.

Consequently, both representative household models of a monetary economy—the money in the utility function model and the cash in advance model—make identical predictions concerning the determination of nominal and real interest rates.

12.7.3 Cash in Advance in an OLG Model

Finally, we examine the determination of nominal and real interest rates in the Samuelson OLG model with a cash in advance constraint. From (12.55) and (12.56), it follows that

$$1+i_t = \frac{1}{1+\beta}\frac{Y_t - T_t}{Y_t}\frac{M_t}{M_t - A_t}, \tag{12.67}$$

where $M_t - A_t = P_t C_{1t} > 0$. The nominal interest rate depends only on the current stock of the money supply and not on its expected future increase.

From (12.67), it follows that

$$\frac{\partial i_t}{\partial M_t} = -\frac{1}{1+\beta}\frac{Y_t - T_t}{Y_t}\frac{A_t}{(M_t - A_t)^2} < 0. \tag{12.68}$$

An increase of the current money supply reduces the nominal interest rate, as it increases liquidity in the economy. The effect is similar to the liquidity effect, which we discussed in section 12.3 when analyzing the short-term effects of an increase in the money supply.

10. See Woodford [1990] for a survey of the evolution of the literature on this issue.

12.7.4 The Liquidity Effect in Representative Household Models

The liquidity effect is not so obvious in representative household models. It occurs only as a result of temporary changes in the money supply. This is illustrated by examining the equations for determining the nominal interest rate: (12.63) for the model with money in the utility function and (12.44) for the model with the cash in advance constraint.

Let us confine our analysis to the latter. The nominal interest rate in the cash in advance representative household model is determined by

$$\frac{1}{1+i_t} = \beta E_t\left(\frac{M_t}{M_{t+1}}\right).$$

If there is a temporary increase of the current money supply, which does not affect the expectation of the future money supply, then the impact on the nominal interest rate is given by

$$\frac{\partial i_t}{\partial M_t} = -\frac{1}{M_t E_t\left(\frac{M_t}{M_{t+1}}\right)} < 0. \tag{12.69}$$

Equation (12.69) shows that there is a liquidity effect for temporary increases in the money supply. Similar properties apply to the model with money in the utility function of a representative household (equation (12.63)).

In contrast, if there is a permanent increase in the money supply, which does not affect the expected ratio between M_t and M_{t+1}, then this increase has no impact on the nominal interest rate. There is no liquidity effect for permanent increases in the money supply in representative household models.

Finally, for an increase in the money supply that increases the expected ratio between M_{t+1} and M_t, then not only is there no liquidity effect, but the opposite occurs (i.e., a positive impact on the nominal interest rate by an increase in the money supply), because an increase in the current money supply signals even higher increases in the future money supply.

For example, assume that the growth rate of the money supply follows a linear first-order, stationary autoregressive stochastic process of the form

$$\ln\left(\frac{M_t}{M_{t-1}}\right) = \mu(1-\lambda) + \lambda \ln\left(\frac{M_{t-1}}{M_{t-2}}\right) + \varepsilon_t, \tag{12.70}$$

where $0 < \lambda < 1$, and ε_t is a white noise process. It is simple to prove that a positive disturbance ε_t leads to higher nominal interest rates, because the disturbance causes a temporary increase in the expected ratio between M_{t+1} and M_t. Consequently, a positive (albeit temporary) disturbance in the growth rate of the money supply leads to higher nominal interest rates. The reason is that it increases the expected future increase in the money supply and thus expected future inflation. This effect is often referred to in literature as the liquidity puzzle.

The liquidity puzzle is not the only paradoxical property of money demand models of a representative household. A second paradox is the indeterminacy of the price level when the central bank pegs the nominal interest rates instead of the money supply. This has led to large literature on interest rate pegging.

12.8 Interest Rate Pegging and Price Level Indeterminacy

In the representative household models with money in the utility function and cash-in-advance constraints (such as the ones we have analyzed so far), one can show that if monetary policy pegs the nominal interest rate, then the price level and the money supply cannot be determined uniquely. In contrast, under a policy that pegs the money supply, the price level and its rate of change are uniquely determined.

This result is known as *price level indeterminacy* and was first alluded to by Wicksell [1898] in the context of a static monetary model, and, more recently, by Sargent and Wallace [1975], in the context of an IS-LM macro model with rational expectations. The same indeterminacy applies in the representative household dynamic general equilibrium models with money that we have examined so far. For simplicity, we will assume that there is no uncertainty and that the nominal interest rate is pegged by the central bank to a constant level i_0.

12.8.1 Interest Rate Pegging and Price Level Indeterminacy in Representative Household Models

From the money demand function of the representative household model with money in the utility function, the money demand equation implies that

$$\frac{M_t}{P_t} = \left(\frac{\gamma}{1-\gamma}\frac{i_0}{1+i_0}\right)^{-\frac{1}{1-\varepsilon}} Y_t. \tag{12.71}$$

In (12.71) we have imposed the equilibrium condition in the goods market: $C_t = Y_t$. Given that real income Y_t is exogenous, this condition is satisfied for an infinite number of combinations of M_t and P_t. For given Y_t, if it is satisfied for M_0 and P_0, it is also satisfied for λM_0 and λP_0, for any λ. Thus, both the money supply and the price level are indeterminate.

The reason for the indeterminacy is that, under interest rate pegging, no monetary anchor can determine the price level, as in the case where the central bank determines the money supply. Because the central bank is committed to providing unlimited liquidity at a nominal interest rate i_0, the money supply is determined by the demand for money. Neither the price level nor the money supply can be identified uniquely by the demand for money, as the latter is a demand for real money balances. The equilibrium condition for money demand can be satisfied with both high prices and a consequent high stock of money, and with low prices and a consequent low stock of money (i.e., virtually for any level of prices).[11]

The same problem arises in the cash in advance representative household model. From the Euler equation for consumption (12.42) and the goods market equilibrium condition $C_t = Y_t$ for every t, it follows that

$$P_{t+1}Y_{t+1} = \beta(1+i_0)P_tY_t. \tag{12.72}$$

Because income is exogenous and the nominal interest rate is fixed, (12.72) is satisfied for any price level. Multiplying P_t and P_{t+1} by a coefficient λ means that (12.72) continues to be satisfied, because it is linearly homogeneous in prices. The price level is thus indeterminate.

Again, the reason for the indeterminacy is that, under interest rate pegging, there is no monetary anchor that can determine the price level, as in the case where the central bank determines the money supply. Neither the price level nor the money supply can be identified uniquely under interest rate pegging. The equilibrium condition for consumption can be satisfied with both high prices and a consequent high stock of money, and with low prices and a consequent low stock of money (i.e., virtually for any level of prices).

This, indeterminacy is especially problematic, because the key monetary instrument used by most central banks has not been the money supply, but nominal interest rates. How is it possible for the price level to be determinate if interest rates are the key monetary instrument of central banks?

12.8.2 The Wicksell Solution to the Problem of Price Level Indeterminacy

The main solution of this problem was provided by the monetary economist who first realized its existence, namely Wicksell [1898, p. 189]. Wicksell proposed that

> So long as prices remain unaltered, the banks' rate of interest is to remain unaltered. If prices rise, the rate of interest is to be raised; and if prices fall, the rate of interest is to be lowered; and the rate of interest is henceforth to be maintained at its new level until a further movement of prices calls for a further change in one direction or the other.

Wicksell's interest rate rule can be written as

$$i_t = \rho + \phi\left(\frac{P_t - P_0}{P_0}\right), \tag{12.73}$$

11. As Sargent and Wallace [1975] were the first to recognize, this indeterminacy was first alluded to by Wicksell [1898], in the context of a static monetary model with flexible prices.

where P_0 is the target price level of the central bank, and ϕ a positive coefficient denoting the response of the central bank to deviations of the actual price level from the target price level.[12]

Substituting (12.73) for i_0 in (12.72), assuming that output is constant and taking logs, we get

$$\ln P_t = \frac{1}{1+\phi}\ln P_{t+1} + \frac{\phi}{1+\phi}\ln P_0. \tag{12.74}$$

If ϕ is positive, as Wicksell proposed, then (12.74) is a stable difference equation that fully determines the price level. The price level is uniquely defined, as it adjusts immediately to P_0, the target price level of the central bank. If ϕ is equal to zero, then we have price level indeterminacy, as in equation (12.72).[13]

Wicksell's rule is a good example of a stabilizing interest rate rule that makes the nominal interest rate a function of endogenous variables, such as the price level, about which the central bank is concerned. The nominal interest rate is not pegged but is a positive function of the price level. Such an interest rate rule does not result is price level indeterminacy. Instead, it stabilizes the price level around the target price level of the central bank.

Alternative ways to solve the problem of price level indeterminacy when the policy instrument of the central bank is the nominal interest rate have subsequently been proposed: inflation targeting rules; nominal income rules (McCallum [1988]); and more recently, the Taylor [1993] rule, which is a generalization of the Wicksell rule. We shall examine the properties of such rules, and in particular the Taylor rule, in chapters 14–17 on aggregate fluctuations and in chapter 20 on monetary policy.

12.8.3 The Fiscal Theory of the Price Level

One theoretical development worth mentioning in this context is the *fiscal theory of the price level*, proposed in Leeper [1991], Sims [1994], and Woodford [1994, 1995]. This theory argues that even if monetary policy rules do not suffice to determine the price level, the price level can be determined as the level ensuring that nominal government debt does not follow an explosive path. This requirement is sufficient in such models to determine the price level. The path for the price level ensures a path of nominal government debt that satisfies the intertemporal budget constraint of the government.

12. In fact, Wicksell suggested that the interest rate should change when the price level deviates from the target price level, as he was fully aware of the difficulties in calculating the natural rate of interest. In our treatment here, it is assumed that the natural real interest rate is constant and fully known. As will be seen in chapter 20, uncertainty about the natural rate of interest (or indeed, other variables) entails additional difficulties for monetary policy.

13. The same analysis can be carried out in the context of equation (12.71), the money market equilibrium condition of the representative household model with money in the utility function.

12.8.4 The Pigou Effect and Price Level Determinacy in OLG Models

Note that the problem of price level indeterminacy under interest rate pegging does not arise in OLG models. Unlike the representative household model, where both the current and the future price level are non-predetermined variables, in the OLG models, the price level is determined through the predetermined nominal financial assets of old households. These function as a monetary anchor and help determine the price level.

For example, in the cash in advance version of the Samuelson OLG model, the equilibrium condition in the goods and services market is given by (12.55). Assuming that the nominal interest rate is pegged at i_0 by the central bank, one can solve (12.55) for the price level:

$$P_t = \frac{(1+\beta)(1+i_0)A_t}{(\beta+(1+\beta)i_0)Y_t + T_t}. \tag{12.75}$$

The price level is uniquely defined. Because consumption depends on the real value of financial assets of the old households and these assets are positive, the price level is determined and positive, regardless of the interest rate policy of the central bank.

In static ad hoc monetary models, such dependence of consumption on the financial wealth of households has been called the Pigou effect (see Pigou [1943]), or the real balance effect (see Patinkin [1956]). As Sargent and Wallace [1975] indicated in their original analysis of price level indeterminacy, in the presence of a Pigou or real balance effect, the problem of price level indeterminacy does not arise, even if the central bank pegs the nominal interest rate at a constant level, because nominal financial assets anchor the price level.

12.9 Money Growth, Seigniorage, and Inflation

If the growth rate of the money supply eventually translates into higher inflation, why don't governments and central banks keep the growth rate of the money supply low and stable to tackle the problem of inflation?

The answer is that governments often have other policy motives besides tackling inflation. Perhaps the most important incentive for the issuance of new money by governments is to finance expenditure that they cannot (or do not wish to) finance through other methods, such as higher taxes or higher government debt.

The main cause of all episodes of high inflation or hyperinflation appears to have been the need of governments to use revenue from money creation (seigniorage) to finance wars and war reparations, revolutions, extraordinary costs related to natural disasters, or sudden reductions in their capacity to borrow from financial markets or to raise revenue from taxes and customs revenues.

In this section, we explore the relationship between the growth rate of the money supply, inflation, and the needs of governments to raise revenue through seigniorage. We examine both the case in which the required income from seigniorage can be raised on the balanced growth path (which results in sustained high inflation), and the case in which the required revenue from seigniorage is so high that it cannot be raised on the balanced growth path. In the latter case, the economy is driven into hyperinflation.

The generally accepted definition of hyperinflation is due to Cagan [1956]. Cagan [1956, p. 25] defined a period of hyperinflation as one "beginning in the month in which the rise in prices exceeds 50% and as ending in the month before the monthly rise in prices drops below that amount and stays below for at least a year."

The first modern periods of hyperinflation occurred in Europe in the aftermath of World War I, as well as during and in the aftermath of World War II.

In the past 40 years, very high inflation rates and hyperinflation reappeared in some Latin American countries, some transition economies after the collapse of the Soviet Union, and in some war-torn countries in Asia and Africa. Moreover, without reaching hyperinflation, many countries have experienced high inflation (from 100% to 1,000% per year) for quite long periods.[14]

12.9.1 Relations between Monetary Growth, Seigniorage, and Inflation

To study the relation between the rate of growth of the money supply, inflation and revenue from seigniorage, we start from the general money demand function (12.2). In equilibrium, the demand for money equals the supply of money, so it follows that

$$\frac{M}{P} = m(Y, i). \tag{12.76}$$

To simplify matters, let us use a linear logarithmic form of the money demand function m:

$$\frac{M}{P} = \kappa Y e^{-\eta i}, \tag{12.77}$$

where κ is a constant, e is the base of natural logarithms, and $\eta > 0$ is the semi-elasticity of money demand with respect to the nominal interest rate i.

The nominal interest rate is defined by the Fisher equation

$$i = r + \pi^e, \tag{12.78}$$

where r is the real interest rate, and π^e is expected inflation.

Real output Y is considered exogenous and is assumed to grow at a rate $g + n > 0$. The rate of growth of the nominal money supply M is equal to $\mu > 0$.

Under these assumptions, inflation on the balanced growth path is determined by

$$\pi = \mu - (g + n). \tag{12.79}$$

14. Apart from the study of Cagan [1956], for the hyperinflation episodes of the interwar period and World War II, see Sargent [1982] on how four hyperinflation episodes ended. More recent episodes of high inflation and hyperinflation have been discussed by Sachs and Larrain [1993, chap. 23] and Fischer et al. [2002].

Assuming rational expectations, we can substitute (12.79) in (12.78) and the resulting equation in (12.77). The money demand function can thus be written as

$$\frac{M}{P} = \kappa Y e^{-\eta(r+\mu-(g+n))}. \tag{12.80}$$

To further simplify matters, assume that the golden rule applies on the balanced growth path, which implies that $r = g + n$. Under this additional assumption, (12.80) simplifies to

$$\frac{M}{P} = \kappa Y e^{-\eta\mu}. \tag{12.81}$$

Because of the golden rule, the nominal interest rate is equal to the rate of growth of the money supply μ.[15]

We can now define *seigniorage revenue* S. This is equal to the real resources that the government commands by issuing additional money, and buying goods and services. Seigniorage is thus given by

$$S = \frac{\dot{M}}{P} = \frac{\dot{M}}{M}\frac{M}{P} = \mu\frac{M}{P} = \mu\kappa Y e^{-\eta\mu}, \tag{12.82}$$

where S denotes total seigniorage revenue from money creation. The money demand equation (12.81) has been substituted in the right-hand side of (12.82).

As a proportion of total output, seigniorage revenue is defined by

$$s = \frac{S}{Y} = \mu\frac{M}{PY} = \mu\kappa e^{-\eta\mu}, \tag{12.83}$$

where s is seigniorage revenue relative to total output.

Taking the first derivative of (12.83) with respect to μ, we can see how the seigniorage to output ratio depends on the growth rate of the money supply:

$$\frac{\partial s}{\partial \mu} = (1 - \eta\mu)\kappa e^{-\eta\mu}. \tag{12.84}$$

Equation (12.84) is positive for as long as the growth rate of the money supply μ is smaller than $1/\eta$. When μ exceeds $1/\eta$, the change in seigniorage revenue as a proportion of total output becomes negative when μ increases further. For $\mu > 1/\eta$, a further increase in the growth rate of the money supply has a negative effect on government revenue from money

15. Alternatively, we could assume that the real interest rate equals $\rho + g$, as would apply on the balanced growth path of a representative household model with logarithmic preferences. In this case, the nominal interest rate would be equal to $\rho - n + \mu$. The results of the analysis would not change, as in periods of high inflation and hyperinflation, the growth rate of the money supply is much higher than the difference between the pure rate of time preference ρ and the population growth rate n.

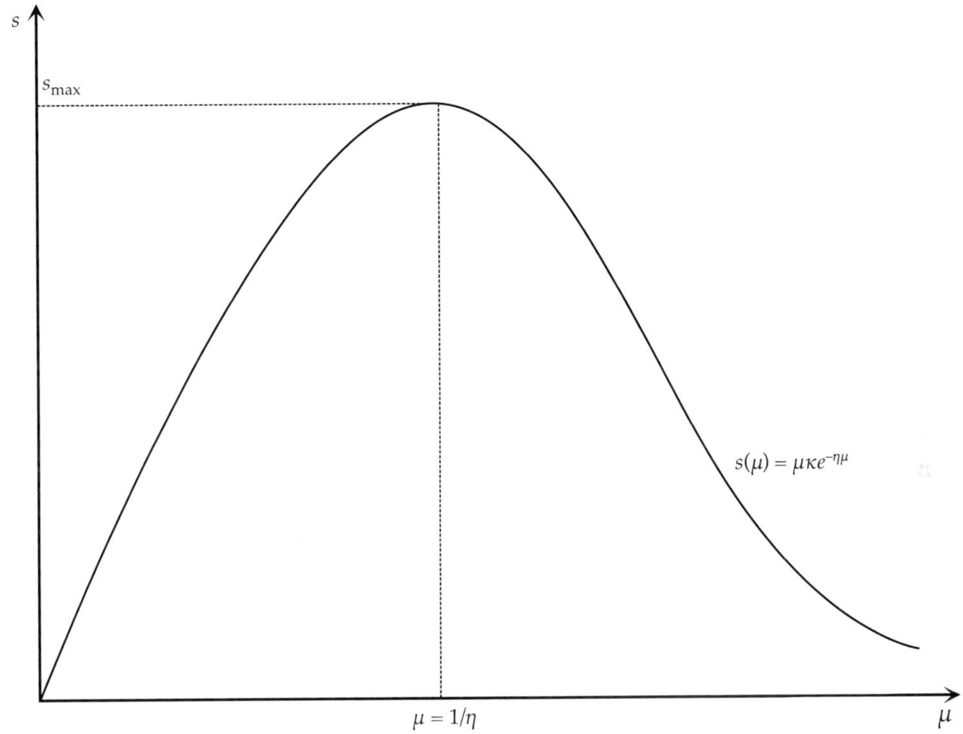

Figure 12.8
The seigniorage Laffer curve.

creation. This happens because the reduction in real money holdings by household and firms, which is the basis of this revenue, is greater than the rise in μ.

12.9.2 The Seigniorage Laffer Curve

Figure 12.8 depicts the revenue from seigniorage as a percentage of total output, as a function of the growth rate of the money supply. As can be seen from the figure, the revenue from money creation is characterized by a *Laffer curve*, because up to a point, the rise in the growth rate of the money supply increases revenues from seigniorage as a percentage of output, but after that point, it begins to reduce them, because the reduction in real money demand exceeds the rise in the rate of growth of the money supply.[16]

16. The term "Laffer curve" derives from Arthur Laffer, an economist who claimed, in a meeting with US administration officials in 1974, that tax revenue after a point becomes a negative function of tax rates, because of the disincentive effects of high taxes. He famously sketched this curve on a napkin in the venue where the meeting took place (Wanniski [1978]). Laffer himself notes antecedents in the writings of the fourteenth-century social philosopher Khaldun and in Keynes (Laffer [2004]).

It is interesting to calculate the percentage of total output at which seigniorage revenue is maximized. The maximum seigniorage revenue $s_{\max}$ that can be extracted occurs when $\mu = 1/\eta$. From (12.83), it follows that

$$s_{\max} = \frac{\kappa}{\eta e}$$

Using annual data, Cagan [1956] estimated that η lies between 1/2 and 1/3. Consequently, he estimated the growth rate of the money supply that maximizes revenues from seigniorage as a percentage of total output (and the corresponding inflation) as between 200% and 300% per year. Assuming that $\kappa = 0.10$ in (12.81), the maximum revenue from seigniorage as a percentage of total output is between 7 and 11%. For the period 1975–1985, Sachs and Larrain [1993] estimated actual revenue from seigniorage at about 5–6.5% for high inflation countries, such as Italy, Bolivia, Turkey, and Peru, and much lower for a series of other countries.

12.9.3 The Demand for Seigniorage and Equilibrium with High Inflation

Let us now consider a government that needs to fund a proportion of its public spending through seigniorage. Assume that this financing requirement, as a proportion of total output, is equal to s_E, which is less than the maximum seigniorage $s_{\max}$ that the government can achieve by setting the growth rate of the money supply at $\mu = 1/\eta$. The equilibrium is depicted in figure 12.9. There are two options to achieve revenue equal to s_E. One is with a growth rate of the money supply $\mu_E < 1/\eta$, and the other is with a growth rate of the money supply $\mu_{E'} > 1/\eta$. Assume that the government dislikes inflation and therefore chooses the lowest growth rate of the money supply that is compatible with the objective of raising revenue s_E from seigniorage.

For as long as the government needs to raise revenue equal to a proportion s_E of its output through seigniorage, the economy is trapped in an equilibrium with a growth rate of the money supply equal to μ_E and the corresponding high inflation rate. For example, if the government wants to raise seigniorage corresponding to 6% of total output, assuming $\eta = 1/2$, then the annual growth rate of the money supply (and corresponding steady state inflation) is equal to about 100%.

12.9.4 The Transition to Hyperinflation

But how can hyperinflation arise? Unlike high inflation, hyperinflation is a disequilibrium phenomenon. It arises when a government tries to raise seigniorage that exceeds the maximum that can be raised in the steady state.

Let us assume that a government needs to raise seigniorage that, as a proportion of total output, is higher than the maximum that can be raised in the steady state. We assume $s_E > s_{\max}$. Obviously, there can be no balanced growth path in which the government can raise revenues from seigniorage that exceeds $s_{\max}$. However, for a time, and as the economy

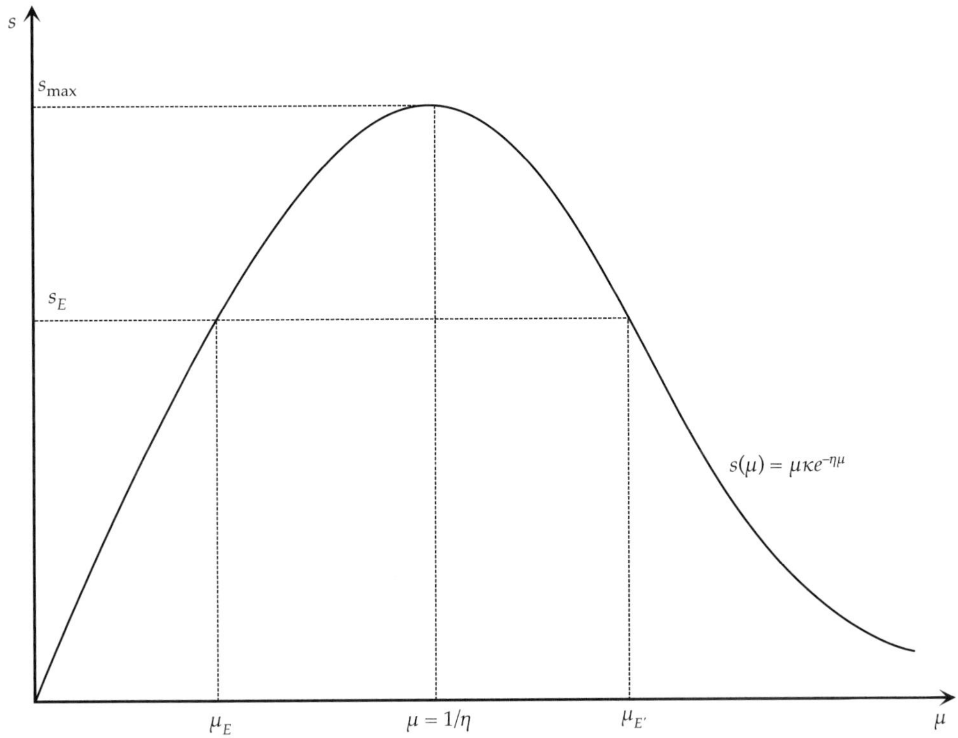

Figure 12.9
Equilibrium with high inflation.

adjusts toward the balanced growth path, the government may be able to raise seigniorage revenues greater than s_{max}. For example, this could happen if there is gradual adjustment in the demand for money or gradual adjustment in inflationary expectations.

Assume that the demand for money does not adjust immediately to its steady state level after a change in the nominal interest rate, but only gradually. Thus, when the nominal interest rate increases, money demand is temporarily higher than in the steady state. In this case, during the adjustment, the monetary base on which the inflationary tax is imposed is higher than the steady state monetary base. Consequently, during the adjustment, as μ increases, seigniorage revenues will exceed s_{max} temporarily, because real money balances are higher than on the balanced growth path. As the demand for money decreases gradually, the government should constantly increase the rate of monetary growth and the consequent inflation, to ensure the required high revenues from seigniorage. This can lead to an explosive path for the growth rate of the money supply and result in hyperinflation.

Let us then assume that (12.81) defines the steady state money demand function and that actual money demand adapts to its steady state level only gradually. We shall continue to assume that real output and the real interest rate are on their exogenous balanced growth paths. From (12.81), the steady state money demand as a percentage of total output m^* depends negatively on the growth rate of the money supply:

$$m^* = \frac{M}{PY} = \kappa e^{-\eta\mu}. \tag{12.85}$$

In the short run, real money demand is assumed to adjust gradually toward its steady state value according to

$$\frac{d \ln m(t)}{dt} = \frac{\dot{m}(t)}{m(t)} = \psi \left(\ln m^* - \ln m(t)\right), \tag{12.86}$$

where $0 < \psi < 1/\eta$.

The concept behind the assumed gradual adjustment is that it is difficult for economic agents to adapt their habits regarding the financing of their transactions or to use alternative means of payment in the short run. Hence, the demand for real money balances adjusts gradually over time. The particular log-linear functional form is chosen for convenience. The parameter ψ, which measures the speed of adjustment, is assumed to be positive but less than $1/\eta$. We thus assume that adjustment is positive but not too fast.

Substituting (12.85) in (12.86) yields

$$\frac{\dot{m}(t)}{m(t)} = \psi(\ln \kappa - \eta\mu(t) - \ln m(t)). \tag{12.87}$$

This describes the evolution of the short-run demand for money. Note that in (12.87), the growth rate of the money supply μ depends on time.

Let us now turn to the government's financing needs. Assume that the government needs revenues from seigniorage that may exceed the maximum that can be raised on the balanced growth path (i.e., $s_E > s_{\max}$). Although such revenues cannot be raised on the balanced growth path, they can be raised along the adjustment path (i.e., before money demand has fully adjusted to its steady state level). We shall see that if indeed $s_E > s_{\max}$, then this requires an ever-increasing rate of growth in the money supply and ever-increasing inflation.

For the government to achieve its seigniorage target s_E, the following relation must hold continuously:

$$s_E = \mu(t)m(t). \tag{12.88}$$

Equation (12.88) with a constant s_E implies that

$$\dot{\mu}(t)m(t) + \mu(t)\dot{m}(t) = 0. \tag{12.89}$$

Equation (12.89) can be written as

$$\frac{\dot{\mu}(t)}{\mu(t)} = -\frac{\dot{m}(t)}{m(t)}. \tag{12.90}$$

This suggests that to keep revenues from seigniorage constant as a percentage of total income at the level s_E, the growth rate of the money supply must keep increasing continuously, at the same rate as the decline of real money demand relative to output. Substituting (12.90) and (12.88) in (12.87), we get

$$\frac{\dot{\mu}(t)}{\mu(t)} = -\psi\left(\ln \kappa - \ln s_E + \ln \mu(t) - \eta\mu(t)\right). \tag{12.91}$$

From the differential equation (12.91), for the growth rate of the money supply to be eventually stabilized, a necessary and sufficient condition is

$$s_E = \mu\kappa e^{-\eta\mu} \leq s_{\max}. \tag{12.92}$$

If $s_E > s_{\max}$, then the right-hand side of (12.91) is positive for all rates of growth of the money supply. Taking the first derivative of (12.91) with respect to $\mu(t)$, we can see that after a point, a higher growth rate of the money supply leads to a higher rate of change in the growth of the money supply. This results in an explosive path for the growth rate of the money supply and inflation.

The relationship between the percentage change in the growth rate of the money supply and the rate of change in the money supply provided from (12.91), for different financing requirements from seigniorage, is depicted in figure 12.10.

When the financing needs of the government from seigniorage are less than or equal to the maximum possible on the balanced growth path, then the growth rate of the money supply is eventually stabilized at a equilibrium rate that may indeed be high, but inflation does not continue evolving into hyperinflation.

However, if the financing needs of government exceed the maximum that is sustainable on the balanced growth path, then, as the government tries to raise the necessary revenue from seigniorage, the growth rate of the money supply gradually accelerates to keep up with the declining monetary base, and the economy falls into a state of hyperinflation. Inflation gradually reduces the demand for money relative to total output, and the government needs an ever-increasing growth rate of the money supply to be able to collect the needed seigniorage revenue.

Our analysis of the link between the needs of a government to raise seigniorage to finance government expenditure and the rate of growth of the money supply can thus help explain episodes of high inflation and even hyperinflation.

12.9.5 How Can High Inflation and Hyperinflation Be Tackled?

Our basic analysis explains why, in many cases, inflation may be driven to very high levels. This is due to the inability of a government to finance its spending from other revenue

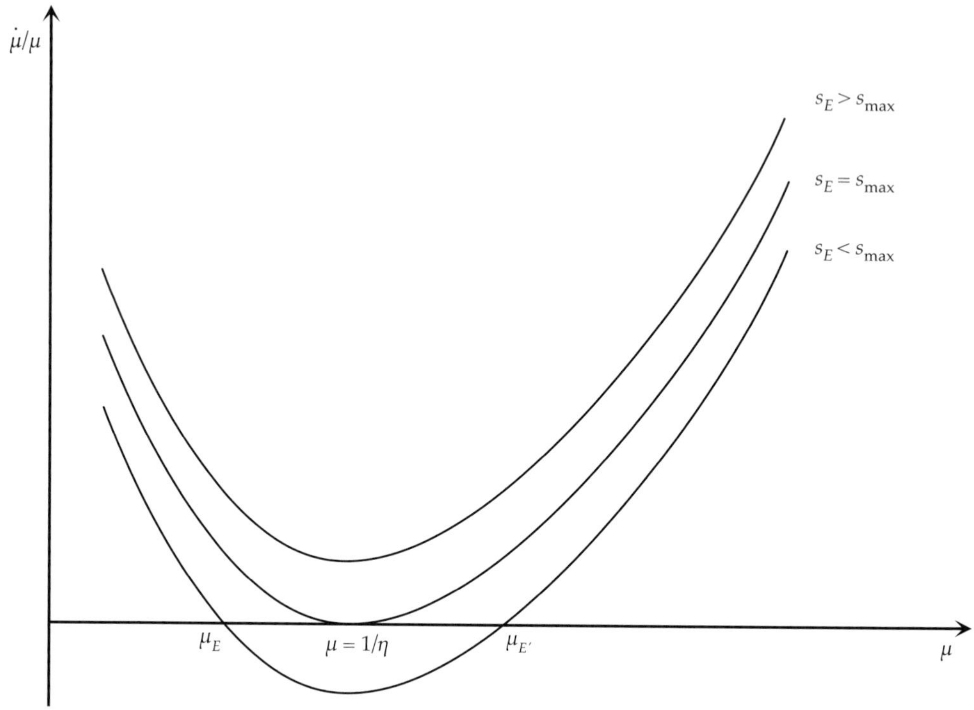

Figure 12.10
Equilibria with high inflation and the transition to hyperinflation.

sources, such as taxation or borrowing from the markets, and its need to use seigniorage (i.e., revenue from money creation).

The analysis also explains why, even though inflation may reach very high levels, it might not evolve into hyperinflation. For hyperinflation to happen, the financing needs of the government must be so high that they exceed the maximum level that can be financed through seigniorage on the balanced growth path.

Finally, the analysis emphasizes the central role of fiscal problems as the main causes of both high inflation and hyperinflation. A significant precondition for tackling high equilibrium inflation rates or hyperinflation is to pursue reforms that address the underlying fiscal problems (Sargent [1982]).

12.10 Conclusion

In this chapter, we have analyzed the role and functions of money and the determination of the price level, nominal interest rates, and inflation.

Money performs three functions. First, it is a unit of account; second, it is a generally accepted means of payment; and third, it is a store of wealth.

We reviewed the basic functions of money and the factors that determine the demand for and supply of money. We analyzed the concept of short-run equilibrium in the money market, assuming that the central bank follows a policy of either targeting the money supply or pegging nominal interest rates. We also discussed the long-run neutrality of money.

We then focused on several dynamic general economic equilibrium models with money, to analyze the determination of the price level and nominal interest rates and also analyzed the long-run relationship between the money supply, the price level, and inflation.

We finally examined the fiscal incentive for increasing the money supply and its effects on inflation. The most important motive for sustained large increases in the money supply by governments has been to finance government expenditure that could not be financed by other methods, such as additional taxes or government bonds. This source of revenue for the government is called seigniorage. The main cause of all episodes of sustained high inflation or even hyperinflation has been the need of governments to use their privilege of printing money to obtain seigniorage.

We investigated the relationship between the growth rate of the money supply, inflation, and government revenue from seigniorage. We examined both the situation where the revenues from seigniorage are adequate for the needs of a government on the balanced growth path, a case in which inflation turns out to be high but stable, and the situation in which the required seigniorage revenues are not sufficient, which may lead to hyperinflation.

13

The Stochastic Growth Model of Aggregate Fluctuations

In previous chapters, we studied the long-run evolution of output and consumption, real interest rates and real wages, and the long-run evolution of the price level and inflation. To focus on long-term trends, we made the assumption that all markets are competitive and in continuous equilibrium through the full adjustment of prices, wages, and interest rates.

However, as noted in chapter 1, economies are characterized by fluctuations in relation to their long-term trends. In some periods, output, consumption, investment, and employment grow at high rates, while at other times, they grow at low or even negative rates. In some periods, unemployment is low and in others it is quite high. Economies experience recessions and upswings. Inflation displays significant fluctuations as well.

Understanding the determinants of aggregate fluctuations is the second main objective of macroeconomics. This chapter and the ones that follow present the main theories regarding the nature of aggregate fluctuations.

This chapter introduces competitive equilibrium models of aggregate fluctuations. These are dynamic stochastic general equilibrium (DSGE) models based on optimizing households and firms, flexible wages and prices, and fully competitive markets. Fluctuations in these models are caused by real shocks (mainly exogenous shocks to productivity). The effects of these shocks are propagated through endogenous dynamic processes, such as consumption, investment, and labor supply.

We start with the stochastic growth model, which is an extended stochastic version of the Ramsey model. The utility function of a representative household depends on both consumption of goods and services and leisure, while random disturbances to real factors, such as productivity, cause aggregate fluctuations.

To be able to arrive at a tractable model, we first make simplifying assumptions regarding production and utility functions. Without such assumptions, the stochastic growth model becomes extremely complicated. The dynamic analysis is conducted in discrete rather than continuous time. Following the analysis of a simplified version of the stochastic growth model, in section 13.4, we analyze the full version of the stochastic growth model.

As the main impulses that generate aggregate fluctuations in the stochastic growth model are real, this model belongs to a class of models often referred to as real business cycle

(RBC) models. In many ways, the stochastic growth model is the modern equivalent of the classical approach to aggregate fluctuations. Hence it is sometimes also labeled as the "new classical" model. Monetary shocks have no real effects on output, employment, and capital accumulation in this class of models; they only affect real money balances and nominal variables, such as the price level, inflation, and nominal wages and interest rates. We postpone the analysis of the impact of monetary shocks in new classical competitive equilibrium models to chapter 14, where we examine a simplified version of the model without capital.

13.1 The Stochastic Growth Model

As we have seen in chapter 1, aggregate fluctuations are not characterized by deterministic cyclical regularities but seem to be characterized by randomness. The prevailing view, which dates back to Frisch [1933] and Slutsky [1937], is that economies are subject to various kinds of random disturbances, which, through the operation of economic transmission mechanisms, affect output, employment, real wages, real interest rates, the price level, and inflation. These disturbances set in motion dynamic stochastic adjustment processes.

The first model we focus on is the *stochastic growth model*. This is a competitive DSGE model without externalities, asymmetric information, frictions, and other imperfections of markets.

This model is essentially a generalization of the Ramsey model. It not only excludes any market imperfections, but also excludes all issues related to the heterogeneity of economic agents. The extended Ramsey model is therefore seen as the natural starting point for the study of aggregate fluctuations, in the same way that the original Ramsey model is seen as the natural starting point for the study of long-run growth.

There are two directions in which the Ramsey model must be extended to account for aggregate fluctuations. First, one should allow for random disturbances, which can cause fluctuations. As we have seen, without random disturbances, the Ramsey model converges to a unique steady state. The disturbances usually introduced in the Ramsey model are disturbances in total factor productivity (technology shocks), as well as real demand shocks, such as shocks to the preferences of consumers or real government expenditure. Because both kinds of shocks are *real*—unlike monetary or nominal shocks—this model is often called the RBC model.

Second, to explain fluctuations not only in total output but also in employment, employment must become endogenous in the Ramsey model. This is achieved through the introduction of leisure in the utility function of a representative household, thus allowing an endogenous labor supply.[1]

1. The original stochastic growth model was presented by Brock and Mirman [1972] and was essentially a Ramsey model, augmented by stochastic shocks to productivity. Later models allowed for endogenous labor supply,

13.1.1 Extending the Ramsey Model to Account for Aggregate Fluctuations

The extended Ramsey model that we end up with is a DSGE model, in which fluctuations are caused by real shocks.

The model assumes identical households and firms, so this is a competitive representative household model. Firms use labor and capital to produce a homogeneous product. They choose investment and employment to maximize their intertemporal profits, while households choose consumption and labor supply to maximize their intertemporal utility.

The key variables and parameters of the model are as follows: Y is aggregate output, K is aggregate physical capital, L is aggregate employment, A is the exogenous efficiency of labor (productivity), C is aggregate private consumption, C^G is aggregate real government expenditure, N is aggregate population, δ is the rate of depreciation of capital, ρ is the pure rate of time preference of households, r is the real interest rate, and w is the real wage per employee.

The economy consists of a large number of identical households and firms that interact through competitive markets. Output and factor prices are thus given for every household and every firm. Households own factors of production, labor, and capital, and they rent them out to firms through competitive factor markets.[2]

13.1.2 The Representative Firm

The representative firm has a production function with constant returns to scale, which takes the Cobb-Douglas form. Thus, the aggregate production function is also Cobb-Douglas:

$$Y_t = K^{\alpha}(A_t L_t)^{1-\alpha}, \tag{13.1}$$

where $0 < \alpha < 1$.

The demand for output consists of private consumption, investment, and government consumption. Government consumption is financed through nondistortionary taxation, and in each period, taxes are equal to government consumption. Thus, the equilibrium condition in the output market is given by

$$Y_t = C_t + C_t^G + K_{t+1} - K_t + \delta K_t. \tag{13.2}$$

Solving (13.2) for K_{t+1}, we get a capital accumulation equation of the form

$$K_{t+1} = K_t + Y_t - C_t - C_t^G - \delta K_t. \tag{13.3}$$

---

encompassing the intertemporal substitution hypothesis of Lucas and Rapping [1969]. The approach analyzed in this chapter follows Kydland and Prescott [1982], Long and Plosser [1983], and Prescott [1986]. It is surveyed in, among others, Plosser [1989], Mankiw [1989], Stadler [1994], and King and Rebelo [1999]. As we shall see in chapters 16 and 17, this approach has also influenced the new Keynesian approach to aggregate fluctuations, which now also relies on DSGE models.

2. In many ways, the model in this section is a generalization of the two-period models analyzed in chapter 2 to allow for an infinite horizon, uncertainty, and stochastic shocks to productivity.

To the extent that aggregate savings $Y - C - C^G$ exceed depreciation investment δK, there is accumulation of capital.

Labor and capital are paid their marginal product, as firms maximize profits taking the real interest rate r and the real wage w as given:

$$w_t = (1-\alpha)\left(\frac{K_t}{A_t L_t}\right)^{\alpha} A_t, \tag{13.4}$$

$$r_t = \alpha\left(\frac{A_t L_t}{K_t}\right)^{1-\alpha} - \delta. \tag{13.5}$$

Equations (13.1)–(13.5) describe the behavior of firms. Firms are assumed to employ workers up to the point where the marginal product of labor is equal to the real wage, and capital up to the point where the marginal product of capital equals the real user cost of capital, assumed to be equal to the real interest rate plus the depreciation rate.

13.1.3 The Representative Household

The economy is inhabited by a large number of identical households, each of which has an infinite time horizon. The representative household maximizes its expected intertemporal utility function, which depends on the path of real consumption of goods and services and leisure. The expected intertemporal utility function is defined by

$$U = E_t \sum_{s=0}^{\infty} \left(\frac{1}{1+\rho}\right)^{t+s} N_{t+s} u(c_{t+s}, 1 - l_{t+s}), \tag{13.6}$$

where E is the mathematical expectations operator, and u is the per capita instantaneous utility of the representative household. Per capita consumption is given by $c = C/N$ and per capita employment by $l = L/N$. Assume that the instantaneous utility function is logarithmic:

$$u_t = \ln c_t + b \ln(1 - l_t), \tag{13.7}$$

where $b > 0$. The assumption of logarithmic preferences is made to arrive at simpler functional relationships. However, like all such simplifications, this assumption implies specific restrictions for the model.

13.1.4 Exogenous Population Growth, Efficiency of Labor, and Government Expenditure

Population increases exogenously at a rate n per period. Consequently,

$$\ln N_t = \bar{n} + nt, \tag{13.8}$$

where $0 < n < \rho$.

The final assumptions of the model concern the behavior of the two main exogenous variables. Both productivity (labor efficiency), and government expenditure are supposed to be exogenous stochastic processes.

The stochastic process describing the evolution of the efficiency of labor is given by[3]

$$\ln A_t = \bar{a} + gt + a_t, \tag{13.9}$$

where

$$a_t = \eta_A a_{t-1} + \varepsilon_t^A. \tag{13.10}$$

It is assumed that $-1 < \eta_A < 1$, and that ε^A is a white noise process. With these assumptions, a_t is a stationary AR(1) process. Equations (13.9) and (13.10) imply that labor efficiency grows at an exogenous rate g, but that it is subject to random disturbances a_t, which follow a stationary first-order autoregressive process. The assumptions about (13.10) imply that the impact of a technological disturbance is gradually reduced over time.

Similar assumptions are made regarding the stochastic process that describes the evolution of real government expenditure. Assume that real government expenditure is growing at an average rate $n+g$ (i.e., on average, it remains constant relative to total output). However, we also assume that real government expenditure is subject to disturbances that follow a stationary first-order autoregressive process. More particularly, assume that

$$\ln G_t = \bar{c}^G + (n+g)t + c_t^G, \tag{13.11}$$

where

$$c_t^G = \eta_G c_{t-1}^G + \varepsilon_t^G. \tag{13.12}$$

It is assumed that $-1 < \eta_G < 1$, and that ε^G is a white noise process. With these assumptions, c_t^G is a stationary AR(1) process.[4]

These elements complete the structure of the stochastic growth model. The two most important differences from the original Ramsey model are first, the introduction of leisure time in the utility function of the representative household (which potentially allows for fluctuations in employment), and second, the introduction of random disturbances to labor efficiency (productivity) and government expenditure (which leads to fluctuations around the long-term trend).

3. Appendix F contains an introduction to stochastic processes.

4. The assumption that the processes driving labor productivity and real government expenditure are AR(1) is made for analytical simplicity and can of course be generalized.

Before we look at the general properties of the model, it is worth considering the implications for the behavior of the representative household of the introduction of leisure in the utility function, as well as the implications of uncertainty in the form of random disturbances.

13.1.5 Labor Supply of the Representative Household

The first difference of this model from the Ramsey model arises from the introduction of leisure time in the utility function of the household, which makes labor supply endogenous. To analyze the importance of this extension, which was first introduced in chapter 2, let us first consider the problem of a household that lives for a single time period and has no assets. The problem of that household is defined as the maximization of

$$\ln c + b\ln(1-l)$$

under the constraint

$$c = wl.$$

The Lagrange function is defined by

$$\mathcal{L} = \ln c + b\ln(1-l) + \lambda(wl - c), \tag{13.13}$$

where λ is the relevant Lagrange multiplier. The first-order conditions for a maximum imply that

$$\frac{1}{c} - \lambda = 0, \tag{13.14}$$

$$-\frac{b}{1-l} + \lambda w = 0. \tag{13.15}$$

From the budget constraint $c = wl$ and from (13.14), it follows that $\lambda = 1/(wl)$. Substituting in (13.15), we get

$$-\frac{b}{1-l} + \frac{1}{l} = 0. \tag{13.16}$$

From (13.16), it is apparent that labor supply is independent of the real wage. This is because of the assumption of logarithmic preferences, implying that the elasticity of substitution between consumption and leisure is equal to unity. Thus, the substitution effect from a change in the real wage is counteracted by the income effect. Labor supply is completely inelastic and is given by

$$l = \frac{1}{b+1}.$$

However, this inelasticity does not mean that temporary changes in real wages do not affect labor supply even in this case. This can be seen if we look at the behavior of a household that lives for two periods, as assumed in chapter 2.

13.1.6 Intertemporal Substitution in Labor Supply

To see how temporary changes in real wages might affect labor supply (even though with logarithmic preferences, permanent changes in real wages have no effect), let us adopt the simplest intertemporal model, which is none other than the two-period model analyzed in chapter 2. Consider the behavior of a household living for two periods that has no initial wealth and no uncertainty about the real interest rate or the real wage of the second period.

The intertemporal budget constraint of the household is given by

$$c_1 + \frac{1}{1+r}c_2 = w_1 l_1 + \frac{1}{1+r}w_2 l_2,$$

where subscripts 1 and 2 refer to the first and second periods of life, respectively.

The Lagrange function of this household is defined by

$$\mathcal{L} = \ln c_1 + b\ln(1-l)_1 + \frac{1}{1+\rho}(\ln c_2 + b\ln(1-l)_2) + \\ + \lambda\left[w_1 l_1 + \frac{1}{1+r}w_2 l_2 - c_1 - \frac{1}{1+r}c_2\right]. \tag{13.17}$$

The household chooses consumption and labor supply for each of the two periods. From the first-order conditions for labor supply, we have

$$\frac{b}{1-l_1} = \lambda w_1, \tag{13.18}$$

$$\frac{b}{1-l_2} = \frac{1+\rho}{1+r}\lambda w_2. \tag{13.19}$$

Dividing (13.19) by (13.18) yields

$$\frac{1-l_1}{1-l_2} = \frac{1+\rho}{1+r}\frac{w_2}{w_1}. \tag{13.20}$$

Equation (13.20) implies that the relative labor supply in the two periods depends positively on the relative real wage in the two periods. The higher the real wage of the first period is in relation to that of the second period, the higher will be the labor supply of the first period in relation to that of the second. The household substitutes labor between periods, depending on relative real wages between periods. Because of the assumption of logarithmic preferences, the intertemporal substitution elasticity is equal to one.

Moreover, the higher the real interest rate r is, the greater will be the labor supply of the first period compared to that of the second period. The increase in the interest rate increases the attractiveness of working in the first period and saving for the second period, compared to working in the second period. It has the opposite effect of the pure rate of time preference rate ρ.

These effects of relative wages over time and the real interest rate on labor supply are the intertemporal substitution effects in labor supply that we analyzed in the two-period model of chapter 2. Such effects obviously generalize to a multiperiod setting. Consequently, fluctuations in real wages and the real interest rate can cause fluctuations in employment, even in a model with logarithmic preferences, in which permanent changes in real wages do not affect labor supply.[5]

13.1.7 Uncertainty and the Behavior of the Representative Household

Apart from the endogeneity of labor supply, the second element that differentiates this stochastic growth model from the deterministic Ramsey model is uncertainty arising from the stochastic disturbances. Therefore, the expectations of the representative household for future developments play a significant role.

It is straightforward to show that, for the general case when the household maximizes the expected intertemporal utility function (13.6) subject to the relevant intertemporal budget constraint, the Euler equation for consumption takes the form

$$\frac{1}{c_t} = \frac{1}{1+\rho} E_t \left[\frac{1}{c_{t+1}} (1 + r_{t+1}) \right]. \tag{13.21}$$

The mathematical expectation of the product of two random variables is not equal to the product of their mathematical expectations. It is equal to the product of their mathematical expectations plus the covariance of the two random variables. Thus, (13.21) implies

$$\frac{1}{c_t} = \frac{1}{1+\rho} \left\{ E_t \left[\frac{1}{c_{t+1}} \right] E_t (1 + r_{t+1}) + \mathrm{Cov} \left(\frac{1}{c_{t+1}}, (1 + r_{t+1}) \right) \right\}. \tag{13.22}$$

However, from the first-order conditions for consumption and labor supply, the ratio of consumption to leisure is a positive function of the real wage of the form

$$\frac{c_t}{1 - l_t} = \frac{w_t}{b}. \tag{13.23}$$

5. The concept of intertemporal substitution in labor supply was first analyzed in an important paper by Lucas and Rapping [1969]. For an empirical investigation of its significance for fluctuations in employment in the United States and the United Kingdom, see Alogoskoufis [1987a,b]. See also Hansen [1985] and Rogerson [1988] for the implications of a generalization of the model to the case where employment is indivisible, and households can work for a minimum number of hours or not work at all.

Equation (13.23) links labor supply (leisure) and consumption with the real wage. It includes only current variables, as there is no uncertainty in the current period. Equations (13.21) and (13.23) are the two basic equations describing the behavior of households in the stochastic growth model.

We can now examine the properties of the model. This model is not easy to solve analytically, as it contains factors that are both linear and log-linear in the endogenous variables. The properties of the model can be described if we simplify it further, or if we use a log-linear approximation around the balanced growth path and solve it numerically for specific values of the parameters.

In section 13.4, we present the Campbell [1994] log-linear approximation of the full model around its balanced growth path. This allows us to describe the full properties of the model through a numerical simulation around the balanced growth path. However, first let us concentrate on the properties of a simplified version of the model to gain a deeper understanding of its structure.

13.2 A Simplified Version of the Stochastic Growth Model

We first consider a special case of the stochastic growth model, without government expenditure and with a depreciation rate of 100%. The equations that describe the accumulation of capital and the determination of the real interest rate then simplify to

$$K_{t+1} = Y_t - C_t, \tag{13.24}$$

$$1 + r_t = \alpha \left(\frac{A_t L_t}{K_t} \right)^{1-\alpha}. \tag{13.25}$$

Because of the assumption of competitive markets and the absence of externalities, the equilibrium of the model is Pareto optimal. We shall examine the properties of the model by solving for the competitive equilibrium.

Let us focus on two variables: labor supply per person l and the savings rate s. Defining the savings rate, we also determine aggregate consumption as $C = (1 - s)Y$.

We focus on both behavioral equations of the representative household (13.21) and (13.23). Once we determine labor supply and the savings rate, the rest follows automatically from either equilibrium conditions or definitions.

The Euler equation for consumption (13.21) can be written as

$$1 + \rho = E_t \left[\frac{c_t}{c_{t+1}} (1 + r_{t+1}) \right].$$

We can substitute for consumption and the real interest rate in the Euler equation by using the relations

$$c_t = (1 - s_t) Y_t / N_t,$$

$$1 + r_{t+1} = \alpha Y_{t+1} / K_{t+1},$$

$$K_{t+1} = s_t Y_t.$$

This allows us to rewrite the Euler equation as

$$\frac{1+\rho}{1+n} = E_t \left[\frac{1-s_t}{1-s_{t+1}} \frac{\alpha}{s_t} \right].$$

Because the left-hand side is constant, the right-hand side must also be constant. Thus, the savings rate is constant and is determined by

$$\bar{s} = \frac{\alpha(1+n)}{1+\rho}. \tag{13.26}$$

The savings rate is independent of the real interest rate and constant in this simplified model because of the assumption of logarithmic preferences.

From (13.23), and by noting that $c_t = (1 - \bar{s}) Y_t / N_t$ and $w_t = (1 - \alpha) Y_t / (l_t N_t)$, we arrive at the conclusion that labor supply per household member is also constant in this simplified model. It is given by

$$\bar{l} = \frac{1-\alpha}{(1-\alpha) + b(1-\bar{s})}. \tag{13.27}$$

Labor supply is constant in this simplified model, because the impact of the shocks in technology (labor efficiency) on the real wage and the real interest rate cancel each other out, so that no intertemporal substitution in labor supply is induced by such shocks.

This result is due to the specific assumptions that we made to simplify the model, and, as one can see from the analysis of the full model in section 13.4, is not a general feature of the model. In fact, the opposite is true. In general versions of the model, intertemporal substitution in labor supply induced by temporary real shocks is the key driver of fluctuations in aggregate employment.

13.2.1 Fluctuations of Output in the Simplified Stochastic Growth Model

We can now determine fluctuations in total output. Taking logs on both sides of the production function (13.1), we get

$$\ln Y_t = \alpha \ln K_t + (1 - \alpha)(\ln A_t + \ln L_t). \tag{13.28}$$

We know that $K_t = \bar{s} Y_{t-1}$ and that $L_t = \bar{l} N_t$. Therefore,

$$\ln Y_t = \alpha \ln \bar{s} + \alpha \ln Y_{t-1} + (1 - a)(\ln A_t + \ln \bar{l} + \ln N_t). \tag{13.29}$$

We can substitute the logarithm of A and N from equations (13.8) and (13.9). This implies

$$\ln Y_t = \alpha \ln \bar{s} + \alpha \ln Y_{t-1} + (1-\alpha)\left[(\bar{a}+gt) + a_t + (\ln \bar{l} + \bar{n} + nt)\right]. \tag{13.30}$$

We can express (13.30) as

$$y_t = \alpha y_{t-1} + (1-\alpha)a_t, \tag{13.31}$$

where $y_t = \ln Y_t - \ln \bar{Y}_t$ denotes the percentage deviation of output from its long-run trend.

The logarithm of trend output in this model is defined by

$$\ln \bar{Y}_t = \frac{\alpha}{1-\alpha} \ln \bar{s} + \ln \bar{l} + \bar{a} + \bar{n} + (n+g)t.$$

Trend output grows at the exogenously given rate of $n+g$, as happens with steady state output in the Ramsey model of growth. From (13.10) and (13.31), we end up with

$$y_t = (\alpha + \eta_A)y_{t-1} - \alpha\eta_A y_{t-2} + (1-\alpha)\varepsilon_t^A. \tag{13.32}$$

Equation (13.32) suggests that the percentage deviations of aggregate real output from trend follow a second-order autoregressive process (AR(2)), depending on the share of capital in the production process and the degree of persistence of productivity shocks. Because α is low (about 1/3), the dynamic behavior of total real output depends primarily on the degree of persistence of productivity shocks. If the persistence of productivity shocks η_A is high, then we have considerable persistence in the fluctuations of output. Otherwise, the persistence of output fluctuations around trend is relatively low.

Note that if the degree of persistence of productivity shocks were zero, then (13.32) would simplify to

$$y_t = \alpha y_{t-1} + (1-\alpha)\varepsilon_t^A. \tag{13.33}$$

Equation (13.33) suggests that if productivity shocks did not persist, deviations of output around trend would follow a first-order autoregressive process, with a degree of persistence equal to α.

13.2.2 The Simplified Stochastic Growth Model and the Evidence on Aggregate Fluctuations

Empirical estimates suggest that percentage deviations of output around trend do indeed follow an AR(2) process. For example, running a regression of the log of US real GDP on a linear trend, and its two lags, using annual data for the period 1890–2014, one gets a fairly good statistical fit. The coefficient on the first lag of output is equal to 1.211, with a standard error of estimate of 0.086, and the coefficient on the second lag of output is equal to −0.319, with a standard error of estimate of 0.087. Both estimates are statistically significant at conventional significance levels, and they imply that $\alpha = 0.386$ (standard error 0.132) and $\eta_A = 0.824$ (standard error 0.082). The estimates of the time trend imply a long-run growth rate of GDP equal to 0.033 (standard error 0.001).

Hence, the econometric estimates of the model parameters are quite sensible, suggesting that, as a first approximation, this simplified model can account for both the long-run growth rate and the aggregate fluctuations of US output.

However, many other features of aggregate fluctuations are not adequately described by this simplified version of the stochastic growth model. The first such feature is the constant savings ratio. This essentially means that consumption will display the same degree of variability as output and investment. As shown by the stylized facts presented by Hodrik and Prescott [1997] and others since the seminal Hodrik-Prescott paper first appeared in 1980, this does not seem to be a property of the data. Empirical estimates suggest that fluctuations in aggregate consumption are much smoother than output fluctuations.

A second counterfactual feature of the simplified model is the constant employment rate. In reality, the employment rate is not constant over the business cycle, whether one looks at total hours or the number of employees. As shown by Hodrik and Prescott [1997], employment and hours worked are pro-cyclical and are very strongly correlated with output.

Finally the behavior of real wages over the business cycle is not as predicted by the simplified stochastic growth model. In the model, real wages would be pro-cyclical and as volatile as GDP per capita, which is not the case in the data, as suggested by, among others, Neftci [1978].

One must thus consider the more general version of the model to assess its empirical significance.

13.3 A Log-Linear Approximation to the General Stochastic Growth Model

In this section, we proceed to analyze the general version of the stochastic growth model without some of the more extreme simplifications introduced in section 13.2. We set out the full stochastic growth model and derive an approximate analytical solution, based on a log-linear approximation around the steady state equilibrium. Following Campbell [1994], the model is thus transformed into a system of log-linear stochastic difference equations, which can be solved by the method of undetermined coefficients. We solve the model assuming that government expenditure is equal to zero.

The first equation of the stochastic growth model is the production function

$$Y_t = K^{\alpha}(A_t L_t)^{1-\alpha}, \tag{13.34}$$

where $0 < \alpha < 1$.

The second equation is the capital accumulation process:

$$K_{t+1} = (1-\delta)K_t + Y_t - C_t. \tag{13.35}$$

The representative household maximizes

$$U_t = E_t \sum\nolimits_{s=0}^{\infty} \left(\frac{1}{1+\rho}\right)^s (\ln C_{t+s} + b\ln(N_{t+s} - L_{t+s})), \tag{13.36}$$

subject to the accumulation process (13.35). Finally, there is a representative perfectly competitive firm that maximizes profits subject to the production function (13.34).

From the first-order conditions for profit maximization, the marginal product of capital and labor are equal to the real interest rate and the real wage, respectively. It thus follows that

$$w_t = (1-\alpha)\left(\frac{K_t}{A_t L_t}\right)^{\alpha} A_t, \tag{13.37}$$

$$r_t = \alpha\left(\frac{A_t L_t}{K_t}\right)^{1-\alpha} - \delta. \tag{13.38}$$

From the first-order conditions for the maximization of the utility of the representative household, it also follows that

$$\frac{1}{C_t} = \frac{1+n}{1+\rho} E_t\left[\frac{1}{C_{t+1}}(1+r_{t+1})\right], \tag{13.39}$$

$$\frac{C_t}{N_t - L_t} = \frac{w_t}{b}. \tag{13.40}$$

Equation (13.39) is a stochastic version of the Euler equation for aggregate consumption, and (13.40) relates current consumption and leisure to the real wage.

13.3.1 The Steady State

In the steady state, aggregate variables such as output, effective labor, capital, and consumption grow at an exogenous rate $g+n$. Thus, from (13.39), the steady state real interest rate is determined by the condition

$$1 + r = (1+\rho)(1+g). \tag{13.41}$$

Equation (13.41) implies that

$$r = (1+\rho)(1+g) - 1 \simeq \rho + g. \tag{13.42}$$

From the marginal productivity condition for capital (13.38), the steady state ratio of output to capital is determined by

$$\frac{Y}{K} = \left(\frac{AL}{K}\right)^{1-\alpha} = \frac{r+\delta}{\alpha} = \frac{\rho+g+\delta}{\alpha}. \tag{13.43}$$

From (13.43), the steady state ratio of effective labor to capital is determined by

$$\frac{AL}{K} = \left(\frac{\rho+g+\delta}{\alpha}\right)^{\frac{1}{1-\alpha}}. \tag{13.44}$$

Finally, from the capital accumulation process (13.35) and (13.43), the steady state consumption to output ratio is given by

$$\frac{C}{Y} = 1-\alpha\left(\frac{n+g+\delta}{\rho+g+\delta}\right). \tag{13.45}$$

Note that the last term in (13.45) is the steady state savings rate.

13.3.2 Log-Linearizing the Model around the Steady State

Let us consider fluctuations of the endogenous variables around the steady state. Outside the steady state, the model is a system of nonlinear equations in the logs of productivity, capital, labor, output, and consumption. Nonlinearities arise because of the depreciation rate, the equation for capital accumulation, the variable savings rate, and the variable employment rate. Unlike the simplified version of the model that we examined in section 13.2, which could be solved fully, let us seek an approximate analytical solution by taking a log-linear approximation of all equations around the steady state.

The Cobb-Douglas production function can be log-linearized directly. From (13.34), it follows that

$$y_t = \alpha k_t + (1-\alpha)(a_t + l_t), \tag{13.46}$$

where lowercase letters denote the difference of the logarithm of the relevant variable from its steady state value.

The capital accumulation equation (13.35) is obviously not log-linear. Dividing by K_t , it can be written as

$$\left(\frac{K_{t+1}}{K_t} - (1-\delta)\right) = \frac{Y_t}{K_t}\left(1 - \frac{C_t}{Y_t}\right). \tag{13.47}$$

Taking logs, (13.47) can be written as

$$\ln[e^{\Delta k_{t+1}} - (1-\delta)] = y_t - k_t + \ln[1 - e^{(c_t - y_t)}]. \tag{13.48}$$

Taking a first-order Taylor approximation of (13.48) around the steady state and using the log-linear version of the production function (13.46), we end up with the following log-linear approximation of the accumulation equation around the steady state:

$$k_{t+1} \simeq \lambda_1 k_t + \lambda_2 (a_t + l_t) + (1 - \lambda_1 - \lambda_2) c_t, \tag{13.49}$$

where $\lambda_1 = \frac{1+\rho+g}{1+g}$, and $\lambda_2 = \frac{(1-\alpha)(\rho+g+\delta)}{\alpha(1+g)}$.

We next turn to the determination of the real interest rate and the Euler equation for consumption. From the marginal productivity condition for capital, (13.38), it follows that

$$1 + r_{t+1} = \alpha \left(\frac{A_{t+1} L_{t+1}}{K_{t+1}} \right)^{1-\alpha} + (1 - \delta). \tag{13.50}$$

Taking a log-linear approximation of (13.50) around the steady state, we get

$$r_{t+1} \simeq \lambda_3 \left(a_{t+1} + l_{t+1} - k_{t+1} \right), \tag{13.51}$$

where $\lambda_3 = \frac{(1-\alpha)(\rho+g+\delta)}{1+\rho+g}$. Substituting (13.51) in the Euler equation for consumption (13.39) and assuming that the variables on the right-hand side are jointly log-normal, the Euler equation for consumption can be written as

$$c_t = E_t c_{t+1} - E_t r_{t+1} = E_t c_{t+1} - \lambda_3 E_t (a_{t+1} + l_{t+1} - k_{t+1}). \tag{13.52}$$

Log-linearizing the marginal productivity condition for labor (13.37) and taking deviations from steady state, we get that deviations of the log of the real wage from steady state are given by

$$w_t = \alpha (k_t - l_t) + (1 - \alpha) a_t. \tag{13.53}$$

Finally, log-linearizing the first-order condition for consumption and leisure (13.40) and using the marginal productivity condition for employment (13.53) to substitute for the logarithm of the real wage, we get

$$l_t = \nu \left(\alpha k_t + (1 - \alpha) a_t - c_t \right), \tag{13.54}$$

where $\nu = \frac{1-(\bar{L}/N)}{(\bar{L}/N)-\alpha(1-(\bar{L}/N))}$. Here, $\bar{L}/N$ is steady state labor supply as a fraction of total available time. Following Prescott [1986], let us assume that this is equal to about one-third.

To close the model, we need only specify the exogenous stochastic process driving productivity a. Let us continue to assume, as in section 13.2, that it follows an AR(1) process of the form

$$a_t = \eta_A a_{t-1} + \varepsilon_t^A, \tag{13.55}$$

where $0 < \eta_A < 1$.

13.4 Solving the Log-Linear Stochastic Growth Model

The model consists of equations (13.46), (13.49), (13.51), (13.52), (13.53), and (13.54). It determines fluctuations around the steady state for output, the capital stock, consumption, employment, the real interest, and the real wage. The exogenous shock driving the fluctuations is a productivity (technological) shock that follows the AR(1) process in (13.55).

We can first solve the subsystem of (13.49), (13.52), and (13.54) for capital, employment, and consumption, and then substitute in the other three equations to determine output, the real interest rate, and the real wage.

The easiest way to solve the model analytically is to use the method of undetermined coefficients. We start from the equation for consumption and conjecture that consumption will be a linear function of the two state variables k and a, of the form

$$c_t = \eta_{CK} k_t + \eta_{CA} a_t, \tag{13.56}$$

where η_{CK} and η_{CA} are coefficients to be determined. Substituting (13.56) in the employment equation (13.54), we get the solution for employment as

$$l_t = \eta_{LK} k_t + \eta_{LA} a_t, \tag{13.57}$$

where $\eta_{LK} = \nu\alpha - \eta_{CK}$, and $\eta_{LA} = 1 - \alpha - \eta_{CA}$.

Substituting (13.56) and (13.57) in the capital accumulation equation (13.49), and making use of the exogenous process (13.55), we get the solution for the accumulation of capital:

$$k_{t+1} = \eta_{KK} k_t + \eta_{KA} a_t, \tag{13.58}$$

where

$$\eta_{KK} = \lambda_1 + (1 - \lambda_1 - \lambda_2)\eta_{CK} + \lambda_2 \eta_{LK},$$

$$\eta_{KA} = \lambda_2 + (1 - \lambda_1 - \lambda_2)\eta_{CA} + \lambda_2 \eta_{LA}.$$

Finally, we can substitute (13.57) and (13.58) in the Euler equation for consumption (13.52) and take the rational expectations solution, using the exogenous process (13.55) as well. We then find that

$$c_t = \frac{\lambda_3 \eta_{KK}(1 - \eta_{LK})}{1 - \eta_{KK}} k_t - \frac{\lambda_3 \left(\eta_A(1 + \eta_{LA}) - \eta_{KA}(1 - \eta_{LK})\right)}{1 - \eta_A} a_t. \tag{13.59}$$

Comparing coefficients between (13.59) and (13.56), we can determine the undetermined coefficients η_{CK} and η_{CA}.

13.4.1 Aggregate Fluctuations around the Steady State

We can now use the solution obtained to characterize the fluctuations of the various aggregates around the steady state. From (13.58) and (13.55), fluctuations in the capital stock are determined by

$$k_{t+1} = (\eta_{KK} + \eta_A)k_t - \eta_{KK}\eta_A k_{t-1} + \eta_{KA}\varepsilon_t^A. \tag{13.60}$$

Logarithmic deviations of the capital stock from its steady state value follow a stationary AR(2) process.

Substituting (13.60) and (13.55) in the consumption equation (13.56), we can see that log deviations of consumption from its steady state follow a stationary autoregressive-moving average, process ARMA(2,1). This takes the form

$$c_t = (\eta_{KK} + \eta_A)c_{t-1} - \eta_{KK}\eta_A c_{t-2} + \eta_{CA}\varepsilon_t^A + (\eta_{CK}\eta_{KA} - \eta_{CA}\eta_{KK})\,\varepsilon_{t-1}^A. \tag{13.61}$$

Substituting (13.60) and (13.55) in the employment equation (13.57), we have that log deviations of employment from its steady state follow a stationary ARMA(2,1) process of the form

$$l_t = (\eta_{KK} + \eta_A)l_{t-1} - \eta_{KK}\eta_A l_{t-2} + \eta_{LA}\varepsilon_t^A + (\eta_{LK}\eta_{KA} - \eta_{LA}\eta_{KK})\,\varepsilon_{t-1}^A. \tag{13.62}$$

Finally, substituting (13.60) and (13.61) in the log-linear version of the aggregate production function (13.46), log deviations of output from its steady state follow:

$$\begin{aligned} y_t = {} & (\eta_{KK} + \eta_A)y_{t-1} - \eta_{KK}\eta_A y_{t-2} + \\ & + (1-\alpha)(1+\eta_{LA})\varepsilon_t^A - (1-\alpha)\left(\eta_{KK}(1+\eta_{LA}) - \eta_{LK}\eta_{KA}\right)\varepsilon_{t-1}^A. \end{aligned} \tag{13.63}$$

Thus, log deviations of output from its steady state follow an ARMA(2, 1) process as well.

13.4.2 A Dynamic Simulation of the Log-Linear Stochastic Growth Model

Figure 13.1 presents the results of a dynamic simulation of the model for a 1% positive shock to productivity a. The parameter values used in the simulation were $\alpha = 0.333$, $\rho = 0.02$, $g = 0.02$, $\delta = 0.03$, $\nu = 2$, and $\eta_A = 0.90$. As can be seen from the simulated impulse response functions, all real variables move procyclically, as innovations in productivity affect output, the capital stock, consumption, and employment in the same direction. Real wages and the real interest rate also move procyclically. Gradually, all variables converge to their original steady state values, unless the system is disturbed by another shock.

Thus, the general stochastic growth model can explain fluctuations in all real variables as a result of stochastic shocks to productivity. However, fluctuations in employment are due to intertemporal substitution in labor supply, and there is no account for unemployment.

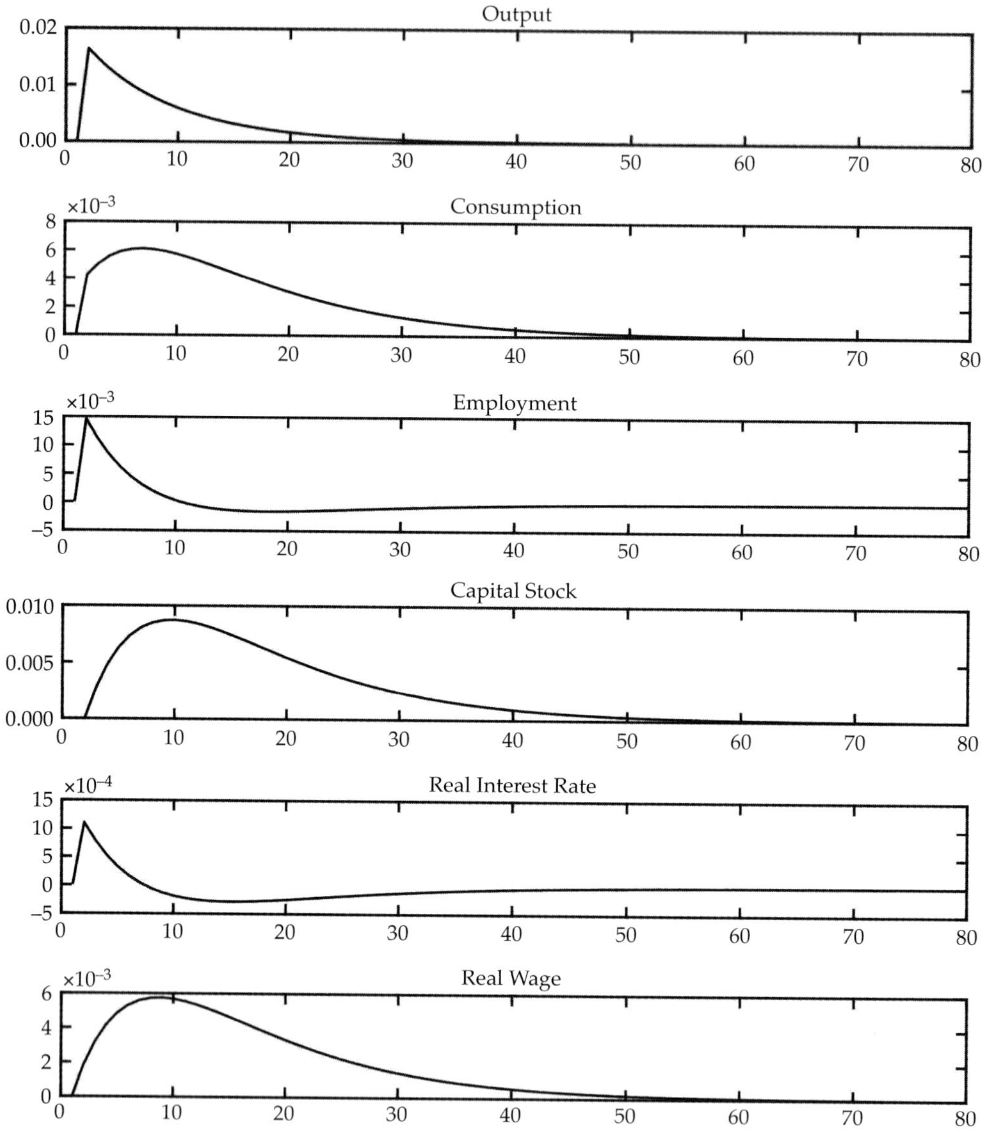

Figure 13.1
Dynamic simulation of the stochastic growth model following a 1% persistent shock to productivity.

13.5 Conclusion

New classical models of aggregate fluctuations, such as the stochastic growth model, imply that aggregate fluctuations are caused by real disturbances, such as productivity shocks. This is why such models are also called RBC models.

New classical models, such as the stochastic growth model analyzed in this chapter, are DSGE models based on optimizing behavior by both households and firms, flexible prices, and fully competitive markets. Households maximize their intertemporal utility, firms maximize the present value of their profits, and markets function efficiently.

If the competitive general equilibrium models of this kind could explain all features of aggregate fluctuations, then there would be little need for models that stress distortions in product and labor markets, or other market inefficiencies. However, new classical models have significant weaknesses as models of aggregate fluctuations.

Before discussing these weaknesses, we first analyze a new classical model without capital, which is simpler to handle and can serve as a basis of comparisons with the new Keynesian models that will be analyzed in chapters 16 and 17.

14

Perfectly Competitive Models with Flexible Prices

This chapter introduces a perfectly competitive model of aggregate fluctuations, in which there is no capital accumulation. This is a DSGE model, based on optimizing households and firms; flexible wages and prices; and fully competitive product, labor, and financial markets. Fluctuations are caused by real shocks to productivity, but we abstract from capital accumulation, which propagates the dynamic effects of such shocks in the stochastic growth model of chapter 13.

This simplified model is introduced without capital, so that we can study the properties of a more tractable new classical model, comparable to the new Keynesian models that we analyze in subsequent chapters. By comparing these models, one gets a better understanding of the similarities and differences between the new classical and the new Keynesian approaches to aggregate fluctuations.

The impulses that generate aggregate fluctuations in this model are also real (i.e., shocks to productivity). However, we also analyze the role of monetary shocks and monetary policy. We will see that monetary shocks have no real effects on output, employment, and other real variables in this model. They only affect real money balances and nominal variables, such as the price level, inflation, and nominal wages and interest rates. Thus, the role of monetary policy in this new classical model is simply to stabilize inflation in the presence of monetary and real shocks.

The short-run neutrality of money implied by new classical models was troublesome for some of their proponents, as these models were not compatible with the evidence suggesting the existence of a positive short-run relation between inflation and employment. Lucas [1972] responded by developing a new classical model, based on imperfect information, which was consistent with a positive short-run relation between inflation and employment even under rational expectations. This model was subsequently analyzed by Barro [1976] and extended to include competitive labor markets by Alogoskoufis [1983]. It was based on the assumption that firms and workers do not have full information about the price level at the time they make their production and employment decisions, and they attribute part of any change in the price level to a change in the relative price of their product or their real wage. Thus, when inflation is unexpectedly high, all producers rationally think that the relative price of their product has gone up, and thus increase production and employment. The opposite happens when inflation is unexpectedly low.[1]

However, this new classical explanation of the short-run relation between inflation and output and employment was still not compatible with involuntary unemployment. It could only account for temporary deviations of output and employment from their "natural" levels, due to intertemporal substitution in labor supply and unanticipated inflation. Its basic premise—that the positive relation between unanticipated inflation and employment is due to misperceptions of actual inflation by workers and producers—was also challenged as a counterfactual assumption, although it has made a comeback through recent models of costly information acquisition in decentralized economies.

14.1 A Perfectly Competitive Model without Capital

In what follows, we focus on a perfectly competitive new classical model of aggregate fluctuations, in which the only variable factor of production is labor. For analytical simplicity, we thus abstract from capital accumulation, which is an important propagation mechanism in the stochastic growth model that we analyzed in chapter 13.

In this analytically simpler model, we allow for a more general approach to the preferences of the representative household and also distinguish between nominal and real variables. This allows us to consider the determination of the level of prices and wages, inflation and nominal interest rates, and the role of monetary factors in new classical models.

14.1.1 The Representative Household

The representative household is assumed to maximize

$$E_t \sum\nolimits_{s=0}^{\infty} \left(\frac{1}{1+\rho}\right)^s u(C_{t+s}, L_{t+s}), \tag{14.1}$$

where C is consumption, and L is labor supply. We assume that

$$u_{C_t} = \frac{\partial u}{\partial C_t} > 0, u_{C_tC_t} = \frac{\partial^2 u}{\partial C_t^2} \leq 0, u_{L_t} = \frac{\partial u}{\partial L_t} \leq 0, u_{L_tL_t} = \frac{\partial^2 u}{\partial L_t^2} \geq 0.$$

The constraints under which the maximization takes place are given by

$$P_t C_t + \frac{1}{1+i_t} B_t \leq B_{t-1} + W_t L_t - T_t, \tag{14.2}$$

$$\lim_{T\to\infty} E_t B_T \geq 0, \tag{14.3}$$

1. This model was implemented empirically and tested by Lucas [1973], Sargent [1973, 1976], and Barro [1977, 1978], among others.

where P is the price level, W is the nominal wage, i is the nominal interest rate, B is a nominal one-period bond, and T is the level of exogenous nominal taxes minus exogenous transfers of nominal income to the household.

From the first-order conditions, it follows that

$$-\frac{u_{L_t}}{u_{C_t}} = \frac{W_t}{P_t}, \tag{14.4}$$

$$\frac{1}{1+i_t} = \frac{1}{1+\rho} E_t \left\{ \frac{u_{C_{t+1}}}{u_{C_t}} \frac{P_t}{P_{t+1}} \right\}. \tag{14.5}$$

Assume that the per period utility function is given by

$$U(C_t, L_t) = \frac{C_t^{1-\theta}}{1-\theta} - \frac{L_t^{1+\lambda}}{1+\lambda}, \tag{14.6}$$

where $\theta > 0$, $\lambda > 0$, $1/\theta$ is the intertemporal elasticity of substitution in consumption, and $1/\lambda$ the Frisch elasticity of labor supply.[2]

The first-order conditions for the problem of the representative household in this case take the form

$$\frac{W_t}{P_t} = C_t^{\theta} L_t^{\lambda}, \tag{14.7}$$

$$\frac{1}{1+i_t} = \frac{1}{1+\rho} E_t \left\{ \left(\frac{C_{t+1}}{C_t} \right)^{-\theta} \frac{P_t}{P_{t+1}} \right\} \tag{14.8}$$

Equations (14.7) and (14.8) can be written in log-linear form as

$$w_t - p_t = \theta c_t + \lambda l_t, \tag{14.9}$$

$$c_t = E_t(c_{t+1}) - \frac{1}{\theta} \left(i_t - E_t(\pi_{t+1}) - \rho \right), \tag{14.10}$$

where $w = \ln W$, $p = \ln P$, $c = \ln C$, $l = \ln L$, and $\pi_t = p_t - p_{t-1}$ is the inflation rate.

14.1.2 The Representative Firm

Production of the representative firm is a positive function of employment and is described by an aggregate production function of the form

$$Y_t = A_t L_t^{1-\alpha}, \tag{14.11}$$

2. The Frisch elasticity of labor supply is defined as the elasticity of labor supply when the marginal utility of wealth is held constant. See Frisch [1932, 1959].

where $A > 0$ and $0 < \alpha < 1$ are exogenous technological parameters; α is a constant, and A follows an exogenous stochastic process.

The representative firm chooses employment to maximize profits, for given nominal wages and prices. Profits are determined by

$$P_t Y_t - W_t L_t. \tag{14.12}$$

Profit maximization implies that employment will be determined so as to equate the marginal product of labor to the real wage:

$$\frac{W_t}{P_t} = (1-\alpha) A_t L_t^{-\alpha}. \tag{14.13}$$

One can solve the marginal productivity condition for employment. The interpretation is that labor demand is a negative function of the deviation of real wages from productivity:

$$L_t = \left(\frac{1}{(1-\alpha)} \frac{W_t}{P_t A_t} \right)^{-\frac{1}{\alpha}}. \tag{14.14}$$

One can also solve the marginal productivity condition for the price level. The interpretation is that the product price is equal to marginal cost:

$$P_t = \frac{W_t}{(1-\alpha) A_t L_t^{-\alpha}}. \tag{14.15}$$

Log-linearizing the first-order condition (14.13), we get

$$w_t - p_t = a_t - \alpha l_t + \ln(1-\alpha), \tag{14.16}$$

where $a = lnA$. Log-linearizing the production function (14.11), we get

$$y_t = a_t + (1-\alpha) l_t. \tag{14.17}$$

Having determined the behavior of households and firms, we can now analyze general equilibrium in this model.

14.1.3 General Equilibrium

Because we have assumed that there is no investment or public consumption, in product market equilibrium, consumption will be equal to total output:

$$y_t = c_t. \tag{14.18}$$

The equilibrium condition (14.18) will determine the real interest rate.

The condition for equilibrium in the labor market will require that labor demand, as implied by (14.16), should be equal to labor supply, as implied by (14.9). This will determine the real wage.

The model consists of equations (14.9), (14.10), (14.16), (14.17), and the equilibrium condition (14.18). It determines employment, output, consumption, real wages, and the real interest rate as functions of the exogenous labor productivity process a.

The real interest rate is defined by the Fisher equation as

$$r_t = i_t - E_t(\pi_{t+1}). \tag{14.19}$$

Solving the model for the five endogenous variables, we get

$$l_t = \eta_{LA} a_t + \bar{l}, \tag{14.20}$$

where $\eta_{LA} = \dfrac{1-\theta}{\theta(1-\alpha)+\alpha+\lambda}$ and $\bar{l} = \dfrac{\ln(1-\alpha)}{\theta(1-\alpha)+\alpha+\lambda}$;

$$y_t = c_t = \eta_{YA} a_t + \bar{y}, \tag{14.21}$$

where $\eta_{YA} = 1 + (1-\alpha)\eta_{LA} = \dfrac{1+\lambda}{\theta(1-\alpha)+\alpha+\lambda}$, and $\bar{y} = (1-\alpha)\bar{l}$;

$$w_t - p_t = \eta_{WA} a_t + \bar{\omega}, \tag{14.22}$$

where $\eta_{WA} = 1 - \alpha\eta_{LA} = \dfrac{\theta+\lambda}{\theta(1-\alpha)+\alpha+\lambda}$, and $\bar{\omega} = (\theta(1-\alpha)+\lambda)\,\bar{l}$; and

$$r_t = \rho + \theta\eta_{YA} E_t(\Delta a_{t+1}). \tag{14.23}$$

Equations (14.20)–(14.23), along with the product market equilibrium condition (14.18), determine the five endogenous variables as log-linear functions of the exogenous labor productivity process a.

Note that fluctuations in employment, output, consumption, and real wages are functions only of fluctuations in exogenous labor productivity a_t, and fluctuations in the real interest rate depend on fluctuations in the expected rate of change of productivity a_t.

Output, consumption, and real wages are positive functions of productivity, whereas employment is a positive function of productivity only if $\theta < 1$ (i.e., if the intertemporal elasticity of substitution of consumption is greater than one). If $\theta > 1$, employment is a negative function of productivity; but if $\theta = 1$, employment is independent of productivity. This is because if $\theta < 1$, the substitution effect dominates over the income effect, after a change in productivity, and real wages, and employment rise. If $\theta > 1$, the income effect dominates over the substitution effect. In the case $\theta = 1$, the two effects cancel each other out, and employment is not affected by the productivity shock.

Only real factors (such as real productivity) affect fluctuations in real variables. As in the stochastic growth model, monetary factors (such as the money supply and nominal interest rates) have no impact on the evolution of real variables.

14.2 Monetary Factors in a Perfectly Competitive Model

To examine the impact of monetary factors in this new classical model, let us assume the existence of a money demand function by households and firms, which in logarithms, takes the form

$$m_t - p_t = y_t - \eta i_t, \tag{14.24}$$

where η is the semi-elasticity of money demand with respect to the nominal interest rate.[3]

From the definition of the real interest rate through the Fisher equation (14.19), the nominal interest rate is equal to

$$i_t = r_t + E_t(\pi_{t+1}), \tag{14.25}$$

where the real interest rate r is determined by (14.23) and is independent of monetary factors.

We will see that, as in the case of the models analyzed in chapter 12, when the central bank follows a rule for the money supply, then the model determines the price level, inflation, and nominal interest rates. If the central bank pegs the nominal interest rate, the price level and the nominal money supply cannot be determined, unless the nominal interest rate reacts sufficiently strongly to changes in the price level.

14.2.1 An Exogenous Path for the Money Supply

If the central bank determines an exogenous path for the money supply, then from (14.24) and (14.25), it follows that

$$p_t = \frac{\eta}{1+\eta} E_t(p_{t+1}) + \frac{1}{1+\eta} m_t - \frac{1}{1+\eta} (y_t - \eta r_t)\,. \tag{14.26}$$

Under the assumption that $\eta > 0$, the rational expectations solution of (14.26) implies that

$$p_t = \frac{1}{1+\eta} \sum_{j=0}^{\infty} \left(\frac{\eta}{1+\eta} \right)^j E_t \left(m_{t+j} - y_{t+j} + \eta r_{t+j} \right). \tag{14.27}$$

3. Equation (14.24) could be derived using the money in the utility function approach, by allowing for real money balances to affect the utility of the representative household. See chapter 12. However, we postulate it directly for reasons of analytical simplicity.

From (14.27), the price level and inflation are determined as functions of the exogenous path of the money supply and the paths of real output and the real interest rate, which, as we have seen, are independent of monetary factors in this new classical model. The nominal interest rate is determined endogenously from (14.27) and (14.25).

14.2.2 An Exogenous Path for the Nominal Interest Rate

If we assume that the central bank follows an exogenous path for the nominal interest rate, then from the Fisher equation (14.25), it follows that

$$E_t(\pi_{t+1}) = i_t - r_t. \tag{14.28}$$

Equation (14.28) determines expected inflation, not actual inflation, given the exogenous path of nominal interest rates. This equation is consistent with any price level path that satisfies

$$p_{t+1} = p_t + i_t - r_t + \xi_{t+1}, \tag{14.29}$$

where ξ is any shock that satisfies $E_t\,(\xi_{t+1}) = 0$. Equation (14.29) suggests that there are multiple equilibria for the price level and inflation, depending on ξ. This price level indeterminacy when the central bank follows an exogenous path for the nominal interest rate is also transferred to the money supply, through the money demand function (14.24). Consequently, neither the money supply nor the price level can be determined uniquely when the central bank follows an exogenous path for the nominal interest rate.

14.2.3 An Inflation-Based Nominal Interest Rate Rule

Central banks predominantly use the nominal interest rate as their preferred monetary instrument. However, they follow policies according to which the path of nominal interest rates is not exogenous but depends on past, current, and expected future economic developments, mainly inflation. For example, if inflation rises, central banks usually raise nominal interest rates to reduce it, and vice versa. After all, this is the essence of the interest rate rule proposed more than a century ago by Wicksell [1898]. Let us therefore assume the following rule for determining nominal interest rates:

$$i_t = \rho + \pi^* + \phi(\pi_t - \pi^*), \tag{14.30}$$

where $\phi > 0$ is the reaction of the central bank nominal interest rate to inflation, and π^* is the inflation target of the central bank (presumably the optimal steady state inflation rate).[4]

4. We have seen how the Wicksell rule results in price level determinacy in the models of chapter 12. Here we use a version of the Wicksell rule for inflation rather than for the price level.

From (14.25) and (14.30), we therefore have that

$$\hat{\pi}_t = \frac{1}{\phi} E_t\left(\hat{\pi}_{t+1}\right) + \frac{1}{\phi}\left(r_t - \rho\right), \tag{14.31}$$

where $\hat{\pi}_t = \pi_t - \pi^*$ is the deviation of the current inflation rate from the target of the central bank. The real interest r depends only on real factors, as implied by equation (14.23) and in fact all new classical models with perfect information.

Solving (14.31) under rational expectations yields

$$\hat{\pi}_t = \sum_{s=0}^{\infty} \left(\frac{1}{\phi}\right)^{s+1} E_t\left(r_{t+s} - \rho\right) \tag{14.32}$$

if $\phi > 1$, and

$$\hat{\pi}_{t+1} = \phi\hat{\pi}_t - \left(r_t - \rho\right) + \xi_{t+1} \tag{14.33}$$

if $\phi \leq 1$. Here ξ is any shock that satisfies $E_t\left(\xi_{t+1}\right) = 0$.

Thus, if the reaction of the central bank nominal interest rates to inflation is sufficiently pronounced ($\phi > 1$), there is no indeterminacy problem for inflation. The fundamental solution is given by (14.32). If the reaction of the nominal interest rates to inflation is not sufficiently pronounced ($\phi \leq 1$), then the problem of inflation indeterminacy and the possibility of price bubbles remains.

14.2.4 Optimal Monetary Policy

Equation (14.32) can be used to determine the optimal ϕ if the objective of the central bank is to stabilize inflation around its steady state target. After all, in this model, real variables are always equal to their equilibrium level, so monetary policy cannot have any other objective.

The optimal monetary policy rule is clearly to let ϕ tend to infinity (i.e., an interest rate policy that, by (14.32), completely stabilizes inflation around the steady state target of the central bank). Thus, optimal monetary policy in a new classical model implies complete stabilization of inflation at the optimal steady state inflation rate π^*.[5]

In any case, as we have already seen, in new classical models of aggregate fluctuations, only real factors affect fluctuations in real variables. Monetary factors and monetary policy only affect real money balances and nominal variables, such as the price level, inflation, nominal interest rates, and the nominal money stock.

5. This was noted immediately after World War I by Fisher [1919], who argued for a policy of complete stabilization of the price level. The modern equivalent of the *Fisher rule* is the complete stabilization of inflation at π^*, the optimal inflation rate of the central bank.

14.3 Imperfect Information and the Nonneutrality of Money

The short-run neutrality of money implied by new classical models was troublesome for some of their proponents, as these models were not compatible with the evidence suggesting the existence of a positive short-run relation between inflation and employment.[6]

Lucas [1972] responded by developing a new classical model that was consistent with a positive short-run relation between inflation and employment, even under rational expectations. His model was subsequently simplified by Barro [1976] and implemented empirically by Lucas [1973], Sargent [1973, 1976], and Barro [1977, 1978]. The Lucas [1972] model was based on the assumption that producers do not have full information about the price level at the time they make their production decisions. What they observe during the production process is only the price of their own product, positively but not perfectly correlated with the price level. Thus, they attribute part of any change in the price level to a change in the relative price of their product. Hence, when inflation is unexpectedly high, all producers simultaneously think that the relative price of their own product has gone up, and so they increase production and employment. The opposite happens when inflation is unexpectedly low.

This model was later extended by Alogoskoufis [1983] to explicitly incorporate competitive labor markets. The assumption in this extended model is that households make their labor supply decisions in the absence of full information about the price level. They are assumed to only observe their nominal wage and the price of the product of the firm for which they work. Hence, when they observe their wage and the price of their firm's output rise unexpectedly, they systematically attribute this rise to a change in the relative price of their output and their real wage. Thus, employment and output rise in response to unanticipated inflation, as labor supply rises in response to the increased labor demand by firms.

It is this extended version of the Lucas [1972] model that we shall examine, as this model incorporates the labor market and is thus compatible with the perfectly competitive model presented in section 14.1.

14.3.1 Competitive Equilibrium under Imperfect Information about the Price Level

Assume a competitive economy that is described by the new classical model of section 14.1. However, following Lucas [1972], let us assume that current production takes place in a continuum of "islands," which are informationally isolated.

Production takes place at the beginning of each period, with producers having only local information about prices and wages. Consumption is decided at the end of each period, under full information about prices and interest rates, and all consumers consume

6. Such a relation is often called a "Phillips curve" or a "Phillips relation" and by the 1960s, had become a major component of Keynesian models. We shall discuss this relation and its properties in chapter 15.

a composite commodity consisting of the products of all islands. Islands are indexed by z, where $z \in [0, 1]$.

Under these assumptions, employment, output, nominal wages, and prices are determined at the local level, with firms and producers having no information about current wages and prices on the other islands when they make their production and labor supply decisions. Employment, output, nominal wages, and nominal prices on island z are determined under imperfect information, by the equality of labor supply with labor demand, and output supply with output demand on island z. They are thus determined by

$$w_t(z) - E_z p_t = \theta E_z c_t + \lambda l_t(z), \tag{14.34}$$

$$w_t(z) - p_t(z) = a_t(z) - \alpha l_t(z) + \ln(1-\alpha), \tag{14.35}$$

$$y_t(z) = a_t(z) + (1-\alpha) l_t(z), \tag{14.36}$$

$$y_t(z) = m_t(z) - p_t(z). \tag{14.37}$$

All variables in these equations are in logarithms. Here $w(z)$ is the nominal wage in island z; $p(z)$ is the competitive price of the good produced in island z; $l(z)$ is employment in island z, determined by the equality of labor demand with labor supply; $y(z)$ is output in island z, determined by the equality of supply and demand; $E_z p_t$ denotes the rational expectation about the end-period price level, based on the local information set for island z at the beginning of period t; $E_z c_t$ denotes the rational expectation about the end-period household consumption, conditional on local information at the beginning of the period; $a(z)$ is labor productivity in island z, and $m(z)$ is the money supply in island z. Note that households are assumed to make their consumption decisions on the basis of full information about the prices of all goods and the economywide interest rate at the end of the period, when they buy their consumption bundle from an economywide market for consumer goods.[7]

Equation (14.34) is the labor supply function of the representative household on island z, derived from the first-order conditions for the maximization of its intertemporal utility derived in the same way as (14.10). Equation (14.35) is the labor demand function of the representative firm on island z derived in the same way as (14.16), by a marginal productivity condition. Equation (14.36) is the log-linearized production function of the representative firm on island z, derived in the same way as (14.17). Equation (14.37) is the demand function for the product of the representative firm on island z. This function depends on the money supply allocated to island z by traders in goods, who collect goods from the various islands at the beginning of the period and sell them to consumers as consumption bundles at the end of the period. The marginal cost of intermediation is assumed constant and is normalized

7. These assumptions are those of Alogoskoufis [1983] and are in the spirit of Lucas [1972].

to zero. The intermediaries are distributed randomly across islands in every period. They are assumed competitive and make zero profits in equilibrium.

Note that imperfect information matters only for the decisions of households regarding their labor supply, because labor supply decisions depend on the expected purchasing power of the locally determined nominal wage (i.e., the nominal wage deflated by the price level that households expect to face at the end of the period). Labor supply also depends on their expected volume of consumption at the end of the period. Neither of the two is known when households decide on their labor supply, but expectations are formed rationally, given the available information. In contrast, the decisions of firms depend on the local real wage (i.e., the nominal wage deflated by the price of the local good), which is known when firms make their production decisions, because local information is fully available.

Productivity and the money supply are assumed to be exogenous stationary stochastic processes that are the sum of two independent components: an aggregate component and an island-specific (local) component. Thus, we assume that

$$a_t(z) = a_t + \varepsilon_a, \tag{14.38}$$

$$m_t(z) = m_t + \varepsilon_m. \tag{14.39}$$

For simplicity, and without significant loss of generality, we shall assume that both the aggregate and the island-specific components are white noise processes. Thus, we assume that

$$a_t \sim N(0, \sigma_a^2), \varepsilon_a \sim N(0, \tau_a^2), m_t \sim N(0, \sigma_m^2), \varepsilon_m \sim N(0, \tau_m^2),$$

where σ^2 denotes the variance of the aggregate component, and τ^2 is the variance of the island-specific component.[8]

Because all households face the same economywide price level for their consumption bundle and the same nominal interest rate, at the end of the period, they will all choose the same level of consumption. The price level, aggregate consumption, and aggregate output will thus be determined by

$$p_t = \int_{z=0}^{1} p_t(z)dz, \tag{14.40}$$

$$c_t = E_t(c_{t+1}) - \frac{1}{\theta}\left(i_t - E_t(\pi_{t+1}) - \rho\right), \tag{14.41}$$

8. We could easily assume that productivity and the money supply follow a more general stationary stochastic process, such as a linear AR(n) process. However, this would not alter our results with regard to the nonneutrality of monetary shocks, as it is only unanticipated changes in the money supply that affect output and employment in this model. Thus, the systematic part of the money supply process would be incorporated in the expectations of households and would not affect labor supply and other real variables.

$$y_t = \int_{z=0}^{1} y_t(z)dz = c_t = m_t - p_t, \tag{14.42}$$

respectively. This completes the presentation of the model.

14.3.2 The Determination of Output and Employment

Under the assumptions we have made, output and employment on each island are determined on the basis of local information only. Aggregate consumption and the nominal interest rate are determined on the basis of full information at the end of the period.

Equating labor supply (14.34) and labor demand (14.35) on each island, we get that employment is determined by

$$l_t(z) = \frac{1}{\alpha+\lambda}\left(\tilde{l} + a_t(z) - \theta E_z c_t + (p_t(z) - E_z p_t)\right), \tag{14.43}$$

where $\tilde{l} = \ln(1-\alpha)$. Employment depends positively on productivity, negatively on estimated aggregate consumption, and positively on the difference of the local price from the estimated aggregate price level. The reason for this relative price effect is that households that supply labor care about the purchasing power of their wage, but firms care about the relation of the wage to the local price. Thus, a higher local price that does not necessarily signify a rise in the general price level causes an increase in both labor demand and labor supply, as it reduces wages deflated by the local price and increases wages deflated by the expected price level. As we shall see, this is the basis for the positive inflation employment (and output) relation in this new classical model. This effect is the main difference between the present model and the full information model of section 14.1.[9]

Substituting the employment equation (14.43) in the local production function (14.36), we find that output supply is determined by

$$y_t(z) = \frac{1+\lambda}{\alpha+\lambda} a_t(z) + \frac{1-\alpha}{\alpha+\lambda}\left(\tilde{l} - \theta E_z y_t + (p_t(z) - E_z p_t)\right). \tag{14.44}$$

In (14.44), we have used (14.42) to write expected consumption in terms of expected aggregate output, because there is no investment in this model, and all output must be consumed. When aggregated across markets, (14.44) denotes a positive short-run relation between aggregate output and unanticipated inflation.

Equating (14.44) with local aggregate demand (14.37) and solving for the local price level, we get

$$p_t(z) = \frac{1-\alpha}{1+\lambda} E_z p_t + \frac{\alpha+\lambda}{1+\lambda} m_t(z) - a_t(z) - \frac{1-\alpha}{1+\lambda}\left(\tilde{l} - \theta E_z y_t\right). \tag{14.45}$$

9. This results from the famous confusion between absolute and relative price changes in the Lucas [1972] model.

Using (14.42) to substitute for expected aggregate output by expected aggregate real money balances $m-p$, we can rewrite (14.45) as

$$p_t(z) = -\frac{1-\alpha}{1+\lambda}\tilde{l} + \frac{(1-\alpha)(1-\theta)}{1+\lambda}E_z p_t + \frac{(1-\alpha)\theta}{1+\lambda}E_z m_t + \frac{\alpha+\lambda}{1+\lambda}m_t(z) - a_t(z). \tag{14.46}$$

Equation (14.46) denotes the local price as a function of the exogenous processes for productivity and the money supply (real and monetary shocks), and the rational expectations of the price level and of the aggregate money supply on the basis of local information.

Given the assumption that productivity shocks and the money supply follow white noise processes of the form of (14.38) and (14.39), the rational expectations of aggregate productivity and the aggregate money supply, given local information, are determined by

$$E_z a_t = \zeta_a a_t(z), \tag{14.47}$$

$$E_z m_t = \zeta_m m_t(z), \tag{14.48}$$

where $\zeta_a = \frac{\sigma_a^2}{\sigma_a^2+\tau_a^2} < 1$, and $\zeta_m = \frac{\sigma_m^2}{\sigma_m^2+\tau_m^2} < 1$. Equations (14.47) and (14.48) denote the *optimal least squares projections* of the aggregate component of productivity and the money supply, given an observation of the local realizations of productivity and the money supply. Given that (14.38) and (14.39) are exogenous linear processes, these are equivalent to the rational expectations of the aggregate component given the local realization.

Note that in the case where there are no relative real and monetary shocks (i.e., when shocks are purely aggregate), $\tau_a^2 = \tau_m^2 = 0$, and it follows that $\zeta_a = \zeta_m = 1$. In this case, there is no confusion between aggregate and relative shocks, and we are back to the full-information new classical model of section 14.1.

Substituting (14.48) in (14.46), the equilibrium local price can be written as

$$p_t(z) = -\frac{1-\alpha}{1+\lambda}\tilde{l} + \frac{(1-\alpha)(1-\theta)}{1+\lambda}E_{zt} p_t + \frac{\alpha+\lambda+(1-\alpha)\theta\zeta_m}{1+\lambda}m_t(z) - a_t(z). \tag{14.49}$$

Equation (14.49)—which expresses the equilibrium local price as a linear function of the expected aggregate price and the two exogenous shocks to productivity and the money supply—can be easily solved by using the method of undetermined coefficients.

14.3.3 The Real Effects of Monetary Shocks in a Rational Expectations Equilibrium

Let us assume that the solution for the local price takes the form

$$p_t(z) = \psi_0 + \psi_1 a_t(z) + \psi_2 m_t(z), \tag{14.50}$$

where the ψs are unknown coefficients to be determined. Then, given our assumptions, the solution for the aggregate price level is given by

$$p_t = \psi_0 + \psi_1 a_t + \psi_2 m_t. \tag{14.51}$$

From (14.51), the rational expectation of the aggregate price level given only local information is given by

$$E_z p_t = \psi_0 + \psi_1 E_z a_t + \psi_2 E_z m_t. \tag{14.52}$$

Substituting (14.47) and (14.48) in (14.52), we get

$$E_z p_t = \psi_0 + \psi_1 \zeta_a a_t(z) + \psi_2 \zeta_m m_t(z). \tag{14.53}$$

Substituting (14.53) in (14.49) and rearranging, we get

$$\begin{aligned} p_t(z) = & -\frac{(1-\alpha)(1-\theta)\psi_0 - (1-\alpha)\tilde{l}}{1+\lambda} + \\ & + \frac{\zeta_a(1-\alpha)(1-\theta)\psi_1 - (1+\lambda)}{1+\lambda} a_t(z) + \\ & + \frac{\zeta_m\left((1-\alpha)(1-\theta)\psi_2 + (1-\alpha)\theta\right) + (\alpha+\lambda)}{1+\lambda} m_t(z). \end{aligned} \tag{14.54}$$

By comparing coefficients between (14.54) and (14.50), we can then determine the ψs as

$$\psi_0 = -\frac{(1-\alpha)\tilde{l}}{1+\lambda-(1-\alpha)(1-\theta)}, \tag{14.55}$$

$$\psi_1 = -\frac{1+\lambda}{1+\lambda-\zeta_a(1-\alpha)(1-\theta)}, \tag{14.56}$$

$$\psi_2 = \frac{\alpha+\lambda+(1-\alpha)\theta\zeta_m}{1+\lambda-\zeta_m(1-\alpha)(1-\theta)}. \tag{14.57}$$

Note that in the case of perfect information, ζ_m is equal to unity, and ψ_2 is then equal to unity. The elasticity of the price level with respect to monetary shocks is equal to unity under full information. Under imperfect information, the elasticity ψ_2 is smaller than unity, as there is also a positive effect on real output, because of the confusion between absolute and relative changes in prices.

To solve for output, we can again use the method of undetermined coefficients. Let us assume that the solution for local output takes the form

$$y_t(z) = \gamma_0 + \gamma_1 a_t(z) + \gamma_2 m_t(z), \tag{14.58}$$

where the γs are unknown coefficients to be determined. From (14.58), aggregate output is determined by

$$y_t = \gamma_0 + \gamma_1 a_t + \gamma_2 m_t. \tag{14.59}$$

From (14.59), the rational expectation of aggregate output given local information is

$$E_z y_t = \gamma_0 + \gamma_1 \zeta_a a_t(z) + \gamma_2 \zeta_m m_t(z). \tag{14.60}$$

From (14.50) and (14.53), the difference between the current local price on island z and the expected aggregate price level is given by

$$p_t(z) - E_z p_t = \psi_1(1-\zeta_a)a_t(z) + \psi_2(1-\zeta_m)m_t(z). \tag{14.61}$$

Substituting (14.60) and (14.61) in (14.44), the solution for output takes the form

$$\begin{aligned} y_t(z) = \frac{1-\alpha}{\alpha+\lambda}\Bigg((\tilde{l} - \theta\gamma_0) + \left(\frac{1+\lambda}{1-\alpha} + \psi_1(1-\zeta_a) - \theta\gamma_1\zeta_a\right) a_t(z) + \\ + \left(\psi_2(1-\zeta_m) - \theta\gamma_2\zeta_m\right) m_t(z)\Bigg). \end{aligned} \tag{14.62}$$

Comparing coefficients between (14.58) and (14.62), we find that

$$\gamma_0 = \frac{1-\alpha}{\theta(1-\alpha)+\alpha+\lambda}\tilde{l}, \tag{14.63}$$

$$\gamma_1 = \frac{1+\lambda+(1-\alpha)\psi_1(1-\zeta_a)}{\theta(1-\alpha)\zeta_a+\alpha+\lambda}, \tag{14.64}$$

$$\gamma_2 = \frac{(1-\alpha)\psi_2(1-\zeta_m)}{\theta(1-\alpha)\zeta_m+\alpha+\lambda}. \tag{14.65}$$

From equations (14.59), (14.63), (14.64), and (14.65), which describe the solution of the model for aggregate output, it is clear that both real and monetary shocks affect fluctuations in aggregate real output. The real effects of monetary shocks depend on ζ_m, the ratio of the variance of aggregate monetary shocks to the variance of both aggregate and relative monetary shocks. Monetary shocks have real effects in this model, because ζ_m is less that unity (i.e., because they cause a confusion between purely nominal and real fluctuations in real wages).

A positive monetary shock causes an increase in both the price level and nominal wages. However, because of imperfect information about the price level, workers rationally attribute part of the increase in the price level to an increase in the relative price of goods on their own island. Hence, they overestimate their real wage, they supply more labor, and employment and output increase. Because of imperfect information, monetary shocks thus have temporary real effects.

These real effects are transmitted to all real variables: employment, real wages, and the real interest rate. Combining the solution for output with the rest of the model, it is easy to show that these real variables are all affected by monetary shocks. The relevant solutions utilizing the rest of the model are given by

$$l_t = \frac{1}{1-\alpha}\left(\gamma_0 + (\gamma_1 - (1-\alpha))\, a_t + \gamma_2 m_t\right), \tag{14.66}$$

$$w_t - p_t = \frac{1}{1-\alpha}\left((-\alpha\gamma_0 - (1-\alpha)\tilde{l}) + (1-\alpha(\gamma_1+\alpha))\, a_t - \alpha\gamma_2 m_t\right), \tag{14.67}$$

$$r_t = \rho - \theta\left(\gamma_1 a_t + \gamma_2 m_t\right). \tag{14.68}$$

One can see from (14.66)–(14.68) that because of imperfect information, monetary shocks also cause fluctuations in employment, real wages, and the real interest rate. Thus, monetary shocks have temporary real effects across the board.

A positive monetary shock causes an increase in prices and nominal wages, but also an increase in employment and output and a reduction in real wages and the real interest rate. The reduction in real wages causes firms to increase employment and output. However, because households underestimate the increase in the price level, they supply more labor, interpreting part of the increase in nominal wages as an increase in real wages. Real interest rates fall to induce households to consume the higher output.

Note that if households had full information about the price level and aggregate shocks, ζ_m would be equal to unity, and γ_2 would be equal to zero. In this case, there would be no real effects from monetary shocks, and we would be back to the model of section 14.1, where only productivity shocks affect real variables. The contribution of the Lucas [1972] imperfect information assumption is that it allows for a short-run nonneutrality of money in an otherwise purely new classical model of aggregate fluctuations.

14.3.4 Optimal Monetary Policy in the Lucas Model

Optimal monetary policy in the Lucas model would not differ from the case of the new classical model with perfect information. If the central bank completely stabilized inflation, households would not confuse relative and aggregate price movements, as they would be able to perfectly forecast the price level. Hence, the short-run trade-off between inflation and real variables would disappear, as inflation would be constant, and all real variables would be at their equilibrium levels. Therefore, optimal monetary policy would again be the Fisher rule of full inflation stabilization.

14.3.5 The New Classical Model and the Great Depression

The explanation of the positive short-run relation between inflation and output and employment offered by the Lucas model is in terms of intertemporal substitution in labor supply and unanticipated inflation. Thus, if it were to account for the Great Depression of the 1930s, it would attribute this event to an unanticipated contraction in the money supply, causing an unanticipated deflation and a rise in real wages, which resulted in lower employment and output. The reason that labor supply fell would be attributed to imperfect information by workers, who mistook the nominal wage deflation for a fall in real wages. The model would not be able to account for the rise in unemployment, unless the rise was interpreted as a temporary fall in labor supply.

In any case, the model would also have problems accounting for the persistence of the Great Depression, as only unanticipated shocks to the money supply have real effects in such a model, and the model would have to invoke a sequence of unanticipated negative monetary shocks.[10]

14.3.6 Models of Informational Frictions and Rational Inattention

The weaknesses of the original classical models based on misperceptions and informational frictions notwithstanding, there has been a recent revival of interest in such models. Mankiw and Reis [2002], Sims [2003], and Woodford [2003b] pioneered this revival by proposing new formalizations of informational frictions and arguing in favor of *rational inattention* by agents to informational frictions. See Angeletos and La'O [2009] and Machowiak and Wiederholt [2009] on recent attempts to explain business cycles in terms of such frictions. Angeletos and Lian [2016] survey this recent literature and its implications for monetary policy. These more recent models are more sophisticated than the original Lucas [1972] model, and some of them emphasize strategic interactions between agents with different information sets. Yet they rest on similar premises as the Lucas model, such as misperceptions of aggregate shocks and intertemporal substitution in labor supply.

14.4 Conclusion

New classical models of aggregate fluctuations imply that aggregate fluctuations are mainly caused by real factors. This is why such models are often called RBC models.

New classical models are DSGE models based on optimizing behavior by both households and firms, flexible prices, and fully competitive markets. Households maximize their intertemporal utility, firms maximize the present value of their profits, and markets function efficiently.

10. See the exchange between Rees [1970] and Lucas and Rapping [1972] on the ability of the Lucas and Rapping [1969] equilibrium labor market model, based on intertemporal substitution in labor supply, to explain unemployment in the Great Depression. Lucas and Rapping [1972] concede that the model has problems explaining the persistence of the rise in unemployment. See also Bernanke [1983] for an econometric investigation of the Great Depression using a model that relies on unanticipated monetary shocks. He finds that such monetary shocks cannot explain the persistence of the Great Depression, and that additional propagation mechanisms are required to explain persistence. He thus proposes a propagation mechanism that relies on the role of financial frictions in the form of a sustained increase of the costs of financial intermediation following the extensive bank failures caused in the first years of the depression. We introduce and discuss financial frictions in chapter 19.

If the competitive general equilibrium models of this kind could explain all the features of aggregate fluctuations, then there would be no need for models that stress distortions in product, financial, and labor markets, or other market inefficiencies. However, new classical models have weaknesses as models of aggregate fluctuations.

First, these models cannot fully account for the real effects of nominal and monetary shocks. For example, it is widely accepted, following the evidence presented by Friedman and Schwartz [1963], that the Great Depression of the 1930s was caused by monetary and not real shocks. Similar views are prevalent regarding the Great Recession of 2008–2009, which was one of the deepest post-World War II recessions.

The imperfect information assumption of Lucas [1972] can be used to account for the real effects of nominal shocks, but the effects of nominal shocks in such a model would be short lived and nonpersistent. However, the more recent models of sticky information, based on persistent informational frictions and rational inattention, are more successful in accounting for persistent effects of monetary shocks. So are the financial frictions models, such as the Bernanke [1983] model.

Second, even though new classical models can in principle account for employment fluctuations, they do so only on the basis of intertemporal substitution in labor supply. However, this explanation is not sufficient to explain the existence and the persistence of unemployment and the widely held view that unemployment is an involuntary condition for those who experience it, and not the result of a voluntary rational choice under imperfect information.

For these reasons—and even though new classical models are internally consistent—many macroeconomists consider them as an incomplete and not persuasive explanation of aggregate fluctuations. The alternative class of models consists of a variety of new Keynesian models. These models are based on product and labor market distortions that hinder nominal wages and prices from adjusting sufficiently in the short run to equilibrate labor and product markets. Thus, following both nominal and real shocks, output and employment deviate from their equilibrium values, resulting in aggregate fluctuations and involuntary unemployment. It is to such models that we now turn, starting with the traditional Keynesian models of aggregate fluctuations.

15

Keynesian Models and the Phillips Curve

As already noted, following the Great Depression of the 1930s, the analysis of aggregate fluctuations evolved into macroeconomics, on the basis of Keynesian models. These models were derived from the *General Theory* of Keynes [1936], who argued against the then-prevailing classical equilibrium theory of employment and aggregate fluctuations.[1]

Keynes proceeded to argue that a general theory of employment, as opposed to the classical theory, ought to be able to explain involuntary unemployment, which he proceeded to duly define as a situation in which the real wage is higher than the marginal disutility of labor. The Keynesian approach was developed through a sequence of models in the *General Theory*, and it very soon took the economics profession by storm.

The first model, the so-called Keynesian cross, focuses on the conditions for short-run equilibrium in the market for goods and services when prices are fixed. A second model, again based on the assumption of fixed prices, focuses on the conditions for simultaneous equilibrium in the market for goods and services and the market for money. This model was codified by Hicks [1937] and has become known as the IS-LM model, following the terminology used by Hansen [1949, 1953]. The IS-LM model was for many years the dominant Keynesian model, both among academic economists and policymakers. A third model combined the IS-LM model with two additional assumptions: first, that the nominal wage is fixed in the short run, and second, that employers determine employment by equating the real wage with the marginal product of labor. This model, analyzed by Modigliani [1944] and later Patinkin [1956], was codified as the AD-AS model, or the neoclassical synthesis model, and was used to determine both unemployment and the price level.

In Keynesian models, the immediate adjustment of prices and wages as equilibrating mechanisms was replaced by the assumption that in the short-term, prices or nominal

1. Keynes' criticism of what he termed the "classical" theory focused on two fundamental postulates: the equality of the real wage to the marginal product of labor and the equality of the real wage to the marginal disutility of labor. See Keynes [1936, p. 5]. It is exactly these two postulates that determine employment in the stochastic growth model we examined in chapter 13 and the competitive models without capital of chapter 14. Keynes himself maintained the first postulate but dropped the second, defining unemployment as involuntary.

wages are not fully flexible. Thus, the level of income and employment become additional adjustment mechanisms for the market for goods and services and the market for labor.

In this chapter, we consider the structure of the basic Keynesian models, initially assuming a constant level of prices or nominal wages. Then we allow for the gradual adjustment of prices and nominal wages based on the *Phillips curve*, a negative relation between inflation and unemployment that was brought to the fore by Phillips [1958], after whom it was named. We also look at the theory of discretionary macroeconomic policy that was developed on the basis of Keynesian models by Tinbergen [1952], Theil [1954], and others.

The negative relationship between inflation and unemployment, which became known as the Phillips curve, was an empirical relationship highlighted by Phillips [1958] for the United Kingdom. It soon became a central reference point for Keynesian models. It was interpreted as evidence of the gradual adjustment of wages and prices and provided the missing link on how a change in aggregate demand would affect both employment and inflation. This relationship was combined with the IS-LM model for the simultaneous determination of both inflation and unemployment.[2]

According to the basic Keynesian model combined with the Phillips curve, an increase in aggregate demand (through government expenditure, a tax cut, or an increase in the money supply) would lead to an increase in real income and employment, a reduction in unemployment, and an increase in inflation. Conversely, a decline in aggregate demand would lead to a decline of real income and employment, an increase in unemployment, and a reduction in inflation.

Following the publication of the Phillips [1958] paper and after estimating a similar relationship for the United States, Samuelson and Solow [1960] argued that the short-term objective of macroeconomic policy could be seen as the appropriate selection of a discretionary mix of monetary and fiscal policies that would deliver the socially desirable combination of unemployment and inflation on the Phillips curve.

In a recession, an increase in aggregate demand would lead to a reduction in unemployment, but at the cost of higher inflation. In an economic boom, inflation could be reduced through a reduction in aggregate demand, but this would also result in higher unemployment. Aggregate fluctuations could thus be smoothed through the appropriate mix of macroeconomic policies. The Keynesian solution to addressing the problem of aggregate fluctuations was thus a prescription for *discretionary aggregate demand policies*. These could be designed, evaluated, and implemented using econometric models based on the IS-LM framework on the demand side and the Phillips curve on the supply side.

2. In many ways, as a primarily empirical relationship, the original Phillips curve was the ultimate macroeconomic relationship without adequate microeconomic foundations. It was one of the first such relationships to break down when policymakers attempted to exploit it.

However, since the mid-1960s, the negative relationship between inflation and unemployment suggested by the Phillips curve began to shift. Higher inflation would lead only to temporary reductions in unemployment, as unemployment tended to return to higher levels without a reduction in inflation. Attempts to keep unemployment low resulted in not only high but also rising inflation. This was soon attributed to the impact of inflationary expectations.

As suggested by Phelps [1967] and Friedman [1968], an increase in average inflation would gradually lead to increased expectations of future inflation on the part of households and firms. Thus, to achieve a reduction in unemployment, inflation would have to increase beyond the revised inflationary expectations of households and firms. Expectations would then gradually adapt to the higher inflation, inflation would have to increase even further, and so on, while unemployment would tend to return to its "natural" rate (a term coined by Friedman [1968] to define equilibrium unemployment).

Phelps [1967] and Friedman [1968] argued that discretionary aggregate demand policies would eventually result in high and possibly unstable inflation, while unemployment would tend to return to its equilibrium (or natural) rate, determined by real factors, such as labor and product market distortions.

The instability of the Phillips curve soon became evident and has since triggered another revolution in the analysis of business cycles and macroeconomic policy. It was this revolution that eventually led to an even greater emphasis on the microeconomic foundations of macroeconomic models, the eventual adoption of the hypothesis of rational expectations (rather than the hypothesis of adaptive expectations that prevailed until then), and a resolution to the debate on rules versus discretion in the determination of aggregate demand policies in favor of rules. The macroeconomic modeling of aggregate fluctuations shifted from the largely ad hoc neoclassical synthesis that prevailed until the mid-1960s to a so-called monetarist counterrevolution in the late 1960s and early 1970s, and eventually to the adoption of the new classical and new Keynesian approaches. The latter approaches are based on explicit dynamic microeconomic foundations and DSGE models.

In the remainder of this chapter, we analyze the original Keynesian models, the Keynesian theory of discretionary monetary and fiscal policy, and the implications of the breakdown of the original Phillips curve. Although these models are not dynamic and stochastic, they are nonetheless useful to understand, as they are representative of the previous generation of macroeconomic models and are also the basis and the inspiration behind the widely used new Keynesian DSGE models.

15.1 The Original Keynesian Models

In the analysis of the *General Theory*, and subsequent Keynesian models, the assumption of the immediate adjustment of wages and prices to equilibrate labor and product markets was replaced by the assumption that there is a short-term rigidity in their adjustment, and that the short-run macroeconomic adjustment mechanism also involves quantities such as the level of real income and employment.[3]

In this section, we look at the three main forms of the original Keynesian model. First, we examine the *Keynesian cross*, which determines real output and employment as a function of real aggregate demand, for an exogenously given price level. Second, the *IS-LM model*, which determines real output and employment and the nominal interest rate as functions of real aggregate demand and monetary conditions, also for an exogenously given price level. Third, we consider the *AD-AS model of aggregate demand and aggregate supply*, which determines real output, employment, and the price level for an exogenously given level of nominal wages. All three forms can be found in successive chapters of the *General Theory*, which develop the Keynesian approach.

15.1.1 The Keynesian Cross

The Keynesian model starts by considering the determination of aggregate demand. The assumption is that total real output and income Y is determined by aggregate demand, consisting of real consumption C, real gross investment I, and real government expenditure G:

$$Y_t = C_t + I_t + G_t. \tag{15.1}$$

In the simplest version, that of the Keynesian cross, investment and government expenditure are considered exogenous, and the only behavioral equation is the consumption function. Consumption is assumed to be a positive function of current real disposable income:

$$C_t = C\left(Y_t - T_t\right), \tag{15.2}$$

where T denotes the real value of taxes, and the first derivative of the consumption function satisfies

$$0 < C_Y = \frac{\partial C}{\partial (Y - T)} < 1.$$

The parameter C_Y is termed the *marginal propensity to consume* and is assumed to be less than unity. Note that the *marginal propensity to save* is given by $1 - C_Y$, and is therefore positive and less than one.

Keynes [1936] devoted a significant number of pages in chapters 8 and 9 of the *General Theory* to the justification of the consumption function. Also, note that the Keynesian

3. Keynes was fully confident of the novelty of the *General Theory*, not only about the equilibrating mechanisms of markets for goods and services and labor, but also about capital markets. For example, in a paper on the role of the interest rate, published after the *General Theory*, Keynes states that "the initial novelty lies in my maintaining that it is not the rate of interest, but the level of incomes which ensures equality between saving and investment." (Keynes [1937, p. 250]).

consumption function differs radically from the Euler equation for consumption we have been relying on so far. It focuses on disposable household income as the main determinant of consumption and explicitly denies a role for the interest rate.[4]

From (15.1) and (15.2), we can determine the equilibrium condition between total output and aggregate demand, which is the *equilibrium condition in the market for goods and services*:

$$Y_t = C(Y_t - T_t) + I_t + G_t. \tag{15.3}$$

The equilibrium condition (15.3) is depicted in figure 15.1, which is also known as the Keynesian cross.[5]

Real output is determined by the equality of aggregate supply and aggregate demand, which is the sum of real consumption, investment, and government expenditure. Prices are assumed to be fixed or sluggish to adjust. Therefore, a change in aggregate demand induces firms to produce more and thus brings about a change in aggregate output and employment.[6]

From equation (15.3), one can derive the *multiplier*:

$$\frac{dY_t}{dI_t} = \frac{dY_t}{dG_t} = \frac{1}{1 - C_Y} > 1. \tag{15.4}$$

An exogenous change in aggregate demand, either through investment or through government expenditure, results in a change in real output that is a multiple of the original change. The multiple is determined by the multiplier, which is the inverse of the marginal propensity to save: $1 - C_Y$. Because the marginal propensity to save is positive and less than one, the multiplier is greater than unity.

When aggregate demand increases because of an autonomous increase in investment or real government expenditure, real output and income initially increases by the same amount. This increase in real output and income induces an increase in private consumption through the consumption function, which brings about a further increase in aggregate demand, real output, and employment. Consequently, a given exogenous rise in aggregate demand has a compound effect on aggregate real income, due to the second (and subsequent) round

4. Whether this is because of an implicit assumption about liquidity constraints or the assumption that the income and substitution effects from the interest rate cancel each other out is unclear from the arguments put forward in chapter 8. A characteristic passage with regard to the role of the interest rate is: "There are not many people who will alter their way of living because the rate of interest has fallen from 5 to 4 per cent, if their aggregate income is the same as before" (Keynes [1936, p. 85]).

5. The diagrammatic depiction of the Keynesian cross is due to Samuelson [1948], the first edition of probably the most successful introductory textbook of economics ever. It was this textbook that first embraced and popularized Keynesian macroeconomics in the United States and the rest of the world.

6. The assumptions here are that output is at less than full employment and that an increase in aggregate demand causes firms to increase labor demand, employment, and output. Implicitly, because of involuntary unemployment, labor supply is assumed perfectly elastic in the short run.

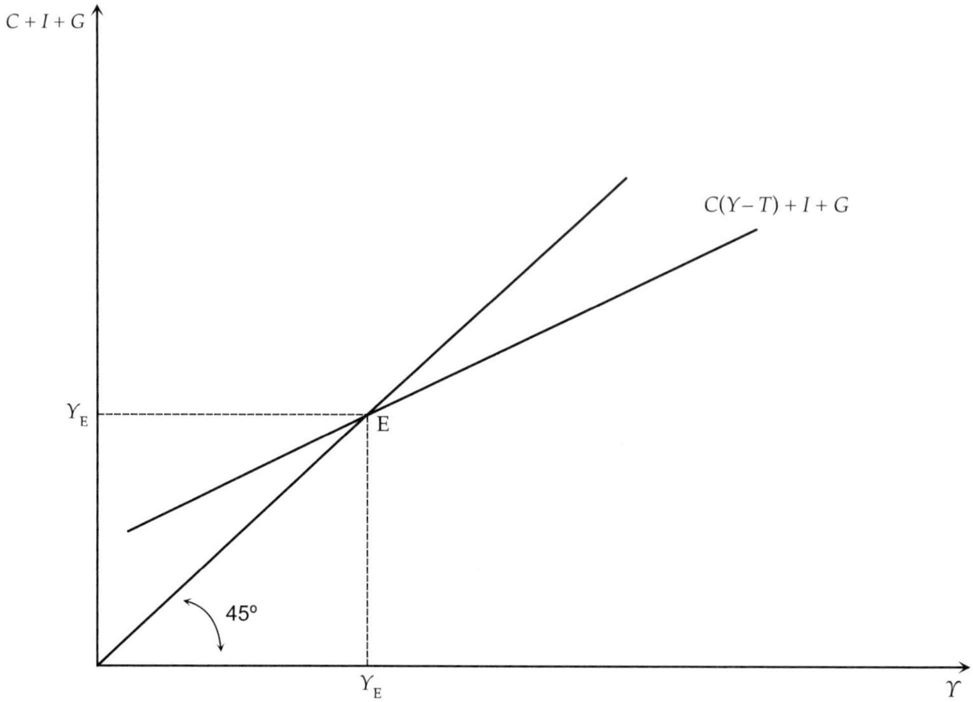

Figure 15.1
Exogenous investment and government expenditure: the Keynesian cross.

effects through aggregate consumption. These produce further increases in real demand, real output, and employment, further rises in private consumption, and so on.[7]

From equation (15.3), one can also derive the *balanced budget multiplier*, that is, the effect of a change in government expenditure and taxes that leaves the budget deficit unchanged. Under the assumption that $dG_t = dT_t$, it follows that

$$\left.\frac{dY_t}{dG_t}\right|_{dG_t = dT_t} = 1. \tag{15.5}$$

An increase in public expenditure, funded by an equal increase in taxes, increases total aggregate expenditure, real output, and income by the same amount. This is something that was proven by Haavelmo [1945]. Government expenditure increases aggregate demand one-to-one, but the tax increase reduces private consumption by less than one-to-one, because the marginal propensity to consume is less than one. Consequently, the initial

7. The explanation of the aggregate consumption function and the multiplier take up chapters 8 to 10 in Keynes [1936] and constitute the most important analytical chapters of the early part of the *General Theory*.

impact on aggregate expenditure is $1 - C_Y$, the inverse of the multiplier, and the overall effect of a change in government expenditure financed by increased taxes is equal to unity.

The model of the Keynesian cross assumes that investment is exogenous. In an important paper, Samuelson [1939] combined this model with an investment function based on the principle of acceleration to derive endogenous business cycles in the Keynesian model. The analysis of the *Samuelson multiplier-accelerator model*, one of the first dynamic Keynesian models of endogenous fluctuations, is presented in section 15.2, after we review all the models discussed in the *General Theory* itself.

15.1.2 The IS-LM Model

A more general form of the basic Keynesian model considers that aggregate investment depends on the real interest rate and introduces the equilibrium condition in the market for money to analyze the simultaneous determination of real output and the interest rate. This form is analyzed in chapters 10–18 of Keynes [1936], and was codified as the IS-LM model, in an important paper by Hicks [1937].[8]

The main difference from the previous model of the Keynesian cross is that investment ceases to be treated as exogenous, and is considered to depend negatively on the real interest rate. Assuming that inflationary expectations are given, investment will depend negatively on the current nominal interest rate. Consequently, the equilibrium condition in the goods and services market takes the form[9]

$$Y_t = C(Y_t - T_t) + I_t(i_t) + G_t, \tag{15.6}$$

where i is the nominal interest rate. The effect of the nominal interest rate on investment is assumed to be negative:

$$\frac{\partial I}{\partial i} < 0.$$

Equation (15.6) describes the combinations of real output and the nominal interest rate that ensure equilibrium in the market for goods and services. It is depicted as the downward-sloping investment-savings (IS) curve in figure 15.2.

When a new endogenous variable (the nominal interest rate) is introduced, one should analyze how it is determined. This is done through introducing the equilibrium condition in

8. This form of the Keynesian model, which is a generalization of the Keynesian cross, is the most popular and best-known version of the Keynesian model, as, following its adoption by Hansen [1949, 1953], it became the dominant model used in most intermediate macroeconomics textbooks.

9. Keynes was fully aware of Fisher's distinction between the nominal and the real interest rate, as is evident in the discussion on pp. 140–143 of the *General Theory*. However, the implicit assumption in his analysis was that inflationary expectations are given. This was, after all, consistent with the assumption of short-run price rigidity.

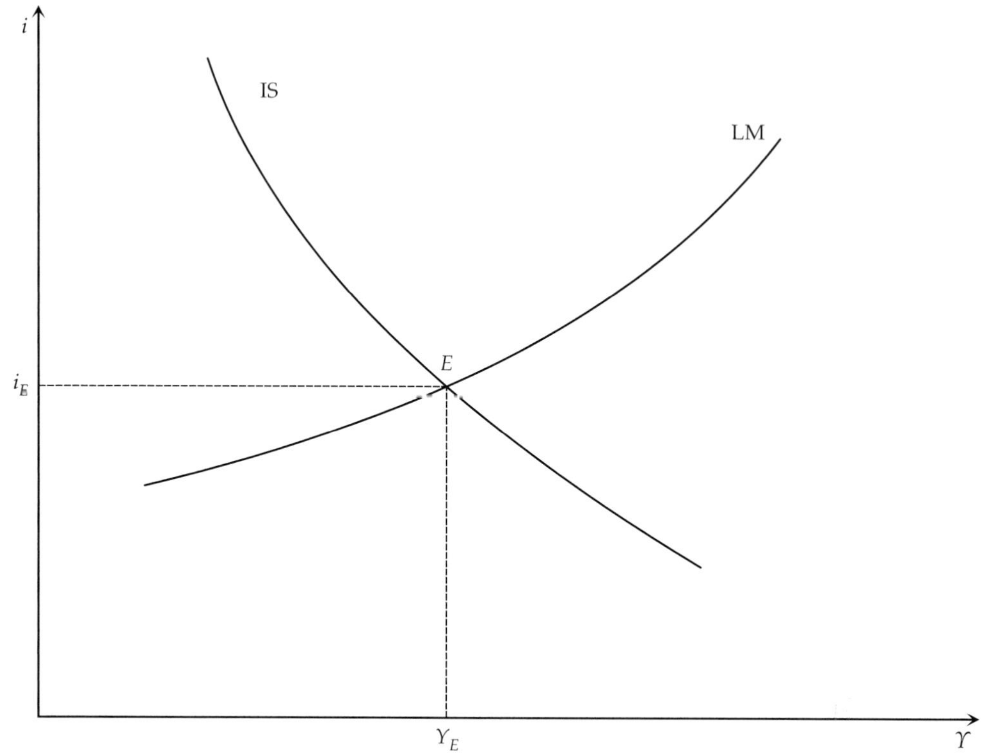

Figure 15.2
Aggregate output and the nominal interest rate: the IS-LM model.

the money market. This condition states that the demand for money (which is assumed to be a positive function of aggregate output and a negative function of the nominal interest rate) is equal to the money supply (as defined by the policy of the central bank). The equilibrium condition in the money market takes the form

$$\frac{M_t}{P_t} = m(Y_t, i_t), \tag{15.7}$$

where M is the nominal money supply, P the price level (which is considered as given in this version of the model), and m the demand function for real money balances (liquidity preference, in the terminology of Keynes).

The properties of the money demand function are described by

$$\frac{\partial m}{\partial Y} > 0, \frac{\partial m}{\partial i} < 0.$$

Equation (15.7) describes the combinations of real output and the nominal interest rate that are consistent with equilibrium in the money market, in the sense that money demand is equal to the exogenous money supply for the given price level. It is depicted as the upward-sloping LM (liquidity-money) curve in figure 15.2.

Real output and the nominal interest rate are determined at the point where both the market for goods and services and the market for money are in equilibrium. At the point of intersection of the IS curve (which describes equilibrium in the market for goods and services) and the LM curve (which describes equilibrium in the money market), the economy is thus in short-run equilibrium. Because the price level is assumed to be fixed, this equilibrium can occur at less than full employment. In fact, this is the assumption usually made in Keynesian models.

It is simple to deduce that an increase in government expenditure or a tax cut shifts the IS curve to the right and causes an increase in real output and the nominal interest rate. It is also simple to deduce that an increase in the money supply shifts the LM curve to the right and causes an increase in real output and a reduction in the nominal interest rate. Both fiscal and monetary policies can thus lead to an increase in aggregate demand and an increase in real output and employment. This is the mechanism through which *aggregate demand policies* affect output and employment in Keynesian models.

The advantage of the IS-LM model over the Keynesian cross is that the IS-LM model can be used to analyze the impact of monetary policy in addition to fiscal policy. An increase in the money supply increases aggregate demand in the short run by reducing interest rates and thus causing an increase in investment. This of course requires that nominal interest rates can in fact be reduced through monetary policy.

If expectations about the future are such that people hoard cash and the demand for money demand becomes infinitely elastic at the current interest rate (or if interest rates are close to zero, and zero is the lower bound), then monetary policy loses its ability to increase aggregate demand through increases in the money supply. Such a situation, which was mentioned in chapters 13 and 15 of the *General Theory*, came to be known as a *liquidity trap*. We shall return to an analysis of such a case when we discuss the role of monetary policy in chapter 20.[10]

10. In chapter 13 (p. 172) of the *General Theory*, Keynes remarks that "Nevertheless, circumstances can develop in which even a large increase in the quantity of money may exert a comparatively small influence on the rate of interest." In chapter 15 (p. 207) he returns to this issue, further remarking that, "There is the possibility … that, after the rate of interest has fallen to a certain level, liquidity-preference may become virtually absolute in the sense that almost everyone prefers cash to holding a debt which yields so low a rate of interest. In this event the monetary authority would have lost effective control over the rate of interest. But whilst this limiting case might become practically important in future, I know of no example of it hitherto." This case, although underplayed by Keynes himself, was given prominence later by Keynesians who favored fiscal rather than monetary policy. As discussed in chapter 20, this case acquired practical significance after the Great Recession of 2008–2009, when short-term interest rates hit the zero lower bound.

15.1.3 The AD-AS Model

The last and most sophisticated form of the basic Keynesian model is analyzed in chapters 19–21 of the *General Theory*. In this form of the model, the price level ceases to be exogenous and is allowed to change in order to equilibrate aggregate demand for goods and services with a less-than-perfectly elastic aggregate supply curve. However, nominal wages are still considered to be fixed in the short run. This version of the model was first formally combined with the IS-LM framework by Modigliani [1944] and has since been known as the *aggregate demand–aggregate supply (AD-AS) model*.

The aggregate demand function AD is derived from the simultaneous satisfaction of the equilibrium condition in the market for goods and services (IS) and the equilibrium condition in the money market. Using (15.6) and (15.7) and substituting out for the nominal interest rate, we get an aggregate demand function of the form

$$Y_t = D\left(\frac{M_t}{P_t}, G_t, T_t\right), \tag{15.8}$$

where $\frac{\partial D}{\partial P_t} < 0$. Equation (15.8) describes aggregate demand as a negative function of the price level. A higher price level, given the money supply, means lower real money balances, higher nominal interest rates, and lower investment demand. Thus, given the money supply, an increase in the price level reduces aggregate demand, and a fall in the price level increases aggregate demand. The aggregate demand function is the negatively sloped AD curve in figure 15.3.

To derive the aggregate supply function AS, we examine the behavior of the representative firm. Assume that the representative firm is competitive and maximizes profits, selecting the level of employment and output, and taking nominal wages and prices as given. Output and employment are determined by solving the following optimization problem:

$$\max\,[P_t Y_t - W_t L_t] \tag{15.9}$$

under the constraint

$$Y_t = F(L_t), \tag{15.10}$$

where F is a concave short-run production function, depending only on the level of employment L.

The maximization leads to a downward-sloping labor demand curve with respect to the real wage. Thus, employment is determined by the condition

$$F'(L_t) = \frac{W_t}{P_t}. \tag{15.11}$$

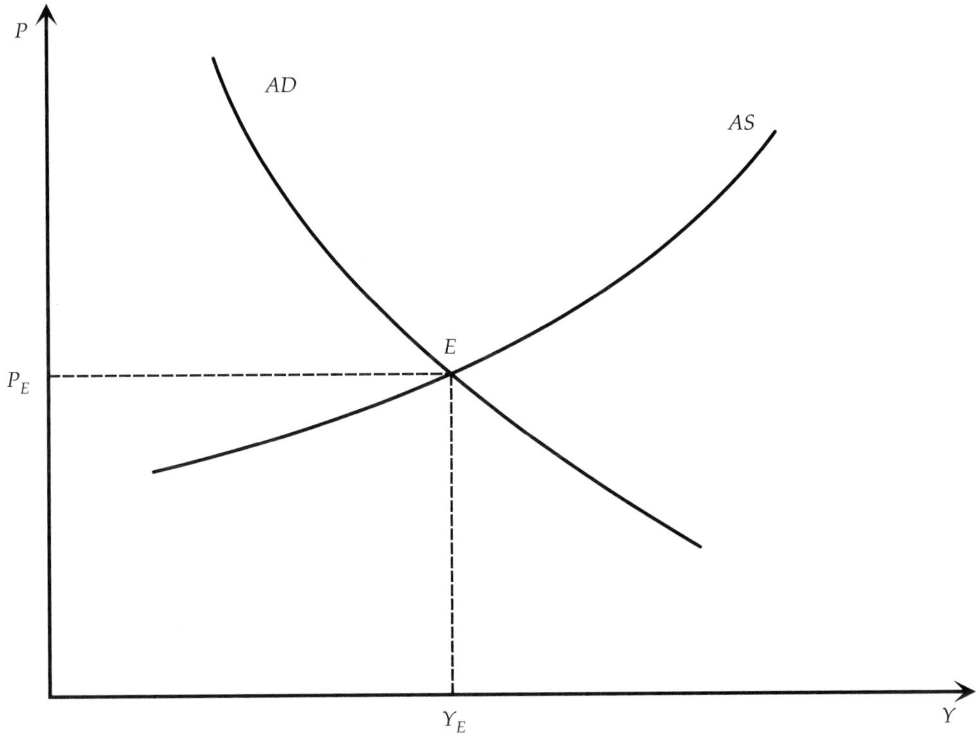

Figure 15.3
Aggregate output and the price level: the AD-AS model.

Because the marginal product of labor is a negative function of the level of employment, the demand for labor is negatively related to the real wage W/P.

Solving (15.11) for employment, and substituting in the production function (15.10), we get an aggregate supply function that is a negative function of the real wage. If the nominal wage is exogenously fixed (as assumed in this version of the Keynesian model), then aggregate supply is a positive function of the price level, as a higher price level is associated with a lower real wage. We thus have

$$Y_t = S\left(\frac{W}{P_t}\right), \tag{15.12}$$

where for a given nominal wage W, it follows that $\frac{\partial S}{\partial P} > 0$.

The higher the level of prices is, the lower the real wage will be, with the result that firms demand more labor and produce more. The aggregate supply function (15.11) is the upward-sloping curve AS in figure 15.3. Short-run equilibrium is at point E.[11]

15.1.4 The Impact of Aggregate Demand Policies

Equations (15.8) and (15.11) and figure 15.3 can be used to analyze economic fluctuations and the impact of macroeconomic policy on both output (employment) and the price level in the standard Keynesian model.[12]

First, for given nominal wages, an economy can be trapped in a short-run equilibrium with high unemployment. Suppose that the entire workforce is equal to N. From the production function (15.10), full employment output and income is given by[13]

$$Y^f = F(N).$$

Consider figure 15.4. The original equilibrium is at full employment output. A negative disturbance in aggregate demand shifts the aggregate demand curve AD to the left. In the new short-run equilibrium E_1, income and employment decline, and the price level falls. Because of the rigidity of nominal wages, the economy moves to an equilibrium with lower real output and employment and positive unemployment.

If nominal wages were not fixed in the short run and adjusted to achieve full employment, the aggregate supply function would be perpendicular to the level of full employment, and changes in aggregate demand would only result in changes in the price level. Consequently, with full flexibility of wages and prices, this model has the same properties as a classical model.[14]

This model can also be used to address the effects of disturbances to aggregate supply. Consider figure 15.5. The original equilibrium is at full employment output. A negative disturbance in aggregate supply, such as a negative productivity shock, shifts the aggregate supply curve AS to the left. In the new short-run equilibrium, income and employment declines, and the price level rises. Because of the rigidity of nominal wages, the economy

11. Again, this aggregate supply function has its origins in the *General Theory*. To quote: "with a given organisation, equipment and technique, real wages and the volume of output (and hence employment) are uniquely correlated, so that, in general, an increase in employment can only occur to the accompaniment of a decline in the rate of real wages. Thus, I am not disputing this vital fact, which the classical economists have (rightly) asserted as indefeasible" (Keynes [1936, p. 17]).

12. This diagrammatic representation of the AD-AS model is due to Patinkin [1956].

13. Here we are discussing full employment output, ignoring frictional or natural unemployment. The definition of the natural rate of unemployment would depend on the particular labor market model employed (Friedman [1968]). We examine the concept of the natural rate of unemployment in section 15.5 and analytical models of the natural rate in chapters 17 and 18.

14. This model forms the basis of the so-called neoclassical synthesis, in the sense that depending on the assumption about the flexibility of nominal wages, one could get either Keynesian or classical results.

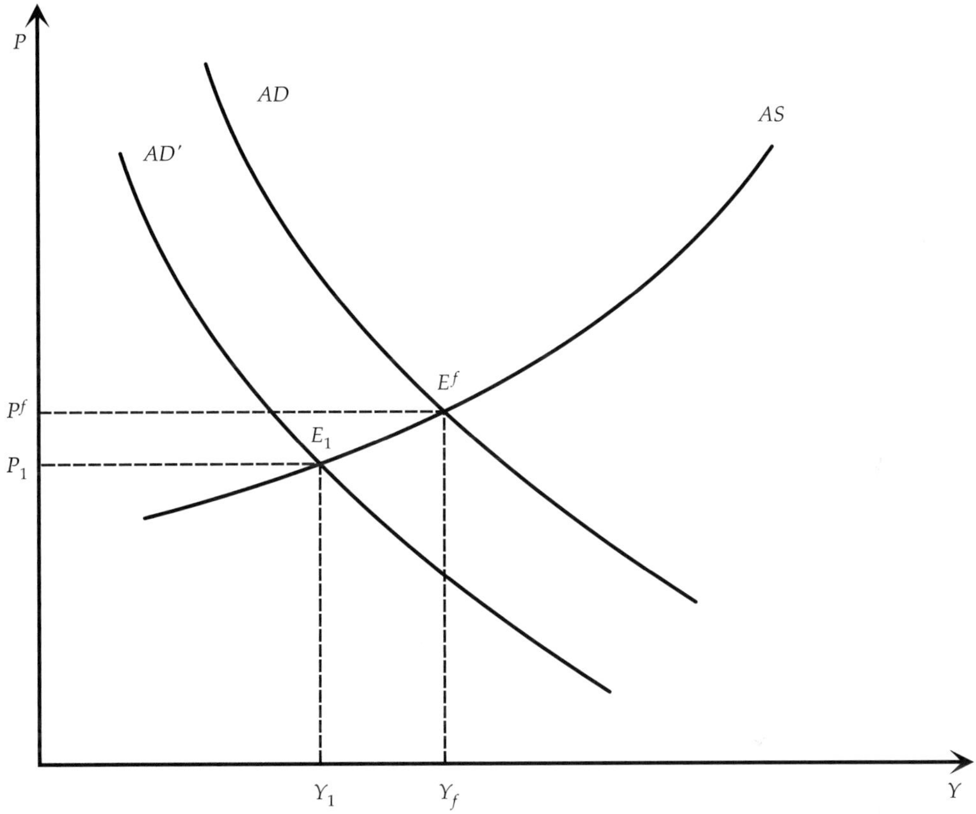

Figure 15.4
Aggregate demand disturbances and their effects on aggregate output and the price level.

moves to an equilibrium with lower real output and employment, a higher price level, and positive unemployment.[15]

In contrast to the classical model of full adjustment of wages and prices, in the Keynesian model with nominal wage rigidity, even monetary disturbances can shift aggregate demand and cause fluctuations in real output, employment, and other real variables (such as real wages and interest rates).

How can the impact of shocks to aggregate demand and supply be addressed? According to the Keynesian approach, an appropriate solution can come from macroeconomic policy. An increase of government expenditure, a reduction in taxes, or an increase in the money

15. Supply shocks are thus not incompatible with the Keynesian approach. Negative supply shocks seem to have been the cause of the problem of stagflation in the 1970s. See Bruno and Sachs [1985].

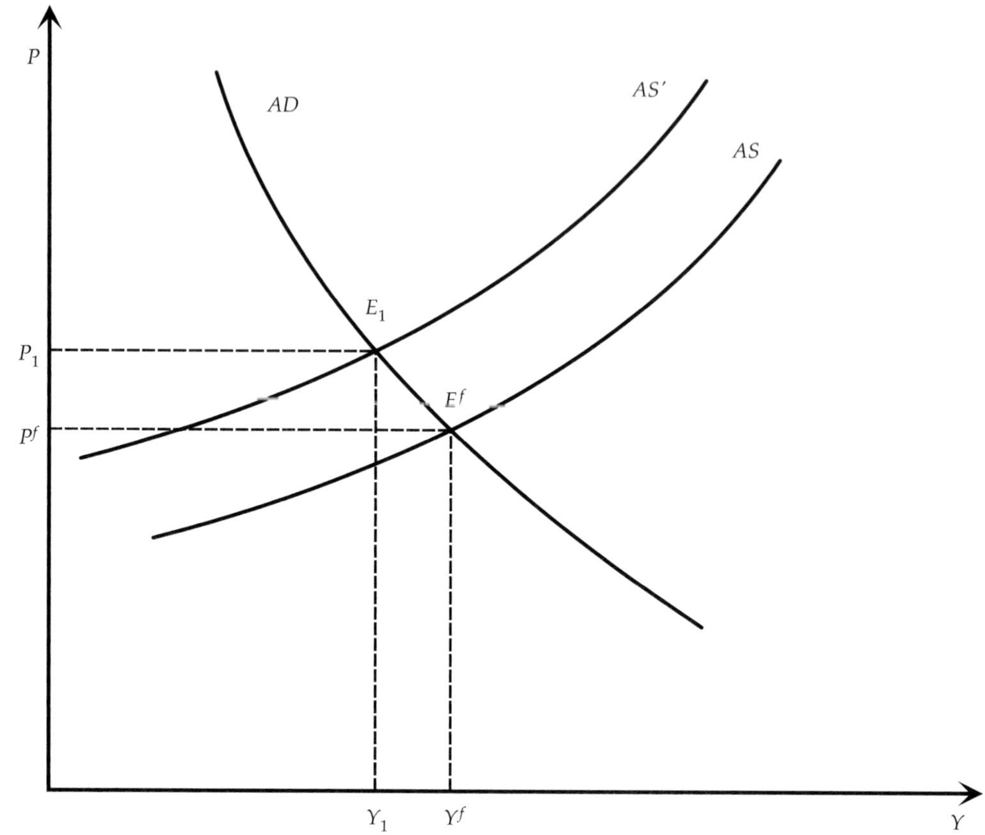

Figure 15.5
Aggregate supply disturbances and their effects on aggregate output and the price level.

supply can move the aggregate demand curve to the right and counteract the consequences of a negative demand or supply shock, on real output and unemployment. In the case of demand shocks, the price level returns to its original equilibrium. In the case of a negative supply shock, there are further upward effects on the price level, so a trade-off occurs between unemployment and price stability. Thus, supply shocks cannot be effectively neutralized through aggregate demand policies, as trying to counteract them through aggregate demand policies has implications for the price level. In the case of a positive demand or supply shock, the opposite would apply.

We shall return to the question of role of aggregate demand policies in Keynesian models after we examine the Samuelson [1939] multiplier accelerator model, which is a dynamic version of the model of the Keynesian cross.

15.2 The Samuelson Multiplier Accelerator Model

All versions of the Keynesian model we have considered so far are essentially static short-run equilibrium models. In an important paper, Samuelson [1939] combined the model of the Keynesian cross with an investment function based on the principle of acceleration to derive a dynamic model of endogenous business cycles. This dynamic Keynesian model is known as the *multiplier accelerator model.*

Samuelson considered the following dynamic version of the model of the Keynesian cross:

$$Y_t = C_t + I_t + G_t, \tag{15.13}$$

$$I_t = a(C_t - C_{t-1}) + b, \tag{15.14}$$

$$C_t = cY_{t-1} + d, \tag{15.15}$$

$$G_t = e, \tag{15.16}$$

where a, b, c, d, and e are constant parameters; a is the accelerator, which determines how a change in consumption affects current investment; b is autonomous investment; $c < 1$ is the marginal propensity to consume; and d is autonomous consumption. Finally, e is government expenditure, assumed exogenous and constant.

The investment function (15.14) is based on the so-called *acceleration principle*, which implies that when there is a positive change in consumption, firms will invest more to produce the higher quantity of consumer goods demanded. When there is a negative change in consumption, firms will reduce investment, as they need less capital to meet the lower demand for consumer goods. The accelerator a measures the sensitivity of investment to changes in aggregate consumption.[16]

Equation (15.15) is a linear Keynesian consumption function, according to which consumption is a function of lagged and not current income. Government expenditure is assumed exogenous and constant at e. Substituting (15.15) in (15.14), the investment function can be written as

$$I_t = ac(Y_{t-1} - Y_{t-2}) + b. \tag{15.17}$$

Investment is a function of the lagged change in income, as the lagged change in income drives the demand for consumption goods.

Substituting the consumption function (15.15), the investment function (15.17), and (15.16) in the equilibrium condition of the market for goods and services (15.13), after

16. The principle of acceleration, as a basis for a theory of investment, has a long history in the analysis of business cycles. It assumes that investment is a positive function of the change in total output or the change in consumption. Aftalion [1909], Bickerdike [1914], and Clark [1917] presented early analyses of business cycles based on this principle. See Knox [1952] for a survey.

collecting terms, one gets

$$Y_t = c(1+a)Y_{t-1} - acY_{t-2} + b + d + e. \tag{15.18}$$

The dynamic path of output in the Samuelson [1939] model is thus determined by the second-order difference equation (15.18).

The particular solution of this equation, which defines equilibrium output, is given by

$$Y^* = \frac{b+d+e}{1-c}. \tag{15.19}$$

Equilibrium output depends only on autonomous expenditure and the multiplier $1/(1-c)$, as suggested by the model of the Keynesian cross. However, the dynamic path of output is determined by the difference equation (15.18), which also depends on the accelerator.[17]

For the difference equation (15.18) to be stable, ac must be less than one, or the accelerator must satisfy $a < 1/c$. If this condition is not satisfied, output will not converge to equilibrium but instead will diverge.

For the roots to be real, we must have $c \geq 4a/(1+a)^2$. Thus, for the roots to be real and for income to converge monotonically to its equilibrium value, the condition is

$$\frac{4a}{(1+a)^2} \leq c < \frac{1}{a}. \tag{15.20}$$

For (15.20) to be satisfied, if the marginal propensity to consume is equal to three-quarters (0.75), the accelerator must be less than or equal to one-third (0.333). In such a case, the difference equation will converge monotonically.

If the accelerator is such that the inequality on left-hand side of (15.20) is strict, the roots will be real, distinct, and less than one. The general solution of (15.18) will then take the form

$$Y_t = \frac{b+d+e}{1-c} + Y_1\lambda_1^t + Y_2\lambda_2^t, \tag{15.21}$$

where Y_1, Y_2 are two boundary (initial conditions). Here $\lambda_1, \lambda_2 < 1$ are the two real and distinct roots of the difference equation, which satisfy

$$\lambda_1 + \lambda_2 = c(1+a), \lambda_1\lambda_2 = ca < 1.$$

Real output will converge monotonically to its equilibrium level Y^*, which is given in (15.19).

If the left-hand side of (15.20) is equal to c, then we have two repeated roots, $\lambda = c(1+a)/2 < 1$. The general solution of (15.18) then takes the form

17. For the solution of second-order linear difference equations, see appendix D.

$$Y_t = \frac{b+d+e}{1-c} + Y_1\lambda^t + Y_2 t\lambda^t. \tag{15.22}$$

Real output will converge monotonically to its equilibrium level Y^*, which is given (15.19).

In the case where the inequality on the left-hand side of (15.20) is not satisfied, then we have two complex roots λ_1, λ_2, and real output will display *damped oscillations* (i.e., endogenous fluctuations) during the convergence to its equilibrium value. This will occur as long as $a < 1/c$. If the accelerator does not satisfy this condition, then the model displays *divergent oscillations*.

The complex roots will take the form of a pair of complex conjugates of the form

$$\lambda_1 = \mu + \nu i, \lambda_2 = \mu - \nu i,$$

where $\mu = \frac{c(1+a)}{2}$, and $\nu = \frac{\sqrt{4ac - c^2(1+a)^2}}{2}$. The general solution will then take the form

$$Y_t = \frac{b+d+e}{1-c} + \left(\sqrt{ac}\right)^t \left((Y_1 + Y_2)\cos(\theta t) + (Y_1 - Y_2)\sin(\theta t)\right), \tag{15.23}$$

where θ is defined by

$$\cos(\theta) = \frac{\mu}{\sqrt{ac}}, \quad \sin(\theta) = \frac{\nu}{\sqrt{ac}}.$$

This solution will display oscillations of a periodic nature. Because we have assumed that $ac < 1$, the oscillations will be dampened, and there will be cyclical convergence to the equilibrium value given by (15.19).

Figure 15.6 shows the dynamic convergence of real output for different values of the accelerator, assuming that the equilibrium value is equal to zero. We assume that $c = 0.75$, and that the accelerator takes three alternative values: (1) $a = 1/10$, (2) $a = 1/3$, and (3) $a = 11/10$. Case 1 results in two real and distinct rules, and monotonic convergence to equilibrium. Case 2 results in repeated real roots and monotonic convergence to equilibrium. Case 3 results in complex roots and cyclical convergence to equilibrium. Thus, if the accelerator is sufficiently high in this model, cyclical convergence (i.e., cyclical fluctuations) occurs.

15.3 The Theory of Discretionary Monetary and Fiscal Policy

The potential for monetary and fiscal policy to achieve full employment is clear in Keynesian models. The question that arises relates to the appropriate use of monetary and fiscal policy. This question was first posed in the important contribution of Tinbergen [1952], who distinguished between *targets* and *instruments* of (macro) economic policy. Tinbergen argued that as long as the policy authorities had as many independent policy instruments as

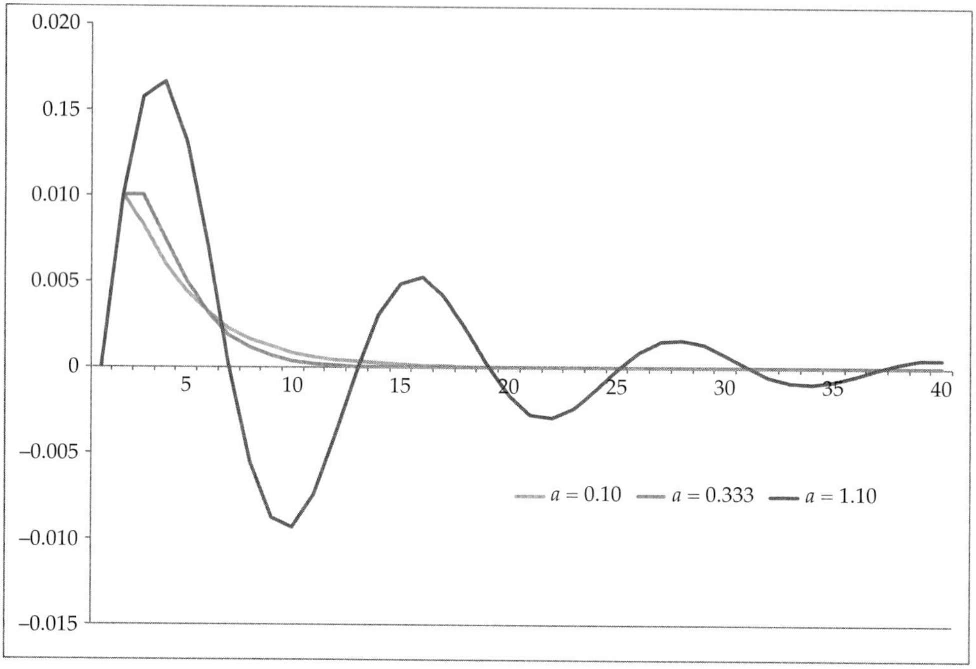

Figure 15.6
Convergence of real output for different values of the accelerator.

they had policy targets, they would be able to fully achieve their targets by using one policy instrument for each target. If they had fewer instruments than targets, then they would not be able to achieve all their targets simultaneously. Moreover, if the policy authorities had access to an econometrically estimated model, they could calculate, with relative precision, the appropriate response of policy instruments to stochastic shocks that shift the economy away from the targets of the authorities.

Tinbergen's ideas were further developed by Theil in a series of contributions (Theil [1954, 1956, 1964]). Theil analyzed how to optimally adjust policy instruments to calculate policy responses, and these ideas gradually became operational through the development of large-scale Keynesian macroeconometric models, which were used for both forecasting and policy evaluation.

The policies that are decided in this way are often referred to as *discretionary policies*, as opposed to rules-based policies, according to which the path of policy instruments is not determined at the discretion of governments but on the basis of restrictive policy rules.

In effect, Keynesian models and the Tinbergen-Theil theory of economic policy tilted macroeconomic policy in the direction of discretion rather than rules.

15.3.1 The Tinbergen-Theil Theory of Discretionary Aggregate Demand Policies

To introduce the Tinbergen-Theil theory of discretionary macroeconomic policy, we shall consider the following simplified stochastic log-linear version of the AD-AS Keynesian macro model:

$$y_t^d = a_0 + a_1 g_t - a_2 i_t + v_t^d, \tag{15.24}$$

$$m_t - p_t = y_t^d - b i_t + v_t^m, \tag{15.25}$$

$$y_t^s = y_t^f - c(\bar{w}_t - p_t) + v_t^s, \tag{15.26}$$

$$y_t^d = y_t^s = y_t, \tag{15.27}$$

where y denotes the logarithm of aggregate real output, which is determined by the equality of aggregate demand y^d with aggregate supply y^s; g is the logarithm of real government expenditure; i is the nominal interest rate; m is the logarithm of the money supply; p is the logarithm of the price level; v^d is an exogenous stochastic shock to aggregate demand; v^m is an exogenous stochastic shock to money demand; v^s is an exogenous stochastic shock to aggregate supply; $\bar{w}$ is the log of the nominal wage, assumed exogenous; and a_0, a_1, a_2, b, and c are exogenous fixed parameters. Equation (15.24) is a log-linear IS curve, (15.25) a log-linear LM curve, and (15.26) a log-linear AS curve (the aggregate supply function). Equation (15.27) is the equilibrium condition in the output market.

In the Tinbergen terminology, the (potential) policy targets are y and p, and the policy instruments are g, m, and i. Because m and i are linearly related through the money demand function, only one of the two can be used as an independent instrument of monetary policy, and the other will be determined endogenously.

Let us initially assume that the monetary policy instrument of the government is the money supply. Then the model determines three endogenous variables, y, p, and i, as functions of the exogenous policy instruments g and m, the exogenous shocks, and the exogenous parameters. Using the money demand function to substitute for the nominal interest rate in the IS curve (15.24), we get the following aggregate demand function:

$$y_t^d = \frac{b}{1+a_2}\left(a_0 + a_1 g_t + v_t^d\right) + \frac{a_2}{1+a_2}\left(m_t - p_t - v_t^m\right). \tag{15.28}$$

Thus, the model consisting of the aggregate demand function (15.28), the aggregate supply function (15.26), and the equilibrium condition (15.27) determines output and the price level as functions of the exogenous shocks and the policy instruments m and g.

15.3.2 Monetary and Fiscal Policy with a Full Employment Target

Let us assume that the sole target of macroeconomic policy is to maintain output at its full employment level. This can be done by using either fiscal policy, monetary policy, or both to ensure that aggregate demand is equal to full employment output y^f. From (15.26) and

(15.28), output and the price level satisfy

$$y_t^f = \frac{b}{1+a_2}\left(a_0 + a_1 g_t + v_t^d\right) + \frac{a_2}{1+a_2}\left(m_t - p_t - v_t^m\right), \tag{15.29}$$

$$p_t = \bar{w}_t - \frac{1}{c} v_t^s. \tag{15.30}$$

Using (15.30) to substitute for the price level in (15.29), we get

$$y_t^f = \frac{b}{1+a_2}\left(a_0 + a_1 g_t + v_t^d\right) + \frac{a_2}{1+a_2}\left(m_t - \bar{w}_t + \frac{1}{c} v_t^s - v_t^m\right). \tag{15.31}$$

From (15.31), we see that the government can use its aggregate demand instruments (i.e., m and g) to achieve the target of full employment output. If m and g satisfy (15.31) for all periods, then output will always be at its full employment target under the discretionary policy.

If the monetary instrument of the government is the nominal interest rate and not the money supply, then (15.31) would be replaced by

$$y_t^f = a_0 + a_1 g_t - a_2 i_t + v_t^d. \tag{15.32}$$

The money supply would then become endogenous, and the price level would still be determined by (15.30).

The above analysis is the justification for discretionary aggregate demand policies in the Keynesian model. In principle, aggregate demand policies can be used to counteract the effects of both demand and supply shocks on aggregate output and unemployment. This ability would imply that aggregate demand policies could in principle be used to stabilize economic activity at the level of full employment and help avoid the repetition of phenomena such as the Great Depression.

15.3.3 Monetary and Fiscal Policy with a Full Employment Target and a Price Level Target

From the preceding analysis, note that if output is stabilized at its full employment level, then the price level cannot be controlled and depends only on the exogenous nominal wage and aggregate supply shocks through equation (15.30). If the government wanted to achieve a price level target as well as full employment, it would not be able to do so, as its monetary and fiscal policy instruments both operate through aggregate demand and are thus linearly dependent. Effectively, the government has only one instrument, aggregate demand policy, and thus can only achieve one target. To affect the price level, it would need an independent instrument (such as an incomes policy) that would affect the nominal wage in (15.30). Without such an additional instrument, it would have to balance deviations from the full employment target against deviations from the price level target.

Let us assume, following Theil [1964], that the government selects monetary and fiscal policy to minimize a loss function that depends on quadratic deviations of output from full employment output and the price level from a socially desirable fixed price level target. This loss function takes the form

$$\Lambda_t = \frac{1}{2}(y_t - y_t^f)^2 + \frac{\zeta}{2}(p_t - \bar{p})^2, \tag{15.33}$$

where $\bar{p}$ is the price level target, and ζ measures the relative marginal social cost of price deviations relative to output deviations in the social welfare ranking of the government.[18]

The problem of discretionary economic policy can be modeled as the minimization of the welfare loss (15.33), subject to the constraint of the model of the economy described by equations (15.26)–(15.28). The outcome of such a policy process is often described as discretionary policy, because the government chooses its policy instruments in every period to minimize its one-period loss function.

From the first-order conditions for a minimum, it follows that

$$c(y_t - y_t^f) = -\zeta(p_t - \bar{p}). \tag{15.34}$$

At the optimum, the government aggregate demand policies equate the marginal social cost of deviations of output from full employment to the marginal welfare cost of deviations of the price level from its target.

If the government possessed enough instruments to eliminate deviations of both output from its full employment level and the price level from its target, then (15.34) would be satisfied for zero deviations from the targets of the government. However, the government essentially has one policy instrument, as both monetary and fiscal policy operate through aggregate demand. Using the aggregate supply function (15.26) to substitute for $y - y^f$ in (15.34), we find that under the optimal policy,

$$p_t - \bar{p} = \frac{c^2}{c^2 + \zeta}(\bar{w}_t - \bar{p}) - \frac{c}{c^2 + \zeta}v_t^s. \tag{15.35}$$

The price level will deviate from the government's target under the optimal policy, unless there is a "divine coincidence," which ensures that the exogenous nominal wage, the price level target of the government, and the supply shock are such that the right-hand side of (15.35) adds up to zero. Aggregate demand policies do not affect (15.35).

Substituting (15.35) in (15.34), we can see that under the optimal policy, output will also deviate from full employment output, and the deviation is determined by

$$y_t - y_t^f = -\frac{\zeta c}{c^2 + \zeta}(\bar{w}_t - \bar{p}) + \frac{\zeta}{c^2 + \zeta}v_t^s. \tag{15.36}$$

18. See Theil [1954, 1964] for a justification and an extensive discussion of such quadratic social welfare functions.

Supply shocks will cause positive deviations of output from full employment output, and wage shocks will cause negative deviations of output from full employment output. The lower the price level target of the government relative to the nominal wage is, the smaller the deviation of output from full employment output will be: Thus, a government with a low price level target, given nominal wages, will end up with lower output and employment compared to full employment under the optimal discretionary policy.

In the presence of wage and supply shocks, discretionary aggregate demand policies can only ensure that the deviation of output from full employment output satisfies (15.34), but no more. Wage and supply shocks induce a trade-off between the employment and price level target of a government. Full employment is not compatible with the optimal discretionary macroeconomic policy, because the government has one instrument (aggregate demand policies) but two targets (output and the price level). The optimal discretionary policy is thus second best, as the government just balances, at the margin, the welfare costs associated with deviations of the price level and output from its targets.

From (15.34), note that if $\zeta = 0$ (i.e., if the government cares only about output and not the price level), this trade-off disappears, and we are back to a full employment equilibrium, as analyzed in sub-section 15.3.2. However, in such a case, the price level is destabilized.

The problem is that monetary and fiscal policy in Keynesian models (such as the AD-AS model we analyzed) can only affect aggregate demand. It is optimal to use them to achieve full employment only if the government cares about output and employment and not the price level. If the government cares about both output and the price level, achieving full employment through discretionary aggregate demand policies is not feasible in the presence of wage and supply shocks, because the optimal policy is second best. The government does not have enough instruments to achieve both targets. Thus, under the optimal discretionary aggregate demand policy, the best a government could do is to equalize the marginal welfare cost of deviations of output from full employment to the marginal welfare cost of deviations of the price level from its target, as suggested by (15.34).

If the government is to be able to achieve both of its targets fully under the discretionary policy, it needs another policy instrument in addition to monetary and fiscal policies. Such an instrument could, for instance, be a price or incomes policy that would operate through controls of nominal wages or prices. Note from (15.35) and (15.36) that if a government could control nominal wages, then it would be able to achieve both full employment and the price level target.

From the 1950s to the 1970s, when many governments tried to implement discretionary aggregate demand policies, conflicts often arose between the targets of full employment and price stability. In such cases, many governments resorted to nominal wage and price controls as an additional policy instrument that would help resolve the conflicts. These conflicts became even more acute with the negative supply shocks of the 1970s, which led to *stagflation*, a combination of recession with a rise in inflation.

We shall return to the dilemma of rules versus discretion after we discuss the evolution of Keynesian models since the 1960s, following the emergence of the Phillips curve.

15.4 The Phillips Curve and Inflationary Expectations

We have already demonstrated that the main difference between the original Keynesian models and the corresponding classical models is the assumption of nominal rigidity in both prices and wages, or (in the case of the AD-AS model) only nominal wages. The assumption of complete nominal rigidity in either prices or wages is clearly not realistic and was rightly considered as one of the main weaknesses of Keynesian models. Economies are characterized by the simultaneous existence of inflation and unemployment, a phenomenon that implies the adjustment of both prices and wages even in the short run.

15.4.1 The Phillips Curve and the Trade-off between Inflation and Unemployment

Since the late 1950s, a central point of reference for Keynesian models has been the Phillips curve, a negative relationship between unemployment and inflation identified and estimated econometrically by Phillips [1958]. The Phillips curve was combined with the IS-LM model of aggregate demand to simultaneously determine both inflation and unemployment. Thus, the Phillips curve essentially replaced the aggregate supply curve of the AD-AS model, which was based on fixed nominal wages, and helped determine both unemployment and inflation.

The curve that Phillips estimated econometrically for the United Kingdom took the form

$$\pi = \varphi(u), \tag{15.37}$$

where $\varphi(u_0) = 0$ and $\varphi'(u) < 0$. In equation (15.37), π denotes inflation, u is the unemployment rate, and u_0 is the zero inflation unemployment rate. The function φ relating inflation and unemployment estimated by Phillips is nonlinear. Its shape is depicted in figure 15.7.[19]

In the context of the basic Keynesian model, combining the IS-LM model of the determination of aggregate demand with the Phillips curve, one could deduce that an increase in aggregate demand would lead to higher real output and employment, lower unemployment, and a rise in inflation along the Phillips curve. Conversely, a decline in aggregate demand would lead to a lower level of real output and employment, higher unemployment, and a reduction of inflation along the Phillips curve.

Inspired by Phillips [1958] Samuelson and Solow [1960] estimated a Phillips curve between price inflation and unemployment for the United States. These authors argued that the short-term problem of macroeconomic policy could be seen as the determination of the level of aggregate demand in order to select the socially desirable combination of inflation and unemployment on the Phillips curve. In times of recession, an increase in aggregate

19. The curve actually estimated by Phillips [1958] had wage inflation and not price inflation on the left-hand side. However, the same negative relationship applied to price inflation. Note that this negative relationship between price inflation and unemployment had already been highlighted in the 1920s in a neglected article by Irving Fisher. See Fisher [1926]. Thus, Fisher could also be credited with the discovery of the Phillips curve, although for more than 30 years, his paper had no impact at all.

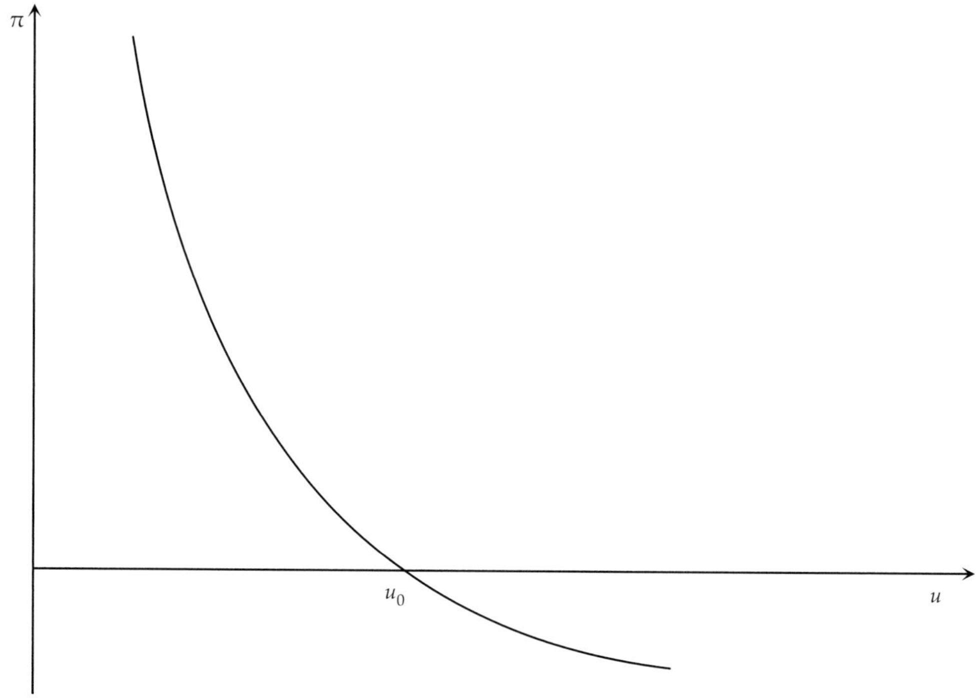

Figure 15.7
The Phillips curve.

demand will lead to a reduction in unemployment, but at the cost of higher inflation. In times of economic boom and high inflation, inflation could be reduced through a reduction in aggregate demand, but this would result in higher unemployment.

The Samuelson-Solow argument can be understood with the help of figure 15.8, which depicts the Phillips curve and the indifference map of policymakers between inflation and unemployment. Because both inflation and unemployment are assumed to be undesirable, the indifference curves are concave to the origin. The closer an indifference curve is to the origin, the higher will be the implied social welfare. Samuelson and Solow argued that because the Phillips curve implies a negative relationship between inflation and unemployment, it acts as a constraint on the options of policymakers. The latter will maximize social welfare at point E in the figure, where the Phillips curve is tangent to the highest-possible indifference curve. Point E is thus associated with the optimal feasible combination of inflation and unemployment under a discretionary macroeconomic policy.[20]

20. In effect, Samuelson and Solow [1960] applied the Tinbergen-Theil framework to an IS-LM model augmented by a Phillips curve, although they did not put their argument in such terms. Also note that Samuelson and Solow

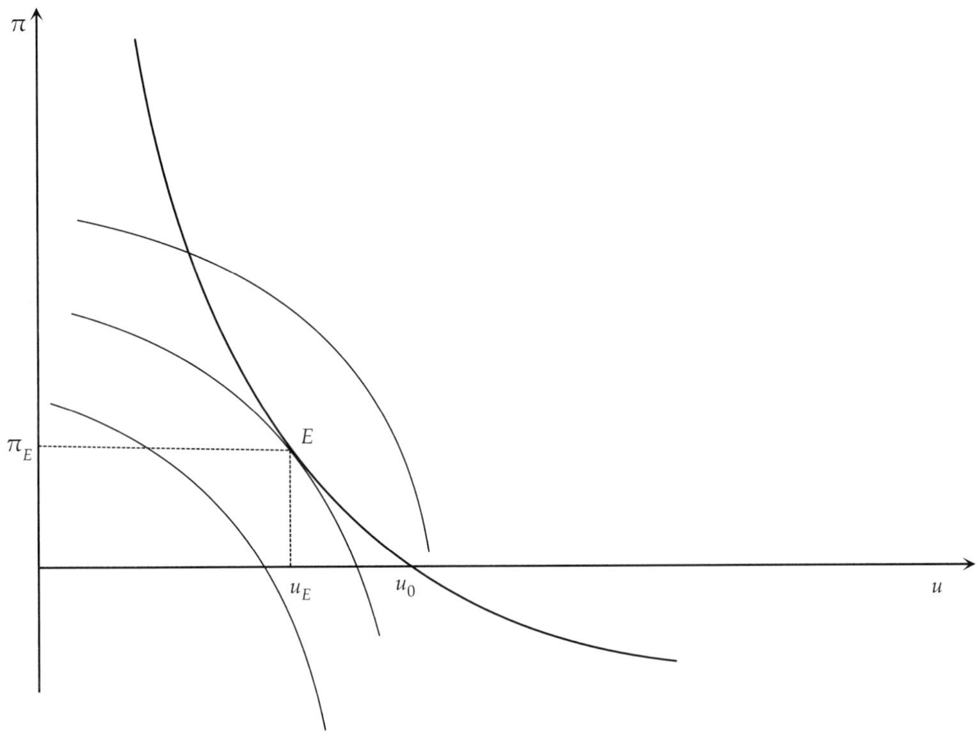

Figure 15.8
The Phillips curve and the socially optimal combination of inflation and unemployment.

Note that at point E, both inflation and unemployment are positive, and policymakers would prefer lower inflation and unemployment. However, an equilibrium with both lower inflation and lower unemployment is not feasible, as the only feasible combinations lie on the Phillips curve, which acts as constraint for macroeconomic policy.

15.4.2 Instability of the Phillips Curve and Inflationary Expectations

Since the mid-1960s, the negative relationship between inflation and unemployment began to shift. Higher inflation led to a reduction of unemployment only temporarily, because unemployment rose after a while to return to its original level without a reduction in inflation. This puzzle was finally attributed to shifts in inflationary expectations.

As argued by Phelps [1967] and Friedman [1968], a sustained increase in inflation would lead to expectations of higher future inflation on the part of households and firms. The result

---

[1960] were very cautious in their interpretations of the evidence. They certainly did not advocate that stabilization policy be conducted as if the Phillips curve were a stable and immutable relationship.

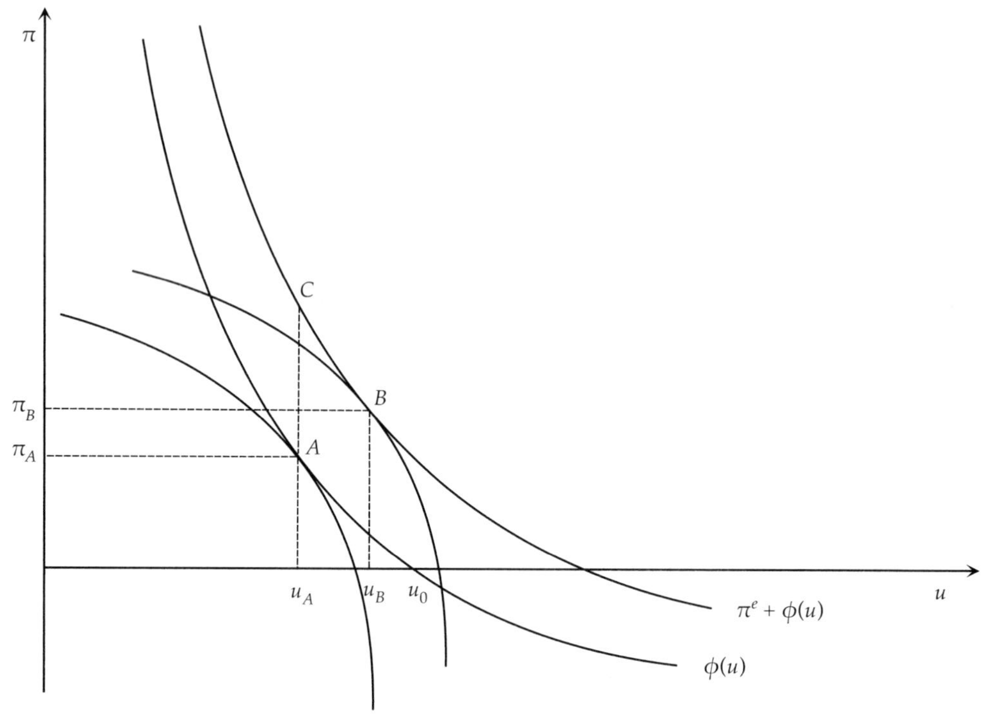

Figure 15.9
Shifts of the Phillips curve due to inflationary expectations.

of this would be that inflation would have to increase even further to achieve a reduction in unemployment. Essentially, Phelps and Friedman argued that the Phillips curve has the form

$$\pi = \pi^e + \varphi(u), \tag{15.38}$$

where $\varphi(u_0) = \pi - \pi^e = 0$ and $\varphi'(u) < 0$, and π^e is expected inflation.

A shift of the Phillips curve (15.38) due to an increase in inflationary expectations is shown in figure 15.9. Assume that initially, inflation and inflationary expectations are equal to zero and unemployment is at u_0. The government and the monetary authorities choose to increase aggregate demand to reduce unemployment, and the economy moves to point A, where unemployment has fallen, but inflation has increased. As inflationary expectations gradually adjust to the higher inflation, the Phillips curve moves up, and thus, the economy moves gradually toward point C. Inflation rises above π_A at the unemployment rate u_A. Point A is no longer feasible. If the government and the monetary authorities want to maximize social welfare, they have to adjust monetary and fiscal policy to move the economy to point B, which implies higher inflation and unemployment relative to A. This would again be temporary, because it would lead to a further gradual upward adjustment in inflationary expectations, a further shift in the Phillips curve, and a further increase in inflation and unemployment.

15.5 The Natural Rate of Unemployment and Aggregate Demand Policies

The instability of the Phillips curve led Milton Friedman to define the concept of the natural rate of unemployment. According to Friedman [1968], a market economy tends to converge toward an equilibrium unemployment rate u_0, which can be labeled as the natural rate of unemployment. The natural rate of unemployment depends only on real factors, including labor market frictions, distortions, and inefficiencies.[21]

Friedman [1968] argued that trying to reduce the unemployment rate below the natural rate, by increasing aggregate demand and inflation, would only meet with temporary success. As inflationary expectations adjust to the higher inflation, unemployment will tend to return to its natural rate. One would need continuous increases in aggregate demand and inflation to keep unemployment below its natural rate. If at some point, the government stopped increasing aggregate demand and inflation, then the unemployment rate would return to its natural rate, and the economy would be saddled with high inflation.

Friedman thus argued against the use of discretion in the determination of aggregate demand policies and in favor of fixed rules for monetary and fiscal policy that would deliver low and steady inflation. In the fullness of time, this proved to be a devastating argument against discretionary policies of the Tinbergen-Theil variety.[22]

To analyze the argument, assume that the Phillips curve is linear and given by

$$\pi_t = \pi_t^e + a - bu_t, \tag{15.39}$$

where a and b are positive constant parameters.

According to the definition of the natural rate of unemployment, the economy is at its natural rate when inflationary expectations are equal to actual inflation. Consequently, the natural rate of unemployment in this simple model is determined by

$$u_0 = \frac{a}{b}. \tag{15.40}$$

21. The concept of the natural rate of unemployment was defined by Friedman [1968, p. 8] as follows: "The natural rate of unemployment ... is the level that would be ground out by the Walrasian system of general equilibrium equations, provided there is imbedded in them the actual structural characteristics of the labor and commodity markets, including market imperfections, stochastic variability in demands and supplies, the cost of gathering information about job vacancies and labor availabilities, the costs of mobility, and so on."

22. To quote again from Friedman [1968, p. 17]: "By setting itself a steady course and keeping to it, the monetary authority could make a major contribution to promoting economic stability." This was a clear argument in favor of policy rules rather than discretion. It is worth noting that Friedman was a consistent advocate of policy rules. His favored policy was a constant rate of growth for the money supply, as he thought that a policy of constant inflation was not feasible. See Friedman [1960].

The natural rate of unemployment is thus constant, as a and b are assumed to be constant parameters.[23]

When analyzing aggregate demand policies in a context in which inflation is determined by the Phillips curve (15.39), a key question that has to be answered is: How are inflationary expectations formed?

15.5.1 The Path of Inflation and Unemployment under Adaptive Expectations

For many years, the dominant approach to the formation of expectations in macroeconomics was the adaptive expectations hypothesis. This was the hypothesis adopted by Phelps [1967] and Friedman [1968]. According to this hypothesis, expectations in each period are adjusted by a percentage of the deviation of the actual from the expected value of a variable in the previous period.[24]

Consequently, the adjustment of inflationary expectations according to this hypothesis would take the form

$$\pi_t^e - \pi_{t-1}^e = (1-\lambda)(\pi_{t-1} - \pi_{t-1}^e), \tag{15.41}$$

where $0 \leq \lambda < 1$. According to (15.41), in each period, inflationary expectations are adjusted by a percentage $1-\lambda$ of the divergence between actual and expected inflation in the previous period.

It is assumed that λ is less than one, because if it is equal to one, then there is no adjustment in expectations, and we have the assumption of nonadaptive or *static expectations*.

What are the properties of this specific hypothesis for the adjustment of expectations? From (15.41), we have

$$\pi_t^e = (1-\lambda)\pi_{t-1} + \lambda\pi_{t-1}^e = \frac{1-\lambda}{1-\lambda L}\pi_{t-1} = (1-\lambda)\sum\nolimits_{i=0}^{\infty} \lambda^i \pi_{t-1-i}. \tag{15.42}$$

Inflationary expectations under the adaptive expectations hypothesis are a geometric distributed lag of past inflation rates. Thus, adaptive expectations are *backward looking*.

Given that $\lambda < 1$, from the difference equation (15.42), if inflation were to be held constant at an equilibrium rate π_A, inflationary expectations would gradually converge to that equilibrium inflation rate π_A. The speed of adjustment is equal to $1-\lambda$. The smaller is λ, the speedier will be the adjustment of inflationary expectations to actual equilibrium inflation. In

23. Equation (15.40) can be consistent with a number of alternative interpretations in analytical terms, as the Phillips curve (15.39) is postulated and not derived from specific analytical microeconomic foundations. In chapter 17, we present a model in which the Phillips curve and the natural rate of unemployment are determined by the behavior of labor market insiders, setting wages in order to secure their own employment, while in chapter 18 we present a much richer matching model of frictions and inefficiencies in the labor market, which also determines the natural rate of unemployment endogenously.

24. See chapter 9 for an introduction to and discussion of the adaptive expectations hypothesis.

the extreme case where $\lambda = 0$, expectations converge after one period. At the other extreme (in the case where $\lambda = 1$), expectations never converge, and we essentially have nonadaptive or static expectations.

Substituting (15.42) in the Phillips curve (15.39) and solving for unemployment, one gets

$$u_t = (1-\lambda)u_0 + \lambda u_{t-1} - \frac{1}{b}(\pi_t - \pi_{t-1}). \tag{15.43}$$

If inflation were held constant at any inflation rate (say, π_A), unemployment would gradually converge to its natural rate u_0 with a speed of adjustment equal to $1-\lambda$ (that is, the speed of adjustment of inflationary expectations).

What would happen in the case where the government did not have a fixed target for inflation, but a socially desirable fixed target for unemployment u_A, which happened to be lower than the natural rate of unemployment u_0? In this case, the government and the monetary authorities would presumably use discretionary aggregate demand policies to maintain unemployment below its natural rate u_0 at u_A, where $u_A < u_0$.

From the unemployment equation (15.43), if the government aimed to keep unemployment constant at $u_A < u_0$, inflation would evolve according to

$$\pi_t = \pi_{t-1} + b(1-\lambda)(u_0 - u_A). \tag{15.44}$$

The difference equation (15.44) has a unit root, and thus inflation does not converge. In fact, it increases from period to period by a percentage that depends on the difference between the natural rate of unemployment rate u_0 and the government's target unemployment rate u_A. As the government uses discretionary aggregate demand policies to keep unemployment below its natural rate, it will be causing a constant increase in inflation, so that inflation is always higher than the rising adaptive inflationary expectations. Otherwise, unemployment cannot be maintained below its natural rate.[25]

This case is depicted in figure 15.10. When the government and the monetary authorities seek to maintain unemployment below its natural rate u_0 at the lower rate u_A, inflation and inflationary expectations start increasing. To keep unemployment below its natural rate, actual inflation must be higher than expected inflation. Under adaptive expectations, this can only happen if inflation increases continuously. If the government and the monetary authorities allow the unemployment rate to return to its natural rate, then inflation will stop increasing.[26]

Let us now assume, as in the case of the AD-AS model, that the government and the monetary authorities are not concerned only about inflation or only about unemployment,

25. This case is sometimes referred to as the "accelerationist" hypothesis, as inflation is increasing constantly. It was alluded to by Friedman [1968].

26. Sometimes the natural rate of unemployment is referred to as the "nonaccelerating inflation rate of unemployment," because under adaptive expectations, it is the only unemployment rate at which inflation is not changing continuously but remains constant.

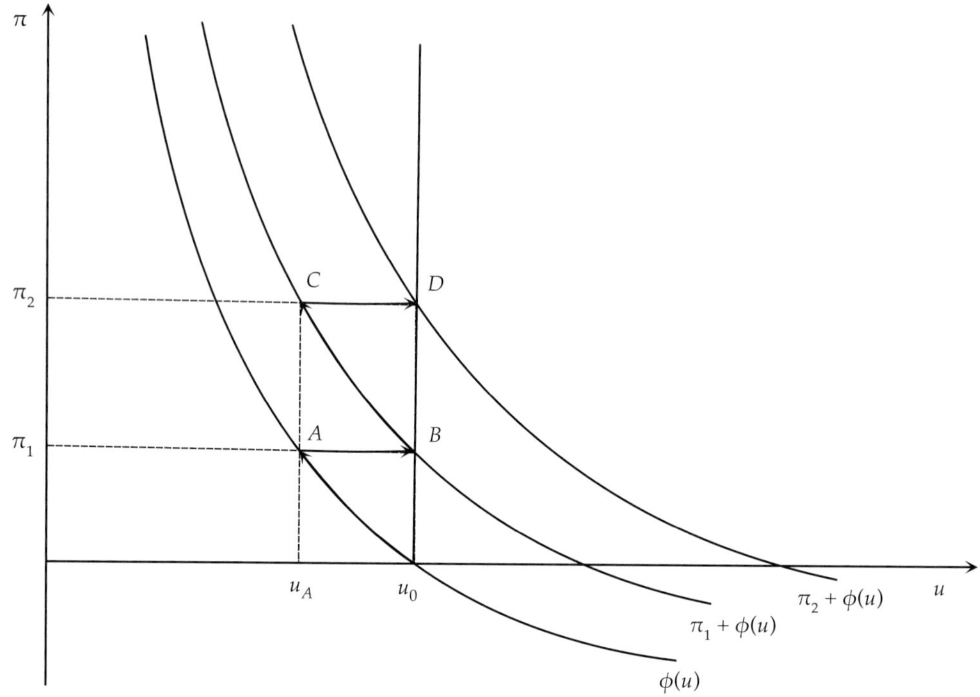

Figure 15.10
Continuous shifts of the Phillips curve due to rising inflationary expectations.

but about both. They use aggregate demand policies to minimize a quadratic loss function that depends on both inflation and unemployment. Assume that this function takes the form[27]

$$\Lambda_t = \frac{1}{2}(u_t - u_A)^2 + \frac{\zeta}{2}(\pi_t - \pi_A)^2, \tag{15.45}$$

where ζ is the relative weight that the government attaches to deviations of inflation relative to unemployment from their socially desirable levels π_A and u_A, respectively. The objective function (15.45) is minimized subject to the Phillips curve (15.39), with the government taking inflationary expectations as given.

From the first-order conditions for a minimum of (15.45), subject to the Phillips curve (15.39), we get

$$(u_t - u_A) = \zeta b(\pi_t - \pi_A). \tag{15.46}$$

27. This is essentially an analysis of the optimal discretionary policy of the Tinbergen-Theil variety.

Under the optimal discretionary aggregate demand policy, the marginal welfare cost of deviations of unemployment from the government target equals the marginal welfare cost of deviations of inflation from target. If both targets could be achieved, (15.46) would be automatically satisfied, but if the government cannot achieve both targets simultaneously, optimal second-best policy must satisfy (15.46).

Using the unemployment equation (15.43) to substitute for unemployment in (15.46), we end up with the following equation for inflation under the optimal policy:

$$\pi_t - \pi_A = \frac{1+\lambda\zeta b^2}{1+\zeta b^2}\left(\pi_{t-1} - \pi_A\right) + \frac{(1-\lambda)b}{1+\zeta b^2}\left(u_0 - u_A\right). \tag{15.47}$$

Substituting (15.47) in the first-order condition (15.46), unemployment under the optimal policy follows

$$u_t - u_A = \frac{1+\lambda\zeta b^2}{1+\zeta b^2}\left(u_{t-1} - u_A\right) + \frac{\zeta b^2(1-\lambda)}{1+\zeta b^2}\left(u_0 - u_A\right). \tag{15.48}$$

From (15.47) and (15.48), inflation and unemployment gradually converge to steady state values equal to

$$\pi^* = \pi_A + \frac{1}{\zeta b}\left(u_0 - u_A\right), \tag{15.49}$$

$$u^* = u_0, \tag{15.50}$$

where π^* and u^* denote steady state inflation and unemployment, respectively.

Equations (15.49) and (15.50) suggest that if the government is using discretionary aggregate demand policies to pursue an unemployment target that is lower than the natural rate of unemployment, but it also cares about inflation ($\zeta > 0$), both inflation and unemployment converge to unique steady state values. However, steady state inflation turns out to be higher than the socially desirable inflation target π_A, and steady state unemployment is also higher than the socially desirable unemployment target u_A and is equal to the natural rate u_0.[28]

Note from (15.49) that the discrepancy between steady state inflation and the socially desirable inflation target π_A is larger,

- the larger the discrepancy is between the natural rate of unemployment and the socially desirable unemployment target u_A,
- the smaller is the weight ζ of inflation relative to unemployment in the social loss function (15.45), and finally,
- the smaller is the impact of unemployment on inflation in the Phillips curve (15.39).

28. Of course, the converse is also true. If the government pursues an unemployment target that is above the natural rate, steady state inflation will be below the government target for inflation.

These parameters reflect the incentives of the government to reduce unemployment and create unanticipated inflation under a discretionary aggregate demand policy.

In the attempt to reduce unemployment below the natural rate, the government drives actual inflation and inflationary expectations above the socially desirable inflation target to a level that balances (1) the marginal welfare cost of deviations of unemployment from the government target with (2) the marginal welfare cost of deviations of inflation from the government target. Note that (15.49) and (15.50) satisfy the first-order condition for the minimization of the social loss function (15.45). Thus, at the steady state inflation rate (15.49), inflation is so high that the government has no further incentive to use discretionary aggregate demand policies to reduce unemployment below its natural rate, because this would bring about a further increase in the already high inflation rate.

We have thus demonstrated that the use of discretionary aggregate demand policies to pursue an unemployment target that is lower than the natural rate does not affect steady state unemployment. This ends up at the natural rate u_0 anyway. But it does affect steady state inflation, which turns out to be higher than the socially desirable government target.

15.5.2 Rules versus Discretion in Aggregate Demand Policy

Because steady state unemployment is equal to the natural rate u_0 anyway, a better policy outcome would be for inflation to be equal to π_A, the socially optimal inflation rate, rather than to the higher π^*.

The *inflationary bias* of discretionary aggregate demand policies arises because policymakers cannot commit to the low, socially desirable inflation π_A: Under discretion, when inflationary expectations are equal to π_A, they have the incentive to create surprise inflation to reduce unemployment. For this reason, under discretion, the economy ends up with both higher inflation and higher unemployment than what is socially desirable.

Suppose that instead of having the discretion to choose aggregate demand policies in every period to minimize (15.45), the government is committed to using aggregate demand policies to keep inflation constantly at the socially optimal rate π_A. Thus for all periods, we have

$$\pi_t = \pi_A. \tag{15.51}$$

Then steady state inflation is also equal to π_A, and steady state unemployment is equal to u_0. The inflationary bias of discretionary aggregate demand policies disappears, as the government is committed to following the rule (15.51). Then it cannot succumb to the temptation to use aggregate demand policies to reduce unemployment and thus create unanticipated inflation. Thus, under commitment to the policy rule (15.51), the economy would end up with unemployment at the natural rate, which is higher than what is socially desirable (but is the same as under the discretionary policy), and inflation that is equal to the socially desirable level π_A and not higher. The inflationary bias disappears, and the policy outcome is better than the policy outcome under discretion.

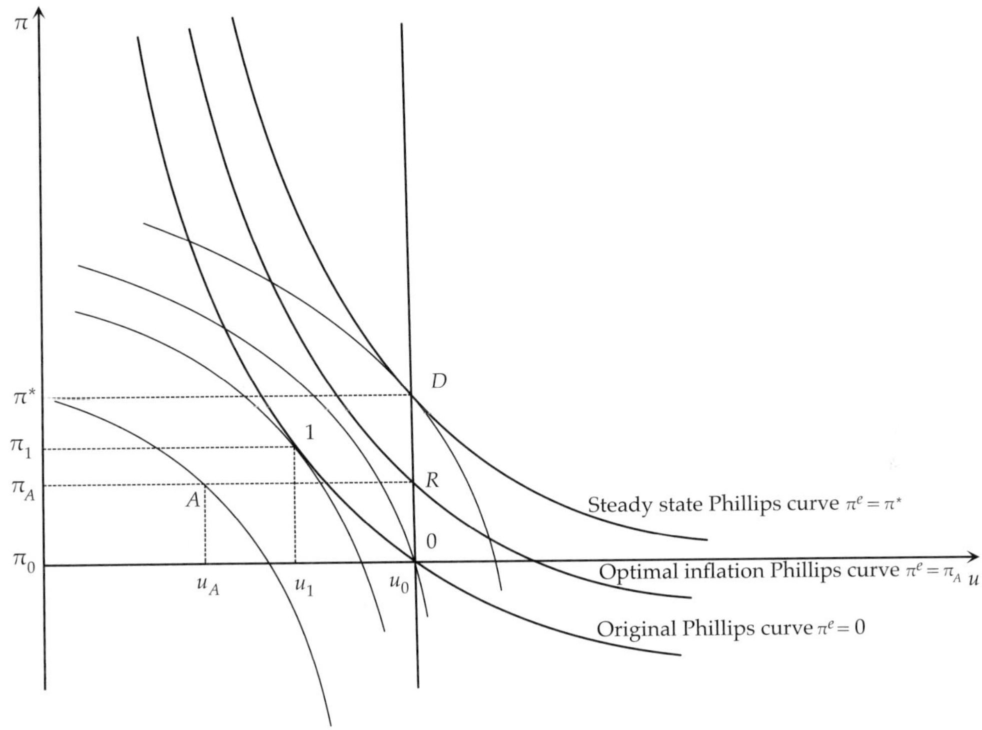

Figure 15.11
Determination of steady state inflation and unemployment under discretion and commitment to an inflation rule.

A graphical illustration of this argument can be seen with the help of figure 15.11. Assume that originally, the economy is at the natural rate of unemployment, with zero inflation (point 0). The government decides to expand aggregate demand to reduce unemployment. This has the effect of increasing inflation along the original Phillips curve. The economy ends up at point 1, where the original Phillips curve is tangent to the highest possible social indifference curve between inflation and unemployment. Point 1 implies lower unemployment and higher inflation. In the short run, the government is better off, as the welfare loss associated with point 1 is lower than that associated with point 0. Note that point A, which implies the lowest-possible welfare loss, cannot be attained. But point 1 is not a stable equilibrium, because inflationary expectations start adapting to the higher inflation π_1, and the Phillips curve starts shifting upward.

Thus, the government will need to further increase aggregate demand to keep unemployment below the natural rate. This will generate a further increase in inflation, further upward revisions of inflationary expectations, and so on.

The process will only stop when the economy ends up at point D (D for "discretion"), and expectations adapt to the inflation rate π^*. At point D, the government no longer has an incentive to further expand aggregate demand to reduce unemployment. The welfare costs from further increases in inflation exceed the welfare benefits from the reduction in unemployment. Thus, D is a stable steady state equilibrium.

Under commitment to a inflation rule that keeps inflation equal to π_A, the economy converges to the steady state equilibrium R (R for "rules"). Point R is preferable to D, because it is associated with lower steady state inflation ($\pi_A < \pi^*$) and the same unemployment rate. The problem is that at R, the government has a short-run incentive to renege on its commitment and expand aggregate demand to reduce unemployment. The short-run marginal welfare gain from the reduction in unemployment is higher than the short-run marginal welfare loss from the rise in inflation. Thus, the commitment mechanism must be binding for the government not to succumb to the temptation of increasing aggregate demand.

These results were first demonstrated by Kydland and Prescott [1977], under the assumption of rational expectations. As we have demonstrated in this section, they hold in the steady state under adaptive expectations too. The discretionary (time-consistent) policy is not intertemporally optimal, in the sense that there is a better policy outcome under commitment to the rule (15.51). However, the rule (15.51) is not time-consistent, because the government has an incentive to deviate from it in every period to minimize (15.45). Thus, the intertemporally optimal steady state policy rule is time inconsistent: It is not optimal in the short run.

This case is an important example of the time inconsistency of optimal policy in dynamic settings, in which policymakers have objectives that conflict with the objectives of private agents (Kydland and Prescott [1977]). The time-consistent policy is not optimal, and the optimal policy is time inconsistent. Thus, binding commitment mechanisms are required to ensure that an optimal policy rule, such as (15.51), is implemented in every period.

15.5.3 Inflation and Unemployment under Rational Expectations

Our analysis so far has been based on the assumption of adaptive expectations. One of the consequences of the realization that the original Phillips curve is unstable was the adoption of the hypothesis of rational expectations. The hypothesis of rational expectations gradually became the key hypothesis regarding the formation of expectations, not only about inflation, but also about all future variables that affect the behavior of households and firms, as well as governments.[29]

In this particular context, rational expectations implies that households and firms form inflationary expectations that take into account the incentives of governments to use discretionary policies to choose between inflation and unemployment. It is thus worth analyzing the implications of the rational expectations hypothesis for this model of the natural rate.

29. See Lucas [1972], who introduced the hypothesis of rational expectations of Muth [1961] to macroeconomics. We have studied models with rational expectations in chapter 9.

From the first-order conditions for a minimum of the social loss function (15.45), subject to the Phillips curve (15.39), we get that under discretionary policies, equation (15.46) must necessarily hold. Using the Phillips curve (15.39) to substitute for unemployment in (15.46), we get

$$\left(u_0 - u_A - \frac{1}{b}(\pi_t - \pi_t^e\right) = \zeta b(\pi_t - \pi_A). \tag{15.52}$$

Because there are no stochastic disturbances, the hypothesis of rational expectations implies that expected and actual inflation will coincide. Thus, (15.52), combined with the rational expectations hypothesis, implies that

$$\pi_t = \pi_t^e = \pi_A + \frac{1}{\zeta b}(u_0 - u_A). \tag{15.53}$$

Under rational expectations, in the absence of stochastic disturbances, inflation is always equal to expected inflation. Thus, inflation jumps to steady state inflation immediately. Consequently, unemployment also jumps to its natural rate immediately. Discretionary aggregate demand policies cannot affect unemployment even in the short run, and they only result in both short-run and steady state inflationary bias, because of the incentives of the government to create surprise inflation and the immediate adjustment of expectations to anticipate these incentives.

In contrast, under commitment to the time-inconsistent policy rule (15.51), inflation is equal to

$$\pi_t = \pi_t^e = \pi_A. \tag{15.54}$$

The unemployment rate is equal to the natural rate u_0 in all periods.

Thus, under rational expectations, the dynamic adjustment to the steady state is immediate, because there are no other sources of persistence in this model. The suboptimality of discretionary policy is even starker in this case, and the argument in favor of commitment to rules such as (15.51) is even stronger.[30]

15.6 Conclusion

In this chapter, we have considered the basic Keynesian approach, which was associated with the development of macroeconomics from the mid-1930s to the end of the 1960s.

30. Note that, following the insights of Kydland and Prescott [1977], Barro and Gordon [1983a,b], Rogoff [1985], and others have provided a detailed analysis of the problem of rules versus discretion for the case of the Phillips curve under rational expectations. We shall return to a more extensive and formal analysis of the rules-versus-discretion debate in chapter 20 on the role of monetary policy.

We have seen that what separates classical from Keynesian models is the assumption of nominal rigidity or gradual adjustment in nominal wages and the price level.

We have looked at the structure of the basic Keynesian models, assuming initially a constant level of prices or nominal wages, and then gradual adjustment of prices and nominal wages, based on the Phillips curve. We also explored the theory of discretionary aggregate demand policy that was originally developed on the basis of these models.

According to the basic Keynesian model, combined with the Phillips curve, an increase in aggregate demand—either through government expenditure (or a tax cut) or through an increase in the money supply—leads to an increase in real income and employment, a reduction of unemployment, and increased inflation. Conversely, a decline in aggregate demand leads to a decline of real income and employment, an increase in unemployment, and reduced inflation. As argued by Samuelson and Solow [1960], the short-term objective of macroeconomic policy can be seen as the appropriate selection of a discretionary mix of monetary and fiscal policies that would deliver the desired combination of unemployment and inflation. Thus, the adoption of the Keynesian approach led to a shift toward discretion in the determination of monetary and fiscal policies.

The instability of the original Phillips curve observed in the late 1960s, and the interpretation given to this instability by Phelps [1967] and Friedman [1968], have since sparked a revolution in the analysis of aggregate fluctuations and the evaluation of aggregate demand policies.

The literature has since moved in three directions. First, great emphasis was placed on the microeconomic foundations of the determination of wages, prices, the supply and demand for goods and services, and the determination of the equilibrium unemployment rate. The result is that today both the new classical and the new Keynesian approaches to aggregate fluctuations are based on DSGE models with consistent dynamic microeconomic foundations.

Second, the instability of the original Phillips curve eventually led to the adoption of the hypothesis of rational expectations: the hypothesis that households and firms form inflationary expectations that take into account the motives of governments and central banks to choose between inflation and unemployment. The hypothesis of rational expectations is currently the key hypothesis regarding the formation of expectations, not only about inflation, but also about all future variables that affect the behavior of households, firms, and governments. This hypothesis is used by both the new classical and the new Keynesian approaches.

Third, the debate on the appropriate use of monetary and fiscal policy has shifted in favor of rules rather than discretion. The problem of macroeconomic policy design is no longer a question of rules versus discretion, but a question of the appropriate design of policy rules.

In the next four chapters, we analyze simplified dynamic stochastic versions of new Keynesian models, highlighting their similarities to and differences from new classical models in accounting for aggregate fluctuations. We also consider the implications of different stabilization policy rules.

16

A Model of Imperfect Competition and Staggered Pricing

The perfectly competitive new classical models that we analyzed in chapters 13 and 14 are examples of DSGE models in which wages and prices are perfectly flexible and equilibrate both the product and labor markets. In such models, only real shocks (such as shocks to productivity) can affect the fluctuations of output, employment, and other real variables. Monetary shocks only affect nominal variables, such as the price level and inflation. Employment fluctuations are based on intertemporal substitution in labor supply, and thus, there is no involuntary unemployment. Nominal shocks can have temporary real effects only if there is imperfect information about aggregate and relative nominal shocks, as in the case of the Lucas [1972] island model.

In this chapter, we introduce an imperfectly competitive macromodel based on staggered price setting. This is a DSGE model based on distortions in product markets. We initially analyze it assuming both full flexibility of wages and prices and, subsequently assuming staggered price adjustment. The model with full flexibility of wages and prices is comparable to the perfectly competitive new classical model presented in chapter 14. The model with staggered pricing allows for a Phillips curve–type relation between inflation and deviations of output and employment from their natural rates, and thus for real effects of nominal shocks and monetary policy. This model differs from the new classical model in that nominal shocks and monetary policy have real effects, not because of imperfect information, but because of the imperfect adjustment of nominal prices.

The imperfectly competitive model introduced in this chapter has two important differences from the typical perfectly competitive new classical DSGE model. First, instead of fully competitive markets for goods and services, it assumes that markets are characterized by conditions of monopolistic competition. Firms have market power and do not take prices as given, but determine prices themselves so as to maximize profits. Because of the market power of firms and the existence of monopolistic competition, the natural rate of employment, real output, consumption, and real wages are determined at lower levels than in the corresponding perfectly competitive model. However, by itself, this difference does not result in major differences from the new classical competitive model regarding the nature of aggregate fluctuations, which again depend solely on real shocks.

Second, this imperfectly competitive model can account for a Phillips curve type of relation, assuming that firms adjust prices only gradually. Two observationally equivalent versions of gradual price adjustment have dominated the literature since the early 1980s. One is the Rotemberg [1982a, 1982b] model of *costly price adjustment*, and the second is the Calvo [1983] model of *staggered pricing*. In the Rotemberg model, firms face convex costs of adjusting prices, which they balance against convex costs of deviating from the profit-maximizing optimal steady state price. They end up gradually adjusting prices toward the profit-maximizing steady state price. In the Calvo model, it is assumed that only a fixed proportion of firms have the freedom to adjust prices in any given period, with the remaining firms not being able to do so. Although optimal pricing by firms takes this restriction into account in advance, the aggregate price level can only adjust gradually to aggregate shocks, because not all firms have the option of adjusting prices to new information in every period.

These two alternative assumptions lead to models with price stickiness, whose properties differ from full-information new classical models. They share some properties of Keynesian models of the Phillips curve and the Lucas [1972] island model. Because they are based on sluggish price adjustment, a key assumption of the original Keynesian models, such models are called new Keynesian models.

In the case of staggered pricing, it turns out that deviations of output from its natural level cause deviations of inflation from expected future inflation, as higher aggregate demand and output causes an increase in nominal marginal costs and hence prices. This results in a Phillips curve–type relation called the *new Keynesian Phillips curve*. This differs from the original expectations-augmented Phillips curve that we analyzed in chapter 15, because current inflation depends on current expectations about future inflation and not on prior expectations of current inflation.

The imperfectly competitive model analyzed in this chapter has the following structure:

- Deviations of inflation from the target of the central bank are determined by the new Keynesian Phillips curve and depend on expected future deviations of inflation from the central bank inflation target, and deviations of real aggregate demand and output from its natural rate. These deviations of output from its natural rate cause a rise in inflation, as they are associated with an increase in nominal marginal costs and hence optimal prices.
- On the demand side, deviations of aggregate demand from the natural rate of real output depend on the new Keynesian IS curve and are driven by deviations of the current real interest rate from its natural rate.
- The nominal interest rate is assumed to be determined by the central bank, which follows a Taylor [1993] interest rate rule. According to the *Taylor rule*, which is a generalization of the Wicksell rule that we discussed in chapters 12 and 14, the nominal interest rate reacts positively to deviations of current inflation from the inflation target of the central bank, as

well as deviations of real output from its natural rate. This is a countercyclical monetary policy rule, aiming to nudge inflation and output toward their equilibrium levels.

After discussing the properties of this model, we analyze the effects of monetary and real shocks on fluctuations in real output and inflation.

The imperfectly competitive new Keynesian model with staggered prices can, unlike the full information new classical model, explain monetary cycles (i.e., aggregate fluctuations caused by monetary shocks). These shocks are transmitted to real variables, and to the extent that they persist over time, they have persistent real effects.

This model is widely considered to be the benchmark new Keynesian model. However, its weakness is that it cannot account for involuntary unemployment but only for underemployment. In this particular model, because of the assumed flexibility of nominal wages, the labor market clears continuously, in the sense that labor demand is always equal to labor supply. Because of imperfect competition, the equilibrium real wage is lower than in a fully competitive model, and thus, equilibrium employment is lower than in a fully competitive economy. However, there is no involuntary unemployment, and fluctuations in employment are due to intertemporal substitution in labor supply, as in the Lucas [1972] misperceptions model.

Furthermore, this model is characterized by the so-called divine coincidence: The stabilization of inflation leads to the stabilization of output and employment around their natural rates as well. There is no trade-off between the stabilization of inflation and employment in this model. Hence, the optimal prescription for monetary policy is to fully stabilize inflation, much like in new classical models.

Thus, the analysis of this new Keynesian model based on staggered pricing eventually leads us to conclude that to account for unemployment, one has to investigate models with distortions in the labor market. We take up this topic in chapter 17.

16.1 An Imperfectly Competitive Model of Aggregate Fluctuations

In this section, we examine in detail the structure of an imperfectly competitive model of aggregate fluctuations. The basic model that we analyze has much in common with the new classical model of chapter 14. It is a DSGE model with two important differences from the new classical model.

First, instead of perfectly competitive markets for goods and services, we assume that markets are characterized by conditions of imperfect (monopolistic) competition. Firms do not take prices as given; instead, they have the power to determine prices that maximize profits. Because of imperfect competition, in equilibrium, employment, real output, consumption, and real wages are determined at a lower level than in the corresponding competitive model, even when there is complete flexibility in prices and wages. By itself, this feature does not result in material differences from the competitive classical model with respect to the nature of aggregate fluctuations. If this was the only difference, we could well talk about an imperfectly competitive new classical model.

Second, we assume staggered price adjustment: Firms do not have the ability to change their prices at all times. This assumption is what leads to a model in which the price level adjusts gradually toward the equilibrium price level. As a result of gradual price adjustment, real variables deviate from their natural rates, and monetary shocks can have real effects.

16.1.1 The Representative Household

The problem of the representative household under monopolistic competition has one difference from the corresponding problem under perfect competition. The difference is that because of monopolistic competition, the household consumes differentiated products.

The representative household maximizes

$$E_t \sum\nolimits_{s=0}^{\infty} \left(\frac{1}{1+\rho}\right)^t u(C_{t+s}, L_{t+s}), \tag{16.1}$$

where C is consumption, L is labor supply, and ρ is the pure rate of time preference. Consumption consists of all produced goods, which are defined on the basis of a constant index j in the interval [0, 1]. The consumption bundle is thus given by

$$C_t = \left(\int_{j=0}^{1} C_t(j)^{\frac{\varepsilon-1}{\varepsilon}} dj\right)^{\frac{\varepsilon}{\varepsilon-1}}, \tag{16.2}$$

where ε is also a parameter of the preferences of the representative household; more precisely, it is the elasticity of substitution between goods. We assume that $\varepsilon > 1$.

The sequence of budget constraints under which the household maximizes intertemporal utility is given by

$$B_{t+1} = (1+i_t)B_t + W_t L_t + T_t - \int_{j=0}^{1} P_t(j)C_t(j)dj. \tag{16.3}$$

The household must also satisfy the transversality condition:

$$\lim_{T\to\infty} E_t B_T \geq 0, \tag{16.4}$$

where $P(j)$ is the price of good j, W is the nominal wage, i is the nominal interest rate, B is a nominal one-period bond, and T is an exogenous transfer of nominal income to the household (dividends, government transfers, or taxes).

In addition to the decision about aggregate consumption and labor supply (which we have analyzed in section 14.1.1 of chapter 14), the household must now decide on the distribution of its consumption expenditure among the various goods. This requires the maximization of the consumption bundle (16.2) for any level of monetary expenditure. One can easily deduce that this implies

$$C_t(j) = \left(\frac{P_t(j)}{P_t}\right)^{-\varepsilon} C(t) \tag{16.5}$$

for any good j in the interval [0, 1], where P is the average price level, defined as

$$P_t = \left(\int_{j=0}^{1} P_t(j)^{1-\varepsilon} dj\right)^{\frac{1}{1-\varepsilon}}. \tag{16.6}$$

In addition, when the household follows this optimal allocation policy, we also have that

$$\int_{j=0}^{1} P_t(j)C_t(j)dj = P_tC_t. \tag{16.7}$$

Equation (16.7) suggests that total consumption expenditure can be written as the product of the aggregate consumption index and the aggregate price index. Substituting (16.7) in the sequence of budget constraints (16.3), we get

$$P_tC_t + \frac{1}{1+i_t}B_t \leq B_{t-1} + W_tL_t - T_t. \tag{16.8}$$

This sequence of budget constraints is the same as the sequence of budget constraints of the representative household in the competitive classical model of chapter 14. As a result, the first-order conditions for consumption and labor supply are analogous to the ones for the new classical model analyzed in chapter 14:

$$-\frac{u_{L_t}}{u_{C_t}} = \frac{W_t}{P_t}, \tag{16.9}$$

$$\frac{1}{1+i_t} = \frac{1}{1+\rho}E_t\left\{\frac{u_{C_{t+1}}}{u_{C_t}}\frac{P_t}{P_{t+1}}\right\}. \tag{16.10}$$

We assume, as in the new classical model without capital of chapter 14, that the per period utility function is additively separable and defined by

$$U(C_t, L_t) = \frac{C_t^{1-\theta}}{1-\theta} - \frac{L_t^{1+\lambda}}{1+\lambda}, \tag{16.11}$$

where $1/\theta$ is the intertemporal elasticity of substitution in consumption, and $1/\lambda$ the Frisch elasticity of labor supply. Assuming that preferences take the form of (16.11), the first-order conditions (16.9) and (16.10) can be written in log-linear form as

$$w_t - p_t = \theta c_t + \lambda l_t, \tag{16.12}$$

$$c_t = E_t(c_{t+1}) - \frac{1}{\theta}\left(i_t - E_t(\pi_{t+1}) - \rho\right), \tag{16.13}$$

where lowercase letters denote the logarithms of the corresponding variables, and π is the rate of inflation. Equations (16.12) and (16.13) are analogous to the ones in the new classical model in chapter 14.

16.1.2 The Representative Firm and Optimal Pricing

Assume that output is produced by a set of firms denoted by a continuous index j defined in the interval [0, 1]. Each firm produces a differentiated product under conditions of monopolistic competition. All firms have access to the same production technology, denoted by the production function

$$Y_t(j) = A_t L_t(j)^{1-\alpha}, \tag{16.14}$$

where $A_t > 0$ and $0 < \alpha < 1$ are exogenous technological parameters common to all firms, $L(j)$ is employment of labor by firm j, the parameter α is constant, and A_t is assumed to follow an exogenous stochastic process.

The optimal price of each firm (if it can choose its price in every period) is given by the maximization of its profits under the constraint of the production function (16.14) and the demand function for its product (16.5). Each firm takes the average price P, the average wage W, and the level of total demand C as given.

The per period profits of firm j are given by

$$P_t(j)Y_t(j) - W_t L_t(j). \tag{16.15}$$

From the first-order conditions for a maximum of (16.15) under the constraints (16.14) and (16.5), the optimal price is determined as

$$P_t(j) = \frac{\varepsilon}{\varepsilon - 1}\left(\frac{W_t}{(1-\alpha)A_t L_t(j)^{-\alpha}}\right). \tag{16.16}$$

The optimal price is a fixed markup on the firm's marginal cost, which equals the expression in large parentheses. The markup depends on the elasticity of substitution between goods in the preferences of consumers, which determines the price elasticity of demand of their product and therefore the profit margin of the firm. In the case of perfect competition that we examined in chapter 14, the elasticity of substitution tends to infinity, and the price tends to marginal cost. In the case of monopolistic competition with $\varepsilon > 1$, as we have assumed, the optimal price is higher than the marginal cost of labor.[1]

1. This model of monopolistic competition, with a constant elasticity of demand, is due to Dixit and Stiglitz [1977].

As all firms have the same production function and face the same nominal wage and the same demand function for their product, they will all choose the same price. Consequently, the price level is defined as

$$P_t = \frac{\varepsilon}{\varepsilon - 1}\left(\frac{W_t}{(1-\alpha)A_t L_t^{-\alpha}}\right). \tag{16.17}$$

Taking the logarithm of the production function (16.14) for the representative firm and equation (16.16) for the optimal price, we get

$$y_t = a_t + (1-\alpha)l_t, \tag{16.18}$$

$$w_t - p_t = a_t - \alpha l_t - \mu, \tag{16.19}$$

where $a_t = \ln A_t$, $\mu = \ln\left(\frac{\varepsilon}{\varepsilon-1}\right) - \ln(1-\alpha)$, a is the logarithm of the exogenous productivity shock, and the constant μ is the logarithm of the markup on marginal cost minus the logarithm of the coefficient of decreasing returns to labor (which is equivalent to scale in this model).

16.1.3 Full Price Flexibility and the Natural Rate

Solving the model under the assumption of full flexibility of prices and wages, one can show that fluctuations in employment, output, consumption, and real wages are functions only of the exogenous shocks to productivity, while fluctuations in the real interest rate are a function of the expected change in productivity, just as in the new classical model under the assumption of perfect competition. Thus, under the assumption of full price flexibility, we can derive the natural rate solution of the model.

Because we have assumed that there is no investment or public consumption, equilibrium implies that labor supply would be equal to labor demand by firms, and consumption would be equal to output:

$$\theta c_t + \lambda l_t = a_t - \alpha l_t - \mu, \tag{16.20}$$

$$y_t = c_t. \tag{16.21}$$

Equation (16.20) is the equilibrium condition in the labor market: The real wage makes labor supply by households equal to labor demand by firms. Equation (16.21) is the equilibrium condition in the output market: Output is equal to aggregate demand, which depends only on consumption.

The full model consists of equations (16.12), (16.13), (16.18), (16.19), and the equilibrium conditions (16.20) and (16.21). The model determines the natural rate solutions of employment, output, consumption, real wages, and the real interest rate as functions of the exogenous shock to productivity a.

The real interest rate is defined by the Fisher equation as

$$r_t = i_t - E_t(\pi_{t+1}). \tag{16.22}$$

Solving the model for the five endogenous variables, we get

$$l_t^N = \phi a_t + \bar{l}, \tag{16.23}$$

where $\phi = \frac{1-\theta}{\theta(1-\alpha)+\alpha+\lambda}$, and $\bar{l} = -\frac{\mu}{\theta(1-\alpha)+\alpha+\lambda}$;

$$y_t^N = c_t^N = \psi a_t + \bar{y}, \tag{16.24}$$

where $\psi = 1 + (1-\alpha)\phi = \frac{1+\lambda}{\theta(1-\alpha)+\alpha+\lambda}$, and $\bar{y} = (1-\alpha)\bar{l}$;

$$(w-p)_t^N = \chi a_t + \bar{\omega}, \tag{16.25}$$

where $\chi = 1 - \alpha\phi = \frac{\theta+\lambda}{\theta(1-\alpha)+\alpha+\lambda}$, and $\bar{\omega} = (\theta(1-\alpha)+\lambda)\,\bar{l}$; and

$$r_t^N = \rho + \theta\psi E_t(\Delta a_{t+1}). \tag{16.26}$$

Equations (16.23)–(16.26), along with the equilibrium conditions (16.20) and (16.21), determine the five endogenous real variables as functions of the exogenous productivity shock. Superscript N (for "natural") denotes the equilibrium values of the relevant variables, which, according to the Friedman definition, are their natural rates.

Output, consumption, and real wages are positive functions of the productivity shock a, and employment is a positive function of the productivity shock only if $\theta < 1$ (i.e., only if the elasticity of intertemporal substitution is greater than one). If $\theta > 1$, employment is a negative function of productivity, and if $\theta = 1$, employment is independent of productivity. This applies because if $\theta < 1$, the intertemporal substitution effect dominates the income effect, following a change in productivity and real wages. If $\theta > 1$, the income effect dominates the intertemporal substitution effect, whereas in the case $\theta = 1$, the two effects cancel each other out, and employment is not affected.

No other factor affects fluctuations in real variables. We see that, as in the competitive real business cycle (RBC) model of chapter 14, monetary factors (such as the money supply and nominal interest rates) have no effect on the evolution of real variables.

16.1.4 Inefficiency of the Natural Rate

However, this model has one significant difference from the competitive model of chapter 14. Because of monopolistic competition, which implies a positive margin of prices over marginal costs of firms, both employment and output (as well as consumption and real wages) are determined at a lower level than in the case of perfect competition. Monopolistic competition implies a distortion in the market of goods and services, which leads to lower equilibrium employment and output and to lower real wages than under perfect competition.[2]

If the productivity shock follows a stationary stochastic process with mean zero, then from (16.23), the log of the steady state employment level will be

$$\bar{l} = -\frac{\mu}{\theta(1-\alpha)+\alpha+\lambda} = \frac{\ln(1-\alpha) - \ln(\varepsilon/(\varepsilon-1))}{\theta(1-\alpha)+\alpha+\lambda}. \tag{16.27}$$

If $\varepsilon > 1$, the steady state employment level will be lower than in the case of perfect competition.

Under perfect competition, goods are perfect substitutes in the preferences of consumers. Thus, steady state employment is

$$\lim_{\varepsilon \to \infty} \bar{l} = \frac{\ln(1-\alpha)}{\theta(1-\alpha)+\alpha+\lambda}. \tag{16.28}$$

Because of imperfect competition, this model implies underemployment relative to a fully competitive model, even when there is full flexibility of prices and wages. Through (16.24) and (16.25), this underemployment implies that steady state output and steady state real wages will also be lower compared to perfect competition.

In all other respects, this model resembles the new classical competitive RBC model analyzed in chapter 14.

16.2 Staggered Price Adjustment and Aggregate Fluctuations

In contrast to the new classical models, in new Keynesian models, the assumption of fully flexible wages and prices is replaced by the assumption of gradual and only partial adjustment of nominal wages and prices toward their equilibrium values. This is in accordance with the approach in the *General Theory* itself, as discussed in chapter 15. In this section, we assume gradual adjustment of prices and fully flexible wages in a competitive labor market.

Various alternative new Keynesian models of gradual price adjustment under monopolistic competition have been developed in the literature. Let us concentrate on one of them, the Calvo [1983] model, which is based on staggered pricing.[3]

2. See Akerlof and Yellen [1985], Mankiw [1985], Blanchard and Kiyotaki [1987], and Ball and Romer [1990] for the first generation of new Keynesian models that relied on monopolistic competition.

3. An observationally equivalent model, the Rotemberg [1982a,b] model of quadratic costs of adjusting prices, is briefly analyzed in section 16.3 of this chapter. The concept of staggered price and wage adjustment was first introduced to macroeconomics by Akerlof [1969]. Versions of staggered nominal wage contracts were used to study the role of monetary policy under rational expectations by Fischer [1977a] and Taylor [1979, 1980]. These contracts were fixed-term contracts. Calvo [1983] generalized the Taylor fixed-term contracts to contracts with a stochastic duration.

Following Calvo [1983], let us assume that firms cannot freely adjust their prices in every period at a rate different than steady state (or *core*) inflation. All firms are assumed to automatically adjust prices at the core inflation rate. However, for any firm, the probability of adjusting prices in any period at a rate different than core inflation is equal to $1-\gamma$, which is constant and independent of the length of time that has elapsed since the last such a price adjustment by the firm. Thus, in each period, a proportion $1-\gamma$ of all firms adjust their prices freely at a rate different than core inflation, and the remaining proportion γ adjust their prices automatically at the rate of core inflation. This assumption has critical implications for the properties of the model, the nature of aggregate fluctuations, and the effects of monetary shocks and monetary policy.[4]

Under these assumptions, in period t, the expected future duration of any price contract is given by

$$(1-\gamma)\sum\nolimits_{s=0}^{\infty} s\gamma^{s} = \frac{\gamma}{1-\gamma}. \tag{16.29}$$

From the definition of the price level in (16.6) and the fact that all firms that reset their prices in period t set the same price, it follows that

$$\hat{P}_t = \left(\gamma\left(\hat{P}_{t-1}\right)^{1-\varepsilon} + (1-\gamma)\left(\bar{P}_t\right)^{1-\varepsilon}\right)^{\frac{1}{1-\varepsilon}}, \tag{16.30}$$

where $\hat{P}$ is the price level relative to the steady state price level, and $\bar{P}$ is the price set by the firms that reset their prices in the current period relative to the steady state price level.

From (16.30), one can show that the dynamic adjustment of the price level relative to the steady state price level is determined by

$$\left(\frac{\hat{P}_t}{\hat{P}_{t-1}}\right)^{1-\varepsilon} = \gamma + (1-\gamma)\left(\frac{\bar{P}_t}{\hat{P}_{t-1}}\right)^{1-\varepsilon}. \tag{16.31}$$

In the steady state with inflation equal to π^*, we have that $\hat{P}_t = \bar{P}_t = 1$, and the price level is given by

$$P_t = (1+\pi^*)P_{t-1}. \tag{16.32}$$

A log-linear approximation of (16.31) around the steady state price level yields

4. In most models of staggered pricing, it is assumed that the firms that are constrained cannot adjust their prices at all. Yun [1996] is probably the first analysis of a new Keynesian DSGE model, such as the one in this section, using the Calvo [1983] assumption of staggered pricing. However, in the case that one does not allow for indexation to the steady state inflation rate, and steady state inflation is positive, the model violates the natural rate property. Increasing steady state inflation would affect steady state output and employment. See, for example, Ascari and Sbordone [2014].

$$\hat{p}_t - \hat{p}_{t-1} \simeq (1-\gamma)\left(\bar{p}_t - \hat{p}_{t-1}\right). \tag{16.33}$$

From (16.33), it follows that inflation exceeds its steady state rate if firms that set prices in the current period set them at a higher level than the average price of the previous period adjusted for steady state inflation.

16.2.1 Optimal Pricing with Staggered Price Adjustment

To analyze the adjustment of inflation, one has to examine how firms that can freely adjust prices in the current period decide on their optimal price. They must take into account that for a period in the future, they may not be able to readjust their prices freely, while some of their competitors have the option of readjusting their own prices at a rate different than core inflation.

The problem of the firm that decides on the price it is about to set in period t is to set the price that maximizes the expected present value of its profits, given that the probability of readjusting its price in any future period is equal to $1-\gamma$. Thus, all firms that readjust their prices in period t maximize

$$E_t \sum_{s=0}^{\infty} \gamma^s \left(I(s)\left(\bar{P}_t Y_{t+s}^t - \hat{W}_{t+s} L_{t+s}^t\right)\right), \tag{16.34}$$

where $I(s) = \prod_{z=0}^{s}\left(\frac{1}{1+i_{t+z}}\right)$, and $\hat{W}$ is the nominal wage adjusted for the steady state price level.

The maximization takes place under the constraints of their production function and the demand function for their product. These are given by

$$L_{t+s}^t = \left(\frac{Y_{t+s}^t}{A_{t+s}}\right)^{\frac{1}{1-\alpha}}, \tag{16.35}$$

$$Y_{t+s}^t = \left(\frac{\bar{P}_t}{\hat{P}_{t+s}}\right)^{-\varepsilon} Y_{t+s}, \tag{16.36}$$

where Y_{t+s}^t and L_{t+s}^t are the volume of output and employment, respectively, in period $t+s$ for the firm that has set its prices in period t. The higher the relative price of the firm is in any period, the lower will be the demand for its product and thus the volume of its output and employment.

From the first-order conditions for a maximum, it follows that

$$E_t \sum_{s=0}^{\infty} \gamma^s I(s) \left((\varepsilon - 1)\left(\frac{\bar{P}_t}{\hat{P}_{t+s}}\right)^{-\varepsilon} Y_{t+s} + \right.$$

$$\left. - \frac{\varepsilon}{(1-\alpha)}\left(\frac{\bar{P}_t}{\hat{P}_{t+s}}\right)^{-\frac{1-\alpha+\varepsilon}{1-\alpha}} \left(\frac{\hat{W}_{t+s}}{\hat{P}_{t+s}}\right)\left(\frac{Y_{t+s}}{A_{t+s}}\right)^{\frac{1}{1-\alpha}} \right) = 0. \tag{16.37}$$

Equation (16.37) implies that the expected present value of revenues from the optimal price is equal to the expected present value of the marginal cost of production, augmented by the profit margin $\varepsilon/(\varepsilon-1)$ of the firm.

As we have already shown (equation (16.16)), if the firm could freely determine its prices in every period, the price of the product in each period would be equal to the marginal cost of production plus the same profit margin. However, if the firm cannot adjust prices freely in every period (as is assumed in the Calvo [1983] model), pricing follows the dynamic rule (16.37).

Assuming that in the steady state, inflation is equal to π^* and all prices are equal to steady state prices, (16.37) can be transformed to logarithmic deviations from the steady state equilibrium, using a log-linear Taylor approximation. Thus, in logarithms, we have that

$$\bar{p}_t \simeq (1-\beta\gamma)\sum_{s=0}^{\infty}(\beta\gamma)^s E_t\Bigg(\hat{p}_{t+s}+\omega\mu+ \\ +\omega\left(w_{t+s}-p_{t+s}+\frac{1}{1-\alpha}(\alpha y_{t+s}-a_{t+s})\right)\Bigg), \tag{16.38}$$

where $\beta=\frac{1}{1+\rho+\pi^*}$, and $\omega=\frac{1-\alpha}{1+\alpha(\varepsilon-1)}$.

Consequently, firms that freely reset their prices in period t will choose a price that corresponds to a weighted average of the current and expected future price levels (relative to the steady state price level) plus a margin μ on a weighted average of the current and expected future levels of real marginal costs. The discount factor of a future period $t+s$ depends on the probability that the firm will not be able to reset its price in the future period $t+s$ (which equals γ^s) times the discount rate β^s. Furthermore, the part of pricing that depends on the expected marginal cost of the firm depends negatively on the elasticity of demand for the product of the firm, through the parameter ω.

Using the future mathematical expectations operator F, (16.38) can be rewritten as

$$\bar{p}_t \simeq \frac{1-\beta\gamma}{1-\beta\gamma F}\hat{p}_t+\omega\left(\mu+\frac{1-\beta\gamma}{1-\beta\gamma F}\left(w_t-p_t+\frac{1}{1-\alpha}(\alpha y_t-a_t)\right)\right). \tag{16.39}$$

Substituting (16.39) in the equation for the adjustment of the average price level (16.34) we get that

$$\hat{p}_t=\gamma\hat{p}_{t-1}+(1-\gamma)\Bigg(\frac{1-\beta\gamma}{1-\beta\gamma F}\hat{p}_t+ \\ +\omega\left(\mu+\frac{1-\beta\gamma}{1-\beta\gamma F}\left(w_t-p_t+\frac{1}{1-\alpha}(\alpha y_t-a_t)\right)\right)\Bigg). \tag{16.40}$$

Multiplying both sides of (16.40) by $1-\beta\gamma F$, after some rearrangements we get that

$$(1+\beta)\hat{p}_t-\hat{p}_{t-1}-\beta E_t\hat{p}_{t+1}=$$

$$= \frac{(1-\gamma)(1-\beta\gamma)}{\gamma}\omega\left(\mu+\left(w_t-p_t+\frac{1}{1-\alpha}(\alpha y_t-a_t)\right)\right). \tag{16.41}$$

Equation (16.41) is the equation of adjustment of the price level toward the steady state price level, which is a constant markup on the marginal cost of production.

To examine the full model, we must introduce the equilibrium conditions in the markets for goods and services, labor, and money.

16.2.2 Equilibrium in the Market for Goods and Services and the New Keynesian IS Curve

Equilibrium in the market for good j implies that

$$Y_t(j) = C_t(j).$$

As a result, equilibrium in the market for all goods requires that

$$Y_t = C_t, \tag{16.42}$$

where Y is aggregate output, defined in the same way as aggregate consumption C in equation (16.2).

Substituting the equilibrium condition (16.42) in the Euler equation for consumption (16.13), the logarithm of real output is determined by

$$y_t = E_t(y_{t+1}) - \frac{1}{\theta}(i_t - E_t\pi_{t+1} - \rho). \tag{16.43}$$

Equation (16.43) is often referred to as the new Keynesian IS curve, as it is derived from the equilibrium condition for the market for goods and services. Recall that this is nothing more than the Euler equation for consumption, supplemented by the assumption that all output is consumed, and the same relation was derived in the new classical model of chapter 14. However, in contrast to the new classical model, where output is determined by aggregate supply, in this model, because of staggered pricing, output is determined by aggregate demand. Thus, it is the IS curve that drives output fluctuations.[5]

Compared to the conventional IS curve, (16.43) contains the rational expectation about future real output and explicitly depends on the real and not the nominal interest rate. Its theoretical advantage over the conventional IS curve is that it has been derived from explicit microeconomic foundations. Thus, its parameters depend on deep structural parameters, such as the pure rate of time preference of the representative household ρ and the intertemporal elasticity of substitution of consumption $1/\theta$, which are assumed to be invariant to

5. In view of the emergence of a new neoclassical synthesis around DSGE models, highlighted by Goodfriend and King [1997], (16.43) is often labeled as the new neoclassical synthesis IS curve, as it characterizes both new classical and new Keynesian models.

policy. Hence, the new Keynesian IS curve is not subject to the Lucas [1976] critique, unlike the traditional IS curve.

16.2.3 Labor Market Equilibrium and the New Keynesian Phillips Curve

We next turn to the equilibrium condition in the labor market. Assume that, in contrast to product prices, which adjust gradually, nominal wages adjust immediately to equate the demand and supply of labor in each period. This assumption is made for reasons of analytical simplicity. Thus, the only nominal stickiness analyzed in this version of the new Keynesian model is the gradual adjustment of prices rather than wages. This means that fluctuations in employment are the result of intertemporal substitution by households and that no involuntary unemployment exists.[6]

Due to the gradual adjustment of prices, firms produce so as to satisfy aggregate demand at the given prices in each period. Aggregate output is determined by aggregate demand and differs from its natural rate, which is the level that would prevail if there was immediate price adjustment by all firms.

As a result, aggregate output, employment, consumption, real wages, and the real interest rate differ from their natural rates and display fluctuations that, as we shall show, depend on nominal as well as real disturbances.

From the price adjustment equation (16.41), we can deduce an equation for fluctuations in inflation. Expressing (16.41) as an inflation equation, we have that

$$\pi_t = (1-\beta)\pi^* + \beta E_t \pi_{t+1} + \\ + \frac{(1-\gamma)(1-\beta\gamma)}{\gamma}\omega\left(\mu + \left(w_t - p_t + \frac{1}{1-\alpha}(\alpha y_t - a_t)\right)\right), \tag{16.44}$$

where $\pi_t = p_t - p_{t-1}$ is the rate of inflation. Equation (16.44) implies that deviations of current inflation from steady state inflation are greater than discounted expected deviations of future inflation from steady state inflation, if the current marginal cost of labor plus the margin μ is higher than the current price level p. The reason is that firms able to set prices in the current period post larger price increases than (discounted) expected future inflation, to offset the higher current marginal cost of labor.

The assumption of equilibrium in the labor market means that we can substitute the real wage in (16.44) from the first-order condition (16.12) for the representative household. Using (16.12), the condition for equilibrium in the market for goods and services ($c = y$), and the production function (16.18), (16.44) can be rewritten as

$$(\pi_t - \pi^*) = \beta(E_t \pi_{t+1} - \pi*) + \kappa\left(y_t - y_t^N\right), \tag{16.45}$$

6. Starting with Erceg et al. [2000], various papers in the new Keynesian tradition have analyzed this model with the additional assumption of staggering of nominal wages. In this case, there are additional fluctuations in output and employment, because wages do not equate the demand with the supply of labor in each period, as is assumed here. See, for example, Gali [2008, 2011b].

where y^N is the natural rate of real output (i.e., the output that would be produced if there was full flexibility of prices); y^N is given by (16.24). The parameter κ is defined by

$$\kappa = \frac{(1-\gamma)(1-\beta\gamma)}{\gamma}\frac{\theta(1-\alpha)+\lambda+\alpha}{1-\alpha+\varepsilon}. \tag{16.46}$$

Equation (16.45) is referred to as the *new Keynesian Phillips curve* and constitutes the second key behavioral equation of this imperfectly competitive new Keynesian DSGE model.

Deviations of output from its natural rate cause inflation to rise relative to expected future inflation because higher output implies a higher current real marginal cost of labor. This induces firms that have the opportunity to change their current price to post price increases that exceed discounted expected future inflation.

Like the new Keynesian IS curve, the new Keynesian Phillips curve has been derived from explicit microeconomic foundations, and its parameters are functions of the deep structural parameters describing the preferences of households, the technology of production, and the price-setting technology. One can confirm this by looking at the parameters that determines κ in (16.46).

Thus, the new Keynesian Phillips curve is also relatively impervious to the Lucas [1976] critique, although one could argue that the parameter γ of the price-setting technology may not be invariant to radical shifts in monetary policy.

16.2.4 The Imperfectly Competitive Model with Staggered Pricing and the Taylor Rule

Equations (16.43) and (16.46), along with equations (16.24) and (16.26) for the natural rate of real output and the real interest rate, constitute the basic structure of the imperfectly competitive new Keynesian model.

Deviations of current inflation from discounted expected future inflation are determined by the new Keynesian Phillips curve (16.45) as a function of deviations of real aggregate demand and output from the natural rate of output.

Deviations of real output from its natural rate are determined by the new Keynesian IS curve, which depends on deviations of the real interest rate from its own natural rate. The new Keynesian IS curve can be expressed as

$$y_t - y_t^N = E_t\left(y_{t+1} - y_{t+1}^N\right) - \frac{1}{\theta}\left(i_t - E_t\pi_{t+1} - r_t^N\right), \tag{16.47}$$

where the natural levels of output y^N and the real interest rate r^N are determined by (16.24) and (16.26), respectively.

To close the model, we must consider the determination of the nominal interest rate. In contrast to the full information new classical model, due to staggered price adjustment, fluctuations in real variables cannot be determined without reference to monetary factors. Monetary factors and monetary policy determine not only the price level and inflation, as in the new classical model, but also fluctuations in real variables, such as real output, consumption, employment, real wages, and the real interest rate.

We shall analyze the model under the assumption that the central bank follows a Taylor [1993] rule of the form

$$i_t = \rho + \pi^* + \phi_\pi \left(\pi_t - \pi^*\right) + \phi_y (y_t - y_t^N) + v_t, \tag{16.48}$$

where ϕ_π and ϕ_y are positive coefficients, and v is an exogenous stochastic disturbance in the nominal interest rate rule. Note that the constant in this rule is equal to $\rho + \pi^*$, the target steady state nominal interest rate consistent with steady state inflation equal to π^*.[7]

This monetary policy rule, which plays the role of the LM curve in traditional Keynesian models, implies a countercyclical monetary policy. When inflation is above π^*, the central bank increases nominal interest rates to reduce aggregate demand and nudge inflation toward π^*. When employment is low (i.e., when output is lower than its natural rate), the central bank reduces nominal interest rates to increase aggregate demand and nudge output and employment toward their natural rates.

As in the case of the Wicksell rule analyzed in chapter 14, this feedback interest rate rule does not result in inflation and price level indeterminacy if the *Taylor principle* is satisfied (i.e., if the reaction of nominal interest rates to inflation is sufficiently pronounced).[8]

Equations (16.45), (16.47), and (16.48) constitute the three key equations of the new Keynesian model with staggered pricing. These three equations—the new Keynesian Phillips curve, the new Keynesian IS curve, and the Taylor rule for nominal interest rates—determine deviations of output from its natural rate, deviations of inflation from the target of the central bank π^*, and the nominal interest rate i. All other nominal and real variables in the model are functions of these three variables.

16.2.5 Real and Monetary Shocks and Aggregate Fluctuations

Having now fully described the new Keynesian model with staggered pricing, we can analyze how nominal and real disturbances induce aggregate fluctuations.

The stochastic disturbance in the nominal interest rate is assumed to follow a stationary AR(1) process of the form

$$v_t = \eta_v v_{t-1} + \varepsilon_t^v, \tag{16.49}$$

where $0 < \eta_v < 1$, and ε_t^v is a white noise process.

7. In the Taylor rule (16.48), the nominal interest rate does to react to shocks that cause fluctuations in the natural real rate of interest, such as productivity shocks. The rule is only conditioned on the steady state real interest rate ρ and core inflation (i.e., the steady state inflation target of the central bank π^*). Thus, productivity shocks turn out to affect deviations of output from its own natural rate and deviations of inflation from the central bank's target. Obviously, one can also analyze the imperfectly competitive new Keynesian model under the assumption that monetary policy follows a rule for the money supply and not nominal interest rates. See Gali [2008].

8. See chapters 12 and 14 for discussions of the properties of interest rate rules. Clarida et al. [1999], Woodford [2003a] and Gali [2008] contain extensive discussions of interest rate rules in new Keynesian models. We shall discuss the properties of the Taylor [1993] rule more fully in chapter 20, on the role of monetary policy.

The productivity shock a is also assumed to follow a stationary AR(1) process of the form

$$a_t = \eta_a a_{t-1} + \varepsilon_t^a, \tag{16.50}$$

where $0 < \eta_a < 1$, and ε_t^a is a white noise process.[9]

The full model consists of the new Keynesian Phillips and IS curves (16.45) and (16.47), the Taylor rule (16.48), the exogenous stochastic processes (16.49) and (16.50), and the equation for the determination of the natural real interest rate (16.26). Thus, the model can be written as

$$\hat{\pi}_t = \beta E_t \hat{\pi}_{t+1} + \kappa \hat{y}_t, \tag{16.51}$$

$$\hat{y}_t = E_t \hat{y}_{t+1} - \frac{1}{\theta}\left(i_t - \pi^* - E_t \hat{\pi}_{t+1} - r_t^N\right), \tag{16.52}$$

$$i_t = \rho + \pi^* + \phi_\pi \hat{\pi}_t + \phi_y \hat{y}_t + v_t, \tag{16.53}$$

where $\hat{\pi}_t = \pi_t - \pi^*$, and $\hat{y}_t = y_t - y_t^N$ denote the deviations between current and target inflation and between the current (log) real output and its natural rate.

The percentage deviation between current real output and its natural rate is often referred to as *excess output*, and its opposite is referred to as the *output gap*. When excess output is positive, the economy produces more than its natural rate; when it is negative (i.e., the output gap is positive), it produces less than its natural rate.

The natural real rate of interest r^N is determined by (16.26) and depends only on the expected change in the productivity shock and the pure rate of time preference.

The dimensions of the model can be reduced by substituting the Taylor rule for the nominal interest rate in the new Keynesian IS curve (16.52) and solving for excess output. This substitution results in an aggregate demand function of the form

$$\hat{y}_t = \frac{\theta}{\theta + \phi_y} E_t \hat{y}_{t+1} - \frac{\eta_\pi}{\theta + \phi_y} \hat{\pi}_t + \frac{1}{\theta + \phi_y} E_t \hat{\pi}_{t+1} - \frac{1}{\theta + \phi_y} \left(\theta \psi (1 - \eta_a) a_t + v_t\right). \tag{16.54}$$

Combined with the new Keynesian Phillips curve (16.51), (16.54) can help determine excess output and inflation as functions of the productivity shocks affecting the natural real rate of interest and the monetary shocks affecting the nominal interest rate rule.

One way to solve the dynamic system of (16.51) and (16.54) is the *method of substitution*, which requires substituting out for one of the endogenous variables, solving for the other, and then determining the variable that was originally substituted out. Another method is to express the two equations as a system, and use a *systems method* like the Blanchard and

9. The assumption of AR(1) processes for the exogenous disturbances is again made for analytical simplicity and could easily be generalized.

Kahn [1980] method. Both methods yield the same results; thus, we shall confine ourselves to the more intuitive substitution method.[10]

The substitution method involves substituting out for excess output from (16.54) into (16.51). After some rearrangement, this will result in an inflation equation of the form

$$\hat{\pi}_t = \frac{\beta(\theta+\phi_y)+\theta+\kappa}{\theta+\phi_y+\kappa\phi_\pi} E_t\hat{\pi}_{t+1} - \frac{\beta\theta}{\theta+\phi_y+\kappa\phi_\pi} E_t\hat{\pi}_{t+2} - \frac{\kappa}{\theta+\phi_y+\kappa\phi_\pi}\left(\theta\psi(1-\eta_a)a_t + v_t\right). \tag{16.55}$$

As can be seen from (16.55), deviations of inflation from steady state inflation depend on expectations about future inflation deviations, productivity shocks (which affect the natural real rate of interest), and nominal interest rate shocks. Recalling the definition of κ in (16.46), one can see that the parameters determining the inflation process depend on the preferences of the representative household θ, λ, ε, and ρ; the technology of production α; market structure ε; the price adjustment mechanism γ; and the parameters of the Taylor rule ϕ_π and ϕ_y.

Because inflation is a non-predetermined variable, both roots of (16.55) must be less than unity (inside the unit circle), which requires that the sum of the coefficients of the future expectations of inflation in (16.55) is less than one. Thus, for a stable inflation process, a necessary and sufficient condition is

$$\frac{\beta(\theta+\phi_y)+\theta+\kappa-\beta\theta}{\theta+\phi_y+\kappa\phi_\pi} < 1. \tag{16.56}$$

Under the assumption that the coefficients of the Taylor rule ϕ_π and ϕ_y are positive, after some rearrangement of (16.56), one can see that a necessary and sufficient condition for a stable inflation process is

$$\phi_\pi > 1 - \frac{(1-\beta)}{\kappa}\phi_y. \tag{16.57}$$

Hence, for a stable inflation process, the Taylor principle, as implied by (16.57) must hold. The reaction of nominal interest rates to current inflation must be sufficiently high to satisfy (16.57). For example, if the reaction of the nominal interest rate to excess output is zero ($\phi_y = 0$), then the reaction of nominal interest rates to inflation must exceed unity.

Assuming that the central bank policy satisfies (16.57), (16.55) can be solved forward for inflation, which is a non-predetermined variable. Inflation will be determined by

10. See chapter 9 for solution methods of dynamic models with rational expectations.

$$\hat{\pi}_t = -\frac{\kappa}{\beta\theta}\frac{1}{\lambda_1\lambda_2}E_t\sum_{s=0}^{\infty}\left(\frac{1}{\lambda_1}\right)^s\sum_{q=0}^{\infty}\left(\frac{1}{\lambda_2}\right)^q\left(\theta\psi(1-\eta_a)a_{t+q}+v_{t+q}\right), \tag{16.58}$$

where $1/\lambda_1$ and $1/\lambda_2$ are the two roots of the inflationary process (16.55), which are both less than one if the Taylor principle (16.51) is satisfied. The inverses of these roots, λ_1 and λ_2, are both greater than one and are defined by

$$\lambda_1+\lambda_2=\frac{\beta(\theta+\phi_y)+\theta+\kappa}{\beta\theta}>2, \tag{16.59}$$

$$\lambda_1\lambda_2=\frac{\theta+\phi_y+\kappa\phi_\pi}{\beta\theta}>1. \tag{16.60}$$

Inflation depends on future expectations of deviations of the natural real rate of interest from ρ and future expectations about nominal interest rate shocks v.

The closed-form solution for inflation, assuming that the two shocks follow AR(1) processes as in (16.49) and (16.50), takes the form

$$\hat{\pi}_t=-\theta\psi\kappa(1-\eta_a)\Lambda_a a_t-\kappa\Lambda_v v_t, \tag{16.61}$$

where

$$\Lambda_a=\frac{1}{(1-\beta\eta_a)(\phi_y+\theta(1-\eta_a))+\kappa(\phi_\pi-\eta_a)}, \tag{16.62}$$

$$\Lambda_v=\frac{1}{(1-\beta\eta_v)(\phi_y+\theta(1-\eta_v))+\kappa(\phi_\pi-\eta_v)}. \tag{16.63}$$

Note that the coefficients Λ_a and Λ_v depend negatively on the Taylor rule parameters ϕ_π and ϕ_y, which are in the denominator of both fractions. The larger the Taylor rule parameters are, the lower will be the impact of real and nominal shocks on deviations of inflation from the central bank target.

By substituting the solution for inflation in the new Keynesian Phillips curve (16.51), one can get the corresponding solution for the evolution of excess output. Excess output will be determined by

$$\hat{y}_t=-\theta\psi(1-\eta_a)(1-\beta\eta_a)\Lambda_a a_t-(1-\beta\eta_v)\Lambda_v v_t. \tag{16.64}$$

From (16.63), because the coefficients Λ_a and Λ_v depend negatively on the Taylor rule parameters ϕ_π and ϕ_y, the larger the Taylor rule parameters are, the lower will be the impact of real and nominal shocks on deviations of output from its natural rate.

Both monetary and real shocks affect fluctuations of real output and inflation in this model. Thus, the classical dichotomy does not hold. Persistent shocks to either nominal interest rates or productivity result in persistent deviations of inflation from the target of the central bank and persistent deviations of output from its natural rate. This new Keynesian model, unlike full information new classical models, can explain aggregate fluctuations caused by monetary shocks. These shocks are transmitted to real variables and persist over time through staggered pricing. Such monetary cycles cannot result from models with immediate and full adjustment of wages and prices, unless there is imperfect current information, as in models in the spirit of Lucas [1972].

16.2.6 The Divine Coincidence and Optimal Monetary Policy in the New Keynesian Model with Staggered Pricing

How different is the new Keynesian model with staggered pricing from the new classical models examined in chapter 14? Clearly, there are some key differences. For example, the natural rate of output and employment is suboptimally low because of imperfect competition; and there is staggered price adjustment, which results in short-run deviations of output, employment, and other real variables from their natural rates.

However, there are some important similarities as well. In the version of the model that we have examined, because nominal wages have been assumed fully flexible, employment fluctuations are only due to intertemporal substitution in labor supply, as in the new classical model. Thus, this version of the new Keynesian model cannot explain involuntary unemployment but only fluctuations of employment, much like the new classical model.

A second important similarity relates to optimal monetary policy. As we have seen in chapter 14, in a new classical model, optimal monetary policy is the one that continuously achieves the inflation target of the central bank, π^*. The same is true of the new Keynesian model with staggered pricing.

To see this, let us consider the new Keynesian Phillips curve (16.51). If the central bank could eliminate deviations of inflation from its target inflation rate π^*, then deviations of output from its natural rate would also be eliminated. Tackling fluctuations in inflation in this model has the effect of eliminating fluctuations in real variables as well. There is no trade-off between the stabilization of inflation and the stabilization of real variables around their natural rates. Blanchard and Gali [2007] have termed this property of the model the "divine coincidence." In fact, to tackle the divine coincidence, they proposed that the new Keynesian model with staggered pricing be augmented with some form of exogenous real wage rigidity, which would break the link between the stabilization of inflation and the stabilization of output and employment.[11]

The divine coincidence has important implications for optimal monetary policy and the Taylor rule. In fact, the optimal interest rate rule is one in which ϕ_π, the response of the interest rate to deviations of inflation from target, tends to infinity. This can be confirmed

11. In fact, the model of Erceg et al. [2000] is not characterized by the divine coincidence, as there is additional staggering for nominal wages. We return to this issue in chapter 17, where we present a model of unemployment and nominal wage contracts that is also not characterized by the divine coincidence.

by examining (16.61) and (16.64), which are the closed-form solutions for inflation and the output gap, respectively. By allowing ϕ_π to tend to infinity in the Taylor rule, neither real nor monetary shocks cause deviations of inflation from target, and therefore output from its natural rate. The coefficients Λ_a and Λ_v tend to zero, and both inflation and the output gap are fully stabilized. This is the same as the optimal monetary policy rule in the new classical models of chapter 14.

Exercise 16.1 Solve the model consisting of equations (16.45), (16.47), and (16.48) using the Blanchard-Kahn method, and compare the solution to the results obtained by the substitution method. Assume that the exogenous shocks follow AR(1) processes, as in (16.49) and (16.50).

16.2.7 A Dynamic Simulation of the Model

To visualize the dynamic properties of the model summarized in (16.51)–(16.53), it is worth simulating it for particular parameter values and presenting the relevant impulse response functions.

Figures 16.1 and 16.2 present the dynamic effects of both monetary and real shocks for commonly used values of the parameters. The parameter values for this simulation are: $\theta = 1$, $\lambda = 1, \rho = 0.01, \alpha = 0.333, \varepsilon = 6, \gamma = 0.667, \phi_\pi = 1.50, \phi_u = 0.125$, $\eta_a = 0.75$, and $\eta_v = 0.50$. All real variables are defined as percentage deviations from their natural rates, and inflation is defined as percentage deviation from the target inflation of the central bank π^*.

Figure 16.1 depicts the dynamic effects of a 1% positive shock ε^v in the nominal interest rate. This shock is a contractionary monetary shock, which leads to an increase of the nominal and the real interest rate and reduces excess output and inflation. This nominal shock does not affect the natural rate of real output, employment, real wages, or the real interest rate. However, actual real output, employment, and real wages decline relative to their natural rate, due to the reduction of aggregate demand and the staggered adjustment of prices. The economy gradually returns to its natural rate, as the effects of the monetary shock gradually die out.

Figure 16.2 depicts the dynamic effects of a 1% shock ε^a to productivity. This shock leads to a persistent rise in the natural rate of output, employment, and real wages, and a temporary fall in the natural real interest rate. However, due to the staggered adjustment of prices, actual real output, employment, and real wages do not rise as much as their natural rates. Hence, their deviations from their natural rates, depicted in figure 16.2, become negative. Inflation also falls below the target rate of the central bank. The negative discrepancy of output relative to its temporarily higher natural rate and the fall of inflation relative to the central bank target prompt a decline in nominal and real interest rates. Again, the economy gradually returns to its steady state equilibrium, as the effects of the real disturbance gradually die out.

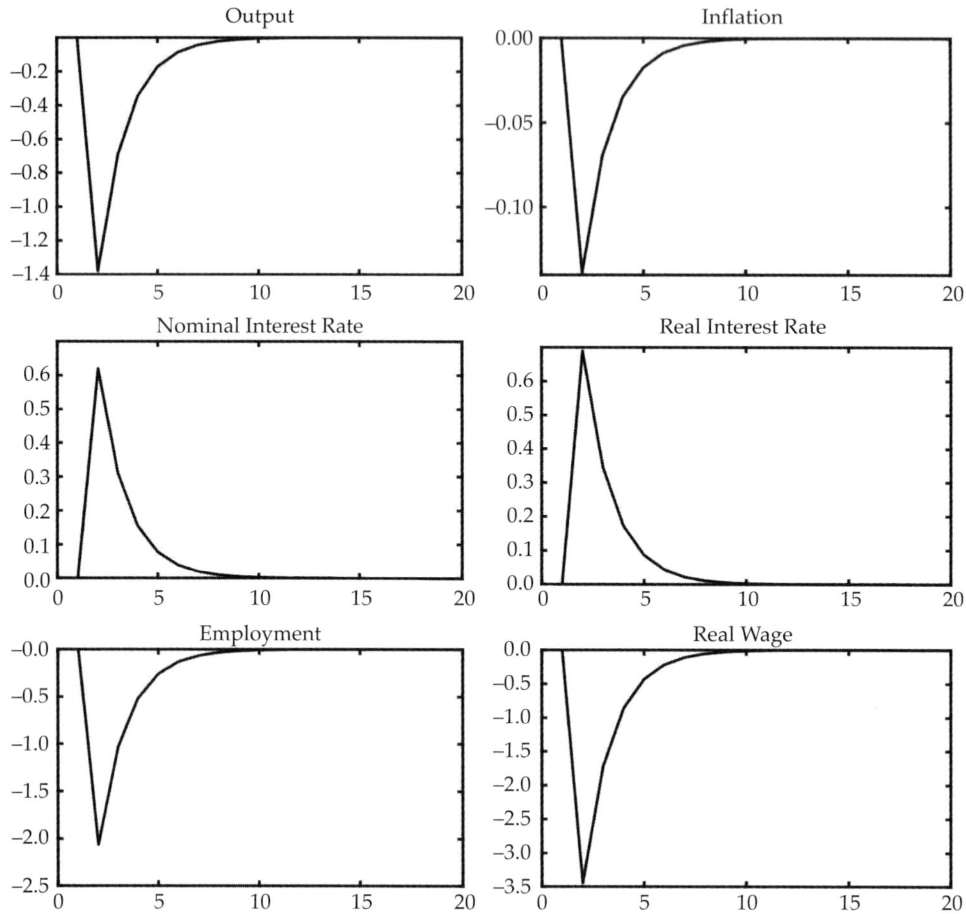

Figure 16.1
Impulse response functions of the staggered pricing model following a contractionary monetary shock.

Note the positive correlation between deviations of output from its natural rate and inflation from target, irrespective of the nature of the shocks hitting the economy. This is a result of the divine coincidence characterizing this model.

16.3 The Rotemberg Model of Convex Costs of Price Adjustment

An alternative to the Calvo [1983] model of staggered pricing is the Rotemberg [1982a,b] model of convex costs of price adjustment. For the representative monopolistically competitive firm, such as the one examined in section 16.1, the optimal price is given by

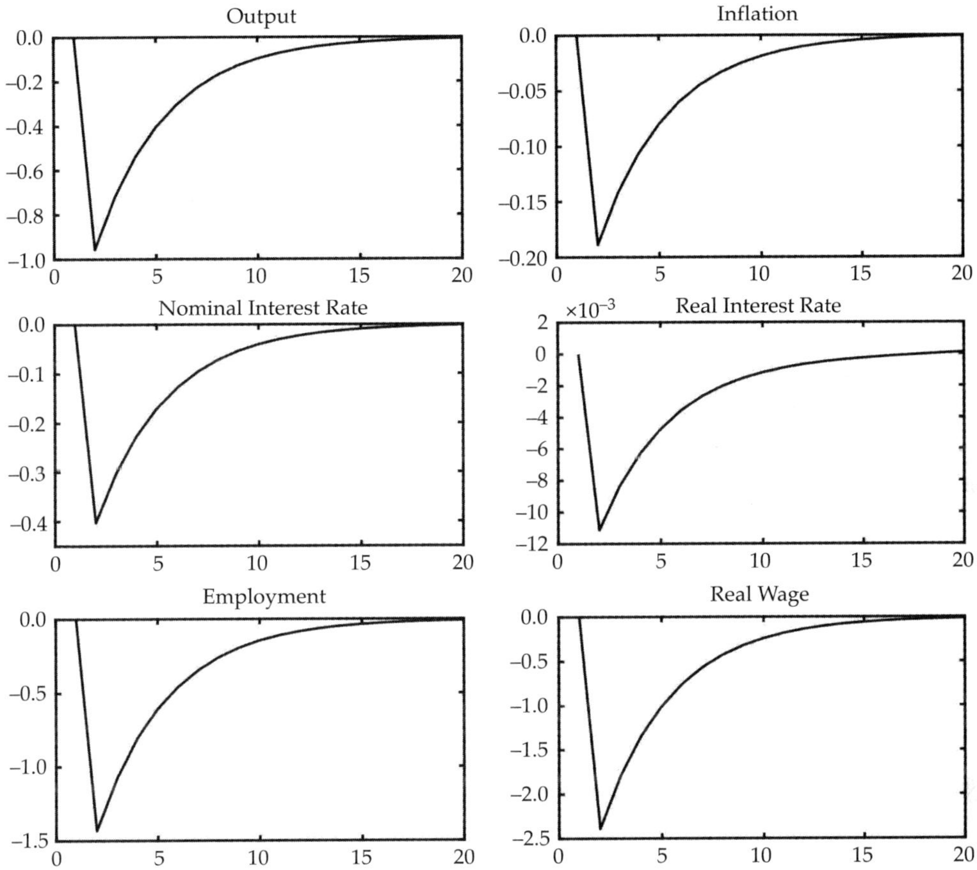

Figure 16.2
Impulse response functions of the staggered pricing model following a positive productivity shock.

$$\bar{P}_t = \frac{\varepsilon}{\varepsilon - 1}\left(\frac{W_t}{(1-\alpha)A_t L_t{}^{-\alpha}}\right). \tag{16.65}$$

The optimal price is a constant markup on marginal costs. Marginal costs are equal to wage costs over the marginal productivity of labor. Note that because of decreasing returns to employment, increasing employment and output implies declining marginal productivity of labor and increasing marginal costs of production. Using the production function to substitute out for labor, (16.65) can also be expressed as

$$\bar{P}_t = \frac{\varepsilon}{\varepsilon - 1}\left(\frac{W_t (Y_t)^{\frac{\alpha}{1-\alpha}}}{(1-\alpha)(A_t)^{\frac{1}{1-\alpha}}}\right). \tag{16.66}$$

An increase in output increases the marginal costs of production for given wages because of the declining marginal productivity of labor. Hence, with higher output, the optimal price must rise.

In logs, (16.65) and (16.66) imply

$$\bar{p}_t = \mu + w_t - a_t + \alpha l_t = \mu + w_t + \frac{1}{1-\alpha}\left(\alpha y_t - a_t\right), \tag{16.67}$$

where $a_t = \ln A_t$, and $\mu = \ln\left(\frac{\varepsilon}{\varepsilon-1}\right) - \ln(1-\alpha)$. Here, a is the logarithm of the exogenous productivity shock, and the constant μ is the logarithm of the markup on marginal cost minus the logarithm of the coefficient implying decreasing returns to labor.

All firms are assumed to be facing convex costs of adjusting their posted prices. Rotemberg [1982a] assumes that firms balance the costs of deviating from their optimal price against the costs of changing their prices. In the model presented below, following Rotemberg, we assume that firms set current prices minimizing a quadratic cost function that penalizes both deviations of prices from the optimal price and the adjustment of prices over steady state inflation from period to period. This takes the form

$$E_t \sum_{s=0}^{\infty} \beta^s \left(\frac{1}{2}(p_{t+s} - \bar{p}_{t+s})^2 + \frac{\xi}{2}(p_{t+s} - p_{t+s-1} - \pi^*)^2\right), \tag{16.68}$$

where p is the log of the actual price of the representative firm, and ξ is a parameter measuring the cost of price adjustment relative to the cost of deviations from the optimal price.

From the first-order conditions for the minimization of (16.68), it follows that

$$p_t = \frac{1}{1+\xi(1+\beta)}\bar{p}_t + \frac{\xi}{1+\xi(1+\beta)}p_{t-1} + \frac{\xi\beta}{1+\xi(1+\beta)}E_t p_{t+1} + \frac{\xi(1+\beta)}{1+\xi(1+\beta)}\pi^*. \tag{16.69}$$

The current price, in logs, is a weighted average of the optimal price, the past price, and the expected future price. The firm is forward looking and anticipates the future costs of adjusting prices, so its current price depends not only on its past price but also on its expected future price. Because this is the representative firm, we can take p to be equal to the log of the price level.

Expressing (16.69) as an inflation equation, we get

$$\pi_t - \pi^* = \beta\left(E_t\pi_{t+1} - \pi^*\right) + \frac{1}{\xi}\left(\bar{p}_t - p_t\right), \tag{16.70}$$

where $\pi_t = p_t - p_{t-1}$ is the rate of inflation.

Inflation deviates from expected future inflation to the extent that the optimal price exceeds the current price. Substituting for the optimal price from (16.67), we get

$$\hat{\pi}_t = \beta E_t \hat{\pi}_{t+1} + \frac{1}{\xi}\left(\mu + w_t - a_t + \alpha l_t - p_t\right), \tag{16.71}$$

where $\hat{\pi}_t = \pi_t - \pi^*$ is the deviation of inflation from steady state inflation.

From (16.71), deviations of current inflation differ from expected deviations of future inflation to the extent that the marginal cost of production plus the optimal price markup exceeds the current price. Using the labor and product market equilibrium conditions to substitute out for the real wage and employment, as well as the definition of the natural rate of output, we can express (16.71) as

$$\hat{\pi}_t = \beta E_t \hat{\pi}_{t+1} + \kappa \hat{y}_t, \tag{16.72}$$

where $\kappa = \frac{\theta(1-\alpha)+\alpha+\lambda}{\xi(1-\alpha)} > 0$ and $\hat{y}_t = y_t - y_t^N$. Equation (16.72) has exactly the same form as the new Keynesian Phillips curve (16.45) derived from the Calvo [1983] model of staggered pricing. The only difference is in the definition of κ, which is now in terms of the paramcter ξ of the Rotemberg model, instead of the parameter γ of the Calvo model. Thus, the two models of sluggish price adjustment—the Rotemberg model of costs of adjustment of prices and the Calvo model of staggered pricing—are observationally equivalent at the aggregate level, as they both result in the same form of a new Keynesian Phillips curve.

Hence, the analysis of the effects of monetary and real shocks in a new Keynesian model based on the Rotemberg model of costly price adjustment would be exactly the same as in the model based on Calvo-type staggered pricing.

16.4 Conclusion

In this chapter, we have analyzed the structure and the properties of a new Keynesian model based on monopolistic competition and staggered pricing. Unlike traditional Keynesian models, in which the basic relations are not derived explicitly from microeconomic foundations, this new Keynesian model is a DSGE model based on explicit microeconomic foundations, analogous to those of new classical models.

After presenting the properties of this model, we analyzed the effects of monetary and real shocks with regard to fluctuations in excess output and inflation. This new Keynesian model can explain aggregate fluctuations caused by monetary shocks. These shocks are transmitted to real variables and persist over time through staggered pricing. Such monetary cycles cannot result from models with immediate and full adjustment of wages and prices, unless there is imperfect information, as in the Lucas [1972] misperceptions model.

As in the fully competitive new classical models, when there is full flexibility of prices and wages, monetary shocks affect only nominal and not real variables, such as output, consumption, employment, real wages, and real interest rates. The assumption of monopolistic competition does not affect the issue of the neutrality of money.

Note that there is no unemployment in this model. Output deviates from its natural rate because of staggered pricing, but fluctuations in employment are due to intertemporal substitution in labor supply, because the labor market is assumed fully competitive. This is a significant weakness of this particular model, a weakness shared with the Lucas [1972] new classical model. An additional weakness of the model is that there is no trade-off between the stabilization of inflation and the stabilization of output and employment. One leads to the other, as if by a divine coincidence.

These weaknesses can be addressed if one allowed for labor market distortions that can account for unemployment. In the next chapter, we examine a model with labor market distortions that can account for both involuntary unemployment, the real effects of nominal shocks, and a trade-off between the stabilization of inflation, output, and employment.

17

A Model of Unemployment and Nominal Wage Contracts

The explanation of unemployment and its cyclical fluctuations is one of the central tasks of macroeconomics. In fact, it was the existence and persistence of interwar unemployment that prompted Keynes to embark on producing the *General Theory*.

Two types of questions need to be asked. The first type asks what determines the equilibrium (or natural) rate of unemployment in an economy, what its properties are, and to what extent equilibrium unemployment reflects frictions and distortions in the labor market. The second type concerns the fluctuations of the unemployment rate during the economic cycle.[1]

Cyclical fluctuations in unemployment can be explained by and large by new Keynesian models with labor market frictions and nominal wage and price contracts. In this chapter, we analyze a model of aggregate fluctuations that is based on *periodic nominal wage contracts* and can explain unemployment and its fluctuations. The model is based on Gray [1976], Fischer [1977a], and Taylor [1979], who emphasized the periodic adjustment of nominal wages rather than the periodic adjustment of prices.

In the Gray-Fischer-Taylor model, nominal wage contracts are assumed to be negotiated at the beginning of every period or at the beginning of alternate periods. In addition, nominal wages are assumed to remain fixed for at least part of the duration of the contract. Nominal wages depend on prior expectations about the evolution of the price level, productivity, and all other shocks. If inflation turns out to be higher than expected, then real wages fall, firms demand more labor, and employment rises. The opposite happens when inflation turns out to be lower than expected when the contract was negotiated.[2]

1. For comparative empirical studies of the determinants of unemployment in the industrial economies, see, among others, Bean et al. [1986], Blanchard and Summers [1986], Newell and Symons [1987], Alogoskoufis and Manning [1988], and the important book by Layard et al. [1991]. More recent surveys are in Blanchard and Wolfers [2000] and Blanchard [2006].

2. The Gray [1976] contracts are one-period nonindexed nominal wage contracts, whereas the Fischer [1977a] and Taylor [1979] models are models of multiperiod *staggered wage contracts*. There are differences among these models, but they share the assumption that wages have been negotiated before full information about the evolution of the price level, productivity, or other shocks was available. For reasons of analytical simplicity, we shall use

The model builds on one of the key insights of the *General Theory*, namely, the short-run rigidity of nominal wages, due to nonindexed labor market contracts. In all other respects, it is based on intertemporal optimization on the part of both households and firms.[3]

The specific model introduced in this chapter is a DSGE model in which nonindexed nominal wage contracts are negotiated periodically by "insiders" in the labor market. There are two distortions in the model compared to the new classical model without capital that we analyzed in chapter 14, or to the new Keynesian model of staggered pricing in chapter 16. The first is a *real distortion*, arising from the fact that the unemployed are disenfranchised "outsiders" in the labor market and cannot affect the determination of nominal wages. As a result, wage contracts, which are negotiated by employed insiders, do not seek to maintain full employment and there is a positive natural rate of unemployment, reflecting the pool of unemployed outsiders. The second is a *nominal distortion*, arising from the assumption that nominal wage contracts are not indexed and can only be reopened at the beginning of each period, before current nominal and real shocks are observed. Thus, nominal wages are set on the basis of prior rational expectations about the various unobserved shocks that may affect output, employment, and inflation.[4]

The real distortion in our model makes the natural rate of unemployment inefficiently high and involuntary, in the sense that outsiders would prefer to work at the current wage. The nominal distortion allows for nominal shocks to have temporary real effects. Thus, nominal shocks (and by extension, monetary policy) are able to affect fluctuations in both inflation and real variables, such as output, employment, unemployment, real wages, and the real interest rate.

The product market is assumed imperfectly competitive as in the model of chapter 16. We analyze the model under both the assumption that prices are perfectly flexible and are set as a constant markup over unit labor costs, and the assumption of staggered pricing.

Even under fully flexible prices, because of nominal wage contracts, the model is characterized by an expectations-augmented Phillips curve. Deviations of current inflation from inflation expected at the beginning of the period depend on deviations of output and employment from their natural rates. They also depend on unanticipated productivity shocks, which affect the hiring decisions of firms. This is because the predetermined nominal wage contracts are set on the basis of expected and not actual inflation and productivity. Staggered pricing introduces an additional trade-off between inflation and unemployment through the nominal distortion in the pricing decisions of firms.

---

the simplest possible of these models, which is the Gray-Fischer model of one-period synchronized nominal wage contracts.

3. An alternative way to introduce nominal wage rigidity is to use the assumption of staggered wages à la Calvo, as has been done in some papers, following Erceg et al. [2000].

4. See Blanchard and Summers [1986], Lindbeck and Snower [1986], and Gottfries [1992] for insider-outsider models of the labor market.

Aggregate demand is determined by the optimal behavior of a representative household that has access to competitive financial markets and chooses the path of consumption and real money balances to maximize its intertemporal utility function. Thus, both the consumption function and the money demand function are derived from intertemporal microeconomic foundations. The model is also characterized by exogenous shocks to productivity and preferences for consumption and money demand.

Thus, the model is in essence a new Keynesian DSGE model that incorporates some of the key features of the AS-AD version of the Keynesian model discussed in chapter 15.

We analyze aggregate fluctuations in this model under a Taylor rule (i.e., a feedback interest rate rule). According to this rule the nominal interest rate deviates from its natural rate in response to deviations of current inflation from the inflation target of the central bank, and deviations of output from its natural rate.

Contrary to the full information new classical model, monetary shocks affect real variables in this model, causing temporary but persistent deviations of output, employment, unemployment, real wages, and the real interest rate from their natural rates. Persistence in deviations of unemployment and output from their natural rates arises from the dynamic evolution of the group of insiders in the labor market, as this group consists of those who were recently employed, as well as "core" insiders in each firm. The propagation mechanism that causes unanticipated nominal and real shocks to produce persistent deviations of unemployment and output from their natural rate is the partial adjustment of the number of labor market insiders to employment shocks.

Under a Taylor rule, the only shocks that cannot be completely neutralized by monetary policy are productivity shocks and, of course, shocks to the nominal interest rate rule of the central bank. Fluctuations of deviations of unemployment and output from their natural rates display persistence and are driven by these two types of shocks. Because of the endogenous persistence of deviations of unemployment from its natural rate, the equilibrium inflation rate also displays persistence around the inflation target of the central bank.

17.1 Alternative Views of the Labor Market and Equilibrium Unemployment

Before proceeding to discuss the model used in this chapter, it is worthwhile to briefly survey alternative approaches to the modeling of unemployment. This will help put the model in its proper context.

There are many alternative approaches to modeling the labor market that differ from the competitive model of the labor market implicit in new classical and some new Keynesian models (e.g., the model of chapter 16). All these approaches offer an alternative explanation as to why, despite unemployment and vacancies, real wages do not adjust sufficiently to induce firms to hire the unemployed and eliminate unemployment.

One approach consists of the so-called *efficiency wage theories*. In these theories, there is asymmetric information between firms and workers. Firms cannot observe either the productivity or the effort of workers directly. Thus, firms offer wages above the average productivity of low productivity job seekers, or existing employees, in order to attract workers with above-average productivity or to provide incentives to their employees to work more intensively. Therefore they are not prepared to reduce real wages, or to replace workers already in jobs with the unemployed, even if the unemployed offered to work at lower wages.[5]

A second class of theories are theories of *long-term contracts*. These contracts prevent firms from undertaking unilateral changes to wages in response to shocks, if such changes are not provided for or allowed in the long-term contract. The contracts can be explicit (such as collective, industry, and individual employment contracts) or informal and implicit.[6]

Finally, there are theories that highlight the search costs of looking for an appropriate job by unemployed job seekers, and for an appropriate employee by firms with vacancies. In these theories, a costly search process is required for the matching of job seekers with appropriate vacancies to create a new job. These theories are called *search or matching theories* of the labor market and seek to explain unemployment flows as well as unemployment rates. We examine a key model in this category in chapter 18.

Let us now examine the specific model we use in this chapter.[7]

17.2 Households and Optimal Consumption and Money Demand

Assume that the economy consists of a continuum of identical households i, where $i \in [0, 1]$. Each household member is constrained to supply one unit of indivisible labor, and unemployment impacts all households in the same manner.[8]

The representative household chooses (aggregate) consumption and real money balances to maximize

$$E_t \sum_{s=0}^{\infty} \left(\frac{1}{1+\rho}\right)^s \left(\frac{1}{1-\theta}\left(V^C_{t+s} C^{1-\theta}_{t+s} + V^M_{t+s}\left(\frac{M}{P}\right)^{1-\theta}_{t+s}\right)\right), \tag{17.1}$$

5. See Weiss [1980] and Shapiro and Stiglitz [1984] for the two most important early models based on this approach.

6. For the original implicit contract theories, see Baily [1974], and Gordon [1974], Azariadis [1975]. These theories viewed employment contracts as insurance contracts between risk-neutral employers and risk-averse employees, against adverse shocks to employment. For theories based on explicit bargaining, see McDonald and Solow [1981]. For theories that distinguish between insiders and outsiders in the labor market, see Lindbeck and Snower [1986], Blanchard and Summers [1986], and Gottfries [1992]. The model we use in this chapter, where the nominal wage is determined by periodic nominal contracts between firms and labor market insiders, is a simple stylized model of this latter category.

7. Surveys of alternative theories of unemployment can be found in, among others, Solow [1980]; Nickell [1990, 1997]; Bean [1994], and Blanchard [2006].

8. These assumptions can be justified in terms of models of indivisible labor, as in Hansen [1985] and Rogerson [1988].

where ρ denotes the pure rate of time preference, θ is the inverse of the elasticity of intertemporal substitution, C is consumption, and M/P is real money balance. In addition, V^C and V^M denote exogenous stochastic shocks in the utility from consumption and real money balances, respectively, and can be thought of as preference shocks.

Consumption consists of differentiated goods and services indexed by a continuous index j, where $j \in [0, 1]$. The consumption bundle is thus given by

$$C_t = \left(\int_{j=0}^{1} C(j)_t^{\frac{\varepsilon-1}{\varepsilon}} dj \right)^{\frac{\varepsilon}{\varepsilon-1}}, \tag{17.2}$$

where ε is also a parameter of the preferences of the representative household, and more precicely, the elasticity of substitution between goods. We assume that $\varepsilon > 1$.

Expected utility is maximized subject to the sequence of expected budget constraints

$$E_t \Bigg(F_{t+s+1} = (1 + i_{t+s}) \times \left(F_{t+s} - \frac{i_{t+s}}{1+i_{t+s}} M_{t+s} + P_{t+s} \left(Y_{t+s} - T_{t+s} \right) - \int_{j=0}^{1} P(j)_{t+s} C(j)_{t+s} dj \right) \Bigg), \tag{17.3}$$

where $F_t = B_t + M_t$, denotes the financial assets held by the representative household, i is the nominal interest rate, B denotes one-period nominal bonds, M represents nominal money balances, Y is real noninterest income, T is real taxes net of transfers, and $P(j)$ is the price of good j.

The household must also satisfy the transversality condition

$$\lim_{T \to \infty} E_t F_{t+T} \geq 0. \tag{17.4}$$

The household must decide on the distribution of its consumption expenditure among the various goods and the intertemporal allocation of its total consumption expenditure and money demand. The first problem requires the maximization of the consumption bundle (17.2) for any level of monetary expenditure. One can easily deduce that this implies

$$C(j)_t = \left(\frac{P(j)_t}{P_t} \right)^{-\varepsilon} C(t) \tag{17.5}$$

for any good j in the interval $[0, 1]$, where P is the average price level, defined as

$$P_t = \left(\int_{j=0}^{1} P(j)_t^{1-\varepsilon} dj \right)^{\frac{1}{1-\varepsilon}}. \tag{17.6}$$

Equation (17.5) defines the demand for good j as a function of its relative price and the level of aggregate demand C.

In addition, when the household follows this optimal allocation policy, we also have that

$$\int_{j=0}^{1} P(j)_t C(j)_t dj = P_t C_t, \tag{17.7}$$

which suggests that total consumption expenditure can be written as the product of the aggregate consumption index and the aggregate price index. Substituting (17.7) in the sequence of expected budget constraints (17.3), we get

$$E_t \left(F_{t+s+1} = (1+i_{t+s}) \left(F_{t+s} - \frac{i_{t+s}}{1+i_{t+s}} M_{t+s} + P_{t+s} \left(Y_{t+s} - T_{t+s} - C_{t+s} \right) \right) \right). \tag{17.8}$$

The solution to the intertemporal problem of the household can thus be derived from the first-order conditions for a maximum of (17.1), subject to (17.8). We then get

$$V_t^C C_t^{-\theta} = \lambda_t (1+i_t) P_t, \tag{17.9}$$

$$V_t^M \left(\frac{M}{P} \right)_t^{-\theta} = \lambda_t i_t P_t, \tag{17.10}$$

$$E_t \lambda_{t+1} = E_t \left(\frac{1+\rho}{1+i_{t+1}} \right) \lambda_t, \tag{17.11}$$

where λ_t is the Lagrange multiplier in period t. Equations (17.9)–(17.11) have the standard interpretations. Equation (17.9) suggests that at the optimum, the household equates the marginal utility of consumption to the value of savings. Equation (17.10) suggests that the household equates the marginal utility of real money balances to the opportunity cost of holding money. Equation (17.11) suggests that at the optimum, the real interest rate, adjusted for the expected increase in the marginal utility of consumption, is equal to the pure rate of time preference.

Eliminating λ from (17.9), (17.10), and (17.11) implies that

$$\left(\frac{M}{P} \right)_t = C_t \left(\frac{V_t^C}{V_t^M} \frac{i_t}{1+i_t} \right)^{-\frac{1}{\theta}}, \tag{17.12}$$

$$E_t \left(\frac{V_{t+1}^C (C_{t+1})^{-\theta}}{P_{t+1}} \right) = \left(\frac{1+\rho}{1+i_t} \right) \left(\frac{V_t^C (C_t)^{-\theta}}{P_t} \right). \tag{17.13}$$

Equation (17.12) is the money demand function, which is proportional to consumption and a negative function of the nominal interest rate, and (17.13) is the familiar Euler equation for consumption.

Taking the logarithms of (17.12) and (17.13) yields

$$m_t - p_t = c_t - \frac{1}{\theta}\ln\left(\frac{i_t}{1+i_t}\right) + \frac{1}{\theta}\left(v_t^M - v_t^C\right), \tag{17.14}$$

$$c_t = E_t c_{t+1} - \frac{1}{\theta}(i_t - E_t\pi_{t+1} - \rho) + \frac{1}{\theta}(v_t^C - E_t v_{t+1}^C), \tag{17.15}$$

where lowercase letters denote natural logarithms, and $\pi_t = p_t - p_{t-1}$ is the rate of inflation.[9]

We next turn to the behavior of firms in product markets.

17.3 Firms and Optimal Pricing and Production

Assume that output is produced by a set of firms denoted by a continuous index j defined in the interval [0,1]. Each firm produces a differentiated product under conditions of monopolistic competition. All firms have access to the same production technology, denoted by the production function

$$Y(j)_t = A_t L(j)_t^{\,1-\alpha}, \tag{17.16}$$

where $A_t > 0$ and $0 < \alpha < 1$ are exogenous technological parameters, common to all firms; $L(j)_t$ is employment of labor by firm j in period t. The parameter α is constant, and A_t, exogenous productivity, is assumed to follow an exogenous stochastic process.

The optimal price of each firm, if it can choose its price in every period, is given by the maximization of its profits under the constraint of the production function (17.16) and the demand function for its product (17.5). Each firm takes the average price P, the nominal wage $W(j)$, and the level of aggregate demand C as given.

The per period profits of firm j are given by

$$P(j)_t Y(j)_t - W(j)_t L(j)_t. \tag{17.17}$$

From the first-order conditions for a maximum of (17.17), under the constraints (17.16) and (17.5), the optimal price is determined as

$$P(j)_t = \frac{\varepsilon}{\varepsilon - 1}\left(\frac{W(j)_t (L(j)_t)^{\alpha}}{(1-\alpha)A_t}\right). \tag{17.18}$$

9. Technically, because the logarithm of the expectation of a product (or ratio) of two random variables is not equal to the sum (or difference) of the expectations of the logarithms of the relevant random variables, (17.15) must also contain second-order terms, depending on the covariance matrix of consumption, inflation, and shocks to preferences for consumption and money. Assuming that all exogenous shocks are independent stationary stochastic processes, these second-order terms are constant and can be ignored.

The optimal price is a fixed markup on the firm's marginal cost, which equals the expression in the outer parentheses.

The marginal cost of production is the wage divided by the marginal product of labor. Because the marginal product of labor is decreasing with the level of employment, the marginal cost of production is an increasing function of employment and output.

The markup depends positively on the elasticity of substitution between goods in the preferences of consumers, which determines the price elasticity of demand of their product and therefore the profit margin of the firm. In the case of perfect competition, the elasticity of substitution tends to infinity, and the price tends to marginal cost. In the case of monopolistic competition with $\varepsilon > 1$, as we have assumed, the optimal price is higher than the marginal cost of labor.[10]

As all firms have the same production function and the same demand function for their product, they will all choose the same price if they face the same nominal wage W. Consequently, the price level will be defined as

$$P_t = \frac{\varepsilon}{\varepsilon - 1}\left(\frac{W_t L_t^{\alpha}}{(1-\alpha)A_t}\right). \tag{17.19}$$

If firms face different wages $W(j)$, then they will choose different prices, and (17.19) denotes the average price as a function of the average of marginal unit labor costs. In either case, the price level is a fixed markup on marginal unit labor costs. It thus depends positively on nominal wages and employment, and negatively on exogenous productivity shocks.

Taking the logarithm of the production function (17.16) for the representative firm and equation (17.19) for the optimal price, we get

$$y_t = a_t + (1-\alpha)l_t, \tag{17.20}$$

$$p_t = \mu + w_t - a_t + \alpha l_t, \tag{17.21}$$

where $a_t = \ln A_t$, and $\mu = \ln\left(\frac{\varepsilon}{\varepsilon-1}\right) - \ln(1-\alpha)$. Here a is the logarithm of the exogenous productivity shock, and the constant μ is the logarithm of the markup on marginal cost minus the logarithm of the coefficient of decreasing returns to the employment of labor.

From (17.21), we see that the higher the level of employment is, the higher will be the price level relative to nominal wages, as higher employment implies lower marginal productivity of labor. Because employment is positively related to output by the production function (17.20), higher output also implies higher prices relative to nominal wages. This can be seen by using (17.20) to substitute for employment in (17.21). One finds that

10. This model of monopolistic competition, with a constant elasticity of demand, is due to Dixit and Stiglitz [1977].

$$p_t = \mu + w_t - \frac{1}{1-\alpha} a_t + \frac{\alpha}{1-\alpha} y_t. \tag{17.22}$$

From (17.22), for given exogenous productivity a_t, firms will only produce more if prices rise relative to wages. The reason is that an increase in output results in higher unit labor costs, because of the diminishing marginal productivity of labor.

We next turn our attention to the labor market and the determination of nominal wages.

17.4 Wage Setting and Employment in a Model with Insiders and Outsiders

Nominal wages are set in a decentralized manner by insiders in each firm. Wages are set at the beginning of each period, before current productivity, current aggregate demand, and the current price level are known. Nominal wages remain constant for one period, and they are renegotiated at the beginning of the following period.[11]

Thus, this model is characterized by nominal wage stickiness of the Gray [1976] and Fischer [1977b] variety. Prices are determined ex post by firms, given the contract wage, aggregate demand, the price level, and exogenous productivity a_t.

Following Blanchard and Summers [1986], assume that the number of insiders in each firm (who at the beginning of each period determine the contract wage) consists of an exogenous number of core insiders and those who were employed by the firm in the previous period. The objective of insiders is to set the maximum nominal wage, which—given their rational expectations about aggregate demand, the price level, and exogenous productivity—will minimize expected deviations of employment from the target level of the number of insiders. This target level is a weighted average of all those who were employed in period $t-1$, and the exogenous set of core employees of each firm. Thus, this model is characterized by a state-dependent pool of insiders, as in Blanchard and Summers [1986]. The employment target of insiders in period t is determined by

$$\bar{n}(j)_t = \delta l(j)_{t-1} + (1-\delta)\bar{n}(j), \tag{17.23}$$

where $l(j)_{t-1}$ is the logarithm of the number of those who were actually employed in the previous period; $\bar{n}(j)$ is the logarithm of the number of core employees of firm j, assumed exogenous; and δ is the weight of those recently employed relative to core employees, in the employment target of insiders. This formulation is the one proposed by Blanchard and Summers [1986].

The expectations on the basis of which wages are set depend on information available until the end of period $t-1$, but not on information about aggregate demand, prices, and

11. The wage setting model in this section was put forward by Alogoskoufis [2018] in the context of an analysis of optimal monetary policy in an economy characterized by labor market distortions but perfectly competitive product markets and flexible prices.

exogenous productivity in period t. On the basis of the above, let us assume that the objective of wage setters is to choose the path of maximum wages that would minimize deviations of the expected employment path from the expected path of the employment target of current insiders.

This can be modeled as a maximin problem. Insiders are assumed to choose the expected employment path that minimizes deviations from their target and to select the maximum wage path that satisfies their optimal employment path, subject to the optimal pricing decisions of firms. Thus, the first stage of the problem can be formalized as choosing the path of current and expected future wages that minimizes the following quadratic intertemporal loss function:

$$\min E_{t-1} \sum\nolimits_{s=0}^{\infty} \beta^s \frac{1}{2} \left(l(j)_{t+s} - \bar{n}(j)_{t+s} \right)^2. \tag{17.24}$$

This is minimized subject to the sequence of optimal prices (17.21) and employment targets $\bar{n}(j)_t$, as defined in (17.23). Here, $\beta = 1/(1+\rho) < 1$ is the discount factor, with ρ being the pure rate of time preference. As can be seen from (17.24), outsiders (i.e., the unemployed) have no influence on the wage-setting process.

We shall assume that the total number of core employees in the economy is always strictly smaller than the labor force. This assumption ensures that the natural rate of unemployment is strictly positive. We thus assume that

$$\int_{j=0}^{1} \bar{n}(j) dj = \bar{n} < n, \tag{17.25}$$

where n is the log of the labor force.

From the first-order conditions for a minimum of (17.24), wages are set at the maximum level that ensures that expected (log) employment by each firm satisfies

$$E_{t-1} l(j)_t = \frac{\beta\delta}{1+\beta\delta^2} E_{t-1} l(j)_{t+1} + \frac{\delta}{1+\beta\delta^2} l(j)_{t-1} + \frac{(1-\beta\delta)(1-\delta)}{1+\beta\delta^2} \bar{n}(j). \tag{17.26}$$

The implied contract wage can be derived by using the log-linear version of the optimal pricing condition (17.18) to substitute for employment in (17.26).

Integrating over j, *expected aggregate employment* must then satisfy

$$E_{t-1} l_t = \frac{\beta\delta}{1+\beta\delta^2} E_{t-1} l_{t+1} + \frac{\delta}{1+\beta\delta^2} l_{t-1} + \frac{(1-\beta\delta)(1-\delta)}{1+\beta\delta^2} \bar{n}, \tag{17.27}$$

which is the same as (17.26) without the j index. Wage contracts that satisfy (17.27) encompass Gray-Fischer wage contracts and Blanchard-Summers wage contracts as special cases.

With the standard Gray-Fischer contracts, $\delta = 0$, as past employment does not exert any separate influence on the wage-setting process. Only core employees would matter in

Gray-Fischer contracts. Setting $\delta = 0$ in (17.23), nominal wages in Gray-Fischer contracts would be set at the maximum level that ensures

$$E_{t-1} l_t = \bar{n}.$$

With Blanchard-Summers contracts, there is no consideration of the effects of current contracts on expected employment beyond period t. This is equivalent to setting $\beta = 0$ in (17.27), that is, to assuming myopic behavior. Setting $\beta = 0$ in (17.27) implies that nominal wages would be set to ensure that

$$E_{t-1} l_t = \delta l_{t-1} + (1 - \delta)\bar{n}.$$

This equation is identical to equation (3.2) in Blanchard and Summers [1986]. Nominal wages with Blanchard-Summers contracts would be set at the maximum level that ensures that expected employment equals a weighted average of core employees and those recently employed, without consideration for the effects on future employment.

In our more general dynamic model, wages are set at the maximum level that ensures that expected employment in period t is given by (17.27), which also depends on expected employment in period $t + 1$. This is because expected employment at t will affect the number of insiders who will negotiate wages for period $t + 1$. Thus, in our model, current labor market insiders are forward looking, in that they set nominal wages to achieve an employment target that depends on core employees, those previously employed, but also on those expected to be employed in the future. Expected future employment will affect the future number of insiders and thus future wage setting behavior. As a result, this dynamic model is more general than the standard Gray-Fischer and Blanchard-Summers models.

17.4.1 Wage Determination, Unemployment Persistence, and the Phillips Curve

To solve (17.27) for expected employment, define the forward expectations operator F as

$$F^s l_t = E_{t-1} l_{t+s}. \tag{17.28}$$

We can then rewrite (17.27) as

$$\left((1 + \beta\delta^2)F^0 - \beta\delta F - \delta F^{-1}\right) l_t = (1 - \beta\delta)(1 - \delta)\bar{n}. \tag{17.29}$$

Equation (17.29) can be rearranged as

$$-\beta\delta F^{-1}\left(F^2 - \frac{1 + \beta\delta^2}{\beta\delta}F + \frac{1}{\beta}\right) l_t = (1 - \beta\delta)(1 - \delta)\bar{n}. \tag{17.30}$$

It is straightforward to show that if $0 < \beta < 1$ and $0 < \delta < 1$, the characteristic equation of the quadratic in the forward shift operator (in large parentheses) has two distinct real roots, which lie on either side of unity. The two roots satisfy

$$\lambda_1+\lambda_2=\frac{1+\beta\delta^2}{\beta\delta}, \lambda_1\lambda_2=\frac{1}{\beta}. \tag{17.31}$$

Using (17.31), we can rewrite (17.30), as

$$(F-\lambda_1)(F-\lambda_2)l_t=-\frac{(1-\beta\delta)(1-\delta)}{\beta\delta}\bar{n}. \tag{17.32}$$

Assuming λ_1 is the smaller root, we can solve (17.32):

$$E_{t-1}l_t=\lambda_1 l_{t-1}+(1-\lambda_1)\bar{n}. \tag{17.33}$$

Equation (17.33), which is the rational expectations solution of (17.27), determines the path of expected employment aimed at by the wage setting behavior of insiders.

It is straightforward to show that λ_1, the coefficient that determines the persistence of expected unemployment, is equal to δ, the relative weight of recent employees in the wage-setting process. From (17.31), which defines the two roots, it follows that because $\lambda_2 = 1/\beta\lambda_1$, it follows that

$$\lambda_1+\frac{1}{\beta\lambda_1}=\frac{1+\beta\delta^2}{\beta\delta}=\delta+\frac{1}{\beta\delta}. \tag{17.34}$$

Thus, the degree of persistence of employment λ_1 is equal to the weight of recent employees relative to core employees in the wage-setting process δ, exactly as suggested by Blanchard and Summers [1986].

The expected employment equation (17.33) can be transformed into an expected unemployment equation in a straightforward manner. Subtracting (17.33) from the log of the labor force n, after some rearrangement, we get

$$E_{t-1}u_t=\delta u_{t-1}+(1-\delta)\bar{u}, \tag{17.35}$$

where $u_t \simeq n-l_t$ is the current unemployment rate, and $\bar{u}\simeq n-\bar{n}>0$ is the natural rate of unemployment. The natural rate of unemployment in this model is defined in terms of the difference between the labor force and the number of core employees. This is the equilibrium rate toward which the economy would converge in the absence of shocks. Note that (17.35) also uses the fact that $\lambda_1=\delta$.

Actual employment is determined from the pricing and employment decisions of firms, after information about aggregate demand and productivity shocks has been revealed.

From the optimal pricing equation (17.21), to achieve the employment target (17.33), insiders will set the nominal wage to

$$w_t=E_{t-1}p_t-\mu+E_{t-1}a_t-\alpha\left(\delta l_{t-1}+(1-\delta)\bar{n}\right). \tag{17.36}$$

Equation (17.36) uses the fact that $\lambda_1=\delta$. Substituting the wage-determination equation (17.36) in the optimal pricing equation of firms (17.21), the (log) price level will be determined by

$$p_t = E_{t-1}p_t - (a_t - E_{t-1}a_t) + \alpha\,(l_t - \delta l_{t-1} - (1-\delta)\bar{n})\,. \tag{17.37}$$

Thus, prices will differ from the expectations of wage setters to the extent that there are unanticipated shocks to exogenous productivity and unanticipated shocks to aggregate demand. These shocks cause firms to determine employment at a different level than the one aimed at and expected by wage setters.

It is straightforward to transform (17.37) into an expectations-augmented Phillips curve. Subtracting p_{t-1} from both sides, and adding and subtracting the log of the labor force multiplied by α on the right-hand side, we get

$$\pi_t = E_{t-1}\pi_t - \alpha\,((u_t - \bar{u}) - \delta(u_{t-1} - \bar{u})) - (a_t - E_{t-1}a_t)\,, \tag{17.38}$$

where $\pi_t = p_t - p_{t-1}$ is the inflation rate, $u_t \simeq n - l_t$ is the unemployment rate, n is the log of the labor force, and $\bar{u} \simeq n - \bar{n}$ is the natural unemployment rate. Equation (17.38) is the expectations-augmented Phillips curve in this model. It is a dynamic version of a traditional expectations-augmented Phillips curve, in the sense that inflation depends on prior inflationary expectations but also on both current and past deviations of unemployment from its natural rate.

According to (17.38), current inflation differs from prior expectations of inflation to the extent that there are unanticipated shocks to exogenous productivity and unanticipated shocks to aggregate demand. These shocks cause the unemployment rate to differ from the target unemployment rate of wage setters. The dynamics arise because of the assumption that the target unemployment rate of wage setters is a weighted average of the past and the natural unemployment rate, due to the composition of labor market insiders. Note that when there is no persistence in the number of labor market insiders (i.e., when $\delta = 0$), (17.38) takes the form of a standard expectations-augmented Phillips curve, like the one analyzed in chapter 15.

17.4.2 The Relation between Output and Unemployment Persistence

It is also clear from this model that only unanticipated shocks to exogenous productivity and aggregate demand cause unemployment to deviate from its expected path, as determined by the behavior of wage setters and summarized in (17.35). Note that if (17.35) holds, and wage setters have rational expectations, the unemployment rate follows

$$u_t = \delta u_{t-1} + (1-\delta)\bar{u} + \zeta_t^u, \tag{17.39}$$

where ζ_t^u is a white noise process, encompassing unanticipated productivity and demand shocks.

Hence, deviations of current unemployment from its natural rate will display persistence equal to δ, the weight of past employees on the wage-setting process. In fact, deviations of unemployment from its natural rate will follow an AR(1) process of the form

$$(u_t - \bar{u}) = \delta(u_{t-1} - \bar{u}) + \zeta_t^u. \tag{17.40}$$

The persistence of employment and unemployment will also be translated into persistent output fluctuations.

Adding and subtracting $(1-\alpha)(n-\bar{n})$ to the aggregate production function (17.20), we get

$$y_t = \bar{y}_t - (1-\alpha)(u_t - \bar{u}), \tag{17.41}$$

where

$$\bar{y}_t = (1-\alpha)\bar{n} + a_t \tag{17.42}$$

is the log of the natural rate of output. Equation (17.41) is an Okun [1962] type of relation, which suggests that fluctuations of output around its natural rate will be negatively related to fluctuations of the unemployment rate around its own natural rate. Because deviations of employment and unemployment from their natural rates display persistence, so will fluctuations in output. The propagation mechanism is the state dependence of the employment target of insiders in the labor market. Hence, deviations of output from its own natural rate will follow

$$(y_t - \bar{y}_t) = \delta(y_{t-1} - \bar{y}_{t-1}) - (1-\alpha)\zeta_t^u. \tag{17.43}$$

Deviations of output from its natural rate will follow an AR(1) process as well, with the same degree of persistence δ as unemployment.

17.4.3 The Phillips Curve in Terms of Deviations of Output from Its Natural Rate

Substituting the Okun-type relation (17.41) in the expectations-augmented Phillips curve (17.38), we get an expectations-augmented Phillips curve defined in terms of deviations of output from its natural rate. This takes the form

$$\pi_t = E_{t-1}\pi_t + \frac{\alpha}{1-\alpha}\left((y_t - \bar{y}_t) - \delta(y_{t-1} - \bar{y}_{t-1})\right) - (a_t - E_{t-1}a_t). \tag{17.44}$$

To the extent that deviations of output from its natural rate are higher than what was anticipated at the time when wages were set, inflation is higher than anticipated, because employment and unit labor costs are higher than what was anticipated. Hence, firms increase prices by more than was previously expected.

Also note that when there is no persistence in the number of labor market insiders (i.e., when $\delta = 0$), (17.44) takes the form of a standard expectations-augmented Phillips curve in terms of deviations of output from its natural rate.

17.5 The Implications of Staggered Pricing

Up to now we have assumed predetermined wage contracts and flexible prices. We can augment the model by introducing price stickiness as a additional nominal distortion. As in chapter 16, we shall concentrate on the Calvo [1983] model of staggered pricing.[12]

All firms are assumed to be able to automatically index their prices to the steady state inflation rate. However, following Calvo [1983], let us assume that the probability of adjusting prices freely, at a rate different than steady state inflation, is equal to $1-\gamma$. This probability is constant and independent of the length of time that has elapsed since the last such price adjustment by the firm. Thus, in each period, a proportion $1-\gamma$ of all firms adjust their prices freely, and the remaining proportion γ are constrained to index their prices only to the rate of steady state inflation.[13]

Under these assumptions, in period t, the expected future duration of any price contract is given by

$$(1-\gamma)\sum_{s=0}^{\infty} s\gamma^{s} = \frac{\gamma}{1-\gamma}.$$

From the definition of the price level in (17.6) and the fact that all firms that freely reset their prices in period t set the same price, it follows that

$$\hat{P}_t = \left(\gamma\left(\hat{P}_{t-1}\right)^{1-\varepsilon} + (1-\gamma)(\bar{P}_t)^{1-\varepsilon}\right)^{\frac{1}{1-\varepsilon}}, \tag{17.45}$$

where $\hat{P}$ is the price level relative to the steady state price level, and $\bar{P}$ is the price set by the firms that freely reset their prices in the current period relative to the steady state price level.

From (17.45), one can show that the dynamic adjustment of the price level relative to the steady state price level is determined by

$$\left(\frac{\hat{P}_t}{\hat{P}_{t-1}}\right)^{1-\varepsilon} = \gamma + (1-\gamma)\left(\frac{\bar{P}_t}{\hat{P}_{t-1}}\right)^{1-\varepsilon}. \tag{17.46}$$

In the steady state with inflation equal to π^*, we have that $\hat{P}_t = \bar{P}_t = 1$, and the price level evolves as

$$P_t = (1+\pi^*)P_{t-1}. \tag{17.47}$$

12. Alternatively, one can use the observationally equivalent model of Rotemberg [1982a,b] based on convex (quadratic) costs of adjusting prices. This model was introduced in chapter 16.

13. As in the model of chapter 16, automatic indexation to steady state inflation ensures that the model does not violate the natural rate property. See, for example, Ascari and Sbordone [2014].

A log-linear approximation of (17.46) around the steady state price level yields

$$\hat{p}_t - \hat{p}_{t-1} \simeq (1-\gamma)\left(\bar{p}_t - \hat{p}_{t-1}\right). \tag{17.48}$$

From (17.48), it follows that inflation exceeds its steady state rate if firms that set prices in the current period set them at a higher level than the average price of the previous period adjusted for steady state inflation.

17.5.1 Optimal Pricing with Staggered Price Adjustment

To analyze the adjustment of inflation, one has to examine how firms that can freely adjust prices in the current period decide on their optimal price, taking into account that for a period in the future, they may not be able to readjust their prices freely, while some of their competitors will have the option of readjusting their own prices at a rate different than core inflation.

The problem of the firm that decides on the price it is about to set in period t is to set the price that maximizes the expected present value of its profits, given that the probability of readjusting its price in any future period is equal to $1-\gamma$. Thus, all firms that readjust their prices in period t maximize

$$E_t \sum_{s=0}^{\infty} \gamma^s \left(I(s)\left(\bar{P}_t Y_{t+s}^t - \hat{W}_{t+s} L_{t+s}^t\right)\right), \tag{17.49}$$

where $I(s) = \prod_{z=0}^{s}\left(\frac{1}{1+i_{t+z}}\right)$, and $\hat{W}$ is the nominal wage divided by the steady state price level.

The maximization takes place under the constraints of their production function and the demand function for their product. These are given by

$$Y_{t+s}^t = A_{t+s}\left(L_{t+s}^t\right)^{1-\alpha}, \tag{17.50}$$

$$Y_{t+s}^t = \left(\frac{\bar{P}_t}{\hat{P}_{t+s}}\right)^{-\varepsilon} Y_{t+s}, \tag{17.51}$$

where Y_{t+s}^t and L_{t+s}^t are respectively the volume of output and employment in period $t+s$ of the firm that has set its prices freely in period t. The higher the relative price of the firm is in any period, the lower will be the demand for its product and thus the volume of its output and employment.

From the first-order conditions for a maximum, it follows that

$$E_t \sum_{s=0}^{\infty} \gamma^s I(s)\left((\varepsilon-1)\left(\frac{\bar{P}_t}{\hat{P}_{t+s}}\right)^{-\varepsilon} - \frac{\varepsilon}{(1-\alpha)}\left(\frac{\bar{P}_t}{\hat{P}_{t+s}}\right)^{-\frac{1-\alpha+\varepsilon}{1-\alpha}}\left(\frac{\hat{W}_{t+s}}{\hat{P}_{t+s}}\right)\left(\frac{L_{t+s}^{\alpha}}{A_{t+s}}\right)\right) = 0. \tag{17.52}$$

Equation (17.52) implies that the expected present value of revenues from the optimal price is equal to the expected present value of the marginal cost of production, augmented by the price markup $\varepsilon/(\varepsilon-1)$ of the firm.

Note that, as we have already seen in equation (17.19), if the firm could determine its prices in every period, the price of the product in each period would be equal to the marginal cost of production augmented by the same markup. However, if the firm cannot adjust prices freely in every period, as is assumed in the Calvo [1983] model, pricing follows the dynamic pricing rule (17.52).

Assuming that in the steady state, inflation is equal to π^* and all prices are equal to steady state prices, (17.52) can be transformed into logarithmic deviations from the steady state equilibrium, using a log-linear Taylor approximation. Thus, in logarithms, we have that

$$\bar{p}_t \simeq (1-\beta\gamma)\sum_{s=0}^{\infty}(\beta\gamma)^s E_t\left(\hat{p}_{t+s}+\omega\left(\mu+w_{t+s}-p_{t+s}+\alpha l_{t+s}-a_{t+s}\right)\right), \tag{17.53}$$

where $\beta=\frac{1}{1+\rho+\pi^*}$, and $\omega=\frac{1-\alpha}{1+\alpha(\varepsilon-1)}$. It follows that $0<\beta,\omega<1$.

Consequently, firms that freely reset their prices in period t will choose a price that corresponds to a weighted average of the current and expected future price levels, relative to the steady state price level, plus a margin μ on a weighted average of the current and expected future levels of real marginal costs. The discount factor of a future period $t+s$ depends on the probability that the firm will not be able to reset its price in the future period $t+s$, which equals γ^s, times the discount rate β^s. Furthermore, the part of pricing that depends on the expected marginal cost of the firm depends negatively on the elasticity of demand for the product of the firm, through the parameter ω.

Using the future mathematical expectations operator F, (17.53) can be rewritten as

$$\bar{p}_t \simeq \frac{1-\beta\gamma}{1-\beta\gamma F}\hat{p}_t+\omega\left(\mu+\frac{1-\beta\gamma}{1-\beta\gamma F}\left(w_t-p_t+\alpha l_t-a_t\right)\right). \tag{17.54}$$

17.5.2 Inflation and Unit Labor Costs under Staggered Pricing

Substituting (17.54) in the equation for the adjustment of the average price level (17.48), we get

$$\hat{p}_t=\gamma\hat{p}_{t-1}+(1-\gamma)\left(\frac{1-\beta\gamma}{1-\beta\gamma F}\hat{p}_t+\omega\left(\mu+\frac{1-\beta\gamma}{1-\beta\gamma F}\left(w_t-p_t+\alpha l_t-a_t\right)\right)\right). \tag{17.55}$$

Multiplying both sides of (17.55) by $1-\beta\gamma F$ and rearranging, we get

$$(1+\beta)\hat{p}_t-\hat{p}_{t-1}-\beta E_t\hat{p}_{t+1}=\frac{(1-\gamma)(1-\beta\gamma)}{\gamma}\omega\left(\mu+\left(w_t-p_t+\alpha l_t-a_t\right)\right). \tag{17.56}$$

Equation (17.56) is the equation of adjustment of the price level toward the steady state price level, which is a constant markup on the marginal cost of production.

From the price adjustment equation (17.56), we can deduce an equation for fluctuations in inflation. Expressing (17.56) as an inflation equation, we have

$$\pi_t = (1-\beta)\pi^* + \beta E_t \pi_{t+1} + \frac{(1-\gamma)(1-\beta\gamma)}{\gamma} \omega \left(\mu + (w_t - p_t + \alpha l_t - a_t)\right), \tag{17.57}$$

where $\pi_t = p_t - p_{t-1}$ is the rate of inflation. This equation implies that deviations of current inflation from steady state inflation are greater than discounted expected deviations of future inflation from steady state inflation, if the current marginal cost of labor plus the margin μ is higher than the current price level p. The reason is that firms able to set prices freely in the current period post larger price increases than the (discounted) expected future inflation, to offset the higher current marginal cost of labor.

Note that if all firms can adjust their prices freely and $\gamma = 0$, then the price level is always equal to the marginal cost of production augmented by the fixed markup μ, and inflation is equal to steady state inflation in all periods. Hence, the existence of a positive relation between inflation and employment in (17.57) requires staggered pricing in the form of a positive γ.

17.6 An Extended New Keynesian Phillips Curve: Combining Staggered Pricing with Periodic Nominal Wage Contracts

We can now combine staggered pricing with periodic nominal wage contracts set by insiders, such as the ones introduced in section 17.4. Wages in period t are set at the beginning of the period, based on information available until the end of $t-1$, to ensure that expected employment is equal to the target of labor market insiders:

$$E_{t-1} l_t = \delta l_{t-1} + (1-\delta)\bar{n}. \tag{17.58}$$

Hence, from (17.57), the nominal wage in period t satisfies

$$w_t = \frac{\gamma}{(1-\gamma)(1-\beta\gamma)\omega} \left(E_{t-1}(\pi_t - \pi^*) - \beta(E_{t-1}\pi_{t+1} - \pi *)\right) + \\ + E_{t-1} p_t - \mu + E_{t-1} a_t - \alpha \left(\delta l_{t-1} + (1-\delta)\bar{n}\right), \tag{17.59}$$

which is the equivalent of equation (17.36) in the case of staggered pricing. Note that if we set $\gamma = 0$ in (17.59), we recover (17.36).

Substituting (17.59) for the nominal wage in the new Keynesian Phillips curve (17.57) and rearranging, we get

$$\pi_t = E_{t-1}\pi_t + \beta \left(E_t \pi_{t+1} - E_{t-1}\pi_{t+1}\right) - \frac{(1-\gamma)(1-\beta\gamma)\omega}{\gamma} (\pi_t - E_{t-1}\pi_t) \\ + \frac{(1-\gamma)(1-\beta\gamma)}{\gamma} \omega \left(\alpha \left(l_t - \delta l_{t-1} - (1-\delta)\bar{n}\right) - (a_t - E_{t-1} a_t)\right). \tag{17.60}$$

Noting that, $l_t - \delta l_{t-1} - (1-\delta)\bar{n} \simeq -(u_t - \delta u_{t-1} - (1-\delta)\bar{u})$, (17.60) can be expressed as

$$\pi_t = E_{t-1}\pi_t + \frac{\beta\gamma}{\gamma + (1-\gamma)(1-\beta\gamma)\omega}(E_t\pi_{t+1} - E_{t-1}\pi_{t+1}) +$$
$$- \frac{(1-\gamma)(1-\beta\gamma)\omega}{\gamma + (1-\gamma)(1-\beta\gamma)\omega}(\alpha((u_t - \bar{u}) - \delta(u_{t-1} - \bar{u})) + (a_t - E_{t-1}a_t)). \tag{17.61}$$

Equation (17.61) is an extended new Keynesian Phillips curve, which encompasses both the new Keynesian Phillips curve and the original expectations-augmented Phillips curve (17.38) as special cases.

For example, by dropping the assumption of staggered pricing and setting $\gamma = 0$, (17.61) is transformed to

$$\pi_t - \pi^* = \left(E_{t-1}\pi_t - \pi^*\right) - \alpha((u_t - \bar{u}) - \delta(u_{t-1} - \bar{u})) - (a_t - E_{t-1}a_t).$$

This is the same as (17.38), which determines inflation only as a function of previously expected inflation, unanticipated productivity shocks, and current and lagged deviations of unemployment from its natural rate.

Equation (17.61) allows for both current expectations of future inflation (due to the assumption of staggered pricing) and past expectations of current inflation (due to the assumption of predetermined nominal wage contracts). It also allows for the effects of both the current and the past unemployment rate, because of the dynamics in the objectives of labor market insiders.

From the Okun-type relation (17.41), it follows that

$$u_t - \bar{u} = -\frac{1}{1-\alpha}(y_t - \bar{y}_t), \tag{17.62}$$

where $\bar{y}_t$ is the natural rate of output, given by (17.42).

Through the use of (17.62), the extended new Keynesian Phillips curve (17.61) can be expressed in terms of deviations of output from its natural rate:

$$\pi_t = E_{t-1}\pi_t + \frac{\beta\gamma}{\gamma + (1-\gamma)(1-\beta\gamma)\omega}(E_t\pi_{t+1} - E_{t-1}\pi_{t+1}) +$$
$$+ \frac{(1-\gamma)(1-\beta\gamma)\omega}{\gamma + (1-\gamma)(1-\beta\gamma)\omega}\left(\frac{\alpha}{1-\alpha}((y_t - \bar{y}_t) - \delta(y_{t-1} - \bar{y}_{t-1})) - (a_t - E_{t-1}a_t)\right). \tag{17.63}$$

In what follows, we shall use this version of the extended new Keynesian Phillips curve. When determining unemployment, we shall use the Okun-type equation (17.62).

17.7 Inflation and Aggregate Fluctuations under a Taylor Rule

Because there is no capital and investment in this model, and no distinction between private and government consumption expenditure, product market equilibrium implies that output is equal to consumption:

$$Y_t = C_t. \tag{17.64}$$

This product market equilibrium condition allows us to substitute output for consumption in the money demand function and the Euler equation for consumption, and derive optimal aggregate money and output demand functions.

17.7.1 New Neoclassical Synthesis IS-LM Functions

Substituting (17.64) in (17.14) and (17.15), we get the following money and output aggregate demand functions:

$$m_t - p_t = y_t - \frac{1}{\theta} \ln\left(\frac{i_t}{1+i_t}\right) + \frac{1}{\theta}\left(v_t^M - v_t^C\right), \tag{17.65}$$

$$y_t = E_t y_{t+1} - \frac{1}{\theta}(i_t - E_t\pi_{t+1} - \rho) + \frac{1}{\theta}(v_t^C - E_t v_{t+1}^C). \tag{17.66}$$

Equation (17.65) can be seen as the money market equilibrium condition, the equivalent of the LM curve in the traditional models of the neoclassical synthesis. Equation (17.66) is the product market equilibrium condition, the equivalent of the IS curve. Because (17.65) and (17.66) are derived from an explicit problem of intertemporal optimization by the representative household, let us refer to them the new neoclassical synthesis LM curve and IS curves, respectively.[14]

17.7.2 The Natural and Equilibrium Real Interest Rate

The real interest rate is defined by the Fisher [1896] equation, first introduced in chapter 2:

$$r_t = i_t - E_t\pi_{t+1}. \tag{17.67}$$

As with other real variables, let us distinguish between the current and the natural real interest rate. The natural real interest rate is determined by the product market equilibrium condition, when output is at its natural rate. From (17.42) and (17.66), the natural real interest rate is thus determined by

$$\bar{r}_t = \rho - \theta\,(a_t - E_t a_{t+1}) + \left(v_t^C - E_t v_{t+1}^C\right). \tag{17.68}$$

14. We could alternatively call them the new Keynesian IS and LM curves, but these would take the same form even in a new classical model, such as the one in chapter 14. We thus adopt the new neoclassical synthesis terminology of Goodfriend and King [1997].

The natural real interest rate is equal to the pure rate of time preference, but it also depends positively on deviations of current shocks to consumption from anticipated future shocks, and negatively on deviations of current productivity shocks from anticipated future shocks. Hence, the natural real interest rate is affected by real shocks, such as productivity and consumption preference shocks. Productivity shocks, which cause a temporary increase in the natural level of output, lead to a reduction of the natural real rate of interest, inducing a corresponding increase in consumption and maintaining product market equilibrium. Real consumption preference shocks, which cause a temporary increase in consumption, require an increase in the natural real rate of interest, reducing consumption back to the natural level of output and maintaining product market equilibrium.

Because of the existence of predetermined one-period nominal wage contracts, and because of staggered pricing, the current equilibrium real interest rate deviates from its natural rate to the extent that current output deviates from its own natural rate. Solving the new neoclassical synthesis IS curve (17.66) for the real interest rate and using (17.42) for the natural rate of output, we get that the current real interest rate is given by

$$r_t = i_t - E_t\pi_{t+1} = \bar{r}_t - \theta(1-\delta)(y_t - \bar{y}_t). \tag{17.69}$$

Deviations of the current real interest rate from its natural rate depend negatively on deviations of output from its own natural rate. Because deviations of output from its natural rate tend to persist, deviations of the real interest rate from its own natural rate will tend to persist as well.

Shocks to inflation or productivity, which cause a temporary rise in current output relative to its natural rate, affect output by reducing the current real interest rate relative to its natural rate.[15]

17.7.3 Equilibrium Fluctuations with Exogenous Preference and Productivity Shocks

In what follows, let us assume that the logarithms of the exogenous shocks to preferences and productivity follow stationary AR(1) processes of the form

$$v_t^C = \eta_C v_{t-1}^C + \varepsilon_t^C, \tag{17.70}$$

$$v_t^M = \eta_M v_{t-1}^M + \varepsilon_t^M, \tag{17.71}$$

$$a_t = \eta_A a_{t-1} + \varepsilon_t^A, \tag{17.72}$$

where the autoregressive parameters satisfy $0 < \eta_C, \eta_M, \eta_A < 1$, and ε^C, ε^M, ε^A, are white noise processes.[16]

15. This is the well-known Wicksellian mechanism, emphasized for the first time by Wicksell [1898].

16. The assumption of AR(1) processes could easily be generalized to AR(n) processes without affecting the nature of the results in this chapter, as, eventually, it is only the unanticipated component of these shocks that affects deviations of real and nominal variables from their natural rates.

With these assumptions, for a given nominal interest rate, fluctuations in output and inflation will be determined by the new neoclassical synthesis IS relation (17.66), and the extended new Keynesian Phillips curve (17.63). Expressing these as deviations from natural rates, we get

$$y_t - \bar{y}_t = -\frac{1}{\theta(1-\delta)} \left(i_t - E_t\pi_{t+1} - \bar{r}_t\right), \tag{17.73}$$

$$\pi_t = E_{t-1}\pi_t + \frac{\beta\gamma 1}{\gamma + (1-\gamma)(1-\beta\gamma)\omega} \left(E_t\pi_{t+1} - E_{t-1}\pi_{t+1}\right) +$$

$$+ \frac{(1-\gamma)(1-\beta\gamma)\omega}{\gamma + (1-\gamma)(1-\beta\gamma)\omega} \left(\frac{\alpha}{1-\alpha} \left((y_t - \bar{y}_t) - \delta\left(y_{t-1} - \bar{y}_{t-1}\right)\right) - \varepsilon_t^A\right). \tag{17.74}$$

The natural rates of real variables, such as output, $\bar{y}_t$, and the real interest rate $\bar{r}_t$, evolve as functions of the exogenous real shocks only. Using (17.70) and (17.72) to substitute for productivity and real consumption shocks in (17.42) and (17.68), we get

$$\bar{y}_t = (1-\alpha)\bar{n} + a_t, \tag{17.75}$$

$$\bar{r}_t = \rho - \theta\left(1-\eta_A\right) a_t + \left(1-\eta_C\right) v_t^C. \tag{17.76}$$

Thus, deviations of real output from its natural rate depend on the current nominal interest rates, expected future inflation, and shocks to the natural real rate of interest; inflation is determined through the dynamic stochastic Phillips curve (17.74).

To solve the model, one needs an assumption about the determination of the nominal interest rate. Let us assume that this is determined by the central bank, which follows a Taylor rule of the form

$$i_t = \bar{r}_t + \pi^* + \phi_\pi\left(\pi_t - \pi^*\right) + \phi_y(y_t - \bar{y}_t) + \varepsilon_t^i, \tag{17.77}$$

where $\phi_\pi, \phi_y > 0$ are policy parameters, and ε_t^i is a white noise monetary policy shock. According to this rule, the central bank aims for a nominal interest rate that is equal to the natural real rate of interest, plus a target inflation rate equal to the steady state inflation rate π^*. If actual inflation is higher than the target π^*, then the central bank raises interest rates to reduce inflation toward its target. In addition, if output is higher than its natural rate, then the central bank increases nominal interest rates to reduce aggregate demand and bring output back to its natural rate.[17]

17. We have expressed the Taylor rule in terms of deviations of output and not unemployment from its natural rate. This does not affect the results, as through the Okun type relation (17.41), deviations of unemployment from its natural rate are a negative linear function of deviations of output from its own natural rate. We have also assumed

We can use the Taylor rule (17.77) to substitute for the nominal interest rate in the aggregate demand equation (17.73), and then substitute for deviations of output from its natural rate in the dynamic stochastic Phillips curve (17.74), to derive an inflation equation that depends only on inflation terms and on real and nominal shocks. Proceeding with these substitutions we get a transformed inflation process of the form[18]

$$\hat{\pi}_t = E_{t-1}\hat{\pi}_t + \kappa_1\left(E_t\hat{\pi}_{t+1} - E_{t-1}\hat{\pi}_{t+1}\right) + \\ -\kappa_2\left(\kappa_3\left(\phi_\pi\left(\hat{\pi}_t - \delta\hat{\pi}_{t-1}\right) - \left(E_t\hat{\pi}_{t+1} - \delta E_{t-1}\hat{\pi}_t\right) + \varepsilon^i_t - \delta\varepsilon^i_{t-1}\right) + \varepsilon^A_t\right), \tag{17.78}$$

where $\hat{\pi}_t = \pi_t - \pi^*$ is the deviation of current inflation from steady state inflation (the target of the central bank), and the κ coefficients are defined as

$$\kappa_1 = \frac{\beta\gamma}{\gamma + (1-\gamma)(1-\beta\gamma)\omega}, \\ \kappa_2 = \frac{(1-\gamma)(1-\beta\gamma)\omega}{\gamma + (1-\gamma)(1-\beta\gamma)\omega}, \\ \kappa_3 = \frac{\alpha}{1-\alpha}\frac{1}{\theta(1-\delta)+\phi_y}. \tag{17.79}$$

To solve for inflation, we first take expectations of (17.78) conditional on information available up to the end of period $t-1$. This yields

$$E_{t-1}\hat{\pi}_t = \frac{1}{\delta+\phi_\pi}E_{t-1}\hat{\pi}_{t+1} + \frac{\delta\phi_\pi}{\delta+\phi_\pi}\hat{\pi}_{t-1} + \frac{\delta}{\delta+\phi_\pi}\varepsilon^i_{t-1}. \tag{17.80}$$

The process (17.80) will be stable if and only if

$$\frac{1+\delta\phi_\pi}{\delta+\phi_\pi} < 1. \tag{17.81}$$

It is straightforward to show that a necessary and sufficient condition for (17.81) to hold is

$$\phi_\pi > 1. \tag{17.82}$$

that the central bank interest rate adjusts to shocks that affect the natural real rate of interest, which is not treated as a constant.

18. Once we solve for inflation, we can also determine deviations of output from its natural rates as well as deviations of all other nominal and real variables, such as the nominal interest rate and the unemployment rate. Note that under a nominal interest rate rule, such as (17.77), the money supply becomes endogenous and is determined through the money demand function (17.65).

Condition (17.82) reflects the *Taylor principle*. It requires that nominal interest rates react sufficiently strongly to deviations of current inflation from target inflation to affect real interest rates and aggregate demand in the desired direction. This is a necessary and sufficient condition for a stable and determinate process for expected (and actual) inflation.[19]

If (17.82) is satisfied, then it is straightforward to show that the expected inflation process has two roots that lie on either side of unity. The smaller root is δ, and the larger root is ϕ_π. Thus, the solution for the expected inflation process (17.80) is given by

$$E_{t-1}\hat{\pi}_t = \delta\hat{\pi}_{t-1} + \frac{\delta}{\phi_\pi}\varepsilon^i_{t-1}, \tag{17.83}$$

where $\delta < 1$ is the smaller root of the characteristic polynomial of (17.81). From (17.83), it follows that

$$E_{t-1}\hat{\pi}_{t+1} = \delta E_{t-1}\hat{\pi}_t,$$

$$E_t\hat{\pi}_{t+1} = \delta\hat{\pi}_t + \frac{\delta}{\phi_\pi}\varepsilon^i_t. \tag{17.84}$$

Substituting (17.83) and (17.84) in the inflation process (17.78), the rational expectations solution for inflation is given by

$$\hat{\pi}_t = \delta\hat{\pi}_{t-1} - \psi_1\varepsilon^A_t - \psi_2\varepsilon^i_t + \psi_3\varepsilon^i_{t-1}, \tag{17.85}$$

where

$$0 < \psi_1 = \frac{\kappa_2}{\phi_\pi\kappa_2\kappa_3 - \delta(\kappa_1 + \kappa_2\kappa_3) + 1} < 1,$$

$$0 < \psi_2 = \frac{(\phi_\pi - \delta)\kappa_2\kappa_3 - \delta\kappa_1}{\phi_\pi\,(\phi_\pi\kappa_2\kappa_3 - \delta(\kappa_1 + \kappa_2\kappa_3) + 1)} < 1, \tag{17.86}$$

$$0 < \psi_3 = \frac{\delta}{\phi_\pi} < 1.$$

From (17.85), fluctuations of inflation around the target of the monetary authorities π^* are as persistent as fluctuations of unemployment and output around their natural rates. They are driven by the current innovation in productivity and current and past monetary policy shocks, as the central bank is using the short-run trade-off between inflation and unemployment to partly counteract the real effects of such shocks.

19. Clarida et al. [1999], Woodford [2003a], and Gali [2008], among others, contain detailed discussions of the Taylor principle and its significance for the resolution of the price level and inflation indeterminacy problem, which affects noncontingent interest rate rules.

Note that the inflationary process displays persistence only because of the persistence of unemployment. This is because under the Taylor rule, the central bank seeks to counteract deviations of unemployment and output from their natural rates, something that conflicts with the objectives of wage setters, who are seeking to maintain persistent deviations of unemployment and output from their natural rates. It is because of the clash in the objectives of wage setters and the central bank that inflation persists.[20]

It is also worth noting that all structural parameters (including the parameters of the Taylor rule) affect the inflation process, through the expectations of consumers, wage setters, and firms, and through deviations of unemployment, output, and the real interest rate from their natural rates.

Because of the persistence of deviations of output from its natural rate, both current and past monetary policy shocks affect the inflationary process. The effects of productivity and monetary policy shocks on inflation also depend on all structural parameters, including the parameters of the Taylor rule.[21]

Having solved for inflation, the solution of the rest of the model is straightforward. Substituting the Taylor rule (17.77) into the new neoclassical synthesis IS relation (17.73), which determines deviations of output from its natural rate, and solving for $\hat{y}_t$, we get

$$\hat{y}_t = -\frac{1}{\theta(1-\delta)+\phi_y}\left(\phi_\pi \hat{\pi}_t - E_t\hat{\pi}_{t+1} + \varepsilon_t^i\right) =$$

$$= -\frac{1}{\theta(1-\delta)+\phi_y}\left((\phi_\pi - \delta)\hat{\pi}_t + (1-\psi_3)\varepsilon_t^i\right), \tag{17.87}$$

where $\hat{y}_t = y_t - \bar{y}_t$ denotes deviations of output from its natural rate.

Substituting (17.85) in (17.87) and solving out for $\hat{y}_t$, we get

$$\hat{y}_t = \delta\hat{y}_{t-1} + \frac{1}{\theta(1-\delta)+\phi_y}\left(\xi_1\varepsilon_t^A - \xi_2\varepsilon_t^i + \xi_3\varepsilon_{t-1}^i\right), \tag{17.88}$$

where

$$\xi_1 = (\phi_\pi - \delta)\psi_1,$$

$$\xi_2 = 1 - \psi_3 - (\phi_\pi - \delta)\psi_2, \tag{17.89}$$

$$\xi_3 = \delta(1-\psi_3) - (\phi_\pi - \delta)\psi_3.$$

20. See Alogoskoufis [2018] for a detailed analysis of this point in the context of a related model.

21. Because equation (17.85) is the inflationary process from a DSGE model, in which the policy rule of the monetary authorities is taken into account when agents form their expectations, it does not suffer from the Lucas [1976] critique. Changing the parameters of the policy rule would also change the parameters of the inflationary process in a predictable manner.

Finally, using the Okun relation (17.62) in conjunction with (17.88), we can solve for the fluctuations of the unemployment rate around its natural rate:

$$\hat{u}_t = \delta\hat{u}_{t-1} - \frac{1}{(1-\alpha)\left(\theta(1-\delta)+\phi_y\right)}\left(\xi_1\varepsilon_t^A - \xi_2\varepsilon_t^i + \xi_3\varepsilon_{t-1}^i\right). \tag{17.90}$$

Fluctuations in both nominal variables (such as the inflation rate) and real variables (such as deviations of real output and the unemployment rate from their natural rates) display the same degree of persistence. This is a result of the clash in the objectives of central bankers and labor market insiders. The central bank, through the Taylor rule, seeks to stabilize both inflation and deviations of output from its natural rate. Labor market insiders seek to secure the maximum wage consistent with their own employment, which depends partly on lagged employment and partly on the natural rate.

To the extent that the short-term employment objectives of wage setters and the central bank differ, with the central bank seeking to minimize persistent deviations of unemployment from its natural rate, the only way for wage setters to ensure that the central bank does not surprise them is to adapt their inflationary expectations to the central bank rule. Because nominal interest rates react to the persistent fluctuations of deviations of output from its natural rate, inflation and inflationary expectations adapt too. Hence, inflation displays the same degree of persistence as output and unemployment.[22]

17.7.4 Does Staggered Pricing Matter for Inflation Persistence?

It is important to demonstrate that most of the results go through even in the absence of staggered pricing. Inflation displays persistence under a Taylor rule, even in the case where prices are fully flexible, as long as nominal wage contracts are predetermined, as assumed by the model.

To demonstrate that staggered pricing does not matter for inflation persistence, assume that $\gamma = 0$. Then, it follows that the dynamic stochastic Phillips curve (17.74) takes the form

$$\pi_t = E_{t-1}\pi_t + \frac{\alpha}{1-\alpha}\left((y_t - \bar{y}_t) - \delta\left(y_{t-1} - \bar{y}_{t-1}\right)\right) - \varepsilon_t^A. \tag{17.91}$$

Deviations of output from its natural rate still cause unanticipated inflation, but the extra terms involving expected future inflation drop out.

Using the Taylor rule (17.77) to substitute for the nominal interest rate in the aggregate demand equation (17.73), and then substituting for deviations of output from its natural rate in the Phillips curve (17.91), results in a transformed inflation process of the form

22. This point is elaborated in Alogoskoufis [2018] in the context of a simpler insider-outsider model.

$$\hat{\pi}_t = E_{t-1}\hat{\pi}_t - \kappa_3\left(\phi_\pi\left(\hat{\pi}_t - \delta\hat{\pi}_{t-1}\right) - \left(E_t\hat{\pi}_{t+1} - \delta E_{t-1}\hat{\pi}_t\right) + \varepsilon_t^i - \delta\varepsilon_{t-1}^i\right) + \varepsilon_t^A, \tag{17.92}$$

where κ_3 is defined in the same way as before (equation (17.79)). However, because of the assumption that $\gamma = 0$, it follows from (17.79) that $\kappa_1 = 0$ and that $\kappa_2 = 1$.

The rational expectations solution for expected inflation is the same as before (given by (17.80)), as ex ante expected current inflation does not depend on staggered pricing, but only on the degree of persistence of unemployment δ and the Taylor rule response to inflation ϕ_π.

The rational expectations solution for actual inflation is the same as (17.85), except that the parameters measuring the impact of the unanticipated shocks now simplify to

$$\begin{aligned}
0 < \psi_1 &= \frac{1}{(\phi_\pi - \delta)\kappa_3 + 1} < 1, \\
0 < \psi_2 &= \frac{(\phi_\pi - \delta)\kappa_3}{\phi_\pi\left((\phi_\pi - \delta)\kappa_3 + 1\right)} < 1, \\
0 < \psi_3 &= \frac{\delta}{\phi_\pi} < 1.
\end{aligned} \tag{17.93}$$

Hence, inflation follows a process similar to (17.85), with a degree of persistence equal to δ even in the absence of staggered pricing.

Substituting the modified inflation process in the new neoclassical synthesis IS relation (17.73), using the Taylor rule to substitute for the nominal interest rate, and solving out, the processes determining the fluctuations of real output and unemployment are given by equations similar to (17.88) and (17.90) with the ψ values redefined as in (17.93). Hence, staggered pricing does not matter for the persistence of either inflation or real variables in this model. It only matters for the transmission of current real and nominal shocks, through the ψ parameters.

Exercise 17.1 Consider the model with periodic wage contracts and unemployment persistence, but perfectly flexible prices. The expectations-augmented Phillips curve is given by (17.44). Solve the model for fluctuations in output, unemployment, and inflation, using the new neoclassical synthesis IS curve (17.66), the Taylor rule (17.77), the Okun-type relation (17.62), and the assumptions made about the exogenous shocks in (17.70)–(17.72). Discuss your findings, and compare them to the findings in the main text, in the presence of staggered pricing.

17.7.5 Inflation Stabilization and the Divine Coincidence

Note that, unlike the bechmark new Keynesian model with staggered prices, analyzed in chapter 16, this model is not characterized by the divine coincidence of output stabilization when inflation itself is stabilized. Stabilization of inflation around the target inflation rate of the central bank does not automatically lead to output and employment stabilization around their natural rates. This is because of the labor market distortions implied by the wage-setting behavior of insiders.[23]

To see this, assume that the central bank allows its response to deviations of inflation from its target ϕ_π to become infinite. Then from the definition of the ψ parameters in (17.86), ψ_1, ψ_2, and ψ_3 would be driven to zero, and neither nominal nor real shocks would affect inflation. Inflation would converge to the target rate of the central bank π^*, and the variance of inflation would be driven to zero. Inflation would thus be fully stabilized.

However, from (17.88) and (17.90), real shocks would continue to affect deviations of real output and unemployment from their natural rates, even if ϕ_π is driven to infinity.

Thus, the divine coincidence does not hold in this model. In the presence of real shocks, inflation stabilization does not result in unemployment and output stabilization, as there is always a trade-off between the stabilization of inflation and the stabilization of unemployment around its natural rate in the presence of real shocks.

17.8 The Optimal Taylor Rule

We have shown that in a model with endogenous unemployment persistence, as in the model in this chapter, the Taylor rule results in inflation persistence. One can show that inflation persistence would also be associated with optimal monetary policy if the loss function of the central bank depends on both deviations of inflation from target and deviations of unemployment from its natural rate.[24]

17.8.1 Optimal Inflation Policy

To derive optimal monetary policy, we have to specify an appropriate social welfare function. Assuming that the optimal steady state inflation rate is equal to π^*, the only other distortion in this model is the deviation of unemployment from its natural rate. Thus, we can assume that the central bank would seek to minimize an intertemporal loss function that depends on deviations of inflation from its steady state optimal rate π^*, and deviations of unemployment from its natural rate $\bar{u}$. This can be written as

$$\Lambda_t = E_t \sum_{s=0}^{\infty} \beta^s \left(\frac{1}{2}(\pi_{t+s} - \pi^*)^2 + \frac{\zeta}{2}(u_{t+s} - \bar{u})^2 \right), \tag{17.94}$$

23. See Blanchard and Gali [2007] and chapter 16 for a discussion of the divine coincidence. To deal with this problem in the benchmark new Keynesian model with staggered prices, one has to superimpose ad hoc additional labor market distortions. This is not the case with the model in this chapter, or the model of Erceg et al. [2000], as labor market distortions are part and parcel of these models and are not an afterthought.

24. See Alogoskoufis [2018] for a proof of this proposition and suggested solutions.

where β is the discount factor, $\beta = 1/(1+\rho)$; ρ is the pure rate of time preference; and ζ is the relative weight attached by the central bank to deviations of unemployment from its natural rate, relative to deviations of inflation from target.[25]

The optimal policy is the one that minimizes (17.94) subject to the dynamic stochastic expectational Phillips curve (17.38). This policy is called the *optimal time-consistent contingent policy*, because the central bank has no short-run incentive to deviate from it, and the choice of inflation will depend on the current state of the economy, summarized by the deviations of the current unemployment rate from its natural rate.[26]

Under this policy, there is a clash between the objectives of the monetary authorities and the objectives of wage-setting insiders with regard to unemployment. The central bank seeks to minimize deviations of unemployment from its natural rate, whereas wage setters seek to minimize deviations of unemployment from a weighted average of the natural rate and past unemployment. This clash is what accounts for the persistence of inflation under the contingent optimal policy.

From the first-order conditions for a minimum of (17.94) subject to (17.38), we get

$$\pi_t = \pi^* + \frac{\zeta}{\alpha}(u_t - \bar{u}) + \frac{\zeta\beta\delta}{\alpha} E_t(u_{t+1} - \bar{u}). \tag{17.95}$$

Using (17.38), Okun's Law (17.41), to substitute for current and expected future deviations of the unemployment rate from its natural rate and after rearranging, we get

$$\pi_t = \delta\pi_{t-1} + (1-\delta)\pi^* - \frac{\zeta(1+\beta\delta^2)}{\alpha^2}\left(\pi_t - E_{t-1}\pi_t + \varepsilon_t^A\right). \tag{17.96}$$

The rational expectations solution of (17.96) is given by

$$\pi_t = \delta\pi_{t-1} + (1-\delta)\pi^* - \frac{\zeta(1+\beta\delta^2)}{\alpha^2 + \zeta(1+\beta\delta^2)}\varepsilon_t^A. \tag{17.97}$$

From (17.97), deviations of the optimal, time consistent, contingent inflation rate from the inflation target π^* display the same degree of persistence as the persistence of deviations of

25. In accordance with the conventions of the literature on monetary policy (e.g., Barro and Gordon [1983a], Rogoff [1985]), treat (17.94) as a measure of the intertemporal welfare costs of inflation and unemployment. However, we assume that the central bank does not seek to systematically reduce unemployment below its inefficiently high natural rate. Thus, we abstract from the systematic inflation bias that would result if the central bank also sought to use inflation to reduce unemployment below its natural rate, as in Kydland and Prescott [1977] and Barro and Gordon [1983a]. We further discuss these issues in chapter 20 on the role of monetary policy.

26. Note that the optimal contingent policy is time consistent, in the sense of Kydland and Prescott [1977]. Alogoskoufis [2018] also examines time-inconsistent policy rules that may result in even lower intertemporal losses.

unemployment from its natural rate. The reason is that the central bank allows inflation to fluctuate so as to minimize deviations of unemployment from its natural rate. Because these deviations in unemployment display persistence, deviations of inflation from target will also display persistence under the optimal contingent policy.[27]

Note that the persistence of inflation under the optimal time-consistent contingent monetary policy does not affect the persistence of unemployment. The reason is that wage setters can anticipate the persistent part of the inflation process, incorporate it in their expectations when they set nominal wages, and neutralize the effects of persistent inflation on unemployment. Thus, the only element of monetary policy that matters for unemployment is the unanticipated part, which is a function of the current productivity shock.

17.9 A Dynamic Simulation of the Effects of Monetary and Real Shocks

To visualize the impulse response functions of the model to nominal and real shocks, we review the results of dynamic simulations of the model. The first simulation follows an unanticipated temporary 1% shock to the nominal interest rate, and the second follows an unanticipated 1% shock to productivity. We use the version of the model without staggered pricing.

The simulations are based on the following values of the parameters: $\alpha = 0.333$, $\rho = 2\%$, $\theta = 1$, $\delta = 0.5$, $\phi_\pi = 1.5$, $\phi_u = 0.5$, $\eta_A = 0.75$, and $\gamma = 0$. The natural rate of unemployment is assumed equal to 5%, and the target inflation rate is 2%.

Figure 17.1 presents the impulse response functions of the model following an unanticipated temporary 1% shock to the nominal interest rate. Note that such a nominal shock does not affect the natural rate of real variables, which only depend on real shocks.

Inflation initially falls below the target of 2%, unemployment rises above its natural rate of 5%, and output falls below its own natural rate. The real interest rate and the real wage rise above their natural rates. Because of the fall in inflation and the rise in unemployment, after the initial shock, the nominal interest rate follows a downward path toward its natural rate of 4%, inflation rises, unemployment gradually declines toward its natural rate, and all other real variables adjust toward their natural rates too. Thus, a temporary nominal shock has persistent real effects, because of the persistence of deviations of employment from its natural rate.

Figure 17.2 presents the impulse response functions of the model following an unanticipated 1% shock to productivity a. Inflation initially falls, and so does unemployment and

27. Note from (17.97) that if deviations of unemployment from its natural rate did not persist (i.e., in the case $\delta = 0$), the optimal contingent monetary policy rule would not result in persistent deviations of inflation from target. There would be deviations of inflation from π^* only in response to unanticipated shocks to productivity.

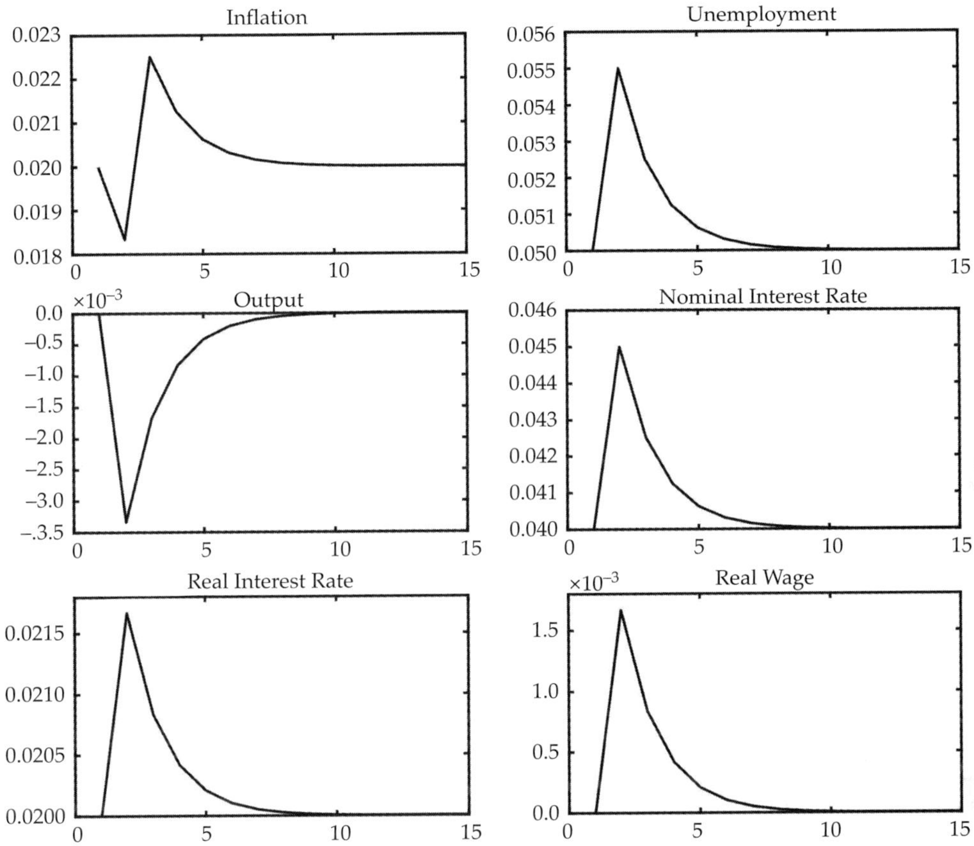

Figure 17.1
Impulse response functions following a 1% unanticipated temporary positive shock to the nominal interest rate.

nominal and real interest rates relative to their steady state natural rates. Output rises above its natural rate, and so do real wages. Following the initial shock, all variables gradually return to their steady state natural rates.

Thus, both nominal and real shocks cause persistent deviations of all variables from their steady state values.

Also note that the correlation of inflation and unemployment (or output) depends on the nature of the shocks. The short-run correlation of inflation and unemployment following a nominal shock is negative, because unanticipated inflation reduces unemployment. But the short-run correlation of inflation and unemployment is positive following a real shock, because higher productivity reduces both inflation and unemployment. Thus, this model could explain stagflation as the outcome of negative real shocks.

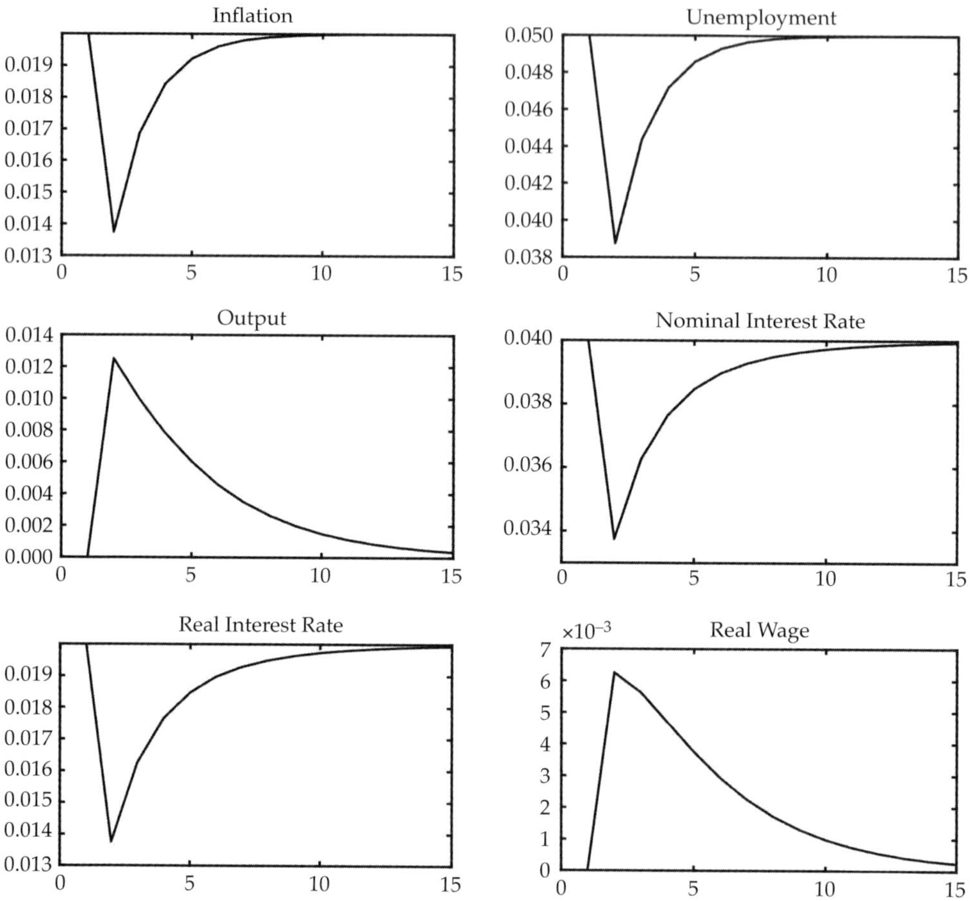

Figure 17.2
Impulse response functions following a 1% unanticipated persistent positive shock to productivity.

17.10 Conclusion

In this chapter, we have considered a dynamic stochastic new Keynesian model, which not only allows for the existence of involuntary unemployment but also for nominal shocks and monetary policy to affect the fluctuations of all real variables.

The model builds on one of the key insights of the *General Theory*: the short-run rigidity of nominal wages, assumed to be due to periodic nominal wage contracts. But in all other respects, it is based on intertemporal optimization on the part of both households and firms.

The full model is characterized by a combination of an expectations-augmented Phillips curve and the new Keynesian Phillips curve. Deviations of output and employment from their natural rates depend on unanticipated current inflation (which reduces real wages relative to productivity) and unanticipated productivity shocks (which also affect the relation between real wages and productivity). However, such deviations cause current inflation to deviate from expected future inflation, as in the new Keynesian Phillips curve.

Nominal shocks and, by extension, monetary policy are able to affect fluctuations in both inflation and real variables, such as output, employment, unemployment, real wages, and the real interest rate.

We analyzed aggregate fluctuations in this model under a feedback interest rate rule, according to which the nominal interest rate responds to deviations of inflation from the target of the central bank, and deviations of output from its natural rate. Such a rule, which is in the spirit of Wicksell [1898], has been proposed and advocated by Taylor [1993].

Contrary to the new classical model under full information, monetary shocks affect real variables in this model, causing temporary and persistent deviations of output, employment, unemployment, real wages, and the real interest rate from their natural rates. Under a Taylor feedback interest rate rule, only productivity shocks and shocks to monetary policy affect aggregate fluctuations. Aggregate fluctuations depend not only on exogenous shocks but also on the parameters of the monetary policy rule followed by the central bank.

18

Matching Frictions and Equilibrium Unemployment

In this chapter, we delve deeper into the microeconomic foundations of models of the determination of the equilibrium (or natural) unemployment rate, assuming that there are matching frictions in the labor market. We focus on one of the most important dynamic models of this category, the Mortensen-Pissarides model.[1]

In this model, employers are incurring costs to create job vacancies, and the process of creating jobs involves the matching of firms that have vacancies with unemployed job seekers. At each instant, there are two flows: into and out of unemployment. Some workers lose their jobs and move from jobs to unemployment, and some of the unemployed find jobs, through the matching process, with firms that have vacancies. Thus, this model explains both equilibrium unemployment and labor market flows in and out of unemployment.

In the simpler versions of the model, the probability of job termination is exogenous. This parameter describes the structural or cyclical shocks affecting the economy, leading to the destruction of jobs.

The probability of filling a vacancy, as well as the probability of an unemployed job seeker finding a job, are endogenous variables in this model. They depend on the degree of *labor market tightness*, which is defined by the ratio of vacancies to the number of unemployed. The higher the tightness of the labor market is, the greater will be the probability that an unemployed job seeker will find a job, and the lower the probability that a firm will fill a vacancy.

In the steady state, the flows to and from unemployment are equalized, and the equilibrium unemployment rate depends (1) positively on the exogenous probability of termination of a job and (2) negatively on the endogenous probability of an unemployed job seeker finding a job. The equilibrium unemployment rate therefore depends negatively on labor market tightness, and of course is determined endogenously. The negative relationship between the

1. See Pissarides [1985], Mortensen [1986], Mortensen and Pissarides [1994], and Pissarides [2000]. Pissarides [2011] provides a historical overview of the development of this approach.

equilibrium unemployment rate and the vacancy rate that is implied by this dependence is known as the *Beveridge curve*.

Real wages are determined in equilibrium by decentralized bargaining between firms that have vacancies and unemployed job seekers. The equilibrium real wage is the result of this negotiation. It depends positively on the relative bargaining power of the unemployed, the level of unemployment benefits, labor productivity, the cost of maintaining a vacancy, and labor market tightness.

In the equilibrium of this model, the unemployed are worse off than the employed. Consequently, unemployment is an undesirable and involuntary condition and is not the result of choice by the unemployed, unlike in competitive models of the labor market without frictions.

The basic idea of *search or matching models of the labor market*, such as the Mortensen-Pissarides model, is that the labor market functions in a decentralized and uncoordinated way, and job creation is a costly process that requires time for both job seekers and firms. Consequently, jobs entail rents, something that does not apply to fully competitive labor market models. This matching class of models is the class we shall focus on in the remainder of this chapter.

18.1 The Matching Function

A key assumption of this class of models is that the number of jobs created at each moment is a positive function of the number of firms looking for employees and the number of unemployed job seekers. The outcome of this process is described by the *matching function*.[2]

The number of jobs created at each moment in time is given by

$$mL = m(uL, vL), \tag{18.1}$$

where L is the size of the labor force, u is the unemployment rate (the unemployed as a proportion of the labor force), v is the vacancy rate (vacancies as a proportion of the labor force), and m is the job creation rate (new jobs as a share of the labor force).

The matching function is assumed to be increasing in every one of its arguments, concave, and linearly homogeneous. Thus, it is characterized by constant returns to scale. These are the same assumptions as those made for the neoclassical production function. The higher the number of unemployed job seekers and the higher the number of vacancies, the higher will be the number of jobs that are created. If the number of the unemployed and vacancies double, then the number of jobs created will also double.

2. The presentation of this model follows Pissarides [2000].

18.1.1 The Probability of Filling a Vacancy and Labor Market Tightness

Assuming that all vacancies have the same probability of being filled, and that all the unemployed have the same probability of being employed, the probability of filling a vacancy will be equal to the ratio of the number of new jobs created over all existing vacancies. If we define this probability as q, then the probability of filling a vacancy is defined by

$$q = \frac{m(uL, vL)}{vL} = m\left(\frac{u}{v}, 1\right). \tag{18.2}$$

This equation assumes that every unemployed job seeker has the same probability of finding a job and that every vacancy has the same probability of being filled. We have thus assumed a *Poisson frequency distribution*.

From (18.2), the probability of filling a vacancy is a function only of the ratio of the number of unemployed to job vacancies, because of the assumption that the matching function is linearly homogeneous. The greater the number of unemployed per vacancy is, the greater will be the likelihood of filling any particular vacancy.

We define θ as the ratio of vacancies to the unemployed:

$$\theta = \frac{v}{u}, \tag{18.3}$$

so θ measures the degree of tightness in the labor market. The higher the number of vacancies is relative to the unemployed, the greater the tightness of the labor market will be. We can thus express (18.2) as a function of labor market tightness:

$$q = q(\theta). \tag{18.4}$$

From the properties of the matching function, it follows that

$$q'(\theta) \leq 0,$$

$$-1 < \eta(\theta) = \frac{\theta q'(\theta)}{q(\theta)} < 0,$$

where $\eta(\theta)$ is the elasticity of q with respect to θ. Higher tightness in the labor market implies a lower probability of filling a vacancy.

Because of the assumption of a Poisson density function, note that the average expected duration of a vacancy is equal to the inverse of q, and is thus a positive function of θ.

18.1.2 The Probability of the Unemployed Finding a Job

The probability of an unemployed job seeker finding a job is correspondingly equal to

$$\frac{m(uL, vL)}{uL} = \frac{v}{u}\frac{m(uL, vL)}{vL} = \theta q(\theta). \tag{18.5}$$

From (18.5), the elasticity of the probability of finding a job with respect to θ is given by

$1-\eta(\theta)>0.$

Therefore, the greater the tightness in the labor market (a higher θ) is, the higher will be the probability of an unemployed job seeker finding a job.

The average *expected duration of unemployment* is given by $1/\theta q(\theta))$ and is a negative function of θ. In models of this type, note that the price mechanism cannot cause the probability of filling a vacancy or the probability of finding a job to be unity, because the labor market does not function only via the price mechanism, but also via the degree of tightness of the labor market. This tightness determines the probabilities of firms to fill their vacancies or of the unemployed to find jobs in any particular instance.

The dependence of the probability of filling a vacancy and the probability of finding a job on the relative number of vacancies to the unemployed (tightness) is an example of a trading externality. These *search externalities* are important determinants of the properties of equilibrium unemployment in this model.

18.2 Flows into and out of Employment, Equilibrium Unemployment, and the Beveridge Curve

The model assumes that some proportion of existing jobs are terminated at every instant. The destruction of jobs and the flow from employment to unemployment are due to either cyclical or structural real disturbances that make the jobs unprofitable. It is assumed that at any instant, the probability of destruction of any job is equal to λ, where λ is an exogenous parameter.[3]

In contrast, job creation occurs when a firm and an employee agree to sign a contract with a wage that is the result of a bilateral negotiation. This leads to a flow out of unemployment.

Therefore, at any given moment, there are two flows in the labor market. One flow is from existing jobs to unemployment (because of job terminations), and the other is from unemployment to newly created jobs. The change of the unemployment rate is thus described by

$$\dot{u}=\lambda(1-u)-\theta q(\theta)u. \tag{18.6}$$

The change in the unemployment rate at each point in time depends on the difference between the proportion of jobs destroyed and the proportion of new jobs created, the proportions being defined relative to the labor force.

3. Mortensen and Pissarides [1994] have generalized this model to make the job termination rate endogenous. This does not fundamentally change the properties of the model. In the interests of simplicity, we shall thus stick to the model with an exogenous job destruction rate λ.

In the steady state, the unemployment rate will be constant. Consequently, the equilibrium unemployment rate is determined by the condition

$$\lambda(1-u)=\theta q(\theta)u, \tag{18.7}$$

which implies that

$$u=\frac{\lambda}{\lambda+\theta q(\theta)}, \tag{18.8}$$

which is the first key equation of this model. The equilibrium unemployment rate depends positively on λ, the exogenous rate of job destruction, and negatively on labor market tightness θ. Labor market tightness is an endogenous variable in this model and is determined in the labor market.

The negative relationship that (18.8) implies between the unemployment rate and labor market tightness θ (or equivalently, between the unemployment rate and the vacancy rate) is usually called the Beveridge curve and is depicted in figure 18.1.[4]

The Beveridge curve only defines a negative relation between vacancies and unemployment. For unemployment to be determined, one needs to determine labor market tightness, which is one of the endogenous variables in this model. Once labor market tightness is determined, then equilibrium unemployment is determined by the Beveridge curve. For example, assume that labor market tightness is equal to θ_E. Then the equilibrium unemployment rate would be determined at u_E, as shown in figure 18.1.

We next turn to analyzing how the behavior of firms and unemployed job seekers results in the endogenous determination of labor market tightness.

18.3 Firms and the Creation of Vacancies

The creation of a new job occurs when a prospective employer and a prospective employee agree to an employment contract. Of course, before this happens, the potential employer has to create a vacancy and search for an employee, and the prospective employee has to be unemployed and looking for a new job. All this involves time and costs and is described by the matching function.

Assume that the instantaneous value of the product of a job is constant and equal to $p>0$. The instantaneous cost of a vacant post to a prospective employer is equal to pc, where $0<c<1$. During the search period, the employer faces a probability $q(\theta)$ of finding a a suitable employee, which is independent of the employer's actions.

The number of vacancies is endogenous and is determined by profit maximization. Any firm can create a vacancy and search for employees. Profit maximization with free entry

4. See Beveridge [1944], who first empirically identified this relationship.

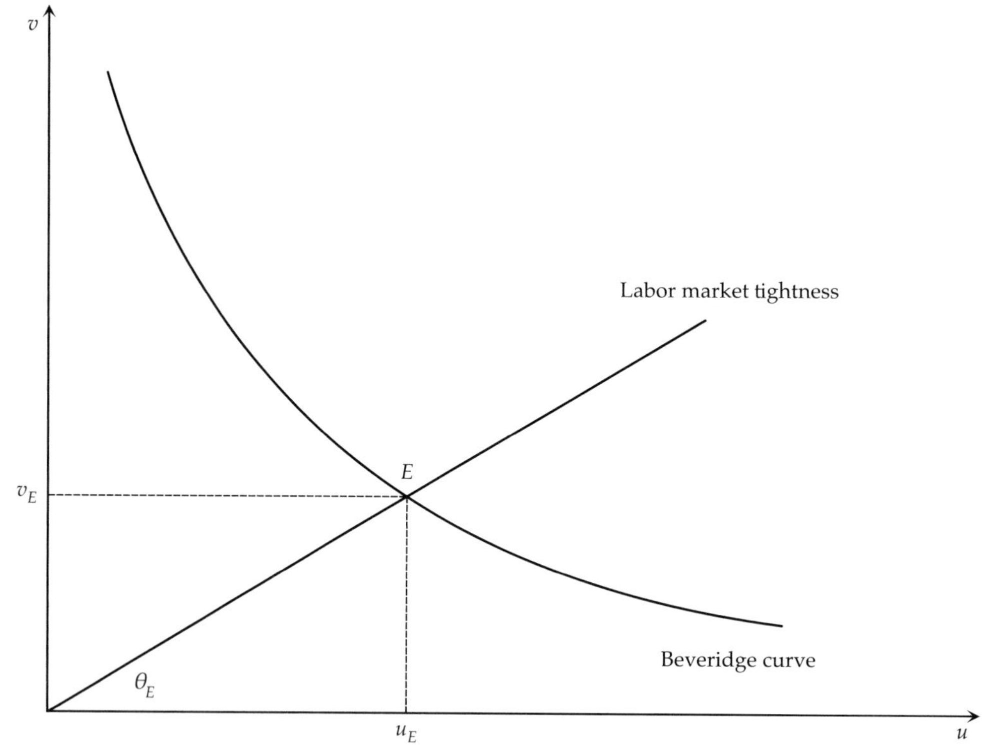

Figure 18.1
The Beveridge curve and equilibrium unemployment.

means that the expected profit from the marginal vacancy should be equal to zero. Otherwise, firms would continue to create vacancies.

18.3.1 The Present Value of Net Expected Profits from an Existing Job

Denote by J the present value of net expected profits from an existing job. The instantaneous gross profit from a job for a firm is equal to the difference $p - w$, where w is the real wage. However, at every instant, there is an exogenous constant probability λ of the job ending and the firm losing the present value of net expected profits from the job. Thus, the instantaneous expected net profit from a job is equal to

$$p - w - \lambda J. \tag{18.9}$$

Assuming a perfect capital market and an infinite horizon, the present value of this expected net profit is equal to

$$J = \int_{t=0}^{\infty} e^{-rt} (p - w - \lambda J)dt = \frac{p - w - \lambda J}{r}, \tag{18.10}$$

where r is the real interest rate, which is assumed exogenous and constant.[5]

From (18.10), the present value J of a job for the employer must satisfy the Bellman equation

$$rJ = p - w - \lambda J. \tag{18.11}$$

Thus, from (18.11), the instantaneous net opportunity cost of a job rJ must be equal to the instantaneous net expected profit from the job, which implies the condition

$$w = p - (r + \lambda)J. \tag{18.12}$$

For a positive net present value of expected profits from an existing job, the real wage will be less than productivity, both because of the interest costs of maintaining a job and the positive probability of termination of the job. Thus, the wedge between productivity and the real wage must reflect these capital and insurance costs.

18.3.2 The Present Value of Net Expected Profits from a Vacancy and the Creation of Vacancies

Denote by V the present value of expected profits from a job vacancy. The instantaneous net expected profit from a vacancy is equal to the probability of filling the vacancy, and earning the difference between the present value of a job and the present value of the vacancy, minus the instantaneous maintenance cost of the vacancy pc:

$$q(\theta)(J - V) - pc. \tag{18.13}$$

Assuming a perfect capital market and an infinite time horizon, the present value of expected net profits from a vacancy V is defined by

$$V = \int_{t=0}^{\infty} e^{-rt} (q(\theta)(J - V) - pc)dt = \frac{q(\theta)(J - V) - pc}{r}. \tag{18.14}$$

Thus, from (18.14), V must satisfy the Bellman equation

$$rV = -pc + q(\theta)(J - V). \tag{18.15}$$

A vacancy is an asset for the firm. In a perfect capital market, the instantaneous expected net yield of this asset, $q(J - V) - pc$, will be equal to its expected opportunity cost, which is equal to rV.

5. See Pissarides [2000] on how the real interest rate can become endogenous.

18.3.3 Free Entry and the Job Creation Condition

In equilibrium with free creation of vacancies (free entry), all profit opportunities by creating new vacancies will be exploited, and the expected profits from the creation of an additional vacancy will be equal to zero. So in equilibrium with free entry, $V=0$. Thus from (18.15), we have that

$$J=\frac{pc}{q(\theta)}, \tag{18.16}$$

which is an important prediction of this model. In equilibrium with free entry, the present value of a job will be equal to the expected cost of hiring an employee. This is equal to the instantaneous cost pc of maintaining a vacancy times the expected duration of the vacancy (which is $1/q(\theta)$). Thus, competition for the creation of vacancies and free entry reduces the present value of profits from a job to the level of the expected cost of hiring a worker.

Equations (18.16) and (18.12) imply that the marginal job must satisfy

$$w=p-\frac{(r+\lambda)pc}{q(\theta)}=\left(1-\frac{(r+\lambda)c}{q(\theta)}\right)p. \tag{18.17}$$

Equation (18.17) is the second key equation of this model and can be called the *job creation condition*. The firm will only hire a worker and create a new job if the real wage is smaller than or equal to the productivity of the worker, minus the marginal hiring cost, which is defined as

$$\frac{(r+\lambda)pc}{q(\theta)}. \tag{18.18}$$

The marginal hiring cost is equal to the gross opportunity cost of maintaining a job. It is the opportunity cost of the expected net present value of profits from the job, which, because of free entry, is equal to the expected cost of hiring an employee. The higher is labor market tightness θ, and the higher is c, the higher will be the marginal hiring cost, because the expected duration and the cost of a vacancy will be greater.

For this model, (18.17) corresponds to the usual condition for hiring in competitive models without hiring costs, which is none other than the real wage must be equal to (marginal) productivity. One can confirm this by setting the cost c of maintaining a vacancy equal to zero. In this case, the real wage is equal to average and marginal productivity p. In the general case, where maintaining a vacancy is costly, the firm will only hire a new worker if the marginal cost of maintaining the vacancy is recouped.

The job creation condition implies a negative relation between labor market tightness and the real wage. The higher is labor market tightness, the higher will be the expected duration of a vacancy and the marginal cost of maintaining a vacancy. Thus, the real wage that the firm would be prepared to pay, relative to productivity, will be lower. The job creation condition

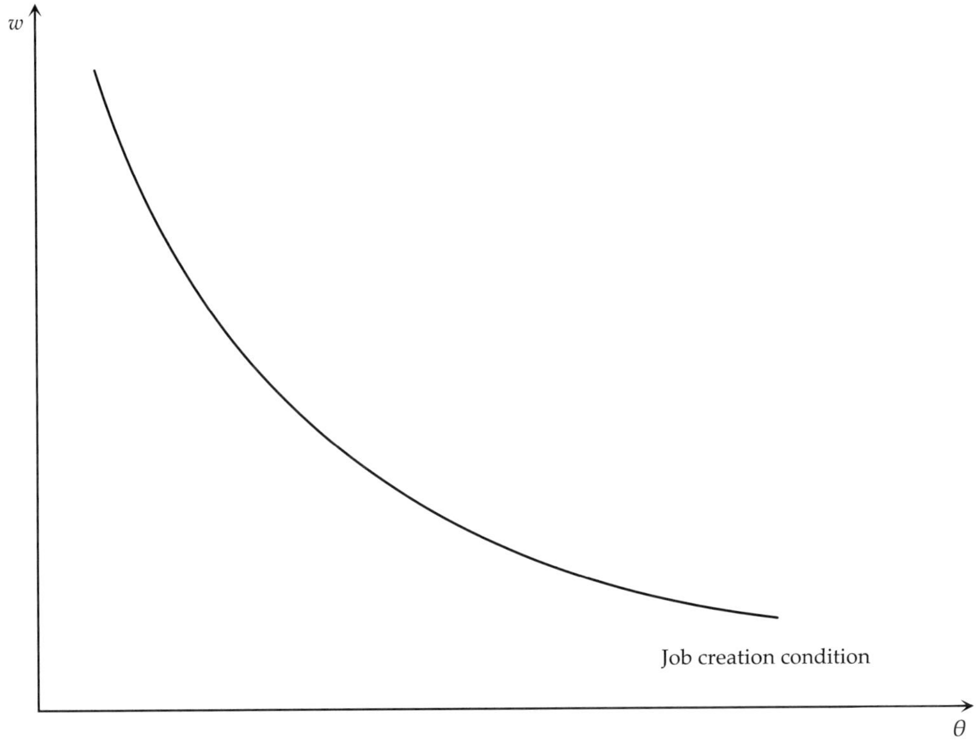

Figure 18.2
The job creation condition.

is depicted in figure 18.2. It is negatively sloped and convex to the origin because of the properties of the matching function.

18.4 The Behavior of Unemployed Job Seekers

Equations (18.8) and (18.17) do not suffice to determine the three endogenous variables u, w, and θ. To determine the real wage, we must now examine the behavior of prospective workers (i.e., the unemployed job seekers).

The typical worker earns a real wage w when employed and is looking for a job when unemployed. For the duration of search, she has an instantaneous real income z, which depends on unemployment benefits and any other income or benefit from the use of free time. For simplicity, let us call z the *unemployment benefit*.

We define U and W as the corresponding present values of expected income for an unemployed and an employed worker, respectively.

18.4.1 The Permanent Income of an Unemployed Job Seeker

An unemployed job seeker has an instantaneous real income equal to z and an instantaneous probability of finding a job equal to $\theta q(\theta)$. As a result, the expected instantaneous income of an unemployed job seeker is equal to

$$z+\theta q(\theta)(W-U). \tag{18.19}$$

From (18.19), the present value of the expected instantaneous income of an unemployed job seeker is defined by

$$U=\int_{t=0}^{\infty} e^{-rt}\,(z+\theta q(\theta)(W-U))dt=\frac{z+\theta q(\theta)(W-U)}{r}. \tag{18.20}$$

The permanent income of an unemployed job seeker is thus given by

$$rU=z+\theta q(\theta)(W-U). \tag{18.21}$$

18.4.2 The Permanent Income of an Employed Worker

In contrast, an employed worker has an instantaneous real income w, the real wage, but at each instant also faces the risk of losing her job with probability λ. Therefore, the present value of her expected income W is equal to

$$W=\int_{t=0}^{\infty} e^{-rt}\,(w+\lambda(U-W))dt=\frac{w+\lambda(U-W)}{r}. \tag{18.22}$$

From (18.22), the permanent income of an employed worker is thus equal to

$$rW=w+\lambda(U-W). \tag{18.23}$$

18.4.3 Comparing the Permanent Income of the Employed and the Unemployed

Equations (18.21) and (18.23) can be solved for the permanent income of the unemployed and the employed:

$$rU=\frac{(r+\lambda)z+\theta q(\theta)w}{r+\lambda+\theta q(\theta)}, \tag{18.24}$$

$$rW=\frac{\lambda z+[r+\theta q(\theta)]w}{r+\lambda+\theta q(\theta)}. \tag{18.25}$$

It is straightforward to see from (18.24) and (18.25) that if $w\geq z$, then $W\geq U$, and the permanent income of an employed worker cannot be lower than the permanent income of an unemployed job seeker. In what follows, let us assume that w exceeds z, which indeed turns out to be the case in equilibrium.

If w exceeds z, no employed worker has an incentive to leave their job voluntarily and become unemployed, while all the unemployed workers would accept any job offer at the prevailing real wage. If the condition $w > z$ is satisfied, unemployment is *involuntary*. The present value of the expected income of an unemployed job seeker is lower that the present value of the expected income of an employed worker. This holds, even though the workers who are employed may, with some probability, lose their jobs and become unemployed. Thus, unlike the competitive real business cycle (RBC) model, unemployment is involuntary in this model, and the unemployed are worse off than the employed.

18.5 Wage Bargaining and the Wage Equation

An unfilled vacancy implies a lower expected net present value of profits than a job, even though with some probability, a job may disappear. Unemployment implies a lower permanent income for those who experience it than for employed workers, even though the workers who are employed may, with some probability, lose their jobs and become unemployed.

A firm with a vacancy will hire an unemployed job seeker if the job creation condition is satisfied (i.e., if the real wage is lower than or equal to productivity minus the marginal hiring cost). An unemployed job seeker will accept a job offer if the real wage is higher than the unemployment benefit.

The real wage for a particular job is determined by a negotiation between a prospective employer (a firm with a vacancy) and a prospective employee (an unemployed job seeker). Because all jobs are equally productive and all unemployed receive the same unemployment benefit, the real wage that is determined by an individual negotiation will be the same as the real wage that prevails in the rest of the economy.

From the assumptions that we have made about productivity and aggregate disturbances, any one employer and any one worker, when they come together through the matching process, will certainly agree to an employment contract and create a job. Otherwise, they must continue searching, with additional costs for both sides.

An employment contract between an employer and an employee is defined by a real wage and the provision that employment will be terminated if there is a disturbance that makes the job untenable.

For a real wage w_i, the expected return for a prospective employer and a prospective employee are given by

$$rJ_i = p - w_i - \lambda(J_i - V), \tag{18.26}$$

$$rW_i = w_i + \lambda(U - W_i). \tag{18.27}$$

Equation (18.26), does not make use of the assumption that competition has reduced the expected present value of a vacancy V to zero. But we have assumed, as it appropriate, that the expected present value of a vacancy (and of the income of the unemployed U) depends on real wages in the rest of the economy and is thus independent of i.

The real wage is determined by a (generalized) Nash bargain that maximizes the weighted product of the surplus of the prospective employer and the prospective employee from the agreement to create a job. An agreement means that the prospective employer gets a surplus $J_i - V$, and the prospective employee a surplus $W_i - U$. Thus, the real wage satisfies

$$w_i = \arg\max\,(W_i - U)^{\beta}(J_i - V)^{1-\beta}, \tag{18.28}$$

where $0 \leq \beta \leq 1$ is a measure of the relative bargaining power of the prospective employee, over and above what results from the "threat" points U and V.[6]

The first-order condition for the maximization of (18.28) implies that

$$W_i - U = \beta(J_i + W_i - V - U). \tag{18.29}$$

Thus, in this model, β turns out to be the share of the prospective employee in the total surplus generated by the creation of a new job.

Using (18.23) and (18.24), and imposing the condition $V = 0$, we get

$$w_i = rU + \beta(p - rU). \tag{18.30}$$

From (18.30), the employee receives a real wage that exceeds the permanent income of an unemployed worker by a multiple β of the difference of productivity and the permanent income of an unemployed worker. From (18.30), it is obvious that real wages will be the same for all workers, as the right-hand side does not depend on i.

From (18.29) and (18.16), for $V = 0$, we can drop i:

$$W - U = \frac{\beta}{1-\beta}J = \frac{\beta pc}{(1-\beta)q(\theta)}. \tag{18.31}$$

From (18.21) and (18.31), we have

$$rU = z + \theta q(\theta)(W - U) = z + \frac{\beta}{1-\beta}pc\theta. \tag{18.32}$$

Using (18.32) to substitute for rU in the wage function (18.30) yields

$$w = (1-\beta)z + \beta p(1 + c\theta) = z + \beta(p - z) + \beta pc\theta. \tag{18.33}$$

Equation (18.33) is the most convenient and easily interpretable form of the wage determination function in this model. Here, p is labor productivity, and $pc\theta$ is the average

6. In a symmetric bargain, as the one we analyze here, a reasonable value of β would be $1/2$, but it is not necessary to assume this particular value.

recruitment cost per unemployed worker. The real wage exceeds the unemployment benefit z. It exceeds it by a proportion β of the difference between productivity and the unemployment benefit, plus a proportion β of the average recruitment cost per unemployed worker.

Higher labor market tightness θ results in a higher real wage, as this increases the average recruitment cost per unemployed person, thereby increasing the threat point of prospective employees versus prospective employers and weakening the effective bargaining position of prospective employers.

The job creation condition (18.12) plays a role analogous to that of a labor demand function in competitive labor market models without hiring costs, the wage function (18.33) plays the role of a labor supply function. Both are needed to determine real wages and labor market tightness.

18.6 Wage Determination and Equilibrium Unemployment

In equilibrium, this model determines the three endogenous variables u, θ, and w, which simultaneously satisfy the Beveridge curve (18.8), the job creation condition (18.17), and the wage equation (18.33). The full model is thus given by

$$u = \frac{\lambda}{\lambda + \theta q(\theta)},$$

$$w = \left(1 - \frac{(r+\lambda)c}{q(\theta)}\right)p,$$

$$w = (1-\beta)z + \beta p(1 + c\theta).$$

From the last two equations, we can establish that the level of real wages w and labor market tightness θ can be determined independently of the unemployment rate u. The job creation condition and the wage equation suffice for the determination of real wages and labor market tightness. Once we determine labor market tightness θ, we can substitute for it in the Beveridge curve (18.8) and determine equilibrium unemployment.

The determination of equilibrium real wages and labor market tightness is presented in figure 18.3. The wage equation (18.33) implies a positive relation between the real wage and labor market tightness. The job creation condition (18.17) implies a negative relation between the real wage and labor market tightness. Equilibrium real wages and labor market tightness are determined at the intersection of these two curves.

As shown in the figure, the wage function has a positive slope, because the higher labor market tightness is, the higher will be the wage that prospective employees can negotiate with employers. The job creation condition has a negative slope, because higher wages make creating vacancies less profitable and thus reduce vacancies relative to unemployment.

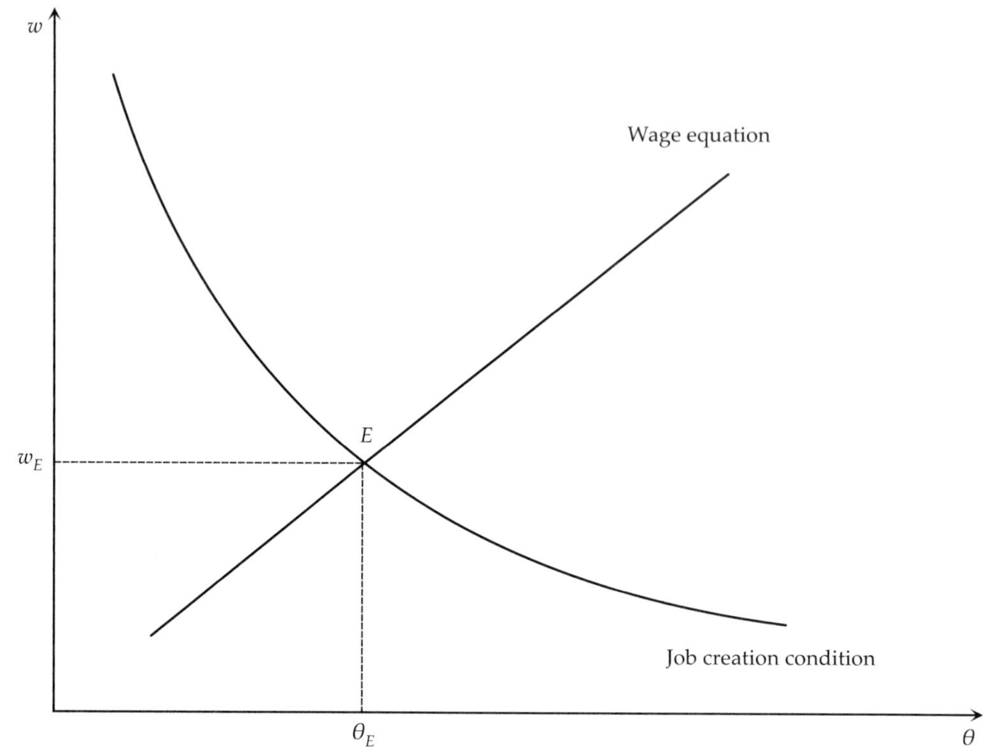

Figure 18.3
The determination of real wages and labor market tightness.

We also see that the determination of real wages and labor market tightness do not depend on the unemployment rate. This is because of the assumption of constant returns to scale in the matching function.

Once θ is determined from the wage equation and the job creation condition, we can substitute it in the Beveridge curve (18.8) and determine the unemployment rate. The solution is shown in figure 18.1.

In figure 18.1, the positively sloped straight line has a slope of θ_E, the equilibrium ratio of vacancies to the unemployed, as analyzed in figure 18.3. The negatively sloped Beveridge curve is derived from equation (18.8), which equates the flows in and out of unemployment. Higher vacancies imply lower unemployment, because the probability of finding a job by an unemployed job seeker is higher. The curve is convex to the origin because of the properties of the matching function. The equilibrium unemployment rate is determined at the intersection of the Beveridge curve with the straight line through the origin, the slope of which is determined by labor market tightness.

18.7 Determinants of Equilibrium Unemployment, Real Wages, and Labor Market Tightness

We can now use the full model to examine how real wages, labor market tightness, and equilibrium unemployment depend on the various exogenous parameters and shocks.

18.7.1 An Increase in Labor Productivity

Let us first consider a permanent increase in labor productivity p. This will shift both the job creation condition to the right and the wage equation upward, as shown in figure 18.4. Because $\beta < 1$, the shift in the job creation condition is greater, and in the new equilibrium A, both real wages and labor market tightness will rise. As a result, equilibrium unemployment will fall.

This effect of labor productivity occurs because of the assumption that the unemployment benefit z is fixed and does not depend on labor productivity. In this case, changes in real wages do not fully reflect changes in labor productivity. Thus, when productivity increases, there are gains from the creation of new job vacancies, new vacancies are then created, and unemployment falls.

However, in many countries, unemployment benefits z are not fixed in real terms and usually are related to the real wages of the employed. Thus, the assumption of an exogenously fixed unemployment benefit z is not very realistic.

Moreover, if the prediction that the growth of labor productivity reduces the unemployment rate is correct, then unemployment would be tending toward zero in the long run because of the continuous increases in labor productivity resulting from economic growth. This prediction is not compatible with the existing empirical evidence, which does not suggest any long-run trends in unemployment rates.

Assuming that unemployment benefits z are a percentage ρ of real wages, where $0 < \rho < 1$, then in our model, we have that $z = \rho w$; ρ is usually called the *replacement rate*. Labor legislation in most industrialized countries provides for an unemployment benefit that is a percentage of the wage received by the unemployed person in his last job, or a percentage of the minimum wage. Therefore, this assumption is more satisfactory and realistic than the assumption of an exogenously determined real unemployment benefit.

In this case, the wage function (18.33) is converted to

$$w = \frac{\beta(1 + c\theta)}{1 - (1 - \beta)\rho} p. \tag{18.34}$$

With the assumption of an exogenous replacement rate, the wage equation (18.33) becomes proportional to labor productivity p. The factor of proportionality depends positively on the bargaining power of prospective employees β, labor market tightness θ, the cost of maintaining a vacancy c, and the replacement rate of the unemployment benefit system ρ.

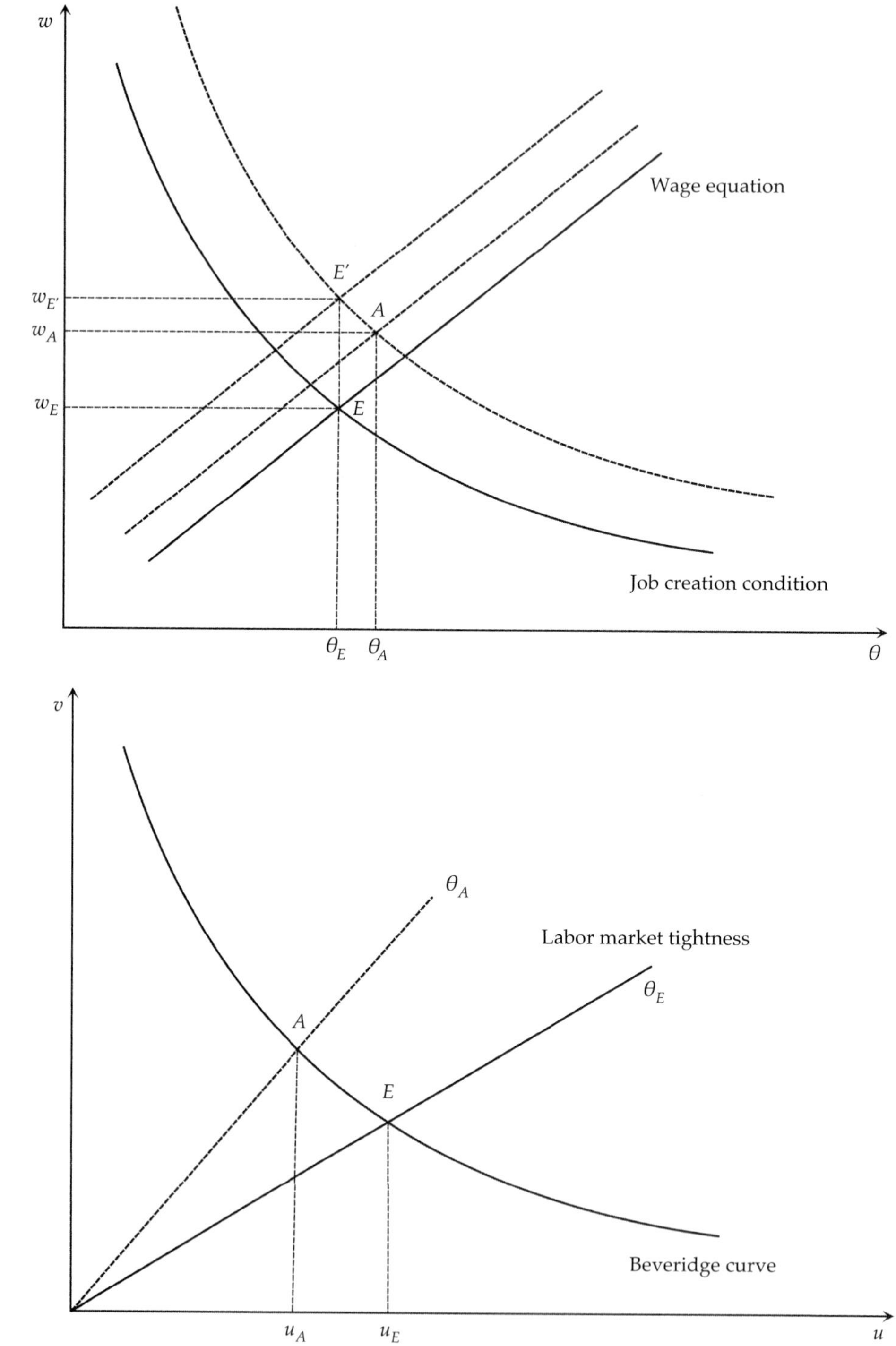

Figure 18.4
Labor productivity and equilibrium unemployment.

For a given labor market tightness, an increase (or fall) in labor productivity results in an equiproportional shift in the wage equation.

From the job creation condition (18.17), a rise in productivity also results in an equiproportional shift in the real wage that satisfies the job creation condition for a given labor market tightness.

This case is also presented in figure 18.4. An increase in labor productivity moves the wage equation and the job creation condition by the same proportion, thus increasing real wages without affecting the degree of labor market tightness. Consequently, the unemployment rate is not affected by an increase in labor productivity in the case where the unemployment benefit is proportional to real wages.

Another way to see the independence of labor market tightness from labor productivity when the unemployment benefit is proportional to the real wage is to equate the right-hand sides of (18.17) and (18.33):

$$1-\frac{(r+\lambda)c}{q(\theta)}=\frac{\beta(1+c\theta)}{1-(1-\beta)\rho}. \tag{18.35}$$

Equation (18.35) implies that in equilibrium, labor market tightness is independent of labor productivity. As a result, the unemployment rate will also be independent of labor productivity.

The independence of labor market tightness (and therefore the equilibrium unemployment rate) from average labor productivity is a desirable property, because unemployment rates do not display a long-term trend, as would be the case if they depended on increases in labor productivity, which have an upward long-term trend.

18.7.2 An Increase in Unemployment Benefits

We can also examine the implications of an increase in unemployment benefits z (or in the case $z=\rho w$, an increase in the replacement rate ρ). This causes an increase in real wages, reduces labor market tightness, and results in higher equilibrium unemployment.

The relevant analysis is shown in figure 18.5. An increase of z (or ρ in the case $z=\rho w$) shifts the wage equation upward, because prospective workers demand higher wages, given that the cost of unemployment is now lower.

When wages are higher, firms create fewer jobs through the job creation condition. Consequently, the unemployment rate increases, and the vacancy rate decreases.

An increase of β, the relative bargaining power of job seekers, would have the same impact for similar reasons. Real wages rise, and labor market tightness is reduced. Consequently, the unemployment rate rises, and the vacancy rate decreases from the Beveridge curve.

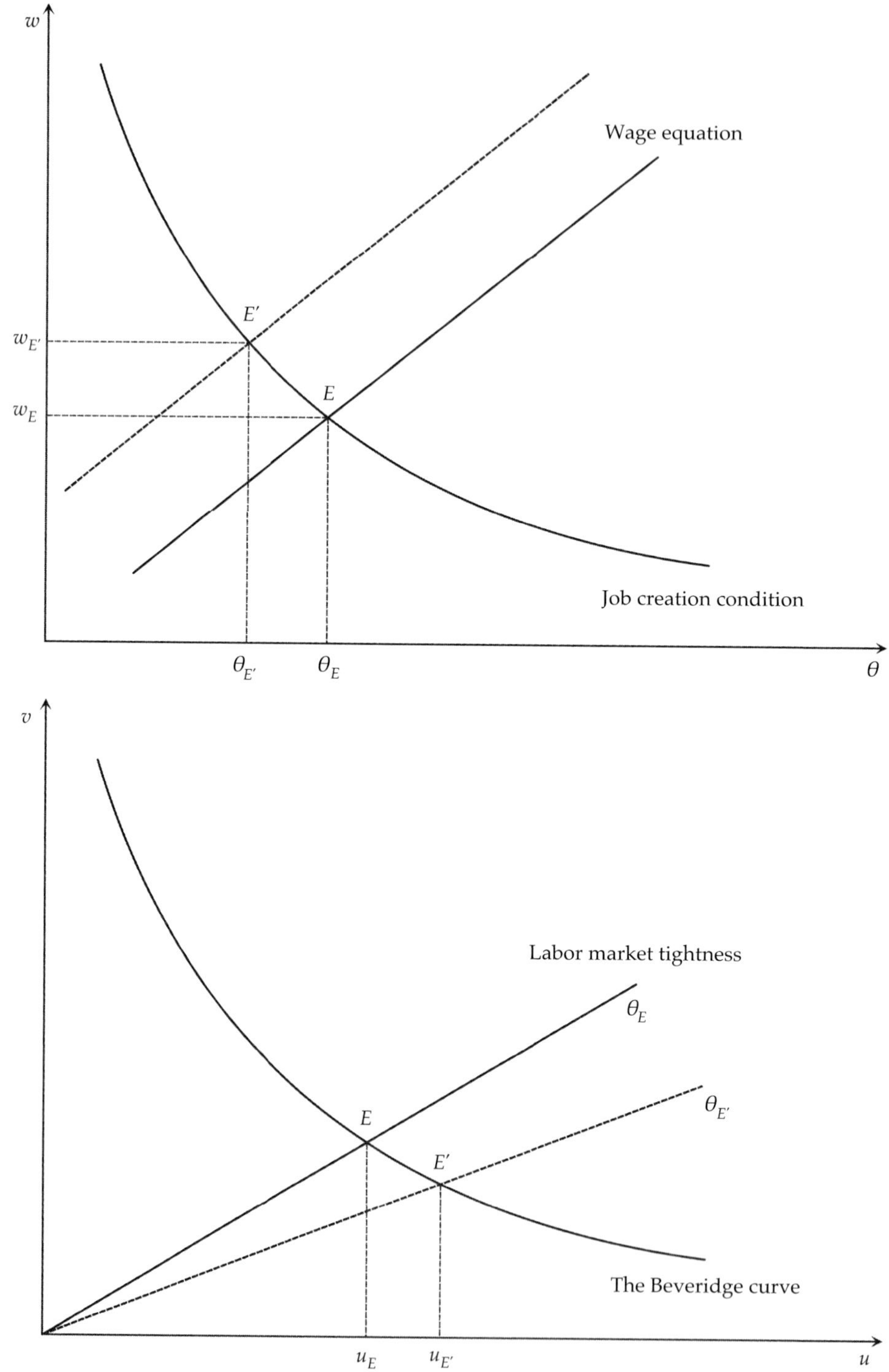

Figure 18.5
Unemployment benefits and equilibrium unemployment.

18.7.3 An Increase in the Real Interest Rate

Figure 18.6 shows the impact of an exogenous increase in the real interest rate. An increase in the real interest rate shifts the job creation condition in figure 18.6 to the left, as it increases the cost of maintaining vacancies. This results in a reduction of both real wages and labor market tightness.

The reason is that with a higher real interest rate, expected future revenues from the creation of a new job have a lower present value, but the cost of creating the new job is paid up front. Therefore, there is less of an incentive to create new jobs. The fall in labor market tightness naturally leads to an increase in the unemployment rate through the Beveridge curve (figure 18.6b).

18.7.4 An Increase in the Probability of Job Destruction

Finally, let us analyze the implications of an increase in λ, the exogenous probability of termination of a job. This case is depicted in figure 18.7.

An increase in λ leads to a reduction in real wages and labor market tightness, because it reduces the expected revenue from the creation of a new job. Consequently, fewer job vacancies are created, labor market tightness is reduced, and flows from unemployment to jobs decrease. This leads to an increase in the unemployment rate (figure 18.7, top).

In this case, equilibrium unemployment also increases, because flows into unemployment also rise. An increase in λ shifts the Beveridge curve to the right (figure 18.7, bottom), as flows from existing jobs to unemployment rise. Consequently, equilibrium unemployment increases both because of the increase of flows from employment to unemployment (resulting directly from the rise of λ) and because of the decrease of flows from unemployment to jobs (resulting from the fall in labor market tightness θ). The impact of an increase in λ on the equilibrium vacancy rate is uncertain, because it depends on the exact values of the parameters of the model.

Thus, the theoretical analysis implies an increase in equilibrium unemployment following a rise in unemployment benefits (or the replacement ratio), real interest rates, and the probability of job destruction. The reason is that all these shocks reduce labor market tightness and the vacancy rate, reducing flows from unemployment to jobs. In addition, an increase in the probability of job destruction also increases flows from jobs to unemployment, further increasing equilibrium unemployment.

18.8 Dynamic Adjustment to the Steady State

Our analysis so far has concentrated on the determination of equilibirum, or steady state, unemployment; almost nothing has been said about the dynamic adjustment of the labor market in the short run. The dynamic adjustment of this model is analyzed in Pissarides [1985, 2000].

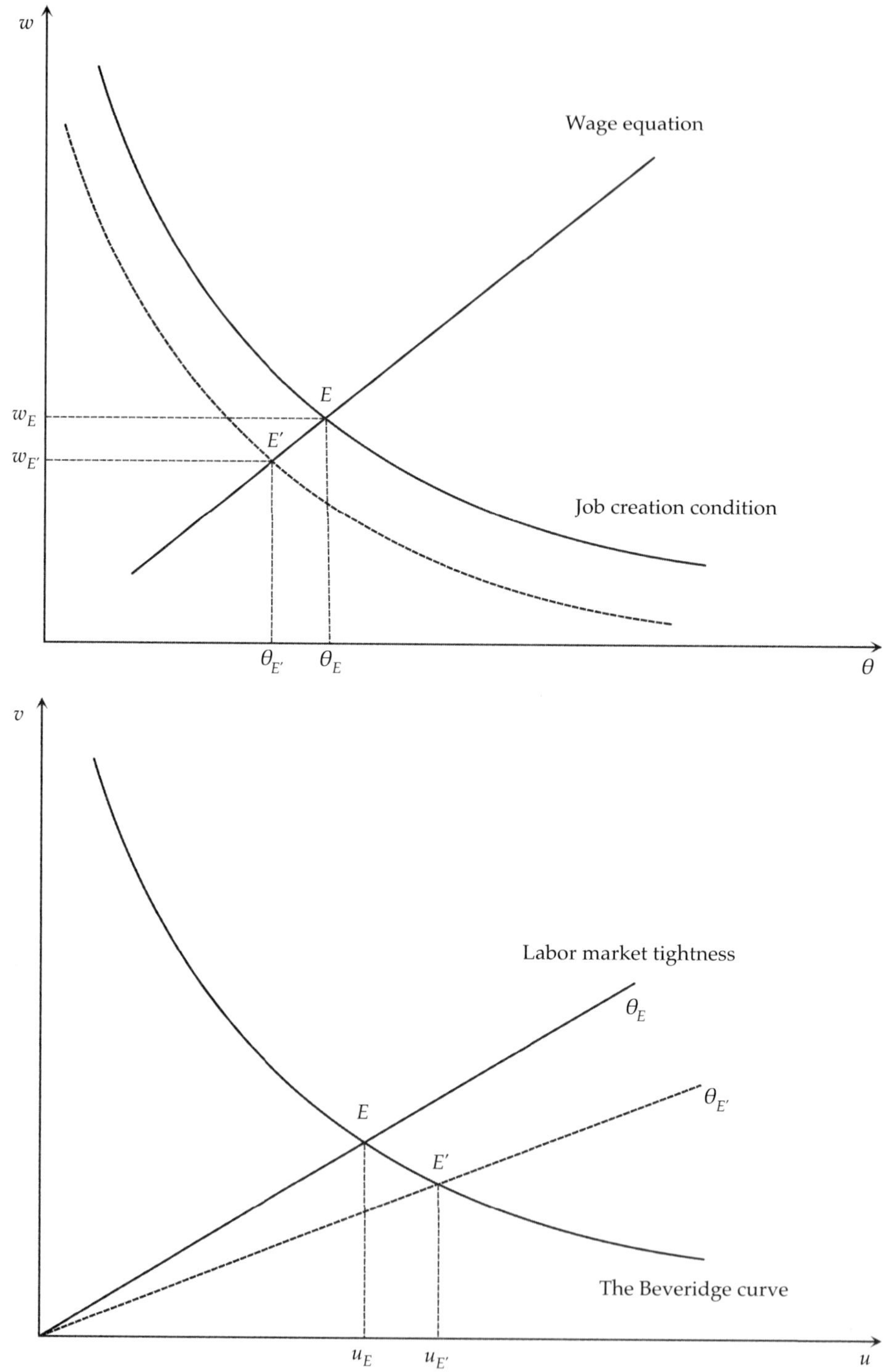

Figure 18.6
The real interest rate and equilibrium unemployment.

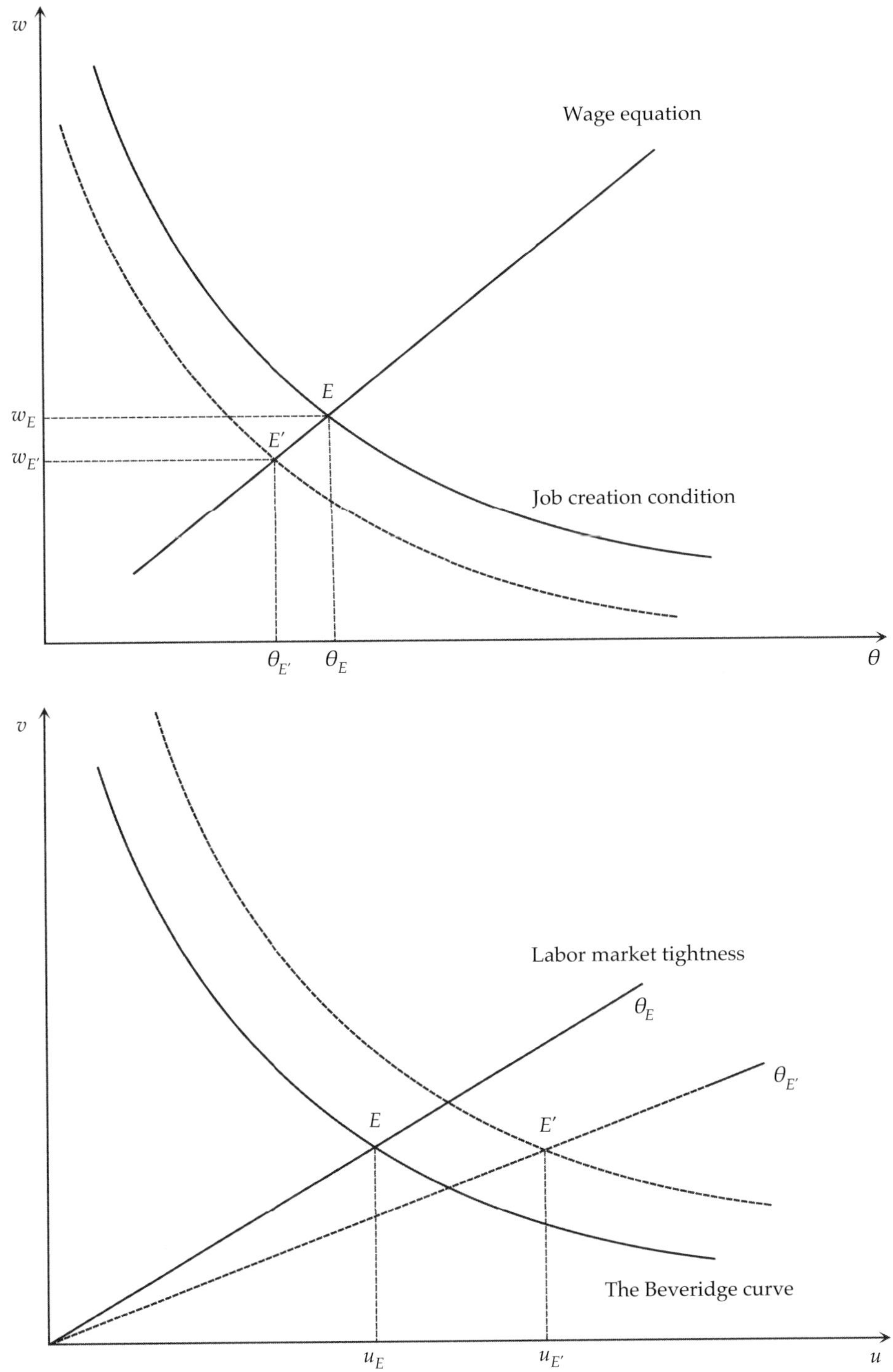

Figure 18.7
The probability of job destruction and equilibrium unemployment.

Assume that vacancies and real wages are non-predetermined variables, because they depend on forward-looking expectations of firms and job seekers. Also assume that unemployment is a predetermined variable, governed by equation (18.6). Then we can show that there is a unique saddle path that leads unemployment to its equilibrium or steady state value.

18.8.1 The Dynamic Adjustment of Unemployment and Vacancies

From (18.6), the unemployment rate evolves according to

$$\dot{u}(t) = \lambda - (\lambda + \theta_E q(\theta_E))u(t), \tag{18.36}$$

where θ_E is the equilibrium labor market tightness determined through the wage negotiations of firms with vacancies and unemployed job seekers, which was analyzed in the previous sections. Because vacancies are a non-predetermined variable, and θ is determined independently of the unemployment rate, θ and real wages w jump immediately to their equilibrium values.

From the solution of the differential equation (18.36), the short-run evolution of unemployment is determined by

$$u(t) = u_E + (u_0 - u_E)e^{-(\lambda+\theta_E q(\theta_E))t}, \tag{18.37}$$

where u_0 is the unemployment rate at time 0, and u_E is the steady state unemployment rate, defined as

$$u_E = \frac{\lambda}{\lambda + \theta_E q(\theta_E)}. \tag{18.38}$$

From (18.37), the unemployment rate will converge to its steady state value from any initial rate, with a speed of adjustment equal to $\lambda + \theta_E q(\theta_E)$. Thus, the model predicts a stable and unique adjustment path for unemployment, following any shock that changes the steady state (natural) unemployment rate.[7]

Because θ_E remains constant along the adjustment path, vacancies will be adjusting at the same rate as unemployment along the adjustment path, implying that

$$\dot{v} = \theta_E \dot{u}. \tag{18.39}$$

The relevant phase diagram in vacancy-unemployment space is shown in figure 18.8. We assume that the labor market is originally in steady state equilibrium (v_0, u_0), and there is a unanticipated permanent shock that changes θ to θ_E. We assume that θ_E implies a higher

7. Note that for the parameter values used in our reference simulation in subsection 18.8.2, the speed of adjustment is equal to 0.49, implying that it takes approximately 1 year to close half of the gap between current and equilibrium unemployment.

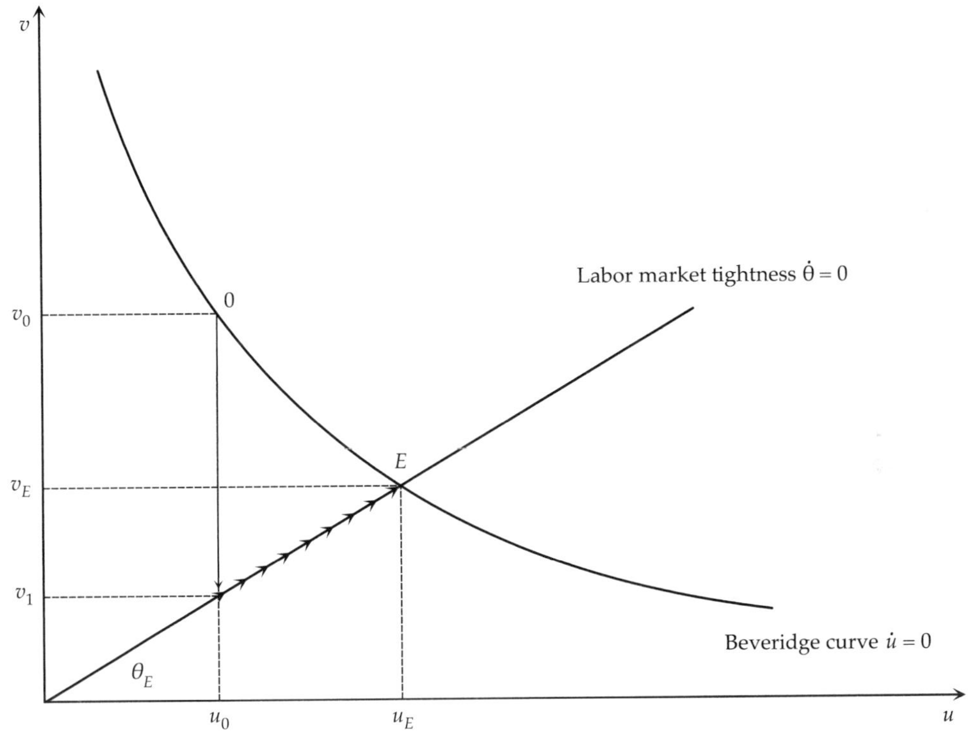

Figure 18.8
Dynamic adjustment of unemployment and vacancies.

steady state unemployment rate u_E and a lower steady state vacancy rate v_E. How will the labor market adjust?

As can be seen from the phase diagram in figure 18.8, vacancies, which are the non-predetermined variable, will jump from v_0 to v_1. There will be an immediate drop in vacancies to ensure that labor market tightness jumps to its new steady state value. Following that, both the unemployment rate and the vacancy rate will gradually adjust upward toward their new steady state values, as described by the differential equations (18.33) and (18.36). Because the unemployment rate is a predetermined variable, the non-predetermined vacancy rate initially overshoots its steady state drop.

Thus, this model explains not only the steady state unemployment rate (i.e., the natural rate of unemployment) but also the dynamic adjustment process of the unemployment rate toward its natural rate, following shocks to the determinants of equilibrium wages and equilibrium tightness in the labor market.

The model has been extended, and applied and tested extensively. An early test the model for unemployment in Britain is in Pissarides [1986]. Blanchard and Diamond [1989,

1990] and Shimer [2005], among others, have estimated and tested the model for US data, with generally mixed results. Merz [1995] and Andolfatto [1996] have introduced the model into an RBC framework with intertemporal substitution of leisure and capital accumulation.

18.8.2 Numerical Simulations of the Model

To get a quantitative sense of the extent to which shifts in the various parameters affect the equilibrium unemployment rate, real wages, and labor market tightness, it is worth simulating the model numerically. The simulations presented here assume that the matching function is Cobb-Douglas with constant returns to scale and is described by

$$mL = M(uL)^{\mu}(vL)^{1-\mu}, \tag{18.40}$$

where $M > 0$ is the efficiency of the matching process, and $0 < \mu < 1$ is the elasticity of job creation with respect to unemployment.

From (18.40), the probability of filling a vacancy is determined by

$$q(\theta) = \frac{mL}{vL} = M\left(\frac{u}{v}\right)^{\mu} = M\theta^{-\mu}. \tag{18.41}$$

Substituting (18.41) in the Beveridge curve (18.8) and the job creation condition (18.17), the model takes the form

$$u = \frac{\lambda}{\lambda + M\theta^{1-\mu}}, \tag{18.42}$$

$$w = p - \frac{(r+\lambda)pc}{M\theta^{-\mu}}, \tag{18.43}$$

$$w = (1-\beta)z + \beta p(1+c\theta) = (1-\beta)\rho w + \beta p(1+c\theta). \tag{18.44}$$

The simulation assumes the following initial parameter values: $\lambda = 2.5\%, M = 1/2, \mu = 1/2, p = 1, c = 1/2, r = 3\%, \rho = 1/2$, and $\beta = 1/2$. Simulating the model for these parameter values, we get $w = 0.95, \theta = 0.85, u = 5.1\%$, and $v = 4.4\%$.

The real wage is 95% of productivity and the unemployment rate is relatively low at 5.1%. If the probability of job destruction λ were to double to 5%, then it follows that $w = 0.93, \theta = 0.79, u = 10.1\%$, and $v = 7.9\%$.

Relative to the original equilibrium, the real wage falls by 2.1%, to 93% of productivity, and the natural rate of unemployment almost doubles, to 10.1%.

The dynamic adjustment of the unemployment rate and the vacancy rate is depicted in figure 18.9. The vacancy rate initially falls and then starts rising as the unemployment and vacancy rates gradually rise toward their higher equilibrium values.

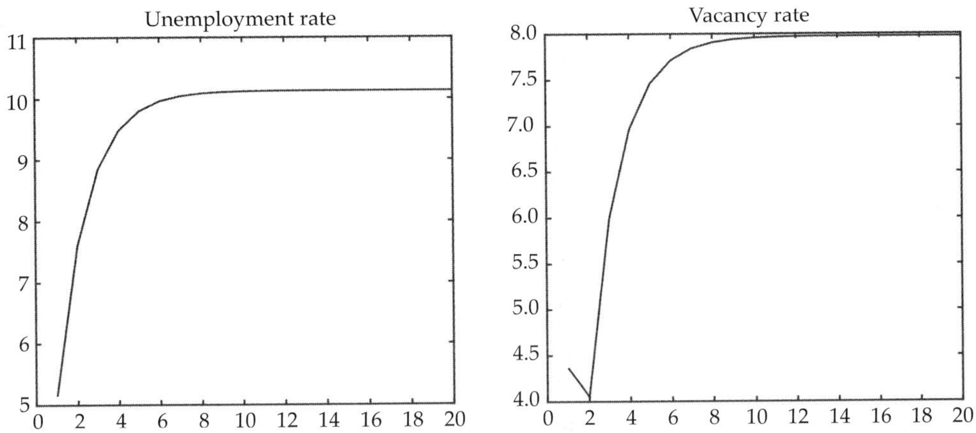

Figure 18.9
Dynamic adjustment of unemployment and vacancies to an increase in the job destruction rate.

If the replacement ratio ρ were to rise from 0.5 to 0.7 (a 40% increase), then it follows that $w = 0.96, \theta = 0.50, u = 6.6\%$, and $v = 3.3\%$.

Relative to the original equilibrium, the real wage rises by roughly 1%, and the unemployment rate rises by 1.5 percentage points, to 6.6%. With a constant labor force, this is equivalent to a 29.4% rise in the number of the unemployed.

The dynamic adjustment of the unemployment rate and the vacancy rate is depicted in figure 18.10. Note the overshooting of the fall in the vacancy rate, relative to its steady state fall, which conforms with the theoretical analysis in figure 18.8. Because of the fall in equilibrium labor market tightness, the vacancy rate initially falls. As the unemployment rate gradually rises toward its higher new steady state value, the vacancy rate gradually rises as well. Thus, the short-run reduction in the vacancy rate exceeds the steady state reduction.

Finally, if the real interest rate r were to double from the original 3% to 6%, it follows that $w = 0.925, \theta = 0.78, u = 5.4\%$, and $v = 4.2\%$.

Relative to the initial equilibrium, the real wage falls by about 2.5%, and the unemployment rate rises by 0.3 percentage points, to 5.4%. With a constant labor force, this is equivalent to a 5.9% rise in the number of the unemployed.

The dynamic adjustment of the unemployment rate and the vacancy rate is depicted in figure 18.11. Note again the overshooting of the fall of the vacancy rate.

We see from these simulations (for the specific values of the parameters chosen) that shifts in the probability of job destruction—as well as shifts of the replacement rate of unemployment benefits—have relatively large effects on the equilibrium unemployment rate and relatively small effects on real wages. However, changes in the real interest rate have a relatively modest effect on both real wages and the unemployment rate.

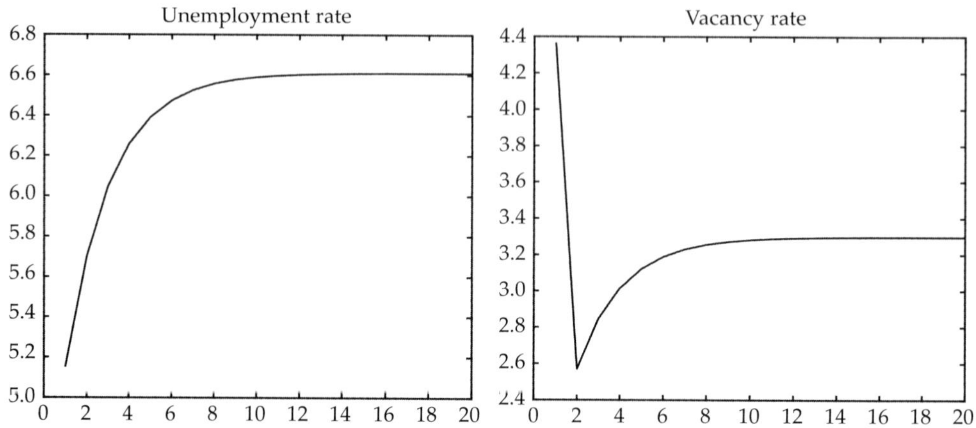

Figure 18.10
Dynamic adjustment of unemployment and vacancies to an increase in the replacement rate.

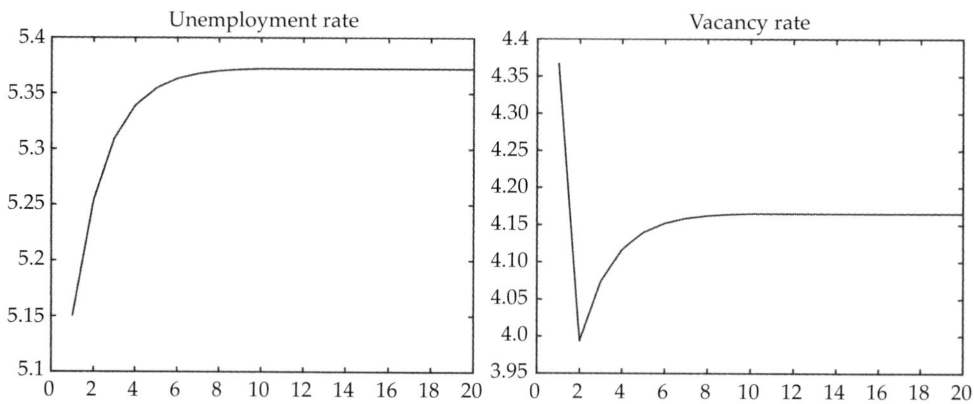

Figure 18.11
Dynamic adjustment of unemployment and vacancies to an increase in the real interest rate.

18.9 Matching Models and Nominal Rigidities

Various authors have attempted to embed matching models in the RBC framework or to incorporate new Keynesian nominal rigidities in matching models.

Merz [1995] and Andolfatto [1996] were the first to introduce labor market frictions in an otherwise standard RBC model. In both cases, the focus was on the dynamic effects of productivity shocks, and in both cases, the model was solved using simulations.

Cheron and Langot [2000], Walsh [2003], and Trigari [2006] have allowed for Calvo staggered pricing by firms, to study the effects of nominal shocks. Those models are also too large to be analytically tractable and so are solved using simulations. Walsh [2005],

Moyen and Sahuk [2005], Andres et al. [2006], and Trigari [2009], among others, introduce extensions that range from habit persistence in preferences, to capital accumulation, to the implications of Taylor rules. The models in these papers are relatively complex DSGE models, which need to be studied through calibration and simulations. Shimer [2005] and Hall [2005] were the first to introduce real wage ridigities. Shimer argued that, in the standard matching model with Nash bargaining, wages are too flexible, and the response of unemployment to productivity shocks is too small. Gertler and Trigari [2009] have explored the implications of introducing real wage staggering à la Calvo. Thomas [2008] and Gertler et al. [2008] have explored models in a staggered nominal wage setting rather than real wage rigidity. Krause and Lubik [2007], Faia [2008], Christoffel and Linzert [2010], and Blanchard and Gali [2010] explore models with matching frictions and both real and nominal wage and price rigidities. More recently, Michaillat [2012] and Michaillat and Saez [2015] have introduced matching frictions in rationing models with nominal wage and price rigidities of the Barro and Grossman [1971] variety. With few exceptions (such as the Blanchard and Gali [2010] model), all these models are quite complicated and can only be solved by using numerical methods.

The quest to produce analytically tractable DSGE models that incorporate both matching frictions and nominal rigidities is an active area of current research.

18.10 Conclusion

In this chapter, we have examined the determination of equilibrium unemployment in a matching model on the labor market. In this model, employers are investing to create job vacancies, and the process of creating jobs involves matching firms that have vacancies with unemployed job seekers.

At each instant, there are two flows: into and out of unemployment. Some workers lose their jobs and move from jobs to unemployment, and some of the unemployed find jobs, through the matching process, with firms that have vacancies.

In the simpler versions of the model, the probability of job destruction is exogenous. This parameter describes the structural or cyclical shocks affecting the economy and leading to the destruction of jobs.

The probability of filling a vacancy, and the probability of an unemployed job seeker to find a job, are endogenous variables. They depend on the degree of labor market tightness, which is defined by the ratio of vacancies to the number of unemployed. The higher the tightness of the labor market is, the greater the probability that an unemployed job seeker will find a job, and the lower the probability that a firm will fill a vacancy.

In the steady state, the flows to and from unemployment are equalized, and the equilibrium unemployment rate (also known as the natural rate) depends positively on the exogenous probability of termination of a job and negatively on the endogenous probability of an unemployed job seeker finding a job. The equilibrium unemployment rate therefore depends negatively on labor market tightness and is, of course, determined endogenously. The negative relationship between the equilibrium unemployment rate and the vacancy rate implied by this dependence is known as the Beveridge curve.

Firms and the unemployed make their decisions rationally, maximizing the expected present value of their profits and income. Firms create new vacancies as long as the expected profits from the investment required to create a vacancy are positive. The condition for a vacancy to be filled (and for a new job to be created) is that the real wage should be equal to labor productivity minus the cost of creating and maintaining a vacancy. By filling a vacancy, in equilibrium a firm must cover both the wage costs and the costs of its investment in the creation of the vacancy.

The job creation condition implies a negative relationship between the wage that the firm is willing to pay and labor market tightness. The higher labor market tightness is, the lower will be the probability of filling a vacancy and the greater the total cost of maintaining a vacancy, because vacancies remain unfilled for longer.

In contrast, an unemployed job seeker will agree to a job offer if the expected present value of income of an employed worker is greater than the expected present value of income of an unemployed job seeker. This condition is satisfied in this model, as long as the real wage is higher than unemployment benefits.

Real wages are determined in equilibrium by decentralized bargaining between firms that have vacancies and unemployed job seekers. The equilibrium real wage is the result of this negotiation, and it depends positively on the relative bargaining power of the unemployed, the level of unemployment benefits, labor productivity, the cost of maintaining a vacancy, and labor market tightness. The equilibrium real wage depends positively on labor market tightness, because this increases the average recruitment cost per unemployed person, thereby increasing the threat point of prospective employees versus prospective employers and weakening the effective bargaining position of prospective employers.

The positive relationship between real wages and labor market tightness (resulting from the negotiation between firms with vacancies and the unemployed) and the negative relationship between real wages and labor market tightness (implied by the job creation condition for firms) jointly determine the equilibrium real wage and equilibrium labor market tightness. For given equilibrium labor market tightness, the equilibrium unemployment rate is then determined by the Beveridge curve, which implies a negative relationship between the unemployment and vacancy rates.

In the equilibrium of this model, the unemployed are worse off than the employed. Consequently, unemployment is an undesirable and involuntary condition and is not the result of choice by the unemployed, as in competitive models of the labor market without frictions.

If unemployment benefits are proportional to the real wage, labor productivity does not affect the equilibrium unemployment rate in this model.

However, the higher the percentage of real wages paid out as unemployment benefits is, the higher will be the equilibrium real wage and the equilibrium unemployment rate. The reason is that higher real wages reduce incentives for creating new jobs, thus reducing the number of vacancies, reducing labor market tightness, and increasing unemployment.

Higher real interest rates also have a positive impact on unemployment in this model, because they increase the cost of maintaining a vacancy, resulting in the creation of fewer job vacancies, lower labor market tightness, and higher unemployment.

A higher exogenous probability of job destruction has a positive impact on unemployment for two reasons: first, because it directly increases the flows from existing jobs to unemployment; and second, because it indirectly reduces the flows from unemployment to jobs. The second effect takes place because the expected profit from the creation and filling of a vacancy decreases, resulting in fewer vacancies and reduced flows from unemployment to jobs.

In this model, equilibrium unemployment depends both on cyclical and structural factors. Moreover, unlike the new classical model of real economic cycles (but like some versions of new Keynesian models), unemployment is involuntary in the sense that the unemployed would always prefer to be in jobs at prevailing real wages.

The adjustment path predicted by the model is stable, because following shocks to the determinants of equilibrium unemployment, the unemployment and vacancy rates follow a unique and stable adjustment path toward the new equilibrium.

Matching models have been incorporated in business cycle models with nominal rigidities, but the resulting models are quite complicated and can only be solved through the use of numerical methods.

19

The Macroeconomic Implications of Financial Frictions

Before the 2008–2009 crisis, financial market frictions were relatively downplayed in dynamic macroeconomics. The underlying assumption in most macroeconomic models (including the models we have analyzed in previous chapters) is that there are two financial assets, noninterest-bearing money and interest-bearing one-period bonds. The central bank is assumed to be able to control the interest rate on bonds through open market operations. This assumption essentially implies that all interest-bearing financial assets are perfect substitutes, and that all interest yields move together with the rate determined by monetary policy.

The financial crisis made it clear that this view is too simplistic. The financial system consists of a multitude of financial instruments (securities) with different risk characteristics and different maturities. In addition, financial intermediaries like banks are heavily leveraged, especially in a fractional reserve banking system. The bulk of the liabilities of financial intermediaries are in relatively safe short-term securities, whereas their assets are in riskier and longer-term securities. In addition, despite the increase in efficiency implied by the presence of financial intermediaries, frictions associated with transaction costs, risk sharing, and asymmetric information between borrowers and lenders persist. As a result, the financial system is subject to risks with major macroeconomic implications.

In this chapter, we briefly discuss the role of finance and financial markets; the nature and implications of financial frictions; and finally, introduce financial frictions in new Keynesian models with staggered pricing and nominal wage contracts to analyze their macroeconomic implications.

19.1 The Role of Finance and Financial Markets

Financial markets perform the essential economic function of channeling funds from households, firms, and governments that have surplus funds (from spending less than their income) to those with a shortage of funds (because they wish to spend more than their income). This could be either for consumption or investment purposes. In addition, financial markets pool different types of risk, reducing the average risk faced by lenders.

Finance can be either direct or indirect. In *direct finance*, borrowers borrow funds directly from lenders by selling them securities (also called financial instruments), which are claims on the borrower's future income or assets. Securities are assets for the lender but are liabilities for the borrower. Securities take the form of either bonds or stocks.

Bonds (and mortgages) are contractual agreements that require the borrower to pay the holder of the instrument fixed amounts at regular intervals (interest and principal payments) until a specified date (the maturity date), when a final payment is made. The maturity of a debt instrument is the number of periods (the term) until the instrument's expiration date. A debt instrument is considered short term if its maturity term is less than a year, and long term if its maturity term is 10 years or longer. Debt instruments with a maturity term between 1 and 10 years are said to be intermediate term. The yield of longer-term securities is characterized by higher interest rate risk, resulting in a *maturity premium*. The longer the maturity of a security is, the higher will be the average yield (return) of a security, even if the other risk characteristics of the borrower are the same.

Stocks are securities that entitle the owner to a share of a company's profits or assets. Equities often make periodic payments (dividends) to their holders and are considered long-term securities, because they do not have a maturity date. Owning common stock means that you own a portion of the firm, which gives you the right to vote on issues important to the firm and on the election of its directors.

The disadvantage of being an equity holder is that you are a residual claimant (i.e., the corporation must satisfy debt holders before equity holders). As an equity holder, one benefits from an increase in the firms profitability, but one also loses from a decrease in the firms profitability. Bond holders receive fixed amounts. In the United States, the bond market is almost twice as large as the equity market.

Financial markets are organized in one of two ways: The first is through *exchanges*, where buyers and sellers of securities (or their agents or brokers) meet in one central location to conduct trades. The New York Stock Exchange (NYSE) and the Chicago Board of Trade for commodities are examples of such organized exchanges. The second is *over the counter (OTC) markets*, where dealers in different locations stand ready to buy and sell securities. OTC markets rely on electronic communication systems, trades and prices are known to everybody, and such markets are thus very competitive.

Many stocks are traded OTC, but the majority of the large corporations have their shares traded at organized stock exchanges. However, the US government bond market, with a trading volume larger than that of the NYSE, is entirely OTC. There are about 40 dealers who establish the market in US government securities, standing ready to buy or sell. Other types of securities (such as negotiable securities of deposit, federal funds, and foreign exchange) are also traded in OTC markets.

By allowing funds to move from those who have no use for them to those who have, financial markets thus contribute to an efficient allocation of resources that increases economic welfare.

In indirect finance, financial intermediaries stand between lenders-savers and borrowers-spenders and help transfer funds from one group to the other. In fact, financial intermediation is the main route for moving funds from lenders to borrowers and is mainly conducted by depository institutions (commercial banks, savings and loans associations, mutual savings banks, and credit unions), by contractual savings institutions (life insurance companies, pension funds, and government retirement funds), and by investment intermediaries (finance companies, mutual funds, hedge funds, and investment banks). To understand the role and significance of financial intermediation, one must understand the role of *financial market frictions*, such as transaction costs, risk sharing, and information costs in financial markets.

19.1.1 Financial Frictions and Financial Intermediation

Financial intermediation implies lower transaction costs because of specialization, economies of scale, and the provision of liquidity services. In addition, because of the scale of their operations, financial intermediaries can reduce the risk of lending by pooling different types of risk. Thus, they can transform individually risky assets into safer composite assets, through *diversification*. By holding a larger and safer portfolio of risky assets, financial intermediaries are thus able to offer savers a safer menu of assets at a lower cost than if savers tried to do the same on a smaller scale.

Another reason for the importance of financial intermediation is *asymmetric information*. Borrowers usually have better information than do lenders about the risk and return of the project they are about to undertake. In addition, lenders cannot usually monitor the behavior of borrowers after they have lent them the funds. Asymmetric information creates two types of problems: Adverse selection and moral hazard.

Adverse selection is the problem created by asymmetric information before the transaction takes place. Adverse selection occurs when the riskier borrowers (those more likely to produce an adverse outcome) are the ones more actively trying to secure a loan. Because of adverse selection, lenders may decide not to make any loans, although good credit risks exist.

Moral hazard is the problem created by asymmetric information after the transaction occurs. It is the risk (hazard) that the borrower might ex post engage in activities that are undesirable (immoral) from the view point of the lender, because they reduce the probability that the loan will be repaid. Hence borrowing and lending may break down because of this risk.

With financial intermediation, small savers can deposit their funds with the financial intermediary who, because of the specialization and the scale of their operations, have better means to address problems of asymmetric information by screening aspiring borrowers and monitoring the behavior of borrowers ex post. Thus, financial intermediaries can mitigate the problems of asymmetric information and thus expand the market. Yet the problems of adverse selection and moral hazard remain, although they may perhaps be less serious than in the case of direct finance.[1]

Most financial intermediaries provide a range of financial services to their customers. Banks take in deposits, offer loans, provide liquidity services through checking accounts, provide insurance services to their customers, and so on. Thus, financial intermediation also implies economies of scope.

Economies of scope create the potential for *conflicts of interest*, a type of moral hazard problem that arises when an agent has multiple objectives (interests), some of which conflict with one another. Conflicts of interest are more likely to occur when a financial institution provides multiple services.[2]

19.1.2 The Risks of Financial Intermediation, Leverage, and the External Finance Premium

Financial intermediation increases the efficiency of the financial system but is not without risks. For a start, the problems of asymmetric information remain. Intermediaries have better information about risks than do their lenders but worse information than their borrowers have. Asymmetric information is reduced but not eliminated. Hence, there is a need for government regulation to reduce the implications of problems of asymmetric information.

In addition, financial markets are vulnerable to systemic risks. A negative systemic shock can destabilize them, especially as financial intermediaries are usually highly leveraged, and there is a discrepancy between the maturity structure of the liabilities and the assets of financial intermediaries.

Leverage is defined as the ratio of assets to own capital. Leverage is simply the inverse of the capital ratio of a firm or a bank. Higher leverage increases the expected profitability of a bank, providing incentives for banks to be highly leveraged. Bank assets typically yield more than the cost of bank liabilities, like deposits, exactly because they are associated with longer maturities and higher risk. However, higher leverage increases the risk of losses for the bank, which may lower the value of its assets below the value of its liabilities and make the bank insolvent. The higher the leverage ratio is, the higher the risk of insolvency for banks will be. These risks apply in case there is a shock that reduces the return of their assets and at the same time shakes the confidence of lenders-savers, leading them to withdraw their deposits. In such a case, financial intermediaries may run into liquidity or solvency problems. Again, the possibility of such systemic risks creates the need for regulation, because in the absence

1. For one of the earlier analyses of the implications of adverse selection and moral hazard in financial markets, see Stiglitz and Weiss [1981].

2. For a comprehensive description and analysis of financial markets, see Mishkin [2016].

of effective regulation, adverse shocks may lead to a destabilization of the financial system and a full-blown financial crisis.[3]

A common way to introduce financial market frictions in theoretical models is to assume an agency problem between borrowers and lenders. There are two basic approaches: postulating some type of informational asymmetry that leads creditors to be more informed than borrowers, or assuming that it is costly for creditors to enforce certain contractual commitments made by borrowers. In either scenario, borrowers potentially can gain at the expense of lenders by acting strategically. Accordingly, rational lenders in this setting will impose constraints on the terms of lending, like credit limits, collateral requirements, and bankruptcy contingencies. Overall, the agency problem makes raising funds externally more expensive than using internal funds. Bernanke and Gertler [1989] call this difference the external finance premium. An increase in the external finance premium is a common feature of financial crises.

Key to the behavior of the external finance premium is the behavior of the borrower's balance sheet–chiefly, its leverage ratio. A stronger balance sheet, in the form of lower leverage, enables the borrower either to self-finance a greater fraction of a project or to provide more collateral to guarantee debt. This basic prediction that credit access improves with the strength of the borrowers' balance sheet is characteristic of many real-world financial arrangements, including restrictions that borrowers post down payments, post collateral, and meet certain financial ratios. In many of these cases, a borrower who is able to take a larger stake in the outcome of the project being financed will have a reduced level of agency conflict with the lender. The external finance premium declines as a consequence.

19.1.3 The Links between the Financial Sector and Real Activity in the Presence of Frictions

The link between borrower balance sheets and the external finance premium leads to mutual feedback between the financial sector and real activity. A weakening of balance sheets raises the external finance premium, reducing borrowing, spending, and real activity. The decline in real activity reduces cash flows and asset prices, which weakens borrower balance sheets, and so on.

This adverse feedback loop between the financial sector and real activity was first alluded to by Fisher [1933] in his debt-deflation theory of the Great Depression. It also played a key role in the Bernanke [1983] explanation of the Great Depression. Subsequent models include the financial accelerator model of Bernanke and Gertler [1989] and Bernanke et al. [1999], the model of bank runs of Diamond and Dybvig [1983], the credit cycle model of Kiyotaki and Moore [1997], and the leverage cycle model of Geanakoplos [2010]. Many derivative models of financial crises have evolved from these approaches to modeling financial frictions.

3. See Geanakoplos [2010] for the role of leverage in financial crises.

This earlier literature had focused largely on constraints faced by nonfinancial firms. In the crisis of 2008–2009, however, it was mainly highly leveraged households and banks that were initially vulnerable to financial distress. Following the crisis, Justiniano et al. [2010], Eggerstsson and Krugman [2012], and Guerrieri and Lorenzoni [2017] incorporated balance sheet constraints on households. The distress in financial markets induced other studies, like Gertler and Kiyotaki [2011], He and Krishnamurti [2013], and Brunnermeier and Sannikov [2014] to incorporate balance sheet constraints on banks. In these studies, the financial accelerator mechanism remains operative, but the transmission of the crisis through the different sectors of the economy is much closer to what actually occurred. In fact, this combination of weak balance sheets and high external finance premia is characteristic of major financial crises. In effect, through its liquidity effects and the rise in risk premia, a financial crisis causes a reduction in aggregate demand and may tilt an economy toward recession.[4]

19.2 Financial Frictions in a New Keynesian Model with Staggered Pricing

In this section, we investigate the macroeconomic effects of a financial shock in the context of the new Keynesian model with staggered pricing. We introduce a financial shock, which, in the presence of financial frictions, results in a rise in the external finance premium. It is assumed that the real interest rate faced by private sector agents, such as households, is the safe real interest augmented by an external finance premium x.

The model consists of the new Keynesian Phillips and IS curves and a Taylor rule. It is the same as the model in chapter 16, although the interest rate relevant for private sector borrowing is no longer equal to the central bank real interest rate: Because of financial frictions, it equals the central bank interest rate augmented by an external finance premium x. For analytical simplicity, let us abstract from productivity shocks and monetary policy shocks, because their effects were analyzed in chapter 16.

The model can be written as

$$\hat{\pi}_t = \beta E_t \hat{\pi}_{t+1} + \kappa \hat{y}_t, \tag{19.1}$$

$$\hat{y}_t = E_t \hat{y}_{t+1} - \frac{1}{\theta}\left(i_t - \pi^* - E_t \hat{\pi}_{t+1} + x_t - \rho\right), \tag{19.2}$$

$$i_t = \rho + \pi^* + \phi_\pi \hat{\pi}_t + \phi_y \hat{y}_t, \tag{19.3}$$

4. A rough proxy for the external finance premium is the interest rate spread between the return on a private debt instrument (such as a corporate bond, a mortgage, or commercial paper) and a similar maturity government bond, which is considered to be the safe asset. These spreads tend to widen across the board during recessions and did so dramatically during the 2008–2009 crisis. Gertler and Gilchrist [2018] is a comprehensive survey of the more recent literature on the relation between financial frictions and financial crises.

where $\hat{\pi}_t = \pi_t - \pi^*$ and $\hat{y}_t = y_t - y_t^N$ denote the deviations between current and target (steady state) inflation and between the current (log) real output and its natural rate, respectively; and x_t is the external finance premium relevant for private borrowing. Thus, the real interest rate on the new Keynesian IS curve (19.2) is the central bank real interest rate, augmented by the external finance premium.

The external finance premium is assumed exogenous and temporary, following an AR(1) process of the form

$$x_t = \eta_x x_{t-1} + \varepsilon_t^x, \tag{19.4}$$

where $0 < \eta_x < 1$ is the degree of persistence of the external finance premium, and ε_t^x is a white noise shock to the external finance premium.[5]

Solving the model under rational expectations in the same manner as in chapter 16, we get that the closed-form solutions for deviations of inflation from its steady state level and deviations of output from its natural rate are given by

$$\hat{\pi}_t = -\kappa \Lambda_x x_t, \tag{19.5}$$

$$\hat{y}_t = -(1 - \beta\eta_x)\Lambda_x x_t, \tag{19.6}$$

where

$$\Lambda_x = \frac{1}{(1 - \beta\eta_x)(\phi_y + \theta(1 - \eta_x)) + \kappa(\phi_\pi - \eta_x)}. \tag{19.7}$$

The deflation and the recession occur despite the fact that, through the Taylor rule, the central bank reduces nominal interest rates. Substituting (19.5) and (19.6) in the Taylor rule (19.3), one can see that the nominal interest rate also reacts negatively to shocks in the external finance premium. However, this reaction is not in general sufficient to neutralize this financial shock:

$$i_t = \rho + \pi^* - \left(\phi_\pi \kappa + \phi_y(1 - \beta\eta_x)\right) \Lambda_x x_t. \tag{19.8}$$

Thus, a financial crisis that raises the external finance premium will cause a fall in inflation and a recession, despite the reduction of nominal interest rates through the Taylor rule.

The typical Taylor rule is clearly suboptimal in the case where a recession is due to financial frictions. The optimal response would have required an infinitely large response of

5. By assuming an exogenously driven external finance premium, we abstract from the possible interdependence of the external finance premium and the state of the economy. In a more comprehensive general equilibrium model of the determination of the external finance premium, one expects that the state of the economy would also affect it. For example, a recession caused by a rise in the external finance premium would tend to raise it through the induced deterioration of private sector balance sheets.

interest rates to deviations of inflation from target, or deviations of output from its natural rate. For example, as ϕ_π tends to infinity, Λ_x tends to zero, and the shock to the external finance premium is completely neutralized, as it does not affect either inflation or output. Thus, in the case of financial frictions, the optimal monetary policy response is the Fisher [1919] response of completely stabilizing inflation at the target inflation rate π^*.[6]

It is also straightforward to prove that higher persistence in the shock to the external finance premium implies both a higher and more persistent deflation and recession under the Taylor rule.

Finally, the real effects of a financial crisis would not occur in a model without nominal rigidities, as for example, the new classical model of chapter 14.[7]

Exercise 19.1 Derive the rational expectations solution of the model consisting of equations (19.1)–(19.4), and prove the results discussed in the text.

Exercise 19.2 In the model consisting of equations (19.1)–(19.4), replace the exogenous process of the external finance premium by the following process:

$$x_t = -\chi \hat{y}_{t-1} + \varepsilon_t^x,$$

where $0 < \chi < 1$, and ε_t^x is a white noise process. Derive the rational expectations solution of the resulting model. How would you interpret the feedback loop between deviations of output from its natural rate and the external finance premium? Discuss your findings.

19.3 Financial Frictions in a Model with Unemployment Persistence and Nominal Wage Contracts

In this section, we introduce financial frictions in the form of an exogenous external finance premium in the model of nominal wage contracts of chapter 17. Assume that prices are fully flexible, but nominal wage contracts are predetermined. We explore the rational expectations solution of the model and analyze the macroeconomic effects of financial frictions. We will see that only unanticipated shocks to the external finance premium affect aggregate

6. However, this policy may not be feasible in the presence of a zero lower bound on interest rates. In such a case, the central bank cannot reduce nominal interest rates below zero, and thus cannot counteract a large enough contractionary financial shock. We shall discuss this case in chapter 20 on the role of monetary policy.

7. Christiano et al. [2014] introduce agency problems associated with financial intermediation into an extended, empirically estimated new Keynesian model of business cycles. Their estimates suggest that fluctuations in the severity of financial shocks account for a substantial portion of business cycle fluctuations over the past two and a half decades. These results highlight the importance of financial shocks for aggregate fluctuations beyond the financial crisis of 2008–2009.

fluctuations in this model. The reason is that anticipated shocks cause wage setters to adjust wages in advance, to counteract the effects of financial shocks on output and employment. Yet deviations of output and unemployment from their natural rates persist, as the degree of persistence depends on the dynamics of the group of insiders.

The model is that presented in chapter 17, simplified so that there is no staggering of prices. It is described by

$$\hat{\pi}_t = E_{t-1}\hat{\pi}_t + \frac{\alpha}{1-\alpha}\left(\hat{y}_t - \delta\hat{y}_{t-1}\right), \tag{19.9}$$

$$\hat{y}_t = E_t\hat{y}_{t+1} + \frac{1}{\theta}\left(i_t - \pi^* - E_t\hat{\pi}_{t+1} + x_t - \rho\right), \tag{19.10}$$

$$i_t = \rho + \pi^* + \phi_\pi\hat{\pi}_t + \phi_y\hat{y}_t. \tag{19.11}$$

Equation (19.9) is the expectations-augmented Phillips curve in the presence of one-period nonindexed wage contracts set by labor market insiders; (19.10) is the new neoclassical synthesis IS curve, determining the demand for output; and (19.11) is the Taylor rule for the determination of the central bank interest rate. In these equations, $\hat{\pi}_t$ denotes deviations of current inflation from the central bank target π^*, and $\hat{y}_t$ denotes deviations of output from its natural rate.

We have simplified the model by abstracting from productivity shocks and shocks to the interest rate rule of the central bank, to concentrate on shocks to the external finance premium x_t. In the model, ρ is the pure rate of time preference, which, in the absence or productivity shocks, is assumed to be equal to the natural real rate of interest, and $1/\theta$ is the intertemporal elasticity of substitution of consumption. The other parameters are as defined in chapter 17. The process determining x_t is given by equation (19.4). Thus, the external finance premium is assumed to follow a zero-mean stationary AR(1) process, as in section 19.1.

The rational expectations solution of the model is straightforward and can be derived in the same way as for the solution in chapter 17. Deviations of inflation from the central bank target and deviations of output from its natural rate are given by

$$\hat{\pi}_t = \delta\hat{\pi}_{t-1} - \psi\varepsilon_t^x, \tag{19.12}$$

$$\hat{y}_t = \delta\hat{y}_{t-1} - \frac{(1-\alpha)\psi}{\alpha}\varepsilon_t^x, \tag{19.13}$$

where

$$0 < \psi = \frac{1}{\phi_\pi\left(1 + \frac{(1-\alpha)(\theta(1-\delta)+\phi_y)}{\alpha(\phi_\pi-\delta)}\right)} < 1. \tag{19.14}$$

In this model, and in the absence of staggered pricing, it is only unanticipated financial shocks that cause negative deviations of inflation from the central bank target and of output from its natural rate. However, the effects of such shocks persist, as they are propagated by the degree of employment persistence δ, which also determines the persistence of output and unemployment from their natural rates.

Obviously, unemployment is also affected by financial shocks in this model. Using the Okun-type relation (17.41), linking deviations of output from its natural rate to deviations of unemployment from its own natural rate, we get the following relation linking financial shocks to fluctuations in the unemployment rate:

$$\hat{u}_t = \delta \hat{u}_{t-1} + \frac{\psi}{\alpha} \varepsilon_t^x. \tag{19.15}$$

Thus, financial shocks, such as shocks to the external finance premium, cause unemployment to rise relative to its natural rate. The rise in unemployment persists because of the degree of persistence in the labor market. The reduction of nominal interest rates through the Taylor rule is not a sufficient response to a financial crisis, as the optimal response would require an infinitely large response of interest rates to deviations of inflation from target, or deviations of output from its natural rate. For example, as ϕ_π tends to infinity, ψ tends to zero, and the shock to the external finance premium is completely neutralized—it does not affect either inflation or output. Thus, as in the case of the model with staggered pricing, the optimal monetary policy response to financial shocks is the Fisher [1919] response of completely stabilizing inflation at the target inflation rate π^*. However, this policy requires an infinitely elastic response of interest rates and may not always be feasible, especially in the presence of a zero lower bound on interest rates.

Exercise 19.3 In the model consisting of equations (19.9)–(19.11), replace the exogenous process of the external finance premium by the following process:

$$x_t = -\chi \hat{y}_{t-1} + \varepsilon_t^x,$$

where $0 < \chi < 1$, and ε_t^x is a white noise process. Derive the rational expectations solution of the resulting model. Derive the response of the unemployment rate to financial shocks, assuming the Okun relation (17.41). How would you explain the feedback loop between deviations of output from its natural rate and the external finance premium? Discuss your findings.

19.4 Conclusion

Understanding the role of financial markets, and financial frictions in particular, is crucial for acquiring a deeper understanding of the nature of aggregate fluctuations. Both the Great Depression of the 1930s and the Great Recession of 2008–2009 appear to have been caused by financial shocks, which propagated through financial and labor market frictions.

The 2008–2009 financial crisis has already led to a change in direction in the modeling of business cycles and views about the role of monetary policy. We shall return to these issues in chapter 20 on the role of monetary policy and chapter 23 on the state of macroeconomics and DSGE modeling.

20

The Role of Monetary Policy

Up to this point in our analysis, we have mostly treated monetary and fiscal variables as exogenous parameters or as determined on the basis of exogenously given policy rules. We have investigated how the parameters of policy rules affect the steady state, the convergence of economies toward the steady state, or fluctuations around the steady state.[1]

We now turn to a deeper discussion of the role of macroeconomic policy, starting with monetary policy. Monetary policy is crucial for the determination of the price level and inflation in both new classical and new Keynesian models. However, for new Keynesian models, monetary policy is also one of the important determinants of aggregate fluctuations in output and employment. And because of its flexibility relative to fiscal policy, it is probably the most important type of stabilization policy.

The analysis of monetary policy in the context of dynamic stochastic general equilibrium (DSGE) models allows us to focus both on the short- and long-run effects of policy, discuss the optimality or suboptimality of alternative policy rules, and consider how alternative institutional arrangements can result in the emergence of policy rules with different macroeconomic implications.

The design of policies that the monetary authorities should follow to control inflation and stabilize the real economy has always been one of the most important concerns of monetary economics and policymaking. There is wide agreement about the key macroeconomic objectives of monetary policy, which are none other than price stability and high and stable output and employment, but disagreements remain regarding the nature of appropriate policies.

1. For example, in chapter 6, we investigated the effects of fiscal policy variables, such as government expenditure, taxes, and government debt, on economic growth. In chapter 7, we investigated the effects of the money supply and monetary growth on economic growth and nominal variables, such as the price level, inflation, and nominal interest rates. In chapter 12, we investigated the implications of monetary growth and central bank interest rate policy on prices and inflation. In chapters 14–17, we investigated the effects of alternative rules for the money supply and nominal interest rates for aggregate fluctuations in real and nominal variables. In chapter 18, we investigated the effects of unemployment benefit systems on equilibrium unemployment. In most cases, the policy variables (or the parameters of the policy rules determining them) were treated as exogenous.

20.1 Rules versus Discretion in Monetary Policy

Disagreements over the appropriate design of monetary policy have existed at least since the nineteenth-century controversy between the *currency* and *banking* schools in the United Kingdom. Although both schools supported convertibility of paper currency to gold, the currency school argued that the quantity of money should vary exogenously, as if all money were gold, whereas the banking school argued for a more flexible approach to the determination of monetary policy. In many ways, the currency school was in favor of strict rules, whereas the banking school favored more discretion.

Although the British Bank Act of 1844 adopted the views of the currency school, the actual operation of monetary policy during the pre-1914 gold standard era entailed significant elements of discretion in the setting of interest rates. This orthodoxy was analyzed in successive editions of Mill [1848] and in Jevons [1875]. In addition, it was gradually recognized that, in periods of financial crisis, central banks should operate as *lenders of last resort* (Bagehot [1873]).

However, the orthodoxy was also challenged, in view of the trend decline of the price level during the gold standard period. Alternative academic proposals for monetary policy emerged toward the end of the nineteenth century, none of which questioned the convertibility of banknotes into precious metals, such as gold or silver. Jevons [1875] favored supplementing gold with indexation to prices, as did Marshall [1871, 1887]. Both Marshall and Edgeworth [1895] advocated symmetallism over the gold standard. Fisher [1896, 1911] put forward a radical academic proposal for the stabilization of the price level, rather than the gold price, as the main rule for monetary policy. Another such proposal was the Wicksell [1898] interest rate rule for changes in the nominal interest rate in accordance with deviations of the price level from a target price level. It is clear that the operation of the gold standard was not considered to be ideal by its contemporaries, and many alternative monetary policy rules were put forward.

Renewed arguments concerning the conduct of monetary policy emerged in the United States, during the operation of the prewar classical gold standard, but especially during and after the Great Depression. Fisher [1936] backed up his earlier proposal for a constant price level objective with a rule for 100% reserves behind bank deposits, and so did Simons [1936]. Simons argued forcefully for rules as opposed to discretion, and favored a fixed money supply rule, although he worried about shocks to the velocity of money. The Simons proposal was later updated by Friedman [1960], who argued for a fixed rate of growth of the money supply as the optimal rule for monetary policy.

After World War II, the dominant Keynesian approach favored a more discretionary monetary policy as discussed in chapter 15. However, the instability of the Phillips curve eventually tilted the discussion again in favor of rules, especially following the important contributions of Friedman [1968] and Kydland and Prescott [1977].

Another argument in favor of rules is the virtual impossibility of perfect knowledge about key parameters of economic models, the difficulties of estimating and forecasting the state of the economy, and the need for robustness. Discretion requires much more knowledge about the workings of the economy than we actually possess, in contrast to abiding by simple rules, as forcefully suggested by Meltzer [1987]. Among others, Orphanides [2003a] has formally investigated the implications of imperfect knowledge for monetary policy.

Very little disagreement exists today about the view that monetary policy should be determined on the basis of rules. Yet there is still a very lively debate about the appropriate design of such rules.[2]

Should rules be contingent on the state of the economy, as, for example, suggested by the Wicksell [1898] rule? Or should they be noncontingent, like the Fisher [1896] price level stabilization rule, or the Simons [1936]–Friedman [1960] rule for the money supply? Contingent rules allow for some flexibility in addressing shocks that affect aggregate fluctuations, whereas noncontingent rules do not.

Another longstanding debate has concerned the appropriate instrument of monetary policy. Should central banks control the money supply or nominal interest rates? In recent years, the debate has tilted in favor of interest rate rather than money supply rules, in view of the practice long followed by most central banks that have to deal with the practical difficulties in controlling (or even defining) the appropriate measure of the money supply.[3]

The literature on interest rate rules in the past 20 years has focused on the analysis of one particular such rule, the Taylor [1993, 1999] rule. This rule has been shown to describe the monetary policy of the United States and other advanced economies relatively well since at least the early 1980s, if not earlier. The Taylor rule, which is a generalized version of the contingent rule proposed more than a century ago by Wicksell [1898], is usually analyzed in the context of new Keynesian models of aggregate fluctuations, such as the models discussed in chapters 16 and 17. It has been compared to optimal monetary policy, and proposals have

2. See chapter 15 for a discussion of the rules versus discretion debate in the context of the Phillips curve. Fischer [1990] surveys the literature on rules versus discretion for monetary policy.

3. Chapters 12 and 15 introduced this discussion. The classic analysis of the appropriate choice of monetary instruments in a Keynesian model was Poole [1970], who conducted his analysis on the basis of the Tinbergen [1952]–Theil [1954] framework, which stressed the distinction between policy instruments and policy targets. Sargent and Wallace [1975] demonstrated that under rational expectations, a noncontingent interest rate target leads to price level indeterminacy and instability (see chapter 12). However, it is now accepted that this problem does not arise in the case of contingent interest rate rules that allow for the nominal interest rate to depend on the price level (McCallum [1981]), or to be a sufficiently sensitive positive function of inflation. See Woodford [2003a], chapter 1 and chapter 12, for the relevant arguments. In any case, central banks have been consistently using interest rates as their main monetary policy instrument. As noted by Bernanke [2006, p. 2], "In practice, the difficulty has been that, deregulation, financial innovation, and other factors have led to recurrent instability in the relationships between various monetary aggregates and other nominal variables."

been put forward for improvements in the choice of parameters and other characteristics of this particular rule.[4]

This chapter analyses the various issues concerning the appropriate design of monetary policy. To analyze monetary policy, let us use the periodic wage contracts model of chapter 17. This is an analytically tractable new Keynesian model in which nominal wages are set periodically by insiders in the labor market and are nonindexed. We shall use this particular model to discuss the question of rules versus discretion and the appropriate use of monetary policy instruments. We will also use it to analyze alternative rules and the design of optimal monetary policy.[5]

20.2 Rules, Discretion, and Credibility in a New Keynesian Model

Let us start with a simple version of the new Keynesian model based on periodic nominal wage contracts that we analyzed in chapter 17. The model can be summarized as follows:

$$\hat{y}_t = E_t\hat{y}_{t+1} - \frac{1}{\theta}(i_t - E_t\pi_{t+1} - r_t^N), \tag{20.1}$$

$$\pi_t = E_{t-1}\pi_t + \frac{\alpha}{1-\alpha}\hat{y}_t - \varepsilon_t^A, \tag{20.2}$$

where $\hat{y}_t = y_t - \bar{y}_t$ is excess output (i.e., the deviation of (the log of) real output from its natural rate), i_t is the nominal interest rate, π_t is the rate of inflation, $1/\theta$ is the intertemporal elasticity of substitution in consumption, $0 < \alpha < 1$ is the exponent of labor in a Cobb-Douglas production with labor as the only factor of production, r^N is the natural real interest rate, and ε^A is a white noise shock to productivity.

Equation (20.1) is the new neoclassical synthesis IS curve, determining aggregate demand, and (20.2) is an expectations-augmented Phillips curve.[6]

4. See Clarida et al. [1999], Woodford [2003a, 2011] Gali [2008, 2011a,b], and Taylor and Williams [2011] for surveys of the findings of this literature. Woodford [2003a] and Orphanides [2003c, 2008] survey the analysis of interest rate rules from Wicksell [1898] to Taylor [1993].

5. One could of course use the staggered pricing model of chapter 16 to analyze optimal monetary policy. For analyses of monetary policy based on this type of new Keynesian model, see Woodford [2003a] and Gali [2011b]. Central banks increasingly use empirically estimated generalized new Keynesian models with both price and wage rigidities to evaluate policy. Such models have been calibrated, estimated, and empirically implemented by Erceg et al. [2000], Smets and Wouters [2003, 2007], Christiano et al. [2005], and others. However, not all of these models are analytically tractable. Simpler models, such as the ones we utilize, are better for highlighting the theoretical basis of the mechanisms at work.

6. Equation (20.2) is the expectations-augmented Phillips curve derived in chapter 17, with the additional restriction of lack of persistence (i.e., by imposing $\delta = 0$).

To focus on the issue of rules versus discretion and simplify matters, assume that the central bank can use its monetary policy instruments to affect aggregate demand and therefore deviations of output from its natural rate.

Recall that in this model, the natural rate of output is lower than full employment output because of the behavior of labor market insiders. The deviation of full employment output from its natural rate is equal to

$$y_t^F - \bar{y}_t = (1-\alpha)(n-\bar{n}) = (1-\alpha)\bar{u}, \tag{20.3}$$

where $\bar{u}$ is the natural rate of unemployment, assumed to be sub-optimally high. If the natural rate of unemployment is positive, then deviations of full employment output from the natural rate of output are also positive.

From (20.2) and (20.3), we can see that deviations of current output from full employment output are determined by

$$\tilde{y}_t = y_t - y_t^F = \frac{1-\alpha}{\alpha}\left(\pi_t - E_{t-1}\pi_t + \varepsilon_t^A\right) - (1-\alpha)\bar{u}. \tag{20.4}$$

To further simplify the analysis, let us initially assume that there are no exogenous stochastic shocks. Thus the natural real rate of interest is constant at ρ, the pure rate of time preference, and the natural rate of unemployment is constant at $\bar{u}$.

In the absence of productivity shocks, the model can thus be written as

$$\pi_t = E_{t-1}\pi_t + \frac{\alpha}{1-\alpha}\hat{y}_t, \tag{20.5}$$

$$\tilde{y}_t = \hat{y}_t - (1-\alpha)\bar{u}. \tag{20.6}$$

Thus, (20.5) and (20.6) describe deviations of inflation from previously expected inflation, and deviations of output from full employment output, in terms of deviations of output from its natural rate and the natural rate of unemployment, assumed positive and constant.

20.2.1 The Social Welfare Loss from Inflation and Unemployment

To evaluate the welfare losses from deviations of output from full employment and from inflation, we need a criterion for social welfare. Assume that the present value of the expected social welfare loss from inflation and unemployment is given by

$$E_t \sum_{s=0}^{\infty} \beta^s \left(\frac{1}{2}(\tilde{y}_{t+s})^2 + \frac{\zeta}{2}(\pi_{t+s} - \pi^*)^2\right). \tag{20.7}$$

We thus assume that the one-period losses from inflation and unemployment are quadratic. We also assume that $\beta = 1/(1+\rho)$ is the discount factor, which depends on the pure rate of time preference ρ; that ζ is the weight of the inflation objective relative to the output objective in the social loss function; and that π^* is the optimal inflation rate. This social welfare function can be justified in terms of the suboptimality of deviations of output from full employment output, and the suboptimality of deviations of inflation from the optimal inflation target of the central bank.

Note that we have assumed that the central bank aims to stabilize output around full employment output and not the natural rate of output, which, because of the distortions in the labor market, is suboptimally low.

20.2.2 Monetary Policy under Discretion: The Problem of Credibility

Assume that the central bank chooses interest rates in each period to minimize the loss function (20.7), subject to system of (20.5) and (20.6) and taking the expectations of wage setters as given. Let us call this behavior the *discretionary policy*. From the first-order conditions for the minimization of (20.7) subject to (20.6), it follows that

$$\pi_t = \frac{(1-\alpha)^2}{(1-\alpha)^2+\zeta\alpha^2}E_{t-1}\pi_t + \frac{\alpha(1-\alpha)^2}{(1-\alpha)^2+\zeta\alpha^2}\bar{u} + \frac{\zeta\alpha^2}{(1-\alpha)^2+\zeta\alpha^2}\pi^*. \tag{20.8}$$

In rational expectations equilibrium, and because there are no exogenous stochastic shocks, actual and expected inflation will coincide. Thus, from (20.8), equilibrium inflation will be equal to

$$\pi^D = \pi^* + \frac{(1-\alpha)^2}{\zeta\alpha}\bar{u}. \tag{20.9}$$

Equilibrium inflation under discretion π^D will be higher than the optimal inflation rate π^*, which is the central bank's target.

In rational expectations, equilibrium output will also fall short of full employment output, because from (20.6), even when deviations of output from its natural rate are zero, deviations of output from full employment output will be negatively related to the natural rate of unemployment:

$$\tilde{y}^D = -(1-\alpha)\bar{u}. \tag{20.10}$$

Thus, equilibrium inflation will be constant and higher than the optimal central bank inflation target π^*. This is because of the incentives of the central bank to reduce unemployment below its natural rate. Inflation will be higher than the optimal inflation target π^*, because wage setters anticipate the incentives of the central bank to increase aggregate demand in order to reduce unemployment below its natural rate. Hence, they raise their inflationary expectations to a level where the central bank no longer has an incentive to create surprise increases in aggregate demand and inflation. Any inflation rate lower than π^D creates

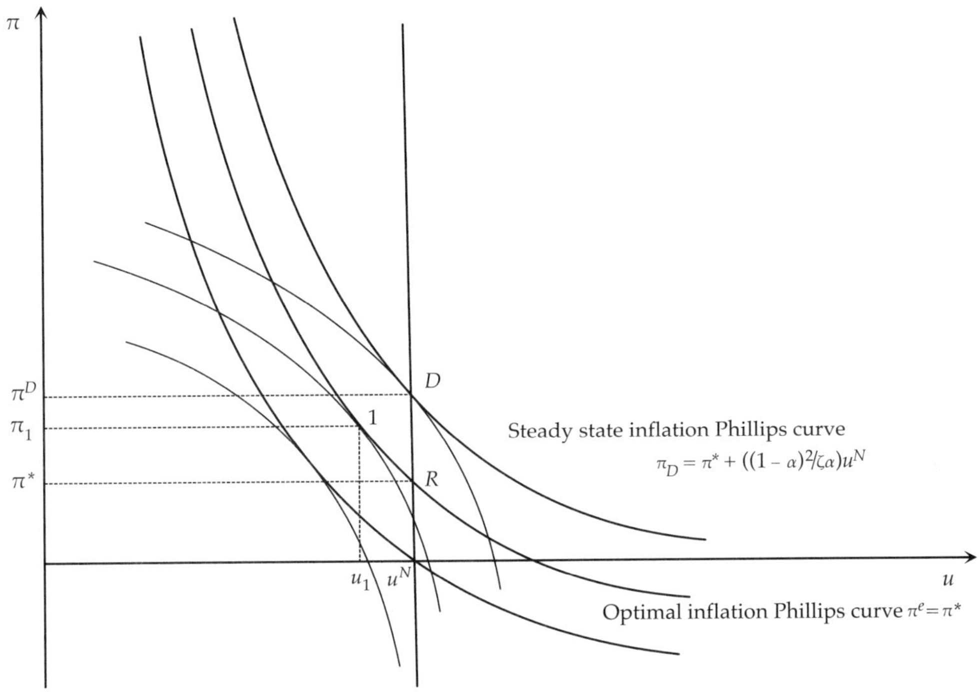

Figure 20.1
Inflation and lack of credibility under a discretionary policy.

incentives for the central bank to push inflation up in the short run, in order to reduce unemployment. Thus, an inflation rate below π^D lacks credibility.

Note that the equilibrium inflation rate depends on the parameter ζ of the social welfare function. The higher is ζ (i.e., the more the social welfare function penalizes inflation relative to output), the lower will be the inflationary bias of discretionary monetary policy. A lower ζ (i.e., a social welfare function that penalizes unemployment more than inflation) will result in a higher inflationary bias.

The inflationary bias of discretionary policy is depicted in figure 20.1. The equilibrium inflation rate under discretion is determined at the point where the highest possible indifference curve of the central bank is tangent to the short-run Phillips curve, at the natural rate of unemployment $\bar{u} = u^N$. Lower inflation rates lack credibility. Assume that the central bank announces that it will stick to an inflation rate equal to π^*. If wage setters believe it, the short-run Phillips curve will be the optimal inflation Phillips curve. If the central bank sticks to its announcement, the equilibrium will be at R, with inflation at π^* and unemployment at $\bar{u} = u^N$. However, under the discretionary policy, the central bank will maximize social welfare in the short run by raising inflation to π_1 so as to reduce unemployment to u_1, below the natural rate $\bar{u} = u^N$. Thus, the initial announcement lacks credibility. The only inflation rate that does not lack credibility is the rate π^D, at which the central bank has no further incentives to increase inflation in order to reduce unemployment.

Under discretion, the central bank does not achieve any of its social objectives. Output and unemployment remain at their natural rates below full employment. Equilibrium inflation turns out to be higher than the optimal inflation rate, because of the rational adjustment of the inflationary expectations of wage setters. As first pointed out by Kydland and Prescott [1977] and Barro and Gordon [1983a] using related models of the expectationally-augmented Phillips curve, if the natural rate of unemployment is inefficiently high, discretionary policy aimed at achieving full employment is characterized by an *inflation bias*. The discretionary policy results in an equilibrium inflation rate higher than the central bank target, without any effects whatsoever on equilibrium unemployment.[7]

The social welfare loss under the discretionary policy is given by

$$\Lambda^D = \frac{1}{2}\frac{(1-\alpha)^2}{1-\beta}\left(1+\frac{(1-\alpha)^2}{\zeta\alpha^2}\right)(\bar{u})^2 > 0, \tag{20.11}$$

where Λ^D denotes the discounted social welfare loss from inflation and unemployment under the discretionary policy.

To the extent that the natural rate of unemployment is inefficiently high, there will be a positive inflation bias in a discretionary monetary policy that aims for full employment. Monetary policy cannot permanently reduce unemployment below its natural rate.[8]

Policies other than monetary policy—such as labor market and tax policies, which can affect the natural rate of unemployment—may be used for that purpose.[9]

Note that this theory of inflation, which is generally considered to be the theory that explains the moderately high inflation rates in the industrial economies in the late 1960s and the 1970s, is different from the theories of high inflation based on the need for seigniorage revenues that we analyzed in chapter 12. Seigniorage-revenue theories of high inflation are generally considered to be more appropriate for economies with weak fiscal systems, such as some less-developed economies, or economies that have emerged from a major economic disruption (for example, a war).

7. As demonstrated in chapter 15, the same outcome would be a feature of an ad hoc model of an expectations-augmented Phillips curve under adaptive expectations. The only difference is that the process of convergence to the equilibrium with high inflation will take more time when expectations are formed adaptively. For a collection of early papers on the issue of credibility of monetary and fiscal policy, see Persson and Tabellini [1994a].

8. As noted by Friedman [1968, p. 13]: "Our economic system will work best when producers and consumers, employers and employees, can proceed with full confidence that the average level of prices will behave in a known way in the future—preferably that it will be highly stable."

9. For example, the Mortensen-Pissarides model that we examined in chapter 18 can be used to suggest some such policies. See Pissarides [2000].

20.2.3 Monetary Policy under a Fixed Inflation Rule

Let us now assume that, although the discounted social welfare loss is described by the loss function (20.7), the government instructs the central bank to follow a fixed inflation target, $\pi = \pi^*$ in every period, by following a rule that minimizes

$$\frac{1}{2}\sum_{s=0}^{\infty} \beta^s (\pi_{t+s} - \pi^*)^2. \tag{20.12}$$

From the first-order conditions for a minimum of (20.12), we have

$$\pi_t = \pi^*, \forall t. \tag{20.13}$$

Inflation is equal to the optimal inflation target rate in every period. Equilibrium output still falls short of full employment output, because it is determined as in (20.10).

The social welfare loss under the constant inflation rule is given by

$$\Lambda^R = \frac{1}{2}\frac{(1-\alpha)^2}{1-\beta}(\bar{u})^2, \tag{20.14}$$

where Λ^R denotes the discounted social welfare loss under the optimal inflation policy rule.

Thus, under a fixed optimal inflation policy rule, social welfare losses are lower than under discretion. There is an improvement in social welfare if the government instructs the central bank to follow the optimal inflation rule irrespective of unemployment. Inflation is at the socially optimal level π^*, and unemployment is at its suboptimally high natural rate, which is the case with the discretionary policy as well.

Although this is not a first-best outcome for the government, or society, it is better than the outcome under discretion, where unemployment is at its suboptimal natural rate anyway, and inflation is higher than optimal inflation. In the absence of alternative policies to reduce the natural rate of unemployment, the optimal monetary policy is the policy under the fixed inflation rule. This rule dominates discretion in the absence of shocks.

20.2.4 Central Bank Constitutions

The question of how to constrain the government to have the central bank follow such an optimal inflation rule (and thus not resort to the discretionary policy) can be addressed by appropriate amendements in the constitution of the central bank.

As Rogoff [1985] has shown, the optimal inflation rule can be implemented by creating a politically independent central bank that is constrained by its constitution to be concerned only with inflation and not with full employment. This can be formally modeled by modifying the loss function of the central bank in either of the following two ways.

The first is to allow the weight ζ on inflation relative to output in the preferences of the central bank to go to infinity. In this case, we end up with the independent central bank instructed to minimize the loss function (20.12), which only depends on inflation and results in the optimal policy rule (20.13).

The second is to modify the output objective in the loss function of the central bank. Instead of the central bank targeting deviations of output from full employment, it can only target deviations of output from its natural rate. The central bank does not seek to keep the economy at full employment, but only at its natural rate. In this case, the loss function minimized by the central bank takes the form

$$E_t \sum_{s=0}^{\infty} \beta^s \left(\frac{1}{2}(\hat{y}_{t+s})^2 + \frac{\zeta}{2}(\pi_{t+s} - \pi^*)^2 \right) \tag{20.15}$$

and is minimized subject to (20.5) rather than to (20.6).

From the first-order conditions for a minimum, we have

$$\pi_t = \psi E_{t-1}\pi_t + (1-\psi)\pi^*, \tag{20.16}$$

where

$$\psi = \frac{(1-\alpha)^2}{\zeta\alpha^2 + (1-\alpha)^2} < 1. \tag{20.17}$$

In rational expectations equilibrium, the inflation rate will be equal to

$$\pi_t = \pi^*. \tag{20.18}$$

Thus, an independent central bank that does not systematically try to reduce unemployment below its natural rate will implement the optimal monetary policy as well. This solution can also be implemented by appropriately modifying the constitution of an independent central bank, so that it will then be constrained to follow the optimal policy by minimizing the objective (20.15). This objective states that the central bank should aim for the optimal inflation rate π^*, unless unemployment deviates from its natural rate.

What is the difference between the objectives (20.12) and (20.15)? In the absence of stochastic shocks to inflation and unemployment, the two objectives lead to the same outcome: the stabilization of inflation at its optimal rate π^*. However, as we shall see below, in the presence of shocks that affect unemployment independently of inflation, the objective (20.15) allows for more flexibility. The central bank can react to shocks that cause deviations of unemployment from its natural rate, something that it would not be able to do if its constitution constrained it to maintain inflation at π^* under all circumstances.

20.2.5 Reputation as a Solution to the Problem of Inflationary Bias

Restrictive constitutions for central banks are not the only solution to the problem of the inflationary bias of discretionary monetary policy. An alternative is for the central bank to commit in advance to the optimal inflation policy π^* and to not succumb to the short-run incentives of following the discretionary policy. This way, the central bank will acquire an *anti-inflationary reputation*, although wage setters know that it has a short-run incentive to follow the discretionary policy. The solution based on the acquisition of an anti-inflationary reputation was first analyzed by Barro and Gordon [1983b]; Backus and Driffill [1985a, b], Tabellini [1985], and Barro [1986].

To analyze this reputational mechanism, we need to explicitly analyze monetary policy as a repeated infinite-horizon game between the central bank and wage setters in the labor market. In this game, the central bank chooses inflation, and wage setters choose their inflation expectations. Such repeated games have multiple equilibria. There are at least two possible equilibria in this case.[10]

The first is the *time-consistent equilibrium*, in which the central bank always follows the discretionary policy. The properties of this equilibrium are that unemployment is equal to its natural rate and inflation is higher than the optimal inflation rate, as in (20.9).

The second is a *time-inconsistent reputational equilibrium*, in which the central bank chooses to continuously follow the optimal inflation strategy (20.13), not succumbing to the short-run incentive to create surprise inflation in order to reduce unemployment below its natural rate. This equilibrium results in the optimal inflation policy, but it is time inconsistent, in the sense that the central bank always has a short-run incentive to depart from the equilibrium policy.

The question that naturally arises is: What is the mechanism that stops the central bank from departing from the reputational policy and reverting to the time-consistent policy, in the absence of a restrictive constitution? The short answer is the risk of the loss of its anti-inflationary reputation.

By sticking to the reputational policy, the gain for the central bank is the difference between the discounted future losses of the time-consistent policy and the reputational policy. From (20.11) and (20.14), this difference is equal to

$$\frac{1}{2}\frac{(1-\alpha)^4}{(1-\beta)\zeta\alpha^2}(\bar{u})^2. \tag{20.19}$$

Expression (20.19) is a measure of the welfare benefits from sticking to the time-inconsistent reputational policy rule. Thus, it measures the cost to the central bank of losing its anti-inflationary reputation.

Suppose that to reduce unemployment, the central bank succumbs to the short-run incentive to follow the time-consistent discretionary policy and thus creates surprise inflation. With inflationary expectations predetermined at π^*, the central bank would reduce

10. The analysis of the significance of reputational mechanisms in repeated games is due to Kreps and Wilson [1982a, b].

unemployment below its natural rate and would gain a one-period welfare benefit equal to

$$\frac{(1-\alpha)^2}{2}\left(\frac{(1-\alpha)^2}{(1-\alpha)^2+\zeta\alpha^2}\right)(\bar{u})^2. \tag{20.20}$$

Thus, if by departing from the optimal policy once, the central bank risked losing its anti-inflationary reputation forever, the net gain would be the difference between the one-period gain (20.20) and the discounted loss (20.19). This difference is equal to

$$\frac{(1-\alpha)^4}{2}\left(\frac{1}{(1-\alpha)^2+\zeta\alpha^2}-\frac{1}{(1-\beta)\zeta\alpha^2}\right)(\bar{u})^2, \tag{20.21}$$

which is always negative for a nonnegative pure rate of time preference, so the central bank would never depart from the reputational equilibrium in this model. The condition for (20.21) to be positive is $(1-\alpha)^2 < -\beta\zeta\alpha^2$, which cannot be satisfied. The threat of the loss of its anti-inflationary reputation forever is sufficient to sustain the reputational equilibrium in this case.

The reputational equilibrium can also be sustained by less extreme threats to the anti-inflationary reputation of the central bank. Thus, if the behavior of wage setters was such that the central bank lost its anti-inflationary reputation only for one period and not forever, then net the gain for the central bank would be equal to

$$\frac{(1-\alpha)^4}{2}\left(\frac{1}{(1-\alpha)^2+\zeta\alpha^2}-\frac{\beta}{\zeta\alpha^2}\right)(\bar{u})^2. \tag{20.22}$$

This would be positive if and only if

$$\frac{1-\beta}{\beta} > \frac{(1-\alpha)^2}{\zeta\alpha^2}. \tag{20.23}$$

The smaller the discount factor β and the higher the relative weight of inflation ζ in the social welfare function, the more likely it is that even the threat of a temporary loss of anti-inflationary reputation can sustain the reputational equilibrium. Thus, reputational mechanisms can also be a solution to the problem of the inflationary bias of monetary policy.

20.3 Optimal Monetary Policy in the Presence of Stochastic Shocks

Up to this point, our analysis of monetary policy has abstracted from the impact of exogenous stochastic shocks. In this section, we allow for the presence of such shocks in order to study the optimal reaction of monetary policy.

The new Keynesian model in the presence of stochastic shocks is described by (20.1) and (20.2). The unemployment objective of the central bank depends on deviations of unemployment from its natural rate. The central bank is thus assumed to choose monetary policy and the inflation rate so as to minimize (20.15), subject to (20.2). This choice would determine the optimal inflation rate. Substituting for the optimal inflation rate in (20.1), one could then determine the optimal path for the nominal interest rate.

From the first-order conditions for a minimum of (20.15) subject to (20.2), the optimal inflation rate satisfies

$$\pi_t = \psi E_{t-1}\pi_t + (1-\psi)\pi^* - \psi \varepsilon_t^A, \tag{20.24}$$

where ψ is defined by (20.17). From (20.24), it follows that

$$E_{t-1}\pi_t = \pi^*. \tag{20.25}$$

Substituting (20.25) in (20.24), we have that the rational expectations solution for optimal inflation is given by

$$\pi_t = \pi^* - \psi \varepsilon_t^A. \tag{20.26}$$

Thus, optimal inflation in the short run is not equal to π^* but also depends on supply shocks. As a result, the optimal monetary policy rule is a contingent inflation target, with mean π^*, but is also dependent on supply shocks. It reacts negatively (but less than one to one) to productivity (supply) shocks. The reason is that such shocks cause a discrepancy between real wages and productivity, because nominal wages are determined before current productivity shocks are known. The optimal reaction of inflation implies that real wages partly adjust to the productivity shocks, thus mitigating the impact of such shocks on deviations of employment and output from their natural rates. In this way, optimal monetary policy partly stabilizes fluctuations of employment and output around their natural rates by inducing appropriate short-run deviations of inflation around the target of the central bank.

Substituting (20.26) in (20.2), under the optimal policy, deviations of output from its natural rate are given by

$$\hat{y}_t = \frac{1-\alpha}{\alpha}(1-\psi)\varepsilon_t^A. \tag{20.27}$$

Thus, optimal contingent monetary policy is *second best* in response to productivity shocks. It cannot completely stabilize both inflation and employment, as it operates through aggregate demand, and productivity shocks are supply shocks that cannot be counteracted directly. Optimal monetary policy can only equate the marginal cost of deviations of inflation from target to the marginal cost of deviations of employment and output from their natural rates. However, in the presence of productivity shocks, this does not completely eliminate fluctuations in employment, output, and inflation.

From (20.17), note that ψ (the optimal response parameter to productivity shocks) depends negatively on ζ (the relative weight that the central bank and society attach to deviations of inflation from target, relative to deviations of output from its natural rate). The higher ζ is, the lower will be the optimal response of inflation to productivity shocks in (20.26), and the higher will be the impact of productivity shocks on fluctuations of output around its natural rate in (20.27).

Thus, in the presence of supply shocks, the optimal monetary policy rule faces a trade-off between the stabilization of inflation at its optimal level π^* and the stabilization of output and employment at their natural rates. One instrument, the nominal interest rate or the money supply, which operates through aggregate demand, does not suffice to achieve both objectives in the presence of supply shocks. The central bank has to resolve this trade-off by choosing a policy that equates the marginal social cost of deviations of inflation from its optimal level to the marginal social cost of deviations of output and employment from their natural rates.

20.4 The Mechanics of Monetary Policy

Up to now we have been assuming that the central bank has been determining inflation by appropriate use of its monetary policy instruments. However, we have not specified the relation between inflation and the monetary policy instruments.

As discussed in chapter 12, the two main instruments of monetary policy are the money supply and the nominal interest rate. These two instruments are not independent, but are related through the money demand function. Thus, if the central bank wishes to achieve a given nominal interest rate target, it must be prepared to supply the stock of money (liquidity) demanded at this nominal interest rate. If the central bank wishes to achieve a given target for the stock of money, then it must be prepared to accept the nominal interest rate that equates the demand with the supply of money.

We have already referred to the classic analysis of the appropriate choice of monetary instrument by Poole [1970] and the demonstration by Sargent and Wallace [1975] that, under rational expectations, a noncontingent interest rate target leads to price level indeterminacy and instability. We have also discussed why this problem does not arise in the case of contingent interest rate rules that make the nominal interest rate depend on the price level (McCallum [1981]), or a sufficiently sensitive positive function of inflation in the context of a Wicksell [1898] or Taylor [1993] rule.[11]

11. See chapter 12, or Woodford [2003a, chapter 1] for the relevant arguments.

In any case, central banks have been consistently using interest rates as their main monetary policy instrument.[12] In the light of this fact, we shall confine our analysis of monetary policy to contingent rules for the nominal interest rate, such as the Taylor [1993] rule.[13]

Before we analyze such rules, it is worth delving a little deeper into the mechanics of monetary policy.

20.4.1 Financial Markets and Open Market Operations

Monetary policy affects the economy through its effects on conditions in financial markets, mainly nominal and real interest rates. In particular, conventional monetary policy operates through interventions in money markets, where short-term debt instruments (such as treasury bills and short-term deposits of financial institutions) are traded. Through buying and selling short-term securities, a central bank can affect short-term interest rates in the market. If it wishes to increase short-term interest rates, then it sells treasury bills or other short-term financial instruments, depressing their prices and causing an increase in their interest yield. If it wishes to reduce short-term interest rates, then it buys short-term financial instruments, causing their price to increase and thus reducing their interest yield.

Consider a one-period discount bond that pays B at the end of period t. Its price (value) at the beginning of the period is equal to $V = B/(1+i)$, where i is the nominal interest rate.

Arbitrage in financial markets thus ensures that the rate of return of a one-period bond will be equal to the short-term interest rate i. Hence, a (risk-neutral) investor who could borrow at the short-term interest rate i would be indifferent between (1) borrowing at the interest rate i and investing in the bond or (2) not borrowing and not investing in the bond. It is clear that for a given bond payment at the end of the period, there is an inverse relation between the bond price and the nominal interest rate. Thus, if the central bank buys more short-term securities in the secondary market and increases their price V, it effectively reduces short-term interest rates. Such operations are called *open market operations*.

For example, the US Federal Reserve aims to affect the so-called federal funds rate, which is an overnight rate. This is the interest rate at which depository institutions, such as commercial banks, trade federal funds (balances held at Federal Reserve Banks) with one another overnight. When a depository institution has surplus balances in its reserve account, it lends to other banks in need of larger balances. In other words, a bank with excess liquidity will lend to another bank that needs to quickly raise liquidity. The rate that the borrowing institution pays to the lending institution is determined by the two banks; the weighted average rate

12. See Capie et al. [1994]. As noted by Bernanke [2006, p. 2], "In practice, the difficulty has been that, deregulation, financial innovation, and other factors have led to recurrent instability in the relationships between various monetary aggregates and other nominal variables."

13. Obviously, these rules can always be expressed as contingent rules for the money supply by substituting for the nominal interest rate in a money demand function and solving for the money supply.

for all of these types of negotiations is called the *effective federal funds rate*. The effective federal funds rate is essentially determined by the market but is influenced by the Federal Reserve through open market operations to reach the federal funds rate target.

The Federal Open Market Committee meets eight times a year to determine the federal funds target rate. This target rate influences the effective federal funds rate through open market operations. More specifically, the Federal Reserve decreases liquidity by selling treasury bills, thereby raising the federal funds rate, because banks then have less liquidity to trade with other banks. Similarly, the Federal Reserve can increase liquidity by buying treasury bills, decreasing the federal funds rate, because banks then have excess liquidity for interbank trades.

Similar procedures are followed by central banks in the other industrial economies with developed financial markets, such as the European Central Bank, the Bank of Japan, and the Bank of England.

20.4.2 The Term Structure of Interest Rates

The federal funds rate is the central interest rate in the US financial market. It influences other interest rates, such as the *prime rate*, which is the rate banks charge their customers with higher credit ratings. Additionally, the federal funds rate indirectly influences longer-term interest rates, such as the yield of government bonds, corporate bonds, mortgages, loans, and savings, all of which are very important to the cost of borrowing, consumer wealth, and confidence.

Interest rates on short- and long-term securities are related through the *term structure of interest rates*. Assume that there are two types of discount bonds, which are perfect substitutes: a short-term bond, which pays an interest rate i^1 at the end of one period, and a long-term bond, which lasts for n periods and pays a rate of return ni^n at the end of n periods. Here i^n is the per period interest rate of the n-period bond.

Assuming that investors are risk neutral, they will be indifferent between investing in a sequence of one-period bonds for n periods and an n-period bond, if the two types of portfolio investment have the same expected rate of return. Hence, at time t, arbitrage would ensure that

$$ni_t^n = i_t^1 + E_t i_{t+1}^1 + \cdots + E_t i_{t+n-1}^1. \tag{20.28}$$

From (20.28), it follows that the per period rate of return of the n-period bond would be equal to the average expected rate of return of one-period bonds between period t and period $t+n$:

$$i_t^n = \frac{1}{n}\left(i_t^1 + E_t i_{t+1}^1 + \cdots + E_t i_{t+n-1}^1\right). \tag{20.29}$$

Thus, open market operations that affect short-term rates would cause long-term rates to move in the same direction. If the change in short-term rates is temporary, then a rise in the short-term rate by one percentage point would raise long-term rates by $1/n$ of a percentage point. If the change is permanent, it will raise long-term rates by one full percentage point as well. If it is expected to persist for m periods, where $m < n$, then the effect on long-term rates will be m/n of a percentage point as well.

This theory of the term structure of interest rates, which results in long-term rates being the average of the expected future short-term rates, is called the *expectations theory of the term structure*.

The theory can be extended to allow for risk-averse investors. In that case, (20.29) is modified to

$$i_t^n = \frac{1}{n}\left(i_t^1 + E_t i_{t+1}^1 + \cdots + E_t i_{t+n-1}^1\right) + \eta_t^n, \tag{20.30}$$

where η_t^n is a positive *term premium* to holding an n-period bond, reflecting the higher uncertainty about the rate of return of the long-term bond.

Hence, on the basis of the expectations theory of the term structure, open market operations that affect short-term rates (such as the federal funds rate) also affect the whole spectrum of interest rates in the same direction.

20.5 Optimal Monetary Policy and the Taylor Rule

We can now analyze interest rate rules and compare them to the optimal monetary policy. Let us focus on the Taylor rule. As discussed in chapters 14–17, the principle of the Taylor interest rate rule requires the central bank to set its target for the nominal interest rate as a function of three variables:

1. the natural nominal interest rate, which is the sum of the natural real interest rate and the inflation target of the central bank,
2. deviations of current inflation from the inflation target of the central bank, and
3. deviations of output from its natural rate.

Assume that this generalized Taylor rule takes the form

$$i_t = r_t^N + \pi^* + \phi_\pi\left(\pi_t - \pi^*\right) + \phi_y \hat{y}_t, \tag{20.31}$$

where $\phi_\pi, \phi_y > 0$.[14]

14. Taylor [1993, 1999] proposed a rule in which the natural real rate of interest was constant at 2% and the inflation target was equal to 2% as well. Let us term this rule the *constant-intercept Taylor rule*. However, in the analysis that follows (as also done in the analysis of chapter 17), we stick to the spirit of the Taylor rule but treat the natural real rate of interest as a stochastic endogenous variable and not a constant.

By substituting (20.31) in the new neoclassical synthesis IS curve (20.1) and then substituting in the expectations-augmented Phillips curve (20.2), we get the following process for inflation:

$$\pi_t = \gamma_1 E_{t-1}\pi_t + \gamma_2 E_t \pi_{t+1} + (\phi_\pi - 1)\gamma_2 \pi^* - \gamma_1 \varepsilon_t^A, \tag{20.32}$$

where

$$\gamma_1 = \frac{(\phi_y + \theta)(1-\alpha)}{\phi_\pi \alpha + (\phi_y + \theta)(1-\alpha)} < 1,$$

$$\gamma_2 = \frac{\alpha}{\phi_\pi \alpha + (\phi_y + \theta)(1-\alpha)}.$$

Note that the inflationary process depends on both parameters of the Taylor rule, because deviations of output from its natural rate cause unanticipated inflation. In addition, the effects of productivity shocks on inflation also depend on the parameters of the Taylor rule.

One can show that the process (20.32) is stable if $\gamma_1 + \gamma_2 < 1$. A sufficient condition for this is

$$\phi_\pi > 1. \tag{20.33}$$

Condition (20.33) is the *Taylor principle* mentioned in the analysis of the new Keynesian models in chapters 16 and 17. If (20.33) is satisfied, then the rational expectations solution of the inflation equation (20.32) is given by

$$\pi_t = \pi^* - \gamma_1 \varepsilon_t^A. \tag{20.34}$$

From (20.34), the fluctuations of inflation around the target of the monetary authorities π^* only depend on the current innovation in productivity, as is the case for the optimal policy analyzed in section 20.3.

The Taylor rule (20.31) would be equivalent to the optimal policy, if γ_1 was equal to the optimal response of inflation to innovations in productivity ψ in equation (20.26). From the definition of ψ in (20.17) and the definition of γ_1 in (20.32), this requires that ϕ_π and ϕ_y must satisfy

$$\frac{(\phi_y + \theta)(1-\alpha)}{\phi_\pi \alpha + (\phi_y + \theta)(1-\alpha)} = \frac{(1-\alpha)^2}{(1-\alpha)^2 + \zeta\alpha^2}. \tag{20.35}$$

As long as the policy parameters are chosen to satisfy (20.35), a Taylor rule can fully replicate the optimal policy in this model.

Solving (20.35) for the optimal ϕ_π, we get

$$\phi_\pi = (\phi_y + \theta)\frac{\alpha}{\psi(1-\alpha)} > 1. \tag{20.36}$$

From (20.36), ϕ_y must be chosen so that $\phi_\pi > 1$, which requires

$$\phi_y > \frac{1-\alpha}{\zeta\alpha} - \theta. \tag{20.37}$$

Thus, any pair of ϕ_π and ϕ_y that satisfies (20.36) results in an optimal Taylor rule.

Note that the Taylor rule specified in (20.31) is not the constant intercept rule proposed by Taylor [1993, 1999] but a rule that also requires the nominal interest rate to respond to changes in the natural real interest rate. The constant intercept Taylor rule is not an optimal rule if there are fluctuations in the natural real interest rate, due to productivity or other real shocks, as in our model.[15]

20.6 Monetary Policy Shocks and the Optimal Policy Rule

Up to now we have been assuming that the monetary policy rules can be implemented without any policy errors. Yet there are two potential policy errors that can creep into the implementation of monetary policy rules, and will affect macroeconomic outcomes.

One is *estimation errors*. If the central bank does not have full information about the model of the economy, the natural rate of interest, the natural rate of output (or unemployment), or even current macroeconomic conditions, it will have to rely on estimates of these variables. Yet even the best estimates will be characterized by estimation and prediction errors, which will affect macroeconomic outcomes. Monetary policy rules must be simple enough to be robust to such estimation errors, as an erroneous assessment of the required policy action may destabilize rather than stabilize the economy.[16]

The second is *implementation errors*. Even an effectively designed monetary policy rule may be subject to implementation errors, such as delays, lags in the transmission mechanism of monetary policy, or other human errors. Such errors will be equivalent to nominal shocks that affect macroeconomic outcomes.

In what follows, we shall examine optimal monetary policy rules in the presence of implementation errors of monetary policy. In the presence of such errors, the optimal inflation rule in response to stochastic shocks is given by

$$\pi_t = \psi E_{t-1}\pi_t + (1-\psi)\pi^* - \psi\varepsilon_t^A + \varepsilon_t^\pi, \tag{20.38}$$

15. This point was first highlighted by Woodford [2001].

16. See Orphanides and Williams [2002] and Orphanides [2003a, b] for theoretical and empirical analyses of the case of such estimation errors.

where ε_t^{π} is a white noise error in the implementation of the optimal inflation rule (20.24). Thus, it can be seen as a nominal (monetary) shock.

The rational expectations solution of (20.38) is given by

$$\pi_t = \pi^* - \psi \varepsilon_t^A + \varepsilon_t^{\pi}. \tag{20.39}$$

Substituting (20.39) in (20.2), which determines deviations of output from its natural rate, we get that fluctuations of output around its natural rate are determined by

$$\hat{y}_t = \frac{1-\alpha}{\alpha}\left((1-\psi)\varepsilon_t^A + \varepsilon_t^{\pi}\right). \tag{20.40}$$

Optimal monetary policy is now third best. It cannot completely stabilize both inflation and employment in response to productivity shocks, because it operates through aggregate demand, and productivity shocks are supply shocks. In addition, because of errors in the determination of the optimal inflation rule, monetary policy shocks also affect fluctuations in both inflation and output.

The same would apply to a Taylor rule, if that rule was subject to implementation errors. Assume that instead of (20.31), the Taylor rule took the form

$$i_t = r_t^N + \pi^* + \phi_\pi \left(\pi_t - \pi^*\right) + \phi_y \hat{y}_t + \varepsilon_t^i, \tag{20.41}$$

where ε_t^i is a white noise error in the implementation of the optimal nominal interest rate rule (20.31). This can be seen as a nominal (monetary) shock. Inflation would then be

$$\pi_t = \gamma_1 E_{t-1}\pi_t + \gamma_2 E_t \pi_{t+1} + (\phi_\pi - 1)\gamma_2 \pi^* - \gamma_1 \varepsilon_t^A - \gamma_2 \varepsilon_t^i. \tag{20.42}$$

The rational expectations solution of (20.42) is given by

$$\pi_t = \pi^* - \gamma_1 \varepsilon_t^A - \gamma_2 \varepsilon_t^i. \tag{20.43}$$

The inflation error in this case is $\varepsilon^{\pi} = -\gamma_2 \varepsilon^i$.

As long as (20.36) is satisfied, the Taylor rule is equivalent to the optimal (third-best) monetary policy rule (20.39). However, as with the optimal inflation rule, in the case of monetary policy shocks, these nominal shocks affect fluctuations of both inflation and real output.[17]

The analysis can be generalized to the version of the model with endogenous unemployment persistence. In this case, not only will deviations of inflation from target and

17. Clarida et al. [1999] analyze monetary policy in a new Keynesian model based on staggered pricing and reach overall conclusions similar to those of this chapter, which uses a model of periodic wage contracts.

unemployment from its natural rate be affected by nominal and real shocks, even under the optimal monetary policy, but they will also display endogenous persistence.[18]

20.7 Monetary Policy, Financial Frictions, and the Zero Lower Bound on Interest Rates

The interest rate rules we have been examining up to now assume that there are no financial frictions and that the central bank can freely adjust the nominal interest rate.

In chapter 19, we discussed the nature of financial frictions and how they can result in financial crises, such as that of 2008–2009 or the Great Depression of the 1930s. We also analyzed the macroeconomic implications of financial frictions, using two alternative new Keynesian models, one with staggered pricing and one with periodic nominal wage contracts. We showed that if the central bank follows a Taylor [1993] rule for interest rates, financial frictions that raise the external finance premium result in recessions and deflations, in the sense that inflation falls below the optimal inflation rate.

We also argued that the normal Taylor rule is not the optimal macroeconomic response to a financial markets shock. The optimal macroeconomic response would be for the central bank interest rate to completely neutralize the rise in the external finance premium, by falling sufficiently so as to completely avert a recession. This can be achieved if the response of the central bank interest rate to inflation became infinitely large, completely stabilizing the inflation rate at its optimal level. However, this may not be possible if there is a zero lower bound on interest rates.

Prior to the Great Recession of 2008–2009, inflation was low and close to official target rates in the advanced economies, so that short-term nominal interest rates tended to deviate relatively little from their long-run average. The only exception was Japan, where short-term nominal interest rates had been close to zero since the 1990s. Central banks in the other industrialized economies responded to the Great Recession by lowering key policy interest rates to, or very close to, zero.

Because the nominal return from holding money in the form of cash is equal to zero, it is generally accepted that central banks cannot sustain their policy interest rates below zero, as cash can always be held as an alternative to negative interest rate bearing assets, such as deposits or bonds. The implication is that nominal interest rates have a zero lower bound even if the state of the economy requires negative nominal and real interest rates to minimize deviations of inflation from target and output and employment from their natural rates. Hence, conventional monetary policy cannot respond effectively to financial or other shocks that tip the economy toward the zero lower bound.

18. Alogoskoufis [2018] analyzes monetary policy when deviations of unemployment from its natural rate display persistence, as in the model of chapter 17.

20.7.1 The Liquidity Trap

Such a situation was referred to as a theoretical possibility by Keynes in the *General Theory* and has since been known as a *liquidity trap*. Keynes [1936, p. 187] argued

> There is the possibility ... that, after the rate of interest has fallen to a certain level, liquidity-preference may become virtually absolute in the sense that almost everyone prefers cash to holding a debt which yields so low a rate of interest. In this event the monetary authority would have lost effective control over the rate of interest. But whilst this limiting case might become practically important in future, I know of no example of it hitherto.

The liquidity trap was analyzed by Modigliani [1944] as a special case of the Keynesian model in which the LM curve becomes flat, and monetary policy is thus ineffective. In such a case, a monetary expansion would fail to further reduce nominal and real interest rates, increase aggregate demand, and counteract deflation and recession.

The liquidity trap can be analyzed with the help of figure 20.2. Assume that the economy is at an initial equilibrium E, and that a negative shock to aggregate demand shifts the IS curve

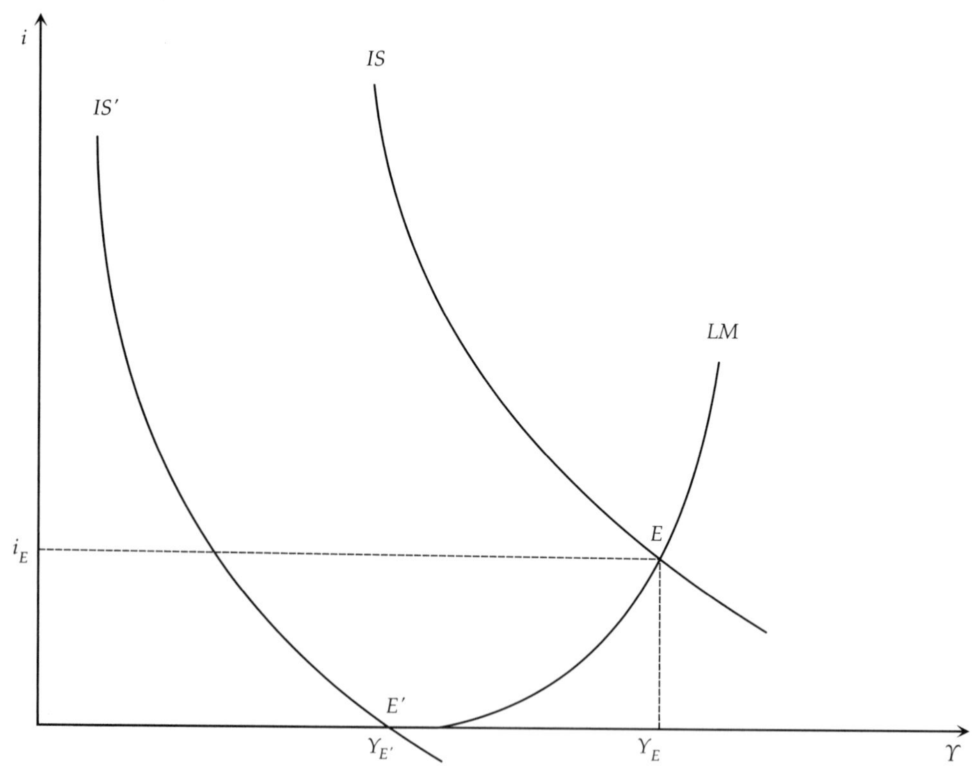

Figure 20.2
The liquidity trap.

to the left. Short-run equilibrium output moves from Y_E to $Y_{E'}$, and the nominal interest rate shifts from i_E to zero.

The central bank cannot counteract the contraction in aggregate demand by increasing liquidity. Increases in liquidity cannot result in further reductions in nominal interest rates, because households and firms prefer to hold money (which has a zero nominal yield) to bonds (which would have a negative nominal yield). Hence, conventional open market operations, in which the central bank increases liquidity by exchanging money for short-term bonds, would have no effect on nominal interest rates. Commercial banks and the nonbank public would be quite happy to exchange zero-yield bonds or deposits for cash, without any effect on the price or yield of these bonds.

20.7.2 Monetary Policy at the Zero Lower Bound

As already mentioned, the theoretical possibility of a liquidity trap became a reality in Japan during the 1990s, and in the other industrial economies in the aftermath of the recession of 2008–2009, when short-term interest rates touched the zero lower bound and in some cases became slightly negative for a brief period.

The analysis of monetary policy at the zero lower bound became an active area of research since Krugman [1998] studied it, prompted by the Japanese experience. Krugman used an intertemporal model of savings and investment with and without price flexibility. Eggerstsson and Woodford [2003], Jung et al. [2005], and others have since extended the analysis to new Keynesian models.

To analyze the conduct of monetary policy at the zero lower bound, consider the model consisting of (20.1) and (20.2), augmented for an external finance premium, as in chapter 19. We abstract from productivity shocks to focus on financial shocks. The modified model thus takes the form

$$\hat{y}_t = E_t\hat{y}_{t+1} - \frac{1}{\theta}(i_t - E_t\pi_{t+1} + x_t - \rho), \tag{20.44}$$

$$\pi_t = E_{t-1}\pi_t + \frac{\alpha}{1-\alpha}\hat{y}_t, \tag{20.45}$$

where x_t is, as in chapter 19, an exogenous external finance premium. This is our financial shock.

Consider the impact of a large x_t. To avert a recession would then require a reduction in the central bank nominal interest rate i_t that would make the real interest rate plus the external finance premium equal to the natural interest rate ρ. Thus, the central bank nominal interest rate would have to be

$$i_t = E_t\pi_{t+1} - x_t + \rho. \tag{20.46}$$

If the shock to the external finance premium is large enough (i.e., if $x_t > \rho + E_t\pi_{t+1}$), then the central bank nominal interest rate ought to become negative. If it cannot become negative because of the zero lower bound, then from (20.44), a recession cannot be avoided.

Hence, the zero lower bound constraint (that the central bank cannot reduce nominal interest rates below zero) results in financial shocks and also other aggregate demand shocks, which could in principle be neutralized by monetary policy, having real effects on output and employment. If the central bank could fully adjust nominal interest rates below the zero lower bound, negative aggregate demand shocks would not affect output and employment in this model. It is only because nominal interest rates may hit the zero lower bound that we end up with real effects for financial and other aggregate demand shocks, even under the optimal policy.

20.7.3 The Zero Lower Bound and Unconventional Monetary Policy

Is there scope for additional action from monetary policy in such a case? Krugman [1998] and Eggerstsson and Woodford [2003] have suggested a potential solution that rests on the central bank announcing that it will not return to its inflation target π^* (at least in the immediate future) and that future inflation will be above target. For example, assume that the central bank announced that its inflation target for $t+1$ would be high enough that the nominal interest rate in (20.46) is positive, despite the shock to the external finance premium. If that was credible, then from (20.46), the recession would be avoided, as the current real interest rate, including the external finance premium, would become equal to the natural rate.[19]

Obviously, if π^* is the optimal inflation rate, then implementing a policy such as that implied by the above discussion would not result in optimal future inflation.

The upshot of this analysis is that managing expectations about future inflation is potentially an important form of unconventional monetary policy at the zero lower bound. The announcement of higher future inflation targets, even temporarily, is a form of unconventional monetary policy called *forward guidance*. As central banks cannot use conventional monetary policy to further reduce short-term nominal interest rates below the zero lower bound, they are using announcements about future monetary policy to affect current expectations about future inflation and thus affect real interest rates; aggregate demand; and through aggregate demand, aggregate income and employment.

To be more credible, forward guidance must be accompanied by action. At the zero lower bound, open market operations (such as further purchases of short-term securities by the central bank) would have no further effect on short-term nominal interest rates. Thus, even if the central bank expands the money supply, the additional money is willingly held by the public, because it is considered a perfect substitute for short-term bonds, which pay an interest rate of zero.

19. Eggerstsson and Woodford [2003], who used a model with staggered pricing, suggested that this can be achieved by announcing a *target price-level path*, instead of a higher inflation path.

An additional unconventional way in which policy can attempt to stimulate the economy is by direct intervention in credit markets that would affect the external finance premium. In 2008 and 2009, the Federal Reserve and other central banks took actions aimed at the markets for specific types of credit, supporting commercial-paper issuance, mortgage lending, and so on. Such actions are clearly most likely to be effective when the particular markets they are aimed at have been disrupted, as in the case of a financial crisis.

The appropriate response of monetary policy is to increase liquidity in order to increase bank lending and reduce interest rates, thereby reversing the effects of the financial crisis and the rise in the external finance premium on aggregate demand. In addition, central banks may be required to act as lenders of last resort to the banking system and to bail out banks, in order to prevent deleveraging, bankruptcies, and further reduction in aggregate demand, output, and employment.

The policy of continuing to expand the money supply at the zero lower bound is usually called quantitative easing and is a policy that was widely adopted in the aftermath of the financial crisis of 2008–2009, when interest rates reached the zero lower bound. By increasing the money supply, quantitative easing makes the commitment to higher future inflation, through forward guidance, more credible.

Another possible way for the central bank to provide stimulus in the face of the zero lower bound is to purchase assets other than short-term government debt in its open market operations. This is another form of unconventional monetary policy, called *asset purchases*. For example, the central bank can purchase long-term government debt or corporate debt, both of which are likely to offer positive nominal returns even when the interest rate on short-term government debt is zero. One can envisage such transactions as conventional open market operations, followed by exchanges of short-term zero-interest government debt for the alternative asset. Such open market operations can reduce long-term rates and the external finance premium directly. These operations thus affect aggregate demand, even when short-term interest rates are at the zero lower bound. Open market operations that involve buying assets other than short-term government debt are an additional form of quantitative easing.[20]

Another type of unconventional open market operation that has attracted considerable attention is exchange market intervention (Svensson [2001]). By purchasing foreign currency or other foreign assets, the central bank can presumably cause the domestic currency to depreciate. An exchange rate depreciation will also stimulate aggregate demand and increase output and employment.

In conclusion, the zero lower bound and financial frictions are serious issues that are likely to constrain monetary policy under particular circumstances, such as a financial crisis. The recent experience of the 2008–2009 financial crisis, and its theoretical analysis,

20. See McGough et al. [2005] for a theoretical analysis of this type of unconventional monetary policy.

have provided important lessons about unconventional forms of monetary policy and its effects and also revived interest in the use of fiscal policy as a tool for stabilizing the economy.[21]

We shall return to how the financial crisis of 2008–2009 has affected not only the analysis of monetary policy but also macroeconomic modeling in general in chapter 23.

20.8 Conclusion

In this chapter, we have delved deeper into policies that the monetary authorities can implement to control inflation and stabilize the real economy. Four conclusions have emerged.

The first is that monetary policy should be determined by politically independent central banks on the basis of rules rather than discretion. Political independence of the central bank and well-defined objectives result in a more credible monetary policy. It helps avoid both the high inflation that could result if the central bank has to fund government deficits through seigniorage and the inflationary bias that would result if the central bank was under political pressure to reduce unemployment below the natural rate. Central bank constitutions should constrain them to pursue a low inflation target, as there is general agreement that the optimal rate of inflation is low.

The second conclusion is that in the presence of stochastic disturbances, policy rules should depend on the state of the economy. Such rules are called contingent. The central bank must be able to react to shocks that cause deviations of real variables from their natural rates, even if this results in temporary deviations of inflation from its medium term target, as is the case with supply shocks. For demand shocks, the optimal reaction of monetary policy does not imply a trade-off between employment and inflation.

A third conclusion is that the appropriate policy instrument of monetary policy is the short-term nominal interest rate, which can be controlled through open market operations. Control of the money supply (to the degree that an appropriate measure of the money supply can be defined) has always been difficult, and it becomes even more difficult if there are financial innovations and money demand shocks. Thus for some years, the focus of monetary policy analysis has been the appropriate contingent rule for short-term nominal interest rates. The Taylor rule has provided the appropriate framework, because it allows for reactions of the central bank policy rate to the natural rate of interest, deviations of inflation from the low-inflation target, and deviations of output or employment from their natural rates. It provides flexibility and allows the central bank to pursue a

21. Williams [2014] provides an assessment of the practical difficulties in pursuing unconventional monetary policy at the zero lower bound. Krugman [2009a, 2012] is the main proponent of a return to a more intensive use of fiscal policy for stabilization purposes.

low-inflation objective over the business cycle, which also results in low nominal interest rates.

A final conclusion is that with a low-inflation objective, there is always the risk that a big enough negative shock to aggregate demand will force monetary policy to hit the zero lower bound of interest rates. In such cases, and especially in the presence of financial frictions, the short-run nominal interest rate ceases to be an effective instrument of monetary policy. Then central banks must follow unconventional monetary policies, such as forward guidance, quantitative easing, and asset purchases.

21

Fiscal Policy and Government Debt

In this chapter, we revisit the role of fiscal policy in macroeconomics, focusing on the government budget constraint and the effects of alternative methods of financing government expenditure, such as taxes and government debt.

We saw in chapters 2 and 6 that if the government has access to financial markets and can borrow and lend freely at the market interest rate, the government budget constraint is defined in a way which is similar to the intertemporal budget constraint of a household that has free access to financial markets. It requires that the present value of current and future tax revenue is greater than or equal to the sum of the current stock of government debt and the present value of current and future primary government expenditure. Primary government expenditure is defined as government expenditure excluding interest payments on government debt, and present values are calculated using market interest rates.

We also saw in chapter 6 that the budget constraint of a government with an infinite horizon does not prevent it from having debt, or even from increasing the level of its debt. However, the limit of the present value of government debt, as time tends to infinity, cannot be positive. For example, if the real interest rate is positive, a positive but constant real government debt—which means that the government never repays it—satisfies the government budget constraint. Even if government debt increases continuously, the government budget constraint is satisfied to the extent that the real interest rate exceeds the growth rate of real government debt.

When the government budget constraint was introduced in the representative household model, it was shown that, if taxes are lump sum, the only aspect of fiscal policy that matters for the choice of the optimal path of private consumption is the present value of primary government expenditure. The method of financing primary government expenditure (i.e., the breakup between government debt and the path of nondistortionary taxes) does not affect the optimal path of consumption of the representative household. This property has become known as Ricardian equivalence between taxes and government debt.

It was also shown that Ricardian equivalence does not apply to overlapping generations (OLG) models. The stock of government debt affects aggregate savings, as current generations realize that part of the present value of future taxes required to finance the stock of government debt will be paid by future generations. In OLG models, current generations are not concerned with the welfare of future generations. Thus, current generations treat part of their holdings of the existing stock of government debt as part of their wealth, because it exceeds the present value of their own future taxes. As a result, debt and tax finance are not equivalent in OLG models, and Ricardian equivalence does not hold.

Taxes are rarely lump sum and nondistortionary, as they affect incentives for savings, investment and labor supply. We investigated the effects of distortionary taxation in chapters 2 and 6, and showed that distortionary taxes have negative effects on both labor supply and capital accumulation. More importantly, Ricardian equivalence breaks down in the case of distortionary taxation.

In this chapter, we focus on models of the determination of the level of distortionary taxes and government debt. We thus endogenize government decisions about the evolution of taxes and debt.

As discussed in chapter 1, government debt has been rising during wars and recessions in both the United States and the United Kingdom. Furthermore, since the early 1980s, government debt has been rising continuously in both countries and in other industrial economies, reversing a trend of falling government debt since the end of World War II. Such trends can be partly explained by the prevalence of distortionary taxation and the attempts of governments to smooth out these distortions. Additional explanations require theories that focus on distributional and political considerations, which we briefly survey.

In the presence of distortionary taxes, the level of government debt matters. In steady state, higher levels of government debt are associated with higher distortionary tax rates, and therefore with higher negative tax distortions. The same obviously applies to higher primary government purchases. In representative household models with nondistortionary taxes, government purchases and government debt do not affect capital accumulation and the dynamic path of output. But distortionary taxation results in negative effects on capital accumulation and labor supply. Hence, if distortionary taxes have to rise to stabilize the government debt-to-output ratio at a higher level (or to finance a higher ratio of government purchases to output), there will be negative effects on steady state per capita income and economic growth.

An additional negative effect of high government debt is the possibility of a debt crisis.

In section 21.6, we analyze the Calvo [1988] model of government debt crises. This is a model in which the interest rate on government debt depends positively on the expected probability of default, and the actual probability of default, depends positively on the interest rate on government debt.

Such a model has multiple equilibria. One equilibrium implies a zero or low probability of default and a low divergence of the interest rate on government debt from the interest rate on safe assets. A second equilibrium implies a probability of default equal to unity and an inability of the government to borrow at any interest rate. A third intermediate equilibrium with a high probability of default exists as well, but it is dynamically unstable. In this model, the equilibrium that prevails depends on the expectations of investors. What equilibrium will prevail is to a large extent a self-fulfilling expectation or prophecy.

In such a model, small changes in the fundamentals can bring about large equilibrium changes and move us from one equilibrium to another. This is because even small changes to the fundamentals can cause large changes in expectations.

When default occurs (say, because of a change in the fundamentals or in expectations), this is unanticipated. It is a jump from a low probability of default equilibrium to an equilibrium with a unitary probability of default.

Thus, in the presence of distortionary taxes, high public debt implies two types of costs:

1. In models with distortionary taxation, higher government deficits and debts, even if sustainable, result in higher distortionary taxes, lower labor supply and employment, lower capital accumulation and growth, and lower steady state per capita income and consumption.
2. In models with potential default, higher government deficits and debts result in a higher probability of default, which brings about an increase in interest rates on government debt and increases the likelihood of a debt crisis.

21.1 Tax Smoothing and Government Debt Accumulation

The simplest explanations of government debt accumulation rely on a representative household economy. In such an economy, the theory of optimal taxation prescribes tax smoothing over time. Because taxes are distortionary, they should not be changed to finance temporary or cyclical changes in the government budget. Debt financing should be used in the case of temporary rises in government purchases (such as during a war) or when tax receipts are temporarily low (such as during a recession); see Barro [1979] and Lucas and Stokey [1983]. Of course, permanent rises in government spending (such as those required for the expansion of the welfare state) ought to be financed through higher taxes, even if taxes are distortionary.

21.1.1 The Barro Tax-Smoothing Model

Let us first explore the general intuition of the tax-smoothing result, using the model of Barro (1979). Assume that a government chooses a sequence of tax rates τ_t to finance a sequence of real primary government purchases C_t^g. Aggregate output Y_t follows an exogenous stochastic process, as does the real interest rate r_t. Taxes are distortionary, and the current aggregate distortion associated with a tax rate τ_t is given by

$$Y_t f(\tau_t), \tag{21.1}$$

where f is a convex function that summarizes the various distortions associated with tax collection. Thus, f satisfies $f' > 0, f'' \geq 0$.

At time t, the government has an inherited stock of real government debt D_{t-1} from the end of period $t-1$. As discussed in chapter 6, the intertemporal budget constraint of a solvent government is given by the requirement that at any time t, the expected present value of tax revenues must be greater than or equal to the expected present value of primary government expenditure, plus the initial level of government debt and its servicing cost. In discrete time, this requirement can be written as

$$E_t\left(\sum_{i=0}^{\infty} R_{t+i}\tau_{t+i}Y_{t+i} \geq (1+r_t)D_{t-1} + \sum_{i=0}^{\infty} R_{t+i}C^g_{t+i}\right), \tag{21.2}$$

where E_t is the mathematical expectations operator, conditional on information available in period t, and R_{t+i} denotes the real discount factor at time $t+i$. It is defined by

$$R_{t+i} = \frac{1}{(1+r_{t+1}) \cdots (1+r_{t+i})}, \quad i=1,2,\ldots, \quad R_t = 1, \tag{21.3}$$

where r_{t+i} is the market real interest rate in period $t+i$.

Assume that the government chooses a sequence of tax rates to minimize the expected present value of the distortions (21.1), subject to the intertemporal budget constraint (21.2), and taking the sequences of aggregate output and aggregate real government purchases as given. The Lagrange function for this problem is given by

$$E_t\left(\sum_{i=0}^{\infty} R_{t+i}Y_{t+i}f(\tau_{t+i}) + \lambda_t\left((1+r_t)D_{t-1} + \sum_{i=0}^{\infty} R_{t+i}\left(C^g_{t+i} - \tau_{t+i}Y_{t+i}\right)\right)\right), \tag{21.4}$$

where λ_t is the Lagrange multiplier.

From the first-order conditions for a minimum, it follows that

$$E_t f'(\tau_{t+i}) = \lambda_t \quad i=0,1,2,\ldots. \tag{21.5}$$

Equation (21.5) implies that

$$\tau_t = E_t\tau_{t+i}, \quad \forall i, \tag{21.6}$$

which implies that the optimal government tax policy is to keep the tax rate constant between periods. This is the basic tax-smoothing result. Under the optimal policy, there cannot be predictable changes in tax policy, and tax rates follow a random walk.

To derive the implications of tax smoothing for debts and deficits, let us consider the dynamic evolution of government debt. From the tax-smoothing first-order condition (21.6) and the government budget constraint (21.2), the tax rate at time t is determined by

$$\tau_t = \frac{1}{E_t\sum_{i=0}^{\infty} R_{t+i}Y_{t+i}}\left((1+r_t)D_{t-1} + E_t\sum_{i=0}^{\infty} R_{t+i}C^g_{t+i}\right). \tag{21.7}$$

The optimal distortionary tax rate is determined by two ratios. The first is the stock of government debt inherited from period $t-1$ plus its servicing cost, divided by the expected present value of aggregate output in period t. The second is the ratio of the expected present value of primary government purchases in period t to the expected present value of aggregate output in period t. The optimal tax rate is equal to the sum of those two ratios only. It is affected by current government purchases or current output only to the extent that these affect their respective present values.

The evolution of government debt over time is determined by current government deficits. From the government budget constraint (21.2), the evolution of real government debt is determined by the following first-order difference equation:

$$D_t = (1+r_t)D_{t-1} + C_t^g - \tau_t Y_t. \tag{21.8}$$

Substituting (21.7) for τ_t in (21.8), after some rearrangement, we get

$$D_t = (1+r_t)\left(1 - \frac{Y_t}{E_t \sum_{i=0}^{\infty} R_{t+i} Y_{t+i}}\right) D_{t-1} + C_t^g - \frac{E_t \sum_{i=0}^{\infty} R_{t+i} C_{t+i}^g}{E_t \sum_{i=0}^{\infty} R_{t+i} Y_{t+i}} Y_t. \tag{21.9}$$

Consider first a temporary increase in C^g in period t, which leaves the expected present value of government purchases unchanged. This could be the effect of a war. It is clear from (21.9) that this increase would cause an increase in the current government deficit and an increase in government debt in period t. Thus, a temporary increase in government purchases causes an increase in government deficits and government debt, because the current optimal tax rate remains unchanged.

Consider next a temporary drop in current aggregate output Y_t that leaves the expected present value of output unchanged. This could be the result of a recession. It is clear from (21.9) that this drop would also cause an increase in the current government deficit and current government debt, because, due to tax smoothing, the current optimal tax rate remains unchanged.

In contrast, a permanent change in either government purchases or output would not affect debt accumulation, because by (21.7), it would result in an increase in the current and expected future tax rates.

21.1.2 Steady State Implications of Tax Smoothing

To determine the steady state implications of the tax-smoothing model, consider a steady state in which the real interest rate is constant at r, output grows at an exogenously determined steady state growth rate $g+n$, and the same applies to real government purchases. The steady state growth rate is equal to the sum of the rate of technical progress g and population growth n. Assume that dynamic efficiency applies (i.e., that $r > g+n$).

The expected present value of output in the steady state is given by

$$E_t \sum_{i=0}^{\infty} R_{t+i} Y_{t+i} = Y_t \sum_{i=0}^{\infty} \left(\frac{1+g+n}{1+r} \right)^i = \frac{1+r}{r-(g+n)} Y_t. \tag{21.10}$$

The expected present value of government purchases is given by

$$E_t \sum_{i=0}^{\infty} R_{t+i} C^g_{t+i} = C^g_t \sum_{i=0}^{\infty} \left(\frac{1+g+n}{1+r} \right)^i = \frac{1+r}{1+(g+n)} C^g_t. \tag{21.11}$$

Substituting (21.10) and (21.11) in (21.7), the optimal tax rate is given by

$$\tau_t = \frac{r-g-n}{1+g+n} d_{t-1} + c^g_t, \tag{21.12}$$

where $d_t = D_t / Y_t$ is the government debt-to-output ratio, and $c^g_t = C^g_t / Y_t$ is the ratio of government purchases to output.

The optimal tax rate is equal to the ratio of government purchases to output plus that part of debt servicing which exceeds economic growth. Thus, the optimal tax rate is sufficient for financing not only permanent government purchases but also part of the servicing of government debt. A permanent increase in the ratio of government purchases to output thus brings about an equal permanent increase in the steady state optimal tax rate. A permanent increase in the government debt-to-output ratio also requires a permanent increase in steady state distortionary tax rates.

To find out how real government debt evolves under optimal tax smoothing, we can substitute (21.10) and (21.11) in (21.9). Real government debt evolves according to

$$D_t = (1+r)\left(1 - \frac{r-g-n}{1+r}\right) D_{t-1} = (1+g+n) D_{t-1}. \tag{21.13}$$

Thus, under the optimal tax-smoothing policy, in the steady state, real government debt is growing at the steady state growth rate $g+n$. As a result, the government debt-to-output ratio remains constant. Dividing (21.13) by real output, it is easy to see that

$$d_t = d_{t-1}. \tag{21.14}$$

Thus, optimal tax policy of a solvent government stabilizes the government debt-to-output ratio in the steady state.

Therefore, this simple tax-smoothing model can explain the relative stability of tax rates, which only depend on the stock of inherited government debt and the present values of aggregate output and government purchases, as well as the positive effects of transitory shocks (such as wars and recessions) on government deficits and debts.

21.2 Keynesian Stabilization Policy, Automatic Stabilizers, and Fiscal Implications of the Zero Lower Bound

An alternative to the tax-smoothing approach is the Keynesian approach to stabilization policy. According to the Keynesian approach, higher government spending or lower taxes during a recession may speed up the recovery. The reason is that under high unemployment and low capacity utilization, higher government spending and lower tax rates can increase aggregate demand and bring output closer to full employment output.

As we saw in chapter 15, Keynesian models would prescribe that deficits should be countercyclical, that is, increase in recessions and become surpluses in booms. However, there is no reason such cyclical deficits should lead to a secular increase in government debt-to-output ratios. Increases in government purchases during recessions could be compensated by discretionary spending cuts during booms, leading to constant government debt to output ratios over the business cycle. Such policies have similar effects in new Keynesian DSGE models as well.

However, there are important counterarguments against this traditional Keynesian fiscal prescription. The main counterargument is the existence of long and variable lags in the design, implementation, and effects of changes in fiscal policy.[1] These lags are particularly important and relate to delays in the recognition of the need for a fiscal stimulus, the political discussion of it, the implementation of the necessary adjustments through the legislative budgetary process, and the ultimate realization of its macroeconomic effects. Such lags also arise in the case of monetary policy, but they are much longer in the case of fiscal policy, as the budgetary process is a long and drawn out political process compared to the relatively swift decision making process for monetary policy. Therefore, by the time a fiscal stimulus is enacted, it may be too late and may even prove counterproductive.

Thus, even for someone who otherwise accepts the theoretical arguments in favor of discretionary Keynesian fiscal policy, the fact that monetary policy is more flexible than fiscal policy (because it has shorter decision and implementation lags) could be reason enough to prefer monetary over fiscal policy. However, in cases where monetary policy has hit the zero lower bound, a more convincing argument can be made for countercyclical changes in fiscal policy.[2]

In any case, even with constant tax rates and expenditure plans, the fiscal system acts in a stabilizing way. This takes place through the operation of the so-called *automatic stabilizers*. If tax rates are constant (say, because of tax-smoothing considerations), a

1. The term "long and variable lags" is due to Friedman [1961], who introduced it in relation to monetary policy.

2. See, for example, Eggerstsson [2010] and Christiano et al. [2011], who comprehensively investigate fiscal policy at the zero lower bound in the context of new Keynesian models. Krugman [2012] also contains a forceful advocacy of this particular position with respect to the Great Recession of 2008–2009.

decline in economic activity reduces aggregate tax revenue and causes fiscal deficits to rise. Government expenditure also increases, because of automatic rises in expenditure for social programs, such as unemployment insurance. Hence, deficits rise in recessions and decline in booms, exerting a stabilizing influence through aggregate demand, even without discretionary changes in fiscal policy.

The operation of automatic stabilizers is consistent with tax-smoothing theories and is an additional reason as to why government deficits and government debt rise in recessions and decline in booms. An additional role for discretionary changes in fiscal policy may arise in cases where monetary policy has hit the zero lower bound.

21.3 Optimal Dynamic Ramsey Taxation

The Barro [1979] model assumes but does not explicitly model the distortions implied by taxation. As we saw in the simple two-period intertemporal models of chapter 2, income taxes imply two main types of distortions. First, they distort the choice between leisure and labor supply in every period. And second, they distort the intertemporal choice between current and future consumption and current and future labor supply. The latter is an intertemporal distortion.

The optimal choice of tax rates in an environment in which a representative household chooses among various consumption goods optimally was first studied formally by Ramsey [1927]. Dynamic versions of this problem have been studied by Lucas and Stokey [1983], Chamley [1986], Aiyagari et al. [2002], and Angeletos [2002]. Chari and Kehoe [1999] and Alesina and Passalacqua [2016] review this literature, which is known as the *dynamic Ramsey approach* to fiscal policy.

Consider an economy with an infinite number of periods and a large number of identical households. There is no uncertainty. The representative household has preferences of the form

$$\sum_{i=0}^{\infty} \beta^i \left[u(c_{t+i}) - v(l_{t+i})\right], \quad 0<\beta=\frac{1}{1+\rho}<1, \tag{21.15}$$

where ρ is the pure rate of time preference, c_{t+i} is consumption in period $t+i$, l_{t+i} is labor supply in period $t+i$, and u and v are twice differentiable concave functions.

All households are initially endowed with $\bar{k}_t$ units of capital. Capital depreciates at a rate δ. In addition, households possess a technology that converts period t consumption goods into period $t+1$ capital goods, and vice versa.

The economy has many competitive firms with a production technology that converts capital k and labor l into y units of consumption goods. This is a production function of the form

$$y_{t+i}=F(k_{t+i}, l_{t+i}). \tag{21.16}$$

This function is quasi-concave and satisfies the usual properties of the neoclassical production function.

Households rent their labor services and capital goods to firms, in competitive factor markets. The returns to labor and capital are sequences of competitive real wages and real interest rates $\{w_{t+i}, r_{t+i}\}$.

The government can convert private goods into public goods one for one. The government is required to create a stream of public goods c^g_{t+i}, $i=0,1,\ldots$. The government needs to raise funds to make its purchases of public goods. It can find the funds through borrowing and lending at the sequence of competitive real interest rates $\{r_{t+i}\}$, levying linear taxes on labor income at rates $\{\tau^l_{t+i}\}$, or levying linear taxes on capital income at rates $\{\tau^k_{t+i}\}$.

The dynamic Ramsey problem consists of the government choosing the sequence of tax rates $\{\tau^l_{t+i}, \tau^k_{t+i}\}$ that maximizes the intertemporal utility function of the representative household, subject to the exogenous sequence of government purchases $\{c^g_{t+i}\}$, the sequences of equilibrium private consumption and employment $\{c_{t+i}, l_{t+i}\}$ resulting from the utility-maximizing choices of households and the profit-maximizing choices of firms, and the sequences of equilibrium real wages and real interest rates $\{w_{t+i}, r_{t+i}\}$. Assume that the government can commit to this choice at the beginning of period t.

One can show that the optimal sequence of tax rates $\{\tilde{\tau}^l_{t+i}, \tilde{\tau}^k_{t+i}\}$ satisfies[3]

$$\tilde{\tau}^l_{t+i} = 1 - \frac{v'(\tilde{l}_{t+i})}{u'(\tilde{c}_{t+i})F_l(\tilde{k}_{t+i}, \tilde{l}_{t+i})}, \tag{21.17}$$

$$\tilde{\tau}^k_{t+i} = 1 - \frac{\left(u'(\tilde{c}_{t+i})/\beta u'(\tilde{c}_{t+i+1})\right) - 1 + \delta}{F_k(\tilde{k}_{t+i}, \tilde{l}_{t+i})}, \tag{21.18}$$

for $i \geq 1$. The sequence $\{\tilde{c}_{t+i}, \tilde{l}_{t+i}, \tilde{k}_{t+i}\}$ is the optimal equilibrium sequence of private consumption, employment, and capital chosen by households and firms, given the optimal tax rates.

As discussed by Chari and Kehoe [1999], the optimal policy has the following two characteristics:

1. Capital income taxes must be high initially and then zero.
2. Tax rates on labor income should be constant.

The intuition behind the first characteristic is straightforward. A high capital income tax initially is optimal, because initial capital is predetermined. However, a positive capital income tax at date t means that the government is essentially taxing consumption in period $t+1$ at a higher rate than consumption in period t. Hence, if the government maintains a positive long-run capital income tax rate, it is essentially taxing consumption at dates $t+i$ at

3. See Chari and Kehoe [1999] or Kocherlakota [2010] for the details of the derivation of the optimal tax rates.

progressively higher rates, as i increases. As a result, the intertemporal distortion becomes progressively higher, and such an outcome is clearly suboptimal. Hence, capital income taxes must converge to zero.

In contrast, the second characteristic results because there is no reason to have time-varying static distortions between consumption and leisure, given the concavity of the utility functions. Hence, the optimal tax rate on labor income is positive and constant.

Tax smoothing is thus a characteristic of dynamic Ramsey taxation as well.

However, these results do not fully carry over to stochastic representative household models. As discussed by Lucas and Stokey [1983], Aiyagari et al. [2002], and Angeletos [2002], tax smoothing is modified in stochastic environments.

Lucas and Stokey [1983] consider a model with complete markets, no capital, exogenous Markov government expenditures, and state-contingent taxes and government debt. In this environment, optimal tax rates and government debt are not random walks, and the serial correlation of optimal taxes is tied closely to that of government purchases. Moreover, they find that taxes should be smooth, not by being random walks but by having a smaller variance than would be implied by a balanced budget. Thus, to some extent, the idea of tax smoothing holds but not in the extreme version of Barro [1979].

Aiyagari et al. [2002] reconsider the optimal taxation problem in an incomplete markets setting. They begin with the same economy as in Lucas and Stokey [1983] but allow only risk-free government debt. Under some restrictions on preferences and the quantities of risk-free claims that the government can issue and own, it is possible to recover Barro's random walk characterization of optimal taxation.

However, by dropping the restriction on government asset holdings (or modifying preferences), one can generate different results, as, for example, in the model of Angeletos [2002], who considers noncontingent debt with varying maturities. The Angeletos model, although based on noncontingent debt, has implications similar to Lucas and Stokey [1983] in the presence of precommitment.

Additional complications arise in overlapping generations (OLG) models or other models with heterogeneous agents. For example, if households differ in their ability, but the government cannot directly observe or tax the ability of households and relies on their wage income instead, then additional distortions are introduced. Kocherlakota [2010] discusses a dynamic extension of the static Mirlees [1971] approach to this problem, as well as other extensions that rely on agent heterogeneity. This approach has been termed *new dynamic public finance*, but it is in many ways an extension of dynamic Ramsey taxation to environments with agent heterogeneity and asymmetric information.

Another weakness of the dynamic Ramsey approach (but also other dynamic public finance approaches) is that without state-contingent government debt, dynamic optimal fiscal plans rely on precommitment. Such approaches have been shown to suffer from the time-inconsistency problem, meaning that at some point in time, the government may have an incentive to deviate from its preannounced ex ante optimal tax policy (Kydland

and Prescott [1977], Calvo [1978]). For example, consider a policymaker (social planner) who, after a war (or a recession), is faced with tackling (reducing) the higher government debt that was accumulated during the war (or the recession). The ex ante optimal policy, on which the accumulation of debt was based, is to create primary surpluses by increasing tax rates after the war or the recession. However, ex post, the policymaker has at least three other options. First, to default on the debt. Second, to impose an extraordinary tax on the wealth of bondholders. Third, to generate unexpected inflation and monetize the debt. These options may appear ex post to imply smaller social costs than the rise in distortionary taxes. Thus, what was optimal before the accumulation of government debt may not appear optimal after government debt has accumulated. This is how the time-inconsistency problem arises. If the government succumbs to the temptation of the options of default, a capital levy, or monetization, it may lose reputation with bondholders and find it extremely difficult to borrow in the future. If the government sticks to the ex ante optimal policy, it does not lose reputation but may incur heavy social and political costs in trying to stabilize the debt that was accumulated through an increase in distortionary taxes. It may thus refrain from increasing future tax rates and follow one of the default options.

The solutions that have been proposed for the time-inconsistency problem resemble those that have been proposed for monetary policy. Binding budget rules and reform of political institutions can help constrain the freedom of governments to deviate from the ex ante optimal policy and thus can address the time inconsistency problem. Alesina and Passalacqua [2016] review the literature on this issue.

21.4 Fiscal Policy and Politics

Things become even more complicated once we allow for the role of politics. If various groups of economic agents have conflicting objectives, then distributional and political considerations will arise as well. These richer models help explain why government debt may also increase for reasons not related to wars or recessions.

21.4.1 Distributional Considerations and Politics

Consider a simple example highlighted by Alesina [1988]. He assumes that there are three groups of agents: rentiers (who hold government debt), entrepreneurs (who hold equity in firms), and workers (who hold human capital). Obviously in reality, a continuum exists between these three groups, as each household may hold different amounts of each particular form of capital.

The three groups will favor different solutions to the government debt problem. Rentiers will oppose default or inflation and will favor reductions in government expenditure or taxes on firms and workers. The entrepreneurs will favor debt default and inflation as well as taxes on labor. Workers will favor default, taxes on capital, and inflation, provided their real wages are protected from inflation. The debt stabilization policies that will actually be followed will be the outcome of a political equilibrium, involving all three groups.

One potential solution is offered by Downsian median voter models (see Downs [1957]). In such models, politics converges to the preferences of the median voter. If the median voter is a worker, a democratic government will tend to favor default, capital taxation, and inflation. If rentiers and entrepreneurs prevail (in the sense of the median voter model), labor taxes will be increased and social expenditure reduced. However, median voter equilibria exist under very restrictive conditions. If every group can block the preferences of the other two but is unable to impose its own preferred solution, then government debt will not be tackled and will continue accumulating well after the war or the initial recession.

Such models provide an explanation as to why we have been observing a bias toward excessive fiscal deficits and rises in debt-to-output ratios in peacetime. Governments are reluctant to make decisions that would stabilize government debt, for fear of alienating one or more of the political groups that stand to lose from an adjustment program. Such decisions are even more difficult in electoral periods. Models of this form are analyzed in the new political economy literature.

Such considerations characterize models that directly try to explain why governments delay adopting effective fiscal adjustment programs. See Alesina and Drazen [1991] and Velasco [1999].

21.4.2 Electoral Factors and Partisan Differences

Electoral factors and partisan politics also play a role. Let us first consider electoral factors. The basic idea is that before the election, decision makers attempt to use fiscal policy to positively influence voters and thus maximize their chance of staying in power. This is called the *opportunistic* or *electoral* incentive. Contrary to what is generally believed, providing theoretical interpretations of such electoral fiscal cycles is not straightforward under the assumption of rational expectations. The question that arises is: Why would rational voters want to reward a government that causes a pre-election budget cycle, when they know that this is for opportunistic reasons?

Rogoff and Sibert [1988] and Rogoff [1990] provide a neat theoretical explanation based on asymmetric information between governments and voters and how governments can exploit this asymmetry. In their model, the effectiveness of government cannot be directly observed by voters. Voters simply observe an electoral improvement in their economic condition, which may result from an increase in government spending or tax cuts. They do not know during the election whether this improvement is artificial and temporary or the result of an effective economic policy. Voters will thus rationally attribute part of the economic improvement they observe to the effectiveness of government policy, and thus the popularity of the government will increase. Consequently, the ruling party has every incentive to increase public spending and reduce taxes before the election to maximize its popularity. Models of asymmetric information can thus explain the expansion of fiscal deficits during elections. Even if voters know that the government has an electoral incentive to reduce taxes and increase public spending, they rationally attribute only part of the economic improvement observed to the opportunism of incumbent governments; the rest is attributed to the effectiveness of government policy.

The model of Rogoff and Sibert for electoral cycles has been enriched by the introduction of partisan differences. Persson and Svensson [1989] and Alesina and Tabellini [1990] introduced partisan differences and the possibility of issuing debt to develop a theory of electoral cycles based on the strategic use of debt.

The basic idea of models based on partisan differences is that policymakers belong to political parties, which have different ideological premises and strive to meet the aspirations of different constituencies. Thus, a "left" leaning government would be aiming for a larger public sector than would a "right" leaning government. Left wing parties would tend to favor the role of the public sector, while right wing parties would tend to rely more on the private sector. Left wing parties would be less averse to high capital income and wealth taxes than right wing parties, having a stronger faith in the redistributive role of taxes. This somewhat stylized and oversimplified distinction is not far from the preferences of voters and parties in most mixed economies and is a key characteristic of partisan models.

Every government knows that, with some probability, voters will replace it at some future election. If it can control a state variable, such as government debt, it will try to use that variable strategically to influence the future choices of its successors in the direction of its own preferences or in the direction of the preferences of its constituents. Of course, for this to be possible, government debt must not be neutral. For example, if taxation is distortionary, a change in the time path of government debt will have permanent effects on the economy, and will even have effects that cannot be fully reversed by future governments.

Persson and Svensson [1989] show that an increase in government debt from a right wing government can be an equilibrium strategy, as it binds its successors to restrain primary public spending in the future. Thus, if a right wing government were to cut taxes today and increase government debt, this puts pressure on its left wing successors to limit future primary expenditure along with a future increase in taxes. The intertemporal distribution of the tax burden may not be optimal, but the future path of fiscal policy will be nearer to the objectives of the right wing incumbent. When the ideological differences between political parties are large, then the trend is for an increase in government debt, even by right wing governments.

A related idea of Tabellini and Alesina [1990] is that governments disagree on the composition of public spending. Again we have an increasing trend in public deficits as the government borrows to increase the type of spending it prefers, knowing that future spending cuts or tax increases to service the debt will come from all areas, including those it does not favor.

Another strand of the literature focuses on the fact that elections result in myopic behavior on the part of incumbent governments. If governments do not care about the state of the economy in case they are not reelected, in election years, they will be more reluctant to incur the costs associated with adjusting government expenditure and taxes, as they discount the future benefits in terms of lower government debt more heavily. Lockwood et al. [1996] set up and estimate models of this nature. Their model is based on the shorter horizon that governments have at election times, which result in a weakening of the incentive to stabilize government debt.

This literature concludes that political institutions matter for the accumulation of government debt. Elections, political instability, and wide ideological differences between the main political parties result in greater deficits and debt.

The literature on the politico-economic causes of high deficits and debts grew exponentially in the early1990s. Among others, see the papers by Cukierman and Meltzer [1989], Alesina and Tabellini [1990], Aghion and Bolton [1990], Alesina and Drazen [1991], Tabellini [1991], and Velasco [1999]. Many cross-country studies have also emerged, focusing on the association between political instability and debt. See Roubini and Sachs [1989] and Grilli et al. [1991], among others. Many of the important early contributions to this literature are collected in Persson and Tabellini [1994b]. An early survey is in Alesina and Perotti [1995]. Comprehensive analyses of the main political economy models of fiscal policy can be found in Persson and Tabellini [2000] and Drazen [2000]. A more recent survey can be found in Alesina and Passalacqua [2016].

21.5 The Burden of High Government Deficits and Debt

Despite extensive research, the burden (i.e., social costs) of high government deficits and debt is not very well understood by macroeconomists. This is not unlike the case for the costs of inflation. Various reasons account for this difficulty.

One reason is that the costs of deficits and government debt depend on the type of macroeconomic model one adopts. In representative household models with nondistortionary taxes, Ricardian equivalence holds, and sustainable government deficits and debts have zero real economic costs. In OLG models, high government debt results in lower savings and investment, lower growth rates, and lower steady state per capita income and consumption. In Keynesian models, higher government deficits during a recession help speed up the recovery and have posititive economic benefits. In models with distortionary taxation, higher government deficits and debts, even if sustainable, result in higher distortionary taxes, lower labor supply and employment, lower capital accumulation and growth, and lower steady state per capita income and consumption.

A second reason is that the costs of deficits and government debt also depend on the differential impact they have on the distribution of income. Welfare analysis is difficult to conduct, as it requires interpersonal and intergenerational comparisons of utility through a social welfare function.

A third reason is that in the presence of uncertainty, it is not straightforward to determine ex ante whether deficits are sustainable or unsustainable. Hence, to the extent that a high government debt is also deemed to be unsustainable, it is also associated with the possibility of a government debt crisis that will force a sudden stop to government borrowing, with possibly significant economic costs. Such a model of government debt crises is presented in the next section.

21.6 A Model of Government Debt Crises

In this section, we consider a simple two-period model of government debt crises. This model is due to Calvo [1988]. We focus on the question of what can cause a government debt crisis, in the sense that investors are not prepared to hold government bonds at a finite interest rate.

The model consists of two equilibrium conditions. The one equilibrium condition is the *debt-holding condition*. This condition requires the expected return on government debt to be equal to the return of a perfectly safe asset. The expected return is the probability of repayment, defined as one minus the expected default probability multiplied by the return on the government bond. The second equilibrium condition is a positive association of the probability of default with the level of government debt and the interest rate on government debt. Let us term this the *debt-default condition*.

21.6.1 The Calvo Model

Consider a two-period model. In period 0, the government wants to issue one-period bonds with a real value of D to finance its budget deficit. In period 1, which is the last period in the model, the government has to repay the debt, using the proceeds from its period 1 primary surplus $S = T - C^g$, where T is real tax revenue, assumed exogenous, and C^g is an exogenously determined amount of real government purchases.

The government offers investors a real interest rate r. Thus, in period 1, it will have to repay RD, where the interest factor R is defined by $R = 1 + r$. The primary surplus S in period 1 is uncertain and is a continuous random variable with a probability density function $f(S)$ and a cumulative distribution function $F(S)$.

If the primary surplus S in period 1 is higher than RD, the government repays the investors and, because this is the last period, returns the remaining revenue to households. If the primary surplus S is smaller that RD, the government cannot repay the full amount and defaults on its debt, returning the primary surplus to households.

Investors have access to a safe asset, which offers a safe rate of return r^*. Thus, the interest factor of the safe asset is equal to $R^* = (1 + r^*)$.

To keep the model tractable, we thus make two simplifying assumptions. First, we assume that if the government cannot pay RD, then it pays nothing and defaults fully. Second, we assume that investors are risk neutral and that the rate of return of the safe asset $R^* - 1$ is independent of R and D.

In asset market equilibrium, the expected rate of return of government debt $r = R - 1$ should be equal to the rate of return of the safe asset, $r^* = R^* - 1$. If investors expect that government debt pays R with probability $1 - p^e$, and zero with probability p^e, they will only buy government debt if $(1 - p^e)R \geq R^*$. Arbitrage will ensure that the expected rate of return of government bonds will be driven down to the rate of return of the safe asset. Thus, with risk neutral investors, equilibrium in financial markets in period 0 will imply

$$(1 - p^e)R = R^*. \tag{21.19}$$

The interest factor on government debt is thus given by

$$R = \frac{R^*}{1 - p^e}. \tag{21.20}$$

The higher the expected probability of default is, the higher the interest factor of government debt will be for a given interest factor of the safe asset. This equilibrium condition is depicted as the *debt holding curve* $R = R^*/(1 - p^e)$ in figure 21.1. The interest factor of government debt R is a positive function of the expected probability of default p^e. As the expected probability of default tends to unity, R tends to infinity.

In fact, as a percentage of the interest factor R, the equilibrium risk premium on government debt is equal to the expected probability of default p^e. Solving (21.20) for p^e, we get

$$p^e = \frac{R - R*}{R}. \tag{21.21}$$

The second key relation of the model comes from the fact that the government defaults if and only if its primary surplus S in period 1 turns out to be lower than RD. Thus, the actual probability of default is equal to the probability that S is less than RD, or that $S/D < R$. Because F is assumed to be the cumulative distribution function of S, the actual probability of default is given by

$$p = F(RD). \tag{21.22}$$

Clearly, for a given D, the higher R is, the higher will be the actual probability of default, because the government requires a higher primary surplus to repay the higher interest charge on its debt.

The actual probability of default as a function of the interest factor R is depicted in figure 21.2 under two alternative assumptions about the density function $f(S)$.

The first assumption is that $f(S)$ is the *continuous uniform distribution*, with support $[S_m, S_M]$, where S_m is the minimum and S_M the maximum possible primary surplus in period 1. The shape of the cumulative distribution function under the assumption of a

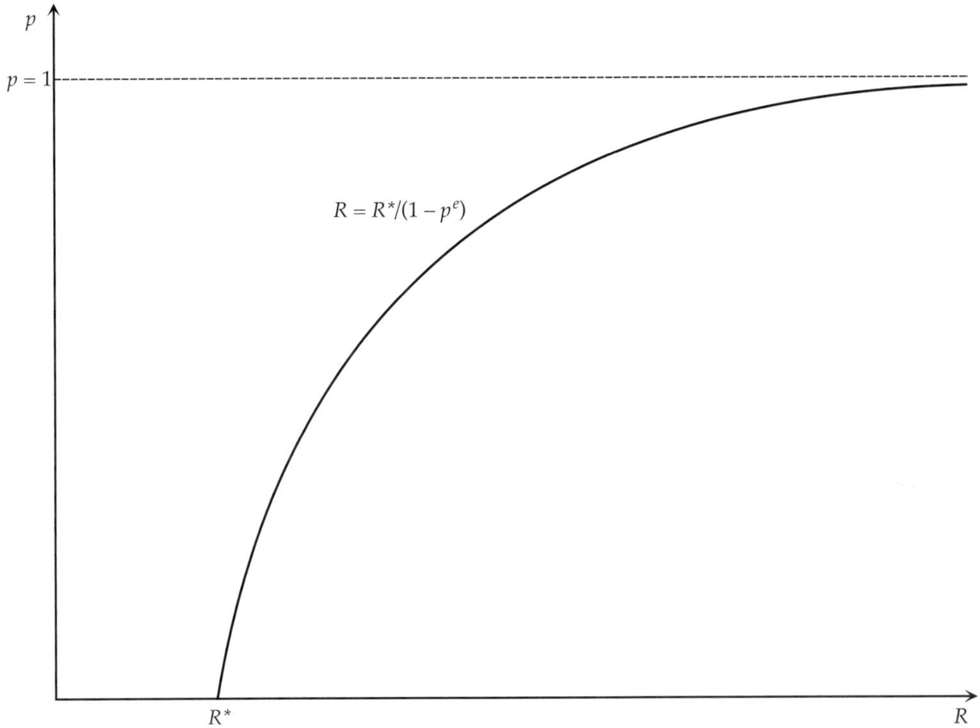

Figure 21.1
Expected default and the debt holding condition.

uniform density function is depicted as $F_U(S)$ in figure 21.2. Between S_m/D and S_M/D, the cumulative distribution function rises at a constant rate from 0 to 1. Thus, if $R < S_m/D$, the probability of default p is equal to zero, and if $R > S_M/D$, the probability of default is equal to unity. In between, the probability of default lies between zero and one and is rising at a constant rate as the interest factor rises.

The second assumption is that $f(S)$ is the *truncated normal distribution*, with support $[S_m, S_M]$, where, again, S_m is the minimum and S_M the maximum possible primary surplus.

The shape of the cumulative distribution function under the assumption of a truncated normal density function is depicted as $F_N(S)$ in figure 21.2. Between S_m/D and S_M/D, the cumulative distribution function rises, at an initially increasing and subsequently decreasing rate, from 0 to 1. Thus, if $R < S_m/D$, the probability of default p is equal to zero, and if $R > S_M/D$, the probability is equal to unity. In between, the probability of default lies between zero and one and is rising at an initially increasing and subsequently falling rate as the interest factor rises.

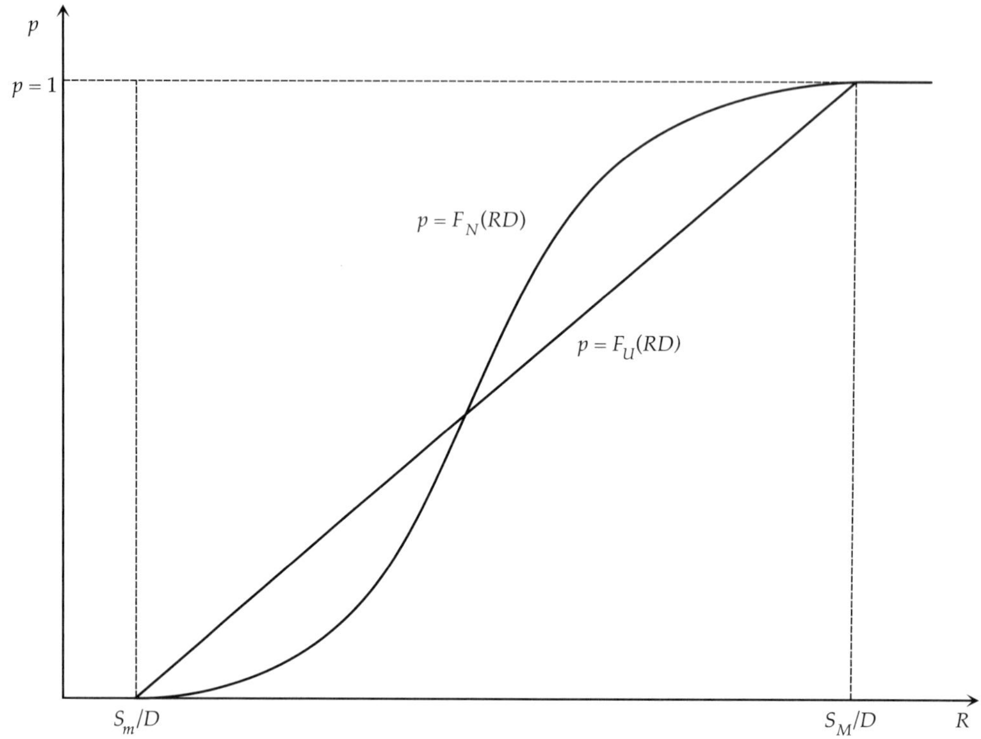

Figure 21.2
The actual probability of default and the cumulative distribution of the primary surplus.

In fact, any symmetric bell-shaped continuous density function would have a cumulative distribution function with a shape similar to the one for the truncated normal distribution depicted in figure 21.2.

Rational expectations equilibrium requires that the expected probability of default is equal to the actual probability of default. Thus, both the debt holding condition (21.21) and the probability of default condition (21.22) must be satisfied simultaneously. Recall that the debt holding condition means that the higher the expected default probability is, the higher will be the interest rate required by investors. In contrast, the dependence of the probability of default on the uncertain primary surplus means that the higher the interest rate required by investors is, the higher the actual probability of default will be, given the distribution of the primary surplus. Because investors move first, a higher expected probability of default may result in a higher actual probability of default, stemming from the higher interest rate on government debt.

Figure 21.3 depicts the possible equilibria for the case of a uniform distribution. The figure shows the case of a low rate of return on the safe asset, in the sense that $R^* < S_m/D$.

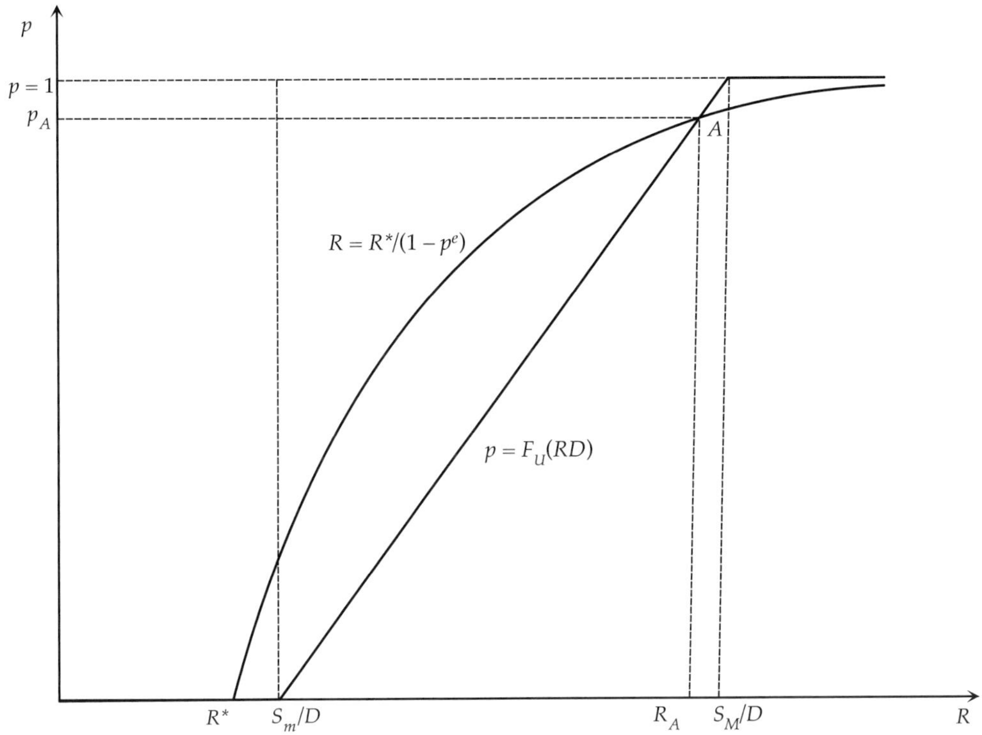

Figure 21.3
Determination of the interest factor and the probability of default for a low rate of return of the safe asset.

The economy depicted in figure 21.3, has three possible equilibria. One has a zero probability of default and a rate of return of government bonds equal to the rate of return of the safe asset r^*. The second, with an equilibrium at A, is characterized by a high probability of default and a high risk premium on government debt. The third has an equilibrium with a probability of default equal to unity and no government debt. This last equilibrium in fact implies a government debt crisis: The government cannot in this case find investors willing to hold government debt D at a finite interest rate.

Which equilibrium will prevail depends on the prior expectations of investors about the probability of default. If investors believe that the default probability is zero, then the interest factor on government debt will be equal to R^*, and the default probability will indeed be zero. If investors believe that the default probability is high (say, p_A), then the interest factor on government debt will be at R_A, at a high premium over the safe asset R^*. The default probability will indeed be high in this case, and equal to p_A. Finally, if investors believe that the government will default with certainty (i.e., if $p^e = 1$), then the government will not be able to borrow at a finite interest rate, and a debt crisis will be the only equilibrium outcome.

Of the three equilibria, one is dynamically unstable in the sense that if investors adapt their expectations to close the gap between the expected and the actual probability of default, the economy will move toward the other two equilibria. In figure 21.3, this is equilibrium A with a high probability of default. If the expectations of investors lead to an interest factor slightly lower than R_A, then the expected probability of default will turn out to be higher than the actual probability of default. This would lead to a reduction in the expected probability of default, and the economy will converge to R^*. But if the expectations of investors lead to an interest factor slightly higher than R_A, then the expected probability of default will be lower than the actual probability of default. This would lead to a rise in the expected probability of default, and the economy will converge to a probability of default equal to unity and undergo a debt crisis. Thus, the only dynamically stable equilibria in this case are the equilibria with a zero and a unitary probability of default.

The equilibrium with a zero default probability and $R=R^*$ is possible only if $R^* < S_m/D$. If $R^* > S_m/D$, this equilibrium is ruled out. The possible equilibria in this case are depicted in figure 21.4. Again there are three possible equilibria. The first is A, with a low probability of default and a rate of return of government bonds slightly higher than the rate of return of the safe asset r^*. The second equilibrium is B, with a high probability of default and a high risk premium on government debt. And the third is an equilibrium with a probability of default equal to unity and a government debt crisis. In the latter case, the government cannot find investors willing to hold government debt D at a finite interest rate. An analysis of the dynamic stability of the three equilibria suggests that the only dynamically stable equilibria are A and the equilibrium with a unitary probability of default; B is dynamically unstable. A similar analysis can be conducted using the truncated normal or any bell-shaped distribution instead of the uniform distribution.

An important characteristic of this model is that, because of the multiplicity of equilibria, the probability of default depends not only on economic fundamentals (such as the size of real government debt and the probability distribution of the government primary surplus) but also on self-fulfilling expectations. If investors expect a zero or low probability of default, the actual probability of default will be zero or low. If investors expect a high probability of default, the actual probability of default will be high, and the government will have to pay a high interest premium. If the expected probability of default is equal to one, then the government will be unable to borrow at all, and a debt crisis will be the only equilibrium outcome.

21.6.2 Multiple Equilibria and Self-Fulfilling Prophecies

Because of nonlinearities in the model and the multiplicity of equilibria, small changes in the fundamentals can bring about large changes in equilibrium default probabilities and interest rates on government debt, or move the economy from one equilibrium to another.

We can draw four basic conclusions from this model. First, there are multiple equilibria. In the examples we have used, one equilibrium implies a zero or low probability of default

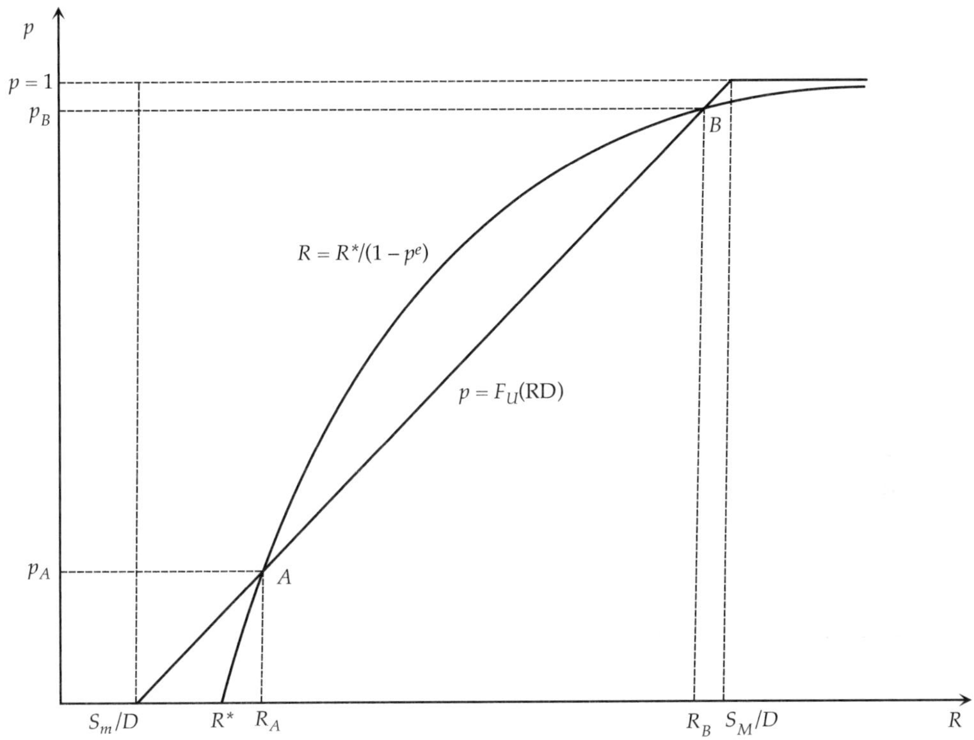

Figure 21.4
Determination of the interest factor and the probability of default for a high rate of return of the safe asset.

and a low divergence of the interest rate on government debt from the safe rate. The second equilibrium implies a probability of default equal to unity and a failure of the government to borrow at any interest rate. A third intermediate equilibrium with a high probability of default exists as well, but it is dynamically unstable.

Second, in this model, the equilibrium that prevails depends on the expectations of investors. If investors expect a zero or low probability of default, the equilibrium will be characterized by a zero or low spread of the interest rate on government debt over the rate of the safe asset. If investors expect that the government will default with certainty, the government will be unable to borrow at any interest rate. Consequently, what equilibrium will prevail is to a large extent a self-fulfilling expectation or prophecy.

Third, small changes in the fundamentals can bring about large equilibrium changes and move us from one equilibrium to another. This is because even small changes to the fundamentals can cause large changes in expectations.

Fourth, when default occurs, it is unexpected. It is a jump from a low probability of default equilibrium to an equilibrium with a unitary probability of default.

The Calvo [1988] model can be extended to multiple time periods or to a monetary economy. In a monetary economy, instead of outright default, the government may choose to issue money to repay its debt, and default may take the form of unexpected high inflation. Again, there are multiple equilibria, such as an equilibrium with a low nominal interest rate and low inflation, or one with a high nominal interest rate and high inflation that wipes out government debt. With multiple time periods, it is of the utmost importance whether investors believe that other investors in the future will be willing to hold government debt.

This model and other stochastic default models interpret debt crises as crises of confidence that are caused by changes in the expectations of investors. These may take place because of changes in fiscal fundamentals, large or small. But they may also occur for other reasons that are purely expectational and not related to the fundamentals of fiscal policy.

21.7 Conclusion

In this chapter, we have surveyed the macroeconomic role of fiscal policy. We have seen that in the presence of distortionary taxes, Ricardian equivalence does not hold, and the level of government debt matters. In steady state, higher levels of government debt are associated with higher distortionary tax rates, and therefore with higher negative tax distortions. The same obviously applies to higher primary government purchases. This applies even in representative household models where, if taxes are nondistortionary, government purchases and government debt do not affect capital accumulation and the dynamic path of output. Distortionary taxation results in negative effects on capital accumulation and labor supply. If distortionary taxes have to rise to stabilize the government debt-to-output ratio at a higher level (or to finance a higher ratio of government purchases to output), there will be negative effects on steady state per capita income and economic growth.

An additional negative effect of high government debt is the possibillity of a debt crisis. In models with an endogenous probability of default, the likelihood of a debt crisis is higher if government debts and deficits are high.

Thus, in the presence of distortionary taxes, high public debt implies two types of costs:

1. In models with distortionary taxation, higher government deficits and debts, even if sustainable, result in higher distortionary taxes, lower labor supply and employment, lower capital accumulation and growth, and lower steady state per capita income and consumption.
2. In models with potential default, higher government deficits and debts result in a higher probability of default, which brings about an increase in interest rates on government debt and increases the likelihood of a debt crisis.

22

Bubbles, Multiple Equilibria, and Sunspots

In most of the models analyzed so far, we have concentrated on unique steady states and unique convergent paths toward the steady state. In both the deterministic models with perfect foresight (such as the ones in the chapters on economic growth) and the stochastic models with rational expectations (such as the ones in the chapters on aggregate fluctuations), we have focused on the *fundamental solutions*. With few exceptions,[1] the solutions were unique and were characterized by the saddle point property.

In this chapter, we focus on solutions other than the fundamental solution, and we delve deeper into models in which there are multiple equilibria.

Let us start with the analysis of bubbles in linear first-order rational expectations models, and then move on to nonlinear dynamic models with multiple equilibria, self-fulfilling prophecies, and sunspots.

Bubbles refer to nonfundamental solutions in rational expectations models, and can even arise in linear models with a unique equilibrium based on fundamentals. In models characterized by the saddle point property, bubbles result in explosive solutions, which in many cases can be ruled out by appropriate transversality conditions. In inherently unstable models which are not characterized by the saddle point property, there are multiple adjustments paths. In such models, bubbles are not explosive and can thus be stabilizing.[2]

Compared to the properties of models with a unique steady state, nonlinear dynamic models possessing multiple equilibria provide a different account of the growth process, the propagation mechanism of business cycles, and the monetary transmission mechanism. Closely related to multiple equilibria in such models is the concept of *sunspot equilibria*, developed by Shell [1977] and Cass and Shell [1983]. This refers to equilibria influenced by extrinsic belief shocks in a general equilibrium setting. Sunspot equilibria can be constructed by randomizing over multiple equilibria. They require deviations from the Arrow-Debreu

1. Examples of exceptions include the Samuelson and Diamond overlapping generations models and the Calvo public debt model.

2. See Blanchard and Watson [1982] for an early analysis of bubbles versus fundamentals under rational expectations. A more recent and comprehensive survey can be found in Brunnermeier [2008].

structure of complete markets, such as those occurring in overlapping generations (OLG) models or models with externalities, informational asymmetries, increasing returns to scale, and money.[3]

In the remainder of this chapter, we explore examples of models with bubbles, multiple equilibria, self-fulfilling prophecies, and sunspots, focusing on models of financial markets and general equilibrium models with money.

22.1 Bubbles in Linear Rational Expectations Models

Consider a linear model in which a non-predetermined endogenous variable y depends on the rational expectation of its future value and on another exogenous variable x. The model, which is the same as the one analyzed in chapter 9 on models with rational expectations, is described by a first-order linear difference equation of the form

$$y_t = aE_t y_{t+1} + bx_t, \tag{22.1}$$

where E_t denotes the rational expectations of a variable, conditional on the information set available in period t, and a and b are constant parameters. The rational expectations hypothesis implies that economic agents know that the variable y is determined by (22.1). We also assume that all economic agents have access to the same information set.[4]

Repeatedly substituting the future expectations of y, until time $t+T$, we get

$$y_t = a^{T+1} E_t y_{t+T+1} + b \sum\nolimits_{s=0}^{T} a^s E_t x_{t+s}. \tag{22.2}$$

To have convergence of the last term in (22.2) as T tends to infinity, the absolute value of a must be less than one (i.e., $|a| < 1$), and the expected value of x should not increase too quickly. If the expected value of x increases exponentially, its growth rate should not exceed $(1/a) - 1$. Under these conditions, it follows that

$$\lim_{T\to\infty} a^{T+1} E_t y_{t+T+1} = 0. \tag{22.3}$$

Then a solution of (22.1) can be derived from (22.2):

$$y_t^f = b \sum\nolimits_{s=0}^{\infty} a^s E_t x_{t+s}. \tag{22.4}$$

Equation (22.4) satisfies condition (22.3) and is thus a solution of (22.1). It suggests that the current value of the endogenous variable y is the discounted sum of the expected future

3. For a comprehensive survey of this literature, see Benhabib and Farmer [1999].

4. This section follows Blanchard and Watson [1982].

values of the exogenous variable x, with a discount factor equal to a. This solution is usually called the *fundamental solution* and is denoted by superscript f.

22.1.1 Bubbles versus Fundamentals

However, note that (22.4) is not the only solution of (22.1). The fundamental solution is based only on the minimum number of variables (x in our case), the so-called fundamentals, and satisfies the convergence condition (22.3). If (22.3) is not satisfied, then a host of other, nonfundamental, solutions exists.

Suppose there is an alternative solution to (22.1) that consists of (22.4) plus an extraneous variable z. This solution takes the form

$$y_t = b\sum_{s=0}^{\infty} a^s E_t x_{t+s} + z_t. \tag{22.5}$$

One can easily demonstrate that for any extraneous variable z that satisfies

$$z_t = aE_t z_{t+1}, \tag{22.6}$$

or equivalently,

$$E_t z_{t+1} = \frac{z_t}{a},$$

(22.5) is also a solution of (22.1). To demonstrate this, express (22.5) as

$$y_t = \frac{b}{1-aF}x_t + z_t = aE_t y_{t+1} + bx_t + z_t - aE_t z_{t+1}, \tag{22.7}$$

where F is the forward shift operator. Substituting (22.6) in (22.7) gives us back the original model (22.1). Hence, (22.5) is also a solution of (22.1).

However, note that because $-1 < a < 1$, the mathematical expectation of the future z explodes over time. This can be proven by taking the limit of the mathematical expectation as time tends to infinity. This limit is given by

$$\lim_{s\to\infty} E_t z_{t+s} = \left(\frac{1}{a}\right)^s z_t = \pm\infty,$$

depending on whether z is positive or negative.

Hence, solutions like (22.5), based on nonfundamental variables such as z, do not satisfy the convergence condition (22.3). Such solutions are called *bubbles*, as opposed to solutions like (22.4), which are based only on the fundamentals.

Any variable z that satisfies (22.6) qualifies as one that can affect the solution of the model in (22.1). Hence, (22.1) admits a multiplicity of solutions, although only the fundamental solution leads to convergence.

22.1.2 Deterministic versus Stochastic Bubbles

Bubbles result in multiple equilibria and can be either deterministic or stochastic. What can be done to exclude solutions involving bubbles? The answer is to impose convergence conditions like (22.3), which ensure that y_t does not explode over time. In almost all the models with perfect foresight or rational expectations that we have analyzed so far, we have ruled out bubbles: Bubbles are explosive and do not satisfy conditions like (22.3), which are required by the models to ensure that agents respect their intertemporal budget constraints.

A *deterministic bubble* z evolves according to the difference equation

$$z_{t+1} = \frac{1}{a} z_t. \tag{22.8}$$

The variable defined by (22.8) clearly satisfies (22.6) and qualifies as a bubble for the model in (22.1). The solution of the difference equation (22.8) is given by

$$z_t = \left(\frac{1}{a}\right)^t z_0. \tag{22.9}$$

Because $|a| < 1$, z_t explodes over time. Figure 22.1 depicts its time path, assuming both a positive a (solid line) and a negative a (dotted line). For a positive a, z_t explodes monotonically; for a negative a, it explodes cyclically.

In a nonfundamental solution that involves z_t, like (22.5), y_t also explodes over time. However, this violates the convergence condition (22.3), because

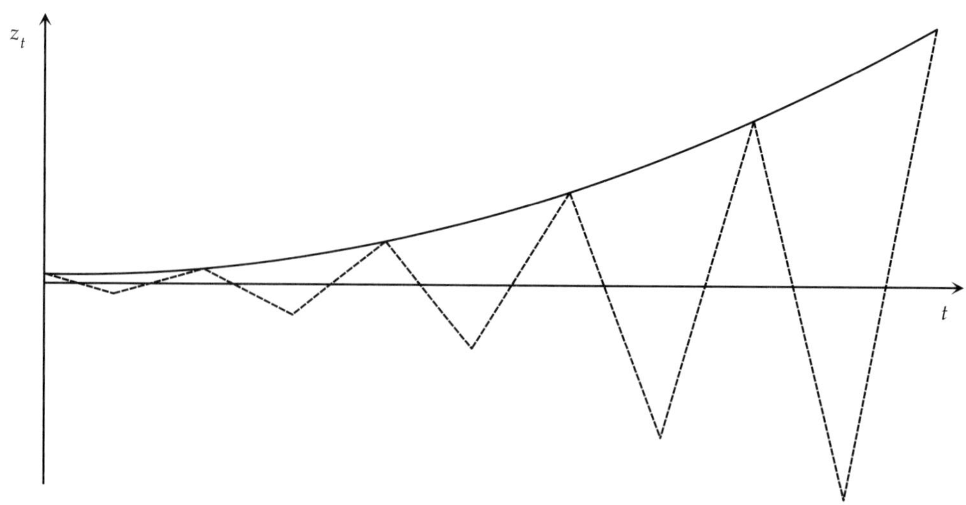

Figure 22.1
Deterministic bubbles.

$$\lim_{T\to\infty} a^{T+1} E_t z_{t+T+1} = z_t \neq 0. \tag{22.10}$$

Hence, even if the fundamental solution converges, the nonfundamental solution does not.

Deterministic bubbles can be ruled out by appropriate transversality conditions that rule out explosive paths. This is the assumption that we adopted in the deterministic growth models of chapters 4–8 to rule out bubbles and concentrate on the fundamental solution.

Another type of bubble is a *stochastic bursting bubble*. Consider the following stochastic process:

$$\begin{aligned} z_{t+1} &= (aq)^{-1} z_t + \varepsilon_{t+1}, \quad \text{with probability } q, \\ z_{t+1} &= \varepsilon_{t+1}, \quad \text{with probability } 1-q, \end{aligned} \tag{22.11}$$

where $0 < q < 1$ is the probability that the bubble will not burst, which is constant for each period, and ε is a zero mean stochastic process that satisfies $E_t(\varepsilon_{t+1}) = 0$. This stochastic process clearly satisfies (22.6), because

$$E_t z_{t+1} = \frac{q}{aq} z_t = \frac{1}{a} z_t. \tag{22.12}$$

A single realization of this stochastically bursting bubble along with the deterministic bubble is presented in figure 22.2 for a positive a. In the absence of white noise disturbances, this bursting bubble has a higher slope than the deterministic bubble to compensate for the probability that the bubble will burst. This stochastically bursting bubble also does not satisfy the convergence condition (22.3) and can therefore be ruled out by appropriate transversality conditions.

If we are prepared to impose a nonexplosion condition like (22.3), bubbles can be ruled out in many models. However, as we shall see below, bubbles cannot always be ruled out.

22.1.3 Bubbles as Self-Fulfilling Prophecies in Inherently Unstable Models

Bubbles may be useful in stabilizing inherently unstable models. Take, for example, the model in (22.1) for the case $|a| > 1$. In this case, the fundamental solution does not necessarily converge. However, an infinity of bubbles z are stable rather than exploding in this case, because $1/|a| < 1$. The multiplicity of solutions is now even more perplexing, as bubbles help convergence to a steady state.

As an example, consider the model in (22.1) and assume that $a > 1$ and that x_t follows a stationary AR(1) process of the form

$$x_{t+1} = \lambda x_t + \varepsilon_{t+1}, \tag{22.13}$$

where $0 < \lambda < 1$, and $E_t \varepsilon_{t+1} = 0$.

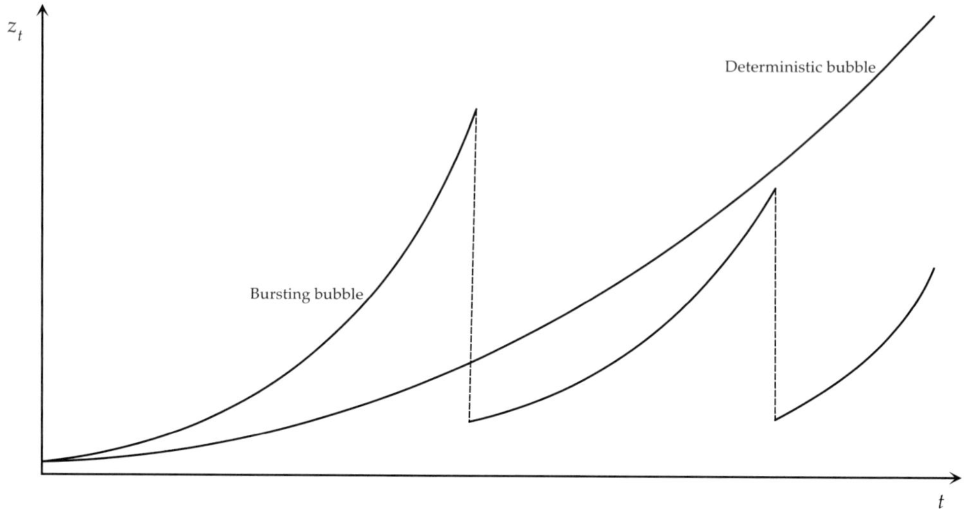

Figure 22.2
A stochastically bursting bubble versus a deterministic bubble.

The fundamental solution of the model in (22.1) when the exogenous variable x_t follows (22.13) is given by

$$y_t^f = \frac{b}{1-aF}x_t = b\sum_{s=0}^{\infty} a^s E_t x_{t+s} = b\sum_{s=0}^{\infty} (a\lambda)^s x_t. \tag{22.14}$$

The fundamental solution converges only if $a\lambda < 1$, or equivalently, if $\lambda < 1/a$. In such a case, the fundamental solution converges to

$$y_t^f = \frac{b}{1-a\lambda}x_t. \tag{22.15}$$

Assume now that $\lambda > 1/a$. Then the model has to be solved backward rather than forward, as it does not satisfy the saddle point property. The fundamental solution takes the form

$$y_t^f = -\frac{b}{a}\frac{1}{1-(1/a)L}x_t = -\frac{b}{a}\sum_{s=0}^{\infty}\left(\frac{1}{a}\right)^s x_{t-s} = -\frac{b}{a\lambda}\sum_{s=0}^{\infty}\left(\frac{1}{a\lambda}\right)^s x_t.$$

A host of other convergent paths exists, depending on bubbles of the type (22.6). Because $a > 1$, these are convergent bubbles, and they do not hinder the convergence of the endogenous variable to its steady state value given by (22.15).

Hence, in inherently unstable models that do not satisfy the saddle point property, there are multiple convergent paths depending on bubbles. Such bubbles are often called *self-fulfilling* prophecies and cannot be ruled out by the usual convergence arguments that we have utilized in the case of inherently stable models.[5]

22.1.4 Higher-Order Linear Models

The first-order linear model (22.1) is inherently stable if $|a| < 1$. Then the fundamental solution is characterized by the saddle point property, and provided the transversality condition (22.3) is satisfied, the economy jumps immediately to its unique fundamental solution, which is a saddle point.

This conclusion generalizes to higher-order linear models, such as the ones examined in chapter 9. In a system with $n+m$ endogenous variables, where n is the number of predetermined (state) variables, and m the number of non-predetermined (or costate) variables, then the system must have exactly m roots outside the unit circle to have a unique nonexplosive solution.

As for the first-order linear model, bubbles can be excluded by appropriate transversality conditions that rule out explosive paths.

Inherently unstable higher-order linear models can be characterized by self-fulfilling prophecies.

22.2 Bubbles in Models of Stock and Money Markets

To reach a deeper understanding of unstable bubbles, it is worth examining some concrete economic examples. We shall look at stock market bubbles and bubbles in the price level and inflation.

22.2.1 Stock Market Bubbles

Assume a capital market in which investors are risk neutral. They choose between a stock and a safe asset with a certain rate of return r. In equilibrium, arbitrage will ensure that the expected rate of return of the stock will be equal to the rate of return of the safe asset:

$$\frac{E_t p_{t+1} - p_t}{p_t} + \frac{d_t}{p_t} = r, \tag{22.16}$$

where p is the price of the stock, and d is the dividend. The expected rate of return of the stock is equal to the expected capital gain plus the dividend as a proportion of the stock price. Equation (22.16) can be rearranged as

5. See Farmer [1999] for an extensive discussion of models with self-fulfilling prophecies. Farmer considers inherently stable models to be the "regular case" and inherently unstable models to be the "irregular case."

$$p_t = \frac{1}{1+r}\left(E_t p_{t+1} + d_t\right), \tag{22.17}$$

which has the form of (22.1), with $0 < a = b = 1/(1+r) < 1$.

The fundamental solution of (22.17) determines the stock price as a function of the expected future stream of dividends:

$$p_t^f = \frac{1}{1+r}\sum_{s=0}^{\infty}\left(\frac{1}{1+r}\right)^s E_t d_{t+s}. \tag{22.18}$$

Under the fundamental solution, the equilibrium stock price is the present value of the expected future stream of dividends, discounted by the rate of return of the safe asset. Assuming that the expectation of future dividends grows at a rate less than r, the present value and hence the equilibrium stock price converges.

To find closed-form solutions, assume first that dividends follow a stationary AR(1) process of the form

$$d_{t+1} = (1-\lambda)\bar{d} + \lambda d_t + \varepsilon_{t+1}, \tag{22.19}$$

where $\bar{d}$ is the steady state dividend, $0 < \lambda < 1$ is the degree of persistence of deviations of current dividends from the steady state dividend, and ε_{t+1} is a white noise process.

From (22.18) and (22.19), the fundamental solution is given by

$$p_t^f = \frac{1}{r}\bar{d} + \frac{1}{1+r-\lambda}\left(d_t - \bar{d}\right). \tag{22.20}$$

Thus, the stock market price based on fundamentals is a stationary stochastic process. Indeed it is an AR(1) process itself, with mean equal to the present value of the steady state dividend $\bar{d}/r$.

If dividends follow a nonstationary process, the stock market price is nonstationary as well. For example, assume that dividends follow a random walk with drift $g > 0$:

$$d_{t+1} = g + d_t + \varepsilon_{t+1}. \tag{22.21}$$

From (22.18) and (22.21), the fundamental solution is given by

$$p_t^f = \frac{1}{1+r}\sum_{s=0}^{\infty}\left(\frac{1}{1+r}\right)^s (sg + d_t) = \frac{1}{r}\left(\frac{g}{r} + d_t\right). \tag{22.22}$$

Thus, the stock market price is a nonstationary variable. Indeed, it is a random walk with drift itself.

Consider now the solutions involving bubbles. The general solution takes the form

$$p_t = p_t^f + z_t = \frac{1}{1+r} \sum_{s=0}^{\infty} \left(\frac{1}{1+r}\right)^s E_t d_{t+s} + z_t, \tag{22.23}$$

where z is a any extraneous variable that satisfies

$$z_t = \frac{1}{1+r} E_t z_{t+1}, \tag{22.24}$$

which is equivalent to $E_t z_{t+1} = (1+r)z_t$.

The general solution is thus equal to the fundamental solution plus the explosive variable z. Even if dividends follow a stationary AR(1) process, the stock market price will display explosive behavior. As long as investors continue investing in the stock, its price keeps increasing, and the expectations of investors are validated. This is what sustains the bubble.[6]

22.2.2 Money Market Bubbles, the Price Level, and Inflation

Consider next the Cagan [1956] model of money demand. This is a model in which consumers decide between holding money and physical commodities. Money is a nominal asset whose value is affected by inflation. In this case, the demand for money is a negative function of expected inflation, and money market equilibrium requires that

$$\frac{M_t}{P_t} = \exp\left(-\alpha\left(\frac{E_t P_{t+1} - P_t}{P_t}\right)\right), \tag{22.25}$$

where M is the nominal money supply, P the price level, and $\alpha > 0$ the semi-elasticity of money demand with respect to expected inflation.

Taking the logarithm of both sides and denoting the logarithm of the nominal money supply by m and that of the price level by p, the model can be written as

$$m_t - p_t = -\alpha(E_t p_{t+1} - p_t). \tag{22.26}$$

Solving for p_t yields

$$p_t = \frac{\alpha}{1+\alpha} E_t p_{t+1} + \frac{1}{1+\alpha} m_t. \tag{22.27}$$

Equation (22.27) has the form of (22.1), with

$$a = \frac{\alpha}{1+\alpha} < 1, b = 1 - a. \tag{22.28}$$

6. See Abreu and Brunnermeier [2003] for a model in which a bubble can be sustained because of unsychronized trading in the presence of informational asymmetries.

The fundamental solution takes the form

$$p_t^f = \frac{1}{1+\alpha} \sum_{s=0}^{\infty} \left(\frac{\alpha}{1+\alpha} \right)^s E_t m_{t+s}. \tag{22.29}$$

The fundamental solution for the current price level depends on the discounted expectations for the evolution of the money supply in the future, with a discount factor equal to $0 < \alpha/(1+\alpha) < 1$.

Assume that the money supply follows a random walk with drift:

$$m_{t+1} = \mu + m_t + \varepsilon_{t+1}, \tag{22.30}$$

where μ is the mean rate of growth of the money supply, and ε is a white noise shock to the money supply.

Then the closed form of the fundamental solution for the level of prices is given by

$$p_t^f = m_t + \alpha\mu. \tag{22.31}$$

The fundamental solution for the price level is a nonstationary stochastic process, but fundamental inflation is stationary, as it is given by

$$\pi_t^f = p_t^f - p_{t-1}^f = m_t - m_{t-1} = \mu + \varepsilon_t. \tag{22.32}$$

Consider now a bubble solution for the price level of the form

$$p_t = m_t + \alpha\mu + z_t, \tag{22.33}$$

where

$$E_t z_{t+1} = \frac{1+\alpha}{a} z_t. \tag{22.34}$$

The price level displays explosive behavior, and inflation is determined by

$$\pi_t = p_t - p_{t-1} = m_t - m_{t-1} + z_t - z_{t-1} = \mu + \varepsilon_t + \frac{1}{\alpha} z_{t-1}. \tag{22.35}$$

Hence, in the presence of a bubble, both the price level and inflation display explosive behavior. The economy eventually reverts to either hyperinflation or hyperdeflation, depending on whether the initial z is positive or negative. This would happen because of the bubble, even though the mean rate of growth of the money supply is constant. As long as households and firms believe that inflation will be increasing, they will reduce their money demand and buy goods at a higher rate, eventually causing an explosive rise in the price level. This may happen even though inflation is higher than its fundamental value, as defined by the rate of growth of the money supply.

22.3 Ruling Out Unstable Bubbles

A positive stock market bubble takes hold because investors expect the stock price to continue increasing, even though the price of the stock exceeds its fundamental value, as defined by the expected present value of dividends. As long as investors continue investing in the stock, the price increases, and the expectations of investors are validated. Hence, a positive bubble may take hold as a self-fulfilling prophecy.

Similarly, a negative stock market bubble takes hold because investors expect the stock price to continue falling, although the price of the stock falls short of its fundamental value, as defined by the expected present value of dividends. As long as investors continue divesting in the stock, the price falls, and the expectations of investors are validated. Hence, a negative bubble may take hold as a self-fulfilling prophecy.

Negative bubbles can be ruled out more easily than positive bubbles. If stocks can be disposed of freely, the price of the stock cannot become negative. But negative bubble implies that the price of the stock will tend to minus infinity. This is ruled out by the free disposal condition; hence, a negative bubble can be ruled out.

Ruling out positive stock market bubbles is more tricky. If there are substitutes for the stock at a finite price, then a positive bubble can be ruled out as well, because in a positive bubble, the price of the stock will tend to infinity, and investors will stop buying the stock, turning instead to lower-valued stocks. In addition, in a positive bubble, shareholders in a listed stock will have a strong incentive to issue more stock at higher prices, which will also tend to eventually depress the price of the stock and rule out positive bubbles. Hence, one would only expect positive bubbles in markets where fundamentals are hard to ascertain, stocks are in short supply, and they do not have close substitutes.

Many of the incidents that have historically been recorded as positive bubbles, such as the tulip mania that crashed in 1637, or the South Sea bubble that crashed in 1720, involved such assets.[7]

A positive inflation bubble may take hold because households and firms expect the level of prices to continue increasing, even though the price level exceeds its fundamental value defined by the path of the money supply. As long as they continue to reduce their money holdings to buy goods, the price level increases, and the expectations of households and firms are validated. Hence, an inflation bubble may take hold as a self-fulfilling prophecy.

Similarly a negative inflation bubble (or deflation bubble) may take hold, because households and firms expect the level of prices to continue falling, even though the price level falls short of its fundamental value, as defined by the path of the money supply. As long as they continue to increase their money holdings and refrain from buying goods, the price level declines, and so the expectations of households and firms are validated. Hence, a deflation bubble may also take hold as a self-fulfilling prophecy.

7. See Kindleberger and Aliber [2005] for a history of what have been termed financial market bubbles.

However, inflation and deflation bubbles have more difficulty gaining traction than do stock market bubbles. Negative inflation bubbles can be ruled out by the fact that the price level cannot become negative. Positive inflation bubbles can be ruled out by the existence of substitutes for money, such as precious metals and other real assets.

The arguments analyzed so far for ruling out bubbles are partial equilibrium arguments. Tirole [1982, 1985] and Weil [1987a] have examined this issue in a general equilibrium context. Their conclusions suggest that whether bubbles can develop on real assets in general equilibrium models depends on whether agents have finite or infinite horizons. They conclude that bubbles on real assets can be ruled out in economies in which agents have infinite horizons. Only in OLG models, in which new agents enter the economy, can bubbles exist, and only when the economy is dynamically inefficient.

The logic of the argument, as expounded by Tirole [1982], is that negative bubbles on real assets can be ruled out because then all individuals will want to buy and keep the asset forever, because its market price will exceed its fundamental price. However, in such a case, there will be excess demand for the asset, and the negative bubble cannot be an equilibrium. In the case of a positive bubble, if short selling occurs, there will be excess supply of the asset, and the positive bubble cannot be an equilibrium. Even without short selling, all agents will plan to sell the asset after a period of time. Hence, a positive bubble cannot be an equilibrium, because the anticipation of its collapse will rule out the bubble in advance. Hence, only in economies where new agents enter the market, such as in OLG models, can a bubble possibly exist. Even for OLG models, Tirole [1985] and Weil [1987a] prove that bubbles can be ruled out, with the exception of the case of dynamic inefficiency.

A large empirical literature, starting with Flood and Garber [1980], Shiller [1981], and others, has concentrated on testing for the existence of inflation and stock market bubbles, with generally mixed results.[8]

22.4 Indeterminacy, Self-Fulfilling Prophecies, and Sunspots

The models we have analyzed in section 22.3 are linear models. Indeed, most of the models we have analyzed formally throughout this text are treated as local linear approximations of nonlinear models around a unique steady state. However, even if a nonlinear model satisfies the saddle point property locally, it may have more than one nonexplosive solution, which implies global indeterminacy. As a result, which solution will apply may depend on extraneous beliefs.

Consider the following model, which is a nonlinear version of the model in (22.1). For simplicity, let us ignore exogenous variables.[9]

8. See Brunnermeier [2008] for a survey of the empirical evidence.

9. This model is a version of an example first used by Azariadis [1981].

$$y_t^2 = aE_t y_{t+1}, \tag{22.36}$$

where $y_t \in [0, 1]$ and $|a| < 1$. This model has two solutions. One obvious solution is

$$y_{t+1} = y_t = a. \tag{22.37}$$

A second solution is that

$$\begin{aligned} y_{t+1} &= y_t^2, \text{ with probability } q = \frac{1-(y_t/a)^2}{1-y_t^2/a} < 1, \\ y_{t+1} &= y_t = a, \text{ with probability } 1-q. \end{aligned} \tag{22.38}$$

Therefore, the model has at least two nonexplosive solutions. In the first, the endogenous variable y is equal to the constant a at all times. In the second solution it follows stochastic cycles, although there is no intrinsic uncertainty.

As suggested by Azariadis [1981], which solution will prevail can be a self-fulfilling prophecy. If economic agents believe in the constant solution, the economy will settle at a. If they believe in the equilibrium with stochastic cycles, the economy will display stochastic cycles.

More generally, as demonstrated by Cass and Shell [1983], in economies with even small departures from the Arrow-Debreu assumptions of full markets, equilibria may display the property that agent's allocations are different across states of nature, even though nothing fundamental is different across these states of nature. Cass and Shell [1983] refer to equilibria with such a property as equilibria where *sunspots* matter. They define sunspots as random variables that have no direct influence on economic fundamentals, such as preferences, endowments, or technologies.[10]

The sunspot theorem of Cass and Shell [1983] has profound implications for DSGE models, because it permits the possibility that sunspots (or "animal spirits," in the terminology of Keynes [1936]) are quite consistent with the existence of a rational expectations equilibrium.

Given that many of the models we have analyzed are essentially nonlinear dynamic models characterized by departures from the Arrow-Debreu assumption of full markets, one cannot exclude multiple equilibria, self-fulfilling prophecies, and sunspots as easily as unstable bubbles. The Calvo [1988] debt model analyzed in chapter 21 is an example of such a model, in which there are multiple equilibria, and self-fulfilling prophecies play a major role in which equilibrium prevails. Other widely used examples of models with multiple equilibria and incomplete markets that we shall consider below are nonlinear OLG models

10. In this definition, Cass and Shell [1983] differ from Jevons [1884], who developed a sunspot theory of agricultural cycles, based on the idea that sunspot activity affected agricultural output, through its impact on the weather. The Jevons theory is based on fundamentals and intrinsic uncertainty and not extrinsic uncertainty as in the case of Cass and Shell [1983] sunspot equilibria.

with money, such as the Samuelson [1958] monetary model. In OLG models, there are no markets for the welfare or future generations, and hence the Arrow-Debreu assumption of full markets is not satisfied.

22.4.1 The Samuelson OLG Model with Money, Revisited

Consider a more general version of the Samuelson [1958] OLG model with money than the one first introduced in chapter 12.

The household born in period t lives for two periods and has a perishable endowment equal to Y_1 in its first period of life and to Y_2 in its second period of life. The only nonperishable asset is money M, held by old households, who were born in period $t-1$, and who are in the second (and last) period of life.

The young households maximize the intertemporal utility function

$$U = E_t\left[\frac{C_{1t}^{1-\theta}}{1-\theta} + \frac{1}{1+\rho}\frac{C_{2t+1}^{1-\theta}}{1-\theta}\right], \tag{22.39}$$

subject to the intertemporal budget constraint

$$C_{1t} + \frac{E_tP_{t+1}}{P_t}C_{2t+1} = Y_1 + \frac{E_tP_{t+1}}{P_t}Y_2, \tag{22.40}$$

where C_1 is the level of consumption of the young; C_2 is the level of consumption of the old; P_t is the price of consumer goods in period t; and E_tP_{t+1} is the rational expectation of the price of consumer goods in period $t+1$, conditional on the information set available in period t. In addition, $\rho > 0$ is the pure rate of time preference, and $1/\theta > 0$ is the elasticity of intertemporal substitution.[11]

First-period savings can only be held in the form of money, which yields no interest. Hence, money demand by the young is given by

$$M_t^d = P_t(Y_1 - C_{1t}). \tag{22.41}$$

Note that from the intertemporal budget constraint, the gross return on savings and money holdings R_t is equal to

$$R_t = \frac{P_t}{E_tP_{t+1}} = \frac{1}{1+E_t\pi_{t+1}}, \tag{22.42}$$

11. Note that this is a more general version of the Samuelson model than the one presented in chapter 12, which relied on logarithmic preferences. The elasticity of intertemporal substitution in the model of this section is allowed to differ from unity.

where π is the inflation rate. Therefore, the gross return on savings and money is inversely related to expected inflation.

The savings of the young are equal to the dissavings of the old, who exchange their money holdings for consumer goods. Hence, the money supply by the old is equal to

$$M_t^s = P_t(C_{2t} - Y_2). \tag{22.43}$$

Equilibrium in the money market implies

$$M_t^s = M_t^d = M, \tag{22.44}$$

where M is the exogenously given money stock. Equilibrium in the money market also implies equilibrium in the goods market, in the sense that aggregate current income, $Y = Y_1 + Y_2$, is consumed by either the young or the old.

The Lagrange function for the problem of the young is given by

$$\mathcal{L} = E_t\left[\frac{C_{1t}^{1-\theta}}{1-\theta} + \frac{1}{1+\rho}\frac{C_{2t+1}^{1-\theta}}{1-\theta}\right] + \lambda\left[Y_1 + \frac{E_tP_{t+1}}{P_t}Y_{2t} - C_{1t} - \frac{E_tP_{t+1}}{P_t}C_{2t+1}\right], \tag{22.45}$$

where λ is the Lagrange multiplier measuring the marginal utility of wealth.

From the first-order conditions for a maximum, we have

$$C_{1t}^{-\theta} = \lambda, \tag{22.46}$$

$$\frac{1}{1+\rho}C_{2t+1}^{-\theta} = \lambda\frac{E_tP_{t+1}}{P_t}. \tag{22.47}$$

Eliminating λ between the two first-order conditions, after some rearrangement, we get the Euler equation for consumption:

$$\frac{C_{2t+1}}{C_{1t}} = \left[\frac{1}{1+\rho}\frac{P_t}{E_tP_{t+1}}\right]^{\frac{1}{\theta}}. \tag{22.48}$$

Figure 22.3 presents the combinations of C_{1t} and C_{2t+1} that satisfy the Euler equation for consumption and the household intertemporal budget constraint as the gross return on money $R_t = P_t/P_{t+1}$ rises. These points trace out the offer curve of young households, which is defined by the points of tangency of the intertemporal budget constraint for different rates of gross return of money (savings) with the highest possible indifference curve.[12]

12. The offer curve approach to the analysis of the Samuelson OLG model with money was introduced by Cass et al. [1979].

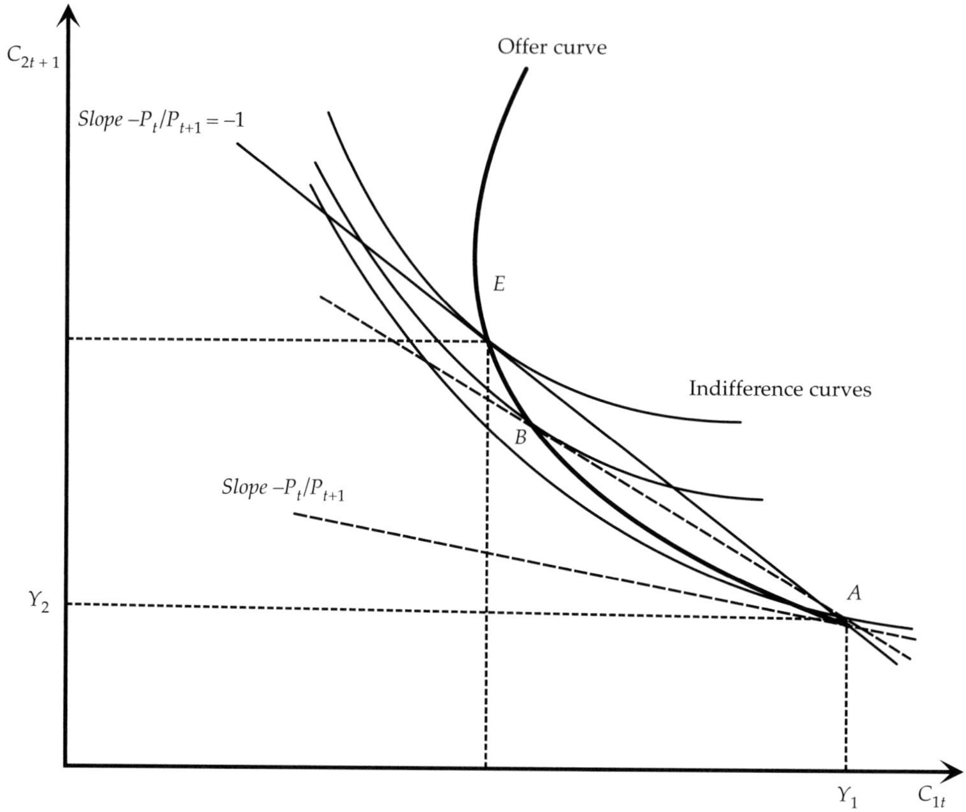

Figure 22.3
Equilibrium consumption in the Samuelson OLG model.

At point A, the gross return of money is sufficiently low, so that the household consumes its current endowment in both periods, and there are no savings and no demand for money. At point B, the gross return of money is sufficiently high to induce the household to save part of its income in its first period of life and thus to hold positive real money balances. At point E, the gross rate of return of money is equal to one, and prices and real money balances are constant.

If the elasticity of intertemporal substitution of consumption is higher than unity, then the offer curve is negatively sloped throughout. If it is lower than unity and the income effect dominates, after some point, the offer curve turns positively sloped, as an increase in the gross return on money causes savings and money demand to decline.

Eliminating C_{2t} between the intertemporal budget constraint and the Euler equation for consumption, we find that the savings of the young is determined by

$$Y_1 - C_{1t} = \frac{Y_1\left(\frac{1}{1+\rho}\right)^{1/\theta}\left(\frac{P_t}{E_tP_{t+1}}\right)^{(1-\theta)/\theta} - Y_2\left(\frac{P_t}{E_tP_{t+1}}\right)^{-1}}{1+\left(\frac{1}{1+\rho}\right)^{1/\theta}\left(\frac{P_t}{E_tP_{t+1}}\right)^{(1-\theta)/\theta}}. \tag{22.49}$$

Because the savings of the young is equal to money demand, it follows that

$$m_t = \frac{M}{P_t} = \frac{Y_1\left(\frac{1}{1+\rho}\right)^{1/\theta}\left(\frac{P_t}{E_tP_{t+1}}\right)^{(1-\theta)/\theta} - Y_2\left(\frac{P_t}{E_tP_{t+1}}\right)^{-1}}{1+\left(\frac{1}{1+\rho}\right)^{1/\theta}\left(\frac{P_t}{E_tP_{t+1}}\right)^{(1-\theta)/\theta}} = s\left(\frac{P_t}{E_tP_{t+1}}\right), \tag{22.50}$$

where m denotes real money balances, and s denotes the savings and money demand function, which depends on the expected gross return on real money balances.[13]

It is straightforward to prove that only if the elasticity of intertemporal substitution of consumption $1/\theta$ is greater than unity does the expected return of money cause money demand to increase throughout. If $1/\theta$ is less than unity, the income effect dominates after some point, and an increase in the rate of return of money (savings) starts reducing savings and money demand. Obviously, in the case where the elasticity of intertemporal substitution of consumption is equal to unity, the income and substitution effects cancel out, and savings and money demand are independent of the rate of return on money holdings.

Because the demand for money by the young is equal to the supply of money by the old, it follows that

$$m_{t+1} = C_{2t+1} - Y_2 = \frac{P_t}{P_{t+1}}m_t = \frac{P_t}{P_{t+1}}(Y_1 - C_{1t}). \tag{22.51}$$

Hence we can translate the offer curves for consumption into offer curves for money demand. The case where the elasticity of intertemporal substitution of consumption is higher than unity is depicted in figure 22.4. The offer curve is positively sloped throughout. There are two possible equilibria, at zero and at point E, with positive real money balances. Only the equilibrium at E is saddle path stable. Hence, the economy will jump immediately to this equilibrium, as the equilibrium with zero money balances is not stable.

The case where the elasticity of intertemporal substitution of consumption is lower than unity is depicted in figure 22.5. At some point, the offer curve for savings and money demand bends backward. If the offer curve crosses the 45° line on its backward-bending part at a slope that is greater than unity, the equilibrium at E is globally stable. This behavior implies that multiple converging paths lead to the equilibrium at E. The economy may thus display cyclical convergence to the equilibrium through a multitude of convergence paths.

13. Note that in the case of logarithmic preferences (i.e., $\theta = 1$), this money demand function reduces to the one analyzed in chapter 12, namely, equation (12.15).

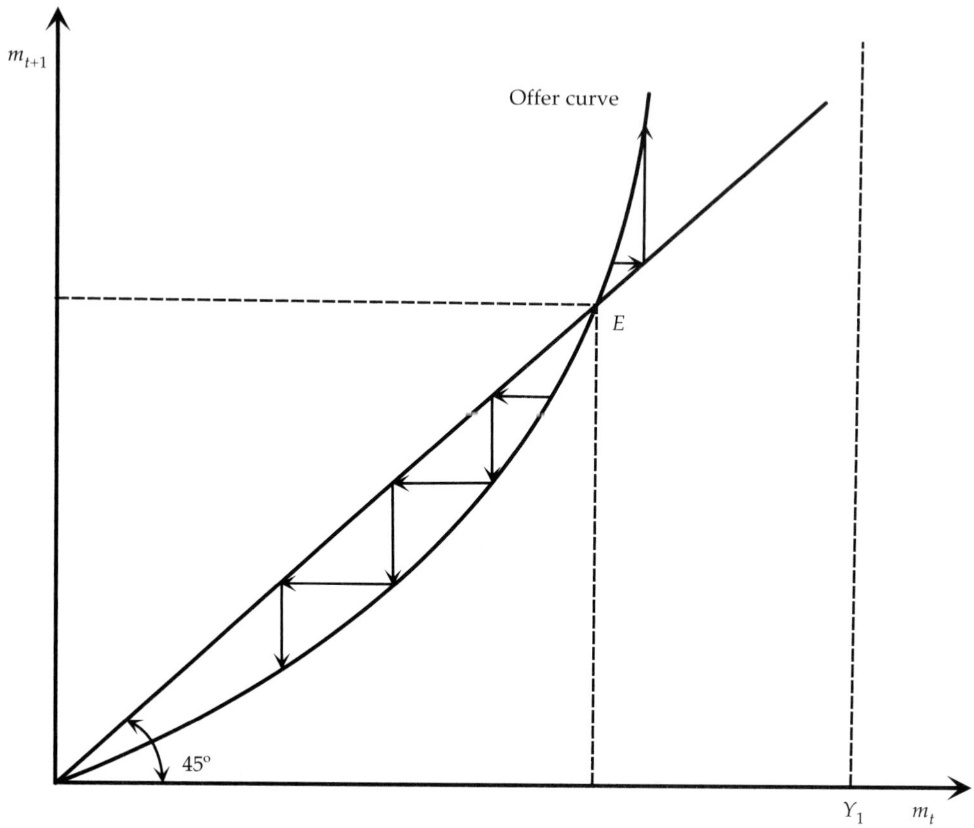

Figure 22.4
Saddle point equilibrium money balances in the Samuelson OLG Model.

The possible existence of multiple convergent paths leading to a unique equilibrium at E is not the only problem of this model. The economy might have multiple equilibria and oscillate cyclically among them. An example of such multiple equilibria, due to Azariadis and Guesnerie [1986], is shown in figure 22.6.

Figure 22.6 depicts two possible equilibria. One is the saddle point at point E, and the second is an equilibrium with cycles between points A and B, which are defined by the intersection of the offer curve with its mirror image reflected through the 45° line. Which equilibrium will prevail will depend on the expectations of the young. Thus, periods of high prices will be followed by period of low prices, and vice versa.

Such equilibria that depend on self-fulfilling prophecies are examples of sunspots. Thus, if consumers believe that high prices will be followed by low prices, and vice versa, the economy will display high-low price cycles. If agents believe that prices will fall at a rate

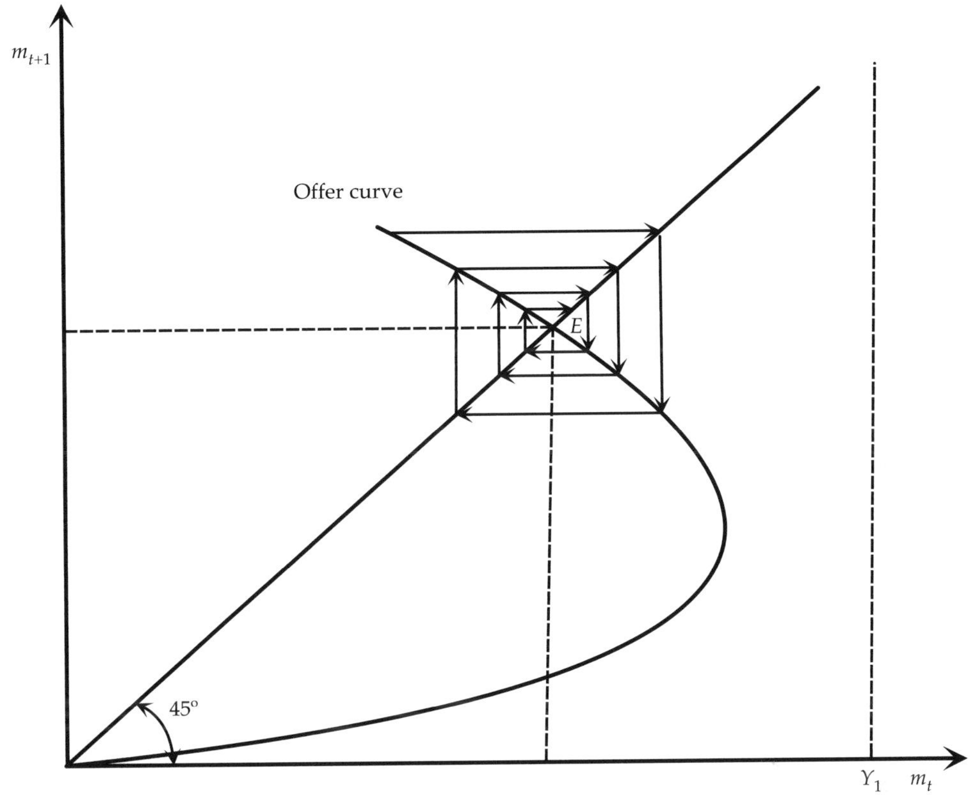

Figure 22.5
Multiple convergence paths for money balances in the Samuelson OLG model.

equal to the pure rate of time preference, then the equilibrium will be at E, with constantly falling prices and steady real money balances.

22.4.2 Other Models of Indeterminacy and Sunspots in Macroeconomics

Sunspot equilibria can be convergent or divergent, and a variety of examples can be constructed. In surveying the relevant literature, Benhabib and Farmer [1999] conclude that it

> can be organized around three strands. First, there is work that uses models with indeterminate equilibria to explain the propagation mechanism of the business cycle. Second, there is a group of papers that uses indeterminacy to explain the monetary transmission mechanism, specifically the fact that prices are sticky, and third, there is work in growth theory that uses indeterminacy to understand why the per capita incomes of countries that are similar in their fundamentals nevertheless save and grow at different rates.

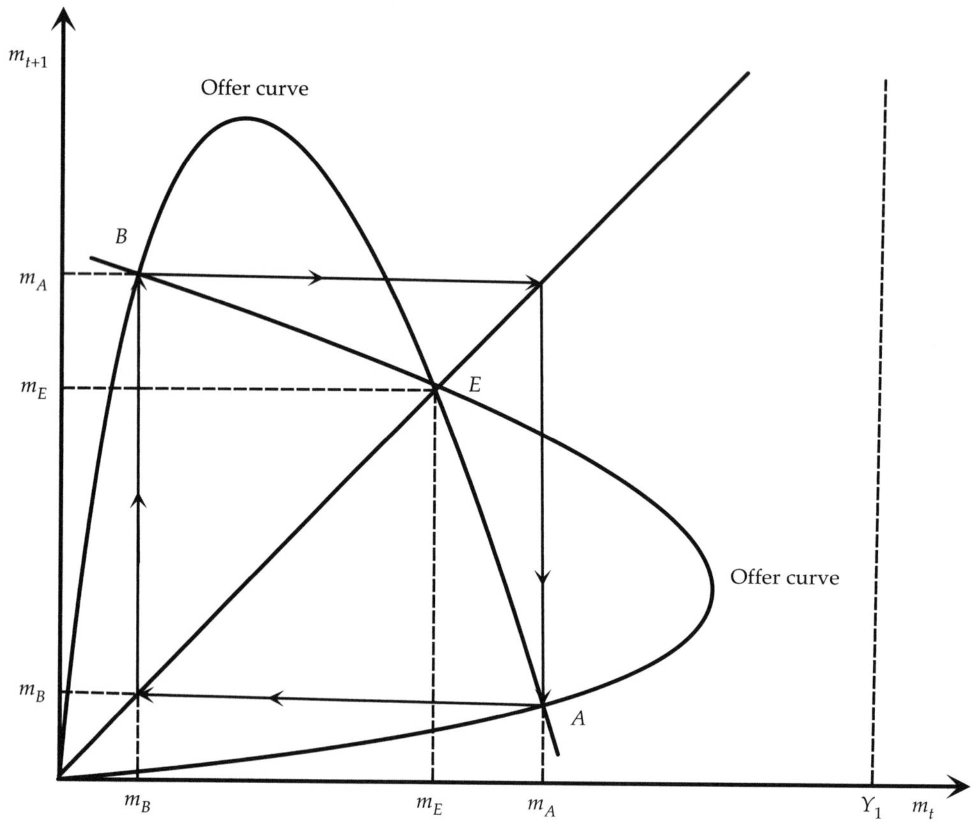

Figure 22.6
Multiple equilibria, sunspots, and cycles in the Samuelson OLG model.

They go on to explain the ideas that underpin each of these strands and compare this literature to the more conventional approach.[14]

22.5 Conclusion

In this chapter, we have investigated bubbles in linear dynamic models and nonlinear models characterized by indeterminacy and sunspot equilibria. These are models in which expectational factors determine the dynamic path of the economy, and in which expectations turn out to be self-fulfilling.

14. Comprehensive treatments of the macroeconomics of self-fulfilling prophecies and sunspots can be found in Azariadis [1993] and Farmer [1999].

We have discussed the conditions under which unstable bubbles can be ruled out in both partial and general equilibrium models, and investigated how sunspot equilibria and endogenous cycles can arise in nonlinear models, such as the Samuelson OLG model.

The examples discussed go beyond the property of uniqueness characterizing the steady state solutions of most of the models used in the rest of this text. Although the approach taken in this chapter does not necessarily invalidate the analytical strategy adopted in the rest of this book, models of bubbles and sunspots can potentially explain why economies sometimes enter unsustainable paths, display endogenous business cycles, or shift from one equilibrium to another.

23

The Interaction of Events and Ideas in Dynamic Macroeconomics

In this final chapter, we discuss recent developments in the interaction of events and ideas and assess their role for the evolution of macroeconomics. Recent developments may be an important determinant of the future evolution of macroeconomics, but readers should be fully aware of the old Danish saying: "It is difficult to make predictions, especially about the future."[1]

Macroeconomics started out in the 1930s based partly on ad hoc Keynesian postulates, quite removed from the axioms of microeconomics. It has come full circle. Modern dynamic macroeconomics is almost fully grounded on microeconomics and general equilibrium theory. It only differs from intertemporal microeconomics in that it assumes markets for homogeneous commodities, labor, capital, and financial assets. This is what allows us to formally define macroeconomic aggregates and analyze economies at the aggregate level.

Macroeconomics has experienced significant progress in the 80 or so years since the publication of the *General Theory*. There has been progress in both growth theory and the theory of aggregate fluctuations. The progress in the theory of economic growth has been largely consensual, focusing on the differences between representative household and OLG models, and the roles of human capital, externalities, and endogenous technical progress. However, the evolution of the theory of aggregate fluctuations has been characterized by sharp divisions and a lot of acrimony. After all, macroeconomics was founded on such a division: that between Keynes and the "classics." New divisions emerged in the 1950s and the 1960s between Keynesians and monetarists. Yet more divisions sprang up following the introduction of the rational expectations hypothesis, and the final set of divisions emerged in the 1980s, following the introduction of new classical and new Keynesian DSGE models.[2]

Over the past 20 years or so, these sharp divisions have been partly bridged, as macroeconomists of different persuasions communicate through the use of models with more

1. The first-known written instance of this quote attributes it to an unidentified Danish parliamentarian of the 1930s. The quote has been repeated in various forms by, among others, the physicist Neils Bohr, the movie mogul Sam Goldwyn, and the baseball catcher Yogi Berra, to each of whom it is sometimes wrongly attributed.

2. For a more detailed discussion of the past evolution of macroeconomics, see chapter 1.

common elements than before. In any case, the old divisions generated more heat than light. Yet differences remain regarding the nature of aggregate fluctuations, unemployment, and of the product, labor, and financial market distortions with macroeconomic consequences that must be addressed by monetary and fiscal policy and structural reforms.

Many of the remaining differences may be further resolved through the emergence of new, richer models and new empirical evidence, but many of the existing differences are due to the inconclusiveness of such evidence, as well as the different interpretations and approaches taken with regard to empirical evaluation, prediction, and policy analysis.

So let us start by reviewing developments in macroeconomics since the financial crisis of 2008–2009, and then go on to discuss the interaction of events and ideas and the role of empirical research in macroeconomics. We will then examine the role of theoretically based empirical models in prediction and policy analysis, and shall end with some tentative conclusions about the likely future evolution of macroeconomics.

23.1 The Financial Crisis and Recent Developments in Dynamic Macroeconomics

Following the financial crisis and the Great Recession of 2008–2009, there was widespread disappointment with the state of economics in general and with macroeconomics and finance in particular. This was mainly because of the failure to forecast or prevent the financial crisis. Macroeconomics was severely criticized, even from within the economics profession, as a set of useless—even harmful—mathematical models incapable of explaining business cycles and contributing to sensible conclusions about economic policy. At the time of the Great Recession, there was widespread concern that the world would experience something similar to the Great Depression of the 1930s.

The relatively effective policy response to the Great Recession, the counterarguments by some prominent macroeconomists in response to the sometimes nihilistic criticism, and subsequent developments in macroeconomic modeling have since restored a more balanced set of views on the current state of macroeconomics.[3]

3. In the context of a widely publicized lecture at the London School of Economics in June 2009, Paul Krugman argued that much of the past 30 years of macroeconomics was "spectacularly useless at best, and positively harmful at worst." The arguments of Krugman and other critics were taken up by the *Economist* magazine on July 16, 2009, in an article called "What Went Wrong with Economics," to which there was a response by Robert Lucas, published in the *Economist* on August 6, 2009. Krugman's criticisms reemerged with an article called "How Did Economists Get It So Wrong?" in the *New York Times Magazine* on September 2, 2009. In this article, Krugman [2009b] argued that "the economics profession went astray because economists, as a group, mistook beauty, clad in impressive-looking mathematics, for truth." A more refined version of these views was presented in Krugman [2009a], a popular book arguing for a return to traditional Keynesian macroeconomics, published at around the same time. See also Skidelsky [2009] for similar arguments from one of the biographers of Keynes. John Cochrane provided a detailed response to Krugman, in an article called "How Did Paul Krugman Get It So Wrong?" published on his blog on September 16, 2009, and eventually in *Economic Affairs* in 2011. This incident is a typical example of an old-style acrimonious exchange that generated more heat than light.

In this section, we consider a critical synthesis of alternative views on the state of macroeconomics since the financial crisis and the responses induced by the crisis.

First, the financial crisis notwithstanding, there is relatively broad agreement among macroeconomists that DSGE models of the kind analyzed in this book are theoretically more satisfactory than the previous generation of largely ad hoc macro models. DSGE models are based on better microeconomic foundations and are characterized by a much higher degree of theoretical consistency and transparency, compared to the models of the original neoclassical synthesis of the 1960s and 1970s. Such models form the basis of an emerging "new neoclassical synthesis," a term coined by Goodfriend and King [1997]. This view is either implicitly or explicitly accepted by macroeconomists of diffferent persuasions, such as Chari and Kehoe [2006]; Mankiw [2006], Blanchard [2009, 2018], Chari et al. [2009], Lucas [2009], Woodford [2009]; Christiano et al. [2018]; Gali [2018]; Ghironi [2018]; Kehoe et al. [2018]; Reis [2018], and Wright [2018]. The evolving new neoclassical synthesis combines elements from both new classical and new Keynesian macroeconomics, although the analogies in the mix differ between adherents to the two schools of thought.[4]

Second, it is also widely accepted that the main existing formal models of the new neoclassical synthesis have theoretical shortcomings. Theoretical consistency and transparency has been largely attained at the expense of both greater analytical complexity and the omission or ex post imposition of important market distortions and mechanisms, such as labor market and financial frictions.[5]

Third, the theoretical shortcomings differ between models of the new classical and the new Keynesian approaches. The benchmark stochastic growth model (chapter 13), favored by the new classical school, contains investment dynamics as the main propagation mechanism of real shocks, but no price dynamics, as prices are assumed to be perfectly flexible. In addition, it relies on perfect competition in all markets, including the labor market. The benchmark imperfectly competitive new Keynesian model (chapter 16) contains price dynamics in the form of staggered pricing, but no capital and investment dynamics. Some of its versions rely on a competitive labor market as well. Labor market frictions in the form of real and nominal wage rigidities can be incorporated, as in the model of chapter 17, but

4. However, note the strong disagreements with this view of, among others, Solow [2008], Krugman [2009b], and Stiglitz [2014, 2018].

5. As a result of the greater complexity of DSGE models, there is a serious dichotomy in the teaching of macroeconomics. Most undergraduate courses and textbooks still by and large rely on the IS-LM, AS-AD models of the previous generation, appropriately extended, but with a marginal role for the intertemporal approach. See, among others, Blanchard [2016b]; Mankiw [2016], and Jones [2017]. In contrast, graduate courses and textbooks rely almost exclusively on the intertemporal approach and DSGE models. See, among others, Blanchard and Fischer [1989]; Romer [2018], and Sargent and Ljungqvist [2018]. DSGE models have some way to go before they become fully accessible to undergraduate students, although Barro [1997b] and Chung [2015] are notable examples suggesting that the task can be accomplished.

matching models of the natural rate of unemployment (of the type analyzed in chapter 18) have proven more difficult to fully incorporate into the DSGE framework.[6]

Fourth, before the financial crisis of 2008–2009, both new classical and new Keynesian models continued to rely on perfect financial markets and the efficient markets hypothesis. Models of financial frictions (such as those based on asymmetric information and agency problems) have since been developed, but financial frictions have not been adequately incorporated into the DSGE framework yet. When they have been incorporated in DSGE macro models, it has been largely through ad hoc additions, such as the addition of an external finance premium. For example, chapter 19 introduced financial frictions to new Keynesian models with nominal rigidities in the form of an exogenous shock to the external finance premium. Use of an exogenous shock to the external finance premium is what is mostly done, in various forms and guises, in the majority of recent papers incorporating financial frictions. The full general equilibrium implications of financial frictions have not been fully investigated in the context of DSGE macro models. This remains an important and difficult challenge for future research.[7]

Despite these shortcomings, DSGE modeling appears to be fully entrenched, and one can expect that the existing models will be extended and improved.[8]

23.2 The Interaction of Events and Ideas and the Role of Empirical Macroeconomics

One of the reasons for the success of macroeconomics in the past 80 years is that it has always been closely connected to real developments. In short, macroeconomics has always been ultimately empirical, and its progress owes much to the interaction of events and ideas.

6. See Shimer [2005, 2009, 2010], Blanchard [2009], Alogoskoufis [2016, 2018], and Christiano et al. [2018] on some of these points. Also note that one can in principle construct a hybrid new neoclassical synthesis model with staggered pricing, labor market distortions, and investment dynamics. Some (mainly empirical) papers have undertaken this task. See, for example, Smets and Wouters [2003, 2007] and Christiano et al. [2016]. Yet this results in even greater complexity and significant losses in the degree of theoretical consistency and transparency compared to the original benchmark models.

7. See Bernanke et al. [1999], Blanchard [2009, 2018], Stiglitz [2014], Ghironi [2018], Wright [2018], Vines and Wills [2018], Christiano et al. [2018], and Gertler and Gilchrist [2018] for discussions of this point. Linde et al. [2016], an example of recent attempts to incorporate financial market imperfections in estimated DSGE models, highlights the inherent difficulties.

8. See Blanchard [2016a, p. 1] who argues that "current DSGE models are seriously flawed, but they are eminently improvable and central to the future of macroeconomics." Christiano et al. [2018, p. 135] argue that "the enterprise of dynamic stochastic general equilibrium modeling is an organic process that involves the constant interaction of data and theory. Pre-crisis DSGE models had shortcomings that were highlighted by the financial crisis and its aftermath. Substantial progress has occurred since then. . . . We don't know where that process will lead. But we do know that DSGE models will remain central to how macroeconomists think about aggregate phenomena and policy. There is simply no credible alternative to policy analysis in a world of competing economic forces operating on different parts of the economy."

The econometric tradition, which initially appeared independently of the *General Theory*, was extended in various directions by econometricians, such as Tinbergen [1937], Haavelmo [1944], and the Cowles Commission and Burns and Mitchell [1946]. It resulted in the development of early Keynesian macroeconometric models by Klein [1950], Klein and Goldberger [1955], and others. These econometric models were used both for prediction and policy analysis.

In addition, many of the major theoretical developments in macroeconomics (such as the microeconomic foundations of the consumption function, the investment function, money demand, and the Phillips curve) were motivated by empirical as well as theoretical considerations. The breakdown of the original Phillips curve is perhaps the most celebrated example. Theoretical advancements were usually tested econometrically by single-equation methods and eventually incorporated into large-scale econometric models.

Empirical macroeconomics changed dramatically following the Lucas [1976] critique and the gradual emergence of DSGE models. One of the approaches that emerged, based on Sims [1980], was entirely atheoretical and sought to model the data-generating process of macroeconomic variables using vector autoregressions.

The second approach, based on Prescott [1986], was based on the calibration of tightly specified DSGE models, the generation of some statistical moments implied by these models through stochastic simulations, and the comparison of these statistical moments to the statistical moments of actual macroeconomic variables. This method was initially applied to the new classical real business cycle (RBC) model, but it was gradually combined with Bayesian econometrics and applied to more general models of the new neoclassical synthesis. The initial application to RBC models is discussed in King and Rebelo [1999]; important examples of early applications based on models of the new neoclassical synthesis can be found in Smets and Wouters [2003, 2007].

These latter models, which combine calibration and Bayesian estimation, are increasingly used by central banks. At the same time, more traditional econometric models, with minor improvements in the treatment of expectations, continued to be used outside academia.[9]

Thus, the modern approach to empirical macroeconomics is a combination of the atheoretical and the structural approaches. The methodology can be briefly described as follows. DSGE models are treated as dynamic systems of equations. Their parameters are nonlinear functions of deep structural parameters. A combination of calibration and Bayesian estimation methods is utilized to derive empirical versions of the models, as maximum likelihood estimation is usually infeasible. VARs are used to describe the properties of the data before a

9. In one sense, the atheoretical approach of Sims [1980] is the modern equivalent of the measurement without theory approach of Burns and Mitchell [1946], while the calibration approach of Prescott [1986], combined with Bayesian econometrics, has evolved into the modern equivalent of the structural econometrics of Klein [1950].

model is estimated and to compare the impulse response functions of the empirical structural model with that of the VAR representation.[10]

However, the rules applied in empirical academic research in macroeconomics may be unnecessarily restrictive. As pointed out by Blanchard [2009, p. 225]:

> A macroeconomic article today often follows strict, haiku-like rules. It starts from a general equilibrium structure, in which individuals maximize the expected present value of utility, firms maximize their value, and markets clear. Then, it introduces a twist, be it an imperfection or the closing of a particular set of markets, and works out the general equilibrium implications. It then performs a numerical simulation based on calibration, showing that the model performs well. It ends with a welfare assessment.

Blanchard [2018] and others have argued in favor of a partial relaxation of these strict rules in the direction of encouraging more empirical research in a partial equilibrium setting, so as to investigate the relevance of particular hypotheses used as building blocks of DSGE models.

23.3 Policy Evaluation and DSGE Models

One of the most forceful condemnations of the previous generation of structural econometric models was the Lucas [1976] critique. It was based on the lack of adequate microeconomic foundations of these models and argued that the estimated parameters were not truly structural, because they consisted of combinations of both structural and policy parameters. Hence, they were not invariant to policy. When there was a change in the policy regime, these models would not be able to trace out the effects of this change, as the estimated parameters would shift once agents realized the change in policy.[11]

In principle, DSGE models should not suffer from the Lucas critique. After all, their parameters are structural and are clearly distinguished from policy parameters. In addition, it is much easier to conduct full-fledged welfare comparisons with DSGE models.

However, in practice, empirical DSGE models fall short of this ideal. The dynamics implied by theoretically consistent DSGE models suggest much faster adjustment toward steady state than the dynamics found in the actual data. As a result, reconciling the models with the data has resulted in significant ad hoc additions of sources of persistence in empirical DSGE models. This approach is not unlike the methodology applied by Klein [1950] in his original Keynesian econometric model, which was initially derived from microeconomic foundations, but in which a data-determined lag structure was allowed.

10. See Favero [2001], Canova [2007], DeJong and Chetan [2011], and Herbst and Schorfheide [2015] for detailed accounts of modern empirical macroeconomics.

11. See Alogoskoufis and Smith [1991] and Alogoskoufis [1992] for the empirical significance of the Lucas critique in the case of estimated Phillips curves.

For example, in estimated DSGE models, habit persistence has been used to explain the slow adjustment of consumption, convex costs of changing investment have been added to account for the dynamics of investment, and indexation on past inflation has been used to account for the dynamics of the Phillips curve. These additional assumptions are neither suggested by the theory, nor do they enjoy independent empirical support. They are introduced simply because they improve the statistical properties of the estimated models. Hence, in practice, estimated DSGE models also contain exogenous nonstructural parameters that are not totally immune to the Lucas critique.

23.4 Conclusion

Macroeconomics was born following a scientific revolution in the sense of Kuhn [1962]. It initially evolved on the basis of the ideas of Keynes [1936], which gained acceptance as a result of the Great Depression, and which were refined and adapted by his many subsequent followers. In the 1960s, the Keynesian theory of aggregate fluctuations faced the monetarist counterrevolution, spearheaded by the rise of inflation and the success of the ideas of Friedman [1956, 1968] and Friedman and Schwartz [1963], in explaining both the Great Depression of the 1930s and the rise in inflation of the late 1960s in monetary terms. For some years, macroeconomics settled into a quieter state, in the form of the neoclassical synthesis, which was accepted as "normal science" by both Keynesians and monetarits. The empirical breakdown of the Phillips curve and the stagflation of the 1970s highlighted the remaining inadequacies of the microeconomic foundations of macroeconomics and resulted in the rational expectations revolution and the eventual emergence of DSGE models. These models were initially new classical competitive models (Lucas [1972], Kydland and Prescott [1982]). Soon, new Keynesian DSGE models, based on short-term price and wage stickiness emerged (Mankiw and Romer [1991]). Divisions around these developments seemed to have entered a quiet phase until the financial crisis of 2008–2009. The new neoclassical synthesis was on its way of becoming the new normal. The financial crisis and the Great Recession of 2008–2009 have disrupted this process and have led to a quest for models that also incorporate financial frictions and their interactions with the real economy.

Growth theory has been following its own path and displaying impressive progress, with fewer divisions and less acrimony. It has focused on the determinants of the accumulation of physical and human capital and endogenous technical progress. In recent years, it has been stressing the role of institutions in fostering these processes.

In this book, we have reviewed the key dynamic general equilibrium models in both growth theory and aggregate fluctuations, including the benchmark dynamic general equilibrium models of growth and the new neoclassical synthesis DSGE models of aggregate fluctuations.

It remains to be seen how dynamic macroeconomic modeling will evolve. A number of avenues for future research appear to exist, including (1) the fuller analysis of the role of institutions for long-run growth, (2) the fuller incorporation of labor market and financial frictions in DSGE models of aggregate fluctuations, and (3) more satisfactory models of the role of political institutions and politics in the determination of monetary and fiscal policy.

One hopes that progress in these directions, and others suggested in this book, will contribute to the emergence of a theoretically more adequate and empirically more relevant dynamic macroeconomics.

APPENDIXES

Appendix A: Variables, Functions, and Optimization

In this appendix, we review some basic mathematical concepts and techniques required for the analysis of macroeconomic models. We focus on calculus and discuss the nature of models, variables, functions, and their derivatives, as well as methods of mathematical optimization under constraints.

This appendix is a review, suitable for those who wish to refresh their knowledge. It is not a complete and rigorous treatment.[1]

A.1 Models, Variables, and Functions

Scientific models can be thought of as simplified versions of that part of that world being studied. Macroeconomic models are thus simplified representations of economies, which allow us to analyse their salient characteristics. Although there is no inherent reason that a model must be mathematical, mathematical models ensure internal consistency in our reasoning about actual economies. They also allow us to handle a greater degree of complexity than nonmathematical models can, and permit us to assess the quantitative significance of various factors. It is for these reasons that macroeconomic models are expressed in mathematical form.

Mathematical macroeconomic models consist of variables, functions, and parameters. They are meant to describe the outcome of the behavior and the interactions of economic agents, such as households, firms, the government, and government agencies (including central banks).

Methods of mathematical optimization allow us to model the behavior of agents that maximize their objective functions, under appropriate constraints. Thus, households are assumed to follow rules that maximize their utility functions under appropriate budget and

1. For rigorous introductions to calculus for economists, see Binmore [1983], or another comprehensive textbook of mathematics for economists, such as Chiang [1974], Simon and Blume [1994], or Klein [2013]. For full discussions of optimization under constraints suitable for economics, see Intriligator [1971] and Dixit [1990].

market constraints, whereas firms are assumed to follow rules that maximize an appropriately defined profit function under the relevant constraints. Similar considerations apply to the government and its agencies.

Mathematical economic models typically consist of systems of equations, designed to describe the structure of the economy in question and the behavior of economic agents, such as households, firms, and the government.

The equations relate two or more variables to one another and are meant to be behavioral relations, accounting identities, or equilibrium conditions. The term *variables* refers to economic magnitudes that can take different values. There is an important distinction between *endogenous variables*(i.e., variables whose values are determined by the model itself) and *exogenous variables* (whose values are determined outside the model).

Another important element of mathematical models is a set of *parameters*, usually assumed constant and exogenously given. Parameters relate to the objective functions and constraints of economic agents. They determine the relations among endogenous and exogenous variables in the model.

Equations in mathematical models take the form of mathematical functions, which describe the relation of a particular variable to other variables in the model. Functions can be linear or nonlinear.

Variables and parameters of functions are usually defined in terms of *real numbers*. In mathematics, a real number is a value that represents a quantity along a line. The adjective *real* in this context was introduced in the seventeenth century by Descartes, who distinguished between real and imaginary roots of polynomials. Modern axiomatic definitions of real numbers are more rigorous than the definition given here, but this simple definition is sufficient for our purposes.

Real numbers include all the rational numbers, such as the integer -5 and the fraction 4/3, and all the irrational numbers, such as 1.41421356..., the square root of 2. Included within the irrationals are transcendental numbers, such as π (3.14159265...).

Real numbers can be thought of as points on an infinitely long line called the number line or real line, where the points corresponding to integers are equally spaced. Any real number can be determined by a (possibly infinite) decimal representation, such as 8.632, where each successive digit is measured in units one tenth the size of the previous one. The real line can be thought of as a part of the complex plane, and complex numbers include real numbers.

A.1.1 Functions

We denote the set of all n-tuples of real numbers by $\mathbb{R}^n$. The elements of this set are referred to as points or vectors. Vectors are indicated by boldface type, for example, $\mathbf{x} = (x_1, x_2, \ldots, x_n)'$. Thus, the ith component of a vector is denoted by x_i.

Formally, a real-valued function is a rule that assigns a unique y, in the set of all real numbers $\mathbb{R}$, to each $\mathbf{x} = (x_1, x_2, \ldots, x_n)'$, in the set of all n dimensional vectors $\mathbb{R}^n$. A function can thus be denoted by

$$y=f(\mathbf{x}), \tag{A.1}$$

where f is a mapping from $\mathbb{R}^n$ to $\mathbb{R}$. Consider the case where n is 1. Then a function f assigns a unique real value y for every real value of a single variable x.

In what follows, let us confine our attention to calculus and continuous functions. Calculus is the mathematical study of continuous change. A *continuous function* is a function for which sufficiently small changes in x result in arbitrarily small changes in y.

An example of such a function is a utility function of the form

$$u=f(c), \tag{A.2}$$

where u denotes consumer utility, and c denotes the consumer's consumption of goods and services. Such a function can be represented graphically as in figure A.1. In the case of a function with n equal to 1, such as (A.2), the graph is a curve in two-dimensional space.

Consider the case where n is equal to 2. Then a function assigns a unique value y for any vector $\mathbf{x}=(x_1,x_2)'$. An example of such a function is the *neoclassical production function* of the form

$$y=f(k,l), \tag{A.3}$$

where y denotes the output produced, k the capital stock, and l the labor force. Such a function can be represented graphically as in figure A.2. In the case of a function with n equal to 2, the graph is a surface in three-dimensional space.

As it is not always easy to draw such three-dimensional graphs, we sometimes describe them by holding one of the three variables constant and using a two-dimensional contour map. For example, figure A.3 depicts such a contour map, consisting of *isoquants* (i.e., combinations of capital and labor that produce a constant volume of output). Higher placed isoquants in the figure correspond to higher output.

Figure A.4 depicts another type of contour map, consisting of production functions for given quantities of labor. Each curve depicts the maximum amount of output produced, as a function of the capital stock, for a given quantity of labor. The higher the quantity of labor is, the greater will be the output that is produced as a function of the capital stock. Hence, the higher curves denote relations between output and the capital stock that correspond to higher employment of labor.

Functions of vectors of order higher than 2 cannot be represented graphically; they can only be analyzed algebraically.

A.1.2 Derivatives and Partial Derivatives of Functions

The (partial) derivative of a function $y=f(\mathbf{x})$ measures the sensitivity of the function value y to a change in its each of its arguments $\mathbf{x}$. Derivatives are a fundamental tool of calculus.

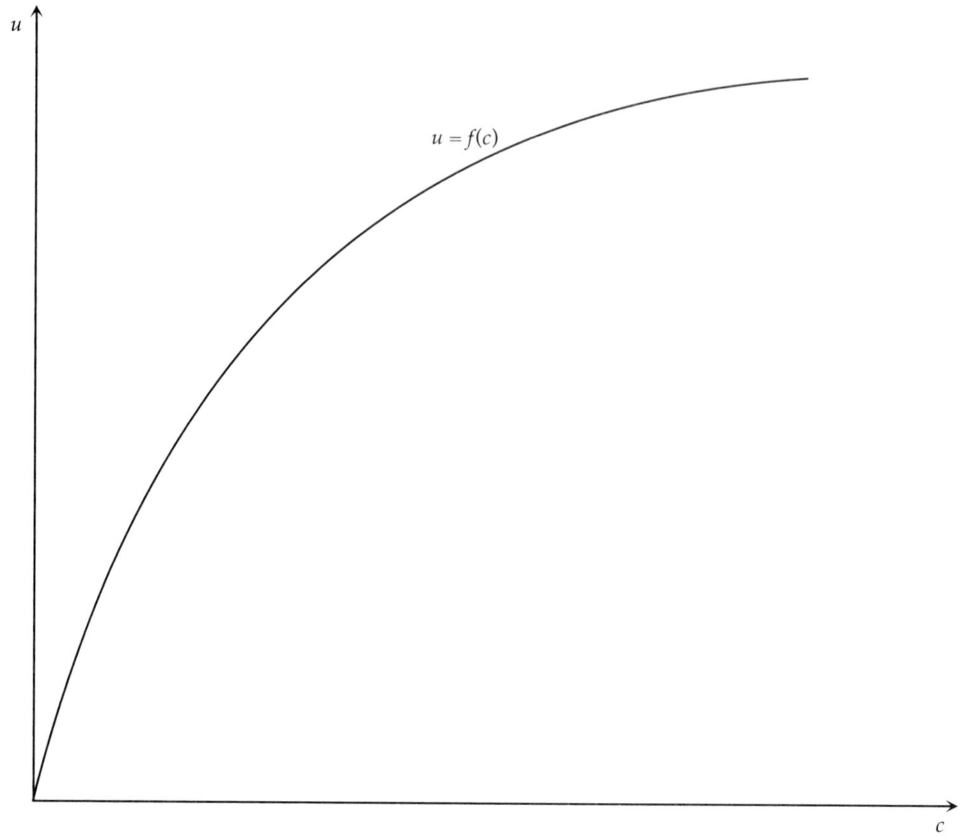

Figure A.1
Utility as a function of consumption.

Consider a function $f : \mathbb{R} \rightarrow \mathbb{R}$. The derivative of the function $f(x)$ evaluated at a point ξ is defined as

$$f'(\xi) = \lim_{h \rightarrow 0} \left(\frac{f(\xi + h) - f(\xi)}{h} \right). \tag{A.4}$$

The derivative of a function, as a function of x itself, is correspondingly defined and usually denoted as

$$f'(x) = \frac{df(x)}{dx}. \tag{A.5}$$

The $f'(x)$ notation is due to Lagrange, and the $\frac{df(x)}{dx}$ notation is due to Leibniz, two of the pioneers of calculus.

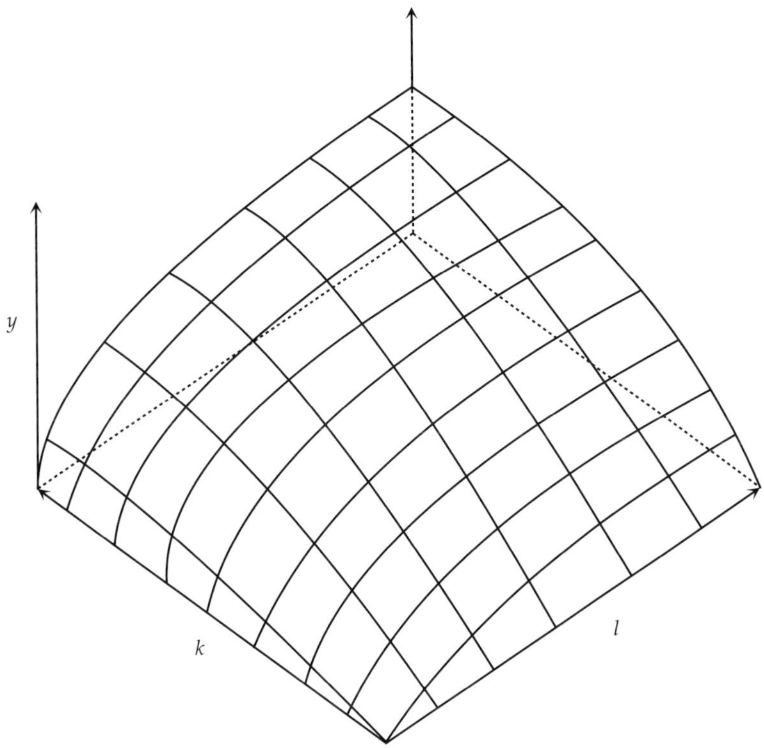

Figure A.2
Output as a function of capital and labor.

Graphically, the derivative is depicted as the *slope* of a function. It measures the change in the value of the function as a result of an infinitesimally small change in the variable x. Such a change is called a *marginal change*.

The derivative of the utility function (A.2) is depicted in figure A.5. It measures the effect on consumer utility of an infinitesimally small change in consumption. The derivative of a utility function is called *marginal utility*. As can be seen from figure A.5, for the utility function depicted, marginal utility is always positive, although declining.

The process of finding a derivative is called *differentiation*. The reverse process is called *integration*. Differentiation and integration constitute the two fundamental operations in calculus.

The derivative of a function can, in principle, be computed from the definition (A.4) by considering the difference quotient and computing its limit. In practice, once the derivatives of a few simple functions are known, the derivatives of other functions are more easily computed using rules for obtaining derivatives of more complicated functions from simpler ones.

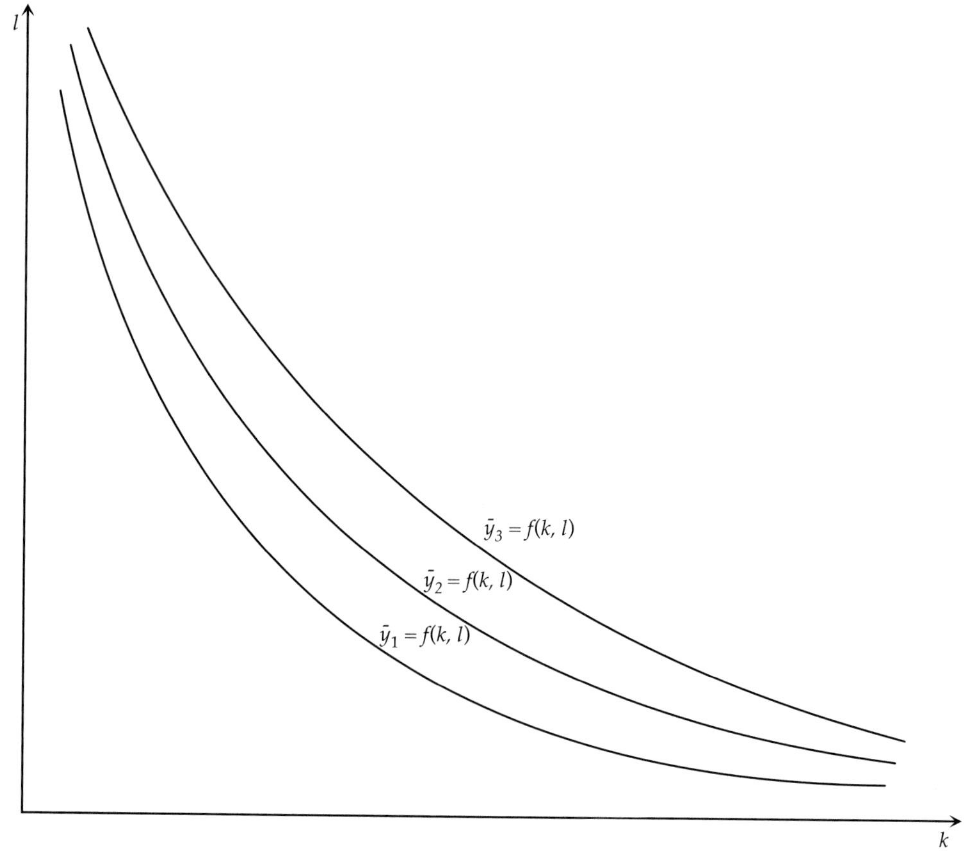

Figure A.3
Isoquants: capital labor combinations that produce given amounts of output.

Note that if a function is differentiable at a point, it must be continuous at this point. However, even if a function is continuous at a point, it may not be differentiable there. In this text, as in macroeconomics in general, we shall be mostly concerned with continuous and differentiable functions.

The following are the derivatives of some basic functions.

The derivative of a linear function, $f(x) = \alpha x$, where α is a constant parameter and x is a real variable, is

$$\frac{d(\alpha x)}{dx} = \alpha. \tag{A.6}$$

The proof of this is straightforward:

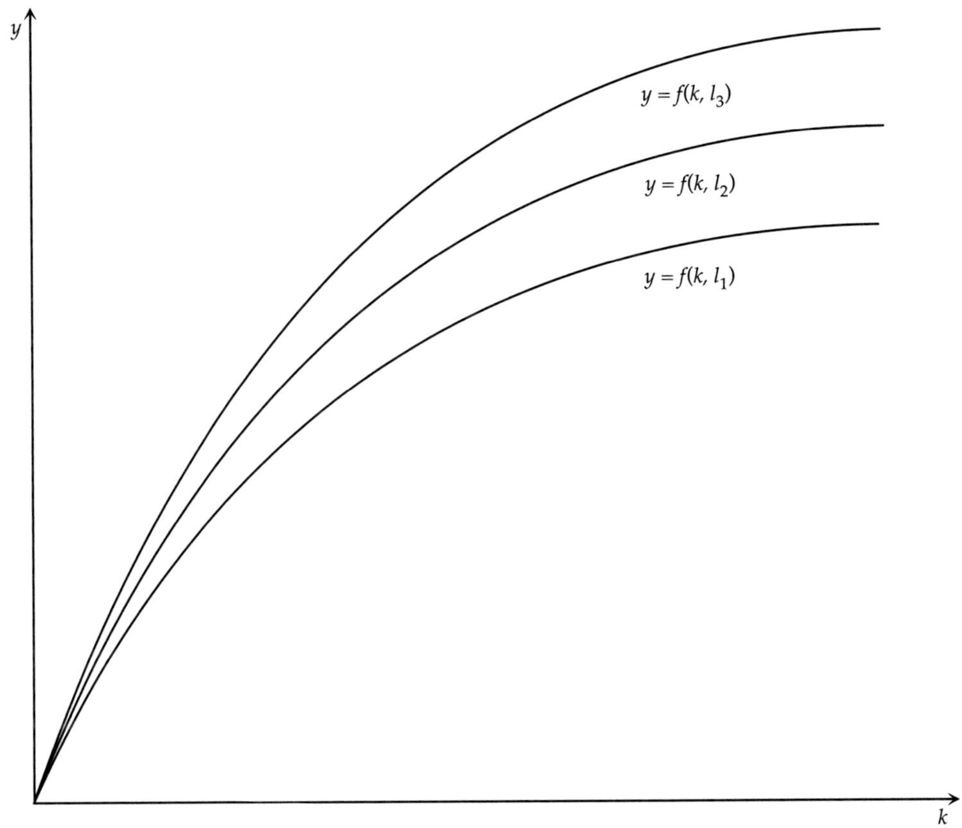

Figure A.4
Output as a function of the capital stock, for a given level of employment of labor.

$$\frac{d(\alpha x)}{dx} = \lim_{h \to 0} \left(\frac{\alpha(x+h) - \alpha x}{h} \right) = \frac{\alpha h}{h} = \alpha.$$

The proofs for the functions below are based on the same procedure, although they are slightly more involved and will be omitted. However, it is worth knowing the derivatives of the following basic functions.

The derivative of the *power function*, x^{α}, where α is a constant parameter and x is a real variable, is

$$\frac{d(x^{\alpha})}{dx} = \alpha x^{\alpha - 1}. \tag{A.7}$$

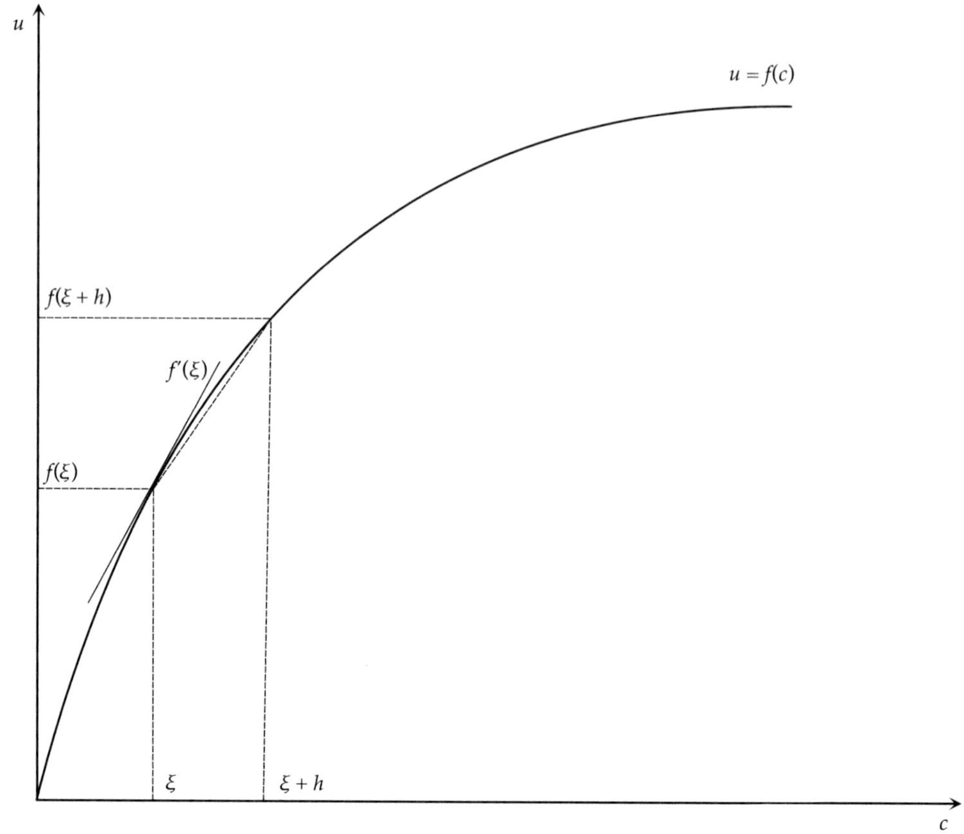

Figure A.5
Utility and marginal utility: the derivative of the utility function.

The derivative of the *exponential function* e^x, where e is the basis of natural logarithms and x is a real variable, is

$$\frac{d\,(e^x)}{dx} = e^x. \tag{A.8}$$

The derivative of the *logarithmic function* $\ln(x)$ is

$$\frac{d\ln(x)}{dx} = \frac{1}{x}. \tag{A.9}$$

The derivatives of the following *trigonometric functions* are

$$\frac{d\cos(x)}{dx} = -\sin(x),$$

$$\frac{d\sin(x)}{dx} = \cos(x), \tag{A.10}$$

$$\frac{d\tan(x)}{dx} = \sec^2(x) = \frac{1}{\cos^2(x)}.$$

The following rules of differentiation can also be proven easily, and they can be applied to sums, products, and ratios of functions, as well as to functions of functions.

The derivative of the *sum of two functions* $f(x)$ and $g(x)$ is given by the sum of the derivatives:

$$\frac{d(f(x)+g(x))}{dx} = \frac{df(x)}{dx} + \frac{dg(x)}{dx}. \tag{A.11}$$

The derivative of the *product of two functions* $f(x)$ and $g(x)$ is given by the sum of the products of each function with the derivative of the other:

$$\frac{d(f(x)g(x))}{dx} = g(x)\frac{df(x)}{dx} + f(x)\frac{dg(x)}{dx}. \tag{A.12}$$

The derivative of the *ratio of two functions* $f(x)$ and $g(x)$ is given by the difference of the product of the function in the denominator, with the derivative of the other, from the product of the function in the numerator, with the derivative of the other, over the square of the function in the denominator:

$$\frac{d(f(x)/g(x))}{dx} = \frac{g(x)\frac{df(x)}{dx} - f(x)\frac{dg(x)}{dx}}{g(x)^2}. \tag{A.13}$$

Finally, the derivative of a function f of a function $g(x)$, with respect to x, is given by the product of the derivative of f with respect to g, times the derivative of g with respect to x:

$$\frac{df(g(x))}{dx} = \frac{df(g(x))}{dg(x)}\frac{dg(x)}{d(x)}. \tag{A.14}$$

Rule (A.14), the rule for differentiating a function of a function, is also called the *chain rule*.

Partial derivatives of a function with two variables (i.e., $f:\mathbb{R}^2 \to \mathbb{R}$) are defined and denoted by

$$\begin{aligned} f_x(x,y) &= \frac{\partial f(x,y)}{\partial x} = \lim_{h\to 0}\left(\frac{f(x+h,y)-f(x,y)}{h}\right), \\ f_y(x,y) &= \frac{\partial f(x,y)}{\partial y} = \lim_{h\to 0}\left(\frac{f(x,y+h)-f(x,y)}{h}\right). \end{aligned} \tag{A.15}$$

The computation of partial derivatives is straightforward. Simply differentiate with respect to one of the variables, treating the other variable as constant.

The above rule applies equally well to the case of functions with n variables: $f:\mathbb{R}^n \rightarrow \mathbb{R}$: Partial derivatives are computed by simply differentiating with respect to one of the variables, treating the other variables as constant.

Partial derivatives can be used to totally differentiate a function of n variables with respect to all the variables. Consider the function $f:\mathbb{R}^n \rightarrow \mathbb{R}$:

$$y=f(x_1,x_2,\ldots,x_n). \tag{A.16}$$

The *total differential* of the function f is determined as

$$dy=\frac{\partial f(x_1,x_2,\ldots,x_n)}{\partial x_1}dx_1+\frac{\partial f(x_1,x_2,\ldots,x_n)}{\partial x_2}dx_2+\cdots\frac{\partial f(x_1,x_2,\ldots,x_n)}{\partial x_n}dx_n. \tag{A.17}$$

A.1.3 Maxima and Minima of Functions

Consider a function $f:\mathbb{R}\rightarrow\mathbb{R}$. A point ξ at which the derivative of the function is equal to zero is called a *stationary point* of the function. The reason is that at this point, the function is neither increasing nor decreasing.

Recall from the definition of derivatives that

$$\frac{df(x)}{dx}=\lim_{h\rightarrow 0}\left(\frac{f(x+h)-f(x)}{h}\right).$$

Hence, if the derivative of a function is equal to zero at a point, the value of the function does not change when x changes.

Figure A.6 shows the stationary points of a general continuous function $f(x)$. The word "stationary" arises from the fact that if one were to place a tiny ball on these points, because the slope is zero and the function is horizontal, the ball would stay in place.

The figure also shows the graph the derivative function $f'(x)$, which denotes the slope of the original function.

The stationary points of well-behaved function fall into three categories: *Local maxima*, *local minima*, and *points of inflection*. The highest local maximum is called a *global maximum*, and the lowest local minimum is called a *global minimum*.

Note that at a local maximum, the slope of the derivative function $f'(x)$ is negative; but at a local minimum, the slope of the derivative function $f'(x)$ is positive. This is equivalent to saying that for a local maximum, the second derivative of the original function f must be negative; for a local minimum, it must be positive. This result is intuitive. For a local maximum, a small change in either direction must result in a reduction in the value of the function. Hence, the derivative function must have a negative slope. For a local minimum, a small change in either direction must result in an increase in the value of the function. Hence, the derivative function must have a positive slope.

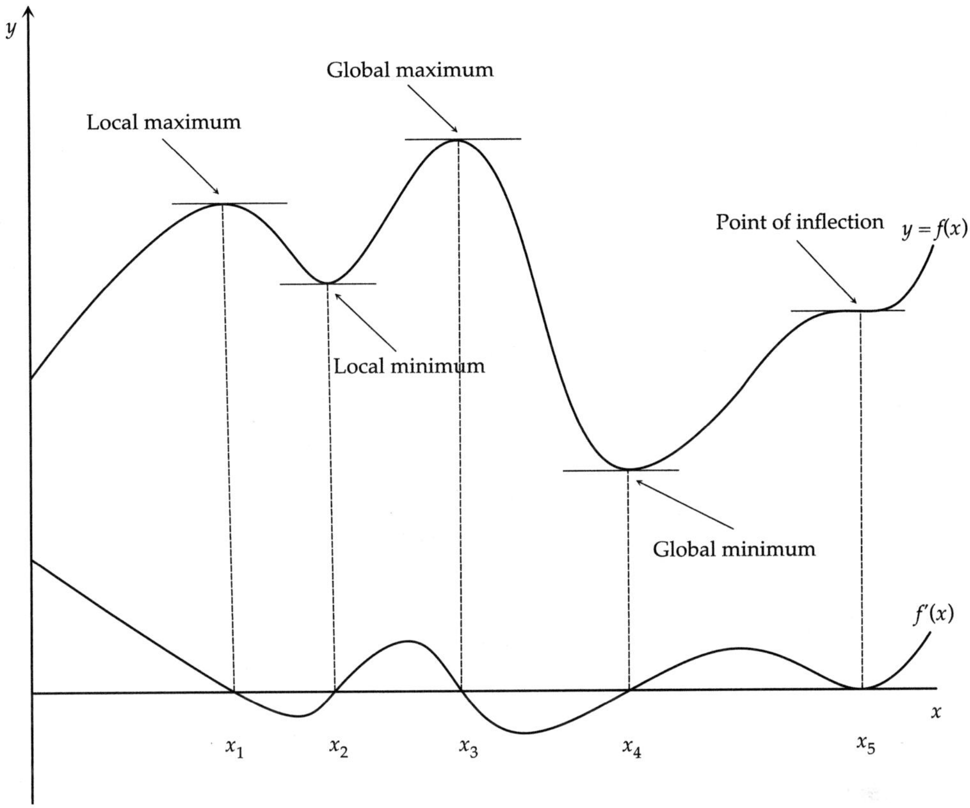

Figure A.6
Stationary points: maxima, minima, and points of inflection.

Hence, the conditions for a local maximum of a twice-differentiable continuous function are

$$\frac{df(x)}{dx} = f'(x) = 0,$$
$$\frac{d^2f(x)}{dx^2} = f''(x) < 0. \tag{A.18}$$

The conditions for a local minimum of a twice-differentiable continuous function are

$$\frac{df(x)}{dx} = f'(x) = 0,$$
$$\frac{d^2f(x)}{dx^2} = f''(x) > 0. \tag{A.19}$$

In most of the applications of calculus in this text, we assume that functions are twice differentiable. Hence, their second derivatives exist and can be computed.

A twice-differentiable function $f(x)$ is *concave* on an interval if and only if its derivative function $f'(x)$ is monotonically decreasing on that interval; that is, $f''(x) < 0$ on that interval. Thus, a concave function has a decreasing slope or first derivative.

A twice-differentiable function $f(x)$ is *convex* on an interval if and only if its derivative function $f'(x)$ is monotonically increasing on that interval; that is, $f''(x) > 0$ on that interval. Thus, a convex function has an increasing slope or first derivative.

These definitions can help us define points of inflection. *Points of inflection* are points where a function turns from concave to convex, or vice versa. Thus, local maxima are likely to be found in concave functions, or concave intervals of functions, while local minima are likely to be found in convex functions, or convex intervals of functions.

The conditions for the existence of stationary points can be generalized to functions of multiple variables. Consider the following function $f: \mathbb{R}^n \rightarrow \mathbb{R}$:

$$y = f(x_1, x_2, \ldots, x_n). \tag{A.20}$$

A stationary point exists where

$$\frac{\partial f(x_1, x_2, \ldots, x_n)}{\partial x_1} = \frac{\partial f(x_1, x_2, \ldots, x_n)}{\partial x_2} = \cdots = \frac{\partial f(x_1, x_2, \ldots, x_n)}{\partial x_n} = 0. \tag{A.21}$$

Whether the stationary point is a maximum or a minimum depends on the whole array of second partial derivatives of the function. This is a discussion that we shall postpone until we discuss the properties of matrices and linear algebra (appendix B).

A.2 Mathematical Optimization under Constraints

Economics is defined as the study of making the best use of scarce resources. Mathematically, this can be implemented by maximizing some objective function, which measures consumer welfare or the profits of firms, subject to another function, which measures the scarcity of resources.

A.2.1 Constrained Optimization in the Case of a Function of One Variable

Let us first consider the problem of choosing a single variable x to optimize an objective function $f(x)$, under a constraint $g(x) \leq 0$. The function to be optimized, called the *objective function*, is denoted by

$$y = f(x). \tag{A.22}$$

Assume that f is a concave function. We shall thus seek to maximize it.

In general, the *constraint* is a function of the form

$$g(x) \leq 0. \tag{A.23}$$

The problem then is to find the value of x that maximizes $f(x)$, subject to the constraint $g(x) \leq 0$.

Assume that the constraint is satisfied with equality at some value $\bar{x}$. Then the maximum is attained at $\bar{x}$ if the first derivative of $f(\bar{x})$ is positive. If the first derivative of the function $f(x)$ becomes equal to zero before $\bar{x}$ is reached (say, at point x_0), then the maximum is attained at x_0, before the constraint becomes binding.

Thus, at the optimum, the slope of the objective function $f'(x)$ is equal to the marginal value of the constraint $g'(x)$. With a binding constraint, this value is positive (i.e., the constraint has value); but with a nonbinding constraint, it is equal to zero (i.e., the constraint has no value).

The rule for finding the maximum of a concave function (such as (A.22)), subject to a constraint (such as (A.23)), is to evaluate the first derivative of the function (A.22) at the value of x for which $g(x) = 0$. If the first derivative is positive, then the constraint is binding and is satisfied with equality. Otherwise, the constraint is nonbinding, and the objective function is maximized before the constraint becomes binding.

Hence, if $f'(\bar{x}) > 0$, the maximum is attained at $x = \bar{x}$, where $\bar{x}$ is the value of x for which $g(x) = 0$. If $f'(\bar{x}) < 0$, the maximum is attained at $x_0 < \bar{x}$, where x_0 is the value of x that satisfies $f'(x_0) = 0$.

This case is depicted in figure A.7. For a binding constraint, the constrained maximum is obtained to the left of x_0, and the value of the objective function is lower than the value when the constraint is not binding. For a binding constraint, the first derivative of the function $f'(x)$ is positive at the optimum, whereas for a nonbinding constraint, it is equal to zero.

A.2.2 Optimal Consumption under an Income Constraint

A typical economic example is consumer choice under an income constraint. Assume that the consumer maximizes the utility function

$$u = f(c), \tag{A.24}$$

subject to the constraint

$$c \leq w. \tag{A.25}$$

The constraint can be expressed as

$$g(c) = c - w \leq 0. \tag{A.26}$$

Assume that $f'(x)$ is positive throughout (i.e., that the preferences of the consumer are characterized by *nonsatiation*) and that marginal utility is always positive. Also assume that

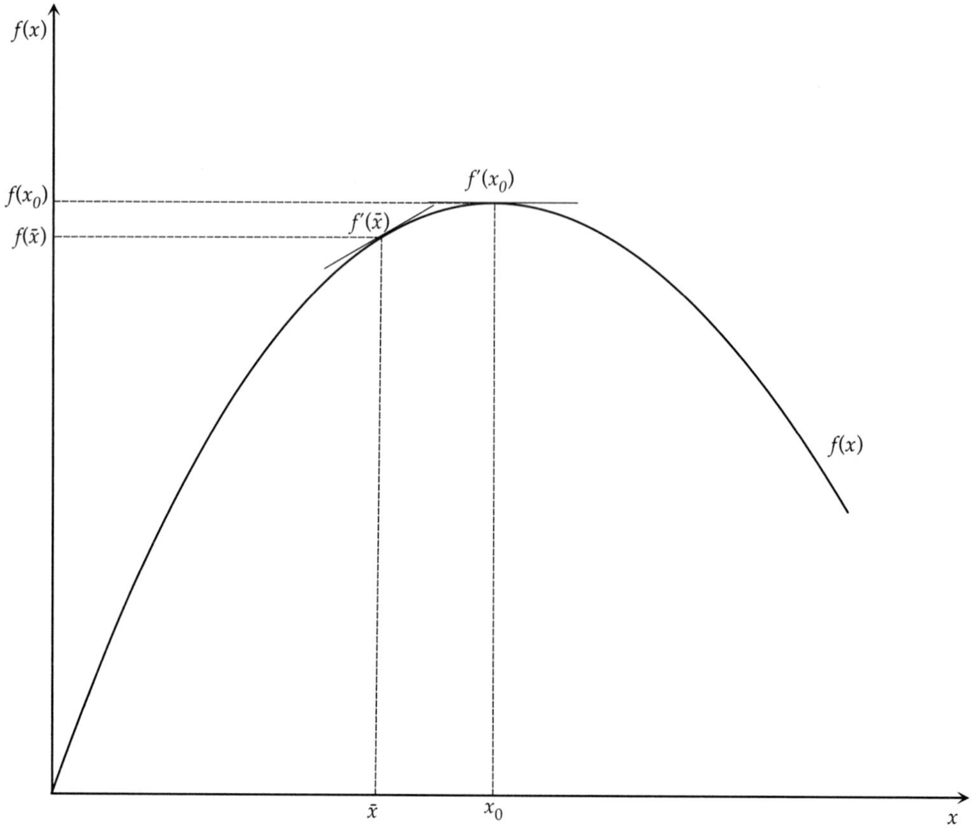

Figure A.7
Maximization with a binding and a nonbinding constraint.

$f''(x) < 0$ (i.e., that marginal utility is diminishing as the level of consumption increases). Then, by consuming all her income w, the consumer maximizes her utility. The income constraint is binding. The consumer chooses $c = w$ to maximize utility.

The case is depicted in figure A.8. At the maximum, the marginal utility of consumption is equal to $f'(w)$, which is positive throughout. The marginal utility of consumption at the maximum measures the marginal value to the consumer of an extra unit of income. If the income of the consumer were to rise from w_0 to w_1, then the consumer would increase her consumption correspondingly, and the marginal utility of consumption would fall. Thus, the marginal value of income to the consumer would also fall.

Under the assumption of nonsatiation (i.e., positive marginal utility of consumption at all levels of consumption), the constraint will always be binding, and the household will consume all its income.

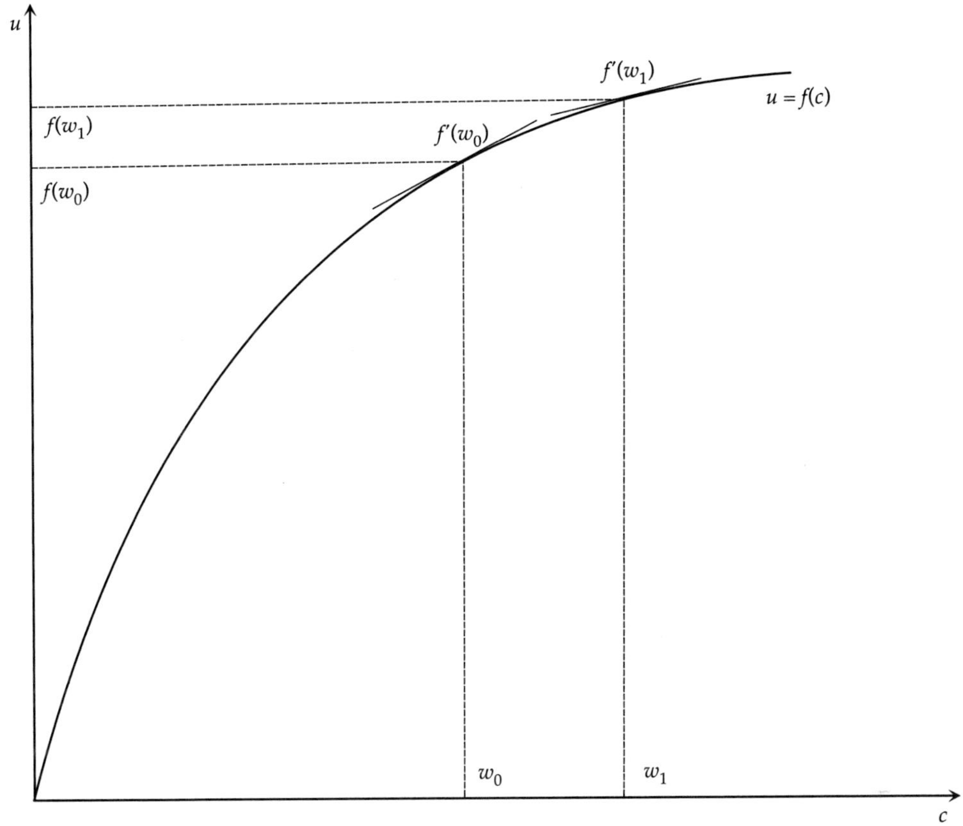

Figure A.8
Maximization of consumer utility subject to an income constraint.

A.2.3 The Lagrange Method

The first-order conditions for a maximum of (A.20), subject to constraints such as (A.21), can be derived by a method proposed by Lagrange, which generalizes to all problems of optimization under constraints.

The method consists of constructing a new function, the Lagrange function:

$$\mathcal{L}(x) = f(x) - \lambda g(x). \tag{A.27}$$

Setting the first derivative of the Lagrange function equal to zero, we get the first-order conditions for an optimum. Here λ is called the Lagrange multiplier, and its interpretation is as the marginal value of the constraint $g(x)$ in terms of the objective function $f(x)$.

Using the chain rule of differentiation, the first derivative of (A.27) is equal to zero when

$$f'(x) - \lambda g'(x) = 0. \tag{A.28}$$

At the optimum, the first derivative of the objective function with respect to x is equal to the Lagrange multiplier λ times the first derivative of the constraint with respect to x.

Applying the Lagrange method to the consumer problem of maximizing the utility function (A.22) subject to the constraint (A.23), we get that at the optimum.

$$f'(c) - \lambda = 0. \tag{A.29}$$

Thus, at the optimum, the marginal utility of consumption $f'(c)$ is equal to the marginal valuation of income λ. If the marginal utility of consumption is always positive (nonsatiation), then the marginal valuation of income is also positive, and the constraint (A.25) is satisfied with equality. The household consumes all of its income w.

Because we have assumed that f is a concave function, the second derivative of the Lagrange function at the optimum is given by

$$f''(c) < 0. \tag{A.30}$$

From (A.30), it follows that the optimum is indeed a maximum. Consumer welfare (A.24) is maximized subject to the income constraint (A.25).

The Lagrange method can be generalized to problems with n variables. Consider the optimization of the objective function

$$y = f(x_1, x_2, \ldots, x_n), \tag{A.31}$$

subject to the constraint

$$g(x_1, x_2, \ldots, x_n) \leq 0. \tag{A.32}$$

Then the first-order conditions for an optimum can be found by optimizing the Lagrange function:

$$\mathcal{L}(x_1, x_2, \ldots, x_n) = f(x_1, x_2, \ldots, x_n) - \lambda g(x_1, x_2, \ldots, x_n). \tag{A.33}$$

The first-order conditions for an optimum of (A.33) are

$$\frac{\partial f(x_1, x_2, \ldots, x_n)}{\partial x_i} - \lambda \frac{\partial g(x_1, x_2, \ldots, x_n)}{\partial x_i} = 0, \tag{A.34}$$

for all $i = 1, 2, \ldots, n$. At the optimum, the first derivative of the objective function with respect to each x_i is equal to the Lagrange multiplier λ times the first derivative of the constraint with respect to each x_i.

We can apply the Lagrange method to a two-variable example from consumer theory. Assume a household who faces exogenous prices of two consumer goods p_1 and p_2, and has an exogenous endowment of money income w. The objective function to be maximized is a utility function given by

$$u = f(c_1, c_2), \tag{A.35}$$

where $f_1, f_2 > 0, f_{11}, f_{22} < 0$ denote its first and second derivatives with respect to the two consumer goods c_1 and c_2.

Assume that the household maximizes utility subject to

$$g(c_1, c_2) = p_1 c_1 + p_2 c_2 - w \leq 0, \tag{A.36}$$

where $p_1, p_2 > 0$ denote the prices of consumption goods 1 and 2, respectively, and $w > 0$ denotes the money income of the household.

We seek the first-order conditions for the maximization of (A.35) subject to the income constraint (A.36). The Lagrange function for this problem is given by

$$\mathcal{L} = f(c_1, c_2) - \lambda\,(p_1 c_1 + p_2 c_2 - w)\,. \tag{A.37}$$

From the first-order conditions for a maximum, we have

$$\begin{aligned} f_1(c_1, c_2) - \lambda p_1 &= 0, \\ f_2(c_1, c_2) - \lambda p_2 &= 0. \end{aligned} \tag{A.38}$$

The first-order conditions (A.38) can be rewritten as

$$\begin{aligned} f_1(c_1, c_2) &= \lambda p_1, \\ f_2(c_1, c_2) &= \lambda p_2. \end{aligned} \tag{A.39}$$

The economic interpretation of (A.39) is straightforward. At the maximum, the marginal utility of each of the two goods is equal to the marginal value of money income λ (the Lagrange multiplier) times the price of each good in terms of money.

Because marginal utilities and prices are assumed positive, the marginal value of money income λ will also be positive. Thus, the constraint will be binding and will be satisfied with equality. The household will spend all of its money income, and we have that

$$p_1 c_1 + p_2 c_2 = w. \tag{A.40}$$

The three unknowns, c_1, c_2, and λ, can be found by solving the system of the three equations (A.39) and (A.40). Thus, optimal consumption and the optimal marginal value of money can be found as functions of the exogenous set of prices p_1 and p_2 and money income w.

The optimality conditions can be given another interpretation, known from intermediate microeconomics. Dividing the first by the second equation in (A.39), we eliminate λ between the two equations, resulting in

$$\frac{f_1(c_1,c_2)}{f_2(c_1,c_2)}=\frac{p_1}{p_2}. \tag{A.41}$$

The economic interpretation of (A.41) is that at the optimum, the ratio of the marginal utilities of goods 1 and 2 is equal to their relative price. The ratio of the marginal utilities is equal to the marginal rate of substitution between the consumption of goods 2 and 1. Hence, at the optimum, the marginal rate of substitution between the two goods is equal to their relative price.

To further delve into this interpretation, we can totally differentiate both the objective function (A.35) and the budget constraint (A.40).

Totally differentiating the objective function (A.35) results in

$$df(c_1,c_2)=\frac{\partial f(c_1,c_2)}{\partial x_1}dc_1+\frac{\partial f(c_1,c_2)}{\partial x_2}dc_2=f_1(c_1,c_2)dc_1+f_2(c_1,c_2)dc_2. \tag{A.42}$$

For a constant level of utility, $df=0$. The marginal rate of substitution between the consumption of good 2 and the consumption of good 1 is thus given by

$$\frac{dc_2}{dc_1}=-\frac{f_1(c_1,c_2)}{f_2(c_1,c_2)}. \tag{A.43}$$

The marginal rate of substitution, (i.e., the marginal change in the consumption of good 2 required to maintain a constant level of utility following an infinitesimally small change in the consumption of good 1) measures the *slope of indifference curves*. It is negative and equal in absolute value to the ratio of marginal utilities of good 1 and good 2.

By totally differentiating the budget constraint (A.40), we get that

$$dw=p_1dc_1+p_2dc_2. \tag{A.44}$$

For a constant level of income, $dw=0$. Therefore, it follows from (A.44) that

$$\frac{dc_2}{dc_1}=-\frac{p_1}{p_2}. \tag{A.45}$$

Equation (A.45) measures the slope of the budget constraint (A.40). It denotes how much of good 2 the household has to sacrifice to buy an extra unit of good 1.

Thus, the optimum is determined at the point where the budget constraint touches the highest possible indifference curve. At this tangency point, the slope of the budget constraint and the indifference curve of the household coincide.

The determination of the optimum is depicted in figure A.9. At the optimum (i.e., point E, the consumption bundle that maximizes the utility of the household), the marginal rate of

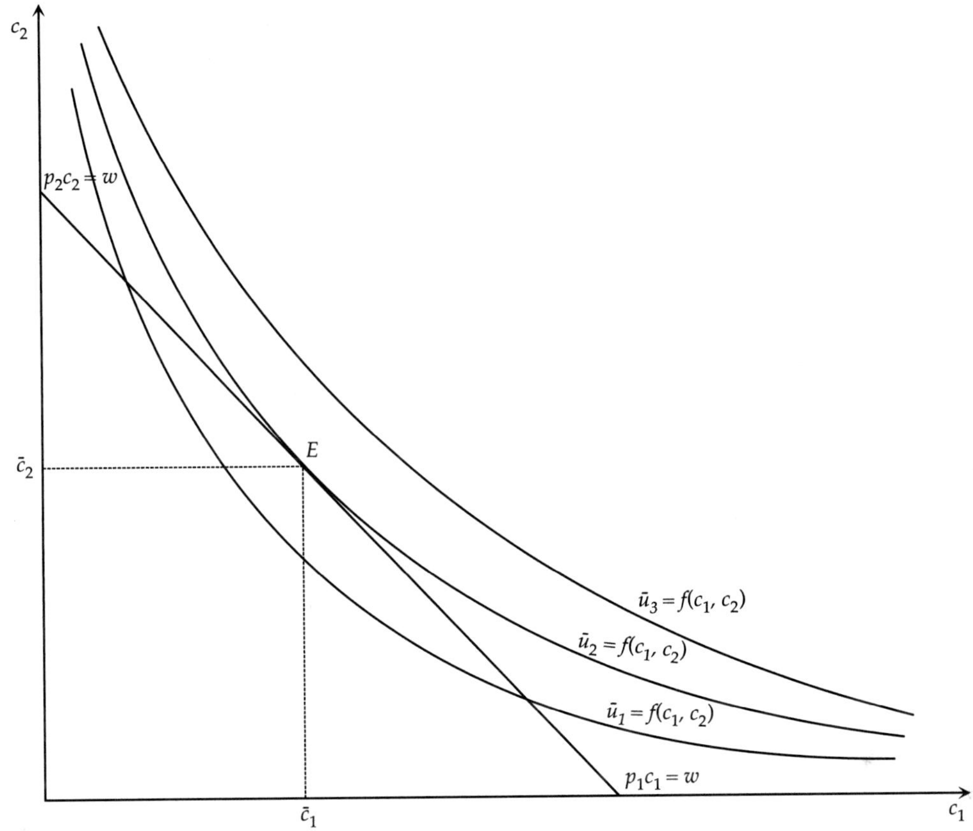

Figure A.9
Optimal choice of a consumption bundle.

substitution (i.e., the slope of the highest possible indifference curve) is the same as the relative price of the two goods, which is the slope of the budget constraint.

A.3 Some Useful Functional Forms

This section introduces some useful functional forms and discusses their properties. These functional forms are widely used to model either the production process or the preferences of households. We shall focus on the constant elasticity of substitution (CES) production and utility functions and the constant elasticity of intertemporal substitution (CEIS) utility function.

The CES functional form contains other functional forms as special cases, such as the Cobb-Douglas, fixed proportions, and linear production and utility functions.

The CEIS functional form is a relatively general *additive* functional form, which is quite useful in modeling intertemporal preferences and uncertainty. It contains the logarithmic, linear, and quadratic utility functions as special cases.

A.3.1 The Two-Factor CES Production Function and the Elasticity of Substitution

The CES production function was introduced by Arrow et al. [1961]. As its name suggests, it is a production function for which the elasticity of substitution between capital and labor is constant. In its most general form, it can be written as

$$Y(t) = F\left(K(t), L(t)\right) = A\left[a(bK(t))^{\psi} + (1-a)((1-b)h(t)L(t))^{\psi}\right]^{\frac{1}{\psi}}, \tag{A.46}$$

where $A > 0$ is total factor productivity, which is assumed to be exogenous and constant. It is assumed that $0 < a, b < 1$ and $\psi < 1$ are constant parameters. Their interpretation will become apparent shortly.

By multiplying both inputs by any positive λ, it is straightforward to confirm that this production function exhibits constant returns to scale.

The *technical rate of substitution* measures how one of the inputs (say, labor) must adjust to keep output constant, when the other input (say, capital) changes. In the two-factor case, it is just the slope of the isoquant and is defined by

$$\left.\frac{dL}{dK}\right|_{Y} = -\frac{F_K}{F_L}, \tag{A.47}$$

where F_K and F_L are respectively the marginal products of capital and labor at output Y.

The *elasticity of substitution* σ between capital and labor is defined as the percentage change in the ratio of labor to capital, divided by the percentage change in the technical rate of substitution, with output being held fixed. It is a measure of the curvature of the isoquants of the production function. The elasticity of substitution σ is thus defined by

$$\sigma = \left(\frac{\partial\left(F_K/F_L\right)}{\partial\left(L/K\right)}\frac{L/K}{F_K/F_L}\right)^{-1}. \tag{A.48}$$

For the CES production function, the technical rate of substitution is given by

$$-\frac{F_K}{F_L} = -(L/K)^{1-\psi} ab^{\psi}\left((1-a)((1-b)h)^{\psi}\right). \tag{A.49}$$

Thus, the elasticity of substitution σ is given by

$$\sigma = \frac{1}{1-\psi}. \tag{A.50}$$

From (A.50), one can confirm that the elasticity of substitution is indeed constant.

A.3.2 Special Cases of the CES Production Function

As ψ tends to minus infinity, the elasticity of substitution tends to zero. Thus, the CES production function contains as a special case the *fixed-proportions production function,* with a zero elasticity of substitution between capital and labor. This takes the form

$$Y(t) = \min\left[bK(t), (1-b)h(t)L(t)\right]. \tag{A.51}$$

Equation (A.51) is a production function that was widely used prior to the introduction of neoclassical production function, by, for example, Harrod [1939], Leontieff [1941], and Domar [1946]. It is often referred to as the *Leontieff* production function.

As ψ tends to zero, the elasticity of substitution tends to one. It is straightforward to show, using L'Hopital's rule, that in this case, the limit of the CES production function is the *Cobb-Douglas* production function. This functional form, due to Cobb and Douglas [1928], is used extensively in macroeconomics. It is worth remembering that it is a special case of the CES production function, with a unitary elasticity of substitution between capital and labor. It takes the form

$$Y(t) = \bar{A}K(t)^a(h(t)L(t))^{1-a}, \tag{A.52}$$

where $\bar{A} = Ab^a(1-b)^{1-a}$

Finally, for $\psi = 1$, the CES production function becomes linear, and the elasticity of substitution between capital and labor becomes infinite. Thus, the CES production function contains the *linear production function* as a special case.

A.3.3 The CES Production Function and the Solow Model of Economic Growth

Expressing the CES production function per efficiency unit of labor, one gets

$$y(t) = f(k(t)) = A\left[a(bk(t))^{\psi} + (1-a)(1-b)^{\psi}\right]^{\frac{1}{\psi}}. \tag{A.53}$$

The marginal product of capital (per efficiency unit of labor) is then given by

$$f'(k(t)) = Aab^{\psi}\left[ab^{\psi} + (1-a)(1-b)^{\psi}k(t)^{-\psi}\right]^{\frac{1-\psi}{\psi}}. \tag{A.54}$$

The average product of capital (per efficiency unit of labor) is given by

$$\frac{f(k(t))}{k(t)} = A\left[ab^{\psi} + (1-a)(1-b)^{\psi}k(t)^{-\psi}\right]^{\frac{1}{\psi}}. \tag{A.55}$$

One can confirm from (A.54) and (A.55) that for any $\psi < 1$, both the marginal and average products of capital (per efficiency unit of labor) fall as capital per efficiency unit of labor increases. Thus, the CES production function is characterized by diminishing returns to capital accumulation. The question that arises is whether the Inada conditions are satisfied in the case of the CES production function.

Consider first the case $0 < \psi < 1$, that is, an elasticity of substitution between capital and labor that is greater than one. The limits of the marginal and average products of capital, as capital tends to zero and infinity, respectively, are given by

$$\lim_{k\to 0} f'(k) = \lim_{k\to 0} [f(k)/k] = \infty,$$

$$\lim_{k\to\infty} f'(k) = \lim_{k\to\infty} [f(k)/k] = Aba^{\frac{1}{\psi}} > 0.$$

Thus, in the case of an elasticity of substitution that is greater than one, the CES production function does not satisfy the second Inada condition, and a steady state capital stock (per efficiency unit of labor) may not exist.

For example, in the Solow model, if

$$Aba^{\frac{1}{\psi}} > \frac{n+g+\delta}{s},$$

then steady state does not exist, and capital per efficiency unit of labor grows continuously. The model becomes one of *endogenous growth*.

Consider next the case $\psi < 0$, that is, an elasticity of substitution between capital and labor which is lower than one. The limits of the marginal and average products of capital, as capital tends to zero and infinity, respectively, are given by

$$\lim_{k\to 0} f'(k) = \lim_{k\to 0} [f(k)/k] = Aba^{\frac{1}{\psi}} < \infty,$$

$$\lim_{k\to\infty} f'(k) = \lim_{k\to\infty} [f(k)/k] = 0.$$

Thus, in the case of an elasticity of substitution that is less than one, the CES production function does not necessarily satisfy the second Inada condition, and a steady state capital stock (per efficiency unit of labor) may not exist.

For example, in the Solow model, if

$$Aba^{\frac{1}{\psi}} < \frac{n+g+\delta}{s},$$

then a steady state does not exist, and capital per efficiency unit of labor is driven to zero.

Only in the case where the constant elasticity of substitution between capital and labor is equal to one (that is, the Cobb-Douglas case) is the satisfaction of both Inada conditions—and hence the existence of a steady state—guaranteed.

A.3.4 The CES Utility Function

The CES functional form can also be used for modeling consumer utility. Assuming a household that has access to two goods, c_1 and c_2, the CES utility function takes the form

$$U(c_1,c_2)=\left[\alpha c_1^{\psi}+(1-\alpha)c_2^{\psi}\right]^{\frac{1}{\psi}}. \tag{A.56}$$

where α is the relative weight of good 1 in the utility of the consumer. Equation (A.56) has the same properties as the two-factor CES production function (A.46).

The elasticity of substitution in the consumption of the two goods is constant and given by $1/(1-\psi)$. As ψ tends to minus infinity, the elasticity of substitution tends to zero. Thus, the CES utility function contains as a special case the *fixed-proportions utility function*, with a zero elasticity of substitution between the two goods. As ψ tends to zero, the elasticity of substitution tends to one. It is straightforward to show, using L'Hopital's rule, that in this case, the limit of the CES utility function is the Cobb-Douglas utility function. Thus, the CES utility function contains the Cobb-Douglas utility function as a special case, with a unitary elasticity of substitution between the two goods. Finally, for $\psi=1$, the CES utility function becomes linear, and the elasticity of substitution between the two goods becomes infinite. Thus, the CES utility function contains the linear utility function as a special case.

The CES functional form can be generalized to n goods. Assuming a household that has access to n goods, a CES utility function in which good i has a weight in consumer utility equal to $\alpha_i>0$, takes the form

$$U(c_1,c_2,\ldots,c_n)=\left[\alpha_1 c_1^{\psi}+\alpha_2 c_2^{\psi}+\cdots+\alpha_n c_n^{\psi}\right]^{\frac{1}{\psi}}. \tag{A.57}$$

The elasticity of substitution in the consumption of any two goods among the n goods is constant and given by $1/(1-\psi)$.

A.3.5 Additively Separable Utility and the CEIS Utility Function

Because utility functions are defined up to any monotonic transformation, we can raise the CES utility function (A.57) to the power ψ. We then end up with a utility function of the form

$$[U(c_1,c_2,\ldots,c_n)]^{\psi}=\alpha_1 c_1^{\psi}+\alpha_2 c_2^{\psi}+\cdots+\alpha_n c_n^{\psi}. \tag{A.58}$$

The difference between the CES utility function (A.57) and the CES utility function (A.58) is that (A.58) is an additively separable utility function. Unlike the original CES utility function (A.57), the marginal utility of consumption of each good in (A.58) is independent of the consumption of the other goods. This property is defined as *additive separability*.

Taking the first derivative of the original CES utility function (A.57) with respect to c_i, the marginal utility of good i is given by

$$\frac{\partial U(c_1,c_2,\ldots,c_n)}{\partial c_i}=U_i(c_1,c_2,\ldots,c_n)=\alpha_i c_i^{\psi-1}\left[\alpha_1 c_1^{\psi}+\alpha_2 c_2^{\psi}+\cdots+\alpha_n c_n^{\psi}\right]^{\frac{1}{\psi}-1}. \quad \text{(A.59)}$$

Taking the first derivative of the transformed CES utility function (A.58) with respect to c_i, the marginal utility of good i is given by

$$\frac{\partial U(c_1,c_2,\ldots,c_n)}{\partial c_i}=U_i(c_i)=\psi\alpha_i c_i^{\psi-1}. \quad \text{(A.60)}$$

In the case of the original CES utility function, the marginal utility of consumption of good i depends on the consumption of all other goods. But in the case of the transformed CES utility function, it only depends on the consumption of the good itself.

However, this does not affect consumer choice. For both the original and the transformed CES functions, the marginal rate of substitution between the consumption of any two goods i and j, and hence the slope of indifference curves, is given by

$$\frac{dc_j}{dc_i}=-\frac{\alpha_i}{\alpha_j}\left(\frac{c_i}{c_j}\right)^{\psi-1}. \quad \text{(A.61)}$$

It is in this sense that utility functions are defined up to a monotonic transformation.

The differences between (A.57) and (A.58) do not matter for the optimal choice of the consumption bundle. Given that at the maximum, the marginal rate of substitution is equal to the relative price of the two goods, consumer choice is the same for both the original and the transformed CES utility functions. For any two goods i and j, it is determined by

$$\frac{\alpha_i}{\alpha_j}\left(\frac{c_i}{c_j}\right)^{\psi-1}=\frac{p_i}{p_j}. \quad \text{(A.62)}$$

Additively separable utility functions are used extensively in intertemporal macroeconomics. The presumption is that the marginal utility of consumption in one period does not depend on the level of consumption in previous or future periods.

Thus, a monotonic transformation of a version of the CES utility function (A.57), in which (A.57) is raised to the power ψ, and multiplied by $1/\psi$, is a widely used functional form for intertemporal utility functions. It takes the form

$$U=\frac{c_0^{1-\theta}}{1-\theta}+\frac{1}{(1+\rho)}\frac{c_1^{1-\theta}}{1-\theta}+\cdots+\frac{1}{(1+\rho)^T}\frac{c_T^{1-\theta}}{1-\theta}=\sum_{t=0}^{T}\frac{1}{(1+\rho)^t}\frac{c_t^{1-\theta}}{1-\theta}, \quad \text{(A.63)}$$

where c_t denotes consumption in different time periods, $t=0,1,\ldots,T$; and $\rho>0$ denotes the rate at which the household discounts the future, which is called the *pure rate of time preference*. Thus, relative to (A.58), in (A.63), $\alpha_t=(1/(1+\rho))^t$. In the equation, $\theta=1-\psi$ is the inverse of the elasticity of substitution, $1/\theta$ is the elasticity of intertemporal substitution in this context, and the utility function of the form of (A.63) is termed the *constant elasticity of intertemporal substitution* (CEIS) utility function.

It is straightforward to show that if θ, and the elasticity of intertemporal substitution $1/\theta$, are equal to unity, then (A.63) is not defined. Because U is not defined when θ is equal to unity, we might as well consider what happens to the first derivative of U with respect to c_t as θ tends to unity. This is the essence of L'Hopital's rule. If the first derivative is defined and is the first derivative of a known function, then the original functions tends to that particular function as θ tends to unity. In this case, we have that the limit of the first derivative of (A.63) is given by

$$\lim_{\theta\to 1} \frac{1}{(1+\rho)^t} c_t^{-\theta} = \frac{1}{(1+\rho)^t}\frac{1}{c_t},$$

where $1/c$ is the first derivative of a logarithmic function. Hence, L'Hopital's rule implies that as θ tends to unity, the CEIS utility function tends to the *intertemporal logarithmic utility function*:

$$U = \sum_{t=0}^{T} \frac{1}{(1+\rho)^t} \ln(c_t). \tag{A.64}$$

This is often used in intertemporal macroeconomics as a special case of the CEIS utility function.

Two extreme cases of (A.63) are worth mentioning, although they are not widely used. The first is the limit of (A.63) as θ tends to 0 and the elasticity of intertemporal substitution tends to infinity. Then the CEIS utility function becomes a *linear intertemporal utility function* of the form

$$U = \sum_{t=0}^{T} \frac{1}{(1+\rho)^t} c_t. \tag{A.65}$$

The second is the limit of (A.63) as θ tends to infinity and the elasticity of intertemporal substitution tends to zero. Then the CEIS utility function becomes independent of consumption.

Appendix B: Linear Models and Linear Algebra

In this appendix, we discuss the solution of linear economic models and introduce the basic elements of linear algebra. *Linear algebra* is the branch of mathematics that analyses vector spaces and linear mappings between such spaces. It essentially studies models consisting of linear functions. Linear algebra is useful in macroeconomics, because it provides efficient solution methods for linear macroeconomic models, especially models with many endogenous variables.

Because linear algebra is such a well-developed branch of mathematics, nonlinear models are sometimes approximated by linear models. Combined with calculus, linear algebra also facilitates the solution of linear systems of differential and difference equations. This appendix provides a review of the main elements of linear algebra.[1]

B.1 Linear Models

Consider the following system of linear equations, where y_i, $i = 1, 2, \dots, n$, denotes an endogenous variable; x_j, $j = 1, 2, \dots, m$, denotes an exogenous variable; and a_{ik} and b_{ij} denote constant parameters, with $k = 1, 2, \dots, n$:

$$\begin{aligned} y_1 &= a_{12}y_2 + \cdots + a_{1n}y_n + b_{11}x_1 + b_{12}x_2 + \cdots + b_{1m}x_m, \\ y_2 &= a_{21}y_1 + \cdots + a_{2n}y_n + b_{21}x_1 + b_{22}x_2 + \cdots + b_{2m}x_m, \\ &\vdots \\ y_n &= a_{n1}y_1 + \cdots + a_{nn-1}y_{n-1} + b_{n1}x_1 + b_{n2}x_2 + \cdots + b_{nm}x_m. \end{aligned} \tag{B.1}$$

The system of equations (B.1) is an example of a linear economic model, with n endogenous variables, and m exogenous variables determined outside the model. Because it contains n

1. This review is neither a complete nor a mathematically rigorous treatment but is adequate for the purposes of this text. For fuller and more rigorous treatments of linear algebra suitable for economists, consult a comprehensive text of mathematics for economists, such as Chiang [1974], Simon and Blume [1994], or Klein [2013].

equations in n unknowns (the n endogenous variables), it could in principle be solved for the values of the endogenous variables as functions of the exogenous variables.

Under what conditions does this model possess a solution? Is the solution unique? How do the exogenous variables affect each endogenous variable?

To answer these types of questions and to be able to derive the solution of the model, we need to use some concepts of linear algebra. The model in (B.1) can be rewritten in *matrix form*. Collecting all the endogenous variables on the left-hand side, the model can be rewritten as

$$\begin{aligned} y_1 - a_{12}y_2 - \cdots - a_{1n}y_n &= b_{11}x_1 + b_{12}x_2 + \cdots + b_{1m}x_m, \\ -a_{21}y_1 + y_2 - \cdots - a_{2n}y_n &= b_{21}x_1 + b_{22}x_2 + \cdots + b_{2m}x_m, \\ &\vdots \\ -a_{n1}y_1 - \cdots - a_{nn-1}y_{n-1} + y_n &= b_{n1}x_1 + b_{n2}x_2 + \cdots + b_{nm}x_m. \end{aligned} \tag{B.2}$$

The system (B.2) can be represented in matrix form:

$$\begin{pmatrix} 1 & \cdots & -a_{1n} \\ \vdots & \ddots & \vdots \\ -a_{n1} & \cdots & 1 \end{pmatrix} \begin{pmatrix} y_1 \\ \vdots \\ y_n \end{pmatrix} = \begin{pmatrix} b_{11} & \cdots & b_{1m} \\ \vdots & \ddots & \vdots \\ b_{n1} & \cdots & b_{nm} \end{pmatrix} \begin{pmatrix} x_1 \\ \vdots \\ x_m \end{pmatrix}, \tag{B.3}$$

where the rectangular arrays of the a_{ik}s and the b_{ij}s are *matrices of coefficients*, and the vertical arrays of the endogenous and exogenous variables are *vectors of variables*.

B.2 Elements of Linear Algebra

A table with n rows and m columns, such as the one containing the b_{ij}s in equation (B.3) is called an $n \times m$ *matrix*. The *elements* of the matrix can be either scalars or variables. For example, b_{11} is the scalar in the first row and the first column of the matrix containing the b_{ij}s.

A matrix with the same number of rows and columns, such as the matrix containing the a_{ik}s in (B.3), is called a *square matrix*. In this case, it is an $n \times n$ square matrix.

A matrix with one column, such as the one containing the endogenous and exogenous variables, is called a *vector*.

The system of equations (B.1) in matrix form, as in (B.3), can be represented more compactly as

$$\mathbf{Ay} = \mathbf{Bx}, \tag{B.4}$$

where $\mathbf{A}$ denotes the $n \times n$ square matrix of the coefficients of the endogenous variables in (B.3), $\mathbf{B}$ denotes the $n \times m$ matrix of the coefficients of the exogenous variables in

(B.3), and $\mathbf{y}$ and $\mathbf{x}$ denote the vectors of the endogenous and the exogenous variables, respectively.

One can perform matrix algebra on matrices and thus analyze systems of equations in matrix form.

B.2.1 Matrix Addition, Subtraction, and Multiplication

One common matrix operation is *scalar multiplication*. If $\mathbf{B}$ is an $n \times m$ matrix, then multiplying $\mathbf{B}$ by a scalar λ entails multiplying each element of the matrix by λ. Thus, $\lambda\mathbf{B}$ is an $n \times m$ matrix with elements λb_{ij}, where b_{ij} is the corresponding element of the $\mathbf{B}$ matrix.

A second type of operation is *matrix addition* and *matrix subtraction*. For these operations to be meaningful, the matrices must be of the same dimension. Thus, if $\mathbf{B}$ and $\mathbf{C}$ are two $n \times m$ matrices, we can define a new matrix $\mathbf{D} = \mathbf{B} + \mathbf{C}$, or an new matrix $\mathbf{E} = \mathbf{B} - \mathbf{C}$. The elements of $\mathbf{D}$ are the sum of the corresponding elements of $\mathbf{B}$ and $\mathbf{C}$, and the elements of $\mathbf{E}$ are the difference between the corresponding elements of $\mathbf{B}$ and $\mathbf{C}$. Thus, element $d_{ij} = b_{ij} + c_{ij}$ in the $\mathbf{D}$ matrix, and element $e_{ij} = b_{ij} - c_{ij}$ in the $\mathbf{E}$ matrix.

A third operation, *matrix multiplication*, requires two compatible matrices as well. To multiply two matrices $\mathbf{B}$ and $\mathbf{C}$, the number of columns of matrix $\mathbf{B}$ must be equal to the number of rows of matrix $\mathbf{C}$. Assume that $\mathbf{B}$ is an $m \times n$ matrix, and $\mathbf{C}$ is an $n \times p$ matrix. Then the product of the two matrices is the $m \times p$ matrix $\mathbf{D} = \mathbf{BC}$, whose element d_{ij} is the *inner product* of the ith row of matrix $\mathbf{B}$ with the jth column of matrix $\mathbf{C}$, defined as $d_{ij} = \sum_{k=1}^{n} b_{ik}c_{kj}$.

These matrix operations also apply to vectors.

It is straightforward to verify that the products $\mathbf{Ay}$ and $\mathbf{Bx}$ in (B.4) exist, because the matrices multiplied are indeed compatible. Both $\mathbf{Ay}$ and $\mathbf{Bx}$ turn out to be $n \times 1$ vectors.

Another useful matrix operation is transposition. The *transpose* of matrix is a new matrix whose rows are the columns of the original matrix, and its columns are the rows of the original matrix. Thus, if $\mathbf{B}$ is an $n \times m$ matrix, its transpose $\mathbf{B}^{\mathrm{T}}$, or $\mathbf{B}'$ is an $m \times n$ matrix.

B.2.2 The Inverse of a Square Matrix

The final, and more involved operation involving matrices is matrix inversion. This is the equivalent of division for scalars, and it only applies to square matrices. To be able to divide by a matrix $\mathbf{A}$, we must define the *inverse* of $\mathbf{A}$.

Consider an n x n square matrix $\mathbf{A}$, defined as

$$\mathbf{A} = \begin{pmatrix} a_{11} & \cdots & a_{1n} \\ \vdots & \ddots & \vdots \\ a_{n1} & \cdots & a_{nn} \end{pmatrix}. \tag{B.5}$$

The *main diagonal* of this matrix consists of all the elements a_{ii}, $i = 1, 2, \ldots, n$. The main diagonal is also the first diagonal of the matrix. *Diagonals* are defined by the n elements on the diagonal of the matrix from left to right, as we go down the rows. The main diagonal is given by $(a_{11}, a_{22}, \ldots, a_{nn})$. The second diagonal is given by $(a_{12}, a_{23}, \ldots, a_{n-1n}, a_{n1})$. The nth diagonal is given by $(a_{1n}, a_{21}, \ldots, a_{n-1n})$. The second diagonal is the main diagonal of a matrix in which the first column has been moved to the end, and the second column has become the first column. The ith diagonal is the main diagonal of a matrix in which the first $i-1$ columns have been moved en block to the end, and the ith column has become first.

The *antidiagonals* of this matrix are defined as the n elements on the diagonals of the matrix from right to left, as we go down the rows. The main antidiagonal is given by $(a_{1n}, a_{2n-1}, \ldots, a_{n1})$. The other antidiagonals are defined analogously. The ith antidiagonal is the main antidiagonal of a matrix in which the first $i-1$ columns have been moved en block to the end, and the ith column has become the first column.

To define the diagonals and antidiagonals, it is sometimes useful to consider the *augmented matrix* $\mathbf{A}|\mathbf{A}$, defined by

$$\mathbf{A}|\mathbf{A} = \left(\begin{array}{ccc|ccc} a_{11} & \cdots & a_{1n} & a_{11} & \cdots & a_{1n} \\ \vdots & \ddots & \vdots & \vdots & \ddots & \vdots \\ a_{n1} & \cdots & a_{nn} & a_{n1} & \cdots & a_{nn} \end{array}\right).$$

It is quite easy to define the n full diagonals and antidiagonals of $\mathbf{A}$ using this augmented matrix.

A special square matrix is the *identity matrix*. This is denoted by $\mathbf{I}$, and is a matrix that has 1s across its main diagonal, and 0s elsewhere:

$$\mathbf{I} = \begin{pmatrix} 1 & \cdots & 0 \\ \vdots & \ddots & \vdots \\ 0 & \cdots & 1 \end{pmatrix}. \tag{B.6}$$

The identity matrix plays the role of unity in matrix algebra. It is straightforward to show that

$$\mathbf{AI} = \mathbf{IA} = \mathbf{A}, \tag{B.7}$$

for any square matrix $\mathbf{A}$.

From (B.7) it follows that, if the inverse $\mathbf{A}^{-1}$ of matrix $\mathbf{A}$ exists, then it should satisfy

$$\mathbf{AA}^{-1} = \mathbf{A}^{-1}\mathbf{A} = \mathbf{I}. \tag{B.8}$$

For the inverse of $\mathbf{A}$ to exist, $\mathbf{A}$ must be a *full rank* matrix. For the moment, it suffices to say that a full rank matrix's rows or columns must be linearly independent. For a square matrix to be full rank, its determinant must be nonzero.

The *determinant* of an $n \times n$ square matrix $\mathbf{A}$ is denoted and defined by the following formula:

$$\det \mathbf{A} = |\mathbf{A}| = \sum_{j=1}^{n} a_{ij}(-1)^{i+j} \left|\mathbf{A}_{ij}\right|, \tag{B.9}$$

where $|\mathbf{A}_{ij}|$ is the minor of element a_{ij}, defined as the determinant of the matrix that results when row i and column j are deleted from matrix $\mathbf{A}$. Hence, the determinant is defined in terms of the elements of row i and the minors of these elements, which are also determinants.

The term

$$(-1)^{i+j}\,|\mathbf{A}_{ij}|$$

is called the *cofactor* of the element a_{ij}. Hence, the determinant is also defined in terms of the elements in the ith row of a matrix, multiplied by their cofactors.

If one were to choose row 1 for i, then the determinant is defined by

$$\det \mathbf{A} = |\mathbf{A}| = \sum_{j=1}^{n} a_{1j}(-1)^{1+j}\,|\mathbf{A}_{1j}|.$$

For example, for a 2×2 matrix, the determinant is defined as

$$\det \mathbf{A} = |\mathbf{A}| = a_{11}a_{22} - a_{12}a_{21}.$$

For a 3×3 matrix, it is defined as

$$\det \mathbf{A} = |\mathbf{A}| = a_{11}\begin{vmatrix} a_{22} & a_{23} \\ a_{32} & a_{33} \end{vmatrix} - a_{12}\begin{vmatrix} a_{21} & a_{23} \\ a_{31} & a_{33} \end{vmatrix} + a_{13}\begin{vmatrix} a_{21} & a_{22} \\ a_{31} & a_{32} \end{vmatrix}.$$

This expression can be expanded as

$$\det \mathbf{A} = |\mathbf{A}| = a_{11}a_{22}a_{23} - a_{11}a_{23}a_{32} - a_{12}a_{21}a_{33} + a_{12}a_{23}a_{31} + a_{13}a_{21}a_{32} - a_{13}a_{22}a_{32}.$$

For higher-order matrices, the calculation is even more complicated, although the principle is quite straightforward.

Armed with these elements from linear algebra, the solution of the linear economic model (B.4) is in principle straightforward. If the inverse of the square coefficient matrix $\mathbf{A}$ exists, then the solution takes the form

$$\mathbf{y} = \mathbf{A}^{-1}\mathbf{B}\mathbf{x}. \tag{B.10}$$

Equation (B.10) expresses the endogenous variables y_i, $i = 1, 2, \ldots, n$, as functions of the exogenous variables x_j, $j = 1, 2, \ldots, m$.

B.3 An Example with Two Endogenous Variables

In this section, let us apply linear algebra to a model with two endogenous and two exogenous variables. The model in matrix form is given by

$$\begin{pmatrix} 1 & -a_{12} \\ -a_{21} & 1 \end{pmatrix}\begin{pmatrix} y_1 \\ y_2 \end{pmatrix} = \begin{pmatrix} b_{11} & b_{12} \\ b_{21} & b_{22} \end{pmatrix}\begin{pmatrix} x_1 \\ x_2 \end{pmatrix}.$$

The **A** matrix is given by

$$\mathbf{A} = \begin{pmatrix} 1 & -a_{12} \\ -a_{21} & 1 \end{pmatrix}.$$

The determinant of the **A** matrix is given by

$$\det \mathbf{A} = |\mathbf{A}| = 1 - a_{12}a_{21}. \tag{B.11}$$

Thus, **A** will be full rank if and only if $a_{12}a_{21} \neq 1$.

The inverse of **A** can be calculated by a number of methods.

B.3.1 Cramer's Rule

The first method is *Cramer's rule*. The inverse is given by

$$\mathbf{A}^{-1} = \frac{1}{\det \mathbf{A}} \begin{pmatrix} \det \mathbf{A}_{11} & \det \mathbf{A}_{12} \\ \det \mathbf{A}_{21} & \det \mathbf{A}_{22} \end{pmatrix}^{\mathrm{T}} = \frac{1}{1 - a_{12}a_{21}} \begin{pmatrix} 1 & a_{12} \\ a_{21} & 1 \end{pmatrix}. \tag{B.12}$$

The matrix premultiplied by the inverse of the determinant of **A** is called the *adjoint matrix* of **A**, and it is the transpose of the matrix of cofactors of **A**. A cofactor of an element a_{ij} of a square matrix **A** is the determinant of the matrix $\mathbf{A_{ij}}$ that results if we eliminate the row and the column containing a_{ij} and multiply by -1^{i+j}.

B.3.2 The Augmented Matrix and Gauss-Jordan Elimination

A second—and computationally more efficient—method for inverting larger matrices is the *augmented matrix* method. This method uses *Gauss-Jordan elimination* to transform the augmented matrix $[\mathbf{A}|\mathbf{I}]$ into the equivalent augmented matrix $[\mathbf{I}|\mathbf{A}^{-1}]$. This is done by transforming the system's augmented matrix into reduced row-echelon form by means of row operations.

The augmented matrix of **A** is given by

$$\left(\begin{array}{cc|cc} 1 & -a_{12} & 1 & 0 \\ -a_{21} & 1 & 0 & 1 \end{array}\right). \tag{B.13}$$

Through successive row operations, such as replacing row 2 by the sum of row 2 and the product of a_{21} and row 1, then dividing the resulting row 2 by $1 - a_{12}a_{21}$, and finally replacing row 1 by the original row 1 minus the product of a_{12} and row 2 of the previous step, we end up with

$$\left(\begin{array}{cc|cc} 1 & 0 & \frac{1}{1-a_{12}a_{21}} & \frac{a_{12}}{1-a_{12}a_{21}} \\ 0 & 1 & \frac{a_{21}}{1-a_{12}a_{21}} & \frac{1}{1-a_{12}a_{21}} \end{array}\right). \tag{B.14}$$

The matrix on the right-hand side of the transformed augmented matrix is the inverse of **A**.

B.3.3 Diagonalization, Eigenvalues, and Eigenvectors

A third method of solving the system (i.e., investing the matrix) is through the diagonalization of **A**, using the *eigenvalues* and the *eigenvectors* of **A**. We postpone the discussion of this method until we discuss the solution of systems of differential equations.

B.3.4 Solving a System with Two Endogenous and Two Exogenous Variables

We can apply these matrix methods to the solution of the system (B.10) with two endogenous and two exogenous variables. This is a system of two equations with two unknowns. The *y*s, can in principle be solved as functions of the exogenous variables, the *x*s.

As this is a low-dimensional system, we can first attempt to solve it through a nonmatrix method, such as the *method of substitution*. This will allow us to check the results of matrix methods, such as Cramer's rule and Gauss-Jordan elimination.

The system in (B.10) can be written in nonmatrix form as a system in the two unknown *y*s. It takes the form

$$\begin{aligned} y_1 &= a_{12}y_2 + b_{11}x_1 + b_{12}x_2, \\ y_2 &= a_{21}y_1 + b_{21}x_1 + b_{22}x_2. \end{aligned} \tag{B.15}$$

The system can be solved by the method of substitution. Using the second equation in (B.15) to substitute for y_2 in the first equation, the solution for y_1 takes the form

$$y_1 = \frac{1}{1 - a_{12}a_{21}}\left((b_{11} + a_{12}b_{21})x_1 + (b_{12} + a_{12}b_{22})x_2\right). \tag{B.16}$$

Note that $a_{12}a_{21} \neq 1$, for y_1 to have a finite solution. Otherwise, y_1 is not defined. This is the same as the condition that the determinant of the matrix of coefficients of the *y*s must be nonzero.

Substituting (B.16) for y_1 in the second equation of (B.15), the solution for y_2 takes the form

$$y_2 = \frac{1}{1 - a_{12}a_{21}}\left((b_{21} + a_{21}b_{11})x_1 + (b_{22} + a_{21}b_{12})x_2\right). \tag{B.17}$$

The system of solved equations (B.16) and (B.17) is called the *reduced form* of the original *structural form* of the system (B.15). There are finite solutions for y_1 and y_2 if and only if $a_{12}a_{21} \neq 1$.

By applying Cramer's rule to the same system in matrix form, the system solution of (B.10) is given by

$$\begin{pmatrix} y_1 \\ y_2 \end{pmatrix} = \frac{1}{1 - a_{12}a_{21}} \begin{pmatrix} 1 & a_{12} \\ a_{21} & 1 \end{pmatrix} \begin{pmatrix} b_{11} & b_{12} \\ b_{21} & b_{22} \end{pmatrix} \begin{pmatrix} x_1 \\ x_2 \end{pmatrix}.$$

Carrying out the matrix multiplications, we get

$$\begin{pmatrix} y_1 \\ y_2 \end{pmatrix} = \frac{1}{1 - a_{12}a_{21}} \begin{pmatrix} b_{11} + a_{12}b_{21} & b_{12} + a_{12}b_{22} \\ b_{21} + a_{21}b_{11} & b_{22} + a_{21}b_{12} \end{pmatrix} \begin{pmatrix} x_1 \\ x_2 \end{pmatrix}. \tag{B.18}$$

Equation (B.18) is identical to the reduced form system (B.16)–(B.17).

It is straightforward to confirm that the same solution applies if one uses the Gauss-Jordan elimination method to find the inverse of the matrix of coefficients of the endogenous variables **A**.

Appendix C: Ordinary Differential Equations

In this mathematical appendix, we review solution methods of linear differential equations and systems of linear differential equations. Knowledge of the properties of differential equations is indispensable for analyzing problems in continuous time in dynamic macroeconomics.

We start with some definitions, and then proceed to examine solution methods of first- and second-order differential equations with both constant and variable coefficients. We finally briefly discuss the generalization of the solution methods to a system of n first-order differential equations.[1]

C.1 Definitions

A *differential equation* is a mathematical equation derived from an unknown function of one or more variables, which connects the function itself and its derivatives of various degrees.

The solution of a simple equation (or a system of equations) is a constant or a set of constants that satisfy these equations. In contrast, the solution of a differential equation (or a system of differential equations) is a function, or a set of functions that, along with their derivatives, satisfy the differential equation or the system of differential equations. The equations we shall consider are all functions of time t, which is assumed to be a continuous variable defined on the set of real numbers $\mathbb{R}$.

For example, the solution to the differential equation

$$\dot{y}(t) = \frac{dy}{dt} = a \tag{C.1}$$

1. This appendix is a review and a toolkit, designed to help students refresh their knowledge. It is not a complete mathematical treatment. For fuller and more rigorous mathematical treatments of ordinary differential equations, see Boyce and DiPrima [1977] or any comprehensive textbook of mathematics for economists, such as Chiang [1974], Simon and Blume [1994], or Klein [2013].

is a function $y(t)$, the first derivative of which with respect to time is equal to a. The general solution to this differential equation is the function

$$y(t) = at + c, \tag{C.2}$$

where c is an arbitrary constant.

A particular solution can be found by using a boundary condition. For example, if we know that at $t = 0$, y is equal to y_0 (known as the *boundary value*), then a particular solution of (C.2) is given by setting c to $c = y_0$.

Another example is the differential equation

$$\ddot{y}(t) = \frac{d^2y}{dt^2} = a, \tag{C.3}$$

whose solution is

$$y(t) = \frac{a}{2}t^2 + bt + c, \tag{C.4}$$

where b and c are two arbitrary constants.

A solution of a differential equation is a function $y(t)$, which, along with its derivatives, satisfies the differential equation. A *general solution* is the full set of solutions of a differential equation. A *particular solution* requires the determination of the arbitrary constant or constants of integration.

Differential equations are classified by their order, which is none other than the order of the highest derivative that appears in the equation. For example, (C.1) is a first-order differential equation, whereas (C.3) is a second-order differential equation.

A differential equation is *linear* if the unknown function $y(t)$ and its derivatives are linear. Otherwise it is *nonlinear*.

A differential equation can be solved by a method known as *separation of variables* if it can be written as a term that contains a function of only y, equated to a term that contains a function only of t. For example, the equation

$$g(y)\dot{y} = f(t) \tag{C.5}$$

can be written as

$$g(y)dy = f(t)dt. \tag{C.6}$$

The variables are separated, and the solution is

$$\int g(y)dy = \int f(t)dt + c, \tag{C.7}$$

where c is an arbitrary constant.

Finally, a differential equation

$$f(t,y)+g(t,y)\frac{dy}{dt}=0, \tag{C.8}$$

which is equivalent to

$$f(t,y)dt+g(t,y)dy=0 \tag{C.9}$$

is called *exact* if there is a function $U(t,y)$ that satisfies

$$dU\equiv U_t dt+U_y dy\equiv fdt+gdy. \tag{C.10}$$

Thus, a differential equation is exact if it constitutes exactly the total differential of a function.

C.2 First-Order Linear Differential Equations

First-order linear differential equations are categorized as equations with constant coefficients, or those with variable coefficients.

C.2.1 Constant Coefficients

A first-order linear differential equation with constant coefficients takes the form

$$\dot{y}(t)+ay(t)=b, \tag{C.11}$$

where a and b are given constants. To find the function $y(t)$ that satisfies (C.11), note that

$$\frac{d(e^{at}y(t))}{dt}=ae^{at}y(t)+e^{at}\dot{y}(t)=e^{at}\left[\dot{y}(t)+ay(t)\right]. \tag{C.12}$$

If the differential equation (C.11) is multiplied by e^{at}, its left-hand side is an exact differential equation) (i.e., the total differential of a function with respect to t). The function e^{at} is called the *integrating factor*. Multiplying both sides of (C. 12) by dt, we get

$$d\left(e^{at}y(t)\right)=be^{at}dt,$$

whose integral is

$$e^{at}y(t)=e^{at}\frac{b}{a}+c,$$

where c is the constant of integration. Multiplying both sides of this expression by e^{-at}, we get

$$y(t) = \frac{b}{a} + ce^{-at} \tag{C.13}$$

as the family of functions that satisfy the differential equation (C.11). This family is called the *general solution* of (C.11).

To determine the constant of integration c, we need to know the value of the function at some point in time. For example, if we know that at time $t = 0$, $y(0) = y_0$, then

$$y_0 = \frac{b}{a} + c,$$

which implies

$$c = y_0 - \frac{b}{a}.$$

The general solution of the differential equation (C.11) that satisfies $y(0) = y_0$ is then given by

$$y(t) = y_0 e^{-at} + (1 - e^{-at})\frac{b}{a} = \frac{b}{a} + (y_0 - \frac{b}{a})e^{-at}. \tag{C.14}$$

In conclusion, to solve a linear first-order differential equation with constant coefficients, multiply it by the integrating factor and integrate it. To calculate the constant of integration, use the value of the function at some point. The point that is used is called an *initial condition* or a *terminal condition*, or more generally, a *boundary condition.*

C.2.2 Variable Right-Hand Side

If the right-hand side of (C.11) is not constant but a known function of time, the solution method is similar. We multiply by the integrating factor and take the integral.

For example, for the differential equation

$$\dot{y}(t) + ay(t) = be^{\lambda t}, \tag{C.15}$$

multiplying by the integrating factor and separating the variables results in

$$d\left(e^{at}y\right) = be^{(a+\lambda)t}dt. \tag{C.16}$$

Taking the integral of both sides of (C.16) yields

$$e^{at}y(t) = \frac{b}{a+\lambda}e^{(a+\lambda)t} + c. \tag{C.17}$$

Dividing both sides by the integrating factor, we get the solution

$$y(t) = \frac{b}{a+\lambda} e^{\lambda t} + ce^{-at}. \tag{C.18}$$

Equation (C.18) is the family of functions satisfying (C.15). The unknown constant c can again be determined by a boundary condition.

C.2.3 Variable Coefficients

The general form of a first-order linear differential equation is

$$\dot{y}(t) + a(t)y(t) = b(t), \tag{C.19}$$

where $a(t)$ and $b(t)$ are known functions, and we seek the function $y(t)$. The function $b(t)$ is often called a *forcing term* and is considered exogenous. The integrating factor in this case is $e^{\int a(t)dt}$, because

$$\frac{d(y(t)e^{\int a(t)dt})}{dt} = e^{\int a(t)dt}\,[\dot{y}(t) + a(t)y(t)] \tag{C.20}$$

Thus, multiplying (C.19) by this integrating factor and taking the integral, we get

$$y(t)e^{\int a(t)dt} = \int b(t)e^{\int a(t)dt}dt + c. \tag{C.21}$$

Dividing (C.21) by the integrating factor, we finally get

$$y(t) = e^{-\int a(t)dt} \int b(t)e^{\int a(t)dt}dt + e^{-\int a(t)dt}c, \tag{C.22}$$

where c is the constant of integration. (C.22) is the general solution of (C.19). A particular solution requires a boundary condition that will determine the unknown constant c.

Note that it is not advisable to apply the solution (C.22) to any equation. It is simpler in many cases to multiply by the integrating factor and take the integral.

C.2.4 Homogeneous and Nonhomogeneous Differential Equations

If $b = 0$ in (C.11), the differential equation to be solved is called *homogeneous*. Otherwise, it is called *nonhomogeneous*.

The general solution of a differential equation consists of the sum of the general solution to the relevant homogeneous differential equation (i.e., setting $b = 0$ and solving, and then adding to this solution a particular solution of the general equation (C.11).

For example, the homogeneous equation derived from (C.11) is

$$\dot{y}(t) + ay(t) = 0. \tag{C.23}$$

The general solution of (C.23) is

$$y(t) = ce^{-at} \tag{C.24}$$

A particular solution (setting, for example, $\dot{y}(t) = 0$) is

$$\bar{y} = \frac{b}{a}. \tag{C.25}$$

Consequently, the general solution of the nonhomogeneous differential equation (C.11) is the sum of (C.24) and (C.25), that is, the general solution of the relevant homogeneous differential equation (sometimes called the *complementary function*) plus the particular solution for a constant y (otherwise known as the *particular integral*). The general solution is thus given by

$$y(t) = \frac{b}{a} + (y_0 - \frac{b}{a})e^{-at}. \tag{C.26}$$

This methodology is not generally necessary for solving first-order linear differential equations, but it becomes very useful for differential equations of order higher than one or for systems of first-order linear differential equations.

C.2.5 Convergence and Stability of First-Order Differential Equations

In many economic applications, we are interested in the behavior of the solution of a differential equation as the independent variable, usually time, tends to infinity. The value to which the solution converges is referred to as a *stationary state*, or *steady state*, or *equilibrium state*.

For example, from (C.13), which is the general solution of (C.11), for $a > 0$, we get

$$\lim_{t\to\infty} y(t) = \lim_{t\to\infty} \left(\frac{b}{a} + ce^{-at}\right) = \frac{b}{a}.$$

The particular integral of the differential equation (C.11) can therefore be interpreted economically as the equilibrium state (or the steady state), which is the state toward which the variable y converges as time goes to infinity. This equilibrium is called a *stable node*. It is a stable equilibrium if y is a predetermined variable and only changes gradually, as postulated by the law of motion (C.26).

Assume now that $a < 0$. In this case, if the boundary condition y_0 is different from the steady value $\bar{y}$, then $y(t)$ (as determined by (C.26)) moves to plus or minus infinity, farther and farther away from the steady state. The only case in which this does not happen is when the boundary condition y_0 is equal to the steady state value $\bar{y} = b/a$. Then y remains constant at $\bar{y}$. However, this is an unstable equilibrium, called a *saddle point*. There is only one adjustment path that leads to it and this is for y to jump immediately to the steady state. If y is a non-predetermined variable (for example, a financial variable or any variable that can change abruptly and not gradually), then it can jump immediately to its steady state value.

C.3 Second-Order Linear Differential Equations

A second-order linear differential equation has the form

$$\ddot{y}(t)+a(t)\dot{y}(t)+b(t)y(t)=h(t), \tag{C.27}$$

where $a(t)$, $b(t)$, and $h(t)$ are known functions, and what is sought is the function $y(t)$. The forcing term in this case is the function $h(t)$. Equation (C.27) is referred to as the *complete equation* and is nonhomogeneous. Related to (C.27) is a homogeneous differential equation in which $h(t)=0$:

$$\ddot{y}(t)+a(t)\dot{y}(t)+b(t)y(t)=0, \tag{C.28}$$

which is called the *reduced equation*. The complete equation is nonhomogeneous, whereas the reduced equation is homogeneous. The reduced equation is of interest because of the following two theorems.

Theorem 1 The general solution of the complete equation (C.27) is the sum of any particular solution of the complete equation and the general solution of the reduced equation (C.28).

Theorem 2 Any solution $y(t)$ of the reduced equation (C.28) on $t_0\le t\le t_1$ can be expressed as a linear combination, $y(t)=c_1y_1(t)+c_2y_2(t)$, $t_0\le t\le t_1$, of any two particular solutions y_1, y_2 that are linearly independent.

C.3.1 Homogeneous Equations with Constant Coefficients

We first examine the differential equation (C.27), with constant coefficients, that is, $a(t)=a$, $b(t)=b$. Assume that $h(t)=0$. The differential equation then takes the form

$$\ddot{y}(t)+a\dot{y}(t)+by(t)=0. \tag{C.29}$$

Inspired by the general solution of the first-order linear differential equation with constant coefficients, let us try the general solution

$$y(t)=ce^{rt},$$

with unknown constants c and r. This solution method is called the *method of undetermined coefficients*. This solution implies that

$$\dot{y}(t)=rce^{rt}, \ddot{y}(t)=r^2ce^{rt}.$$

Substituting these expressions in (C.29), we get

$$ce^{rt}(r^2+ar+b)=0. \tag{C.30}$$

For a nonzero c, our trial solution satisfies (C.30) only if r is a root of the quadratic equation

$$r^2 + ar + b = 0. \tag{C.31}$$

Equation (C.31) is called the *characteristic equation* of (C.29). It has two roots:

$$r_1, r_2 = \frac{-a \pm \sqrt{a^2 - 4b}}{2}. \tag{C.32}$$

We distinguish three cases, depending on the value of the discriminant $a^2 - 4b$ of the characteristic equation (C.31).

Case 1 $a^2 > 4b$ The discriminant is positive, and the roots are *real and distinct*. The general solution of (C.29) takes the form

$$y(t) = c_1 e^{r_1 t} + c_2 e^{r_2 t}, \tag{C.33}$$

where r_1, r_2 are the roots of the characteristic equation (C.31), and c_1, c_2 are arbitrary constants.

Case 2 $a^2 < 4b$ The discriminant is negative, and the roots are a pair of *complex conjugates*:

$$r_1, r_2 = -\frac{a}{2} \pm i\frac{\sqrt{4b - a^2}}{2} = \alpha \pm i\beta,$$

where $\alpha = -\frac{a}{2}$, and $\beta = \frac{\sqrt{4b-a^2}}{2}$. The general solution in this case is

$$y(t) = e^{\alpha t}(k_1 \cos \beta t + k_2 \sin \beta t), \tag{C.34}$$

where k_1, k_2 are arbitrary constants.

Case 3 $a^2 = 4b$ The discriminant is equal to zero, and the two roots are the same and equal to $-a/2$. One can show that the general solution of (C.29) in this case takes the form

$$y(t) = c_1 e^{rt} + c_2 t e^{rt} = e^{rt}(c_1 + c_2 t), \tag{C.35}$$

where $r = -a/2$ is the double root of the characteristic equation (C.31), and c_1, c_2 are arbitrary constants.

C.3.2 Nonhomogeneous Equations with Constant Coefficients

We have already derived the solution of any homogeneous second-order linear differential equation with constant coefficients. To find the solution of a nonhomogeneous equation, we need a particular solution of the complete equation. If the complete equation is of the form

$$\ddot{y}(t) + a\dot{y}(t) + by(t) = h,$$

then a particular solution is the constant function

$$\bar{y} = \frac{h}{b}.$$

The full solution is thus the sum of the general solution to the homogeneous equation plus the particular solution to the complete equation.

For differential equations with variable coefficients, more advanced methods, such as the method of variation of parameters, can be utilized for their solution.

C.4 A Pair of First-Order Linear Differential Equations

We next examine a case with extensive applications in macroeconomics: a pair of first-order linear differential equations of the form

$$\begin{aligned} \dot{x}(t) &= a_1 x(t) + b_1 y(t) + p(t), \\ \dot{y}(t) &= a_2 x(t) + b_2 y(t) + g(t), \end{aligned} \tag{C.36}$$

where a_1, a_2, b_1, b_2 are given constants, and $p(t), g(t)$ are given functions. The solution of the system of differential equations (C.36) will be two functions $x(t)$ and $y(t)$ that satisfy both differential equations.

The homogeneous system that corresponds to (C.36) is given by

$$\begin{aligned} \dot{x}(t) &= a_1 x(t) + b_1 y(t), \\ \dot{y}(t) &= a_2 x(t) + b_2 y(t). \end{aligned} \tag{C.37}$$

C.4.1 The Method of Substitution

One solution method is the method of substitution. Substituting $y(t)$ and its derivatives in the equation determining $x(t)$, we end up with a second-order linear differential equation that contains only $x(t)$ and its derivatives:

$$\ddot{x}(t) - (a_1 + b_2)\dot{x}(t) + (a_1 b_2 - b_1 a_2)x(t) = 0. \tag{C.38}$$

Equation (C.38) is a linear homogeneous second-order differential equation. It can be solved using the method of undetermined coefficients. Its characteristic equation is given by

$$r^2 - (a_1 + b_2)r + (a_1 b_2 - a_2 b_1) = 0. \tag{C.39}$$

If the roots of (C.39) are real and distinct, the solution of (C.38) is given by

$$x(t) = c_1 e^{r_1 t} + c_2 e^{r_2 t}. \tag{C.40}$$

Solving the first equation of (C.37) with respect to $y(t)$, we get

$$y(t) = \frac{1}{b_1}\left(\dot{x}(t) - a_1 x(t)\right).$$

Substituting the solution (C.40) for $x(t)$ and its first derivative, we get

$$y(t) = \frac{1}{b_1}\left((r_1 - a_1)c_1 e^{r_1 t} + (r_2 - a_1)c_2 e^{r_2 t}\right). \tag{C.41}$$

Consequently, the solution of the system (C.37) consists of equations (C.40) and (C.41), if the roots of (C.39) are real and distinct. We can solve the system in an analogous way if we have complex or repeated roots.

However, there is a second and more direct solution method of the homogeneous system (C.37). This method also generalizes to higher-order systems of differential equations.

C.4.2 The Method of Eigenvalues

Our experience with first-order differential equation suggests that we use the pair of equations

$$x(t) = Ae^{rt}, y(t) = Be^{rt}$$

as particular solutions for (C.37). Here A, B, and r are undetermined coefficients. Substituting these solutions in (C.37), we get

$$\begin{aligned} rAe^{rt} &= a_1 Ae^{rt} + b_1 Be^{rt}, \\ rBe^{rt} &= a_2 Ae^{rt} + b_2 Be^{rt}. \end{aligned} \tag{C.42}$$

Dividing both equations by e^{rt}, we can rewrite the system (C.42) in matrix form:

$$\begin{pmatrix} a_1 - r & b_1 \\ a_2 & b_2 - r \end{pmatrix}\begin{pmatrix} A \\ B \end{pmatrix} = \begin{pmatrix} 0 \\ 0 \end{pmatrix}. \tag{C.43}$$

For (C.43) to hold, the determinant of the matrix of coefficients must be zero:

$$\begin{vmatrix} a_1 - r & b_1 \\ a_2 & b_2 - r \end{vmatrix} = 0. \tag{C.44}$$

Calculating the determinant, we get a quadratic equation in r:

$$r^2 - (a_1 + b_2)r + (a_1 b_2 - a_2 b_1) = 0. \tag{C.45}$$

Equation (C.45) is the characteristic equation of the system (C.37). Equation (C.45) is identical to (C.39), the equation we ended up with when using the method of substitution. The solutions of the characteristic equation (C.45) are called the *eigenvalues* of the matrix of coefficients:

$$\begin{pmatrix} a_1 & b_1 \\ a_2 & b_2 \end{pmatrix}.$$

The two roots are given by

$$r_1, r_2 = \frac{(a_1 + b_2) \pm \sqrt{(a_1 + b_2)^2 - 4(a_1 b_2 - a_2 b_1)}}{2}. \tag{C.46}$$

For future use, note that

$$\begin{aligned} r_1 + r_2 &= a_1 + b_2, \\ r_1 r_2 &= a_1 b_2 - a_2 b_1. \end{aligned} \tag{C.47}$$

If the roots are real, and $r_1 \neq r_2$, then the general solution of the homogeneous system (C.37) is given by

$$\begin{aligned} x(t) &= A_1 e^{r_1 t} + A_2 e^{r_2 t}, \\ y(t) &= B_1 e^{r_1 t} + B_2 e^{r_2 t}, \end{aligned} \tag{C.48}$$

where A_1, A_2 are determined by boundary conditions; the roots are determined by (C.46); and B_1, B_2 are determined by (C.42) as

$$\begin{aligned} B_1 &= \frac{r_1 - a_1}{b_1} A_1, \\ B_2 &= \frac{r_2 - a_1}{b_1} A_2. \end{aligned} \tag{C.49}$$

The solution is identical to (C.40) and (C.41). In the case of complex or repeated roots, the solution is analogous.

Having found the general solution to the homogeneous system (C.37), it remains to find a particular solution of (C.36), using, for example, the method of variation of parameters.

For the special case where p and g are constants, a special solution with constant x and y can be found by solving the system of equations

$$\begin{aligned} a_1 \bar{x} + b_1 \bar{y} + p &= 0, \\ a_2 \bar{x} + b_2 \bar{y} + g &= 0. \end{aligned} \tag{C.50}$$

Expressing (C.50) in matrix form and solving for $\bar{x}$ and $\bar{y}$, we get

$$\begin{pmatrix} a_1 & b_1 \\ a_2 & b_2 \end{pmatrix} \begin{pmatrix} \bar{x} \\ \bar{y} \end{pmatrix} = - \begin{pmatrix} p \\ g \end{pmatrix}.$$

The solution is then given by

$$\begin{pmatrix} \bar{x} \\ \bar{y} \end{pmatrix} = - \begin{pmatrix} a_1 & b_1 \\ a_2 & b_2 \end{pmatrix}^{-1} \begin{pmatrix} p \\ g \end{pmatrix}, \tag{C.51}$$

where $\bar{x}$ and $\bar{y}$ can be regarded as *steady state*, or equilibrium points. Whether the system converges globally to equilibrium depends on whether both roots are real and smaller than zero. In this case, the equilibrium is a *fixed node*. If both variables are predetermined, this is a stable equilibrium.

If we have a positive and a negative root, the equilibrium is called a *saddle point*. There is only one unique path that leads to this equilibrium, and this path is called the *saddle path*. The economy will converge to equilibrium if one variable is predetermined and the other not predetermined. The non-predetermined variable will jump to the unique adjustment path leading to equilibrium. Technically, the negative root corresponds to the predetermined variable (for which we solve backward), and the positive root corresponds to the non-predetermined variable (for which we solve forward).

Thus, a system with one predetermined and one non-predetermined variable has an equilibrium (a saddle point) if the matrix of coefficients has one positive and one negative eigenvalue.

C.5 A System of *n* First-Order Linear Differential Equations

Finally, we turn to a more general case with extensive applications in macroeconomics: a system of n first-order linear differential equations of the form

$$\begin{aligned}\dot{x}_1(t) &= a_{11}x_1(t) + a_{12}x_2(t) + \cdots + a_{1n}x_n(t) + g_1(t),\\ \dot{x}_2(t) &= a_{21}x_1(t) + a_{22}x_2(t) + \cdots + a_{2n}x_n(t) + g_2(t),\\ &\vdots\\ \dot{x}_n(t) &= a_{n1}x_1(t) + a_{n2}x_2(t) + \cdots + a_{nn}x_n(t) + g_n(t),\end{aligned} \tag{C.52}$$

where $x_1, x_2, \ldots, x_n$, a_{ij} for $i, j = 1, 2, \ldots, n$ are given constant parameters, and $g_1, g_2, \ldots, g_n$ are exogenous forcing functions of time.

In matrix form, this system can be written as

$$\begin{pmatrix} \dot{x}_1(t) \\ \vdots \\ \dot{x}_n(t) \end{pmatrix} = \begin{pmatrix} a_{11} & \cdots & a_{1n} \\ \vdots & \ddots & \vdots \\ a_{n1} & \cdots & a_{nn} \end{pmatrix} \begin{pmatrix} x_1(t) \\ \vdots \\ x_n(t) \end{pmatrix} + \begin{pmatrix} g_1(t) \\ \vdots \\ g_n(t) \end{pmatrix},$$

or

$$\dot{\mathbf{x}}(t) = \mathbf{A}\mathbf{x}(t) + \mathbf{g}(t), \tag{C.53}$$

where bold letters denote vectors and matrices; $\mathbf{A}$ is the square $n \times n$ coefficient matrix, which is assumed to be nonsingular.

C.5.1 Eigenvalues and Eigenvectors

Before we proceed to discuss the solution of the system of differential equations (C.52), it is worth delving a little more into linear algebra, and in particular, into the concepts of *eigenvalues* and *eigenvectors*.

Let $\mathbf{A}$ be a square matrix, like the one multiplying the $\mathbf{x}$ vector in the right-hand side of (C.53). An eigenvalue of $\mathbf{A}$ is a number ρ, which when subtracted from each of the diagonal elements of $\mathbf{A}$ converts $\mathbf{A}$ into a singular (i.e., noninvertible) matrix. Subtracting a scalar ρ from each of the diagonal elements of $\mathbf{A}$ is equivalent to subtracting from $\mathbf{A}$ ρ times the identity matrix $\mathbf{I}$. Therefore, ρ is an eigenvalue of $\mathbf{A}$ if and only if $\mathbf{A} - \rho\,\mathbf{I}$ is singular.

Because a matrix is singular if its determinant is equal to zero, ρ is an eigenvalue of $\mathbf{A}$ if and only if

$$\det|\mathbf{A} - \rho\mathbf{I}| = 0.$$

For an $n \times n$ matrix $\mathbf{A}$, the determinant of $\mathbf{A} - \rho\,\mathbf{I}$ is an nth-order polynomial in ρ, called the *characteristic polynomial* of $\mathbf{A}$. An nth-order polynomial has at most n roots. Therefore, an $n \times n$ square matrix has at most n eigenvalues.

It follows from the above that the diagonal entries of a diagonal matrix $\mathbf{D}$ are eigenvalues of $\mathbf{D}$, and that a square matrix $\mathbf{A}$ is singular if and only if 0 is an eigenvalue of $\mathbf{A}$.

Recall from elementary linear algebra that a square matrix $\mathbf{B}$ is nonsingular if and only if the only solution of $\mathbf{Bx} = \mathbf{0}$ is $\mathbf{x} = \mathbf{0}$. Conversely, $\mathbf{B}$ is singular if and only if the system $\mathbf{Bx} = \mathbf{0}$ has a nonzero solution.

The fact that $\mathbf{A} - \rho\,\mathbf{I}$ is singular when ρ is an eigenvalue of $\mathbf{A}$ means that the system of equations $(\mathbf{A} - \rho\,\mathbf{I})\mathbf{v} = 0$ has a solution other than $\mathbf{v} = 0$.

When ρ is an eigenvalue of $\mathbf{A}$, a nonzero vector $\mathbf{v}$ such that $(\mathbf{A} - \rho\,\mathbf{I})\mathbf{v} = \mathbf{0}$, is called a (right) eigenvector of $\mathbf{A}$, corresponding to the eigenvalue ρ.

Thus, eigenvectors are nonzero vectors $\mathbf{v}$ that satisfy

$$(\mathbf{A} - \rho\mathbf{I})\mathbf{v} = \mathbf{0},\ \ \mathbf{Av} - \rho\mathbf{Iv} = \mathbf{0},\ \ \mathbf{Av} = \rho\mathbf{v}.$$

These three statements are equivalent.

C.5.2 Solving the *n*th-Order System of Linear Differential Equations

Let us now turn to the solution of the nth-order system of linear differential equations represented by (C.52). The general solution of the nonhomogeneous system of differential equations (C.52) will be the sum of the general solution of the relevant homogeneous system of differential equations plus the particular solution for constant xs.

We shall concentrate on the solution of the homogeneous system

$$\begin{pmatrix} \dot{x}_1(t) \\ \vdots \\ \dot{x}_n(t) \end{pmatrix} = \begin{pmatrix} a_{11} & \cdots & a_{1n} \\ \vdots & \ddots & \vdots \\ a_{n1} & \cdots & a_{nn} \end{pmatrix} \begin{pmatrix} x_1(t) \\ \vdots \\ x_n(t) \end{pmatrix}, \tag{C.54}$$

or simply, $\dot{\mathbf{x}} = \mathbf{Ax}$, where $\mathbf{x}$ is the column vector on the right-hand side of (C.54).

Assume first that $\mathbf{A}$ is a diagonal matrix, for which $a_{ij} = 0$ for $i \neq j$. Then (C.54) becomes a system of n independent self-contained equations of the form

$$\dot{x}_i(t) = a_{ii}x_i(t).$$

We thus have a system of independent first-order linear differential equations that can be solved one by one:

$$x_i(t) = c_i e^{a_{ii}t}.$$

If the off-diagonal elements a_{ij} differ from zero, so that the equations are linked to each other, then we can use the eigenvalues and eigenvectors of the coefficient matrix of (C.54) to transform it to a system of n (or fewer) independent equations. We can use the eigenvalues and eigenvectors of $\mathbf{A}$ to transform the system to a system that has a diagonal coefficient matrix.

Let us assume that $\mathbf{A}$ has n distinct real eigenvalues $\rho_1, \rho_2, \ldots, \rho_n$, with corresponding eigenvectors $\mathbf{v}_1, \mathbf{v}_2, \ldots, \mathbf{v}_n$. It then follows from the definition of eigenvalues and eigenvectors that

$$\mathbf{Av}_i = \rho_i \mathbf{v}_i, i = 1, 2, \ldots, n. \tag{C.55}$$

Let $\mathbf{P}$ be the $n \times n$ matrix whose columns are these n eigenvectors. Thus $\mathbf{P}$ is defined as

$$\mathbf{P} = [\mathbf{v}_1 \cdots \ \mathbf{v}_n]. \tag{C.56}$$

The system of equations (C.55) can thus be written as

$$\mathbf{AP} = \mathbf{PJ}, \tag{C.57}$$

where

$$\mathbf{J} = \begin{pmatrix} \rho_1 & & 0 \\ & \ddots & \\ 0 & & \rho_n \end{pmatrix}.$$

Because eigenvectors for distinct eigenvalues are linearly independent, $\mathbf{P}$ is nonsingular and therefore invertible. We can write

$$\mathbf{P}^{-1}\mathbf{AP} = \mathbf{J}. \tag{C.58}$$

Thus, we can use (C.56) to transform the system (C.52), defined in the variables $\mathbf{x}$, to a system in the variables $\mathbf{y} = \mathbf{P}^{-1}\mathbf{x}$, which means that $\mathbf{x} = \mathbf{Py}$. It follows that

$$\dot{\mathbf{y}} = \mathbf{P}^{-1}\dot{\mathbf{x}} = \mathbf{P}^{-1}\mathbf{Ax} = \mathbf{P}^{-1}\mathbf{APy} = \mathbf{Jy}. \tag{C.59}$$

Because $\mathbf{J}$ is a diagonal matrix, the solution of the system (C.59) can be obtained very easily as the vector of solutions to each variable y_i:

$$\begin{pmatrix} y_1(t) \\ \vdots \\ y_n(t) \end{pmatrix} = \begin{pmatrix} c_1 e^{\rho_1 t} \\ \vdots \\ c_n e^{\rho_n t} \end{pmatrix} \tag{C.60}$$

Finally, we can use the transformation $\mathbf{x} = \mathbf{P}\mathbf{y}$ to return to the original variables $x_1, \ldots, x_n$:

$$\mathbf{x}(t) = \mathbf{P}\mathbf{y}(t) = [\mathbf{v}_1 \cdots \ \mathbf{v}_n] \begin{pmatrix} c_1 e^{\rho_1 t} \\ \vdots \\ c_n e^{\rho_n t} \end{pmatrix} = c_1 e^{\rho_1 t}\mathbf{v}_1 + c_2 e^{\rho_2 t}\mathbf{v}_2 + \cdots + c_n e^{\rho_n t}\mathbf{v}_n. \tag{C.61}$$

Thus, under the assumption that the $n \times n$ matrix $\mathbf{A}$ has n distinct real eigenvalues $\rho_1, \rho_2, \ldots, \rho_n$, with corresponding eigenvectors $\mathbf{v}_1, \mathbf{v}_2, \ldots, \mathbf{v}_n$, the general solution of the homogeneous linear system (C.52) is given by

$$\mathbf{x}(t) = c_1 e^{\rho_1 t}\mathbf{v}_1 + c_2 e^{\rho_2 t}\mathbf{v}_2 + \cdots + c_n e^{\rho_n t}\mathbf{v}_n. \tag{C.62}$$

The solution in the cases of complex eigenvalues or multiple eigenvalues without enough eigenvectors is analogous to the solution of the second-order homogeneous system analyzed in section C.4.

Steady states and stability conditions are defined in an analogous way to those for first- and second-order differential equations. Assuming that the vector of gs consists of constants, one gets the nonhomogeneous system:

$$\begin{pmatrix} \dot{x}_1(t) \\ \vdots \\ \dot{x}_n(t) \end{pmatrix} = \begin{pmatrix} a_{11} & \ldots & a_{1n} \\ \vdots & \ddots & \vdots \\ a_{n1} & \ldots & a_{nn} \end{pmatrix} \begin{pmatrix} x_1(t) \\ \vdots \\ x_n(t) \end{pmatrix} + \begin{pmatrix} g_1 \\ \vdots \\ g_n \end{pmatrix}. \tag{C.63}$$

The steady state, if it exists, can be derived by setting the change in the xs equal to zero. A steady state exists if $\mathbf{A}$ is nonsingular and is given by

$$\begin{pmatrix} \bar{x}_1 \\ \vdots \\ \bar{x}_n \end{pmatrix} = -\begin{pmatrix} a_{11} & \ldots & a_{1n} \\ \vdots & \ddots & \vdots \\ a_{n1} & \ldots & a_{nn} \end{pmatrix}^{-1} \begin{pmatrix} g_1 \\ \vdots \\ g_n \end{pmatrix}, \tag{C.64}$$

where $\bar{x}_i$ denotes the steady state value of x_i. These values can be regarded as equilibrium points. If the x_is are predetermined variables, for the system to converge to equilibrium, all eigenvalues must be less than zero. In this case, the equilibrium is a *fixed node*. When the x_is consist of p predetermined and q non-predetermined variables, where $p + q = n$, the equilibrium (if it exists) is a *saddle point*. For the system to converge to equilibrium, there must be p negative eigenvalues and q positive eigenvalues. The negative eigenvalues correspond to the predetermined variables, which are solved for backward, and the positive eigenvalues correspond to the non-predetermined variables which are solved for forward.

Thus, a system with p predetermined and q non-predetermined variables has a stable equilibrium (a *saddle vector*) if the matrix of coefficients has p negative and q positive eigenvalues. The adjustment path is unique and is called a *saddle path*.

Appendix D: Difference Equations

In this appendix, we briefly review the properties and solution methods of first- and second-order difference equations, as well as of systems of first-order difference equations.

Difference equations are the analog of differential equations when time is a discrete variable defined in terms of integers. They are an indispensable tool for the study of dynamic economic problems in discrete time. We shall thus assume that time is an integer $t = \dots, -2, -1, 0, 1, 2, \dots$, instead of t being a real continuous variable.

After defining lag operators, we then proceed to present solution methods for first- and second-order linear difference equations and for systems of interdependent linear difference equations.[1]

D.1 Lag Operators and Difference Equations

To define and analyze difference equations, it is useful to first define lag operators. The value of a variable x in period t is denoted by x_t. The lag operator L for a variable x_t is defined by

$$L^n x_t = x_{t-n}, \tag{D.1}$$

for $n = \dots, -2, -1, 0, 1, 2, \dots$.

Thus, the multiplication of x_t by L denotes the value of the variable in the previous period, and the multiplication of the variable by L^n denotes the value of the variable in period $t - n$. Note than if n is negative (i.e., $n < 0$), the lag operator shifts the variable n periods into the future.

This definition is mathematically somewhat loose. More formally, let us assume a sequence

1. This appendix is meant as a review and is not a full and rigorous analysis of difference equations. For more complete treatments, the student is referred to comprehensive textbooks on mathematics for economists, such as Chiang [1974], Simon and Blume [1994], or Klein [2013]. A very good treatment of difference equations can be found in Sargent [1987].

$$\{x_t\}_{t=-\infty}^{\infty}$$

that links a real number x with every integer t. Applying the operator L^n to this sequence, we get a new sequence:

$$\{y_t\}_{t=-\infty}^{\infty} = \{x_{t-n}\}_{t=-\infty}^{\infty}.$$

The operator L^n projects one sequence onto another.

Let us now examine a polynomial in the lag operator:

$$A(L) = a_0 + a_1 L + a_2 L^2 + \cdots = \sum_{j=0}^{\infty} a_j L^j. \tag{D.2}$$

Applying the polynomial $A(L)$ to variable x_t, we get a moving sum of xs in different time periods:

$$A(L)x_t = \sum_{j=0}^{\infty} a_j L^j x_t = \sum_{j=0}^{\infty} a_j x_{t-j}. \tag{D.3}$$

Let us confine ourselves to *rational functions* (i.e., polynomials) that can be expressed as the ratio of two finite polynomials in L. Assume that

$$A(L) = \frac{B(L)}{C(L)}, \tag{D.4}$$

where

$$\begin{aligned} B(L) &= \sum_{j=0}^{m} b_j L^j, \\ C(L) &= \sum_{j=0}^{n} c_j L^j, \end{aligned} \tag{D.5}$$

and b_j and c_j are constants. The combination of (D.4) and (D.5) imposes a more economical and restrictive form on a_j, without serious loss of generality.

A special case of (D.4) and (D.5) is the so-called *geometric polynomial*, which takes the form

$$A(L) = \frac{1}{1 - \lambda L}. \tag{D.6}$$

From the properties of geometric progressions, the geometric polynomial can be expanded in two ways:

$$A(L) = \frac{1}{1 - \lambda L} = 1 + \lambda L + \lambda^2 L^2 + \cdots, \tag{D.7}$$

$$A(L) = \frac{1}{1 - \lambda L} = -\frac{1}{\lambda L}\left(1 + \frac{1}{\lambda}L^{-1} + \frac{1}{\lambda^2}L^{-2} + \cdots\right). \tag{D.8}$$

The expansion (D.7) is used when $|\lambda| < 1$, and the expansion (D.8) when $|\lambda| > 1$.

If we multiply the geometric polynomial (D.6) by some variable x_t, we get

$$A(L)x_t = \frac{1}{1 - \lambda L}x_t. \tag{D.9}$$

With the expansion (D.7) for $A(L)$ we get

$$A(L)x_t = \frac{1}{1 - \lambda L}x_t = \sum_{i=0}^{\infty} \lambda^i L^i x_t = \sum_{i=0}^{\infty} \lambda^i x_{t-i}. \tag{D.10}$$

If $|\lambda| < 1$, and $\{x_t\}_{t=-\infty}^{\infty}$ is a finite sequence of real numbers, then (D.10) defines a finite sequence of real numbers as well.

In contrast, we have the alternative expansion of (D.9). Using (D.8), we get

$$A(L)x_t = \frac{1}{1 - \lambda L}x_t = (\lambda L)^{-1} \sum_{i=0}^{\infty} \lambda^{-i} L^{-i} x_t = \sum_{i=0}^{\infty} \lambda^{-i} x_{t+i}. \tag{D.11}$$

If $|\lambda| > 1$, and $\{x_t\}_{t=-\infty}^{\infty}$ is a finite sequence of real numbers, then (D.11) defines a finite sequence of real numbers as well, because we have $\left|\lambda^{-1}\right| < 1$.

In economics, because we usually seek convergence to some equilibrium, we seek the analysis of finite sequences. Thus, we select the backward expansion when $|\lambda| < 1$, and the forward expansion when $|\lambda| > 1$.

A difference equation (or *recurrence relation*) equates a polynomial in the various iterates of a variable—that is, in the values of the elements of a sequence—to zero.

An nth-order linear difference equation with constant coefficients takes the form

$$a_0x_t + a_1x_{t-1} + a_2x_{t-2} + \cdots + a_nx_{t-n} - b = \sum_{j=0}^{n} a_jL^jx_t - b = 0, \tag{D.12}$$

where $a_j, j = 0, 1, 2, \ldots, n$ and b are constant coefficients.

By equating the right-hand side of the geometric polynomial (D.10) to zero, we get

$$\sum_{i=0}^{\infty} \lambda^i x_{t-i} = x_t + \lambda x_{t-1} + \lambda^2 x_{t-2} + \cdots = 0. \tag{D.13}$$

This is an example of an infinite-order linear difference equation.

D.2 First-Order Linear Difference Equations

Let us first consider the first-order linear difference equation with constant coefficients:

$$x_t = a + bx_{t-1}. \tag{D.14}$$

Using lag operators, (D.14) can be written as

$$(1 - bL)x_t = a. \tag{D.15}$$

Dividing both sides of (D.15) by $(1 - bL)$ and adding cb^t, we get

$$x_t = \frac{a}{1 - bL} + cb^t = \frac{a}{1 - b} + cb^t, \tag{D.16}$$

where c is an arbitrary constant. We include the term cb^t because for any c,

$$(1 - bL)cb^t = cb^t - bcb^{t-1} = 0.$$

Hence, if we multiply (D.16) by $(1 - bL)$, we get back (D.15). Equation (D.16) determines the *general solution* of the linear first-order difference equation (D.14).

To find a particular solution, we must determine c. Assume that in period $t = 0$, x had the value x_0. From (D.16), it follows that

$$c = x_0 - \frac{a}{1 - b}. \tag{D.17}$$

Thus, the particular solution of (D.14) is given by

$$x = \frac{a}{1 - b} + \left(x_0 - \frac{a}{1 - b}\right) b^t. \tag{D.18}$$

If the boundary condition is such that $x_0 = a/(1 - b)$, then (D.18) implies that

$$x_t = x_0, \forall t \geq 0.$$

Thus, $a/(1 - b)$ can be seen as an equilibrium value. If $x = a/(1 - b)$, then x tends to stay at this level.

In addition, x_0 if $|b| < 1$, (D.18) implies that for any x_0, we have

$$\lim_{t \to \infty} x_t = \frac{a}{1 - b}. \tag{D.19}$$

Equation (D.19) implies that the difference equation is stable, because x tends to approach its equilibrium value over time from any initial condition. In this case, the equilibrium value is a *stable node*.

If $|b| > 1$, the only path that leads to the equilibrium value is the immediate jump of x to the equilibrium value $a/(1-b)$. This solution requires

$$c = 0, x_t = a/(1-b), \forall t.$$

The equilibrium value in this case is a *saddle point.*

D.3 Second-Order Linear Difference Equations

We next turn to the second-order linear difference equation with constant coefficients, of the form

$$x_t = a + bx_{t-1} + cx_{t-2}. \tag{D.20}$$

Using the lag operator, (D.20) can be written as

$$(1 - bL - cL^2)x_t = a. \tag{D.21}$$

Equation (D.21) can be expressed as

$$(1 - \lambda_1 L)(1 - \lambda_2 L)x_t = a, \tag{D.22}$$

where

$$\lambda_1 + \lambda_2 = b, \tag{D.23}$$

$$\lambda_1 \lambda_2 = -c, \tag{D.24}$$

and λ_1 and λ_2 are the two roots of the second-order linear difference equation (D.20).

There are three possible cases, depending on the discriminant of the characteristic equation of (D.20).

Case 1 $b^2 > -4c$ The discriminant is positive, and the roots are real and distinct, taking the form

$$\lambda_1 = \frac{b + \sqrt{b^2 + 4c}}{2},$$

$$\lambda_2 = \frac{b - \sqrt{b^2 + 4c}}{2}.$$

From (D.22), the general solution of (D.20) takes the form

$$x_t = \frac{a}{(1-\lambda_1)(1-\lambda_2)} + d_1\lambda_1^t + d_2\lambda_2^t = \frac{a}{(1-b-c)} + d_1\lambda_1^t + d_2\lambda_2^t, \tag{D.25}$$

where d_1 and d_2 are two arbitrary constants. To determine the arbitrary constants, one needs two boundary conditions, depending on the values of the two roots.

As in the case of a first-order difference equation, $a/(1-b-c)$ can be seen as the equilibrium value of x.

We have convergence to the equilibrium value if $|\lambda_1|<1$ and $|\lambda_2|<1$. In this case, the equilibrium value will be a stable node, and to determine the two arbitrary constants, d_1 and d_2, we need two initial conditions $x_1, x_2 \neq 0$.

If the two roots lie on either side of unity (i.e., if $|\lambda_1|<1$ and $|\lambda_2|>1$), then the equilibrium value will be a saddle point. In this case, to determine the two arbitrary constants d_1 and d_2, we need one initial and one final condition. The final condition can be none other than the equilibrium value. As a result, we shall have convergence to the equilibrium value only if $d_1 \neq 0$ and $d_2 = 0$.

If both roots are greater than unity (i.e., if $|\lambda_1|>1$ and $|\lambda_2|>1$), then the only solution is the immediate jump of x to the equilibrium value $a/(1-b-c)$. This solution requires $d_1=0, d_2=0$, and $x_t = a/(1-b-c)$ for all t.

Case 2 $b^2=-4c$ The discriminant is equal to zero, and we have two equal real roots of the form

$$\lambda_1=\lambda_2=\lambda=\frac{b}{2}.$$

The general solution takes the form

$$x_t=\frac{a}{(1-b-c)}+d_1\lambda^t+d_2t\lambda^t. \tag{D.26}$$

If $|\lambda|<1$, to determine the two arbitrary constants d_1 and d_2, we need two initial conditions.

If λ is greater than unity in absolute value (i.e., if $|\lambda|>1$), then the only solution is the immediate jump of x to the equilibrium value $a/(1-b-c)$. This solution requires $d_1=0$, $d_2=0$, and $x_t=a/(1-b-c)$ for all t.

Case 3 $b^2<-4c$ The discriminant is negative, and we have two complex roots, which take the form of a pair of complex conjugates:

$$\lambda_1=\mu+\nu i,$$

$$\lambda_2=\mu-\nu i,$$

where $\mu=\frac{b}{2}$, and $\nu=\frac{\sqrt{-4c-b^2}}{2}$.

Using De Moivre's theorem and the Pythagorean theorem the solution takes the form

$$x_t=\frac{a}{1-b-c}+R^t\left((d_1+d_2)\cos(\theta t)+(d_1-d_2)\sin(\theta t)\right), \tag{D.27}$$

where R and θ are defined by

$$R=\sqrt{\mu^2+\nu^2}=\sqrt{\frac{b^2-4c-b^2}{4}}=\sqrt{-c},$$

and

$$\cos(\theta)=\frac{\mu}{\sqrt{-c}}=\frac{b}{2\sqrt{-c}},\quad \sin(\theta)=\frac{\nu}{\sqrt{-c}}=\frac{\sqrt{-4c-b^2}}{2\sqrt{-c}}.$$

This solution will produce oscillations of a periodic nature. The oscillations will be dampened if and only if $|c|<1$. In such a case, there will be cyclical convergence to the equilibrium value. In the case $|c|<1$, there will be continuous oscillations of a constant periodicity. And if $|c|>1$, there will be divergent oscillations, unless x jumps immediately to its equilibrium value.

D.4 A Pair of First-Order Linear Difference Equations

We next turn to a second-order system of two linear first-order difference equations. The system is described by

$$\begin{aligned} x_t &= a_{10}+a_{11}x_{t-1}+a_{12}y_{t-1}, \\ y_t &= a_{20}+a_{21}x_{t-1}+a_{22}y_{t-1}. \end{aligned} \tag{D.28}$$

As in the case of a system of two first-order differential equations, the first method of solving this system is the substitution method. We can use the second equation to substitute for y_{t-1} in the first equation, and thus obtain a second-order difference equation in x:

$$x_t=a+bx_{t-1}+cx_{t-2}, \tag{D.29}$$

where $a=(a_{10}(1-a_{22})+a_{12}a_{20})$, $b=a_{11}+a_{22}$, and $c=-(a_{11}a_{22}-a_{12}a_{21})$.

Equation (D.29) has the same form as (D.20) and can be solved as an ordinary second-order linear difference equation with constant coefficients. Making use of the lag operator, the homogeneous equation corresponding to (D.29) can be written as

$$\left(L^2-\frac{a_{11}+a_{22}}{a_{11}a_{22}-a_{12}a_{21}}L+\frac{1}{a_{11}a_{22}-a_{12}a_{21}}\right)x_t=0. \tag{D.30}$$

The two roots of the polynomial in the lag operator must satisfy the characteristic equation

$$\lambda^2-\frac{a_{11}+a_{22}}{a_{11}a_{22}-a_{12}a_{21}}\lambda+\frac{1}{a_{11}a_{22}-a_{12}a_{21}}=0. \tag{D.31}$$

By going through the alternative substitutions, a similar second-order difference equation can be obtained for the second variable y_t.

Alternatively, one can rewrite the system (D.28) in matrix form as

$$\begin{pmatrix} x_t \\ y_t \end{pmatrix} = \begin{pmatrix} a_{11} & a_{12} \\ a_{21} & a_{22} \end{pmatrix} \begin{pmatrix} x_{t-1} \\ y_{t-1} \end{pmatrix} + \begin{pmatrix} a_{10} \\ a_{20} \end{pmatrix}. \tag{D.32}$$

The homogeneous system corresponding to (D.32), with $a_{10} = a_{20} = 0$, takes the form

$$\begin{pmatrix} x_t \\ y_t \end{pmatrix} = \begin{pmatrix} a_{11} & a_{12} \\ a_{21} & a_{22} \end{pmatrix} \begin{pmatrix} x_{t-1} \\ y_{t-1} \end{pmatrix}. \tag{D.33}$$

Using the lag operator L, (D.33) can be rewritten as

$$\begin{pmatrix} x_t \\ y_t \end{pmatrix} \begin{pmatrix} 1 - a_{11}L & -a_{12}L \\ -a_{21}L & 1 - a_{22}L \end{pmatrix} = \begin{pmatrix} 0 \\ 0 \end{pmatrix}. \tag{D.34}$$

For (D.33) to have a solution, the matrix in the lag operator must be singular. Therefore, its determinant must be equal to zero. Thus, for a solution to exist, we must have

$$\det \begin{pmatrix} 1 - a_{11}L & -a_{12}L \\ -a_{21}L & 1 - a_{22}L \end{pmatrix} = 0.$$

This condition implies a polynomial in the lag operator with characteristic equation

$$\lambda^2 - \frac{a_{11} + a_{22}}{a_{11}a_{22} - a_{12}a_{21}}\lambda + \frac{1}{a_{11}a_{22} - a_{12}a_{21}} = 0, \tag{D.35}$$

which is identical to (D.31), the characteristic equation of the second-order difference equation (D.29), and will of course give the same solution for the two roots.

However, even this solution method becomes unwieldy for higher-order systems when there are more than two variables. It is thus desirable to investigate other solution methods. To do so, it is worth generalizing the system to one of n first-order linear difference equations.

D.5 A System of *n* First-Order Linear Difference Equations

Let us consider the following system of n first-order difference equations. Such systems arise quite often in dynamic macroeconomics:

$$x_{1,t} = a_{10} + a_{11}x_{1,t-1} + a_{12}x_{2,t-1} + \cdots + a_{1n}x_{n,t-1},$$

$$x_{2,t} = a_{20} + a_{21}x_{1,t-1} + a_{22}x_{2,t-1} + \cdots + a_{2n}x_{n,t-1},$$

$$\vdots \tag{D.36}$$

$$x_{n,t} = a_{n0} + a_{n1}x_{1,t-1} + a_{n2}x_{2,t-1} + \cdots + a_{nn}x_{n,t-1}.$$

In matrix form, the system (D.36) can be written as

$$\begin{pmatrix} x_{1,t} \\ \vdots \\ x_{n,t} \end{pmatrix} = \begin{pmatrix} a_{11} & \cdots & a_{1n} \\ \vdots & \ddots & \vdots \\ a_{n1} & \cdots & a_{nn} \end{pmatrix} \begin{pmatrix} x_{1,t-1} \\ \vdots \\ x_{n,t-2} \end{pmatrix} + \begin{pmatrix} a_{10} \\ \vdots \\ x_{n0} \end{pmatrix}. \tag{D.37}$$

By defining the vector of xs as $\mathbf{x}$, the matrix of multiplicative parameters as $\mathbf{A}$, and the vector of the constants as $\mathbf{a}_0$, the system can be written as

$$\mathbf{x}_t = \mathbf{A}\mathbf{x}_{t-1} + \mathbf{a}_0. \tag{D.38}$$

If $a_{ij} = 0$ for $i \neq j$ in the system (D.37), then the n equations are uncoupled, and the system can be solved as n independent first-order linear difference equations with solutions

$$x_{i,t} = \frac{a_{i0}}{1 - a_{ii}} + \left(x_{i,0} - \frac{a_{i0}}{1 - a_{ii}}\right)(a_{ii})^t, \tag{D.39}$$

where $x_{i,0}$ is a boundary value for x_i.

Thus, if we could transform the system (D.37) into one with a coefficient matrix that is diagonal, we could easily calculate the solution. The question is how to transform the system into one with a diagonal coefficient matrix.

We know from the properties of matrices that the coefficient matrix $\mathbf{A}$ can be transformed as

$$\mathbf{A} = \mathbf{P}\mathbf{J}\mathbf{P}^{-1}, \tag{D.40}$$

where $\mathbf{J}$ is a diagonal matrix with the eigenvalues of $\mathbf{A}$ on its diagonal, and $\mathbf{P}$ is a matrix consisting of the corresponding (right) eigenvectors. Equation (D.40) implies that

$$\mathbf{A}\mathbf{P} = \mathbf{P}\mathbf{J}. \tag{D.41}$$

We can use these properties to rewrite the system (D.38) as

$$\mathbf{x}_t = \mathbf{A}\mathbf{x}_{t-1} + \mathbf{a}_0 = \mathbf{P}\mathbf{J}\mathbf{P}^{-1}\mathbf{x}_{t-1} + \mathbf{a}_0. \tag{D.42}$$

Multiplying both sides of (D.42) by $\mathbf{P}^{-1}$, we get

$$\mathbf{P}^{-1}\mathbf{x}_t = \mathbf{J}\mathbf{P}^{-1}\mathbf{x}_{t-1} + \mathbf{P}^{-1}\mathbf{a}_0. \tag{D.43}$$

Defining a new vector of variables $\mathbf{X_t} = \mathbf{P}^{-1}\mathbf{x_t}$, and a new vector of constants $\mathbf{A_0} = \mathbf{P}^{-1}\mathbf{a_0}$, we can rewrite (D.38) as

$$\mathbf{X}_t = \mathbf{J}\mathbf{X}_{t-1} + \mathbf{A}_0. \tag{D.44}$$

Thus, by using the matrix consisting of the eigenvectors of the original coefficient matrix **A** to define new variables and new constants, we can transform the original coupled system of difference equations to a system of decoupled difference equations in the newly defined variables, as in the case of differential equations. The decoupled system can be solved for each of the transformed variables in **X**. We can then find the solutions for the original vector of variables by using the reverse transformation

$$\mathbf{x}_t = \mathbf{P}\mathbf{X}_t. \tag{D.45}$$

By using the diagonal matrix of the eigenvalues of **A** and the matrix of the corresponding (right) eigenvectors, we can solve the system of n first-order linear difference equations (D.36). The solution method is similar in spirit to the one for a system of n first-order differential equations discussed in appendix C.

Appendix E: Methods of Intertemporal Optimization

Optimization in dynamic economic problems, which are problems in which variables change over time, does not require new principles vis-à-vis static problems. However, dynamic problems have a special structure that allows us to say more about their solution methods.

The most important part of this special structure is the relation between *stocks* and *flows*. Some variables, which we shall denote by y, have the form of stocks, changing gradually over time. Other variables, which we shall denote by x, have the form of flows, which can change freely at any instant. In mathematical terminology, stocks are called *state variables*, and flows are called *control variables*.

In this appendix, we briefly review methods of intertemporal optimization.[1]

E.1 The Form of Dynamic Optimization Problems

The change in stocks depends on the evolution of both stocks and flows. Mathematically, control variables control changes in state variables. For example, savings in period t determine the change in household wealth from period t to period $t+1$. The determination of the evolution of state variables has the form

$$y_{t+1} - y_t = Q(y_t, x_t, t), \tag{E.1}$$

where $t, t+1, \ldots$ are discrete time periods, y is a state variable (stocks), x is a control variable (flows), and Q is a vector function.

Apart from the restrictions that determine the evolution of state variables, there may be other restrictions between all variables that refer to a specific time period. Such restrictions

1. This brief review is meant to refresh one's knowledge and does not aim to be either comprehensive or fully rigorous. Methods of dynamic optimization are fully analyzed in comprehensive texts of mathematics for economists, such as Chiang [1974], Simon and Blume [1994], or Klein [2013]. Some mathematical texts that specialize in intertemporal optimization for economists are also useful such as Intriligator [1971], Kamien and Schwartz [1981], and Dixit [1990].

take the form

$$G(y_t, x_t, t) \leq 0, \tag{E.2}$$

where G is a vector function.

In most dynamic economic problems, we assume that economic agents optimize an objective function of the form

$$\sum_{t=0}^{T} F(y_t, x_t, t), \tag{E.3}$$

subject to restrictions of the form of (E.1) and (E.2). Functions like (E.3) are called *additively separable*, as they have the form of a sum of functions that depend on variables in the same time period.

Note that the period of optimization begins at $t=0$ and ends at $t=T$. The value of the initial stock in period 0 is taken as given, and the same applies to the value of stocks in period $T+1$. One needs an *initial* and a *final*, or *transversality*, condition to solve such problems.

E.2 The Method of Optimal Control

The problem is to select the variables y_t and x_t for $t=0, 1, 2, \ldots, T$, to find the optimal solution of (E.3) under the constraints (E.1) and (E.2).

One can define multipliers (shadow values) and construct the Lagrange function. Define as μ_t the multipliers for the constraints (E.2). These have the usual interpretation of shadow values for the constraints in period t. The multipliers (shadow values) for the constraints (E.1) are different from those of the static constraints. They define the first-order change in the objective function if the constraint in the change of the stock is loosened (i.e., if we have a marginal increase in the stock variable y_{t+1}). Thus, they are the shadow values of the stock variables in period $t+1$, and we denote them by λ_{t+1}.

We define as $\mathcal{L}$ the Lagrange function of the full intertemporal problem:

$$\mathcal{L} = \sum_{t=0}^{T} \{F(y_t, x_t, t) - \lambda_{t+1}[y_{t+1} - y_t - Q(y_t, x_t, t)] - \mu_t G(y_t, x_t, t)\}. \tag{E.4}$$

The first-order conditions for the optimization of the Lagrange function with respect to the control variables x are relatively straightforward:

$$\frac{\partial \mathcal{L}}{\partial x_t} \equiv F_x(y_t, x_t, t) + \lambda_{t+1} Q_x(y_t, x_t, t) - \mu_t G_x(y_t, x_t, t) = 0, \tag{E.5}$$

for $t=0, 1, \ldots, T$, where F_x, Q_x, G_x denote the first derivative of the relevant functions with respect to x.

With respect to the state variables y, the first-order conditions are more complex, because each y appears in two terms of the sum: in the term for period t and also in the term for period $t-1$. We can rearrange the Lagrange function (E.4), so that each y appears in a single term of the sum. The rearranged Lagrange function takes the form

$$\mathcal{L}=\sum_{t=1}^{T}\{F(y_t,x_t,t)+\lambda_{t+1}Q(y_t,x_t,t)+y_t(\lambda_{t+1}-\lambda_t)-\mu_t G(y_t,x_t,t)\}+$$
$$+F(y_0,x_0,0)+\lambda_1 Q(y_0,x_0,0)+y_0\lambda_1-y_{T+1}\lambda_{T+1}. \tag{E.6}$$

The final four terms in (E.6) refer to y_0 and y_{T+1} which are taken as given. The first-order conditions for the optimum of $\mathcal{L}$, for y_t, $t=1,2,\ldots,T$ are

$$\frac{\partial\mathcal{L}}{\partial y_t}\equiv F_y(y_t,x_t,t)+\lambda_{t+1}Q_y(y_t,x_t,t)+\lambda_{t+1}-\lambda_t-\mu_t G_y(y_t,x_t,t)=0. \tag{E.7}$$

Equation (E.7) can be written as

$$\lambda_{t+1}-\lambda_t=-\left[F_y(y_t,x_t,t)+\lambda_{t+1}Q_y(y_t,x_t,t)-\mu_t G_y(y_t,x_t,t)\right]. \tag{E.8}$$

These conditions can be written in a more comprehensive and economically useful way. Define a new function, the *Hamilton function* $\mathcal{H}$, as follows:

$$\mathcal{H}(y_t,x_t,\lambda_{t+1},t)=F(y_t,x_t,t)+\lambda_{t+1}Q(y_t,x_t,t). \tag{E.9}$$

Equation (E.5) suggests that the control variables x must be selected to optimize $\mathcal{H}(y,x,\lambda,t)$, under the constraint $G(y,x,t)\leq 0$.

Define the rearranged Lagrange function $\tilde{\mathcal{L}}$ in the following way:

$$\tilde{\mathcal{L}}=\mathcal{H}(y_t,x_t,\lambda_{t+1},t)-\mu_t G(y_t,x_t,t). \tag{E.10}$$

Then (E.8) can be written more simply as

$$\lambda_{t+1}-\lambda_t=-\tilde{\mathcal{L}}_y(y_t,x_t,\lambda_{t+1},\mu_t,t). \tag{E.11}$$

Finally, from (E.1) and (E.9), taking into account the envelope theorem, we get

$$y_{t+1}-y_t=\mathcal{H}_\lambda(y_t,x_t,\lambda_{t+1},t)=Q(y_t,x_t,t). \tag{E.12}$$

These properties of the Hamilton function are summarized in the *maximum principle*.

Maximum Principle The necessary first-order conditions for the optimization of (E.3), under the constraints (E.1) and (E.2), are the following: (1) For each t, the control variables x_t optimize the Hamilton function (E.9) under the static constraints (E.2). (2) The changes of y_t and λ_t over time are determined by the difference equations (E.11) and (E.12).

The maximum principle, which was proposed by Pontryagin et al. [1962], greatly facilitates the determination of the first-order conditions for intertemporal optimization problems. In addition, it also has a great advantage for economic applications, as it facilitates the economic interpretation of the first-order conditions.

Obviously, we do not want the control variables x to optimize the function F, because this would not take into account the impact of the choice of x on the evolution of the state variables y in the next period. The impact is accounted for optimizing (E.9). The impact of x_t on y_{t+1} is equal to its impact on Q. The change in the objective function is found by multiplying the impact of x on Q with the shadow value λ_{t+1} of y_{t+1}. The Hamilton function (E.9) accomplishes this. The Hamilton function provides a simple way of converting the one-period objective function F to account for the future impact of the current choice of the control variables x.

A similar economic interpretation can be given to the first-order conditions for the state variable y. A marginal change in y in period t gives the marginal change $F_y - \mu G_y$ in period t, given the shadow value of the static restriction G, and an additional Q_y in the next period, with a value of λ_{t+1}. The right-hand side of (E.8) may be interpreted as a dividend. The change $\lambda_{t+1} - \lambda_t$ is like a capital gain. Equation (E.8) tells us that the dividend plus the capital gain should be equal to zero: At the optimum point, there can be no excess return from y.

E.3 The Optimal Control Method in Continuous Time

Until now we have treated time as a sequence of discrete periods. However, in many applications, it is more convenient to treat time as a continuous variable.

We can think of continuous time as the limit of discrete periods of length Δt, where Δt tends to zero. For example, (E.1) can be written as

$$y(t+\Delta t) - y(t) = Q(y(t), x(t), t)\Delta t.$$

Dividing by Δt and letting it tend to zero, we get

$$\dot{y}(t) = \frac{dy}{dt} = Q(y(t), x(t), t), \tag{E.13}$$

where as usual, a dot above a variable denotes its first derivative with respect to time. Let us also use the widespread convention that t is written as a subscript in the analysis of discrete time, and in parentheses in the analysis of continuous time.

Equation (E.2), which denotes the constraints in the control variables, does not change. In continuous time, it is written as

$$G(y(t), x(t), t) \leq 0. \tag{E.14}$$

The transformation of the sum (E.3) in continuous time is somewhat more complicated. Total time between 0 and T is divided into $T/\Delta t$ small discrete time intervals. Equation

(E.3) can then be written as

$$\sum_{i=0}^{T/\Delta t} F(y(i\Delta t), x(i\Delta t), i\Delta t)\Delta t.$$

The limit of the above sum, as Δt tends to zero, is the integral

$$\int_0^T F(y(t), x(t), t)dt. \tag{E.15}$$

We can use the Hamilton function as we did in (E.9):

$$\mathcal{H} = F(y(t), x(t), t) + \lambda(t)Q(y(t), x(t), t). \tag{E.16}$$

The first-order conditions for the optimization of the Hamilton function (E.16) under the static constraints (E.14) are

$$\frac{\partial \mathcal{H}}{\partial x} - \mu \frac{\partial G}{\partial x} = 0,$$

$$\frac{\partial \mathcal{H}}{\partial y} = -\dot{\lambda}. \tag{E.17}$$

$$\frac{\partial \mathcal{H}}{\partial \lambda} = \dot{y},$$

Equations (E.17) are the corresponding conditions in continuous time of the discrete time conditions (E.5), (E.11), and (E.12).

E.4 Dynamic Programming and the Bellman Equation

Dynamic programming is an alternative method of solving the problem of the optimization of a function such as (E.3) under the constraints (E.1) and (E.2). Dynamic programming proves to be extremely useful in problems that combine time and uncertainty, as often happens in economics.

Our problem is the optimization of

$$\sum_{t=0}^{T} F(y_t, x_t, t)$$

under the constraints

$$y_{t+1} - y_t = Q(y_t, x_t, t)$$

and

$$G(y_t, x_t, t) \leq 0,$$

for $t = 0, 1, 2, \dots, T$. The vectors of initial and final stocks y_0 and y_{T+1} are taken as given.

We can define the optimal value that comes out of this problem as a function of the initial stocks y_0. Denote this function as $V(y_0)$. The vector of the first derivatives of this function, $V_y(y_0)$, is the vector of the shadow values of these initial stocks.

The separability of the objective function (E.3) and the constraints allow us to make an important generalization of the above idea. Instead of starting off at time zero, let us assume that we start off at time $t = \tau$. For the decisions that start at τ, the only thing that matters from the past is the vector of stocks y_τ, which is the result of past decisions. Our problem is to optimize an objective function such as (E.3), under the constraints (E.1) and (E.2), with time starting from τ and not from 0. We define $V(y_\tau, \tau)$ as the optimal value that emerges as a function of stocks y_τ and period τ. The vector of the first derivatives $V_y(y_\tau, \tau)$ denotes the marginal increase in the optimal value for a small increase of stocks in period τ, which is the vector of shadow values of the initial stocks for the optimization problem that starts in period τ. This applies for all t.

Let us then select any t and examine the decision of choosing the values of the control variables for that period. Any choice of the control variables x_t will lead to stocks y_{t+1} through (E.1). What remains is to solve the subproblem for period $t+1$, and to find the optimal value $V(y_{t+1}, t+1)$. The total value in period t of a choice for the control variables x_t, starting off with stocks y_t, can be separated into two terms: $F(y_t, x_t, t)$, which occurs in the current period; and $V(y_{t+1}, t+1)$, which comes about in future periods. The choice of x_t must optimize the sum of these two terms under the relevant constraints. In other words we have

$$V(y_t, t) = \max_{x_t} \{F(y_t, x_t, t) + V(y_{t+1}, t+1)\} \tag{E.18}$$

under the constraints (E.1) and (E.2) for the specific t.

This method of intertemporal optimization, as a succession of static optimization problems, was proposed by Richard Bellman and is called *dynamic programming*. The idea that whatever the choice in period t, the choices for the subproblem that begins from period $t+1$ should be optimal, is known as Bellman's *principle of optimality*. The optimal value function $V(y_t, t)$ is called the Bellman *value function*, and equation (E.18) the *Bellman equation*.

The Bellman equation gives us a recursive method for solving the original optimization problem. The idea is to start from the end and go backward recursively. In period T there is no future, only the requirement for a given final stock y_{T+1}. Therefore

$$V(y_T, T) = \max_{x_T} F(y_T, x_T, T)$$

under the constraints

$$y_{T+1} = y_T + Q(y_T, x_T, T),$$

$$G(y_T, x_T, T) \leq 0.$$

This is a simple problem of static optimization, which gives us the optimal value function $V(y_T, T)$. This function can in turn be used in the right-hand side of (E.18) for $t = T - 1$. This equation is then another static problem, which gives us the optimal value function $V(y_{T-1}, T-1)$. We can continue in this way, until we reach period 0. In practice, this process provides results for the simplest problems. Analytical solutions exist when the functions F, G, and Q have a very simple form. Where analytical solutions do not exist, we can use numerical solutions.

For many economic applications we have better methods than the recursive method to find or characterize the solution.

Note that in the presence of uncertainty, the Bellman equation (E.18) takes the form

$$V(y_t, t) = \max_{x_t} \{F(y_t, x_t, t) + E_t V(y_{t+1}, t+1)\},$$

where E is the mathematical expectations operator.

To find the Bellman equation in continuous time, note that from (E.18), we have

$$V(y(t), t) = \max_{x(t)} \{F(y(t), x(t), t)\Delta t + V(y(t+\Delta t), t+\Delta t)\}, \tag{E.19}$$

where Δt is a small time interval. Using a Taylor expansion of the last right-hand side term of (E.19), we get

$$V(y(t+\Delta t), t+\Delta t) = V(y(t), t) + V_y(y(t), t)\,[y(t+\Delta t) - y(t)] + V_t(y(t), t)\Delta t. \tag{E.20}$$

From (E.1), we have

$$y(t+\Delta t) - y(t) = Q(y(t), x(t), t)\Delta t. \tag{E.21}$$

Substituting (E.21) in (E.20), and the equation that results in (E.19) yields

$$V(y(t), t) = \max_{x(t)}\{F(y(t), x(t), t)\Delta t + V(y(t), t) + V_y(y(t), t)Q(y(t), x(t), t)\Delta t$$
$$+ V_t(y(t), t)\Delta t\}.$$

Dividing by Δt and noting that $V(y(t), t)$ cancels out from both sides results in

$$0 = \max_{x(t)} \left\{F(y(t), x(t), t) + V_y(y(t), t)Q(y(t), x(t), t)\right\} + V_t(y(t), t) \tag{E.22}$$

under the static constraint

$$G(y(t), x(t), t) \leq 0.$$

Equation (E.22) is the Bellman equation for problems in continuous time.

E.5 An Example Based on Optimal Savings in Continuous Time

Let us apply these techniques to one specific example. The example is the Ramsey [1928] problem of the choice of optimal savings in continuous time. This example will also allow us to investigate the role of discounting of the future, which applies to most dynamic optimization problems in economics.

Assume a household that has a exogenous flow of income equal to w per instant and that can borrow and lend freely in the capital market, at an interest rate r. The household has an finite horizon T and initial interest-yielding assets equal to $a(0)$. The household is assumed to maximize the following inter-temporal utility function:

$$U=\int_{t=0}^{T} e^{-\rho t}u(c(t))dt, \tag{E.23}$$

subject to

$$\dot{a}(t)=ra(t)+w-c(t), \tag{E.24}$$

$$a(0)\geq 0, \tag{E.25}$$

$$a(T)\geq 0. \tag{E.26}$$

In these equations, u is the instantaneous utility function of the household, which depends on consumption of goods and services and is assumed to be twice differentiable and concave; and ρ is the pure rate of time preference, the rate at which the household discounts future utilities. Equation (E.24) is the instantaneous asset accumulation equation, describing how savings in each instant lead to a change in the assets of the household. Equaion (E.25) defines its initial assets, and (E.26) is a terminal condition that ensures that the household respects its intertemporal budget constraint (transversality condition). Equation (E.26) essentially rules out the possibility that the household has negative assets (i.e., debts) at the end of the horizon.

The Hamilton function for this problem is

$$\mathcal{H}(t)=e^{-\rho t}u(c(t))+\mu(t)\,(ra(t)+w-c(t)), \tag{E.27}$$

where μ is the multiplier of the Hamilton function; μ can be interpreted as the discounted value of marginal assets. Note that because utility at t is discounted, (E.27) is the present-value Hamilton function, viewed from the initial time 0. Correspondingly, μ is the discounted, or present-value multiplier at time 0.

The first-order conditions for a maximum are

$$\frac{\partial\mathcal{H}(t)}{\partial c(t)}=0\Rightarrow e^{-\rho t}u'(c(t))=\mu(t), \tag{E.28}$$

$$-\frac{\partial \mathcal{H}(t)}{\partial a(t)} = \dot{\mu}(t) \Rightarrow \dot{\mu}(t) = -r\mu(t), \tag{E.29}$$

$$\frac{\partial \mathcal{H}(t)}{\partial \mu(t)} = \dot{a}(t) \Rightarrow \dot{a}(t) = ra(t) + w - c(t). \tag{E.30}$$

Equation (E.28) implies that at the optimum, the discounted marginal utility of consumption is equal to the discounted marginal value of assets μ. Equation (E.29) implies that the rate of change of the discounted marginal value of assets μ is equal to minus the real interest rate. Equation (E.30) is just the asset accumulation equation.

Conditions (E.25) and (E.26) must be satisfied as well. In fact, (E.26) must be satisfied as an equality. If assets at the end of the horizon were positive, this would not be a maximum, as the household could increase its utility by consuming the remaining assets just before the end of the horizon.

The economic interpretation of these conditions is more intuitive if everything is expressed in current rather than discounted values. Equation (E.28) implies that

$$u'(c(t)) = e^{\rho t}\mu(t) = \lambda(t), \tag{E.31}$$

where $\lambda(t)$ is defined as the current value multiplier (i.e., the nondiscounted marginal value of assets at instant t). From (E.31), at the optimum, the current value multiplier $\lambda(t)$ is the marginal utility of current consumption. From (E.31), it follows that

$$\dot{\lambda}(t) = e^{\rho t}\left(\dot{\mu}(t) + \rho\mu(t)\right). \tag{E.32}$$

Substituting the first-order condition (E.29) in (E.32) yields the following first-order condition for the current value multiplier:

$$\dot{\lambda}(t) = -(r-\rho)\lambda(t). \tag{E.33}$$

From (E.33), along the optimal path, the current marginal value of assets declines at a rate equal to the difference between the real interest rate and the pure rate of time preference of the household. By rearranging (E.33), we get

$$r + \frac{\dot{\lambda}(t)}{\lambda(t)} = \rho.$$

The real interest rate plus the expected rate of change of the marginal value of assets is equal to the pure rate of time preference. Hence, at the optimum, the household is indifferent between asset accumualation and consumption.

Equations (E.31) and (E.33) express the first-order conditions in terms of the current rather than the discounted value multiplier. These conditions can be derived directly if one forms the current-value Hamilton function:

$$\hat{\mathcal{H}}(t) = e^{\rho t}\mathcal{H}(t) = u(c(t)) + \lambda(t)\left(ra(t) + w - c(t)\right). \tag{E.34}$$

The conditions for the maximization of the current-value Hamilton function will be the same as the conditions for the maximization of the present-value Hamilton function, as one is a monotonic transformation of the other. These conditions are

$$\frac{\partial \hat{\mathcal{H}}(t)}{\partial c(t)} = 0 \Rightarrow u'(c(t)) = \lambda(t), \tag{E.35}$$

$$-\frac{\partial \hat{\mathcal{H}}(t)}{\partial a(t)} = \dot{\lambda}(t) - \rho\lambda(t) \Rightarrow \dot{\lambda}(t) = -(r-\rho)\lambda(t), \tag{E.36}$$

$$\frac{\partial \hat{\mathcal{H}}(t)}{\partial \lambda(t)} = \dot{a}(t) \Rightarrow \dot{a}(t) = ra(t) + w - c(t). \tag{E.37}$$

From (E.35), on the optimal path, the multiplier $\lambda(t)$ (which is the current value of the marginal increase in assets) is equal to the marginal utility of consumption. Thus, the household is indifferent between one extra unit of consumption and one extra unit of savings. From (E.36), on the optimal path, the real interest rate plus the expected capital gain on assets is equal to the pure rate of time preference. Finally, (E.37) is the asset accumulation equation.

Dynamic economic optimization problems usually include discounting. In such problems, one can use the current-value Hamilton function (E.34) and the first-order conditions (E.35)–(E.37), as these first-order conditions are more easily interpretable than the first-order conditions (E.28)–(E.30) for the discounted-value Hamilton function (E.27).

Let us use the first-order conditions (E.35) and (E.36) to characterize the behavior of consumption along the optimal path. From (E.35), differentiating with respect to time, we get

$$\dot{\lambda}(t) = u''(c(t))\dot{c}(t). \tag{E.38}$$

Substituting (E.35) and (E.38) in (E.36) yields

$$\dot{c}(t) = -\frac{u'(c(t))}{u''(c(t))}(r-\rho). \tag{E.39}$$

Equation (E.39) is termed the *Euler equation for consumption*. Because the second derivative of the instantaneous utility function is negative (due to the concavity assumption), the change in consumption will have the same sign as the difference between the real interest rate and the pure rate of time preference. If the real interest rate is higher than the pure rate of time preference, consumption will be continuously increasing. In the opposite case, consumption will be continuously decreasing. If the real interest rate is equal to the pure rate of time preference, consumption will be constant on the optimal path. A full analysis of this dynamic problem is contained in chapter 4. A solution of this problem under uncertainty, using dynamic programming, is contained in chapter 10.

Appendix F: Random Variables and Stochastic Processes

This appendix introduces the concepts of probability, random variables, and stochastic processes. Such concepts are extremely useful for analyzing macroeconomic models characterized by uncertainty. After introducing the key concepts we briefly discuss their mathematical treatment.[1]

F.1 Probability

Probability is the measure of the likelihood that an event will occur. Probabilities are quantified as real numbers between 0 and 1, where, loosely speaking, 0 indicates impossibility and 1 indicates certainty. The higher the probability of an event, the more likely it is that the event will occur.

A simple example is the tossing of a fair (unbiased) coin. Because the coin is fair, the two outcomes ("heads" and "tails") are both equally probable. The probability of heads equals the probability of tails. Because no other outcomes are possible, the probability of either heads or tails is 1/2, which can also be written as 0.5 or 50%.

The concepts discussed here have been given an axiomatic mathematical formalization in probability theory, which is used widely in many areas of applied study, including economics.

The mathematical theory of probability has its roots in attempts to analyze games of chance by Gerolamo Cardano in the sixteenth century and by Pierre de Fermat and Blaise Pascal in the seventeenth century. Christiaan Huygens published a book on the subject in 1657, and in the nineteenth century, Pierre Laplace completed what is today considered the classic interpretation of probability.

Initially, probability theory mainly considered discrete events, and its methods were mainly combinatorial. Eventually, analytical considerations compelled the incorporation of

1. This is a review meant for readers who have already taken courses in mathematical statistics. As a result, it is neither comprehensive nor fully rigorous. For a fuller treatment, consult a comprehensive text on mathematical statistics, such as Larsen and Marx [2014].

continuous variables into the theory. This effort culminated in modern probability theory, based on foundations laid by Andrey Nikolaevich Kolmogorov. Kolmogorov combined the notion of *sample space*, introduced by Richard von Mises, and *measure theory*. Kolmogorov presented his axiomatic treatment of probability theory in 1933, which became the basis for modern probability theory.

Although probability is interpreted in several different ways, probability theory treats the concept in a rigorous mathematical manner by expressing it through a set of axioms. Typically these axioms formalize probability in terms of a *probability space*, which assigns a measure taking values between 0 and 1, termed the probability measure, to a set of outcomes called the sample space. Any specified subset of these outcomes is called an event.

Central subjects in probability theory include discrete and continuous random variables, probability distributions, and stochastic processes. These concepts provide mathematical abstractions of nondeterministic or uncertain processes or measured quantities that may either be single occurrences or evolve over time in a random fashion.

F.2 Random Variables and Probability Distributions

A *random variable* (or *stochastic variable*) is a variable whose possible values are outcomes of a random phenomenon. A random variable is defined as a function that maps outcomes to numerical quantities, typically real numbers. A random variable has a probability distribution, which specifies the probability that its value falls in any given interval.

Random variables can be discrete or continuous. Discrete random variables take any of a specified finite or countable list of values, and they are endowed with a probability mass function characteristic of the random variable's probability distribution. Continuous random variables take any numerical value in an interval or collection of intervals, via a probability density function, which is characteristic of the random variable's probability distribution. Random variables can also be a mixture of both types.

The formal mathematical treatment of random variables is a topic in probability theory. In that context, a random variable is understood as a function defined on a sample space whose outputs are numerical values.

F.2.1 Discrete Probability Distributions

Discrete probability theory deals with events that occur in countable sample spaces, such as tossing a coin, throwing dice, or experiments with decks of cards.

Initially, the probability of an event was defined as the number of cases in which the event occurred, divided by the number of total outcomes possible in an equiprobable sample space.

The modern axiomatic definition starts with a finite or countable set called the *sample space*, which relates to the set of all possible outcomes, denoted by Ω. It is then assumed that for each element $x \in \Omega$, one can attach an intrinsic probability value $f(x)$, which satisfies the following properties:

$$f(x) \in [0, 1], \forall x \in \Omega,$$

$$\sum_{x \in \Omega} f(x) = 1.$$

The probability function $f(x)$ lies between zero and one for every value of x in the sample space Ω, and the sum of $f(x)$ over all values of x in the sample space Ω is equal to 1.

An *event* is defined as any subset E of the sample space Ω. The probability of the event E is defined as

$$P(E) = \sum_{x \in E} f(x).$$

Therefore, the probability of the entire sample space is 1, and the probability of the null event is 0. The function $f(x)$, mapping a point in the sample space to the probability value, is called a *probability mass function*.

F.2.2 Continuous Probability Distributions

Continuous probability theory deals with events that occur in a continuous sample space. If the outcome space of a random variable X is the set of real numbers $\mathbb{R}$ or a subset thereof, then a function F can be defined so as to satisfy

$$F(x) = P(X \leq x).$$

Such a function is called a *cumulative distribution function* (CDF) and returns the probability that X will be less than or equal to x.

The CDF F is a monotonically nondecreasing right continuous function that satisfies the following two properties:

$$\lim_{x \to -\infty} F(x) = 0,$$

$$\lim_{x \to \infty} F(x) = 1.$$

If F is continuous everywhere (i.e., its derivative exists and integrating the derivative gives us the CDF back again), then the random variable X is said to have a *probability density function* PDF, or simply *density* $f(x)$, which is defined as the first derivative of the cumulative distribution function $F(x)$:

$$f(x) = \frac{dF(x)}{dx}.$$

For a set E that is a subset of $\mathbb{R}$, the probability of a random variable being in E is given by

$$P(X \in E) = \int_{x \in E} dF(x).$$

If the PDF exists, then the above can be written as

$$P(X \in E) = \int_{x \in E} f(x)dx.$$

Whereas the PDF exists only for continuous random variables, the CDF exists for all random variables (including discrete random variables) that take values in $\mathbb{R}$. These concepts can be generalized for multidimensional cases on $\mathbb{R}^n$ and other continuous sample spaces.

F.2.3 Mathematical Expectation, Variance, and Higher Moments

In probability theory, the *expected value* of a random variable is, intuitively, the long-run average value of repetitions of the experiment it represents. For example, the expected value in rolling a six-sided die is 3.5, because the average of all the numbers that come up in an extremely large number of rolls is close to 3.5. The expected value is also known as the *mathematical expectation*, *mean value*, *mean*, or *first moment* of the random variable.

The expected value of a discrete random variable is the probability-weighted average of all possible values. In other words, each possible value that the random variable can assume is multiplied by its probability of occurring, and the resulting products are summed to produce the expected value. The same principle applies to a continuous random variable, except that an integral of the variable with respect to its probability density replaces the sum. The formal definition subsumes both of these ideas and also works for distributions that are neither discrete nor continuous.

The mathematical expectation of a discrete random variable is defined as

$$E(x) = \sum_{x \in \Omega} f(x)x.$$

For a continuous random variable, it is defined as

$$E(x) = \int_{x \in \Omega} f(x)xdx.$$

The expected value is a key aspect of how one characterizes a probability distribution. It is one type of *location parameter*.

By contrast, the *variance* is a measure of dispersion of the possible values of the random variable around the expected value. The variance itself is defined in terms of two expectations: It is the expected value of the squared deviation of the variable's value from its expected value. For a discrete random variable, it is defined as

$$Var(x) = E(x - E(x))^2 = \sum_{x \in \Omega} f(x)\,(x - E(x))^2.$$

For a continuous random variable, it is defined as

$$Var(x) = E(x - E(x))^2 = \int_{x \in \Omega} f(x)(x - E(x))^2 dx.$$

Third and higher moments can be defined accordingly and are measures of the *skewness* and *kurtosis* of probability distributions. The first and second moments, as used in the mean and variance, are examples of low-order statistics.

F.2.4 Some Useful Probability Distributions

Certain probability distributions occur very often in probability theory, because they are deemed to be good descriptions of many natural or physical processes. Their distributions therefore have gained special importance in probability theory.

Some fundamental discrete distributions are the discrete uniform, Bernoulli, binomial, negative binomial, Poisson, and geometric distributions. Important continuous distributions include the continuous uniform, normal, exponential, gamma, and beta distributions.

Let us briefly discuss a few of these probability distributions.

The *discrete uniform distribution* is a symmetric probability distribution whereby a finite number of values are equally likely to be observed. Every one of n values has equal probability $1/n$. Another way of describing it would be that a known, finite number of outcomes are equally likely to happen.

A simple example of the discrete uniform distribution is throwing a fair die. The possible values are 1, 2, 3, 4, 5, 6, and each time the die is thrown, the probability of a given score is $1/6$.

The discrete uniform distribution itself is inherently nonparametric. It is convenient, however, to represent its values generally by all integers in an interval $[a, b]$, so that a and b become the main parameters of the distribution. Often one simply considers the interval $[1, n]$ with the single parameter n. With these conventions, the CDF of the discrete uniform distribution can be expressed, for any $x \in [a, b]$, as

$$F(x; a, b) = \frac{x - a + 1}{b - a + 1}.$$

The expected value of a uniformly distributed discrete random variable X, with n integers in the interval $[a, b]$, is given by

$$E(X) = \Pr(X = a)a + \cdots + \Pr(X = b)b = \frac{n(a + b)}{2n} = \frac{a + b}{2}.$$

The variance is given by

$$Var(X) = E(X - E(X))^2 = E\left(X^2\right) - E(X)^2 = \frac{(b-a+1)^2 - 1}{12}.$$

The *Bernoulli distribution*, named after the Swiss scientist Jacob Bernoulli, is the probability distribution of a random variable that takes the value 1 with probability p and the value 0 with probability $q = 1 - p$.

The expected value of a Bernoulli random variable X is given by

$$E(X) = \Pr(X = 1) \times 1 + \Pr(X = 0) \times 0 = p \times 1 + (1 - p) \times 0 = p.$$

The variance of a Bernoulli random variable X is given by

$$Var(X) = E(X - E(X))^2 = p - p^2 = p(1 - p) = pq.$$

We next move to continuous distributions. The *continuous uniform distribution* or *rectangular distribution* is a family of symmetric probability distributions such that for each member of the family, all intervals of the same length on the distribution's support are equally probable. It is the continuous equivalent of the discrete uniform distribution. The support is defined by two parameters, a and b, which are the distribution's minimum and maximum values. The distribution is often referred to by the expression $U(a, b)$.

The probability density function of the continuous uniform distribution is given by

$$U(a, b) = f(x\,|a, b) = \begin{cases} \frac{1}{b-a} & a \leq x \leq b, \\ 0 & x < a \text{ or } x > b. \end{cases}$$

The probability density function of the continuous uniform distribution is presented in figure F.1 for three values of the support $[a, b]$.

For $a = 0$ and $b = 1$, the resulting distribution $U(0, 1)$ is called the *standard uniform distribution*. The standard uniform distribution is also depicted in figure F.1.

The mean and variance of the uniform distribution are given by

$$E(X) = \frac{a+b}{2},$$

$$Var(X) = \frac{(b-a)^2}{12}.$$

The probability that a uniformly distributed random variable falls within any interval of fixed length is independent of the location of the interval itself; it is only dependent on the interval size, so long as the interval is contained in the distribution's support.

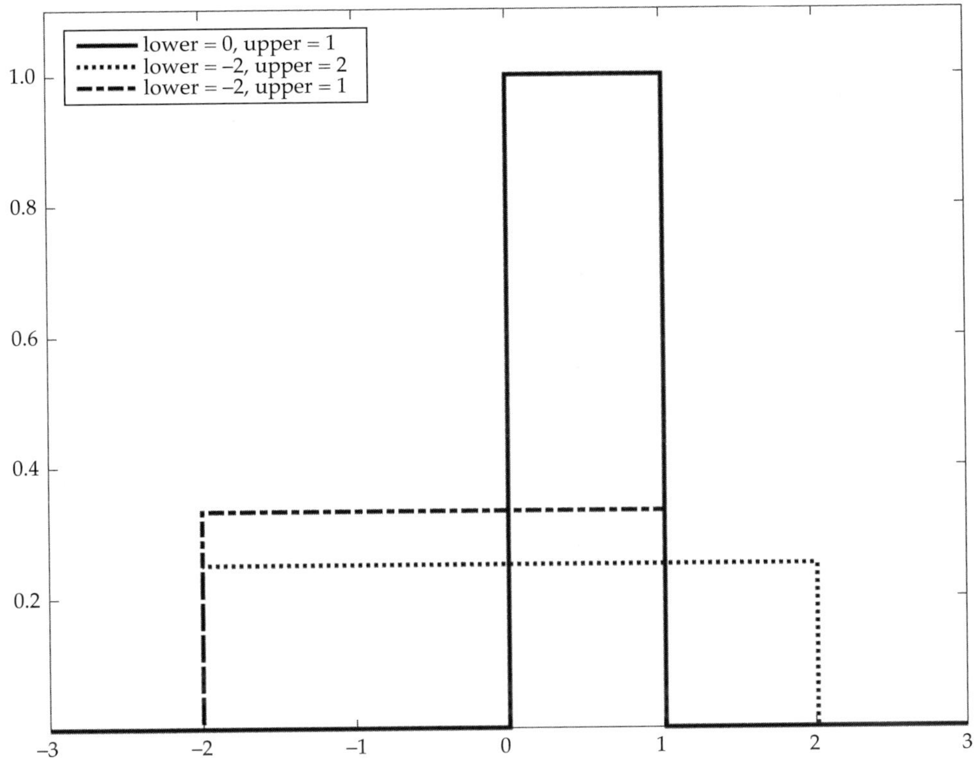

Figure F.1
The uniform distribution.

To see this, if $X \sim U(a,b)$, and $[x, x+d]$ is a subinterval of $[a,b]$ with fixed $d > 0$, then

$$P(X \in [x, x+d]) = \int_{X=x}^{x+d} \frac{1}{b-a} dX = \frac{x+d-x}{b-a} = \frac{d}{b-a},$$

which is independent of x. In fact, this is what motivates the distribution's name.

The CDF of the continuous uniform distribution is given by

$$F(x \mid a,b) = \begin{cases} 0 & x < a, \\ \frac{x-a}{b-a} & a \le x \le b, \\ 1 & x > b. \end{cases}$$

The CDF of the continuous uniform distribution is depicted in figure F.2.

As a final example, let us consider the *normal distribution*. The probability density function of this distribution is given by

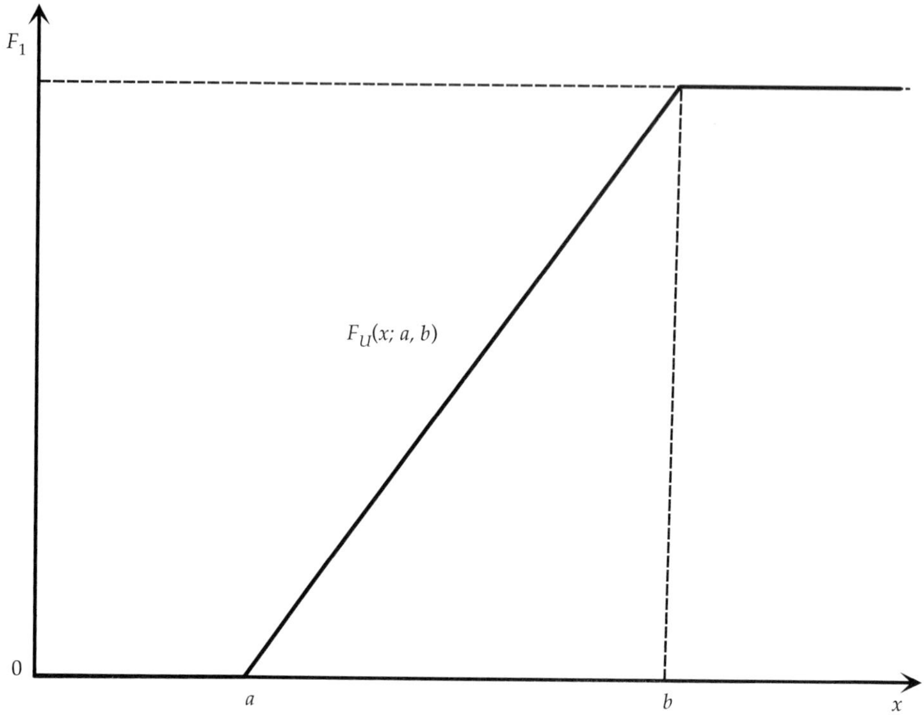

Figure F.2
The CDF of the continuous uniform distribution.

$$N(\mu, \sigma^2) = f\left(x \middle| \mu, \sigma^2\right) = \frac{1}{\sqrt{2\pi\sigma^2}} e^{-\frac{(x-\mu)^2}{2\sigma^2}},$$

where μ is the mean of the distribution, and σ^2 is its variance.

The special case when $\mu = 0$ and $\sigma^2 = 1$ is known as the *standard normal distribution*. It is given by

$$N(0, 1) = f(x) = \frac{1}{\sqrt{2\pi}} e^{-\frac{x^2}{2}}.$$

This special case is depicted in figure F.3, along with two other normal distributions with higher variances.

The factor $\sqrt{2\pi}$ in the denominator ensures that the total area under the curve is equal to one. The factor 1/2 in the exponent ensures that the distribution has unit variance and therefore also has unit standard deviation. This function is symmetric around $x = 0$, where it attains its maximum value, and it has inflection points at $x = 1$ and $x = -1$.

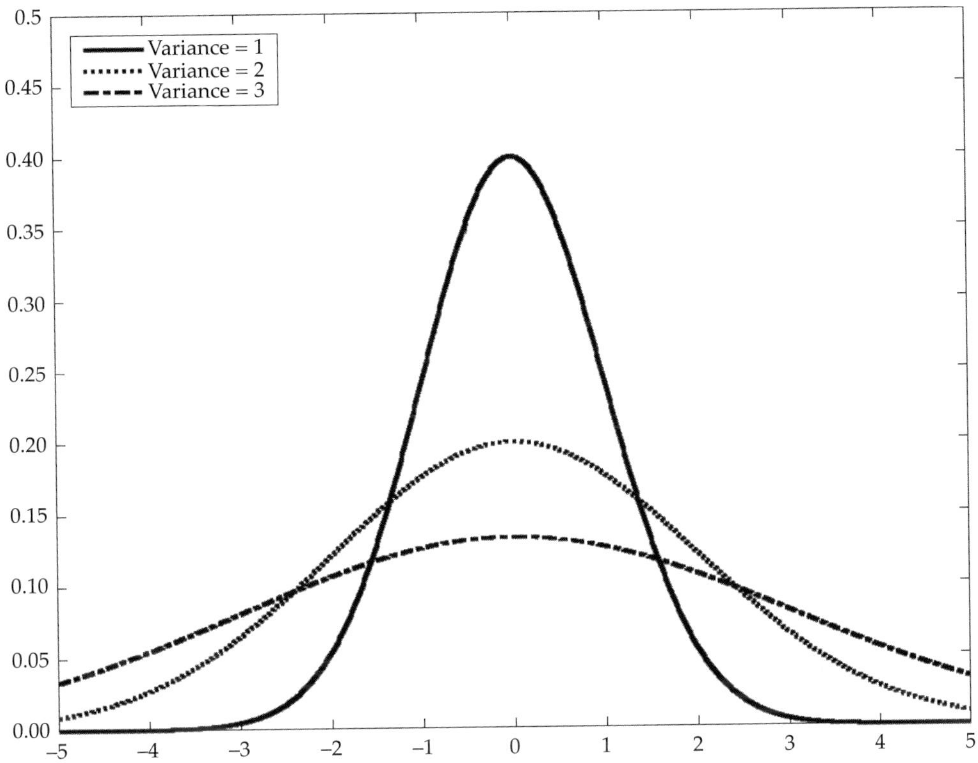

Figure F.3
The normal distribution.

In fact, every normal distribution is a version of the standard normal distribution whose domain has been stretched by a factor σ and moved in a parallel fashion by μ. The relationship between the general normal distribution and the standard normal distribution is given by

$$f\left(x\,\middle|\,\mu,\sigma^2\right)=\frac{1}{\sigma}f\left(\frac{x-\mu}{\sigma}\right).$$

The PDF must be scaled by $1/\sigma$ so that the integral is still 1.

The CDF of the standard normal distribution, often denoted by Φ, is given by

$$F_N(x;0,1)=\Phi(x)=\frac{1}{\sqrt{2\pi}}\int_{-\infty}^{x}e^{-\frac{z^2}{2}}\,dz.$$

The CDF of the standard normal distribution is depicted in figure F.4.

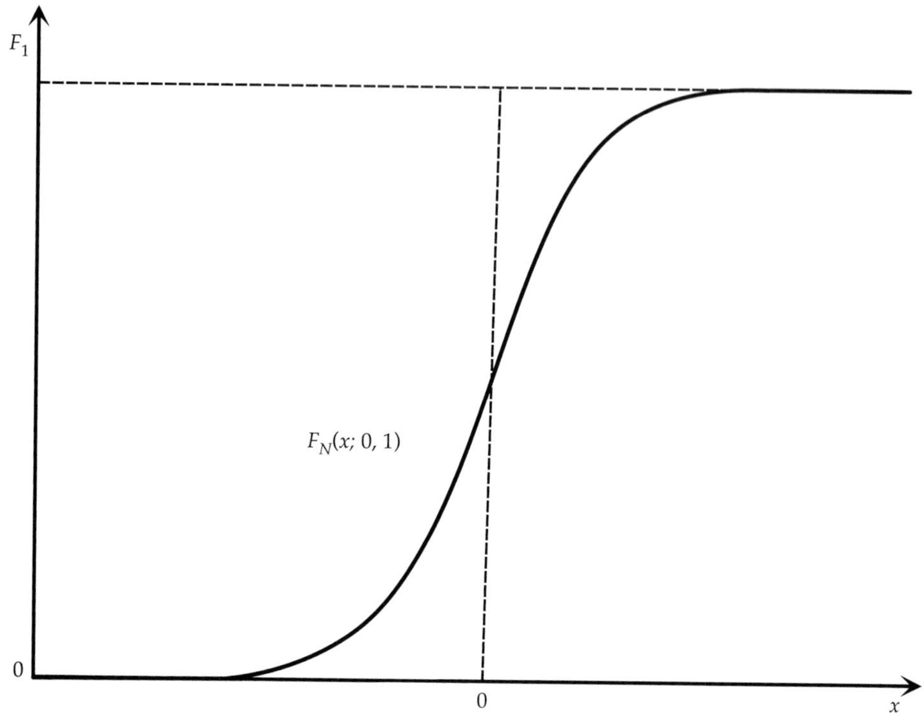

Figure F.4
The CDF of the standard normal distribution.

The normal distribution is extremely important because of the *central limit theorem*. In its most general form, this theorem states that under some conditions (which include a finite variance), averages of samples of observations of random variables that are independently drawn from independent distributions, converge in distribution to the normal. In other words, the averages become normally distributed when the number of observations is sufficiently large.

The central limit theorem is one of two major results in probability theory providing some structure for random events. The second is the *law of large numbers*, which is discussed in subsection F.2.6.

To understand these results, we must first discuss the different concepts of convergence of random variables.

F.2.5 Convergence of Random Variables

In probability theory, there are several notions of convergence for random variables. They are listed below in order of strength, ranging from weak to strong convergence.

Weak convergence: A sequence of random variables $X_1, X_2, \ldots,$ converges weakly to a random variable X if their respective cumulative distribution functions $F_1, F_2, \ldots,$ converge to the cumulative distribution function F of X, wherever F is continuous. Weak convergence is also called *convergence in distribution*.

Convergence in probability: A sequence of random variables $X_1, X_2, \ldots,$ converges in probability to the random variable X if

$$\lim_{n\to\infty} P(|X_n - X| \geq \varepsilon) = 0$$

for every $\varepsilon > 0$.

Strong convergence: A sequence of random variables $X_1, X_2, \ldots,$ converges strongly to the random variable X if

$$P\left(\lim_{n\to\infty} X_n = X\right) = 1.$$

Strong convergence is also known as *almost sure convergence*.

F.2.6 The Law of Large Numbers

Intuition suggests that if a fair coin is tossed many times, then roughly half of the time, it will turn up heads, and the other half, it will turn up tails. Furthermore, the more often the coin is tossed, the more likely it should be that the ratio of the number of heads to the number of tails will approach unity.

Modern probability theory provides a formal version of this intuitive idea, known as the *law of large numbers*. This law is remarkable, because it is not assumed in the foundations of probability theory but instead emerges from these foundations as a theorem. Because it links theoretically derived probabilities to their actual frequency of occurrence in the real world, the law of large numbers is considered a pillar in the history of statistical theory and has been widely influential.

The law of large numbers states that the sample average of a sequence of independent and identically distributed random variables X_k converges toward their common expectation μ, provided that the expectation of $|X_k|$ is finite.

The sample average is defined as

$$\bar{X}_n = \frac{1}{n}\sum\nolimits_{k=1}^{n} X_k.$$

The weak law of large numbers is based on convergence in probability. It states that

$$\lim_{n\to\infty} P\left(\left|\bar{X}_n - \mu\right| \geq \varepsilon\right) = 0.$$

The strong law of large numbers is based on almost sure convergence. It states that

$$P\left(\lim_{n\to\infty} \bar{X}_n = \mu\right) = 1.$$

F.2.7 The Central Limit Theorem

The central limit theorem is one of the great results of mathematical statistics. It explains the ubiquitous occurrence of the normal distribution in nature. The theorem states that the average of many independent and identically distributed random variables with finite variance tends toward a normal distribution, irrespective of the distribution followed by the original random variables.

Formally, let $X_1, X_2, \ldots,$ be independent random variables with mean μ and variance $\sigma^2 > 0$. Then the sequence of random variables

$$Z_n = \frac{\sum_{i=1}^{n} (X_i - \mu)}{\sigma \sqrt{n}}$$

converges in distribution to the standard normal variable.

For some classes of random variables—for example, the distributions with finite first, second, and third moments from the exponential family—the classic central limit theorem works rather fast. However, for some random variables of the heavy tail and fat tail variety, it works very slowly or may not work at all: in such cases, one may use the generalized central limit theorem.

F.2.8 Joint Probability Distributions

Up to now we have dealt with probability distributions of a single random variable. Given at least two random variables $X, Y, \ldots,$ that are defined on a probability space, the *joint probability distribution* for $X, Y, \ldots$ is a probability distribution that gives the probability that each of $X, Y, \ldots$ falls in any particular range or discrete set of values specified for that variable. In the case of only two random variables, this is called a *bivariate distribution*, but the concept generalizes to any number of random variables, giving a *multivariate distribution*.

The joint probability distribution can be expressed either in terms of a joint cumulative distribution function or in terms of a joint probability density function (in the case of continuous variables) or joint probability mass function (in the case of discrete variables). These in turn can be used to find two other types of distributions: the marginal distribution, giving the probabilities for any one of the variables with no reference to any specific ranges of values for the other variables; and the conditional probability distribution, giving the probabilities for any subset of the variables conditional on particular values of the remaining variables.

The *joint probability mass function* of two discrete random variables X, Y is given by

$$P(X = x, Y = y) = P(X = x \mid Y = y) \cdot P(Y = y) =$$

$$= P(Y = y \mid X = x) \cdot P(X = x),$$

where $P(X = x \mid Y = y)$ is the *conditional probability mass function*, which gives the probability that $X = x$, conditional on the fact that $Y = y$; $P(Y = y)$ is the *marginal probability mass function*, giving the probability that $Y = y$, irrespective of X. The other conditional and marginal probabilities are defined similarly.

The property that a joint probability distribution can be expressed as the product of the relevant conditional and marginal distributions generalizes to any number of variables n and is known as the *chain rule of probability*. Joint probability density functions for continuous variables are defined accordingly.

A useful measure of the joint variability of two random variables is the covariance. The *covariance* between two jointly distributed real-valued random variables X and Y, with finite second moments, is defined as the expected product of their deviations from their individual expected values:

$$\mathrm{Cov}(X, Y) = E\left((X - E(X))\,(Y - E(Y))\right).$$

If higher values of one variable mainly correspond with higher value of the other variable, and the same holds for lower values (i.e., if the variables tend to show similar behavior), then the covariance is positive. In the opposite case, when the higher values of one variable mainly correspond to lower values of the other (i.e., the variables tend to show opposite behavior), then the covariance is negative. The sign of the covariance therefore shows the tendency in the linear relationship between the variables.

The magnitude of the covariance is not easy to interpret. The normalized version of the covariance, the *correlation coefficient*, however, shows by its magnitude the strength of the linear relation. The correlation coefficient, due to Pearson, is the covariance of two random variables divided by the product of their standard deviations and is unit free. The correlation coefficient ranges from -1 to 1.

F.3 Stochastic Processes

A *stochastic process* or random process can be defined as a collection of random variables that is indexed by some mathematical set, meaning that each random variable of the stochastic process is uniquely associated with an element in the set. The set used to index the random variables is called the *index set*. Historically, the index set was some subset of the real line, such as the natural numbers, giving the index set the interpretation of time. Each random variable in the collection takes values from the same mathematical space known as the *state space*. This state space can be, for example, the integers, the real line, or n-dimensional Euclidean space.

An increment is the amount that a stochastic process changes between two index values (often interpreted as two points in time). A stochastic process can have many outcomes, due to its randomness, and a single outcome of a stochastic process is called, among other names, a sample function or *realization*.

Thus, for our purposes, a stochastic process will be defined as a collection of random variables evolving over time. It is a process that evolves over time according to probabilistic rules.

Dynamic stochastic models can be contrasted with deterministic models. A deterministic model is specified by a set of differential or difference equations that describe exactly how the system will evolve over time. In a stochastic model, the evolution is at least partially random, and if the process is run several times, it will not give identical results. Different runs of a stochastic process are different realizations of the process.

Thus, instead of describing a process that can evolve in only one way, as in the case of solutions of systems of ordinary differential or difference equations, in a stochastic process, there is potential indeterminacy. Even if the initial conditions (or starting points) are known, there are several (often infinitely many) directions in which the process can evolve.

Like random variables, stochastic processes can be defined in both continuous and discrete time. In the case of discrete time, a stochastic process is a sequence of random variables. The random variables corresponding to various time periods may be completely different, the only requirement being that these different random quantities all take values in the same space. The approach we take is to model these random variables as random functions of the time index. Although the random values of a stochastic process at different times may be independent random variables, in most commonly considered situations, they exhibit complicated statistical dependence.

In the remainder of this appendix, let us confine our attention to linear stochastic processes in discrete time. Such processes are extremely useful tools for studying dynamic stochastic economic problems that combine time and randomness. Aggregate fluctuations are an important example of the application of these tools.

As Lucas [1977, p. 9] observed: "Movements about trend in gross national product in any country can be well described by a stochastically disturbed difference equation of very low order." Stochastically disturbed difference equations are nothing more than difference equations that are affected by random shocks. They are examples of stochastic processes in discrete time.

F.4 Univariate Linear Stochastic Processes in Discrete Time

A stochastic process y_t is defined as a collection of random variables that depend on the time index. One random variable corresponds to each moment of time $t \in T$.

Assume that the probability law that corresponds to each stochastic process is characterized by the set of mathematical expectations (means) of the stochastic process y_t and by the set of covariances of y in different time periods.

The mathematical expectation (or mean) of the stochastic process y_t is given by

$$E(y_t) = \mu_t$$

for $t \in T$, where E is the mathematical expectations operator.

The covariances are given by

$$E((y_t - \mu_t)(y_s - \mu_s)) = \sigma_{t,s}.$$

A stochastic process is considered *stationary* when the mean μ_t is independent of t, and the covariance $\sigma_{t,s}$ only depends on $t - s$.

F.4.1 The White Noise Process

The basic stochastic process, which is the building block of all the stochastic processes that we analyze here, is the *white noise process*. In this process, the mean is equal to zero, the variance is constant, and the covariance is equal to zero for $t \neq s$.

Thus, the white noise process ε satisfies the following properties:

$$E(\varepsilon_t) = 0, \quad \forall t,$$

$$E(\varepsilon_t^2) = \sigma^2, \quad \forall t,$$

$$E(\varepsilon_t \varepsilon_s) = 0, \quad \forall t \neq s,$$

In the white noise process, there is no time dependence, as the covariances are equal to zero for different time periods. Zero mean normal distributions are examples of white noise processes, as are uniform distributions with support $[-a, a]$.

F.4.2 Moving Average Stochastic Processes

Another category of linear stochastic processes in discrete time is the category of *moving average processes*. The first-order moving average stochastic process (MA(1)) is defined by

$$y_t = \varepsilon_t - \theta\varepsilon_{t-1} = (1 - \theta L)\varepsilon_t, \tag{F.1}$$

where ε_t is a white noise process.

For this process, it follows that

$$E(y_t) = (1 - \theta)E(\varepsilon_t) = 0, \quad \forall t,$$

$$E(y_t^2) = (1 + \theta^2)\sigma_\varepsilon^2, \quad \forall t,$$

$$E(y_t, y_{t-s}) = \begin{cases} -\theta\sigma_\varepsilon^2 & \forall t \quad |s| = 1, \\ 0 \quad \forall t & \forall |s| > 1. \end{cases}$$

It is straightforward to confirm that this stochastic process is stationary.

A more general linear moving average stochastic process can be defined as

$$y(t) = y_0 + \theta_0\varepsilon_t + \theta_1\varepsilon_{t-1} + \cdots + \theta_n\varepsilon_{t-n} = \Theta(L)\varepsilon_t, \tag{F.2}$$

where $\Theta(L)$ is an nth-order polynomial in the lag operator L. Equation (F.2) defines an MA(n) stochastic process.

F.4.3 Autoregressive Stochastic Processes

Another category of linear stochastic processes is the category of autoregressive stochastic processes.

The zero mean first-order linear autoregressive process AR(1) is defined by

$$y_t = \lambda y_{t-1} + \varepsilon_t, \tag{F.3}$$

where $\lambda \leq 1$, and ε_t is a white noise process.

An AR(1) process (F.3) is essentially a stochastic first-order difference equation (i.e., a first-order difference equation plus a white noise stochastic process).

Using the lag operator, it follows that

$$y_t = \frac{1}{1-\lambda L}\varepsilon_t = \sum\nolimits_{s=0}^{\infty} \lambda^s \varepsilon_{t-s}. \tag{F.4}$$

We can deduce that this stochastic process has the white noise process ε as its building block. Equation (F.3) is the moving average representation of the AR(1) process (F.4). Thus the AR(1) process is an example of an infinite-order moving average process with geometrically declining weights. It follows that

$$E(y_t) = \frac{1}{1-\lambda}E(\varepsilon_t) = 0, \ \ \forall t,$$

$$E(y_t^2) = \frac{1}{1-\lambda^2}\sigma_\varepsilon^2, \ \ \forall t,$$

$$E(y_t, y_{t-s}) = \frac{\lambda^{|s|}}{1-\lambda^2}\sigma_\varepsilon^2, \ \ \forall t, s.$$

The AR(1) process is stationary if $|\lambda| < 1$. If $|\lambda| \geq 1$, this AR(1) process is *nonstationary*. In the case $\lambda = 1$, it is nonstationary and takes the form

$$y_t = y_{t-1} + \varepsilon_t. \tag{F.5}$$

The nonstationary stochastic process (F.5) is called a *random walk*. The first difference of a random walk is a white noise process, because from (F.5), it follows that

$$\Delta y_t = y_t - y_{t-1} = \varepsilon_t, \tag{F.6}$$

where Δ is the first difference operator.

The random walk is a special case of the class of *homogeneous nonstationary stochastic processes*, which become stationary when we transform them by taking their first differences one or more times.

The *second-order linear autoregressive process* (AR(2)) has the form of a second-order linear difference equation plus a white noise stochastic process:

$$y_t = a + by_{t-1} + cy_{t-2} + \varepsilon_t, \tag{F.7}$$

where ε_t is a white noise process, and a, b, c are constant parameters. Using the lag operator, (F.7) can be rewritten as

$$(1 - bL - cL^2)y_t = a + \varepsilon_t. \tag{F.8}$$

Equation (F.8) can be transformed into

$$(1 - \lambda_1 L)(1 - \lambda_2 L)y_t = a + \varepsilon_t, \tag{F.9}$$

where $\lambda_1 + \lambda_2 = b$ and $\lambda_1\lambda_2 = -c$ are the two roots of the characteristic polynomial of the difference equation (F.7).

The conditions for (F.7) to be stationary are analogous to the conditions for convergence in a standard second-order linear difference equation. There are three possible cases.

Case 1 $b^2 > -4c$ The roots are real and distinct, and they take the form

$$\lambda_1 = \frac{b + \sqrt{b^2 + 4c}}{2}, \quad \lambda_2 = \frac{b - \sqrt{b^2 + 4c}}{2}.$$

We have stationarity if $|\lambda_1| < 1$, and $|\lambda_2| < 1$. The solution takes the form

$$y_t = \frac{a}{(1 - \lambda_1)(1 - \lambda_2)} + \frac{\varepsilon_t}{(1 - \lambda_1 L)(1 - \lambda_2 L)}. \tag{F.10}$$

Case 2 $b^2 = -4c$ We have two equal real roots of the form

$$\lambda_1 = \lambda_2 = \lambda = \frac{b}{2}.$$

We have stationarity if $|\lambda| < 1$, which requires $|b| < 2$.

Case 3 $b^2 < -4c$ We have two complex roots, which take the form of a pair of complex conjugates. We have stationarity if $|c| < 1$, which also implies in this case that $|b| < 2$.

A more general autoregressive process AR(m) takes the form

$$y_t = \lambda_0 + \lambda_1 y_{t-1} + \cdots + \lambda_m y_{t-m} + \varepsilon_t = \Lambda(L)y_t + \varepsilon_t = \frac{1}{1 - \Lambda(L)}\varepsilon_t, \tag{F.11}$$

where $\Lambda(L)$ is a polynomial in the lag operator.

F.4.4 Autoregressive Moving Average Stochastic Processes

Autoregressive and moving average processes can be combined. For example, the combined first-order autoregressive moving average process is called ARMA(1,1) and is defined by

$$y_t = \lambda y_{t-1} + \varepsilon_t - \theta\varepsilon_{t-1} = \frac{1-\theta L}{1-\lambda L}\varepsilon_t. \tag{F.12}$$

This ARMA process is stationary if $|\lambda| < 1$.

For a more general and detailed treatment of linear stochastic processes in discrete time, see chapter 11 in Sargent [1987].

F.5 Vector Stochastic Processes and Vector Autoregressions

Let us now consider the following system of n first-order stochastic difference equations. Such systems arise quite often in dynamic macroeconomics and are a generalization of the deterministic system of difference equations examined in appendix D:

$$\begin{aligned} x_{1,t} &= a_{10} + a_{11}x_{1,t-1} + a_{12}x_{2,t-1} + \cdots + a_{1n}x_{n,t-1} + \varepsilon_{1t}, \\ x_{2,t} &= a_{20} + a_{21}x_{1,t-1} + a_{22}x_{2,t-1} + \cdots + a_{2n}x_{n,t-1} + \varepsilon_{2t}, \\ &\vdots \\ x_{n,t} &= a_{n0} + a_{n1}x_{1,t-1} + a_{n2}x_{2,t-1} + \cdots + a_{nn}x_{n,t-1} + \varepsilon_{nt}. \end{aligned} \tag{F.13}$$

The xs are observable variables, and the εs are white noise stochastic disturbances. Such a system is called a *vector autoregression* and is a widely used example of a vector stochastic process.

In matrix form, the system (F.13) can be written as

$$\begin{pmatrix} x_{1,t} \\ \vdots \\ x_{n,t} \end{pmatrix} = \begin{pmatrix} a_{11} & \cdots & a_{1n} \\ \vdots & \ddots & \vdots \\ a_{n1} & \cdots & a_{nn} \end{pmatrix} \begin{pmatrix} x_{1,t-1} \\ \vdots \\ x_{n,t-2} \end{pmatrix} + \begin{pmatrix} a_{10} \\ \vdots \\ a_{n0} \end{pmatrix} + \begin{pmatrix} \varepsilon_{1t} \\ \vdots \\ \varepsilon_{nt} \end{pmatrix}. \tag{F.14}$$

By defining the vector of xs as $\mathbf{x}$, the matrix of multiplicative parameters as $\mathbf{A}$, the vector of the constants as $\mathbf{a}_0$, and the vector of the disturbances as $\mathbf{e}$, the system can be written as

$$\mathbf{x}_t = \mathbf{A}\mathbf{x}_{t-1} + \mathbf{a}_0 + \mathbf{e}_t. \tag{F.15}$$

The coefficient matrix $\mathbf{A}$ can be transformed as

$$\mathbf{A} = \mathbf{PJP}^{-1}, \tag{F.16}$$

where **J** is a diagonal matrix with the eigenvalues of **A** on the diagonal, and **P** is a matrix consisting of the corresponding (right) eigenvectors.

This vector stochastic process is stationary if all eigenvalues of **A** are inside the unit circle. Sims [1980] pioneered the use of vector autoregressions as a theory-free way of modeling dynamic interactions between macroeconomic time series. Since then, vector autoregressions have become a widely used tool in empirical macroeconomics.

References

Abel, A. B. 1982. "Dynamic Effects of Permanent and Temporary Tax Policies in a q Model of Investment." *Journal of Monetary Economics* 9(3):353–373.

Abel, A. B., N. G. Mankiw, L. H. Summers, and R. J. Zeckhauser. 1989. "Assessing Dynamic Efficiency: Theory and Evidence." *Review of Economic Studies* 56(1):1–20.

Abreu, D., and M. K. Brunnermeier. 2003. "Bubbles and Crashes." *Econometrica* 71(1):173–204.

Acemoglu, D. 2009. *Introduction to Modern Economic Growth*. Princeton University Press, Princeton, NJ.

Acemoglu, D., S. Johnson, and J. A. Robinson. 2001. "The Colonial Origins of Comparative Development: An Empirical Investigation." *American Economic Review* 91(5):1369–1401.

Acemoglu, D., S. Johnson, and J. A. Robinson. 2005. "Institutions as a Fundamental Cause of Long-Run Growth." In P. Aghion and S. Durlauf, eds., *Handbook of Economic Growth*, vol. 1A, pp. 385–472. Elsevier, Amsterdam.

Acemoglu, D., and J. A. Robinson. 2012. *Why Nations Fail*. Crown, New York.

Aftalion, A. 1909. "La realite de surproductions generales." *Revue d' Economie Politique* 22:219–220.

Aghion, P., and P. Bolton. 1990. "Government Domestic Debt and the Risk of a Default: A Political-Economic Model of a Strategic Role of Debt." In R. Dornbusch and M. Draghi, eds., *Public Debt Management: Theory and History*, pp. 315–345. Cambridge University Press, Cambridge.

Aghion, P., and S. Durlauf, eds. 2005. *Handbook of Economic Growth*, vol. 1. North Holland, Amsterdam.

Aghion, P., and S. Durlauf, eds. 2014. *Handbook of Economic Growth*, vol. 2. North Holland, Amsterdam.

Aghion, P., and P. Howitt. 1992. "A Model of Growth through Creative Destruction." *Econometrica* 60(2):323–351.

Aghion, P., and P. Howitt. 2009. *The Economics of Growth*. MIT Press, Cambridge, MA.

Aiyagari, S. R., A. Marcet, T. J. Sargent, and J. Seppala. 2002. "Optimal Taxation without State-Contingent Debt." *Journal of Political Economy* 110(6):1220–1254.

Akerlof, G. A. 1969. "Relative Wages and the Rate of Inflation." *Quarterly Journal of Economics* 83(3):353–374.

Akerlof, G. A. 2007. "The Missing Motivation in Macroeconomics." *American Economic Review* 97(1):5–36.

Akerlof, G. A., and J. L. Yellen. 1985. "A Near-Rational Model of the Business Cycle with Wage and Price Inertia." *Quarterly Journal of Economics* 100(suppl.):823–838.

Alesina, A. 1988. "The End of Large Public Debts." In F. Giavazzi and L. Spaventa, eds., *High Public Debt: The Italian Experience*, pp. 34–89. Cambridge University Press and CEPR, Cambridge.

Alesina, A., and A. Drazen. 1991. "Why Are Stabilizations Delayed?" *American Economic Review* 81(5):1170–1188.

Alesina, A., and A. Passalacqua. 2016. "The Political Economy of Government Debt." In J. B. Taylor and H. Uhlig, eds., *Handbook of Macroeconomics*, vol. 2B, pp. 2599–2651. Elsevier, Amsterdam.

Alesina, A., and R. Perotti. 1995. "The Political Economy of Budget Deficits." *IMF Staff Papers* 42(1):1–37.

Alesina, A., and G. Tabellini. 1990. "A Positive Theory of Fiscal Deficits and Government Debt." *Review of Economic Studies* 57(3):403–414.

Allais, M. 1947. *Economie et Interet*. Imprimerie National, Paris.

Alogoskoufis, G. 1983. "The Labour Market in an Equilibrium Business Cycle Model." *Journal of Monetary Economics* 11(1):117–128.

Alogoskoufis, G. 1987a. "On Intertemporal Substitution and Aggregate Labor Supply." *Journal of Political Economy* 95(5):938–960.

Alogoskoufis, G. 1987b. "Aggregate Employment and Intertemporal Substitution in the UK." *Economic Journal* 97(386):403–415.

Alogoskoufis, G. 1992. "Monetary Accommodation, Exchange Rate Regimes and Inflation Persistence." *Economic Journal* 102(412):461–480.

Alogoskoufis, G. 2016. "Unemployment Persistence, Inflation and Monetary Policy in a Dynamic Stochastic Model of the Phillips Curve." Working Paper 4-16, March. Athens University of Economics and Business, Athens.

Alogoskoufis, G. 2018. "The Clash of Central Bankers and Labor Market Insiders, and the Persistence of Unemployment and Inflation." *Economica* 85(337):152–176.

Alogoskoufis, G., and A. Manning. 1988. "On the Persistence of Unemployment." *Economic Policy* 3(7):427–469.

Alogoskoufis, G., and R. Smith. 1991. "The Phillips Curve, the Persistence of Inflation and the Lucas Critique: Evidence from Exchange Rate Regimes." *American Economic Review* 81(5):1254–1275.

Andolfatto, D. 1996. "Business Cycles and Labor Market Search." *American Economic Review* 86(1):112–132.

Andres, J., R. Domenech, and J. Ferri. 2006. "Price Rigidity and the Volatility of Vacancies and Unemployment." Unpublished paper. University of Valencia.

Angeletos, M. 2002. "Fiscal Policy with Noncontingent Debt and the Optimal Maturity Structure." *Quarterly Journal of Economics* 117(3):1105–1131.

Angeletos, M., and J. La'O. 2009. "Noisy Business Cycles." *NBER Macroeconomics Annual* 24:319–378.

Angeletos, M., and C. Lian. 2016. "Incomplete Information in Macroeconomics: Accommodating Frictions in Coordination." In J. B. Taylor and H. Uhlig, eds., *Handbook of Macroeconomics*, vol. 2A, pp. 1065–1240. Elsevier, Amsterdam.

Arrow, K. J. 1962. "The Economic Implications of Learning By Doing." *Review of Economic Studies* 29(3): 155–173.

Arrow, K. J. 1964. "The Role of Securities in the Optimal Allocation of Risk Bearing." *Review of Economic Studies* 31(2):91–96.

Arrow, K. J., H. B. Chenery, B. S. Minhas, and R. M. Solow. 1961. "Capital-Labor Substitution and Economic Efficiency." *Review of Economics and Statistics* 43(3):225–250.

Arrow, K. J., and G. Debreu. 1954. "Existence of Equilibrium for a Competitive Economy." *Econometrica* 22(3): 265–290.

Ascari, G., and A. M. Sbordone. 2014. "The Macroeconomics of Trend Inflation." *Journal of Economic Literature* 52(3):679–739.

Attanasio, O. 1999. "Consumption." In J. B. Taylor and M. Woodford, eds., *Handbook of Macroeconomics*, vol. 1B, pp. 741–812. North Holland, Amsterdam.

Azariadis, C. 1975. "Implicit Contracts and Underemployment Equilibria." *Journal of Political Economy* 83(6): 1183–1202.

Azariadis, C. 1981. "Self Fulfilling Prophecies." *Journal of Economic Theory* 25(2):380–396.

Azariadis, C. 1993. *Intertemporal Macroeconomics*. Blackwell, Oxford.

Azariadis, C., and R. Guesnerie. 1986. "Sunspots and Cycles." *Review of Economic Studies* 53(5):725–737.

Bachelier, L. J. B. A. 1900. *Theorie de la Speculation*. Gauthier Villars, Paris.

Backus, D. and J. Driffill. 1985a. "Inflation and Reputation." *American Economic Review* 75(3):530–538.

Backus, D. and J. Driffill. 1985b. "Rational Expectations and Policy Credibility following a Change in Regime." *Review of Economic Studies* 52(2):211–221.

Backus, D., and P. J. Kehoe. 1992. "International Evidence on the Historical Properties of Business Cycles." *American Economic Review* 82(4):864–888.

Bagehot, W. 1873. *Lombard Street: A Description of the Money Market*. King P. S., London.

Bailey, M. J. 1956. "The Welfare Cost of Inflationary Finance." *Journal of Political Economy* 64(2):93–110.

Baily, M. N. 1974. "Wages and Employment under Uncertain Demand." *Review of Economic Studies* 41(1):37–50.

Bairoch, P. 1993. *Economics and World History*. University of Chicago Press, Chicago.

Ball, L., and D. Romer. 1990. "Real Rigidities and the Non-neutrality of Money." *Review of Economic Studies* 57(2):183–203.

Barro, R. J. 1974. "Are Government Bonds Net Wealth?" *Journal of Political Economy* 82(6):1095–1117.

Barro, R. J. 1976. "Rational Expectations and the Role of Monetary Policy." *Journal of Monetary Economics* 2(1):1–32.

Barro, R. J. 1977. "Unanticipated Money Growth and Unemployment in the United States." *American Economic Review* 67(2):101–115.

Barro, R. J. 1978. "Unanticipated Money, Output, and the Price Level in the United States." *Journal of Political Economy* 86(4):549–580.

Barro, R. J. 1979. "On the Determination of Public Debt." *Journal of Political Economy* 87(5):940–971.

Barro, R. J. 1986. "Reputation in a Model of Monetary Policy with Incomplete Information." *Journal of Monetary Economics* 17(1):3–20.

Barro, R. J. 1989. "The Ricardian Approach to Budget Deficits." *Journal of Economic Perspectives* 3(2):37–54.

Barro, R. J. 1997a. *Determinants of Economic Growth: A Cross Section Empirical Study*. MIT Press, Cambridge, MA.

Barro, R. J. 1997b. *Macroeconomics*. MIT Press, Cambridge, MA, fifth edition.

Barro, R. J., and D. Gordon. 1983a. "A Positive Theory of Monetary Policy in a Natural Rate Setting." *Journal of Political Economy* 91(4):589–610.

Barro, R. J., and D. Gordon. 1983b. "Rules, Discretion and Reputation in a Model of Monetary Policy." *Journal of Monetary Economics* 12(1):101–121.

Barro, R. J., and H. Grossman. 1971. "A General Disequilibrium Model of Income and Employment." *American Economic Review* 61(1):82–93.

Barro, R. J., and R. G. King. 1984. "Time-Separable Preferences and Intertemporal Substitution Models of Business Cycles." *Quarterly Journal of Economics* 99(4):817–839.

Barro, R. J., and X. Sala-i Martin. 2004. *Economic Growth*. MIT Press, Cambridge, MA, second edition.

Basu, S., and A. M. Taylor. 1999. "Business Cycles in International Historical Perspective." *Journal of Economic Perspectives* 13(2):45–68.

Baumol, W. J. 1952. "The Transactions Demand for Cash: An Inventory Theoretic Approach." *Quarterly Journal of Economics* 66(4):545–556.

Bean, C. R. 1994. "European Unemployment: A Survey." *Journal of Economic Literature* 32(2):573–619.

Bean, C. R., P. R. G. Layard, and S. J. Nickell. 1986. "The Rise in Unemployment: A Multi-Country Study." *Economica* 53(supplement):1–32.

Begg, D. K. H. 1982. *The Rational Expectations Revolution in Macroeconomics*. Philip Allan, London.

Benhabib, J., and R. E. A. Farmer. 1999. "Indeterminacy and Sunspots in Macroeconomics." In J. B. Taylor and M. Woodford, eds., *Handbook of Macroeconomics*, vol. 1A, pp. 387–448. North Holland, Amsterdam.

Bernanke, B. S. 1983. "Nonmonetary Effects of the Financial Crisis in the Propagation of the Great Depression." *American Economic Review* 73(3):257–276.

Bernanke, B. S. 2006. "Monetary Aggregates and Monetary Policy at the Federal Reserve: A Historical Perspective." In Board of Governors of the Federal Reserve System, ed., *4th ECB Central Banking Conference*, pp. 1–6. Washington, DC.

Bernanke, B. S., and M. Gertler. 1989. "Agency Costs, Net Worth and Business Fluctuations." *American Economic Review* 79(1):14–31.

Bernanke, B. S., and M. Gertler. 1995. "Inside the Black Box: The Credit Channel of Monetary Policy Transmission." *Journal of Economic Perspectives* 9(4):27–48.

Bernanke, B. S., M. Gertler, and S. Gilchrist. 1999. "The Financial Accelerator in a Quantitative Business Cycle Framework." In J. B. Taylor and M. Woodford, eds., *Handbook of Macroeconomics*, vol. 1, pp. 1341–1393. Elsevier, Amsterdam.

Bernheim, D. B. 1987. "Ricardian Equivalence: An Evaluation of Theory and Evidence." *NBER Macroeconomics Annual* 2:263–304.

Bernheim, D. B. 1989. "A Neoclassical Perspective on Budget Deficits." *Journal of Economic Perspectives* 3(2): 55–72.

Beveridge, W. H. 1944. *Full Employment in a Free Society*. George Allen and Unwin, London.

Bickerdike, C. F. 1914. "A Non-monetary Cause of Fluctuations in Employment." *Economic Journal* 24(95): 357–370.

Binder, M., and M. H. Pesaran. 1995. "Multivariate Rational Expectations Models: a Review and Some New Results." In M. H. Pesaran and M. Wickens, eds., *Handbook of Applied Econometrics*, pp. 139–187. Basil Blackwell, Oxford.

Binmore, K. G. 1983. *Calculus*. Cambridge University Press, Cambridge.

Blackburn, K., and M. O. Ravn. 1992. "Business Cycles in the United Kingdom: Facts and Fictions." *Economica* 59(236):383–401.

Blanchard, O. J. 1985. "Debts, Deficits and Finite Horizons." *Journal of Political Economy* 93(2):223–247.

Blanchard, O. J. 2000. "What Do We Know about Macroeconomics that Fisher and Wicksell Did Not?" *Quarterly Journal of Economics* 115(4):1375–1409.

Blanchard, O. J. 2006. "European Unemployment: The Evolution of Facts and Ideas." *Economic Policy* 21(45): 7–59.

Blanchard, O. J. 2009. "The State of Macro." *Annual Review of Economics* 1:209–228.

Blanchard, O. J. 2016a. "Do DSGE Models Have a Future?" Policy Brief 16-11, August. Peterson Institute for International Economics, Washington, DC.

Blanchard, O. J. 2016b. *Macroeconomics*. Pearson, New York, seventh edition.

Blanchard, O. J. 2018. "On the Future of Macroeconomic Models." *Oxford Review of Economic Policy* 34(1–2): 43–54.

Blanchard, O. J., and P. Diamond. 1989. "The Beveridge Curve." *Brookings Papers on Economic Activity* 1989(1): 1–76.

Blanchard, O. J., and P. Diamond. 1990. "The Cyclical Behavior of the Gross Flows of U.S. Workers." *Brookings Papers on Economic Activity* 1990(2):85–155.

Blanchard, O. J., and S. Fischer. 1989. *Lectures on Macroeconomics*. MIT Press, Cambridge, MA.

Blanchard, O. J., and G. Gali. 2007. "Real Wage Rigidities and the New Keynesian Model." *Journal of Money, Credit, and Banking* 39(Supplement 1):35–65.

Blanchard, O. J., and G. Gali. 2010. "Labor Markets and Monetary Policy: A New Keynesian Model with Unemployment." *American Economic Journal: Macroeconomics* 2(1):1–30.

Blanchard, O. J., and C. Kahn. 1980. "The Solution of Linear Difference Equations under Rational Expectations." *Econometrica* 48(5):1305–1311.

Blanchard, O. J., and N. Kiyotaki. 1987. "Monopolistic Competition and the Effects of Aggregate Demand." *American Economic Review* 77(4):647–666.

Blanchard, O. J., and L. H. Summers. 1986. "Hysteresis and the European Unemployment Problem." *NBER Macroeconomics Annual* 1:15–78.

Blanchard, O. J., and M. W. Watson. 1982. "Bubbles, Rational Expectations, and Financial Markets." In P. Wachtel, ed., *Crisis in the Economic and Financial Structure*, pp. 295–315. Lexington, Lexington, MA.

Blanchard, O. J., and J. Wolfers. 2000. "The Role of Shocks and Institutions in the Rise of European Unemployment: The Aggregate Evidence." *Economic Journal* 110(462):1–33.

Bolt, J., and J. L. van Zanden. 2014. "The Maddison Project: Collaborative Research on Historical National Accounts." *Economic History Review* 67(3):627–651.

Box, G. E. P., and G. M. Jenkins. 1976. *Time Series Analysis: Forecasting and Control*. Holden Day, San Francisco, revised edition.

Boyce, W. E., and R. C. DiPrima. 1977. *Elementary Differential Equations and Boundary Value Problems*. Wiley, New York.

Breeden, D. 1979. "An Intertemporal Asset Pricing Model with Stochastic Consumption and Investment." *Journal of Financial Economics* 7(3):265–296.

Brock, W. A. 1974. "Money and Growth: The Case of Long Run Perfect Foresight." *International Economic Review* 15(3):750–777.

Brock, W. A. 1975. "A Simple Perfect Foresight Monetary Model." *Journal of Monetary Economics* 1(2):133–150.

Brock, W. A., and L. J. Mirman. 1972. "Optimal Economic Growth and Uncertainty: The Discounted Case." *Journal of Economic Theory* 4(3):479–513.

Brunnermeier, M. K. 2008. "Bubbles." In S. Durlauf and L. E. Blume, eds., *New Palgrave Dictionary of Economics*. Macmillan, London, second edition.

Brunnermeier, M. K., and Y. Sannikov. 2014. "A Macroeconomic Model with a Financial Sector." *American Economic Review* 104(2):379–421.

Bruno, M., and J. D. Sachs. 1985. *The Economics of Wordwide Stagflation*. Harvard University Press, Cambridge, MA.

Buchanan, J. M. 1976. "Barro on the Ricardian Equivalence Theorem." *Journal of Political Economy* 84(2): 337–342.

Buchanan, N. S. 1939. "A Reconsideration of the Cobweb Theorem." *Journal of Political Economy* 47(1):67–81.

Buiter, W. 1988. "Death, Birth, Productivity Growth and Debt Neutrality." *Economic Journal* 98(391):279–294.

Burns, A. F., and W. C. Mitchell. 1946. *Measuring Business Cycles*. National Bureau of Economic Research, New York.

Caballe, J., and M. S. Santos. 1993. "On Endogenous Growth with Physical and Human Capital." *Journal of Political Economy* 101(6):1042–1067.

Caballero, R. J. 1990. "Consumption Puzzles and Precautionary Savings." *Journal of Monetary Economics* 25(1): 113–136.

Cagan, P. 1956. "The Monetary Dynamics of Hyperinflation." In M. Friedman, ed., *Studies in the Quantity Theory of Money*. University of Chicago Press, Chicago.

Calvo, G. A. 1978. "On the Time Consistency of Optimal Policy in a Monetary Economy." *Econometrica* 46(6): 1411–1428.

Calvo, G. A. 1983. "Staggered Prices in a Utility Maximizing Framework." *Journal of Monetary Economics* 12(3):383–398.

Calvo, G. A. 1988. "Servicing the Public Debt: The Role of Expectations." *American Economic Review* 78(4): 647–661.

Campbell, J. Y. 1994. "Inspecting the Mechanism: An Analytical Approach to the Stochastic Growth Model." *Journal of Monetary Economics* 33(3):463–506.

Campbell, J. Y., and N. G. Mankiw. 1989. "Consumption, Income and Interest Rates: Reinterpreting the Time Series Evidence." *NBER Macroeconomics Annual* 4:185–216.

Campbell, J. Y., and N. G. Mankiw. 1991. "The Response of Consumption to Income: A Cross Country Investigation." *European Economic Review* 35(4):723–756.

Canova, F. 2007. *Methods for Applied Macroeconomic Research*. Princeton University Press, Princeton, NJ.

Capie, F., C. A. E. Goodhart, and N. Schnadt. 1994. "The Development of Central Banking." In F. Capie, S. Fischer, C. A. E. Goodhart, and N. Schnadt, eds., *The Future of Central Banking*, pp. 1–261. Cambridge University Press, Cambridge.

Cass, D. 1965. "Optimum Growth in an Aggregative Model of Capital Accumulation." *Review of Economic Studies* 32(3):233–240.

Cass, D., M. Okuno, and I. Zilcha. 1979. "The Role of Money in Supporting the Pareto Optimality of Competitive Equilibrium in Consumption-Loan Type Models." *Journal of Economic Theory* 20(1):41–80.

Cass, D., and K. Shell. 1983. "Do Sunspots Matter?" *Journal of Political Economy* 91(2):193–227.

Chamley, C. 1986. "Optimal Taxation of Capital Income in General Equilibrium with Infinite Lives." *Econometrica* 54(3):607–622.

Chari, V. V., and T. J. Kehoe. 1999. "Optimal Fiscal and Monetary Policy." In J. B. Taylor and M. Woodford, eds., *Handbook of Macroeconomics*, vol. 1C, pp. 1671–1745. North Holland, Amsterdam.

Chari, V. V., and T. J. Kehoe. 2006. "Modern Macroeconomics in Practice: How Theory Is Shaping Policy." *Journal of Economic Perspectives* 20(4):3–28.

Chari, V. V., T. J. Kehoe, and E. R. McGrattan. 2009. "New Keynesian Models: Not Yet Useful for Policy Analysis." *American Economic Journal: Macroeconomics* 1(1):242–266.

Cheron, A., and F. Langot. 2000. "The Phillips and Beveridge Curves Revisited." *Economics Letters* 69(3): 371–376.

Chiang, A. 1974. *Fundamental Methods of Mathematical Economics*. McGraw-Hill, New York.

Christiano, L. J. 2002. "Solving Dynamic Equilibrium Models by a Method of Undetermined Coefficients." *Computational Economics* 20(1–2):21–55.

Christiano, L. J., M. Eichenbaum, and C. Evans. 2005. "Nominal Rigidities and the Dynamic Effects of a Shock to Monetary Policy." *Journal of Political Economy* 113(1):1–45.

Christiano, L. J., M. Eichenbaum, and S. Rebelo. 2011. "When Is the Government Spending Multiplier Large?" *Journal of Political Economy* 119(1):78–121.

Christiano, L. J., M. Eichenbaum, and M. Trabant. 2016. "Unemployment and Business Cycles." *Econometrica* 84(4):1523–1569.

Christiano, L. J., M. Eichenbaum, and M. Trabant. 2018. "On DSGE Models." *Journal of Economic Perspectives* 32(3):113–140.

Christiano, L. J., R. Motto, and M. Rostagno. 2014. "Risk Shocks." *American Economic Review* 104(1):27–65.

Christoffel, K., and T. Linzert. 2010. "The Role of Real Wage Rigidity and Labor Market Frictions for Inflation Persistence." *Journal of Money, Credit, and Banking* 42(7):1435–1446.

Chung, S. K. 2015. *Modern Macroeconomics*. MIT Press, Cambridge, MA.

Clarida, R., G. Gali, and M. Gertler. 1999. "The Science of Monetary Policy: A New Keynesian Perspective." *Journal of Economic Literature* 37(4):1661–1707.

Clark, J. M. 1917. "Business Acceleration and the Law of Demand: A Technical Factor in Economic Cycles." *Journal of Political Economy* 25(3):217–235.

Clower, R. 1965. "The Keynesian Counter-Revolution: A Theoretical Appraisal." In F. Hahn and R. Brechling, eds., *The Theory of Interest Rates*, pp. 103–125. Macmillan, London.

Clower, R. 1967. "A Reconsideration of the Microfoundations of Monetary Theory." *Western Economic Journal* 6(1):1–9.

Cobb, C. W., and P. H. Douglas. 1928. "A Theory of Production." *American Economic Review* 18(1):139–165.

Cochrane, J. D. 2005. *Asset Pricing*. Princeton University Press, Princeton, NJ, revised edition.

Crafts, N., and K. H. O'Rourke. 2014. "Twentieth Century Growth." In P. Aghion and S. Durlauf, eds., *Handbook of Economic Growth*, vol. 2A, pp. 263–346. Elsevier, Amsterdam.

Cukierman, A., and A. Meltzer. 1989. "A Political Theory of Government Debt and Deficits in a Neo-Ricardian Framework." *American Economic Review* 79(4):713–732.

Darby, M. 1976. "Three and a Half Million US Employees Have Been Mislaid, or, An Explanation of Unemployment, 1934–1941." *Journal of Political Economy* 84(1):1–16.

Debreu, G. *Theory of Value*. 1959. Yale University Press, New Haven, CT.

DeJong, D. N., and D. Chetan. 2011. *Structural Macroeconometrics*. Princeton University Press, Princeton, NJ, second edition.

DeVroey, M. 2016. *A History of Macroeconomics from Keynes to Lucas and Beyond*. Cambridge University Press, Cambridge.

Diamond, D., and P. Dybvig. 1983. "Bank Runs, Deposit Insurance, and Liquidity." *Journal of Political Economy* 91(3):401–419.

Diamond, P. 1965. "National Debt in a Neoclassical Growth Model." *American Economic Review* 55(5): 1126–1150.

Dixit, A. K. 1990. *Optimization in Economic Theory*. Oxford University Press, Oxford, second edition.

Dixit, A. K., and J. E. Stiglitz. 1977. "Monopolistic Competition and Optimum Product Diversity." *American Economic Review* 67(3):297–308.

Domar, E. D. 1946. "Capital Expansion, Rate of Growth and Employment." *Econometrica* 14(2):137–147.

Downs, A. 1957. *An Economic Theory of Democracy*. Harper and Row, New York.

Drazen, A. 2000. *Political Economy in Macroeconomics*. Princeton University Press, Princeton, NJ.

Dreze, J., and F. Modigliani. 1972. "Consumption Decisions under Uncertainty." *Journal of Economic Theory* 5(3):308–335.

Edgeworth, F. Y. 1895. "Thoughts on Monetary Reform." *Economic Journal* 5(3):434–451.

Eggerstsson, G. B. 2010. "What Fiscal Policy Is Effective at Zero Interest Rates?" In D. Acemoglu and M. Woodford, eds., *NBER Macroeconomics Annual*, vol. 25, pp. 59–112. University of Chicago Press and National Bureau of Economic Research, Chicago.

Eggerstsson, G. B., and P. R. Krugman. 2012. "Debt, Deleveraging, and the Liquidity Trap: A Fisher-Minsky-Koo Approach." *Quarterly Journal of Economics* 127(3):1469–1513.

Eggerstsson, G. B., and M. Woodford. 2003. "The Zero Bound on Interest Rates and Optimal Monetary Policy." *Brookings Papers on Economic Activity* 2003(1):139–211.

Erceg, D. J., D. W. Henderson, and A. T. Levine. 2000. "Optimal Monetary Policy with Staggered Price and Wage Contracts." *Journal of Monetary Economics* 46(2):281–313.

Evans, G. W., and S. Honkapohja. 1999. "Learning Dynamics." In J. B. Taylor and M. Woodford, eds., *Handbook of Macroeconomics*, vol. 1A, pp. 449–542. North Holland, Amsterdam.

Evans, G. W., and S. Honkapohja. 2001. *Learning and Expectations in Macroeconomics*. Princeton University Press, Princeton, NJ.

Ezekiel, M. 1938. "The Cobweb Theorem." *Quarterly Journal of Economics* 52(2):255–280.

Faia, E. 2008. "Optimal Monetary Policy Rules with Labor Market Frictions." *Journal of Economic Dynamics and Control* 32(5):1600–1621.

Faig, M. 1995. "A Simple Economy with Human Capital Accumulation: Transitional Dynamics, Technology Shocks and Fiscal Policies." *Journal of Macroeconomics* 17(3):421–447.

Fama, E. F. 1965. "The Behavior of Stock Market Prices." *Journal of Business* 38(1):34–105.

Fama, E. F. 1970. "Efficient Capital Markets: A Review of Theory and Empirical Work." *Journal of Finance* 25(2):383–417.

Fama, E. F. 2014. "Two Pillars of Asset Pricing." *American Economic Review* 104(6):1467–1485.

Farmer, R. E. A. 1999. *Macroeconomics of Self-Fulfilling Prophecies*. MIT Press, Cambridge, MA.

Favero, C. A. 2001. *Applied Macroeconometrics*. Oxford University Press, Oxford.

Feenstra, R. C. 1986. "Functional Equivalence between Liquidity Costs and the Utility of Money." *Journal of Monetary Economics* 17(2):271–291.

Fischer, S. 1977a. "Long Term Contracts, Rational Expectations and the Optimal Money Supply Rule." *Journal of Political Economy* 85(1):191–205.

Fischer, S. 1977b. "Wage Indexation and Macroeconomic Stability." *Carnegie Rochester Conference Series on Public Policy* 5(1):107–147.

Fischer, S. 1981. "Towards an Understanding of the Costs of Inflation: II." *Carnegie Rochester Conference Series on Public Policy* 15(1):5–41.

Fischer, S. 1990. "Rules versus Discretion in Monetary Policy." In B. M. Friedman and F. Hahn, eds., *Handbook of Monetary Economics*, vol. 2, pp. 1155–1184. Elsevier, Amsterdam.

Fischer, S. 1994. "Modern Central Banking." In F. Capie, S. Fischer, C. A. E. Goodhart, and N. Schnadt, eds., *The Future of Central Banking*, pp. 262–308. Cambridge University Press, Cambridge.

Fischer, S., R. Sahay, and C. Vegh. 2002. "Modern Hyper and High Inflations." *Journal of Economic Literature* 40(3):837–880.

Fisher, I. 1896. "Appreciation and Interest." *Publications of the American Economic Association* 11:1–98.

Fisher, I. 1911. *The Purchasing Power of Money*. Macmillan, New York.

Fisher, I. 1919. "Stabilizing the Dollar." *American Economic Review* 9(1):156–160.

Fisher, I. 1926. "A Statistical Relation between Unemployment and Price Changes." *International Labour Review* 13:758–792.

Fisher, I. 1930. *The Theory of Interest*. Macmillan, New York.

Fisher, I. 1933. "The Debt-Deflation Theory of Great Depressions." *Econometrica* 1(4):337–357.

Fisher, I. 1936. *"100% Money*." Adelphi, New York.

Flavin, M. 1981. "The Adjustment of Consumption to Changing Expectations about Future Income." *Journal of Political Economy* 89(5):974–1009.

Flavin, M. 1985. "Excess Sensitivity of Consumption to Current Income: Liquidity Constraints or Myopia?" *Canadian Journal of Economics* 18(1):117–136.

Flood, R. P., and P. M. Garber. 1980. "Market Fundamentals versus Price-Level Bubbles: The First Tests." *Journal of Political Economy* 88(4):745–770.

Friedman, B. M. 1975. "Targets, Instruments and Indicators of Monetary Policy." *Journal of Monetary Economics* 1(4):443–473.

Friedman, M. 1956. "The Quantity Theory of Money—A Restatement." In M. Friedman, ed., *Studies in the Quantity Theory of Money*. University of Chicago Press, Chicago.

Friedman, M. 1957. *A Theory of the Consumption Function*. Princeton University Press, Princeton, NJ.

Friedman, M. 1960. *A Program for Monetary Stability*. Fordham University Press, New York.

Friedman, M. 1961. "The Lag in Effect of Monetary Policy." *Journal of Political Economy* 69(5):447–466.

Friedman, M. 1968. "The Role of Monetary Policy." *American Economic Review* 58(1):1–17.

Friedman, M. 1969. "The Optimum Quantity of Money." In *The Optimum Quantity of Money*, pp. 1–50. Aldine, Chicago.

Friedman, M. 1970. "A Theoretical Framework for Monetary Analysis." *Journal of Political Economy* 78(2): 193–238.

Friedman, M., and A. J. Schwartz. 1963. *A Monetary History of the United States*. Princeton University Press, Princeton, NJ.

Frisch, R. 1932. *New Methods of Measuring Marginal Utility*. Mohr, Tübingen, Germany.

Frisch, R. 1933. "Propagation Problems and Impulse Problems in Dynamic Economics." In Gustav Cassel, ed., *Economic Essays in Honour of Gustav Cassel*, pp. 171–205. Allen and Unwin, London.

Frisch, R. 1959. "A Complete Scheme for Computing All Direct and Cross Demand Elasticities in a Model with Many Sectors." *Econometrica* 27(2):177–196.

Gali, G. 2008. *Monetary Policy, Inflation and the Business Cycle*. Princeton University Press, Princeton, NJ.

Gali, G. 2011a. "Monetary Policy and Unemployment." In B. M. Friedman and M. Woodford, eds., *Handbook of Monetary Economics*, vol. 3A, pp. 487–546. Elsevier, Amsterdam.

Gali, G. 2011b. *Unemployment Fluctuations and Stabilization Policies: A New Keynesian Perspective*. MIT Press, Cambridge, MA.

Gali, G. 2018. "The State of New Keynesian Economics: A Partial Assessment." *Journal of Economic Perspectives* 32(3):87–112.

Galor, O. 2005. "From Stagnation to Growth: Unified Growth Theory." In P. Aghion and S. Durlauf, eds., *Handbook of Economic Growth*, vol. 1A, pp. 171–293. Elsevier, Amsterdam.

Galor, O. 2011. *Unified Growth Theory*. Princeton University Press, Princeton, NJ.

Galor, O., and D. Weil. 1999. "From Malthusian Stagnation to Modern Growth." *American Economic Review* 89(2):150–154.

Galor, O., and D. Weil. 2000. "Population, Technology, and Growth: From Malthusian Stagnation to the Demographic Transition and Beyond." *American Economic Review* 90(4):806–828.

Geanakoplos, J. 2010. "The Leverage Cycle." *NBER Macroeconomics Annual* 24:1–66.

Gertler, M., and S. Gilchrist. 2018. "What Happened: Financial Factors in the Great Depression." *Journal of Economic Perspectives* 32(3):3–30.

Gertler, M., and N. Kiyotaki. 2011. "Financial Intermediation and Credit Policy in Business Cycle Analysis." In B. M. Friedman and M. Woodford, eds., *Handbook of Monetary Economics*, vol. 3A, pp. 574–599. Elsevier, Amsterdam.

Gertler, M., L. Sala, and A. Trigari. 2008. "An Estimated Monetary DSGE Model with Unemployment and Staggered Nominal Wage Bargaining." *Journal of Money, Credit, and Banking* 40(8):1713–1764.

Gertler, M., and A. Trigari. 2009. "Unemployment Fluctuations with Staggered Nash Wage Bargaining." *Journal of Political Economy* 117(1):38–86.

Ghironi, F. 2018. "Macro Needs Micro." *Oxford Review of Economic Policy* 34(1–2):195–218.

Goodfriend, M., and R. G. King. 1997. "The New Neoclassical Synthesis and the Role of Monetary Policy." In B. S. Bernanke and J. J. Rotemberg, eds., *NBER Macroeconomics Annual*, vol. 12, pp. 231–296. MIT Press, Cambridge, MA.

Goodhart, C. A. E. 1988. *The Evolution of Central Banks*. MIT Press, Cambridge, MA.

Gordon, D. 1974. "A Neoclassical Theory of Keynesian Unemployment." *Economic Inquiry* 12(4):431–459.

Gottfries, N. 1992. "Insiders, Outsiders and Nominal Wage Contracts." *Journal of Political Economy* 100(2): 252–270.

Gould, J. 1968. "Adjustment Costs in the Theory of Investment of the Firm." *Review of Economic Studies* 35(1): 4–56.

Gray, J. A. 1976. "Wage Indexation: A Macroeconomic Approach." *Journal of Monetary Economics* 2(2):221–235.

Grilli, V., D. Masciandaro, and G. Tabellini. 1991. "Political and Monetary Institutions and Public Financial Policies in the Industrial Countries." *Economic Policy* 6(13):342–392.

Grossman, G. M., and E. Helpman. 1991. *Innovation and Growth in the Global Economy*. MIT Press, Cambridge, MA.

Guerrieri, V., and G. Lorenzoni. 2017. "Credit Crises, Precautionary Saving and the Liquidity Trap." *Quarterly Journal of Economics* 132(3):1427–1467.

Haavelmo, T. 1944. "The Probability Approach in Econometrics." *Econometrica* 12(supplement):1–115.

Haavelmo, T. 1945. "Multiplier Effects of a Balanced Budget." *Econometrica* 13(4):311–318.

Haberler, G. 1937. *Prosperity and Depression*. League of Nations, Geneva, 1937.

Hall, R. E. 1978. "Stochastic Implications of the Life Cycle Permanent Income Hypothesis: Theory and Evidence." *Journal of Political Economy* 86(6):971–988.

Hall, R. E. 2005. "Employment Fluctuations with Equilibrium Wage Stickiness." *American Economic Review* 95(1):50–65.

Hansen, A. H. 1949. *Monetary Theory and Fiscal Policy*. McGraw Hill, New York.

Hansen, A. H. 1953. *A Guide to Keynes*. McGraw Hill, New York.

Hansen, G. 1985. "Indivisible Labor and the Business Cycle." *Journal of Monetary Economics* 16(3):309–327.

Hansen, G., and E. C. Prescott. 2002. "Malthus to Solow." *American Economic Review* 92(4):1205–1217.

Hansen, L. P., and K. J. Singleton. 1982. "Generalized Instrumental Variables Estimation of Nonlinear Rational Expectations Models." *Econometrica* 50(5):1269–1286.

Hansen, L. P., and K. J. Singleton. 1983. "Stochastic Consumption, Risk Aversion and the Temporal Behavior of Asset Returns." *Journal of Political Economy* 91(2):249–265.

Harrod, R. F. 1939. "An Essay in Dynamic Theory." *Economic Journal* 49(193):14–33.

Hawtrey, R. G. 1919. *Currency and Credit*. Constable and Company, London.

Hayashi, F. 1982. "Tobin's Marginal q and Average q: A Neoclassical Interpretation." *Econometrica* 50(1): 213–224.

He, Z., and A. Krishnamurti. 2013. "Intermediary Asset Pricing." *American Economic Review* 103(2):732–770.

Helpman, E. 1981. "An Exploration in the Theory of Exchange Rate Regimes." *Journal of Political Economy* 89(5):865–890.

Herbst, E. P., and F. Schorfheide. 2015. *Bayesian Estimation of DSGE Models*. Princeton University Press, Princeton, NJ.

Hicks, J. R. 1937. "Mr Keynes and the Classics: A Suggested Interpretation." *Econometrica* 5(2):147–159.

Hicks, J. R. 1939. *Value and Capital*. Oxford University Press, Oxford.

Hodrik, R. J., and E. C. Prescott. 1997. "Post War U.S. Business Cycles: An Empirical Investigation." *Journal of Money, Credit, and Banking* 29(1):1–16.

Hume, D. 1752. *Essays, Moral, Political and Literary*. Longmann Green, London.

Humphrey, T. M. 1984. "Algebraic Quantity Equations before Fisher and Pigou." *Federal Reserve Bank of Richmond Economic Review*, pp. 13–22, September/October.

Humphrey, T. M. 1991. "Nonneutrality of Money in Classical Monetary Thought." *Federal Reserve Bank of Richmond Economic Review*, pp. 3–15, March/April.

Humphrey, T. M. 1997. "Algebraic Production Functions and Their Uses before Cobb-Douglas." *Federal Reserve Bank of Richmond Economic Quarterly* 83:51–83, Winter.

Inada, K. 1964. "Some Structural Characteristics of Turnpike Theorems." *Review of Economic Studies* 31(1): 43–58.

Intriligator, M. D. 1971. *Mathematical Optimization and Economic Theory*. Prentice-Hall, Englewood Cliffs, NJ.

Jevons, W. S. 1875. *Money and the Mechanism of Exchange*. Kegan Paul and Co., London.

Jevons, W. S. 1884. "The Solar Period and the Price of Corn." In *Investigations in Currency and Finance*, pp. 194–205. Macmillan, London.

Johnson, H. G. 1971. "The Keynesian Revolution and the Monetarist Counter-Revolution." *American Economic Review* 61(2):1–14.

Jones, C. I. 1995. "R & D-Based Models of Economic Growth." *Journal of Political Economy* 103(4):759–784.

Jones, C. I. 2002. *Introduction to Economic Growth*. W. W. Norton, New York.

Jones, C. I. 2016. "The Facts of Economic Growth." In J. B. Taylor and H. Uhlig, eds., *Handbook of Macroeconomics*, vol. 2A, pp. 3–69. Elsevier, Amsterdam.

Jones, C. I. 2017. *Macroeconomics*. Norton, New York, fourth edition.

Jones, C. I., and P. Romer. 2010. "The New Kaldor Facts: Ideas, Institutions, Population and Human Capital." *American Economic Journal: Macroeconomics* 2(1):224–245.

Jorgenson, D. 1963. "Capital Theory and Investment Behavior." *American Economic Review* 53(2):247–259.

Judd, K. L. 1998. *Numerical Methods in Economics*. MIT Press, Cambridge, MA.

Jung, T., Y. Teranishi, and T. Watanabe. 2005. "Optimal Monetary Policy at the Zero Interest Rate Bound." *Journal of Money, Credit, and Banking* 37(5):813–835.

Justiniano, A., G. Primiceri, and A. Tambalotti. 2010. "Investment Shocks and Business Cycles." *Journal of Monetary Economics* 57(2):132–145.

Kaldor, N. 1934. "A Classificatory Note on the Determinateness of Equilibrium." *Review of Economic Studies* 1(2):122–136.

Kaldor, N. 1961. "Capital Accumulation and Economic Growth." In F. A. Lutz and D. C. Hague, eds., *Proceedings of a Conference Held by the International Economic Association*. Macmillan, London.

Kamien, M. I., and N. L. Schwartz. 1981. *Dynamic Optimization: The Calculus of Variations and Optimal Control in Economics and Management*. Elsevier, Amsterdam.

Kehoe, P. J., V. Midrigan, and E. Pastorino. 2018. "Evolution of Modern Business Cycle Models: Accounting for the Great Recession." *Journal of Economic Perspectives* 32(3):141–166.

Keynes, J. M. 1923. *A Tract on Monetary Reform*. Macmillan, London.

Keynes, J. M. 1936. *The General Theory of Employment, Interest and Money*. Macmillan, London.

Keynes, J. M. 1937. "Alternative Theories of the Rate of Interest." *Economic Journal* 47(186):241–252.

Keynes, J. M. 1938. "Letter to Roy Harrod," July 1938.

Kindleberger, C. P., and R. Aliber. 2005. *Manias, Panics and Crashes: A History of Financial Crises*. Wiley, New York.

King, R. G., and S. T. Rebelo. 1999. "Resuscitating Real Business Cycles." In J. B. Taylor and M. Woodford, eds., *Handbook of Macroeconomics*, vol. 1B, pp. 927–1007. North Holland, Amsterdam.

Kiyotaki, N., and J. Moore. 1997. "Credit Cycles." *Journal of Political Economy* 105(2):211–248.

Klein, L. R. 1947. *The Keynesian Revolution*. Macmillan, New York.

Klein, L. R. 1950. *Economic Fluctuations in the United States: 1921–1941*. John Wiley, New York.

Klein, L. R., and A. Goldberger. 1955. *An Econometric Model of the United States: 1929–1952*. North Holland, Amsterdam.

Klein, M. 2013. *Mathematical Methods for Economics*. Pearson, New York.

Klein, P. 2000. "Using the Generalized Schur Form to Solve a Multivariate Linear Rational Expectations Model." *Journal of Economic Dynamics and Control* 24(10):1405–1423.

Knox, A. D. 1952. "The Acceleration Principle and the Theory of Investment: A Survey." *Economica* 19(75): 269–297.

Kocherlakota, N. R. 2010. *The New Dynamic Public Finance*. Princeton University Press, Princeton, NJ.

Koopmans, T. 1965. "On the Concept of Optimal Economic Growth." In J. Johansen, ed., *The Economic Approach to Development Planning*, pp. 225–287. North Holland, Amsterdam.

Koyck, L. M. 1954. *Distributed Lags and Investment Analysis*. North Holland, Amsterdam.

Krause, M. U., and T. A. Lubik. 2007. "The (Ir)Relevance of Real Wage Rigidity in the New Keynesian Model with Search Frictions." *Journal of Monetary Economics* 54(3):706–727.

Kremer, M. 1993. "Population Growth and Technological Change: One Million B.C. to 1990." *Quarterly Journal of Economics* 108(3):681–716.

Kreps, D., and R. Wilson. 1982a. "Sequential Equilibria." *Econometrica* 52(4):863–894.

Kreps, D., and R. Wilson. 1982b. "Reputation and Imperfect Information." *Journal of Economic Theory* 27(2): 253–279.

Krugman, P. R. 1998. "It's Baaack: Japan's Slump and the Return of the Liquidity Trap." *Brookings Papers on Economic Activity* 1998(2):137–187.

Krugman, P. R. 2009a. *The Return of Depression Economics and the Crisis of 2008*. W. W. Norton, New York.

Krugman, P. R. 2009b. "How Did Economists Get It So Wrong?" *New York Times Magazine*, September 2.

Krugman, P. R. 2012. *End This Depression Now*. W. W. Norton, New York.

Kuhn, T. S. 1962. *The Structure of Scientific Revolutions*. University of Chicago Press, Chicago.

Kydland, F. E., and E. C. Prescott. 1977. "Rules Rather Than Discretion: The Inconsistency of Optimal Plans." *Journal of Political Economy* 85(3):473–492.

Kydland, F. E., and E. C. Prescott. 1980. "A Competitive Theory of Fluctuations and the Feasibility and Desirability of Stabilization Policy." In S. Fischer, ed., *Rational Expectations and Economic Policy*, pp. 169–198. University of Chicago Press and National Bureau of Economic Research, Chicago.

Kydland, F. E., and E. C. Prescott. 1982. "Time to Build and Aggregate Fluctuations." *Econometrica* 50(6):1345–1370.

Laffer, A. B. 2004. "The Laffer Curve: Past, Present, and Future." *Backgrounder, The Heritage Foundation*, pp. 1–16, June.

Larsen, R. J., and M. L. Marx. 2014. *Introduction to Mathematical Statistics and Its Applications*. Pearson, New York, fifth edition.

Layard, P. R. G., S. J. Nickell, and R. Jackman. 1991. *Unemployment: Macroeconomic Performance and the Labour Market*. Oxford University Press, Oxford.

Leeper, E. M. 1991. "Equilibria under 'Active' and 'Passive' Monetary and Fiscal Policies." *Journal of Monetary Economics* 27(1):129–147.

Leijonhufvud, A. 1968. *On Keynesian Economics and the Economics of Keynes*. Oxford University Press, Oxford.

Leland, H. 1968. "Saving and Uncertainty: The Precautionary Demand for Saving." *Quarterly Journal of Economics* 82(3):465–473.

Leontieff, W. 1941. *The Structure of the American Economy, 1919–1929*. Harvard University Press, Cambridge, MA.

Lindbeck, A., and D. Snower. 1986. "Wage Setting, Unemployment and Insider-Outsider Relations." *American Economic Review* 76(2):235–239.

Linde, J., F. Smets, and R. Wouters. 2016. "Challenges for Central Banks' Macro Models." In J. B. Taylor and H. Uhlig, eds., *Handbook of Macroeconomics*, vol. 2B, pp. 2185–2262. Elsevier, Amsterdam.

Lintner, J. 1965. "The Valuation of Risky Assets and the Selection of Risky Investments in Stock Portfolios and Capital Budgets." *Review of Economics and Statistics* 47(1):13–38.

Lockwood, B., A. Philippopoulos, and A. Snell. 1996. "Fiscal Policy, Public Debt Stabilization and Politics: Theory and UK Evidence." *Economic Journal* 106(437):894–911.

Long, J. B., and C. I. Plosser. 1983. "Real Business Cycles." *Journal of Political Economy* 91(1):39–69.

Lucas, R. E., Jr. 1967. "Adjustment Costs and the Theory of Supply." *Journal of Political Economy* 75(4):321–334.

Lucas, R. E., Jr. 1972. "Expectations and the Neutrality of Money." *Journal of Economic Theory* 4(2):103–124.

Lucas, R. E., Jr. 1973. "Some International Evidence on Output-Inflation Tradeoffs." *American Economic Review* 63(3):326–334.

Lucas, R. E., Jr. 1976. "Econometric Policy Evaluation: A Critique." *Carnegie Rochester Conference Series on Public Policy* 1:19–46.

Lucas, R. E., Jr. 1977. "Understanding Business Cycles." *Carnegie Rochester Conference Series on Public Policy* 5:7–21.

Lucas, R. E., Jr. 1978. "Asset Prices in an Exchange Economy." *Econometrica* 46(6):1429–1445.

Lucas, R. E., Jr. 1980. "Equilibrium in a Pure Currency Economy." In J. H. Kareken and N. Wallace, eds., *Models of Monetary Economies*. Federal Reserve Bank of Minneapolis, Minnesota.

Lucas, R. E., Jr. 1981. "Discussion of: Stanley Fischer, 'Towards an Understanding of the Costs of Inflation II.'" *Carnegie Rochester Conference Series on Public Policy* 15:43–52.

Lucas, R. E., Jr. 1982. "Interest Rates and Currency Prices in a Two Country World." *Journal of Monetary Economics* 10(3):335–351.

Lucas, R. E., Jr. 1988. "On the Mechanics of Economic Development." *Journal of Monetary Economics* 22(1): 3–42.

Lucas, R. E., Jr. 1996. "Monetary Neutrality (Nobel Lecture)." *Journal of Political Economy* 104(4):661–682.

Lucas, R. E., Jr. 2000. "Inflation and Welfare." *Econometrica* 68(2):247–274.

Lucas, R. E., Jr. 2002. *Lectures on Economic Growth*. Harvard University Press, Cambridge, MA.

Lucas, R. E., Jr. 2009. "In Defence of the Dismal Science." *The Economist*, August 6.

Lucas, R. E., Jr., and E. C. Prescott. 1971. "Investment under Uncertainty." *Econometrica* 39(5):659–682.

Lucas, R. E., Jr., and L. Rapping. 1969. "Real Wages, Employment and Inflation." *Journal of Political Economy* 77(5):721–754.

Lucas, R. E., Jr., and L. Rapping. 1972. "Unemployment in the Great Depression: Is There a Full Explanation?" *Journal of Political Economy* 80(1):186–191.

Lucas, R. E., Jr., and N. Stokey. 1983. "Optimal Fiscal and Monetary Policy in an Economy without Capital." *Journal of Monetary Economics* 12(1):55–94.

Machowiak, B., and M. Wiederholt. 2009. "Optimal Sticky Prices under Rational Inattention." *American Economic Review* 99(3):769–803.

Maddison, A. 1982. *Phases of Capitalist Development*. Oxford University Press, Oxford.

"Maddison Project Database 2018." Growth and Development Centre, University of Groningen. https://www.rug.nl/ggdc/historicaldevelopment/maddison/releases/maddison-project-database-2018.

Malinvaud, E. 1987. "The Overlapping Generations Model in 1947." *Journal of Economic Literature* 25(1): 103–105.

Malthus, T. R. 1798. *An Essay on the Principle of Population*. J. Johnson, London.

Mankiw, N. G. 1985. "Small Menu Costs and Large Business Cycles: A Macroeconomic Model of Monopoly." *Quarterly Journal of Economics* 100(2):529–537.

Mankiw, N. G. 1989. "Real Business Cycles: A New Keynesian Perspective." *Journal of Economic Perspectives* 3(3):79–90.

Mankiw, N. G. 2006. "The Macroeconomist as Scientist and Engineer." *Journal of Economic Perspectives* 20(4): 29–46.

Mankiw, N. G. 2016. *Macroeconomics*. Worth, New York, ninth edition.

Mankiw, N. G., and R. Reis. 2002. "Sticky Information versus Sticky Prices: A Proposal to Replace the New Keynesian Phillips Curve." *Quarterly Journal of Economics* 117(4):1295–1328.

Mankiw, N. G., and D. Romer, eds. 1991. *New Keynesian Economics* vols. 1 and 2. MIT Press, Cambridge, MA.

Mankiw, N. G., D. Romer, and D. Weil. 1992. "A Contribution to the Empirics of Economic Growth." *Quarterly Journal of Economics* 107(2):407–438.

Marshall, A. 1871. "Money." In J. Whittaker, ed., *The Early Economic Writings of Alfred Marshall*. Macmillan, London.

Marshall, A. 1887. "Remedies for Fluctuations in General Prices." In A. C. Pigou, ed., *Memorials of Alfred Marshall*. Macmillan, London.

Marshall, A. 1923. *Money, Credit and Commerce*. Macmillan, London.

McCallum, B. T. 1981. "Price Level Determinacy with an Interest Rate Policy Rule and Rational Expectations." *Journal of Monetary Economics* 8(3):319–329.

McCallum, B. T. 1983. "On Non-uniqueness in Rational Expectations Models: An Attempt at Perspective." *Journal of Monetary Economics* 11(1):139–168.

McCallum, B. T. 1988. "Robustness Properties of a Rule for Monetary Policy." *Carnegie Rochester Conference Series on Public Policy* 29:173–204.

McCandles, G. T., and W. E. Weber. 1995. "Some Monetary Facts." *Federal Reserve Bank of Minneapolis Quarterly Review* 19:2–11.

McDonald, I. M., and R. M. Solow. 1981. "Wage Bargaining and Unemployment." *American Economic Review* 71(5):896–908.

McGough, B., G. D. Rudenbusch, and J. C. Williams. 2005. "Using a Long Term Interest Rate as the Monetary Policy Instrument." *Journal of Monetary Economics* 52(5):855–879.

Mehra, R., and E. C. Prescott. 1985. "The Equity Premium: A Puzzle." *Journal of Monetary Economics* 15(2): 145–161.

Meltzer, A. 1987. "Limits of Short Run Stabilization Policy." *Economic Inquiry* 25(1):1–14.

Meltzer, A. 1995. "Monetary, Credit and (Other) Transmission Processes: A Monetarist Perspective." *Journal of Economic Perspectives* 9(4):49–72.

Merton, R. C. 1969. "Lifetime Portfolio Selection under Uncertainty: The Continuous-Time Case." *Review of Economics and Statistics* 51(3):247–258.

Merton, R. C. 1971. "Optimum Consumption and Portfolio Rules in a Continuous-Time Model." *Journal of Economic Theory* 3(4):373–413.

Merton, R. C. 1973. "An Intertemporal Capital Asset Pricing Model." *Econometrica* 41(5):867–888.

Merz, M. 1995. "Search in the Labor Market and the Real Business Cycle." *Journal of Monetary Economics* 36(2):269–300.

Michaillat, P. 2012. "Do Matching Frictions Explain Unemployment? Not in Bad Times." *American Economic Review* 102(4):1721–1750.

Michaillat, P., and E. Saez. 2015. "Aggregate Demand, Idle Time and Unemployment." *Quarterly Journal of Economics* 130(2):507–569.

Mill, J. S. 1833. "The Currency Juggle." *Tait's Edinburgh Magazine*, January, pp. 461–467.

Mill, J. S. 1848. *Principles of Political Economy*. J. W. Parker, London.

Mirlees, J. A. 1971. "An Exploration in the Theory of Optimal Income Taxation." *Review of Economic Studies* 38(2):175–208.

Mishkin, F. S. 1995. "Symposium on the Monetary Transmission Mechanism." *Journal of Economic Perspectives* 9(4):3–10.

Mishkin, F. S. 2016. *The Economics of Money, Banking and Financial Markets*. Pearson, New York, eleventh edition.

Modigliani, F. 1944. "Liquidity Preference and the Theory of Interest and Money." *Econometrica* 12(1):45–88.

Modigliani, F., and R. Brumberg. 1954. "Utility Analysis and the Consumption Function: An Interpretation of Cross Section Data." In K. Kurihara, ed., *Post Keynesian Economics*, pp. 388–436. Rutgers University Press, New Brunswick, NJ.

Modigliani, F., and L. Papademos. 1980. "The Structure of Financial Markets and the Monetary Mechanism." In *Controlling Monetary Aggregates*, pp. 111–155. Federal Reserve Bank of Boston, Boston.

Mortensen, D. T. 1986. "Job Search and Labor Market Analysis." In O. Ashenfelter and P. R. G. Layard, eds., *Handbook of Labor Economics*, vol. 2, pp. 849–919. Elsevier, Amsterdam.

Mortensen, D. T., and C. A. Pissarides. 1994. "Job Creation and Job Destruction in the Theory of Unemployment." *Review of Economic Studies* 61(3):397–416.

Moyen, S. and J.-G. Sahuk. 2005. "Incorporating Labour Market Frictions into an Optimising-Based Monetary Policy Model." *Economic Modelling* 22(1):159–186.

Muellbauer, J., and R. Portes. 1978. "Macroeconomic Models with Quantity Rationing." *Economic Journal* 88 (352):788–821.

Mulligan, C. B., and X. Sala-i Martin. 1993. "Transitional Dynamics in Two-Sector Models of Endogenous Growth." *Quarterly Journal of Economics* 108(3):737–773.

Muth, J. F. 1961. "Rational Expectations and the Theory of Price Movements." *Econometrica* 29(3):315–335.

Neftci, S. N. 1978. "A Time Series Analysis of the Real Wages–Employment Relationship." *Journal of Political Economy* 86(2):281–291.

Nerlove, M. 1958. "Adaptive Expectations and Cobweb Phenomena." *Quarterly Journal of Economics* 72(2): 227–240.

Newcomb, S. 1885. *Principles of Political Economy*. Harper and Brothers, New York.

Newell, A., and J. S. V. Symons. 1987. "Corporatism, Laissez Faire and the Rise in Unemployment." *European Economic Review* 31(3):567–601.

Nickell, S. J. 1990. "Unemployment: A Survey." *Economic Journal* 100(401):391–439.

Nickell, S. J. 1997. "Unemployment and Labor Market Rigidities: Europe versus North America." *Journal of Economic Perspectives* 11(3):55–74.

Nordhaus, W. D. 1969. "An Economic Theory of Technological Change." *American Economic Review* 59(2):18–28.

North, D. C. 1990. *Instititutions, Institutional Change and Economic Performance*. Cambridge University Press, Cambridge.

North, D. C., and R. P. Thomas. 1973. *The Rise of the Western World: A New Economic History*. Cambridge University Press, Cambridge.

Ogilvie, S., and A. W. Carus. 2014. "Institutions and Economic Growth in Historical Perspective." In P. Aghion and S. Durlauf, eds., *Handbook of Economic Growth*, vol. 2A, pp. 403–513. Elsevier, Amsterdam.

Okun, A. M. 1962. *"Potential GNP: Its Measurement and Significance."* Cowles Foundation Paper 190. Cowles Foundation, New Haven, CT.

Orphanides, A. 2003a. "Monetary Policy Evaluation with Noisy Information." *Journal of Monetary Economics* 50(3):605–631.

Orphanides, A. 2003b. "The Quest for Prosperity without Inflation." *Journal of Monetary Economics* 50(3): 633–663.

Orphanides, A. 2003c. "Historical Monetary Policy Analysis and the Taylor Rule." *Journal of Monetary Economics* 50(5):983–1022.

Orphanides, A. 2008. "Taylor Rules." In S. Durlauf and L. E. Blume, eds., *The New Palgrave Dictionary of Economics*. Macmillan, London, second edition.

Orphanides, A., and J. C. Williams. 2002. "Robust Monetary Policy Rules with Unknown Natural Rates." *Brookings Papers on Economic Activity* 2002(2):63–118.

Papademos, L., and F. Modigliani. 1983. "Inflation, Financial and Fiscal Structure and the Monetary Mechanism." *European Economic Review* 21(1–2):203–250.

Patinkin, D. 1956. *Money, Interest and Prices*. Harper and Row, New York, second edition.

Persson, T., and L. E. Svensson. 1989. "Why a Stubborn Conservative Would Run a Deficit: Policy with Time Inconsistent Preferences." *Quarterly Journal of Economics* 104(2):325–345.

Persson, T., and G. Tabellini, eds. 1994a. *Monetary and Fiscal Policy*, vol. 1, *Credibility*. MIT Press, Cambridge, MA.

Persson, T., and G. Tabellini, eds. 1994b. *Monetary and Fiscal Policy*, vol. 2, *Politics*. MIT Press, Cambridge, MA.

Persson, T., and G. Tabellini. 2000. *Political Economics: Explaining Economic Policy*. MIT Press, Cambridge, MA.

Phelps, E. S. 1961. "The Golden Rule of Accumulation: A Fable for Growthmen." *American Economic Review* 51(4):638–643.

Phelps, E. S. 1966. "Models of Technical Progress and the Golden Rule of Research." *Review of Economic Studies* 33(2):133–145.

Phelps, E. S. 1967. "Phillips Curves, Expectations of Inflation and Optimal Unemployment over Time." *Economica* 34(135):254–281.

Phelps, E. S., ed. 1970. *Microeconomic Foundations of Employment and Inflation Theory*. W. W. Norton, New York.

Phillips, A. W. 1958. "The Relationship between Unemployment and the Rate of Change of Money Wages in the United Kingdom, 1861–1957." *Economica* 25(100):283–299.

Pigou, A. C. 1913. *Unemployment*. Williams and Norgate, London.

Pigou, A. C. 1917. "The Value of Money." *Quarterly Journal of Economics* 32(1):38–65.

Pigou, A. C. 1941. *The Veil of Money*. Macmillan, London.

Pigou, A. C. 1943. "The Classical Stationary State." *Economic Journal* 53(212):343–351.

Pissarides, C. A. 1985. "Short Run Dynamics of Unemployment, Vacancies and Real Wages." *American Economic Review* 75(4):676–690.

Pissarides, C. A. 1986. "Unemployment and Vacancies in Britain." *Economic Policy* 1(3):499–559.

Pissarides, C. A. 2000. *Equilibrium Unemployment Theory*. MIT Press, Cambridge, MA, second edition.

Pissarides, C. A. 2011. "Equilibrium in the Labor Market with Search Frictions." *American Economic Review* 101(4):1092–1105.

Plosser, C. I. 1989. "Understanding Real Business Cycles." *Journal of Economic Perspectives* 3(3):51–77.

Pontryagin, L. S., V. G. Boltyanskii, R. V. Gamkrelidze, and E. F. Mishchenko. 1962. *The Mathematical Theory of Optimal Processes*. Wiley, New York.

Poole, W. 1970. "Optimal Choice of Monetary Policy Instruments in a Simple Stochastic Macro Model." *Quarterly Journal of Economics* 84(2):197–217.

Prescott, E. C. 1986. "Theory Ahead of Business Cycle Measurement." *Carnegie Rochester Conference Series on Public Policy* 25:11–44.

Ramey, V. A. 2016. "Macroeconomic Shocks and Their Propagation." In J. B. Taylor and H. Uhlig, eds., *Handbook of Macroeconomics*, vol. 2A, pp. 71–162. Elsevier, Amsterdam.

Ramsey, F. P. 1927. "A Contribution to the Theory of Taxation." *Economic Journal* 37(145):47–61.

Ramsey, F. P. 1928. "A Mathematical Theory of Saving." *Economic Journal* 38(152):543–559.

Rebelo, S. 1991. "Long-Run Policy Analysis and Long-Run Growth." *Journal of Political Economy* 99(3):500–521.

Rees, A. 1970. "On Equilibrium in Labor Markets." *Journal of Political Economy* 78(2):306–310.

Reis, R. 2018. "Is Something Really Wrong with Macroeconomics?" *Oxford Review of Economic Policy* 34(1–2): 132–155.

Ricardo, D. 1817. *Principles of Political Economy and Taxation*. J. Murray, London.

Rodrik, D. 2015. *Economics Rules: The Rights and Wrongs of the Dismal Science*. W. W. Norton, New York.

Rogerson, R. 1988. "Indivisible Labor, Lotteries and Equilibrium." *Journal of Monetary Economics* 21(1):3–16.

Rogoff, K. 1985. "The Optimal Degree of Commitment to an Intermediate Monetary Target." *Quarterly Journal of Economics* 100(4):1169–1189.

Rogoff, K. 1990. "Equilibrium Political Budget Cycles." *American Economic Review* 80(1):21–36.

Rogoff, K., and A. Sibert. 1988. "Elections and Macroeconomic Policy Cycles." *Review of Economic Studies* 55(1):1–16.

Romer, C. 1986. "Spurious Volatility in Historical Unemployment Data." *Journal of Political Economy* 94(1): 1–37.

Romer, D. 2018. *Advanced Macroeconomics*. McGraw Hill, New York, fifth edition.

Romer, P. M. 1986. "Increasing Returns and Long Run Growth." *Journal of Political Economy* 94(5):1002–1037.

Romer, P. M. 1990. "Endogenous Technological Change." *Journal of Political Economy* 98(5,2):71–102.

Rotemberg, J. J. 1982a. "Monopolistic Price Adjustment and Aggregate Output." *Review of Economic Studies* 49(4):517–531.

Rotemberg, J. J. 1982b. "Sticky Prices in the United States." *Journal of Political Economy* 90(6):1187–1211.

Roubini, N., and J. D. Sachs. 1989. "Political and Economic Determinants of Budget Deficits in the Industrial Democracies." *European Economic Review* 33(5):903–933.

Sachs, J., and F. Larrain. 1993. *Macroeconomics in the Global Economy*. Prentice-Hall, Englewood Cliffs, NJ.

Samuelson, P. A. 1939. "Interactions between the Multiplier Analysis and the Principle of Acceleration." *Review of Economics and Statistics* 21(2):75–78.

Samuelson, P. A. 1948. *Economics*. McGraw Hill, New York.

Samuelson, P. A. 1958. "An Exact Consumption-Loan Model of Interest, with or without the Social Contrivance of Money." *Journal of Political Economy* 66(6):467–482.

Samuelson, P. A. 1965. "Proof that Properly Anticipated Prices Fluctuate Randomly." *Industrial Management Review* 6(2):41–49.

Samuelson, P. A. 1969. "Lifetime Portfolio Selection by Dynamic Stochastic Programming." *Review of Economics and Statistics* 51(3):239–246.

Samuelson, P. A. 1978. "The Canonical Classical Model of Political Economy." *Journal of Economic Literature* 16(4):1415–1434.

Samuelson, P. A., and R. M. Solow. 1960. "Analytical Aspects of Anti-inflation Policy." *American Economic Review* 50(2):177–194.

Sandmo, A. 1970. "The Effect of Uncertainty on Saving Decisions." *Review of Economic Studies* 37(3):353–360.

Sargent, T. J. 1973. "Rational Expectations, the Real Rate of Interest, and the Natural Rate of Unemployment." *Brookings Papers on Economic Activity* 2:429–480.

Sargent, T. J. 1976. "A Classical Macro-econometric Model for the United States." *Journal of Political Economy* 84(2):207–238.

Sargent, T. J. 1982. "The End of Four Big Inflations." In R. E. Hall, ed., *Inflation*, pp. 41–98. University of Chicago Press, Chicago.

Sargent, T. J. 1987. *Macroeconomic Theory*. Academic Press, New York, second edition.

Sargent, T. J., and L. Ljungqvist. 2018. *Recursive Macroeconomic Theory*. MIT Press, Cambridge, MA, fourth edition.

Sargent, T. J., and N. Wallace. 1975. "Rational Expectations, the Optimal Monetary Instrument and the Optimal Money Supply Rule." *Journal of Political Economy* 83(2):241–254.

Schmitt-Grohe, S., and M. Uribe. 2004. "Solving Dynamic General Equilibrium Models Using a Second-Order Approximation to the Policy Function." *Journal of Economic Dynamics and Control* 28(4):755–775.

Seater, J. J. 1993. "Ricardian Equivalence." *Journal of Economic Literature* 31(1):142–190.

Shapiro, C., and J. E. Stiglitz. 1984. "Equilibrium Unemployment as a Worker Discipline Device." *American Economic Review* 74(3):433–444.

Sharpe, W. F. 1964. "Capital Asset Prices: A Theory of Market Equilibrium under Conditions of Risk." *Journal of Finance* 19(3):425–442.

Shell, K. 1966. "Toward a Theory of Inventive Activity and Capital Accumulation." *American Economic Review* 56(2):62–68.

Shell, K. 1977. "Monnaie et Allocation Intertemporelle." Seminaire d'Econometrie, Roy-Malinvaud, Centre Nationale de la Recherche Scientifique, Paris, November.

Shiller, R. J. 1981. "Do Stock Prices Move Too Much To Be Justified by Subsequent Changes in Dividends?" *American Economic Review* 71(3):421–436.

Shiller, R. J. 2003. "From Efficient Markets Theory to Behavioral Finance." *Journal of Economic Perspectives* 17(1):83–104.

Shiller, R. J. 2014. "Speculative Asset Prices." *American Economic Review* 104(6):1486–1517.

Shimer, R. 2005. "The Cyclical Behavior of Equilibrium Unemployment and Vacancies." *American Economic Review* 95(1):25–49.

Shimer, R. 2009. "Convergence in Macroeconomics: The Labor Wedge." *American Economic Journal: Macroeconomics* 1(1):280–297.

Shimer, R. 2010. *Labor Markets and Business Cycles*. Princeton University Press, Princeton, NJ.

Shleifer, A. 2000. *Inefficient Markets*. Oxford University Press, Oxford, 2000.

Sidrauski, M. 1967. "Rational Choice and Patterns of Growth in a Monetary Economy." *American Economic Review* 57(2):534–544.

Simon, C. P., and L. Blume. 1994. *Mathematics for Economists*. W. W. Norton, New York.

Simons, H. 1936. "Rules versus Authorities in Monetary Policy." *Journal of Political Economy* 44(1):1–30.

Sims, C. A. 1980. "Macroeconomics and Reality." *Econometrica* 48(1):1–48.

Sims, C. A. 1994. "A Simple Model for the Determination of the Price Level and the Interaction of Monetary and Fiscal Policy." *Economic Theory* 4(3):381–391.

Sims, C. A. 2002. "Solving Linear Rational Expectations Models." *Computational Economics* 20(1–2):1–20.

Sims, C. A. 2003. "Implications of Rational Inattention." *Journal of Monetary Economics* 50(3):665–690.

Skidelsky, R. 2009. *Keynes: The Return of the Master*. Penguin Books, London.

Slutsky, E. E. 1915. "Sulla Teoria del Bilancio den Consumatore." *Giornale degli Economisti* 51(1):1–26.

Slutsky, E. E. 1937. "The Summation of Random Causes as the Source of Cyclic Processes." *Econometrica* 5(2): 105–146.

Smets, F., and R. Wouters. 2003. "An Estimated Dynamic Stochastic General Equilibrium Model of the Euro Area." *Journal of the European Economic Association* 1(5):1123–1175.

Smets, F., and R. Wouters. 2007. "Shocks and Frictions in US Business Cycles: A Bayesian DSGE Approach." *American Economic Review* 97(3):586–606.

Smith, A. 1776. *An Inquiry into the Nature and Causes of the Wealth of Nations*. W. Strachan and T. Cadell, London.

Solow, R. M. 1956. "A Contribution to the Theory of Economic Growth." *Quarterly Journal of Economics* 70(1): 65–94.

Solow, R. M. 1980. "On Theories of Unemployment." *American Economic Review* 70(1):1–11.

Solow, R. M. 2008. "The State of Macroeconomics." *Journal of Economic Perspectives* 22(1):243–246.

Stadler, G. W. 1994. "Real Business Cycles." *Journal of Economic Literature* 32(4):1750–1783.

Stiglitz, J. E. 2014. "Reconstructing Macroeconomic Theory to Manage Economic Policy." NBER Working Paper 20517, September. National Bureau of Economic Research, Cambridge, MA.

Stiglitz, J. E. 2018. "Where Modern Macroeconomics Went Wrong." *Oxford Review of Economic Policy* 34(1–2): 70–106.

Stiglitz, J. E., and A. Weiss. 1981. "Credit Rationing in Markets with Imperfect Information." *American Economic Review* 71(3):393–410.

Summers, R., and A. Heston. 1991. "The Penn World Table (Mark 5): An Expanded Set of International Comparisons, 1950–1988." *Quarterly Journal of Economics* 106(2):327–368.

Svensson, L. E. 2001. "The Zero Lower Bound in an Open Economy: A Foolproof Way of Escaping from a Liquidity Trap." *Monetary and Economic Studies* 19(S-1):277–312.

Swan, T. W. 1956. "Economic Growth and Capital Accumulation." *Economic Record* 32(2):334–361.

Tabellini, G. 1985. "Accommodative Monetary Policy and Central Bank Reputation." *Giornale degli Economisti e Annali di Economia* 44(7/8):389–425.

Tabellini, G. 1991. "The Politics of Intergenerational Redistribution." *Journal of Political Economy* 99(2):335–357.

Tabellini, G., and A. Alesina. 1990. "Voting on the Budget Deficit." *American Economic Review* 80(1):37–49.

Taylor, J. B. 1979. "Staggered Wage Setting in a Macro Model." *American Economic Review* 69(2):108–113.

Taylor, J. B. 1980. "Aggregate Dynamics and Staggered Contracts." *Journal of Political Economy* 88(1):1–23.

Taylor, J. B. 1993. "Discretion versus Policy Rules in Practice." *Carnegie Rochester Conference Series on Public Policy* 39:195–214.

Taylor, J. B. 1995. "The Monetary Transmission Mechanism: An Empirical Framework." *Journal of Economic Perspectives* 9(4):11–26.

Taylor, J. B. 1999. "A Historical Analysis of Monetary Policy Rules." In J. B. Taylor, ed., *Monetary Policy Rules*, pp. 319–348. University of Chicago Press and National Bureau of Economic Research, Chicago.

Taylor, J. B., and J. C. Williams. 2011. "Simple and Robust Rules for Monetary Policy." In B. M. Friedman and M. Woodford, eds., *Handbook of Monetary Economics*, vol. 3B, pp. 829–859. Elsevier, Amsterdam.

Thaler, R. H. 2015. *Misbehaving: The Making of Behavioral Economics*. W. W. Norton, New York.

Theil, H. 1954. "Econometric Models and Welfare Maximization." *Weltwirtschaftliches Archiv* 72:60–83.

Theil, H. 1956. "On the Theory of Economic Policy." *American Economic Review* 46(2):360–366.

Theil, H. 1964. *Optimal Decision Rules for Government and Industry*. North Holland, Amsterdam.

Thomas, C. 2008. "Search and Matching Frictions and Optimal Monetary Policy." *Journal of Monetary Economics* 55(5):936–956.

Thornton, H. 1802. *An Enquiry into the Nature and Effects of the Paper Credit of Great Britain*. J. Hatchard and F. & C. Rivington, London.

Tinbergen, J. 1937. *An Econometric Approach to Business Cycle Problems*. Hermann and Cie, Paris.

Tinbergen, J. 1952. *On the Theory of Economic Policy*. North Holland, Amsterdam.

Tirole, J. 1982. "On the Possibility of Speculation under Rational Expectations." *Econometrica* 50(5):1163–1181.

Tirole, J. 1985. "Asset Bubbles and Overlapping Generations." *Econometrica* 53(6):1499–1528.

Tobin, J. 1956. "The Interest Elasticity of the Transactions Demand for Cash." *Review of Economics and Statistics* 38(3):241–247.

Tobin, J. 1965. "Money and Economic Growth." *Econometrica* 33(4):671–684.

Tobin, J. 1969. "A General Equilibrium Approach to Monetary Theory." *Journal of Money, Credit, and Banking* 1(1):15–29.

Treadway, A. B. 1969. "On Rational Entrepreneurial Behavior and the Demand for Investment." *Review of Economic Studies* 36(2):227–239.

Trigari, A. 2006. "The Role of Search Frictions and Bargaining for Inflation Dynamics." IGIER Discussion Paper 304. Milan.

Trigari, A. 2009. "Equilibrium Unemployment, Job Flows and Inflation Dynamics." *Journal of Money, Credit, and Banking* 41(1):1–33.

Uhlig, H. 1999. "A Toolkit for Analyzing Nonlinear Dynamic Stochastic Models Easily." In R. Marimon and A. Scott, eds., *Computational Methods for the Study of Dynamic Economics*, pp. 30–61. Oxford University Press, Oxford.

Uzawa, H. 1965. "Optimum Technical Change in an Aggregative Model of Economic Growth." *International Economic Review* 6:18–31.

Velasco, A. 1999. "A Model of Endogenous Fiscal Deficit and Delayed Fiscal Reforms." In J. Poterba and J. von Hagen, eds., *Fiscal Rules and Fiscal Performance*, pp. 37–58. University of Chicago Press and National Bureau of Economic Research, Chicago.

Vines, D., and S. Wills. 2018. "The Financial System and the Natural Real Interest Rate: Towards a 'New Benchmark Theory Model.' " *Oxford Review of Economic Policy* 34(1–2):252–268.

von Mises, L. 1912. *The Theory of Money and Credit*. English translation by H. E. Batson. Jonathan Cape, London.

Walsh, C. E. 2003. "Labour Market Search and Monetary Shocks." In S. Altug, J. Chadha, and C. Nolan, eds., *Dynamic Macroeconomic Analysis: Theory and Policy in General Equilibrium*, pp. 451–487. Cambridge University Press, Cambridge.

Walsh, C. E. 2005. "Labor Market Search, Sticky Prices and Interest Rate Policies." *Review of Economic Dynamics* 8(4):829–849.

Walsh, C. E. 2017. *Monetary Theory and Policy*. MIT Press, Cambridge, MA, fourth edition.

Wanniski, J. 1978. "Taxes, Revenues, and the 'Laffer Curve.' " *The Public Interest*, Winter.

Weil, P. 1987a. "Confidence and the Real Value of Money in Overlapping Generation Models." *Quarterly Journal of Economics* 102(1):1–22.

Weil, P. 1987b. "Permanent Budget Deficits and Inflation." *Journal of Monetary Economics* 20(2):393–410.

Weil, P. 1989. "Overlapping Families of Infinitely-Lived Agents." *Journal of Public Economics* 38(2):183–198.

Weil, P. 1991. "Is Money Net Wealth?" *International Economic Review* 32(1):37–53.

Weil, P. 2008. "Overlapping Generations: The First Jubilee." *Journal of Economic Perspectives* 22(4):115–134.

Weiss, A. 1980. "Job Queues and Layoffs in Labor Markets with Flexible Wages." *Journal of Political Economy* 88(3):526–538.

Wicksell, K. 1898. *Interest and Prices*. Macmillan, London, English translation, R. F. Kahn 1936 edition.

Williams, J. C. 2014. "Monetary Policy at the Zero Lower Bound: Putting Theory into Practice." Brookings Institution, Washington, DC, January.

Woodford, M. 1990. "The Optimum Quantity of Money." In B. M. Friedman and F. Hahn, eds., *Handbook of Monetary Economics*, vol. 2, pp. 1067–1152. Elsevier, Amsterdam.

Woodford, M. 1994. "Monetary Policy and Price Level Determinacy in a Cash in Advance Economy." *Economic Theory* 4(3):345–380.

Woodford, M. 1995. "Price Level Determinacy without Control of a Monetary Aggregate." *Carnegie Rochester Conference Series on Public Policy* 43:1–46.

Woodford, M. 1999. "Revolution and Evolution in Twentieth-Century Macroeconomics." Presented at "Frontiers of the Mind in the Twenty-First Century." Library of Congress, Washington, DC, June 1999.

Woodford, M. 2001. "The Taylor Rule and Optimal Monetary Policy." *American Economic Review* 91(2):232–237.

Woodford, M. 2003a. *Interest and Prices: Foundations of a Theory of Monetary Policy*. Princeton University Press, Princeton, NJ.

Woodford, M. 2003b. "Imperfect Common Knowledge and the Effects of Monetary Policy." In P. Aghion, R. Frydman, J. E. Stiglitz, and M. Woodford, eds., *Knowledge, Information and Expectations in Modern Macroeconomics*, pp. 25–58. Princeton University Press, Princeton, NJ.

Woodford, M. 2009. "Convergence in Macroeconomics." *American Economic Journal: Macroeconomics* 1(1): 267–279.

Woodford, M. 2011. "Optimal Monetary Stabilization Policy." In B. M. Friedman and M. Woodford, eds., *Handbook of Monetary Economics*, vol. 3B, pp. 723–828. Elsevier, Amsterdam.

Wright, R. 2018. "On the Future of Macroeconomics: A New Monetarist Perspective." *Oxford Review of Economic Policy* 34(1–2):107–131.

Yaari, M. 1965. "Uncertain Lifetime, Life Insurance and the Theory of the Consumer." *Review of Economic Studies* 32(2):137–150.

Yun, T. 1996. "Nominal Price Rigidity, Money Supply Endogeneity and Business Cycles." *Journal of Monetary Economics* 37(2):345–370.

Index

Abel, A. B., 165, 314
Accelerationist hypothesis, 441, 441n25
Accelerators, Samuelson multiplier-accelerator model, 5, 427–429, 427n16
Accounting identities, equations as, 35
Acemoglu, D., 264, 265, 267
Adaptive expectations, 7
  path of inflation and unemployment under, 440–444
  uncertainty and, 273–275
Adaptive learning, 295
AD-AS (aggregate demand–aggregate supply) model, 413, 422–424
Addition, matrix, 661
Additively separable functions, 60, 655, 694
Adjoint matrix, 664
Adjustment costs, investment with, 313–314
  choice of optimal investment, 314–317
  determinants of *q*, 317–318
  dynamic adjustments, 318–320
  gross investment of firm, 315
  investment function, 317
  marginal product of capital, 317
  Rotemberg model, 450, 457n3, 470–473
  uncertainty, 320–327
  user cost of capital, 317
  zero adjustment costs, 317
Adjustment path
  Blanchard-Weil model, 173–177
  Ramsey model, 143–145
Adjustment speed, 163–164
Adverse selection, 541
Aggregate capital accumulation, 216–218, 231
Aggregate consumption over time, 172
Aggregate demand–aggregate supply (AD-AS) model, 413, 422–424
Aggregate demand policies
  aggregate demand function, 422
  impact of, 421, 424–426
  natural rate of unemployment and, 439–447
  rules versus discretion in, 440–444
Aggregate fluctuations, 375–376. *See also* Perfectly competitive model; Recessions; Stochastic growth model
  exogenous preference and productivity shocks, 494–504
  inflation and aggregate fluctuations under Taylor rule, 492–504
  log-linear stochastic growth model, 386–392
  monetary policy and government debt, 26–30
  monetary policy in postwar period, 31–32
  price level and inflation, 22–26
  recession frequency and duration, 18–19
  simplified stochastic growth model, 383–386
  staggered price adjustment, 457–470
  stochastic growth model, 376–377n1, 376–383
  unemployment rates in booms and recessions, 20–22
Aggregate investment, rational expectations equilibrium and, 325–327
Aghion, P., 258n1, 267n13, 592
Aiyagari, S. R., 586, 588
AK models, 236n2, 237n3, 247–248. *See also* Learning by doing
Akerlof, G., 310n12, 457n2, 457n3
Alesina, A., 586, 589, 591–592
Algebra. *See* Linear algebra
Allais, M., 153n1
Almost sure convergence, 713
Alogoskoufis, G., 382n5, 395, 403, 404n7, 475n1, 483n11, 499n20, 500n22, 502n24, 503n26, 571n18, 626n6, 628n11
Andolfatto, D., 532, 534
Andres, J., 535
Angeletos, M., 411, 586, 588
"Animal spirits." *See* Sunspots
Antidiagonals, 662
Anti-inflationary reputation, 560–562
ARMA (autoregressive moving average), 720
Arrow, K. J., 231, 232–233, 234. *See also* Arrow-Debreu model; Arrow-Romer model
Arrow-Debreu model, 7

Arrow-Romer model
Arrow-Romer-Blanchard-Weil model, 242–244
Arrow-Romer-Ramsey model, 239–241
convergence in, 247–248
defined, 232–233
endogenous growth rate, 238–239
externalities from capital accumulation, 234–237
fiscal policy, 245–247
production function, 233–234
real interest rate, 237–238
real wages, 237–238
savings rate, 238–239
suboptimality of the competitive equilibrium, 241–242
variables, 233
Asset purchases, 575
Asymmetric information, 541
Asymptotic convergence, 99, 99n7
Augmented matrix, 662, 664–665
Automatic stabilizers, 585–586
Autoregression, vector, 720–721
Autoregressive moving average (ARMA), 720
Autoregressive processes
autoregressive stochastic processes, 718–719
first-order linear expectational models, 279–286
multivariate linear models, 291–293
rational expectations for, 277–279
second-order linear expectational models, 286–291
simplified stochastic growth model, 385–386, 389, 391
Average real interest rate, 131
Azariadis, C., 10, 159n5, 478n6, 612n9, 613, 618, 620n14

Backus, D., 18n31, 561
Backward-looking expectations, 440
Bairoch, P., 13
Balanced budget multiplier, 418
Balanced growth path. *See* Steady state
Banking school, 552
Bank of Amsterdam, 333
Bank of England, 31, 333
Banks. *See* Central banks
Barro. R. J., 6, 43n7, 79n15, 153–154n1, 188, 201n6, 232, 248n6, 266, 267n13, 395, 396n1, 403, 447n30, 503n25, 535, 558, 561, 581, 586, 588, 625. *See also* Barro tax-smoothing model
Barro tax-smoothing model, 581–583
Barter, 331
Baumol, W. J., 6, 336n5
Behavioral relations, equations as, 35
Bellman, Richard, 698
Bellman equation, 300, 515, 697–699
Bellman principle of optimality, 303
Bellman value function, 698
Benhabib, J., 602n3, 619
Bernanke, B. S., 333n4, 335, 411n10, 412, 543, 553n3, 565n12, 626n7
Bernoulli, Jacob, 708
Bernoulli distribution, 708
Bernoulli equation, 110–111
Beveridge curve, 510, 513, 514, 521, 522, 524–529, 531, 532, 536
Binder, M., 291, 293
Bivariate distribution, 714
Blanchard, O. J., 4n6, 9, 55, 154, 169, 170, 291–292, 483, 457n2, 468, 475n1, 476n4, 478n6, 478n7, 483–486, 502n23, 531, 535, 601n2, 602n4, 625, 626n6, 628. *See also* Blanchard-Kahn linear model solution method; Blanchard-Weil model
Blanchard-Kahn linear model solution method, 291–294
Blanchard-Weil model
aggregation across generations, 172
assumptions of, 169, 169n8
balanced growth path in, 173–177
discrete time model, 178
dynamic simulations, 177–182, 194–201, 227–229
efficiency units of labor, 173
externalities and endogenous growth in, 242–244
fiscal policy, 191–201
intertemporal utility function, 170–171
monetary growth in, 222–229
time period, 154
variables, 169–170
Bolton, P., 592
Bonds, 77, 540
Borrowing constraints, precautionary savings and, 310–311
Boundary values, 668, 670
Bretton Woods system, 31
British Bank Act (1844), 552
Brumberg, R., 6, 297n1, 307, 311
Brunnermeier, M. K., 544, 601n2, 609n6, 612n8
Bubbles
defined, 281, 601
deterministic, 604–605
versus fundamentals, 603
linear rational expectations model example, 602–603
money market, 609–611
ruling out unstable, 611–612
as self-fulfilling prophecies, 605–607
stochastic bursting, 605
stock market, 607–608
Buchanan, J. M., 188n2
Buchanan, N. S., 271n3, 275n4
Budget constraints
in Blanchard-Weil model, 201
consumer choice under, 645–647
government budget constraint, 185–187
in imperfectly competitive model, 452–453
money in the utility function approach, 351–353
optimization under, 644–651

in Ramsey model, 130–131
in two-period competitive model, 43–44, 57–58, 70, 78
Burns, A. F., 8–9, 627
Bursting bubbles, 605
Business Cycle Dating Committee, 18
Business cycle theory, 55, 68–69
Business gross profits taxation, 203–205

Caballe, J., 254
Caballero, R. J., 310
Cagan, P., 269n1, 283, 365, 368, 609–610. *See also* Cagan model of money demand
Cagan model of money demand, 283–284, 609–610
Calibrated Blanchard-Weil model, 177–182, 194–201, 227–229
Calibrated Ramsey model, 148–149
Calibrated Solow model, 113–114
Calvo, G. A., 450, 458. *See also* Calvo model of government debt crises; Calvo model of staggered pricing
Calvo model of government debt crises, 593–598
Calvo model of staggered pricing
assumptions of, 450, 457–461
divine coincidence and optimal monetary policy in, 451, 468–469
dynamic simulation of, 469–470
equilibrium conditions, 461–462
imperfectly competitive model with, 459–461
new Keynesian Phillips curve, 450, 462–463, 468, 493
optimal pricing with, 459–461
real and monetary shocks, 464–468
Taylor rule, 463–464
unemployment modeling and, 489–493
Campbell, J. Y., 307n6, 383, 386
Capital, cost of, 313–314
convex adjustment costs, 313–320
fixed accelerator models, 314n2
investment rate, 313n1
marginal product of capital, 317
uncertainty, 320–327
user cost of capital, 317
Capital accumulation. *See also* Convex adjustment costs; Human capital accumulation; Learning by doing
Diamond overlapping generations model, 157–159
externalities from, 234–237
log-linear stochastic growth model, 386–387
Ramsey model, 126–128, 216–218
Solow model, 90–95
Capital income taxation
dynamic effects of, 203–205
dynamic simulations of, 205–206
Cardano, Gerolamo, 703
Cash in advance approach
defined, 209n1
overlapping generations (OLG) models, 355–357, 359
representative household growth model, 353–355, 359
two-period competitive model, 69–70, 71n13
Cass, D., 4, 9, 119, 601, 613, 615n12
CDF (cumulative distribution function), 705
CEIS. *See* Constant elasticity of intertemporal substitution (CEIS) utility function
Central banks
anti-inflationary reputation, 560–562
constitutions of, 559–560
function and history, 332–333
money supply and, 210, 333–335
Central limit theorem, 712, 714
CES. *See* Constant elasticity of substitution (CES) production function; Constant elasticity of substitution (CES) utility function
Chain rules
chain rule of probability, 715
defined, 641
Chamley, C., 586
Characteristic equation, 674
Characteristic polynomials, 679
Chari, V. V., 586, 587, 625
Cheron, A., 534
Chicago Board of Trade, 540
China, per capita output and income in, 13–14, 13n27
Christiano, L. J., 291, 293, 546n7, 554n5, 585n2, 625, 626n6
Christoffel, K., 535
Civil War, monetary policy during, 27
Classical dichotomy, 74
Classical money theory, 2–3, 74
Clower, R., 6, 209n1, 353
Cobb, C. W., 40. *See also* Cobb-Douglas production function
Cobb-Douglas production function
defined, 653
in extended Solow model, 249
in ideas-and-innovations growth models, 259–260
in log-linear stochastic growth model, 388
in one-period competitive model, 40
in Ramsey model, 145, 148
in simplified Diamond model, 159–162
in Solow model, 89–90, 110–111
in stochastic growth model, 377
in two-period competitive model, 48–49
Cobweb model
absence of uncertainty in, 272–273
adaptive expectations hypothesis, 273–275
rational expectations hypothesis, 275–277
supply and demand functions, 271–272
Cochrane, John, 309n11, 624n3
Coefficients, matrices of, 660

Coefficients, undetermined
first-order linear expectational models, 282
second-order linear expectational models, 288–289
Cofactors, 663
Commodity money, 69, 332
Competitive equilibrium models. *See* Dynamic stochastic general equilibrium (DSGE) models
Competitive models. *See* Imperfectly competitive model; One-period competitive model; Perfectly competitive model; Two-period competitive model
Complementary function, 672
Complete linear differential equation, 673
Complex conjugates, 674
Concave functions, 644
Conditional convergence, 110–111
Conditional probability mass function, 714
Conflicts of interest, 542
Constant capital stock condition, 318
Constant coefficients, 669–670
Constant elasticity of intertemporal substitution (CEIS) utility function, 655–657
constant relative risk aversion, 46n8
Frisch elasticity of labor supply, 60
in Ramsey model, 123
in two-period competitive model, 46–48, 54
Constant elasticity of substitution (CES) production function, 90n3, 651–654
Constant elasticity of substitution (CES) utility function, 655
Constant gross investment condition, 318
Constant-intercept Taylor rule, 567n13
Constant relative risk aversion utility function, 46n8
Constant returns to scale, 88
Constraints, budget. *See* Budget constraints
Consumer price index (CPI) inflation
in postwar period, 31–32
stagflation, 24, 31, 434
trends and fluctuations in, 22–26
Consumption. *See also* Demand for money; Euler equation for consumption; Keynesian models; Ramsey representative household model; Utility function
aggregate over time, 172
Blanchard-Weil model, 170–171
consumption capital asset pricing model, 298, 302–303, 307–308
consumption-labor supply in two-period model, 62–69
consumption-leisure choice in one-period model, 56–62
Gray-Fischer-Taylor unemployment model, 478–481
under income constraints, 645–647
life cycle theory, 6
life cycle theory of, 6, 307, 311
marginal propensity to consume, 416
optimal intertemporal path of, 121–124
permanent income theory, 6, 306–307, 517–519
portfolio choice under uncertainty, 297–311
random walk model of, 301–302
smoothing, 45, 305
Consumption beta, 307
Consumption capital asset pricing model (CAPM), 298, 302–303, 307–308
Continuous functions, 635
Continuous probability distributions, 705–706
Continuous time analysis, 83–84
optimal control method in, 696–697
optimal savings in continuous time, 700–702
Continuous uniform distribution, 594, 708–709
Contour maps, 635
Contracts, long-term, 478
Control variables, 693
Convergence
almost sure, 713
asymptotic, 99, 99n7
with Cobb-Douglas production function, 110–111
conditional convergence, 110
in distribution, 713
in probability, 713
Ramsey model, 143–145
for random variables, 712–713
speed of, 104–106
strong, 713
weak, 713
Convertibility, currency, 27, 29–30
Convex adjustment costs, 313–314
choice of optimal investment, 313–317
determinants of q, 317–318
dynamic adjustments, 318–320
gross investment of firm, 315
investment function, 317
marginal product of capital, 317
Rotemberg model, 450, 457n3, 470–473
uncertainty, 320–327
user cost of capital, 317
zero adjustment costs, 317
Convex functions, 644
Copernicus, 343
Correlation coefficient, 715
Costly price adjustment, 450, 457n3, 470–473
Cost of capital. *See* Capital, cost of
Covariance, 715
Cowles Commission, 8
CPI inflation. *See* Consumer price index (CPI) inflation
Cramer's rule, 664
Cukierman, A., 592
Cumulative distribution function (CDF), 705
Currency school, 552
Current savings and investment per efficiency unit of labor, 92

Damped oscillations, 429
Debt, government. *See* Government debt

Decentralized competitive equilibrium, 126–128
Deficits, 185–187, 201n6. *See also* Government debt
Demand for money, 6, 336. *See also* Euler equation for consumption; Money supply
aggregate capital accumulation, 216–218
Cagan model of money demand, 283–284, 609–610
cash in advance approach, 69–70, 71n13, 209n1, 353–359
classical money theory, 2–3, 74
factors determining, 329–330, 336–339
first-order conditions for optimum, 212–213
inflation and growth rate of money supply, 214–215
money demand function, 213–214, 336–339, 336n5, 420–421, 480
money in the utility function approach, 71n13, 209n1, 211–212
neutrality of money, 71–74, 209–211
opportunity cost of real money balances, 212
perfectly competitive models, 400
quantity theory of money, 71
real money balances, 336
real versus nominal variables, 69, 209
superneutrality of money, 210, 220–221
welfare costs of inflation, 221–222, 345
De Moivre's theorem, 688
Derivatives of functions, 635–642
Descartes, René, 634
Determinants, 662–663
Deterministic bubbles, 604–605
Deterministic models, 7–10, 273. *See also* Overlapping generations (OLG) models; Representative household growth model
Diagonals and diagonalization, 661–662, 665
Diamond, D., 543
Diamond, P., 4, 9, 55, 119n2, 121, 153, 154, 531, 601. *See also* Diamond overlapping generations model
Diamond overlapping generations model
assumptions of, 153–154
balanced growth path in, 159–160
basis of, 153n1
capital accumulation and dynamic adjustment, 157–159
dynamic inefficiency in, 164–165
dynamic simulations of calibrated Diamond model, 165–168
intertemporal utility function, 155–156
markets and household behavior, 156–157
population growth, 161–162
production function, 155
pure rate of time preference, 160–161
self-fulfilling expectations, 159n5
simplified, 159–164
time period, 154
total factor productivity, 162
variables, 155
welfare implications, 164–165
Difference equations
first-order linear, 686–687, 689–692
lag operators, 683–685
second-order linear, 687–689
Differential equations
boundary values, 668
defined, 667–669
first-order linear, 669–672, 675–682
general solutions, 668
linear versus nonlinear, 668
particular solutions, 668
second-order linear, 673–675
Differentiation, 637
Digital money, 69
Direct finance, 540
Discrete probability distributions, 704–705
Discrete time. *See also* Stochastic processes
Blanchard-Weil model in, 178
intertemporal models in, 82–84
Ramsey model in, 146–148
Solow model in, 112–113
Discrete uniform distribution, 707–708
Discretionary aggregate demand policies, 414
Discretionary monetary and fiscal policy, 429–430
credibility issues, 556
with full employment target, 431–432
Tinbergen-Theil theory, 431
Distortionary taxation, 76, 201–203
Distribution, convergence in, 713
Distributional considerations, politics and, 589–590
Distributions, probability. *See* Probability distributions
Divergent oscillations, 429
Diversification, 541
Divine coincidence, 451, 468–469, 501–502
Dixit, A. K., 454n1, 482n10, 633n1, 693n1
Domar, E. D., 4, 87, 106, 653
Douglas, P. H., 40
Downsian median voter models, 590
Drachma, monetary reform of, 346
Drazen, A., 590, 592
Dreze, J., 310
Driffill, J., 561
DSGE. *See* Dynamic stochastic general equilibrium (DSGE) models
Dybvig, P., 543
Dynamic inefficiency, 101, 164–165
Dynamic programming, 697–699
Dynamic Ramsey approach, 586–587
Dynamic simulations
Blanchard-Weil model, 177–182, 194–201, 227–229
Calvo model of staggered pricing, 469–470
Diamond model, 165–168
Gray-Fischer-Taylor unemployment model, 504–506
log-linear stochastic growth model, 391–392
Ramsey model, 149–152
Solow model, 114–117

Dynamic stochastic general equilibrium (DSGE) models, 7, 375–376. *See also* Gray-Fischer-Taylor unemployment model; Imperfectly competitive model; Perfectly competitive model
history of, 7–10
log-linear stochastic growth model, 386–392
policy evaluation and, 628–629
shortcomings of, 625–626, 626n8
simplified stochastic growth model, 383–386
stochastic growth model, 376–377n1, 376–383
Dynamic stochastic models under rational expectations. *See also* Stochastic processes
characteristics of, 269–271
first-order linear expectational models, 279–286
learning dynamics, 295
multivariate linear models, 291–293
rational expectations for linear autoregressive processes, 277–279
rational expectations hypothesis, 275–277
second-order linear expectational models, 286–291

Econometric models, 5, 627
Econometrics, 8n21
Economic growth process, Kaldor facts of, 107, 265–266
Edgeworth, F. Y., 552
Education, spending on, 249–250
Effective federal funds rate, 566
Efficiency units of labor
in Blanchard-Weil model, 173
in Solow model, 91–92
in stochastic growth model, 378–380
Efficiency wage theories, 477–478
Efficient markets hypothesis (EMH), 308–310
Eggerstsson, G. B., 544, 573, 574, 585n2
Eigenvalues, 665, 676–682
Eigenvectors, 665, 679–682
Elasticity of labor supply, 397
Elasticity of steady state output, 101–102
Elasticity of substitution. *See also* Constant elasticity of intertemporal substitution (CEIS) utility function
constant elasticity of substitution (CES) production function, 90n3, 651–654
constant elasticity of substitution (CES) utility function, 655
Electoral factors, fiscal policy and, 590–592
Elements, matrix, 660
EMH (efficient markets hypothesis), 308–310
Empirical macroeconomics, role of, 626–628
Employment. *See* Labor market; Unemployment modeling; Unemployment rates
Endogenous-growth models, 231–232. *See also* Learning by doing; Solow model
defined, 96
extended Solow model, 249–252
ideas-and-innovations growth models, 258–262
institutions and long-run growth, 263–265
Jones model of human capital accumulation, 252–253
Kaldor facts of economic growth, 265–266
Lucas model, 253–258
savings rate and, 238–239
unified growth theory, 262–263
Endogenous variables, 35, 634, 663–666
Endowment economies, 347–351
Endowments, household, 36–38
Envelope theorem, 300
Equilibrium conditions. *See also* Equilibrium unemployment; General intertemporal equilibrium
in Calvo model of government debt crises, 593
in Calvo model of staggered pricing, 461–462
equations as, 35
with high inflation, 368
in IS-LM model, 419, 420
in labor market, 62, 66
in Lucas model, 403–406
in market for goods and services, 417
in perfectly competitive model, 398–400
in product market, 61–62, 66
rational expectations equilibrium, 325–327
short-run equilibrium in money market, 339–342
in Solow model, 85–86
staggered price adjustment and, 461–462
sunspots, 601–602, 612–620
time-consistent equilibrium, 561
time-inconsistent reputational equilibrium, 561
Equilibrium state. *See* Steady state
Equilibrium unemployment, 509–510
Beveridge curve, 510, 513
dynamic adjustment to steady state, 527–534
firms and creation of vacancies, 513–517
flows into and out of employment, 512–513
job destruction, 527
labor market flows, 512–513
labor market tightness, 509
labor productivity, 523–525
matching function, 510–512
nominal rigidities and, 534–535
numerical simulations of, 532–534
real interest rate and, 527
unemployed job seeker behavior, 517–519
unemployment benefit, 525–526
wage bargaining and wage equation, 519–521
wage determination and equilibrium unemployment, 521–522
Equity premium puzzle, 308
Erceg, D. J., 462n6, 468n11, 476n3, 502n23, 554n5
Estimation errors, 569
Euler equation for consumption, 702
distortionary taxation and, 202–203
monetary model, 215–216
Ramsey model, 122–123, 129–130, 147
stochastic growth model, 383–384, 387
two-period competitive model, 45–46, 50, 64, 72

Euro, creation of, 346
Evans, G. W., 295
Events
defined, 705
interaction with ideas, 623–630
Excess output, 465
Exchanges, 540
Exogenous growth models, 109. *See also Individual models*
Exogenous stochastic shocks, optimal monetary policy in, 562–564
Exogenous variables, 35, 284–286, 634
Expectational models. *See also* Rational expectations hypothesis
adaptive expectations, 273–275
cobweb model, 271–277
expectations theory of the term structure, 567
first-order linear, 279–286
static expectations, 273
Expectations-augmented Phillips curve, 7, 476, 487–488, 501, 547, 554
Expected aggregate employment, 484–485
Expected duration of unemployment, 512
Expected values, 706–707
Expenditure, government. *See* Government expenditure
Exponential function, derivative of, 640
Extended Ramsey model, 377
Extended Solow model, 553n3
balanced growth path in, 250–251
endogenous growth in, 251–252
spending on education/training, 249–250
External finance premium, 542–543
Externalities from capital accumulation. *See also* Learning by doing
Arrow-Romer model, 234–239
Blanchard-Weil model, 242–244
Ramsey model, 239–241
Ezekiel, M., 271n3, 275n4

Factorization
first-order linear expectational models, 281
second-order linear expectational models, 287–288
Faia, E., 535
Fama, E. F., 308n9, 309–310
Farmer, R. E. A., 10, 602n3, 607n5, 619, 620n14
Federal funds rate, 565–566
Federal Open Market Committee, 566
Federal Reserve System, 28, 31, 335, 565–566
Feenstra, R. C., 209n1
Financial accelerator model, 543
Financial intermediation, 541–543
Financial market frictions
finance markets, role of, 539–541
financial intermediation and, 541–543
links between financial sector and real activity, 543–544
in model with unemployment persistence and nominal wage contracts, 546–548
in new Keynesian model with staggered pricing, 544–546
open market operations, 565–566
stock market bubbles, 607–611
zero lower bound on interest rates, 571–576, 585–586
Firm behavior. *See also* Investment decisions of firms; Production functions
creation of vacancies, 513–517
in one-period competitive model, 38–40
perfectly competitive model, 397–398
in stochastic growth model, 377–378
technology and optimal output path, 48–49
in two-period competitive model, 65–66
value of firm under uncertainty, 321–323
First difference operator, 83
First moment of random variable, 706–707
First-order linear difference equations
general solutions, 686–687
n first-order, 690–692
pair of, 689–690
First-order linear differential equations
constant coefficients, 669–670
convergence and stability of, 672–673
homogenous, 671–672
nonhomogenous, 671–672
*n*th-order system of, 678–682
pair of, 675–678
variable coefficients, 671
variable right-hand side, 670–671
First-order linear expectational models
economic examples of, 282–284
exogenous variables, evolution of, 284–286
expectational models and, 286
factorization method, 281
law of iterated expectations, 279
repeated substitutions, 279–281
undetermined coefficients method, 282
Fiscal policy, 183–184. *See also* Government debt
in Blanchard-Weil model, 191–201
business gross profits taxation, 203–206
capital income taxation, 203–206
discretionary, 429–433
distortionary taxation, 201–203
endogenous growth and, 245–247
fiscal theory of price level, 363
government budget constraint, 185–187
government debt, 26–30
implications of, 81–82
income taxes and aggregate savings, 78–81
income taxes and labor supply, 76–77
nondistortionary taxation, 201–203
in one-period economy, 74–76
politics in, 589–592
in Ramsey model, 188–191

Fiscal policy (cont.)
Ricardian equivalence, 78–81, 183–184, 187–191, 188n2, 579–580
in two-period economy, 77–78
Fischer, S., 169n7, 221n4, 333n3, 365n14, 457n3, 475, 483, 553n2. *See also* Gray-Fischer-Taylor unemployment model
Fisher, Irving, 3, 42, 55, 119, 121, 153n1, 154n3, 156, 157n4, 212, 269n1, 402n5, 419n9, 435n19, 543, 546, 548, 552, 553. *See also* Fisher equation; Fisher rule
Fisher equation, 72, 72n14, 212, 218, 220, 400, 401, 456, 494,
Fisher rule, 402n5
Fixed accelerator models, 314n2
Fixed inflation rule, 559
Fixed nodes, 678
Fixed-proportions production function, 653
Fixed-proportions utility function, 655
Flexible accelerator model, 6, 314n2
investment under uncertainty, 323–327
value of firm under uncertainty, 321–323
Flood, R. P., 612
Flows into and out of employment, 512–513
Forcing terms, 671
Foresight, perfect, 272–273
Forward guidance, 574
Forward shift operator, 325
Free entry, 516–517
Friedman, M., 6, 221n4, 269n1, 297n1, 307, 311, 333n4, 336n5, 359, 412, 415, 424n13, 437–441, 448, 456, 552, 553, 558n8, 585, 629
Friedman, Milton, 344, 439
Frisch, R., 1n1, 3, 8–9, 8n21, 58–60, 376
Frisch demand for leisure, 60
Frisch elasticity of labor supply, 60, 67, 76, 397, 453
Full employment target, monetary policy with, 431–432
Full rank matrix, 662
Functions, 633–634. *See also* Production functions; Utility function
additively separable, 694
Bellman value function, 698
complementary, 672
conditional probability mass function, 714
constraints, optimization under, 644–651
continuous, 635
cumulative distribution, 705
defined, 634–635
derivatives and partial derivatives of, 635–642
Hamilton, 695–696, 700–702
joint probability mass function, 714
marginal probability mass function, 715
matching, 510–512
maxima/minima, 642–643
objective, 644
probability density, 705–706
probability mass, 705
rational, 684
slope of, 637
stationary points, 642–643
total differential of, 642
Functions, defined, 35. *See also Individual functions*
Fundamental solutions, 280, 601
Fundamental solutions, defined, 603
Future mathematical expectations operator (F), 281, 287

Gali, G., 7n17, 462n6, 464n7, 464n8, 468, 498n19, 502n23, 535, 554n4, 625
Galor, O., 8n19, 262, 263, 267n13
Garber, P. M., 612
Gauss-Jordan elimination, 664
GDP (gross domestic product). *See* Gross domestic product (GDP)
Geanakoplos, J., 543
General intertemporal equilibrium
concept of, 33
and determination of output and employment, 61–62, 66–68
one-period competitive model, 40–42
perfectly competitive model, 398–400
two-period competitive model, 49–55
Generalized Solow model, 109n13, 232
General solutions, 668, 670
General Theory of Employment, Interest and Money, The (Keynes), 1, 3, 413, 416, 416n3, 475–476, 623. *See also* Keynesian models
Geometric polynomials, 684–685
Gertler, M., 333n4, 535, 543, 544, 626n7
Ghironi, F., 625, 626n7
Global maximums, 644
Global minimums, 644
GNI. *See* Gross national income (GNI) per capita
Goldberger, A., 5, 8, 627
Golden rule capital stock, 100
Golden rule savings rate, 99–101
Gold standard, 23, 26–30, 552
Goodfriend, M., 7, 461n5, 494n14, 625
Gordon, D., 447n30, 478n6, 503n25, 558, 561
Gould, J., 314
Government budget constraints, 185–187
Government debt
in Blanchard-Weil model, 191–194
bonds, 77, 540
burden of, 592–593
Calvo model of government debt crises, 593–598
debt-default conditions, 593
debt-deflation theory, 543
debt-holding conditions, 593
debt-holding curve, 594
Keynesian stabilization policy, 585–586
long-run effects, 201n6
monetary policy and, 26–30

multiple equilibria, 580–581, 599–600
optimal dynamic Ramsey taxation, 586–589
overlapping generations models and, 184
in Ramsey model, 188–191
Ricardian equivalence, 78–81, 183–184, 187–191, 188n2, 579–580
rise in, 580
solvency and, 185–187
tax smoothing, 195, 581–584
in two-period competitive model, 77–82
Government deficits, 185–187, 201n6
Government expenditure. *See also* Fiscal policy
in Blanchard-Weil model, 191–192
in one-period economy, 74–76
primary, 78
in Ramsey model, 188–191
in stochastic growth model, 378–380
in two-period competitive model, 77–78
Government intertemporal budget constraint, 78
Gray, J. A., 475
Gray-Fischer-Taylor unemployment model
alternative views of labor market, 477–478
assumptions of, 475–477
dynamic simulations, 504–506
firm pricing and production, 481–483
household consumption and demand, 478–481
inflation and aggregate fluctuations under Taylor rule, 494–502
monetary and real shocks, 504–506
optimal Taylor rule, 502–504
Phillips curve, 488
staggered price adjustment, 489–492
staggered pricing with periodic nominal wage contracts, 492–494
unemployment persistence and wage determination, 485–488
wage setting, 483–487
Great Depression
causes of, 412
government debt during, 28–29
Lucas model and, 410–411
persistence of, 411n10
severity and duration of, 19
theories of, 543
unemployment rates, 20–21
Great Recession (2008–2009), 28–29, 412, 624
Greece, monetary reforms in, 346
Greenbacks, 27
Grilli, V., 592
Gross domestic product (GDP), 11n26, 28. *See also* Recessions
Grossman, H., 6, 535
Grossman, G.M., 258n7
Gross national income (GNI) per capita
cross-country differences, 11–13
defined, 11n26
economic growth and convergence since 1820, 14–17
evolution over time, 13–14
growth rates, 14n28
Growth theory
new growth theory, 8, 8n19
two-period representative household model and, 55
unified growth theory, 8
Guerrieri, V., 544

Haavelmo, T., 8, 418, 627
Half-life, convergence, 106
Hall, R. E., 535
Hamilton function, 121–122, 128–129, 695–696, 700–702
Hansen, A. H., 3, 3n5, 5, 413, 419n8
Hansen G., 262n10, 382n5, 478n8
Hansen L.P., 307n6,
Harrod, R. F., 4n2, 87, 653. *See also* Harrod–Domar model
Harrod–Domar model, 87, 106
Harrod neutral technical progress, 88
Hayashi, F., 314
Hicks, J. R., 3, 5, 58, 89, 231n1, 333n4, 413, 419
Hicksian substitution effect, 58–59
Higher moments, 707
High-powered money, 334
History of macroeconomics
deterministic and stochastic dynamic general equilibrium models, 7–10
Keynesian macroeconomics, 4–5
microeconomic foundations, 6–7
new classical macroeconomics, 7
pre-Keynesian macroeconomics, 2–4
research focus, 1–2
Hodrik, R. J., 18n31, 386
Homogeneous nonstationary stochastic processes, 718
Homogenous differential equations
first-order, 671–672
second-order, 673–674
Honkapohja, S., 295
Household model. *See* Representative household growth model
Human capital accumulation, 232, 248–249
extended Solow model, 249–252
Jones model, 252–253
Lucas model, 253–258
Hume, D., 2, 3, 25, 343
Huygens, Christiaan, 703
Hyperbolic absolute risk aversion (HARA) utility functions, 303
Hyperinflation
Cagan model of money demand, 283–284, 609–610
causes of, 368–371
tackling, 371–372

Ideas-and-innovations growth models
balanced growth path in, 261–262
characteristics of, 258
key elements of, 259–261

Ideas-and-innovations growth models (cont.)
key features of, 258–259
nonrivalrous ideas, 258
rate of technical progress, 261
Ideas/events interaction, 623–624
empirical macroeconomics, role of, 626–628
financial crisis and, 624–626
policy evaluation and DSGE models, 628–629
Identity matrix, 662
Imperfectly competitive model, 446
assumptions of, 451–452
characteristics of, 449–451
full price flexibility, 455–456
natural rates, 455–457
representative firms, 454–455
representative households, 452–454
Implementation errors, 569
Impulse response function, 98–99, 98n6, 116–117
Inada conditions, 88, 94–96, 654
Income effect, 133
Income taxes
aggregate savings and investment and, 81
distortionary taxation, 76
labor supply and, 76–77
Indeterminacy
price level, 361–364
sunspots and, 612–620
Index sets, 715
Inefficiency, dynamic, 101
Infinite horizon growth models. *See also* Ramsey representative household model; Solow model
infinite-horizon transversality condition, 132
infinite-period intertemporal models, 82–84
Inflation
adaptive expectations, 440–444
central bank anti-inflationary reputation, 560–562
equilibrium, 73
fixed inflation rule and monetary policy, 559
growth rate of money supply, 214–215
hyperinflation, 283–284, 368–372
inflationary bias, 444, 558
inflation-based nominal interest rate rule, 401–402
inflation tax, 216–218
long-run neutrality of money, 343–347
money market bubbles and, 609–611
optimal inflation theory, 502–504
in postwar period, 31–32
rational expectations hypothesis, 446–447
relation with monetary growth and seigniorage, 365–367
social welfare loss from, 555–556
stabilization of, 501–502
stagflation, 24, 31, 434
Taylor rule and, 494–504
trends and fluctuations in, 22–26
in two-period competitive model, 69–74
welfare cost of, 221–222, 346
Informational frictions, 411
Initial conditions, 670
Inner products, 661
Insider-outsider model, wage setting in, 483–488
Institutions, long-run growth and, 263–265
Instruments, policy, 429–430
Integrating factor, 669
Integration, 637
Interest rates
average real, 131
Fisher equation, 72, 72n14, 400–401, 456
interest rate pegging and price level indeterminacy, 361–364
in learning-by-doing models, 237–238
nominal, 357–361, 401–402
opportunity cost of real money balances, 212
prime rate, 566
in Ramsey model with money, 216
real, 357–361
in Solow model, 96–97
Taylor rule, 450–451, 463–464, 464n7
term structure of, 566–567
Wicksell interest rate rule, 362–363, 363n12, 401
zero lower bound on, 571–576, 585–586
Intertemporal budget constraints. *See* Budget constraints
Intertemporal logarithmic utility function, 657
Intertemporal model, infinite-period, 82–84
Intertemporal model, one-period
assumptions of, 33–34
consumption and labor supply, 56–62
general equilibrium, 40–42
government expenditure and taxes, 74–77
nature and components of, 34–35
optimal behavior of households, 36–38
profit-maximizing behavior of firms, 38–40
Intertemporal model, two-period
consumption and labor supply, 62–69
fiscal policy, 74–82
general equilibrium, 49–55
implications for growth and business cycle theory, 55
saving and investment, 42–55
Intertemporal optimization
dynamic programming and Bellman equation, 697–699
form of problems, 693–694
optimal control method, 694–697
optimal intertemporal path of consumption, 121–124
optimal savings in continuous time example, 700–702
Intertemporal substitution effect
Ramsey model, 133
stochastic growth model, 381–382, 382n5
Intertemporal utility function. *See* Utility function
Inversion, matrix, 661–663

Investment decisions of firms, 313–314. *See also* Human capital accumulation; Labor market; Savings and investment
- convex adjustment costs, 313–320
- fixed accelerator models, 314n2
- investment rate, 313n1
- marginal product of capital, 317
- uncertainty, 320–327
- user cost of capital, 317

IS-LM model, 3, 3n5, 5, 413, 419–421
- equilibrium conditions, 419, 420
- neo neoclassical synthesis IS-LM functions, 494

Isoquants, 635, 652
Iterated expectations, law of, 279

Japan, per capita GNI (gross national income), 14–17
Jevons, W. S., 552, 613n10
Jevons sunspot theory, 613n10
Jobs. *See* Labor market
Joint probability distributions, 714–715
Joint probability mass function, 714
Jones, C. I., 11n25, 107n11, 109n13, 111n14, 232, 252, 258n7, 265–267. *See also* Jones model of human capital accumulation
Jones model of human capital accumulation, 252–253
Jorgenson, D., 6, 313, 314
Judd, K. L., 291, 293
Jung, T., 573
Justiniano, A., 544

Kahn, C., 291–293, 466
Kaldor, Nicholas, 107, 107n12, 238, 265–266, 271n3, 274
Kaldor facts of economic growth, 107, 265–266
Kehoe, P. J., 18n31, 586–587, 625
Keynes, John Maynard, 1–4, 123n4, 333n4, 336n5, 344, 367n16, 413, 416n3, 417n4, 418n7, 419, 421n10, 424n11, 475–476, 572, 613, 623, 629. *See also General Theory of Employment, Interest and Money, The* (Keynes); Keynesian models; Keynes-Ramsey rule

Keynesia models, 4–5. *See also* New Keynesian models
- AD-AS model, 413, 422–424
- aggregate demand policies, 414, 421, 424–426, 439–447
- characteristics of, 413–415
- discretionary monetary and fiscal policy, 429–433
- IS-LM model, 413, 419–421
- Keynesian cross, 413, 416–419, 417n5, 419n8
- Keynesian revolution, 4n6
- liquidity preference, 336n5
- liquidity traps, 421, 421n10, 572–573
- new Keynesian Phillips curve, 450
- Phillips curve, 414–415, 435–439, 435n19
- Samuelson multiplier-accelerator model, 5, 419, 427–429
- stabilization policy, 585–586

Keynes-Ramsey rule, 123n4
King, R. G., 7, 377n1, 625, 627
Kiyotaki, N., 457n2, 543, 544
Klein, L. R., 4n6, 5n8, 8, 627–628
Klein, M., 633n1, 659n1, 667n1, 683n1, 693n1
Klein, P., 291, 293. *See also* Klein linear model solution method
Klein linear model solution method, 293
Kocherlakota, N. R., 587n3, 588
Kolmogorov, Andrey Nikolaevich, 704
Koopmans, T., 4, 9, 119
Koyck, L. M., 269n1
Krause, M. U., 535
Krishnamurti, A., 544
Krugman, Paul R., 544, 573, 574, 576n21, 585n2, 624n3, 625n4
Kurtosis, 707
Kydland, F. E., 7, 377n1, 446, 447n30, 503n25, 552, 558, 588, 629

Labor, efficiency units of
- in Blanchard-Weil model, 173
- in Solow model, 91–92

Labor market, 478, 509–510. *See also* Labor supply; Unemployment modeling; Wages
- Beveridge curve, 510, 513
- dynamic adjustment to steady state, 527–534
- equilibrium conditions in, 62, 66
- firms and creation of vacancies, 513–517
- flows into and out of employment, 512–513
- job creation, 513–517
- job destruction, 527
- labor augmenting technical progress, 88
- labor productivity, 523–525
- matching function, 510–512
- nominal rigidities and, 534–535
- real interest rate and, 527
- tightness of, 509
- unemployed job seeker behavior, 517–519
- unemployment benefits, 525–526
- wage bargaining and wage equation, 519–521
- wage determination and equilibrium unemployment, 521–522

Labor supply
- efficiency units of labor, 91–92, 173
- efficiency wage theories, 477–478
- Frisch elasticity of, 60, 397, 453
- income and substitution effects on, 58–60
- income taxes and, 76–77
- intertemporal substitution in, 381–382, 382n5
- long-term contracts, 478
- new Keynesian Phillips curve, 450, 462–463, 468, 493
- in one-period competitive models, 56–62
- search or matching theories, 478
- in stochastic growth model, 380–382
- in two-period competitive model, 62–69

Laffer, Arthur, 367n16

Laffer curve, 367–368, 367n16
Lag operators, 281, 683–685
Lagrange, Joseph Louis, 636
Lagrange method, 647–651
in Lucas-Prescott model, 324
in money in the utility function of representative household, 351–352
in one-period competitive model, 37, 57
optimization of, 694–696
in Ramsey model, 147
in Samuelson OLG model with money, 615
in stochastic growth model, 380, 381
in two-period competitive model, 44–45, 63, 70–71
in unemployment model, 480
Langot, F., 534
La'O, J., 411
Laplace, Pierre, 703
Large numbers, law of, 713
Law of iterated expectations, 279
Law of large numbers, 713
Learning approach to expectations, 295
Learning by doing, 231
Blanchard-Weil model, 242–244
convergence in, 247–248
defined, 232–233
endogenous growth rate, 238–239
externalities from capital accumulation, 234–237
fiscal policy, 245–247
production function, 233–234
Ramsey model, 239–241
real interest rate, 237–238
real wages, 237–238
savings rate, 238–239
suboptimality of the competitive equilibrium, 241–242
variables, 233
Leeper, E. M., 363
Leibniz, Gottfried Wilhelm, 636
Leijonhufvud, A., 6
Leisure
consumption-leisure choice in one-period model, 56–58
Frisch demand for, 60
Marshallian demand for, 58–60
Leland, H., 310
Lenders of last resort, 552
Leontieff, W., 87
Leontieff production function, 87, 90, 106, 653
Leverage, 542–543
L'Hopital's rule, 46, 46n9, 125, 653, 655, 657
Lian, C., 411
Life cycle theory, 6, 307, 311
Linear algebra
example with two endogenous variables, 663–666
matrix addition, 661
matrix elements, 660–661
matrix inversion, 661–663
matrix multiplication, 661
matrix subtraction, 661
Linear autoregressive processes
autoregressive stochastic processes, 718–719
first-order linear expectational models, 279–286
multivariate linear models, 291–293
rational expectations for, 277–279
second-order linear expectational models, 286–291
Linear difference equations
first-order, 686–687, 689–692
second-order, 687–689
Linear differential equations
characteristics of, 668
first-order, 669–672, 675–682
second-order, 673–675
Linear functions, derivative of, 638
Linear intertemporal utility function, 657
Linear models
bubbles in, 281, 601–612
defined, 659–660
Linear production function, 653
Linzert, T., 535
Liquidity effect, 340–341, 360–361
Liquidity preference, 336n5
Liquidity traps, 421, 421n10, 572–573
Lira, monetary reform of, 346
Local maxima/minima, 642–644
Location parameters, 706
Lockwood, B., 592
Logarithmic function, derivative of, 640
Logarithmic preferences
portfolio choice under uncertainty, 303–304
simplified Diamond model, 159–162
Log-linear stochastic growth model
capital accumulation process, 386–387
dynamic simulations, 391–392
production function, 386
steady state, 388–391
Long-run economic growth. *See also* Solow model
cross-country differences in per capita output and income, 11–13
economic growth and convergence since 1820, 14–17
evolution in per capita output and income over time, 13–14
growth rates, 14n28
in pre-Keynesian macroeconomics, 2
Long-run neutrality of money, 25–26, 343–347
Long-term contracts, 478
Lorenzoni, G., 544
Lubik, T. A., 535
Lucas, R. E., Jr., 7–9, 8n19, 25, 64n11, 221n4, 232, 253–254, 262n10, 269n1, 307n7, 314, 323, 325, 327, 353, 377n1, 382n5, 395, 403, 404n7, 406n9, 410, 411n10, 412, 446n29, 449–451, 462–463, 468, 473–474, 499n21, 581, 586, 588, 624n3, 625, 627–629, 716. *See also* Lucas and Raping

equilibrium labor market model; Lucas model; Lucas-Prescott model
Lucas and Raping equilibrium labor market model, 411n10
Lucas model
competitive equilibrium under imperfect information, 403–406
equilibrium conditions, 403–406
Great Depression and, 410–411
history of, 403
human capital accumulation, 253–258
informational frictions and rational inattention, 411
monetary shock effects, 407–410
optimal monetary policy in, 410
output and employment, 406–407
Lucas-Prescott model, 323–327
Lump sum taxes, 75

Machowiak, B., 411
Macroeconomic models, concept of, 33–34, 633–634. *See also Individual models*
Maddison, A., 11n26, 13–14
Maddison Project, 14
Main diagonals, 661
Malthus, T. R., 2
Mankiw, N. G., 7, 106, 109n13, 232, 248n6, 249, 266, 307n6, 377n1, 411, 457n2, 625, 629
Marginal change, 637
Marginal probability mass function, 715
Marginal propensity to consume, 416
Marginal propensity to save, 416
Marginal rate of substitution (MRS), 46
Marginal utility, 637
Marshall, A., 3n3, 40, 552
Marshallian demand for leisure, 58–60
Matching frictions in labor market. *See* Matching models of labor market
Matching function, 510–512
Matching models of labor market, 478, 509–510, 535–537
Beveridge curve, 510, 513
dynamic adjustment to steady state, 527–534
firms and creation of vacancies, 513–517
flows into and out of employment, 512–513
job destruction, 527
labor market flows, 512–513
labor market tightness, 509
labor productivity, 523–525
matching function, 510–512
nominal rigidities and, 534–535
numerical simulations of, 532–534
real interest rate and, 527
unemployed job seeker behavior, 517–519
unemployment benefits, 525–526
wage bargaining and wage equation, 517–519
wage determination and equilibrium unemployment, 521–522
Mathematical expectation, 706
Mathematical functions. *See* Functions
Mathematical macroeconomic models, concept of, 33–34, 633–634. *See also Individual models*
Matrices of coefficients, 660
Matrix addition, 661
Matrix inversion, 661–663
Matrix multiplication, 661
Matrix subtraction, 661
Maturity premiums, 540
Maxima of functions, 642–643
Maximum principle, 695–696
McCallum, B. T., 291, 293, 363, 553n3, 564
Mean values, 706–707
Measure theory, 704
Meltzer, A., 333n4, 553, 592
Merton, R. C., 298, 303, 307n7, 311
Merz, M., 532, 534
Metallic monetary systems, 26
Method of substitution, 465–468, 665, 675–676
Method of undetermined coefficients, 673
Mexico, monetary reforms in, 346
Michaillat, P., 535
Mill, J. S., 2, 3, 343, 552
Minima of functions, 642–643
Mirlees, J. A., 588
Mises, Richard von, 704
Mises, L. von, 3
Mitchell, W. C., 8–9, 627
Models, concept of, 33–34, 633–634. *See also Individual models*
Modified golden rule, 138–139
Modigliani, F., 3, 5n10, 6, 297n1, 307, 310–311, 333n4, 413, 422, 572
Monetarism, 344
Monetary authorities
functions of, 332–333
money supply and, 210, 333–335
Monetary base, 333–334
Monetary policy, 468–469, 551
Bretton Woods system, 31
convertibility, 27, 29–30
discretionary, 429–433
divine coincidence and, 468–469
financial market frictions, 571–576
financial markets and open market operations, 565–566
gold standard, 26–30
government debt and, 26–30
interest rate term structure, 566–567
liquidity traps, 421, 421n10, 572–573
in Lucas model, 410
monetarism, 344
monetary reforms, 346
in new Keynesian models, 468–469, 554–562
optimal policy rules, 569–570
policy errors, 569–570

Monetary policy (cont.)
in postwar period, 31–32
rules versus discretion in, 552–562
staggered pricing mode and, 554n5
stochastic shocks and, 562–564
Taylor rule and, 567–569
transmission mechanisms, 333n4
zero lower bound on interest rates, 571–576, 585–586
Monetary shock effects
new Keynesian models, 464–468
perfectly competitive models, 395, 405n8
in rational expectations equilibrium, 407–410
stochastic growth models, 376
unemployment modeling, 504–506
Monetary theory, 2–3, 74
Money demand function, 213–214, 336–339, 336n5, 420–421, 480
Money in the utility function approach, 71n13, 209n1, 211–212
defined, 209n1
money and price level, 351–353
nominal and real interest rates, 357–359
Money market, 329–330. *See also* Demand for money; Money supply
bubbles in, 609–611
central banks, 210, 332–335, 560–562
commodity money, 332
fiscal theory of price level, 363
functions of money, 331
interest rate pegging and price level indeterminacy, 361–364
liquidity effect, 340–341, 360–361
monetary base, 333–334
nominal interest rates, 339–342, 345, 357–361
price level and, 347–357, 363
quantity theory of money, 337n6, 343–344
real interest rates, 357–361
seigniorage, 27–28, 217, 330
short-run equilibrium, 339–342
Money multiplier, 334
Money supply, 331. *See also* Demand for money; Inflation
Blanchard-Weil model, monetary growth in, 222–229
defined, 334
inflation and, 214–215
liquidity effect, 340–341, 360–361
monetary growth, 364–372
money multiplier, 334
neutrality of money, 71–74, 209–211, 343–347
nominal interest rates, 357–361
in perfectly competitive model, 400–401
in Ramsey model, 218–222
real interest rates, 357–361
seigniorage, 364–372
superneutrality of money, 210, 220–221
Monopolistic competition model, 454n1, 457n2
Montagu, Charles, First Earl of Halifax, 333
Moore, J., 543
Moral hazards, 541
Mortensen-Pissarides model, 509–510, 512n3, 558n9
Beveridge curve, 510, 513
dynamic adjustment to steady state, 527–534
firms and creation of vacancies, 513–517
flows into and out of employment, 512–513
job destruction, 527
labor market tightness, 509–510
labor productivity, 523–525
matching function, 510–512
numerical simulations of, 532–534
real interest rate and, 527
unemployed job seeker behavior, 517–519
unemployment benefits, increase in, 525–526
wage bargaining and wage equation, 517–519
wage determination and equilibrium unemployment, 521–522
Moving average processes, 717
Moyen, S., 535
MRS (marginal rate of substitution), 46
Muellbauer, J., 6
Mulligan, C. B., 254
Multiple balanced growth paths, 159
Multiplication, matrix, 661
Multiplication, scalar, 661
Multipliers
Keynesian cross, 417–419
Samuelson multiplier-accelerator model, 5, 419, 427–429
Multivariate distribution, 714
Multivariate linear models, 291–293
Muth, J. F., 7, 269n1, 271n3, 275, 446

Napoleonic Wars, monetary policy during, 27
National Bureau of Economic Research (NBER), 18
Natural interest rate, 494–495
Natural rate of unemployment, 7. *See also* Rational expectations hypothesis
adaptive expectations, 440–444
discretionary policies, 439–440
full price flexibility and, 455–456
inefficiency of, 456–457
rules versus discretion, 444–446
Neftci, S. N., 386
Neoclassical production function, 635
in Diamond model, 155
in one-period competitive models, 38–40
in Ramsey model, 124–125
in Solow model, 87–89
Neoclassical synthesis, 5–6, 424n14
Nerlove, M., 271n3, 275n4
Net expected profits
from existing jobs, 514–515
from vacancies, 515
Neutrality of money, 71–74, 209–211, 343–347

New classical models, 7, 375–376
log-linear stochastic growth model, 386–392
Lucas model, 403–411
perfectly competitive models, 395–402
simplified stochastic growth model, 383–386
stochastic growth model, 376–377n1, 376–383
New dynamic public finance, 588
New growth theory, 8, 8n19
New Keynesian models, 7
assumptions of, 451–452
characteristics of, 449–451
divine coincidence, 451, 468–469, 501–502
financial frictions in, 544–546
full price flexibility, 455–456
natural rates, 455–457
new Keynesian IS curve, 459–462, 461n5
new Keynesian Phillips curve, 450, 462–463, 468, 493
representative firms, 452–454
representative households, 452–454
Rotemberg model of convex costs of price adjustment, 470–473
rules versus discretion in, 554–562
staggered price adjustment, 457–470
Taylor rule, 450–451, 463–464, 464n7
two-period intertemporal model and, 68–69
New neoclassical synthesis, 625–626, 626n6
New York Stock Exchange (NYSE), 540
n first-order difference equations, 690–692
n first-order linear differential equations, 678–682
Nominal distortion, 476
Nominal interest rates, 339–342, 345
cash in advance in OLG models, 359
cash in advance in representative household model, 359
liquidity effect in representative household models, 360–361
money in the utility function of representative household, 357–359
opportunity cost of real money balances, 212
perfectly competitive model, 401–402
Nominal rigidities, 534–535
Nominal variables, 69, 209
Nominal wage contracts, 492–494
Nonaccelerating inflation rate of unemployment. *See* Natural rate of unemployment
Nondistortionary taxation, 201–203
Nonfundamental solutions, 280
Nonhomogenous differential equations
first-order, 671–672
second-order, 674–675
Nonlinear differential equations, 668
Nonlinear models, 612–619
Nonrivalrous ideas, 258–259
Nonsatiation, 37, 56, 645–646
Nonstationary stochastic processes, 718
Non-Walrasian equilibrium modeling, 6
Normal distribution, 709–710
North, D. C., 263, 264n11
NYSE (New York Stock Exchange), 540

Objective functions, 644
Okun's Law, 503
Okun-type relations, 488, 493, 496n17, 500–501, 548
OLG. *See* Overlapping generations (OLG) models
One-period competitive model
assumptions of, 33–34
consumption and labor supply, 56–62
general equilibrium, 40–42
government expenditure and taxes, 74–77
nature and components of, 34–35
optimal behavior of households, 36–38
profit-maximizing behavior of firms, 38–40
Open market operations, 565–566
Operators
first difference, 83
forward shift, 325
future mathematical expectations (F), 281, 287
lag, 281, 683–685
Opportunistic incentives, 590
Opportunity cost of real money balances, 212
Optimal control method, 694–697
Optimal dynamic Ramsey taxation, 586–589
Optimal intertemporal path of consumption, 121–124
Optimality, principle of, 698
Optimal least squares projections, 407
Optimal savings in continuous time, 700–702
Optimal Taylor rule, 502–504
Optimal time-consistent contingent policy, 503–504, 503n26
Optimization
under constraints, 644–651
intertemporal, 121–124, 693–699, 700–702
Orphanides, A., 553, 554n4, 569n16
Oscillations, 429
OTC (over the counter) markets, 540
Output
AD-AS model, 424–425, 424n13
developed versus less developed economies, 108–109
excess, 465
general equilibrium and, 61–62, 66–68
in Lucas model, 406–407
output gap, 465
in Solow model, 93–95
technology and, 48–49
Overlapping generations (OLG) models, 153–154. *See also* Blanchard-Weil model; Diamond overlapping generations model
characteristics of, 153–154
government debt, 184
history of, 4–5
monetary growth in, 222–229
money and price level, 347–351, 355–357
nominal and real interest rates, 359

Overlapping generations (OLG) models (cont.)
Pigou effect, 364
Ricardian equivalence and, 579–580
Samuelson OLG model with money, 347–351, 614–619
taxation, 184
Over the counter (OTC) markets, 540

Papademos, L., 333n4,
Paper currency, 69, 332–333
Parameters, 35, 634
Partial derivatives of functions, 642
Particular integrals, 672
Particular solutions, 668
Partisanship, fiscal policy and, 590–592
Passalacqua, A., 586, 589, 592
Patinkin, D., 3, 5n10, 6, 209n1, 351, 364, 413, 424
PDF (probability density function), 705–706
Per capita GNI (gross national income)
cross-country differences, 11–13
developed versus less developed economies, 108–109
economic growth and convergence since 1820, 14–17
evolution over time, 13–14
growth rates, 14n28
Perfect competition, assumption of, 259n8
Perfect consumption smoothing, 305
Perfect foresight, 42, 272–273
Perfectly competitive model
equilibrium conditions, 398–400
general equilibrium, 398–400
history of, 395–396
money demand function, 400
money supply, 400–401
nominal interest rates, 401–402
optimal monetary policy, 402
representative firms, 397–398
representative households, 396–397
Periodic nominal wage contracts, 492–494
Permanent income theory, 6, 306–307, 517–519
Perotti, R., 592
Perpetual youth model
aggregation across generations, 172
assumptions of, 169, 169n8
balanced growth path in, 173–177
discrete time model, 178
dynamic simulations, 177–182
efficiency units of labor, 173
intertemporal utility function, 170–171
variables, 169–170
Persson, T., 558n7, 591–592
Pesaran, M. H., 291, 293
Peso, monetary reform of, 346
Phelps, E. S., 6–7, 100n8, 258n7, 415, 437–438, 440, 448
Phillips, A. W., 6, 414. *See also* Phillips curve
Phillips curve, 6, 403n6
deviations of output, 488
expectations-augmented, 7, 476, 487–488, 501, 547, 554
history of, 6–7, 414–415, 627
inflationary expectations from, 435–439, 435n19
new Keynesian, 450, 462–463, 468, 493
staggered pricing and nominal wage contracts, 492–494
Pigou effect, 364
Pissarides, C. A., 509, 515n5, 527, 531. *See also* Mortensen-Pissarides model
Points of inflection, 642–644
Poisson frequency distribution, 511
Policy evaluation, DSGE models and, 628–629
Politics, fiscal policy and
distributional considerations, 589–590
electoral factors and partisan differences, 590–592
Polynomials, geometric, 684–685
Poole, W., 553n3, 564
Population growth
in Diamond overlapping generations model, 161–162
in Ramsey model, 142–143
in Solow model, 90, 104
in stochastic growth model, 378–380
Portes, R., 6
Portfolio choice under certainty. *See* Ramsey representative household model
Portfolio choice under uncertainty, 297–298
Bellman equation, 300
consumption capital asset pricing model, 298, 302–303, 307–308
efficient markets hypothesis, 308–310
envelope theorem, 300
hyperbolic absolute risk aversion (HARA) utility functions, 303
logarithmic preferences, 303–304
permanent-income hypothesis, 306–307
precautionary savings and borrowing constraints, 310–311
quadratic preferences and certainty equivalence, 305–306
random walk model of consumption, 301–302
stochastic dynamic programming, 298–301
Power function, derivative of, 639
Preferences, household, 36–38
Pre-Keynesian macroeconomics, 2–4
Prescott, E. C., 7, 18n31, 262n10, 308n8, 314, 325, 327, 377n1, 386, 389, 446, 447n30, 503n25, 552, 558, 589, 627, 629. *See also* Lucas-Prescott model
Price level. *See also* Calvo model of staggered pricing
costly price adjustment, 450, 457n3, 470–473
fiscal theory of, 363
in Gray-Fischer-Taylor unemployment model, 481–483
in imperfectly competitive model, 452–456
indeterminacy, 361–364

in Lucas model, 403–406
monetary and fiscal policy with price level target, 432–434
money and, 347–357, 614–619
money market bubbles and, 609–611
Rotemberg model, 450, 457n3, 470–473
staggered price adjustment, 450, 457–470
trends and fluctuations in, 22–26
in two-period competitive model, 69–74
Primary government deficit, 186–187
Primary government expenditure, 78
Prime rate, 566
Principle of optimality, 698
Probability
concept of, 703–704
probability density function (PDF), 705
probability mass function, 705
probability space, 704
Probability distributions
Bernoulli, 708
continuous, 705–706
continuous uniform, 708–709
defined, 704
discrete, 704–705
discrete uniform, 707–708
higher moments, 707
joint, 714–715
mathematical expectation, 706
normal, 709–710
standard normal, 710–712
standard uniform, 708–709
variance, 706–707
Production functions. *See also* Cobb-Douglas production function
aggregate capital accumulation, 216
constant elasticity of substitution (CES), 90n3, 651–654
fixed-proportions, 653
in Gray-Fischer-Taylor unemployment model, 481–483
in Jones model, 252–253
in learning-by-doing models, 233–234
Leontieff, 87, 106, 653
linear, 653
in log-linear stochastic growth model, 386
neoclassical, 38–40, 87–89, 124–125, 155, 635
optimal decision of firms and, 61
in Solow model, 653–654
Productivity
shocks, 495–500
total factor, 38, 102–104
Product market, equilibrium conditions in, 61–62, 66
Profit-maximizing behavior of firms, 38–40, 48–49
Pure rate of time preference, 43, 656–657
in Diamond model, 160–161
in Ramsey model, 139–141
Pythagorean theorem, 688

q model of investment, 6, 313–314
convex adjustment costs, 314–320
marginal product of capital, 317
uncertainty, 320–327
user cost of capital, 317
Quadratic preferences
certainty equivalence, 305–306
consumption capital asset pricing model, 307–308
permanent-income hypothesis with, 306–307
Quantity theory of money, 25–26, 71, 337n6, 343–344

Ramsey, F. P., 4, 9, 55, 119–121, 586, 700. *See also* Dynamic Ramsey approach; Keynes-Ramsey rule; Ramsey representative household model; Ramsey representative household model with money
Ramsey representative household model. *See also* Ramsey representative household model with money
adjustment path and speed of convergence, 143–145
aggregate fluctuations in, 377
balanced growth path in, 135–139
business gross profits taxation, 203–206
calibrated, 148–149
capital accumulation and, 126–128
capital income taxation, 203–206
consumption function, 133–135
decentralized competitive equilibrium, 126–128
discrete time model, 146–148
distortionary and nondistortionary taxation, 201–203
dynamic simulations of, 149–152
Euler equation for consumption, 122–123, 129–130, 147
externalities and endogenous growth in, 239–241
fiscal policy, 188–191
history of, 4–5
infinite-horizon transversality condition, 132
interest rate pegging and price level indeterminacy, 361–362
intertemporal budget constraints, 130–131
liquidity effect, 360–361
modified golden rule, 138–139
nominal and real interest rates, 357–361
optimal dynamic Ramsey taxation, 586–589
optimal intertemporal path of consumption, 121–124
population growth rate, 142–143
production function, 124–125
pure rate of time preference, 139–141
Ricardian equivalence and, 187–191
Solow model compared to, 119–120
total factor productivity, 141–142
transversality condition, 121, 131–132
utility function, 125–126
utility maximization, 128–129
variables, 124

Ramsey representative household model with money
aggregate capital accumulation, 216–218
Euler equation for consumption and, 215–216
inflation, 221–222
money supply, 218–222
private consumption and money demand, 211–216
Random variables
Bernoulli distribution, 708
central limit theorem, 712, 714
continuous probability distributions, 705–706
continuous uniform distribution, 708–709
convergence of, 712–713
defined, 704
discrete probability distributions, 704–705
discrete uniform distribution, 707–708
higher moments, 707
joint probability distributions, 714–715
law of large numbers, 713
mathematical expectation, 706
normal distribution, 709–710
standard normal distribution, 710–712
standard uniform distribution, 708–709
variance, 706–707
Random walks, 301–302, 717
Rapping, L., 64n11, 377n1, 382n5, 411n10
Rational expectations hypothesis, 7, 42n6
adaptive learning approach, 295
bubbles in, 602–607
concept of, 269n1, 270–271, 275–277
first-order linear expectational models, 279–286
inflation and unemployment under, 446–447
linear autoregressive processes, 277–279
in Lucas-Prescott model, 325–327
monetary shock effects, 407–410
multivariate linear models, 291–293
second-order linear expectational models, 286–291
Rational functions, 684
Rational inattention, 411
Ratio of two functions, derivative of, 641
Real and distinct roots, 674
Real business cycle (RBC) theories, 3, 7. *See also* Stochastic growth model
Real distortion, 476
Real interest rates
average, 131
cash in advance in OLG models, 359
cash in advance in representative household model, 359
job creation and, 527
in learning-by-doing models, 237–238
liquidity effect in representative household models, 360–361
money in the utility function approach, 357–359
natural and equilibrium, 494–495
opportunity cost of real money balances, 212
in Ramsey model with money, 216
in Solow model, 96–97
Realization, 715
Real money balances, 336
Real numbers, 35, 634
Real shocks, 504–507
Real variables, 69, 209
Real wages
learning-by-doing models, 237–238
Ramsey model with money, 216
Solow model, 96–97
wage bargaining and wage equation, 517–519
Rebelo, S., 7n16, 236n2, 237n3, 377n1, 627. *See also* Rebelo model
Rebelo model, 236n2, 237n3
Recent developments in macroeconomics, 623–624
empirical macroeconomics, role of, 626–628
financial crisis and, 624–626
policy evaluation and DSGE models, 628–629
Recessions. *See also* Great Depression
defined, 18
frequency, severity, and duration of, 18–20
government debt during, 28
Great Recession (2008-2009), 28–29, 412, 624
unemployment rates in, 20–22, 20n33
Rectangular distribution, 708
Recurrence relation, 685
Reduced form, 665
Reduced linear differential equation, 673
Reis, R., 411, 625
Repeated substitutions, 279–281
Replacement rate, 523
Representative firms
concept of, 36
in Gray-Fischer-Taylor unemployment model, 481–483
in imperfectly competitive model, 452–454
in one-period competitive model, 38–40, 56–62
in perfectly competitive model, 397–398
in stochastic growth model, 377–378
technology and optimal output path, 48–49
in two-period competitive model, 62–69
Representative household growth model. *See* Ramsey representative household model
Representative households. *See also* One-period competitive model; Two-period competitive model
concept of, 36
in Diamond model, 156–157
in Gray-Fischer-Taylor unemployment model, 478–481
in imperfectly competitive model, 452–454
in perfectly competitive model, 396–397
in stochastic growth model, 378, 380–383
Reputational equilibrium, 560–562
Research and development (R&D) models. *See* Ideas-and-innovations growth models
Reserve banks. *See* Central banks
Ricardian equivalence, 78–81, 183–184, 187–191, 188n2, 579–580

Ricardo, D., 2, 79, 188n2
Riksbanken, 333
Rogoff, K., 447n30, 503n25, 559, 590–591
Romer, C., 21n34
Romer, D., 7, 457, 625, 629
Romer, P. M., 8n19, 231, 232, 236n2, 239, 243, 258–259, 265–267. *See also* Arrow-Romer model
Rotemberg, J. J., 450. *See also* Rotemberg model
Rotemberg model, 450, 457n3, 470–473
Roubini, N., 592
Rules versus discretion in monetary policy
  central bank anti-inflationary reputation, 560–562
  central bank constitutions, 559–560
  credibility issues, 556–558
  historical debate, 552–553
  new Keynesian model example, 553–554
  policy under fixed inflation rule, 559
  social welfare loss from inflation and unemployment, 555–556

Sachs, J. D., 365n14, 368, 425n15, 592
Saddle paths, 678, 682
Saddle points, 672, 678, 682, 687
Saddle vectors, 682
Saez, E., 535
Sahuk, J. G., 535
Sala-i Martin, X., 111n14, 254, 267n13
Sample space, 704
Samuelson, P. A., 1n1, 2n2, 3–4, 5n10, 6, 119n2, 153n1, 298–299, 308n9, 311, 314n2, 414, 417n5, 435, 436, 448. *See also* Samuelson multiplier-accelerator model; Samuelson OLG model
Samuelson-Diamond model. *See* Diamond overlapping generations model
Samuelson multiplier-accelerator model, 5, 419, 427–429, 427n16
Samuelson OLG model. *See also* Overlapping generations (OLG) models
  money and price level, 347–351
  self-fulfilling prophesies and sunspot equilibria, 612–620
Sandmo, A., 310
Sannikov, Y., 544
Santos, M. S., 254
Sargent, T. J., 327n4, 361, 364–365, 372, 396n1, 403, 553n3, 564, 625, 683n1
Savings and investment. *See also* *q* model of investment; Solow model
  balanced growth path in, 98–99
  dynamic inefficiency, 101
  elasticity of steady state output, 101–102
  in flexible accelerator model, 6
  golden rule, 99–101
  implications of, 97–98
  impulse response function, 98–99, 98n6
  income taxation and, 81
  learning-by-doing models, 238–239
  marginal propensity to save, 416
  in two-period competitive model, 42–55
Scalar multiplication, 661
Schmitt-Grohe, S., 291, 293
Schwartz, A. J., 344n7, 412, 629
Search externalities, 512
Search or matching models of labor market. *See* Matching models of labor market
Second-order linear autoregressive process, 719
Second-order linear difference equations, 687–689
Second-order linear differential equations, 673–675
Second-order linear expectational models, 286–287
  economic examples of, 290–291
  factorization method, 287–288
  undetermined coefficients method, 288–289
Seigniorage
  defined, 217, 330
  equilibrium with high inflation, 368
  history of, 27–28
  Laffer curve, 367–368, 367n16
  relation with monetary growth and inflation, 365–367
Self-fulfilling prophesies
  bubbles as, 605–607, 607n5
  in Diamond model, 159n5
  multiple equilibria and, 598–600
  sunspots, 612–620
Separation of variables, 668
Shell, K., 258n7, 601, 613
Shiller, R. J., 309–310, 612
Shimer, R., 532, 535, 626n2
Short-run equilibrium, 339–342
Sibert, A., 590–591
Sidrauski, M., 210n2, 220, 344, 351
Simons, H., 552–553
Simplified Diamond model
  Cobb-Douglas production function, 159–162
  logarithmic preferences, 159–162
  speed of adjustment in, 163–164
Simplified stochastic growth model, 383–386
Sims, C. A., 291, 293, 363, 411, 627, 721. *See also* Sims linear model solution method
Sims linear model solution method, 293
Skewness, 707
Slope of indifference curves, 650
Slutsky, E. E., 8–9, 58–59, 376. *See also* Slutsky substitution effect
Slutsky substitution effect, 59
Smets, F., 554n5, 626n6, 627
Smith, Adam, 1, 2
Smoothing, consumption, 45, 305
Social welfare costs
  of Diamond model, 164–165
  from inflation and unemployment, 221–222, 346, 555–556
Solow, R. M., 4–6, 10n22, 85–87, 119, 414, 432. *See also* Solow model

Solow model, 110–111. *See also* Generalized Solow model
assumptions of, 4, 106–107
balanced growth path in, 85, 92–93, 104–106
calibrated, 113–114
Cobb-Douglas production function, 89–90, 110–111
competitive markets, 96–97
convergence process, 110–111
discrete-time model, 112–113
dynamic simulations of, 114–117
equilibrium conditions, 85–86
exogenous growth model, 109
extended, 249–252
generalized, 109n13
growth rate of capital and output, 93–95
impulse response function, 98–99, 98n6, 116–117
Inada conditions, 94–96
Kaldor facts of economic growth, 107, 265–266
neoclassical production function, 87–89
per capita output and income, differences in, 108–109
population growth, 90, 104
production function in, 653–654
real interest rate, 96–97
representative household growth model compared to, 119–120
savings and capital accumulation, 90–92, 97–102
strengths and weaknesses, 85–87, 117–118
technical progress, 90
total factor productivity, 102–104
variables in, 87
Solow-Swan model. *See* Solow model
Solutions, fundamental versus nonfundamental, 280
Solvency, government deficits and, 185–187
Square matrices, 660
Stabilization policy, 585–586
Stable nodes, 672, 686
Stagflation, 24, 31, 434
Staggered price adjustment
assumptions of, 450, 457–461
divine coincidence and optimal monetary policy, 451, 468–469
dynamic simulation of, 469–470
equilibrium conditions, 461–462
financial frictions and, 544–546
imperfectly competitive model with, 463–464
new Keynesian Phillips curve, 462–463, 468
optimal pricing with, 459–461
real and monetary shocks, 464–468
Taylor rule, 463–464
unemployment modeling and, 489–494
Staggered wage contracts, 45n2
Standard normal distribution, 710–712
Standard uniform distribution, 708–709
State space, 715
State variables, 693
Static expectations, 273, 440
Stationary points, 642
Stationary state, 672
Stationary stochastic processes, 717
Steady state
in Blanchard-Weil model, 173–177
convergence process, 92–93
defined, 85, 672, 678
in Diamond model, 159–160
elasticity of, 101–102
in extended Solow model, 250–251
in ideas-and-innovations growth models, 261–262
investment per efficiency unit of labor, 92
in log-linear stochastic growth model, 388–391
in matching models of labor market, 527–534
in Ramsey model, 135–139
in Ramsey model with money, 219–220
savings rate and, 98–99
speed of convergence toward, 104–106
steady state capital locus, 137
steady state consumption locus, 136
tax smoothing implications, 583–584
Stiglitz, J. E., 454n1, 478n5, 482n10, 542n1, 625n4, 626n7
Stochastic bursting bubbles, 605
Stochastic dynamic programming, 298–301
Stochastic expectational model. *See also* Dynamic stochastic models under rational expectations
absence of uncertainty in, 272–273
adaptive expectations hypothesis, 273–275
defined, 273
rational expectations hypothesis, 275–277
supply and demand functions, 271–272
Stochastic growth model, 375–376
defined, 376–377
efficiency of labor, 378–380
extended Ramsey model, 377
government expenditure, 378–380
history of, 376–377n1
labor supply of representative household, 380–382
log-linear stochastic growth model, 386–392
representative firms, 377–378
representative households, 378
shortcomings of, 625–626
simplified stochastic growth model, 383–386
two-period intertemporal model and, 68–69
uncertainty and household behavior, 382–383
Stochastic processes
autoregressive, 718–719
autoregressive moving average, 720
defined, 715–716
homogeneous nonstationary stochastic processes, 718
moving average, 717
nonstationary, 718
random walks, 718
stationary, 717
vector, 720–721
white noise, 717

Stochastic shocks, monetary policy and, 562–564
Stochastic variables. *See* Random variables
Stock market
 bubbles, 607–612
 organization of, 540
 stock prices in, 282–283
Stokey, N., 581, 586, 588
Store of value, money as, 331
Strong convergence, 713
Structural form, 665
Stylized facts of economic growth, 107, 265–266
Suboptimality of the competitive equilibrium, 241–242
Substitution. *See also* Constant elasticity of intertemporal substitution (CEIS) utility function
 constant elasticity of substitution (CES) production function, 90n3, 651–654
 constant elasticity of substitution (CES) utility function, 655
 intertemporal substitution effect, 133, 381–382
 labor supply and, 58–60
 method of substitution, 465–468, 665, 675–676
 repeated, 279–281
Subtraction, matrix, 661
Summers, L. H., 483
Sum of two functions, derivative of, 641
Sunspots
 defined, 601–602
 in Diamond model, 159n5
 implications of, 612–614
Superneutrality of money, 210, 220–221
Supply of money. *See* Money supply
Supply shocks, 425–426, 425n15
Sustainability criterion, 186
Svensson, L. E., 575, 591
Sveriges Riksbank, 333
Swan, T. W., 4, 85. *See also* Solow model
Symmetallism, 552
Systems method, 465–466

Tabellini, G., 558n7, 561, 591–592
Target price-level paths, 574n19
Targets, policy, 429–430
Taxation
 in Blanchard-Weil model, 192–194
 business gross profits, 203–206
 capital income, 203–206
 distortionary, 76, 201–203
 inflation tax, 216–218
 nondistortionary, 201–203
 in one-period economy, 74–77
 optimal dynamic Ramsey, 586–589
 overlapping generations models and, 184
 Ricardian equivalence, 78–81, 187–191, 188n2, 579–580
 tax smoothing, 195, 581–584
 in two-period competitive model, 77–78
Tax smoothing, 195
 Barro tax-smoothing model, 581–583
 steady state implications of, 583–584
Taylor, J. B., 18n31, 333n4, 363, 450, 457n3, 475. *See also* Gray-Fischer-Taylor unemployment model; Taylor principle; Taylor rule
Taylor principle, 464, 466–467, 498, 568
Taylor rule
 constant-intercept, 567n13
 equilibrium fluctuations with exogenous shocks, 495–500
 in imperfectly competitive model, 463–464, 464n7
 inflation stabilization and divine coincidence, 501–502
 nominal interest rate and, 450–451
 optimal inflation theory, 502–504
 optimal monetary policy and, 553–554, 567–569
 staggered pricing and inflation persistence, 500–501
Technical progress
 Harrod neutral, 88
 in ideas-and-innovations growth models, 258–262
 labor augmenting, 88
 optimal output path and, 48–49
 in Solow model, 90
Technical rate of substitution, 652
Terminal conditions, 670
Term structure, interest rates, 566–567
Theil, H., 414, 430, 433, 553n3
Theoretical models, 5
Thomas, C., 535
Thomas, R. P., 263
Tightness, labor market, 509
Time. *See also* Discrete time
 continuous time analysis, 83–84
 discrete time models, 82–84, 112–113, 146–148, 178
 time-consistent equilibrium, 561
 time-inconsistent reputational equilibrium, 561
 time separability, 43, 43n7
Tinbergen, J., 8, 414, 429, 553n3, 627
Tinbergen-Theil theory of discretionary policy, 431–434
Tirole, J., 612
Tobin, J., 6, 210n2, 314, 336n5. *See also* *q* model of investment
Total differential, 642
Total factor productivity
 in Diamond overlapping generations model, 162
 in one-period competitive model, 38
 in Ramsey model, 141–142
 in Solow model, 102–104
Training, spending on, 249–250
Transposition, 661
Transversality condition
 in Blanchard-Weil model, 223
 defined, 121, 131
 dynamic optimization and, 694

Transversality condition (cont.)
with infinity time horizon, 132
sustainability criterion for fiscal policy, 186
Treadway, A. B., 314
Trigari, A., 534, 535
Trigonometric functions, derivative of, 640
Truncated normal distribution, 595
Turkey, monetary reforms in, 346
Two-period competitive model
consumption and labor supply, 62–69
demand for money, 69–71
fiscal policy, 74–82
general equilibrium, 49–55
implications for growth and business cycle theory, 55
savings and investment, 42–55
Two-period model of government debt crises, 593–598

Uhlig, H., 291, 293
Uncertainty
adaptive expectations hypothesis, 273–275
consumption under, 297–311
investment under, 323–327
stochastic growth model, 382–383
value of firm under, 321–323
Undetermined coefficients
first-order linear expectational models, 282
method of, 673
second-order linear expectational models, 288–289
Unemployment modeling. *See also* Equilibrium unemployment; Matching models of labor market
alternative views of labor market, 477–478
assumptions of, 475–477
firm pricing and production, 481–483
household consumption and demand, 478–481
monetary and real shocks, 504–506
natural and equilibrium real interest rate, 494–495
permanent income of job seekers, 517–519
Phillips curve and, 488
social welfare loss, 555–556
staggered price adjustment, 489–494
staggered wage contracts, 45n2
Taylor rule and, 494–505
unemployment persistence and financial frictions, 546–548
unemployment persistence and wage determination, 485–488
wage setting, 483–487
Unemployment rates. *See also* Natural rate of unemployment
in AD-AS model, 424–425, 424n13
in booms and recessions, 20–22
defined, 20n33
dynamic adjustment of, 530–532
dynamic simulations of, 504–506
flows into and out of employment, 512–513
general equilibrium and, 61–62, 66–68
in Lucas model, 406–407
monetary and fiscal policy with full employment target, 431–432
natural rate of, 439–446, 455–457
probability of filling vacancies, 511
probability of unemployed job seeker finding job, 511–512
Unified growth theory, 8, 262–263
United Kingdom
government debt in, 26–30
monetary policy in postwar period, 31–32
per capita GNI (gross national income), 14–17
price level and inflation in, 22–26
recession frequency and duration in, 18–20
unemployment rates in, 20–22
United States
government debt in, 26–30
Great Depression, 19
monetary policy in postwar period, 31–32
per capita GNI (gross national income), 14–17
price level and inflation in, 22–26
recession frequency and duration in, 18–19
unemployment rates in, 20–22
Unit of account, money as, 331
Univariate stochastic processes. *See* Stochastic processes
Unstable bubbles, ruling out, 611–612
Uribe, M., 291, 293
US Civil War, monetary policy during, 27
User cost of capital, 317
Utility function. *See also* Utility maximization
in Blanchard-Weil model, 170–171, 223
constant elasticity of intertemporal substitution (CEIS), 46–48, 46n8, 54, 60, 123, 655–657
constant elasticity of substitution (CES), 655
continuous time analysis, 83
in Diamond model, 155–156
fixed-proportions, 655
in imperfectly competitive model, 453
money in the utility function approach, 71n13, 209n1, 211–212, 351–353
in one-period competitive model, 36–38, 56–58, 60
in Ramsey model, 125–126, 128–129, 146
in Samuelson OLG model, 347–348
in stochastic growth model, 378
in two-period competitive model, 43–45, 43n7, 63, 69, 75
Utility maximization
in one-period competitive model, 36–38
in Ramsey model, 128–129
in two-period competitive model, 43–45, 63, 69, 75
Uzawa, H., 253–254, 258n7

Vacancies
creation of, 513–517
dynamic adjustment of, 530–532

net expected profits from, 515
probability of filling, 511
Variables. *See also* Random variables
in Blanchard-Weil model, 169–170
control, 693
defined, 35
in Diamond overlapping generations model, 155
endogenous, 634, 663–666
exogenous, 284–286, 634
in learning-by-doing models, 233
nominal, 69, 209
in Ramsey model, 124
real, 69, 209
separation of, 668
in Solow model, 87
state, 693
variable coefficients, 671
vectors of, 660
Variance, 706–707
Vectors, 634
autoregressions, 720–721
defined, 660
of variables, 660
vector stochastic processes, 720–721
Velasco, A., 590, 592

Wages
efficiency wage theories, 477–478
labor supply and, 58–60
periodic nominal wage contracts, 492–494
permanent income, 517–519
real, 96–97, 216, 237–238, 517–519
staggered wage contracts, 45n2
wage bargaining and wage equation, 517–519
wage determination and equilibrium unemployment, 521–522
wage equation, 517–519
wage setting model, 483–487
Wallace, N., 361, 362n11, 364, 553n3, 564
Walrasian general equilibrium theory, 6
Walsh, C. E., 330n1, 534
Weak convergence, 713
Weil, P., 9, 55, 154, 169–170, 612. *See also* Blanchard-Weil model
Welfare costs
of Diamond model, 164–165
from inflation and unemployment, 221–222, 346, 555–556
White noise process, 717
Wicksell, K., 3, 40n5, 333n4, 361–363, 363n12, 401, 552–554. *See also* Wicksell interest rate rule
Wicksell interest rate rule, 362–363, 363n12, 401, 495, 495n15
Wiederholt, M., 411
Woodford, M., 4n6, 7n17, 359n10, 363, 411, 464n8, 498n19, 553n3, 554n4, 564n11, 569n15, 573, 574, 625
Wouters, R., 554n5, 626n6, 627
Wright, R., 625, 626n7

Yun, T., 458n4

Zero lower bound on interest rates
concept of, 571–576
fiscal implications of, 585–586